YEAR	POPULATION (THOUSANDS)	LABOR FORCE (INCLUDING MILITARY)	LABOR FORCE PARTICIPATION RATE (%)	UNEMPLOYED WORKERS (THOUSANDS)	UNEMPLOYMENT RATE (%)	AVERAGE HOURLY EARNINGS	
						(CURRENT DOLLARS)	(1982 DOLLARS)
1960	180,671	71,489	59.4	3,852	5.5	2.09	6.79
1961	183,691	72,359	59.3	4,714	6.7	2.14	6.88
1962	186,538	72,675	58.8	3,911	5.5	2.22	7.07
1963	189,242	73,839	58.7	4,070	5.7	2.28	7.17
1964	191,889	75,109	58.7	3,786	5.2	2.36	7.33
1965	194,303	76,401	58.9	3,366	4.5	2.46	7.52
1966	196,560	77,892	59.2	2,875	3.8	2.56	7.62
1967	198,712	79,565	59.6	2,975	3.8	2.68	7.72
1968	200,706	80,990	59.6	2,817	3.6	2.85	7.89
1969	232,677	82,972	60.1	2,832	3.5	3.04	7.98
1970	205,052	84,889	60.4	4,093	4.9	3.23	8.03
1971	207,661	86,355	60.2	5,016	5.9	3.45	8.21
1972	209,896	88,847	60.4	4,882	5.6	3.70	8.53
1973	211,909	94,203	60.8	4,365	4.9	3.94	8.55
1974	312,854	93,670	61.3	5,156	5.6	4.24	8.28
1975	215,973	95,453	61.2	7,929	8.5	4.53	8.12
1976	218,035	97,826	61.6	7,406	7.7	4.86	8.24
1977	220,239	100,665	62.3	6,991	7.1	5.25	8.36
1978	222,585	103,882	63.2	6,202	6.1	5.69	8.40
1979	225,055	106,559	63.7	6,137	5.8	6.16	8.17
1980	227,726	108,544	63.8	7,637	7.1	6.66	7.78
1981	229,966	110,345	63.9	8,273	7.6	7.25	7.69
1982	232,188	111,872	64.0	10,678	9.7	7.68	7.68
1983	234,307	113,226	64.0	10,717	9.6	8.02	7.79
1984	236,348	115,241	64.4	8,539	7.5	8.32	7.80
1985	238,466	117,167	64.8	8,312	7.2	8.57	7.77
1986	240,651	119,540	65.3	8,237	7.0	8.76	7.81
1987	242,804	121,602	65.6	7,425	6.2	8.98	7.73
1988	245,021	123,378	65.9	6,701	5.5	9.28	7.69
1989	247,342	125,557	66.5	6,528	5.3	9.66	7.64
1990	249,900	126,424	66.4	6,874	5.5	10.01	7.52
1991	252,671	126,867	66.0	8,426	6.7	10.32	7.45
1992	255,462	128,548	66.3	9,384	7.4	10.58	7.42
1993	258,233	129,525	66.2	8,734	6.8	10.83	7.39

ECONOMIC PRINCIPLES & POLICIES

SIXTH EDITION

RYAN C. AMACHER
Professor of Economics
The University of
Texas at Arlington

HOLLEY H. ULBRICH
Alumni Professor of Economics
Clemson University

SOUTH-WESTERN College Publishing

An International Thomson Publishing Company

Acquisitions Editor: Jack C. Calhoun
Developmental Editor: Alice C. Denny
Production Editor: Sue Ellen Brown
Marketing Manager: Denise Carlson
Production House: WordCrafters Editorial Services, Inc.
Internal Designer: Ellen Pettengell Design
Cover Designer: Sandy Weinstein/Tin Box Studio
Cover Illustration: Jane Sterrett

HB67FA
Copyright © 1995
by South-Western College Publishing
Cincinnati, Ohio

ALL RIGHTS RESERVED
The text of this publication, or any part thereof, may not be reproduced or transmitted in any form or by any means, electronic or mechanical, including photocopying, recording, storage in an information retrieval system, or otherwise, without the prior written permission of the publisher.

1 2 3 4 5 6 7 KI 0 9 8 7 6 5 4

Printed in the United States of America

Library of Congress Cataloging-in-Publication Data
Amacher, Ryan C.
    Economic principles & policy / Ryan C. Amacher, Holley H. Ulbrich. — 6th ed.
      p. cm.
    Prev. ed. cataloged under the title: Principles of economics.
    Includes bibliographical references and index.
    ISBN 0-538-83848-5
    1. Economics. I. Ulbrich, Holley H. II. Amacher, Ryan C. Principles of economics. III. Title.
HB171.5.A397 1995
330—dc20
                                                                            94-17744
                                                                             CIP

I(T)P ITP
    International Thomson Publishing
    South-Western College Publishing is an ITP Company. The
    ITP trademark is used under license.

 This book is printed on acid-free paper that meets Environmental Protection Agency standards for recycled paper.

PREFACE

Each revision of a textbook presents new challenges and opportunities. Authors must decide what to keep, what to change, and what to add in order to make the text responsive to changing ideas, methods, and interests. Today's students demand relevance in their course work and introductory economics provides an excellent means of providing it. Our intent with the sixth edition is to provide a pedagogical framework that fosters the use of economic theory in two important areas: policy issues and critical-thinking skills.

One of the major purposes of studying economics is to understand policy and policy choices, not only in the public sector but in other aspects of life as well. Using economic policy means addressing such questions as: What are the choices? How and why are they made? What are the consequences? This book teaches enough theory to enable students to understand policy, and presents enough policy applications to give them an understanding of how to apply the theory to new or different situations.

The sixth edition strengthens and underscores a policy focus that was present in earlier editions. Chapter 1 clearly outlines the essential elements of economic policy analysis. Throughout the text, policy-oriented examples are used wherever possible. One of the two boxed features in every chapter addresses a contemporary policy issue. To further reinforce the policy emphasis, we have grouped the end-of-chapter questions into review, application, and policy categories, making sure that at least one question is always a policy application.

Economics lends itself very well to critical thinking. Each chapter in our text opens with a real-world situation that requires critical analysis ("Consider this . . ."), and revisits that situation again at the end of the chapter ("Consider again . . ."). The policy examples, boxed features, and end-of-chapter questions also encourage critical thinking skills.

CHANGES IN THE SIXTH EDITION

The changes in this edition are largely within chapters rather than in the order or overall focus of complete chapters. Careful pruning made the sixth edition about fifty pages shorter than its predecessor, as we resisted the temptation to let the book become an encyclopedia. Several pedagogical changes make the text more user friendly. For example, we shortened and focused the learning objectives and linked each to a major heading in the chapter. The numbered summaries at the end of each chapter correspond to these learning objectives. We carefully reworked the end-of-chapter material to provide more application and policy questions. The Global Outlook boxed material in each chapter offers a balanced mix of "what happens when our economy encounters the rest of the world" and "how they do this differently in other countries." These extensions present comparative and international economics with new and updated illustrations, such as hyperinflation in Russia.

Users and reviewers urged us to begin the macroeconomics section with a single chapter on inflation and unemployment followed by separate discussions of GDP and economic growth. That change allows us to provide a more thorough treatment of the major goals and measures of macroeconomics without adding any chapters. Also in response to their suggestions, we simplified the treatment of competing schools of thought to stress the differences in theory and policy between economists in the classical tradition and those in the Keynesian tradition.

Budget policy and the limitations of fiscal policy activism receive added emphasis in Chapters 9 and 10. Those chapters incorporate a variety of perspectives on the role of the budget as a stabilization tool and the continuing problem of the federal budget deficit. The four-chapter monetary section (Chapters 11–14) includes coverage of financial markets and ends with a capstone chapter on monetary policy. The conflicts in theory and policy that characterize macroeconomics today, as well as broad areas of consensus, are detailed in Chapter 15. Contemporary issues addressed there include the insider-outsider model and the natural rate hypothesis. Macroeconomics concludes with a look at growth and development. Chapter 17 was rewritten to address basic questions of what works and what doesn't in economic development, stressing the role of the World Bank and its policy goals.

The microeconomics section of the book begins with the basics of supply and demand, using agricultural policy as the primary case study. The policy emphasis continues throughout the micro section. For example, we cover business choices in response to risk, public policy toward monopoly and labor unions, and the conflict between a market-determined income distribution and the demand for polices to alleviate poverty and reduce inequality.

For microeconomics, the policy capstone section is found in Chapters 31–33. Any text that focuses on policy must offer strong and extended discussion of market failure and governmental failure, as well as case studies that illuminate the hard choices that must be made. These final three micro chapters strengthen this popular feature of earlier editions. We added new material and additional examples on both sides of the debate over when governments should intervene to alter market-determined outcomes. Two case studies, addressing urban problems and the environment, were updated and revised. A third major case problem that addresses the health care policy debate is new to this edition.

The international section of the textbook comprises three chapters (34 to 36). The chapter on international trade now contains a thorough discussion of economic integration with specific attention to NAFTA. The international finance chapter has added material on the failure of the European Monetary Union. The comparative systems chapter was completely rewritten to reflect changes not only in Russia and Central Europe but also in China and Japan, with a new section on Mexico.

IMPORTANT FEATURES OF THE SIXTH EDITION

The following features make this introductory text a useful and unique teaching and learning tool.

ORGANIZATION

1. The text is organized so that microeconomics and macroeconomics can be taught in either order. It allows the student to see the power of economic analysis very quickly. As soon as elementary tools are discussed, they are applied to a wide range of public policy questions.
2. Each chapter begins with a scenario/dilemma that motivates both interest in the chapter and critical thinking about a recognizable situation. In the last section of the chapter, the scenario is revisited and students are asked to draw their own conclusions by applying the material learned in the chapter.
3. Each chapter also includes two boxed inserts. One is a Global Outlook that reconsiders the material in the chapter from a global perspective. The other is a Policy Focus, usually a policy problem or issue, but sometimes a brief biography of an important policy maker. The inserts are placed close to the relevant chapter material and highlight the development of theory or its application to current domestic or global problems.
4. Most chapters include Key Ideas sections—capsule summaries of the preceding section or sections placed at strategic points in each chapter. These summaries help students review the material before moving on to the next topic.
5. The end-of-chapter questions provide a balance of review questions, applications, and policy questions. The application and policy questions encourage critical thinking and foster writing skills. Suggested answers are provided in the *Instructor's Resource Guide.*
6. The carefully annotated Suggestions for Further Reading in each chapter have been updated and expanded to include current policy-oriented material.
7. Key terms appear in boldface type and are defined in the margins of the book. The definitions also appear in a comprehensive Glossary at the end of the book.

TEACHING AND STUDY AIDS

In addition to the teaching and study aids included in the textbook, there is also a *Study Guide,* an *Instructor's Resource Guide,* and a *Test Bank.* The *Study Guide* was prepared by Patricia Pando. The revised *Test Bank* and the *Instructor's Resource Guide* were written by the authors of the textbook.

The *Study Guide* reflects all of the changes in the textbook for the sixth edition. One especially useful feature is an exercise page for each chapter which can be used for homework or quizzes. (Answers are provided in the *Instructor's*

Resource Guide.) We believe that the *Study Guide* will be a real asset for students. Each chapter corresponds to a chapter in the textbook and includes a chapter overview, matching questions based on the important terms and concepts, true/false questions, review problems requiring numerical or graphical solutions (where appropriate), multiple-choice questions for review, a review of the learning objectives for the chapter, and complete answers to all questions in the *Study Guide*. Many chapters also include a section called Taking Another Look which provides the student with a further opportunity for critical thinking.

The *Instructor's Resource Guide* is available to adopters. Each chapter of the *Resource Guide* provides teaching suggestions and supplementary materials for the corresponding chapter in the text. A short discussion of the chapter's purposes, a chapter outline, the learning objectives, chapter summary, key terms with definitions, and suggested answers to all end-of-chapter questions and the *Study Guide* exercises are included. The *Resource Guide* also provides suggestions for lectures and extensions and applications of text material, as well as case studies and biographies of famous economists where appropriate. Transparency masters are also included.

An extensive *Test Bank* is available to adopters. It consists of over 5,500 multiple-choice and true-false questions, including those in the *Study Guide* (marked for those who do not wish to use these questions). Many new multiple-choice and short-answer questions were added to each chapter. To facilitate exam preparation, the *Test Bank* is available both in written form and on disks with the test generator program, MicroExam 4.0. MicroExam 4.0 allows the instructor to create new questions, edit questions, and delete questions.

Computerized study software is available for student use.

ACKNOWLEDGMENTS

We are grateful to the following colleagues who made specific comments and suggestions that were incorporated into this new edition:

Jack Adams, *University of Arkansas*
Ogden Allsbrook, *University of Georgia*
Daniel Biederman, *University of North Dakota*
Greg Brown, *Lincoln Memorial University*
Robert Brown, *Texas Tech University*
Mary Bumgarner, *Kennesaw State College*
David Bunting, *Eastern Washington University*
Robert Catlett, *Emporia State University*
Donald Coffin, *Indiana University, Northwest*
Joyce Cooper, *Boston University*
Barbara Craig, *Oberlin College*
Larry DeBrock, *University of Illinois*
David Denslow, *University of Florida*
Pat Dumoulin, *Elgin Community College*

Jonathan Edelman, *Grand Valley State University*
Harold Elder, *University of Alabama*
Gisela Escoe, *University of Cincinnati*
Eleanor Fapohunda, *SUNY College at Farmingdale*
Paul Farnham, *Georgia State University*
Bernard Feigenbaum, *California State University, Northridge*
Ed Gamber, *Lafayette College*
Bob Gillette, *Texas A&M University*
Gayle Heyne Hafer, *Lindenwood College*
David Hames, *University of Hawaii, Hilo*
Stephen Happel, *Arizona State University*
Dannie Harrison, *Murray State University*
Curtis Harvey, *University of Kentucky*
Bruce Horning, *Fordham University*

Thomas Husted, *The American University*
Beth Ingram, *University of Iowa*
Thomas Ireland, *University of Missouri*
Nancy Jianakoplos, *Colorado State University*
David Jobson, *Keystone Junior College*
Randall Kesselring, *Arkansas State University*
Joe Kotaska, *Monroe Community College*
Andrew Larkin, *St. Cloud State University*
Anne Libby, *Washington University*
M. David Low, *University of Texas Health Science Center*
Anton Lowenberg, *California State University, Northridge*
Robert Main, *Butler University*
Robert McAuliffe, *Babson College*
Hal McClure, *Villanova University*
Rob Roy McGregor, *University of South Carolina*
Don McMullen, *Kaskaskia College*
Pat McMurry, *Missouri Western State University*
Michael McPherson, *University of North Texas*
Richard Measell, *St. Mary's College*
Hamid Milani, *University of Wisconsin, Marathon County*
Clark Nardinelli, *Clemson University*
Randy Nelson, *Colby College*
James O'Neill, *University of Delaware*
Eugene Ottle, *McKendree College*
Dennis Placone, *Clemson University*

Gary Quinlivin, *St. Vincent College*
John Rapczak, *Community College of Rhode Island*
John Reid, *Memphis State University*
Terry Riddle, *Central Virginia Community College*
Steve Robinson, *University of North Carolina, Wilmington*
Diane Lim Rogers, *Pennsylvania State University*
Malcolm Russell, *Andrews University*
Tim Schibik, *University of Southern Indiana*
Peter Schwarz, *University of North Carolina, Charlotte*
Dennis Shannon, *Belleville Area College*
Phil Smith, *DeKalb College*
James Starkey, *University of Rhode Island*
Peter Stratton, *Western Illinois University*
Fred Tarpley, Jr., *Georgia Institute of Technology*
Keith Turner, *University of Nebraska, Omaha*
William Ward, *Clemson University and World Bank*
John and Mellie Warner, *Clemson University*
Jim Watson, *Jefferson College*
William Watson, Jr., *Brunswick Junior College*
Bruce Welz, *St. Charles Community College*
Michael White, *St. Cloud State University*
Bernard Widera, *University of Wisconsin, Madison*
Larry Wolfenbarger, *Georgia College*
George Zestos, *Christopher Newport University*
Richard Zuber, *University of North Carolina, Charlotte*

Special thanks go to Robert Catlett of Emporia State University who provided detailed suggestions and insights on the microeconomic graphical presentations. In addition, we owe a significant debt of gratitude to the many users and reviewers of the earlier editions of the textbook for taking the time to pass on numerous suggestions and comments. Finally, we want to thank our spouses, Susan and Carl, who continue to provide encouragement and inspiration.

Ryan C. Amacher
Holley H. Ulbrich

BRIEF CONTENTS

PART 1
INTRODUCTION TO ECONOMICS 1
1 ECONOMICS, ECONOMIC METHODS, AND ECONOMIC POLICY 2
2 MARKETS, GOVERNMENTS, AND NATIONS: THE ORGANIZATION OF ECONOMIC ACTIVITY 32
3 SUPPLY AND DEMAND: THE BASICS OF ECONOMIC ANALYSIS 56

PART 2
INTRODUCTION TO MACROECONOMICS 81
4 UNEMPLOYMENT, INFLATION, AND ECONOMIC FLUCTUATIONS 82
5 THE MEASURE OF OUTPUT, INCOME, AND ECONOMIC GROWTH 106
6 AGGREGATE DEMAND AND AGGREGATE SUPPLY 133

PART 3
DETERMINING OUTPUT AND EMPLOYMENT: KEYNESIAN MACROECONOMICS AND FISCAL POLICY 161
7 CLASSICAL MACROECONOMICS AND THE KEYNESIAN CHALLENGE 162
8 THE KEYNESIAN MODEL 189
9 TAXES, GOVERNMENT SPENDING, AND FISCAL POLICY 221
10 BUDGET DEFICITS AND THE NATIONAL DEBT 249

PART 4
MONEY, FINANCIAL MARKETS, AND MONETARY POLICY 271
11 THE ROLE OF MONEY IN A MARKET ECONOMY 272
12 BANKING AND THE FEDERAL RESERVE SYSTEM 294
13 FINANCIAL MARKETS AND INTEREST RATES 319
14 MONETARY POLICY IN THEORY AND PRACTICE 343

PART 5
POLICY CHALLENGES FOR THE 1990S 373
15 CURRENT ISSUES IN STABILIZATION POLICY 374
16 AGGREGATE SUPPLY, ECONOMIC GROWTH, AND MACROECONOMIC POLICY 400
17 THE CHALLENGE OF ECONOMIC DEVELOPMENT 423

PART 6
DEMAND AND CONSUMER CHOICE 449
18 POLICY APPLICATIONS OF SUPPLY AND DEMAND 450
19 ELASTICITY: THE MEASURE OF RESPONSIVENESS 473
20 DEMAND AND CONSUMER CHOICE 495

PART 7
PRODUCT MARKETS 527
21 FIRMS AND PRODUCTION 528
22 COSTS AND PROFITS 552
23 PERFECT COMPETITION 575
24 MONOPOLY 596
25 MONOPOLISTIC COMPETITION AND OLIGOPOLY 623
26 REGULATION, DEREGULATION, AND ANTITRUST POLICY 648

PART 8
RESOURCE MARKETS 677
27 MARGINAL PRODUCTIVITY THEORY AND LABOR MARKETS 678
28 ORGANIZED LABOR IN THE UNITED STATES 702
29 RENT, INTEREST, AND PROFIT 727
30 POVERTY, INEQUALITY, AND INCOME REDISTRIBUTION POLICIES 742

PART 9
MARKET FAILURE, GOVERNMENT FAILURE, AND PUBLIC CHOICE 769
31 MARKET FAILURE AND GOVERNMENT INTERVENTION POLICIES 770
32 GOVERNMENT FAILURE AND PUBLIC CHOICE 789
33 POLICY STUDIES: CITIES, THE ENVIRONMENT, AND HEALTH CARE 806

PART 10
THE WORLD ECONOMY 833
34 TRADE AMONG NATIONS 834
35 INTERNATIONAL FINANCE AND EXCHANGE RATES 859
36 ECONOMIES IN TRANSITION 881

CONTENTS

PART 1
INTRODUCTION TO ECONOMICS   1

1   ECONOMICS, ECONOMIC METHODS, AND ECONOMIC POLICY   2
    What Is Economics?   2   Economics in Relation to Other Fields   3
    Why Study Economics?   3   Scarcity: Limited Resources, Unlimited Wants   4   Society's Choices: The Production Possibilities Curve   7
    Theories, Hypotheses, and Models   12   Basic Elements of the Economic Approach   15   Making Policy Choices   17   Summary   18
    New Terms   19   Questions: Review, Applications, and Policy   19
    Suggestions for Further Reading   21   Appendix: Economic Relationships and Graphs   21

2   MARKETS, GOVERNMENTS, AND NATIONS: THE ORGANIZATION OF ECONOMIC ACTIVITY   32
    Limited Resources   32   The Basic Economic Questions   34   The Circular Flow of Economic Activity   38   The Economic Role of Government   43   The Role of the Foreign Sector   49   Summary   53   New Terms   53   Questions: Review, Applications, and Policy   54   Suggestions for Further Reading   55

3   SUPPLY AND DEMAND: THE BASICS OF ECONOMIC ANALYSIS   56
    Demand   57   Supply   63   Market Equilibrium   67   A Theory of Price Formation   71   Evaluating the Market Process   73
    Summary   78   New Terms   79   Questions: Review, Applications, and Policy   79   Suggestions for Further Reading   80

PART 2
INTRODUCTION TO MACROECONOMICS   81

4   UNEMPLOYMENT, INFLATION, AND ECONOMIC FLUCTUATIONS   82
    Full Employment and Unemployment   83   Measuring Unemployment   87   Price Stability and Inflation   89   Measuring Inflation: Price Indexes   93   Fluctuations in Output, Employment, and Prices   97

Summary   104   New Terms   104   Questions: Review, Applications, and Policy   104   Suggestions for Further Reading   105

5 **THE MEASURE OF OUTPUT, INCOME, AND ECONOMIC GROWTH**   106
The Circular Flow Model Revisited   106   Basic Accounting Concepts   111   Measuring Gross Domestic Product and National Income   114   Real GDP, the GDP Deflator, and Economic Growth   126   Summary   130   New Terms   130   Questions: Review, Applications, and Policy   131   Suggestions for Further Reading   131

6 **AGGREGATE DEMAND AND AGGREGATE SUPPLY**   133
Aggregate Demand   133   Aggregate Supply   137   Aggregate Equilibrium and Changes in Equilibrium   141   Aggregate Demand and Supply and Unemployment   147   The Classical and Keynesian Traditions and Aggregate Supply and Demand   149   Summary   156   New Terms   157   Questions: Review, Applications, and Policy   157   Suggestions for Further Reading   158   Appendix: A Glossary of Symbols   159

PART 3
DETERMINING OUTPUT AND EMPLOYMENT: KEYNESIAN MACROECONOMICS AND FISCAL POLICY   161

7 **CLASSICAL MACROECONOMICS AND THE KEYNESIAN CHALLENGE**   162
The Classical Tradition and Say's Law   162   Self-Regulating Markets   166   The Quantity Theory of Money   169   Challenges to the Classical Model   176   The Keynesian Alternative   182   Summary   186   New Terms   187   Questions: Review, Applications, and Policy   187   Suggestions for Further Reading   188

8 **THE KEYNESIAN MODEL**   189
The Role of Demand   190   The Aggregate Expenditure Function   191   Adding Government and the Foreign Sector   201   Changes in Aggregate Expenditure and the Expenditure Multiplier   206   The Keynesian Model and Aggregate Demand   211   Summary   214   New Terms   214   Questions: Review, Applications, and Policy   214   Suggestions for Further Reading   215   Appendix: The Algebra of the Keynesian Model   217

9 **TAXES, GOVERNMENT SPENDING, AND FISCAL POLICY**   221
Why Fiscal Policy?   221   How Fiscal Policy Works   223   The Tools of Fiscal Policy: Government Spending and Taxes   229   Implementing Fiscal Policy: Automatic Stabilizers   231   Discretionary Fiscal Policy   234   Limitations of Fiscal Policy   238   Fiscal Policy, Aggregate Demand, and the Price Level   245   Summary   246   New Terms   246   Questions: Review, Applications, and Policy   247   Suggestions for Further Reading   247

10 **BUDGET DEFICITS AND THE NATIONAL DEBT**   249
Debt and Deficits   249   The Growth of the National Debt Since 1980   253   Should the Budget Be Balanced?   256   Do Deficits Matter?   261

Policies to Reduce the Deficit 266   Summary 268   New Terms 268   Questions: Review, Applications, and Policy 269   Suggestions for Further Reading 269

PART 4
MONEY, FINANCIAL MARKETS, AND MONETARY POLICY 271

11 THE ROLE OF MONEY IN A MARKET ECONOMY 272
What Is Money? 272   Banks and Money 278   Demand for Money 282   Equilibrium in the Money Market 287   Money Demand, Money Supply, and Aggregate Demand 289   Summary 291   New Terms 291   Questions: Review, Applications, and Policy 292   Suggestions for Further Reading 293

12 BANKING AND THE FEDERAL RESERVE SYSTEM 294
How Banks Create Money 294   Reserves and the Money Supply 298   Central Banking in the United States 301   Structure and Functions of the Federal Reserve System 304   The Fed and the Money Supply 308   Summary 316   New Terms 317   Questions: Review, Applications, and Policy 317   Suggestions for Further Reading 318

13 FINANCIAL MARKETS AND INTEREST RATES 319
Bank Failures and the Savings and Loan Bailout 320   The Loanable Funds Market and Interest Rates 324   Stocks, Bonds, and Other Financial Assets 331   The Borrower's Side: Investment and Interest Rates 337   Summary 341   New Terms 341   Questions: Review, Applications, and Policy 341   Suggestions for Further Reading 342

14 MONETARY POLICY IN THEORY AND PRACTICE 343
How Monetary Policy Affects Aggregate Demand 343   The Choice of Monetary Policy Targets 349   Problems in Implementing Monetary Policy 354   Monetary Policy Under the Fed, 1914-1993 357   Summary 362   New Terms 362   Questions: Review, Applications, and Policy 362   Suggestions for Further Reading 363   Appendix: A Composite Macroeconomic Model: *IS-LM* 365

PART 5
POLICY CHALLENGES FOR THE 1990S 373

15 CURRENT ISSUES IN STABILIZATION POLICY 374
Which Works Better, Monetary or Fiscal Policy? 375   Government Borrowing, Crowding Out, and Monetary Policy 376   Unemployment, Inflation, and the Phillips Curve 380   Expectations, Markets, and the Natural Rate Hypothesis 386   Honest Disagreement: The Clash of Macroeconomic Ideas 394   Summary 397   New Terms 398   Questions: Review, Applications, and Policy 398   Suggestions for Further Reading 399

16 AGGREGATE SUPPLY, ECONOMIC GROWTH, AND MACROECONOMIC POLICY 400
Demand-Based Growth Strategies 400   Real Business Cycles 403

Shifting the Aggregate Supply Curve   404   Supply Siders: Public Policies to Shift Aggregate Supply   413   Is Industrial Policy the Answer?   418   Summary   420   New Terms   421   Questions: Review, Applications, and Policy   421   Suggestions for Further Reading   421

17 THE CHALLENGE OF ECONOMIC DEVELOPMENT   423
Characteristics of Less Developed Countries   423   Population, Human Capital, and Economic Development   431   Theories and Strategies of Economic Development   435   The Role of Government   439   Help from Outside: Development Assistance   441   Summary   446   New Terms   447   Questions: Review, Applications, and Policy   447   Suggestions for Further Reading   447

PART 6
DEMAND AND CONSUMER CHOICE   449

18 POLICY APPLICATIONS OF SUPPLY AND DEMAND   450
The Economics of Crime: Use of the Self-Interest Assumption   451   Price Ceilings and Price Floors   453   Markets as Allocation Mechanisms   460   A Lesson from Agriculture   462   Summary   471   New Terms   471   Questions: Review, Applications, and Policy   471   Suggestions for Further Reading   472

19 ELASTICITY: THE MEASURE OF RESPONSIVENESS   473
Supply and Demand Revisited   473   Elasticity as a General Concept   475   Price Elasticity of Demand   475   Other Demand Elasticities   484   Price Elasticity of Supply   486   Who Pays the Excise Tax?—An Exercise in the Elasticity of Supply and Demand   488   Summary   493   New Terms   493   Questions: Review, Applications, and Policy   493   Suggestions for Further Reading   494

20 DEMAND AND CONSUMER CHOICE   495
Choice, Value, and Utility Theory   495   Utility and Consumer Behavior   500   Some Applications of Utility Theory   506   Consumer Surplus and Utility   507   Advertising, Marketing, and Demand   508   Experimental Economics: Economics According to Rats   510   Summary   511   New Terms   511   Questions: Review, Applications, and Policy   511   Suggestions for Further Reading   513   Appendix: Indifference Analysis: An Alternative Approach to Consumer Choice   514

PART 7
PRODUCT MARKETS   527

21 FIRMS AND PRODUCTION   528
The Firm in Theory   528   The Business Firm in Practice   531   The Nonprofit Firm   534   Economic Efficiency   536   Production Functions in the Short and Long Run   537   The Choice of Inputs   541   Summary   543   New Terms   543   Questions: Review, Applications, and Policy   544   Suggestions for Further Reading   544   Appendix: Producer Choice   545

22 COSTS AND PROFITS   552
Accounting Profit and Economic Profit   553   Costs in the Short Run   555   Costs in the Long Run   559   Profit Maximization   564   Present Value   566   Risk, Uncertainty, and Choice   569   Summary   572   New Terms   572   Questions: Review, Applications, and Policy   572   Suggestions for Further Reading   574

23 PERFECT COMPETITION   575
Characteristics of Perfect Competition   575   Competitive Adjustment in the Short Run   577   The Shutdown Decision   581   The Long Run: Constant, Increasing, or Decreasing Costs   585   Competitive Equilibrium: What's So Great About Perfect Competition?   588   Economic Rent in Perfect Competition   591   Summary   593   New Terms   594   Questions: Review, Applications, and Policy   594   Suggestions for Further Reading   595

24 MONOPOLY   596
Demand, Marginal Revenue, and Price Output under Monopoly   597   Profits and Barriers to Entry   601   Monopoly Power and Price Discrimination   604   Is Monopoly Bad?   609   The Costs of Monopoly   614   Who Runs the Firm? Alternatives to Profit Maximization   615   Fallacies and Facts about Monopoly   617   Contestable Markets   619   Summary   621   New Terms   621   Questions: Review, Applications, and Policy   621   Suggestions for Further Reading   622

25 MONOPOLISTIC COMPETITION AND OLIGOPOLY   623
Monopolistic Competition   623   Oligopoly   630   Collusion and Oligopolies   632   Market Structures in Review   644   Summary   645   New Terms   646   Questions: Review, Applications, and Policy   646   Suggestions for Further Reading   647

26 REGULATION, DEREGULATION, AND ANTITRUST POLICY   648
What Is an Industry?   649   Industry Structure   650   Concentration and Performance   654   Policies Aimed at Reducing Monopoly Power   659   Monopoly Regulation   660   Antitrust Laws in the United States   665   Competitiveness   672   Alternatives for Controlling Industry   673   Summary   674   New Terms   675   Questions: Review, Applications, and Policy   675   Suggestions for Further Reading   676

PART 8
RESOURCE MARKETS   677

27 MARGINAL PRODUCTIVITY THEORY AND LABOR MARKETS   678
Special Features of the Demand for Labor   678   The Market for Labor with Perfect Competition   680   A Competitive Labor Market with a Monopolistic Product Market   684   Monopsony   686   Determinants of the Demand for Labor   690   Productivity and Earnings Differences   695   Summary   700   New Terms   700   Questions: Review, Applications, and Policy   701   Suggestions for Further Reading   701

28 ORGANIZED LABOR IN THE UNITED STATES   702
   The Economics of Union Goals   703   Types of Unions   705
   Economic Effects of Unions   708   A History of the Labor Movement
   711   Economic Forces and the Future of Unions   722
   Summary   724   New Terms   725   Questions: Review,
   Applications, and Policy   725   Suggestions for Further Reading   726

29 RENT, INTEREST, AND PROFIT   727
   Land and Rent   727   Capital and Interest   729   Enterprise and
   Profits   734   The Distribution of Income   736   Summary   739
   New Terms   740   Questions: Review, Applications, and Policy   740
   Suggestions for Further Reading   741

30 POVERTY, INEQUALITY, AND INCOME REDISTRIBUTION POLICIES   742
   The Personal Distribution of Income   743   Poverty in the United
   States   747   Discrimination and the Distribution of Income   749
   Income Redistribution   755   Government Transfer Programs in
   Practice   758   Summary   765   New Terms   766
   Questions: Review, Applications, and Policy   766   Suggestions for
   Further Reading   767

PART 9
MARKET FAILURE, GOVERNMENT FAILURE, AND PUBLIC CHOICE   769

31 MARKET FAILURE AND GOVERNMENT INTERVENTION POLICIES   770
   Law, Economics, and Government Policy   770   Externalities   772
   Public Goods   782   Public Goods in Practice   785
   Summary   787   New Terms   787
   Questions: Review, Applications, and Policy   788   Suggestions for
   Further Reading   788

32 GOVERNMENT FAILURE AND PUBLIC CHOICE   789
   Public Choice Theory   789   Rent Seeking   791   Rent
   Defending   794   Analysis of the Political Market   794
   Privatization   799   Austrian and Radical Economists and Government
   Failure   800   Summary   804   New Terms   804   Questions:
   Review, Applications, and Policy   804   Suggestions for Further
   Reading   805

33 POLICY STUDIES: CITIES, THE ENVIRONMENT, AND HEALTH CARE   806
   Urban Economics and Policy Issues   807   Environmental Policy Issues
   812   The Health Care Policy Issue   820   Summary   829
   New Terms   830   Questions: Review, Applications, and Policy   830
   Suggestions for Further Reading   831

PART 10
THE WORLD ECONOMY 833

34 TRADE AMONG NATIONS 834
Why Nations Trade 835   Tariffs and Quotas 841   The Rationale for Protection 845   Part Way to Free Trade: Free Trade Areas and Common Markets 850   Movement of Resources: Immigration and Direct Investment 852   Summary 857   New Terms 857   Questions: Review, Applications, and Policy 857   Suggestions for Further Reading 858

35 INTERNATIONAL FINANCE AND EXCHANGE RATES 859
The Balance of Payments 860   The Balance of Payments and the Market for Currencies 863   The Foreign Exchange Market and the Exchange Rate 864   Floating Exchange Rates 871   Fixed Rates: The Gold Standard, Bretton Woods, and the EMU 872   Summary 879   New Terms 879   Questions: Review, Applications, and Policy 879   Suggestions for Further Reading 880

36 ECONOMIES IN TRANSITION 881
Markets, Planning, and Ownership of Property 882   Capitalism, Socialism, and Communism 883   From the Soviet Union to the Russian Republic 886   Transition to a Market System 894   Other Economies in Transition: China, Mexico, and Japan 899   Summary 904   New Terms 904   Questions: Review, Applications, and Policy 905   Suggestions for Further Reading 905

GLOSSARY G–1

INDEX I–1

CHAPTER 1
ECONOMICS, ECONOMIC METHODS, AND ECONOMIC POLICY

LEARNING OBJECTIVES

1. Define economics and discuss how it is related to other social sciences.
2. Recognize the value of studying economics.
3. Explain the relationship between scarcity and choice, and the role of opportunity costs.
4. Use the production possibilities model to identify unemployment of resources and to explain the concept of economic growth.
5. Recognize the difference between theories, hypotheses, and models.
6. List the elements of the economic approach to policy analysis.
7. Understand and develop the steps followed in policy analysis.

Consider this... *Why are some people rich and others poor? Why are the Japanese richer than the Mexicans? Why did the former Soviet Union dissolve into the loose union of states? Why do accountants earn more money than newspaper reporters? Why do Republican congressmen attack the economic policy proposals of the Clinton Administration? Where do these conflicting policy proposals come from anyway? Why do some companies make lots of profits, while others file for bankruptcy? And, perhaps most importantly, why can't you have everything you want—now! These are all important, personal, societal, even global issues. Economics can help you understand the answers to these and many other questions. By the time you finish this chapter you will have some idea about the way economists address these questions, and by the time you finish this course you will be able to develop answers of your own.*

WHAT IS ECONOMICS?

Economics is the study of how people, individually and through institutions, make decisions about producing and consuming goods and services and how they face the problem of scarcity. The study of economics is divided into microeconomics and macroeconomics.

Microeconomics describes the interactions of producers and consumers in individual markets, such as the market for cars. It also examines interactions between such markets; for example, the impact of changes in the demand for steel on the price of aluminum.

The study of the economy as a whole is called **macroeconomics**. Macroeconomics is concerned with **aggregates**, or quantities whose values are

PART 1

INTRODUCTION TO ECONOMICS

The first three chapters serve as an introduction to the economic way of thinking. Together they set the stage for studying economics. In Chapter 1, we explore what economics is, stressing the basic economic problem of scarcity and choice. In order to do that, we introduce you to your first economic model—the production possibilities curve. We then generalize from this model to some accepted characteristics of models. Finally, we explain how economists use models to think about economic problems and develop policies to address those problems. By the end of the first chapter, you will have begun to think like an economist.

Some of the common problems and choices faced by all societies in using their scarce resources to satisfy their wants are explored in Chapter 2. We will also examine the different ways in which choices are made in different societies. Economists and policy makers are well aware of the importance of interactions between national economies. These interactions include trade in goods and services and movements of labor and capital. They affect the growth rate, national output, employment, price level, and other important macroeconomic variables in both countries. Competition from foreign producers, foreign markets for products, and the use of foreign inputs also have important effects on prices and quantities in individual markets. So, another issue we introduce in this chapter is the difference between an isolated, or closed, economy and an open economy. An open economy is one that trades goods, services, and productive resources with other nations.

Chapter 3 introduces the market process. Markets are places where buyers and sellers meet to engage in exchange. The supply and demand model explains how buyers and sellers interact to determine prices and quantities. It is the most basic and most widely used model in economics.

determined by adding across many markets. Macroeconomics studies the behavior of variables that describe the whole economy, such as the value of the total output that the economy produces in a given time period. Macroeconomics also examines the behavior of such aggregates as the price level and total employment or unemployment. Values of these aggregates are derived from many individual markets taken together.

In microeconomics the most important tools are demand and supply. Demand and supply help to explain prices and outputs in individual markets. These tools also explain the relation between prices and outputs in different markets. In microeconomics, you may look at the demand for the output of a single industry, such as bicycle manufacturing. In macroeconomics, you look at the level of prices and output for the economy as a whole, using aggregate demand and aggregate supply as the main tools. Even though microeconomics and macroeconomics are often studied separately, they are closely related.

ECONOMICS IN RELATION TO OTHER FIELDS

Economics is usually classed as a **social science**. This label makes economics an academic relative of political science, sociology, psychology, and anthropology. All of these fields look at the behavior of human beings, individually and in groups. They study different subsets of the actions and interactions of human beings. (For this reason, they are also sometimes termed *behavioral sciences.*)

Economics focuses on the consumption, production, and use of scarce resources by individuals and groups. Economics is also concerned with the processes by which households and firms make decisions about the use of scarce resources. This definition of economics leads to some overlap with the other social sciences. Psychologists and economists share an interest in what causes people to take certain actions. However, economists are primarily interested in actions that are reflected in market activity or in economic decisions made through government. Sociologists are interested in all facets of organized human activity. Economists, however, are interested mainly in organized activities that relate to the production and consumption of goods and services.

WHY STUDY ECONOMICS?

Economics is a required course for many different majors. You may be wondering why this is so. One reason is that economics interacts with almost all other academic subjects. It affects and is affected by current events. Also, it has a major effect on politics, both domestic and international.

A second reason for studying economics is the impact that economic ideas and theories have on world leaders. Much of what political decision makers do is based on economic theory. As John Maynard Keynes, an economist who has had great influence on macroeconomic policy in this century, wrote:

> The ideas of economists and political philosophers, both when they are right and when they are wrong, are more powerful than is commonly understood. Indeed, the world is ruled by little else. Practical men, who believe themselves to be quite exempt from any intellectual influences, are usually the slaves of some defunct economist.

Economics
The study of how people and institutions make decisions about production and consumption and how they face the problem of scarcity.

Microeconomics
The study of individual market interactions, focusing on production and consumption by the individual consumer, firm, or industry.

Macroeconomics
The study of the economy as a whole or of economic aggregates, such as the level of employment and the growth of total output.

Aggregates
Quantities whose values are determined by adding across markets.

Social science
An academic field that studies the behavior of human beings, individually and in groups, and examines their interactions.

Madmen in authority, who hear voices in the air, are distilling their frenzy from some academic scribbler of a few years back.[1]

Keynes was saying that if you want to understand what politicians, great or mad, are trying to do, you must understand the economic theories on which they are acting.

A third reason for studying economics is that it provides a better understanding of how society functions. Economic theory is very useful in understanding behavior because it allows the development of models with predictive power. As Alfred Marshall, another noted economist, wrote, "Economics is the study of mankind in the ordinary business of life."[2]

Finally, economics is useful. People who are trained in economics find rewarding jobs and careers. If you like to think in a logical fashion, you will enjoy studying economics.

GLOBAL OUTLOOK: THE INTERNATIONALIZATION OF STUDYING ECONOMICS

This box, Global Outlook, represents a feature that you will find in every chapter of the book. In Global Outlook, we will examine how an institution, a culture, a product, a policy, or a way of doing business in another country differs from the way it is done in the United States. This chapter is devoted to concepts and ideas that are universal, because scarcity exists in all countries and in all times. Many of the examples in this book are drawn from experiences of people living in the United States. As you read Global Outlooks you will see that some differences in the ways things are done in other countries can be explained by economic incentives.

If you travel to Italy you will be struck by the fact that houses have significantly fewer closets than comparable houses in the United States. Is this because Italians prefer fewer closets than Americans? What if we went into predominately Italian neighborhoods in New York? Would we find fewer closets in these neighborhoods than we would in an oriental neighborhood in New York? Remember, this is a *ceteris paribus* experiment. So the question is, all things being equal, do Italians prefer fewer closets to Americans? If we looked around in the United States, we would conclude that, at least in the United States, Italians don't exhibit any different behavior in building homes with closets than any other ethnic group.

We could then ask if American Italians are different than Italians in Italy. This is something a psychologist might do. An economist would expect that there is some government policy driving these choices. The economist would, therefore, look deeper. What the economist would find is that the Italian government (in part) determines the property tax on a home on the basis of the number of closets it has. Therefore, if you don't build closets, but instead buy armoires (an armoire is a piece of furniture that is a stand-alone closet) you can avoid paying taxes. That's a better explanation than a difference in tastes!

As you study economics and as you read these Global Outlooks, look for examples of your own. As you learn how to see these economic forces at work you will be amazed at the analytical power of economic theory.

SCARCITY: LIMITED RESOURCES, UNLIMITED WANTS

Scarcity
The central economic problem that there are not enough resources to produce everything that individuals want.

Whether you are just taking one course or planning a career in economics, the most important single problem you will address is that of **scarcity**. That is, there are not enough resources to produce all the goods and services people would like to consume. The first tool we will develop is an economic model that is used

1. J. M. Keynes, *The General Theory of Employment, Interest, and Money* (London: Macmillan, 1936), 383.
2. Alfred Marshall, *Principles of Economics,* 8e. (Don Mills, Ontario: Macmillan of Canada, 1920), 323.

to explain how any economic system deals with the basic problem of scarcity. Human wants and desires are vast, relative to the resources available to satisfy them. Thus, in every economic system, there has to be some method for making choices among alternative actions.

We live in a world of limited resources. **Resources** are whatever can be used to produce goods and services for human consumption. Some resources, such as oil and coal, are converted to energy and used up in the course of production or consumption. Others are not used up in that sense but are virtually fixed in quantity. Examples are land, diamonds, and copper. At any given time, even the quantity of resources created by people—roads, factories, machines, and skilled labor—cannot be changed quickly or cheaply.

Resources
Inputs used to produce goods and services.

Limited resources conflict with **unlimited wants**. Human wants are said to be unlimited because no matter how much people have, they always want more of something. You may know people who seem perfectly content with what they have. If you questioned them carefully, however, you would probably find that they would like cleaner air, more time to play tennis or golf, or more shelters for the homeless. Since not all wants can be satisfied, individuals have to choose which ones to satisfy with limited available resources. In fact, every society is faced with the problem of scarcity and choice. Without scarcity, there would be no need to make choices about what desires or needs to satisfy—and thus no need to study economics.

Unlimited wants
The needs and desires of human beings, which can never be completely satisfied.

OPPORTUNITY COSTS

Every decision to produce or consume something means sacrificing the production or consumption of something else. For instance, the cost of going to a football game includes the value of what is given up in order to attend. Economists use the term **opportunity cost** to denote the full value of the best alternative that is given up, or forgone. Part of the cost of attending a football game is the price of the ticket. This price represents the other goods and services you could have purchased with that money instead. However, there is another important part of the cost. This second part is the most valuable alternative use of those three hours. The opportunity cost of attending the game consists of both the price of the ticket and the difference in your test grade that three more hours of studying would have produced. Even if the ticket was given to you, going to the game would still have an opportunity cost.

Opportunity cost
The value of the other alternatives given up in order to enjoy a particular good or service.

Many people have problems grasping the concept of opportunity cost because they are used to thinking of cost only as the amount of money spent on an item or an activity. In economics, however, the concept of cost is much broader. It includes not only the dollar outlay (the other goods you could have purchased) but also the time cost (the earnings or satisfaction you could have produced for yourself in some other activity) and other sacrifices you might have made. Sometimes it is difficult to place a dollar value on these other costs, but they still play an important role in economic decisions.

SOME APPLICATIONS OF OPPORTUNITY COST

Your everyday life provides many illustrations of the concept of opportunity cost. For example, what is the opportunity cost of attending college? It is not simply the dollar figure given in your college's catalog. Money spent on books and tuition is certainly part of the opportunity cost. However, the expense of your room, meals, and clothing is not, because you would have incurred those costs even if you weren't in college. The catalog may list them as costs, but economists don't count them because they are not opportunity costs.

One important opportunity cost not listed in any college catalog is the income you could have been earning during the years you are spending in classes. For most students, that lost income will eventually be made up in higher future earnings. However, right now it is an opportunity cost that should be included. Even if you can earn only $5 an hour, if you have to cut your working hours by 20 hours a week during the 32 weeks a year you are in school, the lost earnings represent a cost of $3,200 a year.

For some students, the opportunity cost of going to college is even higher. Suppose you are a talented athlete who could play professionally right after high school, as many baseball and tennis players do. Your college education may cost as much as $100,000 a year in lost earnings. After two or three years of college, many football and basketball players face this dilemma. Even if they are straight-A students, the opportunity cost of completing a degree in terms of lost income is very high. It is not surprising that many of them choose to "turn pro" and postpone or abandon getting a degree.

OPPORTUNITY COST AND THE CHOICE CURVE

We can illustrate the concept of opportunity cost and its relationship to choice using a very simple example. Assume that you have $40 to spend and you have two choices: pizza and cola. Pizzas cost $8 each, and colas cost $2 for a six-pack. To keep things simple, we assume that you wish to spend the whole $40. Figure 1 shows the various combinations of pizza and cola that you can buy with $40. If

FIGURE 1
CHOICE AMONG ALTERNATIVES
If six-packs of cola cost $2 and pizzas cost $8, a person with $40 to spend has many attainable combinations of cola and pizza. The line PR represents the boundary between attainable and unattainable combinations. Along line PR, the opportunity cost of 1 pizza is 4 six-packs of cola.

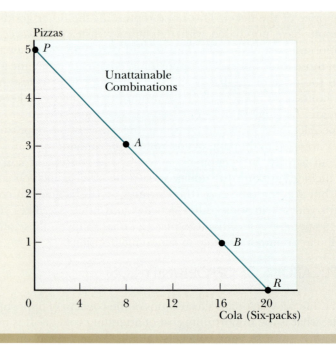

you spend the entire $40 on pizza, you can purchase 5 pizzas (point *P* at the *y*-intercept in Figure 1). On the other hand, you can buy 20 six-packs of cola with $40 (as shown by point *R* at the *x*-intercept in Figure 1). Other possibilities lie along the line that connects these two intercepts. The line represents all possible combinations of pizza and cola that total $40. It is easy to see that points *A* and *B* represent attainable combinations because both contain whole numbers of colas and pizzas. Connecting all these points with a continuous line implies that you can purchase fractional units of cola and pizza. This is merely a convenient assumption.

Of course, all combinations in the shaded area of Figure 1 are also attainable. However, these combinations wouldn't exhaust your entire $40. We have ruled out the possibility of saving part of the $40 because we are assuming only two alternative choices, cola and pizza. Combinations above and to the right of the line are not attainable because they cost more than $40.

Figure 1 illustrates the array of choices and the concept of opportunity cost. The price of 1 pizza is the same as the price of 4 six-packs of cola. The decision to purchase a pizza means the sacrifice of those six-packs that could have been purchased instead. Opportunity cost is measured by the slope of the choice line. If you have forgotten how to measure the slope of a line, refer to the appendix to this chapter.

SOCIETY'S CHOICES: THE PRODUCTION POSSIBILITIES CURVE

From the perspective of the economy as a whole, the choice is not how to spend income between alternative purchases but how to allocate available productive resources between alternative goods that could be produced. This problem is illustrated by a close relative of the choice curve of Figure 1. Society's choice curve is called a **production possibilities curve**. This curve shows the various output combinations of two goods or groups of goods that can be produced in an economy with the available resources. This economic model is based on a few assumptions:

1. All of the economy's productive resources are fully employed. This means that everyone who wants a job has one. Also, factories, land, and other resources are being used to full capacity.
2. There are only two goods (or types of goods) in the economy.
3. The resources used in production are interchangeable. One worker is the same as another, one machine can be substituted for another, and all land is equally useful for producing the two goods.
4. We are looking at the economy at a specific period of time (the short run). During this time period, both the quantity and quality of resources are fixed, and the technology does not change.

Given these four assumptions, we can look at an example of a production possibilities curve. Table 1 shows combinations of missiles and soybeans that an economy can produce. Figure 2 plots the numbers of Table 1 on a graph. Line *PR* in Figure 2 is a production possibilities curve. It represents all the combinations of missiles and soybeans that can be produced in this economy when the available resources are fully employed.

Production possibilities curve
A graph that depicts the various combinations of two goods that can be produced in an economy with the available resources.

In Figure 2, points *A* and *B* represent two different combinations of missiles and soybeans that both lie on the production possibilities curve. Points *A* and *B* are both output combinations that can be attained in this economy with the available resources. Point *C* is also attainable. Since it lies inside of line *PR*, however, it represents unemployed resources. There are points on *PR* that have to be better than *C* because they represent more missiles, more soybeans, or more of both. The economy can do better; that is, can produce more. Therefore, combination *C* is inferior to points on the production possibilities curve.

The line *PR* in Figure 2 can also be used to measure opportunity cost for the economy. Line *PR* is a straight line. This fact implies that the opportunity cost of one product in terms of the other is constant. That is, the number of missiles given up to get another ton of soybeans doesn't change along line *PR*. Each time the production of soybeans is increased by 1 ton, $\frac{1}{4}$ of a missile is sacrificed. The opportunity cost of 1 more ton of soybeans is $\frac{1}{4}$ of a missile. Conversely, the opportunity cost of 1 more missile is 4 tons of soybeans.

Opportunity cost of one good in terms of another is constant along line *PR* in Figure 2 because we assume here that all resources are alike for production purposes. That is, any unit of resources is just as good as any other unit in producing either soybeans or missiles. This assumption produces a straight-line production possibilities curve.

INCREASING OPPORTUNITY COSTS

After an economist has constructed a model, the next step is to go back and vary the assumptions to see what difference they make. Consider what happens when we drop the third assumption stated above—that productive resources are interchangeable. That is, we no longer assume that one unit of labor or land is just as productive as another for producing either good. Table 2 shows a different

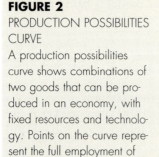

TABLE 1 PRODUCTION POSSIBILITIES SCHEDULE

SOYBEANS (TONS)	MISSILES
20	0
16	1
12	2
8	3
4	4

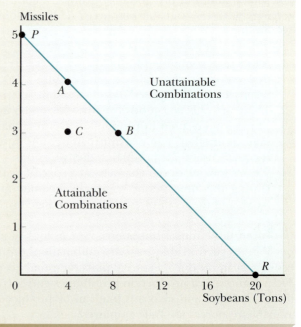

FIGURE 2
PRODUCTION POSSIBILITIES CURVE
A production possibilities curve shows combinations of two goods that can be produced in an economy, with fixed resources and technology. Points on the curve represent the full employment of resources.

set of combinations of missiles and soybeans that can be produced in this economy. These combinations are plotted on the graph in Figure 3. At point A in Figure 3, output is 10 missiles and 200 tons of soybeans. At point B, output consists of more missiles, 100, but fewer soybeans, only 100 tons.

The production possibilities curve in Figure 3 is bowed, or curved, instead of being a straight line. This new shape reflects the change in the assumption that resources are alike. Here we are being more realistic and assuming that some resources are better suited to the production of missiles and others to the production of soybeans. This change in assumptions produces a model that differs from the first one in what it implies about opportunity cost.

If the economy is at point A in Figure 3, we can get another 10 missiles by shifting resources from soybean production to missile production. In moving from point A to point C, we must give up only a small amount of soybeans, 5 units. But to move from point B to point D, producing another 10 missiles requires a larger sacrifice of soybeans, 23 units instead of 5. This curved production possibilities curve illustrates the very important principle of **increasing opportunity cost**. That is, the more missiles that are already being produced, the larger the sacrifice of soybeans required to get additional missiles. Table 2 shows that between points A and C, 10 more missiles cost 5 units of soybeans. Between points B and D, however, 10 more missiles cost 23 units of soybeans.

Increasing opportunity costs are obvious in wartime. As more war goods are demanded, civilian sacrifices increase. Initially, as military production expands, additional labor and other resources are used that are relatively more productive for making missiles and relatively less productive for growing soybeans. As the switch to missiles continues, however, military production takes resources that are relatively less productive for making missiles, although they were highly productive for growing soybeans. Soybean production falls by larger and

Increasing opportunity cost
The principle that as production of one good rises, larger and larger sacrifices of another are required.

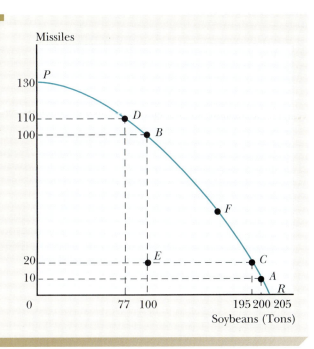

FIGURE 3
PRODUCTION POSSIBILITIES AND INCREASING OPPORTUNITY COSTS
On this production possibilities curve, the opportunity cost of additional units of soybeans increases as the economy becomes more specialized in soybeans: producing each additional unit of soybeans requires a larger sacrifice of missiles than before (increasing opportunity cost). If the economy is inside the production possibilities curve at some point such as E, more of both goods could be produced.

TABLE 2 PRODUCTION POSSIBILITIES SCHEDULE

SOYBEANS (TONS)	MISSILES
205	0
(A) 200 ⎫ −5	10 ⎫ +10
(C) 195 ⎭	20 ⎭
187	30
179	40
169	50
158	60
146	70
133	80
117	90
(B) 100 ⎫ −23	100 ⎫ +10
(D) 77 ⎭	110 ⎭
50	120
0	130
0	130

larger amounts, therefore, because more resources are stripped away from soybeans for every extra missile produced. These resources are increasingly those best suited to producing soybeans and least adaptable to missile production.

UNEMPLOYMENT

The production possibilities curve can also illustrate unemployment and the effect of reducing it. Suppose the economy is at point E in Figure 3. This point is inside the production possibilities curve because some workers, factories, land, and machines are unemployed. If the economy could move from point E to point C, it would be possible to have more soybeans (195 tons instead of 100) with no sacrifice of missiles. Moving from point E to point B would mean producing the same amount of soybeans (100 tons) but more missiles (100 instead of 20). Finally, at point F, more of both missiles and soybeans could be produced simply by putting idle resources to work. At point E, the opportunity cost of both soybeans and missiles is zero because none of either good has to be sacrificed to increase production of the other. However, there is an opportunity cost to being at point E rather than elsewhere on the curve. This cost is equal to the output of either good that could have been produced.

From a macroeconomic perspective, unemployed resources are wasteful. They represent extra production that could be attained simply by putting idle resources to work. The opportunity cost of the goods gained is zero. Thus, economists believe that full employment is an important goal. It is important not just for the individual who needs to work in order to earn income, but also for the aggregate economy.

Both World War II and the Vietnam War made Americans aware of the importance of the full employment of resources. At the beginning of World War II, there were unemployed resources. It was therefore possible to produce more war goods (missiles) without a sacrifice of consumer goods (soybeans). Eventually, all the idle resources were employed. Then further expansion of the production of war goods required the sacrifice of consumer goods. No cars were produced for several years during World War II as auto factories switched to making military tanks and trucks. Other consumer goods were also in short supply. The Vietnam War occurred at a time of relatively low unemployment in the late 1960s. Thus, expanding production of military hardware and diverting labor from civilian activities to soldiering led immediately to reduced production of consumer goods. The economy was already on the production possibilities curve when the United States was drawn into the Vietnam War.

One of the main concerns of macroeconomics is explaining how an economy can find itself inside the production possibilities curve at a point such as E in Figure 3. How can an economic system avoid the idleness and waste of unemployed resources? If an economy finds itself at a point such as E, what policies can be implemented to get back on the production possibilities curve? These are important questions in the study of macroeconomics. The production possibilities curve is a useful technique for identifying these questions.

ECONOMIC GROWTH

Another macroeconomic issue that can be illustrated by the production possibilities model is economic growth. If technology can improve and the quantity of resources can increase, then output can grow beyond the limits of the production possibilities curve. Better technology or more resources means a change in the fourth assumption stated earlier—that both resources and technology are fixed. As labor becomes more skilled and productive, and as producers acquire new machines and plants embodying the latest technology, the production possibilities curve shifts outward.

An outward shift of a production possibilities curve is shown in Figure 4. If the economy is at point A on PR, production consists of D_1 units of soybeans and C_1 units of missiles. With the shift of the curve to P_1R_1, it is possible to reach some point, such as point B, that includes more of both soybeans (D_2 units) and missiles (C_2 units). Other possible combinations on the new production possibilities curve include the same amount of one good and more of the other (such as point E or F) or less of one good and more of the other (such as point H or J). No matter which combination is produced, the important thing about an outward shift of a production possibilities curve is that it increases the economy's capacity to respond to human wants.

KEY IDEAS

THE PRODUCTION POSSIBILITIES CURVE
The production possibilities curve shows:
- Attainable combinations
- Opportunity cost
- Unemployment of resources
- Economic growth

- Points on the curve
- The slope of the curve
- Points below or inside the curve
- A shift of the curve to the right

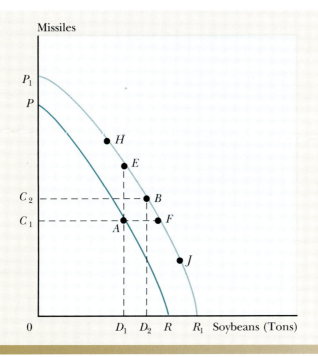

FIGURE 4

SHIFT OF THE PRODUCTION POSSIBILITIES CURVE
An outward shift of the production possibilities curve from PR to P_1R_1 means that the economy can produce more of both goods (economic growth).

Added resources, usually labor or capital, are sources of economic growth. New technology can also shift a production possibilities curve outward and account for economic growth. Invention, innovation, discovery of resources, and improvements in productivity all contribute to economic growth.

THEORIES, HYPOTHESES, AND MODELS

A model represents a scientific approach to examining problems. The production possibilities curve is a theoretical model. Based on certain assumptions (two products, a brief time period, fixed resources, given technology), we theorized that output of one good would change in a predictable way if output of the other good was reduced. The production possibilities curve is just one of many economic models. This book will develop and use a variety of these models. You can use them to understand the workings of markets, the behavior of producers and consumers, and the effects of various policies on a wide range of social problems.

THEORIES AND HYPOTHESES

Theory
A set of principles that can be used to make inferences about the world.

Testable hypothesis
An inference from a theory that can be subjected to real-world testing.

Theories play an important role in everything we do. A **theory** is an abstraction from reality that tries to focus on a cause-and-effect relationship between two variables. The variables can be money supply and prices in macroeconomics or labor costs and prices of cars in microeconomics. A theory is useful in that it simplifies observations by clearing away irrelevant details. In a way, a theory allows you to see the forest instead of the trees. A good theory will develop **testable hypotheses**, which are mini-theories that can be verified or disproved by checking them against facts or experiences. Even small children, for example, quickly develop testable hypotheses based on experience: "My finger will hurt if I touch the hot stove," or "The cat will scratch me if I pull its tail."

MODELS

Economic theorists, like other scientists, develop theories that will yield testable hypotheses. Then they test these hypotheses by comparing them with the facts and seeing if they are consistent.

Model
A set of assumptions and hypotheses that is a simplified description of reality.

A **model** is a formal statement of a theory, usually in the form of graphs or equations. In the model of the production possibilities curve as a straight line, we assumed that all productive resources were alike. As a result, the relationship between outputs of the two goods was a constant one. In the more complex model, we introduced an alternative assumption—that all resources were not alike. The model then predicted that increased production of one good would require increasing sacrifices of the other.

An economic model will generate one or more "if-then" hypotheses about what will happen in the real world. These hypotheses are then tested in real situations or experiments. The production possibilities model offers several such testable hypotheses. For example, according to this model, if a larger share of resources is devoted to production of military goods (missiles), then less will be available for consumer goods (soybeans). During the Vietnam War, President Lyndon Johnson was convinced that there were enough idle resources in the U.S. economy to expand both military and civilian output at the same time. As the economy quickly reached full employment, it became apparent that continuing to produce military goods and to divert some productive resources into fighting could be done only at the expense of producing less housing, education, and other goods and services for consumers.

At the beginning of the 1990s, policy makers were anticipating another test of the above hypothesis—in the opposite direction. If reforms in the Soviet Union and Eastern Europe did indeed lead to reduced spending on defense in the United States, most economists expected that the resources released from military use would lead to a large increase in output of civilian goods. Politicians named those released resources the "peace dividend." The idea of spending this peace dividend for civilian goods was short lived as the political debate in President Clinton's first term focused on the budget deficit.

ASSUMPTIONS

Unlike physical scientists, economists rarely have the chance to conduct controlled experiments to validate their models. Instead, economists most often test hypotheses by looking at actual experiences in markets. Such experiments are often referred to by economists as *ceteris paribus* experiments. *Ceteris paribus* is a Latin phrase that means "all else being equal." An economist changes one variable in a theoretical model (for example, the technology for producing missiles in the production possibilities model). The economist then predicts what would happen *ceteris paribus*, or if everything else remained constant. The **ceteris paribus assumption**, or holding everything else constant, is the most common and most important assumption in economic models. If the technology of soybean production improved but there was no change in the technology of producing missiles, the production possibilities curve would shift out as in Figure 5, from *PR*

Ceteris paribus **assumption** The assumption that everything else will remain constant, used for most economic models. (*Ceteris paribus* is Latin for "all else being equal.")

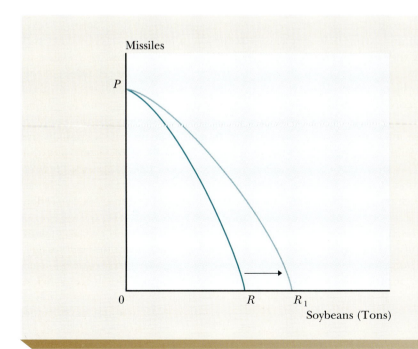

FIGURE 5
TECHNOLOGICAL CHANGE AND THE PRODUCTION POSSIBILITIES CURVE
A change in the technology of producing soybeans shifts the production possibilities curve from *PR* to *PR*$_1$. This shows that if all resources were devoted to soybeans, more could be produced. If all resources were devoted to missiles, however, no increase in output could occur. Increases in both are also possible.

Self-interested behavior
A basic assumption of economic theory that individual decision makers do what is best for themselves.

to PR_1. The economist would predict an increase in output of both commodities, but a relatively larger increase in the output of soybeans. The economist must then untangle the effects of the change in soybean technology on the mix of output (missiles and soybeans) from anything else that changed in the real world in the time period when this model was being tested.

In addition to the *ceteris paribus* assumption, one other assumption is a basic part of most economic models. This assumption is that most people behave in a self-interested way. In general, **self-interested behavior** consists of trying to get the most of something they want (to maximize some goal) out of available resources. For consumers, self-interested behavior means maximizing their satisfaction. For owners of productive resources, self-interest is expressed by seeking to maximize income. For business firms, self-interest means maximizing profits. In the production possibilities model, self-interested behavior will direct the decision as to which combination to produce out of all possible combinations. That combination is the one that maximizes the welfare or satisfaction of consumers.

The self-interest assumption has given economics, and economists, a good deal of undeserved bad press. This has occurred because self-interest is confused with selfishness. Critics of market economies argue that encouraging and rewarding self-interested behavior is a basic flaw in such systems. In fact, concern for others and for the community as a whole is not incompatible with self-interest because individuals define their own self-interest in terms of what is satisfying to them. Some individuals derive their greatest satisfaction from material possessions, others from leisure or enjoyment of the arts, and still others from helping others and building better communities. Some persons may derive satisfaction from all of these! So self-interested behavior is not inconsistent with volunteer work or charitable contributions. Such unselfish activities are not, by our definition, un-self-interested. This definition of self-interest is broad enough to cover the actions of Albert Schweitzer and Mother Teresa as well as those of the most unlovable of "greedy capitalist pigs."

When economists use the self-interest assumption in developing theory, they are simply saying that they expect behavior to be influenced by costs and benefits. If the cost of a course of action declines or the benefits rise, relative to alternatives, more people will choose that course of action. For example, if the price of soybeans rises relative to that of corn, some farmers will switch production from corn to soybeans, attracted by the higher price. If salaries for public school teachers rise relative to those of accountants, more people are likely to prepare for a teaching career and fewer to study accounting. If the penalty for speeding falls, *ceteris paribus*, more people are likely to drive faster than the posted speed limit. If the cost of giving to charity rises because it is no longer tax-deductible, less will be given to charity.

Furthermore, economists do not use the concept of self-interest to predict any one person's or firm's behavior but rather to predict average or group behavior. Such predictions are similar to the use of attributes of certain groups by insurance companies to predict how often certain events will occur. Insurance companies develop norms for various groups—life expectancies, accident rates, or numbers of house fires—and use them to set prices for policies. These norms say nothing about how likely any particular member of a group is to live past the age of 80, run a car off the road, or have a house burn to the ground.

Even economists do not always agree about the best way to develop theories and construct models. Specifically, the role of assumptions has been fiercely debated by two American Nobel Prize winners in economics, Paul Samuelson and Milton Friedman. The traditional view, taken by Samuelson, is that once a theory is demonstrated to be logically correct, its usefulness depends on whether its assumptions are realistic. This view is consistent with the role of theory in the natural sciences. Friedman disagrees, arguing that the true test of the usefulness of a theory is whether it works. That is, does it accurately predict what happens in the real world? In this book, we will look for logically correct theories and models that pass both tests: realistic assumptions and accurate predictions.

BASIC ELEMENTS OF THE ECONOMIC APPROACH

This discussion of theories and models suggests that economics is much like other sciences in its methods. What is unique or different about the economic approach? There are a few emphases and ideas that help set economics apart.

1. *Like the natural sciences, economic theory is positive, or nonnormative.* **Positive statements** are if-then propositions about *what is*. In contrast, **normative statements** describe *what ought to be*. In other words, economic theory strives to be scientific. However, when economists try to apply economic theory to policy questions, they often find it difficult to keep their work positive. Economic theory is value-free. However, appliers of the theory are often tempted to mix in their values in order to favor a preferred outcome or policy. It is a positive statement to say that production of more missiles will require increasing sacrifices of soybeans. It is a normative statement to say that more missiles and fewer soybeans should be produced.

2. *Economic theory cannot predict the future.* It can only explain the effects of certain events. Economic theory consists of statements of the if-*A*-then-*B* type. The prediction that *B* will occur depends on whether or not *A* happens. (Note that theory does not predict the occurrence of *A*. Economists do not have a crystal ball.) In the production possibilities model, an increase in resources will result in economic growth, *ceteris paribus*. In this case, part of the *ceteris paribus* assumption is that the increased resources will be put to work and not left unemployed. There is, however, some difference between what economics *is* and what many economists actually *do*. Many economists, especially macroeconomists, spend a great deal of time forecasting future conditions. To do this, they make use of economic theory. In forecasting, an economist guesses the likelihood that *A* will occur and then uses economic theory to predict the occurrence of *B*. Sometimes, however, forecasts are wrong. This doesn't necessarily mean that the theory is incorrect. The forecaster may have been wrong in expecting *A* to occur.

3. *Most economists look first to market processes for solutions to social problems.* This market bias reflects a preference for the freedom and efficiency arising from decentralized processes. However, most economic theory is applicable to nonmarket systems as well, even though the legal and political institutions differ. Economists can apply tools developed for analyzing market economies to the workings of socialist economies and to a wide variety of nonmarket behavior.

Positive statements
A set of propositions about what is, rather than what ought to be.

Normative statements
A set of propositions about what ought to be (also called value judgments).

4. *Economists pay a great deal of attention to cost.* The emphasis on opportunity cost, scarcity, and choice is fundamental to economics. Nobel Prize winner Milton Friedman underscored the importance of opportunity cost in this famous remark: "There is no such thing as a free lunch. This is the sum of my economic theory. The rest is elaboration." Harping on the subject of cost often puts economists in conflict with policy makers. Environmentalists don't like to hear economists talk about the opportunity cost of environmental purity in terms of forgone output. College admissions officers seeking students don't like economists reminding students that the opportunity cost of a college education includes income not earned while in college.

5. *Economists are very interested in chances to substitute among alternatives.* Substitution and cost are closely related because the decision to substitute is based on the costs of the various alternatives. Sometimes substitutes are obvious, such as plastic for aluminum or electric heat for gas. Other substitutes are less apparent. A tree, for example, can substitute for gas or oil as heat, or for aluminum siding on houses. Trees can also substitute for air conditioning or awnings by providing shade. An important task of economic analysis is identifying alternatives that can serve as substitutes and evaluating the costs of substituting one for another.

6. *Economists think in terms of marginal analysis.* The marginal approach means looking at the effects on other variables of small increases or decreases in one important variable. Should we produce another (marginal) missile? If we do, what will be the (marginal) cost in terms of soybeans not produced? Most

POLICY FOCUS: ECONOMISTS AS POLICY ADVISORS

Milton Friedman and Paul A. Samuelson are two of the best-known contemporary American economists. They both have been very active in the major macro and micro policy debates of the past three decades. Both are winners of the Nobel Prize in economics. The two men represent polar extremes with respect to economic policy. Samuelson sees an important role for government in modern industrial society. Friedman advocates a *laissez-faire* economic policy. He argues that the market economy operates very well and that the interventions Samuelson supports do more harm than good. Samuelson is a leader of the liberal (policy) school of economics. Friedman represents the conservative or free market school, which is sometimes called the Chicago School.

Samuelson, a professor at the Massachusetts Institute of Technology (MIT), has an A.B. degree from the University of Chicago and A.M. and Ph.D. degrees in economics from Harvard University. His Ph.D. dissertation, *Foundations of Economic Analysis*, written when he was only 23 years old, was published as a book. It still ranks as a monumental work in the application of mathematics to economics. Graduate students still study it. Many of today's economists were introduced to economics with Samuelson's textbook, *Economics*. Samuelson is largely responsible for making MIT's economics department one of the best in the country.

Friedman is retired from the University of Chicago, where he taught for 30 years. He is presently a senior research fellow at the Hoover Institution at Stanford University. Friedman received an A.B. degree from Rutgers, an A.M. degree from the University of Chicago, and a Ph.D. degree from Columbia University. He has made notable contributions to economic theory. His policy ideas are readily available in three popular books: *Essays in Positive Economics* (1953), *Capitalism and Freedom* (1962), and *Free to Choose* (1980). Recently, Friedman has angered some of the conservatives who usually agree with him by arguing that illegal drugs should be legalized. He argues that legalizing such drugs will reduce both the profits in selling them and the crime and violence among sellers and users.

decisions in economics are not all-or-nothing choices but are made at the margin. Decisions about how to spend the next hour, whether to eat another slice of pizza, and whether to hire an extra worker are all marginal decisions.

7. *Economists take the individual, rather than the group, the industry, or the community, as the basic decision-making unit.* They regard the behavior of individuals as an important influence on public policy and on decisions made in the private sector. The emphasis on individuals rather than groups reflects the importance of incentives in economics. Changes in prices, costs, profits, wages, substitutes, and opportunities are the driving forces behind individual economic decisions. It is the individual, not the group or community, that responds to incentives.

MAKING POLICY CHOICES

One of the most important uses of economics is to help to analyze possible solutions to public policy problems and to develop recommendations. Some of the most famous economists in history—Adam Smith, David Ricardo, John Maynard Keynes, Milton Friedman, and Paul Samuelson—became interested in economics because it offered tools with which to develop solutions to policy issues. When economic models are applied to public policy issues, it is difficult to decide when the economist's task ends and the policy maker takes over. When economic methods are used for policy analysis, there is a five-step process.

1. *State the problem.* The choice of what problem to consider and how to state it is the task of the policy maker. How a problem is stated often determines what tools the economist applies and what solutions are considered. For example, suppose the problem is illegal parking on campus, especially parking by students in faculty spaces. Let's follow that problem through the next four steps.
2. *Apply the relevant economic model.* The economist turns to the toolkit to select the most useful theoretical model. In this case, there is a fairly simple technique called cost-benefit analysis. This technique simply assumes that people are self-interested, that they are aware of the opportunity costs and benefits of their actions, and that they will choose the course of action that maximizes the excess of benefits over opportunity costs. This simple model predicts that an increase in the opportunity cost of illegal student parking or a reduction in benefits will reduce the amount of such illegal parking.
3. *Identify solutions.* The most common error at this stage is to leave out some alternative solutions. Cost-based solutions to illegal parking might include higher fines. Do you think a student would be less likely to park in a faculty space if the fine were $100 instead of $10? More police officers would raise the cost by increasing the probability of being caught. The university could reduce the benefits of illegal parking by providing more bicycle racks or free bus transportation around campus and to and from commuter parking lots. Campus officials could even sell reserved parking spaces, and let students and faculty bid for parking rights.
4. *Evaluate solutions.* This is the stage where economists are most useful, pointing to costs, substitutes, and incentives. A good economic model predicts how various alternative solutions will affect the amount of illegal parking, who will gain and who will lose, and which solution costs least to imple-

ment. For example, more police officers would be more expensive than higher fines. On the other hand, higher fines are a burden on students, many of whom have limited incomes. Bicycle racks are cheaper than shuttle buses. However racks are not as helpful as buses would be to commuting students, unless they live very close to the campus.

5. *Choose and implement one or more solutions.* This step is *not* the task of the economist, although it is hard to stop after carrying the process this far. The policy maker (who may have been trained as an economist) takes the economist's list of possible solutions and the evaluation and makes a policy choice.

Most arguments among economists occur when they overstep the boundaries of scientific analysis and advocate a particular solution to an economic problem. Newspapers and TV news programs often quote economists who disagree. However, economists agree far more often than they disagree. Disagreements make headlines; agreement isn't news. Throughout this book, we will point out where most economists agree and also where and why they disagree. The models we describe represent a broad range of agreement among most economists on how markets work and how individuals respond to incentives.

Consider again... *You now know why you can't have everything! We live in a world of scarcity. You must make choices, managers of firms must make choices, and leaders of countries must make choices. As we proceed you will become more adept at understanding the trade-offs involved in making choices—personal consumption choices, business decisions, and public policy choices. The policy focus in each chapter will remind you that one of the important functions of economics is to help you understand and improve public policy.*

Economics is an exciting social science. As you begin to understand the economic way of thinking you will gain insights into an endless array of interesting policy questions. We wish you well. Let's get on with it!

SUMMARY

1. Economics is the study of how decisions about producing and consuming goods and services are made and how individuals and groups face the problem of scarcity. Microeconomics looks at the interactions of producers and consumers in individual markets. Macroeconomics is the study of the economy as a whole and is concerned with aggregates, numbers that are determined by adding across many markets.

    Social or behavioral sciences look at the behavior of human beings, individually and in groups. They study different subsets of the actions and interactions of human beings. Together macroeconomics and microeconomics are one of the social sciences.

2. Economics interacts with almost all other academic subjects and much of what both domestic and international political decision makers do is based on economic theory. Economics also provides an understanding of how society functions. Economics is useful; people who are trained in economics find rewarding jobs and careers.

3. Resources are limited, but human wants are unlimited. This conflict is the basic economic problem of scarcity. People cannot have everything they want and must make choices. In order to have more of one good, people must settle for less of another. The cost of extra units of one good is the number of units of the other sacrificed, or the opportunity cost. The principle of increasing opportunity cost says that the more of one good people have, the greater the amount of other goods they must sacrifice to obtain one more unit of that good.
4. The production possibilities curve illustrates the problem of scarcity. The curve shows the various output combinations of two goods or groups of goods that can be produced in an economy with the available resources. Unemployment of resources is shown by a point inside the curve and economic growth is indicated by a shift of the curve to the right.
5. A theory is a set of principles that can be used to make inferences about the world. An hypothesis is an inference from a theory that can be subjected to real-world testing. A model is a set of assumptions and hypotheses that is a simplified description of reality.
6. The economic approach is positive and marginal, and cannot be used to predict the future. Economists tend to look to the market for solutions, pay a great deal of attention to cost, are interested in substitution among alternatives, and look at the individual as the decision-making unit.
7. One of the most important uses of economic theory is to develop models that can be used for policy analysis. An issue is analyzed in five steps: state the problem, apply the relevant economic model, identify solutions, evaluate solutions, and choose and implement solutions.

NEW TERMS

economics
microeconomics
macroeconomics
aggregates
social science

scarcity
resources
unlimited wants
opportunity cost
production possibilities curve

increasing opportunity cost
theory
testable hypothesis
model

ceteris paribus assumption
self-interested behavior
positive statements
normative statements

QUESTIONS: REVIEW, APPLICATIONS, AND POLICY

REVIEW

1. Do you think people exhibit behavior patterns that confirm the self-interest assumption? Does your own behavior confirm this assumption? Is a contribution to charity or volunteer work a contradiction of the self-interest assumption?
2. Why do economists theorize rather than attempt to describe reality exactly?
3. Do assumptions have to be realistic in order for a theory to work?
4. What is the difference between using theory to predict and forecasting?

APPLICATIONS

5. Consider the following simple predictive model: if the speed limit is reduced, fewer highway deaths will occur. What assumptions are being made? What *ceteris paribus* conditions could change and make this prediction invalid?
6. Which of the following quantities are microeconomic and which are macroeconomic? Which might fall between the two?

   a. price of shoes
   b. number of men aged 18 to 24 in the U.S. labor force
   c. level of interest rates
   d. unemployment in Tulsa
   e. production of agricultural products
   f. average level of prices
   g. production of butter
   h. average price of imported goods
   i. unemployment in the United States
   j. total output
   k. unemployment of carpenters
   l. number of nurses in the U.S. labor force
   m. unemployment in the northeastern states

7. What is the opportunity cost of working ten hours a week flipping burgers while in college? If you worked more hours per week, would you experience increasing or constant opportunity cost? That is, would the extra hours require giving up alternative uses of your time that have the same value or an increasing value?
8. a. Given the following data, plot a production possibilities curve and calculate the opportunity cost of bicycles in terms of skateboards.

BICYCLES	SKATEBOARDS
10	0
8	10
6	20
4	30
2	40
0	50

b. Assume that new technology increases the possible output of both skateboards and bicycles by 50 percent. Draw the new production possibilities curve. Calculate the new opportunity cost of bicycles in terms of skateboards.

c. Now assume that new technology increases the amount of bicycles that can be produced by 6 units if all resources are devoted to bicycles, but does not change the amount of skateboards that can be produced. Draw a new curve, and calculate a new opportunity cost.

9. You know that the opportunity cost of books in terms of cassettes not produced is 1 book for 2 cassettes and that available resources can produce a maximum of 100 books. Can you draw the production possibilities curve for these two goods? If so, what is the maximum possible output of cassettes? If you choose to produce 40 books, how many cassettes can be produced?

10. Using the following economic data, plot a production possibilities curve for tomatoes and tomahawks:

TOMATOES	TOMAHAWKS
100	0
80	15
60	30
40	45
20	60
0	75

What is the opportunity cost of a tomato? A tomahawk? If 50 tomatoes are produced, how many tomahawks can be produced?

11. Using the data in Question 10, suppose a change in technology makes it possible to increase tomato production to a maximum of 150 units. There is no change in the technology of producing tomahawks. Draw the new production possibilities curve. Now what is the opportunity cost of each good? If this economy chooses to produce 60 tomatoes, how many tomahawks can it produce?

12. Which of the following statements are normative, and which are positive? Rewrite the normative statements to make them positive and the positive ones to make them normative.
a. "Women earn less than men."
b. "Defense spending has grown too rapidly in the last decade."
c. "Because their child-care duties interfere with their work, women with children should earn less than men."
d. "Twenty-three percent of the federal budget is spent on defense."
e. "An estimated 14 percent of the U.S. population lives in poverty, according to government standards defining poverty."
f. "The government is not doing enough to reduce poverty."

13. The economy of Southland can only produce two goods: food and clothing. Both are subject to constant costs. Draw a production possibilities curve for Southland that shows the maximum output of food as 50 cartons and the maximum output of clothing as 100 suits. Now locate each of the following on your diagram:
a. Output of 25 cartons of food and 25 suits of clothing. Label this point *U*. Does it lie on the curve? What does this point represent? What is the opportunity cost of another suit of clothing at this point?
b. Output of 50 cartons of food and 100 suits of clothing. Label this point *G*. Does this point lie on the curve? Is it attainable? If not, what must happen for *G* to be a possible output combination?
c. Output of 25 cartons of food and 50 suits of clothing. Label this point *A*. Does it lie on the curve? What is the opportunity cost of another carton of food at this point?

14. a. Suppose the two goods in Question 13 are subject to increasing costs, but the end points remain the same. Draw a new production possibilities curve for food and clothing in Southland.
b. Suppose the economy of Southland has a technological change that increases the capacity to produce food but not clothing. How will the production possibilities curve shift? Is it possible to produce more of both food and clothing after this shift?
c. Suppose the economy of Southland has an increase in resources that affects both food and clothing production equally. How will the production possibilities curve shift?

POLICY

15. Try developing a simple economic model to predict how students will respond to an increase in dormitory rents. What are your assumptions? What will happen to the number of dormitory spaces rented? What will happen to the number of off-campus apartments rented and their prices?

SUGGESTIONS FOR FURTHER READING

Henderson, David R. (Editor). *Fortune Encyclopedia of Economics*. New York: Warner Books, 1993. *Fortune* asked 141 leading economists to write short essays on critical economic questions, and Henderson put them together in this volume. A very nice reference book.

Huff, Darrell, and Irving Geis. *How to Lie with Statistics*. New York: W. W. Norton, 1954 (copyright renewed 1982). This classic guide to interpreting and misinterpreting graphs and statistics is must reading for any serious student of the social sciences.

Romer, David. "Do Students Go to Class? Should They?" *The Journal of Economic Perspectives* (Summer 1993): 167–174. The use of a basic economic model to analyze a question of interest to every college student. The answer is yes!

Stigler, George. *Memoirs of an Unregulated Economist*. New York: Basic Books, 1988. A Nobel Prize-winning economist looks at the training of economists and the uses of economics in an account of his own experiences in the field.

Warsh, David. *Economic Principals: Masters and Mavericks of Modern Economics*. New York: Free Press, 1993. This lively book is a collection of columns by a journalist who writes well and understands economic thinking. He conveys the "passion" of policy economics without being highly political.

APPENDIX

ECONOMIC RELATIONSHIPS AND GRAPHS

Economic theories and models are often expressed in the form of mathematical relationships among variables. These relationships can be described by algebraic equations. Economists more often express them visually in the form of graphs. Graphs make it possible to illustrate economic theories and models in ways that make them easier to remember and to apply to the real world. Remember that everything that can be said in graphs can also be said in words. Graphs are only an aid to understanding the theory. Mastering and applying the theory is what you should be trying to achieve. If you can learn to feel comfortable with graphs as visual presentations of economic ideas, reading this textbook and understanding your professor's lectures will be much easier.

RELATIONSHIP BETWEEN TWO VARIABLES

A relationship between two variables, variable x and variable y, can be expressed in a number of ways. One is a table of values of x and y. For example, Table 1A shows the various amounts of fertilizer applied per acre and the corresponding yields of corn per acre. What does this table mean? It means that different amounts of fertilizer were applied to different plots of land and that those plots of land yielded varying amounts of corn.

This relationship could also be expressed in the form of a graph. A graph shows how the quantity of one variable changes when another variable changes. Figure 1A shows the system most commonly used for graphing. The vertical line is referred to as the **y-axis** (or vertical axis). The horizontal line is referred to as the **x-axis** (or horizontal axis). The x-axis and y-axis divide the graph into four quadrants.

y-axis
The upright line in a coordinate system that shows the values of the dependent variable; the vertical axis.

x-axis
The horizontal line in a coordinate system that shows the values of the independent variable; the horizontal axis.

TABLE 1A RELATIONSHIPS BETWEEN TWO VARIABLES

X-VARIABLE, FERTILIZER (100S OF LBS./ACRE)	Y-VARIABLE, CORN (BUSHELS/ACRE)
1	1
2	10
3	40
4	80
5	100
6	110
7	115
8	110
9	100
10	70

Origin
The intersection of the vertical and horizontal axes of a coordinate system, at which the values of both the *x*-variable and the *y*-variable are zero.

The point where the axes cross (or intersect) is the **origin**. At the origin, the values of both the *x*-variable and the *y*-variable are zero. Above the *x*-axis, the *y*-variable has positive values. Below the *x*-axis, the *y*-variable has negative values. To the right of the *y*-axis, the *x*-variable has positive values. To the left of the *y*-axis, the *x*-variable has negative values. Both *x* and *y* have positive values in Quadrant I and negative values in Quadrant III. In Quadrant IV, *x* takes on positive values, and *y* takes on negative values. In Quadrant II, *x* has negative values, and *y* positive values. In this book, most of the graphs will use only Quadrant I because most economic data takes on only positive values.

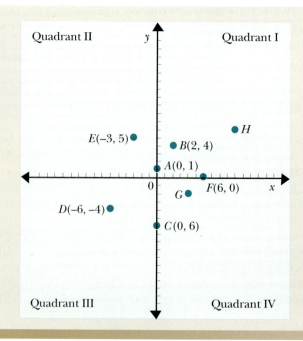

FIGURE 1A
QUADRANT SYSTEM
A four-quadrant system makes it possible to represent combinations of positive and negative values in two dimensions. Point C represents an *x*-value of 0 and a *y*-value of −6. The quadrants are labeled I to IV in the counterclockwise direction.

Each point on a graph has a set of **coordinates**, a pair of numbers representing the *x*-value and the *y*-value. For example, point *B* on Figure 1A represents the value 2 for the *x*-variable and the value 4 for the *y*-variable. The *x*-value is always given first. For example, point *E* represents $x = -3$, $y = 5$. See if you can determine the coordinates of points *G* and *H*.

With this background, we can plot the relationship between fertilizer applied and corn output given in Table 1A. The first decision to make is which variable goes on which axis. If there is a cause-and-effect relationship, we usually put the "causing" variable on the horizontal axis and the variable being affected on the vertical axis. In mathematics, the causing variable is the **independent variable**, and the affected variable is the **dependent variable**. Since we think that fertilizer causes increased corn yields, we plot it on the horizontal axis (*x*-axis). Corn yield is plotted on the vertical axis (*y*-axis).

The next decision concerns establishing a scale for each axis. The scales can be whatever is convenient and do not need to be the same. In this case, the fertilizer units are hundreds of pounds per acre, and the corn units are bushels per acre. Once a scale is established and the axes are labeled, we can plot the coordinates of the points in Table 1A. Then we connect the plotted points with a smooth curve to produce a graph, shown in Figure 2A.

The value of a graph is that it gives you a visual picture of the mathematical relationship between the variables. In Figure 2A, you can easily see that as fertilizer is increased up to 700 pounds per acre, corn output increases. After that level, more fertilizer causes a decrease in output. The corn plants grow too rapidly and don't produce many ears, or the roots suffer fertilizer burn.

Not all relationships produce as tidy a graph as the one for fertilizer and corn yield. Sometimes researchers plot data to see if there is any visual pattern before trying to understand what, if any, is the relationship between the two variables. Such a plot of actual data is called a **scatter diagram**. Scatter diagrams are useful in searching for possible mathematical relationships between two variables.

Coordinates
The values of *x* and *y* that define the location of a point in a coordinate system.

Independent variable
The variable, usually plotted on the horizontal axis, that affects or influences the other variable.

Dependent variable
The variable, usually plotted on the vertical axis, that is affected or influenced by the other variable.

Scatter diagram
A graph that plots actual pairs of values of two variables to determine whether there appears to be any consistent relationship between them.

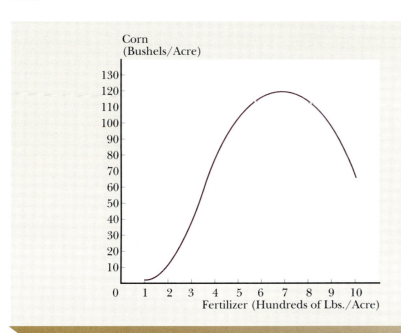

FIGURE 2A
FERTILIZER AND CORN OUTPUT
A graph is usually plotted with the dependent variable on the y-axis and the independent variable on the x-axis. Here, as the independent variable (fertilizer) increases, the dependent variable (corn output) first increases and then decreases.

Positive relationship
A relationship between two variables in which an increase in one is associated with an increase in the other and a decrease in one is associated with a decrease in the other.

Negative relationship
A relationship between two variables in which an increase in the value of one is associated with a decrease in the value of the other.

Slope
The ratio of the change in the dependent variable (*y*) to the change in the independent variable (*x*).

Figure 3A plots actual data on the rate of inflation (vertical axis) and the rate of unemployment (horizontal axis) for the United States from 1980 to 1993. In this diagram, there doesn't seem to be a consistent relationship of any kind between the rate of inflation and the rate of unemployment, at least for the years plotted. Figure 4A plots the relationship between the money supply and total output, or GDP, for the United States from 1980 to 1993. As you can see, there appears to be a more consistent relationship between these two variables.

POSITIVE AND NEGATIVE RELATIONSHIPS AND SLOPES

A graph shows how two variables are related. This relationship may be positive or negative. A **positive relationship** means that an increase in the value of the *x*-variable is associated with an increase in the value of the *y*-variable, as in Figure 4A. A **negative relationship** means that an increase in the value of the *x*-variable is associated with a decrease in the value of the *y*-variable. Some relationships in economics, such as the one between fertilizer and corn output plotted in Figure 2A, are positive for some values of the *x*-variable and negative for others.

Most of the economic relationships you will encounter in this book are represented by straight lines. A straight line can have a positive slope, as in Figure 5A, or a negative slope, as in Figure 6A. The **slope** is a measure of the steepness of the line. It is the ratio of the change in the dependent variable (*y*) to the change in the independent variable (*x*). If the slope is designated by the letter *m*, then the equation of a straight line can be written as

$$y = mx + b,$$

FIGURE 3A
INFLATION AND UNEMPLOYMENT
A scatter diagram plots the coordinates for the values of two variables that may or may not have a consistent relationship. This diagram plots the unemployment rate and the inflation rate for the United States from 1980 to 1993. It shows no consistent relationship between these two variables.

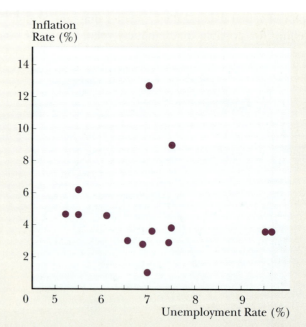

Source: Council of Economic Advisers, *Economic Report of the President* (Washington, DC: U.S. Government Printing Office, 1994).

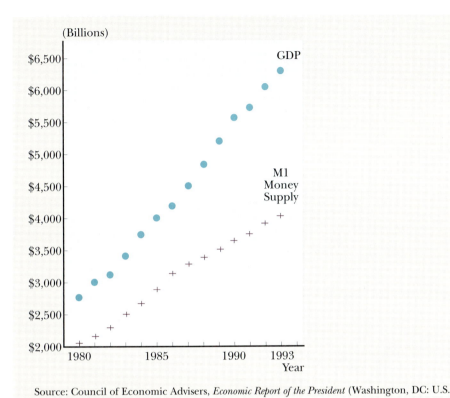

FIGURE 4A
GDP AND MONEY SUPPLY (BILLIONS OF DOLLARS)
This scatter diagram plots the money supply and the GDP for the United States from 1980 to 1993. Unlike the diagram in FIGURE 3A, this one seems to show a rather consistent relationship between the two variables.

where b is the value of y when $x = 0$. (The value b is also known as the y-intercept, because at this value the line crosses the y-axis.)

Even though both lines in Figure 5A are positively sloped, the relationship between the x-variable and the y-variable represented by line A is very different from that represented by line B. The same amount of change in x leads to a larger change in y along line B than it does along line A. In Figure 5A, the slope of line A is equal to $+\frac{1}{2}$ because the y-value changes by one unit for each two-unit change in the x-value. The slope of line B is $+\frac{5}{3}$, or $+1.67$. The steeper slope of line B indicates that a larger change in the value of y will result from a given change in the value of x than along line A. The sign of the slope is also very important. It indicates whether the relationship between the two variables is positive or negative. A slope with a positive sign designates a positive relationship. A slope with a negative sign, as in Figure 6A, indicates a negative relationship. The slope of the line in Figure 6A is $-\frac{1}{2}$.

NONLINEAR GRAPHS AND MAXIMA AND MINIMA

A straight-line graph, such as those in Figures 5A and 6A, has the same slope along the entire line. The slope of a curved line, on the other hand, varies along the curve. The slope of a curve at a particular point is the slope of the straight line tangent to the curve at that point. A **tangent line** is a straight line that touches

Tangent line
A straight line just touching a curve (nonlinear graphic relationship) at a single point. The slope of the tangent line is equal to the slope of the curve at that point.

FIGURE 5A

POSITIVELY SLOPED LINES
The slope of a line is the ratio of the change in the y-value to the change in the x-value. A line sloping upward to the right has a positive slope, indicating a positive relationship between the two variables.

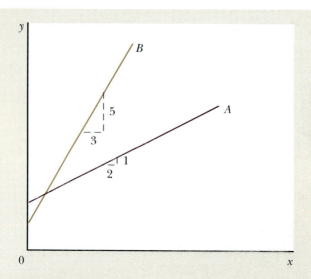

a curve at only one point without crossing it. The slope of the curved line in Figure 7A is +1 at point A and $-3/2$ at point C.

The slope of the curve in Figure 7A at point B is equal to zero. A small change in the value of x results in no change in the value of y along the straight line tangent to the curve at point B. Point B is a **maximum** because the y-variable reaches its highest value at that point. The highest value of y, y_1, is associated with an x value of x_1. Recall that we described self-interested behavior as consumers maximizing satisfaction, resource owners maximizing income, and firms maximizing profit. Being able to find the maximum is very important in economics.

FIGURE 6A

NEGATIVELY SLOPED LINE
A negative slope represents a relationship between the variables in which an increase in the value of the independent variable is associated with a decrease in the value of the dependent variable.

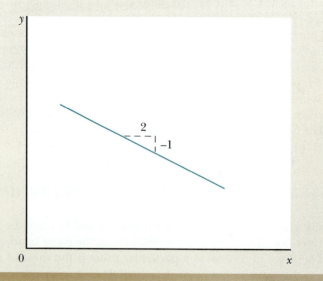

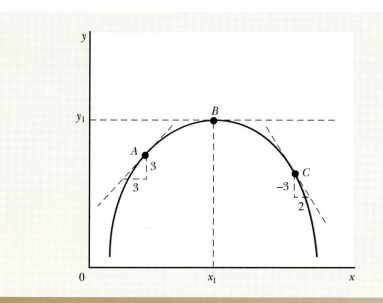

FIGURE 7A

NONLINEAR GRAPHS: SLOPE AND MAXIMUM
On a nonlinear graph, the slope changes along the curve. The slope of the curve at any point is the slope of a straight line tangent to the curved line at that point. When the slope is zero, the value of the y-variable is either at a maximum or at a minimum. At point B, y is at its maximum value, y_1, when x has the value x_1.

Sometimes a slope of zero is associated with a **minimum** rather than a maximum, as in Figure 8A. The y-variable assumes its lowest value, y_1, at point B in Figure 8A. This y-value is associated with an x-value of x_1. A firm that is trying to minimize costs, or losses, may be interested in finding a minimum point. It is also important for many kinds of economic questions to determine whether a point of zero slope is a maximum or a minimum.

Maximum
The point on a graph at which the y-variable, or dependent variable, reaches its highest value.

Minimum
The point on the graph at which the y-variable, or dependent variable, reaches it lowest value.

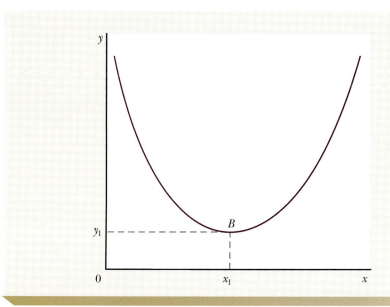

FIGURE 8A

NONLINEAR GRAPHS: MINIMUM
This nonlinear graph also has a slope of zero at point B. In this case, point B represents the minimum value of y, y_1, which is associated with an x-value of x_1.

THE 45° LINE

45° line
A line in the first quadrant, passing through the origin, with a slope of +1, which divides the quadrant in half. If the scales on the axis are the same, the value of the *x*-variable is equal to the value of the *y*-variable along the 45° line.

A geometric construction that proves very useful in economic analysis is a **45° line**. This is a straight line through the origin that divides Quadrant I into two equal sections. If both axes are measured in the same units, the values of the *x*-variable and the *y*-variable will be equal at any point on the line, and the slope will be +1. A 45° line is shown in Figure 9A. Suppose, for example, you want to know whether the value of *x* is less than, equal to, or greater than the value of *y* at point *C*. A 45° line gives you a quick answer to that question. The value of *x* is greater than the value of *y* at point *C* because point *C* lies below the 45° line.

GRAPHS WITHOUT NUMBERS

The graph in Figure 2A and the scatter diagrams in Figures 3A and 4A were constructed from sets of numbers. Other graphs in this section only give a few numerical values from which to calculate slopes. Figures 7A and 8A have no numbers on them at all. In economics, graphs of theoretical concepts often use no numbers. For example, we might theorize that there is a negative relationship between the price of any good that people consume and the quantity demanded. If price is the *y*-variable and quantity demanded the *x*-variable, a negatively sloped line such as the one in Figure 6A could represent this theoretical relationship. It doesn't matter that we don't have specific coordinates to plot. We have instead graphed an abstract idea. Many graphs in economics are of this abstract type.

On graphs without numbers, symbols are used for values, line segments, and areas. For example, Figure 10A is similar to graphs you will study in Chapter 3. The *y*-axis shows the price per loaf of bread, and the *x*-axis shows the quantity of

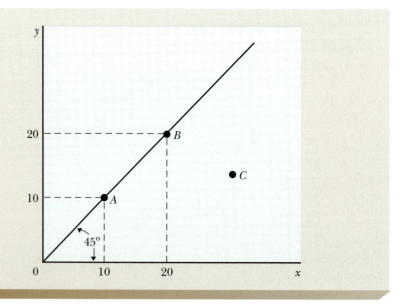

FIGURE 9A
THE 45° LINE
A 45° line drawn in the first quadrant has a slope of +1. If both axes are measured in the same units, the 45° line shows all points where the *x*-value and the *y*-value are equal.

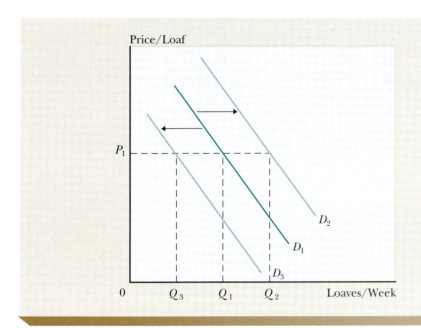

FIGURE 10A

EFFECTS OF CHANGES IN TASTES ON THE DEMAND FOR BREAD

Many graphs in economics use symbols rather than numbers on the axes. The symbol P_1 represents a hypothetical price, and Q_1, Q_2, and Q_3 represent hypothetical quantities.

loaves consumed per week. Particular prices are represented by symbols such as P_1. Quantities consumed are represented by symbols such as Q_1, Q_2, and Q_3.

In addition to using symbols to represent quantities, we will also make frequent use of the symbol delta, Δ, to represent changes in a variable. For example, the symbol ΔQ is a shorthand expression for the change from Q_1 to Q_2 in Figure 10A.

PIE CHARTS AND BAR CHARTS

All of the graphs considered so far, except for the scatter diagrams, represent theoretical relationships of one kind or another. Economists also use graphs to describe the real world. Such graphs display descriptive statistics. These include the allocation of government funds between types of programs, the growth of output or the money supply over time, and the different growth rates of imports and exports.

Two common types of descriptive graphs encountered in economics are pie charts and bar charts. **Pie charts** are used to show the division of some whole into parts, usually designated by percentages. Figure 11A is a pie chart depicting the sources of household income in 1993. Pie charts have become very popular because they are easy to create on a personal computer. This visual representation often conveys a clearer sense of the relative sizes of various components than you could obtain from reading a table of numbers.

Another popular type of descriptive graph is a **bar chart**, such as Figure 12A. This diagram describes the behavior of two variables, federal government revenue and expenditures, in a series of "snapshots" from 1983 to 1993. This graph gives a much more vivid impression of how much expenditures have grown relative to revenues than you could derive from a set of numbers.

Pie chart
A graphic representation in the shape of a pie that expresses actual economic data as parts of a whole. The sizes of the slices of the pie correspond to the percentage shares of the components.

Bar chart
A graphic representation that expresses data using columns of different heights.

FIGURE 11A

PIE CHART OF HOUSEHOLD INCOME FOR THE UNITED STATES, 1993

A pie chart depicts the division of a whole into parts (percentages). This pie chart shows that the largest component of household income is wages and salaries. Transfer payments and interest are much smaller components.

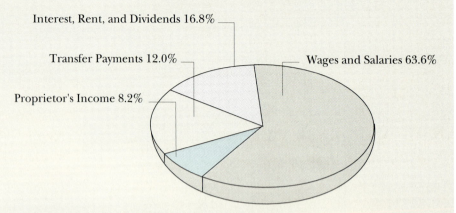

Source: Council of Economic Advisers, *Economic Report of the President* (Washington, DC: U.S. Government Printing Office, 1994).

FIGURE 12A

BAR CHART OF FEDERAL REVENUES AND EXPENDITURES, 1975–1993

A bar chart can be used in a variety of ways to present economic data in a visual fashion. This bar chart compares federal revenues and expenditures for various years.

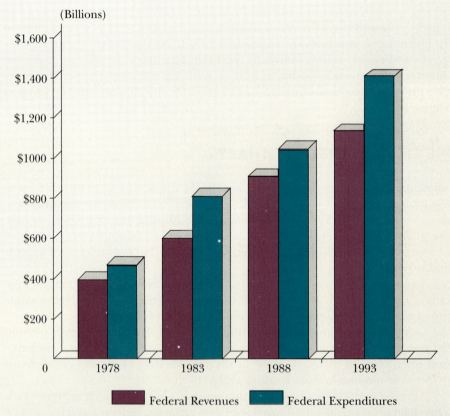

Source: Council of Economic Advisers, *Economic Report of the President* (Washington, DC: U.S. Government Printing Office, 1994).

Theoretical graphs, such as those in Figures 5A through 10A, and descriptive graphs, such as Figures 11A and 12A, are spread throughout this book. Both types are also common in textbooks in social sciences and business and in popular magazines such as *Newsweek*, *Time*, and *Business Week*. Economics is a very visual subject. Be sure that you feel secure with reading and interpreting graphs before proceeding further.

CAUTION: GRAPHS AND NUMBERS CAN MISLEAD AS WELL AS INFORM!

Graphs and statistics can be very informative. They put some concrete, real-world content into abstract models and economic relationships. However, it is very easy to present data in a misleading way. The choice of a scale along an axis can make changes look bigger than they really are. The use of averages conceals a great deal of information about variation. For example, three families with incomes of $24,000, $25,000, and $26,000 have an average income of $25,000. Three incomes of $5,000, $5,000, and $65,000 also average to $25,000. The same average income describes two very different distributions of income.

A classic guide to the use and abuse of numbers and graphs is *How to Lie with Statistics*, by Darrell Huff and Irving Geis. This book has been through numerous paperback editions since it was first published in 1954. It should be required reading for anyone taking courses in the social sciences. It is a useful guide through the pitfalls of the means, medians, averages, bar charts, surveys, samples, and growth rates that are the daily news of the economic and political worlds.

Always be very cautious in accepting someone's graphs or numbers. Consider carefully what that person may be trying to persuade you to think or do and how the statistics could be manipulated to put that position in a more favorable light.

CHAPTER 2

MARKETS, GOVERNMENTS, AND NATIONS: THE ORGANIZATION OF ECONOMIC ACTIVITY

LEARNING OBJECTIVES

1. Identify the four types of productive resources and the income paid to each for its role in producing goods and services.
2. List the three basic economic questions that must be addressed by every economic system.
3. Analyze how traditional, command, and market economies answer the three basic economic questions.
4. Use a circular flow model to show the relationships between firms and households in product markets and in resource markets in a market economy.
5. Explain and give examples of the basic economic functions of government.

Consider this... *Suppose you were hired by Boris Yeltsin to advise him on how he should organize production in Russia. What would you tell him? What things would you tell him the government should do and what things should he let markets do? What goods should the government produce or subsidize, if any? Should the Russian people be allowed to buy goods from foreign firms? How should Yeltsin decide what goods should be imported and what goods should be exported? Reform of the Russian economy appears to be very complicated. The concepts in this chapter will help you develop an understanding of the problems Yeltsin and the Russian people face.*

LIMITED RESOURCES

To examine the process of choice, we can begin by identifying the scarce resources that exist. The productive **resources** are divided into four broad categories: labor, land, capital, and enterprise. All resources used to produce goods and services fit into one of these four categories.

LABOR

Labor is the resource of production with which you are probably most familiar. **Labor** is the physical and mental work of human beings. The efforts of a factory worker, a professional basketball player, a university professor, and a carpenter are all labor.

Wages are the payments labor receives for its productive services. Some labor is valued (and paid) more than other labor. Why? One reason is that some labor is more productive. Workers are born with different talents and abilities. Some are more intelligent. Others are physically stronger or better coordinated. Still others have artistic or musical ability. It is also possible to make labor more productive by devoting money and time to improving skills. Individuals invest in their labor skills by going to college, serving as apprentices, or practicing. Economists refer to this development of labor skills as an investment in human capital. **Human capital** consists of knowledge and skills that increase labor's productivity. A large part of wage differences can be explained by differences in human capital.

LAND

The second resource is land. **Land**, to an economist, is not just rocks and soil, but all natural resources that can be used as inputs to production. By this definition, land includes minerals, water, air, forests, oil, and even rainfall, temperature, and soil quality. The income paid to this resource is called **rent**.

A key distinction between land and other productive resources is that land consists of natural resources or conditions, unimproved by any human activity. For example, acreage in Arizona that has been irrigated represents more than land. It also represents capital, the third resource. Thus, part of the payment that is called rent is a return to land, but part of it may be a return to capital.

CAPITAL

The third resource, **capital**, is defined as all aids to production that are human creations rather than resources found in nature. Capital includes tools, factories, warehouses, and inventories. You have also seen that capital can become attached to land or to labor (human capital) when investment is made in improvements or in skills and training. In common usage, real capital is often confused with financial capital. Financial capital is money lent to purchase real, physical capital. Economists reserve the term *capital* for real inputs to production, not for financial assets.

Capital, like land, receives a flow of income. The payments to capital are called **interest**. Interest is a reward for giving up present consumption in order to make resources available for the creation of more capital for future production. **Investment** is the act of adding to capital. Although the term *investment* is often used for such activities as buying stocks and bonds, to an economist the term means the creation of real, physical assets, such as machines, factories, or inventories that can be used to produce other goods and services.

ENTERPRISE

The last resource is **enterprise**, which consists of the activities of combining the productive resources to produce goods and services, taking risks, and introducing new methods and new products (innovation). Entrepreneurs combine other resources by buying or renting them to produce a saleable product. The reward for innovation, risk taking, and organization is **profit**.

Profit is the most difficult of the four productive reources to measure in practice because it is whatever is left over after paying for land, capital, and labor. Noneconomists frequently count profit as what is left after the bills are

6. Evaluate the benefits of specialization and exchange based on comparative advantage.

Resources
The inputs of land, labor, capital, and enterprise that a firm uses to produce outputs.

Labor
The physical and mental exertion that human beings put into production activities.

Wages
The return to labor, one of the productive resources.

Human capital
The investment made to improve the quality of people's labor skills through education, training, health care, and so on.

Land
Natural resources that can be used as inputs to production.

Rent
The return to land, one of the productive resources.

Capital
The durable inputs into the production process created by people. Machines, tools, and buildings are examples of capital.

33

Interest
The return to capital, one of the productive resources.

Investment
Purchase of real tangible assets, such as machines, factories, or inventories, that are used to produce goods and services.

Enterprise
The input to the production process that involves organizing, innovation, and risk taking.

Profit
The return to enterprise, one of the productive resources of production. Profit is whatever remains after all other resources have been paid.

Market A place where buyers and sellers meet to exchange goods, services, and productive resources.

paid. However, this measure is likely to overlook such opportunity costs as the value of the owner's labor (wages) or the return to the owner's capital (interest).

THE BASIC ECONOMIC QUESTIONS

The process of choosing how to allocate scarce resources can be broken down into three broad economic questions:

- *What* goods and services will be produced and in what quantities?
- *How* will they be produced? (That is, what methods of production and combinations of inputs will be used?)
- *For whom* will they be produced? (That is, who gets what share of the goods and services produced?)

Different kinds of economic systems answer these three questions in different ways. However, people in all economic systems are faced with the problem of how to allocate scarce resources among an unlimited number of wants.

The production possibilities curve introduced in Chapter 1 showed attainable levels and combinations of outputs, or the choices available. The production possibilities curve, however, does not explain how to choose among these combinations. What determines if an economy is at one particular point on the production possibilities curve instead of another, and who makes that choice?

The market provides at least a partial answer to the three basic questions in many societies. A **market** is any setting in which buyers and sellers meet to exchange goods, services, or productive resources. A market system is an economic system that relies primarily on market transactions to answer the three basic economic questions.

WHAT, HOW, AND FOR WHOM

The *what* question asks exactly what mix of goods and services is to be produced—how many tons of wheat, thousands of textbooks, hours of MTV, pairs of jeans, and gallons of milk will make up the total national output. It is a difficult enough question in the simple two-product world of the production possibilities curve. With thousands and thousands of possible combinations of outputs, the *what* question is extremely complex. In a market system, the answer to the *what* question is determined by consumers, who "vote" in the marketplace by using their dollars to obtain particular goods and services. In other economic systems, other methods are used to determine what kinds of goods and services are produced and in what amounts.

A market economy may result in choices about the output mix that some economists or policy makers find peculiar or distasteful. Many policy makers may not share the public's taste for rock videos, gambling palaces, country music, or skateboards. However, unless people's consumption of these items can be shown to be harmful to others, a market society does not pass normative judgment on tastes. Markets produce what people want to buy.

The *how* question asks what input combination will be used to produce the chosen goods and services. Should missiles be produced by combining many workers with a few units of capital or by a more capital-intensive method? Is it better to produce soybeans using lots of tractors and machinery intensely cultivating a few acres of land or using more land and workers and relatively little capital? Should college students be taught in large classes by professors (highly skilled labor) or in small sections by teaching assistants (substituting less-skilled labor)? Such questions must be answered in a systematic way. In a market system, prices guide suppliers and buyers of resources to decisions that maximize profits or minimize costs.

The *for whom* question asks who will get the goods and services produced and how much will each person receive? This is a way of asking which of many possible distributions of income will be chosen. Should the distribution be equal or unequal? Should an individual's share be based on contributions to production, on need, or on some combination of the two? A pure market system answers this question directly: a person's rewards depend on contributions to production. Other systems, including a mixed market system, use a mixture of guidelines to determine the distribution of income.

The answers to the three questions are not independent of one another. The distribution of income will determine whether there is more demand for bread and milk or luxury yachts. The production process chosen may determine the amount of each kind of output that can be produced.

TRADITION, COMMAND, AND THE MARKET

Every society has to find a way to answer the three basic economic questions. The study of the different ways of organizing economic activity, or answering these questions, is called comparative economic systems. There are many ways of classifying economic systems, such as by who owns the productive resources or by the form of government. One useful way of classifying economic systems is by the method used to answer the three basic economic questions. This classification identifies three broad types of economies: the traditional economy, the command (planned) economy, and the market economy. Of course, no economy fits neatly into any one of these categories. All economies are mixed in that they contain elements of traditional, command, and market processes.

THE TRADITIONAL ECONOMY. The **traditional economy** answers the basic economic questions by tradition, or custom. That is, the answers are determined by how the questions have been answered in the past. What is produced is whatever parents have taught their children to produce on the basis of customs developed in the past. A heavily traditional society is usually not highly sophisticated. Most of people's efforts are devoted to production of food, clothing, and shelter. Tradition determines what kinds of food are grown, what kinds of clothing are made, and what kinds of houses are built. It also determines what combination of these three is produced in any given period.

In a traditional economy, the techniques of production (how to produce) are also passed on, with little change, from one generation to the next. In many parts of Asia and Africa, the methods of building houses and of farming have been the same for many generations. These methods use simple materials, much labor, and very little capital equipment.

Traditional societies also have established answers to the distribution question (for whom). If you have studied cultural anthropology, you know that traditional societies often have rules on how to divide the spoils of the hunt or the fruits of the harvest. Medieval Europe was a highly traditional society, with

Traditional economy
An economy in which the three basic questions are answered by custom, or how things have been done in the past.

shares of crops assigned to various claimants. There were also customary duties of military service or payments to the lord of the manor. In such a traditional society, a person's claim on society's resources is determined primarily by status in the hierarchy from peasant to king.

You may recognize elements of tradition that persist even in modern industrial societies. For example, there are still many small, rural communities almost untouched by modern farming techniques. Some ethnic groups have strong traditions of sons following their fathers' occupations. Women's roles and responsibilities continue to follow tradition in many respects. For the most part, however, tradition plays a limited role in the decision-making process in modern industrial economies.

Command economy
An economy in which the three basic questions are answered through central planning and control (also called a planned economy).

THE COMMAND ECONOMY. The **command economy**, or planned economy, answers the basic economic questions through central command and control. A central planning authority makes all decisions regarding what and how to produce. Individual production units receive detailed plans and orders that carry the weight of law. The question concerning income distribution is answered in the process of determining what and how to produce. The central planners also set wage rates and levels of production. This planning process was the primary method of organization in the Soviet Union and other countries in Eastern Europe, before the recent rapid movement toward market economies. Command systems are disappearing very rapidly. North Korea and Cuba still make extensive use of central commands.

In any economy, people plan. That is, they think about the future and prepare for it. In a traditional society, people plan for a future that will be much like the past. In a command economy, the government plays the primary role in planning how to answer the production and consumption questions for society. This kind of planning is very different from the individual planning that goes on in a market economy. Decision making is highly decentralized in a market system.

Market economy
An economy in which the three basic questions are answered through the market, by relying on self-interested behavior and incentives.

THE MARKET ECONOMY. The third type of economic system is the market economy. The **market economy** relies on incentives and the self-interested behavior of individuals to direct production and consumption through market exchanges. Consumers, "voting" with their dollars, determine what is produced. The result of this market process determines what goods and services are available.

Suppliers determine how to produce. Since suppliers are self-interested and seek to maximize their profits, they tend to combine resource inputs so as to produce a good or service at the lowest possible cost. The answer to the *how* question depends on the prices of productive resources. Suppliers will use more of abundant resources because they are relatively cheap.

The goods and services are distributed to consumers who have the purchasing power to buy them. Households that have more purchasing power (because they own more valuable productive resources) receive more goods and services. The quantity and quality of the labor skills the individual sells are the most important determinants of individual income. About 75 percent of the income in the United States is wages and salaries. People with higher earnings have more "votes" in the form of dollars spent in the marketplace. Those with high-quality, scarce skills that are in great demand receive high salaries and have more influence on the output mix.

One essential condition for undirected markets to answer the basic economic questions is the institution of **property rights**. In a command economy, most property belongs to the state. There is very limited private ownership. The process of restoring private ownership and private property rights has been slow in Eastern Europe, requiring changes in the constitutions in many cases. In a market economy, however, private property and property rights play an essential role. Markets will function only if individual buyers and sellers possess the property rights to the goods and services they want to exchange.

In a market economy, productive resources are owned by individuals. Owners of capital will not invest unless they are certain that they can claim the ownership of that capital and the products that it produces. They also need to be assured that their capital and its interest will not be taken away by the state or by force or violence. Workers will not offer their labor for hire if their rights to be paid cannot be enforced or if they know their earnings are likely to be stolen. Agreements to use productive resources and to make payments for them have to be protected from violence or breach of contract. What a market system needs, then, is a legal system that defines property rights and enforces them against any violations. Defining and enforcing property rights is an important function of government even in a pure market economy.

Beyond enforcing property rights, governments undertake some amount of central planning in all economies, including that of the United States. Federal and state governments play a substantial role in determining what is produced and how it is produced. Government policy makers make decisions about highways, schools, public parks, national defense, and other goods and services produced in the public sector. Their actions also change the distribution of income through taxes and social welfare programs. However, politicians and public policy makers are not the primary decision makers in the U.S. economy or in most other modern industrial economies, such as those of Japan, Canada, Australia, and the nations of the European Community. In these countries, most decisions are made by individuals through markets.

Property rights
The legal rights to a specific piece of property, including the rights to own, buy, sell, or use in specific ways, Markets can exist and exchanges can occur only if individuals have property rights to goods, services, and productive resources.

RESPONDING TO CHANGE. One way to compare the workings of these three types of economic systems is to consider how each responds to change. Suppose an earthquake closes some copper mines, and the supply of copper is suddenly cut in half. A traditional economy would only use copper for jewelry and would probably have rules to ensure that the most respected members of the group had first use of any copper. In a command economy, government officials would determine the possible effects of the copper shortage and estimate how long it was likely to last. They would then decide which uses of copper had the highest priority and make sure that the available copper was distributed so that those uses could occur. For example, orders might be sent to firms producing electric generators to substitute some other metal for copper, in order to conserve copper for uses such as house wiring.

Contrast these processes with what occurs in a market economy. When the mines close and less copper is available, copper prices rise. Consumers of copper know immediately that the price has gone up. The high price leads consumers to search for cheaper substitutes. It also attracts a sudden flow of imported copper or scrap copper to the market. The allocation of copper might not meet the traditional economy's criterion of fairness or the command economy's priorities. However, the market response is much faster. Substitution and increased supplies occur very quickly with no need for the government to process and send information. Acquiring relevant information for decisions requires the use of scarce resources. The market system economizes on the amount of costly information needed to make production and consumption decisions.

Clearly, a market system has advantages over command and traditional economies in flexibility and capacity for dealing with change. However, the market system also has some drawbacks. Many observers criticize the distribution of income that results from the workings of the market, which can create extremes of wealth and poverty. Market systems have also been criticized for encouraging self-centered behavior at the expense of community interests.

MIXED ECONOMIES

Because of the advantages of the market system, even primarily traditional or command economies incorporate some elements of markets. Conversely, the pure market system is often modified to soften some of the harshness of pure capitalism.

The blend of tradition, command, and market-decision methods varies, but most modern industrial countries such as Canada, Japan, the United States, Australia, and some of the nations of Western Europe have mixed economies. In a **mixed economy**, the basic decision method is the market, but some economic choices are made by government. These choices are designed to modify the answers to the basic economic questions reached in the course of unregulated market activity while keeping most of the benefits of markets intact. The goal is to leave economic decisions to the market when it works well, but to intervene in the economy when the market outcome is not acceptable. On a macroeconomic level, a high rate of unemployment is an example of an unacceptable market outcome. On a microeconomic level, air pollution caused by coal-fired power plants is an example of an undesirable market outcome. In both instances, some people argue that the government should step in to correct the performance of the market and alter its results.

All noncommunist nations are properly classed as mixed economies. Increasingly, the formerly communist nations of Eastern Europe are moving in that direction as well. The mix varies significantly from country to country. Governments are much more heavily involved in the economy in Poland, Sweden, and France than in the United States and Germany. The differences in the degree of governmental involvement in economic decisions reflect variety in political systems, national values, and historical experiences. Even within economies, the division of labor between the market and the public sector changes from time to time. The movement to privatize certain activities (to shift them from the public sector to the private sector) has taken hold in the formerly communist nations of Eastern Europe as their governments sell off state-owned land and businesses to private individuals.

THE CIRCULAR FLOW OF ECONOMIC ACTIVITY

Chapter 1 discussed the use of models by economists in developing simple descriptions from which wider conclusions and inferences can be made. One model that is often used to describe a mixed economy in which the market is the

Mixed economy
An economy in which the three basic questions are answered partly by market forces and partly through government.

primary source of decisions is the **circular flow model**. This model provides an overview of the central concerns of both macroeconomics and microeconomics. The circular flow model is a visual picture of the relationships between the **resource market**, in which income is earned, and the **product market**, in which income is used to purchase goods and services.

THE TWO-SECTOR CIRCULAR FLOW MODEL

In a pure market economy, there are only two kinds of actors: households and business firms. In reality, sometimes firms and households are one and the same. Family farms fit this description, as do some family-owned grocery stores, day-care centers, and home-based accounting services. We will assume that households own all resources and firms produce all goods and services. Firms and households interact in two types of markets: the resource and product markets. As shown in Figure 1, households purchase goods and services produced by firms, creating a flow of dollars to firms in payment for these goods and services. The individual markets in which these exchanges take place, shown in the upper part of Figure 1, make up the product market. Firms buy resources from households (who own all the productive resources) in order to produce the goods and services they sell to the households. The total of the individual mar-

Circular flow model
A visual representation of the relationships between the resource market (in which income is obtained) and the product market (in which income is used to purchase goods and services).

Resource market
Set of markets in which owners of productive resources sell these to producers.

Product market
Set of markets in which goods and services produced by firms are sold.

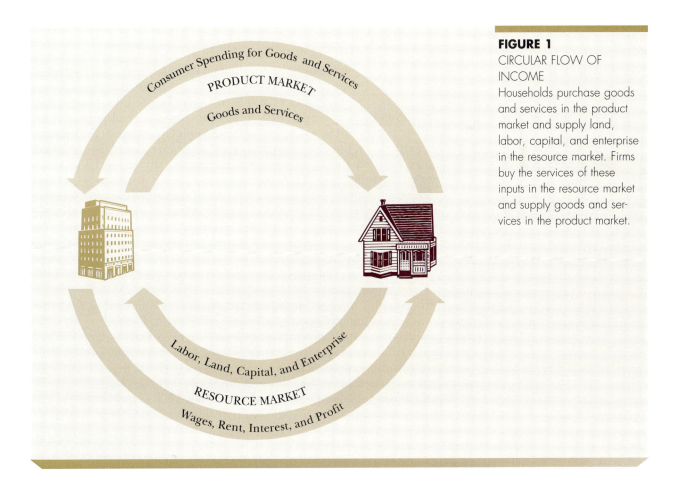

FIGURE 1
CIRCULAR FLOW OF INCOME
Households purchase goods and services in the product market and supply land, labor, capital, and enterprise in the resource market. Firms buy the services of these inputs in the resource market and supply goods and services in the product market.

kets in which these transactions take place, shown in the lower part of Figure 1, is the resources market. The flow of productive resources to firms generates a reverse flow of dollar payments (wages, rent, interest, and profits).

Recall that models are an important part of economic analysis because they permit more orderly thinking about the world. The circular flow in Figure 1 is a very simple model of the way a market economy operates. This model is a broad overview of the economy that you need to keep in mind as we proceed to look at its various specific components. We will add a few simple refinements to the model in this chapter.

Most of macroeconomics is concerned with measuring and changing the sizes of the flows of output and income, represented by the sizes of the shaded arrows in Figure 1. Most of microeconomics is devoted to a closer look at the operation of the individual markets that make up the circular flow and at the behavior of individual actors (households, firms, and governments).

THE CIRCULAR FLOW MODEL WITH SAVING, GOVERNMENT, AND INTERNATIONAL TRADE

We can make the simple circular flow model more realistic in several important ways. To keep things as simple as possible, however, we will limit the model to just the outer flow in each market. The diagrams will show the flow of income payments through the resource market to households, and the flow of purchases through the product market to the business sector.

The first adjustment to our model is to relax the assumption that the flow of income from firms to households (the lower half of Figure 1) and the flow of payments from households to firms (the upper half of Figure 1) are equal. If firms pay out all of their revenues to households and households spend every dollar they receive on purchases of goods and services, then the flows will be equal. But if households save part of their incomes, there is a leakage out of the circular flow. If firms invest (buy new capital equipment), there is an injection into the circular flow. Either an injection or a leakage can change the size of the flow. Figure 2 shows a flow of savings out of the income stream and an injection of investment spending into the income stream.

A second adjustment is to add a government sector. You know that local, state, and federal governments produce, or cause the production of, goods ranging from schools and libraries to missiles and post offices. Governments take part of household incomes in taxes—a leakage out of the spending stream. They also purchase productive inputs from households—an injection, just like investment. Government plays an important microeconomic role because its actions affect the mix of goods and services produced and the distribution of output. At the macroeconomic level, government actions affect the amount of total production, as well as unemployment and economic growth. Figure 3 shows a circular flow diagram with a government that collects taxes from households and purchases goods and services from business firms. Even this model ignores some important government transactions such as taxes on business, transfer payments to households, purchases of labor from households, and borrowing.

Finally, the simple circular flow model describes a closed economy (one that has no interaction with the rest of the world). Most nations are affected by transactions with other countries, so Figure 4 adds one final change. Households purchase imports from the foreign sector (other nations). Business firms sell exports to that sector. Imports are a leakage out of the spending stream. Why?

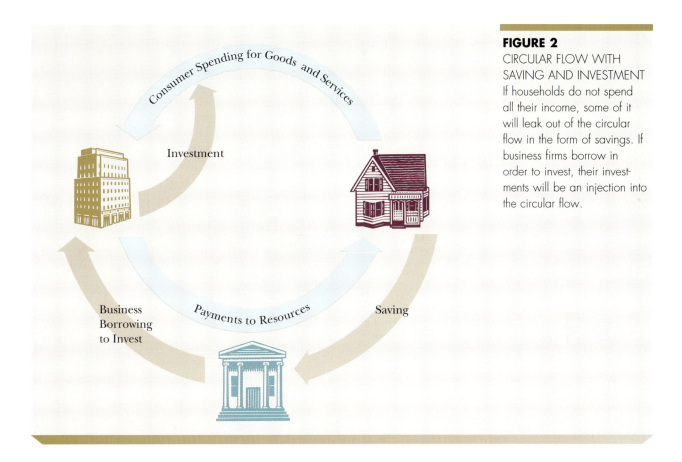

FIGURE 2

CIRCULAR FLOW WITH SAVING AND INVESTMENT If households do not spend all their income, some of it will leak out of the circular flow in the form of savings. If business firms borrow in order to invest, their investments will be an injection into the circular flow.

Income earned within the country, but spent on imports, cannot be used to purchase consumer goods from the domestic business sectors. Exports represent an injection of spending into the flow because the spending comes from outside the country. Exports often represent a large part of sales and income, especially in small countries. Imports may provide a large share of total consumption. In the United States, the ratio of exports to total output is only 12 percent. In some smaller countries, this ratio is much higher. Mexico, for example, exports about 16 percent of its output, and the Netherlands exports 49 percent of what it produces.

In the circular flow diagram, the sizes of the arrows labeled "imports" and "exports" indicate the size of the foreign sector, or the importance of consumers and suppliers in other countries. If the foreign sector is small, the economy is more like a closed economy. With a large foreign sector an economy is more likely to affect and be affected by the rest of the world. It is more vulnerable to the effects of inflation or recession in other countries. Since exports are a large share of total output, when export sales fall, the impact is felt throughout the economy.

The larger its land area, population, and total output or income, the less dependent an economy is likely to be on trade. Trade averages 20 to 40 percent of GDP across the broad range of all countries, but there is tremendous variety within this range. The ratio of exports to total output in 1994 was relatively low for such large countries as India (9 percent) and China (11 percent). Countries

FIGURE 3

CIRCULAR FLOW WITH GOVERNMENT
Government is a third actor in the circular flow model. It interacts with households and firms in collecting taxes from households and purchasing goods and services from firms. Here households have two leakages not spent on consumption. Business firms have three customers for output: households (consumption), other business firms (investment), and government.

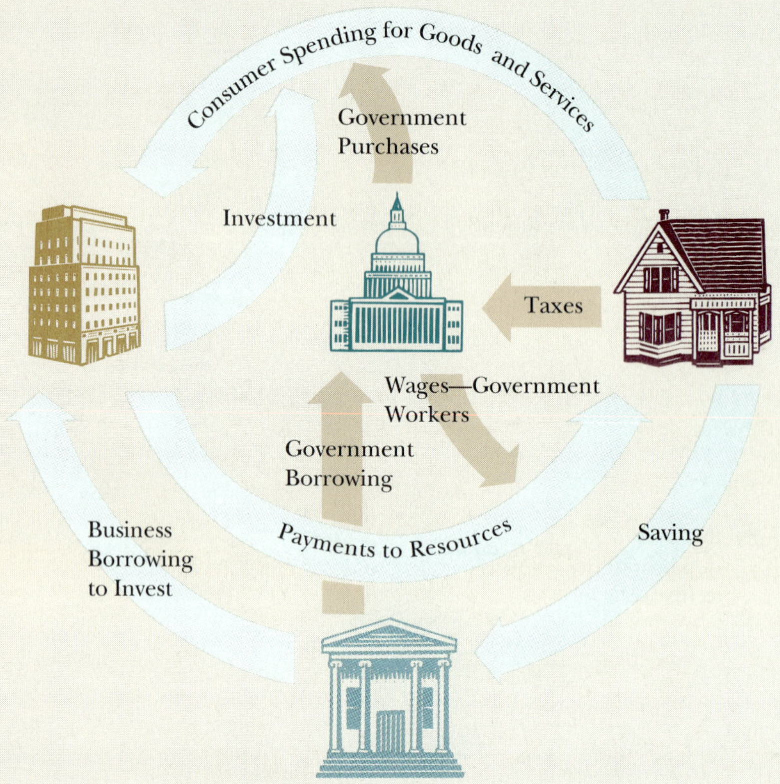

that are geographically isolated, such as Australia (17 percent), also tend to have a lower ratio of trade to total output because the cost of shipping is so high. At the other extreme, small countries that produce primary products (agricultural or mineral) often have very high ratios of trade to total output. The small oil-producing nation of Bahrain exports 92 percent of its total output. The tiny duchy of Luxembourg exports 72 percent of what it produces. The Caribbean nation of Jamaica, whose revenues derive from tourism, exports 62 percent of its total output.

The share of trade in total output is an indicator of how dependent on other nations a nation is. The higher the trade ratio, the more sensitive a country is to events in foreign markets and the more dependent it is on foreign sources of supply. The benefits of trade are substantial, but one of the opportunity costs of this interdependence is less control for policy makers over their own economic destiny.

The government sector and the foreign sector are two very important additions to the circular flow model. The government is what makes the economy a mixed economy, where some decisions are made outside the market. The foreign sector makes the economy an open rather than a closed one. Actions by the three inside actors (households, businesses, and government) will have very different effects from what would occur in a closed economy. We will consider each of these sectors in turn.

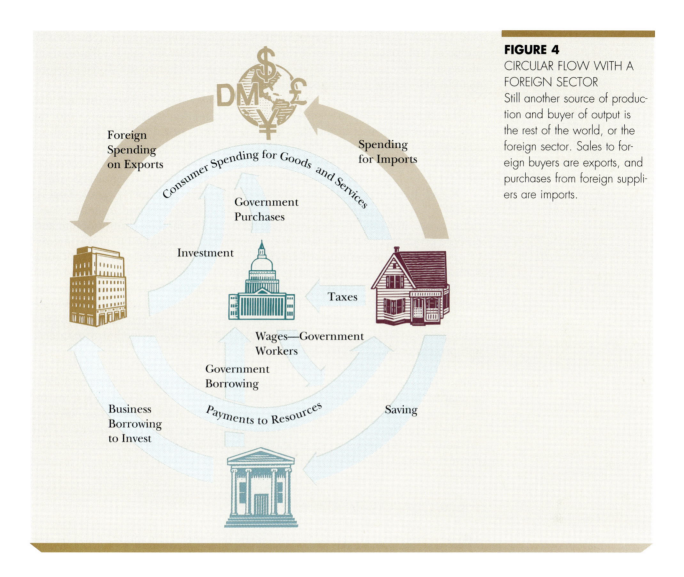

FIGURE 4

CIRCULAR FLOW WITH A FOREIGN SECTOR
Still another source of production and buyer of output is the rest of the world, or the foreign sector. Sales to foreign buyers are exports, and purchases from foreign suppliers are imports.

THE ECONOMIC ROLE OF GOVERNMENT

All markets work in basically the same way in any economy. Supply and demand determine prices and quantities. In some economies or for some kinds of exchanges, however, the market may not be allowed to perform this function. Then some other decision-making process must be used to answer the three basic economic questions.

The most common method other than the market is to allow choices concerning the use of resources to be made by politicians or other agents of government. The kinds of decisions made through governments and the kinds made through the private sector vary among nations. In the United States, health care has been largely private, with government intervention for the elderly and the poor through Medicare and Medicaid. In Canada, it is publicly financed but privately provided. In most European countries, health care is both paid for and provided by government. Some governments (such as Sweden's) use taxes and social welfare programs to greatly modify the market distribution of income. Others (such as Japan's) do very little to change the distribution of income that results from market decisions.

In the United States, the preference is to make most decisions through the market. However, there are some things that the market cannot do or cannot do well. Many economists argue that the market does not do a very good job of addressing such problems as poverty, pollution, inflation, unemployment, and the market power of large firms. It is also difficult for private markets to provide enough of such goods and services as defense, education, and sewer systems.

Recall that a market system requires clearly defined property rights. That is, someone has to decide who owns what goods and services and to define their rights to use and trade those goods and services. The market cannot define and enforce property rights very well, so this role is usually assigned to governments. Citizens in most modern mixed economies cannot legally drive a car without a license, park in a handicapped space without a sticker, or build a fast-food restaurant in a neighborhood zoned residential. These rules represent government restrictions on property rights. An unrestricted market would allow people to do all of these things, whether or not they were considered desirable by the majority. Even in a pure market economy, government is needed to establish and protect property rights.

The activities of government are grouped into three categories: allocation, redistribution, and stabilization. Stabilization and redistribution are conducted primarily through governments in all economic systems. Allocation is a microeconomic activity that is shared by the government and the market to different extents in different systems. Much of the dispute over what government should or should not do relates to its allocation activities. Also, much of the difference between market and command economies involves how allocation is divided between the market and the agencies of government.

THE ALLOCATION FUNCTION

Allocation
Any activities by government or its agents that affect the distribution of resources and the combination of goods and services produced.

Allocation refers to any government activity that affects the quantity and quality of goods and services produced (that is, anything that affects the answer to the *what* question). Allocation activities in a market-based mixed economy may include producing public education, subsidizing higher education, taxing cigarettes, regulating factory and auto emissions, setting safety standards for cars, placing quotas on steel imports, building highways, and setting prices for electric power produced by private firms. In a command economy, the array of government allocation activities is much broader. Some, maybe even most, allocation activities also affect the answer to the *for whom* question because they increase the incomes of some firms and individuals at the expense of others.

Public goods
Goods that are nonrival in consumption and not subject to exclusion.

PUBLIC GOODS AND POSITIVE EXTERNALITIES. In mixed economies, allocation activities are usually assigned to the public sector only when the good or service is considered a public good or when its production or consumption creates substantial external effects. We will explore each of these criteria in turn.

Economists define **public goods** as those goods that are nonrival in consumption and not subject to exclusion. What do these technical phrases mean? *Nonrival* means that a good or service is not used up in consumption. Sunsets and lighthouses are both nonrival in consumption. The fact that you are watching a sunset leaves no less sunset for someone else to enjoy. Sunsets and light-

GLOBAL OUTLOOK: PRIVATIZATION IN GREAT BRITAIN

The division of economic activity between public and private spheres in a mixed economy is not fixed. In wartime, the share of economic activity commanded by government increases. Also, when there are changes in citizens' preferences or political philosophy, government's share of total dollars spent may rise or fall in response. For most Western economies, there has been a gradual upward trend in the share of government spending in total GDP and the share of personal income paid in taxes. In the last decade, however, several mixed economies have tried to reverse that trend and reduce the share of economic activity controlled by government. In particular, there has been a move to spin off some allocation activities of government to the private sector. This change is called **privatization**. In Eastern Europe, a large part of the transition away from communism has consisted of shifting activities from government to the private sector.

Privatization has been strongly advocated in a number of countries. Nowhere was it pushed as far as in Britain under Prime Minister Margaret Thatcher. There the public sector was cut 40 percent in the 1980s. This privatization effort in Britain was stronger than in the United States under President Reagan, in part because there had been more government involvement in economic activity in Britain.

Privatization can mean a variety of things. It may mean that the government continues to provide a service—for example, garbage collection—but is no longer the producer of that service. Instead, the government collects taxes to pay for the service but contracts with a private firm to actually perform it. Alternatively, the government may get out of the business of providing a service altogether. It will either leave provision completely to the private market or limit its role to subsidizing some buyers or producers. For example, instead of owning public housing, the government could meet the housing needs of the poor by providing housing vouchers to allow them to pay for housing and letting the private market respond by producing and managing the housing units. In Britain, a large amount of housing, called council housing, was owned and managed by the local public sector. One big privatization effort in the 1980s was to sell that housing to its occupants. A result of this policy was that, as owners, people have had a stronger vested interest in the maintenance and upkeep of their property.

Much of what was first privatized in Britain is traditionally in the private sector in other market economies. Companies made private included British Steel, British Airways, Rolls-Royce, and Jaguar. (Jaguar was later purchased by Ford Motor Company.) When these companies were privatized, the government issued shares of stock sold to the public, creating private ownership while raising revenue for the public treasury. It was hoped that private, profit-minded managers would be more efficient, lowering costs and prices and increasing output and exports. However, the British government met resistance in trying to privatize such traditionally public services as water, electricity, and roads. The privatization movement has been an important episode in the continuing search for balance between the public and private sectors.

---

houses are also hard to subject to exclusion. *Exclusion* means that nonpayers, or free riders, can be kept from consuming the good. **Free riders** are people or business firms who consume public goods without contributing to the cost of their production. In addition to sunsets and lighthouses, national defense and mosquito spraying are examples of services for which it is very difficult, or at least expensive, to exclude free riders. Because nonpayers cannot easily be excluded, there is not much incentive for a self-interested private firm to produce such goods.

Some economists extend the term *public goods* to include goods with weak rivalry or high costs of exclusion. Examples of such nearly public goods include fire fighting, education, and highways. In all these cases, benefits spill over to nonpayers. These spillover benefits to third parties are called **positive externalities**. Where there are such positive effects, the private market may not produce enough of the good or service because some who benefit can free-ride. Note that this broader group of nearly public goods can imply an expanded role for

Free riders
People or business firms who consume collective goods without contributing to the cost of their production.

Positive externalities
Spillover benefits to third parties (free riders) that result from production or consumption of certain goods.

government. In fact, all of the services mentioned have at some point been produced in the private sector. Volunteer fire departments in some rural areas still will not put out fires in nonsubscribers' homes. Education through the twelfth grade is produced in both the public and the private sector. Private toll roads were the earliest form of highways in New England, and toll bridges still exist today.

Be sure to keep in mind that the concept of public goods is different from the goods that are publicly provided. Local and state governments, and the federal government may supply goods that aren't public goods as we have defined them here. Golf courses and tennis courts are two good examples. Politicians will take action to supply goods to voters if they think this will enhance their electability. These goods, though publicly provided, could be purely private goods. It is also important to note that some goods might be called public, although they are decidedly private. Public television and public radio are good examples. They refer to themselves as public, but almost all their funds come from private donations. There may be small public subsidies, but private fundraising efforts pay for public television.

Negative externalities
Harmful spillovers to third parties that result from production or consumption of certain goods.

Public bads
Negative external effects of production or consumption that impact a large number of individuals—for example, acid rain.

NEGATIVE EXTERNALITIES. When people or firms consume certain goods or engage in certain activities, they pass some of the costs of production or consumption along to others. These costs are **negative externalities**. Those who create noise, litter, hazards, and pollution do not bear the full cost. If the negative externalities are strong enough and widespread enough, they may constitute **public bads**. These are negative effects that impact on everyone to some degree. Public bads are the polar opposite of public goods and include such broad negative effects as global warming, depletion of the ozone layer, and extinction of endangered species. Critics of the pure free market argue that many negative externalities and public bads are produced if all decisions are left to private markets and individuals. Many of the regulatory activities first undertaken in the 1960s and 1970s in the United States were intended to reduce such effects.

THE SCOPE OF ALLOCATION BY GOVERNMENT. Most economists agree that the government does have some responsibility to produce public goods, to encourage the production of goods with positive externalities, and to discourage the production of negative externalities and public bads. But the lines are drawn differently by different individuals within any nation. They are certainly drawn very differently in different countries. How big do spillovers have to be before government gets involved? Does the government itself have to produce public goods, or can their production be contracted out to the private sector or encouraged through subsidies? Do negative externalities have to be addressed by prohibitions or standards, or can taxes and fines do the job? An individual's, or a nation's, answers to these questions will reflect certain underlying values, and ideas about the relative importance of efficiency, equity, and freedom. The answers to these questions also delineate the lines of controversy in almost all debates about public policy.

Figure 5 shows a spectrum from public bads through goods with negative externalities to private goods and then to goods with positive externalities, ending with public goods. In almost all economies, it is agreed that the two ends of the spectrum call for government intervention to promote public goods and deter public bads. It is also fairly generally agreed that the market works best in the middle of the spectrum, producing and distributing private goods and nearly private

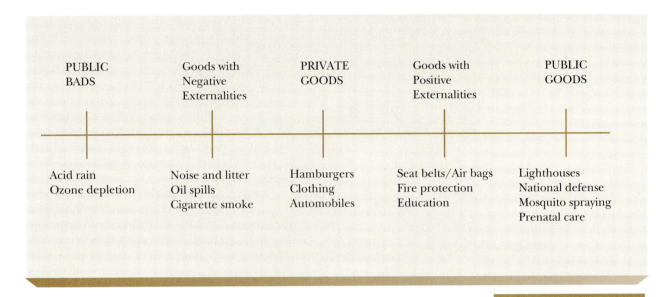

FIGURE 5
PUBLIC GOODS, PRIVATE GOODS, AND PUBLIC BADS
Goods and services fit on a spectrum from pure public goods such as defense through weak public goods, to private goods, and then to goods that cause negative external effects to some parties. At the far end of the spectrum are activities that cause widespread harm, public bads.

goods. Nations disagree on where to draw the lines on either side of the middle, dividing the private from the public sphere.

In the United States, there is another division of responsibility, because the United States has a federal system of government. A federal system has another layer of government (besides the national level) with independent responsibility. In the United States, a large part of allocation by government occurs at the state and local levels. Some public goods are provided on a national scale—defense, for example. But many are provided at the community level. Different cities and towns choose different combinations of public services. One city may choose more street lights and snow removal. Another may vote for public parks and better roads. Allowing this kind of variety in local choices makes governments more responsive to the values and desires of the people who are paying the bills. This diversity is an attractive feature of fiscal federalism, a system in which the economic responsibilities of government are not concentrated at a single level but dispersed among several levels. The United States, Canada, Germany, and Australia are examples of countries in which governments at the state or province level have notable power and responsibility. Economists find a federal system attractive because the autonomous lower levels of governments are in competition for residents and business firms. This competition creates diversity and choice, and perhaps greater efficiency.

THE REDISTRIBUTION FUNCTION

The distribution of income in a market economy is based on each person's contributions to production. There is no denying that the distribution of income determined by the market is quite unequal. Some people are very wealthy, and others are very poor. One way in which economies differ greatly is the extent to which the political process is involved in redistribution. **Redistribution** means taking income from one group and giving it to another through taxes and transfer payments.

Redistribution
Actions by government that transfer income from one group to another.

In any economy, when the government taxes individuals with high incomes, they have less incentive to work, save, and invest to increase output in future years. On the other hand, some individuals cannot earn an income through the market. They may be too old, too young, too sick, or too handicapped. Others work as hard as they can with the skills and resources at their disposal but still cannot earn enough to get by. There is some private redistribution, but private charity is subject to a free rider problem. (Many people will not contribute because they know others will.) Such free-riding behavior makes income redistribution more or less a public good that falls within the domain of government.

How much income should be redistributed? To whom should it go? How can redistribution be managed to minimize the negative effects on work incentives? These are difficult questions to answer. As a result, the answers are very different in different countries. In general, there is more redistribution and greater equality of income in countries at the middle of the mixed economy spectrum than in countries at either the command or the market extreme.

An obvious way to redistribute income is to use taxes and transfer payments. In the United States, transfer payments are streams of income that are received by individuals without any work being done and take the form of Social Security benefits, food stamps, and welfare payments. Taxes that collect relatively more from the rich than the poor, such as the U.S. federal income tax, mean that the rich pay more than the poor do for the same level of public services. This difference is a form of redistribution. In the United States, transfer payments are primarily financed by the federal government rather than state governments. The states do administer the programs and pay part of the cost. Redistributing income at the federal level makes it possible to reduce inequality between rich and poor states, as well as between rich and poor individuals within states.

Transfer payments are the most visible form of income redistribution. However, there is a redistributive side to almost everything the government does. If increased funds are spent on public education, families with school-aged children benefit more than childless households. Increased spending on health care benefits those who are sick. Quotas on steel imports benefit steelworkers but not steel users. Expanded student loan programs help college-aged people who qualify at the expense of all other taxpayers and would-be borrowers. Since it is virtually impossible for the government to spend money on anything without redistributing income, it is difficult to measure how much redistribution takes place.

Indirect kinds of income redistribution often benefit those who are not poor, that is, the middle class or the rich. Income redistribution through taxes and transfer payments is often criticized because of its effect on incentives. However, other government programs are equally vulnerable to criticism as "welfare for the rich." Examples are subsidies for large farms, tax loopholes for real estate owners and developers and oil and gas producers, bailouts for savings and loan institutions, and cost overruns by large defense contractors. This kind of redistribution is a consequence of democracy, where the rich and the middle class have more political clout than the poor. In any economy, however, how much redistribution is enough, from whom it should come, and to whom it should go are very difficult policy questions.

THE STABILIZATION FUNCTION

The last and most recently developed task of government is stabilization. **Stabilization** refers to government policy actions to reduce changes in output, employment, and prices. Until recently, many people believed that stabilization problems were unique to market economies, which tend to go through severe ups and downs in output, employment, and prices. It is now clear, however, that unemployment and inflation were problems for the command economies of Eastern Europe as well.

Stabilization is mainly a macroeconomic function. However, the ways in which stabilization policies are carried out also affect the mix of goods produced (allocation) and the distribution of costs and benefits (redistribution). Government attempts to stabilize the economy consist of increasing spending or cutting taxes to increase output and employment, or cutting spending and increasing taxes to control inflation. In addition, changes in the money supply are used to expand or contract economic activity.

Economists disagree about how stable a market economy would be if it were left alone. Historically, in the U.S. economy (and most market economies) there have been periods of high unemployment combined with low inflation, or occasionally even deflation (falling price level). These downturns have alternated with periods of more rapid inflation (increasing price level) and lower unemployment in a cyclical pattern. Such cycles have been less severe since World War II.

Stabilization
Actions by the government to reduce changes in output, employment, and prices.

THE ROLE OF THE FOREIGN SECTOR

The last of the four sectors is the foreign sector. All nations engage in trade with other nations to some extent, because there are goods and services they cannot produce for themselves or can produce only at a very high cost. In most nations, there is also some inflow and outflow of the productive resources—labor, capital, land, and enterprise. Some nations, including the United States, allow goods and resources to flow relatively freely. Others, especially China, Japan, and the Soviet Union, restrict the movement of one or both with tariffs, quotas, immigration restrictions, capital controls, and exchange controls.

BENEFITS AND COSTS OF INTERNATIONAL TRADE

In general, a nation benefits from trade in both goods and resources. Trade enables households to consume goods that are not produced domestically or would be much more costly to produce there. Trade enables firms to produce for larger markets, often lowering their average costs of production. Trade also forces firms to respond to competitors in other countries that are producing products that are cheaper, more appealing, or safer. A flow of labor or capital may help a country overcome its shortages in certain resources.

Those who work for or own firms whose products compete with imports, as well as workers who compete directly with immigrant workers, may not have a positive attitude toward such trade. These groups are likely to lobby for tariffs and other forms of protection in order to shield themselves from the effects of foreign competition. In addition, an economy that depends on international trade to market its products, or supply needed goods and services, will be affected by the actions of other countries. Interdependence with other countries reduces the amount of control that the government can exert over domestic economic activities.

For a nation as a whole, however, there are substantial gains from trade with other nations. Let's explore one of the main benefits of such trade, the gains that result from specializing on the basis of comparative advantage.

SPECIALIZATION AND COMPARATIVE ADVANTAGE

A major benefit of international trade is that it permits a nation to go beyond its production possibilities curve without acquiring more resources or improving technology. A nation can attain larger combinations of output through specialization and exchange. **Specialization**, or the division of labor, means that individuals will produce more than they intend to consume of one or only a few items and will trade the excess for other things they want.

Specialization allows individuals to take the fullest advantage of their unique talents and skills. Some people who are strong and agile can become professional athletes. Some people who are intelligent and gifted talkers can become lawyers. Specialization allows individuals to concentrate on what they do best and to produce more than they could if they tried to engage in a variety of production activities. For people with very valuable specialized skills, such as basketball stars or brain surgeons, the opportunity cost of using their time for other purposes is very high. Think about the value of the time brain surgeons spend in cooking their own dinner or mowing their lawn!

Nations, states, and regions also specialize. The phrase *banana republic* used to refer to small Central American countries that were heavily specialized in producing bananas for export. These countries used the earnings from bananas to import and consume a wide variety of products that they did not produce. Other small countries are highly specialized in oil, coffee, cocoa, sugar, and other agri-

Specialization
Limiting production activities to one or a few goods and services that one produces best in order to exchange for other goods.

POLICY FOCUS: THE PROBLEM WITH LEVEL PLAYING FIELDS

The one policy issue that almost all economists agree on is the benefit of free trade because of the principle of comparative advantage. In a poll, 97 percent of American economists agreed that impediments to free trade reduce the welfare of the United States.[a] Yet free trade is not a politically popular position. Many politicians propose the extension of free trade agreements to foreign countries. Most recently the North American Free Trade Agreement, which will dramatically increase international trade between the United States, Mexico, and Canada, was a battleground. The treaty was negotiated during the Bush Administration and narrowly passed in 1993 with support from President Clinton. The agreement was being attacked by Ross Perot on the grounds that American jobs will be lost to low-paid, low-skilled Mexican workers.

The arguments against free trade are usually couched in terms of wanting all people in all countries to be on "a level playing field." This is a lofty goal and one that, in at least one political sense, is impossible to argue against.

There are several policy problems with the concept of a level playing field. First, the political problem. When trade takes place, some people (the ones who would have had the business in the absence of international trade) in both countries are hurt. But as we saw, the aggregate benefits exceed the costs. The level playing field argument is a political effort by those who would be damaged by international trade to get government protection. For example, the United Auto Workers wanting governmental protection from foreign autos. Second, you should also keep in mind that there is no such thing as a level playing field. Mexico may have cheap labor, but the United States is rich in natural resources. Finally, the most important point about the level playing field argument is that our theory tells us that even if the fields *aren't* level, both countries gain from specialization and trade. And 97 percent of all economists *agree* on this issue.

Perhaps we shouldn't allow sports analogies in public policy debates!

a. J.R. Kearl, C.L. Pope, G.T. Whiting, and L.T. Wimmer, "A Confusion of Economists," *American Economic Review* (May 1979).

cultural products and raw materials. Within the United States, pineapples come from Hawaii, oranges from Florida and California, wheat from the midwest and plains states, and peaches from Georgia and South Carolina. Nations, states, and regions also specialize in certain types of goods and services. Japan is famous for small cars and electronic products, Switzerland for watches and banking, and France and Italy for wines.

By specializing, individuals, regions, and nations can produce more total output with no increase in resources or breakthroughs in technology. Thus, specialization improves a nation's standard of living and lets it move outside the production possibilities curve. Small countries especially can consume more goods and enjoy a wider range of goods and services through specialization and trade than if they were limited to what they produced. This point was strongly emphasized by the founder of modern economics, Adam Smith. In his 1776 classic *The Wealth of Nations*, he saw specialization and trade as the engine of growth.

SPECIALIZATION AND EXCHANGE. The benefits of specializing require that people or nations engage in exchange. If you choose to specialize, you will have to engage in trade because you will give up producing all the other goods and services you need. If you are concentrating on what you do well, you don't have time to spend cutting your own hair, growing your own vegetables, or repairing your own car. You certainly don't have time to build your house or manufacture your car! One thing that distinguishes modern industrial societies from developing countries is the extent of specialization and exchange. The average American produces very little of what he or she consumes. Instead, individuals specialize in one or two products or services and purchase everything else in the market.

COMPARATIVE ADVANTAGE. How do individuals, regions, or nations decide what products to produce for exchange? How do they answer the question "In what should we specialize?" Sometimes the answer is obvious, determined by climate or other resources. In general, the answer lies in the **principle of comparative advantage**. This principle states that each person, group, or country should specialize in that product or service for which the opportunity cost of production is lowest. If that principle is followed, the total output of a group of people, an entire economy, or, for that matter, the entire world will be maximized. Higher total output will result, with no increase in resources or improvement in technology.

Figure 6 illustrates comparative advantage using two straight-line production possibilities curves. Both George and Karen can produce various combinations of cookies and hamburgers with their available resources, as the curves illustrate. Before specializing, Karen is producing 30 hamburgers and 10 dozen cookies a month for her own consumption (point A in Figure 6). George is producing 10 hamburgers a month and 40 dozen cookies for himself (point R in Figure 6). Karen, who has had some experience working in a fast-food restaurant, is better at making hamburgers. Each hamburger she makes requires that she give up production of only $\frac{1}{2}$ dozen cookies. George's hamburgers cost him 2 dozen cookies per hamburger produced. Karen has a lower opportunity cost for hamburgers, which means that George must have a lower opportunity cost for cookies. Clearly, they should specialize.

If they decide to specialize, Karen will produce 50 hamburgers (point B in Figure 6). George will turn out 60 dozen cookies (point S). Total output in-

Principle of comparative advantage
The idea that output will be maximized if people specialize in producing those goods or services for which their opportunity costs are lowest and engage in exchange to obtain other things they want.

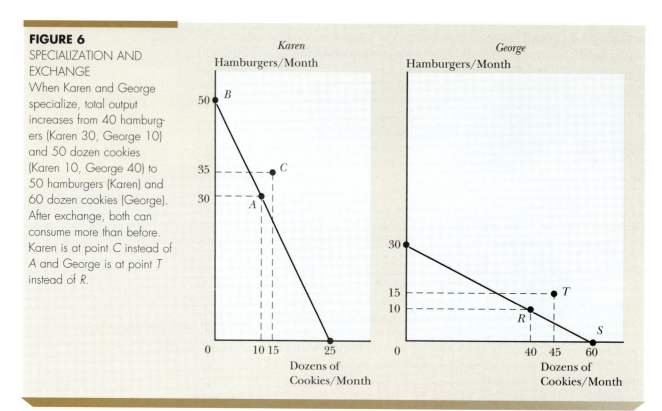

FIGURE 6

SPECIALIZATION AND EXCHANGE

When Karen and George specialize, total output increases from 40 hamburgers (Karen 30, George 10) and 50 dozen cookies (Karen 10, George 40) to 50 hamburgers (Karen) and 60 dozen cookies (George). After exchange, both can consume more than before. Karen is at point C instead of A and George is at point T instead of R.

creases by 10 hamburgers and 10 dozen cookies. All that remains is to divide up the gains. One combination that makes both better off is to split the increase equally. Thus, Karen consumes at point C in Figure 6 and enjoys 35 hamburgers and 15 dozen cookies. George consumes at point T, with 15 hamburgers and 45 dozen cookies. Both have gained because they are consuming more than before. There is more total output with no new resources and no improvement in technology.

The principle of comparative advantage means that both trading partners gain when individuals and nations specialize in the products for which their opportunity cost is lower and trade for what others produce more efficiently. Comparative advantage is the basis of all trade, not just international trade. We will return to comparative advantage in great detail in the chapter on international trade.

Consider again... *You are now on the plane on your way to Moscow to meet with Yeltsin. You have a better understanding of the problems he faces. Trying to reform a previously planned economy that did not engage in international specialization and exchange is not an easy task. It is clear that the Russian people will not adopt a pure market economy, but how much government planning should they retain in their system? Perhaps it is better to ask Yeltsin how much market he wants* *to introduce and how fast. Perhaps when you land you can explain the principle of comparative advantage to the workers who will lose their jobs if the Russian state permits free trade.*

SUMMARY

1. Productive resources consist of labor, land, capital, and enterprise. Labor receives wages, land receives rent, capital receives interest, and enterprise receives profit.
2. Every economy must address three basic economic questions: what to produce, how to produce it, and for whom to produce.
3. The traditional economy answers the basic economic questions by tradition, or custom. In a command economy, a central planning authority makes all decisions regarding what and how to produce. The market economy relies on incentives and the self-interested behavior of individuals to direct production and consumption through market exchanges. Consumers vote with their dollars, and determine what is produced. In different degrees, industrial nations have tried to answer the basic economic questions by using a mixed economy, where the market is the primary method, but with government officials often intervening in the marketplace in an attempt to improve economic performance.
4. The circular flow model is a useful overview of the relations among resources and products in a market economy. The basic model shows the interactions of households and businesses in the resource and product markets. More realistic versions add saving and investment, government, and a foreign sector.
5. There are some necessary functions that the market cannot perform or cannot perform well. These include defining and protecting property rights, providing public goods and correcting for external effects, bringing about a more equal distribution of income, and stabilization. Allocation by government includes not only the production of public goods and the reduction of public bads, but also any activities that affect private decisions about production and consumption. These activities include taxes, subsidies, and regulation. Different societies make different choices about how much allocation is carried out by government. Redistribution changes the unequal distribution of income that results from the market. Redistribution occurs mainly through taxes and transfer payments, but any action of government will have redistributive effects. Stabilization refers to the activities of government aimed at creating full employment, stable prices, and a satisfactory rate of economic growth. These actions include changes in taxes, transfer payments, and spending as well as changes in size of the money supply.
6. International trade in goods, services, and resources benefits both trading partners. Some workers and firms in a nation experience losses because of foreign competition. The gains usually exceed the losses, but the losers may succeed in persuading the government to restrict trade for their protection. Individuals and nations can gain a higher standard of living with the same resources and technology if they engage in specialization and exchange. Total output will be larger if individuals, regions, and nations produce those goods for which their opportunity costs are lowest and trade for other things. This is the principle of comparative advantage.

NEW TERMS

resources
labor
wages
human capital
land
rent
capital
interest

investment
enterprise
profit
market
traditional economy
command economy
market economy
property rights

mixed economy
circular flow model
resource market
product market
allocation
public goods
free riders
positive externalities

negative externalities
public bads
redistribution
stabilization
specialization
principle of comparative advantage

QUESTIONS: REVIEW, APPLICATIONS, AND POLICY

REVIEW

1. Is your college education an investment in human capital? What is the opportunity cost of your degree?
2. How are macroeconomic problems handled in a mixed economy?
3. In what ways are resource markets and product markets similar? In what ways are they different?
4. List all the leakages and all the injections you have observed in circular flow diagrams.
5. Which of the following institutions or actions represent tradition, command, or market processes?
   a. the military draft
   b. the volunteer army
   c. encouraging daughters to be teachers and nurses
   d. requiring women to be teachers and nurses
   e. offering financial incentives to anyone who becomes a teacher or nurse
   f. five generations of farmers tilling the same land
   g. prohibiting the sale of marijuana
   h. taxing the sale of alcoholic beverages
6. Classify each of the following government actions as primarily allocation, redistribution, or stabilization.
   a. cutting taxes to end a recession
   b. making Social Security payments to the elderly
   c. paying farmers not to produce corn
   d. putting restrictions on the amount of sulphur dioxide factories are allowed to emit into the air
   e. buying paper shredders for government offices

APPLICATIONS

7. Why is specialization necessary for exchange, and vice versa?
8. Angela and Arthur have been assigned the tasks of filing folders and grading papers. Angela can file 50 folders an hour and grade 20 papers. Arthur can file 25 folders per hour and grade 25 papers. The total output for these two work-study students is to grade 100 papers and file 200 folders. How long will it take if they divide the task equally? How long will it take if they specialize based on the principle of comparative advantage? How much time do they gain?
9. In Question 8, what is Angela's opportunity cost for filing in terms of grading not done? What is Arthur's? How does this information help you to determine comparative advantage?
10. Use the following information on the production of bushels of peaches and tomatoes in two countries, Upland and Downland. Plot a pair of production possibilities curves like those in Figure 6. Before trade, each country is producing 20 bushels of peaches and 30 bushels of tomatoes. Locate their initial production combinations on the graphs. Determine who should specialize in what, locate the production points after specialization, and determine how much the total output will increase.

UPLAND		DOWNLAND	
PEACHES	TOMATOES	PEACHES	TOMATOES
40	0	50	0
30	15	40	10
20	30	30	20
10	45	20	30
0	60	10	40
		0	50

11. Suppose you own a farm with buildings and machinery, all five members of your family work on the farm, and you take the risks and manage the production. Identify all the productive resources involved and classify them correctly.

POLICY

12. What should be the role of government in providing education? Should it produce, subsidize, or get out of education altogether? Why do you suppose that education through the twelfth grade is "free" (actually, paid for through taxes) but only subsidized beyond that level? Does it have anything to do with who gets the benefits?
13. Can you find examples of services produced in the public sector in your area that are produced in the private sector elsewhere, or vice versa? Can you explain why the choice might not be the same in different sections of the country or in communities of different sizes?
14. Where would you put each of the following items on the spectrum in Figure 5?
    a. hospital wastes that wash up on beaches
    b. noise from a student apartment complex that bothers the neighbors
    c. highways
    d. Christmas decorations that make a house more attractive
    e. flu shots
    Would you expect any of these items to be produced by government as opposed to being public goods? Why?

15. Individuals as well as nations have comparative advantages, which can change. How will going to college and getting a degree change your comparative advantage? Based on your answer, should government

SUGGESTIONS FOR FURTHER READING

Boaz, David, and Edward H. Crane. *Market Liberalism.* Washington DC: Cato Institute, 1993. A collection that calls for less federal involvement in the U.S. economy. Paired with the Schmookler book, you can explore opposite polar ends of the market government debate.

Carson, Robert B. *Economic Issues Today: Alternative Approaches,* 5e. New York: St. Martin's, 1991. The introduction gives an overview of alternative values and approaches underlying different economic systems.

Radford, R. A. "The Economic Organization of a P.O.W. Camp." *Economica* (November 1945): 189–201. This classic article demonstrates how a market economy quickly established itself in a P.O.W. camp during World War II and highlights the gains from exchange.

Schmookler, Andrew Bard. *The Illusion of Choice: How the Market Economy Shapes our Destiny.* New York: State University of New York Press, 1993. An argument that we need more government in the United States. Schmookler believes that in order to save the environment and feed the poor, policy makers in Washington DC must be put in control of the economy.

CHAPTER 3

SUPPLY AND DEMAND: THE BASICS OF ECONOMIC ANALYSIS

LEARNING OBJECTIVES

1. Define demand and list the factors influencing demand. Show how changes in the *ceteris paribus* conditions affect demand.
2. Define supply and list the factors influencing supply. Show how changes in the *ceteris paribus* conditions affect supply.
3. Explain how market equilibrium is reached, and what disequilibrium and equilibrium mean.
4. Use the supply and demand model to illustrate comparative statics, endogenous and exogenous variables, and marginal analysis.
5. Evaluate the functions of prices in a free market and assess how interference with the market distorts its allocative mechanism.

Consider this... *Recently, Garth Brooks announced that he was going to put on a concert in Texas Stadium, where the Dallas Cowboys play football. About 65 thousand seats were going on sale at $17 each. The promoters announced the locations where tickets would go on sale on a particular Saturday at 8:00 A.M. They also announced that lines would not be allowed to form until 7:00 A.M. In addition, the promoters stated that they would sell only six tickets to any one person. The tickets sold out in 93 minutes!*

The next day the newspaper reported that the price of those tickets had skyrocketed to over $300 on the black market. Garth went on the local country-western station and announced that he was not going to allow his fans to be "gouged" by speculators. He therefore would give a second concert the next night. The same procedure would be followed. The places that would sell tickets were announced. The lines could only form one hour before sales commenced, and any one person could buy only six tickets. This concert sold out in less than two hours. The next day there were reports that ticket brokers were selling tickets for both concerts at $150. This made Garth even angrier, and he returned to the radio and announced yet a third concert! His fans were not going to have to pay such high prices for tickets to see and hear him in person. This concert sold out very quickly following the same procedures. However, all of Garth's fans were not so happy. One group of fans, those that got tickets for the first concert, called the radio station and complained that they thought it unfair that they had tickets to the first concert and now there were going to be more concerts. To add insult to injury, the third concert was going to be scheduled before the first (planned) concert because of scheduling availability of Texas Stadium. In addition, those scurrilous ticket brokers were still selling tickets to any of the three concerts for between $75 and $125, depending on the seat location.

What is going on here? Is Garth Brooks really interested in the well-being of his fans? Are the ticket brokers such terrible people? Are the miffed fans being unfair to Garth, or are they just fickle? What is the real price of these tickets, and who is capturing the value of them? This chapter will help you make sense of what is going on with the sale of Garth Brooks tickets and a host of similar interactions between demand and supply.

DEMAND

Markets are places where buyers and sellers meet to engage in exchange. In the process of exchanging, they determine prices and quantities produced. The supply and demand model explains how buyers and sellers interact to determine prices and quantities. It is the most basic and widely used model in economics.

Demand is the quantities of a good or service consumers are willing and able to buy at various prices over a certain time period. Demand is not the same as needs or wants, which can be measured in some social or biological way. Need is a concept reserved for policy makers and political decision making. For needs and wants to be demands, they must be what people will actually do when confronted with different prices. Similarly, **supply** is the quantities of a good or service firms are actually willing and able to produce and offer for sale at various prices over a period of time.

Many things affect the demand for a good or service. As you well know, price is a very important determinant of demand. Thus, we focus first on what happens when the price of a good or service changes relative to the prices of other goods and services. While looking at the relationship between price and quantity demanded, economists hold constant everything else that affects demand.

The **law of demand** states that the *quantity demanded* of a good or service in a given time period is negatively related to its price, *ceteris paribus*. In other words, if everything else is held constant, consumers will purchase more of a good or service at a lower price than at a higher price. As price rises, *ceteris paribus*, consumers will purchase less of a good or service, because its opportunity cost in terms of other goods is higher. Note that we are saying quantity demanded—not demand—is a function of price. This distinction is critical. Demand refers to a whole set of price-quantity combinations. Quantity demanded is the amount consumers want to buy at a particular price.

A **demand schedule** shows the various quantities demanded at various prices during a specified period of time. How can we generate a demand schedule for an individual? We could develop Judy's demand schedule for potato chips by suggesting various prices and asking her how many bags of potato chips she would buy per week at each price. Actual experiments with a variety of subjects support the validity of the law of demand.

The demand schedule in Table 1 shows Fred's demand for doughnuts. As price falls, Fred chooses to consume larger quantities of doughnuts per week as he substitutes doughnuts for other items he might purchase. Table 1 is consistent with the law of demand because Fred demands larger quantities of doughnuts at lower prices. Note that there is a time dimension—a week. We cannot determine how many doughnuts Fred will buy without specifying a time frame— per day, per week, per month, per year, or per lifetime.

We can represent the demand schedule of Table 1 on a graph called a demand curve, as shown in Figure 1. A **demand curve** is a graph representing a

Demand
The desire and ability to consume certain quantities of a good at various prices over a certain period of time.

Supply
The quantity of a good offered for sale at various prices during a certain time period.

Law of demand
The quantity demanded of a good or service is negatively related to its price, *ceteris paribus*.

Demand schedule
A table that shows quantities demanded at various prices during a specific time period.

Demand curve A graph representing a demand schedule and showing the quantity demanded at various prices in a certain time period.

57

demand schedule. When we draw a demand curve, the vertical axis shows the price per unit and the horizontal axis shows the quantity per time period. Note that we usually draw linear curves for convenience (review the Appendix to Chapter 1 if this is confusing).

MARKET DEMAND

Table 1 and Figure 1 show a demand schedule and a demand curve for a single consumer. Sellers, however, are more interested in the market demand curve for a brand of doughnuts or even the market demand curve for all doughnuts. A **market demand curve** shows what quantities will be demanded by all consumers in a certain market at various prices. The market demand curve is the sum of all of the individual demand curves. We add the demand curves for individual consumers horizontally. For example, to determine the market quantity of doughnuts demanded at a price of 40 cents per doughnut, we add the seven doughnuts demanded by Fred to two doughnuts demanded by Betty, a doughnut demanded by Joanna, and so on. We find a total (market) quantity demanded of 10,000 doughnuts at a price of 40 cents per doughnut. These two numbers represent one point on the market demand curve. We then repeat the addition of quantities demanded for every other price. The result is the downward-sloping market demand curve shown in Figure 2, showing a negative relationship between price and quantity. At higher prices, buyers want fewer doughnuts. At lower prices, they want more.

As price changes in the market, the quantity demanded changes in the opposite direction, just as it did for Fred. Figure 2 shows that 13,000 doughnuts are purchased at a price of 35 cents per doughnut. If the price falls to 20 cents

Market demand curve
The sum of all of the individual demand curves. A market demand curve shows what quantities will be demanded by all consumers in a specific time frame in a certain market at various prices.

TABLE 1 FRED'S DEMAND FOR DOUGHNUTS

PRICE PER DOUGHNUT (CENTS)	QUANTITY DEMANDED PER WEEK
50	1
40	7
30	13
20	19
10	25
5	28

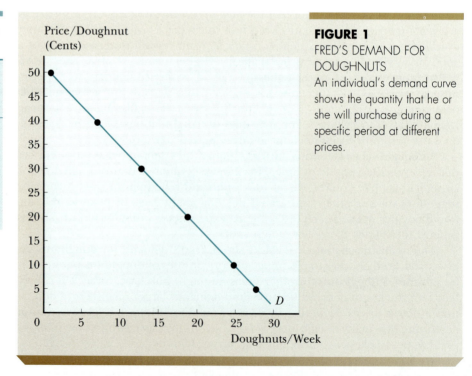

FIGURE 1
FRED'S DEMAND FOR DOUGHNUTS
An individual's demand curve shows the quantity that he or she will purchase during a specific period at different prices.

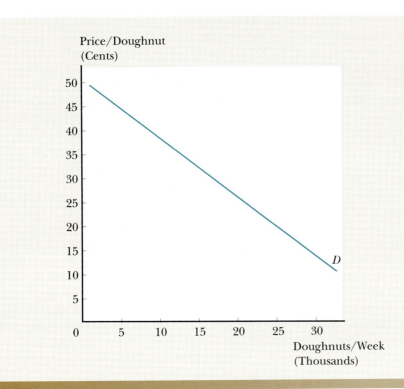

FIGURE 2
MARKET DEMAND FOR DOUGHNUTS
A market demand curve is a graph depicting how much will be purchased in the market at various prices. It is the sum of all of the individual demand curves.

per doughnut, the quantity demanded increases to 25,000 doughnuts. If the price rises to 45 cents per doughnut, the quantity demanded decreases to 5,000 doughnuts.

CETERIS PARIBUS CONDITIONS AND SHIFTS IN DEMAND

Many things can affect the demand for a good or service. Economists separate these factors into two important categories: price, and everything else. Because price is so important, economists express demand as a function of price. The price of a good affects the quantity demanded. Everything else affects demand. So far we have held the nonprice determinants of demand constant while we focused on price. Now we want to look at the nonprice determinants and how they affect the demand curve.

The nonprice determinants of demand are as follows:

1. tastes of the group demanding the good or service,
2. size of the group demanding the good or service,
3. income and wealth of the group demanding the good or service,
4. prices of other goods and services,
5. expectations about future prices or income.

Nearly everything that affects demand does so by working through one of these determinants. Weather, for example, may affect demand for bread by changing tastes. People may eat more cold sandwiches instead of hot meals in warmer weather. Economists study demand by holding all but one of these determinants constant and determining what happens when that one changes. Non-price determinants of demand are the *ceteris paribus* conditions discussed in Chapter 1.

Changes in the *ceteris paribus* conditions change the demand for the good or service. On the graph, a change in demand is a shift of the curve. Economists are careful to distinguish clearly between movements along a demand curve and changes (or shifts) of the curve itself. Movements along the curve are *changes in quantity demanded*, caused solely by a change in the *price* of the good. When the price of bread goes up, fewer loaves are demanded—a change in quantity demanded. Changes (or shifts) of the curve are *changes in demand* caused by changes in any of the *ceteris paribus* conditions. When the weather gets hot or population increases, more loaves are demanded at every possible price—a change in demand.

TASTES. How do changes in the *ceteris paribus* conditions affect the market demand for a good? Suppose people's tastes change in favor of bread because the weather is hot or interest in high-fiber diets increases. As shown in Figure 3, this change in demand shifts the entire demand curve to the right, from D_0 to D_1. An **increase in demand** means that at every price, consumers demand a larger amount than before. The opposite would occur if tastes changed away from bread. Such a change in tastes would cause a decrease in demand, represented by a shift from D_0 to D_2. A **decrease in demand** means that at every price, consumers demand a smaller quantity than before.

SIZE OF THE GROUP The market demand curve, as you saw earlier, is found by adding the individual demand curves. Thus, if the number of individuals in the

Increase in demand
A shift in the demand curve indicating that at every price, a larger quantity will be offered for sale than before.

Decrease in demand
A shift in the demand curve indicating that at every price, consumers demand a smaller amount than before.

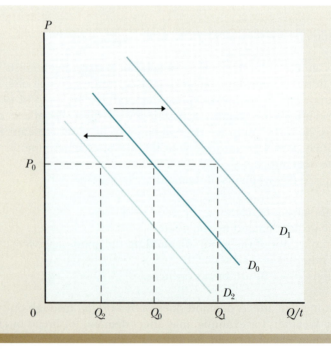

FIGURE 3
EFFECTS OF CHANGES IN THE *CETERIS PARIBUS* CONDITIONS ON DEMAND
If a change causes more of a good to be demanded at every price, the demand curve will shift to the right, as from D_0 to D_1. A change that causes less to be demanded at every price causes a shift to the left, as from D_0 to D_2.

group of potential consumers changes, market demand will also change. Suppose demand curve D_0 in Figure 3 represents the demand for automobiles in a state with a minimum driving age of 16 years. If the law is changed to allow 15-year-olds to drive, the group of potential consumers increases. Some of them, or their families, will want an extra car for the extra driver. The demand curve will shift from D_0 to D_1. The size of the group has increased. Therefore, there has been an increase in the demand for the good, or a larger quantity demanded at every price.

On the other hand, if the size of the group decreases, there will be a decrease in demand, a shift from D_0 to D_2 in Figure 3. The big drop in the birth rate in the late 1960s and early 1970s decreased demand first for baby food and diapers and then for public school teachers. In the 1990s, it is affecting demand for automobiles and college teachers.

INCOME AND WEALTH. Income changes can also shift the demand curve. You might expect that demand for all goods would increase as income increases. However, this is not always true. Whether demand increases in this case depends on whether the good is a normal good or an inferior good. A **normal good** is a good for which demand increases as income increases, *ceteris paribus*. If demand falls when income rises, the good is an **inferior good**. Most goods are normal goods. However, there are a few inferior goods.

Consider, for example, the difference between steak and hamburger. If, as an individual's income increases, the individual consumes less hamburger and more steak, then hamburger is an inferior good and steak is a normal good. However, meat or beef in general is still considered a normal good. Likewise, a mobile home might be considered inferior to a house, but housing in general is a normal good.

For a normal good, an increase in income would cause demand in Figure 3 to shift from D_0 to D_1. For an inferior good, an increase in income would shift demand from D_0 to D_2, as buyers could afford the more expensive substitute. For a normal good, a decrease in income would shift demand from D_0 to D_2 in Figure 3. For an inferior good, a decrease in income would increase demand from D_0 to D_1 as buyers were forced to economize with less appealing goods.

Changes in wealth have the same effect as changes in income. If the value of assets falls, leaving people less wealthy, demand for normal goods will decline. When the stock market crashed in October 1987, many analysts predicted a recession. They expected the decline in wealth to cause consumer spending to decrease. Though there was a decline in wealth, it was not large enough to spark a recession. It did, however, affect the demand for some goods and services.

PRICES OF OTHER GOODS. The fourth nonprice determinant of demand is the prices of other goods and services. There are two classes of other goods: complements and substitutes. **Complementary goods** are goods that are jointly consumed. If consuming two goods together enhances the enjoyment of both, the goods are called complements. Examples are cereals and milk, lamps and light bulbs, or hamburgers and ketchup. Substitute goods have the opposite relationship. Rather than enhancing each other's consumption, **substitute goods** replace each other. Orange juice and grapefruit juice, Coke and Pepsi, and Reebok and Adidas shoes are examples of substitute goods.

If two goods are complements, a rise in the price of one will decrease

Normal good A good for which demand increases as income increases.

Inferior good A good for which demand decreases as income increases.

Complementary goods Goods that are jointly consumed. The consumption of one enhances the consumption of the other.

Substitute goods Goods that can be interchanged. The consumption of one replaces the consumption of the other.

demand for the other. Referring again to Figure 3, consider D_0 as the demand curve for good x (bagels). If the price of complementary good y (cream cheese) goes up, the demand for bagels will decrease, shifting the curve from D_0 to D_2. Buyers will consume less cream cheese because its price is higher, and will thus demand fewer bagels at every price. If the price of cream cheese fell, consumers would want to consume more cream cheese and thus would demand more bagels to go with it at every price. In Figure 3, demand for bagels would shift from D_0 to D_1.

If two goods are substitutes, a rise in the price of one will increase demand for the other. Good x (Coke) and good y (Pepsi) are substitutes. Suppose curve D_0 in Figure 3 represents the demand for good x (Coke). The price of good y (Pepsi) increases relative to the price of Coke. Since this makes the opportunity cost of Coke lower, consumers will demand more Coke at every price. The demand for Coke shifts from D_0 to D_1 in Figure 3. If the price of Pepsi decreased relative to the price of Coke, the opposite would happen. The opportunity cost of Coke would be higher, and consumers would demand less of it at every price as they shifted consumption to Pepsi. The decrease in demand for Coke is shown by a shift from D_0 to D_2 in Figure 3. The shift to substitutes as price rises means that the quantity demanded of the good falls, exactly as predicted by the law of demand.

In a broad sense, all goods are substitutes for each other because they are all alternatives on which people can spend income. Some goods are closer substitutes than others, however. The more easily that good A can be substituted for good B, the more a change in the price of one will affect the demand curve for the other. A rise in the price of watches, for example, would have much less impact on the demand for hot dogs than on the demand for clocks, bracelets, or other substitutes.

KEY IDEAS

REASONS FOR A CHANGE IN THE QUANTITY DEMANDED
- The quantity demanded will *increase* if the price of the good or service *decreases*.
- The quantity demanded will *decrease* if the price of the good or service *increases*.

REASONS FOR A CHANGE IN DEMAND
- The demand for a normal good or service will *increase* if:
    buyers' tastes change to favor that good or service,
    the number of buyers in the market increases,
    the income or wealth of buyers increases,
    the prices of complementary goods fall,
    the prices of substitute goods increase, or
    buyers' expectations for the future cause them to purchase more now.
- The demand for a normal good or service will *decrease* if:
    buyers' tastes change against that good or service,
    the number of buyers in the market decreases,
    the income or wealth of buyers decreases,
    the prices of complementary goods increase,
    the prices of substitute goods decrease, or
    buyers' expectations of the future cause them to delay purchases.

People often make the error of assuming a good has no satisfactory substitutes. How often have you heard someone say, "There is no substitute for victory (or success, steak, a new car…)." In fact, there are substitutes for anything. If the price rises sharply enough, consumers will start searching harder for acceptable substitutes. This point often makes economists seem cynical. Does honesty have a substitute? Yes. If the price becomes too high, many people (not all) will become dishonest.

EXPECTATIONS. The last *ceteris paribus* condition that affects demand is **expectations**. If individuals expect anything important to change in the future, they may take action now that they would otherwise postpone. For example, if you expect that the demand for automobiles will be so high next year that their prices will rise, you may decide to buy a car now to avoid paying a higher price. If you expect your income to be higher in the future, you may demand more goods and borrow to pay for them so that you do not have to delay consumption until your income actually rises.

Expectations
Feelings that individuals have about future conditions.

SUPPLY

A **supply schedule** shows the quantities offered for sale at various prices during a specific period of time. Price is the primary determinant of quantity supplied.

THE (NOT QUITE) LAW OF SUPPLY

Assume everything else is held constant but the price of the good or service. We can then state the **(not quite) law of supply** as follows: the *quantity supplied* of a good or service is *usually* a positive function of price, *ceteris paribus*.

With all else held constant, suppliers usually will supply less of a good or service at lower prices. As prices rise, the quantity supplied will increase, because it becomes more profitable to produce and sell the good. Note also the word *usually*. This relationship is not quite a law because of two exceptions. The first exception occurs when there is no time to produce more units (for example, theater seats at a sold-out performance) or when a unique supplier no longer exists (for example, paintings by Picasso). In these unusual cases, quantity supplied does not respond to price at all. The second exception occurs for certain products for which increased volume allows costs per unit to fall. For example, as a computer software company increases its output of a certain program, its costs per unit typically fall. These lower costs may be passed on to customers in the form of lower prices.

Table 2 shows a hypothetical supply schedule for an individual supplier—Susan's Lemonade Stand. A supply schedule shows the quantities supplied during a period of time at various prices. Like a demand schedule, a supply schedule includes a time frame—in this case, a day. Table 2 is consistent with the law of supply because Susan supplies larger quantities of lemonade at higher prices. The supply schedule of Table 2 can be drawn on a graph as shown in Figure 4. This **supply curve** is a diagram showing the quantity supplied in a particular time and at various prices. It shows a positive relationship—more will be offered for sale at higher prices. Price per unit is on the *y*-axis, and quantity per time period is on the *x*-axis, just as it was for the demand curve. Supply curves usually have a positive *y*-intercept, indicating that at some low price, suppliers may offer none of the good.

Supply schedule
A table that shows quantities offered for sale at various prices over a particular time period.

(Not quite) law of supply
The quantity supplied of a good or service is usually a positive function of price, *ceteris paribus*.

Supply curve
A graph representing a supply schedule and showing the quantities supplied at various prices in a certain time period.

TABLE 2 SUSAN'S SUPPLY OF LEMONADE

PRICE PER GLASS (CENTS)	QUANTITY SUPPLIED PER DAY
10	0
20	5
30	10
40	15
50	20
60	25

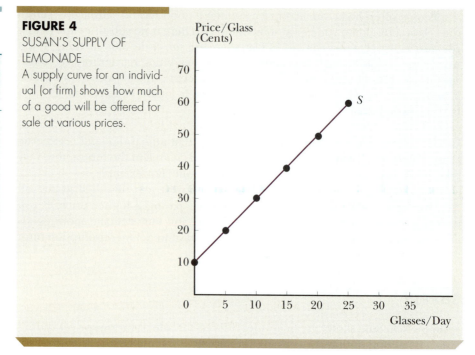

FIGURE 4
SUSAN'S SUPPLY OF LEMONADE
A supply curve for an individual (or firm) shows how much of a good will be offered for sale at various prices.

MARKET SUPPLY

Market supply curve
The sum of all of the individual supply curves. A market supply curve shows what quantities will be supplied by all firms at various prices during a specific time period.

The **market supply curve** is the sum of all of the individual supply schedules. Figure 5 is a market supply curve for lemonade, showing the total quantity supplied over a period of time at various prices. As price changes in the market, quantity supplied changes in the same direction. Figure 5 shows that 5,000 glasses of lemonade are supplied at a price of 20 cents per glass. If price falls to 10 cents per glass, quantity supplied decreases to zero glasses. If price rises to 40 cents per glass, quantity supplied increases to 15,000 glasses. These changes occur because most producers are willing to sell more units if the price rises enough to cover the added costs of production.

CHANGES IN SUPPLY AND THE *CETERIS PARIBUS* CONDITIONS

A supply curve is drawn to show a relationship between price and quantity supplied, with everything else held constant. A change in one of the *ceteris paribus* conditions will cause the entire supply curve to shift. The most important of these are as follows:

1. the state of technology,
2. prices of the productive resources,
3. the number of suppliers,
4. expectations about the future,
5. prices of related goods.

Everything that affects supply works through one of these determinants. For example, if a natural disaster destroys large amounts of capital, it will affect sup-

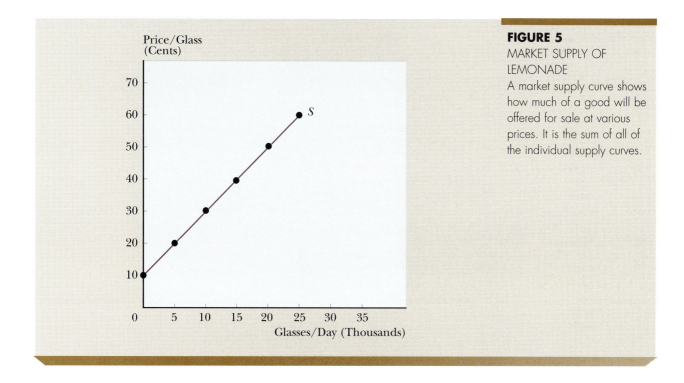

FIGURE 5
MARKET SUPPLY OF LEMONADE
A market supply curve shows how much of a good will be offered for sale at various prices. It is the sum of all of the individual supply curves.

ply by increasing the price of that resource. If the price of corn rises relative to wheat, a farmer might decide to grow corn instead of wheat.

TECHNOLOGY. Suppose technology improves. For instance, agricultural researchers develop a low-cost drug that causes a young steer to double in weight rapidly. This advance in technology means that more beef will be supplied at each price. There is an **increase in supply**, or a shift in the supply curve such that a larger quantity will be provided at every price. In Figure 6, an increase in supply is shown as a shift from S_0 to S_1. A negative change in technology will have the opposite effect. Suppose the government discovers that the drug used to fatten steers has harmful effects on humans who eat the beef. Farmers are forbidden to continue using the drug. Less beef will be supplied at each price. There will be a **decrease in supply**, represented as a shift from S_0 to S_2 in Figure 6.

PRICES OF THE PRODUCTIVE RESOURCES. As you recall from Chapter 2, the productive resources are land, labor, capital, and enterprise. The price paid for the use of land is rent. The price of labor's services is wages. The price for using capital is interest. The return to enterprise is profit. If the price of a resource—such as wages for labor—goes up, the supply of products using that resource will be affected. Suppliers will offer less of the good at each price, because the costs of production have gone up.

Suppose S_0 in Figure 6 represents the market supply of beef. Assume that the wage rate of meat cutters increases. This will mean less beef will be supplied at each price. Supply will decrease from S_0 to S_2. After the increase in wages, suppliers will supply the old amount (Q_0) only at a higher price (P_2). A rise in the price of a productive resource, *ceteris paribus*, causes a decrease in supply. The

Increase in supply
A shift in the supply curve indicating that at every price, a larger quantity will be offered for sale than before.

Decrease in supply
A shift in the supply curve indicating that at every price, a smaller quantity will be offered for sale than before.

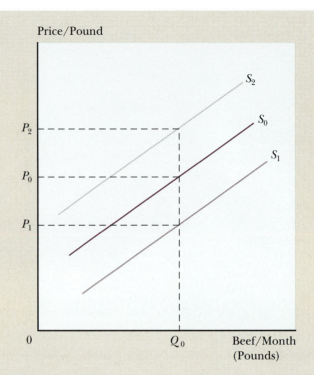

FIGURE 6
CHANGES IN THE *CETERIS PARIBUS* CONDITIONS AND SUPPLY
Changes in a *ceteris paribus* condition can cause the supply curve to shift. A change that would cause more to be supplied at each price is an increase in supply and is represented by the shift from S_0 to S_1. A change that causes the supply to decrease is represented by a shift from S_0 to S_2.

cost of supplying any particular quantity has increased. Thus, less will be supplied at the old price, or the same amount will be supplied at a higher price. The opposite is also true. A decrease in the price of a productive resource will cause an increase in supply, shifting the curve from S_0 to S_1 in Figure 6.

NUMBER OF SUPPLIERS. A change in the number of suppliers will also shift the supply curve. If the number of beef ranchers declines, the supply curve will shift from S_0 to S_2 in Figure 6—a decrease in supply. In contrast, an increase in the number of ranchers will shift the supply curve from S_0 to S_1 in Figure 6—an increase in supply.

EXPECTATIONS. Expectations about any of the *ceteris paribus* conditions or about market price can have an effect on supply. Assume that ranchers expect that the price of beef will fall next year because of an FDA policy statement that links beef consumption to colon cancer. What would this expectation cause ranchers to do? They would bring more cattle to market now, before the price falls. If enough ranchers share this expectation, the supply curve for this year will increase from S_0 to S_1, as shown in Figure 6. The price of beef will fall from P_0 to P_1 because ranchers will be slaughtering more cattle. Next year, with fewer cattle available, the supply curve will shift back to the left.

PRICES OF RELATED GOODS. Changes in the prices of other goods can affect supply. If the price of a good that uses a similar production technique increases, a firm may switch production. A farmer may switch from corn to wheat when the price of corn increases relative to the price of wheat. A sewing factory might switch from men's shirts to babies' nightwear if the price of men's shirts fell and the price of babies' nightwear rose.

KEY IDEAS

REASONS FOR A CHANGE IN THE QUANTITY SUPPLIED
- The quantity supplied will *increase* if the price of the good or service *increases*.
- The quantity supplied will *decrease* if the price of the good or service *decreases*.

REASONS FOR A CHANGE IN SUPPLY
- The supply of a good or service will *increase* if:
  new technology allows the good or service to be produced at lower cost,
  the prices of the productive resources decrease,
  the number of suppliers increases,
  the prices of other goods or services that can be produced with the same resources decrease, or
  suppliers' expectations for the future cause them to produce more now.
- The supply of a good or service will *decrease* if:
  the prices of the productive resources increase,
  the number of suppliers decreases,
  the prices of other goods or services that can be produced with the same resources increase, or
  suppliers' expectations for the future cause them to produce less now.

MARKET EQUILIBRIUM

We can combine market supply and market demand schedules to determine the market equilibrium. **Market equilibrium** occurs at that price for which quantity demanded by consumers is equal to quantity supplied by producers. This equilibrium price is also called the **market-clearing price**.

EQUILIBRIUM AND DISEQUILIBRIUM

In Table 3, at a price of $2, suppliers *want* to supply 4 million pounds of coffee, and consumers *want* to purchase 8 million pounds. A price of $2 is not an equilibrium price because quantity demanded exceeds quantity supplied by 4 million pounds at that price. This situation is one of disequilibrium, in which variables are moving toward equilibrium but are not yet there. This is an unstable position. Some consumers will not be able to purchase the amount they desire at a price of $2. As they search for coffee, they will offer a higher price. As the price rises, quantity supplied will rise, and quantity demanded will fall. This process will continue until the price reaches $3. At $3, the amount consumers wish to purchase is exactly equal to the amount suppliers wish to sell. This quantity is the equilibrium quantity, and $3 is the market-clearing price, because there is no tendency for price or quantity to change.

If the price were $4 per pound, suppliers would offer 8 million pounds of coffee per month, but consumers would only wish to purchase 4 million pounds.

Market equilibrium
A point at which quantity demanded by consumers is equal to quantity supplied by producers. The price at which this occurs is the equilibrium price, or market-clearing price.

Market-clearing price
The equilibrium price, which clears the market because there are no frustrated consumers or suppliers.

TABLE 3 SUPPLY OF AND DEMAND FOR COFFEE

PRICE PER POUND (DOLLARS)	POUNDS SUPPLIED PER MONTH	POUNDS DEMANDED PER MONTH	DIFFERENCE
1	2 million	10 million	8 million excess quantity demanded
2	4 million	8 million	4 million excess quantity demanded
3	6 million	6 million	equilibrium
4	8 million	4 million	4 million excess quantity supplied
5	10 million	2 million	8 million excess quantity supplied

At this price, there is an excess quantity supplied of 4 million pounds per month. Suppliers with unsold coffee will accept a lower price to get rid of it. As price falls, some suppliers reduce their output (a movement along the supply curve), and some consumers buy more (a movement along the demand curve) until the equilibrium price of $3 is reached. This $3 price again clears the market.

Note that the equilibrium price and quantity do not simply represent the point where the amount sold equals the amount bought. Quantities bought and sold are *always* equal, even in disequilibrium. Four million pounds per month were bought and sold at $2 and at $4. Equilibrium occurs at a price for which the quantity supplied and the quantity demanded are equal.

Figure 7 shows market supply and market demand curves for coffee, based on the supply and demand schedules in Table 3. The equilibrium price is $3, and 6 million pounds per month are sold at equilibrium. At $4, there is an excess quantity supplied, and price will fall. This causes the quantity demanded to increase and the quantity supplied to decrease. The opposite happens at a price of $2 per pound.

SUPPLY, DEMAND, AND ECONOMIC MODELS

As you learned in Chapter 1, the primary work of economists is to construct theories and models that explain and predict how the economy works and to use those theories and models to devise policies to make it work better. All theories and models share certain techniques and certain assumptions about how households and firms make decisions about using resources for production and consumption. The supply and demand model can be used to illustrate some of these techniques and assumptions.

EQUILIBRIUM. The supply and demand model represents the first use in this book of the economic concept of equilibrium. In this model, equilibrium is found at that price for which the quantity demanded is equal to the quantity supplied.

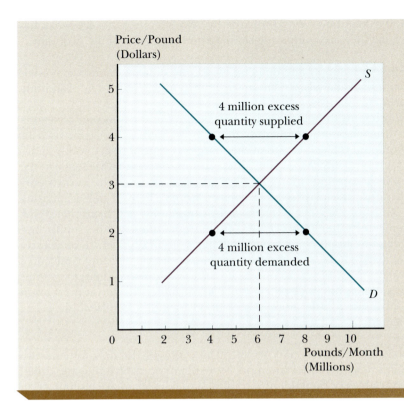

FIGURE 7
SUPPLY OF AND DEMAND FOR COFFEE
At equilibrium, the amount consumers wish to purchase is equal to the amount suppliers wish to sell. The price established at equilibrium is called the market-clearing price. At prices above the market-clearing price, quantity supplied exceeds quantity demanded. At prices below the market-clearing price, quantity demanded exceeds quantity supplied.

Equilibrium (and its counterpart, disequilibrium) is a term that you will encounter often. This book will discuss equilibrium prices, equilibrium quantities, equilibrium levels of employment, equilibrium levels of gross domestic product (GDP), and so forth. Almost every economic model includes a definition of equilibrium. If the model has an equilibrium position, it will have a set of forces that can change that position. There are also forces that move an economy toward a new equilibrium position. In the supply and demand model, sellers' and buyers' responses to price changes will move the economy toward a new equilibrium.

COMPARATIVE STATICS. When a supply curve or a demand curve shifts, the diagram always identifies the original equilibrium and the new equilibrium. Economists are able to describe the process by which a market or economy moves from one equilibrium to another. This kind of analysis is called **comparative statics**. Comparative statics begins by describing the initial equilibrium position of the market (or the economy). This initial state is then compared to some later state in which some element has changed. For example, a change in technology has shifted the supply curve to the right, resulting in a larger quantity supplied and a lower price. That is, comparative statics looks at changes in equilibrium positions between two different times.

Another way of looking at comparative statics is to see the analysis as a comparison of two snapshots of the economy (or of a particular market). We take a snapshot and analyze the relationships that exist. We then change one variable, which causes the economy to move to a new equilibrium. Next, we take another

Comparative statics
A technique of comparing two equilibrium positions to determine the changing relationships between variables.

snapshot of the economy. We compare the two snapshots to see what has changed and why. We are comparing static (frozen) pictures of the economy.

MARGINAL ANALYSIS. Supply and demand is just one of many economic models that involve **marginal analysis**, a technique for analyzing problems by examining the results of small changes.

Marginal refers to the extra, additional, or next unit of output, consumption, or any other measurable quantity that can be increased or decreased by incremental amounts. The concept of the margin is central to economic analysis, although it is probably new to you. Most economic decisions are made at the margin: Should I consume the extra slice of pizza or work the extra hour? Should we produce the extra unit or take on a new client at our accounting firm? These kinds of daily decisions made by households and firms determine prices, output, and other important economic quantities. In the supply and demand model, the supply curve reflects the decisions of suppliers to offer extra or additional (marginal) units for sale at higher prices. The demand curve reflects the decisions of buyers to purchase extra or additional (marginal) units at lower prices. When the price of a good falls, consumers decide at the margin whether to substitute a little more of that good for other goods whose prices have not changed.

ENDOGENOUS AND EXOGENOUS VARIABLES. All economic models contain variables. Variables that a model attempts to explain or determine are called **endogenous variables** or dependent variables. Variables that have an impact on the endogenous variables but are themselves determined outside the model are called **exogenous variables** or independent variables.

In the supply and demand model, both price and quantity are endogenous or dependent variables that affect one another and are determined by the model. For example, the price of oranges is dependent to this model. Some of the other variables in a supply and demand model are independent. For example, in the market for oranges, the weather in Florida is an exogenous variable. The weather affects the price of oranges, but the price of oranges does not affect the weather.

In the supply and demand model, the exogenous variables are the nonprice determinants that cause the position of the supply or demand curve to change. These nonprice determinants are technology, tastes, number of suppliers, income, prices of related goods, and so forth. Most economic models concentrate on just one or two endogenous or dependent variables and explain them by the behavior of a larger number of exogenous or independent variables.

PRIMARY AND SECONDARY EFFECTS. Economists often analyze the effect of a change in one variable on other related variables. The **primary effect** is the dominant effect they seek to analyze. For instance, the demand curve shows how adding a tax that doubles the price of oranges would affect the quantity of oranges consumed. But there are also **secondary effects** in related markets. These effects may not be immediately apparent and may take time to work through the economy. For example, if the price of oranges doubled, the sales of cranberry juice might increase, or the consumption of bacon and eggs might decrease. These are complementary goods whose demand depends on the price of oranges (or orange juice). Such changes would not be as obvious or as immediately apparent as the primary effect.

Marginal analysis
A technique for analyzing problems by examining the results of small changes.

Endogenous variables
Variables that are explained or determined within a model.

Exogenous variables
Variables that are determined outside a model and affect endogenous variables.

Primary effect
The dominant or immediate effect of a change in an economic variable.

Secondary effects
Effects indirectly related to the immediate effect, often smaller and felt after some time.

A THEORY OF PRICE FORMATION

The law of demand and the (not quite) law of supply support a very powerful theory of how markets work to set and change prices. That theory is based on two propositions. The first is that quantity demanded is negatively related to price. The second is that quantity supplied is positively related to price. When these two propositions are combined, they imply several things:

1. When the quantity demanded exceeds the quantity supplied, ($Q_d > Q_s$), price will rise.
2. When the quantity demanded is less than the quantity supplied, ($Q_d < Q_s$), price will fall.
3. When the quantity demanded equals the quantity supplied, ($Q_d = Q_s$), price is at equilibrium.

This theory, combined with the possible shifts in *ceteris paribus* conditions, produces all of the basic elements of a model of how prices (and quantities) are determined in a market system.

CHANGES IN DEMAND AND SUPPLY

When changes occur in any of the *ceteris paribus* conditions that affect demand, the model can be used to trace the effect on market equilibrium. Assume first that there is an increase in demand, that is, an outward shift of the entire curve. This increase in demand could be a result of a change in any of the *ceteris paribus* conditions. It could result from an increase in income (for a normal good), a change in tastes in favor of the good, an increase in the price of a substitute or a decrease in the price of a complement, an increase in the size of the consuming group, or a change in expectations. The increase in demand is shown as an outward shift in the demand curve from D_0 to D_1 in Figure 8. The equilibrium price rises from P_0 to P_1, and the price increase causes quantity supplied to increase to Q_1. Consumers demand a larger quantity of the good at every price than before the shift of the curve.

Now consider a decrease in demand. A decrease in demand means that consumers will demand less of a good at every price. This decrease could result from a fall in income, a change in tastes away from the good, a decrease in the price of a substitute or an increase in the price of a complement, a decrease in group size, or a change in expectations. The decrease in demand is shown as an inward shift in the demand curve from D_0 to D_2 in Figure 8. The decrease in demand causes the equilibrium price to fall from P_0 to P_2, and quantity supplied responds by falling from Q_0 to Q_2.

Changes in any condition that affects supply will shift the supply curve. An increase in supply could result from an advance in technology, a decrease in the price of a resource, an increase in the number of suppliers, or a change in expectations. The increase in supply appears on a graph as a rightward shift of the supply curve, from S_0 to S_1 in Figure 9. This increase in supply would cause the equilibrium price to fall from P_0 to P_1, leading to an increase in the quantity demanded from Q_0 to Q_1.

A decrease in supply could result from an increase in the price of a resource, a decrease in the number of suppliers, or a change in expectations. A decrease in supply is shown as a leftward shift from S_0 to S_2 in Figure 9. This

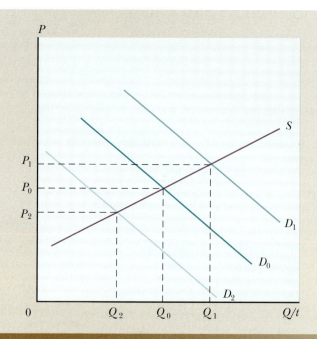

FIGURE 8
CHANGES IN DEMAND
An increase in demand from D_0 to D_1 causes the equilibrium price to rise from P_0 to P_1 and the quantity supplied to increase from Q_0 to Q_1. A decrease in demand from D_0 to D_2 causes the equilibrium price to fall from P_0 to P_2 and the quantity supplied to fall from Q_0 to Q_2.

decrease in supply causes the equilibrium price to rise from P_0 to P_2, causing quantity demanded to decrease from Q_0 to Q_2.

The supply and demand model is very useful in analyzing a variety of economic problems and issues. As you apply this model, keep in mind the difference between changes in demand and supply (that is, shifts in the positions of the curves) and changes in the quantity demanded and quantity supplied (that

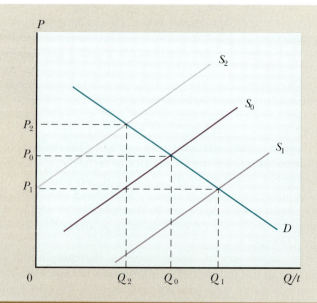

FIGURE 9
CHANGES IN SUPPLY
An increase in supply from S_0 to S_1 causes the equilibrium price to fall from P_0 to P_1 and the quantity demanded to increase from Q_0 to Q_1. A decrease in supply from S_0 to S_2 causes the equilibrium price to rise from P_0 to P_2 and the quantity demanded to fall from Q_0 to Q_2.

is, movements along the curves). The importance of this difference will become very clear as you attempt to untangle situations that involve several changes in *ceteris paribus* conditions.

ARE PRICES FAIR?

The analysis of supply and demand presented in this chapter has been positive rather than normative. No mention has been made of what constitutes a fair or just price. Nor has there been any comment as to whether certain minimal levels of consumption of certain goods are necessary for a fair society. Supply and demand theory predicts how an increase in demand for a good will affect price and quantity. A higher price may mean that some people can no longer afford the item, regardless of how necessary or "basic" it may appear to be. The supply and demand model offers no moral evaluation of what prices should be.

DIFFERENT PRICES FOR DIFFERENT BUYERS

In the real world, people often pay different prices for the same good. In the supply and demand model, the equilibrium price is a single, unique price that is paid by all buyers and received by all sellers. There may be different prices for different buyers and sellers because of transactions costs. **Transactions costs** are costs associated with gathering information about markets (prices and quantities supplied) for consuming or producing. Organizing, negotiating, and searching take time and involve opportunity costs. Firms are organized to reduce transactions costs on the producing side. For consumers, the existence of transactions costs means that different people may pay different prices for the same good or service.

A familiar example of such price differences is that gas stations next to expressways charge higher prices for gasoline than do stations farther away from expressways. Why? Transactions costs. Most users of an expressway are unfamiliar with the area and are in a hurry. They perceive the cost of searching for a lower price to be higher than the potential saving produced by such searching. Think about what gas prices might be in a retirement community. Do you think there would be lower and more uniform gas prices in and around a retirement community because the opportunity cost of the customers' time is lower? If you live near a retirement community, you might want to check on the prices charged for gasoline in nearby areas.

Transactions costs Costs associated with gathering information about markets (prices and quantities supplied) for consuming or producing.

EVALUATING THE MARKET PROCESS

In Chapter 2, you saw that each and every economy must address three basic questions: what, how and for whom? Supply and demand—the market process—provide important signals to inform, direct, and motivate economic agents in answering these questions.

FUNCTIONS OF PRICES

Prices play a central role in a market system in allocating scarce resources and answering the basic economic questions. The primary functions of prices are to inform, direct, and motivate consumers and business firms.

POLICY FOCUS: THE SIMPLE SUPPLY AND DEMAND ANALYSIS OF NAFTA

There is a lot of political debate about international trade. A key policy issue in the Clinton administration's first year was signing the North American Free Trade Agreement (NAFTA) which makes trade between Canada, the United States, and Mexico much freer. We can use the demand and supply model to focus on this policy debate.

A change in the number of suppliers and the number of buyers can shift the supply and demand curves, respectively. With NAFTA, these shifts can result from additional buyers and sellers in Canada and Mexico. Since there already is a free trade agreement between the United States and Canada, we will focus on Mexico.

In an open economy, the market demand curve faced by producers is the sum of the domestic demand for the product and the foreign demand for the product. Consider the market demand for American corn, which is exported to Mexico. If there were no Mexican demand, the market price would settle at P_d, and corn producers would sell Q tons of corn. (See the graph titled "Mexican Demand for Corn.") When Mexican demand, D_m, is added, the price rises to P_{d+m} and the amount sold rises to Q_{d+m}. The price of corn and the amount of corn sold have both increased. U.S. consumers are paying a higher price because they now pay P_{d+m}. Since the domestic demand curve has not shifted and the price has increased, the quantity of corn demanded by U.S. consumers will fall. In this example, domestic consumption falls to Q_d.

It appears that domestic corn producers have gained at the expense of domestic corn consumers. After all, consumers now pay a higher price for less corn. This conclusion is correct, but it ignores the other side of the coin. Mexican consumers can only buy the corn if they sell something that earns the currency necessary to pay for the corn. The domestic supply of the product that Mexicans sell to pay for the corn will have an effect in other markets.

The graph titled "Mexican Supply of Textiles" shows the U.S. market for textiles. Without a Mexican supply, the domestic price and quantity would be P_d and Q_d. Adding Mexican supply, S_m, changes the equilibrium. There is a decline in price to P_{d+m} and an increase in quantity demanded to Q_{d+m}. In this case, the domestic consumption of textiles increased by $Q_{d+m} - Q_d$. U.S. consumers can purchase more textiles at a lower price.

There is an important lesson in this example of supply and demand in an open economy. Relative to the present situation, NAFTA will result in higher prices and less consumption of exported items and lower prices and more consumption of imported items. So there are winners and losers as a result of NAFTA. In this example corn farmers and textile consumers in the U.S. are gainers, while textile producers and corn consumers in the U.S. are losers. In Mexico the situation on gainers and losers is reversed. But, as you learned in Chapter 2, the principle of comparative advantage shows that the net effect of trade is an expansion of choices and an increase in total consumption for consumers in the domestic market. You can use this model to predict who speaks for NAFTA and who speaks against NAFTA in the policy debate. You might also predict that U.S. textile producers may move part of their production to Mexico.

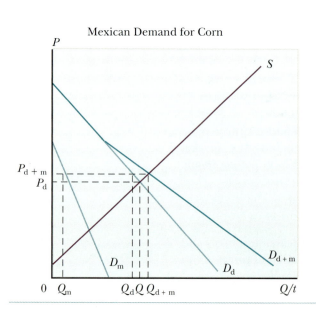

Mexican Demand for Corn

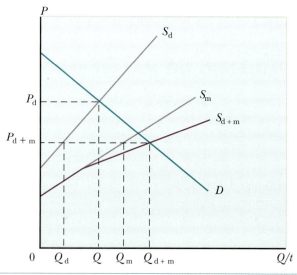

Mexican Supply of Textiles

INFORMING. Market prices condense a great deal of complex information into a simple form. This condensed information is useful to consumers and producers in making decisions. An increase in demand causes a market price to rise. The supplier of a product does not have to know what caused demand to change. All suppliers need to know is that the price has risen. They will respond by increasing the quantity supplied. Likewise, consumers do not need to understand anything about the production process or the associated costs. All they need to know is the market price. If the price rises, consumers decrease the quantity demanded. The market price, then, provides all participants in the market with up-to-the-minute information on the relative scarcity of goods.

DIRECTING. Market participants act on price information. If suppliers are bringing too much of a good to market, its price will fall. The decisions of consumers and producers will move the market to a new equilibrium. Market prices will signal for an increase in the production of those products of which consumers are demanding more. Firms will produce these goods by bringing resources together in a way directed by the market prices of those resources. All of this takes place without any individual or group telling consumers and entrepreneurs how or why to act. All of the necessary information is found in market prices.

MOTIVATING. The *for whom* question is also a reminder that price is a powerful motivator. Supply and demand establish a reward structure for owners and users of productive resources. Households and firms will seek to produce those goods or develop those skills that are highly desired by others, in order to earn rewards in the form of higher incomes. All of this happens without any government agency or central planning bureau telling people what to do. No one has to tell a supermarket owner when to be open or where to build a store, or a bright young person to invest in education. People pursue certain activities because they perceive it to be in their own self-interest.

THE EFFICIENCY OF THE MARKET

According to Adam Smith, the invisible hand informs, directs, and motivates the self-interest of market participants. Suppliers are motivated to guide resources into the production of the goods most wanted by consumers and to produce those goods with the most efficient methods and resource combinations possible. In the words of Nobel Laureate George Stigler, ". . . an economic actor on average knows better the environment in which he is acting and the probable consequences of his actions than an outsider, no matter how clever the outsider may be."[1]

FREEDOM

Finally, an important result of a market system is that individuals enjoy a great deal of freedom to pursue their own self-interest. In a market system, the production and distribution of goods and services take place on a basis of voluntary cooperation in the pursuit of individual self-interest. Nobel Laureate Milton

---

1. George J. Stigler, "Economists and Public Policy," *Regulation* (May/June 1982): 16.

Friedman, like Stigler a champion of the market system, describes this advantage in these terms:

> *So long as effective freedom of exchange is maintained, the central feature of the market organization of economic activity is that it prevents one person from interfering with another in respect to most of his activities. The consumer is protected from coercion by the seller because of the presence of other sellers with whom he can deal. The seller is protected from coercion by the consumer because of other consumers to whom he can sell. The employee is protected from coercion by the employer because of other employers for whom he can work, and so on. And the market does this impersonally and without centralized authority.*[2]

SHORTCOMINGS OF MARKETS AND NONMARKET ALLOCATIONS

Although the market is a highly efficient way to allocate resources, it does have some drawbacks, as we observed in Chapter 2. Some of those drawbacks include failure to provide public goods or to correct negative externalities, stabilization problems, and inequality in the distribution of income. Markets also perform poorly when there is a lack of competition. The quotation from Friedman does not apply when monopolies interfere with freedom of choice. Often the failings of the market lead to government intervention, resulting in a mixed economy rather than a pure market economy.

Critics of the market system range from those who would replace it with complete central direction to those with a more middle-of-the-road approach. The latter see a variety of ways of dividing responsibilities between markets and government. If prices are not allowed to direct resources in certain situations, some other mechanism must be developed for their allocation. Government directives, waiting in line, or appeals to "good behavior" are possible allocative mechanisms. The benefits of government intervention must be weighed against the very strong advantages of markets in terms of efficiency and flexibility. The following examples suggest some areas where government intervention has reduced the efficiency of resource allocation.

ORGAN DONATIONS.
Another example of markets at work occurs in the relatively new medical field of organ transplanting. Certain organs such as hearts, lungs, and eyes are donated only at death, usually from accident victims. Other organs, such as kidneys, can be donated by live donors, because humans have two kidneys and can function with just one. There have also been some successful transplants of part of a liver, since this organ can regenerate itself. As organ transplants have become more popular and more successful, a shortage of organs has developed. Newspapers and television frequently carry heart-rending appeals. Some hospitals even have donor seekers who contact relatives of accident victims. One explanation for the shortage of organs is that the price is

---

2. For a famous discussion of the freedom of markets, see Milton Friedman, *Capitalism and Freedom* (Chicago: University of Chicago Press, 1981): 14–15.

being held at too low a level. In fact, government prevents markets in human organs and the price is zero.

It would be possible to establish a market for some organs. Since individuals can get along quite well with one kidney, it would be possible to let individuals who are cash-poor and kidney-rich sell a kidney to those who are cash-rich and kidney-poor. Some years ago, Congressional hearings were held to consider what could be done about the shortage of kidneys for transplant. Two members of Congress proposed a federal program to fund a computer organ-marketing system and a 24-hour kidney hotline. The program would, however, establish no financial incentives for donors. What do you think might happen if there were a market for kidneys?

Some idea of the possible effect of paying for kidneys comes from an experiment by two British economists, Michael Cooper and Anthony Culver. They tried to determine the supply of blood that would be offered at various prices.[3] They found that there was a moderate supply at a price of zero. At this price, blood was given by those who were motivated by charity, altruism, or other noneconomic reasons. The supply actually fell at a nominal price of about $1.00 a pint, because the payment did not compensate some potential donors for the loss of the good feeling they obtained from giving blood for free. But as the price rose, more and more donors came forward. For many years, some people in American cities have sold their blood when they needed money. The quantity supplied is positively related to price, just as our models would predict. Do you think that kidneys would be any different?

FACULTY OFFICES. A final example of market versus nonmarket allocation comes, appropriately, from an economics department trying to allocate faculty offices in a new building. In this case the "government" was the university administration that did not permit a market to allocate a scarce resource. The other five departments in the school of business used various methods of allocation: seniority; first come, first served; and a roll of the dice. None of these methods reflected the intensity of people's preferences for corner offices, offices with windows, large offices, and so forth. There was great dissatisfaction with the outcomes. Only in the economics department was there an attempt to use the market for allocating office space. Faculty members were invited to submit sealed bids. The highest bidders got to choose first, and the proceeds went to student scholarships. A bid indicated how important the "perks" associated with a particular office were to the bidder. Those who worked at home more or were away from campus more would presumably bid less than those who used their offices more regularly and cared more intensely about aspects of their workplace.

The experiment was quite successful. The highest bidder paid $500 for the first choice of office, and bidders down to $75 were able to secure the more desirable offices with windows. Since those who bid too low were free to recontract with others if they changed their minds, there was general satisfaction with the outcome.[4]

---

3. "Socialized Kidneys," *Fortune* (19 March 1984): 190.
4. William J. Boyes and Stephen K. Happel, "Auctions as an Allocation Mechanism in Academia:

Consider again... *You should now have a pretty good understanding of the market interactions in the market for Garth Brooks concert tickets. The promoters knew at the start that the market was not going to be in equilibrium at a price per ticket of $17. If it were at or near equilibrium there would have been no need to try to control the line or to limit the purchase to six tickets. One should wonder why they didn't price the tickets higher if they only intended to offer one concert! It may well be that the intent from the beginning was to present multiple concerts. But what about the ticket brokers? They were simply bringing together people who wanted tickets, but who did not want to pay the $17 plus the opportunity cost of going to the ticket outlet and standing in line. Indeed, many of the people who bought six tickets and only wanted two were filling the role of speculators. What about the people who had tickets for the first (and what they thought was the only) concert? Should they be upset? Garth increased the supply (twice) and made their tickets less scarce. If they wanted to sell them they were worth less money, but even if they intended to consume the scarce ticket it was now less scarce and therefore less valuable to them. It is easy to understand why they felt cheated. They had bought what they thought was a limited edition and after the fact it became a very common commodity. That is why most collectibles are more valuable after it is impossible to produce more of the same product. Picasso's paintings became more valuable after Picasso died!*

SUMMARY

1. Demand is the quantities of a good or service consumers are willing and able to buy at various prices over a certain time period. Demand depends on the current price of the good or service as well as nonprice determinants. These other influences on demand include the size of the group demanding the good, the tastes of the consuming group, the incomes of that group, the prices of related goods and services, and the expectations concerning the future.

    The law of demand states that the quantity demanded of a good or service is negatively related to its price, *ceteris paribus*. Changes in the price of a good affect the quantity demanded of that good. That is, a price change leads to a movement along the demand curve.

    Changes in the *ceteris paribus* conditions cause demand to either increase or decrease. That is, there is a shift in the position of the entire demand curve. When income increases, the demand for a normal good will increase, and the demand for an inferior good will decrease. Two goods are complements when a price increase in one will cause a decrease in demand for the other. Two goods are substitutes if an increase in the price of one causes an increase in demand for the other.

2. Supply is the quantities of a good or service firms are actually willing and able to produce and offer for sale at various prices over a period of time. Supply depends on the price of the good or service as well as on nonprice determinants. These include the prices of resources, the level of technology, the number of suppliers, and expectations.

    The law of supply states that the quantity supplied of a good or service is usually a positive function of its price, *ceteris paribus*. Changes in a good's price affect the quantity supplied of that good.

    Changes in prices of resources that affect supply cause supply to either increase or decrease. When prices of resources increase, there will be a decrease in supply. An advance in technology or increase in the number of suppliers will usually cause supply to increase.

3. The market-clearing (equilibrium) price is the price at which the amount consumers wish to purchase is equal

to the amount suppliers wish to sell. When supply or demand shifts, the market is in disequilibrium until natural forces determine a new equilibrium price and quantity.
4. The comparison of two equilibrium positions is called comparative statics. The supply and demand model has two endogenous variables—price and quantity—that are determined within the model. The exogenous variables are determined outside the model but influence what goes on in the model by shifting supply and demand. These variables include prices of related goods, tastes, income, expectations, and technology. The supply and demand model, like most economic models, uses marginal analysis. It focuses on decisions about the next unit purchased or sold rather than on aggregate or all-or-nothing decisions.
5. Prices play an important role in informing, directing, and motivating consumers and producers. If left alone, markets maximize individual freedom by allowing individuals to pursue their own self-interest.

NEW TERMS

demand	decrease in demand	(not quite) law of supply	comparative statics
supply	normal good	supply curve	marginal analysis
law of demand	inferior good	market supply curve	endogenous variables
demand schedule	complementary goods	increase in supply	exogenous variables
demand curve	substitute goods	decrease in supply	primary effect
market demand curve	expectations	market equilibrium	secondary effects
increase in demand	supply schedule	market-clearing price	transactions costs

QUESTIONS: REVIEW, APPLICATIONS, AND POLICY

REVIEW

1. How can expectations about economic conditions affect supply?
2. Does the fact that some people appear to buy more of some goods, such as mink coats and diamonds, as their prices go up negate the law of demand?
3. How can belief in a future change in the availability of gasoline affect the demand for automobiles?
4. A market-clearing price is the price at which the amount sold equals the amount purchased. Is this correct?
5. List all of the conditions that can decrease demand or supply.
6. List all of the conditions that can increase demand or supply.
7. Why is it so important to distinguish changes in demand and changes in supply from changes in quantity demanded and changes in quantity supplied?
8. If both the supply and demand curves shift to the right, what happens to price and quantity? What happens if both the supply and demand curves shift to the left?

APPLICATIONS

9. Develop a simple theory to explain (predict) student grades in this course. Identify at least two exogenous variables and one endogenous variable.
10. Pat, a professional student, failed an economics course and decided to sell flowers on a street corner to make ends meet. A second flower seller established a business directly across the street from Pat. Pat, unconcerned, came up with the following hypothesis: "When supply increases, demand will increase. Therefore, I will be just as well off as I was before the second flower seller arrived." Did Pat deserve to fail economics? Why or why not?
11. Why do some people shop at convenience stores, knowing they will pay higher prices, even when a supermarket with lower prices is open in the same block?
12. Draw a supply curve for personal computers that slopes upward and a demand curve for personal computers that slopes downward. They intersect at an equilibrium price of $2,000 and an equilibrium quantity of 6,000 units per month. Now experiment with each of the following:.
    a. A breakthrough in the technology of making chips substantially lowers the cost of production. Which curve shifts, and which way? (Draw it on your diagram.) Find the new equilibrium price and quantity. Did they increase or decrease?
    b. The baby boom generation has bought large numbers of personal computers, and the market is

saturated. The number of potential customers in the following generation is much smaller because the birth rate fell sharply during the late 1960s and early 1970s. Does this affect supply or demand? Which curve shifts, and in which direction? What is the effect on price and quantity?

c. A foreign firm enters the market, adding a new source of supply. How does this change affect the price, quantity, and market supply curve? What is the impact on domestic firms?

13. Explain whether each of the following will shift the supply curve or the demand curve for milk and in which direction.
    a. The birth rate rises. (There are more babies.)
    b. The price of beef is very high, tempting dairy farmers to slaughter their milk cows.
    c. There is a drought, creating a shortage of feed for dairy herds.
    d. Scientists find that drinking too much milk increases the risk of heart disease.
    e. Scientists find that drinking more milk reduces the chances of developing osteoporosis.

POLICY

14. The following table lists market information you gathered about landing slots at the Atlanta airport. Suppose you are asked to make a recommendation to the airport manager about pricing the slots to reduce crowding and delays. What will you recommend?

MARKET FOR LANDING SLOTS FROM 8:00 A.M. to 9:00 A.M.

PRICE ($)	QUANTITY SUPPLIED	QUANTITY DEMANDED
0	12	50
250	12	40
500	12	20
1,000	12	15
1,500	12	8
2,000	12	2

15. In 1994, one of the hot gift items was the Nintendo entertainment system, which was used to play games. Only Nintendo games could be played on this system, and Nintendo games could not be played on other systems. How would a shortage of Nintendo systems affect the demand for Nintendo games? Should governmental policy allow such an arrangement?

SUGGESTIONS FOR FURTHER READING

Friedman, Milton. *Capitalism and Freedom.* Chicago: University of Chicago Press, 1981. This book presents the case for free markets by perhaps the most respected and passionate of their advocates.

Hayek, F. A. "The Use of Knowledge in Society." *American Economic Review* (September 1945): 519–528. This classic, very readable article shows the importance of markets as a source of information and coordination.

Miller, Roger LeRoy, Daniel K. Benjamin, and Douglass C. North. *The Economics of Public Issues,* 8e. New York: Harper-Collins, 1993. An easy-to-read book that uses supply and demand to analyze issues of current interest. North won the Nobel Prize in 1993.

PART 2
INTRODUCTION TO MACROECONOMICS

The next three chapters establish the foundation for the study of macroeconomics. Macroeconomics is concerned with the behavior of economic aggregates, including total output and income, total employment and unemployment, and price levels and inflation. In contrast, microeconomics is focused more narrowly on the quantities and prices of specific goods, such as pizza or textbooks, and the employment of certain resources, such as farmland or textbook writers. If a few people are unemployed, it is probably a microeconomic problem of finding information on job openings or of developing the right skills. If ten million people are unemployed, it is a macroeconomic problem. If the price of eggs rises, it is a microeconomic matter. If the average price of everything rises, it is a macroeconomic problem.

Employment, inflation, and economic growth are the central concerns of macroeconomics. These three chapters provide an overview of some major macroeconomic concerns. Chapter 4 is concerned with employment and unemployment, price stability and inflation and their measurement. Chapter 5 explores the level of output, or GDP, and how it is measured. We begin to look at how these economic aggregates are determined and what makes them change by developing a model of aggregate economic activity called aggregate supply and aggregate demand in Chapter 6.

CHAPTER 4

UNEMPLOYMENT, INFLATION, AND ECONOMIC FLUCTUATIONS

LEARNING OBJECTIVES

1. Define full employment and the various kinds of unemployment, and explain why unemployment is an important policy concern.
2. Explain how unemployment is measured.
3. Define inflation and identify those who gain and lose from inflation, and explain why inflation is an important policy concern.
4. Compute a price index and use it to adjust dollar values for inflation.
5. Explore the relationship between unemployment, inflation, and the business cycle.

Consider this... *What's the number one concern of most college students about life after graduation? Probably finding a job. In 1990–1991 the U.S. economy went through its first recession (a downturn in output and employment) in nine years. As unemployment rose, college graduates in the spring of 1990 and 1991 faced the worst job markets in decades. Even as the economy recovered in 1992, employment did not keep pace. The focus on the 1992 presidential campaign, in fact, was on jobs—good jobs, jobs to re-employ factory workers and middle managers that had been displaced, and jobs for new high school and college graduates.*

When citizens grade the President and Congress on economic performance, they do so with three primary goals in mind. One of those goals is full employment. A second is price stability, or at least a low rate of inflation. A third is economic growth, which means a larger level of output and a higher standard of living. When the economy is performing poorly, as it was in 1980 and again in 1992, voters are likely to turn to a candidate of the opposite party in search of improvement.

What do people want from the economy as a whole? What are the macroeconomic goals? How can a nation measure whether it is better off or worse off than before? One important measure of changes in economic well-being is the amount of output being produced and the amount of income households receive. The level of income and output and the rate at which they grow are the central focus of macroeconomics.

The economic well-being of one household (or of all households taken together) depends on how much income that household earns and what that income can purchase. The ability of a household to earn income is closely tied to employment opportunities. While there are other sources of earnings, like rent and interest, wages and salaries make up most of household income. Households in which people have jobs earn more than households without employed workers, and households with multiple earners have higher incomes that households with just one worker. The purchasing power of the income that these workers earn depends on what is happening to the inflation rate. While growth of total income and output is abstract to most people, the effects of unemployment and inflation on their economic well-being is much more direct and immediate. We begin our study of economics by focusing on employment and unemployment, and the two goals of price stability and inflation. The third goal, economic growth, is discussed in the next chapter.

FULL EMPLOYMENT AND UNEMPLOYMENT

The macroeconomic goal that has received the most attention in recent years is full employment. The precise amounts of employment and unemployment that constitute full employment are difficult to pinpoint. Full employment does not mean that everyone in the population is employed or even that 100 percent of those able are willing to take a job. One way of defining **full employment** is to identify some level of unemployment as "normal" (acceptable or desirable), and only be concerned about unemployment in excess of that amount. A level of 5 to 6 percent is currently considered normal. By this definition, an economy is at full employment when 94 to 95 percent of those who want to work are employed. Another definition of full employment is that the number of job seekers should be approximately equal to the number of job vacancies—the "Help Wanted Index" made famous by former President Reagan. Economists use the 94 to 95 percent standard because it is easier to measure and gives similar results to the other definition.

Unemployment rates since 1950 are shown in Figure 1. Although each decade but the 1960s has seen a recession that drove unemployment up above the norm, you can also see a gradual rise in the average rate of unemployment. Unemployment averaged 4.5 percent in the 1950s, 4.8 percent in the 1960s, 6.1 percent in the 1970s, and 7.3 percent in the 1980s. The first four years of the 1990s averaged 6.6 percent unemployment.

FRICTIONAL AND STRUCTURAL UNEMPLOYMENT

It is not possible to have a situation where everyone is always employed. Some unemployment is normal because there are new entrants into the labor force searching for jobs. Finding a job takes time. During that time, a person will be unemployed. Other workers are between jobs. They have quit one job to look for a better one, are recovering from an illness, or have moved with their families to a different part of the country. Such short-term unemployment is called **frictional unemployment**.

Frictional unemployment is about 3 to 4 percent of the labor force. When immigration is higher, or when there is a large number of high school and college graduates entering the labor force, frictional unemployment may be slightly higher. Immigration, both legal and illegal, is higher in the 1990s than in earlier periods. However, that increase in the labor force is offset by a smaller than average number of high school and college graduates. Frictional unemployment in the 1990s is probably no higher or lower than in earlier decades.

Another normal source of unemployment is a mismatch of workers and jobs. There may be a surplus of aerospace engineers and a need for health care

Full employment
The level of employment at which approximately 94 to 95 percent of those who want to work are employed.

Frictional unemployment
Unemployment caused by workers temporarily between jobs or new entrants to the labor force.

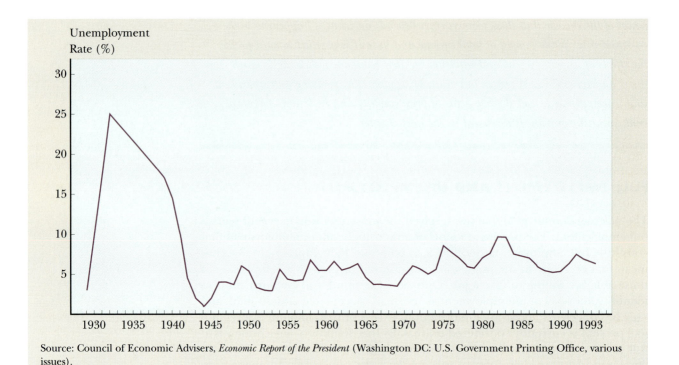

Source: Council of Economic Advisers, *Economic Report of the President* (Washington DC: U.S. Government Printing Office, various issues).

FIGURE 1

U.S. UNEMPLOYMENT RATES (PERCENTAGE OF THE CIVILIAN LABOR FORCE) 1929–1993
Unemployment rates soared between 1929 and 1933. Unemployment remained high until World War II, when war production required almost complete employment of the civilian labor force. Since then, a gradual upward trend in unemployment rates can be observed, with peaks in the recessions of 1959–1960, 1970, 1975, 1980–1982, and 1990–1991.

workers, or excess labor in Montana and a shortage of workers in Virginia. Whenever the available workers do not match the jobs in terms of skills or location, there is **structural unemployment**. This kind of unemployment tends to last longer than frictional unemployment because it takes longer for workers to retrain or relocate to match available jobs. When plants close, either permanently or because the firm is moving production to another place, most of the workers eventually find other work. According to the Bureau of Labor Statistics, 60 percent of workers displaced by plant closings in the 1980–1982 recession were employed again by 1984, but many were working for a lower wage.

Although there is always a certain amount of structural unemployment, it varies more from one time period to the next than frictional unemployment. When economists change the way they define full employment, it usually reflects changes in their estimate of structural unemployment.

Structural unemployment appears to be higher and lasting longer in recent years than in earlier periods because of major changes occurring in the economy. The shift from defense production to civilian production is painful for many workers, firms, and regions, because the products, services, and skills found in firms producing for the military are not easily shifted into civilian uses. The downsizing and restructuring of large firms in the late 1980s and early 1990s put a large number of white collar workers out of jobs, and these displaced workers are only slowly being reabsorbed. The decline in direct manufacturing jobs has been partly offset by growth in service jobs, particularly in health care, but these workers are not easily transferred into very different lines of work.

Some economists argue that both frictional and structural unemployment are higher than necessary because government "subsidizes" unemployment.

Workers take longer to search for a job when they can collect unemployment compensation and other benefits, and the cost of the search falls on taxpayers. Other economists argue that this effect may actually benefit both workers and society as a whole, because workers who search longer may wind up with more suitable jobs, in which they can earn more and be more productive. Regardless of which view you hold, these programs probably do raise the measured rate of unemployment.

In terms of public policy, frictional unemployment calls for better information and employment services. Structural unemployment may imply a need for retraining and assistance in relocating. Since these kinds of policies try to make specific segments of the labor market work more efficiently, they are really closer to being microeconomic than macroeconomic. However, when structural unemployment results from massive shifts in patterns of government spending, such as reduced defense spending in the 1990s, or from major changes in industrial structure, this kind of unemployment can be considered a macroeconomic issue.

Structural unemployment Unemployment caused by a mismatch of the skills or location of unemployed workers and the skills required or locations of available jobs.

CYCLICAL UNEMPLOYMENT

Some unemployment is related to declines in the level of aggregate output. This **cyclical unemployment** is a major policy concern in macroeconomics. Workers are laid off because of a fall in demand generally or specifically for the products they produce. Cyclical unemployment tends to be most severe in heavy industry (manufacturing equipment and some consumer goods such as cars and refrigerators). Macroeconomic policies intended to reduce cyclical unemployment try to create more jobs by increasing demand for total output. There was an increase in cyclical unemployment during the 1990–1991 recession, which lasted from July 1990 to March 1991. Unemployment rose from 5.3 percent in 1989, before the recession, to 5.5 percent in 1990 and 6.7 percent in 1991. However, even after the recession officially ended, unemployment continued to rise, reaching 7.1 percent by the end of 1991 and remaining over 7 percent throughout 1992. This increased unemployment occurred because the very slow economic growth in the recovery created relatively few jobs, while structural changes in both private industry and federal government spending continued to drive up structural unemployment. Only in 1993 did unemployment finally begin to decline.

Cyclical unemployment Unemployment caused by fluctuations in the level of total output, or GNP.

KEY IDEAS

KINDS OF UNEMPLOYMENT

KIND	NORMAL RATE	CAUSE	POLICY
Frictional	4–5%	New entrants Job leavers Returning workers	Improve labor market information
Structural	1–3%	Mismatch between worker and job skills/location	Retraining and relocation assistance
Cyclical	0–?	Downturn in output	Stabilization policy

PRODUCTIVITY AND EMPLOYMENT

Productivity
A measure of year-to-year changes in output per worker hour.

One of the most important influences on long-run trends in employment is changes in worker productivity. **Productivity** is a measure of economic performance that shows changes in output per worker hour from one year to the next. When workers are more productive, firms will hire more of them. Real wages (wages adjusted for inflation) and employment will rise together.

The productivity index for the United States for 1950–1992 is shown in Figure 2. The annual rate of growth of productivity was very high in the early postwar period. It slowed considerably in the 1970s and has remained low since that time, although it has always been higher in the two years immediately following recessions. The 1990–1991 recession showed the same pattern of improved productivity growth coming out of the recession. Much effort has been expended in trying to explain the slowdown in the growth of productivity in recent decades and to suggest ways to improve productivity. Inexperienced or poorly trained workers, low savings rates, and not enough investment in developing new products and technology were all cited as possible causes. Other economists, however, have suggested that the high rates of increase in productivity of the early postwar period were not typical and that current rates are more nearly normal.

COSTS OF UNEMPLOYMENT

Why are macroeconomic policy makers concerned about the level of unemployment? First, unemployment is wasteful. If workers are unemployed, the economy is not operating on the production possibilities curve. These workers could be producing goods and services. Although other resources can also be unemployed, policy makers and the public are usually more concerned about

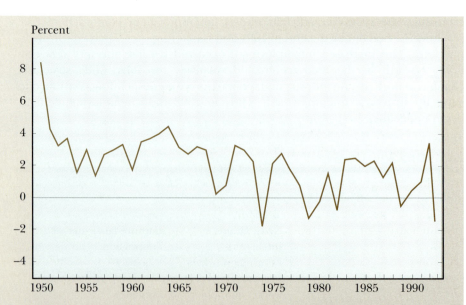

FIGURE 2
PRODUCTIVITY INDEX, 1950–1993
The index of productivity per worker hour in the private sector increased at an average rate of just under 2 percent, doubling in the last 40 years. The rapid growth rates of the early period slowed down in the 1970s but picked up slightly in the 1980s and early 1990s.

Source: U.S. Department of Commerce, *Business Statistics* (Washington DC: U.S. Government Printing Office, various issues).

unemployed labor than idle capital or land, because most households receive the largest share of their income from labor earnings.

The second reason for concern about unemployment is that the system of income distribution in a market economy is very dependent on employment. If people don't have jobs, they earn no income. Employed persons wind up supporting unemployed persons through unemployment benefits, food stamps, and other social welfare programs. For the unemployed, a period without meaningful work or an opportunity to be self-supporting can also be psychologically demoralizing. Sociologists find more depression, addiction, spouse and child abuse, and other social problems in households where workers are unemployed for long periods.

Finally, unemployment is costly to workers in terms of future earnings. Each period of unemployment is a lost opportunity to develop skills and experience that will make a worker more valuable to an employer.

MEASURING UNEMPLOYMENT

The number of unemployed as well as the number of employed will grow with the population and with the fraction of the population that is of working age and employable. In order to make comparisons over time, it is more helpful to measure unemployment as a percentage of the labor force than to just count the number of unemployed. The **unemployment rate** is defined as the percentage of the labor force that wants to work but does not currently have a job. That is,

$$\text{Unemployment rate} = \frac{\text{Unemployed workers}}{\text{Labor force}}$$

where Labor force = Employed workers + Unemployed workers.

Unemployment rate
The percentage of the labor force that wants to work but is not currently employed.

THE LABOR FORCE AND UNEMPLOYED WORKERS

The first step in measuring unemployment is to determine the size of the labor force. Until recently, only the civilian labor force was counted. Those who were employed in the military services were excluded. Newer measures include the military in the labor force.

The **labor force** consists of those who are working and those who are actively seeking work. A full-time homemaker, a child, a retiree, a full-time student, a prisoner, or anyone else not employed is not counted in either the numerator or the denominator of the unemployment rate. People who had been seeking work but have given up and stopped looking are also excluded from the measured labor force.

The measures of both the labor force and the number of unemployed are obtained primarily from door-to-door surveys and payroll data from business firms.[1] Respondents in door-to-door surveys are only considered unemployed if they have made some effort to find work in the last four weeks. Other data comes from filing of unemployment claims at state employment offices. Because the Bureau of Labor Statistics can't count the unemployed directly, sometimes

Labor force
Those who are working or actively seeking work.

---

1. The results of these surveys are not the same because some jobs are held by illegal aliens and some workers have more than one job. See Paul O. Flain, "How Many New Jobs Since 1982? Two Surveys Differ," *Monthly Labor Review* (August 1989): 10–15.

the figures reported immediately are later revised a great deal. An example of this kind of data problem occurred during the 1990–1991 recession, when there appeared to be a major loss of jobs that did not actually occur. The people calculating employment and unemployment from payroll data were confusing the number of payroll checks with the number of people. Many people receive extra checks for bonuses and vacations. When those numbers drop, there appear to be fewer workers on the payroll. This source of error has been corrected, but it illustrates the kinds of problems there are in collecting and interpreting unemployment data.[2]

The unemployment rate is an imperfect indicator for other reasons as well. Discouraged workers (those who sought work for a while, became discouraged, and gave up) are not counted as unemployed. This omission makes unemployment appear lower than it really is. Some workers may be underemployed—working below their ability or fewer hours than they would like. These workers, however, are counted as employed. On the other hand, some workers leave jobs, make a modest effort to find work in order to qualify for unemployment benefits, and avoid taking a job until their unemployment benefits run out. These people should probably not be counted as "actively seeking work." Their inclusion overstates unemployment.

THE LABOR FORCE PARTICIPATION RATE

Labor force participation rate
The fraction of the population over 16 years of age who are employed or actively seeking work.

The major source of short-term changes in unemployment is changes in total demand for labor that result from changes in total output. Over longer periods, total labor supply also affects the unemployment rate. An indicator that is helpful in sorting out the relative importance of these two sources of changes in unemployment is the labor force participation rate. The **labor force participation rate** measures the fraction of the adult population that is employed or actively seeking work.

In 1948, the labor force participation rate was 59 percent. It remained near that level until the 1960s, when it began to rise. By 1993, 66 percent of the population over the age of 16 was in the labor force. The increase in the labor force participation rate resulted partly from the baby boomers coming of age and partly from increased female labor force participation. In the early 1960s, only 38 percent of adult women were in the labor force; by 1993, 58 percent were working or looking for work. This increased fraction of the population in the labor force meant that even though the U.S. unemployment rate was reaching new highs, the employment rate (the percentage of the population with jobs) was fairly stable. Part of the increase in unemployment was caused by the larger fraction of the population that was seeking employment.

In the 1990s, the growth in the labor force participation rate is expected to level off, and the labor force is expected to grow at an average rate of only 1.2 percent a year, compared to 2.3 percent in the 1980s.[3] The main reason for slow growth is fewer new entrants to the labor force, because of a smaller number of people in their late teens and early twenties.

---

2. "The Bureau of Labor Statistics' Case of the Missing Jobs," *Washington Post* (March 10, 1993): F-1.
3. Howard N. Fullerton, Jr., "New Labor Force Projections Spanning 1988 to 2000, *Monthly Labor Review* (November 1989): 3–11.

POLICY FOCUS: FORECASTING AND THE LEADING INDICATORS

Before governments can try to control inflation or unemployment through stabilization policy, they have to be able to forecast the course of the business cycle. Economic forecasting is not very accurate or very timely. Economists are very good at explaining what happened and why, but they are not nearly as successful as weather forecasters in predicting the future. (Remember, though, that weather forecasters only predict for five days ahead!)

The search for a forecasting tool has to be based in theory. Ideally, you would like to find some variable, such as interest rates or grocery store sales or college enrollments, that had some systematic relationship to the ups and downs of the business cycle for some sound theoretical reason. Even better would be a variable that not only moved *with* the business cycle but actually *ahead* of it. Over many decades, forecasters have identified such variables. A group of eleven economic variables called the leading indicators is used for forecasting the ups and downs of the business cycle by policy analysts, business forecasters, and individuals. These indicators are called leading indicators because they lead the business cycle, generally turning down six months before the peak or upper turning point, and turning up six months before the trough or lower turning point. The ups and downs of the average of the leading indicators are reported monthly on the evening news and in the major newspapers.

The variables that make up the leading indicators include the money supply, stock prices, consumer expectations, commodity (raw materials, farm products) prices, the average work week, new unemployment claims, new building permits, new orders for consumer goods, new orders for investment goods, unfilled orders, and backlogged deliveries. You will see the change in the average of these eleven indicators reported in newspapers and on television news the first week of each month. If the average rises for several months in a row, it's forecasting expansion in six months time. If the average points consistently downward, it's hinting at recession. The leading indicators are far from perfect as a forecaster. Economists like to joke that this index forecast eight of the last six recessions! One of the reasons that economists had difficulty in deciding when the 1990–1991 recession ended was that the leading indicators didn't give a clear direction. They went up a little, down a little, and sideways a lot. Economists finally figured out (correctly) that the indicators were pointing to a weak recovery.

Economists have other forecasting tools in their arsenal, including elaborate computer models and other techniques. But for rough estimates of the direction of the economy, policy makers in both government and business find that the leading indicators are a very useful forecasting tool.

PRICE STABILITY AND INFLATION

A second important macroeconomic goal is price stability. Both individual prices and the average level of prices can either rise or fall. In recent years, however, the United States has experienced a continued rise in the general, or average, level of prices, which is **inflation**. The measure of inflation is the change in the price index. A **price index** measures the price level in any year relative to some base year. The best-known such measure is the **Consumer Price Index (CPI)**, popularly known as the cost-of-living index. The CPI measures the cost of a market basket of a selected array of consumer goods each year, much as consumers might compare the cost of the usual contents of their grocery cart each week at the supermarket. The percentage change in the CPI from one year to the next is the inflation rate.

The inflation rate from 1933 to 1993 is shown in Figure 3. You can see that, except for World War II, prices were relatively stable until the 1970s. High inflation in the late 1970s and early 1980s increased awareness of the many problems caused by inflation, especially when it is unexpected. Lower inflation rates in the rest of the 1980s helped to calm fears that high rates of inflation would become

Inflation
A rise in the general, or average, level of prices.

Price index
A measure of changes in price levels from year to year.

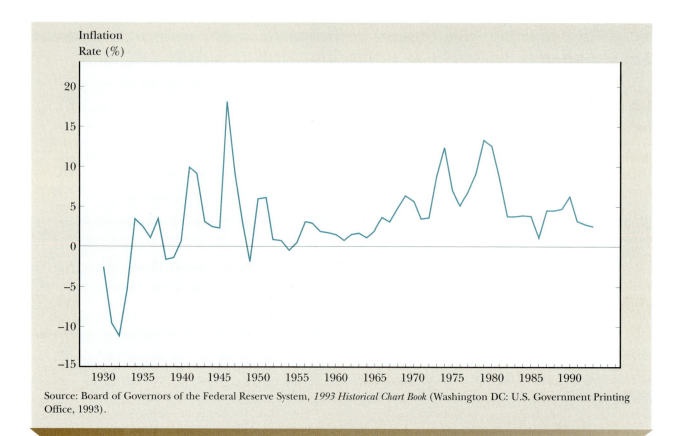

Source: Board of Governors of the Federal Reserve System, *1993 Historical Chart Book* (Washington DC: U.S. Government Printing Office, 1993).

FIGURE 3
INFLATION RATE, 1933–1993
The rate of change in the CPI is shown for each year since 1933. Note the very low inflation rates during the 1950s, then the gradual rise in the 1960s, a sharp increase in 1975–1982, a drop after the 1980–1982 recession, and lower inflation rates since then.

Consumer Price Index (CPI)
A measure of the year-to-year increase in the price level based on the cost of a representative market basket of consumer goods.

a permanent feature of the American economy. Inflation was low in the early 1990s, primarily because of the 1990–1991 recession and the slow recovery.

GAINERS AND LOSERS FROM INFLATION

One reason why governments try to restrain inflation is that it causes unintended and often undesirable redistribution of income and wealth. Redistribution is more likely to occur when inflation is unexpected. People make contracts and decisions on the assumption of an expected rate of inflation. Suppose, for simplicity, you are expecting zero inflation. You lend someone $100 for a year at an interest rate of 5 percent. This rate is enough to cover your risk of not being repaid and the cost of not using the money for a year, assuming no inflation. Then there is unexpected inflation of 10 percent. At the end of a year, you receive $105, but it will only purchase $95.45 in goods and services ($105/1.10). Who gained? The borrower. If you had anticipated the inflation, you would have demanded a higher interest rate to cover the loss of purchasing power. Unexpected inflation redistributes income from lenders to borrowers.

Lenders and borrowers are not the only ones who are affected by income redistribution because of inflation. People who hold any kind of fixed-dollar assets, such as life insurance policies, lose purchasing power. People who hold real, physical assets, such as land, houses, or jewelry, often find that the value of those assets rises faster than the rate of inflation. As more people shift to real assets in response to expected inflation, the increase in demand for those assets will drive their prices up even faster than the inflation rate. Those assets that people buy as "insurance" against inflation are called inflation hedges.

Buying as much house as you could possibly afford was a popular inflation hedge in the 1970s and 1980s. Many home buyers were later able to sell their houses for much more than they paid for them as house prices increased rapidly. This pattern ended in the late 1980s. In the 1990s, the smaller number of new home buyers has meant that average house prices have been fairly stable or even falling. Housing does not look like a good inflation hedge in the 1990s. Generally, common stocks, which represent ownership claims on the real, physical assets of firms, also do better than the inflation rate. However, the future course of the price of any given stock is highly uncertain, making stocks a risky inflation hedge. Hedging against anticipated inflation is an important way to protect the value of assets, but there is no perfect instrument to use for that purpose.

Governments are often winners during times of inflation because state and federal income tax revenues tend to rise faster than the inflation rate. As prices rise, households' dollar incomes also rise, even if the purchasing power of those incomes is unchanged. Taxpayers find themselves in higher tax brackets, paying a higher percentage of their incomes in taxes. Changes in U.S. tax laws since 1986 made federal income taxes less progressive, although some progressivity was restored in the 1993 deficit reduction plan. In the future, the government will stand to gain less from inflation. Since 1990, some aspects of the income tax code (brackets and personal exemptions) have been adjusted for inflation each year, making the federal government even less of a winner from inflation. However, even with these changes, the government will continue to reap gains in the form of increased revenues when there is inflation. This revenue gain will occur because there are still several rates and brackets in the federal income tax code and in many state income tax codes as well. Revenue from other taxes, such as sales taxes and property taxes, tends to lag behind inflation.

THE PRICE LEVEL AND RELATIVE PRICES

It is important to separate the effects of inflation from the effects of changes in *relative* prices. As a worker, you may feel that you are hurt by inflation because your wages aren't rising as fast as the price level. But it's very possible that even if prices were stable your wages might fall. Your wages could fall because of declining demand in your occupation or in your area. Wages of some workers—for example, accountants and health care workers—have been rising faster than the rate of inflation. Wages of other workers—such as retail clerks—have been rising more slowly. In recent years, wages for fast-food work and other entry-level jobs traditionally held by teenagers and college students have been rising sharply because of the relatively small number of people in that age group. Such relative wage changes have been caused by changes in supply and demand in those markets. As long as the average wage keeps pace with inflation, workers are not hurt by inflation, even though some workers may be suffering from a decline in demand for their particular skills.

The same is true of prices of consumer products. Even when most prices are rising, the prices of some goods are falling or rising much more slowly. If the market basket of goods you purchase is very different from that used to compute the CPI, then you will feel the effects of both inflation and changing relative prices. If your basket is full of items whose prices are rising faster than average, both inflation and changing relative prices will hit your budget. But if you are consuming less popular goods such as bicycle tires, granola, and diapers, when most other consumers are driving up the prices of gasoline, oat bran, and college tuition, the cost of your basket may not be rising as fast as the CPI.

MARKET SIGNALS, INFLATION PSYCHOLOGY, AND MENU COSTS

This discussion of the difference between changes in relative prices and changes in the price level suggests another problem due to inflation. Inflation confuses the market signals on which individuals rely to make good decisions about earning, spending, saving, and investing. It is difficult to tell what is happening to relative prices when all prices are moving at once. This confusion of signals due to inflation is a major problem in market economies.

Another problem from high rates of inflation is an inflation psychology that leads people to "buy now before the price goes up." This expectation encourages consumption but discourages saving and investment. Saving and investment are important because they increase the nation's stock of capital and result in a higher rate of economic growth. By discouraging saving and investment, high rates of inflation can have a negative effect on economic growth.

A third problem is the menu cost of inflation. Have you ever gone into a restaurant and seen prices crossed out and written over? Such price changes happen more often with inflation. Firms have to get new menus, price lists, catalogs, and other price information printed more often. All of these adjustments use real resources that could be used more productively in other ways.

KEY IDEAS

WHAT'S WRONG WITH INFLATION?
The costs of inflation are:
- unintended redistribution of income and wealth,
- transfer of resources to government,
- confused market signals,
- lower levels of saving and investment (inflation psychology), and
- menu costs.

A GOAL OF ZERO INFLATION?

Given all these drawbacks to inflation, why not try to reduce the inflation rate to zero? In fact, a target inflation rate of zero has been proposed by Alan Greenspan, the chairman of the Federal Reserve System (the central bank). One of the problems with this target, however, is that the measurement of inflation is not very precise. Therefore, what appears to be modest inflation of about 2 percent might actually be closer to zero inflation if the index were correctly computed.[4] A stronger argument against the goal of zero inflation is that the costs of reducing the inflation rate to zero may be greater than the benefits.

---

4. For an evaluation of Greenspan's proposal, see Michelle Garfinkel, "What is an 'Acceptable' Rate of Inflation?—A Review of the Issues," *Review*, Federal Reserve Bank of St. Louis (July-August 1989):3–15.

Often moderate inflation is associated with rapid economic growth, which is usually considered a desirable goal. Since most of the problems from inflation are related to high rates of inflation, rapid inflation, or unexpected inflation, a low and stable rate of inflation may be desirable.

MEASURING INFLATION: PRICE INDEXES

A price index, like any index, is a weighted average. Index values are composites of many numerical values, which are assigned weights based on their relative importance. The absolute value of any index has little meaning. The *relative value*, especially changes in the relative value, of an index is important. The fact that the Dow-Jones industrial stock index passed the 3,600 mark in 1993, for example, doesn't mean much unless you know what its value was in earlier years.

HOW PRICE INDEXES ARE CONSTRUCTED

A price index can be constructed in two different ways. One is to take a current-year market basket of goods and services and ask what it would have cost to buy the same collection last year or several years ago. This kind of index, a current-weights index, assigns weights to the various items based on the composition of output or the consumption in the current year. The other way to construct a price index is to start with a market basket or output mix in some benchmark, or base, year. Then the behavior of the cost of that market basket is followed in succeeding years.

The most familiar price index, the Consumer Price Index (CPI), uses base-year weights. The current CPI is based on the mix of goods bought by a typical urban family of four in 1987–1988. The base changes every five years based on new consumer surveys, but there is a long lag between when the survey is taken and when the results are available. Data with a base of 1987–1988 just began to be reported in 1993, and the 1992–1993 survey data will not be available to use until 1998.

Suppose that a typical family bought twenty pounds of ground beef, three pairs of jeans, five rolls of paper towels, and eight pounds of apples. Those goods and the amounts of each are used in computing the index. That basket of goods is priced at regular intervals to see what is happening to the CPI, or the "cost of living." Table 1 constructs a price index for those four items after determining their base-year and current-year prices.

TABLE 1 COMPUTING A PRICE INDEX

ITEM	QUANTITY Q	YEAR 1 PRICE P_1	TOTAL VALUE $(Q \times P_1)$	YEAR 2 PRICE P_2	TOTAL VALUE $(Q \times P_2)$
Ground beef	20	$1.10	$22.00	$1.50	$30.00
Jeans	3	16.00	48.00	18.00	54.00
Paper towels	5	.60	3.00	.50	2.50
Apples	8	.25	2.00	.30	2.40
Value of market basket			$75.00		$88.90

Since the items in the market baskets are the same for both years, the increase from $75.00 to $88.90 must be due entirely to price changes. The index is

88.90/75.00 = 1.18,

or, as it is usually written, 118. This number means that prices rose, on the average, 18 percent. Note, however, that two prices rose more than 18 percent, one price rose less, and one price actually fell.

PRICE INDEXES IN PRACTICE

The actual CPI is based on what is happening to the prices of hundreds of items. To find out what is happening to the prices of particular groups of goods or services—such as housing, food, energy, and health care—you can check their price indexes each month in the *Monthly Labor Review*. Indexes for different regions of the country are also available. Some colleges and universities compute and publish a price index for their immediate areas.

Forbes magazine constructs a price index each year called "The Forbes Four Hundred Cost of Living Extremely Well Index." This index includes such items as a Russian sable coat, tuition at Harvard, season tickets to the Metropolitan Opera, a private plane, an Olympic-size swimming pool, Cuban cigars, and other luxury items. In the late 1980s, this index was rising more rapidly than the CPI. However, little sympathy was generated in political circles for the plight of the extremely well-to-do.

Another tongue-in-cheek index was constructed by James Schick for the cost of the equipment that colonists were required to provide in order to accompany Captain John Smith to the New World in 1624.[5] Schick's list of food, clothing, household equipment, tools, and transportation included such now hard-to-find items as powder and shot, swords, and muskets. A careful search for equivalent items led to the conclusion that in 1989 these items would cost $3,190 (plus transatlantic passage for the settler and possessions). John Smith's estimate for the same list of goods was 12 pounds, 6 shillings, and 3 pence, or about $55 at the old dollar/pound exchange rate. Of course, some of the modern items were of better quality, but still, a comparison of these two figures gives you a very rough estimate of inflation over the last 365 years!

USES FOR THE CONSUMER PRICE INDEX

Real income
Income measured in terms of the goods and services it will buy.

Price indexes are useful for a number of purposes. If you are comparing job offers in different parts of the country, you will want to adjust salary offers to take into account differences in the local cost of living in each area. If you want to see if there has been any improvement since last year in your **real income**, or the purchasing power of what you earn, you need to adjust this year's nominal income for price changes. Suppose, for example, that between 1990 and 1991 your nominal income rose from $20,000 to $21,200, a 6 percent increase. How much did your real income increase? Table 2 shows this calculation, using CPI indexes for which the base value is 100 for 1982–1984.

5. James B. M. Schick, "John Smith's Bill: Then and Now," *American Heritage* (November 1989):158–165.

TABLE 2 CONVERTING NOMINAL INCOME TO REAL INCOME

YEAR	INCOME	CPI	INCOME IN 1982–1984 DOLLARS
1990	$20,000	130.7	$15,302
1991	$21,200	136.2	$15,565

Percentage increase in the price level: $(136.2-130.7)/130.7 = 4.21$ percent
Income increase in constant dollars: $263
Percentage increase in real income: $263/$20,000 = 1.32$ percent

Note that the 6 percent increase in nominal income is slightly greater than the sum of the real increase of about 1.32 percent and the price increase of 4.21 percent. This observation offers a shortcut for approximating a change in real income when inflation rates are not too high. You can approximate real income changes using

% change Y_r = % change Y_n − % change P,

where Y_r is the real income, Y_n is the nominal income, and P is the price level. If the change in nominal income (6 percent in this case) and the change in the price level (4.2 percent) are known, then their difference will be approximately equal to the percentage change in real income.

Changes in the CPI are used to adjust poverty income levels, Social Security benefits, and wages for workers who have contracts providing for cost-of-living adjustments. Even where no contract is involved, the CPI plays a role in many wage negotiations and other business and personal decisions. Housing became an attractive investment in the 1970s, for example, because of figures showing that the value of the average house was rising faster than the CPI. (It is expected to fall behind the CPI in the 1990s, however.) Probably no other economic data is quoted as often as the CPI.

PROBLEMS WITH THE CONSUMER PRICE INDEX

Because the CPI is used so widely, it is important to recognize its drawbacks and limits. One of these is the fact that the market basket is fixed or changed very infrequently on the basis of extensive consumer surveys. The current CPI is based on a survey taken in 1987–1988. Since that time, changes in the age distribution of the population, changes in tastes and technology, and development of new products have changed the mix of goods consumers buy. The more time that has passed since the survey that was used to find the weights, the more inaccurate the CPI becomes.

A second problem has to do with changes in relative prices. The CPI measures changes in the *average* price of a representative market basket of goods and services. If your household consumes those goods and services in about that proportion, then the CPI will reflect changes in your cost of living. If, however, you spend more than average amounts on medical care and housing (whose prices have risen rapidly) and less than average amounts on clothing and furniture (whose prices have risen more slowly), then your personal price index will rise faster than the CPI. Using the CPI to compare incomes over time or to adjust wages or Social Security benefits is likely to lead to over adjusting at some times and under correcting for inflation at others.

OTHER PRICE INDEXES

GDP deflator
A current-weights index used to correct for price changes in the GDP.

There are two other widely used price indexes. One is the **GDP deflator**, used to adjust total output for inflation. GDP as a measure of total output will be discussed in the next chapter. This index has a broader base than the CPI because it reflects all of the goods and services produced in the economy, not just consumer goods. Unlike the CPI, the GDP deflator is a current-weights index. The weights for the various components are based on the proportions sold or produced in the current year, not a base year. Because the two indexes are calculated differently, the GDP deflator gives a different measure of inflation than the CPI does. The difference is partly due to the deflator's broader coverage and partly due to the fact that it uses current weights rather than base-year weights. Table 3 compares inflation measured by the CPI and by the GDP deflator for 1975 to 1993.

Producer Price Index
A group of three indexes for raw materials, semifinished goods, and finished goods that shows what is happening to prices paid by producers and wholesalers.

Another major price index, the **Producer Price Index**, is actually a family of indexes. There are three indexes: one for raw materials, one for semifinished goods, and one for finished goods. These indexes show what is happening to prices paid by producers and wholesalers, which will eventually affect the prices of retail goods and services. The Producer Price Index is useful in forecasting changes in the CPI and the GDP deflator.

TABLE 3 COMPARISON OF INFLATION RATES: CONSUMER PRICE INDEX AND GDP DEFLATOR, 1980–1993

YEAR	INFLATION RATE MEASURED BY CPI (PERCENT)	INFLATION RATE MEASURED BY GDP DEFLATOR (PERCENT)
1980	12.5	9.5
1981	8.9	10.0
1982	3.8	6.2
1983	3.8	4.1
1984	3.9	4.4
1985	3.8	3.7
1986	1.1	2.6
1987	4.4	3.2
1988	4.4	3.9
1989	4.6	4.4
1990	6.1	4.4
1991	3.1	3.9
1992	2.9	2.9
1993	2.7	2.6

Source: Council of Economic Advisers, *Economic Report of the President* (Washington DC: U.S. Government Printing Office, 1994); U.S. Department of Commerce, *Survey of Current Business*, (Washington DC: U.S. Government Printing Office, March 1994).

FLUCTUATIONS IN OUTPUT, EMPLOYMENT, AND PRICES

The ups and downs of inflation and employment are not random. In fact, they tend to move in rather systematic fashion, related to changes in total output. In particular, the unemployment rate and growth of output track each other quite closely, though in opposite directions. The inflation rate is less consistently related to the other two. Until the 1970s, inflation rates in the United States tended to be low when growth was slow and unemployment was high. Higher inflation rates went with rapid growth and low unemployment rates. From 1973 to 1982, however, the U.S. economy experienced slow growth, high unemployment, and high inflation all at once. The rest of the 1980s saw steady growth of output with both unemployment and inflation rates lower than the preceding decade, but with unemployment still relatively high. Thus far in the 1990s, there is a pattern of slow growth, low inflation, and relatively high unemployment, with expectations that growth and unemployment will improve in the future while inflation may begin to pick up as well.

Over the course of a longer period, the major macroeconomic variables tend to move together in a rather predictable fashion, although not always in the "right" direction. When there is slow growth or even falling output, rising unemployment, and/or high inflation rates, the government often intervenes to try to "correct" the course of these variables. **Stabilization policy** consists of those actions of government designed to smooth out ups and downs in output, employment, and prices.

An observed and repeated pattern of ups and downs in output, employment, and prices was named the **business cycle** in the nineteenth century. A simplified business cycle is shown in Figure 4. In the expansionary phase of the cycle (from upturn through peak), output increases, prices rise rapidly, and unemployment falls. Productivity tends to increase as the economy emerges

Stabilization policy
Government actions designed to dampen fluctuations in output, employment, and prices.

Business cycle
Fluctuations in economic activity measured by the ups and downs in real output, employment, and prices.

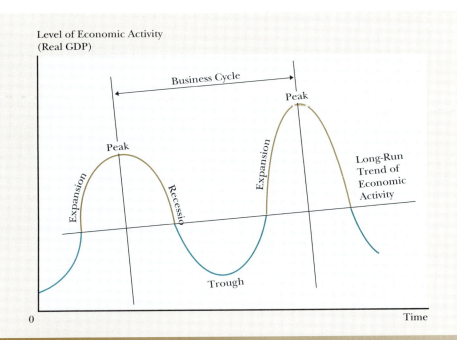

FIGURE 4
A HYPOTHETICAL BUSINESS CYCLE
This typical business cycle shows fluctuations in the level of economic activity over time. In this hypothetical business cycle, the peak and trough are equal in magnitude, and the upturn and downturn take the same length of time. Actual cycles may be less symmetric, with upturns greater or smaller than downturns in size or duration. The cycle is measured from peak to peak. The trend line is the underlying growth rate of GDP.

from the trough of a recession. Firms have kept some workers on during the recession but have not used them fully. As sales increase, firms employ these workers more fully, and productivity rises. As expansion continues, new and less experienced workers are hired. Then the increase in both productivity and output starts to slow, although employment continues to rise.

RECESSIONS, TROUGHS, EXPANSIONS, AND PEAKS

Peak
The highest output level in a business cycle: the upper turning point.

Recession
A decline in real output for two or more successive quarters.

Trough
The lower turning point in a business cycle.

Expansion
A period of growth in real output following a recession.

As output reaches a high point, or **peak**, and turns down, prices tend to fall also, or at least to rise at a slower rate. The downturn of output is called a **recession**. The Commerce Department's rule is that the economy is in a recession when output (adjusted for price changes) declines for two or more successive quarters. Unemployment increases and income and output fall, until the lower turning point, or **trough**, when output reaches its lowest level. Then the process starts over again. The upturn from trough to peak is an **expansion**. A complete cycle goes from peak to peak or from trough to trough.

Each successive peak (and trough) should occur at a higher level of output because the business cycle is a fluctuation around a trend line of growing output over time. For example, a six-year business cycle with a trend growth rate of output of 2 percent a year should see a final peak of output that is 12 to 13 percent above the previous peak.

EARLY BUSINESS CYCLE THEORIES

Much of the early measurement work in macroeconomics was related to the study of business cycles. Researchers identified recurring patterns of upturns and downturns at intervals of eight years (the general business cycle) and twenty years (linked to activity in building construction). In the nineteenth century, macroeconomics meant describing and attempting to explain these business cycles.

These observed ups and downs in economic activity were explained in some rather creative ways. One of these explanations was the sunspot theory, developed by English economist William Stanley Jevons. Unusually severe radioactive storms on the surface of the sun, known as sunspots, seemed to be closely linked to business cycles. This link may sound like a perfect example of the association-causation fallacy discussed in Chapter 1, but there was some plausible logic behind it. Sunspots do affect weather patterns on earth, and the agricultural sector (then the largest single sector of the economy) has always been highly dependent on the weather. However, even with the declining relative importance of agriculture, the business cycle is still a fact of economic life. Sunspots may have contributed to early business cycles, but they do not appear to be the driving force in this century.

Another contributor to the mystique of business cycles was a Russian economist, Nikolai Kondratieff. Other observers noted regular cycles of eight to ten years, with shorter cycles of two to three years and longer cycles of about twenty years. Kondratieff found even longer periods of expansion and contraction of about fifty years. These cycles are called Kondratieff cycles, or long waves. Some observers argue that both the regular eight-year cycle and the long-wave cycle turned down at the end of the 1920s, contributing to the severity of the Great Depression.

It has been suggested that the fifty-year cycles are related to the development of entire new industries and complexes of industries—for example, the development of automobiles, radio and motion pictures, and household appliances in the first few decades of this century. If Kondratieff was right, another downturn in the fifty-year cycle was due in the late 1970s. However, a depression did not occur, although there was slow growth and high unemployment during that period.

Most nineteenth-century economists focused their attention on the shorter eight- to ten-year cycle and the twenty-year cycle. They looked to patterns of consumption and investment for their explanations.

U.S. ECONOMIC FLUCTUATIONS SINCE THE CIVIL WAR

Some recent business cycles in the United States can be identified in Figure 5, which plots both unemployment rates and the rate of change of real output on the same diagram. There was a mild recession in 1953–1954 and again in 1957–1958 and 1970. There were particularly severe downturns in 1974–1975 and 1980–1982, and a modest but identifiable recession in 1990–1991.

The U.S. economy experienced twenty-seven recessions between the end of the Civil War and 1990. On the average, a recession has occurred in the United States every 4.5 years. The 1929–1933 recession was so severe it was given a special name: depression. A **depression** is a very severe recession. President Harry Truman once said that when your neighbor is out of work, that's a recession; but

Depression
A very severe recession.

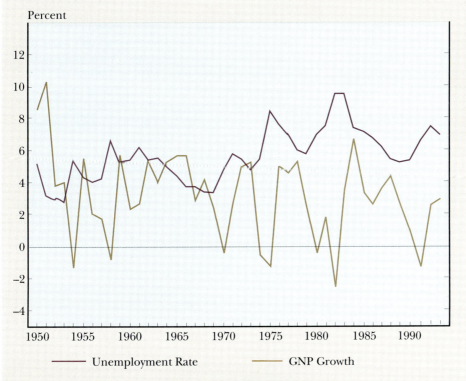

FIGURE 5
ACTUAL BUSINESS CYCLES, 1953–1993
Plotting unemployment and the rate of growth of real output on the same diagram makes it possible to identify fluctuations. Recessions can be identified for 1957–1958, 1970–1971, 1974–1975, 1980–1982, and 1990–1991.

when you lose your job, that's a depression. In a depression, people suffer unemployment, inability to get credit, and losses of their homes, farms, savings, and businesses.

With the outbreak of World War II, prices began a sharp rise, both output and employment rose dramatically, and unemployment almost disappeared. The United States experienced more minor ups and downs in the late 1940s and 1950s, followed by a period of fairly steady growth from 1961 to 1969. The ups and downs resumed with the recession of 1970. There was a severe downturn in 1974–1975 and another in 1980–1982. The most recent recession, 1990–1991, was relatively brief (nine months) and less severe than the two preceding recessions.

In the years since World War II, the most significant change from the prewar period is that declining real output has been much less likely to be accompanied by a fall in prices. When prices have declined, they have not fallen nearly as much as in periods before World War II. A decline in economic activity that is not accompanied by a fall in the price level is referred to as **stagflation**. A combination of the words *stagnation* and *inflation*, this term means that the economy is stagnant (not growing), but there is also inflation at the same time. In the 1974–1975 recession, prices continued to rise sharply. Not until the relatively severe 1980–1982 recession did the rate of inflation fall sharply. Inflation rates remained low through the late 1980s and into the 1990s.

Stagflation
An economic condition of slow growth, high unemployment, and inflation.

GLOBAL OUTLOOK: THE DEPRESSION IN EUROPE AND CANADA

The Great Depression of the 1930s was felt in other countries as well. The triggering event for the United States was the stock market crash of Black Friday, October 29, 1929. For Europeans, it was the collapse of a major bank, the Kredit Anstalt Bank, in Austria in 1930. Other banks failed in its wake.

Two important conditions in the early 1930s made the Depression spread from country to country. The first was the international gold standard, which linked the banking systems of many countries. The gold standard limited the power of national banking systems to expand their money supply unless they had enough gold backing for any added currency. Nations that lost gold to foreigners were forced to contract their money supplies at a time when expansion of the money supply would have been a more suitable policy. As the Depression deepened, one country after another abandoned the gold standard, usually only after the domestic money supply had shrunk to a much smaller size.

The second condition was protectionism. Many countries, including the United States, reacted to falling output and rising unemployment by trying to "keep jobs at home." They tried to substitute domestic production for imported goods by imposing high tariffs and other restrictions—a policy known as "beggar thy neighbor." A few economists even argue that protectionism caused the Great Depression, although most would only argue that protectionism made the Depression even more severe. The physical volume of trade fell by one-third in the early years of the Depression. Because of falling prices, the value of trade fell by two-thirds.

The Depression's effects in each country can be measured by what happened to output and unemployment during the worst period, 1929–1932. Partly because of their great prosperity in the 1920s, the United States and Canada experienced the largest declines in total output, measured in current dollars. The market value of output fell 25 percent in Canada and 26 percent in the United States in that worst period. Part of the decline was in real output and part was due to falling prices. In Europe, where the 1920s had not been as prosperous, declines in the market value of output were less drastic but still striking: 12 percent in France, 16 percent in Germany, and 10 percent in Sweden. The unemployment statistics were even grimmer. (See the table of unemployment rates for 1929 and 1932.)

The political effects of the Great Depression were far-reaching. In the United States, it led to an expanded role for government, including Social Security, unemployment compensation, welfare programs, and bank regulation. In Germany and Italy, the frustrations of the Great Depression led to the rise of fascist governments under Hitler and Mussolini. Canada and many Western European nations followed the same path as the United States in building a social safety net for those who lost their source of income. Most Western European governments, however, went much further, creating welfare states that provided health care, public housing, income support programs, and similar services.

UNEMPLOYMENT RATES FOR 1929 AND 1932

YEAR	GERMANY	SWEDEN	UNITED KINGDOM	CANADA	UNITED STATES
1929	5.9%	2.4%	5.9%	2.9%	3.1%
1932	17.2%	6.8%	13.1	17.6%	23.5%

A CASE STUDY IN BUSINESS CYCLES: THE GREAT DEPRESSION

The Great Depression brought severe economic hardships to a large portion of the U.S. population. Real output fell by more than one-third. Unemployment rose to almost 25 percent of the work force in the depths of the Depression. Many jobs were converted to a part-time basis in order to spread the work among more people. In addition, banks were failing. Between 1929 and 1933, the number of commercial banks in the United States fell by one-third. More than a fifth of all surviving banks had to suspend operations for some time because of financial problems. Few depositors ever recovered any of the funds they lost.

The effect on people went beyond economic hardships. America seemed to have lost its bright promise. People who had worked hard all their lives, who had saved and planned for the future, and who had believed in the work ethic found themselves wiped out. They lost homes, businesses, and jobs—through no fault of their own. Retired people found their stocks and bonds nearly worthless, and their savings vanished in bank failures. Many people's self-images and status depend on their jobs, on their success in the workday world, and on their ability to provide for their families. The Depression sowed doubt and fear among those who lost their jobs and those in danger of losing theirs.

The suffering during the Depression was not eased by programs available today, such as unemployment insurance, welfare, Social Security, and food stamps. These programs were in large part inspired by the experiences of the Depression. In 1933, people out of work had to rely mainly on private charity and relief from state and local governments, which were facing hard times themselves. Many city governments were unable to pay their bills because property owners had defaulted on local property taxes. Local governments were in no position to help their residents.

Economic conditions were no better abroad. The Depression affected every European country. Banks failed, and the European financial system was badly shaken. The United States and European countries raised tariffs and took other anti-trade measures in an effort to create jobs by substituting domestic production for imported goods. As a result, trade fell sharply.

The Roosevelt administration tried to deal with both the immediate emergency and the long-term issues. People had to be put back to work and, in the meantime, had to be given help. To put people back to work, Roosevelt and his advisers experimented with emergency government hiring programs. This policy was one of the early instances of the proposal that government should be the employer of last resort for people who can't find jobs elsewhere.

Beyond the emergency needs, the Roosevelt administration felt that policies had to be adopted to ensure that the Great Depression would never happen again. There should be programs to aid people in hard times as a matter of "right," so they wouldn't have to feel ashamed. The safety net of social welfare programs, such as Old Age and Survivors Insurance (Social Security), Aid to Families with Dependent Children, and unemployment compensation, was created during this period. In addition, deposit insurance and other banking regulations were put in place during the Great Depression to safeguard people's savings.

In economics, the Depression and the resulting policies of the Roosevelt administration set the stage for the new ideas of the Keynesian revolution imported from England. The impact of the Great Depression on policy, programs, and economic thinking far outlasted the decade's soup kitchens and federal relief agencies.

The misery and fear of the Depression led to political changes in many countries. In January 1933, Adolf Hitler became Chancellor of Germany, a country having severe economic problems. The Depression is also credited with helping Mussolini rise to power in Italy. In the United States, unhappy voters rejected Herbert Hoover in the 1932 election in favor of Franklin Roosevelt. The Socialist candidate, Norman Thomas, received almost 900,000 votes in that election. The Communist candidate received more than 100,000 votes.

Despite his campaign promise to balance the federal budget, Roosevelt was a pragmatic politician, willing to try various tactics to solve the pressing economic problems. One such scheme was to put people back to work by employing them on government projects such as constructing dams and public buildings, sewers, and streets. Naturally, the jobless who found work on these projects were pleased. Not only were they making money, but they had also regained the dignity of having worthwhile work and providing for their families. There seemed to be no harm and much good in such projects. Jobless workers were once again providing things people could use. One of the most disturbing aspects of the Depression was the terrible paradox that many people were living in great need of goods and services while many workers couldn't get jobs to produce those things. Despite criticisms of the government's "make work" projects, the majority of the American public supported such efforts to move the country out of the Depression.

STABILIZATION POLICY AND THE GREAT DEPRESSION

The Depression greatly influenced the direction of future macroeconomic policy. Because it was so severe in both length and depth, the Roosevelt administration tried many new programs and experimental policies. However, Roosevelt and his advisers developed their plans for government spending and government jobs to reduce unemployment during the Depression on a trial-and-error basis, with little theory behind them. In the meantime, economists had begun to provide theoretical reasons for the kinds of programs the United States was trying. Swedish economists such as Erik Lindahl and Gunnar Myrdal (who won the 1974 Nobel Prize in Economics) had proposed in the late 1920s and early 1930s that governments abandon the goal of balancing the budget annually. Instead, they argued, the budget should be balanced over the course of the business cycle. When output is falling and unemployment is rising, government should spend more to put people back to work, even if this produces a government deficit. In boom times, the government could run a surplus by cutting back on its projects. This surplus would cool off the boom while paying off the money borrowed during the deficit years. Only over the entire course of a business cycle, then, would the government budget be balanced.

Much more influential than Lindahl and Myrdal was a British economist whose book was published in 1936, the year of Roosevelt's reelection. That book was *The General Theory of Employment, Interest, and Money,* by John Maynard Keynes. At that time, the Depression in the United States still had five more years to run before it would end as the country entered World War II. Recovery from the Depression was already progressing in Great Britain and in some other countries, including Germany. Keynes, his theories, and his followers did not really have much influence on either the British or the American recovery. However, the Depression convinced many people that Keynesian theory was right and that it provided sound guidelines for economic policy making. Not until the 1970s were there serious challenges to Keynesian ideas about macroeconomic policy.

The Great Depression was a painful and difficult experience for almost all Americans. It forced economists and politicians to think more carefully about macroeconomics and economic policy. The Depression set the stage for Keynes's ideas to challenge the theories and models economists had been working with. In order to test these new ideas, it was necessary to have better measures of output and income than had been developed in the past. Beginning in the 1930s, economists devoted much more attention to measuring output and the components of output in order to have the information needed to design and implement stabilization policies. The next chapter will address the measurement of output, employment, and economic growth.

Consider again...There's no way to ensure that you will graduate during good times in the job market. Chances are that if jobs are easy to find, you will have to worry about inflation. Usually if unemployment is low, the inflation rate tends to increase, while low inflation rates may be accompanied by higher than normal unemployment. Inflation and unemployment both affect the economic welfare of individual households in important ways. Inflation reduces the purchasing power of incomes in many households, while others gain. Unemployment means a loss of income both now and in the future because of lost opportunities to polish and upgrade skills on the job.

Inflation and unemployment are important macroeconomic policy issues because both are costly to society as a whole. Inflation confuses important market signals and creates menu costs. Unemployment means lost output and results in a burden on taxpayers to support unemployed workers while they are looking for work. Citizens measure the performance of their federal government by looking at how the economy is performing in terms of unemployment and inflation.

SUMMARY

1. Full employment is usually reached when about 94 to 95 percent of the labor force is employed. That is, there is an unemployment rate of about 5 to 6 percent. Normal unemployment is partly frictional (due to new entrants in the job market or workers between jobs) and partly structural (due to a mismatch between workers and job openings). Some changes in unemployment arise from changes in the size of the labor force relative to the population rather than from changes in total output or the demand for labor. Unemployment in excess of a normal level is usually due to declines in real output. This kind of unemployment is called cyclical unemployment and is a macroeconomic policy concern. Unemployment is an important policy issue because it is costly to the economy as a whole in terms of lost output and income. Workers suffer not only from reduced income but also psychological costs and lost opportunities to develop and maintain skills that increase their productivity and income in the future.
2. Unemployment is measured as the percentage of the labor force not working but actively seeking work. Inflation is measured by changes in a price index such as the Consumer Price Index (CPI) or the GDP deflator.
3. Inflation is a sustained general rise in the price level. Losers from inflation are lenders, people on fixed incomes, and taxpayers; gainers are borrowers, owners of real assets, and the government. Inflation is an important policy issue because it causes a redistribution of income and wealth, confuses market signals, discourages saving and investment, and creates menu costs.
4. Inflation is measured by changes in a price index, which measures the rise or fall in the cost of a market basket of goods and services. The best known index is the consumer price index. This index is used to adjust incomes to correct for inflation and to determine increases in wages and Social Security benefits.
5. Business cycles describe the ups and downs of output, employment, and prices. During recessions, output and inflation fall while unemployment rises. During recoveries and expansion, unemployment falls while output and inflation usually increase. The most significant business cycle in the twentieth century was the Great Depression. It not only had important economic and political effects but also led to many changes in macroeconomic theory and policy.

NEW TERMS

full employment	labor force	real income	recession
frictional unemployment	labor force participation rate	GDP deflator	trough
structural unemployment		Producer Price Index	expansion
cyclical unemployment	inflation	stabilization policy	depression
productivity	price index	business cycle	stagflation
unemployment rate	Consumer Price Index	peak	

QUESTIONS: REVIEW, APPLICATIONS, AND POLICY

REVIEW

1. Which of the following are structurally unemployed, frictionally unemployed, or cyclically unemployed?
   a. a new college graduate seeking a first job
   b. a teenager who quit a fast-food job because she didn't like the hours
   c. farmers in Iowa who had to sell their farms because of inadequate demand for farm products and who are looking for a different line of work in a different area
   d. a person with a Ph.D. in classical languages, a field in which there are a hundred applicants for every available teaching position
   e. a person laid off because of a recession
2. Can you think of any benefits of having high rates of inflation? Of having high rates of unemployment?
3. Suppose another baby boom occurred and a significant number of parents dropped out of the labor force to stay home and do child care. What would happen to the unemployment rate, the labor force participation rate, and the employment rate?
4. Explain this statement: "Everybody's CPI is nobody's CPI."
5. Suppose there is a decline in real output. What would you expect to happen to employment and to the inflation rate? Why?
6. How can you tell when an economy is in a recession?

APPLICATIONS

7. Given the following information, compute the unemployment rate.
   Civilian noninstitutional population 186,393,000
   Civilian labor force 125,557,000
   Total civilian employment 117,342,000
   There were an additional 1,688,000 people in the armed forces. What would happen to the unemployment rate if these persons were counted?

8. Given the information in the table below, compute a price index for a ten-year-old child. This child receives a weekly allowance and would like to request a raise based on the increase in the cost of the market basket of goods purchased. By how much has this consumer's cost of living risen?

ITEM	QUANTITY	LAST YEAR'S PRICE	THIS YEAR'S PRICE
Movie admission	1	$3.00	$3.25
Soft drinks	3	.50	.50
Candy bars	4	.30	.35
Pencils	2	.15	.12
Comic books	2	.75	.85

9. Using Figures 3 and 5 in this chapter, see if you can trace the relationship between changes in output, consumer prices, and unemployment for each of the following years, all of which showed signs of a recession: 1955, 1958, 1961, 1970, 1974–1975, 1980, 1982, 1991.

10. Try constructing an index of your own, using the following data. Suppose that 40 percent of the cost of car repairs is labor, 50 percent is parts, and 10 percent is miscellaneous. Suppose that in the first year the cost of labor is $12 an hour, parts cost an average of $15 each, and miscellaneous costs run about $5. In the second year, labor rises to $15, parts average $20, and miscellaneous costs are unchanged. What is your "price index" for car repairs? By how much has the cost risen?

11. Use the given data to calculate the inflation rate between Year 1 and Year 2.
    Year 1, price index = 140
    Year 2, price index = 155.

POLICY

12. Suppose that the government relaxes the limitations on immigration into the United States. What effect would that have on employment and unemployment? How would that effect be different from a rise in the birth rate?

13. Suggest three ways in which the Great Depression affected economic policy in the United States.

SUGGESTIONS FOR FURTHER READING

Barber, William J. *From New Era to New Deal: Herbert Hoover, the Economists, and American Social Policy.* London: Cambridge University Press, 1985. Examines attempts to stem the flood of decline in the Hoover years before Roosevelt's New Deal.

Briggs, Vernon M., Jr. *Mass Immigration and the National Interest.* Armonk NY: M.E. Sharpe, 1992. A critical look at the effects of immigration on the composition of the labor force, unemployment, and wages.

Hibbs, Douglas A., Jr. *The American Political Economy: Macroeconomics and Electoral Politics.* Cambridge MA: Harvard University Press, 1987. Chapters 2 and 3 of this very readable blend of history, economics, and politics offer a thorough discussion of the costs of unemployment and inflation.

U.S. Department of Labor. *Monthly Labor Review.* Washington DC: U.S. Government Printing Office. Best source of data for both unemployment and changes in the Consumer Price Index.

CHAPTER 5

THE MEASURE OF OUTPUT, INCOME, AND ECONOMIC GROWTH

LEARNING OBJECTIVES

1. Expand the circular flow model as a basis for developing the GDP accounts.
2. Become familiar with income statements and balance sheets and the relationship between income statement flows and balance sheet stocks and the national income accounts.
3. Explain how gross domestic product (GDP), net domestic product (NNP), domestic income (NI), and personal income (PI) are computed.
4. Learn how to compute real GDP and rates of growth of real GDP, and to evaluate the costs and benefits of economic growth.

Consider this... Remember the problem from the last chapter of finding a job when you graduate? Part of the problem in 1990 and 1991 was that the economy was in recession. But that explanation doesn't hold for 1992 and 1993 and beyond. A key factor in the number of jobs available is the rate of economic growth. In fact, if you look at the economics and business shelf in your local bookstore, the word that appears most often in the title of popular economics books in the 1990s is growth. The motto of President Clinton in the 1992 election, "It's the economy, stupid!," was aimed at the goal of economic growth and the effects of growth on jobs. **Economic growth** is defined as an increase in real output per capita. An increase in real output per capita means that the average person has more goods and services and a higher standard of living than before.

Before public officials can develop policies to promote the growth of output, they need to be able to measure output and its growth. Individuals who are assessing their job prospects, making decisions about buying stocks and bonds, or planning for retirement also need to be able to figure what is happening to income and output into their decisions. The measurement of output and output growth really dates from the Great Depression of the 1930s, although some limited measures were developed prior to that period. Because real output or income is the central variable in all macroeconomic models, this chapter is devoted to understanding what real output is and how it is measured.

THE CIRCULAR FLOW MODEL REVISITED

In Chapter 2, we introduced the circular flow model as a way to see the interrelationships in a market economy. The individual markets and actors that make up the circular flow constitute microeconomics. The sums of their actions constitute macroeconomics. In this chapter, we want to focus on circular flow from a macroeconomic perspective.

A simple two-sector circular flow model shows the flow of goods and services from business firms to households in the upper flow as well as a return flow of payments from households for their purchases. In the lower flow, business firms purchase the services of productive inputs from households, creating a flow of income back to households. Even in this very simple two-sector world, it is possible to identify some important macroeconomic relationships. The upper part of the diagram, the product market, represents the aggregate of the individual markets in which final goods and services are bought and sold. The lower half, the resource market, is the aggregate of the individual markets in which the services of productive inputs are bought and sold. These markets represent the total of thousands of individual markets for steelworkers, bread, rental housing, cars, machine tools, and other inputs and outputs. That is, the product market and the resource market are both macroeconomic markets.

Another important macroeconomic concept that is suggested by the circular flow diagram is the view of domestic income or output as a *flow*. The flow of resource income from firms to households becomes a flow back to firms to pay for purchases of goods and services. The upper flow is total output, and the lower flow is total income. The two flows are the same size in the simple circular flow model because all of the income received by households is spent to purchase the output of firms.

SAVING, INVESTMENT, AND THE CREDIT MARKET

Figure 1 is a simplified circular flow model (with just one flow through each market) that adds two additional kinds of economic activity: saving and investment. **Saving** is a flow from households that occurs because people (both as individuals and as owners of business firms) refrain from spending part of their income flow on consumer goods and services. These funds flow into the credit market instead of the product market. **Investment** is a flow between firms. Business firms borrow from households through the credit market in order to purchase new plants or equipment or to add to their inventories. That is, firms use the borrowed funds to purchase new capital goods from other firms or to finance the "purchase" of their own output in the form of increased inventories. The **credit market** consists of financial institutions channeling household savings to business firms that want to invest. The credit market is an important macro market.

Another important pair of macroeconomic concepts illustrated in Figure 1 are leakages out of the income stream and injections into the income stream. **Leakages** are flows out of the circular pattern that occur when resource income is received but not spent directly on purchases from domestic firms. Examples of leakages are saving, taxes, and purchases of imports. Income leaks out of the income stream if households do not spend all of their income on consumption of goods produced by domestic business firms. **Injections** are added flows into the circular pattern that represent spending not paid for out of resource income. Examples of injections are business investment, government expenditures, and sales of exports. There are injections in Figure 1 because the business firms spend income that is not earned but borrowed.

If leakages are greater than injections, the size of the income flow will shrink. If injections are larger than leakages, the income flow will increase. Since the level of output and income (that is, the size of the flow) is a central macroeconomic concern, leakages and injections play important roles in macroeconomic models.

Economic growth
An increase in the level of real per capita output.

Saving
The part of an income flow not spent on purchases of goods and services.

Investment
Business purchases of some real, tangible asset, such as a machine, a factory, or a stock of inventories.

Credit market
The aggregate market consisting of financial institutions that channel household savings to business firms that want to invest.

Leakages
Flows out of the circular flow that occur when resource income is not spent directly on purchases from domestic firms, but goes to savings, taxes, and imports.

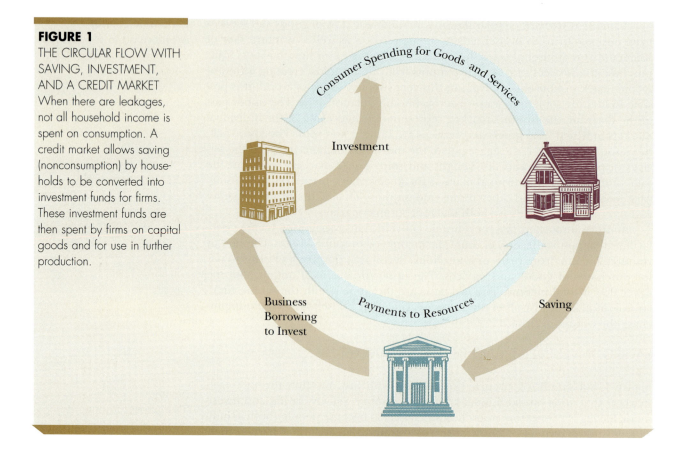

FIGURE 1

THE CIRCULAR FLOW WITH SAVING, INVESTMENT, AND A CREDIT MARKET
When there are leakages, not all household income is spent on consumption. A credit market allows saving (nonconsumption) by households to be converted into investment funds for firms. These investment funds are then spent by firms on capital goods and for use in further production.

Injections
Spending added to the circular flow that is not paid for out of resource income, such as business investment, government expenditures, and exports.

GOVERNMENT IN THE CIRCULAR FLOW

When we add a third actor, government, to interact with households and firms, the picture of the macroeconomy becomes still more realistic. In Figure 2, governments (federal, state, and local) interact with firms and households in several ways. The government buys goods and services produced by firms. It is thus a third "customer" in addition to households, which buy goods for consumption, and business firms, which purchase goods for investment. Government purchases of goods and services are another injection into spending in the product market. The government also employs resources, mainly labor services. Wages paid by government increase the flow of income to households.

Taxes collected by governments are a leakage from household income. (For simplicity, we assume that all taxes fall on households.) Taxes are paid to finance the services governments provide, such as defense, police, fire protection, streets, and education. Taxes reduce households' consumption by lowering their after-tax (disposable) incomes. Therefore, less is available to spend. Taxes may also reduce household saving.

Finally, if the government spends more than it collects in taxes, it must borrow funds in the credit market. There it will compete with business firms for the supply of household savings. A government that spends more than the revenue it takes in is running a *deficit*. A government that collects more in taxes than it spends on wages and purchases is showing a *surplus*.

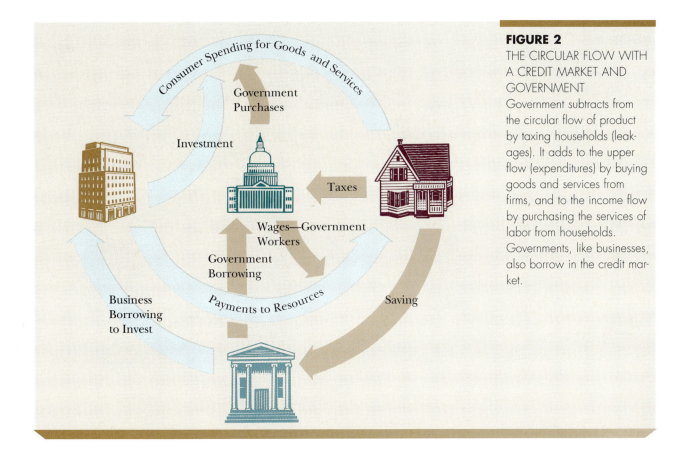

FIGURE 2

THE CIRCULAR FLOW WITH A CREDIT MARKET AND GOVERNMENT
Government subtracts from the circular flow of product by taxing households (leakages). It adds to the upper flow (expenditures) by buying goods and services from firms, and to the income flow by purchasing the services of labor from households. Governments, like businesses, also borrow in the credit market.

The government, then, enters the circular flow model at a number of points. It takes funds out of the stream by taxing households and by borrowing in the credit market. It adds to the spending flow by purchasing goods and services from firms. It adds to the income flow by purchasing labor services from households. Taxes are leakages out of the flow. Government purchases of goods and services are injections.

THE FOREIGN SECTOR: EXPORTS AND IMPORTS

Adding the foreign sector completes the picture of the macroeconomy. As Figure 3 shows, it is not only another "customer" for firms' output but also another supplier of goods and services besides the domestic business sector. Buying from foreign countries and selling to other countries add a new source of leakages and a new source of injections. Purchases from foreign firms are **imports**. Goods and services sold to foreign buyers are **exports**. Purchases of imports are flows out of the stream (leakages). Sales of exports are flows into the stream (injections). Thus, if a country increases its purchases from foreigners, *ceteris paribus*, the size of the flow will shrink. If the same country increases its sales to foreigners, *ceteris paribus*, the size of the flow will increase. The difference between exports and imports for a given country for a given year is called the **balance on goods and services**. A surplus in the balance on goods and services means that injections from the foreign market exceed leakages to it. A deficit in

Imports
Purchases of goods and services from foreign sellers.

Exports
Goods and services sold to foreign buyers.

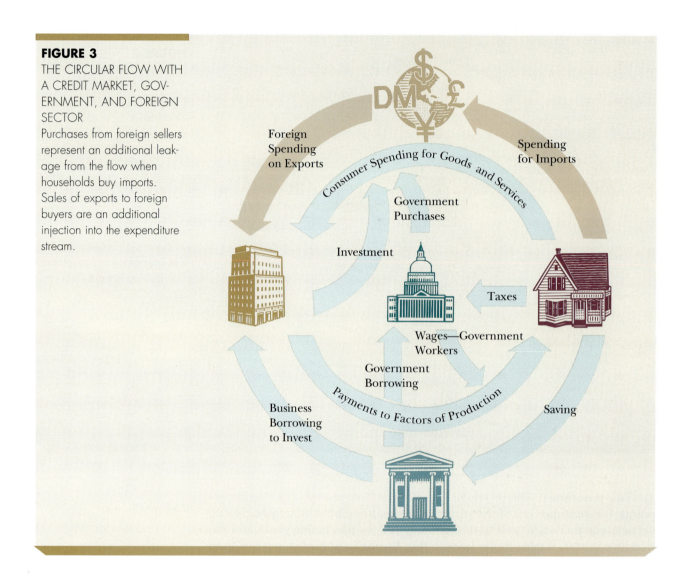

FIGURE 3

THE CIRCULAR FLOW WITH A CREDIT MARKET, GOVERNMENT, AND FOREIGN SECTOR
Purchases from foreign sellers represent an additional leakage from the flow when households buy imports. Sales of exports to foreign buyers are an additional injection into the expenditure stream.

Balance on goods and services
The difference between the value of exports and the value of imports for a country in any given year.

the balance on goods and services means that foreign market leakages are greater than injections.

KEY IDEAS

THE COMPONENTS OF THE CIRCULAR FLOW DIAGRAM			
FOUR MARKETS	FOUR ACTORS	THREE LEAKAGES	THREE INJECTIONS
Product	Households	Saving	Investment
Resource	Firms	Taxes	Government purchases
Credit	Government	Imports	Exports
Foreign	Exports and imports		

BASIC ACCOUNTING CONCEPTS

Two basic kinds of accounting statements are used in economics as well as in all business fields. These statements are balance sheets and income statements. In accounting, balance sheets measure stocks of assets and liabilities at a point in time. Income statements record flows of income and expenditures over time. National income accounts take the form of an income statement.

INCOME STATEMENTS

One widely used tool for measuring economic flows for individuals, firms, government, or the economy as a whole is an income statement. An **income statement** measures the total flow of revenue to a household, individual, or firm over a period of time. It also records where the outflow goes.

For example, Katrina Miller, a college student, has drawn up an income statement for the year 1995, which is shown in Table 1. Katrina had to draw on her savings this year, because her expenditures were greater than her income. If she had earned more than she spent, her saving would have been positive. If Katrina happened to be a business firm instead of an individual, the saving line would be replaced by a line labeled "Net income," equal to income less expen-

Income statement Measures the total flow of revenues to an economic unit, such as a household, individual, or firm over a particular period of time.

TABLE 1 KATRINA MILLER'S INCOME STATEMENT

Katrina Miller's
Income Statement
for Year Ended December 31, 1995

INCOME:	
Scholarships	$3,000
Part-time job	1,800
Parents	2,500
Student loan	800
Gifts and miscellaneous	300
Total income	$8,400
EXPENSES:	
Tuition, room, and board	$6,800
Books and school supplies	300
Clothes and toiletries	500
Travel	100
Weekend meals, recreation	600
Miscellaneous	400
Total expenses	$8,700
Saving	–300
Total expenses plus saving	$8,400

ditures. The difference between income and expenditures plays an important role in national income accounts and in economic models of how the level of total output and income is determined.

An income statement has a variety of uses as a planning and forecasting tool. Katrina can use it to plan her finances for next year, to decide how much money to ask her parents for, or to increase or decrease the amount of her student loan or her hours of work. We will use two kinds of income statements in this textbook. One kind is the national income accounts described in this chapter, which measure aggregate income and expenditures for the whole economy. The other, covered in a later chapter, is the international balance of payments account.

BALANCE SHEETS

The second type of financial statement that economists use is a balance sheet. A **balance sheet** measures stocks. It is a picture of assets owned, debts owed, and the difference between them (called **net worth**) at a specific time. Individuals and firms "stop the clock" at a given time and "take a snapshot" of where they stand financially. Katrina's balance sheet is shown in Table 2. As you can see, her tuition will exhaust most of the funds in her savings account.

Assets are anything of value. *Liabilities* are anything you owe. Katrina's liabilities are the bills she has to pay in the near future and her long-term loans. Assets are listed in order of decreasing liquidity. (Liquidity is a measure of how quickly an asset could be converted to cash.) Liabilities are listed in order of how soon they have to be paid. Katrina has relatively few assets, the largest being her savings account, but she also has relatively few liabilities. If Katrina sold all her assets, even her stereo, clothes, and other personal possessions, she could pay her liabilities with $810 to spare. This sum represents her net worth, or the excess of the value of assets over the value of liabilities. Because her assets exceed her liabilities, Katrina has a small but positive net worth.

Balance sheet
A statement of assets owned, liabilities owned, and the difference between them at a particular point in time.

Net worth
The difference between assets and liabilities for a particular person or firm at a point in time.

TABLE 2 KATRINA MILLER'S BALANCE SHEET

Katrina Miller's
Balance Sheet
December 31, 1995

ASSETS:		LIABILITIES AND NET WORTH:	
Cash	$ 100	Telephone bill	$ 40
Checking account	550	Tuition due	1,500
Savings account	1,500	Student loans	1,500
Stereo	600		
Clothes and other		Total liabilities	3,040
personal items	1,100	Net worth	810
Total assets	$3,850	Total liabilities and net worth	$3,850

Katrina has a major asset that is never included on a balance sheet because it is difficult to assign it a dollar value. That asset is her human capital, or her skills and education as a worker. Most of her liabilities are related to the cost of improving those skills to increase her future earnings potential. Thus, if Katrina's future earnings are taken into account, her financial condition is somewhat better than her balance sheet suggests.

KEY IDEAS

BASIC ACCOUNTING CONCEPTS

INCOME STATEMENTS
- Measure flows,
- Add income and subtract expenditures,
- Have net income as the "bottom line," and
- Identify additions to stocks of savings or assets.

BALANCE SHEETS
- Measure stocks,
- Compare value of assets to value of liabilities,
- Have net worth as the "bottom line," and
- Show year-to-year changes in wealth.

Individuals and firms use balance sheets regularly to assess where they stand. Nations use income statements to measure total output, but we rarely see balance sheets for countries as a whole. A balance sheet will be very useful in Chapter 12, however, when examining money and the banking system.

STOCKS AND FLOWS

The size of the arrows in the circular flow diagram and the total income and total expenditures on Katrina Miller's income statement are all flow variables. A **flow variable** is a variable that is defined over a period of time, such as the year 1995. Flows measure changes in quantities over time. The number of new apartments built from January 1 to December 31 of this year is a flow variable. The length of the period—hour, day, month, quarter, year, or decade—must be specified in order for the size of the flow to have any useful meaning. Different kinds of information are collected at different intervals. The U.S. Census measures flows of population through births, deaths, and migration at ten year intervals, primarily to provide the data for redistricting the U.S. House of Representatives. A speculator in the wheat market, however, requires daily information on crop prospects. The operator of a nuclear reactor wants very frequent readings on the core's temperature. Most economic data is reported at monthly, quarterly, and annual intervals.

A flow can be either gross or net. For example, in your city new houses are built every year while some old ones are torn down. The total number of new houses built is the *gross* flow. The number of new houses built this year minus the number destroyed is the *net* flow of houses. On Katrina Miller's income statement, the net flow of income minus expenses, or saving, was negative, because she spent more than she earned.

Stock variables, which appear on balance sheets, are variables that are defined at a point in time, such as December 31, 1995. Stocks are existing quantities of goods or assets. An example of a stock variable is the number of apart-

Flow variable
A variable that is defined over a period of time.

Stock variable
A variable that is defined at a point in time.

ment units that exist today. Notice the date on this stock—today. A year from today, there will be more or fewer units, depending on how many new apartments are built and how many old ones are torn down.

A positive flow increases the stock, while a negative flow decreases the stock. Suppose there is a stock of 1,000 houses on January 1 in Townville. If 300 new houses are built in Townville this year, and 100 old houses are torn down or boarded up during the year, the net flow of housing is 200. At the end of the year, the stock of houses in Townville is 1,200. The change in the stock of housing is equal to the net flow of new housing.

Like most economic information, the data on housing flows provides an incomplete picture of the state of housing in that community. Two important missing dimensions are size and quality. If the 300 new houses are all very small and the 100 houses destroyed were the largest in town, or if the 300 new houses all have less storage space or fewer bathrooms than the destroyed houses, the figure of a 200-house increase would be misleading as an indicator of better housing conditions. If we want to consider size and quality, the stock and flow of houses are reflected somewhat more accurately in dollar values. Suppose that 300 houses worth $2.5 million are lost through depreciation and 100 houses worth $10 million are built. The number of houses has decreased, but the housing stock has increased in terms of value and quality. Quality measures are an important issue in all kinds of economic data.

How might data such as this be used? The stock of housing or the flow of new housing may be important for several purposes. An increasing housing stock suggests more demand for a variety of house-related services—a hardware store or a lawn-care business, for example. If the net housing stock is declining, this fact may be an indicator of the community's economic health. Macroeconomic data, likewise, provides useful information both for evaluating the nation's economic health and for making personal and business decisions.

All important macroeconomic variables can be classified as stocks or flows. Savings is a stock, but saving is a flow. The amount of money in a savings account is a stock. The amount put into such an account per week, per month, or per year is a flow. Income is a flow, but wealth is a stock. You may be wealthy if you own a large amount of land. In order to convert that wealth to an income flow, however, you must either sell it, plant a cash crop on it, or rent it out. The stock of wealth creates a flow of income. The labor force is a stock, with new entrants being the inflow and retirees and dropouts being the outflow.

The national debt is a stock, but the federal deficit is a flow. The size of the national debt, like the size of your savings account, is fixed at any given time. Whether it increases or decreases depends on the size of the flow variable (the current year's surplus or deficit) affecting the stock variable (the total debt due to previous deficits).

MEASURING GROSS DOMESTIC PRODUCT AND NATIONAL INCOME

Gross Domestic Product (GDP)
The total market value of all final products produced by a country's residents in a given year.

The most important flow variables in the economy as a whole are the total flow of output through the product market in the upper half of the circular flow, and the total flow of income through the resource market in the lower half of the circular flow. The most widely used measure of total output is the Gross Domestic Product (GDP). GDP is the total market value of all final products produced by a country's residents during a given time period, most commonly a year. It measures the size of the spending flow in the upper half of the circular flow diagram that takes place within a nation's borders.

Until 1991, a related measure, Gross National Product (GNP), was the standard measure of output. GNP differs from GDP in counting all production by the resources owned by a nation's *citizens* rather than all production that takes place inside its borders. GDP includes, for example, the value of output produced by a foreign-owned plant or a resident foreigner in the United States, but does not count the value of output of an American firm in Europe or Latin

POLICY FOCUS: WHAT GOES INTO GDP?

There is no standard recipe for GDP. The choice of what to include and what to exclude is a policy decision that is based on the uses of GDP. One major use of GDP is to measure economic well-being. Are Americans better off than last year? Are Americans better off than the Russians or Japanese? You may not think that these international comparisons are important, but politicians and the media pay as much attention to the economic race as they used to give to the arms race.

A second important use of GDP is as a forecasting tool. Changes in GDP affect employment, prices, interest rates, government tax revenues, and exchange rates. The GDP measure that best reflects economic well-being is not necessarily the same one that makes the most reliable forecasting tool. In choosing what to include or exclude, GDP accountants usually base their decision on the usefulness of GDP as a forecasting tool rather than as a measure of economic welfare.

This choice explains why GDP is not adjusted for either depreciation of capital equipment or depletion of natural resources. Neither of those affect employment. Workers do not care if they are employed adding to the capital stock or replacing capital that has worn out. Depletion may affect current jobs, but not present ones. This choice also explains other omissions such as nonmarket production, changes in leisure, and illegal activities.

There are also undesirable activities that increase measured GDP while reducing economic well-being. Suppose there is a rise in the crime rate, resulting in the hiring of more police and the building of more jails. Is the average person better off? Probably not. But the government spending component of the GDP registers an increase in purchases of police services. In the process of producing more goods and services, the economy may be creating more air and water pollution, more noise, more litter, and more congestion. Not only are these side effects of growth not subtracted, but the costs of combating pollution, noise, and litter are added into GDP as production of additional goods and services. These costs are known as "defensive" expenditures. While such costs are hard to calculate, there are scattered estimates of how high they are. For example, one estimate places such defensive expenditures in Germany (actually West Germany before reunification) as high as 10 percent of measured GDP.[a]

To convert GDP from a forecasting tool to a welfare measure, a correction would also have to be made for any increase in negative external effects and public bads, such as noise, water pollution, and global warming. Some economists have actually attempted to develop an alternative to GDP as a measure of changes in the quality of life. In 1972, William Nordhaus and James Tobin developed the first estimates of the value of leisure time, household work and other nonmarket production, and quality improvements to add to GDP.[b] They also estimated negative influences on the quality of life (pollution, crime, etc.) and subtracted those from the GDP. The result was their Measure of Economic Welfare (MEW), an alternative to GDP that focuses more closely on changes in economic welfare. Nordhaus and Tobin found that, in general, MEW appears to have grown more slowly than real GDP.

a. Leipert, Christian, "National Income and Economic Growth: The Concept of Defensive Expenditures," *Journal of Economic Issues* (September 1989): 843–855.
b. Nordhaus, William, and Tobin, James, "Is Growth Obsolete?" *Economic Growth, Fiftieth Anniversary Colloquium V* (Cambridge MA: National Bureau of Economic Research, 1972). A number of other extensions and qualifications to GDP/GNP are summarized in Robert Eisner, "Extended Accounts for National Income and Product," *Journal of Economic Literature* (December 1988): 1611–1684.

America, or an American citizen working abroad. The difference between the two is relatively small (about $20 billion in the early 1990s) for the United States, although it can be quite large for developing countries that are hosts to a large number of foreign firms.

GROSS DOMESTIC PRODUCT BY PRODUCING SECTOR

Table 3 shows GDP by producing sector for the United States in 1993. The business sector's $6,374.0 billion consists of net sales of all business firms. These figures are obtained from sales figures reported in connection with state sales taxes, corporate income taxes, and reports to stockholders. Domestic income accountants try to determine *net* sales, eliminating double counting by subtracting sales to other firms that use the goods in further production. All goods produced should be counted, but only once. The accounts are supposed to consist of only final goods or final sales, not any intermediate goods. **Final goods** are those that will not be further processed or resold. **Intermediate goods** are those that will be further processed into final goods. For example, flour sold to consumers in supermarkets is counted in the GDP, but flour sold to bakers is not, because the bakers will use the flour to make bread. That sale of flour will be counted in the GDP as part of the value of bread produced.

The output of the business sector reflects sales of final product, measured in dollars. Most U.S. output is produced by the business sector, as you would expect in a market economy. Domestic income accountants get a large share of their data from various financial reports of the business sector, such as sales tax returns, income tax returns, and reports by corporations to their stockholders.

Governments—federal, state, and local—also produce services such as public education, police protection, and domestic defense. Data for the public sector is easy to find, because all governments must report to their citizens each year how much money was received and how it was spent. Although the data is easy to come by, the market value of government output is difficult to measure because these services are not sold. Since government agencies hire employees to produce these services, national income accounts measure the value of government output by the compensation paid to employees. The services may actually be worth more or less than this amount. In the absence of a market price, however, labor cost is the only available measure of the value of government output.

Final goods
Goods that do not have to be further processed or resold before final sale.

Intermediate goods
Goods sold to be further processed into final goods.

TABLE 3 U.S. GROSS DOMESTIC PRODUCT BY PRODUCING SECTOR, 1993 (BILLIONS OF DOLLARS)

Business sector		$5,400.6
Government sector		687.1
Federal	$207.0	
State and local	480.1	
Household and nonprofit sector		286.3
Gross Domestic Product		$6,374.0

A relatively small part of the GDP is produced in the household and nonprofit sector. The household and nonprofit sector includes the value of goods and services produced by nonprofit, nongovernmental agencies, such as private schools, museums, charitable organizations, and social clubs, as well as some small in-home businesses, such as family day care. This data is assembled primarily from income tax returns and other sources.

GROSS DOMESTIC PRODUCT BY BUYING SECTOR

The more common way of reporting GDP is by the purchasers rather than the sellers. The upper half of the circular flow diagram sorts out the components of GDP by buying sectors. A basic assumption behind this approach to measuring GDP is that everything that is produced is also sold to someone. If the business sector produces goods that are not sold, these goods must be added to inventories. **Business inventories** are stocks of goods held by firms from which they can make sales to meet demand. The changes in these inventories are counted as "sales" of output to the business sector.

Table 4 shows how U.S. GDP for 1992 was divided among the four groups of buyers to which it could be sold: households, business firms, government, and the foreign sector. These four groups correspond to the four actors in the circular flow model. This second (and more widely used) way of accounting for output also provides a cross check on the data collected for the producing sector.

THE HOUSEHOLD SECTOR. Sales to the household sector are called **consumption expenditures**. Since consumer purchases are final sales, they are all counted as

Business inventories
Stocks of goods held by businesses from which they can make sales to meet demand.

Consumption expenditures
Sales to the household sector.

TABLE 4 U.S. GROSS DOMESTIC PRODUCT BY BUYING SECTOR, 1993 (BILLIONS OF DOLLARS)

			% of GDP
Gross Domestic Product		$6,374.0	100.0
Personal consumption expenditures		$4,390.6	68.9
Consumer durables	$ 537.7		8.4
Consumer nondurables	1,350.2		21.2
Consumer services	2,502.7		39.3
Gross private domestic investment		$ 892.0	14.0
Fixed investment (plant and equipment)	$622.9		9.8
Residential construction	252.3		4.0
Change in inventories	16.8		0.3
Government purchases of goods and services		$1,151.1	18.2
Federal government	$443.4		7.0
State/local government	713.7		11.2
Net Exports of Goods and Services		−65.7	−1.0
Exports	660.1		10.4
Imports	−725.8		−11.4

Source: U.S. Department of Commerce, *Survey of Current Business* (Washington DC: U.S. Government Printing Office, February 1994).

Consumer durables
Goods that last, on average, a substantial length of time.

Consumer nondurables
Goods that last, on average, only a short period of time.

Consumer services
That part of household consumption composed of nontangible activities.

Gross private domestic investment
Business sector purchases of final output in the GDP.

Fixed investment
The part of investment that does not add to inventories; consists of business plant and equipment and residential construction.

part of GDP. Consumption expenditures in turn can be divided into various categories, which are useful because each one responds a little differently to changes in economic conditions. **Consumer durables** are such long-lasting items as refrigerators and washing machines. **Consumer nondurables** are items that have a very short useful life, such as a loaf of bread or a shirt. **Consumer services** are that part of household consumption composed of nontangible activities. Examples of services are haircuts, concerts, being waited on at a restaurant, or having a gardener tend your yard. Services form a large part of total personal consumption, as Table 4 indicates.

THE BUSINESS SECTOR. Purchases of final output by the business sector are called **gross private domestic investment**. Gross investment is measured before subtracting capital goods that have worn out or become so obsolete they aren't worth using. Thus, if the business sector buys 10,000 computers during one year but has to scrap 1,000 old computers that year, the net change in the number of computers is 9,000. The word *gross* in gross private domestic investment means that this figure was calculated before subtracting the value of equipment that was worn out or used up. In this example, gross investment is 10,000 computers; net investment is 9,000 units.

The word *private* means investment by business firms, rather than by the government. The word *domestic* means that the investment was made in the United States, not in another country. Finally, in GDP accounting the term *investment* means the purchase of some real, tangible asset, such as a machine, a factory, or a stock of inventories. To an economist, buying bonds and making deposits in banks are actually forms of lending. When business firms use those borrowed funds to purchase new plants or equipment or expand their inventories, they are investing in the economic sense.

The components of gross private domestic investment are given in Table 4. The largest component of investment consists of **fixed investment**, which is new plants or equipment, such as factories, office buildings, industrial robots, machine tools, and computers. A second major component of gross private domestic investment is residential construction. If you think of investment as something that will be used to provide goods and services in the future, the idea that housing should be classed as investment rather than consumption makes a great deal of sense for several reasons. First, houses—like factories and office buildings—last a long time and produce "shelter services" to consumers over many years. The shelter services produced by houses are counted each year under consumption as part of consumer services.

Second, many housing units, especially apartments, are owned by firms and rented to households. These housing units are similar to other kinds of business investments in that firms build these units in order to generate a future income stream. Even when individuals purchase houses for their own use, this transaction is more like a business investment than an ordinary consumer purchase of a final good. A housing purchase, like a business investment, is a large expenditure, usually of borrowed money, that will provide a stream of services in the future.

The one major difference between rented and owned housing is that there is no market transaction between the owner and the occupant of an owner-occupied house. To determine a dollar value for those shelter services that owners "purchase" from themselves, GDP accountants have to estimate the equivalent rental value. This value is what the owner-occupied housing would rent for in the market. This estimated value is then counted as a purchase of consumption services by the household sector.

The last component of gross private domestic investment is changes in business inventories. Domestic income accountants treat inventory changes as sales by businesses to other businesses or to themselves. Since these inventories aren't used up in the current year, they are treated as final products, not intermediate goods. Inventories are counted in GDP for the year in which they are produced, not the year sold. Whatever firms produce that is not sold to other sectors becomes part of their investment in inventories. This method of accounting for inventories assures that the GDP accounts balance. Every dollar of output produced has a buyer. If no one else wants some output, the accounts show that the firm that produced it has "bought" it to add to its own inventories. Business inventory is an important category to watch in the national income accounts. If firms experience undesired inventory changes, their efforts to restore inventories to desired levels will have a significant impact on output and employment.

THE GOVERNMENT SECTOR. A large part of a nation's income is claimed by government—federal, state, and local—and a substantial share of output is produced by or for government. Total government expenditures are much higher than the figures that appear in the GDP accounts. The federal government alone spent more than $1,400 billion in 1993. State and local governments added another $885 billion. Some of these government expenditures were for **transfer payments**, which are income payments to individuals who provide no goods or services in exchange. Veterans' benefits, welfare payments, unemployment compensation, and Social Security benefits are all examples of transfer payments. Most transfer payments come from the federal level, although many of them are administered by state and local governments. Transfer payments are not counted in GDP because they are not related to production. Only spending by government to produce or to purchase goods and services, such as defense, health care, highways, police, education, and courts, is counted in GDP.

Transfer payments
Income payments to individuals who do not have to provide any goods or services in exchange.

Even with this narrower definition of what to include, purchase of goods and services by governments at all levels is still a major component of GDP—almost one dollar in five. The largest part of government expenditures is for salaries and wages for government employees. Governments produce services such as defense, education, and road repair using the labor of these employees. Governments also purchase goods and services produced by other sectors, mainly the business sector. State and local governments actually purchase more goods and services than the federal government does. Some government purchases are used up almost immediately, such as food for army mess halls. Other government expenditures, such as those for dams or highways, result in goods that will last for years. These can be regarded as a form of "government investment." The national income accounts, however, do not distinguish between government consumption and government investment, but treat all government expenditures alike.

THE FOREIGN SECTOR. The final group of buyers is the foreign sector. The foreign sector consists of business firms who buy from and sell to other countries, as well as a relatively small amount of household purchases abroad. Consumption, investment, and government expenditures all include some imported goods, which must be subtracted from the GDP because they are produced elsewhere. Exports are part of domestic production, so they need to be included in GDP. Thus, exports are added and imports are subtracted to arrive at Gross Domestic Product, or what was produced by a country's own resources. For convenience, GDP accounts usually group these exports and imports together and report the difference between them as net exports of goods and services.

The use of net exports makes the foreign sector look less significant than it really is. Exports and imports are now each approximately 11 percent of GDP. For many years, exports and imports were so small relative to the total flow of income and product in the United States that they were often omitted from the circular flow diagram. In the early 1960s, the ratio of both imports and exports to total domestic output was only about 5 or 6 percent. By the early 1990s, exports were about 9 percent of total output, and imports accounted for 12 percent of spending. Although net exports are usually a fairly small part of GDP, they receive more attention than any of the other three components. The balance on goods and services (another name for net exports) can be either positive or negative. When it is negative, there is much concern about the effects of the "flood" of imports on competing American firms and of reduced export sales on American exporting industries.

TOTAL SPENDING AND GDP. The sum of spending by the four buying sectors is GDP. Adding consumption spending by households (C), investment spending by business (I), purchases of goods and services by government (G), and spending by the foreign sector, or net exports ($X - M$), gives this formula for GDP:

$$GDP = C + I + G + (X - M).$$

This formula states that everything that is produced in a year must be purchased by one of the four buying sectors.

NATIONAL INCOME

The top half of the circular flow diagram measures the flow of output, or GDP. In the process of producing GDP, income is generated. This income is paid to the resources and corresponds to the accounting concept of domestic income. **National income (NI)** is income earned by the resources—land, labor, capital, and enterprise. It consists of wages, rent, interest, profit, and proprietors' net income and is shown on the bottom half of the circular flow.

The key to understanding NI is that all of the income generated in producing GDP must be accounted for in some way. Most of it is paid to the four resources. Thus, NI consists of rent, wages and salaries, interest, and profits. In a very simple economy, all of the value of final goods and services produced (GDP) would become payments to resources. GDP, which measures the flow in the product market of the circular flow diagram, and NI, which measures the flow in the resource market, would be identical. Since the actual economy is not so simple, some adjustments must be made in order to convert GDP to NI.

National income (NI)
Income earned by the resources; consists of wages, rent, interest, profit, and proprietors' net income.

FROM GDP TO GNP. The first adjustment in the process of getting from GDP to NI is to make a small correction for the difference between what is produced by U.S. *residents* (GDP) and what is produced by U.S. *citizens* (GNP). The value of the resource payments to foreign-owned resources within the U.S. national boundaries ($121.9 billion in 1992) is subtracted, and the value of the resource payments to U.S. resources located outside the country ($129.2 billion in 1992)

GLOBAL OUTLOOK: MAKING INTERNATIONAL COMPARISONS

Once statistics are compiled, they are almost always used for comparisons. Is GDP higher than last year? Is U.S. GDP growing faster than GDP in other countries? How does the unemployment rate or inflation rate in the United States compare with that in other developed countries? It is possible to make those comparisons, but it must be done with caution. GDP, unemployment, and price indexes are not computed exactly the same way in all countries. The share of economic activity going through the market is much different in less developed countries. This difference affects all three indicators, but especially GDP and unemployment.

Comparisons of the United States, Canada, Japan, Australia, and the countries of Western Europe are a little more reliable because these countries are all at similar levels of economic development. The share of economic activity passing through the market is roughly the same, and the ways statistics are collected and presented are similar, but differences still remain. For example, unemployment figures for some countries may only include long-duration unemployment (13 weeks or longer), or persons aged 25 or over, or full-time workers only. Others may count as unemployed those workers who hold part-time jobs but would prefer to be full-time.[a] Similar differences exist for GDP figures and for price indexes.

In addition, even in industrial countries the data is not always very accurate. The preliminary figures for GDP are often very different from the final figures, which do not appear until three years later.[b] The unemployment figures that appeared in 1990 and 1991 turned out to have significantly overstated job losses during the recession. The Consumer Price Index was widely criticized for overstating increases in the cost of living by giving too large a weight to newly constructed housing in the 1970s and early 1980s.

With these qualifications, how do the major industrial economies compare on the three principal measures—GDP growth, inflation (measured by the Consumer Price Index), and unemployment rate? *The Economist*, a British weekly news magazine, reports comparative data for 13 industrial countries on a regular basis. The table gives the figures for GDP growth in 1992, unemployment for March 1993, and the inflation rate from March 1992 to March 1993.

COUNTRY	GDP GROWTH RATE (%)	UNEMPLOYMENT RATE (%)	INFLATION RATE (%)
Australia	+2.5	11.0	+1.2
Canada	+1.3	11.1	+1.9
France	+0.7	10.1	+2.2
Germany	+0.2	6.3	+4.3
Japan	+0.2	2.1	+1.2
United Kingdom	+0.6	9.4	+1.9
United States	+2.9	7.3	+3.1

Source: *The Economist* (May 8, 1993): 107.

These figures tell an interesting story. Growth is slow in all the major industrial countries, but highest in the United States. Unemployment is high in all the industrial countries (except Japan, where it is beginning to become a problem), but only Germany and Japan have lower unemployment rates than the United States. Inflation does not appear to be a problem anywhere, but in most cases, prices seem to be rising the fastest where unemployment is lowest (Germany, United States) and much more slowly where unemployment is highest (Australia and Canada). Despite all the complaints about the state of the U.S. economy, compared to other countries, the United States is not doing too badly. As the table shows, the United States is *not* number one, at least not on many measures. The United States is behind Japan and about even with Canada in industrial production. It ranks in the middle of the seven countries in economic growth and inflation and is better than every country but Japan in the unemployment rate.

a. See Constance Sorrentino, "International comparisons of unemployment indicators," *Monthly Labor Review* (March 1993): 3–17 for some of the differences in definition from country to country.
b. Walter B. Wriston, "Off by a Factor of Four," *Forbes* (June 21, 1993): 88.

is added. For 1992, the net difference comes to $7.3 billion, so GNP was $6,045.8 billion compared to GDP of $6,038.5 billion. This adjustment is necessary because the other measures of output and income are still based on the economic activity of the nation's citizens rather than its residents.

DEPRECIATION AND NET NATIONAL PRODUCT. The next adjustment is to reduce GNP to account for the fact that part of the capital stock is used up in the production process. Depreciation (called capital consumption allowance in the GDP accounts) is a cost of production that is not received as income by any resource. The **capital consumption allowance** is the domestic income accountants' estimate of the wear and tear and loss of the nation's capital stock. This estimate may be very different from the sum of what firms report on their tax returns or in their annual reports to stockholders.

In Table 5, GNP minus capital consumption allowance is equal to **net national product (NNP)**. Similarly, **net private domestic investment** is defined as gross private domestic investment minus the capital consumption allowance (depreciation). Net national product is equal to

$$NNP = C + I_n + G + (X - M),$$

where I_n represents net, rather than gross, investment. The only difference between GNP and NNP is that GNP includes gross private domestic investment but the investment term in NNP is net private domestic investment.

NNP is a more meaningful measure of production than GDP or GNP, because it excludes all intermediate products, including capital used up in the course of the year's production. GDP is more widely used, however, for two reasons. First, GDP figures are more precise than NNP figures because depreciation is difficult to measure or even estimate accurately. Second, GDP is more closely related than NNP to the behavior of employment and prices.

Capital consumption allowance (depreciation) The national income accountants' estimate of the amount of the nation's capital stock used up in production during the current year.

Net National Product (NNP) Equal to GDP less capital consumption allowance and adjustments (depreciation).

Net private domestic investment Gross private domestic investment less capital consumption allowances and adjustments (depreciation).

TABLE 5 RELATION OF GROSS DOMESTIC PRODUCT, GROSS NATIONAL PRODUCT, NET NATIONAL PRODUCT, AND NATIONAL INCOME, 1992 (BILLIONS OF DOLLARS)

GDP		$6,038.5
Plus:	Adjustments for citizens v. residents	7.3
Equals:	GNP	6,045.8
Less:	Capital consumption allowance	657.9
Equals:	NNP	5,387.9
Less:	Indirect business taxes and nontax liability and business transfer payments	530.4
Plus:	Net subsidies less surpluses of government enterprises	2.7
Plus:	(or minus): Statistical discrepancy	+23.6
Equals:	NI	$4,836.6

Source: U.S. Department of Commerce, *Survey of Current Business* (Washington DC: U.S. Government Printing Office, February 1994).

The World Resources Institute, a Washington-based environmental organization, has developed still another version of NNP. This version subtracts depletion of natural resources as well as depreciation of capital equipment from GDP. This group argues that if capital used up is subtracted, it makes sense to also subtract nonrenewable resources that are used up. The group's first set of estimates of this new concept was made for Indonesia, because so much of that country's output is based on natural resources, mainly oil and natural gas. The correction reduced the estimate of Indonesia's output by 17 percent and reduced the country's estimated growth rate from 1971 to 1984 from an average of 7 percent to an average of 4 percent.[1]

FROM NET NATIONAL PRODUCT TO NATIONAL INCOME. There are a few more adjustments that must be made to NNP to obtain NI, which are shown in Table 5. The first correction is to subtract costs of production not paid to resources. These costs are indirect business taxes and business transfer payments. The next step is to add payments to resources that are not reflected in market prices. These payments consist of *net* subsidies to farmers and other businesses. Finally, the net surpluses of government enterprises, such as the U.S. Postal Service or a municipal water department, are subtracted. The resulting figure is NI, or that part of NNP that was earned by the resources.

Indirect business taxes, such as license fees, excise taxes, and business property taxes, are subtracted from NNP because they are reflected in the prices of final products but are not earned by any resource. Business transfer payments, such as private pension payments, bad debts, and prizes in promotional contests, are subtracted for the same reason. Also subtracted is the net surplus (or "profit") of any government enterprise that charges for services. Although this surplus is part of the price paid for services of the government enterprise, it is not earned by any owner of resources. Some such enterprises are subsidized, so their market prices reflect less than resource cost. These subsidies are *added* to NNP to determine NI. The sum of these corrections is the *net* amount added to (or subtracted from) NNP to obtain NI.

Statistical discrepancy reconciles errors that arise from the two different data sources used. GDP and GNP are estimated from sales data; NI is estimated from resource income. The discrepancy is the remaining difference in estimates after the "less" and "plus" items have been deducted from or added to GNP.

In Table 6, NI is computed as the sum of resource payments. NI consists of the total of wage and salary income, rental income, corporate profits, net interest earnings, and income of proprietors. (Proprietors are owners of small retail stores, independent farmers, and other businesses that are not corporations.) All of this income is earned by households. However, some of it is not actually paid out—such as the part of corporate profits that firms keep as undistributed profits or pay in corporate income taxes to the government.

Wages, interest, and corporate profits need no explanation, but proprietors' net income is more complicated. Net income for proprietorships consists mostly of wages and profits to the owner-worker. If the proprietor has invested funds in the business, some of this income is interest. Some of the proprietor's income is probably profit to enterprise. It is not possible to separate proprietors' net

---

1. *Wasting Assets: Natural Resources in the National Income Accounts* (Washington DC: World Resources Institute, June 1989).

TABLE 6 NATIONAL INCOME BY RECIPIENT, 1992 (BILLIONS OF DOLLARS)

NATIONAL INCOME	$4,836.6
Wages and supplements (including supplements and contributions to social insurance)	3,582.0
Proprietors' income	414.3
Rental income of persons	−8.9
Corporate profits	407.2
Net interest	442.0

Source: Council of Economic Advisers, *Economic Report of the President* (Washington DC: U.S. Government Printing Office, 1994).

income into these components. Thus, it is listed as a single item in the national income accounts.

The rental income figure is small partly because it has been adjusted for depreciation. Gross rent was $57.4 billion in 1992, but depreciation reduced that amount by $66.3 billion. Net interest is also smaller than one might expect because it omits all payments of interest from one member of the household sector to another. For example, the interest paid to a relative for a loan to buy a car is not included in domestic income. Also, interest on government bonds is treated as a transfer payment. It is included in personal income but not in national income because it is not regarded as a cost of production.

NI measures the value of resource services and provides a useful cross check on the accuracy of the GDP and NNP figures. However, from the standpoint of households, the important income flow is not what they *earn* (NI) but what they *receive*. What they receive is personal income.

Personal income
Equals NI after the subtraction of corporate profits taxes, undistributed corporate profits, and Social Security contributions, and the addition of net transfer payments.

PERSONAL INCOME AND DISPOSABLE INCOME. **Personal income (PI)** is the income *received* by households (whether earned or not). It is different from national income (NI), which is the income *earned* by the household sector. One major difference between NI and PI is that corporate income taxes and undistributed corporate profits are earned by households (stockholders) but are not actually paid to them. A second difference is that payments by workers and their employers into the Social Security system are earned by workers but not received. Finally, transfer payments are added because they are received but not earned. Transfer payments are not a part of NI because they represent only a movement of spending power from one sector to another. They are not related to any current production in the top half of the circular flow model. Although there is a modest amount of business transfer payments (prizes, scholarships, charitable donations, etc.), most transfer payments come from government ($889.7 billion in 1993). Government transfers include Social Security, unemployment compensation, Aid to Families with Dependent Children, and veterans' benefits. Table 7 shows how 1992 national income is converted to personal income for that year.

Disposable income
Income received by households and available to spend or save; equals PI less personal taxes.

As Table 7 indicates, the household sector can use its personal income in three ways: (1) to pay personal taxes to various levels of government, (2) to spend on consumption goods, or (3) to save. The income the household sector has left after taxes is called **disposable income**. Disposable income can be spent

TABLE 7 CONVERTING NATIONAL INCOME TO PERSONAL INCOME AND DISPOSABLE INCOME, 1992 (BILLIONS OF DOLLARS)

NATIONAL INCOME		$4,836.6
Less:	Undistributed corporate profits,	−266.8
	Corporate profits tax and	
	social insurance contributions	−555.6
	Other adjustments	−20.0
Plus:	Net interest payments	+252.3
	Government transfer payments	+836.8
	Business transfer payments	+21.6
Equals: PERSONAL INCOME		$5,144.9
Less:	Personal taxes	−644.8
Equals: DISPOSABLE INCOME		$4,500.2
Used for:		
	Personal consumption	$4,261.5
	Personal saving	238.7

Source: Council of Economic Advisers, *Economic Report of the President* (Washington DC: U.S. Government Printing Office, 1994).

on consumption or saved. It is very useful for forecasting household consumption, the largest component of GDP.

OMISSIONS FROM GDP

A number of kinds of productive activity are not counted in GDP. For instance, nonmarket production is not included in GDP. If you repair your own car, only the parts that you purchase are counted. If you take your car to a service station, all of the repairs enter into GDP. Excluding nonmarket transactions understates economic well-being and also distorts the comparative use of GDP figures. This omission of nonmarket production may not make a big difference in year-to-year comparisons within a country or comparisons of similar countries such as the United States and Canada. It does distort comparisons between 1900 and 1995 or between the United States and India. As a country gets wealthier, there are more professional laundries, for example. Less laundry is done at home. This change says nothing about how clean the clothes of the population are. In the last twenty years, as more women have entered the work force in the United States, a larger share of household services (including laundry, meals, and day care) is being purchased in the market. The change in GDP overstates the actual increase in economic well-being.

On the other hand, activities that are paid for "under the table" or by barter are difficult to track, so GDP accountants are not able to include such transactions. This omission understates economic welfare. Some transactions are excluded on purpose. Since the GDP is limited to legal markets, domestic income accountants exclude illegal activities such as drugs, prostitution, or gambling.

An important aspect of well-being not reflected in GDP is change in leisure time. Since 1900, the average factory work week has dropped from 70 hours to less than 40 hours. That reduction clearly represents an increase in economic well-being, but it is not reflected in GDP. A partial indicator of leisure activity is spending for leisure-type activities (such as travel, theater tickets, and health-club memberships) or equipment (VCRs, tennis racquets, and skis), but these are poor proxies for actual consumption of leisure.

Finally, in many cases what appear to be price increases are actually quality improvements. Products may be safer, more durable, or more useful. However, unless a specific feature can be separated out and assigned a price tag, GDP accountants have no good way of correcting for quality improvements.

REAL GDP, THE GDP DEFLATOR, AND ECONOMIC GROWTH

The most important correction to GDP and other measures of output is to adjust for changes in the price level in order to measure real economic growth. The values of GDP, GNP, NNP, and NI in Tables 4 through 7 are all nominal values. Nominal GDP (uncorrected for inflation) and real GDP can give very different pictures of economic performance. For example, in 1982 (a recession year), nominal GDP rose to $3,069 billion from $2,958 billion in 1981, a modest increase of $111 billion, or 3.6 percent. However, after dividing by the GDP deflator, real GDP actually fell by 2.1 percent between 1981 and 1982. Thus, in order to use GDP to measure economic growth or to forecast output or employment, economists need to know what is happening to real, physical production. The price index used to correct GDP figures for changes in the price level is the GDP deflator introduced in Chapter 4.

COMPUTING REAL GDP AND GROWTH RATES

The GDP deflator is a price index using the current output mix as the "basket" of goods and services. Instead of fixing a market basket and remeasuring the cost of that basket each year, as the Consumer Price Index does, the GDP deflator is computed by working backwards. The current year's output is valued at current prices; then the value of that output is recalculated using last year's prices, and so forth. In order to understand how GDP deflators, real GDP, and growth rates are calculated, consider the hypothetical data in Table 8.

TABLE 8 HYPOTHETICAL DATA FOR REAL GDP COMPUTATIONS FOR 1995

GDP at current prices: $6,500
1995 GDP at prices of earlier years:

1994	$6,200
1993	$5,800
1992	$5,400
1991	$5,200
1990	$5,000

How were these numbers computed? The same items that are actually produced in 1995 were entered at the prices of 1990, 1991, 1992, 1993, and 1994 to develop a series of values that is called 1995 GDP at 1990 prices, 1991 prices, and so on. These figures can now be used to compute a GDP deflator and an inflation rate.

Suppose, for example, that we set the GDP deflator for 1990 equal to 100. By holding the quantity of real output constant at the 1995 level, as in Table 8, we can measure the change in the average price level from year to year. The price index for 1991 is given by

$$(\$5,200/5,000) \times 100 = 104,$$

and for 1992

$$(\$5,400/5,000) \times 100 = 108$$

The GDP deflators for each of the five years, calculated backwards from 1995, are shown in Table 9. The inflation rates in Table 9 are calculated by dividing each index by the previous year's index and subtracting 1. For example, the inflation rate in 1993 is

$$(116/108) - 1 = 7.4\%$$

While price indexes are useful for calculating inflation rates, they are at least equally important in making it possible to measure changes in real output, or economic growth. For example, 1995 real GDP, measured in 1990 prices, is $6,500/1.30 = $5,000. Suppose that actual GDP in 1990, the base year, was $4,750. Then the growth of real GDP from 1990 to 1995 was

$$(\$5,000/\$4,750) - 1 = 1.053 - 1 = 5.3\%.$$

ACTUAL AND DESIRABLE RATES OF GROWTH

The rate of real economic growth for 1950–1993 is shown in Figure 4. As this figure suggests, the United States has experienced periods of rapid growth alternating with stretches of slow growth or even decline in output. The 1970s were

TABLE 9 COMPUTING GDP DEFLATORS AND INFLATION RATES

YEAR	GDP DEFLATOR	INFLATION RATE
1991	104	4.0%
1992	108	3.8%
1993	116	7.4%
1994	124	6.9%
1995	130	4.8%

a period of very slow growth. The rate of growth picked up again by the mid-1980s but slowed at the end of the decade. After a brief recession in 1990–1991, the economy began growing again, but quite slowly. The overall (compounded) rate of growth in Figure 4 has been about 3.6 percent a year, with a wide range from –9 percent a year (briefly) in 1980 to over 12 percent a year in the late 1940s.

It is generally believed that a growth rate of 3 to 4 percent per year is the highest that can be sustained for any length of time. Producing more output requires more productive resources and/or improvements in technology. A rate of growth of 3 to 4 percent corresponds to an attainable combined rate of change in these two important sources of economic growth.

As population grows, output has to grow just to keep per capita output and income from falling. Generally, people want economic growth to provide some improvements in the standard of living as well. Additional capacity to produce means that more of those unlimited wants can be fulfilled, whether they are private wants such as better housing or collective wants such as better roads. Growth creates new jobs to absorb new workers into the labor force, holding down employment.

COSTS OF ECONOMIC GROWTH

In the 1960s many people questioned both the value and the costs of economic growth. As the birth rate dropped in the late 1960s and early 1970s, the need for growth in order to provide for additional population became much less pressing. Critics of continued economic growth pointed out that humanity lives on a finite planet, with limited natural resources. Thus, growth cannot be sustained indefinitely. Growth also creates undesirable by-products, such as solid waste, hazardous wastes, air pollution, noise, congestion, and litter.

FIGURE 4
REAL GDP ANNUAL GROWTH RATE, 1950–1993
Growth rates of real Gross Domestic Product (GDP in constant dollars) show much variation over time. It is easy to identify recessions in this diagram as periods when real output fell (i.e., growth rates were negative).

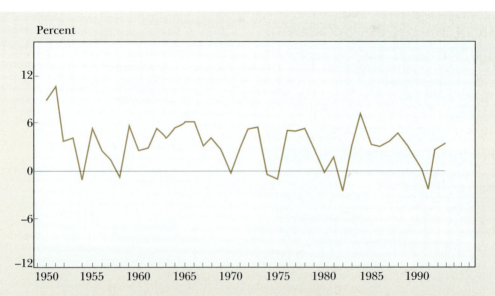

Source: U.S. Department of Commerce, *Survey of Current Business* (Washington DC: U.S. Government Printing Office, various issues).

Doubts have also been raised about whether continued economic growth has really resulted in improvements in the quality of life. Gains in productivity have seemed to go into producing more output instead of more leisure. In the 1980s, the typical European worker had a four- to six-week annual vacation in contrast to the usual two weeks for an American worker. Some Americans asked whether economic growth was worth the cost in terms of lifestyle. At the same time, younger Japanese workers questioned the benefits of their nation's rapid economic growth. Most of them had to put up with cramped housing, long commutes, long work hours, and high prices for consumer goods.

Some of these concerns really point to disagreements about the composition of output rather than about economic growth. If there is an increase in productive capacity, it can be directed toward more output or more leisure, more private goods or more collective goods. With more resources, a society can devote more effort to improving the environment without sacrificing other goods and services. In fact, there is some evidence that wealthier societies devote more resources to protecting and enhancing environmental quality than poorer countries, and enjoy a higher standard of environmental quality. The 1992 *World Development Report* of the World Bank explored the relationship between income levels and the environment, and came up with mixed results. In their findings, as income levels increased, a higher percentage of the population had access to safe water and sanitation, and concentrations of particles in the air and sulfur dioxide declined, but per capita emissions of carbon dioxide and municipal wastes rose.[2] Many of these apparent objections to economic growth are really objections to how output is measured and how priorities are set for using new resources and technology.

The last two recessions, in 1981–1982 and 1990–1991, made Americans more aware of the costs of not growing. When economic growth is slow or stops, tax revenues decline or grow slowly. Rising unemployment further reduces tax revenues and creates pressures on government to spend in order to create jobs. There are even political battles between generations. Retirees want a greater share of the public budget to support them, and younger people want funding for public schools. Thus, for most Americans, a steady and sustainable rate of economic growth, along with attention to the quality of life and the state of the environment, remains a central economic goal.

The debate over economic growth is an ongoing one. Environmentalists and loggers, homeowners and developers, avid consumers and wilderness lovers will continue to disagree about how fast and in what ways the country should grow. Because the desirable rate of growth is a normative issue, it cannot be resolved by economics. All economists can do is point out the costs and benefits of growing and not growing and provide ways to measure output and its growth so that the debate can continue on the basis of reliable data. The GDP accounts exist for that purpose.

Consider again... This chapter didn't solve the problem of making economic growth happen, but it did lay an important foundation. Before policy makers can identify ways to encourage growth, they need to be able to measure output and income and how fast it is growing. Armed with a better understanding of what those

---

2. *World Development Report 1992: Development and the Environment* (World Bank, 1992): 9–11.

numbers for GDP, personal income, saving, and economic growth mean, you as a citizen are better equipped to evaluate the economy's performance and its implications for your future as a consumer, a worker, and a citizen.

Economic growth is more abstract than price stability and full employment, but it is an equally important goal. President Reagan won the 1980 election by asking citizens if they were better off than they were four years earlier. He won again in 1984 with the same question because the economy was on an upswing by the end of his first term. The same question, expressed a little differently, was a critical factor in President Clinton's victory in 1992.

SUMMARY

1. The circular flow model represents the aggregate level of economic activity. Adding a credit market, the government, and a foreign sector provides a more realistic picture of the components of the macroeconomy.
2. Stocks are existing quantities. Flows measure quantities over time. An income statement measures flows. A balance sheet measures stocks. GDP and national income are flows.
3. Gross Domestic Product (GDP) measures final output produced in a country over a given period of time. It can be measured by producing sector or by buying sector. Its value should be the same whether it measures output produced or income created in the production process. Other measures of output and income are domestic income (NI), net domestic product (NNP), personal income (PI), and disposable income. Domestic income corresponds to the flow in the lower half of the circular flow diagram.
4. Economic growth is measured by changes in real output. Economic growth of about 4 percent a year is generally regarded as feasible and desirable because it raises the standard of living and reduces unemployment. However, economic growth often creates costs in terms of environmental quality and leisure forgone.

NEW TERMS

economic growth
saving
investment
credit market
leakages
injections
imports
exports
balance of goods and services

income statement
balance sheet
net worth
flow variable
stock variable
Gross Domestic Product (GDP)
final goods
intermediate goods

business inventories
consumption expenditures
consumer durables
consumer nondurables
consumer services
gross private domestic investment
fixed investment
transfer payments

national income (NI)
capital consumption allowance
net national product (NNP)
net private domestic investment
personal income
disposable income

QUESTIONS: REVIEW, APPLICATIONS, AND POLICY

REVIEW

1. What are the costs and benefits of rapid economic growth?
2. Suppose that during a certain period GDP rises from $3,000 billion to $3,500 billion, while the GDP deflator goes from 100 to 125. What has happened to real GDP?
3. What is a leakage? What is an injection? Identify three kinds of leakages and three kinds of injections.
4. Why is GDP not entirely satisfactory as a measure of economic well-being? Why is it better for comparisons over short time periods or between countries that are similar in economic and social conditions?
5. Why is it unlikely that a rate of economic growth in excess of 3 or 4 percent can be sustained for a long period?

APPLICATIONS

6. How would an increase in Social Security taxes affect GDP, NNP, domestic income, and PI?
7. Draw up a personal income statement. See if it helps you to understand why domestic income accountants wind up with a statistical discrepancy in matching the income side to the expenditure side.
8. Use the following data to compute GDP, NNP, and NI. If NI computed at resource cost is $3,387 billion, what is the statistical discrepancy? (All figures are in billions; any omitted items are zero.)

Consumption	$2,762
Government purchases	865
Gross investment	675
Depreciation	455
Indirect business taxes	349
Net exports	–106

9. Use the data in Question 7 to compute the percentage of GDP going to each buying sector. Present the results as a bar chart or pie chart.

10. Use the following data to compute NI, PI, and disposable income for the year. (All figures are in billions; any omitted items are zero.)

Wages and salaries	$2,499
Personal taxes	513
Government transfers	491
Social insurance taxes	376
Corporate profits	300
Net interest	295
Proprietors' income	279
Corporate profits taxes	103
Dividends	88
Undistributed profits	46
Business transfers	23
Rental income	16

11. Suppose a hurricane struck the coast of New England, destroying millions of dollars' worth of housing. What would be the immediate effect on GDP, NNP, NI, and PI?
12. Identify whether each of the following would be an asset or a liability on your personal balance sheet.
    a. government bonds
    b. car loan
    c. bill due for doctor's care
    d. a TV set
    e. a bicycle
    f. a condominium

POLICY

13. Suppose the government decided not to tax corporate profits, and as a result corporations decide to pay out all the extra funds as dividends to stockholders. How would this change affect GDP, NNP, NI, and PI?
14. Suppose that the government is considering deficit reduction by cutting spending, and is trying to choose between cutting spending for defense (soldiers, weapons, etc.) and cutting spending for transfer programs such as farm price supports and Social Security. For equal dollar amounts, which kind of cuts will have a more direct effect on GDP? NI? PI?

SUGGESTIONS FOR FURTHER READING

Council of Economic Advisers. *Economic Report of the President.* Washington DC: U.S. Government Printing Office, annual. Gives a summary of economic developments and a variety of statistics.

Frumkin, Norman. *Guide to Economic Indicators.* Armonk NY: M.E. Sharpe, 1991. A good reference on the meaning of the major economic data.

U.S. Department of Commerce. *Survey of Current Business.* Washington DC: U.S. Government Printing Office, monthly. The official source of data and analysis of the U.S. GDP accounts.

CHAPTER 6

AGGREGATE DEMAND AND AGGREGATE SUPPLY

Consider this... *In 1992, the year after the collapse of communism, Russia suffered from dramatically falling output (a 13 percent decline in GDP) and 2,000 percent inflation. In the same year, the United Kingdom also had falling output (GDP fell by 2.2 percent), but the British inflation rate fell from 9.5 percent in 1990 to 5.9 percent in 1991. In the same year, Mexico experienced rising output and declining inflation, while Japan enjoyed 3.7 percent growth and a steady inflation rate. In the United States, economic growth was a modest 1 percent, while inflation was relatively low at about 3 percent.*

Why do different countries have such different combinations of inflation and economic growth? Should not the two move together? That is, as output rises and producers find they face more competition for inputs and more demand for their output, should not the price level rise in response? Not necessarily. The key factor in determining what happens to the price level when output grows or shrinks is whether the change in output is due to a shift in aggregate supply, aggregate demand, or some of each. This chapter introduces the aggregate supply and aggregate demand model that economists use to explain changes in the macroeconomy.

LEARNING OBJECTIVES
1. Define aggregate demand and explain why the aggregate demand curve has a negative slope.
2. Discuss the alternative possible slopes of the aggregate supply curve.
3. Identify the factors that can shift aggregate demand or aggregate supply.
4. Explain the relationship between equilibrium output, employment, and unemployment.
5. Relate the aggregate supply and aggregate demand curves to the two major alternative approaches to macroeconomic policy.

AGGREGATE DEMAND

When you think of demand, you probably think of the kinds of demand curves for individual products developed in Chapter 3. Your first thought might be to obtain an aggregate demand (*AD*) curve, or an aggregate supply (*AS*) curve, by adding the supply or demand curves for all the products in the marketplace. Unfortunately, this is not the way to proceed. Why not? First, there are technical problems with adding such unlike goods as cars, toothpaste, and haircuts on the horizontal axis and the prices of each on the vertical axis.

Second, when you add across many markets, many of the effects that can shift the individual supply and demand curves drop out of the picture. For instance, the demand for toothpaste is affected by the prices of mouthwash (a substitute) and toothbrushes (a complement). On the aggregate demand curve, however, it is not possible to distinguish among individual products or individual prices. The vertical axis measures only the aggregate, or average, price level. On the horizontal axis, it does not matter whether consumers are buying toothpaste or mouthwash, as long as they are buying some item. More toothpaste offsets less mouthwash when both goods are combined into total real output on the horizontal axis. The substitution effect between specific products that plays such an important role in individual demand curves has little effect on aggregate demand.

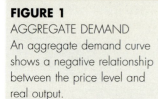

Aggregate demand curve A graph showing the amounts of total real output that all buyers in an economy wish to purchase at various price levels.

A microeconomic market demand curve shows how much of a given product consumers will buy at various prices, *ceteris paribus*. The **aggregate demand curve (AD)** shows the quantity of total real output that all buyers in an economy will purchase at various price levels. Figure 1 shows an aggregate demand curve (AD). On the vertical axis, P represents the price level, measured by a price index. On the horizontal axis, Y represents real output, or the value of output adjusted for changes in the price level. Economists generally believe that the aggregate demand curve has a negative slope, as pictured in Figure 1. For convenience, we will usually use a straight-line aggregate demand curve.

Economists use the symbol Y to stand for several different concepts of the flow of income or output. However, if we overlook some of the smaller differences between GDP and national income (NI), then Y can represent both the

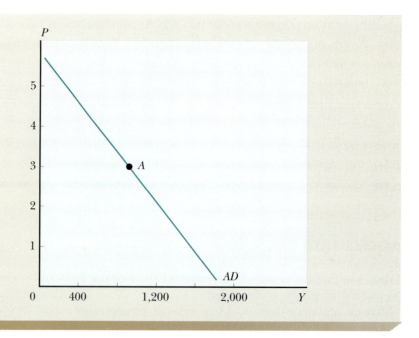

FIGURE 1
AGGREGATE DEMAND
An aggregate demand curve shows a negative relationship between the price level and real output.

flow of output and the flow of income. Nominal GDP or NI is then the product of P and Y at any point. For example, at point A in Figure 1, a price level of 3 and total output of 1,000 combine for a GDP of $3,000. Although Y represents real, physical quantity, it has to be measured in dollars because that is the only way to aggregate across different products—to add autos, pizzas, movie tickets, telephone calls, and college tuition into one useful whole.

WHY AGGREGATE DEMAND SLOPES DOWN

The slope of the aggregate demand curve implies that higher prices have a negative effect on planned purchases of real output. Dollar spending ($P \times Y$) may be higher if P is sufficiently higher, but Y will be lower. People tend to be reluctant to buy as much real output at higher price levels as they do at lower ones. This is especially true if prices rise ahead of wages or more rapidly than wages or income. Several explanations based on the theory of self-interested behavior can be offered for the negative slope of the aggregate demand curve.

TAXES AND THE PRICE LEVEL

If the price level rises, even with no change in employment and real output, nominal income ($P \times Y$) will increase. When nominal income increases and the tax code is progressive, then tax revenues rise more than in proportion to the income increase, even if *real* income (Y) is unchanged. Households' disposable incomes fall relative to total real income and output. Higher taxes, by reducing disposable income, reduce people's ability to buy at higher prices.

NET EXPORTS AND THE PRICE LEVEL

When there is inflation, usually exports fall and imports rise. The resulting change in net exports ($X - M$) will change real quantity demanded. Higher domestic prices mean that a country's exports become more expensive to foreigners. Also, imports become more attractive to residents of the country because they are relatively cheaper. Both foreigners and residents will substitute cheaper foreign products for more expensive domestic ones, reducing exports and increasing imports. A fall in net exports means that real quantity demanded is lower at a higher price level. Conversely, a lower price level, *ceteris paribus*, will lead to substitution of home products for foreign products. Then real quantity demanded will be greater at lower price levels.

ASSETS AND THE PRICE LEVEL

Higher prices also reduce the purchasing power of financial assets owned by households. These assets include savings accounts, bonds, certificates of deposit, pension funds, and insurance policies. As the value of these assets falls, households will cut back on spending in order to rebuild their assets to the desired levels. Changes in aggregate assets or wealth have the same effect on the aggregate demand curve that changes in individual wealth have on the individual demand curve. When the price level falls, the real purchasing power of financial assets rises, making households feel wealthier. Such an increase in wealth means that households are willing and able to purchase more goods and services at every level of real income (Y).

If you are thinking like an economist, it may occur to you that one household's or firm's asset may be another's debt. Your savings deposit (asset) has been loaned by the bank as someone else's mortgage (liability). Your bonds (asset) are the liability of some corporation. When the price level rises, the decreased spending by asset holders may be offset by the increased spending of debtors, who feel less burdened by their debt. This would be true were it not for the fact that the government is a major net debtor. When the price level rises, there is a fall in the value of government debt held by households. As their wealth decreases, households spend less. However, government officials do not necessarily respond by spending more. Similarly, a fall in the price level would increase the value of government debt held by households, raising their spending. Again, there is no reason to expect that public officials would respond by spending less.

STATE AND LOCAL SPENDING AND THE PRICE LEVEL

Spending by state and local governments is also sensitive to price level changes. Many of these governments are constrained by their constitutions or in other ways to limit their spending to what they receive in revenues. When the price level rises, revenues from two of the three major state and local taxes—property taxes and sales taxes—tend to lag behind. These taxes are not highly sensitive to changes in the price level. Therefore, state and local governments must limit their purchases to what they can buy with revenues that are rising more slowly than the price level.

INTEREST RATES AND THE PRICE LEVEL

Finally, higher price levels are associated with higher interest rates, for reasons we will explore in later chapters. Rising interest rates increase the opportunity cost of borrowing by business for investment, by households for purchase of consumer durables, and by state and local governments to finance construction. Lower price levels lead to lower interest rates and more of all three of these kinds of borrowing.

All of the effects described here—taxes, net exports, household wealth, government spending, and interest rates—support the notion of a downward-sloping aggregate demand curve. However, none of them are very powerful—certainly not as powerful as the substitution effect in the demand for individual products. Consider, for example, the effect of a change in the value of households' financial assets. Some estimates suggest that a $1 change in a household's wealth only leads to a $.06 change in its spending. Although all of these effects on price levels are weak, they all work in the same direction—yielding an aggregate demand curve that slopes downward from left to right. Because none of these effects are very powerful, the aggregate demand curve is generally believed to be quite steep.

KEY IDEAS

WHY THE AGGREGATE DEMAND CURVE HAS A NEGATIVE SLOPE

A higher price level reduces
- consumption demand,
- net exports, and
- government (state and local) spending through

    smaller real money supply,
    higher interest rates,
    lower value of households' financial assets,
    higher (progressive) taxes,
    substitution of relatively cheaper foreign goods for domestic goods, and
    slow growth of sales and property tax revenues.

AGGREGATE SUPPLY

The **aggregate supply curve** *(AS)* shows the various quantities of total real output that producers will offer for sale at various price levels. One point on the aggregate supply curve corresponds roughly to NI at resource cost—the point at which NI is equal to GDP, or where aggregate demand intersects aggregate supply. However, the actual value of NI at resource cost only represents one point on the aggregate supply curve, the quantity supplied at the current actual price level. Points on the aggregate supply curve represent possible values of NI that suppliers are willing to produce and offer for sale.

> **Aggregate supply curve**
> A graph showing the amounts of total real output that all producers in an economy will offer for sale at various price levels.

THE SLOPE OF THE AGGREGATE SUPPLY CURVE

What is the slope of the aggregate supply curve? Economists would like to know the answer to that question! Probably no single graphical construction in economists' vast collection has generated as much argument as the aggregate supply curve. A large part of this dispute has to do with how firms and owners of resources respond to changes in the price level, and how quickly. Time plays an even more important role with respect to aggregate supply than with respect to aggregate demand. The dispute over the slope often centers on the difference between what the aggregate supply curve looks like in the short run and in the long run, and how much time is meant in each of these cases.

Since you know that the market supply curve for an individual product slopes upward, you are probably expecting that the aggregate supply curve will also slope up from left to right, like line *AS* in Figure 2(a). However, like the aggregate demand curve, the aggregate supply curve differs from the supply curves for individual products in some important ways. The problems of adding individual prices and outputs also exist for aggregate supply, so the aggregate supply curve is not simply the sum of the market supply curves for all goods and services. One of the reasons for the upward-sloping microeconomic supply curve for a single product is substitution. (Producers switch to more profitable products when prices of those goods rise relative to the prices of other goods the firm could produce.) This reason, however, has no validity at all in explaining why the aggregate supply curve slopes upward. Total real output on the horizontal axis already includes all possible substitute goods.

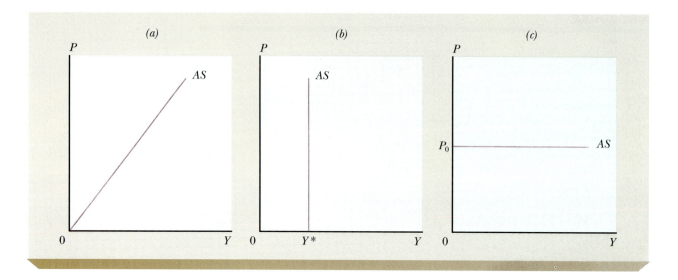

FIGURE 2

AGGREGATE SUPPLY CURVES
(a) An aggregate supply curve with an upward slope, similar to most supply curves. (b) The classical aggregate supply curve, with the economy producing at capacity (or full employment level of output, Y^*). Attempts to increase real output will only drive up the price level. (c) The Keynesian aggregate supply curve, which assumes that there are enough unemployed resources so that real output can increase without driving the price level above P_0.

Full-employment level of output
The level of real output associated with full use of all resources, especially labor.

Nevertheless, many economists expect the aggregate supply curve to slope upward for some of the same reasons that supply curves for individual goods and services slope upward. As firms in general try to produce more output with given resources, some labor has to work overtime at higher pay, driving up costs and prices. Firms are working their capital harder, so it wears out faster and breaks down more often. Competition among producers for scarce resources drives up wages and interest rates. All of these cost increases, for individual products and for aggregate real output, will be reflected in higher prices.

Another reason for an upward-sloping supply curve, either for a single product or for goods and services in the aggregate, is that the lure of higher prices will induce producers to try to expand output. If firms and entrepreneurs can sell their products for more, and if their overall costs have not risen as much as the prices of what they sell, they can make more profit. Profit is the incentive and the reward to which producers respond. If higher prices do indeed mean higher profits, then the aggregate supply curve will slope upward.

A VERTICAL AS CURVE. Before the 1930s, an even simpler view of the aggregate supply curve prevailed. It was seen as a vertical line, running straight up and down. This slope indicates that output does not respond at all to changes in the price level. Most economists before Keynes believed that the economy naturally tended toward the level of output that available resources could support. There was really only one level of real output that could occur in a properly functioning economic system, where supply and demand in labor markets assured full employment. This real output level was defined as the full-employment level of output, or capacity output. The **full-employment level of output** is the level of real output associated with full use of all resources, especially labor. The level of real output associated with full employment is labeled Y^*.

Figure 2(b) shows the aggregate supply curve as a vertical line (AS). This version of aggregate supply is usually referred to as a classical aggregate supply curve, because pre-Keynesian macroeconomics has been labelled classical macroeconomics. In this model, the price level can vary, but changes in the price level will have no effect on real output. A fixed real output level and a variable price level imply a vertical aggregate supply curve.

A HORIZONTAL AS CURVE. John Maynard Keynes, the British economist whose writings in the 1930s had such a great influence on twentieth-century macroeconomic theory and policy, offered a third view of the aggregate supply curve. He suggested that during periods when large amounts of resources were unemployed, the aggregate supply curve could be horizontal, as in Figure 2(c). It would be possible for firms to increase both individual and aggregate output without driving the price level above P_0. They could produce more simply by putting unemployed resources to work. Firms would not have to pay higher prices to compete for scarce resources. They could simply hire idle workers at the going wage and use their factories' idle capacity. A horizontal aggregate supply curve implies that the economy is inside its production possibilities curve, since there is unemployed labor (and other resources) willing to work at the present wage.

A COMPOSITE VIEW. These three views of the aggregate supply curve are sometimes combined in a composite version with three distinct regions, shown in Figure 3. The horizontal region (sometimes known as the Keynesian region) represents a situation in which there are ample idle resources. In this case, output can be increased without driving up prices. This segment corresponds to the Keynesian aggregate supply curve of Figure 2(c).

In the intermediate, upward-sloping region of the composite aggregate supply curve, there are some unemployed resources. Perhaps they are not the right kind for the mix of additional output that firms are trying to produce. Attempting to expand output in this situation will drive up the price level but will also result in more output. This segment corresponds to the upward-sloping curve of Figure 2(a).

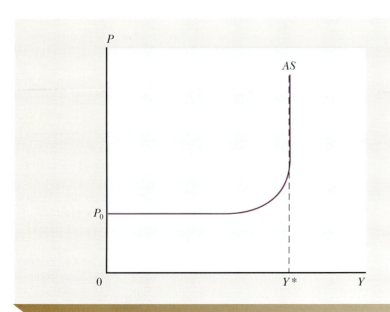

FIGURE 3
A COMPOSITE AGGREGATE SUPPLY CURVE
This composite aggregate supply curve is made up of a horizontal (Keynesian) region, an intermediate region in which prices and output rise or fall together, and a vertical (classical) region.

The last (or classical) segment of the composite aggregate supply curve shows what happens when there are no more unemployed resources available. It is possible to produce more of good *A* only by cutting output of good *B*. As producers of *A* try to bid resources away from other uses, they drive up prices and reduce output of other goods. In this region, the economy is on the production possibilities curve. More of one kind of output can only be obtained by sacrificing output of other goods or services. Attempts to expand total real output will only drive up the price level. This segment corresponds to the vertical (classical) aggregate supply curve of Figure 2(b).

THE SHORT RUN AND THE LONG RUN

The composite aggregate supply curve is one way to reconcile the conflicting views of how the graph should look. Another way of reconciling these conflicting views is to clarify what is meant by the short run and the long run. Part of the debate between Keynes and both his predecessors (the classical economists) and his successors (monetarists) is a matter of defining terms. Most economists would agree that in the long run, the level of output will tend toward full employment, which corresponds to a vertical aggregate supply curve. They disagree about the curve's shape in the short run, however. Even more important, they disagree about the length of time that separates the short run from the long run. If the dividing line between the short run and the long run is six months, a fair amount of unemployment can be tolerated until the economy returns to "normal." If the dividing line is more like ten years, people will be less patient. Keynes and his followers pointed to the length and severity of the Great Depression as evidence of how long an economy can deviate from the long-run equilibrium level of output corresponding to full employment of resources.

GLOBAL OUTLOOK: THE CHINESE MIRACLE?

One of the great mysteries of the early 1990s is how China managed to grow at a rate estimated to be 9 percent a year for the last few years. This high-speed growth has been going on since the late 1980s, but outside observers were slow to catch up with the rapid improvement in the Chinese standard of living. Since developed countries normally manage to shift their aggregate supply curves to the right at a pace in the 2 percent to 4 percent range in good years, China's growth rate is considered truly astounding.

Being impressed with China's leap forward is merely the latest in a series of "other countries' miracles." There was the German miracle in the 1950s and 1960s, followed by the Japanese miracle, followed by the Taiwanese miracle. Mexico and Argentina are two other recent success stories of rapid economic growth. Inevitably, their successes pose the question, "What are they doing that we could borrow and apply in our country?"

The answer may depend on what country you are in, and which model you are considering. Germany and Japan were two successful, developed countries before World War II, who pulled themselves back together after the war because they had an infusion of Western aid as well as a solid base of capital, technology, and skilled labor with which to rebuild. China has been able to succeed in part through introducing market forces and decentralization in a large, bureaucratic economy. Most of the growth in China has been concentrated in the southern provinces where citizens have been given the most freedom to experiment and develop profit-making enterprises. Mexico's success was partly due to privatizing a number of bureaucratic, inefficient state-run enterprises. Argentina, a country rich in natural resources, finally pulled back from years of decline from its peak at the beginning of the century as one of the wealthiest countries in the world. Like Mexico, Argentina got its budget deficit under control to reduce the inflation rate and sold off inefficient state enterprises to the private sector.

Certainly there is a positive lesson to tell here, particularly about the benefits of using markets and rewarding efficiency. But percentage growth rates do not tell the whole story. The experiences of all of these countries must be qualified by two important cautions: First, the important growth rate is per capita GDP. Mexico, in particular, is in a difficult race between growing output and growing population. Part of China's success is due to holding its population growth rate down with restrictive population policies while encouraging growth of output. Second, it's easier to grow at a faster rate when starting from a low base. If China's per capita GDP is indeed about $1,000, as some estimates would indicate, then a 9 percent increase is $90. An equal dollar increase per capita in the United States would amount to less than 0.5 percent increase in per capita GDP—a growth rate closer to embarrassing than miraculous.

AGGREGATE EQUILIBRIUM AND CHANGES IN EQUILIBRIUM

What happens when aggregate supply meets aggregate demand? When the demand curve and supply curve for a specific good are drawn on the same graph, it is possible to determine an equilibrium quantity and price. In the same way, the aggregate demand and aggregate supply curves together determine the level of real output and the price level.

Consider the simplest case, a downward-sloping aggregate demand curve and an upward-sloping aggregate supply curve (Figure 4). Equilibrium occurs at Y_1 and P_1. This output and price combination is an equilibrium in the same sense that the intersection of an individual supply curve and demand curve is. If firms collectively try to produce any other level of output, market forces will tend to push the economy toward the equilibrium level.

Suppose that firms try to produce a real output, Y_2, that is larger than the equilibrium level of output, Y_1. For that level of output, producers will attempt

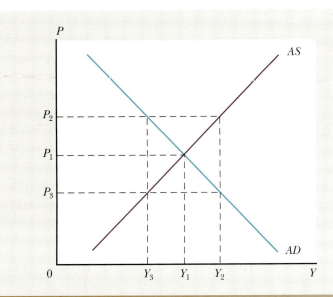

FIGURE 4

EQUILIBRIUM OUTPUT AND PRICE LEVEL
Equilibrium occurs at the intersection of AS and AD. If producers attempt to produce and sell the quantity Y_2, they will have unsold output at the corresponding price level on the AS curve, P_2. As they accumulate unwanted inventory or find that they are paying idle workers, they will cut production. Real output and the price level will fall to Y_1 and P_1.

to charge prices that average out to a price level of P_2. But consumers are only willing to purchase that large quantity of output, Y_2, when the price level is much lower, P_3. At a price level of P_2, consumers are only willing to buy a total quantity of Y_3. At the higher output level, Y_2, producers will find themselves with unsold output (unplanned inventory investment of $Y_2 - Y_3$) and will have to cut prices. As prices fall, there is less incentive to produce additional output. Real output declines until equilibrium is restored. The opposite process occurs if firms try to produce a real output that is less than the equilibrium level. Excess demand will result in falling inventories, and higher prices will encourage firms to expand production to meet demand and rebuild inventories, restoring equilibrium price and output levels.

In Figure 4, as in the diagrams for individual markets, the quantity sold and the quantity bought are always equal. Producers may offer quantity Y_2 at price level P_2, but they only sell quantity Y_3 at that price level. Both NI and GDP, however, are equal to $P_2 \times Y_2$. The unsold output is counted as inventory investment, and the workers and owners of capital who produced that output receive resource incomes. The national income accounts balance (GDP = NI) whether or not the economy is in equilibrium. In the circular flow model, the unplanned investment that firms make in inventory means that they will reduce their inventories in the near future. When that happens, the size of the flow will shrink back to a sustainable level of $P_1 \times Y_1$.

Changes in real output and price level can result from shifts in either aggregate demand or aggregate supply. These curves can shift if there is a change in any of the other variables besides price level, or a change in the *ceteris paribus* conditions.

SHIFTS IN AGGREGATE DEMAND

Two factors that shift individual demand curves are not relevant here. One is changes in the prices of substitutes and complements, which disappear when we aggregate over all goods. Except for the substitution between foreign and domestic goods, there is no substitution along the aggregate demand curve. The other missing factor is changes in income. Since real output is also real income (GDP = NI), income is already represented in the model, so it cannot be an outside source of demand shifts.

The nonprice variables that can shift the aggregate demand include interest rates, expectations, and other familiar demand shifters. These factors affect *AD* through changes in the components of demand—household consumption, government spending, business investment, and net exports.

CONSUMPTION AND INVESTMENT SPENDING. Many of the factors that can shift individual demand curves also affect aggregate demand through consumption spending. These effects are changes in consumer wealth (for reasons other than change in the price level), tastes, population, expectations, and interest rates. An increase in consumption spending because of an increase in wealth or population, a change in tastes, more positive expectations, or lower interest rates will shift aggregate demand to the right. Changes in any of these variables in the opposite direction will shift aggregate demand to the left.

EXPECTATIONS AND INTEREST RATES. Business investment spending is strongly influenced by expectations and interest rates. Positive expectations and low interest rates will increase investment spending at every possible price level and shift *AD* to the right, while pessimistic expectations or high interest rates will shift *AD* to the left.

Another factor that can affect both consumption and investment spending is changes in the money supply. An increase in the money supply means that households and firms have more available to spend and will demand a larger real quantity of goods and services at every possible price level, shifting *AD* to the right. A reduction in the money supply means that households and firms have less available to spend at every possible price level, shifting aggregate demand to the left.

GOVERNMENT PURCHASES. Spending by governments is determined largely by factors other than expectations and interest rates, but even governments are sensitive to their economic surroundings. Interest rates affect borrowing by state and local governments to finance construction of roads, schools, hospitals, prisons, libraries, sewer systems, and other public facilities. When interest rates fall, these governments may borrow more and increase their spending on long-term projects, shifting *AD* to the right. Likewise, when interest rates fall, the federal government finds that its bill for interest on the national debt declines, freeing up funds for other kinds of purchases. Since interest on the debt is a transfer payment, switching those funds to the purchase of goods and services should shift *AD* to the right. Higher interest rates will have the opposite effect on government purchases. For the most part, however, changes in government spending are determined independently of the factors that may influence spending by households and business firms.

NET EXPORTS. Finally, changes in exports or imports can have an effect on output, employment, and the price level by shifting aggregate demand. You might expect that exports would affect aggregate demand, and imports affect aggregate supply, or vice versa. However, the conventional way to reflect exports and imports is to include both in aggregate demand. To understand why, we need to refine the definitions of aggregate supply and aggregate demand a little. In an economy with a foreign sector, aggregate supply is defined as the supply of goods and services *produced* in the country, not the supply of goods and services available for consumption. Aggregate supply is a production concept, not a consumption concept. Aggregate demand means demand for goods and services produced in the country, whether the demanders are residents or foreigners. Higher exports show up in an aggregate supply and demand diagram as an increase in aggregate demand. Imports are shown as a decrease in aggregate demand rather than an addition to aggregate supply. An increase in exports will shift aggregate demand to the right, while an increase in exports shifts aggregate demand to the left.

Some of the factors that affect exports and imports are domestic, and some are foreign, or a combination of the two. Although the price level is already shown in the *AS–AD* diagram, the important consideration for imports and exports is the price level relative to foreign price levels; that is, how prices of U.S. goods compare to prices of foreign goods. An increase in foreign price levels will increase net exports (increase exports, decrease imports) at every possible price level and shift aggregate demand to the right, while a decrease in foreign price levels will reduce net exports and shift aggregate demand to the left. Income and output are also reflected in the AS–AD diagram, but foreign income is not; changes in foreign income will affect demand for this country's exports. Higher foreign income will increase demand for exports, shifting AD to the right; lower foreign income will reduce demand for exports, shifting AD to the left.

One of the most important influences on net exports is the exchange rate, or the price of the country's currency in terms of other currencies. A higher price for the dollar will make foreign goods cheaper and American goods more expensive, reducing U.S. exports and increasing U.S. imports and shifting AD to the left. A lower price for the dollar will increase net exports and shift AD to the right. The exchange rate in turn is influenced by some of the factors mentioned above—relative price levels and income changes and interest rates—as well as tastes and preferences and expectations.

EFFECTS OF SHIFTS IN AGGREGATE DEMAND

If the aggregate supply curve slopes upward, we expect both the price level and output to increase when the aggregate demand curve shifts to the right. How much of the shift is in the price level and how much is in real output depends on the slope of the aggregate supply curve. In Figure 5, the original equilibrium is at P_1 and Y_1 on AD_1. A shift of the curve to AD_2 means that people want to purchase more real output at every possible price level. If the aggregate demand curve shifted to AD_3, this would mean that people were willing to buy less real

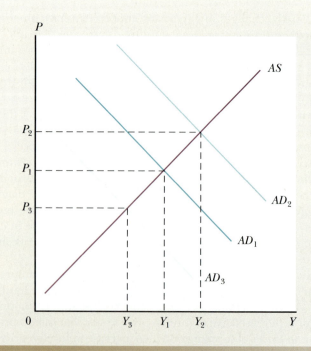

FIGURE 5
SHIFTS IN AGGREGATE DEMAND
An increase in aggregate demand from AD_1 to AD_2 (a shift to the right) drives real output and the price level up. A decrease in aggregate demand from AD_1 to AD_3 (a shift to the left) drives real output and the price level down.

output at every possible price level. Both the price level and total real output would fall. When the aggregate demand curve shifts, prices and real output move in the same direction.

The effect of shifts of the aggregate demand curve on real output and the price level is different if the aggregate supply curve is horizontal or vertical. Along a horizontal aggregate supply curve, increases in aggregate demand drive up real output only. Also, a decline in aggregate demand reduces real output only, with no effect on the price level. With a vertical aggregate supply curve, the price level rises when the aggregate demand curve shifts to the right and falls when it shifts to the left, but real output does not change. You might experiment with the composite aggregate supply curve of Figure 3 to observe these different effects on prices and output.

SHIFTS IN AGGREGATE SUPPLY

Some of the factors that affect individual supply curves, such as the prices of other products the firm could produce, disappear when the horizontal axis measures aggregate output. However, aggregate supply can shift for two of the reasons that individual supply curves shift. One is an increase or decrease in the amount of productive resources available. The other is a change in technology. In addition, there may be shifts in aggregate supply due to special factors such as political changes or natural disasters, such as Hurricane Andrew in Florida in 1992 or the great Mississippi flood of 1993.

RESOURCE AVAILABILITY. The United States has seen some significant changes in the size, the makeup, and the skills of the labor force over the last few decades. More women working outside the home, the baby boom generation hitting the work force, and a change in the level and mix of immigrants have combined to create a very different kind of labor force. The size of the labor force is now a larger fraction of the total population because the share of the population that is in the labor force has risen from 61 percent in 1960 to 67 percent in 1992. In addition, the human capital that those workers bring to the job has changed. A significant part of human capital comes from on-the-job training. The 1970s, in particular, were a period when experienced, skilled workers became relatively scarce, slowing growth of output. In the 1990s the average worker has considerably more skill and experience, increasing the availability of human capital. More workers or more productive workers (workers with more skills or human capital) shifts AS to the right. A decline in labor force participation, or a lower average level of skill and experience, will shift AS to the left.

A second important resource is capital, which comes from the accumulation of savings over time that is invested in plant and equipment. Typically about 15 percent of GDP goes into private sector investment—some for replacement, the rest for new equipment and facilities, including not only factories but also housing, shopping malls, and office buildings. An increase in the stock of capital makes workers more productive and shifts AS to the right. If capital is not replaced as it ages or wears out, AS could shift to the left.

CHANGES IN TECHNOLOGY. A change in the methods of production can shift AS to the right. Most people are familiar with such innovations as industrial robots that increase productivity of existing resources. Other changes are often less visible but can still impact on productivity of labor and capital. For example, new ways of organizing production with more worker participation (including quality circles and production teams) have been found to increase productivity in some industries. The most important technological innovation of the 1980s was the use of computers to manage a variety of tasks in production, ranging from scheduling production to management of inventories.

OTHER SOURCES OF SHIFTS IN AGGREGATE SUPPLY. Aggregate supply can be subject to shocks—wars, earthquakes, floods, hurricanes, major strikes, or terrorist attacks. Except for wars, most of these shocks are fairly short run or localized in their effects. Hurricane Andrew in 1992 had a devastating impact on the south Florida economy for several years, but relatively little impact on the national economy and relatively little long-term impact.

Since aggregate supply represents the sum of all kinds of production, the level of output can be affected by changes in the output mix. The defense cutbacks of the 1990s will affect aggregate supply because shifting resources from military to civilian uses is not costless and not instantaneous. Output is lost in the process of change. One of the short-run effects of reducing military spending in the 1990s is a leftward shift in *AS* during the adjustment process.

Policy actions can affect aggregate supply also. Remember, the goal of the business firm is to make a profit. When tax laws or other regulations change, they affect the profitability of firms and their willingness to supply output at all price levels. Tax policies can impact on both aggregate supply and aggregate demand, although in different ways. Tax breaks that stimulate spending on new capital, development of new capital, or investment in worker training will all shift *AS* to the right. Policies that reduce interest rates make it easier for firms to borrow and invest in new capital, increasing productivity and shifting *AS* to the right. Policies that drive up interest rates have the opposite effect.

KEY IDEAS

SHIFTS IN *AD* AND *AS*

Aggregate demand shifts in response to changes in
- consumer wealth,
- population,
- tastes,
- expectations,
- size/age of the capital stock,
- interest rates,
- money supply,
- taxes,
- foreign price level, and
- exchange rates.

Aggregate supply shifts in response to changes in
- resource availability,
- technology,
- tax incentives, and
- wars, earthquakes, and other shocks.

EFFECTS OF SHIFTS IN AGGREGATE SUPPLY

Shifts in aggregate supply are shown in Figure 6. For simplicity, we use the upward-sloping aggregate supply curve. A shift in aggregate supply to the left (from AS_1 to AS_2) means that producers will be willing to supply a smaller quantity of real output at every possible price level *or* the same real output at a higher price level. Real output falls and the price level rises—the worst of all possible worlds. When aggregate supply shifts to the right (from AS_1 to AS_3), the result is the best of all possible worlds—rising real output and a falling price level.

AGGREGATE DEMAND AND SUPPLY AND UNEMPLOYMENT

The three macroeconomic goals identified in Chapter 4 are steady growth of total output, price stability, and full employment. Since Y represents real output and P represents the price level, two of the three goals are included in the aggregate supply and demand model. This graphic model can be extended to include the third goal of full employment.

THE AGGREGATE PRODUCTION FUNCTION

Figure 7 is an **aggregate production function**. This graph shows how much total real output can be produced by various amounts of labor, given the amount of capital and available technology. An increase in capital or an improvement in technology will shift the production function.

Aggregate production function
A graph showing the relationship between total real output and the number of workers employed.

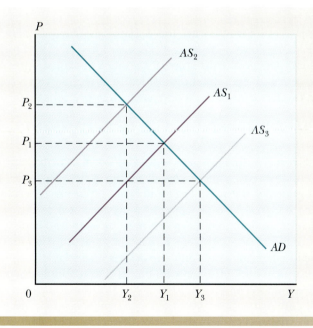

FIGURE 6
SHIFTS IN AGGREGATE SUPPLY
A decrease in aggregate supply from AS_1 to AS_2 (a shift to the left) reduces real output and raises the price level. An increase in aggregate supply from AS_1 to AS_3 (a shift to the right) raises real output and lowers the price level.

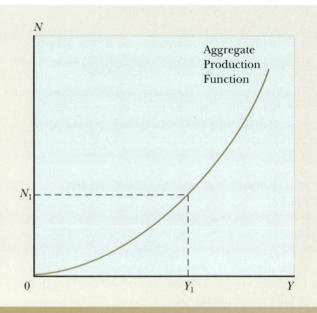

FIGURE 7

THE AGGREGATE PRODUCTION FUNCTION

The aggregate production function shows the relationship between the level of real output and the level of employment. The increase in real output gets smaller as more and more workers are hired.

A production function is normally drawn with labor (the independent variable) on the horizontal axis and real output (the dependent variable) on the vertical axis. The diagram in Figure 7, however, is turned sideways so that the horizontal axis shows real output (Y) and the vertical axis shows the aggregate level of employment of labor (N). Assuming that the size of the labor force is stable, the higher the value of N, the lower the rate of unemployment will be.

There is a positive relationship between the number of workers employed and the level of real output. More workers will produce more output. In Figure 7, output rises as more workers are hired, but as more workers are added, total output grows more slowly. The best workers are hired first, and the last workers hired are usually less productive. Also, if the stock of capital is fixed, each worker added has less and less capital with which to work. So extra workers increase total output, but later ones do not add as much as previous ones.

EQUILIBRIUM OUTPUT AND THE LEVEL OF EMPLOYMENT

Combining Figure 7 with aggregate supply and demand curves provides a view of output, employment, and prices all at once. This is done in Figure 8. Equilibrium values of the price level and real output are determined to be P_1 and Y_1, where AS crosses AD_1. Tracing real output down to the aggregate production function, we find that N_1 workers must be employed in order to produce that level of real output. Aggregate supply and demand combined with a production function determine not only the price level and real output but also the level of employment and, by extension, the level of unemployment.

If N_1 is less than full employment, then the diagram in Figure 8 suggests how to get to full employment. A shift of either AD or AS to the right will cause the two curves to intersect at a higher level of real output. This shift increases employment and reduces unemployment. For example, a shift from AD_1 to AD_2

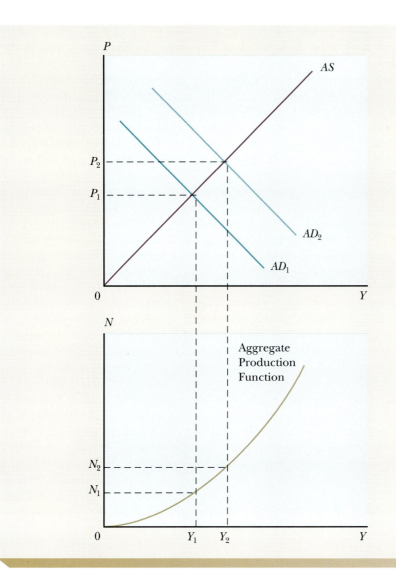

FIGURE 8
OUTPUT, EMPLOYMENT, AND THE PRICE LEVEL
Combining aggregate supply, aggregate demand, and a production function in two parallel graphs shows what is happening to output, employment, and the price level all at once. Shifts in AD or AS affect employment as well as the price level and real output.

will raise output to Y_2, the price level to P_2, and employment to N_2. In this case, statistics would show an increase in both output and employment but at the expense of a higher price level (inflation). You can experiment with other combinations to see how changes in aggregate supply and demand affect employment and unemployment.

THE CLASSICAL AND KEYNESIAN TRADITIONS AND AGGREGATE SUPPLY AND DEMAND

The aggregate supply and demand model is very useful for looking at macroeconomic policy. It is also helpful in understanding some of the disputes over what policy can and cannot do. The competing ideas of different groups of macroeconomists can be interpreted using this simple framework. These ideas will be developed over the next ten chapters, but we can use aggregate supply and demand to develop an overview of how different economists look at the macroeconomy.

Although there are many fine shades of opinion among economists that split them into distinct groups, there are two distinctive traditions, the classical and the Keynesian. Some of the differences between these two groups are disagreements over how aggregate demand shifts, or whether it can be permanently shifted by government policies. Most of the disagreement, however, centers around the slope of the aggregate supply curve and whether and how it can be shifted by public policies.

Although the formal model of aggregate supply and aggregate demand is relatively new, both concepts date from the nineteenth century. Macroeconomics did not get a great deal of attention before the Great Depression. Nineteenth-century economists were mainly interested in microeconomic questions of value, cost, and price; free trade and protectionism; and monopoly and competition. There were, however, two schools of thought that disagreed over the macroeconomic questions of how output, employment, and the price level are determined. These groups were the classical school and the business cycle theorists. Classical economists emphasized aggregate supply rather than aggregate demand, although neither of these terms were actually used until the mid-twentieth century. Business cycle theorists in the nineteenth century are regarded as the intellectual ancestors of the Keynesian tradition.

The conflict between these two schools of thought climaxed during the Great Depression. The outcome of that clash was the Keynesian revolution, which put a new emphasis on aggregate demand and how it could be shifted. As Keynesian policies produced mixed results, new groups of economists challenged Keynes's emphasis on aggregate demand. Although these groups had a wide range of views, most of them adhered to the classical tradition, emphasizing the long run over the short run and preferring minimum government intervention. Other economists refined and modified ideas in the Keynesian tradition but continued to be concerned about short-run problems and in favor of activist government involvement in the macroeconomy.

THE CLASSICAL TRADITION

Classical school
A group of economists in the eighteenth and nineteenth centuries who believed that the economy automatically tended toward the full-employment level of output.

Economists use the term **classical school** to refer to a diverse group of economists, from David Hume in the early eighteenth century to A. C. Pigou in the early twentieth century. What these economists had in common was a belief that the economy automatically tends toward a level of output associated with full employment. The classical tradition dates back to Adam Smith's *The Wealth of Nations* in 1776. Economists in the classical tradition are basically market-oriented, minimal government in their policy recommendations—an approach known as *laissez-faire*, or "let it be." They believe that most government economic policies are ineffective, ill-timed, or downright harmful, and that the market system works best in macroeconomics as well as microeconomics when left to itself.

This group tends to focus its attention on the long-run aggregate supply curve, which they believe is vertical or nearly so. If this is the case, shifting aggregate demand will accomplish little except to change the price level. The important role for policy, if policy has any role at all, is to try to shift aggregate supply

POLICY FOCUS: LIBERALS, CONSERVATIVES, AND POLITICAL ECONOMY

As you may have noticed, some economists support and others are opposed to government intervention to promote output growth and reduce unemployment. In general, those who favor a larger role for government in both macroeconomic and microeconomic policy are known as liberals. Those who wish to minimize the role of government and rely primarily on market processes are labeled conservatives. Ironically, the use of these terms has reversed in the last 100 years. Liberals in the eighteenth and nineteenth centuries took their name from the root of the word *liberal* (*liber*, in Latin, means free), and stood for freeing individuals from government oppression. The origin of the term conservative meant preserving the traditional way of doing things and, by implication, resistance to change.

The old name of economics was political economy, reflecting an emphasis on proposing and evaluating public policy. Although contemporary economists pride themselves on being positive rather than normative, in practice the line between positive and normative is not clearly drawn. Goals, values, and priorities tend to influence economists' thinking, research agenda, development of models, and interpretation of data.

Keynesians are generally liberal in political philosophy, although there are differences among Keynesians. They are concerned about unemployment, somewhat tolerant of inflation, and inclined to look for solutions through government. They are also more inclined to use the political system to change the income distribution toward greater equality; that is, favoring programs giving income or services to the poor. Contemporary representatives of the classical tradition, on the other hand, tend to be conservative. These economists have much more faith in market processes and much less trust in the ability of government to improve outcomes. They also tend to worry more about inflation than unemployment, and to resist using government to redistribute income from the rich to the poor.

The labels "liberal" and "conservative" conceal important and subtle differences within and between groups. It is possible to be conservative and to worry about unemployment—to favor policies that create incentives in the private sector to increase output and jobs. Such policies might include less regulation or tax breaks for job creation, while the liberal solution is more likely to involve increased government spending to accomplish the same goal. Nevertheless, these broad categories are helpful in sorting out who is likely to advocate what kind of policy and why.

---

to the right. Economists in the classical tradition expect that automatic market forces will always push real output (Y) toward the full-employment level, or Y^* in Figure 9. Any attempts to change Y by increasing aggregate demand will only drive up the price level. In Figure 9, an increase in aggregate demand from AD_1 to AD_2 drives the price level up from P_1 to P_2, leaving real output unchanged at Y^*.

Historical data makes it clear that there were extended periods of falling output and unemployment during the time of the classical school. It is difficult to reconcile these data with an aggregate supply curve that is vertical at the full-employment level of output. However, some of the classical economists' ideas reflected their ordering of macroeconomic goals. Inflation was of greater concern to them than unemployment. Also, reducing government intervention was important to classical economists for other reasons. They felt that government intervention in the economy, even on behalf of the worthy goal of full employment, was likely to interfere with the more highly valued microeconomic goals of efficiency and freedom.

Finally, classical economists were primarily concerned with the long run, a time period in which the economy is normally at or near the full-employment level of output. They felt that any deviations from full employment and capaci-

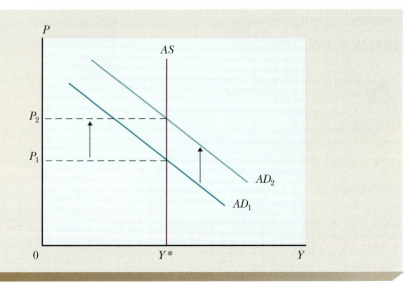

FIGURE 9

AGGREGATE SUPPPLY AND DEMAND: A CLASSICAL VIEW

If the aggregate supply curve (AS) is vertical, shifting AD from AD_1 to AD_2 drives the price level up from P_1 to P_2, leaving real output unchanged at Y^*. Policies aimed at increasing aggregate demand will not be effective.

ty output would be corrected if only people were flexible and willing to wait for natural market forces to operate.

Contemporary economists in the classical tradition believe that the aggregate supply curve is vertical in the long run. Some of them do concede that the AS curve can have a positive slope in the short run, although they expect it to be fairly steep. That is, in the short run, the economy could find itself at a level of output Y_e that is below the full-employment level of output, Y^*, as shown in Figure 10. At least some government policies, such as expanding the money supply, could shift the aggregate demand curve from AD_1 to AD_2. With a positively sloped aggregate supply curve, the price level in the short run would rise from P_1 to P_2. Real output, however, would also increase from Y_e to Y^*. These economists, like their classical predecessors, are also concerned about inflation and generally opposed to government intervention. In addition, some economists in the new classical tradition regard both monetary and fiscal policies as ineffective. These economists argue that individuals find it in their own self-interest to anticipate government actions and respond in ways that offset the impact of those actions. In this case, government policies will only be effective in shifting AD to the right if people are taken by surprise. These effects will last until the private actors in the economy realize what the government is doing. In the long run, private decisions will determine the level of output and employment.

THE KEYNESIAN TRADITION

Nineteenth-century economists who anticipated the work of Keynes were called **business cycle theorists**. Among them were Thomas Robert Malthus and Karl Marx. These economists were concerned about large or prolonged deviations from the full-employment level of output. They challenged the classical view that market forces will return the economy automatically to full employment because this view did not seem to fit the evidence. There were long and painful periods of declining output and widespread unemployment that had to be explained and, if possible, corrected. In addition, cyclical patterns in economic

Business cycle theorists A group of economists in the nineteenth and early twentieth centuries who tried to develop explanations for cyclical patterns in economic activity.

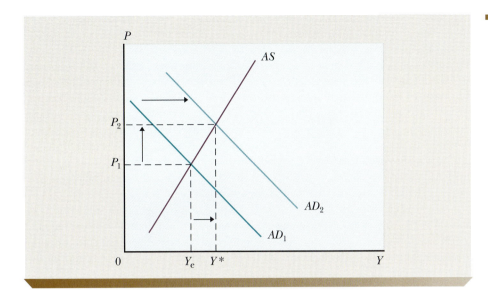

FIGURE 10
AGGREGATE SUPPLY AND DEMAND: A CONTEMPORARY CLASSICAL VIEW
If the economy is operating at a level of output Y_e below the full-employment level of output Y^*, and the AS curve has a slight upward slope in the short run, then it may be possible for government efforts to temporarily increase output and reduce unemployment by shifting AD from AD_1 to AD_2. Most of the effect will be an increase in the price level from P_1 to P_2, but real output does increase slightly from Y_e to Y^*.

activity were clearly observable, such as the business cycle illustrated in Chapter 5. Business cycle theorists argued that cyclical ups and downs in output, employment, and prices occurred with such regularity and frequency that they seemed to be obeying some natural law of the marketplace. Such real-world events were not consistent with an aggregate supply curve that was vertical. The business cycle theorists' picture of the economy is captured by Figure 11, which shows a fairly flat aggregate supply curve. In this model, a shift in aggregate demand from AD_1 to AD_2 drives the price level up from P_1 to P_2, but also results in an increase in real output from Y_1 to Y_2. When Keynes tried to explain one of the most severe downturns in economic activity in modern times—the Great Depression—he built on the work of the business cycle theorists.

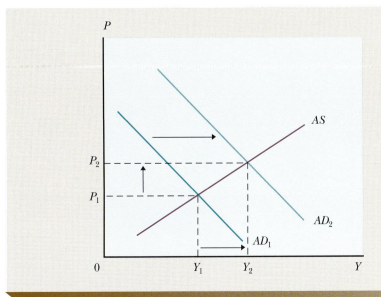

FIGURE 11
AGGREGATE SUPPLY AND DEMAND: THE VIEW OF THE BUSINESS CYCLE THEORISTS
The aggregate supply and demand model can be used to interpret the ideas of business cycle theorists. With a fairly flat AS curve, a shift of AD from AD_1 to AD_2 drives the price level up from P_1 to P_2. Real output also increases from Y_1 to Y_2.

Keynesians
Twentieth-century economists who share the views of Keynes that there could be persistent unemployment and low levels of production that could be corrected only with government intervention.

The greatest challenge to the classical school was the business cycle itself at its worst—the Great Depression. "Wait it out; the economy will correct itself," was not appealing advice in the depths of the Depression. John Maynard Keynes's often quoted answer to the classical economists was, "In the long run we are all dead." He insisted that even if the problems of falling output and unemployment could not last indefinitely, they could last long enough to cause great hardship, lost output, and human suffering. Even if the aggregate supply curve was vertical in the long run, its shape could be much flatter, or even horizontal, in the short run. If aggregate supply was relatively constant, shifts in aggregate demand could have significant effects on real output and employment. Economists whose macroeconomic ideas are based on the work of this famous British economist are called **Keynesians**.

Keynes started with the idea that the aggregate supply curve might be very flat, or even horizontal. In that case, the economy could be in equilibrium, with aggregate supply equal to aggregate demand, at a level of output Y_e that is substantially below the full-employment level of output, Y^*. This situation is pictured in Figure 12.

Keynes argued that private components of aggregate demand (consumption and investment) might not behave so as to restore full employment. He thought that the government should use its power to spend and tax in order to shift aggregate demand to the right, increasing output and employment. Otherwise, he argued, unemployment and low levels of output could persist for a fairly long time. This view challenged the classical position that equilibrium implied full employment. To the classical economists, the situation Keynes described was a disequilibrium that would set in motion automatic corrective forces.

Because the government policies he proposed can be inflationary (depending on the slope of the aggregate supply curve), many people believed that Keynes was more concerned about unemployment than inflation. That is not true. Some of his writings, such as *Treatise on Money* and *How to Pay for the War*, addressed the problem of inflation. In 1936, however, when *The General Theory of Employment, Interest, and Money* was published, unemployment was a very seri-

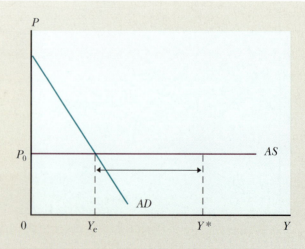

FIGURE 12
AGGREGATE SUPPLY AND DEMAND: A KEYNESIAN VIEW
This diagram shows an equilibrium situation in which aggregate supply is equal to aggregate demand. Note that the resulting level of output, Y_e, is substantially below the full employment level of output, Y^*.

ous concern, and the price level had been falling for several years. What really set Keynes apart from the classical school was not so much his concern for unemployment as his willingness to sacrifice *laissez-faire* principles. Unlike classical economists, Keynes thought that government officials could and should intervene to speed up the process of getting back to full employment. The alternative might be a communist or fascist government.

Again, it is not difficult to draw some inferences about Keynes's values and priorities from what he had to say. He was concerned primarily with unemployment, at least in 1936. He was not willing to let hardship, suffering, and lost output persist while the economy slowly corrected itself. Finally, Keynes was not committed to *laissez-faire* policies and a minimal role for government. He believed that the benefits of intervention in the business cycle would exceed the cost. This argument led to a political revolution with respect to the economic role of government. That change was as important as the intellectual revolution Keynes's ideas caused in the field of economics.

After declining in popularity in the 1970s and 1980s, Keynesian ideas are very much a part of the macroeconomic debate in the 1990s. In fact, every recession brings a resurgence in the popularity of Keynesian ideas, because he offered a specific prescription for appropriate government intervention during periods of falling output and rising unemployment. Over time, however, the emphasis has changed. Keynes focused on the role of aggregate demand. Modern economists in the Keynesian tradition take pains to explain why they

KEY IDEAS

HOW TO TELL CLASSICAL FROM KEYNESIAN

	CLASSICAL	KEYNESIAN
1. What determines the level of output?	Available resources which determine the position of aggregate supply	Aggregate demand
2. What determines the price level?	Aggregate demand	Price level does not change
3. What should the government do if there is substantial unemployment?	Wait for the economy to correct itself	Increase government purchases to shift aggregate demand
4. What is the most important macroeconomic problem?	Inflation	Unemployment
5. Should policy makers be more concerned about the short run or the long run?	The long run	The short run

think that aggregate supply is relatively flat. They are skeptical about the responsiveness of markets, the flexibility of wages and prices, and the speed of the adjustment process. Like Keynes, they see an important role for government in smoothing out ups and downs and, in particular, in reducing unemployment by shifting aggregate demand.

Consider again... *The tools developed in this chapter should enable you to answer the questions posed at the beginning. Rather than the level of output and the level of prices, which appear in the aggregate supply and aggregate demand diagram, these questions were expressed in terms of rates of output growth (or decline) and rates of inflation. However, we can still interpret these changes with aggregate supply and aggregate demand. If Russia suffered from dramatically falling output (a 13 percent decline in GDP) and 2,000 percent inflation, the only explanation in terms of aggregate supply and aggregate demand is that AS must have shifted to the left. Uncertainty about ownership of property and lack of incentives to work during the transition from communism to a market economy clearly discouraged production efforts.*

In the United Kingdom, falling output and declining inflation can be explained by a leftward shift in the aggregate demand curve. Mexico's outstanding performance suggests that its aggregate supply curve shifted to the right, while Japan's growth at steady inflation suggests that both AS and AD shifted to the right. How would you explain a small amount of growth and steady inflation in the United States? You can see that aggregate supply and demand is a simple and handy tool for thinking about growth rates and inflation around the world.

SUMMARY

1. The aggregate demand curve shows the amounts of total real output that consumers will buy at various price levels. This curve slopes down from left to right. A higher price level is associated with less demand for real output. This negative relationship is due to the effects of changes in price level on tax revenues, interest rates, exports and imports, and household assets.

2. The aggregate supply curve shows the amounts of total real output that the economy will produce at various price levels. An upward-sloping aggregate supply curve results from higher costs of production as firms compete for increasingly scarce supplies of resources. Alternatively, an upward-sloping aggregate supply curve reflects the incentive that higher profits associated with higher prices gives to producers to increase output. Alternatively, the aggregate supply curve could be horizontal or vertical. A composite aggregate supply curve has a horizontal region at low levels of output, followed by an upward-sloping range, and finally a vertical segment as output reaches capacity.

3. Aggregate demand will shift if there is a change in consumption, investment, government spending, or net exports at every price level or if there is a change in the money supply. Aggregate supply will shift if there is a change in resource availability, technology, special

factors such as war or earthquakes, or certain kinds of government policies.
4. The aggregate supply and demand curves, taken together, determine the price level and the level of real output. Adding an aggregate production function also indicates the level of employment.
5. The two competing traditions in macroeconomics are the classical tradition and the Keynesian tradition. Classical economists thought that the economy tended naturally toward full employment. The classical aggregate supply curve was vertical. The classical school advocated a *laissez-faire* approach. The business cycle theorists were concerned about the ups and downs of the market economy, which had long periods of unemployment and falling output. Business cycle theorists put more emphasis on the role of what contemporary economists call aggregate demand. Keynes challenged the classical school during the Great Depression. He suggested that the aggregate supply curve could be horizontal, or at least very flat, in the short run. Periods of unemployment could persist for a long time without automatic correction. He advocated government intervention in the form of fiscal policy to shift aggregate demand.

NEW TERMS

aggregate demand curve (AD)
aggregate supply curve (AS)
full-employment level of output
aggregate production function
classical school
business cycle theorists
Keynesians

QUESTIONS: REVIEW, APPLICATIONS, AND POLICY

REVIEW

1. Which variables rise during the upswing of the business cycle? Do any fall? Which ones rise and which ones fall during a downturn?
2. How does Keynes's famous remark "In the long run we are all dead" relate to the debate between classical economists and Keynesians?
3. Why does the aggregate demand curve slope down from left to right?
4. Explain how Figure 8 makes it possible to consider all three macroeconomic goals at once.
5. What kinds of changes can shift the aggregate supply curve to the right? What kinds of changes can shift the aggregate demand curve to the right?

APPLICATIONS

6. Practice using the aggregate supply and demand curves. What kind of shift would produce a rise in both P and Y? A fall in both? A rise in P and a fall in Y? A rise in Y and a fall in P?
7. How can you shift aggregate demand and/or aggregate supply so that real output increases while prices remain stable?
8. Identify whether each of these statements is most likely to be made by an economist in the classical tradition or the Keynesian tradition.
   a. "If the government does not do something about unemployment, it is not going to go away any time soon."
   b. "If the government tries to increase employment, all it will wind up doing will be driving up the price level."
   c. "Whatever the government does, smart people will figure it out in advance and take actions that will wind up offsetting the effect of government policy."
   d. "If we just encourage production by making it worthwhile for business to produce, we will get out of this recession. Demand is not the problem."
9. Assume an upward-sloping aggregate supply curve. How will an increase in foreign demand for exports affect aggregate supply and demand, output, prices, and employment? Use aggregate supply and demand curves and a production function in your answer.

10. How would your answer to Question 9 be different if the aggregate supply curve were vertical? What if it were horizontal?
11. Suppose the aggregate demand curve is a straight line. One point on it is represented by a price level of $3 and a quantity of 1,500 units, and another point by a price level of $5 and a quantity of 1,000 units. What quantity of real output is associated with a price level of $4? Can you locate other points on this line?

POLICY

12. Suppose the President proposes to increase federal spending in order to reduce unemployment. Show the effect of this change on the diagram of Figure 8. What would be the reaction to this policy by an economist of the classical tradition? A Keynesian?

SUGGESTIONS FOR FURTHER READING

Backhouse, Roger. *Economists and the Economy: The Evolution of Economic Ideas, 1600 to the Present Day.* Oxford and New York: Basil Blackwell, 1988. Development of economic ideas in a context of economic history; particularly strong in the development of ideas about inflation, employment, and business cycles.

Breit, William, and Roger L. Ransom. *The Academic Scribblers: Economists in Collision,* 2e. Hinsdale IL: Dryden Press, 1982. Biographical sketches and contributions of a number of famous economists of the past.

Warsh, David, *Economic Principals: Masters and Mavericks of Modern Economics.* New York: Free Press, 1993. An economic journalist offers thumbnail sketches of the personalities and contributions of some of the economists described in this and later chapters.

APPENDIX

A GLOSSARY OF SYMBOLS

Chapters 4 through 6 have introduced a number of symbols. More will appear in the next few chapters. Here, for handy reference, is a list of symbols you have already encountered.

GDP	gross domestic product
GNP	gross national product
NNP	net national product
NI	national income
PI	personal income
Y	real output
Y^*	full-employment level of real output
N	level of employment
C	consumption
I	gross private domestic investment
G	government purchases of goods and services
T	taxes
X	exports
M	imports
P	price level
AD	aggregate demand curve
AS	aggregate supply curve

Here are some additional symbols you'll encounter in the next few chapters.

C_0	that part of consumption that is independent of the level of income
b	marginal propensity to consume (also MPC)
M_s	money supply
M_d	demand for money
V	velocity of money
t	marginal tax rate
T_0	that part of taxes collected that is independent of the level of income
R	transfer payments
K	capital stock
k	the fraction of money income people want to hold in cash; equal to $1/V$
a	marginal propensity to invest

m marginal propensity to import
RR required bank reserves
ER excess bank reserves
rr reserve ratio
i_n nominal, or market, interest rate
i_r interest rate after correcting for inflation

PART 3

DETERMINING OUTPUT AND EMPLOYMENT: KEYNESIAN MACROECONOMICS AND FISCAL POLICY

The four chapters in this section of the book will introduce you to the theory and practice of fiscal policy. Fiscal policy consists of the use of the taxing and spending powers of government to affect the level of output, employment, and prices. Chapter 7 highlights the confrontation between economists in the classical tradition and those in the Keynesian tradition, a conflict that continues into the policy debates of the 1990s. Chapter 8 develops the Keynesian model as an explanation of why an economy might come to rest at an output level that is considerably below the full employment level and how that output level might change.

Chapter 9 develops the tools of fiscal policy, showing how government can use its taxing and spending powers to influence the levels of output, employment, and prices. This is a practical chapter that not only looks at the theory of fiscal policy but also the myriad practical problems and issues raised by using the government's budget as a macro policy tool. Chapter 10, finally, focuses on the most significant fiscal policy issue of the last decade: the budget deficit and the national debt. This chapter looks at the source of the deficit, what its effects are, and what options exist for addressing the deficit and the national debt.

CHAPTER 7

CLASSICAL MACROECONOMICS AND THE KEYNESIAN CHALLENGE

LEARNING OBJECTIVES

1. State Say's law and explain why this law led classical economists to conclude that periods of overproduction or high unemployment would be temporary and self-correcting.
2. Describe the roles of the self-regulating product, resource, and credit markets in ensuring that the economy will tend toward the full-employment level of output.
3. State the quantity theory of money and use it to explain how increases in the money supply lead to proportional increases in the price level.
4. Identify and explain the Keynesian criticisms of the classical model.
5. List the basic ideas behind the Keynesian alternative to the classical model.

Consider this... *In 1992, the two major party candidates for president spent a lot of time arguing what government should be doing about the recession and continued high employment, or indeed, if government should be doing anything at all. President Bush argued that the economy was on the path to recovery and should be left alone. Candidate Clinton called for the federal government to play a more active role in creating jobs and moving the economy toward full employment.*

The 1992 campaign was not the first time that "to act or not to act" was the center of a macroeconomic debate. Among economists, this often-repeated debate took place over and over between economists of the classical tradition and the Keynesian tradition. Among presidential candidates, the debate in 1992 was a repeat of 1932, when Franklin Roosevelt defeated Herbert Hoover during the depths of the Great Depression. Every recession or depression brings a demand to "do something!" from the public. Economists in the classical tradition find themselves on the defensive because "just wait and the economy will right itself" is not a very satisfactory answer to a demand for action.

THE CLASSICAL TRADITION AND SAY'S LAW

There are several reasons to begin the study of macroeconomic theory with the classical school. First, classical macroeconomics represents the best efforts of early economists to develop a theoretical system to explain the aggregate level of economic activity and to predict the effects of changes of various kinds on economic activity. Second, classical macroeconomics provided the background against which John Maynard Keynes, the great British economist, developed his new ideas. Finally, the ideas of the classical school have received renewed attention in the economic debates of the last two decades.

The aggregate supply and demand model, although not used until well into this century, is helpful in understanding the ideas of the classical school. Specifically, Figure 1 shows a vertical aggregate supply (*AS*) curve and a down-

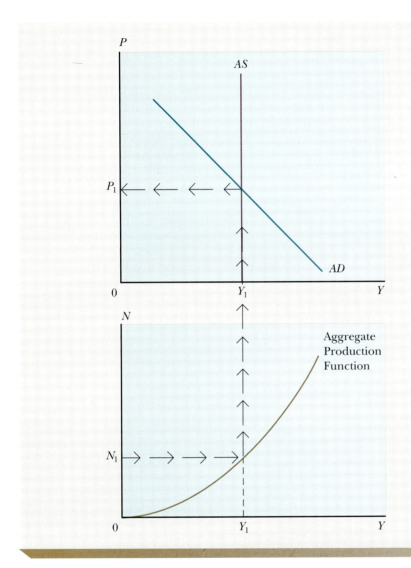

FIGURE 1
A CLASSICAL VIEW OF OUTPUT, EMPLOYMENT, AND PRICES
The level of employment (N_1), established in the labor market, determines the level of real output (Y_1), and thus the location of the aggregate supply curve (AS). Aggregate demand (AD) only affects the price level. It has no influence on output or employment.

ward-sloping aggregate demand (AD) curve in the upper panel, and the aggregate production function in the lower panel. Classical economists believed that the interaction of labor supply and labor demand determines the real wage and the level of employment. The level of employment (N) then determines how much total real output (Y) will be produced. In Figure 1, N_1 is determined in the labor market (not shown). N_1 is the level of employment capable of producing a real output of Y_1. Output does not vary with the price level because the level of real output is determined by the interaction of labor supply and labor demand. Thus, the AS curve is vertical at Y_1. The AD curve has no influence on real output. It only serves to determine the price level, P_1. Shifts in aggregate demand will change the price level only.

Classical macroeconomics does not describe a single approach but rather a rich and diverse group of ideas. Within that group, however, there are several recurring themes. The foundation of classical macroeconomics lay in three ideas: Say's law, the quantity theory of money, and self-regulating markets.

SAY'S LAW

A central idea of nineteenth-century classical macroeconomics was Say's law, which says that "supply creates its own demand." This law is named for Jean-Baptiste Say, a nineteenth-century French economist who pointed out that enough income is created in the process of production to buy everything that is produced. He agreed that individual goods can be overproduced if suppliers fail to read correctly the signals from the market. These suppliers will be penalized for producing the wrong things by incurring losses. Meanwhile, those who read the market signals correctly will be rewarded with profits. General overproduction for any length of time, however, is not possible.

The statement "supply creates its own demand" means that the production of goods and services generates an amount of income equal to the value of the products produced. If firms produce output with a value of $1,000, then they also create incomes for the resources equal to $1,000. Since the income created is the same as the value of output, the production process creates the amount of income necessary to purchase the goods and services produced. Say further argued that the only reason people offer their labor or other productive resources in the resource market is to earn income to use for consumption spending. Production generates income, which is all spent to purchase what was produced.

SAY'S LAW WITH SAVING AND INVESTMENT

This simple form of Say's law implies that a market economy will not be subject to severe or prolonged periods of overproduction. Say himself realized that this view was rather simplistic. What would happen if households let part of their income "leak" out of the circular flow in order to save, instead of spending it all on consumption? If people save a part of their incomes, spending can be less than the value of what is produced. This level of spending results in unsold goods. As producers pile up inventories, they cut back on production and lay off workers. Output falls and unemployment rises. Thus, Say's law is not correct if there is any saving.

The circular flow model offers a good way to visualize this objection to Say's law. In the circular flow diagram in Figure 2, firms produce $1,000 in products and generate $1,000 in incomes. Households, however, choose to save $200 of their income, so there is not enough spending to purchase all the output. Left with unsold products ($200 worth) on their hands, firms will decrease production and employment.

Say had an answer for that objection. Household saving would flow into banks and be lent to business firms that would inject it back into the income stream as investment. In an economy with small government and foreign sectors, saving (leakages) and investment (injections) would be equal. In the national income accounts, investment consists of some combination of business plants and equipment, residential construction, and changes in inventories. In our example, the $200 of unsold output, or a change in inventories, is the investment that matches the saving of households. Thus, actual, or realized, saving has to be equal to realized investment. In Figure 2, $200 in realized saving is matched by $200 in realized investment in the form of added inventory.

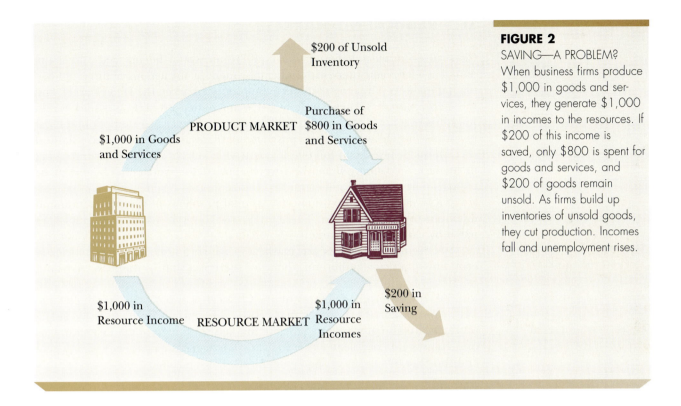

FIGURE 2

SAVING—A PROBLEM? When business firms produce $1,000 in goods and services, they generate $1,000 in incomes to the resources. If $200 of this income is saved, only $800 is spent for goods and services, and $200 of goods remain unsold. As firms build up inventories of unsold goods, they cut production. Incomes fall and unemployment rises.

ACCOUNTING BALANCE VERSUS EQUILIBRIUM

Defining unsold output as inventory investment merely balances the accounts. It does not result in an equilibrium level of output and employment. Even in Say's time, economists recognized the distinction between a balancing of accounts and the concept of macroeconomic equilibrium. **Macroeconomic equilibrium** is the level of output at which there is no tendency to change. The amount that buyers wish to buy is exactly equal to what is being produced. If firms build up unwanted inventories, their initial response may be to cut prices. However, after cutting prices to unload excess inventories, firms are likely to cut back production in the next period. Then the size of the flow of income and output will shrink.

As long as unplanned and unwanted inventory changes are occurring, the economy is in disequilibrium. Realized saving and realized investment are always equal. In equilibrium, however, planned saving and planned investment must also be equal. The saving desired by consumers must be exactly offset by desired business investment or other planned injections so that the size of the flow is neither shrinking nor growing. What ensures that saving will be equal to investment? The incentive to save is the interest that can be earned. Interest is the reward for saving. Interest is also the price of investment. The biggest obstacle to borrowing in order to invest is the interest that must be paid. Changes in the interest rate, like changes in any price, ensure that the supply of funds (saving) will be equal to the demand for borrowing (investment).

Macroeconomic equilibrium
The level of output at which there is no tendency to change. The amount that buyers wish to buy is exactly equal to what is being produced.

SELF-REGULATING MARKETS

Classical economists believed that equilibrium would be reached and maintained at a level consistent with full employment by the actions of three self-regulating markets. These markets were the product market, the labor market, and the credit market. If these three markets functioned properly, Say's law would hold in the sense that the sum of planned spending for consumption and for investment would be enough to purchase all that was being produced. Classical economists believed that full employment of resources was almost a sure thing in a market economy if markets were allowed to operate freely and given enough time. They did not claim that the economic system would *always* operate at a level of full employment. Occasional problems of overproduction and unemployment would occur. These problems, however, would be quickly eliminated by self-regulating markets.

Self-regulating markets are markets in which automatic forces move the economy to a new equilibrium whenever there is a shift in supply or demand. Equilibrium will be restored by adjustments in either prices or output, or both, without any government intervention. Classical economists believed that the same kind of corrective forces that restore equilibrium in markets for single products are also at work in aggregate markets. Although temporary shortages or surpluses are possible in either individual or aggregate markets, a lasting general shortage or surplus of aggregate output is not possible.

THE PRODUCT AND LABOR MARKETS

The two primary markets in the circular flow diagram are the product market (upper flow) and the resource market (lower flow). The labor market is the largest part of the resource market. Classical economists believed that flexible prices and wages in the product and labor markets were the first line of defense against unemployment and recession.

The labor market played a central role in the classical model. The supply and demand for labor together determined both the wage level and the amount of labor employed. If there were unemployed workers, the quantity supplied must be more than the quantity demanded. This was a clear indication that the market price (the wage) was too high for equilibrium.

If firms find that they have unsold output, they can dispose of it by cutting prices. The idea of cutting prices when there is a surplus of wheat, autos, or plane tickets is familiar. How do price and wage adjustments work when there is an excess of output in general? Figure 3 shows the usual *AD* curve and a classical (vertical) *AS* curve. In this diagram, there is an excess of aggregate supply over aggregate demand at price level P_1, resulting in unsold output. The unsold output is reflected in the fact that Y_1 exceeds Y_2 (distance *AB*). This diagram seems to suggest that if all firms cut prices, the price level will fall to P_2. Output will remain at the full-employment level, Y_1.

Suppose, however, that firms respond to the piling up of unwanted inventories by cutting output to Y_2 instead of cutting prices. Then employment will fall to N_2. There will be excess labor in the labor market. Competition among workers for jobs will drive down both real and nominal wages (wages with and without adjustments for changes in the price level). With lower wages, a wheat farmer or auto producer will find it possible to produce the same output at

---

Self-regulating markets Markets that quickly resolve problems of shortage and surplus through price changes, quantity adjustments, or a combination of the two.

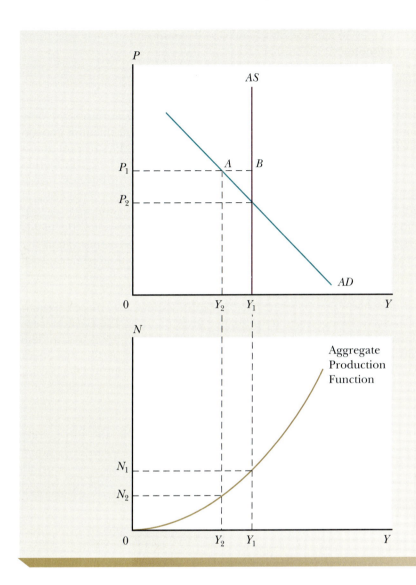

FIGURE 3

EXCESS AGGREGATE SUPPLY

Excess aggregate supply (AB in this diagram) will put downward pressure on the price level, either directly or through wages and the labor market. This process will continue until full employment output is restored.

lower cost. Firms will choose to hire more workers at the lower wages. Although sellers will have to cut prices to sell the extra output, they can afford to because of lower labor costs. The fall in output is temporary, because flexible wages and prices will always restore output to the full-employment level. In fact, some advisers to President Hoover recommended wage and price cuts in 1930 during the first stage of the Great Depression as a solution to growing unemployment, although Hoover himself did not advocate that policy.

You may have noticed a subtle flaw in this reasoning. If all firms cut prices to sell excess output, they will have to cut wages in order to avoid losses. When producers of toothpaste cut the price of their product and the wages of their workers, the wage cut has almost no impact on the market for their product. The firms' workers make up a very small part of the total toothpaste market. What is true of a single good, however, is not necessarily true of aggregate output. If all firms cut wages, the workers (who are also the customers) will have less purchasing power with which to buy the output. Therefore, sales will fall in real terms. (Remember to beware of the fallacy of composition when you think about macroeconomics!)

THE CREDIT MARKET

Flexible wages and prices in the labor and product markets were not the only weapon in the classical armory. The classical answer to the problem of general overproduction was to recognize that, in addition to a product market and a resource market, there is a third market—the credit market. The credit market is where the saving of households is used to provide funds for business investment. A self-regulating credit market was another important part of the classical explanation of why unemployment and unsold output would not persist. Through the credit market, household income that is saved flows into the hands of business firms, which in turn spend it on investment. The interest rate is the incentive to lend and the price of borrowing. Changes in the interest rate assure that planned saving and planned investment spending will be equal.

SUPPLY AND DEMAND FOR LOANABLE FUNDS. Figure 4 shows how the credit market works to make saving available to finance investment. In the classical view, the supply of credit (loanable funds) comes from people's decisions to save. The demand for credit reflects the desire by business firms to borrow for investment purposes. The supply curve has a positive slope. This slope indicates that saving is directly related to the interest rate. People save (give up some spending) only

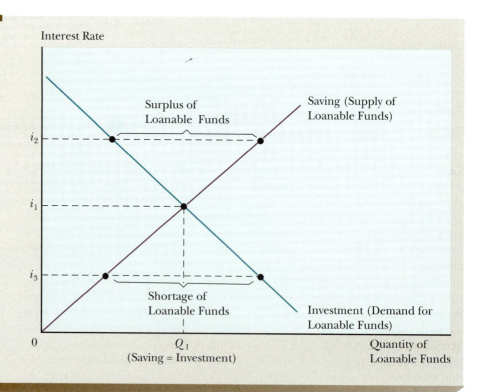

FIGURE 4

THE CLASSICAL VIEW OF THE CREDIT MARKET
In the classical view, changes in the interest rate ensure that the quantity of loanable funds supplied (saving) and the quantity demanded (investment) will be equal. Saving and investment are equal (at Q_1) when the interest rate is i_1. There would be a surplus of loanable funds at higher interest rates such as i_2 and a shortage at lower rates such as i_3.

if there is an incentive to do so. The interest rate is the incentive for saving. By saving now, individuals can earn interest and accumulate larger sums of money to spend in the future. When the interest rate rises, saving will increase because the same amount of current saving will provide more future consumption. Thus, a higher interest rate will call forth more saving, or a greater supply of loanable funds. Lower interest rates, on the other hand, will lead to less saving, or a smaller supply of loanable funds. There is less incentive to save instead of consume at lower interest rates.

The demand curve in Figure 4 shows the amount of loanable funds borrowers want at various interest rates. It has the familiar negative slope. The price of borrowing is the interest rate that firms pay to obtain credit. Investment spending increases when the interest rate declines. It decreases when the interest rate rises. Projects or purchases of investment goods that would be profitable at lower rates of interest may not look as attractive at higher interest rates. Thus, planned investment spending will be lower at higher rates of interest.

THE ROLE OF INTEREST RATES. According to classical economists, the interaction of borrowers and lenders in the credit market should establish an equilibrium interest rate. At this interest rate, the quantity of planned saving will be equal to planned investment spending. This interest rate, i_1 in Figure 4, is determined by the intersection of the saving and investment curves. At higher interest rates, such as i_2, the quantity of loanable funds supplied exceeds the quantity demanded. The surplus of saving over planned investment spending will push the interest rate downward toward i_1. At lower interest rates, such as i_3, the quantity of loanable funds demanded exceeds the quantity supplied. This shortage causes the interest rate to be bid up to i_1 as would-be borrowers compete for the limited amount of credit.

Either the supply curve or the demand curve can shift to create a disequilibrium. Either way, natural forces will restore equilibrium in a self-regulating market. Suppose a fear of recession or a high level of consumer debt causes people to suddenly become more thrifty. The amount of saving will increase at every possible interest rate. That is, the saving curve will shift to the right. The new equilibrium interest rate will be lower than i_1. An increase in saving puts downward pressure on the price of loanable funds. The lower interest rate leads to an increase in the amount of investment spending. Thus, changes in the interest rate ensure that any income not spent on consumption will be channeled into desired investment.

THE QUANTITY THEORY OF MONEY

The classical idea that the workings of markets will eliminate unemployment is one that is still widely held. Classical economists believed that individual prices were explained by the market forces of supply and demand. Even they would have agreed, however, that a more complex explanation is needed for the determination of the general price level.

The classical explanation of the price level is based on the equation of exchange and the quantity theory of money. The **quantity theory of money** states that changes in the price level are proportional to changes in the money supply. This theory, like many theories in macroeconomics, developed as a way to explain certain economic events.

Quantity theory of money The theory that changes in the price level will be proportional to changes in the money supply.

GLOBAL OUTLOOK: THE QUANTITY THEORY AND RUSSIAN INFLATION

In 1992, Russia experienced 1,200 percent inflation. That figure means that the average good was selling for 12 times as much at the end of 1992 as it did at the beginning. When inflation hits such high rates, it's called hyperinflation. Hyperinflation is relatively rare, occurring mostly after wars, revolutions, or other disasters. Russia in 1992 was in a post-revolution mode that was a prime situation for hyperinflation. But any kind of inflation can be interpreted in terms of the equation of exchange. If the price level is rising rapidly, something has to be happening to the other components of the equation of exchange (V, M_S, and Y).

Part of the explanation for Russian inflation is the same as for the Spanish inflation after the discovery of the New World, except that gold didn't play much of a role in Russia. Russia is, in fact, a net exporter of gold. But gold isn't money in the twentieth century as it was in the sixteenth. Like citizens of other countries, Russians get their rubles from the printing presses of their central bank. In July, Viktor Geraschenko replaced Georgy Matyukhin as the chairman of the Russian Central Bank, and immediately began to issue more currency in order to provide funds to failing state enterprises—$4.3 billion worth in the first two months alone.[a] Expansion of the money supply was an important part of the explanation of hyperinflation in Russia.

Hyperinflation, however, rarely occurs without some other element besides monetary expansion. In the case of Russia, the second important element was a decline in real output. As factories closed, exports fell, and uncertainty about the long-range future discouraged any enterprises except the most short-term ones. Russia's real output fell by at least 13 percent. In the equation of exchange, when an increasing money supply encounters falling real output, there is a double source of upward pressure on the price level. If, for example, the money supply expanded by 50 percent while output fell by 10 percent, the price level would rise by 67 percent.

Finally, there is velocity (V). Once inflation sets in, citizens spend their money quickly before it declines in value. Holding cash is foolish. Even with interest rates as high as 85 percent, lenders are unwilling to tie up their rubles for very long because the purchasing power they get back is so much less than what they lend.[b] Workers spend their wages on the way home for fear they will be worth less when they wake up the next morning. Although we have no data on velocity in Russia, we can infer that velocity is higher from the fact that the rate of inflation is greater than the equation of exchange would predict from just changes in the money supply and real output.

One of the reasons why people are afraid of inflation is that they expect it to develop into hyperinflation. That rarely happens. Hyperinflations have occured in Germany after World War I, Hungary after World War II, and several Latin American countries in the last two decades. But they only occur under fairly extreme circumstances. It takes a triple hit from all three of the other components of the equation of exchange in order for hyperinflation to take off.

a. "Project Capitalism," *Business Week* (September 28, 1992): 104–108.
b. Ibid.

THE EQUATION OF EXCHANGE

Equation of exchange
An identity based on the quantity theory of money that states that the money supply times the velocity of money is equal to the price level times the level of real output.

Classical economists believed that there was a very simple relationship between the money supply and the price level:

$$M_S \times V = P \times Y.$$

This relationship is called the **equation of exchange**. The idea behind this relationship is that the value of spending must be equal to the value of what was bought. M_S is the money supply, and V is the velocity of money, or the number of times the average dollar is spent per year. Thus, $M_S \times V$ equals total spending.

For example, if the money supply is $2,000 and $V = 3$, then total spending will be $6,000. If dollars turn over more often, then the same amount of spending could be supported by a smaller money supply. For example, with $V = 5$, the same $6,000 in spending could be sustained by a money supply of only $1,200. Classical economists generally believed that velocity (V) was quite stable. Therefore, any change in the money supply would result in a proportional change in spending ($P \times Y$).

The variables on the right-hand side of the equation of exchange should look familiar. P is the price level, and Y is real output, so $P \times Y$ is (nominal) national income. If $M_s \times V$ is what was spent, $P \times Y$ is what was bought, and the two have to be equal. In fact, the equation of exchange is an identity. It states that what was spent has to equal the market value of what was bought.

The equation of exchange implies that a fixed money supply (M_s) combined with a stable velocity (V) will yield a constant value of nominal GDP, which is equal to $P \times Y$. That is, a fixed amount of money available to spend and a fairly stable frequency of spending for each unit of currency each year will determine nominal GDP. However, for any given nominal GDP, various combinations of P and Y are possible. For example, the combinations of money supply and velocity that resulted in total spending of $6,000 could imply a price level of $1 and real output of 6,000 units, or a price level of $4 and real output of 1,500 units, or various other combinations. If Y is at the equilibrium levels determined by Say's law and self-regulating markets, however, this equation becomes an explanation of the link between the money supply and the price level.

INFLATION, DISCOVERY OF THE NEW WORLD, AND THE QUANTITY THEORY OF MONEY

The quantity theory of money, like many theories in macroeconomics, developed as a way to explain certain economic events. Among the early writers on this theory was the Scottish philosopher David Hume (1711–1776). Hume was interested in the very practical problem of explaining the inflation that followed the discovery of the New World.

Gold and silver were the main forms of money in Europe until the nineteenth century. The New World was discovered in the late fifteenth century and colonized by several European nations in the next two centuries. The Spaniards seized the gold and silver of the Aztecs in Mexico and the Incas in Peru and brought it to Europe. As this gold and silver flowed in, Spaniards went on a spending spree. They bid against other potential buyers and drove up the prices of goods and services all over Europe. Hume and other theorists sought to explain the link between the inflow of money and the rising price level.

Although these early theorists did not have the tools of demand and supply, their reasoning can be expressed in those terms. In the supply and demand diagram of Figure 5, an inflow of gold and silver has caused the demand for a specific good, woolen goods, to increase while the supply curve remains unchanged. In the seventeenth century, the newly wealthy Spanish demanded more woolens from both Spanish and British suppliers. Of course, the people who sold woolens then had extra money, so they too demanded more goods of all kinds. As demand for a broad range of products increased, aggregate demand shifted to the right, as shown in Figure 6.

The story didn't end there. People who supplied all kinds of goods found that the prices of their inputs were rising. Higher prices for inputs meant that

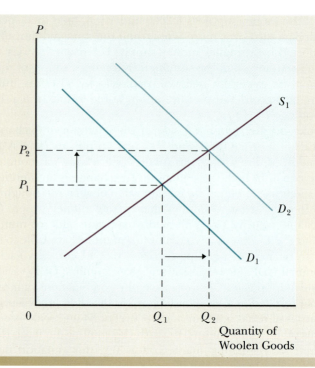

FIGURE 5

A SEVENTEENTH-CENTURY SHIFT IN THE DEMAND CURVE FOR WOOLENS
An inflow of gold and silver from the New World led Europeans to increase their demand for various goods, such as woolen goods. The rightward shift of the demand curve drove up the price of woolen goods from P_1 to P_2. Quantity increased along the supply curve from Q_1 to Q_2 in response to the higher price.

their costs were rising. For example, the new, higher prices for woolens attracted more people into the business of raising sheep. Competition for grazing land drove up the lease payments that the sheep herders had to pay, raising the price of raw wool. Eventually these increased production costs caused the individual supply curves for wool and other goods to shift to the left. Thus, aggregate supply shifted to the left, as shown in Figure 6. A leftward shift in aggregate supply means that producers will offer the same amount for sale at a higher price than

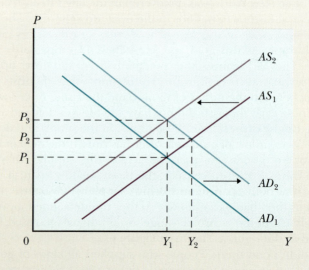

FIGURE 6

ADJUSTING TO AN INFLOW OF MONEY
The general increase in demand for goods drives up both prices and costs. The rise in costs shifts the aggregate supply curve to the left. Both P and Y increase, but equilibrium output ultimately returns to Y_1. When all prices have adjusted (the supply curve has shifted as well as the demand curve), there will have been no change in real output but an increase in the price level to P_3.

before because their costs have risen. (We are using an upward-sloping short-run aggregate supply curve here. As you will see shortly, however, the long-run aggregate supply curve will still be vertical. Classical economists tended to concentrate on the long run.)

As long as money was flowing into Spain and from there to the rest of Europe, prices were destined to go on rising. Aggregate demand kept shifting to the right and aggregate supply to the left. Since rising demand spilled over from Spain to other countries, the aggregate demand and supply curves in all of these countries continued to shift. Thus, the money inflow to Spain led to higher price levels throughout Europe.

CHANGES IN THE MONEY SUPPLY AND CHANGES IN THE PRICE LEVEL

When would such a rise in the price level come to an end? If the inflow of money never stopped, classical economists could see no end to rising prices. However, suppose the money inflow did end. After both aggregate demand and aggregate supply adjusted to changes in the price level, the equilibrium quantity of real output would be the same as before the inflow of money. The inflow of gold and silver to Europe in the seventeenth century did not increase any of the economy's productive resources or improve its technology. Thus, there was no reason why total output would change once the economy adjusted fully to the larger money supply.

With more money but no more real output, classical economists argued, the increase in the price level would be proportional to the increase in the money supply. A money supply that was twice as large would lead to a price level that was twice as high. A money supply that was four times as large would mean a price level that was four times as high. Land prices and wages would also rise in proportion to increases in the money supply.

Changes in the price level may not be exactly proportional to the rise in the money supply. While the money supply is rising, other things that affect the price level may also be changing. For example, the productivity of labor may rise. Like most economic predictions, those based on the quantity theory are subject to *ceteris paribus* conditions.

The insight that the long-run level of prices is directly related to the money stock was a notable insight of classical economics. To the question, "How much will the price level change when the money supply increases?," it gives a reasonably precise answer: The price level changes in proportion to the change in the money supply. However, the quantity theory could not predict how long it would take the price level to change. Furthermore, you should have noticed in Figure 5 that output of a particular good will initially increase when demand increases. (Figure 6 shows that this also holds for goods in general.) Thus, in the short run, changes in the money supply may affect real output as well as the price level. In the long run, real output returns to the level that existed before the added money came into the system.

How much will output increase at the start? How long will it take output to settle back to its old level? Classical economists could not find answers to these questions in the quantity theory. The quantity theory offered an explanation for long-run changes in the price level, but did little to explain the short-run effects of changes in the money supply on real output and employment.

THE QUANTITY THEORY AND MONEY DEMAND

The quantity theory of money underwent some changes in the late nineteenth century because of the work of British economist Alfred Marshall (1842–1924). One of Marshall's most important contributions was to reinterpret the equation of exchange ($M_s \times V = P \times Y$) as a theory of the demand for money. The **demand for money** is the amount of money that people want to hold in the form of currency or checking account balances. The demand for money is not that different from the demand for other goods and services. People demand money because it is useful in making market transactions. Holding money has a price, however. Choosing to hold money means giving up the things that it could buy or giving up the interest that could be earned if it were converted into other kinds of financial assets. Money is also unique in certain respects, especially in its almost total acceptance in transactions for all other goods and services. Thus, although the demand for money is similar to the demand for other goods and services, money plays a special role in a market economy.

Marshall argued that people normally want to hold part of their wealth in the form of money. He assumed that the amount of wealth that individuals choose to hold in the form of currency or checking account balances (as opposed to stocks, bonds, and other financial assets) is positively related to their incomes. The higher a person's income, the higher the average amount of money balances that person will want to hold to meet day-to-day transaction needs. For the economy as a whole, the total demand for money should be positively related to the aggregate level of income and output.

Marshall observed that the public had to hold whatever amount of money was being supplied. That is, actual M_d had to equal actual M_s. If the money supply is $1,000, then the public collectively has to hold (demand) $1,000. Based on this observation, Marshall rearranged the equation of exchange, obtaining

$$M_d = k \times P \times Y = k \times \text{GDP}.$$

Money supply has been replaced by money demand because in equilibrium the two should be equal. The velocity of money, V, has been replaced by k on the other side of the equation, because $k = 1/v$ by definition. Marshall explained k as the fraction of income people desire to hold in the form of cash balances. Like V, the size of k depends on such factors as how often people get paid and have to make payments and what other forms of assets are available. Marshall expected that k, like V, would be fairly stable over long periods of time. If one accepts the classical arguments that Say's law is valid and markets are self-regulating, then Y will be stable at the full-employment level. In that case, Marshall's revised equation of exchange becomes an explanation of what determines the price level.

Suppose there is more money supplied than the amount people want to hold. The money market will be in disequilibrium. That is, $M_s > M_d$. Finding that they have larger cash balances than they wish to hold, individuals will spend more, driving up the price level (P). The rise in the price level will increase the nominal value of output ($P \times Y$), which determines the amount of money people want to hold. The public will finally be satisfied to hold exactly the amount of money being supplied at the higher price level. Similar forces are set in

---

Demand for money
The amount of money that people want to hold in currency or checking accounts.

motion when the money supply is less than the amount people want to hold, or $M_s < M_d$. Reductions in spending as people try to rebuild their cash balances will drive down the price level until the money supply is once again equal to the money demand. Thus, a self-regulating market for money, working through the price level, should assure that the equilibrium condition, $M_d = M_s$, will be satisfied. In equilibrium, money supply and money demand must be equal. That is,

$$M_s = M_d = k \times P \times \bar{Y} = k \times \text{GDP}.$$

The bar over Y in this expression indicates that real output is constant at the full-employment level. The proportional relationship between the money supply and the price level is the same as before. This version of the equation offers an explanation of the price level in terms of money demand and the behavior of households.

A simple example will show how the behavior of households translates an increase in the money supply into an increase in the price level. Assume that the economy is at the full-employment level of output, with 500 units of output being produced ($\bar{Y} = 500$). Also, assume that the fraction of their income that people desire to hold as money is stable and equal to 25 percent of their annual income ($k = 0.25$). Finally, assume that the money supply is initially $1,000 ($M_{S1} = \$1,000$) and that the annual value of output ($P \times \bar{Y}$) is such that the public is satisfied to hold $1,000 in money ($M_d = M_s$). The initial price level (P_1) can be found by substituting these numbers in

(1) $M_{S1} = k \times P_1 \times \bar{Y}$

and solving for P_1, which gives the following:

$$P_1 = \frac{M_{S1}}{k \times \bar{Y}} = \frac{\$1,000}{(0.25)(500)} = \frac{\$1,000}{125} = \$8.$$

The equilibrium price level is $8. That is, the average price for a unit of output is $8. The annual value of output is $4,000 ($8 × 500).

What would happen if, as a result of an influx of gold into the economy, the money supply doubled? Substituting the new value of the money supply ($M_{S1} = \$2,000$) into equation (1) determines that equilibrium occurs at a new price level, P_2:

$$P_2 = \frac{M_{S1}}{k \times \bar{Y}} = \frac{\$2,000}{(0.25)(500)} = \frac{\$2,000}{125} = \$16.$$

According to these calculations, a doubling of the money supply (from $1,000 to $2,000) would cause a doubling of the equilibrium price level (from $8 to $16). Therefore, the annual value of nominal output would also double to $8,000 ($16 × 500), even though real output is unchanged.

How and why do prices rise in response to increases in the money supply? Given an initial equilibrium ($M_{D1} = M_{S1}$), an increase in the money supply puts people in the position of having larger money balances than they wish to hold. That is, $M_{S2} > M_{D1}$, relative to the value of total output $P_1 \times \overline{Y}$. Individuals who find themselves with more dollars than they wish to hold will increase their spending for consumer goods and services. Although individuals can decrease their money holdings through spending, the economy as a whole cannot. The excess dollars are passed from person to person. If one person puts his or her cash into financial assets such as stocks or bonds, these assets are purchased from another person who is now holding more cash. The increased spending, therefore, shifts aggregate demand to the right (see Figure 6). The resulting shortages of goods and services cause price increases. Eventually, wages and other costs also rise, shifting aggregate supply to the left. The level of output returns to the original level (Y_1 in Figure 6) and the price level rises further (to P_3). At the higher price level, the public is willing to hold the entire money supply. The money market is again in equilibrium (quantity supplied equals quantity demanded).

Classical economists favored a strictly *laissez-faire* approach to most markets. Many of them did agree, however, that regulation of the money supply would help control ups and downs in output and employment. If a temporary decline occurred in output, falling prices and wages could be avoided by expanding the money supply. An increase in the money supply could lead to at least a short-run improvement in the level of real output as well as (or instead of) a rise in the price level.

The quantity theory of money, Say's law, and the idea of self-regulating markets provided a complete classical model of macroeconomics. This model explained the level of employment, output, and prices. According to this model, recessions would be temporary and self-correcting. Thus, the role of the government should be limited to careful management of the money supply.

KEY IDEAS

ELEMENTS OF CLASSICAL MACROECONOMIC THEORY
- Employment is determined by the forces of supply and demand in the labor market.
- Output is determined by equilibrium in the labor market.
- The aggregate supply curve is vertical at the full-employment level of output.
- The price level is determined by the supply of and demand for money.
- An economy always tends toward the full-employment level of output because enough income is created during production to purchase the output (Say's law) and self-regulating markets correct temporary disequilibria.
  In the product market, falling prices ensure that all output is sold.
  In the labor market, adjustments in wages clear the labor market.
  In the credit market, changes in interest rates make saving equal to investment.

CHALLENGES TO THE CLASSICAL MODEL

In the nineteenth century, the main critics of the quantity theory of money were the business cycle theorists. They called attention to the reality of ups and downs in the economy. The classical model showed with perfect logic that prolonged unemployment was impossible. Actual unemployment seemed to defy the model by lasting for long periods of time. The classical model said that output would always be at, close to, or tending toward the full-employment level. Real-world experience showed that large and prolonged deviations from the full-employment level of output not only were possible, but occurred with alarming frequency.

BUSINESS CYCLE THEORISTS

Business cycle theorists, from Thomas Malthus in the nineteenth century to Wesley Mitchell and Joseph Schumpeter in the early twentieth century, observed regular cyclical patterns in economic activity. They sought to explain these patterns in terms of the nature of the market economy. Unlike the classical school, the business cycle theorists did not offer a complete model of how output, employment, and the price level are determined. Classical economists stressed natural forces that would tend to restore equilibrium. Business cycle theorists were more interested in what happened during the period when the economy was moving from one equilibrium to another. Schumpeter even described economic downturns as periods of "creative destruction." *Creative* meant that the old worn-out capital of declining industries was being replaced by new, improved capital in emerging industries.

The ideas of business cycle theorists such as Schumpeter are important because they offer a bridge from classical to Keynesian macroeconomics. Two important themes of this school of thought play an important role in Keynes's *General Theory*:

1. *The notion of underconsumption, or inadequate aggregate demand.* Malthus and other business cycle theorists argued that an unequal distribution of income affects the ability of consumers to purchase all that is produced. A small number of wealthy households consume a great deal less than their income and save a large amount. Workers earning very low wages spend most or all of their income. This amount is not enough, however, to purchase the rest of what is produced. If the saving of the wealthy few is not channeled into investment, then leakages from the circular flow will exceed injections. The size of the flow will decrease.

2. *The instability of investment.* If the government and foreign sectors are small and there is not enough consumption, then the burden of purchasing the rest of output falls on business firms. Firms must increase their demand for funds to invest. Both Schumpeter and Keynes, writing in the 1920s and 1930s, emphasized the fact that investment demand is extremely unstable. Investment depends on changes in technology, development of new industries, interest rates, final demand, and investor psychology. All of these variables are unpredictable and highly volatile. In addition, new plants and equipment last for a long time and continue to produce consumer goods during that time. Once an increase in consumption demand has been filled by investing in new plants and equipment, very little further investment is needed in order to have enough productive capacity for current consumption. As a result, demand for investment goods tends to depend on consumer demand. If consumer demand is growing, new investment is

needed to meet that demand. If consumer demand is stable, no new investment is needed. If consumer demand falls, the appropriate level of new investment may be negative as producers work off and wear out excess productive capacity.

Although business cycle theorists identified other influences, inadequate demand from both consumers and investors played the central role in explaining recessions. Business cycle theorists were concerned about aggregate demand, even though they didn't use that term. Both the government and the foreign sector played minor roles in nineteenth-century economics. Thus, the business cycle theorists focused on two major actors in the macroeconomic drama: consumers and investors. In doing so, they laid the groundwork for the Keynesian revolution.

POLICY FOCUS: KEYNES AND THE POLITICS OF THE KEYNESIAN REVOLUTION

John Maynard Keynes was born in Cambridge, England, the son of a well-known economist who taught at Cambridge University. The young Keynes grew up in an atmosphere of intense debates over the public policy issues of the day. Keynes divided his life between teaching at Cambridge and active involvement in government and business affairs. He worked for the British Treasury, where he rose rapidly during World War I. In fact, Keynes was a British delegate to the Versailles Peace Conference, which drafted and signed the peace treaty ending World War I in 1919. He was disillusioned by the negotiations at Versailles and the harsh conditions imposed on the losers, especially Germany.

In a very critical book, *The Economic Consequences of the Peace*, Keynes argued that the harsh economic conditions imposed on Germany would lead to more problems with that country in the future. This book ended Keynes's employment by the Treasury because he criticized British policy. He returned to Cambridge and turned to business, making a great deal of money with shrewd investments. He managed the investment funds of King's College at Cambridge, to the college's great benefit. Keynes wrote essays on policy topics and biographical essays on many people, including economists, as well as a treatise on the theory of probability.

Along with his other activities, Keynes did some revolutionary work in macroeconomics. During the 1920s, he wrote the two-volume *Treatise on Money*, which was published in 1930, after the beginning of the Great Depression. The *Treatise* was basically a quantity theory approach to macro problems in the spirit of Keynes's teacher, Alfred Marshall. By the time the *Treatise* was published, Keynes was unhappy with this approach and had begun what he called his "long struggle" to see macro questions from a different perspective. The new view Keynes was working toward was contained in *The General Theory of Employment, Interest, and Money*, published in 1936. This book presented an alternative macroeconomic model aimed at explaining how economies had fallen into the Great Depression and how they could get out of it.

Keynes's ideas were considered radical by many at the time. Keynes considered his proposals conservative. During a period when communism, fascism, and other antimarket philosophies were very popular, Keynes saw his economic policy as a way to rescue the market economy from its most serious weakness—persistent and recurring downturns in output and employment. Recessions and depressions offered fertile ground for socialist or communist proposals to shift to a more centrally planned economy. Keynes wanted to salvage the market economy by reducing its tendency to go into recessions.

After World War II, Keynesian ideas were more widely accepted. The Keynesian revolution was a huge political and economic success. The Great Depression had brought a great deal of suffering. Classical economic theory offered no immediate relief. Classical economists advised people to wait until prices fell, markets readjusted, and equilibrium was restored. In short, their policy was to do nothing until, in the long run, the economy returned to its full-employment equilibrium. Keynes offered a policy that could make things better in the short run. This option was much more appealing to both politicians and the unemployed. At the same time, Keynes offered frustrated economists a plausible explanation of the Great Depression. Today, most government officials still adhere to at least part of the Keynesian view. They believe it is better to do something about economic conditions than to wait for the economy to correct itself—especially if the correction may not take place until after the next election!

THE KEYNESIAN REVOLUTION

When Keynes attacked the ideas of the classical school in *The General Theory of Employment, Interest, and Money* (1936), he was attacking the mainstream of nineteenth-century economic thought. In doing so, he ignored some important work by other economists of that period such as Henry Simons and Irving Fisher, who were working in the classical tradition. The ideas that Keynes criticized were those that drove the macroeconomic policies of his time. His contributions changed the policy approach to recessions and depressions for decades to follow.

The Great Depression challenged the classical model with the reality of a long depression and high unemployment. In *General Theory*, Keynes attacked the classical model in two important ways. First, he identified some flaws in the model. Second, unlike the business cycle theorists, he offered a well-developed alternative model of the macroeconomy. This model was the basis for the **Keynesian revolution**, the change in macroeconomic theory and policy that occurred when Keynes's ideas displaced the classical explanation of how output and employment are determined. The Keynesian model begins with aggregate demand and works from there to employment, instead of the other way around.

KEYNES ON SAY'S LAW. Keynes was critical of Say's law. Classical economists argued that the existence of saving by households and investment by firms does not invalidate Say's law because changes in the interest rate will ensure that planned saving is equal to planned investment at the full-employment level of output. If planned saving is always exactly offset by planned investment, then all output will be sold to willing buyers for either consumption or investment. In that case, overproduction or lasting unemployment is not possible. Keynes argued that even though the interest rate does influence planned saving and planned investment, other important influences can keep the credit market from perfectly matching these two flows.

Keynes identified several reasons why individuals save besides the desire to earn interest: (1) to build reserves in case of unforeseen future needs, (2) to develop a nest egg for retirement, (3) to establish a financial base for an increased standard of living in the future, (4) to gain economic independence, (5) to build reserves for speculative purposes, (6) to leave an inheritance, and (7) to satisfy the urge to accumulate. These motives, he argued, generate considerable saving that is relatively independent of the interest rate.

Keynes also argued that the interest rate was only one influence on investment decisions. He argued that firms invest in new plants and equipment only if they expect to make a profit. Based on their expectations of the profit from a given investment project, businesses often borrow even when interest rates are high or refuse to borrow when they are low. According to Keynes, final demand

Keynesian revolution The change in macroeconomic theory and policy that occurred when Keynes's ideas displaced the classical theory of how output and employment are determined.

by consumers, the size and age of existing capital stock, and new technology all play more important roles than the interest rate in determining investment.

Since both saving and investment respond more strongly to other influences than the interest rate, Keynes argued, planned saving *could* exceed planned investment at the full-employment level of output. Thus, Say's law would be invalid. According to the classical model, if planned saving exceeds planned investment, the interest rate will fall. Keynes said that a fall in interest rates may have little effect on either saving or investment, but excess saving will lead to a decline in the level of output and income. Thus, if credit markets fail to work as the classical model describes, severe depression and unemployment can persist for long periods in a market economy.

KEYNES ON SELF-REGULATING MARKETS. According to classical theory, temporary overproduction and unemployment in individual markets would be eliminated as unemployed workers competed for jobs and drove down wages. To a firm, falling wages mean lower costs. The firm could profitably cut prices and increase sales. Falling wages and prices would eliminate overproduction and restore full employment.

Keynes argued that neither the product nor labor market would adjust quickly and automatically to eliminate unemployment and overproduction. He believed that labor unions and large corporations had enough market power to keep wages and prices from falling. Faced with rising unemployment, labor unions would fight to keep wages from declining in order to protect their members who were still working. Without declining wages, business firms would not be willing to cut their prices. Furthermore, when facing overproduction, large corporations are likely to choose to reduce production levels rather than prices. Price cutting risks cutthroat price competition. Keynes felt that in a mature, capitalistic economic system, it would be difficult to reduce either prices or wages. According to him, prices and wages are "sticky downward." Since prices and wages are not fully flexible, there will be no automatic adjustment process in product and labor markets to restore full-employment equilibrium.

Finally, Keynes pointed out that even if wages and prices could fall, the result would not necessarily be to restore output to the full-employment level. Falling prices mean that buyers can purchase more output, but falling wages mean that workers can buy less. In a macroeconomy, supply and demand are not entirely independent because they are parts of the same circular flow.

KEYNES ON THE QUANTITY THEORY OF MONEY. Keynes admitted that the quantity theory of money was useful in describing the long-run movement of the economy from one equilibrium to another. He saw the theory as much less useful in the short run. The quantity theory was based on the assumption that, in the equation of exchange, the velocity of money was stable. That is, V was constant. Data from the early 1930s, as well as other periods, showed that this assumption did not hold in the short run. (Some economists prior to Keynes, such as Henry Simon and Irving Fisher, did not share this simplistic view. They recognized the instability of velocity over the course of the business cycle, and recommended active changes in the money supply to offset changes in velocity and keep the price level and real output stable.)

Keynes pointed out that a theory that only explains what happens in the long run is not very useful. He reminded his readers that we live in the short run and "in the long run we are all dead." Keynes was more interested in developing a theoretical model to explain short-run economic activity and recommending policies to improve short-run economic conditions.

The velocity of money (and therefore k) was especially unstable during the Great Depression. Between 1929 and 1933, V fell sharply, and k increased. (Remember that $k = 1/v$.) A rise in the value of k meant that the amount of money people wanted to hold, relative to GDP, had increased. The quantity theory of money offered no explanation for the sudden increase in the demand for money implied by the sharp drop in V.

Building on Marshall's analysis of money demand, Keynes reasoned that the demand for money was strongly influenced by more than the level of GDP. In addition to demanding money for making transactions, as Marshall claimed, people also want to hold money as a safeguard against changes in interest rates on bonds and other financial assets. If interest rates are low, people will avoid buying bonds and hold more of their wealth in the form of money while waiting for interest rates to rise. When interest rates are low, the opportunity cost of holding money is also low. Thus, very little is sacrificed by holding money instead of bonds or other securities. In addition, people who buy bonds when interest rates are low run a risk of locking in those rates and being stuck with low-yield assets when the rates rise.

When market interest rates are high, people will prefer to hold more of their wealth in interest-earning securities and less in money because the opportunity cost of holding money is high. Much interest is lost by holding money, which earns little or no interest, instead of interest-earning assets. In addition, if interest rates are high compared to the immediate past, people will expect them to fall rather than to rise further. Buying securities when interest rates are high enables the holder to lock in those rates for the life of the assets.

Keynes called the motive for holding money as an asset the "speculative demand for money." Today many economists prefer the term **asset demand for money**, which is the demand for money to hold in order to protect oneself against losses due to changes in interest rates. The asset demand for money is negatively related to interest rates. The motive for holding money identified by Marshall is called the **transactions demand for money**—the demand for money in order to make purchases and carry out other day-to-day market transactions. Transactions demand is positively related to income. Keynes added a third source of demand for money, called the precautionary demand for money, which is cash for a "rainy day" or emergency fund. Since this demand is also related to the level of income, later economists combined it with transactions demand.

Keynes argued that the interest rate would strongly influence the demand for money. If the interest rate declined, the quantity of money demanded relative to GDP ($P \times Y$ in the equation of exchange) might increase, even if GDP were stable or declining. In the equation of exchange, this change in people's desire to hold money would appear as an increase in k or a decline in V. Thus, changes in V and k during the Great Depression could be explained by including the interest rate as an important influence on the demand for money.

Asset demand for money
Demand for money to hold in order to protect the value of one's assets against changes in interest rates. The asset demand for money is negatively related to the interest rate.

Transactions demand for money
Demand for money in order to make purchases and carry out other day-to-day market activities. The transactions demand for money is positively related to income.

KEY IDEAS

KEYNESIAN CRITICISMS OF THE CLASSICAL MODEL
- Say's law is not necessarily valid. Just because enough income is created does not mean it will be spent.
- Self-regulating markets do not necessarily guarantee full employment.
  In the credit market, saving and investment are influenced by much more than the rate of interest.
  In the labor market, unions and other influences can make it difficult to adjust wages downward. If wages do fall, that will also reduce demand.
  In the product market, large corporations may cut output rather than prices.
- Instead, in the Keynesian model:
  Employment is determined by output.
  Output is determined by the intersection of the aggregate supply and demand curves (by demand for final output).
  The aggregate supply curve can be horizontal.

THE KEYNESIAN ALTERNATIVE

Keynes criticized the quantity theory because it neglects the role of interest rates and fails to explain short-run changes in V and k. He argued that Say's law was not valid and that long periods of overproduction and unemployment *were* possible. Without Say's law and self-regulating markets, no automatic forces would bring the economy back to equilibrium during a recession. Without a stable velocity of money, even an increase in the money supply might not work. Having criticized the classical view of the way the macroeconomy worked, Keynes offered a different model. In his view, only government intervention could bring the economy out of a downturn as severe and prolonged as the Great Depression.

During the Great Depression, the U.S. economy experienced severe and lasting unemployment, along with falling prices and a sharp decline in real output. Table I shows some of the dramatic changes in spending, output, and unemployment between 1929 and 1939. Classical theory could not account for such conditions. In developing an alternative theory, Keynes and his followers focused on the question, "What determines the level of employment in a market economy?" They knew that if they could explain employment, the same model would explain unemployment.

BUILDING BLOCKS OF THE KEYNESIAN MODEL

In attempting to identify the cause of employment, Keynes reasoned as follows:

1. The level of employment is directly related to the level of production, or output (Y).
2. In a market economy, planned spending on the output of the business sector will determine the level of production. Firms adjust their levels of production to meet demand for their products. Put simply, "supply adjusts to demand." (In contrast, Say's law said "supply creates its own demand.")

TABLE 1 CONSUMPTION AND INVESTMENT EXPENDITURES DURING THE DEPRESSION (BILLIONS OF DOLLARS)

YEAR	CONSUMPTION EXPENDITURES	INVESTMENT EXPENDITURES	TOTAL GDP	UNEMPLOYMENT RATE
1929	$79.0	$16.2	$103.9	3.2%
1930	71.0	10.3	90.4	8.7%
1931	61.3	5.5	75.8	15.9%
1932	49.3	.9	58.0	23.6%
1933	46.4	1.4	55.6	24.9%
1934	51.9	2.9	65.1	21.7%
1935	56.3	6.3	72.2	20.1%
1936	62.6	8.4	82.5	16.9%
1937	67.3	11.7	90.4	14.3%
1938	64.6	6.7	84.7	19.0%
1939	67.6	9.3	90.5	17.2%
1940	71.9	13.2	100.4	14.6%
1941	81.9	18.1	125.5	9.9%

Source: Council of Economic Advisers, *Economic Report of the President* (Washington DC: U.S. Government Printing Office, various years).

3. Since employment depends on production and production responds to spending, the level of employment in a market economy depends on the level of planned spending in the economy.

Note how Keynes reversed the sequence of events from the classical model. In the classical model, the labor market determined employment, and employment determined the level of output. Therefore, the position of the aggregate supply curve is vertical. Recall from Chapter 6 that the aggregate supply curve can be very flat, even horizontal, if many resources are unemployed (the economy is operating inside its production possibilities curve). The Keynesian model of the Depression economy has ample unemployed resources and a horizontal aggregate supply curve. If aggregate supply is constant (horizontal), then aggregate demand determines the level of output. In turn, the level of output determines the level of employment. Aggregate demand, which determined only the price level in the classical model, has the starring role in Keynes's model. It determines the level of real output. In Figure 7, the price level is given at P_1, and aggregate demand determines the level of output, Y_1. Output, in turn, determines the level of employment, N_1.

KEYNES AND POLICY SOLUTIONS TO UNEMPLOYMENT

Consider how this model might apply to the situation in the 1930s. Unemployment was high because planned spending was too low to generate the level of output (Y^* in Figure 7) that would result in full employment (N^*). Thus, too little spending was identified as the cause of unemployment. To reduce unemployment, planned spending had to increase. In the language of aggregate supply and aggregate demand (a model developed after Keynes), aggregate demand had to shift to the right.

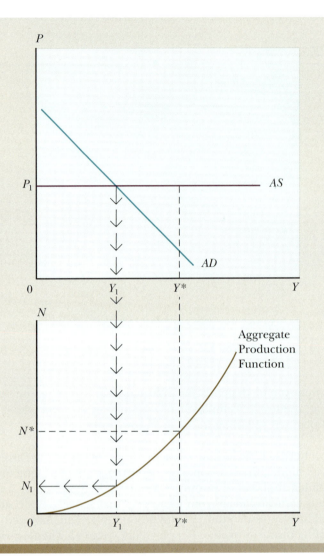

FIGURE 7
A KEYNESIAN VIEW OF AGGREGATE SUPPLY AND AGGREGATE DEMAND
When there are unemployed resources, the aggregate supply curve is horizontal. Aggregate demand determines the level of real output (Y_1). The price level (P_1) is not affected by changes in demand. The level of real output (Y_1) determines the number of workers needed to produce it (N_1) through the production function in the lower graph.

How could aggregate demand be shifted to ensure a level of output that would result in higher employment and lower unemployment? Keynes's answer goes back to the circular flow model. He identified the groups of purchasers (households, firms, government, and the foreign sector) in the spending stream and considered what determines the amount of planned spending by each group. Keynes was very interested in determinants of planned consumption spending and planned investment spending. (If Keynes were still alive in the 1990s, he would have added net export spending.) He concluded that sometimes these two sources of spending would be inadequate to lead the economy to the full-employment level of output. At such times, the government, as a third major spending sector, should step in and boost planned spending (and aggregate demand) to the desired level.

What determines planned consumption and investment spending? According to Keynes, consumer spending (and saving) depends primarily on the level of income. Keynes believed that household spending habits are relatively stable and that households will spend a specific fraction of any increase in income. Investment demand, or planned investment spending, however, is much less stable. Investment depends on such factors as expectations, interest rates, and changes in final consumer demand. Expectations are especially prone to sharp swings. Thus, Keynes believed that investment spending would shift a great deal and would be the major source of changes in output and employment. Government can offset those changes by increasing its spending when investment demand is low and by cutting it back when investment demand is high.

This emphasis on determinants of planned spending highlights a basic difference between the Keynesian and classical models. In the classical model, investment and saving both depend on the interest rate, which ensures that leakages are equal to injections in the circular flow. In the Keynesian model, however, the interest rate plays a much smaller role. The interest rate has little influence on investment. Investment is instead dominated by changing expectations about final sales and consumer demand. The interest rate also has almost no effect on saving (which responds mainly to income). Since investment and saving are determined by different forces, there is no reason to expect that planned saving will be equal to planned investment. Therefore, there is no reason to expect the economy to move automatically toward an equilibrium at a full-employment level of output.

THE KEYNESIAN EXPLANATION OF THE GREAT DEPRESSION

The Great Depression resulted from many complex forces and cannot be explained by a single cause or event. Since the Depression, many economists have looked for explanations and key causes. These causes include the Smoot-Hawley Tariff of 1930, international monetary problems relating to the collapse of the gold standard, long-wave business cycles, and the Federal Reserve's mismanagement of the money supply. At the time, however, economists trained in the classical tradition could not explain what was happening. Keynes was able to offer a direct and plausible explanation of why planned spending by consumers and investment by firms fell so dramatically from 1929 to 1933, as was shown in Table 1. He also explained why the economy did not recover automatically, as classical macroeconomics predicted.

Keynes observed that, after several years of rising consumption and investment spending during the 1920s, the rate of expansion began to slow. With enough plants and equipment to meet current demand, firms reduced their levels of investment spending, leading to a decline in output and employment. When employment declined, household income declined. Consumption spending also declined. Falling consumption further discouraged investment spending because of firms' expectations of poor future sales. Investment spending fell further, causing more declines in employment, income, and consumption spending. The spiral continued, and output and sales plummeted.

Consumer spending fell because there were fewer jobs and less income. Business firms reduced output because they couldn't sell their products. They weren't spending for investment because they had little confidence in the future. In fact, firms were so pessimistic about the future that they weren't even replacing machinery as it wore out. To many people, it seemed as though the whole system had broken down.

This view of what was happening also suggested that the way to end the Great Depression was simple: The government should intervene in the market economy by using its power to tax and spend to increase aggregate demand. That is, the government should spend more or tax less, or both. Keynes's prescription was followed to a very limited extent until World War II. Table 1 shows that the process of recovery was very slow, especially in employment. Consumption, investment, and total GDP did not reach the pre-Depression levels of 1929 until twelve years later, in 1941. Unemployment remained high until the war was fully under way in 1942.

Preparations for war forced the U.S. government to increase its defense spending. Congress chose to raise taxes, but by less than the amount needed to pay for the war. By 1943, the unemployment rate in the United States had fallen to 1.9 percent. Keynesian economic policy of increasing spending more than taxes had finally ended the Great Depression, but not as Keynes expected. The massive increase in government spending in the 1940s was not an exercise in Keynesian macroeconomic policy. It occurred in order to pay for World War II.

Consider again...*The 1990–1991 recession had a somewhat happier ending than the one that began in 1930, although not for incumbent President George Bush, who lost the election. This recession was short and shallow; in fact, it was apparently already ended by the time of the 1992 election campaign, although the recovery that followed was weak and unemployment remained high. Compared to the experience of the Great Depression, however, the 1990–1991 recession didn't require massive doses of Keynesian policy response to bring it to an end. The classical "wait and see" prescription seemed to fit the most recent recession much better than it did seventy years earlier in the Great Depression.*

SUMMARY

1. The view of the classical school was that the economy always tends toward the full-employment level of output. The classical aggregate supply curve is vertical. Changes in aggregate demand affect only the price level. Deviations from the full-employment level of output are temporary and self-correcting because of Say's law, which states that enough income will be created in the process of production to purchase all that is produced.
2. Any temporary overproduction or unemployment will be corrected through price adjustments in the self-regulating product, resource, and credit markets. The interest rate ensures that planned saving is equal to planned investment.
3. The quantity theory of money explains how changes in the money supply are translated through household behavior into changes in the price level and/or real output. In the classical model, the velocity of money (V) and real output (Y) are constant. According to the equation of exchange, $M \times V = P \times Y$, changes in the money supply lead to proportional changes in the price level.
4. Keynes criticized the three central elements of classical theory: Say's law, the quantity theory of money, and self-regulating markets. He argued that factors other than interest rates determine saving and investment, that prices and wages can be sticky downward, and that the demand for money is unstable.
5. Keynes stressed the role of planned spending in determining the levels of output and employment. He argued for government intervention to deal with persistent recession and unemployment.

NEW TERMS

macroeconomic equilibrium
self-regulating markets
quantity theory of money
equation of exchange
demand for money
Keynesian revolution
asset demand for money
transactions demand for money

QUESTIONS: REVIEW, APPLICATIONS, AND POLICY

REVIEW

1. Why is the classical aggregate supply curve vertical? Why is the Keynesian aggregate supply curve horizontal?
2. What was revolutionary about Keynes's ideas?
3. According to classical economists, how do interest rates help to ensure that the economy will always return to the full-employment level of output?
4. What reason did Keynes give for the instability of money velocity?
5. Sometimes the Keynesian revolution is described as a switch from "supply creates its own demand" to "demand creates its own supply." Explain this statement.
6. Why, according to Keynes, do self-regulating markets not solve the problem of falling output?

APPLICATIONS

7. In the equation of exchange, suppose V is stable (constant) with a value of 4, and the money supply is $200 billion. What combinations of P and Y are possible? Identify about a dozen combinations, and plot them on a graph. Does your graph look like an aggregate demand curve? Why or why not?
8. Suppose the money supply in Question 7 increases to $300 billion. Identify some new possible combinations of P and Y. Plot the new combinations. Which way has the curve shifted?
9. Marshall's form of the equation of exchange is $M_d = k(P \times Y)$. Let $k = \frac{1}{4}$. Suppose money national income is $3,000. What must the money supply be in order to be equal to the money demand? Suppose the money supply increases to $1,000. What must the value of total output be? What are some possible divisions of that total between P and Y?
10. Keynes argued that k was not stable, especially in the short run. Suppose when you increase the money supply to $1,000 in Question 9, k rises from $\frac{1}{4}$ to $\frac{1}{3}$. That is, people decide to hold a larger fraction of their money income in cash balances. What happens to $P \times Y$ when M_s increases in this case? What does that imply for monetary policy?
11. The variables V and k are not calculated directly but are inferred from the value of M_s and $P \times Y$ (nominal GDP). Given the following data on money supply and GDP (both in billions of dollars), compute V and k for the United States for the years shown.

YEAR	MONEY SUPPLY	GDP
1959	$141	$488
1960	143	507
1961	147	525
1962	149	565
1963	155	597
1964	162	638
1965	170	691
1966	174	756
1967	185	800
1968	199	873
1969	206	944
1970	217	993

You can repeat this exercise for other periods with data from the *Economic Report of the President*. What do you conclude about the stability of k and V during this period?

12. Using the data from Table 1 in this chapter, compute the ratio of consumption to GDP and the ratio of investment to GDP for each year. Present the data as a graph. What conclusions can you draw about which form of spending is more stable?
13. Indicate whether each of the following statements about the Great Depression would be likely to be made by a business cycle theorist, a classical economist, or a Keynesian.
   a. "Left alone, the economy would have corrected itself."
   b. "Unequal distribution of income meant that the rich bought too little and the poor could not buy the rest, leaving a glut of unsold goods."
   c. "Instability of investment means that the government has to step in to stabilize demand."

14. If you expect interest rates to rise, will you hold money in cash or buy bonds? Why? What if you expect interest rates to fall?
15. Suppose there are 100 million workers in the economy, and full employment is defined as 96 percent of them being employed. Also suppose that, given current technology, each $10 billion in output employs one million workers. What is the full-employment level of output? If actual output is $850 billion, what would you expect the unemployment rate to be?

POLICY

16. Suppose an economy has suffered two years of falling output and rising unemployment. How would this be explained by an economist in the classical tradition? a Keynesian? What would each recommend doing?
17. Suppose that in the last six months real output has fallen by 3 percent, with a sharp rise in unemployment. What would a classical economist recommend as policy? Why? What would a Keynesian recommend?

SUGGESTIONS FOR FURTHER READING

Clarke, Peter. *The Keynesian Revolution in the Making, 1924–1936.* Oxford UK: Oxford University Press, 1988. Examines the British economic conditions in the 1920s and 1930s as a major influence on the development of Keynes's ideas.

Garraty, John A. "The Big Picture of the Great Depression," *American Heritage* (August/September 1986): 90–97. A good account of one of the most significant economic events of the twentieth century.

Hollander, Samuel. *Classical Economics.* Oxford and New York: Basil Blackwell, 1987. Traces the development of the ideas of the classical school.

Lekachman, Robert. *The Age of Keynes.* New York: McGraw-Hill, 1975. The best-known account of the life, times, and contributions of the most famous economist of the twentieth century.

Terkel, Studs. *Hard Times: An Oral History of the Great Depression.* New York: Random House, 1970. A classic retelling of personal experiences of individuals and families during the Depression.

CHAPTER 8

THE KEYNESIAN MODEL

Consider this... *What caused the 1990–1991 recession? Were those causes different from the factors that led to the 1980–1982 recession, or earlier ones? Why was the 1990–1991 recession so short compared to earlier ones, and why was the recovery so slow and weak, when the economy seemed to bounce back with rapid growth and falling unemployment after the 1980–1982 recession? Could the government have done something in each case to minimize the recession or speed the recovery? These are the same kinds of questions that Keynes was trying to answer in 1936.*

LEARNING OBJECTIVES
1. Explain the relationship between consumption and investment spending as sources of demand, and between national income and demand, as a factor in determining the level of income and output.
2. Describe the central elements of the two-sector aggregate expenditure function, the consumption function and investment demand, and how this model determines the equilibrium level of income and output.
3. Expand the aggregate expenditure function to incorporate the government and foreign sectors and determine equilibrium in a four-sector model.
4. Use the multiplier to calculate the change in the equilibrium national income that results from a

In order to approach recessions and expansions in a systematic way, it is necessary to have a more complex model than just aggregate supply and aggregate demand. Classical economists had a more elaborate model, involving Say's Law, self-regulating markets, and the quantity theory of money. Unfortunately, that model was a long-run model. It didn't really offer much insight into the behavior of the economy in the periods between the peaks of the business cycle. It was those periods between the peaks, recessions and recovery, that caught Keynes's attention and have been a major conern of macroeconomists ever since.

Keynes did not agree with the classical view that the output level associated with full employment was the only possible equilibrium for the economy. He pointed out that the predictions of classical theory did not match the experience of the 1930s. In the Great Depression, the economy appeared to be at an equilibrium level of national income and output far below that required for the full employment of resources. Keynes did agree with the classical view that the economy would move automatically to an equilibrium level of national income and output. At that level, total planned spending and actual output would be equal. However, Keynes argued that it was quite possible for this equilibrium level to be a relatively low one, associated with a high level of unemployment. The Keynesian model explains how it is possible to reach an equilibrium level of income and output that is not the full-employment level.

given change in planned spending.
5. *Explain the relationship between the Keynesian aggregate expenditure function and the aggregate demand curve.*

THE ROLE OF DEMAND

Keynes argued that supply adjusts to demand. That is, businesses will adjust their level of output to meet the demand as long as there are idle resources to expand production. The key to determining the level of output, then, is the factors that determine the spending plans of households and firms. Keynes believed that expenditures, especially consumption expenditures, are strongly influenced by the level of income. All income (wages, salaries, rent, interest, and profit) is received by the owners of resources. There is a continuous flow from income to demand to output and back to income. Planned spending by households and firms determines the level of national income and output, but planned spending itself is influenced by national income. The levels of planned spending and national income are jointly determined.

THE KEYNESIAN VIEW OF AGGREGATE SUPPLY

In the language of aggregate supply and demand, the Keynesian model has a downward-sloping aggregate demand (*AD*) curve and a horizontal aggregate supply (*AS*) curve. Remember, the AS curve can be horizontal when there are a lot of unemployed resources, which make it possible to expand output without driving up wages and prices. With a horizontal *AS* curve, the position of the *AD* curve determines the equilibrium level of national income and output. Unlike equilibrium in the classical model, the equilibrium level of real output (Y) in this model does not necessarily ensure full employment.

CONSUMPTION, INVESTMENT, AND AGGREGATE EXPENDITURES

Keynes, however, did not use the terms *aggregate supply* and *aggregate demand*, at least not in the way they are used today. When Keynes wrote about demand, he was looking at factors that underlie the aggregate demand curve that we have been using. In his model, the central focus was the relationship between consumption expenditures and disposable income. This relationship is known as the consumption function.

Investment demand also plays an important role in the Keynesian model. In a two-sector economy, with just households and business firms, the sum of the two sources of planned spending—consumption and investment—is the aggregate expenditure (*AE*) function. This function determines the equilibrium level of national income and output. The addition of government purchases and export and import spending provides a complete Keynesian model of the macroeconomy.

SIMPLIFYING ASSUMPTIONS

In this chapter and the next, we make a few simplifying assumptions. First, we initially ignore the distinctions among GDP, GNP, NNP, NI, and PI. We treat these output measures as though they were all equivalent to Y, or real income and output. The only important distinction we will need to make later on is between income before taxes and after-tax, or disposable, income (Y_d). Second, we assume that the price level is fixed. When the price level does not change, consumption, investment, output, and income have the same values whether they are expressed in current market terms or in real (price-adjusted) terms. For periods of high unemployment when there is little upward pressure on prices, a fixed price level is a convenient and plausible assumption. (This second assumption will be relaxed toward the end of this chapter.)

Third, we initially ignore government and the foreign sector to concentrate on a simple two-sector economy with just households and business firms. Once we have built a working model of this simple economy, we can relax each assumption and bring the model closer to the real world.

THE AGGREGATE EXPENDITURE FUNCTION

The Keynesian model uses a measure of planned spending that is different from aggregate demand. **Aggregate expenditure (*AE*)** is defined as total planned spending by all sectors for an economy's total output. Planned expenditures are distinguished from actual expenditures, because sometimes households or firms will find that actual spending does not equal what was planned.

In the circular flow, there are four sectors in the economy: households, business firms, government, and a foreign sector. In the upper half of the circular flow, the business sector sells output to each of the four sectors, including business firms that are making investment purchases. Aggregate expenditure for a four-sector economy is the sum of the purchases of all sectors:

$$AE = C + I + G + (X - M).$$

In a complete model, the components of *AE* are *C* (planned consumption spending), *I* (planned investment spending), *G* (government purchases of goods and services), and *X* and *M* (exports and imports). This breakdown is not the only way of sorting planned spending into components. It is useful, however, because the factors that influence planned spending are different for each of the sectors of the economy. These four purchasers of output correspond to the four categories of purchasers used in national income accounting and to the four sectors in the circular flow model. With no government and no foreign trade, however, planned expenditures have just two components: consumption and investment. It is useful to start with these two to develop a model of income determination and then add the others to make the model more realistic.

Aggregate expenditure (*AE*)
Total planned spending for an economy's total output.

THE CONSUMPTION FUNCTION

Since the largest component of spending is consumption, Keynes began building his model by examining the behavior of consumption. He argued that the amount consumers choose to spend depends mainly on their disposable income. Keynes called this relationship the consumption function and made it a key part of his theory.

The **consumption function** is any equation, table, or graph that shows the relationship between the income of consumers (disposable income) and the amount they plan, or desire, to spend on currently produced final output.

Consumption function
Any equation, table, or graph that shows the relationship between income received by consumers and the amount they plan to spend on currently produced final output.

Consumption spending depends on the level of disposable income, not national income. The distinction between these two income concepts is not important in a simple economy with no government and thus no taxes. However, it will be important later on to relate consumption to disposable income, so we present the consumption function here in the same form in which it will appear when government is included in the model.

The equation for the consumption function is

$$C = C_0 + bY_d$$

where C is consumption expenditures and Y_d is disposable income. This expression says that consumption is positively related to income. That is, consumption rises when income rises and falls when income falls. The expression also indicates that there is a component of consumption (C_0) that is not related to the level of income. In the simple Keynesian model, any variable that is not dependent on income is said to be autonomous, or determined by other variables not included in the model. On a graph, the consumption function is a positively sloped straight line that crosses the vertical axis at C_0. The slope of this line is b.

As an example, assume that the consumption function for a simple economy is expressed as

$$(1) \quad C = C_0 + bY_d = \$200 + 0.8Y_d,$$

with all values in billions of dollars. Table 1 shows some specific values for this consumption function. The first column lists different levels of national income ($Y = Y_d$). The values for planned consumption spending (C) are then obtained by substituting the values of Y_d into equation (1). That is, the table answers this question: "If disposable income is equal to Y_d, then how much will households spend out of that income on consumption?" For example, if

$Y_d = \$1,200$ billion, then
$C = \$200$ billion $+ 0.8(\$1,200$ billion$) = \$1,160$ billion.

Subtracting consumption from income in each row gives the values for planned saving (S) in the fifth column of Table 1. Remember, saving is that part of income that is not spent. Note that saving is negative at very low levels of income. Households will draw on their past savings in order to maintain some minimum level of consumption.

THE MARGINAL PROPENSITIES TO CONSUME AND TO SAVE. The values in Table 1 show a consistent relationship among income, consumption, and saving. In the table, every time income increases by $200, consumption increases by $160 and saving by $40. Keynes believed that consumers were creatures of habit. When disposable income changed, he expected consumer spending to change by a constant fraction of the change in income. This behavior is important in deter-

TABLE 1 PLANNED CONSUMPTION EXPENDITURES (C) AND PLANNED SAVING (S) AT VARIOUS LEVELS OF NATIONAL INCOME (Y) (BILLIONS OF DOLLARS)

(1) NATIONAL INCOME (DISPOSABLE INCOME) $Y=Y_d$	(2) CHANGE IN DISPOSABLE INCOME ΔY_d	(3) PLANNED CONSUMPTION SPENDING C	(4) CHANGE IN CONSUMPTION SPENDING ΔC	(5) PLANNED SAVING S	(6) CHANGE IN SAVING ΔS
$ 0	$ —	$ 200	$ —	$ -200	$ —
200	200	360	160	-160	40
400	200	520	160	-120	40
600	200	680	160	-80	40
800	200	840	160	-40	40
1,000	200	1,000	160	0	40
1,200	200	1,160	160	40	40
1,400	200	1,320	160	80	40
1,600	200	1,480	160	120	40
1,800	200	1,640	160	160	40

mining the level of output because consumption spending is such a large share of total spending.

Keynes called this ratio of the change in consumption to the change in income the **marginal propensity to consume (MPC)**. It corresponds to b in the equation for the consumption function. The marginal propensity to consume (MPC) is the ratio of the change in consumption spending (ΔC) to the change in disposable income (ΔY_d):

$$\text{MPC} = \frac{\Delta C}{\Delta Y}.$$

Once you have calculated the MPC, it's very easy to compute its twin, the **marginal propensity to save (MPS)**, which describes how saving responds to income changes. The marginal propensity to save (MPS) is the ratio of the change in saving (ΔS) to the change in disposable income (ΔY_d):

$$\text{MPS} = \frac{\Delta S}{\Delta Y}.$$

Values of MPC and MPS are not shown in Table 1 but can be calculated easily from the values given there. For instance, when Y_d increases from $1,000 bil-

Marginal propensity to consume (MPC)
The fraction of any change in income that is consumed; the MPC is greater than zero and less than one.

Marginal propensity to save (MPS)
The fraction of any change in income that is saved; the MPS is greater than zero and less than one, and MPC + MPS = 1.

lion to $1,200 billion, C increases from $1,000 billion to $1,160 billion and S increases from $0 to $40 billion. Thus, for $\Delta Y_d = \$200$ billion, $\Delta C = \$160$ billion and $\Delta S = \$40$ billion. The values of MPC and MPS are

$$MPC = \frac{\Delta C}{\Delta Y} = \frac{\$160 \text{ billion}}{\$200 \text{ billion}} = \frac{4}{5} = 0.8, \text{ and}$$

$$MPS = \frac{\Delta S}{\Delta Y} = \frac{\$40 \text{ billion}}{\$200 \text{ billion}} = \frac{1}{5} = 0.2.$$

If you calculate MPC and MPS from other values in Table 1, you will get the same values each time. Table 1 was created using Keynes's assumption that the marginal propensity to consume is constant.

In this example, MPC is $\frac{4}{5}$ and MPS is $\frac{1}{5}$ of the change in income, and their sum equals 1. In an economy with no taxes, MPC and MPS will always add up to 1 because all consumer income that is not spent on final goods and services must be saved. (If MPC and MPS are computed as fractions of changes in disposable, or after-tax, income, then they will sum to 1 even if taxes are included in the model.) When income rises by $500 billion, the additional consumption spending is the marginal propensity to consume times $500 billion. If MPC is 0.8, consumption spending rises by $400 billion. The amount *not* spent on consumption (that is, the amount saved) is (1 − MPC) times $500 billion, or $100 billion. Thus, when income rises by $500 billion, the change in saving is equal to the marginal propensity to save times $500 billion. Since all the added income must be either spent or saved, we can conclude that

MPS = 1 − MPC, or MPC + MPS = 1.

If MPC is 0.9, then MPS must be 0.1. If MPC is 0.6, then MPS must be 0.4.

Figure 1 is a graphic presentation of the numbers in Table 1 and the corresponding consumption function,

$C = \$200 + 0.8Y_d$,

and the savings function,

$S = Y_d - C = Y_d - \$200 - 0.8Y_d = -\$200 + 0.2Y_d$.

The marginal propensity to consume is equal to b, the slope of the consumption function. Recall that the slope of a line is the ratio of the change in the variable on the vertical axis to the change in the variable on the horizontal axis, moving from left to right along the horizontal axis. In Figure 1, the slope is the ratio of the change in C to the change in Y. In symbols, $b = \Delta C/\Delta Y =$ MPC. Similarly, the slope of the saving function is $\Delta S/\Delta Y =$ MPS. When consumers receive more income, a much larger share of it normally goes to consumption than to saving. Thus, the slope of the consumption function is much steeper than the slope of the saving function in Figure 1.

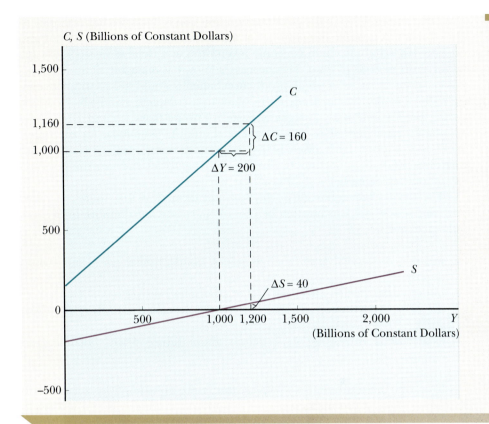

FIGURE 1
PLANNED CONSUMPTION AND PLANNED SAVING SCHEDULES
The consumption function shows the relationship between planned consumption and national income, and the saving function shows the relationship between planned saving and national income. The slope of the consumption function is the MPC; the slope of the saving function is the MPS.

Keynes believed that the marginal propensity to consume would be relatively constant, at least over a modest range of values of income and output. That is, he expected that a rise in disposable income from $1,000 billion to $1,200 billion would lead to the same increase in consumption as a rise in disposable income from $1,200 billion to $1,400 billion. Since Keynes wrote *General Theory*, economists have studied the behavior of consumption more closely. When consumption functions are estimated from annual data for total consumption and national income for the United States, they appear to be fairly stable, with a nearly constant marginal propensity to consume. When the consumption function is estimated from year-to-year, data for the United States show a value of C_0 that is close to zero and a slope (MPC) between 0.8 and 0.9.

THE CONSTANT TERM IN THE CONSUMPTION FUNCTION. It is easy to understand why consumption would rise as income rises. But where does that constant term, C_0, come from in the equation for the consumption function? If we insert a value of zero for Y_d into the consumption function, $C = C_0 + bY_d$, this equation seems to say that there is a positive level of consumption, C_0, even when no output is currently being produced and no income is being earned. For Table 1, C_0 had a value of $200 billion. This value indicated that consumers would buy $200 billion worth of goods and services even if there were no production taking place and no income coming into households.

Dissaving
Consuming by drawing on accumulated stocks (inventories) or financial assets.

The constant term in the consumption function reflects two important facts. One is that it is possible to consume for a short while even with no current production. An economy could consume inventories and deplete its stock of capital for short periods of time. This process is known as **dissaving**. If an economy was in a crisis situation in which production halted, it could still continue to consume for a while. No economy ever comes to a complete standstill. However, during the revolutionary changes in Eastern Europe from 1989 to 1991, some economies came very close to a complete shutdown (Romania, for example). What does happen fairly often is that economies temporarily consume more than they produce in wartime by drawing on inventories and wearing out capital without replacing it.

The second fact reflected in the constant term C_0 is that there are many other influences on consumption besides income. The most important of these influences are

1. wealth (consumers' assets such as stocks, bonds, houses, cars, and savings deposits),
2. interest rates (which affect the cost of consumer borrowing),
3. the price level (discussed in Chapter 6 in connection with the *AD* curve), and
4. expectations (including expectations about future prices, income, and employment).

If one of these influences changes, the entire consumption function will shift up or down. Consumers will want to purchase more goods and services at every income level. This shift in the consumption function will also be reflected as a change in the value of C_0. For example, if consumers acquired more wealth and assets over time and thus felt they did not need to save as much out of any level of income, they would increase their consumption at every possible value of Y_d. The value of C_0 might increase from $200 billion to $250 billion, and the entire consumption function would shift upward.

KEY IDEAS

BASIC FEATURES OF THE KEYNESIAN CONSUMPTION FUNCTION
- Consumption (*C*) depends on the level of disposable income (Y_d).
- Part of consumption is independent of the level of income. This constant term (C_0) changes in response to changes in such other influences as wealth, interest rates, the price level, and expectations.
- The rest of consumption (bY_d) is positively related to income. The marginal propensity to consume (MPC = *b*) is the fraction of an additional dollar of income that will be spent on consumption: $0 < b < 1$.

INVESTMENT EXPENDITURES

Classical economists believed that the most important determinant of planned investment spending was the interest rate. Keynes thought that profit expectations were a much more important influence on investment. Other influences on investment are the interest rate, the size and age of the existing stock of capital, changes in corporate taxes, and changes in technology. Some of these influences are subject to drastic and sudden changes.

Investment has three components: fixed investment in business plants and equipment, residential construction, and inventories. All three of these components are responsive to changes in both expectations and interest rates, but to different degrees. Buildings and equipment have a long useful lifetime. Thus, there may be a large existing stock to be used up before there will be much replacement. The same is true of residential construction. Also, housing demand is very sensitive to changes in construction costs and patterns of population growth. If a larger proportion of the population is twenty to forty years old, there is higher demand for new housing as new families are formed.

Because inventories are very sensitive to actual and expected final sales, they tend to fluctuate more in the short run than other types of investment. Unplanned changes in inventories, in fact, play a very important role in moving an economy toward equilibrium. Sudden increases or decreases in inventories signal producers that they need to change their level of output.

In general, all three types of investment fluctuate much more than consumption. Because inventories are more likely than other types of investment spending to exceed or fall short of desired levels, we assume that other investment spending plans as well as consumption plans are realized, and any gap between planned and actual spending will consist of unplanned changes in inventories. This is not always the case, however. Prior to the fall of communism, actual consumption in Eastern European countries frequently fell short of planned consumption because stores' shelves were empty and there were no inventories on which to draw.

Keynes assumed that the investment demand curve would shift so frequently that the relationship between planned investment spending and the level of income or the rate of interest would not be as important as the causes of its shifts. For this reason, we will follow Keynes for now and treat investment demand as an exogenous variable, or a given value that is determined outside the model.

EQUILIBRIUM IN A TWO-SECTOR MODEL

The consumption function along with investment demand are all the basic elements of a two-sector model that determines the equilibrium value of national income and output (Y). Along with the consumption function from Table 1, there is now an investment demand of $160 billion, which is autonomous (independent of the level of income). The sum of consumption and investment demand is shown in Table 2. Figure 2 graphs the data in Table 2 and adds a reference line with a slope of 45°. This reference line locates those points where the value measured on the horizontal axis (total output or income) is equal to the value on the vertical axis (aggregate planned expenditure, or $C + I$). Where the AE (or $C + I$) curve crosses the 45° line, aggregate expenditure is equal to total output. This value of output is the equilibrium level. In Figure 2, equilibrium occurs at $Y_e = \$1,800 = C + I$.

An output level of $1,800 is equilibrium because unplanned changes in inventory would occur at any other other level. These changes direct business firms to adjust production levels in order to make output equal to aggregate planned expenditure.

TABLE 2 THE AGGREGATE EXPENDITURE (AE) SCHEDULE (BILLIONS OF DOLLARS)

(1) NATIONAL INCOME Y	(2) CONSUMPTION C	(3) BUSINESS INVESTMENT I	(4) AGGREGATE EXPENDITURE AE = C + I
$ 0	$ 200	$160	$ 360
200	360	160	520
400	520	160	680
600	680	160	840
800	840	160	1,000
$1,000	$1,000	$160	$1,160
1,200	1,160	160	1,320
1,400	1,320	160	1,480
1,600	1,480	160	1,640
1,800	1,640	160	1,800
2,000	1,800	160	1,960
2,200	1,960	160	2,120
2,400	2,120	160	2,280
2,600	2,280	160	2,440

Table 3 shows the important role played by unplanned inventory changes, using a few of the values from Table 2. For example, if Y were equal to $1,400 billion, aggregate planned expenditure (AE) would be $1,480 billion. Planned spending for output would exceed current production by $80 billion. As firms tried to fill orders, their inventories would begin to decline. Firms would respond to unplanned declines in inventories by increasing their levels of output. The expansion in output to rebuild inventories would increase the level of output to the equilibrium level of $1,800 billion.

On the other hand, if Y were equal to $2,200 billion, AE would be only $2,120 billion. In this case, current production would exceed aggregate planned expenditure by $80 billion, resulting in an unplanned buildup of inventories. Firms would reduce output in order to bring inventories back to the desired levels. The level of output would fall steadily until the equilibrium level of $1,800 billion was reached.

ADJUSTMENTS THROUGH INVENTORIES AND LAYOFFS

Firms maintain inventories because they do not want to risk losing sales to competitors by not having a desired item in stock. What did you do the last time you tried to purchase an item in a store and that item was sold out? You went to a competitor. Not only did the first store lose a sale, they may also have lost a customer for future sales.

Most firms choose a desired level of inventory that is related in some way to expected sales. For instance, a firm may plan to maintain an inventory of goods equal to twice the amount usually sold in a month. Inventories act as a safety cushion or buffer between production and sales. When the actual level of inven-

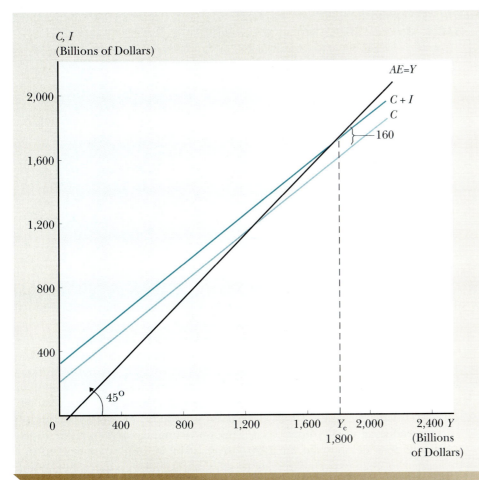

FIGURE 2
THE AGGREGATE EXPENDITURE LINE AND EQUILIBRIUM OUTPUT
Adding investment to the consumption function gives aggregate expenditures ($AE = C + I$) at every possible level of output. The 45° reference line shows the points where total expenditures (measured on the vertical axis) equal total output (measured on the horizontal axis). The total expenditure ($C + I$) line crosses the 45° line at the equilibrium level of output (Y_e).

tory is different from the level desired by the firm, unplanned inventory changes have occurred. Such changes are a signal that the amount being produced is not equal to the amount that purchasers want to buy.

When sales are greater than current production, firms find that they do not have enough inventory to fill all their customers' orders. When production is greater than sales, firms find that they are piling up unwanted inventory. Business firms, therefore, find that it is in their self-interest to respond to unplanned changes in inventories by expanding or contracting their output levels.

Two important changes in the last decade have modified the role of inventories in the Keynesian model. The first is "just in time production" and "quick response" management strategies. Both of these strategies attempt to minimize inventory of not only final goods but also raw materials, parts, and semifinished goods while still trying to respond quickly to consumer demand. These new methods have been made possible by such technological innovations as computerized inventory management and overnight delivery services. While inventories are smaller, however, changes in inventories are still an important adjustment factor between expected and actual sales, and between planned and realized spending.

TABLE 3 UNINTENDED INVENTORY CHANGES AND THE EQUILIBRIUM LEVEL OF NATIONAL INCOME (BILLIONS OF DOLLARS)

(1) NATIONAL INCOME Y	(2) AGGREGATE EXPENDITURE AE	(3) UNINTENDED INVENTORY CHANGES (Y - AE)	(4) BUSINESS RESPONSE	(5) EFFECT ON NATIONAL INCOME
$1,400	$1,480	$-80	Increase Output	Increase
1,600	1,640	-40	Increase Output	Increase
1,800	1,800	0	Maintain Output	No Change
2,000	1,960	+40	Decrease Output	Decrease
2,200	2,120	+80	Decrease Output	Decrease

The second important change is the shift from manufacturing to services as the major source of new jobs and output. Service firms do not maintain much inventory of goods. Instead, they maintain an inventory of workers. For example, a hairdressing salon maintains a staff of hairdressers so that customers can be served when they come in. If sales are below expectations, the unplanned inventory adjustment applies not to extra goods on the shelves, but to workers with nothing to do. Initially, the firm may use those workers to catch up on other tasks, like cleaning, or use the slack time to encourage workers to upgrade their skills. Eventually, however, firms will respond to reduced demand by laying off workers, reducing worker hours, or relying on temporary workers to fill in the periods of peak demand. In the 1990s, there is still an output adjustment to a difference between expected and actual sales, but it shows up more quickly and more directly in employment as an output in an economy where services account for a larger share of output.

LEAKAGES AND INJECTIONS IN A TWO-SECTOR MODEL

The aggregate expenditure approach is the most common method for explaining what determines the level of output and income. However, there is another approach that will give the same result, the leakages and injections approach, which derives from the circular flow. Equilibrium national income occurs at the level at which planned leakages from the circular flow (saving in this two-sector model) equal planned injections (or planned investment, excluding unplanned inventory changes). Think of the level of income as the water in a bathtub, injections as the water flowing in from the faucet, and leakages as water going down the drain. If leakages are greater than injections, the size of the flow (or the water level in the tub) will decline. If injections are greater than leakages, the size of the flow (or the amount of water in the tub) will increase. The level of income or the water level is stable only when planned leakages and planned injections are equal.

Table 2 shows that the level of income for which $C + I = Y$ is the same level of income at which leakages (planned saving, or S) are equal to injections (planned investment, or I). At the equilibrium level of income ($Y = \$1,800$), consumption is $1,640. Thus, the amount of planned saving (equal to income minus consumption) must be $160. Planned investment takes up the slack in demand not filled by consumption and is also equal to $160. In Table 2, leakages are equal to injections at $Y = \$1,800$.

Figure 3 plots the values of investment and saving from Table 2 to find the equilibrium level of national income (Y or Y_d). Equilibrium occurs where leakages in the form of planned saving (S) are equal to injections in the form of planned investment (I). The equilibrium level of output and income in Figure 3, as in Figure 2, is $1,800 billion.

ADDING GOVERNMENT AND THE FOREIGN SECTOR

A more complete Keynesian model includes all four sectors from the circular flow and the national income accounts. Adding government and the foreign sector makes the model more realistic.

GOVERNMENT SPENDING AND TAXES

Government adds another leakage from the circular flow in the form of taxes (T) and another injection of spending in the form of government expenditures (G). Government expenditures, like investment expenditures, are assumed to be determined by factors other than income. That is, they are autonomous. There may be some linkage to levels of income and output, but government

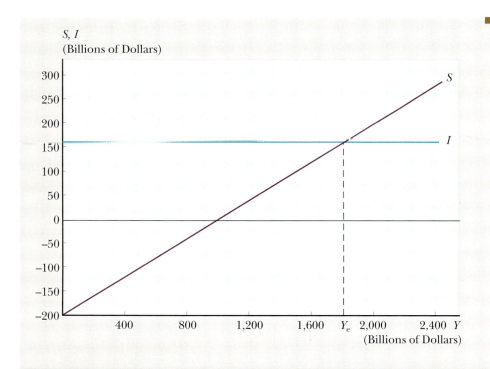

FIGURE 3
DETERMINING EQUILIBRIUM OUTPUT WITH LEAKAGES AND INJECTIONS
Another way to determine equilibrium national income is the leakages and injections method. In a two-sector economy, saving (S) is the only leakage, and investment (I) is the only injection. They are equal at $S = I = \$160$ billion, which occurs at $Y_e = \$1,800$ billion.

spending is determined through the political process. Thus, we treat its value (G) as a given constant, like C_0 in the consumption function. When we add government expenditures, aggregate planned expenditure becomes

$$AE = C + I + G.$$

Taken by itself, the addition of government expenditures to planned aggregate expenditure would increase the equilibrium level of income and output by a multiplier effect. However, there is a downside to this addition. Government purchases must be paid for, at least in part, by collecting taxes. For simplicity, we assume that taxes are independent of the level of income and that all taxes are paid by consumers. (In practice, tax collections are definitely linked to the level of income. We will explore this complication in Chapters 9 and 10.)

Taxes are a leakage from the circular flow. A part of income received by households is not available to spend on consumption because it has been claimed by the government in taxes. Taxes (T) do not enter into aggregate expenditures directly because they do not represent planned spending for output. Instead, taxes work indirectly by reducing disposable income and consumption, which depends on disposable income. A rise in taxes will reduce disposable income and consumption. A fall in taxes will increase disposable income and consumption. With taxes, the consumption function can be written

$$C = C_0 + b(Y - T),$$

where $Y - T$ is disposable income (Y_d).

THE FOREIGN SECTOR

The fourth actor in the complete circular flow model is the foreign sector. The purchases of the foreign sector are exports (X), which add to aggregate expenditure. The foreign sector also competes with domestic business firms when imported products are bought by households, firms, and government. Any spending by these groups for imports (M) reduces the level of planned spending for domestic output (AE). For the United States, both exports and imports are currently about 12 percent of total GDP. For convenience, we assume that both export and import spending are autonomous, like investment and government spending, so that net exports ($X - M$) can be treated as a given constant. In practice, imports are somewhat consistently related to domestic income and output, while exports depend on income and output in the rest of the world. With the foreign sector in the model, the complete aggregate expenditure function looks like this:

$$AE = C + I + G + (X - M).$$

Changes in exports or imports can shift the aggregate expenditure function and change the level of income and output. Suppose, for example, that a crop failure in another country leads to a large increase in exports of wheat, soybeans, and beef from the United States. If imports are unchanged, there will be an increase in net exports ($X - M$). This change shifts the AE curve upward and causes an increase in the equilibrium value of Y. A decrease in net exports would have the opposite effect. The AE curve would shift down, and the equilibrium value of Y would decrease.

Changes in net exports can result from changes in prices and incomes between countries, or from tariffs, quotas, or other trade restrictions. The exchange rate (the price of a nation's currency) is another major influence on exports and imports. Weather, natural disasters, and wars can also have an effect. For instance, if severe winter weather in Russia ruins the wheat crop, Russians may turn to foreign suppliers for grain, as they have in the past. If they purchase wheat in large quantities from the United States, U.S. net exports increase. In Figure 4, such an increase shifts the aggregate expenditure curve upward from AE_1 to AE_2, and equilibrium national income rises to Y_2.

The Smoot-Hawley Tariff of 1930, right at the beginning of the Great Depression, was designed to increase net exports by reducing imports rather than increasing exports. Fewer imports, policy makers reasoned, would create jobs in the production of import substitutes and thus increase aggregate demand. Another type of shift in net exports from the import side originates with a sudden rise in the price of an imported good. An example is the increase in the price of OPEC oil in the 1970s and again during the Gulf War in 1990. In both cases, expenditures for imported oil increased, and net exports fell. In Figure 4, a decrease in net exports causes the aggregate expenditure curve to shift downward from AE_1 to AE_0. As a result, the equilibrium level of national income falls to Y_0. A decline in the price of oil, such as the one in the mid–1980s, has the opposite effect, shifting the AE curve upward and increasing the equilibrium level of national income.

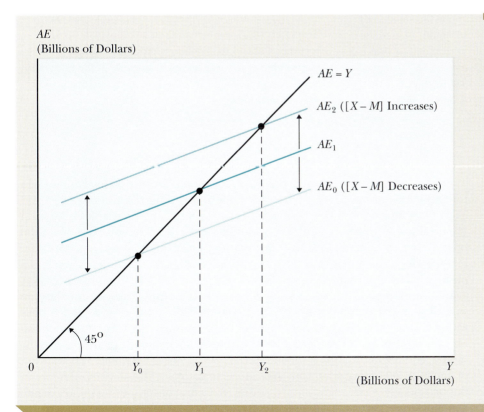

FIGURE 4
EQUILIBRIUM INCOME AND NET EXPORTS
With aggregate expenditures and national income initially at AE_1 and Y_1, an increase in wheat sales to Russia causes aggregate expenditures to shift up to AE_2. National income increases to Y_2. When OPEC raises the price of oil, aggregate expenditures shift downward to AE_0. National income decreases to Y_0.

POLICY FOCUS: CAN GOVERNMENT INFLUENCE EXPORTS?

The next chapter will explore the various tools that the government uses to influence the level of consumption, investment, and government spending. Actions by the government to influence all of these kinds of spending will also affect spending by the nation's citizens on imports. Exports, however, are autonomous. In fact, they are largely influenced by economic conditions abroad. Yet politicians put a lot of effort into finding ways to create jobs in export production. If economic conditions in other countries are the main influence on exports, is there anything the home government can do to stimulate exports?

Most governments have some microeconomic tools that they use to promote specific export products. Export subsidies for farm products and tourism promotion to increase exports of tourist services may increase sales of these products enough to have an impact on total export sales. Another tool is to promote exports using political leverage to remove barriers to our export sales in other countries. Negotiations with Japan to open their markets to U.S. products have been going on for decades with mixed success.

A third tool is general negotiations through GATT (General Agreement on Tariffs and Trade) to increase both exports and imports, usually with the hope that U.S. exports will increase more than imports. The Uruguay Round, which dragged on from 1986 to 1993, was the latest of seven rounds of trade negotiations designed to reduce trade barriers among nations. A fourth tool is the formation of regional trading blocs such as NAFTA (North American Free Trade Area), which increases both imports and exports but may increase exports more than imports. The problem with the last two policies is that it is hard to stimulate exports through trade negotiations without also stimulating imports. If the target is an increase in net exports, this approach has very unpredictable effects!

Exports are also sensitive to relative prices in a macro sense—the prices of U.S. products relative to foreign products, which depends on the U.S. price, the foreign price, and the exchange rate. At the macro level, anything that influences the U.S. price level and the exchange rate will impact on both exports and imports. So policies to restrain inflation or any policy aimed at reducing the price of the dollar would encourage exports while reducing imports. A cheap dollar is good for exporters (but not for those who want to buy imported goods).

Strong export sales played an important role in keeping the 1990–1991 recession short and shallow. As the U.S. economy recovered, unfortunately, Europe, Canada, and Japan were sliding into recessions that dampened their demand for U.S. exports and put a damper on the U.S. recovery. Policies to encourage exports, although of limited usefulness, can play an important role at the margin in cushioning recessions and strengthening expansions in the U.S. economy.

EQUILIBRIUM IN A FOUR-SECTOR MODEL

Table 4 and Figure 5 show how the level of national income is determined in a four-sector economy. Table 4 adds government spending (G) and taxes (T) and a foreign sector (X and M) to the numbers of Table 2. These variables have been given values: $G = \$200$ billion, $T = \$200$ billion, $X = \$200$ billion, and $M = \$100$ billion. The constant term in the consumption function, C_0, is still equal to $200 billion. The government has a balanced budget ($G = T$), and the nation has a positive balance of trade ($X > M$). As before, $I = \$160$ billion. Equilibrium occurs at an output level of $Y = AE = \$2,500$ billion, where output is exactly equal to the sum of planned purchases by the four sectors. The addition of a government with a balanced budget and net exports that are positive has increased the equilibrium level of income compared to the two-sector model. In the two-sector model, equilibrium national income was $1,800. Here it is $2,500. The addition of more purchasers for output has more than offset the negative effects of imports on aggregate expenditure and of taxes on consumption and aggregate expenditure.

TABLE 4 EQUILIBRIUM Y WITH GOVERNMENT AND A FOREIGN SECTOR (BILLIONS OF DOLLARS)

(1) NATIONAL INCOME Y	(2) PERSONAL INCOME TAXES T	(3) DISPOSABLE INCOME $Y_d = (Y - T)$	(4) CONSUMPTION C	(5) INVESTMENT I	(6) GOVERNMENT PURCHASES G	(7) NET EXPORTS $(X - M)$	(8) AGGREGATE PLANNED EXPENDITURE $AE = C + I + G + (X - M)$	
0	200	−200	40	160	200	100	$500	$AE > Y$
500	200	300	540	160	200	100	1,000	$AE > Y$
1,000	200	800	840	160	200	100	1,300	$AE > Y$
1,500	200	1,300	1,240	160	200	100	1,700	$AE > Y$
2,000	200	1,800	1,640	160	200	100	2,100	$AE > Y$
2,500	200	2,300	2,040	160	200	100	2,500	$AE = Y$
3,000	200	2,800	2,440	160	200	100	2,900	$AE < Y$
3,500	200	3,300	2,840	160	200	100	3,300	$AE < Y$
4,000	200	3,800	3,240	160	200	100	3,700	$AE < Y$
4,500	200	4,300	3,640	160	200	100	4,100	$AE < Y$
5,000	200	4,800	4,040	160	200	100	4,500	$AE < Y$

LEAKAGES AND INJECTIONS IN A FOUR-SECTOR MODEL

In the four-sector economy, when aggregate expenditure equals total output, planned leakages from the circular flow will be equal to planned injections. However, there are now three leakages (saving, taxes, and imports) and three

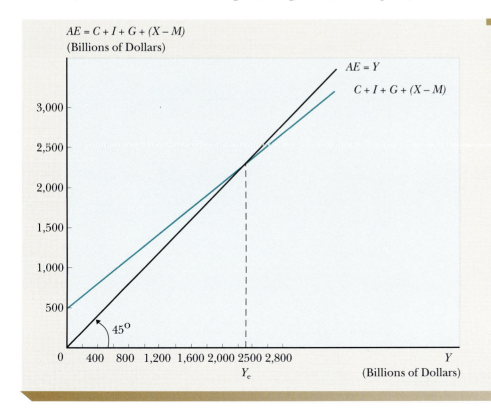

FIGURE 5

EQUILIBRIUM WITH THE GOVERNMENT AND FOREIGN SECTORS
Equilibrium occurs where aggregate expenditure, $C + I + G + (X - M) = AE$, is equal to current output, Y_e.

injections (investment, government purchases, and exports). At equilibrium income, the condition that leakages equals injections becomes

$$S + T + M = I + G + X.$$

Saving consists of income that is not consumed, paid in taxes, or spent on imports. At the equilibrium level of income ($Y = \$2,500$), consumption takes $2,040 billion of income and taxes $200 billion, leaving $260 billion for saving. Saving plus taxes plus imports gives total leakages of $560 billion. With investment of $160 billion, government purchases of $200 billion, and exports of $200 billion, injections also total $560 billion. Notice in Table 4 that leakages and injections are equal *only* at the equilibrium level of income. Below that level, injections exceed leakages, causing income to rise. Above that level, leakages exceed injections, causing income to fall. Figure 6 shows the equilibrium level of income of $2,500 billion determined by the leakages and injections method, the same value as that obtained by the aggregate expenditure method.

CHANGES IN AGGREGATE EXPENDITURE AND THE EXPENDITURE MULTIPLIER

Suppose that the economy is in equilibrium at $2,500 billion, when one of the components of aggregate expenditure changes. A change in C, I, G, or $(X - M)$ shifts the AE curve and changes the equilibrium level of income. The size of the

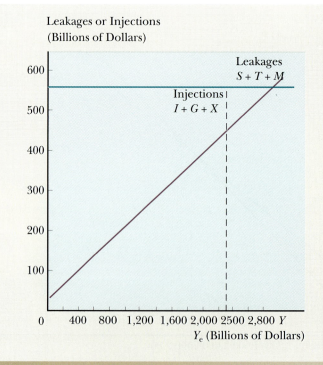

FIGURE 6

LEAKAGES AND INJECTIONS IN A FOUR-SECTOR ECONOMY

In a four-sector economy, equilibrium income occurs where the sum of the three leakages ($S + T + M$) is equal to the sum of the three injections ($I + G + X$) into the circular flow. The equilibrium income, $2,500 billion, is the same as in Figure 5.

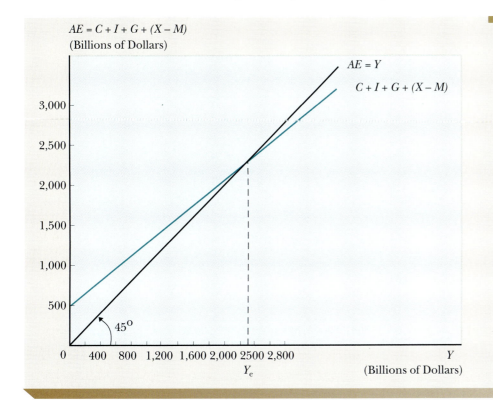

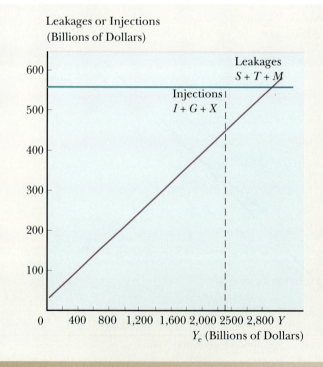

change in income depends on the magnitude and direction of the change in C, I, G, or $(X - M)$.

Suppose investment expenditures (I) increase by $200 billion to a new level of $360 billion at each level of national income. The aggregate expenditure curve shifts upward by $200 billion from AE_1 to AE_2, as shown in Figure 7. The original equilibrium income of Y_1 ($2,500 billion) no longer holds. At this level of national income, planned spending (AE) is now $2,700 billion and exceeds Y_1 by $200 billion. Unplanned reductions in inventories occur. Business firms respond by increasing output, which increases national income.

The final increase in income and output is much greater than the initial $200 billion increase in investment. The new equilibrium in Figure 7 occurs where AE_2 intersects the 45° line. At that point, national income is at Y_2, or $3,500 billion, which is $1,000 billion higher than the original equilibrium level. Thus, the $200 billion upward shift in aggregate expenditure results in a $1,000 billion increase in equilibrium income and output because of the multiplier effect. The expenditure multiplier measures the impact of a given initial change in aggregate expenditure on equilibrium income and output. This multiplier is an important and powerful tool of Keynesian economic theory.

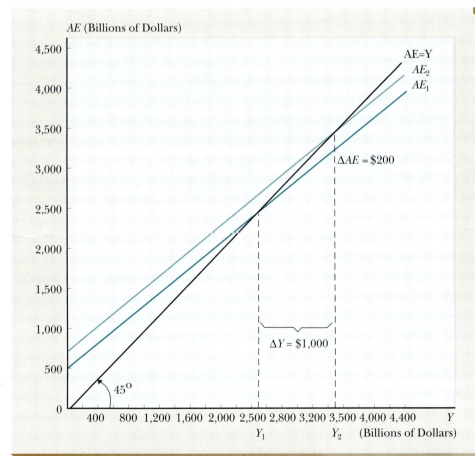

FIGURE 7
A SHIFT IN AGGREGATE EXPENDITURE
With equilibrium national income at Y_1, business investment spending increases by $200 billion ($\Delta I = \$200$). The aggregate expenditure schedule shifts up (from AE_1 to AE_2) by $200 billion. Equilibrium national income increases by $1,000 billion, from Y_1 to Y_2.

THE MULTIPLIER AND CHANGES IN INVESTMENT

Suppose that, as a result of changed expectations, firms increase investment expenditures (I) by $200 billion. Aggregate expenditure (AE) initially increases by the same amount. The additional investment spending creates additional income for those who produce investment goods. Suppose, for example, the investment consists of building an apartment complex. The plumbers, carpenters, and electricians earn additional income, which they in turn spend to buy groceries, movie tickets, and new cars. Grocers, farmers, theater operators, actors, auto workers, and auto dealers all receive more income, which they in turn spend. According to the consumption function, when Y changes, C also changes, but by a smaller amount. The marginal propensity to consume describes the relationship between changes in income and the *induced* changes in consumption spending. Thus, an additional business investment of $200 billion causes incomes to increase by $200 billion.

This increase is the round one effect. As a result of receiving this additional income ($200 billion), households will increase their spending by an amount dependent on the marginal propensity to consume. The round-two spending will increase aggregate expenditure further. If MPC is 0.8, the round-two increase in AE will be $160 billion ($200 billion × 0.8). But this spending also becomes additional income to those who receive it, setting off a round-three increase in spending. This round-by-round process is shown in Figure 8. Each change in output and income causes a change in spending in the next round, which changes output and income. The process continues, with smaller increases in each successive round.

How long does this income-spending process go on? Figure 8 traces the process through the first five rounds and then summarizes the remaining rounds. Although in theory the process goes on forever, a shortcut is available to quickly determine the total change in output and income. Note that after round one, each column entry in Figure 8 is 80 percent of the entry above it. Thus, the numbers in the columns that show each round of increase in spending and income are declining at a uniform rate of 80 percent—or 0.8, the value of the marginal propensity to consume. There is clearly a relationship between

FIGURE 8

THE MULTIPLIER PROCESS
In each successive round of spending, the multiplier makes another addition to the spending flow. However, the additions get smaller and smaller in each successive round.

ROUND	CHANGE IN AGGREGATE EXPENDITURE (BILLIONS)	CHANGE IN NATIONAL INCOME (BILLIONS)
1	$200 (initial change)	$200
2	160	160
3	128	128
4	102.40	102.40
5	81.92	81.92
All following rounds	327.68	327.68
Total	$1,000.00	$1,000.00

income growth and the size of the marginal propensity to consume. It turns out that the overall effect of the round-by-round changes in national income is shown by

(2) $\Delta Y_f = \Delta AE_1 \times$ expenditure multiplier,

where ΔY_f is the sum of all the changes in the level of national income and ΔAE_1 is the initial change in planned aggregate expenditure. The **expenditure multiplier** is defined as

$$\frac{1}{1 - MPC} = \frac{1}{1 - b}.$$

It is possible to compute the change in the equilibrium level of national income (ΔY_f) if the initial change in aggregate expenditure (ΔAE_1) and the marginal propensity to consume (MPC) are known. First, we substitute the actual value of MPC in the expression for the multiplier:

$$\text{Expenditure multiplier} = \frac{1}{1 - 0.8} = \frac{1}{0.2} = 5.$$

Expenditure multiplier Measure of the impact of a given initial change in total expenditures on equilibrium national income; equal to $1/(1 - MPC)$.

Second, we solve equation (2) for ΔY_f by substituting the known values for ΔAE_1 and the expenditure multiplier:

$$\Delta Y_f = \$200 \text{ billion} \times 5 = \$1{,}000 \text{ billion}.$$

This result corresponds to the change in the level of national income in Figure 7. This change in output and income is also the value that would result from summing the effects of an infinite number of rounds in Figure 8.

The expenditure multiplier applies to a change in any of the components of aggregate expenditure: C, I, G, or $(X - M)$. For instance, a $50 billion increase in net exports, multiplied by an expenditure multiplier of 5, would cause an increase of $250 billion in the equilibrium level of national income. The expenditure multiplier is the same no matter where the change in spending originates. A government dollar multiplies as well as a dollar from the foreign sector. If the C_0 term in the consumption function can shift up or down with changes in consumer wealth or population or other influences, it will have the same kind of multiplier effect. The size of the multiplier, however, is usually somewhat smaller than the value we have been using here, because of a variety of leakages and other effects. The multiplier for the U.S. economy is generally believed to be about 3. That is, over a period of about two years, a $1 change in the level of autonomous spending will raise equilibrium by about $3.

THE MULTIPLIER AND CHANGES IN CONSUMPTION

Although economists generally expect changes in AE to come from changes in planned investment, government purchases, or net exports, occasionally there are shifts in the consumption function. Normally the consumption function is the most stable component of aggregate expenditure. Government spending is unpredictable, investment is volatile, and exports and imports have swings. Consumers, however, seem to buy food, cars, clothing, and other necessities and conveniences with great regularity. Once in a while, however, consumers take forecasters by surprise. They did so when forecasting output and income with the Keynesian model was in its infancy.

During World War II, output was high and unemployment was low because of massive government spending for the war effort. Since so much output consisted of military goods and so many workers were in the military, few consumer goods were being produced. Consumers worked long hours and earned big paychecks. But they were encouraged to be patriotic and purchase war bonds (save) instead of spending on the limited supply of consumer goods.

Economists had predicted a serious recession at the end of the war as government spending dropped back to normal levels. There was eventually a mild recession, but not until about four years after the war ended. What was wrong with the forecast? The consumption function shifted upward because consumers had amassed large amounts of financial assets in the form of boxes full of war bonds. After the war, they were ready to cash in these bonds to satisfy their pent-up demand for cars, houses, new clothes, and other consumer goods. Many of the ex-soldiers went to college on the GI Bill, further offsetting the decline in planned government spending for national defense. Cuts in government spending were offset by an upward shift in the consumption function. In terms of the Keynesian model, the downward multiplier effect of reduced government spending was offset by the upward multiplier effect of an increase in C_0.

More recently, consumption played an important role in the 1991 recession for the opposite reason—there had been an increase in consumer debt during the 1980s. As consumers worked off their debt for mortgages, car loans, and credit cards during the late 1980s and early 1990s, they reduced their spending for cars, houses, and other big ticket items. The average age of cars rose sharply in the 1980s. The downward multiplier effect of reduced consumption spending was an important factor in the 1990–1991 recession. By the end of the recession, consumer debt was down closer to normal levels relative to income, and consumers again began buying refrigerators, cars, computers, and new homes.

THE MULTIPLIER AND CHANGES IN PLANNED SAVING

The expenditure multiplier can also be used to describe the effect of an increase in planned saving on equilibrium income and actual or realized saving. Keynes questioned the value of increasing saving when an economy is operating well below the full-employment level of output. An upward shift in the saving function implies an equal and opposite downward shift of the consumption and aggregate expenditure functions. The equilibrium level of national income must fall because aggregate expenditure has fallen. The increase in planned saving does not necessarily result in much increase in actual saving. As income falls, households are forced to consume less and save less out of their smaller incomes. It is possible that households may wind up saving no more than before out of a lower level of income and output.

GLOBAL OUTLOOK: DOES THE KEYNESIAN MODEL WORK IN DEVELOPING COUNTRIES?

The Keynesian model was developed to describe ups and downs of income and output in developed, industrial economies. For such economies, it can be assumed that the components of aggregate expenditure—consumption, investment, government spending, and net exports—are largely independent of each other. The Keynesian model was constructed on the assumption of such independence. In a small economy with a single major export product, however, this assumption may not be valid.

Consider the economy of Ghana, an African country whose main crop is coffee. Coffee represents 60 percent of the value of Ghana's exports and 40 percent of total output. Suppose there is a large drop in Ghana's coffee sales due to changes in tastes abroad. In a developed economy, this fall in net exports would be duly entered in the aggregate expenditure function. It would then have a larger impact on output and employment through the expenditure multiplier and induced declines in consumption.

In Ghana, however, such ripples will be larger and more serious. In addition to the induced decline in consumption, the fall in coffee sales means a loss of revenue to the government. (Taxes on the export crop are often a major source of government revenues in small one-crop economies.) With little capacity to borrow, the government will be forced to reduce government purchases (G). The decline in government purchases has an additional downward multiplier effect on income and output.

Furthermore, most of the investment occurring in Ghana is probably linked to the production of coffee. With poor sales prospects for their major crop, investors in Ghana are likely to cut back on their investment spending (I). This fall has a third downward multiplier effect on income and output.

During a boom in coffee sales, the reverse is true. Net export sales have a multiplier effect. They also create a stimulus to government spending from the additional revenue from export taxes and a stimulus to investment in the coffee industry in anticipation of future boom years. These two injections of new spending have their own multiplier effects on consumption and, through consumption, on income and output.

Thus, for such an economy, changes in economic activity are likely to be much more intense than for economies that are more diversified and less dependent on international trade. The same dependence is seen in some of the states in the United States; Texas and oil, Hawaii and tourism, Connecticut and defense procurement. A modest dip in the level of economic activity in the country or countries to which Ghana exports its coffee could have a major impact on the level of income and output in this small, highly specialized economy. This kind of effect was responsible for a saying heard often during the first two decades after World War II: "When the United States sneezes, the rest of the world catches pneumonia."

THE KEYNESIAN MODEL AND AGGREGATE DEMAND

Our working model for macroeconomics up until now has been the aggregate supply and aggregate demand model. This chapter has developed a Keynesian model in which an aggregate expenditure function determines the level of income and output. The price level receives no attention in the Keynesian model. The price level and real output receive equal billing in the aggregate supply and demand model. How are these two models connected?

The relationship between the aggregate demand (*AD*) curve of Chapter 6 and the aggregate expenditure (*AE*) curve of the Keynesian model is shown in Figure 9. The *AE* curve is drawn for a given, fixed price level. Higher price levels are associated with lower aggregate expenditure at every level of income. Chapter 6 suggested many reasons why total demand for goods and services will be lower at higher price levels. Higher price levels discourage consumption by

FIGURE 9

DERIVING AN AGGREGATE DEMAND CURVE FROM A FAMILY OF AGGREGATE EXPENDITURE CURVES

Each aggregate expenditure function determines a unique equilibrium level of real income, Y. There is a different aggregate expenditure function for each possible price level. The price level, P, and the unique equilibrium level of output, Y, corresponding to each AE schedule are plotted in Panel (b) to trace out an aggregate demand curve.

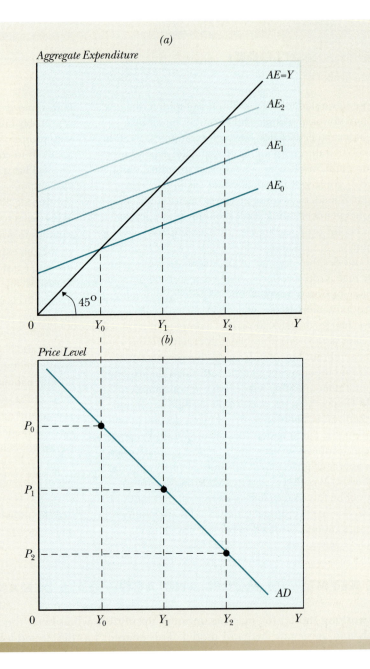

reducing the value of household financial assets. Higher price levels are associated with higher interest rates, discouraging both investment and purchases of consumer durables. Higher price levels also discourage exports and stimulate imports, reducing the net exports ($X - M$) component of aggregate expenditure. The same reasons that explain why the AD curve slopes down from left to right also explain why there will be a different AE curve corresponding to each different price level. Thus, AE_0 is associated with a high price level, P_0; AE_1 with a lower price level, P_1; and so forth.

Figure 9 derives an AD curve by plotting the various P and Y combinations derived from the set of AE curves in the upper panel. For example, along AE_0, price level P_0 is associated with equilibrium real income level Y_0. Remember, the *AE* curve shows the amount consumers and business firms will plan to spend on consumption and investment at various *income* levels. The *AD* curve in the lower panel of Figure 9 shows the amounts of real output (*Y*) that will be demanded by households and business firms (and, in a four-sector economy, government and the foreign sector) at various *price* levels.

Both the *AE* curve and the *AD* curve represent demand for total output. The *AE* curve shows the relationship between demand and income. The *AD* curve shows the relationship between demand and the price level. The individual demand curves in Chapter 3 were specifically defined as showing a price-quantity relationship. The phrase *demand curve* is therefore reserved for those graphs that plot quantity against price. A shift in aggregate expenditure for any reason *other than a change in the price level* will shift the *AD* curve. An increase in consumer wealth, a change in firms' expectations, a reduction in government spending, a surge in exports, or a shift away from buying imported goods can shift both the *AE* and *AD* curves. An upward shift of the *AE* curve due to any of these events will lead to a rightward shift of the *AD* curve. A downward shift of *AE* will shift *AD* to the left.

Whether you use an aggregate supply and demand model or an aggregate expenditure model, the equilibrium level of national income occurs where total output and planned aggregate expenditure are equal. In the Keynesian model, equilibrium does not mean that the economy will necessarily be at full employment with stable prices. If the economy does reach equilibrium with high unemployed resources (as during the Great Depression) or with rampant inflation (as during the late 1970s), what can be done to alter the situation? The next chapter will discuss the tools government can use to deal with undesirable equilibrium conditions.

Consider again...*How does the Keynesian model help us to understand what caused the 1990–1991 recession and why the recovery was so weak? The Keynesian model refocused attention on the role of demand and the components of demand in causing fluctuations in economic activity. Declining consumption because of high levels of consumer debt (a reduction in C_0) played an important role in the 1990–1991 recession. Because of poor sales, investment followed consumption into decline. Rather than offsetting declining consumption and investment spending, governments at all levels were tightening their belts, raising taxes and cutting spending in order to reduce budget deficits or (in the case of state and local governments) balance their budgets. All of these actions had multiplier effects downward. As the economy began to recover, one of the factors that held back recovery was a decline in net exports. Imports rose as the economy recovered, but recession in Europe, Canada and Japan (our major export markets) meant that our exports fell.*

The 1980–1982 recession was quite different. High interest rates discouraged investment spending while a rising price for the dollar reduced net exports. This decline in net exports and investment spending precipitated a recession, with multiplier effects reducing consumption. A major federal tax cut in 1981 resulted in increased consumption and investment and helped to fuel the recovery. In both cases, however, the Keynesian model provided a framework in which to interpret the forces that led to the recession and also determined the strength of the recovery.

SUMMARY

1. Because aggregate supply is horizontal in the Keynesian model, demand plays a central role. Keynes focused on the two-way relationship between income and spending, especially consumption and investment spending.
2. The simple two-sector aggregate expenditure function has two components. The consumption function shows how consumption expenditures (C) vary with disposable income (Y_d). The second component is investment demand, which is independent of the level of income. The equilibrium level of national income occurs where output equals aggregate expenditure, at the intersection of the AE curve and the 45° line. At nonequilibrium levels of income, differences between aggregate expenditure and income result in unplanned changes in business inventories. These changes act both as a signal and as an incentive, causing firms to adjust their level of output to the level of spending.
3. The expanded aggregate expenditure function is the sum of four components: consumption expenditures (C), investment expenditures (I), government purchases of goods and services (G), and net exports (X – M). Equilibrium is determined in the same way as in the two-sector model.
4. Through the multiplier process, any initial change in planned spending will result in a larger change in the equilibrium level of national income.
5. The AE curve shows the relationship between planned spending and income. The AD curve shows the relationship between planned spending and the price level. Shifts in the AE curve for any reason except a change in the price level will shift the AD curve.

NEW TERMS

aggregate expenditure (AE)
consumption function

marginal propensity to
consume (MPC)

marginal propensity to save
(MPS)

dissaving
expenditure multiplier

QUESTIONS: REVIEW, APPLICATIONS, AND POLICY

REVIEW

1. Why did aggregate expenditure and aggregate demand play a more important role in the Keynesian model than in the classical model?
2. How is it possible to consume without any income?
3. How do unplanned inventory changes ensure that actual saving and investment are always equal in a two-sector economy, even if planned saving and investment are not?
4. If a point on the AE curve is above the 45° reference line, are unplanned inventory changes positive, negative, or zero at that level of Y? Why?

APPLICATIONS

5. Suppose C_0 is $300 billion and MPC is 0.5. Create a table relating C and S to Y_d for values of Y_d between 0 and $5,000 billion (by $500 billion intervals).
6. Use the following information to construct a table similar to Table 4:
C is $200 billion when Y_d = 0 and MPC = 0.75; T = $300 billion; I = $100 billion; G = $400 billion; X = $50 billion; and M = $150 billion.
7. Use the information in Question 6 to construct a graph of the AE curve. Indicate the equilibrium level of national income on the graph. What is the dollar value of that equilibrium income?

8. Use the information from Question 6, but change I to $200 billion. Determine the new equilibrium income level and the value of the expenditure multiplier.
9. Use each of the following to find the value of the expenditure multiplier: (a) MPC = 0.40; (b) MPS = 0.25; (c) MPC = 0.67; (d) MPS = 0.50; (e) MPC = 0.90; (f) MPC = 0.75.
10. Assume the initial equilibrium level of national income is $4,800 billion and MPC = 0.9. What will be the new equilibrium level of Y if I decreases $100 billion from its initial level?
11. Suppose the consumption function is $C = \$300 + 0.85Y$.
    a. What is the value of the multiplier?
    b. What are the values of C_0, MPC, and MPS?
    c. Determine the level of consumption for $Y = \$100$, $300, $500, $700, $1,000, $1,200, $1,500, $2,000, and $3,000.
12. Discuss what would happen to the consumption function in Question 11 in each of the following situations:
    a. Consumers experience an increase in wealth.
    b. Taxes increase.
    c. Consumers expect prices to rise rapidly in the future.
    d. Interest rates fall.
13. In what directions would the AE curve and the AD curve shift in each of the following cases?
    a. Worried about a recession, business firms reduce their investment spending.
    b. A high birth rate means that families increase their consumption at every level of income to pay for diapers, pediatricians, and day care.
    c. Real income increases.
    d. The government reduces taxes.
14. If a rise in the price of the dollar reduced sales of American exports and increased Americans' purchases of imports, what would be the effect on the level of income and output? What about the price level?

POLICY

15. In order to influence the level of output, governments need to know how changes in the level of various kinds of spending affect AE and AD. In what direction will each of the following government or business policy actions shift the AE curve? How will the AD curve shift? In what direction will income change?
    a. As a result of U.S. restrictions on foreign goods, there is an exogenous fall in the level of imports (M).
    b. The government launches a new program to improve highways and bridges. That is, government purchases (G) increase.
    c. Banks are offering such attractive interest rates that consumers decide to save a larger part of their incomes and spend less.
    d. Businesses decide to change the ratio of inventories to sales from 30 percent to 25 percent. Therefore, there is a planned reduction in inventory investment.

SUGGESTIONS FOR FURTHER READING

Dimand, Robert W. *The Origins of the Keynesian Revolution: The Development of Keynes' Theory of Employment and Output.* Stanford CA: Stanford University Press, 1988. An overview of how Keynes's ideas about output and employment evolved during the 1930s and into the 1940s.

Temin, Peter. *Lessons from the Great Depression.* Cambridge MA: The MIT Press, 1991. The first chapter explains the causes of the Great Depression in Keynesian terms and draws implications for the 1990s.

APPENDIX
THE ALGEBRA OF THE KEYNESIAN MODEL

The Keynesian model has been presented in this chapter largely in graphs and numbers. However, the model can be written in algebraic form, providing a formal derivation of the equilibrium level of income and the expenditure multiplier. In this appendix, we derive a series of four versions of the Keynesian model, each more complex than the last.

MODEL 1

The simplest Keynesian model is the two-sector model in which there is no distinction between disposable and national income because there is no government. In symbols,

$$Y = C + I,$$

where $C = C_0 + bY$, and $I = I_0$.
  Substituting,

$$Y = C_0 + bY + I_0, \text{ or}$$

$$Y - bY = C_0 + I_0.$$

Solving for the equilibrium level of Y results in

$$(1) \quad Y_e = \frac{1}{1-b}(C_0 + I_0).$$

This relationship can also be used to show the effects of the multiplier. A change in equilibrium income resulting from a change in investment spending (or a change in C_0) is given by

$$(2) \quad \Delta Y_e = \frac{1}{1-b}(\Delta I_0).$$

MODEL 2

The second model adds a government sector, with three activities: government purchases (G), taxes (T), and transfer payments (TR). All of these new variables are autonomous—that is, not related to the level of income. With these additions, the model becomes

$$Y = C_0 + b(Y - T_0 + TR_0) + I_0 + G_0, \text{ or}$$

$$Y - bY = C_0 - bT_0 + bTR_0 + I_0 + G_0.$$

Solving for the equilibrium value of Y gives the same multiplier as with the first model. There are now more variables in the expression being multiplied that can shift aggregate expenditures:

$$(3) \quad Y_e = \frac{1}{1-b}(C_0 - bT_0 + bTR_0 + I_0 + G_0).$$

The basic multiplier is unchanged, but there are more sources of shifts in the aggregate expenditure function. For example, a change in government expenditures would affect equilibrium income as follows:

$$(4) \quad \Delta Y_e = \frac{1}{1-b}(\Delta G_0).$$

However, the impact of a given change in T or TR is less than the impact of an equal change in C_0, I, or G because taxes and transfer payments work through the consumption function. This smaller impact is indicated by the fact that T_0 and TR_0 are multiplied by the marginal propensity to consume, b, which always has a value of less than 1. Thus, the multipliers for a change in taxes or transfers are given, respectively, by the following equations:

$$(5) \quad \Delta Y_e = \frac{-b}{1-b}(\Delta T_0)$$

and

$$(6) \quad \Delta Y_e = \frac{b}{1-b}(\Delta TR_0).$$

MODEL 3

The third model makes T and TR dependent on the level of income, because taxes rise and transfers fall as income rises. That is,

$$T = T_0 + tY, \text{ and } TR = TR_0 - rY.$$

In these equations, t is called the marginal tax rate and r is called the marginal transfer rate, or the change in transfers per additional dollar of income. Equilibrium is given by

$$Y = C_0 + b(Y - T_0 - tY + TR_0 - rY) + I_0 + G_0, \text{ or}$$

$$Y - bY + btY + brY = C_0 - bT_0 + bTR_0 + I_0 + G_0.$$

The solution to the model is given by

$$(7) \quad Y_e = \frac{1}{1 - b + bt + br}(C_0 - bT_0 + bTR + I_0 + G_0).$$

The multiplier is smaller than in the second model. The effects of a change in C_0, I_0, or G_0 on the equilibrium level of income (we use G_0 to represent any one of these three) is given by

$$(8) \quad \Delta Y_e = \frac{1}{1 - b + bt + br}(\Delta G_0).$$

The effects of a change in T_0 or R_0 on equilibrium income is given by

$$(9) \quad \Delta Y_e = \frac{-b}{1 - b + bt + br}(\Delta T_0), \text{ and}$$

$$(10) \quad \Delta Y_e = \frac{b}{1 - b + bt + br}(\Delta TR_0).$$

This model can be used in connection with Chapter 9 to describe the effects of fiscal policy by changing the tax rate.

MODEL 4

The fourth model adds two important complications. First, it allows investment expenditures to be at least partly responsive to the level of final demand, rather than being totally autonomous. This change makes investment expenditures, like taxes and transfer payments, a function of the level of income and output. This model uses an investment demand function of the form

$$I = I_0 + aY,$$

where a is defined as the marginal propensity to invest.

The second change is to incorporate the foreign sector, or net exports. Exports (X_0) are independent of the level of income, but imports are not. The import demand function takes the form

$$M = M_0 + mY,$$

where m is the marginal propensity to import. This change gives the final form of the model:

$$Y = C_0 + b(Y - T_0 - tY + TR_0 - rY) + I_0 + aY + G_0 + X_0 - M_0 - mY, \text{ or}$$

$$Y - bY + btY + brY - aY + mY = C_0 - bT_0 + bTR_0 + I_0 + G_0 + X_0 - M_0.$$

Again, solving for the equilibrium value of Y gives the following expression:

$$(11) \quad Y_e = \frac{1}{1 - b + bt + br - a + m} (C_0 - bT_0 + bTR + I_0 + G_0 + X_0 - M_0).$$

The multiplier may be larger or smaller than the one in the third model because there is an additional leakage of funds into spending on imports in every additional round of spending, but also an additional injection in each round from induced investment spending. Equation 12 shows the change in equilibrium income resulting from a change in government spending. The other equations for changes in consumption, taxes, transfers, exports, or imports, are left to the reader as an exercise.

$$(12) \quad \Delta Y_e = \frac{1}{1 - b + bt + br - a + m} (\Delta G_0).$$

Equations 11 and 12 provide a fairly complete form of the basic Keynesian model. The multiplier reflects induced changes in consumption, taxes, transfers, investment, and imports. The aggregate expenditure function can be shifted by autonomous changes in consumption (C_0), taxes (T_0), transfer payments (TR_0), investment spending (I_0), government spending (G_0), exports (X_0), or the autonomous component of export demand (M_0).

This model can be used as a basis for a microcomputer simulation of economic activity. There are much larger and more complex models that include interest rates, prices, the money supply, and other variables to forecast output and employment. However, you can get an idea of how these variables are interrelated by putting this model on a microcomputer with some initial values for each variable. You can then change one variable and see how the others respond.

CHAPTER 9
TAXES, GOVERNMENT SPENDING, AND FISCAL POLICY

Consider this...*In 1980, President Reagan was elected with a promise of "morning in America." In the unpoetic language of economics, this was a stimulus program to increase economic growth. He took office in the midst of a two-part recession, with a sharp drop in 1980 (just before the election), a brief recovery, and a second and longer drop before the economy started upward in 1983. The centerpiece of Reagan's stimulus/recovery program was the 1981 tax cut, a 25 percent reduction in taxes phased in over two and one-half years, with numerous special provisions to encourage saving and investment. The tax cut was billed as "supply side economics"—a collection of policies intended to shift aggregate supply to the right by encouraging investment. Keynesians argued, however, that this tax cut was actually Keynesian fiscal policy, designed to increase aggregate expenditures, aggregate demand, and the level of output and employment. Who was right? This chapter may not provide the answer, but it will help you to understand both sides of the argument.*

LEARNING OBJECTIVES
1. Summarize the Keynesian argument for active fiscal policy as the only way to assure full employment with stable prices.
2. Describe the use of an appropriate fiscal policy to promote growth and full employment through both demand and supply effects.
3. Distinguish between automatic stabilizers and discretionary fiscal policy, and give examples of each.
4. Describe experience with discretionary fiscal policy in the United States since 1960.
5. Critically analyze the arguments for and against active fiscal policy.

WHY FISCAL POLICY?

Fiscal policy is based on the Keynesian model in Chapter 8. **Fiscal policy** consists of changes in government expenditures (G) or taxes (T) in order to influence the level of economic activity, inflation, and economic growth. Government spending and taxes existed, of course, long before the development of Keynesian economic theory. Fiscal policy is *intentional* use of taxing or government spending to affect the level of output, employment, and prices. Even when governments change their levels of spending or taxes for other reasons, policy makers are very conscious of the effects these actions will have on output, employment and the price level.

Fiscal policy
The use of government spending and taxes to try to influence the levels of output, employment, and prices.

Most economists in the classical tradition consider fiscal policy to be of limited benefit, sometimes even harmful. Keynesians, however, regard active fiscal policy as a valuable tool for stabilizing economic activity. Both groups of economists agree that the economy automatically moves to a level of national income where total output equals aggregate expenditure (or where leakages equal injections). In the Keynesian model, however, this equilibrium level may not result in full employment of resources. Keynes argued that governments should respond to unemployment with fiscal policy. That is, government should increase aggregate expenditure (AE) enough to ensure a socially desirable equilibrium level of income and output.

Aggregate expenditure consists of consumption demand, planned investment spending, government purchases of goods and services, and net exports. An increase in any of these four components can stimulate output and employment. Keynesians, however, do not think it is realistic to expect private demand (consumption and investment) alone to restore full employment.

Households and businesses are motivated more by self-interest than by social interest. Individual persons or firms cannot be expected to act in the interest of society as a whole if those actions would conflict with their own self-interest. In a recession, social interest calls for households to increase consumption spending and business firms to increase investment spending in the face of stagnant demand for their products. Self-interest, however, dictates that it would be foolish for these individual households or business firms to "swim against the tide" by expanding production or consumption while others are contracting. Instead, households tend to save more and spend less because of uncertainty about future income and employment. Business firms invest less because of pessimistic expectations about future income, employment, and sales. During expansionary periods, upbeat expectations of job security, pay raises, and increasing sales and profits stimulate more private spending, pushing the economy further beyond full-employment equilibrium. Thus, the self-interested behavior of households and business firms makes economic fluctuations worse.

The foreign sector also offers little help in ending prolonged downturns. Net exports ($X - M$) are highly variable. Export demand (X) depends on changes in the price level in the United States and abroad, exchange rates, economic conditions abroad, and trade restrictions. Imports (M) reflect changes in the price levels at home and abroad, exchange rates, trade restrictions, consumer tastes, and the domestic income level. A higher level of income stimulates all kinds of private spending, including spending on imported goods.

The government has some policy tools to increase net exports in order to shift the AD curve to the right. Most of these policies are aimed at limiting imports. The government can try to put downward pressure on the price of its currency to encourage exports and discourage imports. Tariffs and quotas will reduce imports of foreign goods and services. Such solutions were popular in the early years of the Great Depression and have been proposed in almost every economic downturn since that time. Since these actions are taken at the expense of a nation's trading partners, they are referred to as beggar-thy-neighbor policies. One country may increase its level of employment by limiting imports, which will add jobs in producing substitutes. However, the problem is then passed on to the trading partner, which sees a fall in exports and thus in employment. In any case, the effects on the domestic economy are usually short-lived. Other countries retaliate with similar policies, negating any gains.

With little help from the other three sectors, Keynesians see government spending as the only hope for stabilization. They argue that only the government can be expected to act in the social interest by using its taxing and spending powers to offset changes in private demand.

HOW FISCAL POLICY WORKS

The aggregate expenditure function is very unstable. As consumption spending (C), investment (I), or net exports ($X - M$) fluctuate, aggregate expenditure changes. Through the multiplier process, the resulting changes in income, output, and employment are larger than the initial change in C, I, or ($X - M$). Upward shifts in the AE curve result in rightward shifts in the AD curve, as you saw at the end of Chapter 8. Shifts in aggregate demand lead to changes in the price level as well as in real output and employment. We will work mostly with the aggregate supply and demand model in this chapter. You should keep in mind, however, that changes in government spending and taxes work by shifting the AE curve, which in turn shifts the AD curve.

Although some forms of fiscal policy may also shift the aggregate supply curve, fiscal policy is mainly directed at shifting aggregate demand. If government spending (G) increases only temporarily or taxes (T) are reduced temporarily, then when they return to their original level, the AE and AD curves will return to their original positions. Real output and income will also fall back to the original level.

Figure 1 shows how an increase in government spending works in a combined $AE/AS/AD$ model. In part (*a*), an increase in government spending (G) by an amount of $10 billion shifts the AE curve from AE_1 to AE_2, increasing the equilibrium level of output from Y_1 to Y_2. In part (*b*) of Figure 1, the shift in AE means a corresponding shift of the AD curve to the right by a horizontal distance corresponding to $10 billion. With an upward-sloping supply curve, however,

FIGURE 1

AGGREGATE EXPENDITURE, AGGREGATE DEMAND, AND FISCAL POLICY
(a) An increase in aggregate expenditure from AE_1 to AE_2 because of increased government spending will raise equilibrium output from Y_1 to Y_2 if there is no change in the price level.
(b) The shift in AE also shifts the AD curve from AD_1 to AD_2, increasing Y by a smaller amount (from Y_1 to Y_3) and also increasing the price level (from P_1 to P_3). At the higher price level, the economy's AE curve will be AE_3, corresponding to an equilibrium level of output Y_3.

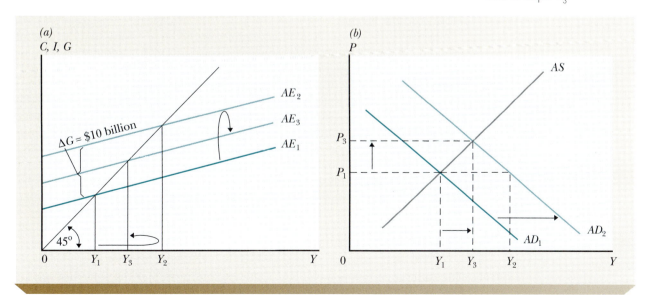

the impact of the added spending is divided between a change in output (from Y_1 to Y_3) and a change in the price level (from P_1 to P_3). Each *AE* curve is associated with a given price level. Thus, when the price level rises, aggregate expenditure will be lower. As the higher price level feeds back into the aggregate expenditure function, the economy finds itself on a lower *AE* curve (AE_3) in part (*a*), corresponding to a higher price level. The final level of output in both diagrams is Y_3.

Keynesian economists do not advocate government intervention to offset every shift in aggregate expenditure, only those shifts that have substantial and prolonged effects on output, employment, and prices. In reality, major fiscal policy actions have been relatively infrequent during the last fifty years, although minor adjustments to tax schedules, transfer programs, and government purchases with an eye to the economic impact take place in almost every session of Congress.

THE GOAL: FULL EMPLOYMENT WITH STABLE PRICES

In order to use fiscal policy wisely, policy makers must identify a target level of national income. If this target is far from the current equilibrium level, then the government should adjust taxes or spending. The goal is an equilibrium level of national income that generates full employment with price stability. This level is represented by the symbol Y^*. In reality, Y^* is a range of values clustered around that level rather than a precise, specific number.

In the Keynesian model, the aggregate expenditure function is the sum of the four components of planned spending—*C*, *I*, *G*, and (*X* – *M*)—at each level of national income. Consumption expenditures were represented by the equation $C = \$200$ billion $+ 0.8Y_d$. In this consumption function, the marginal propensity to consume (*MPC*) is 0.8, giving a value of 5 for the expenditure multiplier. The economy in Figure 2 is at full employment with stable prices when national income is \$3,500 billion ($Y^* = \$3,500$ billion). Above \$3,500 billion lie inflationary pressures. Below \$3,500 billion lies unemployment. The equilibrium level of output, which in this case is equal to Y^*, is found at the intersection of AE_2 and the 45° line.

In this situation, the goal of fiscal policy would be to ensure that the level of spending in the economy is AE_2 (the level that results in Y^*) and not some other level, such as AE_1 or AE_3. If the level of aggregate expenditure is lower than AE_2, unemployment will result. If aggregate expenditure and aggregate demand are above the levels required to bring the economy to full employment, there will be a shortage of workers. Then competition for workers and other scarce resources will result in inflationary pressures. The Keynesian model with a given price level is not as useful in addressing the situation represented by AE_3, because this model is based on idle resources and a horizontal *AS* curve, not excess demand for resources and a vertical *AS* curve. Fiscal policy is still useful in such a situation, but the model must be modified to include a variable price level.

THE RECESSIONARY GAP

Recessionary gap
The difference between aggregate expenditure and the full-employment level of output.

The difference between the aggregate expenditures and the full-employment level of output is called the **recessionary gap**. A recessionary gap exists when

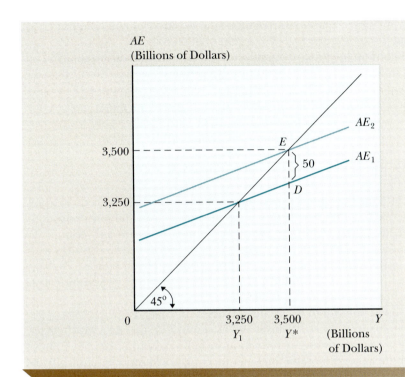

FIGURE 2
THE RECESSIONARY GAP
The full employment level of national income, Y^*, is achieved when aggregate expenditure is AE_2. If aggregate expenditure is AE_1, the recessionary gap is DE.

equilibrium national income is *less* than the desired level Y^*. In Figure 2, planned spending measured by AE_1 results in a recessionary gap because the resulting equilibrium level of income is only $3,250 billion. The recessionary gap (measured at Y^*) is equal to the vertical distance that AE would have to shift to get from AE_1 to AE_2. This gap, distance DE, measures how much aggregate expenditure must rise to bring national income up to the desired level. The difference between actual income (Y_1) and full employment income (Y^*) is called the **income gap**. The income gap is equal to the recessionary gap times the multiplier.

A recessionary gap exists when buyers are unwilling to purchase as much output as the economy would supply at the full-employment level of output (Y^*). If firms attempt to produce at the full-employment level of output, they will see unplanned increases in inventories and respond with cutbacks in production. Thus, the economy in Figure 2 is in equilibrium at Y_1.

A recessionary gap such as DE calls for expansionary fiscal policy. **Expansionary fiscal policy** consists of cutting taxes, raising transfer payments, and/or increasing government purchases to try to increase the level of output and employment. The tools of government purchases (G) and taxes (T) are already familiar. Transfer payments, first introduced in Chapter 5, are payments from governments to individuals for which no goods or services are expected in exchange. Many of these payments are made to those unable to earn enough to meet their basic needs—the elderly, single mothers of small children, or the disabled, for example. Changes in transfer payments work like negative taxes. An increase in transfer payments has the same effect on consumption as a reduction in taxes, although the individuals affected are usually a different group. For

Income gap
The difference between the equilibrium level of output and the full-employment level of output; equal to the recessionary gap times the multiplier.

Expansionary fiscal policy
Cutting taxes, raising transfer payments, or increasing government purchases to try to increase the level of income and employment.

the economy in Figure 2, an upward shift of the AE curve of $50 billion increases equilibrium income from Y_1 to Y^*, a gain of $250 billion.

The $250 billion increase in equilibrium income that results from a $50 billion upward shift in aggregate expenditure is a result of the multiplier effect discussed in Chapter 8. With MPC = 0.8, the final change in real output (Y) is equal to the multiplier of 5 times the upward shift in planned spending (AE) of $50 billion. If there is any effect on the price level (in the aggregate supply and demand diagram), then the change in real output will be smaller.

CHANGING THE LEVEL OF OUTPUT WITH FISCAL POLICY

Fiscal policy attempts to close a recessionary gap by increasing aggregate expenditure. In Figure 2, an increase in national income of $250 billion (from Y_1 to Y^*) requires an upward shift in aggregate expenditure of $50 billion. To increase spending by $50 billion at each level of national income (to shift from AE_1 to AE_2), government expenditures must increase by $50 billion. Through the multiplier process, a $50 billion change in aggregate expenditure causes national income to change by $250 billion.

Another fiscal policy tool is a change in taxes or transfers (T_{net}). Changes in transfer payments and personal taxes affect disposable income, which determines consumption spending. A reduction in taxes or an increase in transfer payments will increase disposable income, increase consumption, and shift the AE curve upward and the AD curve to the right. An increase in taxes or a decrease in transfer payments will reduce disposable income and consumption, shifting the AE curve downward and the AD curve to the left.

Suppose we want to cut taxes enough to shift AE upward by $50 billion in Figure 2. For simplicity, we will assume that taxes are not linked to the level of income, but are some arbitrary value, T, that is determined by Congress. Since the marginal propensity to consume (MPC) is 0.8, consumption (C) will increase by 80 cents for every dollar of tax cut. A $10 billion tax cut will increase disposable income by $10 billion and consumption by $8 billion. The change in C is equal to the change in taxes multiplied by MPC:

$\Delta C = \text{MPC} \times \Delta Y_d = \text{MPC} \times \Delta T$, or

$50 billion = 0.8 \times \Delta T$.

Taxes must be cut by $62.5 billion at each level of national income in order to generate an initial change in consumption of $50 billion. After the initial change, the multiplier process will generate an increase in income (Y) of $250 billion (the multiplier of 5 times the shift in aggregate expenditure of $50 billion). It takes a $62.5 billion decrease in taxes to accomplish the same change in national income as a $50 billion increase in government spending.

FISCAL POLICY AND THE MULTIPLIER

Why is the multiplier smaller for a tax change than for a change in government spending? Think about how taxes and government spending enter the income stream. Every dollar of additional government spending immediately contributes another dollar to aggregate expenditure. On the other hand, every dollar not taken by personal taxes is split between saving and consumption. When the marginal propensity to consume is 0.8, every $1 reduction in personal taxes results in an 80 cent increase in consumption spending and a 20 cent increase in saving.

Recall from Chapter 8 that the equilibrium level of national income is given by

$$AE = Y_e = C_0 + b(Y - T) + I + G + (X - M),$$

where b is the marginal propensity to consume (MPC) and disposable income (Y_d) is equal to $Y - T$. We can rearrange this expression:

$$Y_e = \frac{1}{1 - b}(C_0 - bT + I + G + (X - M)).$$

In this rearranged expression, we have separated equilibrium income into two terms. The first term, $1/(1 - b)$, is the multiplier from Chapter 8. The second term, in parentheses, contains all the factors that can shift aggregate expenditure: C_0, T, I, G, and $(X - M)$.

Note that the investment, government spending, net exports, and consumption terms are all multiplied by the multiplier, but the tax term is also multiplied by $-b$. This difference between the tax term and the others reflects two important facts. First, changes in taxes work in the opposite direction from changes in all of the other terms. An increase in taxes reduces aggregate expenditure, and a reduction in taxes increases aggregate expenditure. Changes in all of the other terms move aggregate expenditure in the same direction. Second, because b is always less than 1, taxes have a smaller effect on output and employment than an equal change in any of the others. We can express this difference by writing two multipliers:

$$\text{consumption } (C_0) \text{ multiplier,}$$
$$\text{government expenditure } (G) \text{ multiplier,} = \frac{1}{1 - b}$$
$$\text{and investment } (I) \text{ multiplier}$$

and

$$\text{Tax change multiplier} = -b\left(\frac{1}{1 - b}\right) = \frac{-b}{1 - b}$$

For example, with MPC = b = 0.8, the government expenditure multiplier is 5 and the tax change multiplier is –4.

THE BALANCED BUDGET MULTIPLIER

Suppose the government wanted to pursue an expansionary policy but did not want to unbalance the budget or increase an existing deficit. Since a given dollar amount of change in government spending has a greater impact than the same amount of change in taxes, equal changes in both government spending and taxes would still have some net effect on the equilibrium level of income. Suppose the government increases both spending and taxes by $20 billion, leaving the budget deficit or surplus unchanged. The change in government spending (G) increases the level of income (Y) by the expenditure multiplier, $1/(1 - b)$, times the change in G. If b is equal to 0.8, then Y increases by 5 times $20 billion, or $100 billion. Likewise, the $20 billion increase in taxes (T) is multiplied by the tax multiplier of -4, which is equal to $-b/(1 - b)$. So the reduction in Y resulting from the tax increase is -$80 billion.

Thus, the net change in Y from these two offsetting actions is $20 billion—exactly the same as the equal-sized changes in G and T! Is this a coincidence? No. If we add the two multipliers, +5 and −4, we get 1. Adding the algebraic expressions for the two multipliers also gives 1:

$$\frac{1}{1-b} + \frac{-b}{1-b} = \frac{1-b}{1-b} = 1.$$

The balanced budget multiplier is always equal to 1 as long as taxes are independent of the level of income. Equal increases in government spending and taxes will have a modest net impact on the level of output and employment, but this effect will be much smaller than the impact of a change in only G or only T with the other held constant.

BUSINESS TAX CUTS AS FISCAL POLICY

Sometimes there have been changes in business income taxes designed to stimulate investment. One such change was the Investment Tax Credit (ITC), first introduced as part of the Kennedy tax cut in 1964. This credit offers tax savings over and above depreciation for business firms investing in new plants or equipment. Firms can subtract a percentage of the investment made from their tax liability. The ITC has been a political football—being modified, removed, or restored many times. Each time, Congress weighs the revenue loss against the current perceived need to stimulate investment. Business firms complain that the ITC is less effective in encouraging investment when it is uncertain. They say it should be permanent rather than on and off. In 1992, both candidates Bush and Clinton proposed different forms of the ITC as part of their platforms for the presidential campaign.

The ITC, along with other features of the 1981 tax cut, was designed to stimulate investment. Investment is not only a market for sales of investment goods, but also an addition to the productive capacity of the economy. Thus, both aggregate demand and aggregate supply shift to the right, reducing the inflationary effect of fiscal policy. It is not clear how much additional investment resulted, but there was a definite decline in revenues from the corporate income tax.

SUPPLY SIDE EFFECTS

While fiscal policy is aimed at shifting AD and AE, the composition of government spending and the structure of taxes also affect aggregate supply. In the late

1970s and early 1980s, a number of economists, journalists, and politicians (known as supply siders) focused on the impact of changes in spending, taxes, and transfers on the aggregate supply curve. This group greatly influenced the thinking of President Reagan, especially in the structure of the tax cut.

SUPPLY SIDE EFFECTS OF TAXES. A reduction in corporate income taxes could make business more profitable and stimulate investment, job creation, and output. This reduction could be general (a cut in the corporate income tax rate) or it could be targeted (investment incentives, capital gains tax reductions, etc.) in such a way as to reward firms that invested or created jobs. A reduction in personal income taxes should stimulate both consumption and saving. This reduction can be targeted specifically to savers (for example, tax deductions for retirement savings) or to investment in one's own human capital (such as deductions for educational expenses).

A tax reduction may also stimulate work effort if workers get to keep a larger share of their earnings, although this effect is less clear cut. President Reagan and his advisers argued that it was particularly important to cut the tax rate for the highest income workers because they are the most productive and their extra work effort will greatly increase output. Others, inside and outside the Reagan administration, argued that tax cuts at the lower end were also important in getting people off welfare and into work, because tax cuts meant that these workers could keep a larger share of their earnings. All of these effects would increase labor supply and the stock of capital, shifting aggregate supply to the right.

SUPPLY SIDE EFFECTS OF GOVERNMENT SPENDING. While President Reagan stressed the supply side effects of tax cuts, President Clinton in the 1992 election campaign emphasized the supply side effects of certain types of government spending. The kinds of spending most likely to stimulate private investment and production are improvements in infrastructure (roads, airports, sewer systems) and investment in human capital (mainly education at all levels). Public sector infrastructure increases the productivity of private capital investment, because private firms need the transportation system, the water and sewer system, and other infrastructure as inputs to their production and distribution activities. Investment in human capital also increases the profitability of firms and encourages increases in output. Thus, while changes in the *level* of public spending impact on aggregate demand, changes in the *composition* of spending can shift aggregate supply.

THE TOOLS OF FISCAL POLICY: GOVERNMENT SPENDING AND TAXES

Fiscal policy relies on changes in government spending and taxes (and transfer payments, which can be treated as negative taxes). In general, conservative Keynesians prefer tax changes, leaving the level of government spending constant. Liberal Keynesians are more likely to favor changes in government spending or transfer payments. Fiscal policy cannot be considered outside the context of the level and composition of existing government spending.

In the United States, a large share of the nation's income is claimed by government, and a substantial share of output is produced by or for government.

Government spending has been growing faster than the economy as a whole. Between 1950 and 1992, the federal government's expenditures rose from 15 percent of GDP to 23 percent. State and local governments' expenditures rose from 8 percent of national income to 15 percent. Because government plays such a major role in the economy, changes in its taxing and spending levels can be a very effective tool for influencing the level of income and output.

GOVERNMENT PURCHASES AND TRANSFER PAYMENTS

Total government expenditures—federal, state, and local—account for more than one-third of national income in the United States. The federal government alone spent $1,493 billion in fiscal 1993 (the fiscal year running from October 1, 1992 to September 30, 1993). State and local governments added another $885 billion. Table 1 summarizes the major types of spending by levels of government.

About two-thirds of these funds were spent to produce or to purchase goods and services, such as defense, health care, highways, police, education, and courts. The rest were transfer payments to individuals who provided no goods or services in exchange. These payments included veterans' benefits, welfare payments, unemployment compensation, and Social Security benefits. Most transfer payments originate at the federal level, although some are administered by state and local governments. Defense and Social Security are the two biggest expenditures for the federal government. Education is the largest item in state and local budgets. Interest on the national debt takes a growing share of the federal budget because of continuing large budget deficits.

PAYING FOR GOVERNMENT

Table 2 lists revenue sources for all three levels of government. Major federal taxes are income taxes and social insurance taxes (Social Security taxes, workers' compensation taxes, and unemployment insurance taxes). The main revenue sources at the state and local levels are sales taxes and property taxes, respectively. Another revenue source for state and local governments is grants. Federal grants to states accounted for 17 percent of state and local revenue in 1991.

TABLE 1 GOVERNMENT EXPENDITURES (FISCAL YEARS)

FEDERAL (1993)		STATE AND LOCAL (1991)	
Income security	36.3	Education	32.7
Defense	20.7	Public welfare	14.4
Interest payments	14.1	Highways	7.1
Transfers to state and local governments	13.2	Interest	5.7
		Health, hospitals	8.9
All other	15.7	All other	31.2
Total	100%	Total	100%

TABLE 2 GOVERNMENT REVENUES

FEDERAL (1993)		STATE (1991)		LOCAL (1991)	
Income taxes	48.4%	Income taxes	12.4%	Property taxes	11.7%
Social insurance		Sales taxes	10.7	Income taxes	0.8
taxes	29.7	Fees/charges	4.9	Sales taxes	1.6
Other	10.5	Other	47.5	Fees/charges	9.0
Borrowing	11.4	Federal grants	24.5	Fed/state grants	37.2
				Other	39.7
Total	100%	Total	100%	Total	100%

IMPLEMENTING FISCAL POLICY: AUTOMATIC STABILIZERS

There are two kinds of fiscal policy. One kind is put into place and left to respond automatically to changes in the level of economic activity. The second kind, used less frequently, is deliberate action to change tax laws or enact new spending programs so as to influence the level of output, employment, and prices.

Congressional legislation over the years, much of it enacted during the Great Depression, has created a system of tax collections and transfer payments that change automatically in response to changes in national income. These **automatic stabilizers** partially offset changes in private spending and tend to reduce fluctuations in output and employment. They include changes in income tax collections, agricultural support payments, Social Security and welfare benefits, unemployment compensation claims, and imports. Because these automatic stabilizers are triggered by changes in the economy, they do not require further action by Congress.

Automatic stabilizers Changes in tax collections and transfer payments that are automatically triggered by changes in national income and tend to reduce changes in output and employment.

GLOBAL OUTLOOK: RECESSION AND FISCAL POLICY IN GERMANY AND JAPAN

For more than four decades, the economies of Germany and Japan have performed very well. Japan has had spectacular growth in output and is legendary for lifetime employment and low unemployment. Budget deficits were offset by high levels of private saving. High prices have been the prime complaint. Germany has also had excellent growth, low unemployment, and low inflation. Both countries have had strong export performances, excellent productivity growth, reputations for quality products, and strong currencies. But no country is immune to economic downturns.

Japan's recession in the early 1990s was partly imported—as a nation dependent on export markets, Japan felt the effects of a worldwide recession. Part of Japan's recession, however, was home-grown, resulting from a speculative bubble in stock and real estate prices that collapsed in 1990. As the Nikkei (the Japanese equivalent of the Dow Jones averages) plunged, and real estate along with it, a lot of family wealth fell as well. Consumers cut back their purchases, and reduced sales and lowered expectations took their toll of output and eventually even employment. Unemployment approaching 3 percent may not sound like much to Americans, but the Japanese are accustomed to a rate of 2 percent or less.

Germany's recession was mostly the result of the unification of East and West Germany in 1990. The prosperous

West took on the problems of the East—high unemployment, aging factories with no marketable products, obsolete technology, decaying infrastructure, and none of the necessary features of a market system, like private ownership, banks, and marketing networks. High labor costs in former West Germany led to substantial job losses in 1992 and 1993, with unemployment rising to almost 8 percent. Germany experienced unaccustomed budget deficits, and tried to stave off inflation with tight monetary policy that resulted in high interest rates, which discouraged borrowing for investment and consumer durables.

The responses of these two countries were different not only from the U.S. response to the recession but also from each other. Unlike the United States, Japan has little in the way of a social safety net to cushion the downturn and provide automatic stabilizers. The Japanese government tackled its first recession in quite some time with a healthy dose of expansionary fiscal policy, adding some $80 million dollars in increased government spending to aggregate expenditures and aggregate demand. This traditional Keynesian response to a recession saw Japan through the worst of the downturn. Japan kept unemployment from going higher while waiting for domestic spending to recover and for the rest of the world to emerge from recession and once again increase their imports from Japan.

Like other Western European nations, Germany has an extensive social welfare system that triggers automatic changes in benefit payments over the course of the business cycle. These automatic stabilizers were part of the reason for the budget deficits in 1990 and 1991. With the central government budget already deep in the red before the recession, the government felt that there was little additional opportunity to respond with tax cuts or government spending increases. The German central bank reluctantly agreed to reduce interest rates in order to encourage borrowing for consumption and investment. Germany also made some effort to trim extensive social benefits (unemployment compensation, day care, health care, and retirement). These cuts would make the economy worse in the short run (remember, a cut in transfer payments is like an increase in taxes in its effect on disposable income and consumption), but in the long run would reduce labor costs and make Germany more competitive in manufacturing.

Faced with a recession, different countries respond with different policy mixes, based on their own situation and their own values. Economic theory can tell you how the economy will respond to a particular policy, but it cannot tell you which policy to choose and implement.

PROGRESSIVE INCOME TAXES

In the Keynesian model of Chapter 8, taxes (T) were independent of level of income. If you have ever filled out Form 1040 to pay income taxes to the Internal Revenue Service, you know that as your income goes up, your taxes go up even faster. That is, your taxes rise as a percentage of income. The federal income tax is progressive, as are some state income taxes.

An income tax, or any tax, can be regressive, proportional, or progressive. Table 3 shows examples of how each type of tax affects three income earners. A **regressive tax** is a tax that takes a smaller share (percentage) of income as income rises. In the second column of Table 3, Jones pays a higher share of his income (5 percent) than does Brown (1 percent). Note that a tax can be regressive even if the tax does not decline in absolute dollars as income rises. In Table 3, Brown paid $5,000, and Jones paid only $500. For Brown, however, the tax represented a smaller percentage of income.

Regressive tax
A tax that takes a smaller share (percentage) of income as income rises.

Many people object to regressive taxes because of the burden they place on low-income families. General sales taxes, used by 45 states, are levied on most purchases of goods but very few services. These taxes are regressive, because a larger share of a household's income goes to saving and purchases of services rather than tangible goods as income rises.

Proportional tax
A tax that takes the same share (percentage) of income from all taxpayers.

A **proportional tax** takes the same share (percentage) of income from all taxpayers. The proportional tax of 5 percent in Table 3 takes the same share of income from each person, but the dollar amount increases as income increases.

TABLE 3 COMPARISON OF AMOUNTS PAID UNDER THREE TYPES OF TAXES

	INCOME	REGRESSIVE TAX	PROPORTIONAL TAX	PROGRESSIVE TAX
Jones	$10,000	$500 = 5%	$500 = 5%	$500 = 5%
Smith	$80,000	$1,600 = 2%	$4,000 = 5%	$20,000 = 25%
Brown	$500,000	$5,000 = 1%	$25,000 = 5%	$250,000 = 50%

A **progressive tax** takes a larger share (percentage) of income as income rises. In Table 3, the progressive tax takes not only more dollars from Brown than from Smith or Jones, but a higher share of Brown's income. The federal personal income tax in the United States is a moderately progressive tax, with rates ranging from 15 percent to 31 percent. The range of rates was reduced by the 1986 tax reform and again in 1990, but an extra rate (36 percent) was added on incomes over $140,000 in 1993. Thus, the federal income tax is still moderately progressive, although less so than before 1981.

Progressive tax
A tax that takes a larger share (percentage) of income as income rises.

If tax collections rise or fall more than in proportion to changes in national income, then consumption (which depends on after-tax, or disposable, income) will rise or fall *less* than in proportion to changes in national income. Suppose that at an income level (Y) of $3,000 billion, taxes are $300 billion, or 10 percent. Disposable income (Y_d) is then $2,700 billion. Substituting $2,700 billion for Y_d in the equation for the consumption function gives a value of consumption at that income level of

$$C = \$200 \text{ billion} + 0.8 Y_d = \$200 \text{ billion} + 0.8(\$2,700 \text{ billion}) = \$2,360 \text{ billion.}$$

What happens if equilibrium Y increases by $1,000 billion (from $3,000 billion to $4,000 billion)? With a marginal propensity to consume of 0.8, you might expect consumption to rise by 80 percent of the income increase of $1,000 billion, or $800 billion. However, taxes will limit the rise in consumption. If taxes take 10 percent of income, a rise in Y of $1,000 billion will raise Y_d by only $900 billion. Consumption will increase by 0.8 times $900 billion, or $720 billion. If the tax system is progressive, taxes may increase from 10 percent ($300 billion) at the old level of income to 12 percent ($480 billion) of the new income. In this case, national income rises by $1,000 billion, but disposable income will rise by only $820 billion, from $2,700 billion to $3,520 billion. Substituting this value of Y_d in the consumption function, we find that consumption (C) is now $3,016 billion. This increase of $656 billion, or 28 percent, in C is less than the 33 percent increase in Y. Thus, when income rises, progressive taxes rise more than in proportion to the increase in income. The effect is to dampen consumer demand.

With progressive income taxes, a fall in national income will lead to a more-than-proportional fall in tax collections. The disposable income of households will be a larger fraction of total income and output when income falls. Thus, the fall in consumption will be less than proportional to the decline in output and income.

The mildly progressive corporate income tax is also an automatic stabilizer. The corporate income subject to this tax consists of profits. Revenues from corporate income taxes still increase sharply during economic expansions and fall sharply during contractions. Profits and corporate income tax revenue are both highly sensitive to changes in the level of economic activity.

TRANSFER PAYMENTS

Transfer payments, many of them dating from the Great Depression, also act as automatic stabilizers. Transfer programs include unemployment compensation, Social Security, farm price supports, food stamps, and welfare benefits. All of these programs involve payments for which no production is expected in exchange.

Transfer programs such as food stamps usually set rules that determine who is eligible, rather than specifying a dollar amount to be spent. The number of families eligible for transfer programs rises during recessions and falls during periods of expansion. During recessions, more people qualify for unemployment benefits, apply for food stamps, go on welfare, and retire early on Social Security. As the economy recovers, some people—even some of those who retired early—go back to work. Transfer payments fall. In addition, farm prices will be higher during expansionary periods so less will be spent on farm price supports. During recessions, farm prices usually fall, which triggers a rise in support payments.

Think of transfer payments as negative taxes. They work in the same way as progressive income taxes in stabilizing output and employment by cushioning fluctuations in disposable income. Instead of changes in average tax rates paid as the level of income in the economy rises and falls, there are changes in the number of persons who qualify for benefits.

IMPORTS

Along with changes in taxes and transfer payments triggered by changes in output and income, changes in imports also serve to reduce fluctuations in output and employment. When income rises, consumers spend more on everything, including imports. Imports are a leakage out of the spending stream, so increased imports hold down the multiplier effects in the upward direction. During recessions, consumers spend less on everything, including imported goods. Declining imports help to cushion the fall in output and employment.

DISCRETIONARY FISCAL POLICY

Discretionary fiscal policy Deliberate changes in tax rates, transfer programs, or government purchases designed to change the equilibrium level of national income.

Automatic stabilizers might be considered Keynesian fiscal policy because they lead to changes in transfer payments and tax revenues that offset changes in private economic activity. For small changes in output and employment, automatic stabilizers may be sufficient to cushion the fluctuations until the economy corrects itself. For major swings in aggregate expenditure, however, automatic stabilizers are not enough. Policy makers turn to discretionary fiscal policy. **Discretionary fiscal policy** consists of changes in tax rates, in levels of transfer payments, or in government purchases of goods and services in order to change the equilibrium level of national income.

Congress changes tax rates, transfer programs, and government purchases almost every year for various reasons. The collapse of communism has led to a sharp decline in defense spending. Social problems such as AIDS and homelessness put pressure on policy makers to increase spending in those areas. Congress tinkers with the income tax code regularly to change incentives to save, invest, or give to charity. These actions may affect the level of economic activity, but they are not really fiscal policy, because their primary purpose is not to influence the level of output and employment.

The Employment Act of 1946 requires the federal government to actively promote full employment, steady growth, and stable prices through the use of fiscal and monetary policy. Nobel Prize winner James Tobin argues that this mandate is still as important today as it was almost fifty years ago. Clear examples of pure, large-scale discretionary fiscal policy are relatively rare. We will examine five fiscal policy actions that took place in the last thirty years to illustrate the political and economic processes at work in discretionary fiscal policy.

THE KENNEDY TAX CUT

The most famous act of discretionary fiscal policy was the 1964 Kennedy tax cut. During the 1960 presidential campaign, Kennedy criticized the lack of active fiscal policy in the two recessions of the 1950s. Although the 5.4 percent unemployment rate and 2.2 percent economic growth rate for 1960 look good compared to current figures, they were worse than in earlier years. In terms of the Keynesian model, the economy was in equilibrium in 1960, but national income was below the full-employment level. There was a recessionary gap. President Kennedy proposed both a decrease in personal and corporate income taxes and an increase in government spending. The proposal was designed to cause an increase in all three domestic components of aggregate expenditure: consumption, investment, and government spending. Congress was slow to respond, but after Kennedy was assassinated, the tax cut passed in 1964.

Did the Kennedy tax cut work? From Table 4, you can see that the unemployment rate declined and the economic growth rate rose for several years after 1964. These statistics do not prove that discretionary fiscal policy was responsible for the rapid economic expansion between 1964 and 1968. However, Keynesian economists felt that in this case fiscal policy had worked as theory predicted. Other economists in the classical tradition were not so sure. They argued that the gains came primarily from the effects of tax reductions on aggregate supply by providing greater incentives to work, save, and invest.

THE JOHNSON TAX SURCHARGE

By 1966, as the unemployment rate continued to fall (Table 4), concern had shifted from slow growth and high unemployment to inflationary pressures and labor shortages. Spending for both the Vietnam War and President Johnson's War on Poverty provided more stimulus than the economy needed. The time had come for the first (and only) experiment in using contractionary fiscal policy to "put on the brakes"—to reduce the level of aggregate expenditure and the equilibrium level of income and output. **Contractionary fiscal policy** consists of decreases in government purchases, decreases in transfer payments, or increases in taxes in order to reduce the equilibrium level of output to one that can be produced with available resources.

Contractionary fiscal policy
Raising taxes, lowering transfer payments, or reducing government purchases in an attempt to reduce the equilibrium level of output to one that is attainable with available resources.

TABLE 4 UNEMPLOYMENT, ECONOMIC GROWTH, AND INFLATION IN THE UNITED STATES, 1959–1971

YEAR	UNEMPLOYMENT RATE	REAL GDP GROWTH RATE	INFLATION
1959	5.3%	5.8%	1.7%
1960	5.4	2.2	1.4
1961	6.5	2.6	0.7
1962	5.4	5.3	1.3
1963	5.5	4.1	1.6
1964	5.0	5.3	1.0
1965	4.4	5.8	1.9
1966	3.7	5.8	3.5
1967	3.7	2.9	3.0
1968	3.5	4.1	4.7
1969	3.4	2.4	6.2
1970	4.8	-0.3	5.6
1971	5.8	2.8	3.3

Source: Council of Economic Advisers, *Economic Report of the President* (Washington DC: U.S. Government Printing Office, various years).

The contractionary policy was a one-time 10 percent surcharge on income taxes (with an option to extend it to a second year). Policy makers expected the surcharge to dampen demand and reduce inflationary pressures. The tax surcharge was requested by the President in 1967 but was not passed by Congress until 1968. Unemployment rose, but the inflation rate did not fall. However, the policy involved only a temporary change rather than a sustained increase in taxes, and its impact was blunted by a monetary policy that was expansionary at the same time. Both of these facts make it difficult to assess whether or not contractionary policy can be effective.

THE FORD TAX REBATE

By the mid–1970s, the economy suffered from both high unemployment and high inflation. During the administration of President Ford, income tax changes were again used as expansionary policy, in the form of a $23 billion tax rebate in 1975. As the Ford tax rebate took effect, planned spending and aggregate demand increased, and the unemployment rate fell. By 1976, unemployment had fallen slightly, to below 8 percent from a high of over 9 percent in 1975. Once again, fiscal policy appeared to produce the intended results. However, the improvement was not enough to get Ford reelected! In fact, because of the temporary nature of the rebate, it had far less impact on income and employment than the Kennedy tax cut a decade earlier.

THE REAGAN TAX CUT

In 1981, President Reagan proposed and Congress passed a major tax cut. This tax cut was not billed as traditional Keynesian fiscal policy for three reasons. First, the Reagan tax cut, like the Ford tax rebate, came at a time when both unemployment and inflation were very high. Discretionary fiscal policy is designed to address either unemployment (expansionary policy) or inflation (contractionary policy), but not both. Second, the tax cut was accompanied by some modest spending cuts. For maximum impact, a Keynesian would generally recommend cutting taxes without cutting spending in order to combat unemployment. Third, the tax cut was designed so as to affect aggregate supply rather than aggregate demand. However, any tax cut, especially one that is larger than spending cuts, will also shift aggregate expenditure and aggregate demand. We can consider the Reagan tax cut from the perspective of expansionary fiscal policy and examine its effects on output and employment.

Personal taxes were cut by 25 percent over a three-year period, with the largest effects on disposable income from mid–1982 on. The main component of the business tax cut was accelerated depreciation for new business investment, which greatly shortened the time period over which new plant and equipment purchases could be depreciated for tax purposes. Most of the original business tax cut was later offset by increases in business taxes enacted in 1982 and 1986.

From a Keynesian standpoint, the timing of the tax cut was appropriate. It came in the midst of a major recession. Unemployment peaked in November of 1982 at 10.8 percent. At the bottom of the recession in late 1982, real GDP had fallen 3 percent from its previous peak in the third quarter of 1981. By mid–1984, unemployment had fallen to 7.2 percent, and real GDP had bounced back to 7.7 percent above the 1981 peak. From 1985 until the start of the recession in 1990, unemployment continued to decline, reaching a low of 5.3 percent. Real income also grew, although at a slower rate of about 2 to 4 percent. Thus, whether or not the Reagan administration considered its actions to be discretionary fiscal policy, the tax cut was successful by Keynesian standards in increasing output and employment.

THE BUSH-CLINTON TAX INCREASES

As the national debt grew and the annual budget deficit failed to decline, two tax increases and spending cuts were enacted to try to reduce the deficit. The first was the 1990 budget agreement, which occurred at the beginning of the 1990–1991 recession. The second was the Clinton deficit reduction program enacted in 1993, which also involved both tax increases and spending cuts. Neither of these actions was billed as contractionary fiscal policy, even though they look like such a policy in a Keynesian model. Both were aimed strictly at controlling the federal budget deficit, which did begin to decline in 1993—partly because of the 1990 budget agreement and partly because of improving economic conditions. Nevertheless, like the Reagan tax cut, they can be analyzed as if they were contractionary fiscal policy.

The agreement reached by Congress and President Bush in 1990 to raise taxes and reduce spending generated a great deal of controversy because President Bush was forced to give up his "no new taxes" pledge from the 1988 presidential campaign. Conservative critics, who are normally skeptical about the effectiveness of expansionary fiscal policy, blamed the 1990–1991 recession on the tax increase as contractionary fiscal policy. While the recession was already under way when the tax increase was passed, it may have had some impact on the weak recovery.

President Clinton was aware that his proposals to reduce the deficit with tax increases and spending cuts amounted to contractionary fiscal policy during a period of weak recovery when growth was slow and unemployment was still high. For that reason, at the beginning of his term in 1993, he proposed a modest ($16 billion) stimulus package (spending for roads, summer jobs for youth, and extended unemployment benefits) for the first six months of his term. This stimulus was to be followed by deficit reduction as the economy began to improve. As the economy appeared to be recovering in early 1993, Congress only approved about one-third of the stimulus program, but it did approve a substantial program of tax increases and spending cuts over a five year period. It is too early to assess the impact of this deficit reduction program on output, employment, and the price level.

LIMITATIONS OF FISCAL POLICY

Advocates of fiscal policy as a way to affect output and employment claim that government spending and taxes can be used to reduce, if not eliminate, the social costs of unemployment and inflation. Furthermore, increased government expenditures intended to close a recessionary gap can provide needed social goods, such as schools, parks, and highways. However, discretionary fiscal policy has been criticized since its beginnings in the 1930s. Some critics question its effectiveness. Other critics point to the use of fiscal policy for political gain, an increase in the size of government, and budget deficits and the national debt. Because deficits and the national debt have been a key issue for the last ten years and promise to continue to be at least until the end of the century, they are discussed separately in Chapter 10.

THE PERMANENT INCOME HYPOTHESIS

The centerpiece of the Keynesian model is the consumption function, $C = C_0 + bY_d$, which is the source of the expenditure multiplier, $1/(1-b)$ or $1/(1-\text{MPC})$. In order to increase the level of income and output, the government can cut taxes (raising Y_d directly) or increase government spending. The multiplier effect results in further rounds of consumption spending. If the consumption function is very stable, the value of the expenditure multiplier derived from the consumption function will also be stable.

One modification to the simple consumption function was developed by Franco Modigliani, who pointed out that the consumption behavior of individuals and households depends on where they are over their life cycles. Consumption behavior is very different for young families with small children, parents of teenagers and college students, and retired persons. Modigliani hypothesized that young families would dissave (borrow) to acquire their start-up capital of houses and cars while their current earnings were low but their potential future earnings were high. In the middle years of higher earnings, households would pay off debt and save for retirement. During retirement years, households would again become dissavers, drawing on their pool of accumulated savings as their consumption needs exceeded their income.

Modigliani's ideas were further developed into a critique of the multiplier analysis of fiscal policy by Nobel Prize winner Milton Friedman. This critique was based on Friedman's permanent income hypothesis. The **permanent income hypothesis** is the view that consumption does not depend on current income alone, but on past income and expected future income as well. Think about your own consumption. Today's spending is not based just on today's income. If you are paid every other week, you don't consume very heavily on payday and then not at all for the next thirteen days! Some people may come close to that pattern, but a household's consumption usually depends on its expected income over time. Friedman argues that consumption depends on permanent income, which consists of past, present, and expected future income.

Observations of how people act, as well as some more formal economic research, seems to support Friedman's idea. Seasonal workers, such as farmers and construction workers, may only work six to eight months a year, but consume at a fairly constant level throughout the year. Striking or laid-off workers can maintain their consumption if the strike or layoff doesn't last too long. If these households do not have enough liquid assets (cash or other assets easily turned into cash) or access to credit, they may have to cut back. But in general, Friedman argues, consumption is much more stable than actual current income because it is not based on that income alone.

Another way of understanding the permanent income hypothesis is to think about what you would do if you had less income for a short time. You would probably continue to pay those expenses that are fixed in the short run, such as house payments, car payments, and utility bills. You would still eat meals and put gas in the car but might give up seeing new movies and buying tapes or new clothes. You might cut back a little on food by eating out less, and spend less on recreation and other nonessentials. In the short run, you may have few options to cut spending. If your income fell permanently, however, you might decide to sell your house and car and move to smaller quarters or make other big changes in your consumption patterns. You might drop out of school, move out of an apartment and back home or into the dorm, or make other large adjustments.

It is more difficult to argue that individuals won't increase their consumption in response to a temporary increase in income. But people will usually increase consumption less with a temporary increase in income than with a permanent increase. Thus, the permanent income hypothesis seems to make good sense in terms of how people behave.

POLICY IMPLICATIONS. The permanent income hypothesis has some important implications for fiscal policy. If consumers fail to respond to a temporary increase in disposable income by spending a large fraction of it, then fiscal policy will have less effect on output. A temporary change in government spending or taxes will still have a first-round effect on output and employment, but subsequent (multiplier) changes in spending will be very small. Temporary changes in taxes or spending will have little impact on consumer spending, because a one-time tax cut or a one-year spending increase will affect permanent income much less than current income. For example, a person who expects to live twenty-five more years would not respond to a one-time tax cut of $1,000 as an increase in her permanent income of that amount. Ignoring interest, her permanent income increases by only $40 a year! Experience supports this view. The 1964 and 1981 income tax cuts, which were enacted as permanent changes, appear to have had more effect on income and consumption than the 1968 temporary surcharge or the 1975 one-time tax rebate.

Permanent income hypothesis
The view that consumption does not depend on current income alone, but on past income and expected future income as well.

PROBLEMS OF MEASUREMENT. The debate on the consumption function cannot be easily settled by statistical testing. In order to test whether the consumption function works better with current income than with permanent income, economists would have to be able to measure permanent income. A household's permanent income depends on both experience and expectations, which change over time. Economists have much more trouble trying to measure permanent income for the entire economy than for one household. They can only offer examples that suggest that temporary income changes have less effect on consumption than permanent income changes.

GOVERNMENT SPENDING

Public choice economics
A branch of economic theory that attempts to integrate economics and politics by examining the motives and rewards facing individuals in the public sector.

Public choice economics attempts to integrate politics and economics by examining the motives and rewards for different types of behavior in the public sector. Economists in this tradition argue that fiscal policy actions tend to increase the size of the government sector relative to the private sector. James Buchanan, a Nobel Prize winner, and his colleague Richard Wagner see rising deficits and resistance to collecting the taxes to pay for spending as logical outcomes of the U.S. political system. Buchanan and Wagner argue that policies that hurt a few citizens very intensely and benefit most others very slightly are not likely to be enacted, even if the total benefits exceed the costs. Conversely, it is politically easy to enact programs that benefit a few very greatly at a small cost to each taxpayer, even if total costs exceed total benefits.[1]

Spending programs benefit specific interest groups: defense firms, colleges, welfare clients, hospitals, farmers, or industries that would like to export more. For example, an export subsidy may be designed to benefit the aircraft industry or soybean farmers. Such a policy benefits workers and owners in those industries at the expense of domestic consumers of air travel or soybean products. The costs of many spending programs, such as farm price supports or cost overruns by defense contractors, are likewise borne by citizens in general as either higher current taxes, more inflation, or higher future taxes to finance deficits.

Recessions provide an excuse to fund such programs by borrowing rather than by raising taxes. When the recession ends, the program has acquired a constituency and cannot be axed. Over time, then, the government sector grows relative to the private sector.

Keynesian economists, including Nobel Prize winner James Tobin, tend to be less concerned about the growth of government. They argue that the large size of the government sector relative to the private sector is a force for stability. Investment and net exports are quite unstable, as are some components of consumption—especially consumer durables. Government purchases, however, are quite stable from one year to the next. The share of total output that is bought by or produced by government is much larger now than it was in Keynes's day. With this big, stable sector providing an anchor, the economy is less likely to drift into recession. These economists argue that the growing share of economic activity passing through government is the primary reason why there has not been another Great Depression.

---

1. James Buchanan and Richard E. Wagner, *Democracy in Deficit: The Political Legacy of Lord Keynes* (New York: W. W. Norton, 1977).

Most economists would agree that it is inefficient to make production decisions through government when there are no compelling reasons such as public goods or strong externalities. The market does a better job of allocating resources in response to consumer demand. Thus, if a larger share of economic activity in the public sector offers the benefit of greater stability, there will be a difficult trade-off between stability and efficiency.

POLICY FOCUS: THE COUNCIL OF ECONOMIC ADVISERS

At the end of World War II, political and business leaders feared that the transition from wartime to peacetime production would send the economy into another depression. In response to these concerns, Congress passed the Employment Act of 1946. The Employment Act of 1946 reflected Keynesian ideas about the role of discretionary fiscal policy in keeping the economy on a steady path. This legislation made the U.S. government responsible for achieving and maintaining full employment, steady growth, and stable prices through the use of fiscal (and monetary) policy. To provide policy-making advice, Congress created the three-member Council of Economic Advisers.

Officially, the Council's three members, appointed by the President, are the chief economic policy advisers. The functions of the Council are to advise the President on the course of the economy, and to participate in decision making on economic, budget, and financial policy (international as well as domestic).[a] The President is also required (with the aid of the Council) to prepare an annual economic report, the *Economic Report of the President*. This report, sent to Congress every January, describes the state of the economy and explains the administration's policy decisions.

Some presidents rely heavily on the Council for economic advice, while others depend more heavily on the Secretary of the Treasury or the Director of the Office of Management and Budget. When Kennedy undertook the tax cut that was the most significant fiscal policy action of his administration, he acted on the advice and counsel of the chair of his Council of Economic Advisers, Walter Heller. Heller represented the ascendant Keynesian views of the 1950s and 1960s. He believed that it was possible to target a particular combination of inflation and unemployment and structure expenditures, transfer payments, and taxes so as to achieve that target. He even gave this kind of policy a name: fine-tuning.

President Clinton appointed the first woman to head the Council, and only the second woman to serve as a member, Laura D'Andrea Tyson of the University of California at Berkeley. Tyson, who has a Ph.D. in economics from the Massachusetts Institute of Technology, was an unusual choice not only as the first female but also because her research work has been in areas other than macroeconomics. She is well known for her studies of Japanese industrial policy, which provides selective aid to high technology firms, and also for her studies of worker-managed firms in former Yugoslavia.

U.S. News and World Report describes the role of the Council in the Clinton administration as a "good government idea factory—looking for constructive ways to correct instances of market 'imperfections,' such as the lack of broadly affordable long-term care insurance for the elderly."[b] The new chair favors higher taxes on the wealthy to reduce the deficit and more investment in education, training, and research.[c] Tyson is also working on trade policy issues and reworking the government's economic statistics to make them more accurate measures of the state of the economy. Like most academic economists who have been chosen for this post, however, her most important job is a teacher with a class of one—the President. It's an opportunity most economists would love to have.

a. Murray Weidenbaum, "The Role of the Council of Economic Advisers," *Journal of Economic Education* (Summer 1988): 237–244; and Martin Feldstein, "How the CEA Advises Presidents," *Challenge* (November-December 1989): 51–55.
b. "Practicing What She Teaches," *U.S. News and World Report* (June 14, 1993): 75–76.
c. "Clintonomics is Looking a Lot Like Tysonomics," *Business Week* (May 24, 1993): 60–64.

INTERNATIONAL SPILLOVERS

An important limit to the effectiveness of fiscal policy is that much of the intended impact spills over to other nations. When Nation A increases its output level, its citizens demand more imports. Imports are a leakage. Every extra dollar spent on imports instead of domestic goods reduces the multiplier effects of expansionary fiscal policy. In small countries, such as Guyana, Chad, Luxembourg, or Belgium, trade is a large share of total spending. In these countries, most of the impact of fiscal policy may spill abroad. Even for a nation like the United States, where imports are only about 13 percent of GDP, international spillovers can weaken the impact of fiscal policy.

The situation of small countries is very similar to that of the individual states in the United States, which find little benefit in trying to pursue an expansionary fiscal policy. (The large and isolated state of Alaska did consider this option to address its local recession in the late 1980s.) If Minnesota runs a budget deficit to try to increase the state's output and employment, a large share of the multiplier effect will be felt in Wisconsin, North Dakota, and even as far away as New York and California—all places that supply a substantial amount of Minnesota's "imports."

Price level changes represent another challenge to expansionary fiscal policy in an open economy. Expansionary policy shifts AD to the right, driving up the price level. With higher domestic prices, citizens want to buy more cheap foreign goods, while foreigners are less interested in the nation's high-priced exports. The value of net exports $(X - M)$ falls. There are fewer injections (X) and more leakages (M). A higher price level does even more than a higher level of income to offset the initial expansionary effect of fiscal policy. Prices affect both exports and imports, but rising real income only affects imports.

What about contractionary fiscal policy? Falling income reduces imports, while a falling price level will stimulate exports and reduce imports. Again, the effect of being part of a global economy is to offset some of the contractionary impact of fiscal policy.

LAGS IN FISCAL POLICY

Recognition lag
The length of time it takes to determine that an economic problem exists.

Lags in making policy decisions provide another limitation on discretionary fiscal policy. The first lag is in identifying the problem. The **recognition lag** is the length of time required to become aware of, or recognize, an economic problem. Statistical measures (unemployment rate, CPI, and GDP) take from one to three months to compile. When these measures become available, they describe economic conditions for the previous month or previous quarter. These measures provide the basis for forecasting whether a recession will continue or end, whether unemployment will rise, fall, or remain the same, how fast output will grow, or what the rate of inflation will be. Such forecasts are difficult to make and prone to errors. An inaccurate forecast can result in the wrong fiscal policy.

Once a problem is recognized, more time passes as the President and Congress choose a fiscal policy solution and enact it into law. Policy makers must decide what kind of action to take—taxes, transfers, or government spending—and at what level. They must decide whose taxes to cut, what kinds of spending programs to undertake, and what section of the country should get the initial benefit. This **implementation lag** is the time it takes after a problem is recognized to choose and enact a fiscal policy in response.

After a fiscal policy has become law, further time passes before the economy improves. Tax changes can be implemented fairly quickly through payroll withholding, but most spending programs take time to design and carry out. Once the initial round of spending takes place, then the multiplier effects are felt over a period of eighteen to twenty-four months. The **impact lag** is the time that elapses between the implementation of a fiscal policy and its full effect on economic activity.

Taken together, the recognition, implementation, and impact lags add up to a long period of time. It is quite possible that the combined lags can take up so much time that the full impact of a tax cut or an increase in spending will not be felt until after the economy has begun to move out of the recession by itself. In Figure 3, the points labeled R, I_1, and I_2 are, respectively, the end points of the recognition, implementation, and impact lags. As you can see, the delays mean that the policy's effect on economic activity is not actually felt until the economy is well into the recovery phase. The dashed line from point I_2 shows what the path of economic activity is likely to be as a result of poorly timed discretionary policy. The expansionary fiscal policy intended to combat recession will simply fuel inflation. Similar mistiming on contractionary policy could aggravate a recession. Discretionary fiscal policy combined with lags can actually make an economy less stable.

THE POLITICAL BUSINESS CYCLE

Public choice economists have also suggested that fiscal policy combined with the American political system can create a political business cycle. In many other countries, the political system is parliamentary. The legislative branch and executive branch are united under a prime minister. In such systems the prime minister usually has some say about when elections are called, and campaigns are

Implementation lag
The time it takes after a problem is recognized to choose and enact a fiscal policy in response.

Impact lag
The time that elapses between implementation of a fiscal policy and its full effect on economic activity.

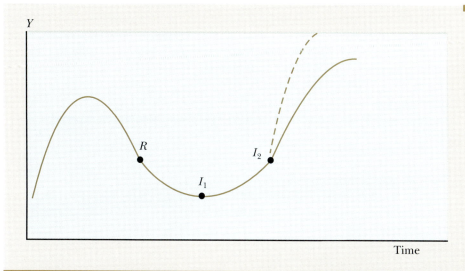

FIGURE 3
LAGS AND DESTABILIZING FISCAL POLICY
Recognition that the economy is in a recession occurs at point R. Fiscal policy is implemented at point I_1, and its impact on the economy is finally felt at point I_2. Because the expansionary policy was delayed, the economy takes on the course indicated by the dashed line rather than the solid line. Fiscal policy has made the economy less stable.

relatively brief. In the U.S. political system, however, there are only two years between elections. All members of the House of Representatives and one-third of the Senate are elected every two years, and presidents are elected every four years. Consequently, the next election is never very far from the mind of anyone in Congress or the White House.

The dominant party has a strong incentive to try to reduce unemployment and inflation so that economic conditions look good at the time of the next election. Such political maneuvers give the economy a series of short-run policies and rapid reversals to meet political needs, rather than a consistent pursuit of long-run policies. For example, the 1981 tax cut had its first substantial effect on withholding in 1982, a Congressional election year, and the final impact was felt in the 1984 presidential election year. In fact, it is hard to find a tax cut that took effect in an odd-numbered year or a tax increase that took effect in an even-numbered year!

Some economists have suggested that politicians may control the business cycle so that it peaks just before elections. This **political business cycle** results from the use of fiscal (and monetary) policy to influence the outcome of elections. A downturn can follow an election, as long as there is another peak, or at least an upturn, in time for the next election. According to this view, the level and timing of tax and spending changes (and, when the Federal Reserve is willing to cooperate, changes in the money supply) tend to respond less to changes in economic activity than to the timing of elections. Presidents Carter and Bush, however, can testify that they were not able to control the business cycle closely enough to ensure their own reelections. Both lost elections in part because of economic conditions in 1980 and 1992, respectively.

Economist Donald Hibbs offers evidence that favorable or unfavorable economic conditions at the time of an election have a definite effect on the success or failure of the incumbent party.[2] President Reagan saw his party lose many congressional seats in the recession-year election of 1982. Economic conditions had improved by the 1984 presidential election, no doubt contributing to Reagan's landslide reelection. As expansion continued to the end of the decade, low unemployment and only moderate inflation undoubtedly helped Reagan's Vice President, George Bush, win the 1988 election, but deteriorating economic conditions by 1992 played an important factor in his loss to President Clinton. Although economic conditions can influence political outcomes, thus far no economist has been able to show that politicians are actually able to create a political business cycle for their own benefit.

Political business cycle
A business cycle that results from the use of fiscal (or monetary) policy to influence the outcome of elections.

KEY IDEAS

PROBLEMS WITH FISCAL POLICY
- Instability of the multiplier
- Increase in the relative size of government
- Spillovers of impact of policy to other countries
- Lags (recognition, implementation, and impact)
- Political business cycles

---

2. Donald A. Hibbs, *American Political Economy* (Cambridge MA: Harvard University Press, 1988).

FISCAL POLICY, AGGREGATE DEMAND, AND THE PRICE LEVEL

The analysis of fiscal policy in this chapter has used the aggregate expenditure (Keynesian) model, with a fixed price level. When the price level can change, this simple Keynesian model needs to be blended with the aggregate supply and demand model.

Figure 4 shows how the slope of the AS curve affects the impact of expansionary fiscal policy. Expansionary fiscal policy shifts the AE curve upward for all price levels and thus shifts the AD curve to the right. Only the shifting of the AD curve is shown in Figure 4. If aggregate demand remains in the horizontal range of the AS curve (AD_1 and AD_2), all of the impact of expansionary policy falls on real output. A shift to AD_3 in the upward-sloping range of the AS curve means that expansionary policy will affect both real output and the price level. If the AD curve intersects AS in its vertical range, expansionary fiscal policy will only affect the price level. Because classical and new classical economists believe the AS curve is vertical, they would not expect fiscal policy to affect real output at all.

For most of this chapter (except for the Johnson surcharge), we have concentrated on expansionary fiscal policy. Higher taxes, lower transfers, or reduced government spending is contractionary fiscal policy. Such policy is rarely undertaken, usually only in response to severe inflation. Contractionary fiscal policy affects both real output and the price level. Which of the two is affected more depends on the range of the aggregate supply curve in which the economy is operating. Contractionary fiscal policy will have its main impact on the price level when equilibrium output exceeds Y^* on the AE diagram. This situation corresponds to aggregate demand curves AD_4 and AD_5 in Figure 4.

Three decades of largely expansionary fiscal actions, whether aimed at stimulating output or in response to other pressures, have resulted in a large budget deficit. This problem of fiscal policy is a major focus of public debate in the 1990s. The next chapter will complete our understanding of fiscal policy by considering the problem of deficits and debt.

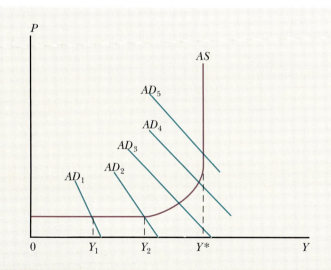

FIGURE 4
AGGREGATE DEMAND, AGGREGATE SUPPLY, AND FISCAL POLICY
Expansionary fiscal policy shifts aggregate demand to the right. A shift in aggregate demand from AD_1 to AD_2 will increase Y with no effect on P. At higher levels of output, shifts in AD will drive up the price level as well. Once real output reaches Y^*, further increases in AD will only increase the price level.

Consider again...*However President Reagan sold his program, it clearly fit the traditional model of Keynesian expansionary fiscal policy, with the expected results. Unemployment fell, and output expanded. However, the structure of his tax and spending cuts, combined with tight monetary policy, probably did help to reduce the inflation rate by shifting aggregate supply to the right. So both groups were correct. The policies shifted both aggregate demand and supply to the right. However, they also contributed to the growing budget deficit, the most hotly debated macroeconomic issue of the 1990s. We will address that issue in the next chapter.*

SUMMARY

1. Keynesian fiscal policy is based on three assumptions: (a) The economy can be in equilibrium with either high unemployment or inflation. (b) Changes in private or foreign-sector spending may result in an equilibrium that is not satisfactory. (c) Only the government can be counted on to change its spending and taxing to move the economy toward a more acceptable equilibrium. A recessionary gap occurs when aggregate expenditure is too low to purchase an economy's full-employment output. Fiscal policy can be used to close a recessionary gap.
2. An appropriate fiscal policy in a recession would be a reduction in taxes or an increase in government spending and transfer payments. An appropriate fiscal policy in an economy with low unemployment and high inflation would be the opposite. A careful design of the mix of changes in taxes and spending can also shift aggregate supply to the right.
3. Automatic stabilizers reduce fluctuations in economic activity without requiring legislation. Discretionary fiscal policy requires deliberate action by the executive branch or by Congress.
4. Major examples of discretionary fiscal policy in the United States were the Kennedy tax cut, the Ford tax rebate, and the Johnson tax surcharge. The Reagan tax cut and the Bush and Clinton deficit reduction actions can also be analyzed as discretionary fiscal policy.
5. The permanent income hypothesis says that consumption is based on permanent income and income expectations, not just current income. By this hypothesis, the Keynesian expenditure multiplier is unstable and fiscal policy is less effective. Public choice economists argue that active fiscal policy leads to inefficiency because it results in a larger public sector and creates an opportunity for political business cycles. International spillovers reduce the domestic impact of fiscal policy. Discretionary fiscal policy is also limited by lags in recognition, implementation, and impact.

NEW TERMS

fiscal policy
recessionary gap
income gap
expansionary fiscal policy
automatic stabilizers

regressive tax
proportional tax
progressive tax
discretionary fiscal policy

contractionary fiscal policy
permanent income
  hypothesis
public choice economics

recognition lag
implementation lag
impact lag
political business cycle

QUESTIONS: REVIEW, APPLICATIONS, AND POLICY

REVIEW

1. Why did Keynes not expect the private sector to offer much help in stabilizing economic activity?
2. What are the costs and benefits of having a larger government sector and a smaller private sector?
3. How does the permanent income hypothesis challenge the effectiveness of fiscal policy?
4. Why is fiscal policy less effective in an economy with a large foreign sector?
5. Why does a tax cut have less effect on the level of income and output than an equal change in government spending? What about a change in transfer payments?
6. Do you think that economists who adhere to classical macroeconomic theory would recommend the use of fiscal policy to eliminate a recessionary gap? Why or why not?
7. How would you identify a political business cycle?
8. Under what conditions will expansionary fiscal policy be inflationary?

APPLICATIONS

9. Suppose MPC = 0.9, C_0 = $300 billion, and I, G, T, and $(X - M)$ are each equal to $100 billion. What are the equilibrium values of Y, C, and S?
10. If G in Question 9 rises to $150 billion, *ceteris paribus*, by how much will the equilibrium levels of Y, C, and S change? What would happen to the equilibrium levels of Y, C, and S if T were reduced by $50 billion, *ceteris paribus*?
11. Use the information in Question 9, and suppose Y^* is $5,600 billion. By how much would G have to change to bring the economy to full employment? By how much would T have to change?
12. According to the permanent income hypothesis, which of the following would have the greatest effect on your consumption? Why?
    a. a Christmas bonus
    b. a promotion
    c. a six-week layoff
    d. getting married to someone who is also employed
13. Classify each of the following as a recognition, implementation, or impact lag:
    a. The numbers on GDP are slow in arriving from the Department of Commerce.
    b. Congress takes a recess to think things over.
    c. A new spending program has finally been put in place, and the dollars are starting to trickle through the economy.

POLICY

14. If the United States changed its political system so that elections were held less often and called by the President at a time that he or she chose, how do you think macroeconomic policy would be affected?
15. Why are economists concerned about the lags associated with fiscal policy actions? What solutions can you suggest?
16. Using the latest issue of the *Economic Report of the President*, list the rates of unemployment, inflation, and real output growth since 1981, the year of the Reagan tax cut. What conclusions can you draw about possible effects of that tax cut as expansionary fiscal policy?

SUGGESTIONS FOR FURTHER READING

Blinder, Alan. *Hard Heads, Soft Hearts*. New York: Addison-Wesley, 1987. Blinder looks at fiscal policy from a perspective of efficiency and incentives (hard heads) as well as equity in distribution of the benefits and burdens (soft hearts).

Council of Economic Advisers. *The Economic Report of the President*. Washington DC: U.S. Government Printing Office, annually. Gives a summary and explanation of fiscal actions on an annual basis.

Federal Reserve Bank of Chicago. *Economic Perspectives*. This quarterly publication, as well as those of the other Federal Reserve banks, follows developments in fiscal policy closely and relates developments to regional economic activity.

Stein, Herbert. *Presidential Economics: The Making of Economic Policy From Roosevelt to Reagan and Beyond*. New York: Simon & Schuster, 1985. A well-written account of the ins and outs of fiscal policy in practice, with thorough coverage of its weaknesses and limitations, by an economist who was a Washington insider for several decades. More recently, Stein has also written *Governing the $5 Trillion Economy* (Oxford and New York: Oxford University Press, 1989).

CHAPTER 10
BUDGET DEFICITS AND THE NATIONAL DEBT

Consider this... *Presidential election campaigns offer a chance to debate economic policy, especially macroeconomic policy. The 1992 presidential election campaign offered an exceptional opportunity because of both the recession and the deficit. Traditionally, the incumbent President defends his policies and promises minor course corrections, while the challenger offers an alternative vision and a different course. This time, however, it was one of those rare three-candidate races, and the third candidate was more interested in the deficit than the recession. Ross Perot, the third-party candidate, forced both President Bush and his challenger, Governor Clinton, to shift their attention away from the recession and propose policies to deal with the deficit. Perot received 19 percent of the vote to Clinton's 43 percent and Bush's 38 percent, an exceptionally high figure for a third candidate. After the election, the issue, and Ross Perot, did not go away. Because of Perot's challenge and increasing concern over the deficit, President Clinton was forced to rethink his economic plan and put much stronger emphasis on the budget deficit.*

How did Perot manage to enlist such a following and get so many votes without the backing of a major party? Why did the deficit issue catch fire with the American people in 1992 when it hadn't really caught on as an issue before? And is it possible to cut the deficit without precipitating another recession? This chapter attempts to answer these questions.

LEARNING OBJECTIVES
1. Distinguish between a federal budget deficit and the national debt.
2. Explain the links between fiscal policy and the national debt, and why the national debt grew so rapidly during the 1980s.
3. Distinguish among the actual deficit, the structural deficit, and the cyclical deficit.
4. Discuss the pros and cons of running deficits and having a large national debt.
5. Explain why it is so difficult to reduce the deficit.

DEBT AND DEFICITS

Citizens, the media, and even politicians often get confused by the difference between the national debt, which is a stock concept, and a budget deficit, which

Deficit
The difference between the federal government's revenues and expenditures in a given year (the fiscal year), when the government spends more than it collects in taxes.

National debt
The total of all past budget deficits minus all past surpluses, or the net amount owed to bondholders by the federal government.

is a flow concept. A **deficit** is the amount by which the federal government's expenditures exceed its revenues in a given year (the fiscal year, which runs from October 1 to September 30). The **national debt** is the cumulative total of all past budget deficits minus all past surpluses. It is the amount owed to lenders by the federal government.

Deficits are nothing new. The United States began its history with a national debt. The Revolutionary War was financed by printing money—before there was a government with taxing power. One of the major problems facing the first Congress in 1789 was the retirement of $79 million in national debt, about two-thirds of it from the Revolutionary War. By the second term of President Andrew Jackson in the 1830s, the entire debt had been repaid.[1]

The U.S. government ran budget surpluses for much of the nineteenth century. However, both the Union and the Confederacy ran large deficits to finance the Civil War. Except for periods during the Civil War and World War I, federal budget deficits were quite small before the 1930s. In 1929, just before the Great Depression, the national debt stood at $16.9 billion, or about 16 percent of GDP. Comparing the size of the debt to the size of the economy by using the percent of GDP is more meaningful than just looking at the absolute value of the debt, because the capacity to repay the debt grows as the economy grows.

Three years into the Great Depression (1932), the federal budget had become unbalanced by a sharp drop in output, employment, and the price level. Both Herbert Hoover and Franklin Roosevelt ran for President in that year on a campaign promise to balance the budget. By 1939, at the outbreak of World War II, the national debt had nearly tripled to $48.2 billion, or 55 percent of GDP. World War II brought a large increase in output but an even larger increase in government borrowing. At the end of the war, the national debt stood at $260.1 billion, or 122 percent of GDP. The debt was reduced slightly in the next few years. Then it began to grow very slowly, much more slowly than GDP. By 1970, the national debt had risen to $380.9 billion. Because GDP had also grown, the national debt was only 38 percent of GDP.

DEFICIT GROWTH, 1970–1993

In the 1970s, the debt grew rapidly along with nominal GDP, so the ratio of debt to GDP was relatively stable. By 1980, the national debt held by the public stood at $908.5 billion, but had fallen to 34 percent of GDP. The 1980s saw a rapid rise in both the national debt and GDP. Between 1980 and 1993, the size of the national debt tripled, from less than $1 trillion to over $4 trillion, or 72 percent of GDP. The estimated 1993 debt held by the public was $3,247, or 55 percent of GDP, the highest ratio since just after World War II.

Table 1 shows the budget deficit and the gross national debt over the last two decades, with a few earlier years included to provide a benchmark. Note that the budget deficit does not fully account for the increase in the debt in most years, because some of the debt is sold to the Social Security system and other government agencies rather than the public and thus "washes out" in the com-

---

1. For a good survey of the history of U.S. debt and deficits, see Benjamin Friedman, *Day of Reckoning* (New York: Random House, 1988), Chapter 5.

TABLE 1 GROSS FEDERAL DEBT AND BUDGET DEFICITS FOR THE UNITED STATES, 1945–1993

YEAR	FEDERAL DEFICIT (BILLIONS OF DOLLARS)	NATIONAL DEBT (BILLIONS OF DOLLARS)	DEBT/GDP (%) NET
1945	$47.6	$260.1	$122.5%
1955	3.0	274.4	71.0
1965	1.4	322.3	35.9
1970	2.8	380.9	37.7
1971	23.0	408.2	37.2
1972	23.4	435.9	36.1
1973	14.9	466.3	34.6
1974	6.1	483.9	33.2
1975	53.2	541.9	34.2
1976	73.7	629.0	35.6
1977*	53.6	706.4	35.8
1978	59.2	776.6	34.8
1979	40.2	828.9	33.3
1980	73.8	908.5	33.5
1981	78.9	994.3	32.8
1982	127.9	1,136.8	36.1
1983	207.8	1,371.2	40.2
1984	185.3	1,564.1	41.4
1985	212.3	1,817.0	45.0
1986	221.2	2,120.1	49.7
1987	149.8	2,345.6	55.0
1988	155.2	2,600.8	53.1
1989	152.5	2,867.5	54.6
1990	221.4	3,206.3	58.1
1991	269.5	3,598.3	63.4
1992	290.4	4,001.9	67.0
1993	254.7	4,351.2	72.0

Source: Council of Economic Advisers, *Economic Report of the President* (Washington DC: U.S. Government Printing Office, 1994).
*The third quarter of 1977 (July–September) is included in the debt figure for the end of fiscal 1977, but this extra quarter is not reflected in the 1977 budget deficit. In 1977 the federal government changed its budget (fiscal) year from July 1–June 30 to October 1–September 30. Fiscal 1977 ended June 30, 1977. Fiscal 1978 ran from October 1, 1977 to September 30, 1978.

bined federal budget. Figure 1 plots national debt relative to GDP for the entire post-World War II period.

The current national debt actually understates the financial obligations of the U.S. government, because of other obligations besides debt repayment that could prove costly in the near future. The federal government has guaranteed not only the safety of deposits in federally insured banks but also mortgage loans, student loans, and other private sector borrowing. If default rates on loans or bank failures are higher than expected, these guarantees could represent a serious drain on the Treasury.

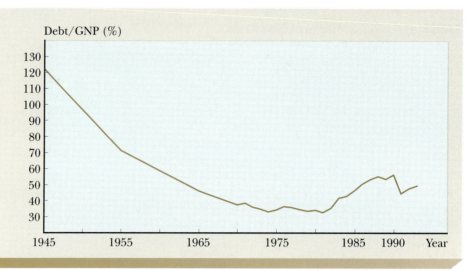

FIGURE 1
THE RATIO OF DEBT TO GDP, 1953–1993
After falling steadily until 1981, the ratio of debt to GDP climbed steadily through the 1980s before falling slightly in the early 1990s.

FISCAL POLICY AND DEFICITS

Critics of Keynesian fiscal policy claim that it is at least partly responsible for deficits in the federal budget and increases in the national debt. These economists might be less opposed to Keynesian fiscal policy if budget surpluses offset deficits over the long run. They point out that from 1950 through 1993, budget surpluses totaled less than $20 billion, and budget deficits totaled almost $5,000 billion. During what might be considered the heyday of Keynesian policy, the period from 1960 to 1980, the national debt tripled from $290.5 billion to $908.5 billion, even though the debt did decline as a share of GDP.

During the Great Depression, even before Keynes's *General Theory*, there was support for spending more on social projects during economic downturns and cutting back when the economy returned to full employment. However, it is politically very difficult to cut back spending or increase taxes during the expansionary phase of the business cycle. Thus, many economists fear that Keynesian policy provides a ready excuse for the long-run expansion of the relative size of the government sector.

Households and business firms are limited in their ability to spend more than their income for any length of time because of the threat of bankruptcy. Bankruptcy is a remote possibility for a central government. Sometimes local governments—cities, counties, school districts, and water systems—have been unable to pay the interest and principal on bonds and have filed for bankruptcy. The difference between a national government and a household, firm, or local government is the power to tax a broad range of persons in order to raise funds to pay off debts. For nations, any threat of bankruptcy comes from abroad. If a national government finances its spending through foreign loans, then it may be unable to come up with the "hard currency" (acceptable foreign currencies) to repay them. This kind of bankruptcy is not a serious concern for the United States at present, but it has been an important problem for a number of developing countries.

The deficits of the 1970s and 1980s are largely due to political decisions: the expansion of spending programs and several cuts in taxes. Once spending programs are created, they acquire clients and supporters. Thus, it is difficult to reduce or eliminate them. For example, it is difficult to close military bases because nearby towns will lose income and population. The uproar over base closings in 1993 made it clear that there is great resistance to such spending cuts. Social Security and Medicare, two of the fastest growing categories of federal spending, are politically untouchable. On the other hand, voting for higher taxes is also politically unpopular. President Clinton started out in 1993 with ambitious plans for raising taxes and cutting spending in order to reduce the deficit, but wound up with much smaller tax increases and spending cuts after his proposals went through the political process.

Recent budget deficits did not result primarily from discretionary fiscal policy actions to fight recessions, but rather from perennial political problems with raising taxes and cutting spending. The deficits and the debt are mainly the result of political decisions to spend more than the government takes in. Only a small portion of the current national debt is due to deficits incurred as a result of deliberate fiscal policy actions. Furthermore, most Keynesians argue strongly that the benefits of active fiscal policy (increased employment and economic growth) more than offset the costs (budget deficits). The problem is that many politicians have used Keynesian arguments to avoid making difficult budget decisions. Keynes may have created a politically acceptable excuse for increasing spending without raising taxes.

THE GROWTH OF THE NATIONAL DEBT SINCE 1980

Between 1980 and 1993, budget deficits grew steadily in dollar terms, and the size of the national debt tripled. The most striking change, however, was in the ratio of debt to GDP, as shown in Table 1 and Figure 1. That ratio reached a ten-year low in 1981 at 32.8 percent, only to shoot up to 72 percent in 1993. The current intense concern about the deficits and debt is not based only on the fact that both are large and growing. More serious is the unpleasant reality that both have risen much more rapidly than total output in recent years.

GLOBAL OUTLOOK: CANADA'S DEBT AND DEFICITS

Americans may take comfort that their national debt is not the only one that has been growing at a rate comparable to those of some less developed nations. Our neighbor to the north has an even worse record. Canada ranks 40th among 174 countries surveyed by the World Bank in the ratio of government debt (federal, provincial, and local) to GDP, currently about 85 percent. While the 1993 deficit of $60 billion may look small by U.S. standards, Canada is a much smaller country, with a GDP only about 10 percent that of the United States. A much larger share of Canada's debt is held externally. One-third of Canada's debt is held by foreigners.[a]

How did Canada get so deeply in debt? Some of the debt was incurred to build infrastructure, particularly transportation, which is an important asset in a country that covers so much land area. Canada has also had a long spell of high unemployment and sluggish growth alternating with recession. The Canada-United States free trade area, which was initiated in 1988, has cut into manufacturing in southern Canada as U.S. firms have moved back across the border when they no longer needed to be inside Canada to avoid trade barriers. While Canada's health care costs per capita are still low by U.S. standards, they have been rising rapidly, and in Canada the government shoulders the entire burden. All of these factors have led to a steady increase in the deficit. Canadian officials have been reluctant to take strong actions—tax increases, spending cuts—to reduce the deficit while the nation is still in recession, with unemployment still over 10 percent in 1993. There's some comfort in knowing that in our debt and deficit problems, the United States has plenty of company.

a. Peter C. Newman, "Our Place of Shame: Right behind Burundi," *McLean's* (July 5, 1993): 22.

REAGAN'S POLICIES AND THE DEFICIT

Most of the growth in deficits in the 1980s was not based on Keynesian theory or justified as expansionary fiscal policy. There are various ideas as to exactly what Reagan's advisers had in mind in 1981 when they proposed a 30 percent reduction in personal income taxes (and an even bigger cut in corporate profits taxes). The actual cut in personal income taxes was 25 percent. Some supply siders argued that the increased incentives to work, save, and invest would actually result in increased tax revenues. Although there may have been some supply side effects on tax revenue, they were not enough to offset the original tax cut. A second group (including David Stockman, Reagan's first director of the Office of Management and Budget) argued that the purpose of the tax cut was to cut off the revenue source that was feeding government spending. Lower revenues would force a reduction in spending and in the size of government. This expectation was not realized, as the budget kept spending high and simply accommodated lower revenues with a larger deficit. A third group claimed that the growth of the deficits was due not to the tax cut but to excessive spending, which they blamed on Congress. It is true that Congress generally did increase spending, but the budgets they received from the executive branch had large deficits when they arrived at Congress's doorstep.

A balanced view of the deficits of the early 1980s would suggest that they were the result of attempting the impossible—cutting taxes while increasing defense spending and failing to control growth of income transfers, especially Social Security and Medicare. Even attempts to reduce other categories of spending could not bridge the gap. In addition, there were two other contributing factors. One was the recession of 1980–1982, and the other was high interest rates.

THE 1980–1982 RECESSION

The United States entered a recession in 1980, with a sharp drop in GDP during the second quarter. The economy then rebounded, only to see a second sharp decline in output and a rise in unemployment in 1982. Real output fell by 2.5 percent in 1982, and unemployment rose to 9.5 percent in 1982, remaining at that level during 1983. During the recession, the automatic stabilizers did their job. Tax revenues fell even further than they would have with the tax cut alone, and payments for food stamps and unemployment compensation rose. Temporarily, the deficit increased more than it would have under more normal conditions. However, cyclical increases in the deficit are normally corrected by an ensuing expansion. Thus, the recession can only absorb a small part of the blame for the high deficits.

HIGH INTEREST RATES

A second factor contributing to the deficit problem was the fact that both nominal interest rates and real interest rates (nominal rates corrected for inflation) remained high throughout the early 1980s. From 1979 to 1983, the interest rate on a three-month Treasury bill (a very short-term, riskless investment) was over 10 percent. Although interest rates fell in the latter part of the 1980s, the T-bill rate was still higher than it had been for most of the preceding three decades. Interest rates were slow to fall even in nominal terms. In real terms, interest rates remained high until the 1990–1991 recession, when first short-term rates and then longer term rates finally began to decline.

When the government borrows money, it must pay interest. Interest must be paid not only on new debt (the deficit) but on all outstanding debt as well (the national debt). In 1980, net interest payments amounted to 8.9 percent of total federal spending. By 1991, interest payments had risen to 14.7 percent of spending. A combination of a larger debt and high interest rates accounted for the increase in the interest payments from $53 billion in 1980 to $195 billion in 1991. As interest rates fell, the share of the budget going to interest payments dropped a little to 14.1 percent in 1993, although total interest paid continued to rise. This large annual commitment of funds to interest payments makes it much harder for the President and Congress to cut spending.

EFFORTS TO REDUCE THE DEFICIT

The rapid growth of the national debt alarmed some politicians and created pressure for restricting Congress's unlimited ability to spend. After many years of proposing a balanced budget amendment to the Constitution, which would require a balanced budget on an annual basis, Congress passed the Gramm-Rudman-Hollings Act in 1985. This act set a timetable for reducing the deficit from over $200 billion in 1986 to zero in 1990. Targets were set for each year. Failure to meet the targets would automatically trigger painful across-the-board cuts in most federal spending programs. However, the President and Congress were required to meet the targets only in the projected budget (based on assumptions about economic conditions), not the actual budget.

The size of the deficits did decrease for several years, partly as a result of spending cuts and partly due to gradual increases in tax revenues from economic growth. Part of the deficit reduction consisted of accounting tricks, sales of assets, and increased revenues in the Social Security Trust Fund. On the other hand, the unexpectedly high cost of the savings and loan bailout offset some of the other forces working to reduce the deficit.

As deficits began to rise again, President Bush reached an agreement with Congress in 1990 to reduce the deficit with a combination of tax increases and caps on spending. However, the 1990–1991 recession and the huge cost of the savings and loan bailout sharply increased deficits in 1989 and afterwards. By 1992, the deficit had become a serious concern in the eyes of most voters, and was a central issue in the election campaign, largely because of Ross Perot. The outcome of that election campaign was the deficit reduction program of the Clinton administration, a combination of tax increases and spending cuts designed to reduce the deficit by $500 billion over a five-year period.

SHOULD THE BUDGET BE BALANCED?

The debate over balancing the budget arises from the conflicting needs for appropriate fiscal policy and some degree of budgetary control. This debate is far from new. Before Keynes, the conventional wisdom called for balancing the budget every year. An annually balanced budget would force Congress to collect taxes to pay for spending programs and thus restrict the growth of government. It would not allow the use of any kind of fiscal policy.

Some Keynesian economists suggested, instead, that the budget should be balanced over the course of the business cycle. Surpluses during the expansion phase of the business cycle would offset deficits incurred in the recession phase. A cyclically balanced budget was a nice idea in theory but hard to apply in practice. For example, a prolonged recession followed by a weak and brief expansion would generate a large deficit and then a small surplus. Other economists wanted to throw out the whole idea of balancing the budget and simply let a surplus or deficit emerge from the need to stabilize the economy. The problem with this approach was that it ignored the importance of putting some limits on government spending.

THE STRUCTURAL DEFICIT AND THE CYCLICAL DEFICIT

In the 1960s, a new goal was established to reflect the concern about balancing taxes with spending, the need for fiscal policy, and the role of the newly recognized automatic stabilizers. The goal that would balance these three conflicting views was a budget that would balance only if the economy was at the full-employment level of output (Y^*). The actual budget need not be balanced, but tax rates and transfer programs should be set so that the budget would be in deficit if the economy was in recession, balanced at full employment, and in surplus if the economy was trying to produce beyond capacity.

The actual deficit is a poor measure of fiscal policy because it reflects not only decisions about taxing and spending but also the state of the economy. If output (Y) falls far below the full-employment level (Y^*), progressive income taxes and transfer programs will create a deficit as tax revenues fall and transfer payments rise. This deficit is acceptable from a Keynesian standpoint because it helps to stabilize the level of income and output. But if the economy were producing at Y^*, even with no action by Congress, there might not be a deficit. What policy makers need to look at is not the actual deficit but what the deficit would be at Y^*.

Figure 2 shows the various levels of taxes (T) and spending (G) that a particular set of tax rates, transfer programs, and spending programs will generate at various national income (Y) levels. At an equilibrium level of income (Y_e = $2,500), the deficit is $70 billion. If the economy were at full employment (Y^* = $3,500), there would be a surplus of $25 billion.

The notion of a budget that balances at full employment gives policy makers both a goal to work toward and a measure of the direction of fiscal policy (whether it is contractionary or expansionary). Just because a deficit exists doesn't necessarily mean that the government is pursuing an expansionary fiscal policy. The President and Congress may even be pursuing a contractionary policy. The deficit may simply be the result of automatic stabilizers and recessionary conditions. When economists want to measure the direction of fiscal policy, they

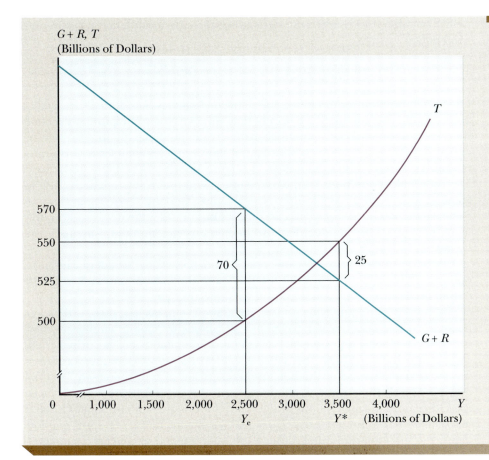

FIGURE 2
BALANCING THE BUDGET AT THE FULL EMPLOYMENT LEVEL
The budget surplus or deficit is equal to government purchases (G) plus transfer payments (R) minus taxes (T). When income rises, transfers fall and taxes rise. There is a surplus at the full-employment level of output ($Y^* = \$3,500$ billion) but a deficit at the current equilibrium income ($Y_e = \$2,500$ billion).

look at changes in the high-employment budget surplus or deficit rather than the actual deficit. The adoption of a high-employment balanced budget as a policy goal was a major victory for Keynesian ideas.

Two new terms were created in the 1980s to distinguish between the part of a deficit related to a downturn of the economy and the part of a deficit that would persist even at full employment. The **structural deficit** is the part of a deficit that would persist even if the economy were at the full-employment level. A structural deficit of zero would reflect the goal of policy makers in the 1960s and 1970s, and suggest that fiscal policy is neutral. A deficit greater than zero would imply the the direction of fiscal policy is expansionary, while a deficit less than zero would imply that fiscal policy is contractionary. The **cyclical deficit** is that part of a deficit that is due to a downturn in economic activity.

Both these concepts take their meaning from the comparison of potential output to actual output. **Potential output** is another name for the output the economy could produce if all its resources were fully employed. Potential output is thus a number or range of numbers that corresponds to the full-employment level of output (Y^*) from the aggregate supply and demand and Keynesian models. If the structural deficit is zero, then all of the budget deficit is due to the economy falling short of its potential—that is, there are many idle resources. With unemployment hovering around 7 percent in 1993, the cyclical

Structural deficit
The part of a deficit that would persist even if the economy were at the full-employment level of output.

Cyclical deficit
The part of a deficit that is due to a downturn in economic activity.

Potential output
The output an economy could produce if all of its resources were fully employed.

deficit accounted for part of the deficit, but the structural deficit was still over $150 billion in 1993.

THE PROJECTED DEFICIT AND THE ACTUAL DEFICIT

One of the problems with taming the deficit is that its size is difficult to predict and control. The automatic stabilizers that appear to be so helpful in directing the economy toward a more stable path create problems in forecasting the deficit. When Congress enacts a budget, it does not legislate a level of revenue but rather a tax structure that will yield varying amounts of revenue under varying economic conditions. Similarly, entitlement programs such as Aid to Families with Dependent Children, food stamps, veterans' benefits, and Social Security are budgeted not as precise dollar sums but as estimates based on how many people will be eligible. If more people are eligible than estimated, the deficit will be larger than expected.

To make budget proposals look rosier, Congress or the President can make optimistic assumptions about the levels of output, employment, and prices. If output grows rapidly and unemployment is low, then tax revenues will be higher and transfer programs will cost less. If inflation remains low, there will be less pressure to increase transfer payments or salaries for public employees, and smaller cost-of-living adjustments for federal retirees and Social Security beneficiaries. Inflation also affects the revenue side. With low inflation rates, taxpayers do not find themselves in higher tax brackets because of increased nominal income. For all these reasons, the budget surplus or deficit projected by both the Office of Management and Budget and the Congressional Budget Office is likely to be very different from the actual surplus or deficit. Output, employment, and inflation rates often differ from what the budget makers assumed.

Another source of error in estimating the deficit is changes in interest rates. With interest payments on the national debt accounting for about 14 percent of federal spending, market interest rates have an important influence on the spending side of the budget. When the Treasury has to sell newly issued bonds, interest rates that are higher than expected will add to the deficit, and lower than expected rates will reduce it.

Long-range projections of the deficit are even more prone to error. They must anticipate changes in output, exchange rates, labor force participation, investment, productivity, and other determinants of government revenues and expenditures. Forecasts of declining deficits in the late 1980s did not anticipate how expensive it would be to bail out failed savings and loans, a major drain on the federal budget in recent years. By 1989, some economists were projecting that, in the absence of a recession, the budget deficit would gradually decline if the President and Congress held firm on new spending programs while tax revenues continued to rise with economic growth. The combination of a recession and the unexpectedly large cost of the savings and loan bailout made their predictions far off the mark.

Political factors play a role in forecasts as well. For most of the 1980s, the executive branch (home of the Council of Economic Advisers (CEA)) was under the control of one political party, while Congress (home of the Congressional Budget Office (CBO)) had a majority from the other. The forecasts by the CEA were often more optimistic than those of the CBO. The CEA projected higher real growth and lower unemployment. (However, a careful comparison to private forecasts shows that, while both the CEA's and the CBO's forecasts are prone to error, neither shows any permanent bias toward erring on the side of optimism or pessimism.[2]) In 1993, President Clinton tried to overcome this problem by basing his budget projections on the CBO's more conservative assumptions about growth and employment.

Balancing fiscal policy with controlling the size of the public sector and limiting the size of the deficit is a tough political task. It is made much more difficult by the fact that the actual deficit is not known until after the fiscal year is over. Obviously, there is a political incentive for the administration to use clever accounting to conceal or reduce the apparent size of the deficit. Presenting the actual deficit as well as the budget in such a way as to make the deficit look smaller is an old practice. Beginning in 1967, the Johnson administration changed the way the budget was presented to a unified format that included Social Security revenues and expenditures. This change was made at least partly to gloss over the deficit by making it appear smaller. When the President and Congress came up with the savings and loan bailout plan in 1989, they put large parts of it "off budget." That is, the bailout was financed largely outside the regular budget and not counted in the deficit. When the government sells assets, as it did often in the late 1980s in an effort to at least approach the Gramm-Rudman-Hollings targets for deficit reduction, the proceeds help to reduce the deficit, but only in the current year.

SOCIAL SECURITY AND THE DEFICIT

The federal budget deficits peaked in 1986, then declined steadily in nominal terms before rising again in the early 1990s. A large part of the improvement in 1986–1989 was due not to direct Congressional action or better economic conditions, but rather to reforms in the Social Security system that were enacted in 1983. Noting that there would have to be increased outlays in the period after the year 2000, as the baby boomers began to reach retirement age, a special presidential commission proposed increasing Social Security taxes to build up a surplus in the Social Security Trust Fund. Since Social Security taxes are collected and benefits are paid out by the federal government, the taxes appear as revenue and the benefits as expenditures in the combined federal budget. Technically, Social Security funds are separate, but the reported overall budget deficit or surplus has included these funds since 1967. As a result, a large part of the debt is not held by the public. In 1993, of the gross federal debt of $4,351 billion, only $3,472 billion (75 percent) was held by the public. The rest was held by federal agencies, chiefly the Social Security Trust Fund.

When the Social Security Trust Fund runs a surplus, those funds are invested in federal government bonds until they are needed to pay benefits. What will happen when the baby boomers start to retire? In theory, other taxes will be increased or other spending decreased in order to provide the revenue to retire those bonds and pay the benefits. In other words, Social Security revenues are being used to finance a part of the regular budget deficit. There will have to be future budget surpluses to repay the "loan" from the Social Security Trust Fund.

---

2. Michael T. Belongia, "Are Economic Forecasts by Government Agencies Biased? Accurate?" *Review*, Federal Reserve Bank of St. Louis (November/December 1988): 15–23.

TABLE 2 FEDERAL REVENUES, EXPENDITURES, AND DEFICITS WITH AND WITHOUT SOCIAL SECURITY FOR FISCAL YEARS 1980–1993 (BILLIONS OF DOLLARS)

YEAR	FEDERAL REVENUES		FEDERAL EXPENDITURES		FEDERAL DEFICIT	
	WITH SS	WITHOUT SS	WITH SS	WITHOUT SS	WITH SS	WITHOUT SS
1980	$517.1	$359.3	$590.9	$240.8	$73.8	$118.5
1981	599.3	416.6	678.2	538.6	78.9	112.0
1982	617.8	416.3	745.7	589.7	127.9	173.4
1983	600.6	391.6	808.3	637.6	207.8	246.0
1984	666.5	427.1	851.8	673.6	185.3	246.5
1985	734.1	547.9	946.3	757.7	212.3	209.8
1986	769.1	485.2	990.3	791.5	221.2	306.3
1987	854.1	550.8	1,003.8	796.4	149.8	246.4
1988	900.0	574.7	1,064.1	844.7	155.2	270.0
1989	990.7	727.0	1,144.2	915.9	152.5	188.1
1990	1,031.3	749.6	1,252.7	1,007.7	221.4	258.1
1991	1,054.3	760.4	1,323.8	1,057.4	269.5	297.0
1992	1,091.6	789.2	1,381.8	1,094.3	290.2	305.1
1993	1,153.5	842.6	1,408.2	1,109.8	254.7	267.2

Source: Council of Economic Advisers, *Economic Report of the President* (Washington DC: U.S. Government Printing Office, 1994).

There are other special funds and off-budget categories, but Social Security is by far the largest. Table 2 shows federal revenues, expenditures, and deficits, with and without Social Security, from 1980 to 1993. As you can see, the apparent reduction in the deficit in 1987 and 1988 was partly due to increased net revenues in the Social Security system. Social Security revenues were increasing more rapidly than other federal revenues, while Social Security expenditures were rising more slowly. Since 1990, the gap between the two deficits (with and without Social Security) has become smaller, but including Social Security in the total budget does tend to mask the size of the gap between discretionary revenues and discretionary expenditures.[3]

The Social Security Trust Fund represents a real policy challenge. The balance in the fund is projected to rise by a large amount in the next thirty years, then drop sharply until about 2050. One option for public policy is to ignore these changes in Social Security revenue and expenditures and balance the rest of the budget. This policy would call for severe cuts in spending or increases in other taxes until about 2020—a contractionary fiscal policy. Another option, more or less the one that has been pursued for the last twenty-five years, is to treat the federal budget as a single entity. Thus, current Social Security revenues are used to offset deficits in the rest of the budget. In terms of the current

---

3. The relationship between Social Security and the deficit is a politically controversial issue. For two views on this issue, see Lee Smith, "Trim that Social Security Surplus," *Fortune* (August 29, 1988): 84–89; and Alan S. Blinder, "Congress Should Keep its Hand off this Nest Egg," *Business Week* (July 4, 1988): 20.

impact of federal spending and taxing on the economy, this approach makes a great deal of sense. But unlike other revenues, Social Security revenues carry a deferred commitment to pay benefits. Paying those benefits (by repaying the Trust Fund) will require higher taxes or less spending for other purposes in the future.

DO DEFICITS MATTER?

It is difficult to convince citizens that the deficit impacts on them directly. Its effects are slow and insidious, while the impact of tax increases or spending cuts is immediate and painful. One major advantage of being able to run deficits is that they make it possible to use fiscal policy in order to stabilize the level of output and unemployment. However, there are costs associated with running deficits. A number of problems have been attributed to deficits and the growing national debt. Are deficits a problem? Economists differ on this question.

YES: THE GROWTH OF THE PUBLIC SECTOR

When deficits are not controlled, there is no constraint on the size of the public sector. If the government had to finance all its spending out of tax revenues, it would have to weigh the pleasure citizens derive from spending programs against their pain in paying taxes. The necessity to tax would be a constraint on spending. With deficits, legislators can adopt a "spend now, pay later" approach. And "later" is likely to be after they have left office. When the cost of spending programs is not immediately apparent as higher taxes, both legislators and citizens may underestimate the cost of government programs. The expansion of government programs may then take too large a share of total resources. Being able to spend without taxing, at least in the short run, means that added spending has zero opportunity cost for politicians.

YES: HIGHER INTEREST RATES AND INTEREST PAYMENTS

When the government runs a deficit, it borrows by issuing bonds, just as corporations do. In selling bonds, the government competes for funds in the credit market, driving up interest rates for all borrowers. The real interest rate measures the actual cost of repaying a loan in dollars at the time the loan is repaid. The real interest rate is the market interest rate minus the expected rate of inflation. Through the 1980s, this rate remained high relative to the past.

The large deficits of recent years have made many economists concerned that competition from the federal government in the credit market and the resulting high real interest rates (interest rates adjusted for inflation) have discouraged borrowing for private investment. This effect is known as **crowding out**. In fact, high interest rates attracted foreign funds to the United States until the early 1990s, which limited the crowding out of private investment.

High interest rates, especially in the early 1980s, also increased the fraction of federal spending going to interest payments on the national debt from 8.9 percent in 1980 to 14.1 percent in 1993. With more and more funds diverted to interest payments, Congress has less choice about the use of funds or about budget cutting. Cutting the size of the deficit in any given year has almost no impact

Crowding out
The negative effect on borrowing for private investment due to competition from the federal government in the credit market.

on the interest liability. Only surpluses that actually reduce the debt and/or lower interest rates can reduce this large piece of the budget. In the early 1990s, as interest rates finally began to decline during the recession, the federal government saw some slowing in the growth of interest costs.[4]

POLICY FOCUS: CROWDING OUT WITHIN THE BUDGET

A group of U.S. economists told a Joint Economic Committee hearing in 1989 that the budget deficit was causing a reduction in public investment in two areas critical to the nation's future. Those two areas were physical infrastructure and children. They named this failure to invest the "third deficit." This viewpoint became a cornerstone of the Democratic platform in the 1992 election.

During the 1980s, budget makers had to hold the line on nondefense spending because of a political commitment to higher defense spending without any increase in taxes. As a result, funding for existing nondefense programs was scarce, and that for new programs almost nonexistent. These economists argued that failure to spend in certain key areas could have a long-term impact on productivity and economic growth. One group of neglected expenditures, in their view, includes spending for highways, bridges, mass transit, airports, water supply, and waste disposal. All of these facilities are important to industry as well as to households. The other area of concern to these economists is investment in education for low-income children and youth. Not enough is being done in teaching basic skills, dropout prevention, and job training.

Total government spending just about doubled (without adjusting for inflation) between 1981 and 1992. Spending on the areas identified by the concerned economists grew much more slowly. Their first area of concern fits into the budget category of transportation and community and regional development. Their second concern matches with the budget heading of education, training, employment, and social services. These two categories have fallen from 10 percent to 6.2 percent of the budget between 1981 and 1992. Spending in these categories grew by only 27 percent. Since the price level rose by 56 percent during the same time period, this small nominal increase translates into a substantial decrease after correcting for inflation.

The debate on the "third deficit" highlights two important aspects of the budget. The first is that the budget is an expression of priorities and values as well as a fiscal policy tool. In the 1980s, there appeared to be a strong consensus for lower taxes and more defense spending. Cuts had to come from somewhere. Some of the trade-off has clearly come out of the kinds of nondefense spending that this group of economists has identified. The second is that crowding out occurs within the budget as well as between public and private spending. Rising interest payments on the national debt had to be met. Those interest payments were rising both because the debt was larger and because interest rates were higher than normal, reflecting the impact of increased government borrowing. As more of the budget went to interest payments, Congress was forced to limit spending in the few discretionary areas available.

YES: THE TRADE DEFICIT

The budget deficit is also blamed for a higher trade deficit, which means an excess of imports over exports in the balance of payments. A trade deficit means that Americans bought more currently produced goods and services from foreigners than they sold to the rest of the world. A trade deficit also means that

---

4. See *Federal Debt and Interest Costs: A CBO Study,* Congressional Budget Office (Washington DC: U.S. Government Printing Office, May 1993).

net exports are negative, depressing aggregate expenditures and aggregate demand, so that output, employment, and prices are lower than they would otherwise be.

Both the balance of trade and the current account have been mostly in deficit since the early 1970s. The deficits were modest at first, and there were a few surplus years. The current account was in surplus in six of the eleven years from 1971 to 1981. The main reason for these surpluses was the fact that Americans received more interest and dividend payments from the rest of the world than U.S. firms and government paid to foreigners. The balance of trade took a big turn for the worse in the late 1970s, mostly due to higher prices for imported oil. From 1980 to 1987, the balance of trade deficit rose from $25 billion to $160 billion before declining to $96 billion in 1992. The current account balance shifted from a modest $2.3 billion surplus in 1980 to a $167 billion deficit in 1987. Except for 1991, when payments from allies in the Gulf War helped the current account, these deficits have remained high into the 1990s.

Are the two deficits related? Some economists argue that they are. If the budget deficit drives up interest rates, funds will be attracted from abroad to earn high interest. The inflow of funds will cause a demand for U.S. dollars to invest in the United States, driving up the price of the dollar. A high price for the dollar makes exports more expensive and imports cheaper. Thus, interest rates provide a link between the budget deficit and the trade deficit. Lower interest rates in the United States in the 1990s, combined with higher interest rates in Europe and elsewhere, have combined to improve the trade balance somewhat in the 1990s. As long as the deficit is high, however, we can expect a link between deficits, interest rates, and imports and exports.

KEY IDEAS

THE COSTS OF THE NATIONAL DEBT
- The private sector output given up at the time the debt was incurred
- Lack of constraint on the growth of the public sector
- Higher interest rates that discourage private investment, reduce the future capital stock, and indirectly discourage exports
- Future repayment of debt held by foreigners
- Income redistribution when the debt is repaid

MAYBE: A BURDEN ON OUR GRANDCHILDREN?

The burden of the debt usually means the problems that will arise when it is repaid. President Eisenhower was the first to worry publicly about passing a burden of debt to our grandchildren. Often the size of the national debt is given per person. People who worry about the burden of the debt on the next generation point out that every child born today assumes a national debt burden of more than $11,000.

How valid is this concern? Does a free-spending generation pass on a heavy burden to the next? Not necessarily. Basically, the burden of the national debt falls on the generation in which the debt is incurred. These people are the ones who give up consumption in order to make resources available for government spending. Deficit financing of government spending, just like taxation, takes resources away from the private sector and transfers them to the government. The loss of current consumption is borne by the generation that lent to the government, not their grandchildren. During World War II, the government ran large deficits to finance the war effort. The cost was borne by those who were working, paying taxes, and buying war bonds between 1941 and 1945. They paid by consuming fewer goods and services, because the output mix was skewed toward military production.

Running deficits can create some future problems, however. If funds are borrowed by the government during a period when the economy is close to full employment, such as the last half of the 1980s, then resources may be diverted away from productive investment. As the government drives up interest rates in the credit market, some private borrowers who wanted funds to build housing, factories, and shopping centers are priced out of the credit market. (We will look more closely at the relationship between deficits, interest rates, and private investment in Chapter 13.) Thus, future generations may be worse off as a result of current borrowing, because of the productive capital that was not created during this period.

If the government borrows to expand the productive capacity of the economy and put idle resources to work, then future generations will inherit a larger capital stock and enjoy a higher output. They will benefit from the borrowing and spending activity that created the debt. When the time comes to repay the debt, it can be repaid more easily out of the higher national income that will result from the productive use of borrowed funds in an earlier time. Future generations can benefit from debt incurred through expansionary fiscal policy.

Sometimes the national debt is incurred in ways that benefit the next generation even if the spending is not for productive investments. For example, fighting World War II created benefits for the next generation in terms of the kind of world they inherited. If the government had not borrowed money to fight the war, you might not have been born into a democratic society.

When and if the government repays part of the debt, some citizens will be taxed to repay the maturing bonds owned by others. If most bond holders are rich, repaying the debt will mean some redistribution of income from the poor to the rich. In addition, if the government must cut spending programs in order to use tax revenues to repay the debt, the people who would benefit from those spending programs will essentially be "taxed" to pay back the debt.

Finally, Americans no longer simply owe the debt to themselves. High interest rates in the United States during most of the 1980s attracted foreign lenders. Many of them bought U.S. government bonds. About 20 percent of the national debt owed to individuals is owed to foreigners, mostly Japanese. Currently, about $35 billion in interest payments on the national debt is sent abroad. When those bonds are redeemed, the United States will have to transfer real goods and services away from domestic uses in order to pay back the bond holders. Repaying the debt to foreigners is a burden that will fall on future generations.

NO: RICARDIAN EQUIVALENCE

Economist Robert Barro has argued that the choice of deficit spending versus tax financing doesn't matter. According to Barro, rational consumers will recognize that debt financing simply means higher future taxes to pay off the debt. Thus, any increase in their current spending because of higher disposable income would be offset by a reduction in current spending because of anticipated lower future disposable income. That is, they will consume less and save more because of anticipated higher future taxes. This concept is called *Ricardian equivalence*.[5]

Few economists accept Barro's argument in its pure form, which implies that the impact of tax and debt financing is exactly the same. However, Barro does offer a useful insight: The difference in impact between different methods of government financing may be smaller than expected.

NO: THE REAL DEFICIT ARGUMENT

Another argument that minimizes the importance of deficits is the real deficit argument. Some economists, most notably Robert Eisner, claim that the deficit that matters is not the nominal deficit but the real deficit.[6] The **real deficit** measures the federal budget deficit as the change in the real (inflation-adjusted) value of the national debt from one year to the next. During a period of inflation, the real value of the debt falls. Thus, a budget deficit during an inflationary period could occur at the same time as a fall in the real value of the national debt. If the deficit is measured as the change in that real value, what was a deficit by usual measures might turn out to be a surplus!

This may sound like lying with statistics. We can make the argument more concrete with some numbers. Suppose the national debt at the beginning of a year is $200 billion, and the current-year deficit is $10 billion. Prices rise by 10 percent. The real deficit is equal to the change in the real value of the outstanding debt. At the end of the year, the $210 billion in debt (including $10 billion in new debt from the current deficit) is worth, in real terms, only $210 billion/1.10 = $190.9 billion. When the deficit of $10 billion is measured in real terms, it becomes a surplus of $9.1 billion!

Some of the deficits of the 1980s do look a little less frightening when measured either in real terms or as a fraction of GDP. The sleight-of-hand trick in the preceding paragraph cannot convert the deficits of the 1980s into surpluses, but it does bring them down to less alarming levels. However, no adjustments can change the fact that the deficit grew in the 1980s—in nominal terms, in real terms, and as a percentage of GDP. Furthermore, however the debt and deficits are measured, the basic problem remains. The ability to run unlimited deficits frees politicians from the need to raise the money in taxes for programs they want to fund. That political reality has contributed to the growth of government beyond what taxpayers might choose if they were paying the bill directly. In that sense, deficits are still a matter for concern.

NO: THE STATE AND LOCAL SURPLUS

The total impact of government taxes and spending on output involves the combined actions of all governments—federal, state, and local. Local governments usually come quite close to balancing their budgets. State governments rather

Real deficit
A measure of the federal budget deficit as the change in the real (inflation-adjusted) value of the national debt from one year to the next.

---

5. Robert Barro, "Are Government Bonds Net Wealth?," *Journal of Political Economy* (December 1974), 1094–1118; and "The Ricardian Approach to Budget Deficits," *Journal of Economic Perspectives* (Spring 1989): 37–54.
6. Robert Eisner, "Budget Deficits: Rhetoric and Reality," *Journal of Economic Perspectives* (Spring 1989): 73–93. Eisner also suggests a number of other adjustments of the deficit, such as separating out investment-type spending and not counting sales of governments assets.

consistently ran surpluses throughout the 1980s. From 1980 to 1990, these surpluses totaled $511.0 billion, or about 52 percent of the federal deficits during that period.

To some extent this argument mixes apples and oranges. State governments are quite different from the federal government. For one thing, states are much more limited in their ability to run long-term deficits. Many of them are constrained by their constitutions. Even those that do not have balanced budget requirements find their bonds harder to sell if they keep running deficits. Even if states could run deficits for long periods, there is no way to integrate those deficits into fiscal policy. Congress can influence state and local spending through changes in federal grants but cannot exercise any direct control over state and local budgets. As a tool of fiscal policy, only the federal budget is under the control of the policy makers.

Furthermore, the states' surpluses appear to have been temporary. The combined surpluses dropped from $38.4 billion in 1988 and $44.8 billion in 1989 to $30.1 billion in 1990, $17.1 billion in 1991, and $15.3 billion in 1992. A large part of the surpluses in earlier years was accounted for by contributions to state retirement systems. As state employees begin to retire in larger numbers in future years, those surpluses will shrink. Declining federal defense spending, especially base closings, has hit certain states hard. Falling incomes and declining property values in some states during the 1990–1991 recession turned budget surpluses into deficits and forced tax increases. In most states, there are increased pressures to build prisons, combat homelessness, take care of Medicaid patients, and replace parts of the infrastructure (especially roads and schools). These demands on the states, which have been receiving smaller and smaller amounts of federal aid, mean that their surpluses are projected to be smaller in the 1990s. State and local budget surpluses may help to mitigate federal deficits, but they seem likely to be of less help in the near future than they were in the last decade.

POLICIES TO REDUCE THE DEFICIT

There are no painless options to reduce the deficit. However, the deficit has begun to fall because of two circumstances not entirely under the control of policy makers. Low interest rates have reduced the amount of federal spending to pay interest on the national debt. Reduced international tensions have made it possible to cut defense spending. These two factors should help to reduce the deficit for the near future.

OBSTACLES TO DEFICIT REDUCTION

Two factors are pushing in the opposite direction. One is rising health care costs, especially for Medicaid and Medicare. No policy will be successful unless it can contain cost increases in health care, which continue to rise much faster than the general rate of inflation. Controlling health care costs will have to be part of any long-term deficit reduction plan.

The second is entitlements, particularly Social Security benefits, which have continued to increase as a share of the budget. During the 1993 budget debate, both parties shied away from controlling entitlements, but it is clear that this big budget item will have to be attacked.

THE POLITICS OF DEFICIT REDUCTION

Remember, the deficit can only be reduced if we raise taxes, cut spending, or some of each. Politicians prefer to wait for the deficit to go away, so that growth of revenues while holding the line on spending will gradually whittle the deficit down to size. That process is very slow and undependable.

Politically, raising taxes is very unpopular. In 1984, Democratic candidate Walter Mondale admitted that, if elected, he would raise taxes. He carried two states and the District of Columbia. In 1988, George Bush promised no new taxes. He was elected, agreed to raise taxes, and lost the election in 1992. Members of Congress face the same resistance in their districts. Even the modest 4.3 cent increase in gasoline taxes in 1993 generated great opposition.

Cutting spending sounds attractive until you try to find something to cut. Every program, every subsidy, every agency has a constituency—the employees, customers, and suppliers that depend on its survival for their economic futures. They contact their representatives in Congress, and members of Congress trade votes to protect programs in their districts by doing the same for each other. Even the cuts in defense spending, made possible by the end of the Cold War, have run into great resistance.

THE ECONOMY AND DEFICIT REDUCTION

In addition to the political economy of deficit reduction, there are at least two other important considerations. One is that the economy in 1993 was not very strong, and projections for growth to the end of the decade are not very promising. When the federal government makes massive shifts in spending from defense to other public uses, or just cuts programs, there is a lot of structural unemployment and temporary declines in output. Increases in taxes discourage certain kinds of economic activity, also reducing output and employment. Cutting the deficit is definitely contractionary fiscal policy, not necessarily the best choice in a weak economy. Out of a lower level of output, tax revenues will fall and transfer payments will rise as the automatic stabilizers kick in. Thus, the planned deficit reduction may be larger than the actual result, and the economy may suffer from slow growth and high unemployment.

On the bright side, success in deficit reduction combined with continued low inflation is likely to bring interest rates even lower, making it easier to borrow for cars, homes, and business investment. Lower interest rates will reduce the price of the dollar and stimulate export sales while curtailing import purchases. These effects may offset some of the negatives from contractionary fiscal policy.

Consider again...The choices facing the President and Congress in addressing the deficit are not very attractive. The deficit can only be reduced by cutting transfers, reducing federal spending, or increasing taxes—or some combination of the three. None of these choices are popular. Every program has a constituency, every military base has a community anxious to protect jobs and incomes, every tax has an army of opponents, and every transfer program from veterans' benefits to subsidies for mohair goat ranchers has people who count on that program to survive.

Looking at the overall effects of deficit reduction, it is easy to see why progress is slow and Congress is so resistant to change. If it weren't for Ross Perot and his followers insisting that the deficit must be addressed, the task might be even harder. Even without getting elected, Perot changed the political climate and priorities for the mid–1990s.

SUMMARY

1. The federal budget deficit, which is the difference between the current year's revenue and expenditures, has grown rapidly in the last decade. A brief reduction in the mid–1980s was followed by another upturn in the deficit. The national debt, or the sum total of past deficits and surpluses, is now about 74 percent of GDP.

2. Fiscal policy can lead to a larger national debt if deficits exceed surpluses. Most deficits are at least partly due to politicians' reluctance to raise taxes or cut spending. The growth of the national debt in the early 1980s was the result of the 1981 tax cut, increased defense spending, the 1981–1982 recession, and high interest rates. Efforts to control the deficit, such as the Gramm-Rudman-Hollings Act in 1985, have been relatively ineffective.

3. The actual deficit is the difference between current revenues and current spending. The actual deficit is difficult to control because it depends on economic conditions. In forecasting the expected deficit, politicians may use optimistic assumptions to make it look smaller. The structural deficit is that part of the deficit that would persist even at full employment, and exists because of the structure of tax rates, transfer programs, and spending commitments. The cyclical deficit is the part of the deficit due to economic conditions. The structural deficit is a measure of the direction of fiscal policy.

4. Deficits are a matter of concern because they may increase the size of government, drive up interest rates, and impose a burden on future generations because of lost productive investment and higher debt to foreigners. One argument that deficits do not matter is based on the idea of Ricardian equivalence—that people will save more in anticipation of higher future taxes. Another argument stresses the real deficit, or changes in the inflation-adjusted value of the debt. State and local surpluses also partly offset the federal deficit.

5. It is difficult to reduce the deficit because of opposition to new taxes and constituencies for agencies and programs that organize to protect their budgets. While lower interest rates and decreased defense spending will help hold down the deficit, rising entitlements (Social Security and Medicare) and slow economic growth work in the opposite direction.

NEW TERMS

deficit
national debt
structural deficit
cyclical deficit
potential output
crowding out
real deficit

QUESTIONS: REVIEW, APPLICATIONS, AND POLICY

REVIEW

1. What is the real deficit? What are the risks of using this measure instead of the nominal deficit?
2. Does Keynesian fiscal policy necessarily mean deficits?
3. Did the federal borrowing in the 1980s impose a burden on future generations? Why or why not? How was it different from federal borrowing during the 1930s?
4. What would happen to the real deficit if there was high inflation but no change in the nominal deficit?
5. Why does the actual deficit almost always turn out to be very different from the projected deficit?
6. What is a structural deficit? A cyclical deficit? Which is of greater concern?
7. Why is the structural deficit rather than the actual surplus or deficit used to determine the direction of fiscal policy?

APPLICATIONS

8. Suppose the consumption function is $C = \$300$ billion $+ 0.9Y_d$ and the values of I, G, and $(X - M)$ are each $\$100$ billion. Taxes (T) and transfer payments (TR) are dependent on the level of income according to $T = -\$40$ billion $+ 0.15Y$, and $TR = \$500$ billion $- 0.1Y$. Since you know that $Y_d = Y - T + TR$, the new consumption function is $C = \$300 + 0.9(Y + \$40 - 0.15Y + \$500 - 0.1Y)$, where all figures are in billions. Use this relationship to determine the equilibrium value of Y. What is the actual surplus or deficit in the government budget? If $Y^* = \$4,000$ billion, what is the high-employment surplus or deficit? Does this indicate that fiscal policy is expansionary or contractionary?
9. Given the following relationships, develop a table that shows the surplus or deficit in the government budget at Y values (in billions) of $\$500$, $\$1,000$, and $\$1,500$. At what level of Y will the government's budget balance?
   $G = \$150$
   $T = -\$25 + 0.2Y$
   $TR = \$125 - 0.1Y$

POLICY

10. Why do some politicians advocate balancing the budget on an annual basis? What problems would this policy create?
11. Why do some economists say the budget deficit should be measured as the combined federal, state, and local deficit? What problems would this create?
12. Suppose businesses in the United States adopt early retirement plans on a large scale. As a result, a much higher proportion of workers decide to retire at sixty-two (when they are first eligible for Social Security benefits) rather than at sixty-five. What would happen to the federal budget deficit?
13. Which measure of the deficit would you use for each of the following purposes?
    a. determining the direction of fiscal policy
    b. measuring the inflation-adjusted deficit
    c. estimating the deficit that would persist even at full employment
    d. determining the part of the deficit due to unfavorable economic conditions

SUGGESTIONS FOR FURTHER READING

Aaron, Henry J., Barry P. Bosworth, and Gary Burtless. *Can America Afford to Grow Old?* Washington, DC: Brookings Institution, 1989. A close look at the demographics, economics, and politics of the Social Security system.

Baker, Dean, and Todd Schafer. "Putting Deficit Reductions First?" *Challenge* (May–June 1993): 4–10. A critical look at Clinton's deficit reduction policies from the perspective of investment in infrastructure and human capital.

Friedman, Benjamin. *Day of Reckoning*. New York: Random House, 1988. A critical look at U.S. policies in the 1980s that led to the increase in federal budget deficits and an outline of policies to address those concerns in the 1990s.

Savage, James D. *Balanced Budget and American Politics*. Ithaca, NY: Cornell University Press, 1988. A historical and political look at the controversy over balancing the federal budget.

PART 4

MONEY, FINANCIAL MARKETS, AND MONETARY POLICY

The inner portion of the circular flow showed the money flows—the payments for goods and services and for the use of productive resources—in the economy. The expanded circular flow also included the credit market, where the savings of households are channeled into investment by business firms. In Part 3, we put the monetary side of the economy on hold while we explored some of the relationships among real variables. Now we need to complete the picture of the economy by bringing in money, the banking system, and financial markets. This side of the economy provides yet another tool with which to influence economic activity, monetary policy. Monetary and fiscal policy taken together represent the government's best possibility to influence output, employment, and the price level.

Chapter 11 starts by exploring money, what it consists of, why people hold it, and where it comes from. Chapter 12 expands on where money comes from by introducing the banking system and the central bank, the Federal Reserve, and how they work together to create money and control its supply. Chapter 13 puts banking in a context of a broader system of financial institutions and financial markets, including stock and bond markets, to look at what determines interest rates and investment decisions. Finally, Chapter 14 examines the theory and practice of monetary policy in the U.S. economy.

CHAPTER 11

THE ROLE OF MONEY IN A MARKET ECONOMY

LEARNING OBJECTIVES

1. Describe the three functions of money and the properties that money should have in order to perform those functions well.
2. Discuss the role of banks in the production of money and the main components of the U.S. money supply.
3. Explain why people hold money and how they decide how much money to hold.
4. Determine equilibrium in the money market.
5. Analyze the relationship between changes in the demand for and supply of money and aggregate demand.

Consider this... *Yap, one of the Caroline Islands, lies in the western Pacific Ocean, north of the equator and the island of New Guinea and east of the Philippines. The fame of Yap lies in its stone money, called* fei, *which are large, heavy wheel-shaped stones with holes in the center so that they can be carried on poles. Each stone is quite valuable. Together they represent most of the island's financial wealth.*

As you can imagine, the stones aren't used in everyday transactions. The usual currencies are tridacna shells, used for large transactions, and mother-of-pearl, used for smaller transactions. The stones are mainly used as a store of wealth rather than to settle accounts between buyers and sellers. The larger stones are well known, and possession can change hands without changing location. Indeed, even stones that are now under the sea (lost in shipment between islands) maintain their value, and their ownership can change. The stone on display in the Smithsonian Institution is probably still a part of Yap's money stock!

Who decides what is money, and what determines its value? Why do people hold money, and how do they decide how much they want to hold? Until now, we have focused on the real flows of goods and services in the circular flow diagram. However, the circular flow diagram also shows flows of money payments and even a credit market. Starting in this chapter, we will expand the model to include money, financial instruments, banks, and financial markets.

WHAT IS MONEY?

The word *money* means different things to different people. The variety of meanings often leads to misunderstandings between economists and noneconomists.

Here are some ways in which economists *don't* use the word money:

1. How much money (income) did you earn last year?
2. Most of his money (wealth) is tied up in bonds.
3. It's almost impossible to get mortgage money (loans) in today's market.
4. This country does not have enough money (productive resources) to increase both military and social spending.

Money is not income, wealth, loans, or productive resources, although it is sometimes confused with each of those. When economists use the word *money*, they usually mean items (cash and checking account balances) that are used to make purchases in a market economy. For example, "If I didn't keep some money on hand, I'd have to go to the bank every time I wanted to buy a candy bar."[1]

Let's start with a working definition: Money is something that people accept as payment for a good or service. Later, after looking at the properties of money, the functions of money, and the reasons for holding money, we will be able to give a more precise definition. This working definition draws attention to a basic requirement for anything that serves as money. It must be generally acceptable to those who are exchanging goods and services in markets.

If you go into a store and buy some socks or rent a video, chances are you pay with dollar bills, or Federal Reserve notes. Paper money has been used in the United States for nearly 300 years, since colonial times. The paper by itself is worth only a few cents, but you know you can exchange the bills for goods and services in stores, restaurants, and theaters. Other people are willing to accept these pieces of paper in trade for goods and services because they know they can, in turn, spend the money and pass it on to someone else. If you believed that no one would take the money, you wouldn't be interested in having it. If everyone thought the money was worthless, no one would take it. Then it really would be worthless because it couldn't be used to buy anything. Money has value because it is accepted as the means of exchange.

BARTER AND THE INVENTION OF MONEY

Your professors make a living by providing you with high-quality teaching services. They teach, not out of altruism, but because they want to get things in return, such as housing, food, books, and vacations. Professors, like other workers, sell their services in the resource market in order to make purchases in the goods market. And professors, like most people in modern industrial economies, specialize in producing just one or a few goods or services but want to purchase many different ones.

In societies that have only a few goods, trade can be carried out fairly easily. Certain tribes of pygmy hunters in Zaire trade ivory from their elephant hunts for the metal they need to make arrows and spears. They also trade for a few agricultural goods. Because most of their trade is in metal and tusks, prices are measured not in money but in terms such as arrow tips per tusk. Money is not needed here because few goods are traded. People can easily arrange to trade what they have for what they want. This type of direct trade of goods and services is called **barter**.

Barter
Direct exchange of one good or service for another without the use of money.

1. Adapted from Ira Kaminow, "The Myth of Fiscal Policy: The Monetarist View," *Business Review*, Federal Reserve Bank of Philadelphia (December 1969).

Consider a barter economy in which a potter wants to buy a pizza. Such trades require that each trader find a trading partner who wants what he or she offers and offers what he or she wants. If the potter goes to the market and the pizza maker wishes to exchange a pizza for a ceramic bowl, all is well. But what if the pizza maker isn't interested in pottery and wants a shirt instead? The potter then has to find someone who wants to trade a shirt for a bowl before going to trade with the pizza maker. In addition, a pizza or a shirt may not be equal in value to a bowl, raising the problem of making change. Barter is costly in terms of the time and effort required to find a trading partner.

A large or highly specialized economy cannot function by barter. A better system eliminates the need for the double coincidence of wants by finding one commodity that everyone will accept in trade. The most common solution to the problems of barter is to use money. This solution is extremely efficient because using money saves on the search and transactions costs that are involved in bartering. Although money has other uses, carrying out transactions is its most important role.

Even in modern industrial economies, people still engage in barter. Newspapers sometimes report creative barter transactions made to avoid taxes. Barter is common among friends and neighbors. Lawn mowing is traded for babysitting, or the use of tools for some help with a fix-up project. Doctors have been known to perform operations in exchange for a two-week vacation at a beachfront condominium. Most transactions in the United States and other developed countries, however, are made with money rather than by barter.

THE FUNCTIONS OF MONEY

Medium of exchange
A function of money in simplifying transactions by allowing people to exchange the goods and services they produce for money and then exchange money for other goods and services they want.

Standard of value
A function of money in providing a measuring unit in which goods can be valued and compared with each other and in providing a medium in which to write contracts for future payment.

Because barter can be inconvenient, money has developed as a means for trading in goods and services. That is, money serves as a **medium of exchange**. As a medium of exchange, money simplifies transactions by allowing people to exchange the goods and services they produce for money and then exchange money for other goods and services they want. People receive their wages in the form of money and use it to buy clothes, food, housing and other items. In the jargon of economics, money reduces transactions costs. This function is so important that it is the first part of our definition of money: In order for something to be money, it must be used to carry out transactions.

A second function of money is to serve as a **standard of value**, a way to compare the costs, values, or prices of various goods. In this function, money is the equivalent of such measures as lengths or weights. If people did not have prices and money as a way of making comparisons, they would have to keep track of the value of each good in terms of all other goods. The price of an apple might be 2/3 of an orange, or 1/500 of a pair of shoes. For example, in an economy that had only 100 goods, there would be 4,950 prices without money. (Since 100 items would each have 99 prices in terms of the other goods, you might think that there would be 9,900 prices—but the price of apples in terms of oranges is just the reciprocal of the price of oranges in terms of apples, cutting the number of different prices in half.) Having money to serve as a unit of account reduces those 4,950 prices to a more manageable 100 prices.

Money as a standard of value also allows people to make contracts that extend into the future. As a standard of value, money gives borrowers and lenders a medium in which to express the repayment of debt in the future. If you work for someone today, you may be paid two weeks later. If you charge something on your credit card, you are agreeing to make a future payment. (If you don't know that, read the fine print on the back of the card!) In this way, money allows an economic link to the past and the future. It is easier to specify a repayment in terms of money than as a list of a number of goods and services.

The third and final function of money is to serve as a **store of wealth**, or financial asset. As a store of wealth, money provides a general form of purchasing power that can be held in order to buy goods and services in the future. A decision to store your wealth as automobiles works well only if you happen to need a car in the future or can easily and quickly find a car buyer when you need cash. Not knowing what their future needs will be, people usually want to store some wealth in a form that can serve as a medium of exchange. Then they will be able to easily convert their wealth into goods and services. The ease with which an asset can be converted into the medium of exchange is called **liquidity**. Money is the ultimate liquid asset because it already is the medium of exchange. In its function as a store of value, money competes with other (substitute) financial assets such as savings bonds or certificates of deposit. These assets offer interest but do not serve as a medium of exchange.

This list of functions makes it possible to replace the working definition of money with a more precise definition. Money is what money does. That is, anything that performs all three of the functions just listed is money. **Money** is any financial asset that serves as a medium of exchange, a standard of value, and a store of wealth.

DESIRABLE PROPERTIES OF MONEY

Money can take all kinds of physical forms. What should be used for money? Fishhooks? Stones? Shells? Beads? Tobacco? All of these have served as money at some time. Some of the desirable properties of money can be inferred by considering the forms of money that have been used for long periods and those that haven't made the grade. Experience suggests that a good candidate for serving as money should be somewhat scarce (but not too scarce), portable, durable, uniform, divisible, and generally acceptable.

SCARCITY. The general level of prices tends to increase directly with the quantity of money in circulation. Scarcity keeps the price level from rising too rapidly. Sand, for example, meets many of the other criteria for money but is too easy to scoop up in large quantities. Scarcity was one reason for the popularity of precious metals as money in the past. The difficulty of finding and transporting the large stones ensured that Yap money would be scarce. Today, governments try to maintain the scarcity of the money stock by limiting the quantity of money they produce.

PORTABILITY. Medieval Swedish copper coins and the stone money of the Island of Yap were both very heavy. In general, however, money is portable. In fact, portable forms of money—usually gold—have been very useful in crises. Refugees fleeing political upheaval or persecution know how important portability is when they have to convert their assets to a form that can be carried and concealed.

Store of wealth
A function of money in providing purchasing power in a generalized form that can be held in order to buy goods and services in the future.

Liquidity
The measure of how quickly a financial asset can be converted into the medium of exchange.

Money
Any financial asset that serves as a medium of exchange, a standard of value, and a store of wealth.

DURABILITY. Perishable commodities such as apples or fragile commodities such as glass would not serve well as money. Paper money is not extremely durable, but it is easy to replace. The average U.S. dollar bill has a useful lifetime of only about sixteen months. Coins, in contrast, last about twenty years, a fact that has led some U.S. officials to advocate replacing the dollar bill with a more durable dollar coin, as Canada has done.

UNIFORMITY. Variations in quality complicated the use of tobacco as money in the south during colonial times. Cows can be fat or thin, healthy or sick, and their value as money would vary accordingly. The advantage of paper money or precious metals is that it is easy to verify its value because it is uniform. The purity of gold and silver can be tested by weight or vouched for by a stamp of approval, as on coins.

DIVISIBILITY. Divisibility of money means it is possible to make change. Small denominations and coins are needed for this purpose. Divisibility as well as portability makes cows, houses, and other large, heavy assets very unsatisfactory forms of money, and helps to explain the long-term popularity of precious metals such as gold and silver.

ACCEPTABILITY. To be useful, money must be acceptable; people must be willing to take it in payment for goods and services. A person will accept money only because of the belief that others will also accept it. If the substance used as money is also a commodity with nonmonetary uses (such as gold), its value as a commodity sets its minimum value, which gives it some general acceptability. If the money is not itself a commodity but is always redeemable in a commodity, the acceptability and value of the commodity transfer to the money. Such money is known as **representative money**. The gold certificates and silver certificates used as currencies in the United States until 1933 and 1963, respectively, were representative monies. The acceptability of representative money depends on whether people believe it will be redeemed as promised.

Modern money, however, is normally neither a commodity nor redeemable as a commodity. It is usually **fiat money**, which is whatever the government declares to be money. What gives such money its value and acceptability? By law, certain forms of money (currency in the United States) are "legal tender for all debts, public and private." That phrase is printed on all U.S. bills. If something is **legal tender**, all persons are required to accept it in payment of debts. Governments must also accept paper money for the payment of taxes if it is designated as legal tender. This legal backing somewhat replaces the commodity backing of earlier times.

FORMS OF MONEY

An incredible variety of items have served as money throughout history. All monies have had at least some of the desirable properties of money but in different degrees. Milk—a very nondurable item (but liquid!)—has been used as money. Cattle and slaves have also served as money, though they are neither very homogeneous nor divisible. Even cannons have been used as money, despite the fact that they are not very portable.

Representative money
Money that is redeemable in a commodity such as gold.

Fiat money
Money that is not a commodity and not redeemable in commodity.

Legal tender
Money that, by law, must be accepted by private parties and governments in payment of debts and obligations.

GLOBAL OUTLOOK: CURRENCIES AROUND THE WORLD

Each country's currency is unique in appearance, size, and value. There is the peso in Mexico, the yen in Japan, the franc in France and Switzerland, the mark in Germany, and the lire in Italy. Often the unit has a historic name. The franc is a name going back to the Dark Ages, when the tribe inhabiting the area that is now France was the Franks. The bolivar in Venezuela is named for a Latin American hero, Simon Bolivar. The krone of several Scandinavian countries simply means "crown," indicating that it is issued by the king or queen. The pound sterling originally was worth one pound of sterling silver. Sometimes the name is changed in a currency reform. In 1986, Brazil called in its cruzeiros and replaced them with a new currency, the cruzado, at a ratio of 1 cruzado for 1,000 cruzeiros. By 1993, another effort at currency reform restored the name cruzeiro.

The basic currency unit may be very large or very small. That is, it may take a large number or a small number of currency units to buy a newspaper or a loaf of bread. In most cases, the size of the currency unit says nothing about the currency's value or stability. The pound sterling is a large currency unit but has much smaller purchasing power relative to other currencies than it had ten, twenty, or forty years ago. The yen is a small currency unit but has a stable value and was increasing in value relative to most other currencies throughout the 1980s and into the 1990s. From World War II until 1973, the official price of the dollar in terms of yen was 360 yen = $US1.00. That value was set by General MacArthur when he was in charge of the occupation of Japan, because the Japanese symbol for the yen also stands for a circle, and there are 360 degrees in a circle.

Sometimes a currency unit changes from large to small as a result of severe inflation. For example, in early 1989, it took 78,000 australs to buy a car in Argentina. A year later, 78,000 australs bought dinner for four at a nice restaurant in Buenos Aires.[a] The ruble was at one time supposed to be the equivalent of one US dollar; in 1993, the value was about 1,000 rubles to $US1.00.

The value of the currencies of the major industrial countries is determined by supply and demand in the international marketplace. You can check on currency prices in most major daily newspapers. Here are the currency values in terms of U.S. dollars for the nation's major trading partners in March 1994:

CURRENCY	UNITS PER U.S. DOLLAR
Dollar (Canada)	1.356
Franc (France)	5.841
Mark (Germany)	1.719
Peso (Mexico)	3.244
Pound (United Kingdom)	.671
Ruble (Russia)	1,691.0
Yen (Japan)	105.8

a. *Washington Post National Weekly Edition* (March 4–10, 1990):39.

Various precious metals, such as gold and silver (and copper, though it is not as rare), have frequently served as money. The value of coins made from precious metals can be reduced by clipping, chipping, or shaving, either by private citizens or by the issuing governments. Precious metals can also be combined with less expensive (base) metals. In the Middle Ages, it was not uncommon for a monarch to call in all the coins, melt them, add base metals, recast them, and redistribute twice as many coins. The increased number of coins drove up the prices of goods and reduced the value of each coin. This debasement of money made the value of coins suspect. How much gold (or silver) was really in a coin?

During World War II, prisoners of war in German detention camps used cigarettes as money. They received cigarettes as part of their rations from the Red Cross and elsewhere. There were more cigarettes than people wanted to smoke, so they were traded for other goods. The supply was well known, so cigarettes gradually became recognized as a form of money with a fairly stable value. Toward the end of the month, before new cigarette rations arrived, many of the cigarettes had been smoked. The value of a cigarette in terms of most other goods, such as chocolate bars, tended to rise until a new shipment came in.[2]

Money in the form of coins has been around for a long time. Originally, coins were made out of precious metal, and the stamp of the royal authority (often complete with a flattering profile) certified to their value. Such coins were **full-bodied money**, with a value in other uses equal to their monetary value. Modern coins are **token money**, because their value as money is greater than the value of the metal they contain. Currency and checks, mostly issued by banks, are somewhat more recent than coins but still have a long history.

In the United States, the **money stock** consists of coins, currency, and checkable deposits. The term money stock refers to the amount of financial assets in existence at a particular time that perform the function of money as a medium of exchange. The term money stock is used somewhat interchangeably with the money supply, but the latter term is used more often in connection with changes in the money stock because of actions of banks or the Federal Reserve. **Currency** is paper money with a specified value. In the United States, official currency is now issued solely by the central bank (the Federal Reserve System). In the past, paper money has been issued by the Treasury (gold and silver certificates), private banks, and even state governments. In some countries, private banks continue to issue currency. Traveler's checks, a form of money issued by U.S. banks, are a safe and acceptable medium of exchange that is very close to currency. **Checkable deposits**, the principal component of the money stock, consist of balances in checking accounts at banks and other depository institutions. All of these forms of U.S. money have the desired properties of money.

BANKS AND MONEY

Banks have always played an important role in the creation of money. Modern banking evolved from the services provided in the Middle Ages by goldsmiths. Goldsmiths made jewelry and decorative objects and kept a stock of gold for their own use. Because they maintained safe storage facilities, goldsmiths began storing other people's gold. They issued receipts for the gold left with them. Depositors often found it more convenient to use those receipts as money than to retrieve the gold. The receipts began to circulate as currency, fully redeemable in gold. Goldsmiths were thus the earliest bankers.

The emergence of banks resolved several problems with existing forms of money. Coins were bulky, inconvenient to carry in large amounts, and easy to

Full-bodied money
Money that has a value in other uses equal to its monetary value.

Token money
Money whose monetary value is greater than its commodity value.

Money stock
The amount of financial assets in existence at a particular time that perform the function of money as a medium of exchange.

Currency
Paper money with a specified value, issued by the government or a central bank.

Checkable deposits
Balances in accounts at depository institutions against which checks can be drawn.

---

2. Radford, R. A., "The Economic Organization of a P.O.W. Camp." *Economica* (November 1945): 189–201. Many times reprinted, a classic article that looks at the use of cigarettes as money in an actual situation.

steal. Paper money, on the other hand, needed some guarantee of its value. One form of guarantee was its convertibility into coins. Thus, banks could provide safe storage for and convenient access to coins and could issue currency that had some guarantee of value. Another need fulfilled by banks was the need for a credit market—a way of transferring money balances from those individuals who did not wish to use them at the moment to those who did. Your local bank or savings and loan still offers these basic banking services today.

BANK NOTES, CHECKING ACCOUNTS, AND OTHER FORMS OF MONEY

By the late eighteenth century, bank notes like the receipts issued by goldsmiths had become a substantial part of the money stock in England and many other countries. Such bank notes carried a promise to give the bearer the specific sum of gold stated on the face. Sometimes banks failed because they could not meet their obligations to redeem these notes in gold as promised.

Governments also issued notes redeemable in gold or silver on demand. Like banks, governments were sometimes unable to keep their promise to redeem this paper money for gold or silver. During the Civil War, the U.S. government issued notes called greenbacks that were not redeemable in gold. The Confederate States of America also issued nonredeemable notes. When the war was going well for the Union forces, greenbacks traded at close to their face value in gold. Greenbacks fell in value during periods when the war was going badly for the North. Confederate notes became virtually worthless toward the end of the war. It became clear that the Confederacy would lose, and the notes would not be redeemed. Confederate notes are now popular collectors' items, but you would have a hard time getting anyone to accept them in payment!

Until 1863, most U.S. banks were chartered by individual states. In that year, the National Banking Act imposed a federal tax on bank notes issued by state-chartered banks. This act was an attempt to force banks to obtain federal charters and come under federal regulation. Instead, it virtually drove bank notes out of existence and encouraged the development of checking accounts as a substitute for gold and bank notes in the United States.

Checking accounts first appeared in fifteenth-century Italy. They have some advantages over bank notes. There is no problem of making change, because a check can be written for the exact amount. Checking accounts are easier to protect from theft than cash because you can stop payment on checks if your checkbook is stolen. Checking accounts have one important drawback, however. The person who accepts a check has no easy way to verify that the check will be accepted by the bank on which it is written. If the check writer doesn't have enough funds on deposit, the check will "bounce"—right back to the person who accepted it in payment. Thus, especially if you are young, move around a great deal, or don't have satisfactory identification, your check is not always as widely accepted as currency or coins.

Before the development of such new financial instruments as certificates of deposit and money market accounts, there was a wide gap between checkable deposits, which are considered money by even the strictest definition, and savings-type accounts, which cannot be used directly for transactions. Changes in the banking system have filled this gap with certificates of deposit, money market accounts, credit union share draft accounts, and automated funds transfers between accounts. There is a much wider variety of checkable deposits offered by all types of depository institutions, each with different regulations, interest rates, and service charges. These changes have come about because the federal government eliminated many of the regulations on the kinds of accounts banks could offer and the interest rates they could pay.

MEASURING THE MONEY SUPPLY

Before 1980, there was a clear line that separated money from near money. A financial asset—coin, currency, CD, or bond—was either a medium of exchange (money) or an interest-earning asset (near money). With a whole new array of interest-bearing checking accounts, the dividing line became blurred. Economists have had to decide where these new kinds of deposits fit into the various definitions of the money stock (more commonly known today as the money supply).

Liquidity is the most important criterion for deciding what financial assets are a part of the money supply. Since money is highly liquid, the amount of liquidity that a financial asset has is useful for deciding whether it should be considered money or near money. **Near money** is a financial asset that is a close but not perfect substitute for money as a medium of exchange.

Today, the **M1 money supply** is defined as the total of those kinds of financial assets that function as a medium of exchange. It includes currency in circulation (outside banks), traveler's checks, and checkable deposits at commercial banks, savings banks, and credit unions.

The **M2 money supply** is equal to M1 plus small time and savings deposits, money market accounts at banks and other financial institutions, and a few other specialized monetary assets. Time and savings deposits are those on which you can earn interest and on which you cannot write a check. Money market accounts with banks or mutual fund companies are deposits invested in short-term liquid assets (such as Treasury bills), on which the owner can write only a limited number of checks. A still broader measure, the **M3 money supply**, adds large time deposits, repurchase agreements, and a few other items to M2. Table 1 gives exact definitions and current magnitudes of these three widely used measures.

THE MONEY SUPPLY AND THE EQUATION OF EXCHANGE

The equation of exchange, $M_s \times V = P \times Y$, describes the relationship between money supply and the money value of total output. Which measure of the money supply do economists use for M_s in this equation? This decision is important because the equation is used to predict changes in the price level and real output (and, as we will see later, changes in interest rates as well). The choice is not easy. Suppose you decide to use M1 for the money supply in the equation of exchange. Everything not a part of M1 is then near money. However, savings and time deposits at banks, which are a part of M2 but not M1, are very good substitutes for checking accounts. With an automatic teller card, it is possible to withdraw cash from a money market account just as easily as from a checkable deposit.

Near money
Highly liquid financial assets that are very similar to those assets that are included in the money stock.

M1 money supply
The total of all financial assets in the United States that function as a medium of exchange: currency, traveler's checks, demand deposits, and other checkable deposits.

M2 money supply
The total of M1 and small denomination time and savings deposits at all financial institutions, money market accounts, and a few other items.

M3 money supply
The total of M2 and large-denomination time and savings deposits and a few other items.

TABLE 1 MONEY SUPPLY MEASURES AND COMPONENTS, 1993 (BILLIONS OF DOLLARS)

MEASURES	
M1	$1,078.7
M2	$3,509.5
M3	$4,163.3

COMPONENTS

M1 money supply: currency held by the public plus commercial bank demand deposits, travelers' checks of nonbank issuers, and other checkable deposits, including NOW and ATS accounts, and checkable accounts at credit unions and thrifts.

M2 money supply: M1 plus small-denomination savings and time deposits at all depository institutions, money market deposit accounts and money market mutual funds (except those owned by institutions), overnight repurchase agreements at commercial banks, and overnight Eurodollars.

M3 money supply: M2 plus large denomination savings and time deposits at all depository institutions, term repurchase agreements at commercial banks and savings and loans, term Eurodollars, and money market mutual funds (institutions only). (There is another correction for interbank deposits.)

Source: *Survey of Current Business* (Washington DC: U.S. Government Printing Office).

Clearly, there will always be some near money that is close to the money concept you choose. If you use M2 in the equation of exchange, you will find that deposits at savings and loan associations, which are not included in M2, are not very different from similar accounts at commercial banks. If you choose M3, which includes negotiable certificates of deposit (CDs), you will find that short-term U.S. government obligations, such as Treasury bills, are fairly good substitutes for those CDs because there are active resale markets for Treasury bills.

In order to use the money supply as a policy tool or a forecasting tool for prices, employment, and real output, it is important to agree on the best measure. Some economists use the one that is the most accurate in predicting the money value of GDP. That measure is usually M2. M2 is also more stable than M1. When individuals look for higher-yielding assets, they often switch to some of the interest-bearing accounts included in M2. Such changes make M1 fluctuate a great deal more than M2.

Other economists argue for M1 because it corresponds to money's function as the medium of exchange, which is the basis for the equation of exchange. M2 incorporates more of money's function as a store of value, which is more important in the Keynesian tradition than the classical tradition because of the link between money as an asset and interest rates. By the 1990s, the preference among model builders and policy makers had shifted from M1 to M2, but not all economists agreed with the change.

DEMAND FOR MONEY

Now that you have a working definition of what money is, what it does, and what the money supply consists of, we can use the equation of exchange to see the effects of changes in money supply and demand on output, employment, and the price level. The demand for money is very important to monetary policy because it tells policy makers just how people are likely to respond to changes in the money supply. As we will see in the next chapter, the monetary authorities can control the supply of money fairly well, but demand is determined by the choices of individual citizens.

The demand for money is based on the quantity theory of money and the equation of exchange. The supply of money is closely linked to the banking system, which we will describe in the next chapter. Changes in the supply and demand for money are important to the macroeconomy because these changes can shift the aggregate demand curve and thereby affect the levels of output, employment, and prices.

MOTIVES FOR HOLDING MONEY

Two of the three functions of money—as the medium of exchange and a store of wealth—relate directly to its uses by individuals and business firms. People hold money because it is convenient for market transactions. They also may hold money as one of many forms in which to store wealth.

According to the Marshallian explanation of money demand, individuals decide how much money to hold in the same way they decide which goods and services to buy. That is, they compare the satisfaction obtained from holding money with the satisfaction obtained from holding alternative assets. Money is useful for two important purposes: making transactions and storing purchasing power for future use. Whenever money is used to carry out transactions or held in anticipation of transactions in the near future, those funds are satisfying the transactions demand for money, or the desire for cash balances to meet day-to-day spending needs. The transactions demand for money is positively related to income.

The classical quantity theory of money was based on the role of money as a medium of exchange, or the transactions demand for money. If people hold money mostly for making transactions, the amount they wish to hold is related to the volume of transactions they expect to make. For an individual, the amount of money held for transactions is proportional to income. For the economy as a whole, the amount of money demanded for transactions is proportional to the aggregate volume of transactions, which is roughly equal to GDP (or $P \times Y$). The equation of exchange can be written as either

$$M_d = k \times P \times Y = k \times \text{nominal income}$$

or

$$M_s \times V = P \times Y,$$

where $k = 1/V$. Classical economists expected that k and V would be constant, or at least stable, because transactions demand reflects patterns of earning and spending that do not change very rapidly. Think about your own spending and earning. The money you receive—from a part-time job, from scholarships, or from your parents—comes in at regular intervals and you spend it at a rather steady and predictable pace.

During the Great Depression, however, there was a large decline in the velocity of money that took many economists by surprise. In the 1930s, people wanted to hold more money at every level of GDP. In the equation of exchange, this change in preferences meant that k increased and V fell. When people attempted to increase their money holdings, they engaged in fewer transactions and, on average, held each dollar longer. As they spent less, both GDP ($P \times Y$ in the equation of exchange) and V declined. Keynes attempted to explain changes in people's desired cash balances in terms of other reasons for holding money besides transactions demand.

INTEREST RATES, RISK, AND THE ASSET DEMAND FOR MONEY

Despite the advantages of money for transactions purposes, individuals don't choose to keep all of their financial assets in cash or checking accounts. There are opportunity costs associated with holding money. A major opportunity cost is the higher interest that could be earned by holding other assets, such as bonds, instead of money. The asset demand for money is the amount of money people wish to hold as a store of wealth in preference to other kinds of financial assets. This demand for money depends on the interest rates available on other kinds of financial assets. When interest rates in general rise, the opportunity cost of holding money that earns little or no interest rises. People rethink the division of their assets between money and other financial assets, and are likely to shift some of their wealth into bonds. When interest rates fall, it is cheaper (in terms of opportunity cost) to hold money, and since money offers some advantages like safety and convenience, people may switch back to more cash and less bonds (or other financial assets). Consequently, the asset demand is negatively related to the interest rate.

The relationship between the interest rate and the demand for money depends not only on the current interest rate, but also on how that rate compares to past and expected future rates. Suppose that for the past decade the yield on bonds had averaged 6 percent, but this year it dropped to 4 percent. You would tend to increase your holdings of cash balances (currency and checkable deposits) relative to your holdings of bonds because the opportunity cost of holding cash is lower. But there is another reason to stay away from bonds. If you think that 6 percent interest is "normal" and the 4 percent yield is temporary, then you expect the yield on bonds to go back up to 6 percent in the near future. If you buy bonds now, not only will you get a low yield, but you will be risking a capital loss. A bond that you purchase for $1,000 at 4 percent will decline in value if the interest rate rises to 6 percent. If you tried to sell it, you would get considerably less than $1,000, because it pays only $40 in interest a year while a newly issued $1,000 bond pays $60 a year.

If interest rates are very low, people will accumulate cash and checkable deposits while waiting for rates to rise. If there is an increase in the money supply, banks and individuals will just add the new funds to their current holdings of cash and checkable deposits. Thus, if interest rates are already low relative to past experience, an increase in the money supply has little effect on lending, interest rates, and investment. Velocity will fall, as it did during the Great Depression.

EXPECTED PRICE LEVEL CHANGES AND THE DEMAND FOR MONEY

A third factor in determining the demand for money is the price level, including changes in both actual and expected prices. Changes in price expectations influence the demand for money because changes in the price level affect the purchasing power of money. When prices rise, a dollar buys less. When prices fall, it buys more. People will be concerned that a rising price level will cause their money holdings to decline in value.

If the price level were expected to rise, this would provide an incentive for people to shift part of their assets out of money and into other kinds of financial assets that might be less vulnerable to losing value through inflation. Such assets are called inflation hedges. People might try to purchase real assets (such as land, coins, stocks, or houses) whose value is expected to rise with the price level. Or they might purchase financial assets with yields high enough to offset the expected loss of purchasing power. As people try to exchange their money for other kinds of assets, such as stocks and bonds, desired money balances fall relative to GDP ($P \times Y$ in the equation of exchange). Velocity (V) increases, or k declines.

An expected drop in the price level would have just the opposite effect. As money increases in purchasing power and is expected to increase further in the future, people will expect the value of their money holdings to rise. They cut spending to build up their cash balances and plan to buy later when prices fall. With reduced spending, GDP falls. Since the money supply is unchanged, the equation of exchange must be balanced by a decline in V or a rise in k.

KEY IDEAS

WHY PEOPLE HOLD MONEY

MOTIVE	CHARACTERISTICS
Transactions demand for money	• To meet day-to-day expenses • Reflects money's function as the medium of exchange • Positively related to level of income
Asset demand for money	• As a store of wealth or as one asset among many • Reflects money's function as a store of wealth • Negatively related to interest rate

THE STABILITY OF VELOCITY

If V and k are unstable, it is much more difficult for monetary authorities to predict the effects of changes in the money supply on GDP. The combined influence of interest rates and price expectations on the demand for money explains why k and V vary in the short run. It is easy to verify that this was the case in the 1930s when V fell and k rose. After the stock market crash of 1929 and the many

POLICY FOCUS: KEEPING THE VALUE OF THE CURRENCY STABLE

In the 1992 election campaign, one of the more telling arguments offered by Republicans against electing a Democrat was that inflation would take off again. Inflation had been high at the end of the term of the previous Democratic President, Jimmy Carter, who left office in 1980 with double-digit inflation. This threat reminded citizens that one of the responsibilities of governments is to protect the value of the currency from the ravages of counterfeiting, debasement, and inflation. Of these three, the most important threat to the stability of a currency's value in this century has been inflation.

Stability of value means that purchasing power of money held in currency or checkable deposits doesn't change very rapidly. Inflation means that money is losing purchasing power. A dollar that you set aside in the mattress in 1960 would purchase only 23 percent as many goods and services in 1990 because of inflation. This decline in purchasing power may sound bad, but it is a better record than that of many other countries. Latin American governments are notoriously unstable in part because of citizens' frustration at their inability to protect the purchasing power of their currencies. A major problem in the nations of Eastern and Central Europe in the early 1990s has been rampant inflation that has eroded the value of the small amount of savings people had managed to accumulate.

If the value of a currency is stable, one currency unit (such as a dollar) buys about the same amount of goods and services over time, even though the prices of some items may rise or fall in response to changes in supply and demand in individual markets. This domestic purchasing power value must be distinguished from the exchange rate, which measures the value of a currency in terms of other currencies and is influenced by other factors. However, if a currency's domestic purchasing power is falling, usually its exchange rate will fall also.

Stability of value is especially important if money is to function as both a store of wealth and a standard of value. If further inflation is expected, money will be viewed as a poor store of wealth. If you fear that the value of your money is in danger of being rapidly eroded by price increases, you may be tempted to switch some of your store of wealth into land, buildings, fine art, rare coins, diamonds, or gold. These other assets are real goods whose value rises when prices increase. Owning them thus partly protects you against inflation. The amount of money you hold as a store of wealth will depend on what you expect to happen to its future value. Money whose value is being eroded by inflation is also not a satisfactory standard of value for determining future loan repayment, because the money repaid will have less value than the money borrowed.

Although other factors affect a currency's purchasing power, the key to maintaining stability of value lies in controlling the money supply. The government's role as an issuer of currency and a guarantor of its value is sufficiently important that it was spelled out in the U.S. Constitution, which grants to the federal government the right to issue currency and regulate its value. Today, that role is interpreted broadly as the authority to supervise and regulate the banking system as well as the exclusive right to issue coins and currency.

---

bankruptcies of the early 1930s, many people wanted to hold a larger fraction of their assets in the form of money. The interest rates on bonds and other financial assets were very low. In 1933, the yield on a three-month Treasury bill was only 0.5 percent, compared to about 3 percent in 1993 and 6 to 7 percent in the late 1980s. Furthermore, the price level was falling in the early 1930s and was expected to fall further.

Velocity, measured by comparing GDP to M1, declined sharply again in the late 1980s. However, this time the decline in velocity was not tied to a recession. A gradual decline in interest rates played some role. The decline in velocity was also related to changes in financial markets and the emergence of new forms of near money. These changes made M1 a less satisfactory measure of the money supply as more close substitutes appeared for its components. An imperfect measure of the money supply would give an imperfect measure of velocity, since $V = GDP/M_s$.

How often and how much does the velocity of money change? Figure 1 plots two values of V ($V_1 = GDP/M1$ and $V_2 = GDP/M2$) as well as the interest rate on a Treasury bill for the period from 1970 to 1993. You can see from this diagram that V_1 is less stable than V_2, but that both seem to be related to the interest rate. We will consider the stability of velocity and its implications in Chapter 14.

KEY IDEAS

DETERMINANTS OF VELOCITY

The velocity of money (V) is determined by
- Interest rates — Higher interest rates increase velocity. Lower interest rates reduce velocity.
- Price expectations — Inflationary expectations increase velocity. Deflationary expectations reduce velocity.
- Institutional changes — Different forms of money or payment periods will change spending habits and affect velocity.

FIGURE 1

VELOCITY OF MONEY, 1970–1993

Velocity is equal to GDP divided by the money supply (M1 or M2). In the last twenty-three years, V_1 has increased, but with fluctuations around an upward trend. Presently, the value of V_1 (GDP/M1) is in the range of 5.5 to 7.0. The value of V_2 (GDP/M2) is around 1.5 to 2.0.

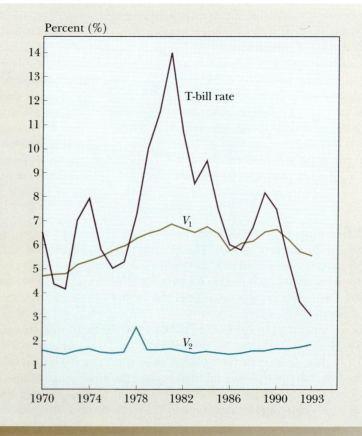

EQUILIBRIUM IN THE MONEY MARKET

The money supply is largely under the control of the central bank, which uses tools that are described in Chapter 12. Until now, we have treated the amount of money in the economy as an exogenous variable or a given number. Money demand, however, is subject to many influences, including (1) the interest rate, which determines the demand for money as a store of wealth, (2) the level of income, which determines transactions demand, and (3) the price level and price expectations. Money demand is positively related to the level of money income ($P \times Y$). The money market, like any other market, will be in equilibrium when money demand is equal to money supply. The price of money is the interest rate.

Figure 2 shows the relationship of money demand and money supply to interest rates at a given level of nominal income. The money supply is largely independent of the level of interest rates (with qualifications to be discussed in later chapters), so the money supply is drawn as a vertical line. Money demand is negatively related to interest rates. Equilibrium in the money market occurs at an interest rate of i_1.

SHIFTS IN MONEY DEMAND

Since the demand for money is shown as a function of the interest rate, all other influences on money demand will shift the demand curve. In particular, an

FIGURE 2
MONEY SUPPLY AND MONEY DEMAND
The money supply is considered independent of the interest rate, but money demand is negatively related to the interest rate. Equilibrium occurs where i_1 ensures that money demand is equal to money supply. An increase in money demand to M_{d2} because of an increase in nominal GDP will drive up the interest rate to i_2, while a decline in money demand to M_{d3} because of a decrease in nominal GDP will drive the interest rate down to i_3.

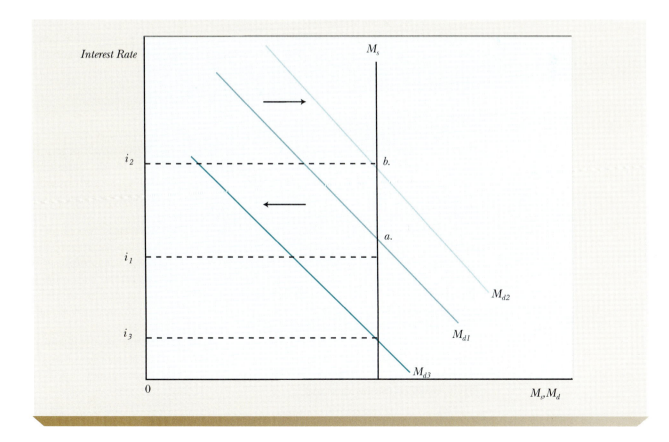

increase in $P \times Y$ will shift the demand curve from M_{d1} to M_{d2} in Figure 2. People require larger transactions balances. At the old interest rate, i_1, the quantity of money demanded exceeds the quantity supplied by amount ab. Lenders who are swamped with borrowers will start raising the rates that they charge on loans. With a higher opportunity cost of holding money, people will choose to hold smaller cash balances for asset purposes, freeing up funds to use for transactions purposes to support the higher level of money income and spending. Since V and k measure the relationship between money demand and money income, another way of saying the same thing is that velocity has risen.

A decline in the level of income and output has the opposite effect, shifting money demand to M_{d3} in Figure 2. At that lower income level, individuals will demand smaller cash balances. Money supply will exceed money demand. Lenders seeking to find outlets for their funds will offer lower interest rates. At lower interest rates, people will move along the money demand curve, increasing their asset balances because the opportunity cost is lower while reducing their transactions balances because they are at a lower level of money income. As funds shift from transactions to asset balances, equilibrium is restored at a lower interest rate.

Not all of the burden of adjustment falls on interest rates. As interest rates rise in the first case, some spending will be discouraged—housing purchases, cars, business investment. This decline in spending will result in a multiplier effect on the value of output. As nominal income declines, the money demand curve will shift back to the left, reducing the impact of the original change in nominal income on the level of interest rates. Similarly, a decline in nominal income leads to a fall in interest rates which stimulates some spending and restores some of the initial decline.

The issue of the relationship between interest rates and spending has been particularly important in the 1980s (when interest rates were very high) and the 1990s (when interest rates fell sharply). We will explore this issue in more detail in Chapter 14.

SHIFTS IN MONEY SUPPLY

Suppose, instead, the money supply increases. In Figure 3, this development is shown as a shift in the vertical money supply curve from M_{s1} to M_{s2}. Note that there is now too much money in the system. Quantity supplied exceeds quantity demanded. When the money supply increases, how do individuals respond? If money demand is unchanged, people have larger money balances than they want. When people have excess money balances, they have only two choices about what to do with the money: spend it or lend it. (If they choose to leave the money in their bank accounts, the bank will lend it to someone.) Lending the money drives down interest rates. The economy moves along the money demand curve to a larger quantity of money demanded at a lower level of interest rates, i_2. At lower interest rates, people will be willing to hold larger cash balances (lower velocity of money).

Lower interest rates (as well as excess cash balances themselves) will stimulate spending, which drives up output and prices. A combination of lower interest rates and a higher level of $P \times Y$ will ensure that the larger money supply is again equal to money demand.

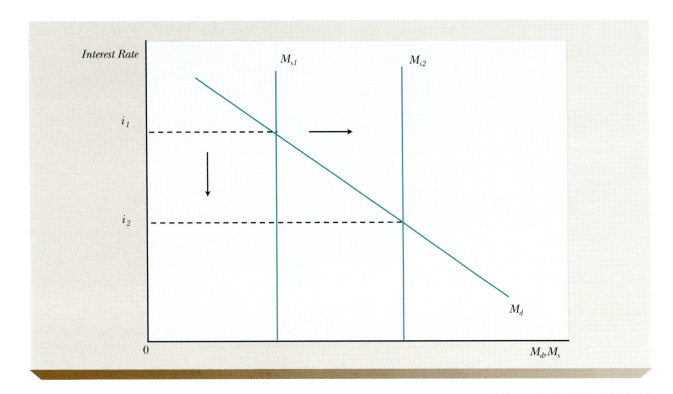

FIGURE 3

AN INCREASE IN THE MONEY SUPPLY

An increase in the money supply shifts the money supply curve from M_{s1} to M_{s2}. The result is a decline in interest rates from i_1 to i_2 as households increase their cash balances and banks increase their lending.

MONEY DEMAND, MONEY SUPPLY, AND AGGREGATE DEMAND

One of the reasons why the aggregate demand curve slopes downward is based on the equation of exchange. If $M_s V = PY$, this relationship implies that a given money supply will buy various combinations of P (price level) and Y (real output). In terms of the aggregate demand curve, the equation of exchange implies that a fixed money supply (M_s) combined with a stable velocity (V) will yield a constant value of nominal GDP, which is equal to $P \times Y$. That is, a fixed amount of money available to spend and a fairly stable frequency of spending for each unit of currency each year will determine nominal GDP. However, for any given nominal GDP, various combinations of P and Y are possible. For example, the combinations of money supply and velocity that resulted in total spending of $6,000 could imply a price level of $1 and real output of 6,000 units, or a price level of $4 and real output of 1,500 units, or various other combinations. An increase in the money supply would permit a higher P with the same Y, or a higher Y with the same P, or higher levels of both.

If we add aggregate demand to the analysis above, we can determine how much of the impact of a change in money demand or supply will be on real output and how much on the price level. There are other factors that affect the slope and position of the aggregate demand curve, but money supply and demand are both important. If M_s increases, and that increase is not entirely offset by a rise in interest rates and a resulting decline in V, there will be an increase in aggregate demand for goods and services. The AD curve shifts to the right, as shown in Figure 4. The result is an increase in P or Y or both. The exact combi-

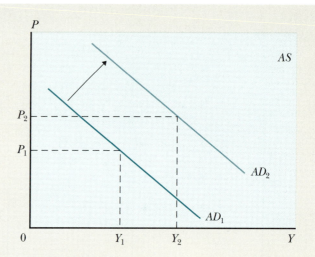

FIGURE 4

MONEY AND AGGREGATE DEMAND

An increase in the money supply (or a decrease in the demand for money) creates an excess supply of money. As it is spent on consumption or lent to investors, aggregate demand shifts to the right (from AD_1 to AD_2), driving up the price level (from P_1 to P_2) and real output (from Y_1 to Y_2).

nation depends on the slope of the AS curve. In Figure 4, the price level rises from P_1 to P_2, and real output rises from Y_1 to Y_2. The supply and demand for money are reflected in aggregate demand and therefore affect output, employment, and prices.

The addition of money to the aggregate supply and demand model identifies another source of shifts in aggregate demand besides fiscal policy or changes in consumption or investment habits. The fiscal policy tools used to shift aggregate demand are under the control of Congress and the executive branch. The money supply is under the control of the banking system, mainly the Federal Reserve System. In order to understand how this tool for shifting aggregate demand can be used, you need to know more about the banking system and how it works. The Federal Reserve System and the creation of money are described in the next chapter.

Consider again... *Yap's experiences with modern currencies explain why the stones have retained their monetary role. The Spanish first claimed Yap, but after defeat in the Spanish-American War, they sold the island to Germany in 1899. After Germany's defeat in World War I, Yap was transferred as a League of Nations trust territory to Japan. The Japanese controlled it until the end of World War II, when it came under the jurisdiction of the United States. All these nations introduced their currencies to Yap. Upon the introduction of U.S. currency, a Yap chief said, "First Spanish money no good, then German money no good, now Japanese money no good. Yap money always good!"*[3]

---

3. "The Trust Territory: Its 2,130 Islands Form a New U.S. Domain in the Pacific," *Life* (April 25, 1949):100.

When the people of Yap were allowed to choose what is money, they preferred the old familiar currency because it offered a stability that the changing currencies of colonial powers did not. Its value was determined by scarcity—the difficulty of procuring and transporting the stones ensured that counterfeiting would not be easy. While it isn't a particularly useful currency for carrying in your wallet and making change (the medium of exchange function), it is an excellent way of storing wealth for future use—it is not subject to rust, rot, or decay, and is too large and ungainly to steal.

SUMMARY

1. The functions of money include its use as a medium of exchange, standard of value, and store of wealth (asset). A variety of items have been used as money. Desirable properties of money include portability, durability, acceptability, recognizability, divisibility, and scarcity.

2. Banking developed from goldsmiths' acceptance of deposits for safekeeping. Over time, the goldsmiths began to issue written promises to return a certain amount of gold. These promises were an early form of paper money. Bank notes gradually replaced gold and were in turn replaced by checking accounts. Today, checkable deposits issued by banks are the largest part of the U.S. money supply. Several different measures of the money stock are used today in the United States. Whatever measure is used, money will have close substitutes, called near money.

3. People hold money because it can be exchanged for other things they want. Barter is extremely costly and inefficient. The use of money allows people to carry out market transactions more economically. The demand for money is expressed by the equation $M_d = k \times P \times Y$; another form of the equation of exchange, $M_s \times V = P \times Y$. Transactions demand for money is related to the level of income. Money is also demanded as an asset. Asset demand for money is higher when the interest on other financial assets is low.

4. Equilibrium in the market for money occurs at that interest rate at which money supply is equal to money demand. Money supply is drawn as vertical. Money demand is downward sloping because of the negative relationship between money demand and interest rates. An increase in the price level or the level of real output will shift money demand to the right, while a decrease will shift money demand to the left.

5. Changes in money demand and money supply affect output and prices by shifting the aggregate demand curve. Excess money balances will be spent or lent, increasing aggregate demand and driving up the price level and/or output.

NEW TERMS

barter
medium of exchange
standard of value
store of wealth
liquidity

money
representative money
fiat money
legal tender
full-bodied money

token money
money stock
currency
checkable deposits

near money
M1 money supply
M2 money supply
M3 money supply

QUESTIONS: REVIEW, APPLICATIONS, AND POLICY

REVIEW

1. In terms of the desirable properties of money, why have precious metals (gold and silver) been such popular choices for money? Why would each of the following be a poor choice: peanuts, seashells, glass, diamonds, teeth, cows, and trees?
2. Part of the U.S. money supply (M1) is currency, and part of it is checkable deposits. Why might the ratio of currency to checkable deposits change? That is, why might people prefer to keep more of their money in currency or more of it in checkable deposits?
3. Draw a line labeled "Liquid" at one end and "Not very liquid" at the other end. Place the following financial assets along the line from most liquid to least liquid: currency, twenty-year bonds, money market accounts, NOW accounts, savings accounts, checkable deposits, certificates of deposit, real estate, and Treasury bills (short-term obligations that mature in less than a year). Explain how this continuum relates to the problem of defining the money supply.
4. Classify each of the following as transactions demand, precautionary demand, or asset demand for money:
   a. lunch money in your wallet (cash)
   b. money set aside in your checking account to pay next week's bills
   c. a coin bank in the kitchen for emergencies
   d. the proverbial stock of money kept in the mattress because of fear of banks
   e. funds in a NOW account that will be put into bonds when interest rates rise
5. Why did the velocity of money fall so sharply during the Great Depression?
6. Why, according to Keynes, is the relationship between current interest rates and "normal" interest rates important in determining how much money to hold as an asset?
7. "If you have excess money balances, your only choices are to spend the money or lend it." What does this statement mean? Can people collectively get rid of excess money balances?
8. If it is not possible for people as a group to get rid of excess money balances, how is equilibrium restored in the money market when people have more money than they currently wish to hold?

APPLICATIONS

9. Do you sort out your money on hand into transactions money, precautionary money, and asset money? Why do you think economists make these distinctions?
10. In each case, solve for the missing term in the equation of exchange.
    a. $M_s = \$500$, $V = 3$, $Y = \$750$, $P =$ _____
    b. $M_s = \$600$, $P = 3$, $Y = \$500$, $V =$ _____
    c. $M_s = \$800$, $V = 2$, $P = 0.75$, $Y =$ _____
    d. $V = 4$, $Y = \$1,400$, $P = 1.5$, $M_s =$ _____
11. In the *Federal Reserve Bulletin*, find the most recent figures for the sizes of M1, M2, and M3. List the components (for example, currency and checkable deposits) of each. What is the largest component of the money supply?
12. What are the benefits of holding cash? What are the costs or risks?
13. Take a bill from your wallet and answer the following questions:
    a. How do you know it is legal tender?
    b. Whose signatures are on it?
    c. By whom and in what city was it issued?

POLICY

14. How would each of the following affect people's demand for money?
    a. A reduction in the federal budget deficit results in lower interest rates.
    b. Floods in the midwest reduce the harvest and result in a higher price level.
    c. Election of a President with a reputation for big spending leads to an expectation of a higher inflation rate.
    d. Defense conversion leads to higher unemployment and a lower real income level.
15. Using the equation of exchange and the quantity theory of money, explain how each of the following would affect the money value of GDP.
    a. A new federal law requires that workers be paid more often. (*Hint*: What happens to the average balance in their checking accounts?)
    b. A big promotional campaign by the Treasury persuades individuals to buy more government bonds. Thus they hold smaller cash balances.
    c. The minority political party convinces people that rampant inflation is coming back soon.

SUGGESTIONS FOR FURTHER READING

Galbraith, John K. *Money: Whence It Came, Where It Went.* New York: Bantam Books, 1976. A delightfully readable account of money by one of the most talented writers in economics.

Polanyi, K., M. Arenseberg, and H. W. Pearson, eds. *Trade and Markets in the Early Empires.* Chicago: Regnery Gateway, 1971. Looks at the history of money.

Romer, Christina D., "The Nation in Depression," *Journal of Economic Perspectives* (Spring 1993): 19–39. This nontechnical discussion of the Depression by a prominent young economist includes examination of the behavior of money demand during the Depression.

Mishkin, Frederick. *Economics of Money, Banking, and Financial Markets*, 3e. New York: HarperCollins, 1992. A good intermediate text with thorough coverage of money demand.

CHAPTER 12

BANKING AND THE FEDERAL RESERVE SYSTEM

LEARNING OBJECTIVES

1. Explain how banks create money.
2. Analyze the role of reserves in money creation and control of the money supply.
3. Explain why a central bank is needed, and what functions the Fed performs for the banking system.
4. Describe the Fed's monetary policy tools and how they are used to influence the money supply and interest rates.

Consider this... Have you ever noticed that banks seem to like senior citizens better than college students? People over 50 can get special accounts with no service charges, free checks, sometimes no minimum balance, and even a little interest. Students, on the other hand, are offered accounts with monthly service charges and have to pay for checks. You probably know that landlords discriminate against student renters because they expect them to be noisy and careless, but those problems shouldn't matter to banks. In fact, you would think that banks would want to build customer loyalty by getting students into their banks early so they would be lifelong customers. Why the difference in treatment? Why do banks seem to have a policy of favoring older customers?

This chapter looks at the role of banks, including the central bank, in managing the monetary side of the economy. Once you have a better understanding of how banks operate, you may also see why many of them prefer older customers. Banks are in the business of "making money" (in the double sense of making a profit and creating a medium of exchange). Banks provide the answer to the questions left unanswered in Chapter 11 about exactly where money comes from and how the supply can be changed.

HOW BANKS CREATE MONEY

As you learned in Chapter 11, goldsmiths developed the first paper currency and were also the first modern bankers. The notes issued by goldsmiths as receipts for gold deposits began to circulate as currency. It didn't take the goldsmiths long to discover that they had few day-to-day requests from depositors to redeem these notes for gold. They could safely lend out some of the depositors' gold (as well as their own), earning interest and eventually paying interest on deposits.

Suppose a prosperous medieval baron deposited 100 florins in gold with a goldsmith in exchange for a paper receipt, or note, which is redeemable as gold. This paper note serves as money. The goldsmith could lend someone else 50 florins of the baron's gold, which would also be money. The baron's deposit expanded the money supply by 50 florins. The original deposit of 100 florins was still money, but so was the 50 florins lent by the goldsmith. This kind of transaction by goldsmiths illustrates fractional reserve banking, the basis of all modern banking systems. **Fractional reserve banking** is the practice of holding a fraction of money deposited as reserves and lending the rest.

The development of banking was as great an innovation as the development of money. By replacing barter, money solved the problem of matching what you had to offer with what the seller wanted to buy. With banking, it was no longer necessary to hunt for an individual who was willing to lend as much as the borrower wanted to borrow for the desired time and on acceptable terms. Just as money simplified the problem of matching traders, banks simplified the problem of matching lenders with borrowers. The most important function of a bank is to be a wholesaler (intermediary) in the lending business, gathering up small sums from depositors and lending larger amounts to borrowers. Banks pay some interest to depositors, charge more interest to borrowers, and make their profit and pay their expenses out of the difference.

It is risky for individual lenders to deal with individual borrowers because a lender loses the entire amount of the loan if the borrower fails to repay. If individuals lend through a bank rather than directly, they are "buying" a piece of the whole range of loans made by the bank. Although one or two borrowers may default, most of the loans will be repaid.

THE BANK'S BALANCE SHEET

A bank is a business firm, just like a grocery store or a shirt factory. It is in business to earn a profit for its owners, who are stockholders. The balance sheet of any firm provides a picture of its financial situation. The balance sheet of a bank lists its assets in order of liquidity (from most liquid to least liquid), its liabilities (or claims against it to be paid in the future), and its net worth. Table 1 is a balance sheet for Amacher National Bank. The first thing you should notice is that the balance sheet balances. That is, assets equal liabilities plus net worth. A balance sheet must always balance. The fact that it balances says nothing about how well the bank is doing. To determine the bank's condition, we must look at some individual assets and liabilities.

For Amacher National, reserves are the most liquid asset. **Reserves** are bank assets that can be used to pay depositors when checks are presented for payment. Reserves consist of currency on hand (vault cash) and deposits at the central bank. It is important for a bank to keep some reserves to meet the day-to-day withdrawals of customers. However, a bank does not want to keep any more reserves than necessary because reserves do not earn interest, and loans do.

Amacher National's interest-earning assets are government bonds and loans to the public. Government bonds range from T-bills (short-term obligations) to notes (medium term) to bonds (long term). Note that a bank's assets are some-

Fractional reserve banking The practice of holding a fraction of money deposited as reserves and lending the rest.

Reserves Bank assets that can be used to pay depositors when checks are presented for payment, consisting of currency and reserve deposits at the central bank.

TABLE 1 BALANCE SHEET, AMACHER NATIONAL BANK

ASSETS		LIABILITIES	
Vault cash*	$1,000	Checkable deposits	$50,000
Reserves*	19,000	Other deposits	5,000
Bonds	15,000	Loans from the Fed	2,000
Loans to public	20,000		
Building, misc.	10,000	TOTAL LIABILITIES	$57,000
		NET WORTH	$ 8,000
TOTAL ASSETS	$65,000		
		TOTAL LIABILITIES AND NET WORTH	$65,000

*These two items are usually combined as "reserves."

one else's liabilities. Government bonds are liabilities of the U.S. Treasury. Loans are liabilities of households and businesses who borrowed the money. Amacher National's fixed assets consist of the bank's building, furnishings, and other equipment. This kind of asset is the least liquid because it is very difficult to convert to cash.

This bank's largest liability is checkable deposits of $50,000. Savings deposits and loans that the Fed has made to this bank (which will be explained later in the chapter) make up the rest of the bank's liabilities. The net worth of $8,000 represents the value of the bank to its stockholders.

Balance sheets of banks and savings and loans (thrifts) have received a great deal of public scrutiny in the last few years, because many depository institutions found that the value of their assets had fallen below the value of liabilities, resulting in negative net worth. We will examine this banking crisis in the next chapter. For now, we are mainly interested in balance sheets as a tool to help describe money creation.

T-ACCOUNTS AND MONEY CREATION

T-accounts
Partial balance sheets showing changes in assets and/or liabilities resulting from a transaction or group of transactions.

Several items on a bank's balance sheet play an important role in the money creation process. Rather than relisting all assets and liabilities, it is simpler to look at only those that change. A partial balance sheet, called a **T-account**, shows changes in assets and/or liabilities resulting from one or more transactions. The only items listed on a T-account are those that change. If the balance sheet balances at the start, then as long as the changes on the T-account offset each other, the balance sheet will still balance after the transaction.

Table 2 shows how T-accounts are used to record changes in Amacher National's balance sheet for two sample transactions. Suppose Susan Smith deposits $100 in cash in her checking account, which the bank places in its vault. The T-account shows a $100 increase in assets (vault cash, or reserves) and a $100 increase in liabilities (checkable deposits). The balance sheet still balances. In the second transaction, Amacher National sells a $1,000 bond and uses the proceeds to make a loan. The balance sheet would still balance after this transaction because an increase in one asset (the loan) is exactly offset by a decrease

TABLE 2 SAMPLE TRANSACTIONS AND T-ACCOUNTS

TRANSACTION #1: Susan Smith puts $100 in cash in her checking account; Amacher National adds the $100 to its reserves.

ASSETS	LIABILITIES
Reserves +$100	Checkable deposits +$100

TRANSACTION #2: Amacher National Bank sells a bond and makes a loan.

ASSETS	LIABILITIES
Loans +$1,000	
Bonds − 1,000	

in another (the bond). T-accounts are useful for following the process of money creation in banks.

Plus and minus signs in the T-accounts denote increases and decreases in assets or liabilities. The +$100 represents an increase in reserves in transaction 1, and the −$1,000 refers to a reduction in bonds in transaction 2.

Modern banks create money in much the same way that medieval goldsmiths created money—by making loans with the money others had deposited for safekeeping. The goldsmiths discovered that on any given day, most depositors did not withdraw any gold. A fractional amount was all goldsmiths had to hold to meet daily demand. Although gold has ceased to play much of a role in the money supply, banks still lend part of the reserves created by deposits. Banks' checkable deposits serve as money, just as the notes issued by the goldsmiths served as money.

How much can Amacher National lend? The balance sheet in Table 1 shows that this bank already has $20,000 in loans outstanding, as well as reserves of $20,000 (including vault cash) and checkable deposits of $50,000. To keep it simple, we will assume that banks keep reserves only to back up checkable deposits. Amacher National's reserves are 40 percent of its checkable deposits, a fairly high level of reserves. This bank can lend more and still have enough reserves to meet demands of depositors.

Assume that Amacher National has decided to reduce reserves to 20 percent of deposits. Twenty percent of $50,000 in checkable deposits is $10,000. Amacher National can expand its loans by $10,000. Remember, reserves do not earn interest, but loans do. When the next deserving borrower comes in, the bank will make a $10,000 loan. The bank will probably issue the loan by crediting the borrower's checking account, increasing checkable deposits (liabilities) by $10,000. The T-account for this transaction is shown in Table 3.

The balance sheet of Amacher National still balances. The money supply has increased by $10,000 in new checkable deposits. It appears that Amacher National could lend still more because the note at the bottom of the T-account points out that reserves are still $20,000 and checkable deposits are $60,000. The bank only needs to keep $12,000, or 20 percent, in reserves to back up $60,000 in checkable deposits.

Amacher National lent only $10,000 because the loan officer knew that Joe's Barber Shop intended to spend the money very quickly. Joe will spend the

TABLE 3 AMACHER NATIONAL BANK LENDS TO JOE'S BARBER SHOP

ASSETS		LIABILITIES	
Loans	+$10,000	Checkable Deposits	+10,000

Note: Total reserves = $20,000; Total checkable deposits = $60,000.

money on equipment for his shop, and Joe's supplier will probably deposit Joe's check in another bank, such as Ulbrich Savings. When a check drawn on one bank is deposited in another, the first bank loses reserves and checkable deposits. The bank that receives a check drawn on another bank gains reserves and checkable deposits. The receiving bank can now make loans and expand the money supply. When Joe's supplier deposits the check in Ulbrich Savings Bank, the effect on the T-accounts for the two banks is shown in Table 4.

After this transfer of reserves, Amacher National is "all loaned up." It cannot make any new loans until it acquires more reserves. However, Ulbrich Savings can make new loans. If this bank also keeps a 20 percent reserve behind checkable deposits, then it needs only $2,000 in reserves behind the $10,000 in new checkable deposits. Ulbrich Savings can safely lend the other $8,000 of newly acquired reserves.

RESERVES AND THE MONEY SUPPLY

Excess reserves
Reserves above the level required by law.

Amacher National lent $10,000 in **excess reserves**, which are reserves above the level required by law. Then Ulbrich Savings Bank expanded its lending by $8,000. It's not hard to see that this bank's lending will create new reserves for a third bank, which will in turn lend and create new reserves for a fourth bank, and so on. How long will this process continue? If you knew what ratio of reserves to deposits banks wish to maintain, you could identify the upper limit of money expansion.

TABLE 4 TRANSFER OF RESERVES FROM ONE BANK TO ANOTHER

AMACHER NATIONAL BANK			
ASSETS		LIABILITIES	
Reserves	−$10,000	Checkable Deposits	−$10,000
ULBRICH SAVINGS BANK			
ASSETS		LIABILITIES	
Reserves	+$10,000	Checkable Deposits	+$10,000

Note: Total reserves = $10,000; total checkable deposits = $50,000.

A bank can expand loans as long as it has excess reserves. The banking system as a whole can expand loans as long as there are excess reserves in the system. Expansion of the money supply must stop only when there are no more excess reserves in the banking system. The only way to get rid of excess reserves is for banks to lend them.

THE RESERVE RATIO

Suppose all banks in the system hold reserves of 20 percent of checkable deposits, either voluntarily or because this ratio is required by law. Each bank wants to lend out any excess reserves (ER) to earn interest. Money creation stops only when there are no more excess reserves. That is, no more money will be created when all bank reserves (BR) in the entire banking system have been converted to required reserves (RR). The **reserve ratio** (rr) is the fraction of deposits that banks are required to hold in reserves. Banks' required reserves are $rr \times D$, where D = checkable deposits. The banking system (as well as any individual bank) is fully loaned up when RR equals BR, or

Reserve ratio
The fraction of deposits that banks are required to hold in reserves.

$$(1) \ RR = BR = rr \times D.$$

Dividing equation (1) by rr gives

$$(2) \ D = \frac{1}{rr} \times BR$$

The steps in money creation are shown in Table 5 for the first five banks as well as the totals for the process. Note that the bottom line satisfies equation (2): newly created checkable deposits are equal to the initial excess reserves multiplied by the deposit multiplier, $1/rr$. The **deposit multiplier** is the ratio between the maximum increase in the money supply and a given increase in excess reserves. It equals the reciprocal of the reserve ratio. The deposit multiplier depends only on the ratio of required reserves to checkable deposits.

Deposit multiplier
The ratio between the maximum increase in the money supply and a given increase in excess reserves. It equals the reciprocal of the reserve ratio.

TABLE 5 INCREASE IN MONEY SUPPLY WITH INITIAL EXCESS RESERVES OF $10,000 AND A RESERVE RATIO OF 20 PERCENT

BANK	ΔDEMAND DEPOSITS	ΔRESERVES	AMOUNT THE BANK LENDS
Amacher National	$ 0	$ 0	$10,000
Ulbrich Savings	+$10,000	+2,000	8,000
Bank C	+8,000	+1,600	6,400
Bank D	+6,400	+1,280	5,120
Bank E	+5,120	+1,024	4,096
All others	+20,480	+4,096	16,384
All Banks	$50,000	$10,000	$50,000

According to equation (2), checkable deposits (*D*) can change only if the reserve ratio (*rr*) changes or if all bank reserves (*BR*) change. Using the symbol Δ to represent "change in," the change in deposits (and the change in the money supply) is given by:

$$\Delta D = \frac{1}{rr} \Delta BR = \Delta M_S$$

The change in checkable deposits will be equal to the reciprocal of the reserve ratio (*rr*) multiplied by the change in bank reserves (Δ*BR*). In our example, *rr* = 0.20, so the value of $1/rr$ is 5. If the Δ*BR* equals $10,000, then Δ*D* = 5 × $10,000 = $50,000.

Expansion of checkable deposits can occur only when there are excess reserves. If all reserves are being held to meet the desired ratio of reserves to deposits, there are no excess reserves available. In that case, the money supply cannot increase.

WHY EXPANSION MAY BE LESS THAN THE MAXIMUM

Currency drain
An increase in currency holdings by the public that causes a dollar-for-dollar decline in bank reserves.

The actual money supply may be less than the maximum determined by existing bank reserves for two reasons. First, the public may decide to hold more of its financial assets in currency and less in checkable deposits. Individuals may hold more cash because of concerns about bank safety or because they are using cash transactions to avoid income taxes or to hide illegal activities (such as drug dealing). A **currency drain** is an increase in cash held by the public. Since currency is part of reserves when it is in the banking system, a currency drain reduces bank reserves. When reserves fall, the banking system cannot support as many checkable deposits. For every dollar of currency flowing out of the banks and into circulation, bank reserves (*BR*) fall by $1. With a 20 percent reserve ratio (*rr*), $5 of potential new deposits are eliminated.

Second, banks may choose to hold more reserves than are legally required. Reserves not only meet the legal requirement, but also provide a cushion against above-average withdrawals. Usually banks like to hold reserves to the required minimum because reserves earn no interest. But if economic conditions are depressed, loan prospects are risky, or interest rates on loans are very low, banks may choose to hold some excess reserves until conditions improve. Banks may also hold more reserves if they expect larger cash withdrawals, because they will lose more reserves than they are legally allowed to lose. Even if banks are willing to lend, households and firms may not be anxious to borrow if they are already heavily in debt or have gloomy expectations.

LOSS OF RESERVES AND MONEY CONTRACTION

Contracting the money supply is just like expansion in reverse. Suppose that a customer of Amacher National withdraws currency from her account in the amount of $2,000. If the bank was all loaned up before this withdrawal, this withdrawal will put the bank below the required reserve level. Amacher has lost $2,000 in reserves and $2,000 in deposits. With a 20 percent reserve ratio, the bank was holding only $400 in reserves behind that deposit. The shortfall of

$1,600 must be made up by reducing loans or by selling bonds. As Amacher works to rebuild its reserves, however, it gains reserves at the expense of the other banks in the system. Table 6 shows the first few stages of this process. The deposit multiplier is the same here as for the expansion process. The initial loss of $2,000 in reserves will lead to a maximum contraction of the money supply of $10,000 if no banks had any excess reserves before the first transaction.

RESERVES AND THE CENTRAL BANK

This description of the money expansion and contraction process raises two important questions. Where do reserves come from, and who sets the required reserve ratio? Deposits and withdrawals of currency by the public are one source of changes in bank reserves, but these flows are relatively small in the U.S. banking system. The major source of bank reserves, including cash in the form of Federal Reserve notes, is the central bank, the Federal Reserve System. The Fed has the power to create reserves and set the required reserve ratio.

CENTRAL BANKING IN THE UNITED STATES

The United States was one of the last modern industrial countries to establish a central bank. The Fed was modelled partly on the Bank of England, which is almost 400 years old. The **Federal Reserve System (Fed)**, established in 1914, is the U.S. central bank. Congress created the Fed in response to two perceived needs. The first was to regulate banks to keep them from making risky loans that threatened the safety of deposits. The second was for a lender of last resort to rescue basically sound banks that were threatened with failure and bankruptcy because of temporary economic conditions. Later, a third role was established: managing the size of the money supply so as to promote economic growth, high employment, and a stable price level. This goal is now the Fed's most important function, but it was not part of the original design of the system.

Federal Reserve System (Fed)
The central bank of the United States.

BANKING POLICY AND PROBLEMS, 1791–1913

The U.S. Constitution gave the federal government the power to "coin money and regulate the value thereof. " It said nothing, however, about establishing banks. Two early attempts to establish a central bank failed. The Bank of the

TABLE 6 DECREASE IN MONEY SUPPLY FOLLOWING A LOSS OF RESERVES OF $2,000

BANK	ΔDEMAND DEPOSITS	ΔRESERVES	CHANGE IN BANK LENDING
Amacher National	$ 0	$ −2,000	$ −1,600
Ulbrich Savings	−1,600	−1,600	−1,280
Bank C	−1,280	−1,280	−1,024

United States, established in 1791, was privately owned but chartered by the federal government. It supervised other banks, promoted bank safety, and served as a lender of last resort until its charter expired in 1811. In 1816, the Second Bank of the United States was created, but its charter was not renewed in 1835. Opponents of both banks felt that these banks had used governmental power to benefit the banks' owners, their friends, and business associates.

PANICS AND LIQUIDITY. The nineteenth century was marked by frequent bank panics. **Bank panics** are sudden waves of fear that banks will not be able to pay off their depositors. Nineteenth-century banks did not issue checkable deposits. They made loans by issuing bank notes, which were supposed to be redeemable in gold. As long as note holders believed they could redeem their notes, very few would actually do so on any given day. The day-to-day demand for redemption in gold could easily be met with fractional gold reserves.

During bank panics, some banks had problems of liquidity—not enough reserves to meet current demand. Most of their loans would eventually be repaid, but not quickly enough to meet depositors' current withdrawals. Other banks had more serious problems of solvency. These banks had so many bad loans that the value of their assets was less than the value of their deposits.

Banks that followed unsound lending practices eventually found that too many notes would be presented for redemption at once, and reserves would be too low to redeem them all. When one bank could not meet demand for withdrawals, people sometimes panicked and tried to redeem notes at other banks as well. At the height of bank panics, many sound and well-managed banks were unable to redeem large numbers of notes presented in a single day. These banks failed, or closed, even though they were basically sound. People lost funds they had deposited in failed banks, and people who needed loans could not get them. Even banks that didn't fail had to greatly reduce their lending to build reserves against a run of withdrawals.

A run could occur at a perfectly sound bank. All that was needed was a rumor of possible failure. A lender to banks was needed to prevent sound banks from going under in a panic. A **lender of last resort** is a source of funds for rescuing sound banks by lending them what they need to meet temporary high demand from depositors. If sound banks could obtain funds from such a lender, depositors would be less likely to panic. Panics would be less likely to occur in the first place and would be less severe when they did occur.

Does this description of bank panics sound like the banking crisis of the late 1980s? There are some similarities, but also some important differences. Because of federal deposit insurance (discussed later in this chapter), few depositors in the 1980s crisis suffered losses. Bank failures in the 1980s were due to problems of solvency, not liquidity. These banks had made risky loans and investments. When the value of those investments fell, many banks became insolvent. We will examine the banking crisis in the next chapter.

EARLY ATTEMPTS AT CONTROL. Without a central bank to regulate unsound banking practices in the nineteenth century, some larger private banks tried to fill the void. A major bank, or group of banks, that was concerned about Bank A's overissue of notes and unsound loan practices could exert pressure by presenting Bank A's notes to be redeemed in gold. This action drained gold from Bank A and slowed its lending. (Such a process was carried out with some success by

Bank panics
Sudden waves of fear that banks will not be able to pay off their depositors.

Lender of last resort
A source of funds for rescuing sound banks by lending them funds to meet temporary high demands from depositors.

the Suffolk Bank and its affiliated banks in New England.) Control through private banks did not work well or last long, because banks did not have the legal authority to examine another bank's books and lending practices or to force it to stop making bad loans. They also weren't financially strong enough themselves to withstand a major panic.

Only the federal government had the effective power to regulate banks, as well as the financial resources to act as the lender of last resort. However, political battles over whether to give central banking powers to the federal government went on for nearly a century. One reason for resistance was the fear that the centralized power would be used to benefit rich and powerful bankers. Another source of resistance was disagreement about the importance of sound money and the dangers of inflation. Conservative bankers wanted a central bank to limit expansion of loans for fear it would lead to inflation. If that happened, the value of the loan repayments they received would fall. Other groups who wanted loans—for example, farmers on the western frontier or small businesses in the east—looked on the expansion of loans and a little inflation as a good thing. Interest payments on loans were fixed in dollar terms. In times of rising prices, debtors had increasing incomes with which to make their payments. In times of falling prices, they had to make fixed payments out of a falling income. Borrowers and debtors were afraid that a central bank would pursue a conservative policy that would make life more difficult.

THE NATIONAL BANKING SYSTEM. During the Civil War, Congress tried again to make banks safer. The National Banking System, established in 1863, allowed banks to apply for federal instead of state charters (formal permission to incorporate and operate). Banks that receive charters from the federal government are called national banks. A state bank is chartered and regulated by one of the states.

The Comptroller of the Currency in the Department of the Treasury charters and regulates national banks. State banks are regulated by various state agencies and commissions. After 1863, state banks continued to exist alongside national banks. Since state regulation was weak and ineffective, the National Banking Act did not substantially improve the stability of banks. Furthermore, there was still no lender of last resort. That situation changed with passage of the Federal Reserve Act in 1913.

GLOBAL OUTLOOK: BANKING IN BULGARIA

Like other nations of Eastern and Central Europe, Bulgaria lacked a modern banking system after the collapse of communism in 1989. Bulgaria has nothing like commercial banks that offer small business loans, mortgages, and auto loans; collect deposits in checking and savings accounts; and dispense money at drive-up windows and electronic tellers. As the nation moves toward a mixed market economy, one of its most pressing tasks is to develop a banking system to support a market economy.

Prior to the revolution, Bulgaria had a three-part banking system. The Bulgarian National Bank was a super-central bank, which served both the government and all of the enterprises (controlled by the government) with investment financing, credit, and deposit services. The Bulgarian Foreign Trade Bank was responsible for all foreign transactions. The State Savings Bank was the only bank with which households had any contact, collecting savings deposits and financing housing credits. (In Bulgaria, there was substantial private ownership of housing, although not of any commercial or industrial establishments). Reforms in the 1980s created additional banks to finance business activities, with banks specialized in certain industrial sectors, such as electronics, chemicals, and construction.

After the revolution, the government created fifty-nine new commercial banks out of the branches of the Bulgarian National Bank. New banking laws eliminated the requirement that existing banks specialize by sector. However, none of these banks were really private banks. Although they issued stock, most of the stock was held by the Bulgarian National Bank and the Foreign Trade Bank. In late 1991, these shares were transferred to a newly created agency, the Bank Consolidation Company (BCC), which is wholly owned by the Bulgarian National Bank. Shares are now being sold to private investors in order to create genuinely private banks. Part of the BCC agenda is to merge some of the seventy-four banks now in existence into about eight to ten larger and stronger banks. This process is slow because the existing banks are small, have weak loan portfolios, and cannot find employees with the needed banking and financial skills.

The biggest problem facing these banks is that their assets consist largely of the debt of state-owned enterprises, many of which are not likely to pay their debt. Of an estimated total debt of state-owned enterprises of 100 billion leva (about $4.3 billion), about half is held by Bulgarian commercial banks. As a result, at least some of the banks are technically insolvent.

A second set of problems has to do with the mechanics of banking. It will take some time to set up loan processing, credit reporting, and the other banking procedures and services that Westerners take for granted. Borrowers have no credit histories in a society that did not encourage the use of consumer credit. Business borrowers are operating in a very uncertain environment that makes almost any loan very risky. Banks, as well as commercial and industrial enterprises, find it difficult to produce basic financial statements such as balance sheets. What value do you put down for land, buildings, machinery, and cars when there has been little past history of buying and selling these assets to provide an estimate of market selling prices? Most of these enterprises also have outstanding loans, but bankers know that some loans will have to be written off as never likely to be paid. Which ones? At what percentage of their value?

Finally, most Bulgarians have no experience with checks, consumer loans, electronic tellers, or any of the other wonders of modern banking. Right now, the typical Bulgarian is paid weekly in cash and makes purchases in cash, rarely having occasion to visit a bank. Credit cards are used in a few tourist hotels, but checks are totally unknown. Because wages were low in the past and the state guaranteed education, health care, housing, and pensions, there was no incentive to save. As a result, there is no pool of savings to channel into loans and investments. This situation is changing as the social safety net begins to weaken, and households have begun to save for education, housing, or retirement.

Bulgaria can expect to have a banking network available for consumers and small enterprises as well as financing foreign trade, governments, and industrial producers by the end of the decade. Then they will have to figure out how to use it. We can expect that, before too long, Bulgarians, too, will have the opportunity to borrow money, pay interest, and even bounce checks!

STRUCTURE AND FUNCTIONS OF THE FEDERAL RESERVE SYSTEM

The panic of 1907 and the recession that followed convinced Congress to hold hearings on banking problems. After a series of compromises designed to quiet some of opponents' fears, the Federal Reserve Act was passed in 1913, and the Fed began operating in November 1914. The Federal Reserve System was intended to regulate banks and serve as a lender of last resort. It would also serve as a banker to the Treasury, clear checks, and issue currency. Only later did monetary policy become its major function.

When the Fed was created, national banks were required to be members. State-chartered banks were allowed but not required to join. In 1980, the law was changed to place all depository institutions under the Fed's control.

STRUCTURE OF THE FED

The Federal Reserve System was designed to allay fears about concentrating financial power at the federal level. The United States is divided into twelve

Federal Reserve districts with their own Reserve Banks (see Figure 1). The purpose of districts was to keep management in closer touch with the people, instead of concentrating power in Washington DC or New York City. In addition, the board of directors of each district bank includes specific numbers of representatives of the banking industry, agriculture, and the general public in order to prevent domination by bankers.

A **Board of Governors** is the governing body of the Federal Reserve System. Seven members are appointed by the President for fourteen-year, staggered terms, with no more than one governor from any of the twelve districts. Most governors have a background in law, banking, or economics.

Within the Fed, the most powerful group is the **Federal Open Market Committee (FOMC)**, which supervises the conduct of monetary policy. The FOMC consists of the Board of Governors plus the presidents of five district banks, always including the president of the New York Federal Reserve Bank. When the FOMC meets regularly to decide changes in bank reserves and the money supply, all district bank presidents attend.

FIGURE 1

THE FEDERAL RESERVE SYSTEM
There are twelve Federal Reserve districts, each with its own bank. Most of these banks have branches. The Board of Governors of the Federal Reserve System is located in Washington DC.

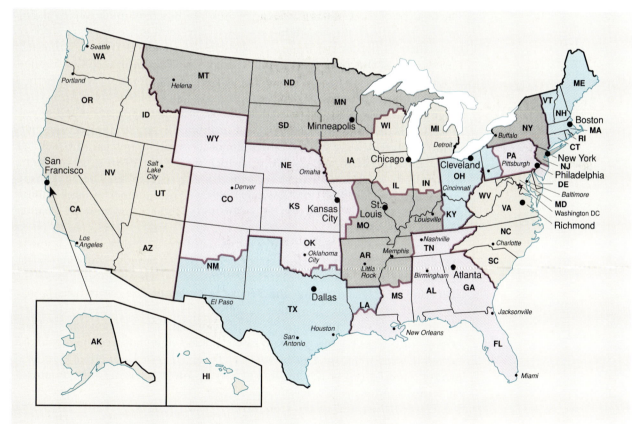

★ Board of Governors of the Federal Reserve System
● Federal Reserve Bank Cities
· Federal Reserve Branch Cities

Source: Board of Governors of the Federal Reserve System, *Federal Reserve Bulletin* (Washington DC: U.S. Government Printing Office, February 1994).

Board of Governors
The central governing body of the Federal Reserve System.

Federal Open Market Committee (FOMC)
The committee that supervises the conduct of monetary policy.

CHECK CLEARING

Check clearing is carried out by the district banks. Suppose you write a check for $100 on your account at Student Union Bank in Boston and send it to a firm in Georgia. The firm deposits your check in its account in Georgia National Bank. Georgia National records $100 in the firm's account and sends the check to the Atlanta Federal Reserve Bank, which credits the Georgia National reserve account with $100 and forwards the check to the Boston Federal Reserve Bank. The Boston Fed transfers $100 from the reserve account of Student Union to the account of the Atlanta Fed. Finally, the check is returned to Student Union, which loses $100 in reserves (an asset) and deposits (a liability). Complex as this process sounds, it is more efficient than what happened before the Fed existed. Checks were passed from bank to bank to bank until they returned to the point of origin, often months later.

BANK SAFETY

Bank safety was a primary reason for establishing the Federal Reserve System. The first test of the Fed was the Great Depression. Based on numerous bank failures in 1930–1933, the Fed didn't receive a very good grade as a guarantor of bank safety. Two deposit insurance agencies, the Federal Deposit Insurance Corporation (FDIC) and the Federal Savings and Loan Insurance Corporation (FSLIC), were created in 1935. These two insurance corporations were designed to protect bank depositors, not banks or bank stockholders, from insolvency. Originally deposits were insured up to $2,500, but the ceiling was raised several times and is currently $100,000. Deposit insurance is required for all members of the Federal Reserve System and is financed by premiums paid by member banks. Both the FDIC and the FSLIC (which merged in 1990) supervise member banks for safety and compliance with banking regulations. The bank insurance system worked well until the late 1980s, when a number of bank failures shifted the burden of protecting depositors to the federal government. Chapter 13 will address this issue in more detail.

The two sources of bank failures in the nineteenth century are still a source of policy concern today. One reason why banks fail is a liquidity problem—a lack of ready cash to meet large withdrawals by the public. Deposit insurance by the FDIC and FSLIC and having the Fed as a lender of last resort have largely resolved that problem. The other problem is insolvency—a bank with assets whose value is not enough to cover its liabilities, such as deposits. A bank becomes insolvent if it has too many assets in loans that may never be repaid. An insolvent bank will go out of business or be taken over by another bank in a merger, often forced by the insuring agency. Insolvency has been the dominant bank problem for the last decade.

The FDIC as well as the Comptroller of the Currency regulate kinds of investments that banks can make. This regulation provides stockholders and depositors some protection against insolvency. Even in a regulated industry such as banking, it is important to allow unsuccessful firms to fail and leave the industry if the market system is to function effectively. However, a very high failure rate, such as occurred in the late 1980s, overstrains the capacity of the regulatory authorities and the resources of the insurance corporations.

There were some spectacular failures of major banks in the late 1970s and early 1980s, including Franklin National Bank in New York City, Continental Illinois in Chicago, and Penn Square in Oklahoma. After a two-year wave of failures (79 banks in 1984 and 120 in 1985) and "shotgun" mergers, most surviving state-chartered banks became members of the FDIC or FSLIC. By the late 1980s, bank failures were less spectacular but more numerous, threatening the soundness of the FDIC and FSLIC. A number of banks—especially savings and loans—developed solvency problems. The value of their assets had fallen below the value of liabilities. Some banks were mismanaged by owners who made loans to themselves and their friends on the basis of property with inflated values. Bank supervisors were often careless in reviewing bank financial conditions, allowing problems to persist and multiply. Other banks ran into regional economic problems. Banks serving rural agricultural communities saw the value of loan collateral drop sharply with falling prices for farmland and high bankruptcy rates among farmers. Similar problems affected banks in Texas and Oklahoma with many loans to oil companies. A number of large banks had to write off bad loans to less developed countries. In 1990 and 1991, several major New England banks failed as the recession and falling real estate prices hit that region harder than the rest of the country.

KEY IDEAS

FUNCTIONS OF THE FED
- Preventing bank crises and panics by serving as the lender of last resort
- Supervising banks for safety
- Providing currency and check-clearing services
- Providing banking services to the Treasury
- Conducting monetary policy

THE BALANCE SHEET OF THE FED

Like all banks, the Fed has a balance sheet, shown in simplified form in Table 7. Note that member banks' reserves are liabilities of the Fed. Federal Reserve notes, now the only legal form of U.S. currency, are another major liability. Treasury deposits are a relatively small entry on the liability side, because most Treasury deposits are placed in commercial banks. The main assets of the Fed are government bonds of various maturities, which are used in open market operations. The Fed also holds gold certificates, issued by the Treasury when it acquires gold. A small amount of the Fed's assets consists of loans outstanding to banks.

On a balance sheet, the best measure of financial health is net worth, or assets minus liabilities. For a corporation, net worth represents the value of ownership rights of stockholders. Who owns the Fed? Member banks do, and they earn a guaranteed return on their shares. Any earnings in excess of that guaranteed return go to the U.S. Treasury, since the Fed is both a privately owned firm and an agency of the government.

The same kind of T-accounts used for bank transactions can also be used to describe the transactions of the Fed. The main transactions of interest are those

TABLE 7 FEDERAL RESERVE BALANCE SHEET, DECEMBER 1993 (MILLIONS OF DOLLARS)

ASSETS		LIABILITIES AND NET WORTH	
Government securities	$326,680	Reserves	$31,931
Loans to depository institutions	236	Federal Reserve notes	328,125
		Treasury deposits	7,975
Gold certificates	11,057	Other liabilities	9,577
OTHER ASSETS	47,387	TOTAL LIABILITIES	$377,608
		NET WORTH	7,956
TOTAL ASSETS	$385,364	TOTAL LIABILITIES AND NET WORTH	$385,364

Source: Board of Governors of the Federal Reserve System, *Federal Reserve Bulletin* (Washington DC: U.S. Government Printing Office, November 1993).

that change member bank reserves, because bank reserves determine bank lending and the size of the money supply. The important items for this purpose are government securities, loans to banks, and reserves of banks.

Table 8 shows the T-account summaries of two Fed transactions. In Transaction 1, the Fed buys a $10,000 bond from Amacher National Bank. In Transaction 2, the Fed makes a $20,000 loan to Ulbrich Savings Bank. When the Fed buys the bond, Amacher National is paid by a credit to its reserve account at the Fed. When the Fed makes the loan to Ulbrich Savings, this bank requests the funds in Federal Reserve notes.

THE FED AND THE MONEY SUPPLY

Transactions involving bonds, reserves, loans to banks, and Federal Reserve notes are the tools of monetary policy. The Fed uses the money supply and

TABLE 8 SAMPLE TRANSACTIONS FOR THE FED

TRANSACTION 1: The Fed buys a bond from Amacher National.

ASSETS		LIABILITIES	
Government bonds	+$10,000	Reserves	+$10,000

TRANSACTION 2: The Fed makes a loan to Ulbrich Savings.

ASSETS		LIABILITIES	
Loans to banks	$20,000	Federal Reserve notes	+$20,000

interest rates to affect output, employment, and the price level. The Fed has three ways to influence the money supply: open market operations, changes in the reserve ratio, and changes in the discount rate. Open market operations involve buying and selling bonds to affect banks' reserves. Changes in the reserve ratio affect excess reserves. The discount rate affects the level of bank borrowing from the Fed.

OPEN MARKET OPERATIONS

The Fed's preferred tool is open market operations. **Open market operations** are purchases and sales of bonds by the Fed on the open market in order to affect bank reserves. Open market operations are a very flexible tool. The impact on reserves can be precisely determined to be as large or as small as desired. Open market operations can be reversed if necessary and can be done without any fanfare.

> **Open market operations** Purchases and sales of U.S. Treasury securities on the open market by the Fed in order to affect bank reserves.

Open market operations are carried out by the Federal Reserve Bank of New York. Bonds are bought and sold through brokers in New York City. The New York district bank has this responsibility because New York is the financial center of the country. The New York Fed, however, does not buy and sell on the basis of its own decisions. It carries out the directives of the FOMC.

How do open market operations affect bank reserves? Suppose Bank A has reserves of $1,000,000 in the form of deposits with the Fed. The Fed buys $100,000 worth of government bonds from Bank A, paying for them by writing on its books that Bank A has $100,000 more in deposits (reserves) with the Fed. Bank A's reserves are now $1,100,000. These changes are shown on the T-accounts of Bank A and the Fed in Table 9. If the Fed buys a bond from an individual or a business firm, the seller will deposit the check from the Fed in a bank. The bank will clear the check through the Fed, and its reserves with the Fed will increase by the amount of the sale. No matter where the Fed buys bonds, bank reserves increase by the amount of the Fed purchase. Likewise, open market sales of securities by the Fed decrease the reserves of banks. Through open market operations, the Fed can directly affect the reserves of banks.

FIRST-ROUND EFFECTS OF OPEN MARKET OPERATIONS. Assume that the required reserve ratio is 20 percent of checkable deposits and that all of Bank A's reserves were required reserves prior to the purchase of $100,000 in government bonds by the Fed. As shown in Bank A's T-account in Table 9, the bank's interest-earn-

TABLE 9 EFFECTS OF OPEN MARKET OPERATIONS ON BANK A AND THE FED

BANK A			FED			
ASSETS		LIABILITIES	ASSETS		LIABILITIES	
Reserves	+$100,000		Government bonds	+$100,000	Reserves	+$100,000
Government bonds	− 100,000					

ing assets in government bonds have fallen by $100,000 while its reserves have risen by $100,000. Now its excess reserves, total reserves *minus* required reserves, are $100,000.

This change in the makeup of Bank A's assets is only the first-round effect of the open market operation. What will Bank A do with its excess reserves? It now has fewer interest-earning assets after selling the $100,000 bond to the Fed. When the next customer asks for a $100,000 loan, it will be granted if that customer is a good risk. Further, the bank may be willing to make loans on easier terms, perhaps even at a lower interest rate. The new loan of $100,000 is shown in Table 10 as an increase in both checkable deposits (liabilities) and loans (assets) of Bank A.

Bank A has new deposits of $100,000 and new reserves of $100,000. Twenty percent of these new deposits, or $20,000, are required reserves. Bank A can safely lend its excess reserves because it can afford to lose these reserves and still meet the reserve ratio. As long as a bank lends only reserves that are in excess of its required reserves, it will be able to meet its reserve requirement, even if all loaned funds leave the bank.

OPEN MARKET OPERATIONS AND THE DEPOSIT MULTIPLIER. What happens to funds that the borrower spends? Bank A will lose reserves and deposits, but another bank will gain both. The new reserves will remain in the banking system until the Fed withdraws them (perhaps by an open market operation in the opposite direction). These reserves can be passed around from bank to bank, but banks cannot create new reserves. As long as reserves are in the banking system, they can support additional checkable deposits and a larger money supply. The amount of additional deposits these reserves can support depends on the reserve ratio, according to the relationship developed earlier in this chapter:

$$\Delta D = \frac{1}{rr} \Delta BR.$$

The change in checkable deposits (ΔD) from the $100,000 open market operation ($\Delta BR = \$100,000$) with a reserve ratio ($rr$) equal to 0.20 can be as much as $100,000/0.20, or $500,000. How did this happen? Initially, member bank reserves increased by $100,000. Since the reserve ratio was unchanged, all of these additional reserves were excess reserves, available for lending. As loans and deposits expand, however, excess reserves become required reserves behind newly created checkable deposits. This process continues until all of the new reserves are serving as required reserves.

CONTRACTING THE MONEY SUPPLY. Open market purchases of bonds by the Fed are expansionary. When the Fed purchases bonds, it pays for them by increasing member banks' reserves. If the Fed wishes to contract the money supply or

TABLE 10 T-ACCOUNT FOR BANK A'S LOAN EXPANSION OF $100,000

ASSETS		LIABILITIES	
Loans	+$100,000	Checkable Deposits	+$100,000

prevent banks from expanding the money supply, it will offer to sell bonds to the banks. If banks do not wish to buy the bonds, their customers will, and the effect on reserves will be the same. When the Fed sells bonds, it accepts payment by decreasing the bank's reserve account.

Sales of government bonds by the Fed reduce bank reserves. The deposit

---

POLICY FOCUS: WHO SHOULD CONTROL THE FED?

Governments in many other parts of the world do not face a major political problem that confronts the President and Congress in the United States. U.S. monetary policy is controlled by an agency that operates independently of both the executive and legislative branches of the U.S. government. Central banks in many other countries are a part of the government and are under political control. This arrangement makes it easier to coordinate monetary and fiscal policy. Among major industrial countries, only Germany gives its central bank more independence than the Fed, although in practice the Bank of Japan has as much freedom or more.[a]

Because members of the Board of Governors serve such long terms, even a two-term President rarely appoints more than a bare majority of the board. Long terms give the Fed a degree of political independence. The Fed is accountable to its regional boards, its stockholders, and the banks, but there is no effective way for the President or Congress to exercise any control except by appointments to the Board. Because of this independence, political insiders in Washington have labeled the chair of the Fed's Board of Governors, currently Alan Greenspan, the second most powerful person in Washington.

Until the end of World War II, the Fed's independence did not pose major problems for the President and Congress. With the advent of active fiscal policy, however, some observers felt a need for better coordination of monetary and fiscal policy, which could be achieved if the Fed answered to the President. The first conflict surfaced over interest rates in the period immediately after World War II, when the government wanted the Fed to keep interest rates low in order to reduce the interest cost on the huge federal debt incurred during the war. The Fed accommodated the Treasury until 1951, when an agreement was reached to let the Fed focus on monetary policy concerns rather than Treasury financing problems. Conflict arose again in 1979 when the Fed's concern about inflation led to a sharp slowdown in monetary growth that resulted in record high interest rates and contributed to the 1980–1982 recession. During the 1980s, an expansionary fiscal policy was partly offset by Fed actions that limited growth of the money supply and kept interest rates high, but this policy had the approval of the Reagan administration.

The Fed is sensitive to concerns of the banking and business communities. As a result, the Fed is more focused on inflation than unemployment, while Congress tends to worry more about unemployment than inflation. Congress is also more sensitive to pressure from industries that like low interest rates, such as the auto and housing industries. The tension between these two goals would be there whether or not the Fed were independent of the President. Having an independent monetary authority puts some constraints on the President and Congress, who tend to have a shorter term perspective than the appointed long-term governors at the Fed. Most of the time there is considerable dialogue, negotiation, and compromise between monetary and fiscal authorities that may result in a better combination of policies. After lengthy debates spanning several decades, most economists would conclude that the advantages of the Fed's independence probably outweigh the drawbacks.

a. "Central Banks: America vs. Japan," *The Economist* (January 25, 1992): 19–21.

---

multiplier works on this reduction in reserves in the same way it works on an expansion. The money supply that existing reserves can support is smaller than before. If banks were fully loaned up before this transaction, there would be a decrease in the money supply.

CHANGING THE RESERVE RATIO

The second tool used by the Fed is setting and changing the reserve ratio. There are two kinds of assets that a bank can count toward meeting the required reserve. One is currency and coins, or vault cash. The second, and larger, consists of funds the bank has on deposit with its district Reserve Bank. The Fed requires depository institutions to hold reserves equal to certain fractions of the different kinds of deposits they have. The reserve ratio is higher for banks with deposits over $40 million. One reason why banks collapsed during panics before the Fed was created was that their reserves were too small or not readily available. In practice, reserves now have little to do with the safety of checking and savings account deposits. Their safety is ensured by deposit insurance. However, reserves do ensure that banks will have some ready funds to meet withdrawals.

THE RESERVE RATIO AND THE DEPOSIT MULTIPLIER. A change in the reserve ratio changes the maximum size of the money supply, not by changing bank reserves (BR), but by changing the deposit multiplier ($1/rr$). The deposit multiplier is the reciprocal of the reserve ratio. When the reserve ratio changes from 20 percent to 10 percent, the deposit multiplier increases from 5 to 10. A reduction in the reserve ratio has a double impact on the money supply. First, it converts some required reserves into excess reserves. Second, it increases the size of the deposit multiplier. An increase in the reserve ratio works in the opposite way. The higher reserve ratio creates a shortfall of excess reserves and also reduces the size of the deposit multiplier.

A change in the reserve ratio is more complex than open market operations because of this double impact. Because it is such a powerful tool, changes in the reserve ratio are made rarely and in small amounts. Even a change of a fraction of 1 percent can have a very large (and somewhat uncertain) impact on the economy and can be very unsettling to banks. In the last two decades, the Fed made adjustments to the reserve ratio an average of three times a year, most of them affecting only one or two types of deposits.[1]

THE RESERVE RATIO AND BANK LENDING. The reserve ratio is less important to ensure a cushion of liquidity than as a means for the Fed to control the ability of banks to lend and create money. To see how this works, assume that banks have to hold reserves equal to 20 percent of their checkable deposits. Suppose Bank A has exactly the reserves required: deposits of $1,000,000 and reserves of $200,000. If people withdraw $100,000 from their checkable deposits, Bank A will have only $100,000 left in reserves supporting deposits of $900,000. Required reserves behind that level of deposits are $180,000. Bank A's reserves are now $80,000 below the level required by the Fed. The bank must make up these reserves or face fines by the Fed. When Bank A, and other banks, are forced to contract lending to make up reserves, the money supply will shrink.

A change in the reserve ratio increases or decreases banks' ability to lend. With a given level of reserves, an increase in the reserve ratio from 20 percent to 25 percent would create a reserve shortage and make bankers less willing to lend. A reduction in the reserve ratio from 20 percent to 15 percent would con-

---

1. A list of these changes is given by Michelle R. Garfinkel and Daniel L. Thornton in "The Link Between M1 and the Monetary Base in the 1980s," *Review*, Federal Reserve Bank of St. Louis (September–October 1989): 35–52.

vert some required reserves to excess reserves and make bankers more willing to make loans. (Normally changes in the reserve ratio are much smaller than that, no more than 0.5 percent at a time.)

Both open market operations and changes in the reserve ratio affect the amount of checkable deposits by changing excess reserves. The difference is that changes in the reserve ratio leave the amount of reserves the same but convert some required reserves to excess reserves, or vice versa. A reduction in the reserve ratio increases the size of the money supply that can be supported by any given amount of bank reserves. An increase in the reserve ratio reduces the size of the potential money supply.

The impact of a lower reserve ratio on Bank A is shown in Table 11. When the Fed reduces the reserve ratio from 20 to 10 percent, Bank A's reserves are still $200,000, but required reserves have fallen to $100,000, and excess reserves have risen to $100,000. With $100,000 in excess reserves, Bank A will expand its lending, just as it did when an open market operation increased its reserves. Table 11 traces the response by Bank A.

Whether excess reserves result from an open market operation or a change in the reserve ratio, they are still something of a "hot potato." Reserves move from bank to bank until they gradually become required reserves through the lending process.

If excess reserves are initially zero, an increase in the reserve ratio results in a reserve deficit. Checkable deposits fall as banks are forced to contract loans. The maximum money supply that a given volume of reserves can support will be smaller because the deposit multiplier is smaller.

DISCOUNTING AND THE DISCOUNT RATE

One way for banks to correct a shortage of required reserves is to borrow from the Fed. This lending power is the Fed's third tool of monetary control. It derives from the role of the central bank as a lender of last resort. Borrowing from the Fed by banks is called "using the discount window." The interest rate the Fed charges banks is called the **discount rate**. Changing the discount rate is

Discount rate
The interest rate the Fed charges on loans to banks.

TABLE 11 BANK A RESPONDS TO A CHANGE IN THE REQUIRED RESERVE RATIO FROM 20 PERCENT TO 10 PERCENT

ASSETS		LIABILITIES	
Reserves	$200,000	Checkable deposits	$1,000,000
Loans and government bonds	$800,000		

After the change in the reserve ratio, Bank A makes a loan of $100,000. When the borrower spends the funds, Bank A loses reserves and deposits to another bank.

ASSETS		LIABILITIES	
Reserves	$100,000	Checkable deposits	$1,000,000
Loans and government bonds	900,000		

another tool of monetary policy. The higher the rate, the less eager banks are to borrow. The Fed may deny use of the discount window to banks that have made unwise loans. The discount rate is normally lower than other interest rates at which banks could borrow.

THE DISCOUNT WINDOW AND CHANGES IN THE RESERVE RATIO. Recall what happens when an increase in the reserve ratio leaves banks with too little reserves. Banks have to contract their deposits by selling interest-earning assets or eliminating loans. Such a forced contraction creates a difficult situation for both banks and their loan customers. It takes time to adjust. For this reason, the Fed may cushion the impact of a decline in bank reserves by keeping the discount window open—standing ready to make loans to banks as needed. With an open discount window, instead of immediately calling in loans and selling bonds, banks can borrow reserves from the Fed. However, banks have taken out loans with the Fed that they will eventually have to repay. They will still have to reduce their loans, but they have bought some time in which to adjust more gradually.

Each Federal Reserve Bank sets a discount rate for the depository institutions of its district, but the rates are usually the same in all twelve districts. Normally the discount rate is slightly below the market interest rate. To keep banks from borrowing from the Fed at low rates and lending to customers at high rates, district banks ration their loans and warn banks about abusing their borrowing privileges. Many people are under the impression that the Fed sets market interest rates, but the discount rate is the only rate the Fed sets directly. The Fed's indirect effect on market interest rates is discussed in Chapter 14.

The discount rate functions as a signal more than as a direct tool of monetary control. An increase in the discount rate indicates to banks that the Fed wants to cool down the economy by reducing bank lending. A decrease signifies the Fed's desire to stimulate the economy. Changes in the discount rate also alter the profitability of borrowing from the Fed in order to relend. Raising the rate makes it more expensive to borrow. In that case, banks are expected to borrow less and hold larger excess reserves in order to avoid borrowing. A lower rate makes borrowing from the Fed more attractive and encourages banks to hold fewer excess reserves. They know they can easily borrow from the Fed if necessary.

The discount rate is not as powerful a tool as changes in the reserve ratio or open market operations. Its impact is hard to measure, since the magnitude of the effect depends on bankers' reaction to the change. If this tool were used too often, it would lose its effectiveness as a signal of the Fed's policy direction.

THE FEDERAL FUNDS MARKET. Banks can borrow reserves from each other as well as from the Fed. Loans between banks are made in the **federal funds market**. If Bank A has excess reserves, it can lend some of these (for one day at a time) to Bank B. The rate charged is the **federal funds rate**. If the annual rate is 12 percent, it costs the borrowing bank approximately 0.03 percent for a one-day loan.

The Fed does not directly set the federal funds rate, but it does set a target range for that rate, such as plus or minus .125 percent around 12 percent. If the federal funds rate drops to 11.875 percent, the Fed will sell bonds to drain reserves from the banking system. As excess reserves of member banks fall relative to the demand for them, the federal funds rate will be driven up. Similarly, if the rate rises to 12.125 percent, the Fed will buy bonds to inject reserves into

Federal funds market
The market in which banks borrow reserves from each other.

Federal funds rate
The interest rate charged in the federal funds market.

banks. The supply of reserves increases relative to demand, driving the federal funds rate back down toward 12 percent. Many economists think that this indirect control of the federal funds rate plays an important role in monetary policy. The federal funds rate is usually slightly above the discount rate because banks prefer to borrow from other banks rather than from the Fed.

OTHER TOOLS OF THE FEDERAL RESERVE SYSTEM

The Fed has a few more specialized tools. From time to time, the Fed has been authorized to set maximum repayment periods and minimum down payments for consumer credit. It can also set the fraction of stock purchases that a buyer can finance with credit (the margin requirement). These tools, called selective credit controls, are not used very frequently. They have become less useful in the last few decades with the growth of alternative sources of funds (nonbank financial institutions) to which borrowers can turn.

The Fed can also use **moral suasion**. That is, it can try to convince banks to do what it favors. For example, the Fed may think that the money supply is growing too quickly. The Board of Governors will urge banks not to make as many new loans in order to hold down the rate of growth. Since the Fed regulates banks and controls their access to the discount window, banks have to pay some attention to such requests. Although the Fed has some success in persuasion, this approach is generally less effective than open market operations as a way of controlling the money supply.

Moral suasion Attempts by the Fed to convince depository institutions to do what the Fed favors.

KEY IDEAS

FEDERAL RESERVE TOOLS			
TOOL	PLUSES AND MINUSES	FREQUENCY OF USE	WORKS THROUGH
• Open market operations	Flexible Broad impact	Used frequently	Changing bank reserves
• Changes in the reserve ratio	Broad impact Extremely powerful	Used rarely	Changing excess reserves
• Changes in the discount rate	Useful as signal	Used occasionally	Changing the amount of borrowing by banks Affects interest rates
• Selective credit controls	Limited effectiveness	Used infrequently	Changing terms of consumer loans and borrowing to buy stock
• Moral suasion	Limited effectiveness	Used occasionally	Persuading banks to change amount of lending

Both economists and politicians have disagreed over the effectiveness of the Fed in using its monetary policy tools. The debates of the nineteenth century over how freely banks should lend are still alive. There is still support for a policy of easy money, unlimited credit, and inflation among those who are in debt and want to be able to borrow more and pay it back with cheaper dollars. There are also groups who support a hard-money policy, ranging from those who simply want monetary growth carefully controlled to those who would like to return to full-bodied money, usually a gold standard.

Developments in banking and financial markets in the last fifteen years have changed the nature of banking in the United States. The next chapter will take a closer look at some of these changes as part of a broader examination of financial markets and interest rates.

Consider again...*Now that you understand how the banking system works, perhaps you will take discrimination by banks against students a little less personally. The big difference between older adults and college students is the average balance that each group keeps in checkable accounts. Older people tend to spend less often and leave a larger balance. Students get their monthly check from home, promptly spend most of it, and are down to the prospect of bouncing checks by the end of the month. It is those average balances that matter to banks, because those are the funds that banks can lend out to earn interest.*

Banks operate on the spread—the difference between the interest earned on their loans and investments and interest paid their depositors. If depositors would just leave a little more of their funds on deposit on a regular basis, instead of constantly visiting the electronic teller machine for a little more cash, banks could get by with less excess reserves, which earn no interest, and have more available to lend. Naturally, banks are going to favor depositors who leave idle cash in their accounts and frown on the "in-and-out" patterns typical of younger people with limited incomes and lots of opportunities to spend. It may not be fair, but your turn as a favored senior citizen will come if you wait long enough.

SUMMARY

1. The banking system in the United States is based on the principle of fractional reserve banking, first developed in the Middle Ages by goldsmiths. Depository institutions make loans, which expands the money supply. The upper limit on such expansion is determined by the amount of reserves banks must keep to back up deposits. Changes in reserves lead to changes in the money supply through bank lending.

2. The amount banks can lend depends on excess reserves. Required reserves are equal to deposits multiplied by the reserve ratio. These reserves must be held in some combination of vault cash and deposits in a Federal Reserve Bank. Excess reserves are total reserves minus required reserves. As excess reserves expand, banks can increase their loans and, thus, the money supply. Reductions in excess reserves force contractions of loans and the money supply.

3. The Federal Reserve System was created to protect the economy from the kinds of bank panics that occurred in the nineteenth and early twentieth centuries. It was designed to serve as a regulator and lender of last resort to member banks, to provide banking services to the Treasury, and to manage check clearing between banks. The Fed supplies reserves to member banks in

the form of Federal Reserve notes and reserve deposits at the Fed. The twelve Federal Reserve districts in the United States each have a Federal Reserve District Bank. The central authority is the Board of Governors in Washington DC. The Fed is responsible for monetary policy, which is carried out by actions that influence interest rates and the money supply.
4. The Fed has three tools of monetary policy: open market operations, changes in the reserve ratio, and lending at the discount rate. Open market operations, the main tool, are purchases and sales of government bonds by the Fed on the open market, which change the level of bank reserves. Changes in the reserve ratio alter banks' excess reserves. Banks can borrow from the Fed at the discount rate to cushion reductions in reserves. Changes in the discount rate affect banks' willingness to borrow from the Fed to increase their reserves. Both the reserve ratio and the discount rate are changed infrequently.

NEW TERMS

fractional reserve banking
reserves
T-account
excess reserves
reserve ratio

deposit multiplier
currency drain
Federal Reserve System (Fed)
bank panics

lender of last resort
Board of Governors
Federal Open Market Committee (FOMC)
open market operations

discount rate
federal funds market
federal funds rate
moral suasion

QUESTIONS: REVIEW, APPLICATIONS, AND POLICY

REVIEW

1. Why are there twelve Federal Reserve districts? In which district are you? What is the Board of Governors?
2. Which of the following items appear on the Fed's balance sheet? For each item that appears on the balance sheet, indicate whether it is an asset or a liability.
   a. government bonds
   b. reserves of banks
   c. deposits by the Treasury
   d. deposits by the public
   e. loans to banks
   f. currency
3. Which of the following items appear on a bank's balance sheet? For each item that appears on the balance sheet, indicate whether it is an asset or a liability.
   a. government bonds
   b. reserves
   c. deposits by the Treasury
   d. deposits by the public
   e. loans to the public
   f. currency
4. What are the three main tools of the Fed? Which one is used most often? Why?
5. List the steps by which a sale of government bonds by the Fed affects output and the price level through aggregate supply and demand.
6. Why do banks borrow from one another instead of from the Fed?
7. How does the Fed's role differ from what was originally envisioned?
8. Why did it take the United States so long to establish a permanent central bank?
9. List all of the actions the Fed can undertake to try to increase lending, the money supply, and the level of economic activity.

APPLICATIONS

10. Suppose the reserve ratio is 20 percent. If an extra $2 billion in excess reserves are injected into the banking system through an open market purchase of T-bills by the Fed, by how much can checkable deposits rise? What would your answer be if the reserve ratio were 10 percent? Does the total of checkable deposits have to rise?

11. Would it make a difference in your answers to Question 10 if the increase in excess reserves came about because the Fed lowered the discount rate and thus induced banks to borrow $2 billion?
12. Suppose bank reserves are $100 billion, the reserve ratio is 20 percent, and banks are fully loaned up (that is, excess reserves are zero). Now suppose the reserve-ratio is lowered to 10 percent and banks once again become fully loaned up. What is the new level of checkable deposits? Do this problem again, but assume the reserve ratio rises to 25 percent.
13. If the Fed sells bonds, what is likely to happen to each of the following?

a. bank reserves
b. interest rates
c. the money supply
d. output and/or prices (money GDP)

POLICY

14. Should the Fed be independent of the President and Congress? Why or why not?
15. How are the effects of changes in the reserve ratio on bank lending and the money supply different from the effects of open market operations? How do these differences affect the Fed's choice of policy tools?

SUGGESTIONS FOR FURTHER READING

Board of Governors of the Federal Reserve System. *The Federal Reserve System: Purposes and Functions.* Washington DC: U.S. Government Printing Office, annually. Describes the structure and operations of the Fed.

Goodhart, Charles. *The Evolution of Central Banking.* Cambridge MA: MIT Press, 1988. Explains why and how central banks evolved, drawing on the experiences of several countries.

Humphrey, T. "Lender of Last Resort: The Concept in History." *Economic Review,* Federal Reserve Bank of Richmond (March/April 1989): 8–16.

CHAPTER 13
FINANCIAL MARKETS AND INTEREST RATES

Consider this...*From 1990 through 1993, the stock market was booming. The Dow-Jones average, which stood at about 2,400 in mid–1990, had risen to over 3,500 by mid–1993. Money kept flowing into the market, and stocks kept rising. Yet the economy itself wasn't doing anything very exciting. Coming out of the 1990–1991 recession, growth was slow, inflation was low, and unemployment remained high. Normally stock prices take off in response to growth (which means the value of stocks will appreciate as firms enjoy higher sales and profits) and inflation (because stock prices typically rise as fast as or faster than the inflation rate). Why a stock market boom in a sluggish economy? The answer to the puzzle lies in the relationship between stock prices, bond prices, and interest rates.*

LEARNING OBJECTIVES

1. Explain the problems that led to the policy decision to bail out failing banks in the late 1980s and early 1990s.
2. Identify the various kinds of interest rates, the factors that result in different rates on different financial instruments, and the relationship between bond prices and bond yields.
3. Describe the role of the stock and bond markets in transforming saving into investment.
4. Discuss the effect of interest rates on investment spending, output, and income.

The Fed is interested in lending, borrowing, and interest rates mainly as a channel of monetary policy. But it cannot ignore the close links between the market for stocks and the market for loanable funds in which banks operate. The role of financial markets, or the credit market, is to gather funds from households and other savers and channel them to borrowers (households, government, or business firms) or to firms that sell ownership rights (stock). Interest rates are the prices at which firms borrow in the credit market (by issuing bonds). Ownership claims, or stocks, convey a right to a share in the profits of the firm. Since firms raise funds by issuing both stocks and bonds, these two markets are closely linked to each other as well as to the banking system and the money market. After we explore the lender's side of financial markets, we will turn to the borrower's side and look at the relationship between investment decisions and interest rates.

BANK FAILURES AND THE SAVINGS AND LOAN BAILOUT

The last two decades have seen dramatic changes in financial markets. There are more kinds of institutions offering more kinds of deposits, financial instruments, and services. High inflation rates and high market interest rates in the 1970s led to some major changes in regulations governing the nation's banking system. Most of the bank regulations that were eliminated in the 1980s had been enacted in the 1930s as part of a policy of preventing bank failures. Banks did not object to regulation as long as they had no serious competition from other firms offering deposit accounts. Regulation kept banks from competing with each other to attract deposits by offering interest on checking accounts. They could lend funds deposited in checking accounts without having to pay depositors any interest. Consumers, whether they liked it or not, were being protected from bank failure at the sacrifice of higher yields and a greater array of accounts and services.

THE MOVE TO DEREGULATE

In the 1970s, inflation drove up market interest rates and widened the gap between what banks were allowed to pay and what competing nonbank institutions were willing to pay. Banks lost deposits to other institutions where depositors could earn higher rates. Deregulation let banks fight back and regain some of the lost deposits. High interest rates also resulted in the loss of member banks by the Federal Reserve System, because member banks had higher required reserve ratios and were losing potential interest earnings at increasingly higher market rates. Banks began exchanging their federal charters for state charters. With fewer banks under its direct control, the Fed was finding it more difficult to carry out monetary policy.

The policy response to these developments was legislation to deregulate banks so that they could compete more aggressively with nonbank financial institutions. In 1980, all depository institutions—commercial banks (with either state or national charters), savings banks, savings and loan associations, and credit unions—were placed under the control of the Fed. All gained access to Fed services and became subject to the same reserve ratios for the same types of deposits. At the same time, banks were allowed to offer interest-bearing checking accounts, and savings banks and savings and loan associations were allowed to offer a full range of accounts and invest in a greater variety of assets. In 1982, Congress allowed banks to issue checkable, interest-bearing deposit accounts similar to the money market mutual funds available from nonbank institutions.

Bank deregulation made it possible for banks to offer a wider range of services and more attractive interest rates to small depositors and middle-income households. Although interest rates on all assets had fallen by the 1990s, depositors still had a choice among a much wider variety of accounts than before. Armed with these new types of accounts, banks could compete more effectively with nonbank institutions in attracting deposits.

THE BANKING CRISIS

Although the benefits of deregulation were apparent, the costs of this policy change were slower to appear. Freed from interest rate ceilings, banks began to compete aggressively for deposits. With fewer restrictions on the kinds of assets they could hold, some banks—especially savings and loans—began to make riskier investments. When the 1981–1982 recession hit, interest rates fell on the loans they were making, but funds deposited in CDs were locked in for periods up to seven years at the old high interest rates. In addition, many bank loans were in default (borrowers were not making payments).

Banks earn income by charging more interest on loans than they pay on deposits. Banks' earnings fall when there is a decline in the **spread**, the difference between the average interest rate earned on loans and the average interest rate paid on deposits. Banks are tempted to make riskier loans in order to earn higher interest rates and restore earnings. In the early 1980s, when market interest rates dropped sharply, the average interest rate on banks' loan portfolios fell very quickly, because banks hold a large amount of short-term assets, such as T-bills and commercial paper (very short-term business loans). As these assets matured, banks tried to replace them with loans and assets that earned as much or more, but most such assets involved greater risk. Average bank earnings on investments fell. Unable to reduce the average interest paid on deposits as quickly, the spread also fell. For some banks, the spread was not enough to cover operating expenses, so they suffered losses (negative net earnings). Since the net worth of banks grows or shrinks depending on their earnings, negative net earnings reduced many banks' net worth.

Spread
The difference between the average interest rate earned on bank loans and the average interest rate paid on deposits.

At the same time, there was a decline in the market value of banks' assets. Banks in Texas, Oklahoma, and Louisiana had made many loans to oil companies. The value of these loans declined sharply in value with the fall in oil prices. The drop in the price of oil affected earnings of oil workers and oil firm owners, affecting the prices of houses in Houston and other oil centers and threatening mortgage holders (usually savings and loans) with losses. As owners defaulted, the houses abandoned to the bank usually had a resale value less than the balance owed on the mortgage. Office buildings in large cities in these three states, especially in Houston, had few tenants. When rental income was not enough to meet mortgage payments, developers abandoned buildings to the bank. Problems spread to other states. In addition to other problems, defaults on loans to Third World countries hit some of the larger banks.

Savings and loans, even more than commercial banks, had taken advantage of the freedom created by deregulation combined with the safety net of deposit insurance to make some very risky loans. Banks that were close to insolvency were tempted to make such loans. If the loans paid off, at high interest rates, the bank could become solvent again. If the gamble failed, depositors were protected by deposit insurance.

To understand the nature of the insolvency problem, consider the balance sheet of Petroleum Savings and Loan (Table 1). As you can see, this bank has $100 million in assets, consisting of reserves, mortgages, and commercial loans. It has $94 million in deposits as liabilities and a net worth of $6 million. This bank exceeds the current capital requirements imposed on banks by regulatory agencies. Its capital is 7 percent of its loans ($6 million divided by $85 million). Capital requirements have been raised, but are still only 3 percent of loans. (In this chapter, we are using the term capital in its financial or balance sheet sense of net worth rather than its proper economic use of producer goods.)

TABLE 1 BALANCE SHEET OF PETROLEUM SAVINGS AND LOAN (BILLIONS OF DOLLARS)

ASSETS		LIABILITIES	
Reserves	$15	Deposits	$94
Mortgages	40		
Commercial loans	45		
TOTAL ASSETS	$100	TOTAL LIABILITIES	$94
		NET WORTH	6
		TOTAL LIABILITIES AND NET WORTH	$100

Suppose a weak housing market forces Petroleum S&L to foreclose on a number of mortgages. The bank takes over some of the houses and sells them to pay off the mortgages. Assume that the bank forecloses on $10 million in mortgages, but distress sales of those properties bring in only $5 million. The value of the mortgage part of the bank's portfolio of assets drops to $30 million. The bank adds the $5 million received from property sales to its reserves. At the same time, suppose some of the bank's commercial loans are in trouble. A few borrowers go bankrupt, paying only a small fraction of what they owe. The value of commercial loans drops to $38 million. Now the bank's balance sheet looks like Table 2.

This bank is still liquid—in fact, its reserves have increased. However, it is no longer solvent—the value of its liabilities is greater than the value of its assets. Unless matters improve quickly, this bank will have to file for bankruptcy. Its assets will be sold to pay the claims of depositors. After the bank pays off $88 million worth of deposits, the remaining $6 million (of deposits up to $100,000) will be paid by the Federal Deposit Insurance Corporation (FDIC).

The experience of Petroleum Savings and Loan is typical of what happened to many banks in the 1980s. From 1980 to 1990, 1,039 banks were closed because of solvency problems. In comparison, 80 commercial banks and 43 sav-

TABLE 2 REVISED BALANCE SHEET OF PETROLEUM SAVINGS AND LOAN (BILLIONS OF DOLLARS)

ASSETS		LIABILITIES	
Reserves	$20	Deposits	$94
Mortgages	30		
Commercial loans	38		
TOTAL ASSETS	$88	TOTAL LIABILITIES	$94
		NET WORTH	−6
		TOTAL LIABILITIES AND NET WORTH	$88

ings and loans closed during the 1970s, and 58 commercial banks and 43 savings and loans closed during the 1960s. Clearly something had happened to the banking system. Although the vast majority of both commercial banks and savings and loans remained solvent, those that failed rolled up huge losses. The payoffs to depositors far exceeded the financial resources of the deposit insurance agencies, the FDIC and the FSLIC.

GLOBAL OUTLOOK: BANKING IN JAPAN

Each country's system of banks and financial markets is unique, but most have some features in common. Japan's financial system provides an interesting comparison to that of the United States.

Japan has had a central bank, the Bank of Japan, since 1882. Like the Fed, the Bank of Japan issues currency, serves as a bankers' bank and a depository bank for the government, and conducts monetary policy. The banking system consists of city and regional banks, *sogo* banks, *shinkin* banks, and postal savings. There are only twelve city banks, which hold 20 percent of all deposits of financial institutions and lend to large corporations. (The Japanese government also invests directly in business ventures.) The sixty-four regional banks, located in medium-sized cities, hold individual deposits (mostly time deposits for one year or more). Thus, one major difference is the smaller number of what are called commercial banks in the United States.

Sogo banks are roughly equivalent to U.S. savings banks or savings and loans. *Shinkin* banks are the Japanese equivalent of credit unions. These banks are much more numerous than the city and regional banks and serve the needs of individuals. Partly for cultural reasons and partly because there is no social security system, Japanese households save a much larger share of their incomes than American households do. Japanese households also maintain large deposits in postal savings (deposits at the post office). Such deposits were important in the United States at one time but no longer exist. Like the United States, Japan has deposit insurance. However, the government protects the Japanese deposit insurance system from large demands by imposing strict collateral requirements on most loans in order to ensure bank solvency.

Japan deregulated its banks at about the same time as the United States did, and for a similar reason. The development of medium-term government bond funds with higher yields than bank deposits led to an outflow of deposits from the banking system. Interest rates were then allowed to rise. More generous funding of the deposit insurance system and stricter collateral requirements have helped Japan to avoid bank failures.

THE BANK BAILOUT

A policy response to the crisis in the banking industry was slow to emerge. Legislation was finally passed in 1989, merging the FDIC with its savings and loan counterpart, the FSLIC. It also set up a new agency, the Resolution Trust Corporation (RTC), to deal with the problems of insolvent banks, including the sale of their assets.[1] The RTC held sales of bank assets — buildings, land, equipment, cars, boats, household furnishing, even works of art. Some of these assets were part of the bank's own buildings and furnishings, but most were assets pledged as collateral on loans that were never repaid. The goal of the RTC was to recover as much as possible as quickly as possible, because the difference

---

1. For a description of this legislation and the events leading up to it, see Dwight M. Jaffee, "Symposium on Federal Deposit Insurance for S & L Institutions," *Journal of Economic Perspectives* (Fall 1989): 3–10.

between the money recovered from selling these assets and the amount owed to depositors in failed banks had to be made up by the taxpayers. The total cost to taxpayers for cleaning up the banking mess over a period of five years came to $182 billion, plus about $40 billion spent prior to 1989.

Other policy steps were taken to avoid repeating the banking disasters of the 1980s. The insurance premiums banks pay for deposit insurance were increased, and banks were made subject to higher capital-to-loan ratios to provide a larger cushion for solvency. These higher ratios mean that the bank's stockholders have more to lose from risky loans. Concerns of stockholders should force banks to be more cautious and less likely to become insolvent in the future.

The recovery of the banking industry has moved more quickly than expected. By 1992, 94 percent of banks were making a profit, and the banking industry as a whole racked up an impressive profit of $31.5 billion.[2] The retained profits enabled banks to rebuild their capital as a percentage of their assets to an average of over 7 percent. The major source of increased bank profits was the unusually high spread between the rate on safe long-term investments, such as Treasury bonds, and short-term rates, including rates paid on CDs and other deposits. A second source of profits for banks with substantial mortgage lending was the fees from refinancing loans as mortgage rates fell. When a bank refinances a loan, the bank's processing fees range from 1 to 3 percent of the amount of the loan. When the average rate on a thirty-year, fixed-rate mortgage fell from over 10 percent in 1989 and 1990 to under 7 percent in 1993, there was a tremendous volume of refinancing resulting in large fees. Consolidation of banks through mergers (in addition to mergers forced by failure) also helped to strengthen the banking system. In 1991 there were 428 such voluntary mergers.

THE LOANABLE FUNDS MARKET AND INTEREST RATES

Banks are only one group of players, although a very important group, on the lending side of financial markets. The other major lenders in the loanable funds market are stockbrokers, bond dealers, insurance companies, pension funds, credit unions, and mutual funds. The borrowers are business firms, households, and governments. The **market for loanable funds** is the market in which transactions between borrowers and lenders determine an interest rate that ensures that the quantity of loanable funds offered is equal to the quantity demanded. The interest rate is an important policy concern because it influences lending and borrowing decisions and thus affects the level of output and employment.

Like most demand curves, the demand for loanable funds (to invest) is negatively related to the interest rate, as shown in Figure 1. More will be borrowed at lower rates, *ceteris paribus*, and less at higher rates. The supply of loanable funds rises with the interest rate. The interest rate is the price of loanable funds. Like any price, this rate rises and falls to clear the market and make quantity demanded equal to quantity supplied. The interest rate is a very important macroeconomic variable because it affects business investment decisions, household purchases of consumer durables, demand for the U.S. dollar, and the cost of servicing the public debt. Because of its importance, we will explore interest

Market for loanable funds The market in which transactions between borrowers and lenders determine the interest rate and the volume of loans.

---

2. "Profits and Balance Sheet Developments at U.S. Commercial Banks in 1992," *Federal Reserve Bulletin* (July 1993): 649–654.

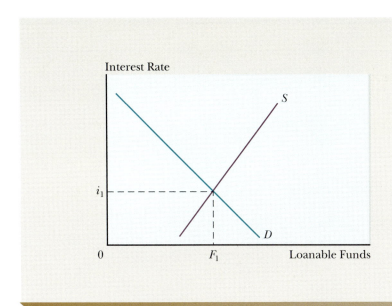

FIGURE 1
THE MARKET FOR LOANABLE FUNDS
The demand curve for loanable funds slopes downward because at lower nominal interest rates borrowers want to borrow more. The supply curve slopes upward because lenders are willing to lend more at higher nominal interest rates. Equilibrium occurs at F_1 and i_1, where the amount borrowers want to borrow is equal to the amount lenders are willing to lend.

rates more carefully before returning to other aspects of the loanable funds market.

THE RANGE OF INTEREST RATES

We have been using the term *interest rate* as if there were a single interest rate paid by all borrowers in the market. In fact, there is a whole complex of interest rates. A few of these are

- interest rates on home mortgages and car loans,
- interest rates on bonds (ranging from the lowest on T-bills to the highest on junk bonds),
- interest rates that banks pay the Fed (the discount rate) and each other on borrowed reserves (the federal funds rate), and
- interest rates banks pay on checking and savings accounts and CDs.

The interest rate on a loan depends on how risky the borrower is as well as the length of the repayment period. Short-term loans carry lower rates than long-term loans. Risky borrowers pay more than safe, dependable borrowers. Table 3 lists interest rates from 1981 to 1993 on a variety of loans, including bonds. The lowest rate is usually the discount rate, followed by the T-bill rate and the rate on municipal bonds. Interest rates on municipal bonds are low because the interest is exempt from federal income taxes. In general, interest rates rise and fall together. In the late 1970s and the beginning of the 1980s, all interest rates rose to levels that were very high compared to past experience. Home mortgage rates, which had been in the 6 to 8 percent range, rose to 14 percent and higher. T-bills, which had been paying interest at a rate ranging from 4 to 6 percent in previous decades, peaked at 14 percent in 1981. Since that time interest rates have all fallen, although not at the same speed.

TABLE 3 INTEREST RATES, 1981–1993

YEAR	GOVERNMENT BONDS			CORPORATE BONDS		MORTGAGES	DISCOUNT RATE
	T-BILLS	3-YEAR	MUNICIPAL	AAA	BAA		(NEW YORK FED)
1981	14.0%	14.4%	11.2%	14.2%	16.0%	14.7%	13.4%
1982	10.7	12.9	11.6	14.8	16.1	15.1	11.0
1983	8.6	10.5	9.5	12.0	13.6	12.6	8.5
1984	9.6	11.9	10.2	12.7	14.2	12.4	8.8
1985	7.5	9.6	9.2	11.4	12.7	11.6	7.7
1986	6.0	7.1	7.4	9.0	10.4	10.2	6.3
1987	5.8	7.7	7.7	9.4	10.6	9.3	5.7
1988	6.7	8.3	7.8	9.7	10.8	9.2	6.2
1989	8.1	8.6	7.2	9.3	10.2	10.1	6.9
1990	7.5	8.3	7.3	9.3	10.4	10.1	7.0
1991	5.4	6.8	6.9	8.8	9.8	9.3	5.5
1992	3.5	5.3	6.4	8.1	9.0	8.2	3.3
1993	3.0	4.4	5.6	7.2	7.9	7.2	3.0

Source: Council of Economic Advisers, *Economic Report of the President 1994* (Washington, DC: U.S. Government Printing Office).

RISK AND INTEREST RATES

Although interest rates rise and fall together, the differences among them will vary over the course of a business cycle. During downturns, some private borrowers have a higher risk of default as their businesses teeter on the edge of bankruptcy. As private borrowers begin to look riskier relative to the government, lenders will be more inclined to buy safer assets such as T-bills. The rate that lenders charge private borrowers rises relative to the T-bill rate. The difference between interest rates charged to the safest borrowers and those charged to less safe borrowers for the same length of time is called the **risk premium**. Risk premiums vary from borrower to borrower, but they generally rise during recessions and fall during expansions.

With so many interest rates, it is difficult to choose one to serve as an indicator of how the market is doing. Generally the interest rate on T-bills is used as the market indicator. The T-bill rate is the interest rate the U.S. government, the safest borrower of all, pays on its short-term borrowing.

REAL AND NOMINAL INTEREST RATES

Why did interest rates rise so sharply in the late 1970s and early 1980s, and then fall steadily through the early 1990s? To answer this question, we need to distinguish between the real and nominal rates of interest. The rate that people observe, or the market rate, is the nominal rate. The **nominal rate of interest** is the rate of interest actually charged, without any correction for inflation. The real rate of interest is not observed. The **real rate of interest** is the nominal rate of interest minus the expected rate of inflation or the actual rate of inflation. If

Risk premium
The difference between the interest rate charged the safest borrowers and those charged to less safe borrowers for the same length of time.

Nominal rate of interest
The rate of interest actually charged, without correction for inflation (also known as the market rate of interest).

Real rate of interest
The nominal rate of interest minus the expected rate of inflation.

the price level is rising, the dollars repaid on a loan will be worth less and less with each successive payment. Lenders aren't interested in just getting their dollars back. They want to be repaid the purchasing power they lent plus some interest. Similarly, borrowers make calculations as to what a loan really costs them, considering that they can repay with depreciating dollars. Thus, an inflation premium is included in the interest rate.

KEY IDEAS

COMPONENTS OF THE INTEREST RATE

THE MARKET INTEREST RATE CONSISTS OF:	WHICH IS:
• the real rate of interest	the amount people are willing to pay for the right to spend now instead of later *or* the rate of return on investment
• plus the risk premium	a measure of the probability that the borrower will fail to repay the loan
• plus the inflation adjustment	the expected rate of inflation over the life of the loan

Consider what happens when Joan lends Peter $100 for a year, charging him 5 percent interest. At the end of the year, Peter repays Joan $105. Suppose, however, that the price level rose by 10 percent that year. The $105 that Joan gets back at the end of the year will purchase $105/1.10 = $95.45 worth of goods and services. Instead of earning a positive real return, Joan has less purchasing power. If she had added an inflation premium of 10 percent, Peter would have paid back $115, which would have purchased $104.54 worth of goods. Joan wouldn't have made quite 5 percent in real terms, but she would have come close.

Some estimated values of real interest rates from 1970 to 1993 are shown in Table 4. (We assume that expected inflation rates were equal to the actual inflation rates for each period.) Real rates are computed by subtracting the percent change in the GDP deflator from the interest rate on T-bills. Note that the real rate of interest is quite small but is also much more stable than the nominal rate. There were seven years in the 1970s when the real rate was negative. Negative real interest rates occur when lenders do not correctly anticipate inflation and charge too small an inflation premium. When negative real interest rates occur, there is a surge in loan demand. Negative interest rates are a good reason to borrow! In the 1970s, borrowers were offered loans at 8 percent interest when the inflation rate was over 10 percent. The opposite problem occurred in the early 1980s when lenders overestimated inflation and added too much of an inflation premium to interest rates. As a result, real interest rates rose sharply.

EXPECTED INFLATION AND THE MARKET FOR LOANABLE FUNDS

Changes in expected inflation rates will shift both the demand and supply of loanable funds and lead to a new equilibrium value of i, the nominal interest

TABLE 4 REAL AND NOMINAL INTEREST RATES, 1970–1993

YEAR	T-BILL RATE	INFLATION RATE*	REAL INTEREST RATE
1970	6.46%	5.4%	1.06%
1971	4.35	5.4	−1.05
1972	4.07	4.6	−0.53
1973	7.04	6.4	0.64
1974	7.89	8.7	−0.81
1975	5.84	9.6	−3.76
1976	4.99	6.3	−1.31
1977	5.27	6.9	−1.63
1978	7.22	7.9	−0.68
1979	10.22	8.6	1.62
1980	11.51	9.5	2.01
1981	14.03	10.0	4.03
1982	10.69	6.2	4.49
1983	8.63	4.1	4.53
1984	9.58	4.4	5.18
1985	7.48	3.7	3.78
1986	5.98	2.6	3.38
1987	5.82	3.2	2.62
1988	6.69	3.9	2.79
1989	8.12	4.4	3.72
1990	7.51	4.3	3.21
1991	5.42	4.4	1.02
1992	3.45	2.7	0.75
1993	3.02	2.5	0.52

*Percent change in GDP deflator.
Source: Council of Economic Advisers, *Economic Report of the President* (Washington, DC: U.S. Government Printing Office, 1994).

rate. Suppose people come to expect a higher rate of inflation. The demand curve for loanable funds shifts to the right, from D_1 to D_2 in Figure 2. Individuals want to borrow more at any given interest rate because they think the inflation rate is going to be higher. The higher the inflation rate, the less valuable are the dollars the borrower must repay. Exactly the same sort of reasoning applies to business demand for borrowing. Business firms will be much more willing to borrow at any given interest rate if they expect to be able to charge higher prices for the goods they produce.

The supply curve for loanable funds will shift to the left if there is an increase in the expected inflation rate. Lenders look at the purchasing power they will have when they get their funds *plus interest* back from the borrower. For example, if you lend $100 at 10 percent interest for one year, you will get back $110 at the end of the year. If the price level is the same as it was at the start of the year, you will be able to buy 10 percent more real goods. But if the price level also rises by 10 percent, then the $110 you get back will buy only the same amount of goods that $100 would have bought at the beginning. If lenders

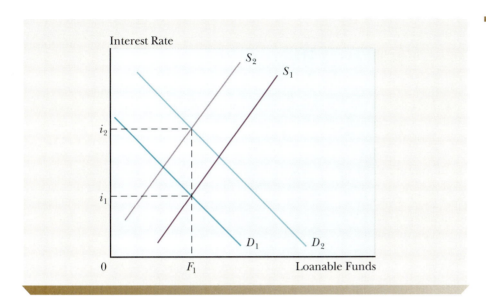

FIGURE 2
EXPECTED INFLATION AND THE LOANABLE FUNDS MARKET
An increase in the expected rate of inflation increases demand for loans at every market interest rate (the demand curve shifts from D_1 to D_2) because loans are cheaper to repay. The supply of loanable funds falls (the supply curve shifts from S_1 to S_2) because each market rate on the vertical axis now represents a lower real rate of interest. The demand and supply curves shift the same distance, intersecting at a market interest rate that reflects higher expected inflation. The volume of loanable funds, F_1, is the same as before.

demand 10 percent more in real goods in order to give up the current use of their funds, they won't lend at 10 percent interest if they expect 10 percent inflation. In fact, to get a 10 percent return in terms of real goods, lenders will demand an interest rate of 20 percent. The supply curve shifts to the left because lenders are willing to lend the same amount only at a higher nominal interest rate.

When expected inflation rises, both the demand and supply curves shift, driving up the equilibrium nominal interest rate. In fact, the nominal interest rate should rise by about the same amount as the increase in the expected rate of inflation. Lenders and borrowers will adjust the market rate they are willing to accept or pay to correct for the rising price level.

INTEREST, DIVIDENDS, AND YIELD ON AN ASSET

Interest is not the only form in which lenders receive a return on their funds. Suppose you purchase one share of stock in AT&T. You probably will receive some dividends, although you can't be sure how much. Also, the value of your share may go up, although there is no guarantee that it will. Suppose you come out $10 ahead in a given year for an initial investment of $100, a return of 10 percent. That $10 may be all in the form of dividends, all in the form of an increase in the price of a share, or some combination of the two.

The **yield** is the rate of return on funds invested in an asset. In this case, 10 percent is the actual yield. Yields of various assets tend to rise and fall together. Many yields are measured by interest rates. Others are measured by dividends or by increases in the value of the asset. When you try to decide whether to hold your funds in cash or in IBM stock, you want to look at what you can expect to get out of either investment in the future over and above what you paid for it. This figure is the expected yield.

The **expected yield** is the rate of return on an asset that includes expected interest or dividends and the expected increase or decrease in its price. Expected yield is heavily influenced by the degree of perceived risk of the investment. **Risk** is a measure of how much the actual yield on an asset may vary from

Yield
The return on funds invested in an asset measured as a percentage of the price paid for the asset.

Expected yield
The rate of return on an asset that includes expected interest or dividends and the expected increase or decrease in price.

Risk
A measure of how much the actual yield on an asset may vary from the expected yield.

POLICY FOCUS: INTEREST RATES IN AN OPEN ECONOMY

Interest rates are a macroeconomic variable of great importance to investors, banks, bond markets, and the stock market. Consequently, the Fed—like most central banks—pays close attention to interest rates. When the economy is in recession, the Fed tries to put downward pressure on interest rates in order to encourage spending by business firms (for investment), consumers (for houses and consumer durables), and state and local governments (for school buildings, sewer systems, and other projects financed by borrowing). The amount of control that the central bank has over interest rates, however, is inversely related to the degree of openness in an economy. A country with a large volume of international transactions will be less able to control interest rates than a country that is relatively isolated from the rest of the world.

Until the last decade or two, international borrowing and lending was too complicated and too risky for all but the most sophisticated borrowers and lenders. In a world where markets are separated, interest rates can be high in one county and low in another without generating a substantial flow of funds between the two. In such a world, the central bank could exert considerable control over domestic interest rates. If the Fed engaged in open market operations to expand the money supply, or lowered the discount rate, interest rates would fall in the United States with relatively little impact on interest rates in the rest of the world. If interest rates rose in Germany or Canada, their impact on U.S. interest rates would be minimal.

Improvements in communication technology, the growth of multinational enterprises, and the internationalization of banking have changed that situation. Loanable funds flow freely among most countries. Today, if one country is offering attractive yields on bonds, money will flow in from abroad, tending to equalize yields between nations. If another country is offering low rates on borrowed money, borrowers will flock there to take advantage of the opportunity. Germany's high interest rates from tight monetary policy have spread tight money and recession throughout the European Community, and tight money and recession in Europe spilled over to the United States, both in higher bond yields and in declining demand for U.S. exports. For a small, open economy, such as Costa Rica or Belgium, the yields on financial assets for all but the smallest loan and deposit activities are determined in global markets rather than at home.

The Fed still exerts more power over interest rates, domestically and internationally, than any other central bank. As we will see in the chapter on international finance, floating exchange rates have helped to preserve some of that power. But in a global economy, even with floating exchange rates, the Fed's power over interest rates and bond yields is gradually declining. The interest you pay on your car loan or receive on your bonds is influenced at least in part by the actions of the Bundesbank and the Bank of Japan as well as by millions of borrowers and lenders around the globe.

---

the expected yield. A high-risk asset may have a large yield in some years and a low or even negative yield in others. A low-risk asset will have a much more stable yield. The risk for a given asset can change depending on market conditions. An increase in the actual yield or a decrease in risk will increase the expected yield. A decrease in the actual yield or an increase in risk will reduce the expected yield.

Because other financial assets are substitutes for money, anything that increases demand for those other assets will lead to a decrease in demand for money. An increase in yield will cause people to increase their holdings of stocks or bonds and reduce their holdings of money. Why? Think of the yield on stocks or bonds as the opportunity cost of holding money. When people hold money, they are giving up earnings they could gain from other assets. When yields on other assets increase, the opportunity cost of holding money also rises. Individuals respond by holding more stocks and bonds and less money. The opposite is true when yields on other assets decline. Thus, interest rates and yields on competing financial assets are important to the Fed in trying to influence the demand for money.

STOCKS, BONDS, AND OTHER FINANCIAL ASSETS

Changes in interest rates played an important role in bank deregulation and the rise of new types of financial assets in the 1970s. Banks are increasingly aware of competition from other institutions. In fact, many banks have moved into providing brokerage services and in-house mutual funds to attract some of that activity.

Taken together, banks and nonbank financial institutions make up the credit market at the bottom of the circular flow diagram (see Figure 3). The principal nonbank financial institutions are stockbrokers and the stock market, bond dealers and the bond market, mutual funds, insurance companies, and pension funds. There are other players in financial markets, but these major ones should be enough to give you a sense of how financial markets work. Stockbrokers and bond dealers each deal in one type of financial asset. Mutual funds, insurance companies, and pension funds are more like banks in that they collect funds at "retail" and place them in a diversified portfolio of assets.

STOCKS AND THE STOCK MARKET

The **stock market** is a financial market in which ownership claims on corporations are bought and sold. Most daily trades involve just one stockholder selling shares to another. However, new stock is also issued. Individuals make invest-

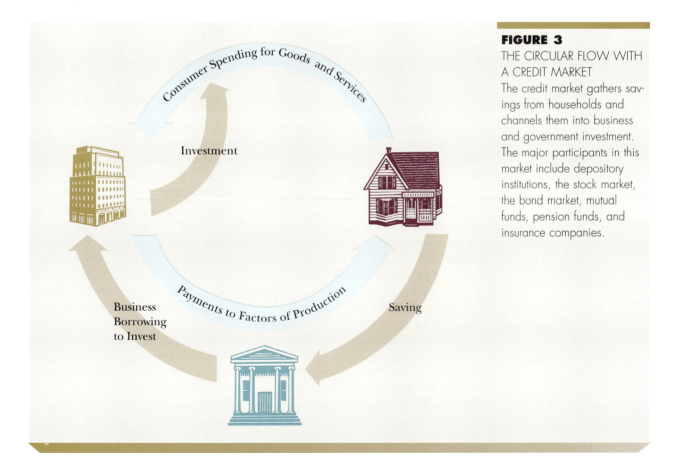

FIGURE 3

THE CIRCULAR FLOW WITH A CREDIT MARKET
The credit market gathers savings from households and channels them into business and government investment. The major participants in this market include depository institutions, the stock market, the bond market, mutual funds, pension funds, and insurance companies.

ment funds available to corporations by purchasing the newly issued shares of stock. The performance of the market is measured daily in terms of several indexes of stock prices as well as the daily volume of shares traded. To an economist, the stock market is a mechanism for channeling loanable funds to corporations and allowing individuals to share the risks of losses in the hope of gain.

STOCKHOLDERS AND STOCK EXCHANGES. Only corporations can issue stock. A share of **stock** is an ownership claim in a corporation. Stockholders, who own shares of stock, have a claim on the profits of the corporation after all expenses are paid. Stockholders are therefore risk takers. They are taking the chance that there will be no profits and thus no earnings. If the corporation goes bankrupt, the value of their stock will fall sharply, perhaps to zero. Then they will lose their capital as well as their earnings. If the corporation succeeds, however, stockholders gain both by an increase in the value of their shares and by higher earnings. Some of a corporation's net earnings are paid as dividends to stockholders. Other parts of net earnings are reinvested to increase future earnings. Such reinvestment normally increases the net worth of the corporation and therefore increases the value of a share of stock.

Stockholders also enjoy voting rights in corporations. They can attend the annual meeting to vote on the board of directors and comment on company policy. Few stockholders take advantage of this privilege. Some, however, have chosen to vote their shares to change a corporation's leadership, to redirect its market strategy, and sometimes even to involve it in social policy. In the 1980s, the focus of many corporate annual meetings was shifted by a minority of stockholders to issues such as environmental awareness, disinvesting in South Africa, and increasing opportunities for minorities and women. Other stockholders are more interested in such bread-and-butter issues as new product development, marketing strategy, and profitability.

The organized stock market in the United States has its primary center in the New York Stock Exchange, where ownership shares of large corporations are traded. Other exchanges are the American Stock Exchange and the Pacific Stock Exchange. Stocks that are not traded as frequently or that are issued by smaller corporations are traded through brokers in the over-the-counter market. Buyers may also invest through foreign exchanges, such as the London or Tokyo stock exchange.

The average price of a share on the New York Stock Exchange is considered a leading indicator, forecasting downturns and upturns in the business cycle. There are several indexes that provide a handy guide to the performance of the market on any particular day. The Dow-Jones Industrial Average and Standard and Poor's 500, for example, follow the prices of a fixed group of stocks and measure the change in the average price.

Although individuals see the stock market as an opportunity for gain through sharing corporate risk, the most important economic function of the stock market is to provide equity funds for corporations. Equity refers to ownership. In contrast, debt, or borrowed funds, has a fixed interest rate and must be repaid at some future date. Stock ownership provides a way to share the risks of new ventures, new technology, new products, or expanding in an uncertain market among a large number of individuals holding shares in the corporation.

Stock
An ownership claim in a corporation.

STOCK MARKET CRASHES, FORECASTING, AND RECESSIONS. In October 1987, the major indexes that measure the average price of a stock on the New York Stock Exchange all dropped sharply, the largest decline since 1929. That 1929 crash marked the beginning of the Great Depression. In 1987, the Dow-Jones Industrial Average dropped 30 percent in about three weeks, from its September level of 2,571 to a December low of 1,910. Standard and Poor's 500 index fell about 22 percent. It took almost two years for the market to recover to pre-crash levels. The 1929 stock market crash was even more severe. The market fell by 34.8 percent from its peak in September 1929 to the end of that year. At its low point in 1932, the average price of a share was down 89 percent from its peak value.

How does a stock market crash affect the rest of the economy? The links between the stock market and overall economic activity run through four channels. First, when stock prices fall, it is more difficult for firms to raise equity capital in order to invest. Thus, a weak stock market discourages investment by making it difficult to market new stock issues. Second, stocks are part of the assets of households. When the value of household assets falls, households experience a decline in wealth and respond by cutting back consumption. Both these actions will shift the *AD* curve to the left, reducing output and the price level. Third, investors often borrow in order to finance their stock purchases. When the value of the stocks that serve as collateral for their loans falls, they have to come up with some cash to reduce the size of the loan in line with the lower value of their stocks. The reduction in loans also tends to reduce output and prices.

Finally, the market both reflects and creates expectations about the current and future condition of the economy. A stock market crash may reflect generally negative expectations, or it may create them. Negative expectations tend to reduce lending, borrowing, and spending, thus having the effect of lowering economic activity.

Because the stock market is one of the dozen leading indicators used to predict downturns and upturns in economic activity, the crash in 1987 was widely heralded as a forecast of an impending recession. However, there was no recession until 1990. Both nominal and real GDP continued to rise and unemployment continued a slow decline for almost three years. A major reason for this positive outcome was that the Fed rushed to pump loanable funds into financial markets. In fact, stock market declines are not very reliable as a forecaster. During the period from the end of World War II through 1993, there have been eight major stock market declines, of which only three were associated with a recession.

In 1929, stocks were among the few financial assets available to small investors. Today, individuals have access to many types of assets, and stocks make up a smaller part of their portfolios. Thus, the impact of a stock market crash on consumption is much weaker. In addition, requirements about borrowing to buy stocks are much stricter now than they were in the 1920s. Fewer stock buyers are caught with large loans on stocks that have fallen in value.

When the average price of a stock, or prices of stocks in general, rise more rapidly than is justified by the underlying value of the companies issuing the stocks, a correction eventually takes place. Stock prices will fall to more realistic levels. Many large institutional investors (such as mutual funds and pension funds) have programmed trading plans that respond automatically to price changes. These investors may thus tend to overreact and buy or sell too much.

Bond market
A market in which the debt instruments of governments and corporations are traded.

Bond
A debt instrument issued by a corporation or government agency with a fixed face value, annual interest payment, and maturity date.

The stock market tends to show larger and larger swings because these large buyers and sellers increasingly dominate the market and have great influence on prices.

BONDS AND THE BOND MARKET

The second major financial market is the **bond market**, in which the debt instruments of governments and corporations are traded. Sometimes governments and corporations borrow by taking out a loan from a bank or other financial institution at a specified interest rate. Such loans involve formal agreements about regular payments of capital and interest until the sum is repaid. More often, however, governments and corporations issue bonds. A **bond** is a debt instrument issued by a corporation or a government agency and having a fixed face value, annual interest payment, and maturity date. The face value is the dollar amount for which the bond can be redeemed at maturity. The maturity date tells how long a time period will elapse between when the bond is issued and when it is redeemed.

CORPORATE AND GOVERNMENT BONDS.
Corporations issue bonds in order to raise money to invest. The federal government issues bonds in order to finance the deficit in the federal budget. As you learned in Chapter 12, such bonds are a major asset of the banks as well as the Federal Reserve System. These bonds are attractive because they are safe, offer reasonably good yields, can be readily marketed if necessary, and have a wide range of maturities. In addition, federal agencies such as the Federal National Mortgage Association issue bonds (called agency bonds) in order to help finance mortgage loans and for other purposes. State and local governments also issue bonds in order to finance capital projects, such as school buildings and sewer systems. These bonds are called municipal bonds regardless of whether they are issued by a state, city, county, or school district. They are attractive to investors because the interest on them is not subject to federal (and sometimes state) income tax.

Governments are major borrowers in the bond market. In 1989, about 25 percent of all the funds raised in the U.S. credit market went to finance the borrowing of federal, state, and local governments. Some critics of government borrowing argue that competition from the government makes it harder for private firms to sell their bonds or to borrow. If funds are limited, the federal government will have its demand satisfied first because it is a safer borrower. Private borrowers may have to settle for borrowing less at higher interest rates. When government borrowing drives up interest rates and chokes off some private borrowing, crowding out has occurred.

Bonds are usually considered a safer investment than stocks because bonds have a prior claim on a corporation's assets. Bond prices do fluctuate with changes in interest rates but are generally more stable than stock prices. Interest payments on bonds are safer and more certain than dividends from stock shares.

BOND YIELDS, INTEREST RATES, AND BOND PRICES.
The annual interest rate is fixed when the bond is sold, but the yield is not. The yield on a bond is the annual income from it (the annual interest payment plus any change in its market

price) divided by the current selling price of the bond. Since the selling price of the bond can go up or down, the yield varies with that price. When interest rates are high, buying bonds is a way to lock in high yields. Even if you have to sell the bonds before they mature, you will get some of the high yield in the form of a **capital gain**, an increase in the market price of the asset (bond). If your bond is yielding 12 percent when newly issued bonds are paying only 9 percent, buyers will bid up the price of your higher yielding bond.

Capital gain
An increase in the market price of an asset.

The advantage of bonds when interest rates are high becomes a disadvantage when interest rates are low. If you buy bonds when interest rates are low, not only are you getting a low yield, you may also suffer a capital loss if interest rates rise. When interest rates are low, two other assets are more attractive than bonds: stocks and money. Stocks are more attractive because the dividend and the potential for capital gains look better when bonds are offering low yields. Money is more attractive because its opportunity cost (the bond interest forgone) is lower and the risk of capital loss on bonds is higher if interest rates go back up.

There is a fairly simple relationship between the price of a bond and its yield. Higher bond prices mean lower yields, and vice versa. An example will illustrate this relationship. Assume that the federal government issues bonds maturing in ten years with a face value of $10,000 and an annual interest payment of $900. At this price, their yield is 9 percent. Now suppose the Fed engages in open market operations (normally carried out with Treasury bills). The Fed buys so many of these bonds that their price rises by $100. (In the bond market, like any other market, an increase in demand with no change in supply will drive up the price.) This price increase will reduce the current yield on government bonds to 8.91 percent ($900/$10,100).

Because financial markets are interrelated, lower yield rates on government bonds will spread to other assets. If both government and low-risk corporate bonds are priced at $10,000 with yields of 9 percent, most buyers would not prefer one to the other. But if the price of a government bond rises to $10,100, its yield will fall. Corporate bonds, whose yield remains at 9 percent, then become more attractive than government bonds. As buyers shift from government to corporate bonds, corporate bond prices will also be driven up, and their yields will fall. Lower yields and interest rates spread from asset to asset.

NONBANK FINANCIAL INTERMEDIARIES

There are some nonbank financial institutions that also collect funds from households and pass them on to borrowers and to firms raising equity capital (issuing stock). Recall that one of the major reasons for bank deregulation was the competition for both loan customers and depositors from nonbank financial institutions. Although these nonbank competitors cannot provide a substitute for money as a medium of exchange, they can provide good substitutes for money as a store of wealth. Individuals who hold deposits in banks can shift those deposits to other specialized financial assets, such as shares of mutual funds. Individuals may also own financial assets that are serving several purposes, such as deposits in pension funds and life insurance policies. These financial assets are a store of wealth providing funds for retirement income or to take care of dependents in case of death.

Institutional investors
Large investors, including insurance companies, mutual funds, and pension funds, whose purchases and sales have a significant impact on the prices of investment assets.

Pension funds, insurance companies, and mutual funds are known as **institutional investors**. Because these investors deal in much larger volume than the individual investor, their purchases and sales can affect the market price of a stock or bond. If institutional investors become more cautious and switch from stocks to bonds, the stock market suffers a decline. If institutional investors become bullish (optimistic about stocks), stock market indicators will rise. Institutional investors have become much more important players in the stock market in the last few decades. Some market watchers attribute the wider swings in average stock prices to the increased role of institutional investors.

MUTUAL FUNDS. Mutual funds compete directly with banks for the deposits of households and small businesses. Like banks, mutual funds invest in a variety of assets. The most common assets held by mutual funds are stocks and bonds. A **mutual fund** is a financial institution that pools money from many individuals in order to invest in a diversified portfolio of assets. Through a mutual fund, a small investor can own a small share of a wide array of assets instead of concentrating his or her assets in the stock or a bond of one corporation. Mutual funds charge a small fee for their management services, but often offer an excellent return with some diversification of risk.

Mutual fund
A financial institution that pools money from many individuals in order to invest in a diversified portfolio of assets.

KEY IDEAS

PLAYERS IN THE LOANABLE FUNDS MARKET

- Depository institutions — Offer checkable deposits, certificates of deposit, and other services
  Make loans to consumers, as well as mortgage and business loans
  Buy government bonds
- Stock market/Stockbrokers — Buy and sell ownership shares in corporations
- Bond market/Bond dealers — Buy and sell debt instruments of governments and corporations
- Mutual funds — Gather up funds from investors to create a diversified portfolio of financial assets
- Insurance companies — Use their reserves to purchase stocks, bonds, and mortgages and make short-term loans to business firms
- Pension funds — Generally purchase safer and lower-yielding assets

INSURANCE COMPANIES. Insurance companies sell policies covering homes, automobiles, health care, disability, and death. These companies accumulate investment funds in reserves against expected future losses. The insurance companies with the largest sums to invest are the life insurance companies, which sell several types of policies that accumulate a cash value. Life insurance companies invest these cash reserves in a variety of assets. Property insurers also have large reserves accumulated to pay off losses that are available to invest in the interim. Most commonly, insurance companies invest in major construction projects, stocks, bonds, and short-term loans to business firms. Earnings on these assets, along with premiums paid by policyholders, provide enough funds to pay off present and estimated future claims as well as the costs of operation and profit for stockholders.

PENSION FUNDS. Pension funds are very similar to insurance companies in that they take in large amounts of cash that they hold and invest. The cash reserves are used for payments to pensioners. Because workers normally pay into the fund for many years before collecting benefits, pension funds have very large sums available to invest. They are generally quite cautious in their investments, preferring a safe low yield to a riskier higher one.

THE BORROWER'S SIDE: INVESTMENT AND INTEREST RATES

We have examined the motives of lenders and the structure of financial markets. Now we need to complete the picture by looking at why firms and individuals borrow. Households borrow in order to finance the purchase of houses, cars, and consumer durables. Chapter 10 explored government borrowing in some detail. This section concentrates on borrowing by businesses for investment purposes. Bear in mind, however, that borrowing by households and state and local governments is very similar to business borrowing. Like business firms, these borrowers seek loans in order to buy durable assets that will yield a stream of services in the future.

THE INVESTMENT DEMAND SCHEDULE

A business firm makes a decision to invest by comparing the expected rate of return on the investment to the market interest rate. Assume that a small manufacturing firm, Karl's Kayaks, is considering three investment projects for the coming year: (1) an industrial robot to paint the kayaks that costs $60,000, (2) a computerized inventory management software system that costs $20,000, and (3) a delivery truck that costs $30,000. The firm has calculated the expected revenues and costs of operation for each piece of equipment over its useful life to the firm. These calculations also took into account the initial cost and salvage value. With this information, the firm's accountants have calculated that the expected rate of return on investment is 14 percent for the industrial robot, 22 percent for the inventory management system, and 8 percent for the delivery truck. Each of these rates of return is compared to the market interest rate to determine whether or not the investment should be undertaken.

Based on this information, Figure 4 shows an investment demand schedule for Karl's Kayaks. An **investment demand schedule** ranks all possible investment projects for a firm in order of decreasing expected rate of return. The schedule looks like a set of steps rather than a smooth line because the firm is considering three separate projects, each of which requires a lump sum expenditure.

For the economy as a whole, aggregate business investment spending will also depend on how the interest rate compares to the expected rate of return on investments. An investment demand schedule that sums the schedules of

Investment demand schedule
A graph that ranks possible investment projects for a firm in order of decreasing expected rate of return.

Marginal efficiency of investment (MEI) curve A graph that represents the combined investment demand schedules for all firms in the economy, showing the volume of investment demand as a function of the expected rate of return.

every firm in an economy is a smooth line, as shown in Figure 5. The economy's investment demand schedule in Figure 5 is also known as the **marginal efficiency of investment (MEI) curve**. This diagram ranks all investment possibilities for all firms according to their expected rates of return.

THE ROLE OF INTEREST RATES

Given the MEI curve for an economy, the market interest rate will determine the amount of investment spending. Every investment with an expected rate of return equal to or exceeding the market interest rate will be undertaken. For instance, at an interest rate of 20 percent, the level of investment spending for the entire economy will be $50 billion in Figure 5. There are $50 billion worth of investment projects with an expected rate of return exceeding 20 percent. At an interest rate of 20 percent, Karl's Kayaks in Figure 4 would invest in the inventory management system because its expected rate of return (22 percent) exceeds that interest rate. Karl's Kayaks would not purchase either the industrial robot or the delivery truck. At an interest rate of 12 percent, Karl's Kayaks would invest in the industrial robot as well as the accounting system. For the entire economy, a 12 percent interest rate would result in $100 billion of investment spending.

HOW STEEP IS THE INVESTMENT DEMAND CURVE?

Investment demand and interest rates are negatively related. Higher interest rates raise the cost of investing so that only the most desirable investments will be undertaken. Less promising projects may become cost-effective at lower interest rates. The market interest rate is relevant whether the firm is borrowing or

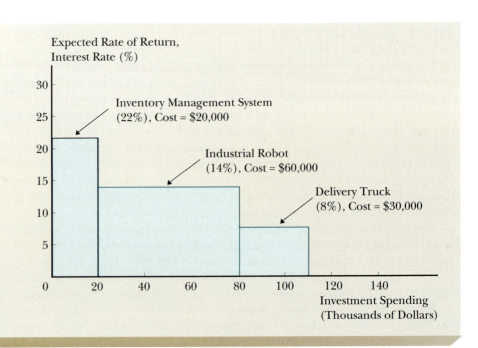

FIGURE 4
INVESTMENT DEMAND SCHEDULE FOR A FIRM
The three possible investment alternatives for Karl's Kayaks are ranked according to their expected rates of return. The firm decides which investment to undertake by comparing their expected rates of return to the market interest rate.

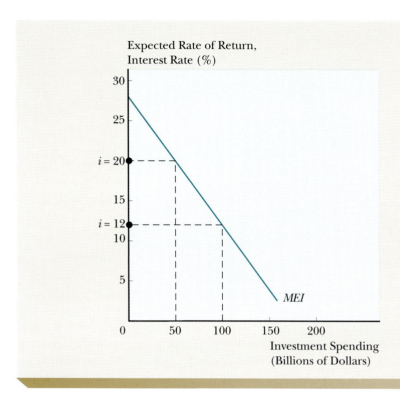

FIGURE 5

INVESTMENT DEMAND SCHEDULE FOR THE ENTIRE ECONOMY

Aggregate investment expenditures depend on the interest rate (i). If i is 20 percent, then total investment will be $50 billion. If i declines to 12 percent, investment will increase to $100 billion. Investment demand is negatively related to the interest rate.

not. When a firm borrows funds to invest, it wants to be sure that it will earn enough to pay all costs and interest, with some profit left over. If the firm is using its own funds to finance a project, there is still an opportunity cost. The firm must consider whether investing those funds in financial assets (bonds or other corporations' stock, for example) instead would offer a higher return than investing in new physical capital.

The steepness of the investment demand curve indicates how responsive investment demand is to changes in the rate of interest. In Figure 6, the investment demand curve labeled I_1 is relatively flat. A small decline in interest rates leads to a big change in investment demand along this curve, from I_A to I_C. The investment demand curve labeled I_2 is relatively steep. Here the same fall in interest rates increases investment demand only from I_A to I_B. Keynesians argue that the investment demand curve is closer to I_2, which shows interest rates having little influence on investment demand.

It is very difficult to measure the responsiveness of investment demand to changes in the interest rate. Both investment demand and interest rates are highly sensitive to changes in demand, expectations, and other economic conditions that vary over the course of the business cycle. Thus, investment demand and interest rates may move in the same direction because of other influences that offset or hide any negative relationship between the two. Other things being equal, lower interest rates do seem to stimulate spending on new homes, factories, business equipment, and state and local government projects.

In the early 1990s, this stimulus took a roundabout route. Lower interest rates made it possible for households, business firms, and state and local governments to reduce their payments on debt by refinancing their borrowing at

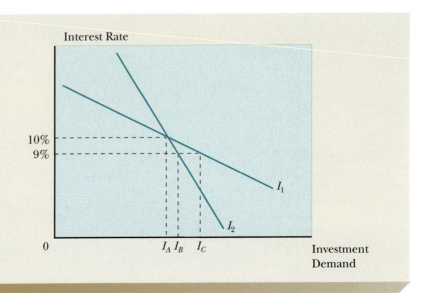

FIGURE 6

INTEREST RATES AND THE SLOPE OF THE INVESTMENT DEMAND CURVE When the interest rate falls from 10 to 9 percent, the change in the quantity of investment is greater along the more responsive investment demand curve, I_1, than along the steeper investment demand curve, I_2.

lower interest rates. These lower monthly or annual payments freed up some income for those who refinanced to use for both current expenditures and long-term investments. However, weak economic conditions meant that the stimulus to investment from lower interest rates was relatively modest.

At least some evidence suggests that the impact of interest rates on housing demand has declined.[3] A study by Randall J. Pozdena of the San Francisco Fed indicates that changes in T-bill rates were a factor in 60 percent of the changes in housing starts from 1960 to 1982. In the 1983–1989 period, only 31 percent of housing starts were influenced by changes in the T-bill rate, which is widely used as an indicator of overall interest rates. The development of a secondary (nonbank) mortgage market, adjustable-rate mortgages, and easier refinancing when interest rates fall all contributed to the diminishing influence of current interest rates on housing.

Consider again…*The stock market surge from 1990 to 1993 was primarily due to falling interest rates. These falling interest rates were the result of an expansionary monetary policy as the Fed tried to encourage economic growth and reduce unemployment in a period where the inflation rate remained relatively low. As interest rates declined on mortgages, bonds, and other long-term investments (and had earlier fallen on short-term investments, like certificates of deposit and Treasury bills), investors started searching for better rates of return.*

As more funds poured into the stock market, stock prices began to rise (a matter of simple supply and demand). Rising stock market prices made stocks look like a better investment. For stocks that were paying regular dividends, as the stock prices rose,

---

3. "The Fed's Clout Just Ain't What it Used to Be." *Business Week* (October 1, 1990): 24.

the dividend as a percentage of the stock price fell until returns on stocks were again comparable to the new, lower yields on bonds.

SUMMARY

1. The inflation of the 1970s and accompanying high interest rates led to a loss of deposits by banks and a demand for bank reform to make it easier for banks to attract and retain deposits. Bank reforms in the early 1980s greatly reduced the differences among types of depository institutions, expanded the kinds of accounts they could offer, and eliminated regulations on the interest banks could pay. Bank deregulation combined with conditions in the oil industry and the real estate market contributed to the failure of a large number of banks in the 1980s. The bailout has been costly to taxpayers and has led to more stringent regulations of bank investments and capital. By 1993, the bailout was essentially completed and banks were in much better financial condition.

2. The real rate of interest is the nominal, or market, rate of interest adjusted for the expected rate of inflation. When lenders guess wrong about inflation, the real rate of interest they earn can be negative. The real rate, not the nominal rate, governs money demand and investment decisions. The rates of interest on various assets are all related, but they differ because of differences in risk and maturity. A higher inflation rate will shift the demand curve for loanable funds to the right and the supply curve to the left, driving up the market interest rate.

3. The two major financial markets are the stock market and the bond market. Buyers and sellers exchange ownership shares in corporations in the stock market and debt instruments of governments and corporations in the bond market. Bonds are generally less risky than stocks. The yield on a bond is inversely related to its current market price. When a bond's price rises, its yield falls. The major nonbank financial institutions, or institutional investors, are mutual funds, insurance companies, and pension funds. These institutions gather funds from households and other sources and invest them in stocks, bonds, or major construction projects. They also invest in commercial paper and provide capital for new business firms.

4. Business firms compare the expected rate of return on an investment to the market rate of interest in deciding whether to undertake that investment. The ranking of investments by their expected rates of return is a firm's investment demand schedule. For the economy as a whole, the investment demand schedule is the sum of the demand schedules of all firms and is called the marginal efficiency of investment (MEI) curve.

NEW TERMS

spread
market for loanable funds
risk premium
nominal rate of interest
real rate of interest
yield
expected yield
risk
stock market
stock
bond market
bond
capital gain
institutional investors
mutual fund
investment demand schedule
marginal efficiency of investment (MEI) curve

QUESTIONS: REVIEW, APPLICATIONS, AND POLICY

REVIEW

1. In terms of a balance sheet, what does it mean to say that a bank has become insolvent?
2. What is the difference between a stock and a bond? Which would you prefer to own if you were willing to take risks in hope of profits? Which would you prefer if you wanted safety and interest income?
3. What are institutional investors? Why are they so important in financial markets?
4. Why is the level of investment for a firm or an economy negatively related to the interest rate? Does it make any difference whether the firm borrows or uses its own funds?
5. How would a decline in the interest rate affect aggregate demand?

APPLICATIONS

6. Suppose you were the manager of Petroleum Savings and Loan, and you knew that federal regulators were aware of your problems and would soon be checking your books and deciding whether to close your bank down. What might you do? How is your self-interested behavior likely to make the problem worse?

7. A one-year bond issued today will pay $1,000 at maturity. Calculate the yield on this bond for prices of $999, $975, $950, $925, $900, $850, and $800.

8. Suppose the equilibrium real rate of interest is 3 percent and that people always try to earn this rate. If they believe inflation will be 5 percent, what should the nominal rate of interest be? What if they believe inflation will be 12 percent? Suppose they believe inflation will be 12 percent, but it turns out to be 15 percent. What is the actual real rate of interest that people will receive? (*Hint:* When people try to earn the equilibrium real rate in every period, the difference between the expected real rate of interest and the actual real rate is the expected inflation rate minus the actual inflation rate.)

9. Is it possible for the real rate of interest to rise while the market rate is falling? How would this happen?

10. In Table 3, why is the interest rate on Baa corporate bonds always higher than the rate on T-bills?

11. You own a bond with a face value of $1,000 and a yield of 6 percent. That is, it pays interest of $60 a year. Now the nominal rate of interest rises to 8 percent. In order for your bond to yield 8 percent, to what level must its price rise or fall?

12. What would happen to the price of the bond in Question 11 if the market interest rate fell to 5 percent?

13. Using the investment demand schedule in Figure 5, assume that *i* declines from 20 percent to 15 percent. How much would investment spending change?

POLICY

14. How did government regulation and deregulation contribute to the banking crisis of the last decade?

15. If the government enters the market as an additional borrower by issuing more bonds, what would you expect to happen to bond prices, bond yields, and interest rates?

SUGGESTIONS FOR FURTHER READING

Day, Kathleen, *S&L Hell: The People and the Politics Behind the $1 Trillion Savings and Loan Scandal.* New York: W.W. Norton, 1993. A *Washington Post* reporter's account of how the banking crisis and bank bailout unfolded from 1982 to 1992.

Kane, Edward J. *The S&L Insurance Mess: How Did It Happen?* Washington DC: Urban Institute Press, 1989. A good history of how the savings and loan problem evolved and evaluation of the bailout policy.

Lewis, Michael. *Liars' Poker: Rising through the Wreckage on Wall Street.* New York: W. W. Norton, 1989. A fast-paced account of the action in the New York bond market, written by a Wall Street insider.

Seidman, William D. *Full Faith and Credit: The Great S&L Debacle and Other Washington Sagas.* New York: Times Books, 1993. A former chair of the FDIC gives an inside account of the bailout.

CHAPTER 14

MONETARY POLICY IN THEORY AND PRACTICE

Consider this...*In February 1993, Alan Greenspan, Chairman of the Federal Reserve Board of Governors, made headlines in an unusual way. He sat next to the President's wife at President Clinton's State of the Union address to a joint session of Congress. Why should that seating arrangement be of interest to anyone besides* People *magazine?*

President Clinton's message was about fiscal policy, deficit reduction, unemployment, and economic growth—standard fare for the State of the Union address. His policy proposals called for a short-term stimulus followed quickly by deficit reduction, which has the effect of contractionary fiscal policy. This was a risky fiscal policy mix during a period of slow growth and high unemployment. In order to minimize the negative effects on the economy, President Clinton needed the cooperation of the central bank and easy monetary policy. Hillary Rodham Clinton's task was to help persuade Alan Greenspan to cooperate.

Why was monetary policy so important to President Clinton's plans? Does monetary policy really have all that much impact on economic activity? This chapter will help you find the answers to those questions.

LEARNING OBJECTIVES

1. Explain how monetary policy works both directly and through changes in the interest rate to affect output, employment, and the price level.
2. Identify some of the difficulties in making monetary policy effective.
3. Summarize the debate over the appropriate targets for monetary policy.
4. Describe the main policy actions of the Fed over the last few decades.

HOW MONETARY POLICY AFFECTS AGGREGATE DEMAND

Economists, politicians, investors, and business people keep a close eye on the Fed because the actions of the Fed change the money supply and interest rates. Changes in money supply and interest rates affect household assets, the amount of funds available to borrow, the return on various assets, and the terms of new loans. Through these changes in the credit market the Fed influences spending.

343

Changes in planned spending will shift AE and AD and affect output, employment, and the price level.

The Fed's impact on the economy through the credit market operates through two different channels. Recall that there are only two things that individuals can do when they have more money than they wish to hold: spend it or lend it. (If you leave money in a checking or savings account, the bank will lend it for you.) Classical theory puts a strong emphasis on spending as the way to get rid of extra money. Classical economists point to the role of demand for cash balances (transactions demand) and the equilibrium between money supply and money demand. The Keynesian model puts an equally strong emphasis on lending. Economists in the Keynesian tradition emphasize the role of interest rates (asset demand for money).

These explanations are not necessarily in contradiction. Both mechanisms can be at work to translate changes in the money supply into shifts in aggregate demand, resulting in changes in output, employment, and the price level. However, the impact of monetary policy on the economy tends to be stronger through the spending route than the lending route, because there are so many more things that can go wrong on the longer lending route.

THE CLASSICAL VIEW

The classical tradition stressed the effects of monetary policy through excess money balances. In this view, when the Fed engages in open market operations, both bank reserves and the money supply increase. When the Fed buys bonds from banks, there is an increase in bank reserves. When the Fed buys bonds directly from the public rather than from banks, the switch from bonds to money increases the money supply directly. If the public deposits their payments from the Fed in checkable deposits, bank reserves will also increase.

According to the quantity theory, when the money supply (M_s) expands, both individuals and private banks find that they are holding larger money balances than they want. Demand for money to hold for transactions depends mainly on money income. When the Fed increases the money supply, at the current level of money income, money supply will exceed money demand. People attempt to spend their excess cash balances. This increase in planned spending is represented by a rightward shift in the AD curve. Either the price level or real output or some combination of the two will rise, depending on the slope of the AS curve. Money income, which is $P \times Y$, will rise. This process will continue until people are satisfied with their larger cash balances as a fraction of a larger money income. Thus, classical economists saw changes in the money supply as affecting spending directly, rather than working indirectly through interest rates.

The process of translating money supply changes into changes in demand, output, and the price level is called the **transmission mechanism**. Figure 1 shows the classical view of the transmission mechanism.

Transmission mechanism The process by which a change in the money supply is transformed into changes in demand, output, and the price level.

THE KEYNESIAN VIEW

The Keynesian transmission mechanism is longer and more complicated than the classical view. In a Keynesian model, financial markets are linked to aggregate supply and aggregate demand primarily through changes in planned

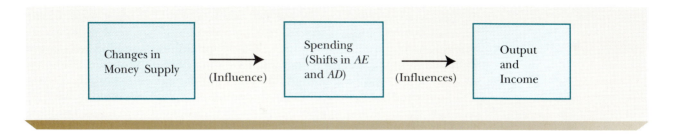

FIGURE 1

A CLASSICAL VIEW OF THE TRANSMISSION MECHANISM

In the classical tradition, an increase in the money supply creates excess money balances. As these balances are spent, the increase in planned spending shifts AD to the right, driving up real output and the price level.

investment, which is a highly volatile component of aggregate demand. Other borrowing decisions (by households and governments) are also translated into changes in aggregate demand. An increase in the money supply will reduce interest rates, at least initially, because more funds will be available for banks to lend. The lower interest rates will stimulate investment demand (which Keynes emphasized) as well as other kinds of spending that depends on borrowed funds (which is much more important in the 1990s than it was in the 1930s). Changes in both kinds of spending shift the *AE* and *AD* curves, causing changes in output and income. Depending on the slope of the *AS* curve, perhaps there will be an increase in the price level as well. Figure 2 shows the Keynesian view of the transmission mechanism.

FROM MONEY TO INTEREST RATES. When the Fed creates money by buying bonds, the initial effect is to create excess bank reserves. Banks will want to lend these reserves in order to earn interest. To entice borrowers, banks may have to offer lower interest rates. In fact, the process of monetary expansion itself will tend to lower interest rates, at least in the short run. Recall the relationship between bond prices and bond yields. When the Fed uses open market operations to expand the money supply, it buys bonds. The increased demand for bonds drives their prices up and their yields down. As the lower yields on bonds spread to other assets and other financial markets, interest rates in general tend to fall.

Modern macroeconomists have tried to build their theories and models on a solid foundation of microeconomics. That is, they have sought to develop models that are firmly anchored in the self-interested behavior of individuals. The response of banks and individuals to money creation is based on how they respond to changes in interest rates as the opportunity cost of holding money.

FIGURE 2

A KEYNESIAN VIEW OF THE TRANSMISSION MECHANISM

In the Keynesian tradition, when the Fed buys bonds, the money supply increases, and interest rates fall. Lower interest rates stimulate spending, especially investment, and drive up aggregate expenditure, shifting AD to the right. The result is higher real output and a higher price level.

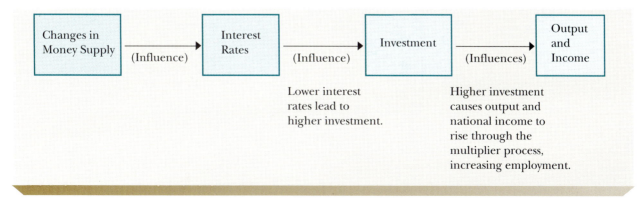

If open market operations by the Fed result in banks holding more excess reserves than they would like to, bankers will be eager to lend those excess reserves even at lower interest rates. If individuals find themselves with larger cash balances than they need, they will make some of them available for lending in order to earn interest. Both of these actions will increase the supply of loanable funds and tend to put downward pressure on the market interest rate.

The lower interest rates brought about by monetary policy may be short-lived, however, because market interest rates reflect expected inflation. If investors, banks, and households think that expansion of the money supply will increase the inflation rate, they will build a higher expected inflation rate into the interest rates that they ask from borrowers or are willing to pay on loans. Thus, expectations of higher inflation can weaken the impact of monetary policy at this stage.

FROM INTEREST RATES TO PLANNED SPENDING. The next step in the transmission mechanism is from interest rates to planned spending, especially for investment. Chapter 13 introduced a relationship between investment demand and the interest rate, the *MEI* curve. In Figure 3(*a*), we assume that the *MEI* curve, representing private investment demand, is the only source of demand for borrowing. When the supply of loanable funds increases due to expansion of the money supply, the interest rate falls from 15 percent to 12 percent and the quantity of loanable funds demanded for investment purposes increases from $100 billion to $125 billion.

Since investment is an important component of aggregate expenditure, the *AE* curve will shift from AE_1 to AE_2 as shown in Figure 3(*b*). The vertical shift will equal the $25 billion increase in investment demand. The upward shift in the *AE* curve will shift the *AD* curve to the right in Figure 3(*c*), increasing output and the price level. Thus, in the Keynesian version, monetary policy works through

FIGURE 3
FROM LOANABLE FUNDS TO AGGREGATE DEMAND
(a) The process of translating changes in the money supply into changes in output begins in the market for loanable funds. An increase in loanable funds depresses the interest rate, increasing investment demand from $100 billion to $125 billion. (b) Increased investment demand shifts aggregate expenditure upward, from AE_1 to AE_2. (c) An increase in aggregate expenditures shifts aggregate demand to the right, from AD_1 to AD_2, driving up output and the price level.

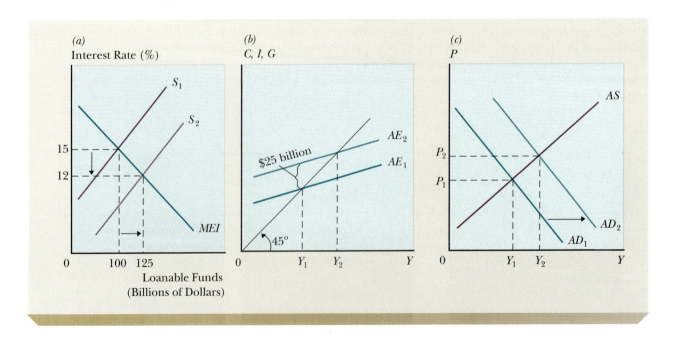

interest rates and investment demand to influence the levels of output and prices.

PROBLEMS WITH THE TRANSMISSION MECHANISM

In the Keynesian view, however, several things could go wrong in translating changes in the money supply into changes in output. Banks may not lend, interest rates may not fall, or borrowers may not respond to lower interest rates. This last issue, how sensitive borrowing is to changes in interest rates, was addressed in Chapter 13. The other two issues are examined here.

BANK LENDING AND EXCESS RESERVES. Banks might choose to hold excess reserves, especially if the economy is in recession, when interest rates are already low and potential borrowers look risky. If the Fed buys bonds from the public rather than banks, the individuals who sell the bonds might choose to hold currency instead of depositing the funds from selling the bonds in their checking accounts. If interest rates are low, the opportunity cost of holding money instead of interest-bearing assets is also low. Both banks and individuals may hold on to their monetary assets, expecting that interest rates will go back up and not wanting to lock in their assets in bonds at low current interest rates. Thus, currency drains and excess bank reserves can reduce the expansionary effect of open market operations on the money supply.

Keynes believed that banks would be more likely to hold excess reserves and households would be more likely to increase their money holdings when the money supply increase takes place under recessionary conditions of low interest rates and pessimistic expectations. He thought that the demand for excess reserves by banks and for cash balances by households would be very sensitive to interest rates, at least during recessions.

MONEY DEMAND AND INTEREST RATES. Even if banks or individuals lend some of the newly created money in the form of bank loans or purchases of other financial assets, it is possible that the interest rate might not fall very much. Figure 4 shows two views of the negative relationship between money demand and interest rates. The demand curve in both cases slopes down from left to right because interest is the opportunity cost of holding money, and when that cost is lower, more money will be demanded. The real issue between Keynesians and monetarists is not the negative slope but the steepness of the money demand curve.

The curve labelled D_K is a Keynesian money demand curve, on which the quantity of money demanded is very sensitive to interest rates. The curve labelled D_C is a money demand curve in the classical tradition, on which the quantity of money demanded does not respond very much to changes in interest rates. When the money supply expands from M_{s1} to M_{s2}, interest rates fall much more along D_C than D_K. When money demand is highly sensitive to interest rates, a given expansion of the money supply will bring about a smaller decline in interest rates. A very small drop in interest rates is enough to induce banks and households to hold much more cash and fewer other financial assets, such as loans and bonds.

The responsiveness of money demand to interest rates is a major point of disagreement between economists in the Keynesian tradition and economists in the classical tradition. Numerous studies have attempted to determine the rela-

FIGURE 4

MONEY DEMAND, MONEY SUPPLY, AND INTEREST RATES

In the Keynesian view, money demand (D_K) is very flat (sensitive); an increase in the money supply from M_{s1} to M_{s2} only reduces interest rates from i_1 to i_2, because it only takes a small drop in interest rates to bring about a large change in desired cash balances. In the classical view, money demand (D_C) is very steep (insensitive); an increase in the money supply from M_{s1} to M_{s2} reduces interest rates from i_1 to i_3, because it takes a very large drop in interest rates to bring about the same change in desired cash balances.

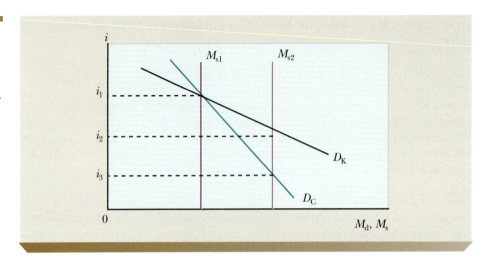

tive importance of changes in money income and interest in money demand. These test results suggest that both the "spend it" and the "lend it" channels of monetary policy are important routes through which monetary policy can affect output, employment, and prices.[1]

IS MONETARY POLICY EFFECTIVE?

Suppose banks do not lend, or the public holds cash, or interest rates do not fall very much, or investment demand does not respond to lower interest rates. If any one of these occurs, a very large increase in the money supply will be needed to bring about much change in aggregate expenditure, output, and employment. Thus, the possibility that money demand is very sensitive to interest rates while investment demand is not is a serious drawback to monetary policy. Keynesians argue that you can lead investors to money, but you can't make them spend. In their view, monetary policy should play a supporting role for fiscal policy, keeping credit available and interest rates low when fiscal policy is expansionary and keeping credit tight when fiscal policy is contractionary. If fiscal policy is successful in inducing investors and other spenders to borrow, however, then it is important that funds be available to them. Keynesians do not deny that monetary policy is important, but they think it clearly takes a back seat to fiscal policy, especially during recessions. To Keynesians, money matters, but not as much as fiscal policy.

Modern macroeconomists in the classical tradition who focus their attention on monetary policy are called **monetarists**. This group of economists feels that monetary policy is very important in affecting the level of employment, output, and prices—especially prices. Most monetarists regard recessions and depressions as well as inflation as results of bad monetary policy rather than some sort of normal, regular fluctuations in a market economy.

Monetarists
Economists who emphasize the role of money and monetary policy as the important influence on the price level and inflation.

1. See Stephen M. Goldfeld, "The Demand for Money Revisited," *Brookings Papers on Economic Activity* (Washington DC: Brookings Institution, 1973); and Dennis Hoffman and Robert H. Rasche, "Long Run Income and Interest Elasticities of Money Demand in the United States," National Bureau of Economic Research Working Paper No. 2949, April 1989.

Monetarists argue that Keynesians put too much emphasis on the importance of interest rates in money demand and not enough stress on the importance of the interest rate to investment decisions. Keynesians are firmly grounded in microeconomic behavior with respect to money demand and interest rates. But economists in the classical tradition have the solid microeconomic foundation in their view of what determines investment demand. Interest is the price that firms must pay for the use of funds now rather than later. Firms compare that interest rate to the rate of return on the investment, whether they are borrowing funds or using their own funds that could be earning interest.

The debate over the role of interest rates in affecting lending and borrowing has important policy implications. If the Keynesian view is correct, then monetary policy will be relatively ineffective, especially during recessions. If monetarists are correct, monetary policy is an important and powerful tool with which to influence the price level and real output.

Economists in the classical tradition, who tend to unite in their doubts about the usefulness or desirability of activist fiscal policy, are more likely to split on the issue of monetary policy. Some economists in this tradition think that the aggregate supply curve is so close to vertical, even in the short run, that all monetary policy can do is to influence the price level, not real output. Others feel that monetary policy can be an effective tool for influencing output in the short run, but often they argue that in practice monetary policy has done more harm than good.

KEY IDEAS

TWO VIEWS OF MONETARY POLICY

Economists in the Keynesian tradition believe:
- Money demand is sensitive to interest rates.
- The velocity of money is unstable.
- Investment is insensitive to interest rates.
- Monetary policy is not very effective in changing aggregate demand, output, and employment.

Economists in the classical tradition believe the opposite:
- Money demand is insensitive to interest rates.
- The velocity of money is stable.
- Investment responds to changes in interest rates.
- Monetary policy is effective in influencing aggregate demand, output, and employment in most cases.

THE CHOICE OF MONETARY POLICY TARGETS

Keynesians argue that monetary policy works mainly through interest rates. As a result, some economists argue that the target of monetary policy should be controlling interest rates. Monetarists place less emphasis on interest rates and more on the direct effects of changes in the money supply on spending. They believe that the Fed should emphasize controlling the size of the money supply. Interest rates and the money supply are alternative targets for monetary policy, and there has been an ongoing dispute about which policy works better.

This dispute is important for two reasons. First, the Fed's impact on market interest rates is limited and temporary. If the Fed tries to reduce interest rates by expanding the money supply, there will eventually be upward pressure on the price level. Inflationary expectations will spread. Since these expectations are an important influence on interest rates, market interest rates will rise.

The second reason why the dispute is important is that the Fed cannot pursue both targets at once. If the Fed tries to control interest rates, it must adjust the money supply to whatever level is needed to maintain the desired rates. If interest rates rise above the desired level, the Fed must buy bonds and increase bank reserves to stimulate lending and bring interest rates back down. If interest rates fall below the desired level, the Fed must cut back on the money supply to try to bring them back up. If the Fed tries to control the money supply, then it cannot control interest rates. When the Fed chooses one target, it loses control of the other.

The Fed can direct its attention to controlling the growth of the money supply or to controlling the level of interest rates. Monetarists usually favor controlling the size of the money supply and its rate of growth. Keynesians usually prefer an interest rate target. This choice reflects the Keynesian belief that interest rates exert an important influence on business activity.

In addition, some Keynesians argue that it is difficult, if not impossible, for the Fed to control the growth of the money supply within narrow limits. This argument is based on the fact that the Fed does not exercise direct control over the money supply. The Fed affects the money supply indirectly through its control of bank reserves and currency (Federal Reserve notes). Banks' decisions about excess reserves and individuals' decisions about cash balances will affect how large a money supply a given monetary base supports.

THE MONEY SUPPLY AS TARGET

The Humphrey-Hawkins Act of 1978 requires the Fed to report monetary growth targets for the year to Congress. The target is not a precise number or a specific rate of growth but a range of growth rates for the various monetary aggregates: the monetary base, M_1, M_2, and related measures. One of the problems in pursuing a money supply target is choosing among the different measures of that supply. With more kinds of financial institutions and deposits, the Fed has shifted its monetary target from M_1 to M_2. This change was made partly because the link between the monetary base and M_2 seems to be slightly more stable and partly because M_2 seems to be more closely linked to the level of economic activity (money income, or $P \times Y$).

THE MONETARY BASE AND THE MONEY MULTIPLIER

Monetary base
The currency in the hands of the public plus reserves held by banks.

The Fed can influence bank lending by influencing bank reserves, but it cannot directly control lending and the money supply. What the Fed can control is the **monetary base**, which consists of currency in the hands of the public plus reserves held by banks. (Currency in people's hands is part of the monetary base because it becomes bank reserves if it is deposited in banks.) Thus, the monetary base is used either as cash holdings for the public or as reserves to support bank deposits. The monetary base can support a money supply up to the maximum determined by the deposit multiplier. The actual money supply may be less than that amount, depending on currency withdrawals and bank excess reserves. The measure of the relationship between the monetary base and the actual money supply is given by the **money multiplier**, m, which is measured by

$$m = \frac{M_s}{B}$$

Money multiplier The ratio of the actual money supply to the monetary base.

where B is the monetary base.

Suppose, for example, that the reserve ratio was 12.5 percent. The deposit multiplier would be 8, and a monetary base of $200 billion could support a maximum money supply of $1,600 billion. The value of m, however, is calculated from the actual money supply and the monetary base. There are different money multipliers that correspond to the different measures of the money supply. For example, suppose M1 = $400 billion, M2 = $1,000 billion, and B = $200 billion. Then the M1 money multiplier is

$$m_1 = \frac{M1}{B} = \frac{\$400 \text{ billion}}{\$200 \text{ billion}} = 2,$$

and the M2 money multiplier is

$$m_2 = \frac{M2}{B} = \frac{\$1{,}000 \text{ billion}}{\$200 \text{ billion}} = 5.$$

Both the size and the stability of the money multiplier are important because the Fed can only control the monetary base, not the money supply. Changes in the money supply can result from changes in the monetary base, the money multiplier, or both. The value of m is influenced by the required reserve ratio but is really not under the Fed's control. Part of an increase in the monetary base could result in increased holdings of currency, with a smaller increase in bank reserves. In this case, the public's decision to hold more currency and coins instead of checkable deposits would keep M_s from rising as much as it otherwise would. The value of m would fall. If an increase in B goes entirely to reserves, banks could decide not to lend all these reserves, and again there would be a fall in m, partly frustrating the Fed's attempt to increase the money supply.

If the money multiplier is not constant, changes in its value can affect the money supply even with no change in the monetary base. Suppose B is $200 billion and m is initially 2.5. Then M_s equals $500 billion (2.5 × $200 billion). A fall in m of only 0.1, to 2.4, means that M_s becomes $480 billion (2.4 × $200 billion), a fall of $20 billion. Thus, a very small change in m has a large effect on M_s.

Monetarists argue that the money multiplier is fairly stable and that most changes in the money supply are therefore caused by changes in the monetary base. Thus, to monetarists, controlling the money supply is very important. Controlling the monetary base can allow the Fed to control the money supply fairly well.

Table 1 gives the values of m for two measures of the money supply, M1 and M2, for the period 1970–1993. In each case, m was calculated by dividing the

TABLE 1 MONEY MULTIPLIERS, 1970–1993

YEAR	M1 MONEY MULTIPLIER	M2 MONEY MULTIPLIER
1970	3.30	9.66
1971	3.31	10.31
1972	3.32	10.71
1973	3.24	10.62
1974	3.14	10.38
1975	3.06	10.90
1976	3.02	11.47
1977	3.00	11.66
1978	2.98	11.53
1979	2.92	11.42
1980	2.88	11.48
1981	2.93	12.03
1982	2.96	12.19
1983	2.97	12.46
1984	2.95	12.68
1985	3.05	12.62
1986	3.24	12.57
1987	3.13	12.13
1988	3.06	11.95
1989	2.97	12.05
1990	2.82	11.38
1991	2.83	10.84
1992	2.93	10.08
1993	2.93	9.20

money supply by the monetary base. The numbers in each column look deceptively stable. But note that the spread from the lowest value of the M1 multiplier (in 1990) to the highest (in 1972) is 0.5/2.8, or about 18 percent. For the M2 multiplier, the maximum spread is even higher—27 percent—suggesting that overall, the M1 multiplier is more stable. During the 1980s, however, the M2 multiplier was more stable than the M1 multiplier. The M2 multiplier shows the effects of higher interest rates in the early 1980s as individuals economized on cash balances and banks cut their excess reserves to a minimum in order to earn high rates on interest-bearing assets.

Because the money multiplier is less than perfectly stable, when the Fed is pursuing a money supply target, the target is usually set in terms of the growth of the money supply rather than the monetary base. The monetary base is then adjusted to offset undesired changes in the money supply from week to week.[2]

2. The link between the monetary base and M1 in the 1980s was affected by reforms that brought all depository institutions under the Fed and provided for uniform reserve requirements. For a discussion of this relationship, see Michelle R. Garfinkel and Davnel L. Thornton, "The Link Between M1 and the Monetary Base in the 1980s," *Review*, Federal Reserve Bank of St. Louis (September–October 1989):35–52.

INTEREST RATES AS TARGET

Until the late 1970s, the Fed paid more attention to interest rates than to the money supply. Letting interest rates rise too high could discourage investment and cause a recession. The decision to target interest rates instead of the money supply was reinforced by the fact that the Treasury has to borrow by selling U.S. government securities to the public. The government budget deficit is financed through these bond sales, and the Treasury prefers low, stable interest rates to high, unstable ones.

When the Fed pursues an interest rate target, the Open Market Committee attempts to keep the federal funds rate (the interest rate banks charge each other when lending and borrowing reserves) within a certain range. If, for example, Bank A needs $1 million in reserves to meet the reserve requirement, it can borrow them from Bank B and pay that bank interest at the federal funds rate. Bank B notifies the Fed to transfer $1 million from its reserve account to Bank A's account. If banks want to borrow more reserves in the federal funds market than other banks have available to lend, there will be upward pressure on the interest rate, the federal funds rate.

When the Fed targets interest rates, the normal specific target is a range of values for the federal funds rate, such as 7 to 7.5 percent. If the demand for reserves rises, driving up the federal funds rate to 7.5 percent or higher, the Fed will buy government bonds. The prices of bonds will rise, and their yields will fall. Lower interest rates spread from bonds to other assets, making bank lending less attractive and banks less anxious to borrow reserves from other banks in order to expand their loans. As a result, the federal funds rate is kept from rising above 7.5 percent. If demand for reserves falls, and the federal funds rate seems likely to fall below 7 percent, the Fed will sell government bonds. Open market sales of bonds will depress bond prices and put upward pressure on interest rates.

An interest rate target requires the Fed to keep adjusting the monetary base to whatever is demanded in the market for loanable funds. Thus, the Fed cannot control both the money supply and interest rates at the same time. The Fed was widely criticized by monetarists in the 1970s for giving interest rate targets priority over money supply targets. In an abrupt shift, the Fed changed its priorities from interest rates to the money supply in the fall of 1979. This change, under the leadership of chairman Paul Volcker, was regarded as a milestone in monetary policy and a victory for monetarist ideas. The policy of focusing on the money supply remained in place until 1982, but pressure on the Fed during the recession then forced it to moderate that policy. In addition, changes in the banking system have made it more difficult to forecast and control relationships between the size of the monetary base and the money supply. Finally, the link between both M1 and M2 and GDP has weakened as more substitutes for traditional forms of money have developed.

CURRENT DEBATES OVER TARGETS

In recent years, the Fed has added **GDP targeting** to its range of policy targets. This policy calls for the Fed to aim at some level of nominal GDP by influencing a number of variables that affect it. These variables include the measures of the

GDP targeting
A monetary policy that calls for the Fed to aim at some level of nominal GDP by influencing a number of variables that affect GDP.

money supply as well as total credit and interest rates. However, even if changing GDP is the ultimate goal, the Fed must choose intermediate targets that are within its control to try to attain that goal.[3] Those targets are still some combination of money supply and interest rates.

Since 1982, the Fed has been using a mix of targets: a range of growth rates for the several measures of the money supply and a range of market interest rates. In 1993, after working with a changing array of targets for six years, Chairman Alan Greenspan announced that the policy of the Fed would emphasize real (inflation-adjusted) interest rates as a policy target. This choice of targets was partly influenced by a weakening relationship between the M2 money supply and the price level.[4] As both short-term and long-term real interest rates fell sharply in the early 1990s, the real interest rate on Treasury bills was close to zero by 1993. Greenspan's goal was to slow the growth of bank reserves and put the brakes on bank lending so that the expansion would continue, but not at a pace that would result in accelerating inflation.

KEY IDEAS

POSSIBLE MONETARY POLICY TARGETS

MONEY SUPPLY TARGETS
- Monetary base — Currency plus bank reserves
- M1 or M2 money supply — Currency, checkable deposits, travelers' checks, other items

INTEREST RATE TARGETS
- Federal funds rate — Rate banks charge each other to borrow excess reserves
- Real interest rate — Federal funds or T-bill rate adjusted for inflation

GDP TARGET
- GDP or growth rate — Nominal output

PROBLEMS IN IMPLEMENTING MONETARY POLICY

In addition to theoretical difficulties in how monetary policy affects the economy, and the problems associated with a choice of targets, there are also some practical difficulties in implementing monetary policy. Like fiscal policy, monetary policy is subject to lags. Monetary policy impacts heavily on a few sectors of the economy, rather than being spread evenly throughout the economy. And finally, the management of monetary policy has been complicated by the increasing globalization of financial markets. This section examines each of these problems in turn.

---

3. For a more detailed discussion of GDP targeting (originally GNP targeting), see Michael D. Bradley and Dennis W. Jansen, "Understanding Nominal GNP Targeting," *Review*, Federal Reserve Bank of St. Louis (November–December 1989):30–40.

4. For a discussion of this policy change, see John B. Carlson, "Assessing Real Interest Rates," *Economic Commentary*, Federal Reserve Bank of Cleveland (August 15, 1993).

LAGS IN MONETARY POLICY

Monetary policy is affected by the same kinds of lags as fiscal policy: recognition, implementation, and impact. The recognition lag is probably about the same length for both monetary and fiscal policy. Unlike fiscal policy, however, monetary policy has a very short implementation lag. The Federal Open Market Committee (FOMC) meets regularly and makes decisions about changes in the money supply. Because of the Fed's independence from Congress and the executive branch, it can move quickly without asking anyone's permission.

In discussions of monetary policy, the recognition and implementation lags are combined and known as the inside lag. The impact lag—known as the outside lag in monetary policy—can be quite long. In the 1960s, it was estimated that it took one to two years for money supply changes to be fully reflected in prices and output. By the 1980s, the lag appeared to be getting shorter. The inflation of the late 1970s had made lenders and borrowers more sensitive to the need to acquire and use current information to form correct expectations about inflation. Shorter lags also reflect increased competition in financial markets as a result of bank deregulation.

The length of the outside lag depends on how quickly people recognize and respond to a change in the money supply. It takes time for banks to increase or decrease their lending or for individuals to adjust their spending. In general, it is estimated that, because of the outside lag, it takes at least two quarters for monetary policy to have half its ultimate impact and eighteen to twenty-four months for the full effect to be felt.

Lags can cause monetary policy to have the wrong effect, just as they can for fiscal policy. Between 1945 and 1982, cycles of economic activity were brief, with the average recession lasting only eleven months. A policy that cannot be implemented quickly and have a rapid impact may be worse than no policy at all.

DOMESTIC SECTORAL EFFECTS

Monetary policy does not affect all sectors of the economy equally. When monetary policy is tight, economic activities that depend on borrowing are affected more heavily. Business investment in plants and equipment, housing, consumer durables (especially automobiles), and state and local government capital projects are very dependent on borrowing and sensitive to changes in monetary policy. Consumers, the auto industry, and the construction industry resent being singled out to bear more than their share of the battle against inflation when monetary policy is tightened. Adjustable-rate mortgages (ARMs) and other innovations in home financing have somewhat lessened the impact of monetary policy on housing. However, this and other parts of the private sector are still sensitive to changes in interest rates and the availability of funds.

MONETARY POLICY IN A GLOBAL ECONOMY

The transmission mechanism model of monetary policy is based on a closed economy. That is, this model ignores the rest of the world. However, the fraction of U.S. output entering international trade has grown in recent decades. Flows of money and financial assets between countries have also expanded. It has become increasingly clear that neither monetary policy nor fiscal policy can ignore the rest of the world.

Since 1973, when nations switched to floating exchange rates, monetary policy has been more closely tied to changes in the foreign sector. A tight monetary policy that drives up interest rates attracts funds from abroad and drives up the price of the dollar. When the price of the dollar rises, exporters find it harder to sell their goods abroad. Also, import-competing firms find that their foreign competitors can more easily undersell them because their goods are cheaper in dollar terms. Thus, the international sector of the economy has become increasingly sensitive to monetary policy.

Suppose the Fed is pursuing an expansionary policy. According to the monetarist model, there will be an excess supply of money. As people try to spend it, their purchases will drive up both real output and the price level, in some combination. In an open economy, however, some of their purchases will be imported goods rather than domestic products. As the price level starts to rise, sales of exports will fall, and imports of relatively cheaper foreign goods will rise. A fall

GLOBAL OUTLOOK: THE BUNDESBANK AND THE EUROPEAN RECESSION

For Europeans, a lasting memento of the end of the Cold War will be the recession of the early 1990s. When the Berlin wall came down, East and West Germany were united into a single country. The west was prosperous, thriving, cautious, efficient. West Germany had an unparalleled record of price stability, low unemployment, and economic growth stretching back to the 1950s. The east, although a showcase of communist success, was far behind its larger western counterpart in technology, infrastructure, communications, housing, and other necessary elements of a modern industrial economy. The West German government vowed to help bring the rest of Germany up to par with the west with investment in modernizing the economy in the east. The transition in former East Germany also meant high unemployment, and the government was committed to a generous program of unemployment benefits as well as other elements of a social welfare system. For the first time, the central government, always a model of fiscal conservatism, began to run large deficits.

Germany has always pursued very conservative monetary policies in order to minimize the prospect of inflation. From 1967 to 1991, the U.S. consumer price index rose more than 300 percent; Canada's, 357 percent; the United Kingdom's, 748 percent. Even Japan's price index rose 257 percent over the twenty-four-year period. Germany had the best inflation record of any major industrial nation, with prices rising 126 percent in twenty-four years, an average inflation rate of well under 2 percent a year. Fiscal deficits were a threat to that price stability. The Bundesbank responded with very tight monetary policy. The result was a sharp rise in interest rates in 1991 through 1993 as the central government increased its borrowing in a very tight credit market.

The story might have ended there with a German recession if it weren't for the fact that Germany is part of the twelve-nation European Community (EC), whose currencies and credit markets are very closely linked. High interest rates in Germany attracted funds from other member countries and drove up their interest rates. Recession in Germany led to a decline in German imports, a big market for other members of the EC. Some members of the EC dropped out of the currency system in order to partly disconnect from high German interest rates, but they still felt the effect of the decline in German import demand.

The experience of the EC with German unification points up one of the costs of a closely integrated economic system. If there are hard times in California, they are felt in Delaware. If there is a hurricane that devastates Florida, some of the costs are felt in Minnesota. If the dominant partner of the EC pursues a restrictive monetary policy, the rest of the EC shares in the consequences. All of the twelve members of the EC have helped to shoulder the costs of German reunification.

in exports and a rise in imports mean that the aggregate demand curve shifts to the left. This shift reduces the impact of expansionary monetary policy on output and the price level. Some of the extra money is, in effect, exported, increasing demand in the rest of the world as well as at home.

In the Keynesian model, monetary policy works mainly through interest rates. In the international economy, the emphasis shifts from interest rates to yields on assets. Most of the difference between yields and interest rates comes from the fluctuations in exchange rates. For countries with a common currency, or a currency agreement, such as some of the members of the European Community, yields and interest rates will be the same, as they are among the states of the United States.

As interest rates start to fall in an open economy, domestic firms will want to borrow more in response to the lower rates. Lenders, however, are more likely to want to make loans in other countries where higher yields are offered. Some of the newly created money goes abroad in search of higher yields. In addition, the inflow of funds from abroad shrinks as domestic interest rates fall. The net increase in loanable funds is fairly small, and there is little effect on investment.

The same problems occur with contractionary monetary policy in a Keynesian model. Spending falls, but some of the decline is in spending for imports, rather than domestic goods and services. Thus, there is less impact on aggregate demand, output, and the price level. Higher interest rates will attract an inflow of foreign funds, frustrating any attempts to reduce investment demand.

Thus, although Keynesians and monetarists disagree about the process, they concur that monetary policy is less effective in an open economy. Regardless of whether monetary policy works directly through spending or indirectly through interest rates, it will be less effective in an economy that is very open (has a lot of economic interactions with other countries). Small countries, such as Guyana, Taiwan, the Netherlands, and Costa Rica, find it virtually impossible to pursue an independent monetary policy because most of the effects leak out of the economy instead of staying at home.

MONETARY POLICY UNDER THE FED, 1914–1993

When the Federal Reserve System was established in 1913, one of its primary functions was to keep the United States in compliance with the international gold standard. The Fed had to allow the size of the U.S. gold stock held by the Treasury to set an upper limit on the size of the money supply. Such a requirement severely limited the Fed's freedom to expand the money supply.

The Fed's first challenge was helping the Treasury finance the budget deficit during and after World War I. The Fed cooperated in keeping interest rates low and buying any government bonds that could not find a buyer. These actions were inflationary. When the Fed recognized that the ratio of money to gold was getting too high, it began to contract the money supply. That action played a role in bringing about the 1920–1921 recession.

THE FED AND THE DEPRESSION

The biggest controversy over the Fed's policy centers on its actions from 1929 to 1937. The money supply fell by 25 percent from August 1929 to March 1933, in part because of widespread bank failures. Such a wave of failures was exactly what the Fed was intended to prevent. The Fed, aided by large inflows of gold, did keep the discount rate low during the early years of the Depression. It was the money supply, not the monetary base, that fell sharply. The monetary base remained stable while the ratio of currency to deposits rose (as people withdrew cash from the banking system) and the ratio of deposits to reserves fell (as banks held more excess reserves). Widespread bank failures led to large cash withdrawals from banks. Thus, the same monetary base supported fewer deposits. Banks saw few good loan prospects, so they chose to hold large excess reserves. Cash withdrawals combined with excess reserves meant that the money multiplier was smaller.

Milton Friedman and Anna Schwartz are the best-known critics of the Fed's actions in this period. In a thorough study of these actions, Friedman and Schwartz argued that the Fed was too passive, failing to pump up reserves to offset what was happening in the private sector.[5] The Fed did not shrink the monetary base but did not allow it to expand either. However, the Fed was constrained with respect to the size of the money supply by the gold standard until 1934. The most controversial policy decision by the Fed during the Depression took place after the United States went off the gold standard. The Fed chose to raise reserve requirements in 1936, trying to "mop up" excess bank reserves. This action was widely blamed for sparking an economic downturn in 1937.

Peter Temin argued that Friedman and Schwartz came down too hard on the Fed.[6] The money supply can change from either the supply side or the demand side. The return on investment was low during the early years of the Depression. If there is low return on investment and weak consumption demand, interest rates will fall. That fall will lead both individuals and banks to hold more cash and make less available to borrowers. The opportunity cost of holding currency and excess reserves will be low because of demand factors, which are largely outside the Fed's control.

The Fed did not cause the Depression, but perhaps a more aggressive expansionary monetary policy would have made it shorter and milder. Bear in mind, however, that the Fed had had only seventeen years of experience when the Depression occurred, and monetary theory was not as well developed as it is today. Also, some of the Fed's actions prior to 1935 were restricted by its need to comply with the gold standard.

THE ACCORD

The Accord
The 1951 agreement between the Fed and the Treasury that the Fed was no longer obliged to hold interest rates low in order to assist with the Treasury's debt financing.

During and after World War II, the Fed's main task was helping the Treasury finance the enormous debt incurred during the war at acceptably low interest rates. The Fed abandoned monetary targets in order to hold down interest rates. The result was inflation, because every time the Fed bought Treasury obligations to keep interest rates down, it expanded bank reserves. In 1951, the Fed and the Treasury reached an agreement. This agreement, called **The Accord**, stated that the Fed was no longer obliged to hold interest rates low to assist with the Treasury's debt financing. In 1952, the Fed was finally free to turn its monetary policy in the direction of stabilizing economic activity.

5. Milton Friedman and Anna J. Schwartz, *A Monetary History of the United States* (Princeton, NJ: Princeton University Press, 1963).
6. Peter Temin, *Did Monetary Forces Cause the Great Depression?* (New York: W. W. Norton, 1976).

POLICY FOCUS: ALAN GREENSPAN

The four year term of the chair of the Federal Reserve Board of Governors overlaps the term of the President in a peculiar fashion. About a year and a half before leaving office or running for reelection, the President finally gets to choose the person who controls the nation's monetary policy. In 1979, President Carter appointed Paul Volcker, whose sharp reversal to tight monetary policy contributed to both the 1980–1982 recession and Carter's defeat. Despite some controversy over his policies, President Reagan reappointed Volcker because the chair of the Fed commanded so much respect internationally.

In 1987, near the end of his term, Reagan finally got his own choice. Alan Greenspan, a conservative economist with a strong anti-inflationary bent, was named to head the Federal Reserve. Greenspan, who was reappointed by President Bush in 1991, is only the second economist (after Arthur Burns) to have served both as chair of the Council of Economic Advisers (under President Ford) and head of the Federal Reserve System. His anti-inflationary policies under both Ford and Bush probably contributed to their respective losses in 1976 and 1992!

Greenspan's career has been largely in the private sector, interspersed with stints of government service in a variety of capacities. With a Ph.D. from New York University, Greenspan ran a private consulting firm with a variety of big-name clients who relied on his gift for tearing into statistics and teasing a story and significant trends out of seemingly insignificant numbers. A political conservative, he is less interested in politics than in keeping the Fed on an anti-inflationary course. Greenspan is not an advocate of zero inflation, just inflation low enough so that it is no longer a significant factor in financial decisions. Greenspan feels that this goal requires frequent adjustments in the Fed's goals and targets, a course that earns him much criticism from monetarist supporters of a monetary rule and a steady monetary growth policy.

Under Greenspan, the Fed has gradually shifted back in the direction of interest rate targeting, but still pursues monetary targets as well. A conservative manager with a penchant for fine tuning rather than laissez-faire monetary policy raises the hackles of conservatives and liberals alike. Greenspan seems to have the ability to chart his own course without succumbing to political pressures, an essential attribute in a central banker.

For most of the rest of the 1950s, the Fed used free reserves as its policy target. **Free reserves** consist of bank excess reserves less bank loans from the Fed. If free reserves were large, the Fed took that as a signal of too much slack in the credit market. The Fed defined its role during this time as "leaning against the wind." That is, the Fed was assessing the direction of economic activity and trying to steer the economy back toward a middle ground of steady growth, stable prices, and high employment.

Free reserves
Excess bank reserves minus loans from the Fed to member banks.

MONETARY POLICY IN THE 1960S AND 1970S

The inflation rate began to creep up in the late 1960s and rose faster in the 1970s. From 1965 to 1979, the CPI rose 130 percent. For most of this period, monetary policy was expansionary. The 1970s began with a financial crisis, a sharp drop in the stock market combined with the failure of Penn Central. That railroad was a major borrower from commercial banks. The Fed earned some of its highest marks ever for monetary policy during this crisis. It announced that the discount window was open and lowered reserve requirements.

By the late 1970s, after flip-flopping between targeting the money supply and targeting interest rates, the Fed began to move more in a monetary direction, while keeping an eye on interest rates. An abrupt change of direction in October 1979 was later named the "Saturday night special." Instead of interest rates, the Fed decided to make the growth of the various measures of the money supply, especially M1, the focus of its policy actions. The Fed cut the monetary growth rate sharply at the end of 1979, which drove interest rates to all-time highs. This action contributed to the recession (and drop in the inflation rate) of the early 1980s. The 1979 shift marked a firm choice of money supply targets over interest rate targets.

RECENT MONETARY POLICY

Through most of the 1980s, the Fed, under chair Paul Volcker, pursued a fairly restrictive monetary policy. This policy was credited with helping to reduce both the inflation rate and nominal (but not real) interest rates. Part of the decrease in inflation and interest rates, however, was the result of a decline in velocity rather than a slowing of the growth of the money supply. Monetary policy in the 1980s was complicated by rapid growth in the federal debt, an influx of foreign lending, changes in bank regulations, and more numerous bank failures. In 1982, the Fed backed off from its 1979 decision to focus solely on money supply targets and began to pursue interest rate targets as well. In addition, M1 competed with other measures of money and credit for the role of primary money supply target.

In 1987, Volcker was succeeded by Alan Greenspan as chair of the Fed. A combination of changing leadership and experience has changed the Fed's operating style and priorities. The experience of the 1970s and 1980s made the Fed much more concerned about inflation and also much more aware of the effects of high interest rates on the economy. Bank deregulation, increasing involvement of foreigners in U.S. money and credit markets, and the gradual weakening of the close link between M1 and GDP have made the Fed much more uncertain about the effects of its actions on the economy.

RULES VERSUS DISCRETION

Many economists, especially monetarists, have not been happy with the Fed's performance. Monetarists blame the Fed for both recessions and inflation, as the course of monetary policy zigzags between expansion and contraction. The Fed has come under criticism in recent years for monetary tightness during the Great Depression. The same criticism was leveled at the Fed during the 1980–1982 recession. A proposed regulation requiring the Fed to chart a course of growth in the money supply at some predetermined, steady rate is called a **monetary rule**. Such a regulation would replace discretionary monetary policy.

The most commonly suggested form of monetary rule is to allow the money supply to grow about as fast or just slightly faster than real output over the long run, keeping inflation at a tolerable rate of 1 to 2 percent a year. This rule would call for a growth rate of 4 to 5 percent a year for the money supply. Under such a rule, monetary policy would be mildly inflationary when output growth slows down because of a recession. Suppose, for example, that the rule calls for M_s to grow at 4 percent a year. If velocity is stable, then $P \times Y$ must grow at the same rate. If Y is growing more slowly than 4 percent, P will rise to make up the difference. If the economy is overheated and demand is fueling growth of 7 percent a year, this monetary rule would be contractionary. Proponents of such a rule argue that attempting to respond to imperfect information from the mar-

Monetary rule
A proposed regulation requiring the Fed to make the money supply grow at some predetermined, steady rate.

ketplace, with the added hindrance of lags, is worse than having no monetary policy at all. Nobel Prize winner Milton Friedman is probably the best-known advocate of having a monetary rule.

The Fed is not likely to adopt such a binding rule voluntarily. It has, however, tried to stabilize the monetary growth rate and give more emphasis to the money supply as target rather than interest rates in recent years. Although monetarists are still unhappy with the Fed's performance in the last decade, especially with rapid monetary growth in the early 1980s, this change in targets represents a victory for monetarist ideas.

Another proposed "rule" is to return to a gold standard. Being on a gold standard requires a nation to have enough gold to redeem its currency in gold on demand. The stock of gold would place limits on the size of the money supply, and the Fed's discretionary policy role would be greatly reduced. The United States went off the gold standard in 1934 and is not likely to return, but some people find the idea of an automatic limit on monetary expansion very attractive.

Consider again...*As you have seen, seating Alan Greenspan next to Hillary Clinton was not the first time that a President has tried to subtly influence the direction of Federal Reserve policy. Even though the Fed is technically independent, it is not immune from political pressures. Congress has pressured the Fed to keep interest rates low, often in response to the construction and auto industries and others who want low interest rates. The Fed has often been pressured by Congress or the President to ease monetary conditions in election years. With a large national debt, lower interest rates are politically very appealing as a relatively painless way to reduce the interest cost in the federal budget. The Fed is also under pressure from banks, which would like to be able to lend freely (and borrow freely from the Fed) during times of high loan demand.*

All these forces tend to push the Fed in the direction of monetary expansion. It was only after some painful experience with the resulting inflation that the Fed was able to fight back and tighten monetary conditions in the late 1970s and early 1980s. The Fed kept money relatively tight during the 1980s and early 1990s, easing up only as the recession hit. As the economy expands, we can expect continued pressure on the Fed to pursue a more expansionary monetary policy than their own prudent, anti-inflationary goals would dictate.

Greenspan has made it clear that he supports deficit reduction and is willing to help make it possible with expansionary monetary policy as long as there is no serious threat of inflation. Containing inflation, however, remains his number one priority. Even Hillary Rodham Clinton is not likely to persuade the head of the Fed to shift gears in order to make life easier for the President.

SUMMARY

1. Monetarists believe that monetary policy works directly by creating a money supply that exceeds money demand. The excess money is spent, driving up prices and/or output. The Keynesian view of monetary policy is that it works by lowering interest rates. In turn, lower interest rates stimulate investment and increase aggregate expenditure and aggregate demand. In this case, the effectiveness of monetary policy depends on how sensitive money demand is to interest rates and how responsive investment demand is to changes in interest rates. Keynesians do not think that monetary policy is always very effective at lowering interest rates or that lower interest rates are very effective in stimulating investment.

2. The Fed can attempt to control either the money supply or interest rates, but not both. From 1979 until the early 1990s, more emphasis has been placed on targeting the money supply. More recently, the Fed has been looking at other targets, including real interest rates.

3. Monetary policy suffers from lags, regional effects, and political pressures. Because of these problems with monetary policy, some economists support a monetary rule that would set a fixed rate of growth for the money stock. Monetary policy is less effective in a global economy because financial markets are integrated among countries.

4. The Fed has been criticized for its role in the Great Depression, for failing to provide enough reserves to banks to keep the money supply from contracting. Since World War II, the Fed has been pursuing multiple and changing goals. A switch to tight money in 1979 was blamed in part for the 1980–1982 recession. Monetary policy remained tight through the 1980s because of expansionary fiscal policy.

NEW TERMS

transmission mechanism   monetary base   GDP targeting   free reserves
monetarists   money multiplier   The Accord   monetary rule

QUESTIONS: REVIEW, APPLICATIONS, AND POLICY

REVIEW

1. The monetarist transmission mechanism accepts "spend it" as the explanation of what happens to an increase in the money supply. The Keynesian transmission mechanism follows the "lend it" route. Explain the difference.
2. Why can't the Fed control both the money supply and interest rates at the same time? Discuss the advantages and disadvantages of each target.
3. Which sectors are most affected by changes in monetary policy? Why?
4. Why does Milton Friedman advocate a monetary rule instead of discretionary fiscal policy?
5. What are the inside lag and the outside lag? How do they affect the usefulness of monetary policy?

APPLICATIONS

6. If $MPC = 0.75$, what change in Y would occur if i decreased from 20 percent to 15 percent? Use Figure 3 to determine your answer.
7. Let $i = 15$ percent and $MPC = 0.9$. Further, suppose the economy is in equilibrium and $Y = \$2,000$ billion. If $Y^* = \$2,200$ billion, what change in i would be necessary to bring the economy to the full-employment level of national income? Use Figure 3 to determine your answer.
8. Let B be $200 billion. If m is 3 and then rises to 3.2, what is the change in M_s? What is the dollar change in M_s if B rises from $200 billion to $225 billion, and m is constant at 3?

POLICY

9. Why do Keynesians think that monetary policy is likely to be less effective than fiscal policy?
10. If money demand is sensitive to changes in interest rates and investment demand is not, how would that affect the relative effectiveness of monetary and fiscal policy? What if money demand is not sensitive to interest rate changes but investment demand is?
11. How might each of the following have differed if the Fed had been following a 4 percent monetary growth rule?

a. the 1936–1937 recession (during the Depression)
b. the postwar interest rate agreement with the Treasury
c. the 1966 credit crunch

12. If you were in charge of the Fed and concerned about inflation, would you pursue an interest rate target or a money supply target? Why?

SUGGESTIONS FOR FURTHER READING

Friedman, Milton. *Money Mischief.* New York: Harcourt, Brace, Jovanovich, 1992. One of contemporary economics' best writers, Nobel Prize winner Milton Friedman looks at policy proposals to reform the banking system.

Greider, William. *Secrets of the Temple: How the Federal Reserve Runs the Country.* New York: Simon and Schuster, 1989. A critical and highly controversial look at how the Fed has conducted monetary policy in recent years.

Heller, Robert. "Implementing Monetary Policy." *Federal Reserve Bulletin* (July 1988): 419–429. Reviews monetary policy making in the 1970s and 1980s.

Review, Federal Reserve Bank of St. Louis. An annual review of the previous year's monetary policy. All of the regional Federal Reserve Banks put out regular newsletters that comment on monetary policy issues.

APPENDIX
A COMPOSITE MACROECONOMIC MODEL: *IS-LM*

In the last eight chapters we have examined both real and monetary variables, as well as monetary and fiscal policies. Not long after the Keynesian revolution, a composite model integrating interest rates into the Keynesian model was developed; it is called the *IS-LM* model. The model incorporates both interest rates and real income as central variables, but not the price level, which is held constant. The *IS-LM* model illustrates the feedback between the *real* (goods) world of investment, government spending, saving and taxes, and the *monetary* world of money supply and the transactions and asset demands for money.

THE *IS* CURVE

We begin with the real side. Figure 1A shows the relationship of leakages (savings, taxes, and imports) to the level of income. At low enough levels of income, the sum of savings, taxes, and imports may be negative, but as incomes rise, all three leakages rise as well.

Figure 2A shows the relationship of injections (investment, government spending, and exports) to the level of interest rates. While government spending is largely independent of interest rates, investment demand and exports are not. We have already explored the negative relationship between investment

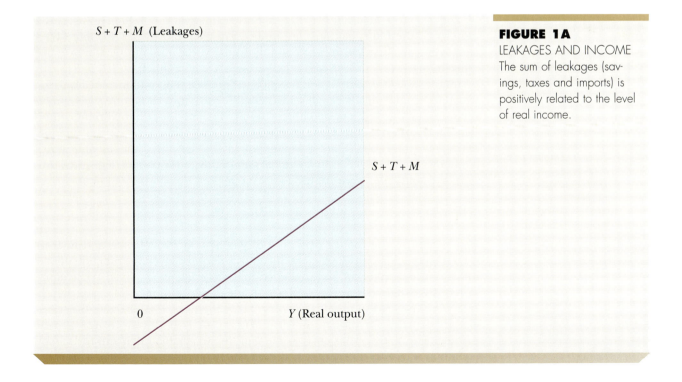

FIGURE 1A
LEAKAGES AND INCOME
The sum of leakages (savings, taxes and imports) is positively related to the level of real income.

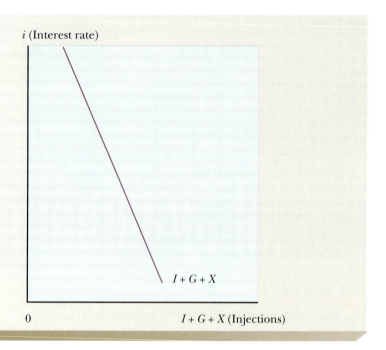

FIGURE 2A

INJECTIONS AND THE INTEREST RATE

The sum of injections (investment, government spending and exports) is negatively related to the real interest rate.

demand and interest rates using the *MEI* curve. Exports are negatively related to interest rates through a more complex mechanism. High interest rates attract funds from abroad, raising the exchange rate, which makes exports more expensive. Consequently, exports have an indirect negative relationship to interest rates.

In equilibrium, leakages must equal injections. To link Figures 1A and 2A, we add two more quadrants to make a four-part diagram shown in Figure 3A. To aid clarity, the four quadrants are numbered. Quadrant II is a 45° line which simply ensures that leakages, measured on the vertical axis in Quadrant I, are equal to injections, measured on the horizontal axis in Quadrant III. The fourth quadrant shows the various combinations of interest rates and income levels for which injections will be equal to leakages. We have traced out one such combination (i_1, Y_1) with the dotted line in Figure 3A. This set of equilibrium combinations is known as the *IS* curve (for investment = saving, or more generally, leakages = injections). Any combination of interest rates and income levels along the *IS* curve will result in equilibrium in the goods market. Figure 3A presents the complete *IS* part of the *IS-LM* model.

THE *LM* CURVE

Equilibrium in the money market also depends on real income and interest rates. Figure 4A shows the demand for transactions balances as a function of real income. (Remember, we have assumed that the price level is fixed.) The equation of exchange tells us that transactions demand for money, M_{dT}, is positively related to the level of nominal income. Since the price level is fixed, the transactions demand for money shown in Figure 4A is positively related to real income. The slope of this curve is the k in the Marshallian demand for money equation, where $k = 1/V$.

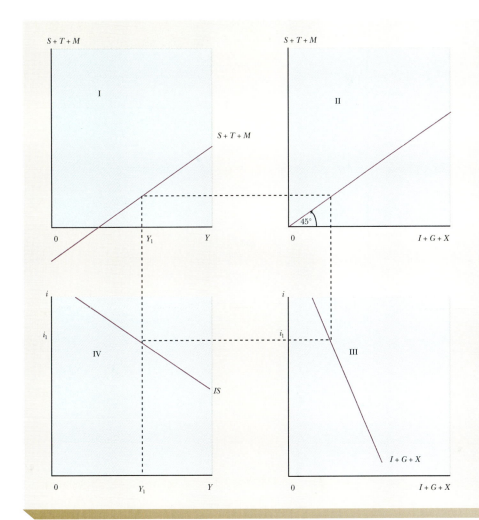

FIGURE 3A
DERIVING THE *IS* CURVE
This figure combines the leakages of Figure 1A in Quadrant I, the injections of Figure 2A in Quadrant III, and the equilibrium condition that leakages must equal injections (Quadrant II), to develop a set of possible combinations of real output and real interest rates that will result in equilibrium in the goods market. The *IS* curve in Quadrant IV shows those possible equilibrium combinations.

The asset demand for money, M_{d2}, is negatively related to the interest rate, i. The steep slope of this function, shown in Figure 5A, reflects the relatively low interest-elasticity of the demand for money.

Equilibrium in the money market requires that money supply equals money demand. To illustrate this equilibrium, we will use Figure 6A, where the quadrants are again numbered for clarity. In Quadrant VI of Figure 6A, there is a line with a negative slope of 45° that represents the money supply. A given money supply can be divided into transactions and asset balances in any combination, but the total of the transactions balances (shown in Quadrant V) and the asset balances (shown in Quadrant VII) have to add up to the fixed money supply. For example, at point *A* in Quadrant VI, all of the money supply is in asset balances; at point *B*, all of the money supply is in transactions balances.

The division of a given money supply between transactions and asset balances will be determined by the level of real income and the rate of interest. A high interest rate and a high level of income will mean that most money holdings will be transactions balances, while a low interest rate and a low level of income will ensure that most money will be held as asset balances. The various

FIGURE 4A
MONEY DEMAND AND INCOME
The transactions demand for money is positively related to the level of real income.

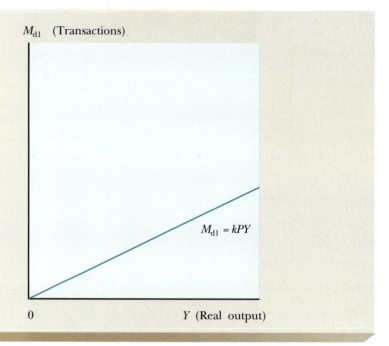

FIGURE 5A
MONEY DEMAND AND THE INTEREST RATE
The asset demand for money is negatively related to the real interest rate.

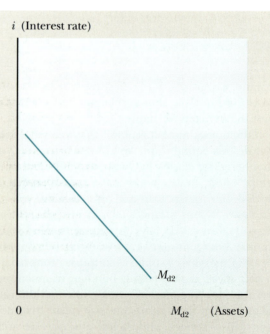

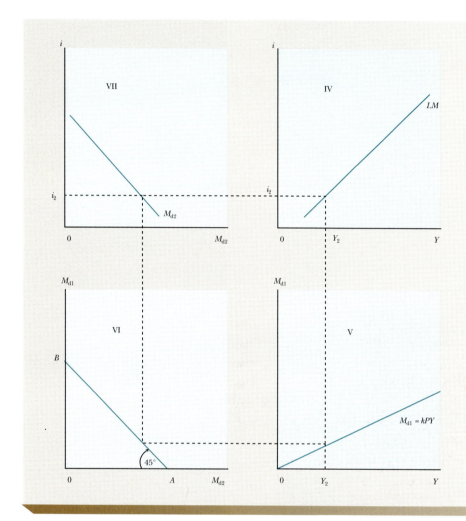

FIGURE 6A

DERIVING THE *LM* CURVE
This figure combines the transactions demand for money of Figure 4A in Quadrant V, the asset demand for money injections of Figure 5A in Quadrant VII, and the equilibrium condition that money demand must equal money supply (Quadrant VI), to develop a set of possible combinations of real output and real interest rates that will result in equilibrium in the money market. The *LM* curve in Quadrant IV shows those possible equilibrium combinations.

combinations of interest rates and real income levels that ensure equilibrium in the money market are given in Quadrant IV. This set of equilibrium combinations is known as the *LM* curve.

The *LM* curve is found in the same way as the *IS* curve, by choosing an arbitrary income level such as Y_2, which determines the level of transactions balances, M_{d1}, in Quadrant V. Quadrant VI determines how much of the money supply is left for asset balances, M_{d2}, and Quadrant VII tells us that an interest rate of i_2 is needed for people to be satisfied with that level of asset balances. Thus, Y_2 and i_2 represent one possible equilibrium combination for the money market. Figure 6A presents the complete *LM* part of the *IS-LM* model.

Although there are many combinations of *Y* and *i* that will result in equilibrium in the money market, and many combinations that will ensure that leakages equal injections in the goods market, there is only one combination that will satisfy both markets at once. Figure 7A includes both markets and shows that the equilibrium combination is Y_e and i_e.

The complete *IS-LM* model is very useful for analyzing the effects of changes in any of the underlying variables. We will consider one example here and illustrate it with Figure 8A. Suppose that a tax increase is initiated in order to reduce

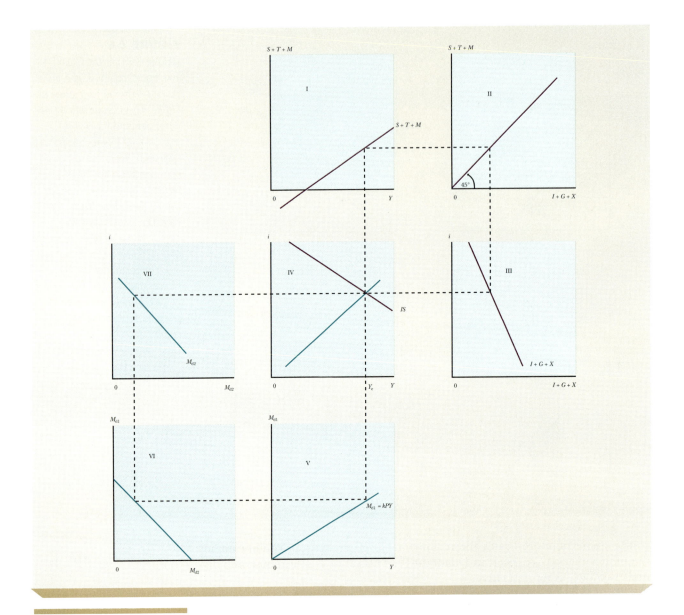

FIGURE 7A

EQUILIBRIUM IN BOTH MARKETS: IS-LM

This figure combines Figures 3A and 6A to determine a unique combination of real output (Y_e) and real interest rates (i_e) that will ensure equilibrium in both the goods market and the money market.

the budget deficit. The increase in T shifts the $S + T + M$ line upward in Quadrant I, causing IS to shift to the left in Quadrant IV. The lower level of economic activity puts downward pressure on both income, Y, and interest rates. The lower level of income reduces demand for transactions balances (M_{d1}, in Quadrant V) but the lower level of interest rates increases demand for asset balances (M_{d2}, in Quadrant VII). Equilibrium is restored in both markets with a decline in real income and interest rates. The effect of the tax increase on real income is smaller than one might conclude from a simple multiplier analysis, because of the downward pressure on interest rates.

The *IS-LM* model can be adapted for use with variable price levels, but we will not attempt to do so here. Even with the limitation of a fixed price level, the *IS-LM* model is a powerful tool for analyzing the effects of fiscal and monetary policy changes on output, employment, and interest rates.

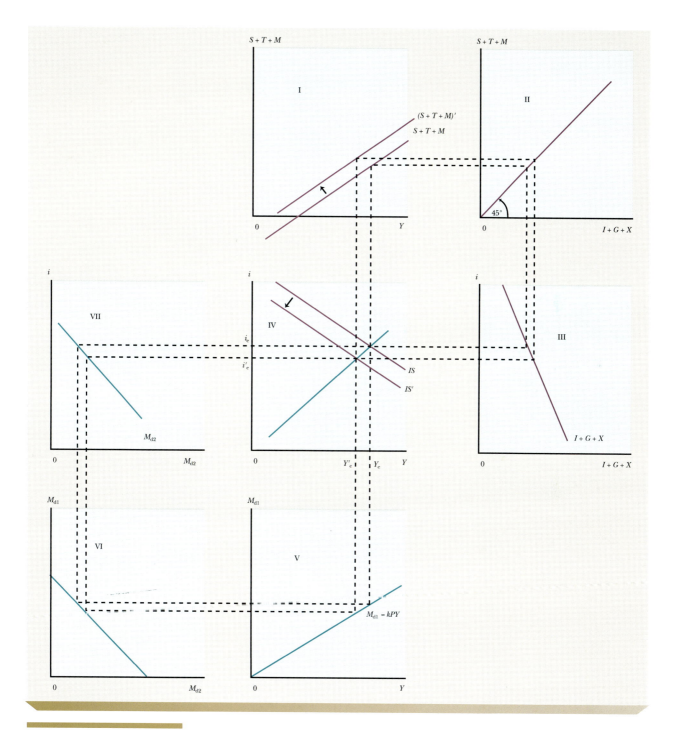

FIGURE 8A

CHANGE IN EQUILIBRIUM: AN INCREASE IN TAXES

An increase in taxes shifts the $S + T + M$ function upward and the IS curve back to the left. At a lower level of Y and i, the goods market is again in equilibrium. The lower Y means a reduction in demand for transactions balances, while the lower i means a higher demand for asset balances, so the existing money supply still equals money demand, but now with a different mix of transactions and asset balances.

PART 5

POLICY CHALLENGES FOR THE 1990S

The three chapters in this section look at a number of current challenges facing macroeconomic policy makers as they address the goals of full employment, price stability, and steady economic growth. Chapter 15 summarizes several current challenges and controversies relating to the implementation of demand management policies, including the idea of an inflation-unemployment trade-off and a revisit to the crowding-out debate. An important issue in this chapter is whether the market should be left alone or whether intervention is appropriate and effective.

Chapter 16 tackles the dominant issue of the decade, economic growth, and explores the recent experience with growth, the sources of economic growth, and some of the policy tools used to shift aggregate supply outward. Chapter 17 takes the growth issue abroad to look at the problem of economic development in less developed countries. This chapter looks at the theory of economic development, the policy alternatives, and the role of the high-income nations in promoting and encouraging economic development in the Third World.

CHAPTER 15
CURRENT ISSUES IN STABILIZATION POLICY

LEARNING OBJECTIVES

1. Explain why the relative stability of velocity and the multiplier is important for the relative effectiveness of monetary and fiscal policy.

2. Discuss the impact of a policy of financing increased government spending by taxes rather than by borrowing from the public or expanding the money supply.

3. Describe the shape of the Phillips curve and explain its usefulness and limitations as a way to guide or interpret demand management policy.

4. Explain why the differences between rational and adaptive expectations, and auction and contract markets, are important for the effectiveness of stabilization policy.

Consider this... *Remember the last time you were on a crowded freeway, wishing you had taken another route? Have you ever visited a neighborhood going downhill one house at a time, because as one or two were allowed to run down, it wasn't worth the effort and expense for the neighbors to keep their property up? When's the last time you arrived late for a concert or a play to find that the only seats available were in the front row, where you had to obstruct everyone's view to get to a seat? These may not sound like economic policy problems, especially macroeconomic policy, but they are related to the problems facing macroeconomic policy makers.*

Economist Thomas Schelling has analyzed the aggregate results of individual choices. In one of his many books, *Micromotives and Macrobehavior*, he offers a wide range of examples of what happens when individuals make choices without considering the choices of others, including choosing seats at a concert, picking a route when commuting to work, and buying or selling a house in a declining neighborhood.[1] The outcomes are likely to be an empty front row at a concert, overcrowding on some roads and little use of others, or panic selling. Outcomes are often less satisfactory for everyone when people are unable to devise policies to cope with the effects of interdependence.

Consider what might happen in an economy where everyone had pessimistic expectations and decided to save more as a hedge against recession. Under such conditions, it is likely that some of the added savings would not be invested. With increased saving (and lower consumption), demand and income would both fall. Fear of recession and a self-interested response to that fear would help to cause a recession.

Members of a small group—a family, a club, a small town, or a class—are well aware of their interdependence. Their individual contributions to an outcome

---

1. Thomas Schelling, *Micromotives and Macrobehavior* (New York: W.W. Norton, 1978).

are large enough to make a difference. In a larger group, however, each member has a small effect on the aggregate outcome. When individuals make self-interested decisions without considering the effects of interdependence, the outcome may be unsatisfactory for everyone.

To avoid an aggregate outcome that is unsatisfactory to the majority of citizens is the central policy concern of macroeconomics. The sum of individual and collective decisions can lead to a rate of inflation and a level of unemployment that few people find satisfactory. Citizens expect government policy to offset the effects of these choices and to provide a better outcome. Demand management (fiscal and monetary) policies are the tools governments use to offset some of the undesirable macro effects of self-interested private decisions. This chapter will look at some of the challenges and problems in using demand management policies.

5. Summarize the main differences and areas of agreement between contemporary economists in the Keynesian tradition and the classical/monetarist tradition.

WHICH WORKS BETTER, MONETARY OR FISCAL POLICY?

In the last chapter, we examined Keynesian arguments that monetary policy is ineffective. Now it is time for a word from the other side. Monetarists argue that monetary policy is really more effective than fiscal policy because of the way households respond to changes in the money supply and changes in real income. If households respond in predictable ways to changes in the money supply, the velocity of money (V in the equation of exchange) must be stable.

Velocity and the marginal propensity to consume cannot both be stable. If V is stable, MPC is unstable, and so is the expenditure multiplier. If, as monetarists claim, the marginal propensity to consume, MPC (and therefore the expenditure multiplier), is not stable, then the impact of fiscal policy is much less certain. To understand why both V and MPC can't be stable at the same time, consider how households respond to an increase in the money supply. The Keynesian consumption function shows a supposedly stable relationship between real disposable income and real consumption. An increase in the money supply will have no impact on consumption unless it is accompanied by an increase in real income. According to the equation of exchange, an increase in the money supply without an increase in real income will either drive down interest rates, reducing velocity, or raise the price level. Keynesians believe that velocity is unstable; it is likely to change in response to a change in the money supply. Monetary policy is therefore ineffective, because it only affects velocity and the price level, not real output.

Not so, argue the monetarists. An increase in cash balances creates an excess supply of money. People will spend more to get rid of the excess cash balances, increasing consumption out of their given real income. In this case, the fraction of money income spent will increase even if there is no change in real income, so the marginal propensity to consume and the multiplier are unstable, responding to changes in the money supply. Monetary policy works, and fiscal policy does not.

When economists look at annual data for consumption spending and the marginal propensity to consume, they find that the fluctuations in MPC are quite large. Despite its year-to-year ups and downs, however, MPC stays pretty close to an average of 89% of disposable income over the long run. Long-term velocity relative to M_1 has become increasingly unstable, while velocity relative to M_2 has remained somewhat more stable. Like the marginal propensity to consume, both measures of velocity are quite unstable in the short run, rising during expansions and falling during recessions.

The evidence of the last fifteen years suggests that both the multiplier and velocity are unstable in the short run, especially over the course of the business cycle. An unstable Keynesian expenditure multiplier makes the effects of fiscal policy less certain. An unstable velocity of money that is sensitive to interest rates makes monetary policy less effective.

GOVERNMENT BORROWING, CROWDING OUT, AND MONETARY POLICY

A second dispute between economists in the classical and Keynesian traditions comes at the point where monetary and fiscal policy are most closely linked. Financing government borrowing involves both monetary and fiscal policy, because the Treasury must consider the effects of deficit financing on interest rates and private investment while the Fed may need to increase the money supply to prevent crowding out.

Economists in the classical tradition argue that increased government spending (G) may not affect aggregate demand much, because it will be offset by a decline in private spending (probably investment). If government spending is financed by borrowing, interest rates rise and private investment is crowded out. In extreme cases, aggregate spending may not increase at all, and fiscal policy will be completely ineffective.

Figure 1 shows how crowding out occurs. The demand curve, D_0, reflects only demand for loanable funds for purposes of private investment. The government is not borrowing at all. The interest rate is i_0, and the volume of lending and borrowing is I_0. Now the government adds its demand in order to finance an increase in G with no additional taxes. The combined demand curve shifts to D_1. The horizontal distance between the two demand curves at the ini-

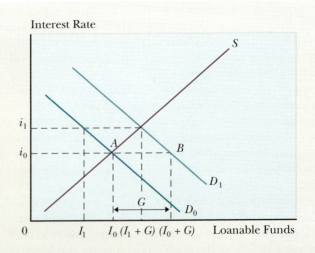

FIGURE 1

SUPPLY AND DEMAND FOR LOANABLE FUNDS AND CROWDING OUT

Increased demand for loanable funds to finance government spending shifts demand from D_0 to D_1. Increased demand drives up interest rates and reduces private borrowing. Total borrowing rises to $I_1 + G$, but private investment falls from I_0 to I_1.

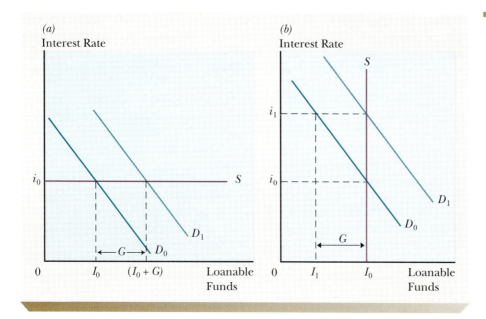

FIGURE 2

THE SUPPLY CURVE FOR LOANABLE FUNDS (a) In the Keynesian view, there are ample loanable funds available at the current interest rate. When G increases, no crowding out occurs, interest rates do not rise, and aggregate expenditures rise by the full amount of G. Aggregate demand shifts to the right (from D_0 to D_1). Real output and/or the price level rises. (b) In the monetarist view, the rise in G is fully offset by a decline in I as interest rates rise sharply. Aggregate expenditure is unchanged, and there is no effect on aggregate demand, real output, or the price level.

tial interest rate is AB, the amount of increased G financed by borrowing in the loanable funds market.

At the new equilibrium interest rate, i_1, private borrowers (still represented by D_0) only want to borrow I_1. Total demand for loanable funds has risen, but actual lending increases only by the difference between I_0 and $(I_1 + G)$, which is much smaller than the increase in G, and private investment has fallen.

How much crowding out occurs? Figure 2 diagrams two extreme cases: a horizontal supply curve of loanable funds in part (*a*) and a vertical supply curve in part (*b*). The horizontal version represents the extreme Keynesian view. With excess reserves, banks are reluctant to lend to risky private borrowers, but will lend freely to the government because they are certain of being repaid. Government borrowing has no effect on interest rates because funds are available at the existing rate. No crowding out occurs. Aggregate demand will rise by the full amount of G, the distance between I_0 and $(I_0 + G)$.

Part (*b*) of Figure 2 represents an extreme classical view. Since banks are already all loaned up when the government issues new bonds, government borrowing comes at the expense of other borrowers, including business investors, state and local governments, and consumers. The rise in G is offset by an equal fall in I from I_0 to I_1 as interest rates rise from i_0 to i_1. Part (*b*) shows total crowding out. Expansionary fiscal policy has no effect on the level of real output. Aggregate demand does not shift because the rise in G is offset by an equal and opposite fall in I.

THE SUPPLY OF LOANABLE FUNDS

The slope of the supply curve for loanable funds depends on the sensitivity of demand for money to changes in interest rates. Money that households do not wish to hold becomes available to lend in the loanable funds market. If money demand is very responsive to interest rates, the supply curve for loanable funds will be relatively flat (the Keynesian view). A small rise in interest rates will induce individuals to switch from holding money to lending it. In this case, interest rates hardly change at all when the government enters the market as a borrower.

The classical supply curve for loanable funds is close to vertical, implying that money demand is not very responsive to interest rates. When increased demand for loanable funds drives up the interest rate, funds lent to the government are exactly offset by a reduction in business borrowing, with no increase in aggregate expenditure or aggregate demand.

Both sides are partly correct. Money demand is moderately responsive to changes in interest rates. If money demand responds to changes in interest rates, higher interest rates will call forth more loanable funds as banks lend excess reserves and individuals cut down on their cash balances. Under normal circumstances, there should be partial but not total crowding out.

The 1980s did not provide a good test of the crowding out hypothesis because of foreign lending. A part of both government and private borrowing was financed by foreign funds flowing into the United States, which reduced direct competition between government borrowing and business borrowing for the same pool of funds. Instead, the inflow of foreign funds drove up the price of the dollar and made U.S. exports more expensive and U.S. imports cheaper. Instead of crowding out investment, government borrowing in the 1980s appears to have crowded out net exports.

ALTERNATIVES TO BORROWING

Borrowing from the public is not the only way to finance increased government spending. Other choices are raising taxes and borrowing from the central bank, which expands the money supply. Only raising taxes is pure fiscal policy. The other two methods involve a blend of monetary and fiscal policy.

A tax-financed increase in G may be slightly expansionary, according to the Keynesian model. As you learned in Chapter 9, the government expenditures multiplier $(1/(1 - b))$ is a little larger than the tax multiplier $(-b/(1 - b))$. However, the effect of expansionary fiscal policy on output and employment is much larger when the increase in G is not accompanied by higher taxes (T). A fiscal policy of equal changes in G and T requires a very large change in both to have any effect.

Another option is to expand the money supply. In order to keep interest rates from rising when the government borrows, the Fed buys the excess government bonds. When the Fed buys bonds, bank reserves increase, and the money supply expands—a solution often referred to as "printing money." Monetary expansion that is undertaken to help the Treasury finance deficits without driving up interest rates very much is called **accommodating monetary policy**. Economists in the classical tradition argue that expansionary fiscal policy supported by accommodating monetary policy is not fiscal policy at all, but monetary policy. If an increased deficit results in increased output, the higher output is caused by monetary expansion, not fiscal policy. When an increased deficit is financed with a larger money supply, it is difficult to tell how much of the change in output and the price level is due to monetary policy and how much to fiscal policy.

Accommodating monetary policy
Monetary expansion that is undertaken to help the Treasury to finance deficits without driving interest rates up too much.

POLICY FOCUS: THE BUDGET DEFICIT AND THE EXCHANGE RATE

The huge U.S. government budget deficits in the 1980s and early 1990s appear to have resulted in very little crowding out of investment. Between 1981 and 1985, the flow of funds into the loanable funds market in the United States rose sharply, attracted by high interest rates, an appealing business climate, and other factors. As a result, international capital flows provided funds for investment, and the crowding out effects of large deficits were less than expected.

When foreigners purchase U.S. bonds, stocks, or whole firms or make bank deposits, they must first convert their currency (yen, pounds, francs, Canadian dollars, or whatever) into U.S. dollars. As foreigners demand more dollars, the price of the dollar, or the exchange rate, rises. Between 1981 and 1985, the price of the U.S. dollar rose 60 percent.

Was this development good or bad? Both. A higher price for the dollar is great if you want to visit Europe or buy a foreign car. American dollars will buy more foreign currency and thus more foreign goods. A more expensive dollar is also good news on the inflation front. Relatively cheap imports will keep the CPI from rising as rapidly. If, however, you are an exporter or compete with imported products, a higher dollar price presents problems. When dollars are expensive, American goods are expensive, and foreign goods are relatively cheap. It is hard to sell goods abroad or to compete at home. Exports fell steadily as the dollar rose during the early 1980s. Slow growth of real output and employment was blamed on the high price of the dollar, the flood of imported goods, and the decline in U.S. exports. Thus, some of the pressures for protection against competition from imports in the first half of the 1980s reflected the high price of the dollar.

The rising tide of foreign investment in the United States and the rising price of the dollar both slowed in 1985. These changes occurred partly because there were better investment opportunities elsewhere and partly because federal deficits stabilized and began to fall, reducing interest rates. Between 1985 and 1990, the price of the dollar fell 38 percent. The dollar remained at about the same level through the early 1990s. Despite a relatively cheap dollar, however, exports lagged behind growth of imports in 1991–1993 because of recession in the countries that are the United States' main trading partners: Canada, Western Europe, and Japan.

If the lower price for the dollar holds in the next few years, while these nations recover from recession, the United States can expect more exports, fewer imports, more jobs—and higher prices. Either an increase or a decrease in the inflow of foreign funds into the market for U.S. stocks, bonds, and bank accounts brings both costs and benefits. In economics, there is no free lunch and no unmixed blessing.

DO FINANCING METHODS MATTER?

Economist Robert Barro of the University of Rochester argues that the method of financing government spending has no impact on private spending.[2] People will perceive that increased government spending now, financed by borrowing, will mean higher taxes in the future to pay off the debt. If citizens are consuming on the basis of permanent income, they will consume less now because they must save to pay higher expected future taxes. The effect of higher government spending will be to increase current income, decrease future income, and leave permanent income unchanged.

Barro's argument is based not only on the permanent income hypothesis but also on the idea that people have rational expectations. That is, people make economic decisions using all available information and they avoid repeating previous errors. According to this view, developed by economists Thomas

---

2. Robert Barro, "Are Government Bonds Net Wealth?" *Journal of Political Economy* (November/December 1974):1095–1117.

Sargent and Robert Lucas, temporary policy changes will not mislead people into changing their behavior. Barro's view that financing methods do not have any effect on output has produced a great deal of debate, but is difficult to prove or disprove. While few economists accept his argument in its extreme form, the ideas of rational expectations have greatly influenced contemporary macroeconomic theory.

KEY IDEAS

QUESTIONS ABOUT THE EFFECTIVENESS OF FISCAL POLICY	
CLASSICAL CRITICISM	KEYNESIAN RESPONSE
The expenditure multiplier is unstable.	Velocity is unstable.
Tax-financed changes in G do not change AD.	The balanced budget multiplier is positive (but very small).
Borrowing crowds out private investment demand.	Investment demand is not that sensitive to interest rates.
Changes in G financed by borrowing are really monetary policy.	Monetary and fiscal policy need to be coordinated.
Higher government spending does not change permanent income.	People respond to transitory income changes.
People have rational expectations and will increase savings in anticipation of higher future taxes to pay for current deficits.	People have imperfect foresight.

UNEMPLOYMENT, INFLATION, AND THE PHILLIPS CURVE

According to the Keynesian model, too low a level of aggregate expenditure results in unemployment. When aggregate expenditure is too high, relative to full-employment output (Y^*), the result is inflation. In this model, it is only possible to experience both inflation and unemployment at the same time if there is a shift in the aggregate supply curve. As long as aggregate supply is stable and upward sloping, shifts in aggregate demand create a policy trade-off between inflation and unemployment.

AGGREGATE DEMAND AND INFLATION

Although the aggregate supply and demand models have been a useful way to visualize macroeconomic policy choices, they are not very satisfactory for exploring the relationship between unemployment and inflation. The variables on the axes of the aggregate supply and demand graph are not the same ones we are looking for, but they are related to unemployment and inflation. Changes in employment and unemployment are very closely linked to changes in production, or real output. The inflation rate is a measure of the rate of change in the price level. The aggregate supply and demand model shows changes in the price level, not inflation rates. A one-time change in the price level is *not* inflation, which consists of a sustained and continuous rise in the price level. It would take continuous shifts in aggregate demand to the right to result in sustained inflation.

Suppose that aggregate demand is continuously shifting to the right with a growth in population and output (from AD_1 to AD_2 to AD_3 in Figure 3), while aggregate supply shifts to the right at a slower pace (from AS_1 to AS_2 to AS_3 in Figure 3). This continuous rightward movement of both curves at an unequal pace will produce more output but also a rising price level. If the labor force is growing at a faster rate than real output, there will also be higher unemployment.

IS THERE AN UNEMPLOYMENT-INFLATION TRADE-OFF?

In the 1960s, economists generally believed that there was a consistent negative relationship between the inflation rate and the unemployment rate. That kind of relationship between inflation and unemployment is shown in Figure 4. The vertical axis measures the inflation rate, and the horizontal axis measures the unemployment rate. A zero inflation rate is found at high levels of unemployment (points *a* and *b*). As the economy moves toward point *c*, the further decline in unemployment is associated with a higher rate of inflation. As the economy approaches very low levels of unemployment, the inflation rate becomes much higher (points *d* and *e*).

Shifts in aggregate demand alone will not result in both higher inflation and higher unemployment. A series of rightward shifts of the aggregate demand curve will result in a higher price level, but also higher output and lower unemployment. A leftward shift of the aggregate demand curve will increase unem-

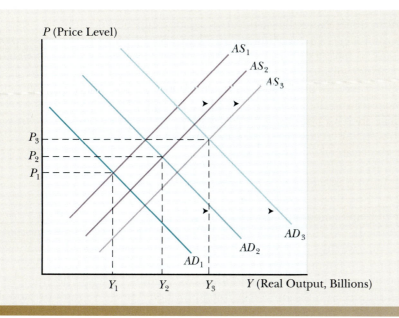

FIGURE 3
BOTH AGGREGATE SUPPLY AND AGGREGATE DEMAND SHIFT TO THE RIGHT
When both aggregate demand and long-run aggregate supply shift to the right, the effect on output is clearly an increase. The effect on unemployment depends on whether output grows faster or more slowly than the labor force, and the effect on the price level depends on which curve shifts farther or faster.

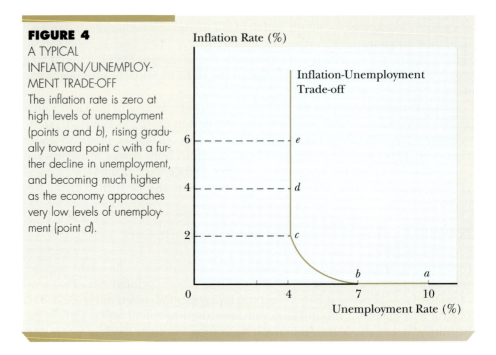

FIGURE 4
A TYPICAL INFLATION/UNEMPLOYMENT TRADE-OFF
The inflation rate is zero at high levels of unemployment (points a and b), rising gradually toward point c with a further decline in unemployment, and becoming much higher as the economy approaches very low levels of unemployment (point d).

ployment, but it should reduce the price level (along with the inflation rate). Thus, if aggregate supply is stable, there does appear to be a trade-off between unemployment and price stability.

Figure 5(a) shows the actual unemployment and inflation rates for 1961 to 1970. With one exception, these points seem to lie on or fairly close to a smooth curve with the expected negative slope. Until the late 1960s, a relatively stable composite aggregate supply curve, combined with changes in aggregate demand, offered a plausible description of the relationship between unemployment and inflation. Figure 5(b) plots the unemployment and inflation rates for 1970 to 1993. Note that a negative relationship between the two rates is not apparent here. In fact, during the late 1970s, inflation and unemployment seemed to have a positive relationship! Most observers attribute the change in the relationship between inflation and unemployment to shifts in the aggregate supply curve. By the 1980s, aggregate supply seemed to have stabilized somewhat, restoring the inflation-unemployment link. The late 1980s and early 1990s appear to have returned to the pattern of the late 1960s and early 1970s. However, the relationship was still not as close and consistent as it was two decades earlier.

THE DEVELOPMENT OF THE PHILLIPS CURVE

The unemployment-inflation relationships plotted in Figures 4 and 5 originated in the work of British economist A. W. Phillips. In 1958, Phillips reported a negative relationship between the rate of wage increases and the level of unemployment in Great Britain for the period 1861–1913. Since both wages and production costs are closely related to prices, Phillips's original diagram was transformed into an inflation versus unemployment curve. A graph of the relationship between the rates of inflation and unemployment for a particular country over a specified period of years is called a **Phillips curve**.

Phillips curve
A graph showing the relationship between the rates of inflation and unemployment for a country over a specified period of years.

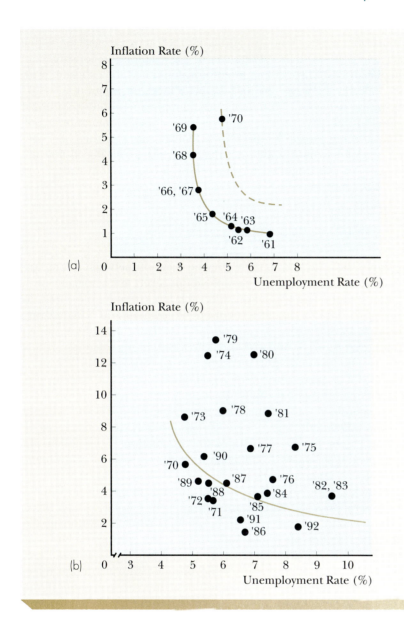

FIGURE 5
INFLATION AND UNEMPLOYMENT IN THE U.S. ECONOMY
(a) The data for 1961–1970 show a consistent negative relationship, except for 1970. For 1970, this point appeared to lie on a new Phillips curve that had shifted to the right (the dashed line).
(b) The data since 1970 seems to show a much less consistent relationship between unemployment and inflation than in earlier periods. It is possible to trace one relationship for 1970–1973, and another for 1974–1983 that is to the upper right, with more recent data returning to the 1970–1973 pattern.

In the early 1960s, Paul Samuelson and Robert Solow, two Nobel Prize winners in economics, reinterpreted this diagram, labeled a Phillips curve, as representing choices, or trade-offs, between various combinations of inflation and unemployment. For example, along the Phillips curve in Figure 4, a society could opt for low unemployment, such as point *c* or *d*, and pay the price of rapid increases in the price level. On the other hand, it could keep the inflation rate low, as at point *a* or *b*, at the cost of higher unemployment.

Phillips presented evidence suggesting that a trade-off existed between inflation and unemployment, but he offered no theoretical explanation. Early explanations for the Phillips curve focused on how changes in labor market conditions influenced prices. When aggregate demand is increasing, business firms expand output and increase employment. As the unemployment rate falls, it becomes increasingly difficult to hire qualified workers at the prevailing wage rates. Firms must offer higher wages to attract new workers. Because aggregate demand is increasing, those higher wages can be passed along to consumers in the form of higher prices. Thus, falling unemployment rates are associated with continuous increases in the wage rate and the price level, or inflation.

In the 1960s, the behavior of inflation and unemployment rates reinforced the idea that the Phillips curve represented a menu of choices for economic policy makers. Take another look at Figure 5(a), a Phillips curve for the U.S. economy showing unemployment and inflation data for 1961–1970. Recall that the 1964 Kennedy tax cut was intended to reduce the unemployment rate. From 1965 through 1969, lower unemployment rates were traded for higher inflation rates.

SHIFTS IN THE PHILLIPS CURVE

If the Phillips curve shifts up and to the right, the trade-off between unemployment and inflation worsens. Higher unemployment levels are associated with each rate of inflation, or higher inflation with each level of unemployment. In 1970, the United States had a higher level of unemployment and a higher rate of inflation than in earlier years, as you can see in Figure 5(a). One way to explain this point that is out of line with the others is to argue that a previously stable Phillips curve had shifted up to the right.

Why did the Phillips curve shift? Early explanations looked at random supply shocks and changes in the makeup of the labor force. Several supply shocks affected the U.S. economy in the early 1970s, increasing the price level without lowering the unemployment rate. These shocks, which affected aggregate demand as well as aggregate supply, included the devaluation of the dollar with respect to other currencies in 1971 and again in 1973 and a series of dramatic increases in oil prices beginning in 1973.

Devaluation means a higher dollar price for imports. Higher import prices contributed to general price increases in the economy. Because the physical volume of imports declined very little, however, there was no reduction in the unemployment rate. Higher oil prices had an even wider effect on the U.S. economy. Gasoline prices quadrupled between 1973 and 1980. In addition, because oil is used for many other purposes, including heating and as raw materials, rapidly rising prices for imported oil set off price increases throughout the economy.

As total spending on imports increased, net exports $(X - M)$ fell, shifting aggregate demand to the left. According to the Keynesian model, this reduction in total spending should have resulted in a decrease in national income and output and an increase in unemployment. Higher oil prices, however, also affected the price level, a result that could not be accounted for in a simple Keynesian framework. The Phillips curve provided a modification of that model to account for this result. Price increases resulting from random economic shocks cause the inflation rate associated with any given unemployment rate to be higher than before the shocks. That is, the Phillips curve shifts to the right in response to such random shocks.

Changes in the makeup of the U.S. labor force were another random shock that was blamed for the higher unemployment rates and inflation rates in the 1970s. From 1960 to 1980, women and young people made up the largest share of new entrants into the labor force. These workers had higher unemployment rates and also increased the size of the labor force as a fraction of the total population. Thus, the unemployment rate rose relative to the level of output, because of the changing makeup of the labor force. In this case, higher rates of unemployment will be observed at each inflation rate. In contrast, the explanation based on random shocks suggested a higher inflation rate at each unemployment rate. In both cases, however, the Phillips curve shifts up and to the right.

THE INSIDER-OUTSIDER MODEL AND THE PHILLIPS CURVE

Another explanation of the worsening inflation-unemployment trade-off is based on the power of insiders (employed union members) relative to outsiders (nonunion members).[3] The **insider-outsider model** rests on the assumption that, with a union, those already employed (insiders) will bargain for a higher wage even at the expense of employment for those on the outside. Unemployment will rise, but inflation will not fall. During economic downturns, some workers are laid off and become outsiders. When economic activity increases, insiders will bargain for a higher real wage in preference to more jobs. Unemployment will be higher than before at each inflation rate. If union bargaining is widespread, an upturn in economic activity will be accompanied by more inflation and less reduction in unemployment than would otherwise be the case. The insider-outsider model offers an explanation for stagflation that was missing in the simpler Keynesian model. It also offers a policy challenge in finding ways to reflect the concerns of both potential and actual employees in labor negotiations.

Insider-outsider model An explanation of labor market behavior that assumes that insiders (employed union members) will negotiate for higher wage rates for themselves at the expense of outsiders, thus worsening the inflation-unemployment trade-off.

KEY IDEAS

SHIFTS IN THE PHILLIPS CURVE
Sources of a changing unemployment-inflation trade-off over the last twenty-five years include:
- oil price shocks (higher prices in the 1970s, lower in the 1980s)
- changes in demand for U.S. exports
- changes in the makeup of the labor force
- the insider-outsider model

THE PHILLIPS CURVE AND MARKET IMPERFECTIONS

Economists who believe that there is a stable trade-off between inflation and unemployment for fairly long periods of time tend to be policy activists, or in the Keynesian tradition. Contemporary Keynesians, particularly in the United Kingdom, stress market power and market imperfections as the reasons why self-correcting forces may be weak and policy actions may be needed.

---

3. Assar Lindbeck and Dennis Snower, "Wage Setting, Unemployment, and Insider-Outsider Relations," *American Economic Review Papers and Proceedings* (May 1986):235–239.

When demand is weak, firms in concentrated industries with considerable market power cut output instead of prices. This response to a decline in aggregate demand leads to more unemployment rather than a falling price level. When aggregate demand increases, firms with market power are likely to raise prices instead of output. Thus, since prices are flexible upward but not downward, it is possible to experience chronic unemployment along with inflation during periods of expanding demand. Demand management policies that keep aggregate expenditures and aggregate demand stable by offsetting changes in demand originating in the private sector can reduce these fluctuations in employment and the price level.

Some modern Keynesians who support demand management policies are still concerned that policies to expand demand will reward powerful firms with higher prices and profits. Expansionary policies appear to benefit monopolistic firms. Contractionary policies put the burden on workers in the form of higher unemployment.

EXPECTATIONS, MARKETS, AND THE NATURAL RATE HYPOTHESIS

Economists in the classical/monetarist tradition have severe reservations about a stable trade-off between unemployment and inflation and a resulting menu of policy choices. In 1967, Milton Friedman offered another view of the Phillips curve in his presidential address to the American Economic Association. Friedman argued that any trade-off was purely short run, that no real trade-off between inflation and unemployment existed in the long run.[4]

THE NATURAL RATE OF UNEMPLOYMENT

Natural rate of unemployment
The rate of unemployment that is determined by frictional and structural factors and toward which the economy tends to return.

Friedman argued that the economy tends to return to a level of output and employment determined by the economy's capacity to produce—the vertical aggregate supply curve of the classical tradition. This output level (Y^*) is determined by the **natural rate of unemployment**, which is the rate of unemployment determined by frictional and structural factors. These kinds of unemployment result from changes in the number, location, and job skills of people in the labor force and to changes in the location and job skills that firms demand.

Friedman, together with Edmund Phelps and other economists in the classical/monetarist tradition, used the idea of the natural rate of unemployment to challenge the Keynesian view that the Phillips curve represents a stable menu of attainable combinations of inflation and unemployment. In his words, "There is always a temporary trade-off between inflation and unemployment; there is no permanent trade-off." Friedman stated that the short-run trade-off between inflation and unemployment exists only because some workers and managers have mistaken expectations. In the long run, when people adjust their expectations to reflect changed economic conditions, Friedman's version of the Phillips curve is also vertical at the natural rate of unemployment.

---

4. Milton Friedman, " The Role of Monetary Policy," *American Economic Review* (May 1968):1–15.

GLOBAL OUTLOOK: UNEMPLOYMENT AND INFLATION IN EASTERN EUROPE

During the transition to a market economy in Eastern Europe, one striking development has been the emergence of both inflation and unemployment as serious macroeconomic problems. In Poland, the price level rose 70 percent in early 1990 while wages fell and unemployment rose sharply. Workers in Russia saw steadily rising unemployment through 1992 while inflation soared to 1,200 percent. What has happened? Did restructuring these economies toward greater decentralization and use of markets shift the aggregate supply curve back to the left, resulting in severe stagflation?

No. Stagflation in Eastern Europe can be interpreted in an aggregate supply and demand framework, but not as a sudden decrease in aggregate supply at the time of the change. For many years, the economies of Eastern Europe suffered from repressed inflation and disguised unemployment. An inefficient system of production failed to produce enough output to keep pace with the growth of aggregate demand. When aggregate demand exceeds aggregate supply at a given price level, the price level is normally expected to rise. However, price controls in Eastern European countries kept the price level from rising. Instead, there was a chronic gap between aggregate supply and aggregate demand at the artificially low price level maintained by the state. That gap showed up as empty shelves, chronic shortages of consumer goods, long lines, and long waiting lists for telephones, apartments, and other goods and services. When prices were allowed to adjust, they rose quickly. As output begins to expand under a more efficient system, prices should stabilize. In the meantime, shelves are full again at the higher, more realistic prices.

The rising unemployment in Eastern Europe also represents a surfacing of unemployment that had previously been disguised. The communist governments guaranteed a job and a paycheck for everyone who was able and willing to work. Those workers were not necessarily productive, however. (A standing joke in Eastern Europe went like this: "The government pretends to pay us, and we pretend to work.") Incentives to work and to manage and use workers effectively were missing because of the lack of market signals. Now that some production is being privatized, most of the new owners and managers get to choose how many workers to employ and what to pay them. They may even be allowed to fire those who do not earn their keep.

Many Eastern Europeans are fearful about the transition to a market-based economy where there is no job security. The trade-off between a higher standard of living and job security is one that workers in market-based economies have always faced. It is one of the costs of a productive market system.

RESPONDING TO EXPANSIONARY POLICY

Suppose the government attempts to reduce unemployment by increasing the money supply. The larger money supply shifts the demand for output to the right, from AD_1 to AD_2 in Figure 6. Initially, business firms keep prices at P_1 and produce total output of Y_1. However, at P_1, people will demand the larger quantity of output Y_2, even though firms would like to supply only Y_1. Firms will sell a total of Y_2 by using up part of their inventories. Output has not yet changed, but inventories fall because sales have risen.

If firms were satisfied with their initial inventories, they will try to rebuild them to that desired level. Inventory is important in building a clientele. In order to attract and retain customers, firms implicitly promise to sell as many units as buyers demand at the price set in the short run. For example, if you go to a hardware store for a doorknob, you expect to find doorknobs in stock at the usual price. If the store doesn't have them, you will probably go to another store. The first store runs a good chance of losing a customer, perhaps permanently.

FIGURE 6

AN INCREASE IN AGGREGATE DEMAND: LONG-RUN AND SHORT-RUN EFFECTS

An increase in the money supply shifts the demand for output from AD_1 to AD_2. At P_1, people will demand Y_2, and firms will draw down inventories. As firms expand output to replenish inventory and meet demand, unemployment falls and prices rise to P_2. As market forces drive up the prices of inputs, suppliers charge higher prices, shifting the aggregate supply curve from AS_1 to AS_2. The economy is again on the long-run vertical aggregate supply curve, AS^{lr}, corresponding to the natural rate of unemployment.

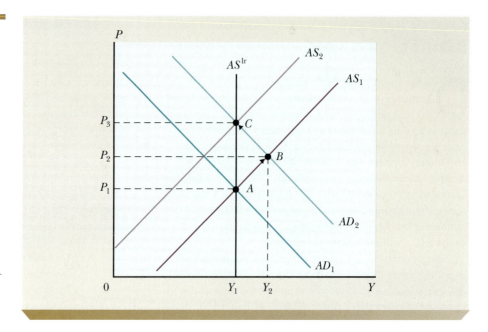

In a service establishment—a restaurant, perhaps, or a hairdresser, or a bank—the inventory takes the form of available workers to meet demand as it arrives. If the restaurant is short of cooks or waiters, or all the barbers or hair stylists are hard at work and booked up for hours or days ahead, or the bank tellers each have a long line of customers waiting, you are likely to go elsewhere. Maintaining extra staff helps these firms meet peak demand. As demand rises, service firms will add to their staff rather than to their inventory of physical commodities.

The rightward shift of the aggregate demand curve causes temporary shortages at the current price level. Excess aggregate demand begins to pull the price level upward. Rising prices result in rising profits for business firms, which respond by increasing output. In order to produce more output, more workers must be hired. The newly employed workers take jobs at the prevailing wage rate. Even though prices have begun to rise, wage rates do not respond at once to the changed conditions.

The price increases are initially perceived as changes in particular prices, not in the general price level. Even after people recognize that there is an increase in the general price level, wages are slow to adjust because many wage rates are determined by contracts that are renegotiated only once every two or three years. During the lag between rising prices and the upward adjustment of wage rates, firms earn higher profits.

The increase in demand means that many firms will experience falling inventories or shortages of available staff. If they sell or produce tangible goods, they will order new inventories from their suppliers or begin to produce more themselves. These firms hire more workers to produce the extra output, reducing unemployment. Output will start to rise. Eventually, prices will also start to rise. Any business firm that holds its prices at P_1 will find inventory falling steadily. As firms replenish their inventories by buying more inputs or semifinished goods, they find themselves competing for limited supplies. As firms seek to hire more workers, wages start to go up. Market forces drive up the prices of inputs. Suppliers will be charging higher prices. The aggregate supply curve will eventually shift to the left, from AS_1 to AS_2 in Figure 6.

Thus, while there was a temporary trade-off of lower unemployment and a higher price level, the final equilibrium has the economy back to the natural rate of unemployment associated with Y_1 at a higher price level. The economy is once again operating on the long-run vertical aggregate supply curve, AS^{lr}, corresponding to the natural rate of unemployment.

FROM PRICE LEVEL INCREASES TO INFLATION

Figure 7 converts this one-time rise in the price level into an explanation of inflation. Suppose the economy is initially in equilibrium at Y^* and a price level P_1. Then a money supply increase or a tax cut shifts aggregate demand to the right, from AD_1 to AD_2. The quantity of real output demanded at the old price level, P_1 exceeds the economy's full-employment level, Y^*. Real output may expand at first without a rise in the price level because expectations of inflation have not yet changed. However, as people adjust to higher prices, aggregate supply shifts to the left. At AS_2, suppliers and workers have fully adjusted to the change in the price level. Suppliers have made their full price adjustments. Workers have made the full wage demands that they will make when they completely anticipate the new, higher price level.

In Figure 7, the shift to AS_2 restores the economy to long run equilibrium. The market has settled back at the initial level of real output (Y^*), but at a new, higher price level (P_2). However, policy makers are disturbed by the increase in unemployment after a temporary decline. They try again.

If government uses expansionary monetary or fiscal policy again, the same thing will happen. Real output will always return to the full-employment level,

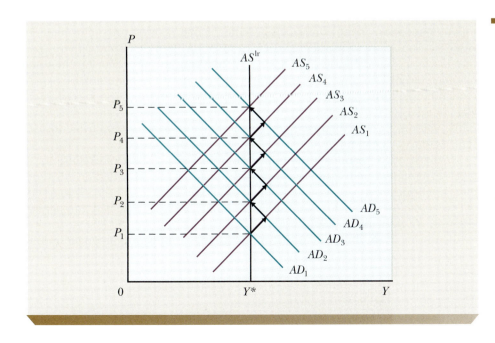

FIGURE 7
REPEATED SHIFTS IN AGGREGATE DEMAND AND AGGREGATE SUPPLY
The arrows trace a path of shifts in the short-run aggregate demand curve to the right, followed by shifts in the short-run aggregate supply curve to the left as workers and other owners of inputs react to higher prices and wages. Output always returns to the level (Y^*) associated with the natural rate of unemployment. There is a series of temporary increases in output and decreases in unemployment, and continued increases in the price level.

Y^*, corresponding to the natural rate of unemployment but at a higher price level. The "Christmas tree" pattern of changes in Y and P in Figure 7 is the result of successive doses of expansionary policy. The heavy arrows trace the path of output and prices in response to successive doses of expansionary fiscal (or monetary) policy shifting the aggregate demand curve up and to the right. Thus, attempts to reduce unemployment below its natural rate using demand management policies may have temporary success but will ultimately only drive up the price level. A series of successive increases in the price level becomes inflation.

According to Friedman, an upward slope of the short-run aggregate supply curve is based on incorrect expectations about inflation and on temporary profits as wages lag behind price increases. Workers are willing to supply more labor and firms more output only as long as they do not realize that the higher wages and prices are general, rather than specific to their labor or their product. Once workers realize that the price level as a whole is rising and the purchasing power of their wages is falling, they will demand higher nominal wages in order to maintain the value of the real wage. Costs will rise, eroding the temporary profits of business firms. As the cost-profit relationship returns to its original level, firms will want to produce the same real output at the new higher prices, and the aggregate supply curve shifts back to the left.

According to Friedman, there is a short-run trade-off between inflation and unemployment only if actual inflation is different from what was expected. If inflation is fully anticipated (as is more likely in the long run), no trade-off will occur. The current rate of unemployment might change in the short run in response to monetary and fiscal policies, but the natural rate of unemployment would not be affected.

THE NATURAL RATE AND POLICY INEFFECTIVENESS

In the short run, expansionary policy buys a reduction in the unemployment rate at the cost of an increase in the inflation rate. But, Friedman argues, the new inflation-unemployment combination is not stable. Lower unemployment is achieved only because workers expect no inflation. Workers eventually realize that prices in general have risen and are continuing to rise, reducing the purchasing power of their wages. They adjust their expectations about inflation and demand higher wages to restore the purchasing power of their earnings. Higher wages cut business profits back to their original levels. Business firms reduce output to the old level at the new higher price level, and the unemployment rate returns to its original level.

If aggregate demand continues to shift to the right because of expansionary fiscal or monetary policy, the economy will remain at the new, higher inflation rate. Unemployment will remain at the natural rate. These rates represent a stable combination of inflation and unemployment because expected and actual inflation are the same.

This view of the Phillips curve and the ineffectiveness of policy actions has been reinforced by the work of new classical economists. These economists reinforce the natural rate model by arguing that expectations adapt very quickly because it is in people's self-interest to acquire, interpret, and respond to information that affects their economic well-being.

If producers, workers, consumers, and investors have accurate information about present and future price levels and other relevant data, and if they know how to act on that information, they will adjust their wage demands, money holdings, and purchases very quickly when conditions change. Not only policy makers but also participants in labor, product, and financial markets quickly acquire, process, and act on correct information. In this case, the short run will be quite short, and a vertical or nearly vertical aggregate supply curve will be the appropriate model.

THE KEYNESIANS STRIKE BACK

Keynesians find this account of the response to demand shifts to be too dependent on the accuracy of expectations and the smooth workings of markets. In their view, there are two important market imperfections that make the aggregate supply curve slope upward for long periods of time. Whether the *AS* curve is vertical in the long run is not important to Keynesians because they focus on short-run policy concerns.

These imperfections are inaccurate information or incorrect expectations and inability to respond quickly and correctly to accurate information. If the process of acquiring and responding to information works quite slowly, the upward-sloping aggregate supply curve may be a better model than the vertical *AS* curve of Friedman and others.

RATIONAL OR ADAPTIVE EXPECTATIONS?
Acquiring and acting on accurate economic information could be slow because information is not free. It takes real resources and time to produce and distribute information. These lags became much shorter in the last decade (aptly labeled the start of the "Information Age") because of increasing use of telecommunications networks, personal computers, and other information technology. However, information is still not widely available on an instantaneous basis.

Even if people learn from their mistakes, they do not always learn immediately or adapt fully. For example, they may expect next year's rate of inflation to be the same as this year's, rather than adjusting their forecasts upward or downward on the basis of changes in the money supply, the unemployment rate, and other relevant information. On the other hand, they may keep in mind an average of the last few years' data, to which they add some current information about changes in policy and market conditions in order to form expectations about next year. People will adjust their behavior in the right direction, but not completely. They may not correctly anticipate the actual rate of inflation. Individuals acquire, process, and act on relevant economic information in their own self-interest, but they never have information that is entirely accurate or complete. This view of how expectations are formed is called **adaptive expectations**.

The experience of the late 1970s and early 1980s supported the adaptive expectations argument. That experience also suggested that people adapt more quickly as the payoff from acquiring and using accurate information gets higher. Throughout the 1950s and 1960s, inflation rates were low and steady, so past experience was a good guide to the future. Conditions changed in the mid–1970s. Many people—mortgage lenders, investors, workers, and pro-

Adaptive expectations
Expectations about the future that are formed by economic actors on the basis of current and recent past experience and that adjust slowly to changing conditions.

ducers—were surprised by high inflation rates. Their real wages and the value of their assets fell because they had not correctly anticipated the inflation. By the end of the 1970s, cost-of-living adjustment clauses in contracts, variable-rate mortgages, and other developments allowed markets to react more quickly to changes in the inflation rate. The short-run aggregate supply curve shifted upward more quickly and also became steeper as many price adjustments became automatic.

In the 1980s, as the rate of inflation began to fall, the opposite problem arose. The real rate of interest rose sharply because the market rate that was fixed in many contracts now included inflation premiums that were too high. Wage contracts based on higher inflation rates had to be quickly renegotiated. Within a few years, however, people were incorporating lower expected rates of inflation in their economic decisions.

While economists argue over adaptive versus rational expectations, psychologists have studied how people actually form expectations. Their work suggests that expectations typically consist of a mixture of recent past experience, current experience, and some projections of future events. That is, they are closer to adaptive than to rational expectations. Work with psychologists may help economists clarify how expectations are formed and how rapidly they adjust.

The extreme rational expectations view of how market participants behave requires individuals to obtain large quantities of information quickly, sort out the relevant information, and process it through a sophisticated economic model about how changes in some variables will impact on others. However, this view offers useful insights. Rational expectations theory is helpful in understanding the long-run adjustment process. When the payoff for obtaining and using correct information is high enough, people will make the effort to seek out information and act on it to the greatest extent possible. When the costs of ignorance and the benefits of possessing accurate information rise, people will react faster. Furthermore, it is not necessary that each and every market participant acquire and respond to information. It is only necessary that the search for and use of information take place at the margin.

AUCTION MARKETS OR CONTRACT MARKETS? Even if expectations are rational, the aggregate supply curve will not be vertical if wages and prices change slowly. When aggregate demand increases, a slow response of wages and prices means that output may expand for a fairly long period of time before the short-run aggregate supply curve shifts up. A decline in aggregate demand may lead to long periods of low output and high unemployment until prices finally respond.

Even if people have accurate information, they may not be able to act on it immediately. In some cases, it may not be desirable to act at all because the cost of responding is too high. Acting on accurate information may require changing jobs, selling assets, or other drastic actions. Thus, some people may choose to wait until the rate of inflation falls back to what they had expected. Often the costs of responding depend on the kinds of product markets and resource markets in which individuals are buying and selling. People will be more likely to relocate, for example, if their houses can be sold quickly at acceptable prices and if new jobs at satisfactory wages are easy to find.

Markets characterized by good information, many buyers and sellers, and rapid adjustments of price to changing conditions are known as **auction markets**. Typically, auction markets have many buyers and sellers making frequent

Auction markets
Markets characterized by good information, many buyers and sellers, and rapid adjustment of prices to changing conditions.

transactions. You may have been to an estate auction, an antique auction, or a livestock auction. At these auctions, a fixed stock of goods is offered for sale, one item at a time. The price moves up the demand curve until one buyer pays the final price bid. Price bears all the burden of adjustment, and price changes rapidly.

Other markets are **contract markets**. In contract markets, buyers and sellers enter into long-term agreements at fixed prices. Contracts protect both buyer and seller from risks of price changes or other uncertainties. Typical contract markets can be found in housing (with long-term fixed-rate mortgages), college faculty appointments (because of tenure), apartments rented on leases, unionized labor, and major construction projects. Contracts of pro athletes or college football coaches reflect past performance. Such contracts may run for several years and be very expensive to change if the player or coach fails to live up to expectations. Prices move slowly in contract markets because it takes time for old contracts to expire. During that time, the cost of changing a contract is very high.

If auction markets are typical, then prices will adjust quickly to changes in demand at both the micro and macro level. A relatively small increase in aggregate demand will drive the price level up quickly with little effect on real output. The aggregate supply curve will be vertical, or nearly so. If contract markets are typical, price adjustments will be slow and the aggregate supply curve flatter. In the long run, even contract markets become auction markets because no contract lasts forever. Rent controls expire. The ninety-nine-year leases in Hong Kong end in 1997 and will not be renewed. The typical contract is much shorter and more flexible.

Contract markets
Markets characterized by imperfect information, few buyers and sellers, long-term contracts, and sluggish price adjustments.

KEY IDEAS

EXPECTATIONS, MARKETS, AND AGGREGATE SUPPLY

• If expectations are rational and markets are efficient (auction),	People are correctly informed about current conditions and form appropriate expectations about the future.
	Prices adjust quickly to changing conditions.
THEN the aggregate supply curve is vertical in the long run and very steep in the short run.	Demand management policies have little if any effect on real output.
• If expectations are adaptive and markets are contractual (contract),	Information is acquired gradually, and expectations adjust slowly.
	Prices cannot change rapidly because it is too difficult to change them.
THEN the aggregate supply curve is upward sloping, at least in the short run (which can be fairly long).	Demand management can have a significant impact on short-run output and employment.

HONEST DISAGREEMENT: THE CLASH OF MACROECONOMIC IDEAS

The macroeconomic events of the last twenty-five years have challenged economists to revisit their models and their policy prescriptions. The public has an image of economics in great disarray, as one group proposes one remedy while another group insists it will not work. In fact, there are broad areas of agreement along with some points of dispute. The issue of whether or not to call for government to improve on market outcomes is the touchstone that most strongly separates economists in the Keynesian tradition from the various groups—classical, monetarist, new classical—that share the classical tradition.

MAJOR POINTS OF DISPUTE

Most economists in the classical tradition argue that unsatisfactory outcomes are only temporary. Market forces would correct such mistakes, just as market forces lead commuters to less congested freeways to save valuable time or make it attractive for a couple to move into a declining neighborhood because the price of housing is relatively cheaper there. They argue that self-interested individuals quickly anticipate and often offset the effects of any demand-expanding policies. Unsatisfactory macro outcomes will be quickly changed because rational individuals will act in their own self-interest. These economists argue that government intervention often makes things worse and that the role of government should be reduced.

Keynesians believe that unsatisfactory outcomes can persist for long periods of time and that corrective market forces are weak and ineffective. They see an active role for government in moving the economy to a more satisfactory outcome. Some contemporary economists in the Keynesian tradition, variously known as post-Keynesians or new Keynesians, put particular emphasis on the role of monopoly power as a contributing factor to inflation and unemployment, and the role of government in managing some of the undesired distributional effects of inflation and unemployment.

The differences among economists can be grouped into four major areas:

1. What determines the level of output and employment?
2. What is the role of interest rates?
3. What are the goals and values that can be inferred from each group's theories?
4. What is the general thrust of policy recommendations of each group?

Table 1 summarizes the conflicting views of the classical and Keynesian traditions, with qualifiers where needed to identify some of the contributions of the newer monetarist and new classical members of the classical tradition.

TO INTERVENE OR NOT TO INTERVENE

This list recalls a basic macroeconomic question raised in Chapter 4. Should the government be asked to try to stabilize economic activity? Should, or can, the government do anything to control unemployment and inflation? If so, what actions should it undertake, and how effective will they be? These are questions

TABLE 1 BASIC AREAS OF DISAGREEMENT BETWEEN THE CLASSICAL AND KEYNESIAN TRADITIONS

	CLASSICAL	KEYNESIAN
What determines the level of output and employment?	Output tends toward the full-employment level, determined by resources/technology. *Monetarist:* Policy can have temporary effects on output. *New classical:* Rational expectations make adjustment very rapid.	Output is determined by planned spending; may be less than full employment.
What is the role of interest rates?	Interest rates fluctuate to make savings and investment equal. *Monetarist:* Interest rates influence investment spending but have little effect on demand for money.	Interest rates have little influence on investment. Interest-sensitive demand for money makes monetary policy ineffective.
What are the most important economic goals and values?	Minimum government, price stability, steady growth.	Full employment, growth, equitable income distribution.
Policy recommendations	None (laissez-faire). *Monetarist:* Monetary policy with stress on stable money growth.	Fiscal policy primarily, with monetary policy in a supporting role.

to which the two groups of economists give very different answers. Despite theoretical differences, the various groups that are part of the classical tradition share a faith in the effectiveness of market processes, the importance of incentives, and the self-correcting nature of the economy, at least in the long run. Contemporary representatives of this tradition go even farther, arguing that activist policy—especially fiscal policy—may do more harm than good.

Keynesians see a larger role for government and more evidence of market failure of various kinds. They also share a concern about the short run as well as the long run. Keynesians believe that policy makers should be concerned about the short run. The long run, or the period in which the economy may adjust to some full-employment equilibrium, is very long. In the interim, there may be an unacceptable amount of suffering from unemployment, inflation, or both.

POLICY AND INCOME DISTRIBUTION

Economist Lester Thurow argues that differences in policy advice are based at least partly on differences in the distributional effects of different kinds of policies—laissez-faire, fiscal, or monetary policy.[5] Thurow believes that the existence of different schools of macroeconomic thought, each holding to different theo-

---
5. Lester Thurow, *The Zero Sum Society* (New York: Penguin Books, 1981) and *Dangerous Currents* (New York: Random House, 1984).

retical models and empirical conclusions, is really the result of differences in distributional preferences.

Groups hurt by inflation are different from those hurt by unemployment, although there is some overlap. Those who benefit from active fiscal policy are different from those who benefit from a laissez-faire approach. Those who gain from supply side policies may or may not overlap with those who benefit from easy or tight monetary policies. Tight monetary policy falls heavily on housing, investment, and industries that export and compete with imports. Selective policies aimed at shifting aggregate supply favor certain groups of investments and entrepreneurs. Benefits to the poor or to average workers may trickle down as the result of increased output, investment, and productivity.

DO ECONOMISTS EVER AGREE?

Although economists disagree about many points of macroeconomic theory and policy, there is also a broad range of consensus among most economists. More than two decades ago, Milton Friedman said, "We are all Keynesians now." That is, most economists use a modified Keynesian framework to discuss macroeconomic issues. Most mainstream economists would add, "We are also all monetarists now." The loanable funds market incorporates both monetarist and Keynesian views. The aggregate supply and demand model is broad enough to encompass both major traditions.

Here are some points of agreement between contemporary economists in the Keynesian and classical traditions:

1. The money supply can affect output as well as prices, although the effects on output may be only short-run.
2. Velocity is more stable in the long run than the short run.
3. Demand for money depends on both income and interest rates, although income has a stronger effect.
4. Expectations about income, prices, and interest rates are an important influence on consumption and investment.
5. Fiscal policy can have some effects on real output in the short run. The long-run effects are much less certain.
6. Both inflation and unemployment beyond a certain minimum are undesirable.
7. Lags may distort the intended effects of monetary and fiscal policy.
8. Some crowding out is a likely result of a deficit-financed increase in government spending.

Note the qualifiers in this list: "may," "some," and "in the short run." Economists have not yet arrived at clear-cut answers that they can agree on with respect to the slope of the aggregate supply curve, the importance of crowding out, and the relative length of the long run and the short run. But even when they disagree, economists in both the Keynesian and classical traditions are using the same ideas: the aggregate expenditure function, the quantity theory of money, and the aggregate supply and demand model.

Consider again... *The problems posed by Thomas Schelling at the beginning of this chapter represent a typical Keynesian view of the role of government. Government steps in because the sum of private choices may not result in a desirable outcome. Even some of Schelling's own examples, however, can be countered with different experiences. Neighborhood declines in urban areas in the 1970s and 1980s have been halted in some areas by processes called gentrification (restoring old inner city homes for young professional families) and urban homesteading (programs sponsored by local governments and private voluntary groups to turn abandoned property over to low-income families who will restore and maintain them). When one route to work gets crowded, creative commuters seek out alternative routes, until the time cost of all the alternative routes is roughly equalized. At large events, promoters sell assigned seats to avoid empty front rows.*

Schelling's observations are accurate, but some of them are short term. Keynesians are people who want to do something. Economists in the classical/monetarist tradition are people who are content to let the problem work itself out, confident that there are corrective forces at work. Neither group is always right or always wrong. The creative tension between these two poles of policy advice may mean that the country shifts between policy activism and laissez-faire, steering a course somewhat between the two extremes.

SUMMARY

1. Economists in the classical tradition believe that the velocity of money is stable (at least in the long run) and the expenditure multiplier is not. Keynesians argue the opposite. Stable velocity means monetary policy is more effective. A stable expenditure multiplier means fiscal policy is more effective. Velocity rises during business expansions and falls during recessions, with a long-term upward trend in the last twenty years.

2. Fiscal policy will not be effective if government borrowing drives up interest rates and crowds out private borrowers. If an increase in government spending is financed by higher taxes, the taxes reduce the impact of fiscal policy. Financing government spending by printing money makes it hard to separate the effects of fiscal and monetary policy.

3. The Phillips curve shows the various combinations of inflation and employment that an economy has experienced in a specific period of time. Early Phillips curves showed a negative relationship, leading economists to view the Phillips curve as a menu of policy choices between inflation and unemployment. The Phillips curve appears to show a trade-off between inflation and unemployment, but the relationship shifted in the 1970s. Experience in the last two decades has led economists to doubt that the Phillips curve offers a stable menu of policy choices.

4. Friedman argues that the long-run Phillips curve is vertical at a level of output corresponding to the natural rate of unemployment. Friedman developed the natural rate hypothesis to explain why there is no long-run trade-off between inflation and unemployment. When expectations about inflation are correct, and markets respond very quickly to changes in signals, expansionary policy will have only a temporary effect on output, driving up the price level only and restoring the natural rate of unemployment. If expectations are adaptive and a large number of markets are contract rather than auction, however, the effect of expansionary monetary or fiscal policy may have a more lasting effect.

5. Although there are various groups within each tradition, most economists can be classified as either in the Keynesian tradition or the classical/monetarist tradition. The two groups differ on certain issues of theory: the shape of the *AS* curve, the stability of velocity versus the stability of the multiplier, the importance of crowding out, the interest sensitivity of investment demand and money demand, and the long-term effectiveness of monetary and fiscal policy. These two groups also differ in their goals and values. Economists in the Keynesian tradition tend to be policy activists, while those in the classical/monetarist tradition tend to rely more on self-correcting market forces.

NEW TERMS

accommodating monetary policy
Phillips curve
insider-outsider model
natural rate of unemployment
adaptive expectations
auction markets
contract markets

QUESTIONS: REVIEW, APPLICATIONS, AND POLICY

REVIEW

1. Why, according to Schelling, are aggregate outcomes more likely to be unsatisfactory as the group size increases?
2. Why can't both velocity and the expenditure multiplier be stable at the same time?
3. If the demand for money is sensitive to interest rates, how is velocity affected?
4. If the government tries to increase the level of output by increasing *G*, what difference does it make how that increase is financed?
5. According to Barro, why should the financing method in Question 4 make no difference?
6. What difference does it make for a Phillips curve whether aggregate supply is stable or not?
7. If the Phillips curve has shifted to the right, what does that suggest about the direction and relative size of shifts in aggregate supply and aggregate demand?
8. What is the natural rate hypothesis? Why does it imply that demand management policy is ineffective in the long run?
9. What determines the slope of the *AS* curve?
10. Economists who believe in rational expectations assume that individuals will acquire and process all relevant information to make economic decisions in their own self-interest. If you watch key variables and expect the inflation rate to rise, how will that affect your consumption, saving, and work behavior?
11. Why are both rational expectations and auction markets necessary in order to have a vertical *AS* curve in the short run?

APPLICATIONS

12. Suppose that a recession in the rest of the world led to a decline in U.S. exports. Would that shift *AD* or *AS*? Trace the process of adjustment along the short-run and long-run aggregate supply and demand curves if (a) the government does nothing, or (b) the government pursues an expansionary fiscal policy to restore demand.
13. Which of the following can be classed as auction markets and which as contract markets?
    a. the stock market
    b. the mortgage market
    c. the labor market
    d. the market for new houses
    e. the market for tickets to a baseball game

POLICY

14. Identify some of the distributional effects of expansionary and contractionary policies.
15. What difference does it make to monetary and fiscal policy whether expectations are adaptive or rational and whether markets are primarily auction or contract?

SUGGESTIONS FOR FURTHER READING

Blinder, Alan. *Hard Heads, Soft Hearts*. New York: Addison-Wesley, 1987. A very readable, fairly Keynesian look at policy options with a concern for distributional effects. Chapters 2 and 3 look at unemployment, inflation, and demand management.

Colander, David. *Why Aren't Economists as Important as Garbagemen?* Armonk NY: M. E. Sharpe, 1991. This thoughtful and entertaining collection of essays includes a chapter on the evolution of contemporary macroeconomic ideas discussed in this chapter.

Schelling, Thomas. *Choice and Consequence*. Cambridge MA: Harvard University Press, 1984. One of several unusual works by an economist with a unique perspective on the collective effects of individual choice.

Sheffrin, Steven M. *The Making of Economic Policy*. Cambridge MA: Basil Blackwell, 1989. Discusses the current state of stabilization policy and the areas of consensus that have emerged in the last two decades.

CHAPTER 16
AGGREGATE SUPPLY, ECONOMIC GROWTH, AND MACROECONOMIC POLICY

LEARNING OBJECTIVES
1. Discuss the importance of the slope of the aggregate supply curve and the length of the short run to demand-based growth strategies.
2. Define real business cycles and explain their relationship to aggregate supply.
3. Identify the sources of economic growth, which are the factors that can shift the aggregate supply curve and improve productivity.
4. Discuss the supply side policies relating to taxes, transfers, and regulation, and evaluate the effectiveness of supply side policies in the 1980s.
5. Explain what industrial policy is and how it is implemented.

Consider this... *From 1989 to 1993, spanning a brief recession and a longer period of slow economic growth, job prospects for the average high school or college graduate were dismal. The class of 1992 had some of the worst experience in trying to land jobs related to their education since the Class of '81 walked off campus eleven years earlier into 9 percent unemployment. The recession of 1990–1991 was much less severe, but recovery of the job market has been slower. What happened to the "good old days" when a college diploma from a respectable college combined with reasonably good grades was a ticket to a good job? Will they ever return?*

Jobs are closely linked to economic growth. In the United States and most other industrial nations, economic growth during the last decade was rather uneven, averaging 2.5 percent in the 1980s and slowing down to a crawl (0.7 percent) in 1990–1992. From 1948 to 1965, real GDP increased an average of 4 percent a year; from 1965 to 1979, by 3.1 percent a year. In this chapter, we will examine the causes of economic growth and policies to encourage growth.

DEMAND-BASED GROWTH STRATEGIES

A steady rate of economic growth is the most central of macroeconomic goals. Like any goal, the goal of economic growth involves some trade-offs. Growth is often accompanied by inflation, which redistributes income. Growth may benefit the rich but fail to trickle down to the poor. Growth may come at a cost in terms of leisure, environmental quality, or security. Against these costs a society must weigh the benefits of growth. Growth allows a society to absorb a growing labor force without rising unemployment. Growth increases the standard of living. Out of the "growth dividend," a society can (if it chooses) provide for the elderly, the homeless, the poor—needs that can be addressed less painfully out of new resources and new income. While there are still concerns about environmental effects, leisure, and quality of life, there appears to be a consensus in favor of encouraging growth by either increasing aggregate demand or increasing aggregate supply.

A **demand-based growth strategy** is an attempt to create a long-term increase in output and employment by shifting aggregate demand to the right. Demand-based growth strategies are based on the long-run effects of the lost output during periods when the economy is operating significantly below its potential. The output that is lost during that time includes some valuable investment in research and development, physical capital, and human capital (both formal education and on-the-job training). These lost investments could be the inputs into future growth. The usefulness of demand-based growth strategies depends on the length of the time period that divides the short run from the long run. Thus, the ideas about the aggregate supply curve discussed in the previous chapter are important not only for stabilization policy but also for demand-based growth policies.

Demand-based growth strategies
Policies attempting to increase the level of output over time by shifting the aggregate demand curve to the right.

THE AGGREGATE SUPPLY CURVE REVISITED

The debate over aggregate supply has concentrated on the alternatives of vertical versus upward sloping. Most economists agree that the short-run aggregate supply curve is upward sloping rather than vertical. The upward slope results from imperfections in the marketplace, such as immobile resources, imperfect information, long-term contractual agreements, incorrect expectations, or delayed responses to information. Rational expectations and auction markets suggest that the short run is not a very long period of actual time, and that the long-run aggregate supply curve is vertical or at least very steep. Adaptive expectations and contract markets suggest that the short-run aggregate supply curve could be fairly flat and that the short run itself may be a long period of time.

SHORT RUN AND LONG RUN

The link between demand management policies and economic growth arises from opportunities for real (short-run) profit created by a rising price level. Workers, entrepreneurs, investors, and consumers who can respond more quickly than others gain from rising prices. Suppose, for example, you are a shoe manufacturer. Prices in general are rising, and you can get a higher price for your shoes. Your contracts with workers and suppliers include prices that are fixed for six months. If, during those six months, you can obtain resources at fixed prices and sell the shoes for higher prices, you can increase your profits. At the end of six months, your contracts will be up for renewal. You know that wages and prices of materials will rise and your temporary profit surge will end in the long run. In the meantime, however, you have an incentive to expand output. In fact, if you expect more such surges in the future, each with a short-run profit opportunity, you may respond by investing more in new equipment, more modern technology, and upgrading employee skills.

The long-run and short-run aggregate supply curves are shown in Figure 1. The long-run aggregate supply curve, AS^{lr}, is vertical at Y^*, which is the real out-

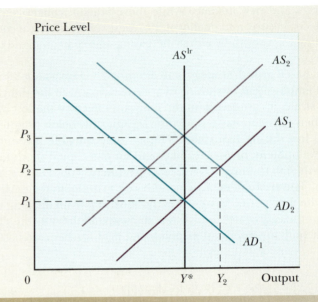

FIGURE 1

SHORT-RUN AND LONG-RUN AGGREGATE SUPPLY

When the AS curve slopes upward in the short run but is vertical in the long run, an increase in aggregate demand (shift from AD_1 to AD_2) raises both real output and the price level. Eventually rising prices drive up input costs, shifting the short-run AS curve (from AS_1 to AS_2). Real output returns to Y^*, and only the price level increases.

put level corresponding to the natural rate of unemployment. The short-run aggregate supply curve, AS_1, is upward sloping. Initially the economy is in short-run and long-run equilibrium at P_1 and Y^*. Then aggregate demand shifts from AD_1 to AD_2. Moving along AS_1, output increases to Y_2, and the price level begins to rise to P_2. Producers raise prices and expand output in response to increased demand.

Eventually, however, the rising price level affects the prices of productive inputs: workers, capital, and raw materials. The real value of workers' earnings falls. As soon as resource owners have an opportunity to renegotiate wages and prices, those wages and prices rise. Rising costs produce an upward shift in the short-run aggregate supply curve to AS_2. Once again the economy is in short-run and long-run equilibrium at a higher price level, P_3. However, there has been no permanent increase in the level of output and employment.

The important question is how widespread these short-run profit opportunities are and how long it takes the market to eliminate them. If imperfections are substantial, and it takes a long time for the market to adapt to change, then an increase in aggregate demand can increase profit opportunities and real output for a fairly long period of time. This higher output represents growth not only of consumption but also of the resource base of human and physical capital acquired during the interim. Expanding aggregate demand can be a growth strategy as well as a stabilization strategy.

The longer the contract period, the longer the original short-run upward-sloping aggregate supply curve will be valid. When contracts expire, the short-run aggregate supply curve will shift upward. A new short run will begin on a new curve at the old level of output associated with the natural rate of unemployment. Once again, economists are faced with this question: How long is the short run? Economists in the Keynesian tradition argue that the short run is very long indeed, because these imperfections are large and the market works slowly to overcome them. Economists of the classical tradition claim that the short run is really not a very long period of time. They are more optimistic about people's ability to acquire and process information and on the ability of buyers and sellers to respond quickly by changing prices, quantities, or suppliers. Consequently, they see little role for demand-based growth strategies, and concentrate instead on shifting aggregate supply.

REAL BUSINESS CYCLES

A growing economy typically exhibits some instability, because innovations resulting from research and development and investment spending do not occur at a steady pace. Thus, such an economy would be expected to exhibit business cycles, as described in Chapter 5. The Keynesian model explains such cyclical fluctuations in output, employment, and the price level in terms of shifts in aggregate demand combined with a relatively stable aggregate supply curve that gradually moves rightward over time.

Another explanation of cyclical fluctuations, in the classical tradition, was developed in the 1980s. Its roots go back to such early twentieth-century economists as Wesley Clair Mitchell (who first measured business cycles) and Joseph Schumpeter. This explanation holds that cyclical economic fluctuations result from changes in aggregate supply rather than in aggregate demand (or changes that affect both at once). The cyclical pattern is called the **real business cycle**. If changes in aggregate supply as a result of technology shocks and other disturbances occur irregularly in large bursts, the result is cyclical fluctuations in output.[1]

These cyclical fluctuations arise because workers and owners of firms take advantage of temporarily high returns to investment, production, and work effort when such shocks occur. Later, when the returns to such efforts are lower, workers will catch up on leisure and firms will slack off until the next shock begins. Intertemporal substitutions of effort (shifting economic activity between periods to take advantage of the time period with higher returns) will lead to fluctuations in output. Note, however, that in this model unemployment is largely voluntary, caused by the substitution of work effort between time periods to take advantage of the higher wages when productivity is higher.

A supply-induced explanation of fluctuations was a response to the experience of the 1970s and early 1980s. At that time, supply influences, such as a less experienced labor force and higher oil prices, seemed to shift the aggregate supply curve to the left. Such a shift would result in the usual decline in output and employment that indicates a recession. Unlike most recessions, however, there would be no fall in the price level (or the inflation rate). In a supply-induced recession, in contrast to a demand-induced recession, real output can fall while the price level rises. A subsequent shift of the aggregate supply curve to the right would expand both employment and real output. What happened to the price level during such an expansion would depend on whether aggregate demand also shifted to the right during that period.

In general, a real business cycle—one based on shifts in aggregate supply—implies rising price levels or higher inflation rates during recessions and lower price levels or lower inflation rates during expansions. This pattern is somewhat

Real business cycle
A cyclical pattern of economic activity resulting from changes in aggregate supply rather than aggregate demand.

---

1. The pros and cons of this highly technical subject are discussed in Charles I. Plosser, "Understanding Real Business Cycles," *Journal of Economic Perspectives* (Summer 1989): 51–78; and N. Gregory Mankiw, "Real Business Cycles: A New Keynesian Perspective," *Journal of Economic Perspectives* (Summer 1989): 79–89.

consistent with the experience of the 1970s but does not generally describe cyclical fluctuations for longer periods. Evidence to support a real business cycle on a regular and recurring basis has not been strong, but certainly some recessions or expansions are triggered by real factors shifting the aggregate supply curve.

SHIFTING THE AGGREGATE SUPPLY CURVE

Although economists disagree about real business cycles, they do agree about what makes aggregate supply shift. The long-run aggregate supply curve will shift to the right in response to increases in the capital stock, improvement in the size and/or quality of the labor force, additional natural resources, improvements in productivity, or technological advances. Increases in resources or productivity will shift the aggregate supply curve to the right. Encouragement of production through reduced taxes or regulations that lower costs to firms will also shift the curve to the right. Anything that shifts the aggregate supply curve to the right is a source of economic growth, because it will produce a rise in real output and income.

The aggregate supply curve can also shift to the left, indicating negative growth, or a decline in a nation's standard of living. Factors that can shift the curve to the left include resource depletion, a decline in the size and/or quality of the labor force, and public policies (taxes or regulations) that discourage productive activity.

Long-term economic growth requires steady rightward shifts of the aggregate supply curve. Economic growth has been a major concern in the United States for at least thirty years. Economists are constantly examining the growth rate of the U.S. economy to make sure that the standard of living is rising, and economic journalists are always comparing that growth rate to economic growth in other nations, such as Japan. Economists are also concerned that output expand fast enough to create enough jobs for a growing labor force. The antigrowth voices of the early 1970s became muted when Americans started realizing the costs of not growing—in terms of inflation, unemployment, and a lower standard of living if population grew faster than real output. During the 1980s and 1990s, the continuing debate has not been over *whether* to grow but rather *how* to grow. Economists try to determine what strategies are most successful for shifting aggregate supply to the right.

GROWTH IN INVESTMENT AND SAVING

Between 1962 and 1992, real output increased 135 percent in the United States. Some of that growth was a result of increased resources, specifically labor and capital. Even coming out of a recession, gross investment in constant dollars was 130 percent higher in 1992 than it was in 1962. However, recall from Chapter 5 that a large (and increasing) part of gross private domestic investment goes to replacement of worn-out capital. After correcting for depreciation, real net investment was actually lower in 1992 than in 1962! Even during the relatively prosperous years of the 1980s, real net investment only averaged about 80 percent higher than in 1962. Thus, the real growth rate of investment has been much lower than the rate of economic growth.

Because investment is so volatile, year-to-year comparisons must be treated carefully. Figure 2 plots both gross and net investment expenditures as percent-

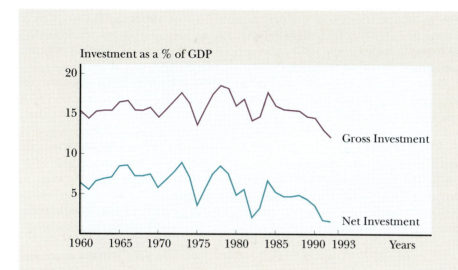

FIGURE 2
GROSS AND NET PRIVATE INVESTMENT IN THE UNITED STATES AS A PERCENTAGE OF GDP, 1960–1993
Gross investment averages about 17 percent of GDP, and net investment about 6 percent, with both dropping sharply relative to GDP during the recessions of 1975, 1982, and 1991.

ages of GDP for 1953 to 1993. The growth of gross investment over that whole period was greater than the growth of total GDP but was very erratic. Net investment, which consists of new plants, equipment, and housing as opposed to replacement of worn-out facilities and equipment, actually fell relative to GDP. Note that in recession years, such as 1975, 1982, and 1991, investment declined even more than GDP, reducing the stock of capital available for future economic growth.

PRIVATE SAVING. The most commonly used indicator of what is happening to saving is the **savings rate**, or saving by households, business, and government combined as a percentage of GDP. The current U.S. rate is low compared to past experience and to savings rates in many other industrial countries. However, saving has fallen in other industrial countries as well in the last two decades. From 1960 to 1980, the United States saved 19.6 percent of GDP, somewhat below the average for seventeen industrial countries, which was 23.4 percent. (Japan, at 35 percent, had the highest ratio.) Demographic factors, such as the maturing of the baby boomers, are just now beginning to contribute to a higher savings rate in the United States.

The national savings rate was the focus of much attention in the 1980s as economists tried to explain why it was so low and policy makers tried to invent creative ways to induce households to save more. The savings rate fell throughout the 1980s in both the United States and other industrial countries. By 1990, the U.S. savings rate was down to 13 percent, compared to an average of 20 percent for other industrial countries. This low rate was largely the result of negative government saving in the form of a large budget deficit. Federal deficits combined with state and local government surpluses reduced the overall savings rate by more than 2 percent of GDP.

Private saving is the major source of funding for investment to expand future output. Saving by households and business firms, which provides the funds for investment, has not kept pace with the growth of GDP in recent years. From 1980 to 1990, business and household saving rose only about two-thirds as fast as

Savings rate
The ratio of combined business, household, and government saving to GDP.

GDP. In addition, much of the private saving in the 1980s was absorbed in financing the large federal budget deficits. The combination of low private saving and negative saving in the public sector resulted in a substantial inflow of funds from abroad to cover the shortfall.

Since 1990, two offsetting developments have changed this pattern. As the baby boomers grow older, they have begun to enjoy higher incomes and finish paying for houses and educating their children. Households have increased their saving as the baby boomers have reached these high savings years, and as they have been able to reduce their debt burdens with the help of lower interest rates. This increased household saving came just at a time when the inflow of foreign funds to the United States slowed in response to higher interest rates in Europe and recession in Japan and Canada. Together with some reduction in the budget deficit, which has been absorbing a large share of private saving, the availability of saving looks more promising for the rest of the decade.

PRIVATE INVESTMENT. A higher level of investment would shift both the aggregate demand curve and the aggregate supply curve to the right. Such a shift would increase employment without more inflation. More specifically, business investment in new equipment is a key source of economic growth. Additional equipment gives each worker more capital with which to work and thus increases productivity. New equipment embodies new technology, which also increases productivity. Thus, the slowdown in investment in the 1970s and 1980s led to a search for policies that would stimulate investment. Tax incentives of various kinds were proposed and implemented. In the 1981 tax law, accelerated write-offs of new investment greatly reduced corporate income taxes. Those revenues were partly restored by reforms in the 1986 tax law.

Since 1986 there have been numerous efforts to restore the special tax treatment of capital gains, which are currently taxed as ordinary income. Capital gains are "profits" that result from the sale of assets at a higher price than they cost. Many policy makers argue that favorable tax treatment of capital gains would stimulate more sales of business firms and corporate stock. All three candidates in the 1992 presidential election favored some special treatment of capital gains as a way to encourage investment.

PUBLIC INVESTMENT. The policy emphasis in the last decade has been on private capital as a way to increase economic growth. However, the role of infrastructure as capital should not be overlooked. Most of this capital is in the state and local public sector, where the growth of the capital stock has slowed considerably from earlier decades. The transportation network of highways and airports on which private business depends is provided in the public sector. Investment in human capital also requires local public sector investments in schools and health care facilities. Economist David Aschauer has examined public sector investment in a number of countries to see whether it enhances growth (because it is complementary to private investment) or discourages growth (by crowding out private investors).[2] His conclusion, which has been challenged by other

---

2. David A. Aschauer, "Does Public Capital Crowd Out Private Capital?" *Journal of Monetary Economics* (September 1989): 171–188. Explores the relationship between public and private capital as both complements and substitutes in promoting economic growth. Aschauer concludes that public sector capital does make a significant contribution to growth.

economists, is that public and private investment are complementary. Public investments, especially in transport facilities (roads, bridges, airports, and mass transit) enhance the productivity of private sector capital and contribute to economic growth.

GROWTH IN THE LABOR FORCE

Another source of economic growth is a larger and/or more skilled labor force. Increases in both the size and the quality of the labor force can contribute to economic growth. If only the size of the labor force increases, as occurred during the 1970s, real GDP may increase but there will be little if any increase in real per capita GDP, which measures improvements in the standard of living. A more skilled and productive labor force, which has more capital and better technology to work with, is the essential ingredient for an increase in real per capita GDP.

THE SIZE OF THE LABOR FORCE. During the 1970s, the labor force grew by 22 percent. A large part of that increase reflected the entry of the baby boom generation into the labor force. In 1970, 16 percent of the population was between sixteen and twenty-four years old, the age group that makes up most of the new entrants to the labor force. Another large part of the increase was due to the increased participation of women, many of whom were entering the labor force for the first time. Thus, labor force growth was much more rapid than before, but the average level of workers' skill and experience fell. This fall slowed the growth of GDP and the rightward movement of the aggregate supply curve.

Since 1980, labor force growth has dropped, increasing only 16 percent between 1980 and 1990. By 1990, those in the sixteen to twenty-four age group made up only 13.4 percent of the population. The plus side is that the average worker now has more experience than a decade ago. Still, a shortage of new workers is on the horizon, leading some economists to recommend reduced barriers to immigration as a way to ensure continued growth in the labor force.

INVESTMENT IN HUMAN CAPITAL. Investment in human capital includes any spending that increases the health or productive skills of the individual worker. Both individuals and firms can invest in human capital. An individual's decision to seek additional education is very similar to an entrepreneur's decision to purchase a new piece of equipment. In both cases, the investment is productive if the return over time exceeds the cost over the same time period.

The largest investment in human capital in the United States is in the public schools, which offer "free" education through grade twelve. This education is supplemented by post-secondary education in colleges, universities, and technical schools; vocational training programs; adult literacy and retraining programs; and on-the-job training. Estimates by Jacob Mincer in the 1970s indicated that as much as half of human capital in the United States was derived from on-the-job training.[3]

The median amount of education (years of schooling completed) of persons twenty-five years old and over has also risen steadily in the United States,

---

3. Jacob Mincer, *Schooling, Experience, and Earnings* (New York: National Bureau of Economic Research, 1974).

from 10.5 years in 1960 to 12.7 years in 1991. In 1991, 78 percent of the adult population had at least a high school diploma. As older workers with less education retire, average worker schooling continues to rise.

The United States spends about 4.2 percent of GDP on education at all levels. A large share of this investment is in elementary and secondary education. In 1959, expenditures per pupil were $1,635 (measured at 1982–1983 prices). By 1992, this figure had risen to $3,206, almost twice as much. This amount compares favorably with educational expenditures in other developed nations. Of other major industrial nations, only Switzerland spends more per pupil. The other nations of Western Europe, Canada, Japan, and Australia all spend less.[4]

The U.S. educational system has come under much criticism for failing to produce a well-educated labor force. Public schools were among the scapegoats for the slow economic growth in the 1970s and early 1980s. Parents, taxpayers, and educators pointed to falling SAT scores and high dropout rates. Employers complained about lack of basic skills in writing and computation.

The result of these complaints has been a careful examination of how effectively resources invested in education are being used. At the elementary and secondary levels, a number of states have enacted reforms in order to use those resources more effectively. Those reforms include tougher attendance laws, stricter teacher certification, basic skills testing for students, and other measures designed to improve the quality of public education. A few business leaders have even offered to provide college funds for those who make it through twelfth grade in certain inner city schools. That guarantee has lowered the dropout rate in those schools. A number of political leaders have expressed an interest in integrating high school with specific, apprenticeship-type training along the lines developed successfully in Germany in order to prepare non-college-bound students for work. All of these steps are attempts to improve the quality of human capital. The result would be an increase in aggregate supply and in the U.S. standard of living.

GROWTH IN NATURAL RESOURCES

The last category of inputs that can shift the aggregate supply curve is natural resources. In the late 1960s, a group of doomsayers called "The Club of Rome" used a computer simulation model to predict massive shortages of natural resources by the end of this century. Many economists are not very concerned about resource shortages because they have observed how market forces have dealt with such problems in the past. The market has several mechanisms to address problems of declining resource availability. When high-grade sources are exhausted, lower-grade sources are substituted. When a given resource becomes scarce, its price rises. Users then turn to natural or synthetic substitutes. Higher prices also stimulate searches for new sources of supply. Finally, technological change has helped to lower extraction costs and make lower-grade deposits worth exploiting.

Economists V. Kerry Smith and John V. Krutilla examined experience with natural resources over a 100-year period. While they acknowledge valid concerns over increased resource scarcity, Smith and Krutilla found the record of the past

---

4. Comparative international data is taken from John Hood, "Education: Money Isn't Everything," *The Wall Street Journal* (February 2, 1990): A-10.

to be encouraging.[5] Higher prices typically called forth the kinds of responses just described.

With one exception, increased resource prices did not have much impact on the slowdown in GDP growth. That exception was oil, which had a tenfold price increase in just seven years, leading to a temporary leftward shift of the aggregate supply curve. Even in that case, with a dramatic price increase of a widely used natural resource, producers and consumers adapted. More fuel-efficient cars, alternative energy sources, insulation, modified production methods, and other responses minimized the long-run effect on the economy. The higher price also ultimately called forth additional oil supplies, and by the early 1990s energy prices were back down to more normal levels. Cheaper energy supplies shifted the aggregate supply curve back to the right to some extent, contributing to very low inflation rates.

RESEARCH AND DEVELOPMENT

Increased productive resources are not the only source of increases in aggregate supply. If new ways of using resources can create more output, then those technological changes can also shift the aggregate supply curve to the right. New technology may be embodied in new capital or in a change in methods of production. Research and development, or R&D, consists of efforts to develop new products and new production methods and put them to use. In the United States, R&D is supported by both the private sector ($81 billion in 1992) and the public sector ($68 billion in federal funds, and $5 billion from universities and colleges, including contributions by state governments). Of that total, $92 billion is for development (mostly new or improved product development), $37 billion for applied research, and $25 billion for basic research.[6]

Total research and development spending, public and private, accounts for about 2.8 percent of GDP. This figure is comparable to levels in Germany and Japan, and higher than the share of GDP that goes to R&D in France and the United Kingdom. However, a large share of that R&D spending in the United States is devoted to military research and technology, with very limited spinoffs in terms of civilian production. Nondefense R&D spending in the United States amounts to about 2 percent of GDP, compared to 2.8 percent for Japan and 2.6 percent in West Germany (before reunification). With defense R&D eliminated, the gap in R&D spending between the United States and France or the United Kingdom is also much narrower—2 percent of GDP in the United States compared to 1.8 percent in both those countries.

Technological change is a two-step process. The first step requires investment in research into new products and new methods. This step results in inventions. The second step is to translate those inventions into something that is commercially feasible and cost-effective. This second step is **innovation**, or the translation of new methods and products into actual production and marketing. A special issue of *Business Week* devoted to innovation suggested that Americans excel at the invention phase, but the Japanese are much more successful in mak-

Innovation
The translation of inventions into products and processes that are commercially feasible and cost-effective.

---

5. V. Kerry Smith and John V. Krutilla, "Economic Growth, Resource Availability, and Environmental Quality," *American Economic Review Papers and Proceedings* (May 1984): 226–230.
6. Data are from *National Patterns of R&D Resources: 1992* (Washington DC: National Science Foundation, October 1992): NSF92–330.

POLICY FOCUS: MILITARY SPENDING, DEFENSE CONVERSION, AND ECONOMIC GROWTH

As the United States reduces its military spending, economists have taken the opportunity to explore the impact of the defense buildup of the last fifty years on economic growth. In 1992, the U.S. federal budget included $265 billion for defense, about 19 percent of total federal expenditures. This figure was lower in real terms than 1991, and lower still than the level of spending during the six-year defense buildup under President Reagan. The projected budgets for the rest of the 1990s include a continuing decline in military spending, partly as a way to control deficits and partly as a result of the end of the Cold War.

Has military spending helped or hindered growth of U.S. output in the past? At least one critic argues that it reduced growth:

> Owing to the disproportionate allocation of scientific and engineering talent to military research, the rate of commercial innovation has declined appreciably since the late 1960s. Rising prices and deteriorating relative quality have made U.S.-produced goods increasingly noncompetitive in both world and domestic markets, forcing production cutbacks and plant closures in the United States and creating additional inflationary pressures.[a]

This observation pinpoints an essential concern about the relationship of military spending to the economy. Has defense spending displaced infrastructure investment or funding for human capital? Has military research and development benefited private industry?

The United States concentrates a much larger share of research and development spending in defense than most other industrial countries. The distinction between military and civilian R&D spending would be less important if there were substantial spillover benefits between the two. The one great success of military R&D that was translated into profitable civilian applications is the transistor. However, other examples are hard to find. In fact, Hewlett-Packard has argued that defense has been a net user of civilian-created technology in electronics, rather than the other way around.[b] The military is generally more interested in performance than in price. The civilian market is sensitive to both concerns. Machine tool manufacturing in the United States has been stimulated by military demand, but the result has been an industry that has been more attentive to high performance than to cost. The more price-sensitive civilian sector of the market has gone to the Germans and the Japanese.

Some military innovations with spinoffs to the private sector have not been in technology but in management. Cost-benefit analysis, operations research, and planning-programming-budget systems originated in the military and spread quickly to private industries. Overall, however, it is difficult to evaluate whether high levels of defense spending have increased, reduced, or had no impact on U.S. economic growth.

These questions are important because defense conversion is already underway. The process is painful for many regions and many workers—cities with military facilities, defense contractors, and military and civilian workers in both. As a result of the 1990 and 1993 budget agreements, this reduction in defense spending will not be offset by an increase in nondefense spending. Consequently, there is a negative effect on aggregate demand that results in short-run cyclical unemployment. The fact that workers and facilities are not easily shifted to peacetime uses also means that structural unemployment will be higher than average during the transition period, which will take most of the decade of the 1990s. The lost output from these workers and facilities during the transition will reduce U.S. current output and thus dampen future growth as well.

Conversion is likely to be slow, judging from past experience. It is not easy to find appropriate employment for ex-military personnel and former employees of defense contractors or to find good uses for old military installations. While defense contractors have a lot of skilled, highly trained personnel and capital equipment in search of other uses, those firms that have tried to develop civilian markets have found that producing for private customers is very different from producing for the Pentagon. Marketing must replace lobbying. Cost overruns are less likely to be tolerated.[c]

Previous efforts to convert defense contractors to civilian producers have had very limited success, although there are some promising adaptations of military to civilian technology. Rockwell International has succeeded as a producer of automotive parts and computer chips. Martin-Marietta is adapting technology developed for the navy to scout Soviet submarines to use for tracking home TV audiences and the programs they watch.[d] Some communities where bases have closed in the past have been successful in converting these facilities into industrial parks, airports, or other productive uses. The federal government has set aside funds to help firms with conversion.

Two of the greatest economic successes of the last fifty years are the defeated powers of World War II, Japan and Germany. Forbidden to rearm, they poured their scientific and engineering talent into civilian uses. Defense conversion may provide the same opportunity for the United States.

a. *The Political Economy of Arms Reduction*, Selected Symposium 80, American Association for the Advancement of Science, 1982.
b. Jacques S. Gansler, *Affording Defense* (Cambridge MA: MIT Press, 1989).
c. Jurgen Brauer and John Teller Marlin, "Converting Resources from Military to Non-Military Uses," *Journal of Economic Perspectives* (Fall 1992): 145–164.
d. John Mintz, "Fitting Defense Pegs into Commercial Holes," *Washington Post National Weekly Edition* (July 5–11, 1992): 20.

---

ing the transition from invention to innovation and exploiting the profit potential of new ideas.[7]

Technological change is difficult to measure in the aggregate. It is possible to measure changes in spending on research and development, and on new equipment that embodies the latest technology. There is no easy way, however, to measure the extra output due to the new technology. The United States does spend heavily on R&D. About 2.8 percent of GDP goes to R&D, much of it funded by the federal government and carried out by industry and universities. In the 1970s and 1980s, however, about 25 percent of U.S. spending on R&D was directed to defense-related research, which has limited applications to other markets. Other countries (especially Japan) have put much more effort directly into industrial research.

Research and development spending usually requires investment in new capital that embodies the newly developed technology. Thus, R&D spending and new capital spending go hand in hand to shift the aggregate supply curve to the right and promote economic growth.

PUBLIC POLICY TOWARD RESEARCH AND DEVELOPMENT

Since the federal government plays a major role in the allocation of research and development funds, it has an important direct influence on the activities of invention and innovation. In addition to direct expenditures, the federal government also finances the education of many scientists and engineers, protects property rights to inventions through the patent system, and offers special tax breaks for R&D spending in the private sector.

Profits are the incentive to engage in research and development. The outcome of an R&D effort will be more profitable if the resulting product reaches the broadest possible market. One effort to increase the return to research and development, therefore, has concentrated on opening foreign markets to new U.S. products and better protecting patents and copyrights on a worldwide basis (protecting rights in "intellectual capital").

THE PRODUCTIVITY DILEMMA

Between recession and slow growth, increases in real per capita GDP have been small—about 2 percent a year from 1979 to 1992, or from $14,183 to $19,250. Even this modest gain resulted largely from putting a larger proportion of the

---

7. "Innovation in America," *Business Week* (special issue, 1989).

KEY IDEAS

SOURCES OF ECONOMIC GROWTH
Aggregate supply shifts to the right and real output grows as a result of
- Increased investment and saving
    - Private saving
    - Private investment
    - Public investment in infrastructure and human capital
- Growth of the labor force
    - Increased numbers of workers
    - Improvements in worker skills
- Growth of natural resources
    - Discovery versus depletion
- Research and development
    - Invention
    - Innovation

Productivity
A measure of output per worker hour.

population to work, not from higher wages. In real terms (1982 dollars), the average weekly earnings for workers in the private sector in the United States fell from a 1972 high of $315.44 to $256.81 in 1992. Increases in real wages depend on increases in productivity. **Productivity** is the measure of real output per worker hour. Like the price level, productivity changes are measured by an index. Table 1 shows the increase in productivity by decade for the United States.

The slow growth of productivity in the last two decades is a dramatic change from earlier periods. The problem is not unique to the United States. A similar slowdown in productivity growth has plagued all of the developed industrial countries. The concern over productivity, slow growth, and the combination of rising prices and rising unemployment led to many efforts to explain what was occurring and to devise suitable policies to get the economy moving again.[8]

8. Issues of productivity growth are discussed in detail in a symposium edited by Stanley Fischer in the *Journal of Economic Issues* (Fall 1988): 3–98.

TABLE 1 U.S. PRODUCTIVITY GROWTH, 1950–1992

PERIOD	PRODUCTIVITY INDEX	AVERAGE ANNUAL INCREASE (%)
	1950 = 50.2	
1950–1960	1960 = 65.5	+2.8
1960–1970	1970 = 86.9	+2.9
1970–1980	1980 = 98.6	+1.3
1980–1990	1990 = 109.7	+1.2
1990–1992	1992 = 113.9	+1.3

Source: Calculated from data in Council of Economic Advisers, *Economic Report of the President* (Washington DC: U.S. Government Printing Office, 1994.)

According to studies by economist Edward Denison, increases in labor productivity accounted for about two-thirds of U.S. economic growth from 1929 to 1982.[9] (The remainder was due to an increase in the size of the labor force.) Increases in the productivity of labor resulted from having more capital with which to work as well as such important factors as education and technological change.

One type of policy to increase productivity consists of various types of incentive, bonus, or profit-sharing schemes to encourage labor to work harder and become more skilled. Under such plans, workers are paid for output rather than input. Their pay is based on what they produce, rather than being an hourly wage or annual salary. After reviewing a number of studies on productivity incentives, economist Alan Blinder (a member of President Clinton's Council of Economic Advisers) concluded that there is some persuasive statistical evidence that such incentives do increase productivity.[10] That shouldn't surprise anyone who has studied economics!

Convincing explanations for the productivity slowdown are not hard to find. Although the labor force has grown, there has been some (short-term) decline in its quality as a result of a fall in the average age, training, and experience of workers, a situation that will gradually improve during the 1990s. The rates of saving and investment and spending for research and development have remained stubbornly low. New and better capital and methods of production are one of the most important sources of increased labor productivity. The pace of technological change has been slow. A great deal of R&D spending has been directed toward defense rather than commercial innovations.

Some economists question the accuracy of the productivity data. Productivity is much harder to measure in services than in goods production, and the share of services in total output is rising. For example, in banking, output is measured by the number of checks processed or deposits taken. With increasing use of automatic teller machines, the number of checks is down, yet productivity is up.[11] Other observers feel that we are at the point of a productivity payoff to the development and adoption of new technology in information processing and management techniques that has taken place over the last fifteen years. The payoff to new technology is delayed because it takes a while for workers to learn to use it and for management to figure out how to adapt the technology to their particular line of production. In 1992, productivity rose by 3 percent, the best figure in twenty years. Eventually, increased productivity should result in more job opportunities, especially for skilled workers who can work with computers.[12]

SUPPLY SIDERS: PUBLIC POLICIES TO SHIFT AGGREGATE SUPPLY

In the late 1970s and early 1980s, a group of economists, policy makers, and business journalists proposed that the United States adopt policies that would be

---

9. Edward F. Denison, *Trends in American Economic Growth, 1929–1982* (Washington DC: Brookings Institution, 1985).
10. Alan S. Blinder (ed.), *Paying for Productivity: A Look at the Evidence* (Washington DC: Brookings Institution, 1990).
11. "More Than Meets the Eye," *The Economist* (December 26, 1992): 91.
12. "The Technology Payoff," *Business Week* (June 1, 1993): 27–35.

Supply side economics
A branch of economics that advocates a specific group of policies relating to deregulation, tax incentives, and work incentives.

aimed at shifting aggregate supply to the right. **Supply side economics** was the work of a group of economists and business journalists who advocated a specific group of policies relating to deregulation, tax incentives, and work incentives.

In designing those policies, supply siders emphasized certain microeconomic foundations of aggregate supply. Supply siders insisted that economic incentives are important and that the driving force behind economic decisions is the self-interested behavior of individuals. Recall the importance of incentives and response to the role of interest rates in money demand, bank lending, and business investment decisions on the aggregate demand side of the market. The responses of individuals in their roles as workers, managers, investors, and savers to changes in the reward structure of their environment is also important for aggregate supply. Supply siders pointed out that the government has a great deal of influence on this reward structure.

In a broader sense, all economists are supply siders in that they believe that factors that can shift the aggregate supply curve are important for long-term economic growth. In fact, a Keynesian or a monetarist is often an advocate of some supply side policies.

For the most part, what President Reagan did in his first term (1981–1985) was a textbook application of supply side economics. Congress and the President reduced some nondefense programs, such as grants to state and local governments, and enacted a three-stage, 25 percent cut in personal income taxes in 1981. Accompanying the tax cuts were some incentives to save and invest. Also, efforts were made to reduce the burden on business of complying with government regulations. The goal was to shift aggregate supply to the right, increasing saving, investment, productivity, output, and employment while reducing inflation.

At first, U.S. supply side policies seemed to be out of step with much of the rest of the world. European countries were committed to demand management policies, and the United States was pursuing supply side policies. In the latter part of the 1980s, however, supply side policies became more popular in France, Denmark, New Zealand, Canada, and the United Kingdom. All of these countries adopted a less progressive tax system aimed more at incentives and less at redistribution of income. These changes may be the most lasting legacy of supply side economics.

REGULATION AND DEREGULATION

Supply siders were very critical of government regulations in environmental and health and safety areas that increase costs of production and drive up prices without increasing output. In addition to the direct costs of compliance, these regulations place a heavy burden of paperwork on industry. Although the purposes of the regulations might indeed be desirable, they divert real resources from producing goods and services to complying with regulations and filing forms. These higher costs shift the aggregate supply curve to the left. Deregulation should shift it back to the right.

Deregulation was a central feature of the policies of the Reagan administration. Some regulations were repealed. Others were simply not enforced. Experiments with deregulation in the 1980s in the airline industry, telephone service, and banking, however, generated mixed results. The enthusiasm for deregulation appears to have peaked in the mid-1980s, except for attempts to make the bureaucracy function more efficiently and reduce paperwork.

TAXES, TRANSFERS, AND INCENTIVES

Supply siders were particularly concerned about the effects of taxes and transfer payments, especially personal income taxes, on incentives and productive activity. They argued that the growth of the tax-transfer system reduces incentives to work, save, invest, and innovate, all of which contribute to productivity. Higher taxes drive up costs of production and consumer prices. Taxes to support government activity create a **tax wedge**, which is the gap between prices paid by consumers and the prices (incomes) received by sellers (resource owners). Thus, the tax wedge discourages both consumption and production. If the government borrows instead of raising taxes to finance additional spending, this action raises the cost of borrowing to private firms. The rise in the cost of borrowing drives up their costs and discourages private-sector investment. Either way, supply siders argue, the growth of government contributes to rising costs.

Tax wedge
The gap between prices paid by buyers and the prices received by sellers.

TAXES AND WORK EFFORT.
High marginal tax rates discourage individuals from putting forth extra effort and encourage tax avoidance. Under a progressive income tax system (and the U.S. federal income tax was fairly progressive until 1986), increases in nominal income push workers into higher marginal tax brackets. As a result, a significant portion of the return to increased effort and productivity is taxed away. Consequently, workers are likely to opt for more leisure (longer vacations, increased absenteeism, less moonlighting, and earlier retirement).

Consider Ruth Perez, a skilled accountant who earns $35 an hour. She is considering either putting in an extra four hours for a client on Saturday morning or spending that time cleaning her carpets. If she works, her gross income will be $140. A commercial carpet cleaner charges $100. Without considering taxes, it makes sense for her to work four hours, pay the carpet cleaner, and come out $40 ahead. Resources would be efficiently allocated. The value of her time as an accountant is higher than the value of her time as a carpet cleaner. However, taxes may change her decision. If her marginal income tax rate (federal plus state) is 40 percent, then after taxes she will earn only $84. It would be cheaper to clean her own carpets. A lower tax rate would induce her to use her time where it is most productive—as an accountant, not as a carpet cleaner. These concerns about the incentive effects of high marginal tax rates were reflected in the 1981 tax cut and the 1986 tax reforms. Both of these policy actions sharply reduced marginal income tax rates for individuals. The 1993 deficit reduction bill raised marginal tax rates for those with taxable incomes over $140,000, but rates were still below their pre-1981 levels.

TAXES, SAVING, AND INVESTMENT.
An individual's reward for saving depends on both the interest rate and the marginal tax rate on the next dollar of income. For any given interest rate, there is less incentive to save additional dollars at a higher marginal tax rate. Less credit will be available to borrowers. Thus, a progressive income tax discourages saving and, indirectly, through the higher cost of borrowed funds, discourages investment.

Supply siders also applied this argument to entrepreneurial or management risk taking. In deciding whether to expand productive facilities or to implement new technologies, owners or managers must weigh the risks that are involved against the expected profits *after taxes*. The higher the marginal tax rate, the smaller the expected profit will be, and the less eager investors will be to assume risks. As a result, less new technology is adopted, and both output and productivity growth are retarded.

TAXATION OF CAPITAL GAINS. In the late 1980s, a modified supply side argument became popular. Some economists and policy makers argued that the special tax treatment of capital gains, eliminated in the 1986 tax reform, should be restored. All three presidential candidates supported some form of a tax break for capital gains in the 1992 election. (Capital gains are earnings that result from an increase in the market value of an asset over its purchase price.) Under a highly progressive tax system, capital gains are likely to push their recipient into a higher tax bracket and generate more tax liability than they would have if they were received over several years instead of all at once. Many economists argue that special tax treatment (a lower rate) for capital gains is an effective incentive to invest in riskier ventures, thus providing capital for innovation and growth. However, there is no conclusive evidence about the effect of this tax break on investment, particularly since the income tax system is much less progressive than formerly.

TRANSFER PAYMENTS AND THE INCOME TAX. Supply siders also argue that transfer payments discourage productive work. Unemployment compensation programs encourage workers to stay unemployed until their benefits are exhausted. Welfare programs, including not only cash transfers but also food stamps, subsidized housing, and Medicaid, discourage people from taking low-wage jobs. The wages they could earn may barely offset the loss of welfare payments plus other benefits. Consider Bruce Thompson, who currently receives $120 a week in welfare benefits. A job becomes available that would require Bruce to work forty hours a week at the minimum wage of $4.25 an hour. If he takes the job, he loses his welfare benefits. He will earn $170 a week instead of $120. The "tax" on his earnings will be $120/$170, or about 71 percent. Is it worth working forty hours a week to earn $50 more? (After Social Security and other taxes, Thompson's net earnings increase may actually be negative.)

This argument was popularized in the early 1980s by Charles Murray in his book, *Losing Ground*.[13] He argued that welfare actually discourages people from investing in human capital. Workfare programs in some of the states and finally on the national level in the late 1980s were designed to overcome this problem by allowing people who go off welfare to accept jobs to keep more of their earnings.

RESOURCE ALLOCATION. Supply siders also argue that progressive taxes cause resources to be allocated inefficiently. Resources flow to certain sectors of the economy, such as real estate, that enjoy tax advantages. All depreciation, taxes, and interest expenses are deductible on real estate investments. Individuals in high marginal tax brackets find that their after-tax yields are higher from investing in real estate than in other assets. Thus, supply siders argue that too many financial resources flow into the real estate market, instead of more productive uses. The 1986 tax reform eliminated some but not all of the special tax provisions for certain types of investments.

13. Charles Murray, *Losing Ground: American Social Policy, 1950–1980* (New York: Basic Books, 1984).

KEY IDEAS

SUPPLY SIDE POLICIES

Supply siders would recommend the following policies:
- Deregulation of industries
- Reduction in taxes on high productivity workers
- Reduction in taxes on business firms
- Reduction in tax disincentives for welfare recipients
- Tax incentives for saving and investment

Supply siders would predict the following results:
- Increased work effort by high income workers
- Increased work effort by former welfare recipients
- Increased saving
- Increased investment and risk taking
- Improved resource allocation
- Reduced tax avoidance

TAX AVOIDANCE. Finally, supply siders stress that high marginal tax rates cause too many scarce resources to be devoted to avoiding taxes. Time spent looking for tax loopholes (by individuals and their hired attorneys and accountants) could be used more productively.

DID SUPPLY SIDE ECONOMICS WORK?

It is difficult to evaluate supply side policies because it is impossible to conduct *ceteris paribus* experiments. Tight monetary policy combined with lower inflation rates drove real interest rates to record highs. The worldwide recession from 1980 to 1982 led to falling output and employment and probably deserves some of the credit for lower inflation rates. Since recovery from a recession is generally associated with rising productivity, it is hard to know how much of the improvement in productivity during the mid-1980s was due to the Reagan program. The most noteworthy changes were the drop in the inflation rate and the steady recovery and expansion since the 1981–1982 recession. The massive budget deficits that followed the tax cut are also at least partly the result of these supply side policies.

There is some support for the argument that marginal tax rates affect those at the bottom of the ladder. There is also some weak support for a similar effect on those in high tax brackets. Economists Gary Burtless and Robert Haveman, summarizing a variety of studies of the effects of taxes and transfers, conclude that the loss of welfare benefits was a deterrent to work effort in some experimental programs to test work incentives. They also found that possible loss of Social Security benefits had a negative effect on work effort among the elderly.[14] Most of the increase in transfers during the 1980s was in Social Security and Medicare rather than in welfare programs. These increases did have some negative effects on work effort among older citizens, as supply siders would predict. Labor supply responses to lower tax rates were also modest, although different researchers find different results. Combining work from several sources suggests a labor supply response to the tax cuts of 2 percent or less.[15]

---

14. Gary T. Burtless and Robert H. Haveman, "Taxes and Transfers: How Much Economic Loss?" *Challenge* (March–April 1987): 45–51.
15. M.A. Akhtar and Ethan S. Harris, "Supply Side Consequences of U.S. Fiscal Policy in the 1980s," *Federal Reserve Bank of New York Quarterly Review* (Spring 1992): 1–22.

There is little evidence from the 1980s to support the view that reductions in the marginal income tax rate stimulate saving or investment. The 1981 tax law even contained some tax breaks for special savings accounts, such as All Savers Certificates and Individual Retirement Accounts (IRAs). Despite these incentives, the share of after-tax income that people saved continued to fall. Investment did not show much response either, growing more slowly than in the preceding decade and shifting into assets with shorter useful lifetimes to take advantage of depreciation rules. Most of these incentives were eliminated in 1986.

Crowding out within the budget, which was impacted by reduced tax revenue and increased Social Security payments, is at least partly responsible for reduced public sector capital formation and reduced spending on nondefense research and development. These two negative effects on growth offset some of the potential gains from work and investment incentives.

The Reagan supply side program was often criticized on distributional grounds. Opponents argued that the package of tax cuts and incentives was "welfare for the rich," who received the biggest tax cuts and benefited the most from saving and investment incentives. Supply siders countered that the rich were paying the most to begin with! In addition, as a group they tend to include the most productive workers (measured by their high salaries) and the individuals most willing and able to save and invest. Thus, any program aimed at encouraging work effort, saving, and investment has to focus on incentives for individuals with higher incomes. But, the defenders argued, the resulting economic growth, lower inflation rates, and higher productivity will eventually benefit everyone.

IS INDUSTRIAL POLICY THE ANSWER?

Industrial policy
A growth strategy consisting of government programs to identify and encourage promising industries and to ease the decline of old industries.

Supply side economics was a politically conservative growth strategy, relying on private market forces. In the last few years, a competing growth strategy has been proposed. This politically liberal strategy, known as **industrial policy**, calls for government to identify and encourage promising industries and to cushion the decline of old industries. Japan has often been cited as an example of the successful use of industrial policy. European countries also pursue similar strategies, but generally less successfully than Japan, because they tend to concentrate on protecting declining industries.

The tools of industrial policy include subsidies, tax incentives, government-sponsored research and development, low-interest loans, and other devices designed to promote a particular industry or group of industries. Often restrictions on imports or promotion of exports is part of the policy. One goal is to identify promising industries and help them to develop to the point where they can continue to grow and prosper on their own. In other cases, industrial policy is a way to avoid the pain of structural change in declining industries by propping them up and helping them to survive. Industrial policy may also attempt to ease the transition of labor and capital out of declining industries and into other areas with more promising futures.

The United States already has an industrial policy of sorts, although it is not deliberate and coordinated. Existing tax, subsidy, and regulatory policies, as well as government spending for research and training programs, favor certain industries at the expense of others. Concentration of research in agriculture, de-

GLOBAL OUTLOOK: INDUSTRIAL POLICY IN EUROPE AND JAPAN

Japan and the European Community (EC) offer good examples of two very different approaches to industrial policy. Japan pursues a more positive policy of identifying and promoting industries that seem to have growth potential. Since Japan had the best record of economic growth of any industrial country from World War II until very recently, other countries have shown much interest in its policies. As a general rule, the nations of the EC have pursued a more negative approach. This approach consists of protecting and supporting declining industries, trying to get them back to a competitive level.

The key to Japan's program has been the Ministry of Trade and Industry (MITI), which selects the industries to assist. Methods used in the 1950s and 1960s included organizing cartels, providing loans at low interest rates to targeted industries, and controlling imports. In the 1970s and 1980s, the government did offer some aid to declining industries in the form of tax breaks and loan guarantees. However, overall industrial policy in Japan has been directed much more at supporting promising industries through accelerated depreciation allowances, tax benefits, research support, and loans. The U.S. government usually makes such benefits available to all firms, but Japan is more selective in deciding which industries to favor. Critics have argued, however, that the MITI is not always successful in identifying which industries to promote. It has backed some losers and missed some potential winners, such as the auto industry. Although the Japanese strategy is mostly positive, selected industries, such as agriculture, are heavily protected.

The EC's primary strategy has been to slow structural changes that cause losses and unemployment in declining industries. Low-interest loans and import restrictions play a key role. Agriculture has benefited from subsidies and import controls, despite its comparative disadvantage. Other declining industries that have been singled out for special treatment are shipbuilding, steel, textiles, and footwear. One exception to the EC pattern has been Italy, which has relied heavily on antitrust policy, deregulation, and reducing the size of the public sector in order to make its industries more competitive within as well as outside the EC. At the same time, Italy is promoting small and medium-sized industries with technical assistance and low-cost loans in order to enable them to compete with larger firms in both Italy and the EC.[a] Italy's strategy, intended to position Italian industry to compete when the EC becomes a single integrated market after 1992, is more forward-looking than those of some of its neighbors. It will be difficult to support, subsidize, and protect specific industries against competition within a unified twelve-nation market with uniform product standards, no trade barriers, and a free flow of goods and productive resources.

American policy makers interested in industrial policy have been attracted to the Japanese model because of Japan's high growth rate over three decades. However, most of the policy proposals as well as actual practice in the United States seem to more closely resemble the EC model. They have emphasized protection from foreign competition and focused on rebuilding declining industries rather than developing promising new ones.

a. "Italy's Industrial Policy Challenged by 1992," *The Wall Street Journal* (June 27, 1988): 15.

---

fense, and space programs favors industries in those areas and suppliers to those industries. The minimum wage, by *not* favoring industries that use large amounts of unskilled labor, has tipped the balance in favor of industries using more capital and/or skilled labor. The Investment Tax Credit and accelerated depreciation, until modified in 1986, favored capital-intensive industries.[16] The list is endless. The point is that every nation has an industrial policy. The real question is whether it is pursued as a deliberate strategy and the results are evaluated to see if the industries the nation wishes to help are indeed the ones benefiting.

16. The results of the Investment Tax Credit are mixed; they tend to favor certain industries on the basis of capital intensity rather than promise of success. For an evaluation of the ITC, see Jane G. Gravelle, "What Can Private Investment Incentives Accomplish? The Case of the Investment Tax Credit," *National Tax Journal* (September 1993): 275–290.

The foremost advocate of industrial policy in the United States has been Harvard political economist (and now Secretary of Labor) Robert Reich, who laid out such a strategy for the United States in his 1983 book, *The Next American Frontier*. Among his recommendations were replacing the income tax with an expenditure tax (to encourage saving), increased federal spending for research and science training, tax incentives for human capital investments, and aid to declining industries to encourage conversion to other areas.

Critics of industrial policy point out that it involves second-guessing the market. The government, rather than the market, is selecting the industries to develop, using its judgment instead of the judgment of consumers, entrepreneurs, and owners of productive resources. In addition, industrial policy creates a field day for lobbyists and special-interest groups trying to make a case that their industry is most deserving of any special benefits.

Consider again...*The American economy is many things to many people, but for most of those over eighteen and under sixty-five, it is first and foremost a job-creating machine. The experience of the late 1980s and early 1990s was very discouraging, not only for new high school and college graduates, but for older workers displaced by downsizing (especially middle managers), blue-collar workers, and unskilled workers. The prospects for the rest of the decade are generally somewhat brighter, although there will be regions of slow growth, particularly those that face closure of defense plants and military installations.*

Brighter prospects come not only from demand factors, like growth in Latin America, recovery in Europe, a backlog of demand for autos and appliances, and low interest rates, but also some long-term supply factors. The labor force is getting more experienced. The productivity payoff from the investment in information technology is being realized. The savings rate is picking up after a decade of abnormally low saving. There is a shift in R&D spending underway from military to civilian uses that should pay off in new products. Companies that went through the trauma of mergers, acquisitions, and bankruptcies in the 1980s are now leaner, more efficient, and ready to invest and grow. Those new workers who have studied the market and matched their skills to emerging job opportunities should be poised to succeed.

SUMMARY

1. Monetary and fiscal policies to stimulate demand can be considered growth strategies because they attempt to increase output by ensuring that what is produced will be sold. Such strategies increase demand in the face of an upward-sloping short-run aggregate supply curve, and will increase both output and the price level.

2. The slope of the aggregate supply curve and the length of the time period that separates the short run from the long run has important implications for the effects of a change in aggregate demand on prices, output, and employment. If the aggregate supply curve is vertical, at least in the long run, and the short run is relatively brief, demand management policies will have little impact on economic growth. If the aggregate supply curve has a flatter slope in the short run and the short run is a fairly long period of calendar time, demand management policies will have more effect on growth of GDP.

3. The aggregate supply curve can be shifted by changes in the quantity and quality of resources available or by changes in technology. Increases in capital, including human capital and improvements in technology, in-

crease worker productivity. Productivity growth in industrial countries has been slower in recent decades than in earlier periods.
4. Supply side economics is a group of policies intended to shift the aggregate supply curve to the right. These policies include work incentives, saving and investment incentives, and deregulation. The Reagan administration implemented a supply side program in the 1980s. These policies had some modest effects on work effort but little impact on investment and saving, and are partly responsible for the growth of the deficit.
5. Industrial policy, like supply side policies, emphasizes tax and production incentives but emphasizes promoting and encouraging a specific industry or a group of industries.

NEW TERMS

demand-based growth strategies
real business cycle
savings rate
innovation
productivity
supply side economics
tax wedge
industrial policy

QUESTIONS: REVIEW, APPLICATIONS, AND POLICY

REVIEW

1. How are demand-based growth strategies different from supply-based growth strategies?
2. What is industrial policy? How is industrial policy different from supply side economics?
3. What are some of the drawbacks to industrial policy?
4. Does business investment shift aggregate supply or aggregate demand? How do you think increased business investment will affect prices and real output?
5. Why have natural resources not been a serious constraint on economic growth?

APPLICATIONS

6. How would each of the following affect measured productivity?
   a. new and better capital equipment for many workers
   b. a sharp rise in the labor force participation rate
   c. higher prices for natural resources in general
7. What are some of the factors that can increase labor productivity?
8. Marilyn Karcher is retired and receiving Social Security benefits, but she is considering working part-time. If she works part-time, she will pay about 15 percent of her earnings in federal income tax, 4 percent in state income tax, and 7.3 percent in Social Security tax. What is her marginal tax rate on earnings? If she works twenty hours a week, she will earn a gross income of $100. What is her net income and her net hourly wage? Should she take the job?
9. Robert Stewart is trying to decide whether to work on Saturday for three hours at an hourly rate of $20 or to spend the three hours cleaning his garage. He can hire two neighborhood boys to clean the garage, but they charge $35. What should he do if his combined tax rate (federal income tax, state income tax, and Social Security tax) on the additional income totals 30 percent? What if the combined tax rate totals 50 percent?

POLICY

10. How can a tax cut be both a demand side (Keynesian) and a supply side policy? Does it make any difference what kinds of taxes are cut?
11. The United States has had an extensive, federally funded program of research and technical assistance to agriculture through the Cooperative Extension Service and the Agricultural Experiment Stations located in each state's land grant universities. Is this industrial policy? Do you think it was successful?
12. Were supply side policies successful in the 1980s? Why or why not?

SUGGESTIONS FOR FURTHER READING

Blinder, Alan S. (ed.). *Paying for Productivity: A Look at the Evidence.* Washington DC: Brookings Institution, 1990. Examines the potential for increasing workers' productivity through various types of pay incentives.

Council of Economic Advisers. *The Economic Report of the President.* Washington DC: U.S. Government Printing Office, annual. Policies to promote growth are always emphasized. The 1993 edition (the final one from the Bush administration) and the 1994 edition (the first from the Clinton administration) offer two moderately different perspectives on growth policy.

"The Great Refrigerator Race," *Business Week* (July 15, 1993).

78–83. A well-told story of product research and development in a competitive environment.

Thurow, Lester. *Head to Head: The Coming Economic Battle Among Japan, Europe, and America.* New York: Time Warner Books, 1992. The most recent of Thurow's many books for a popular audience looks at strategies (including industrial policy) to strengthen the American economy in an increasingly competitive global environment, emphasizing research and development, infrastructure, and worker skills.

CHAPTER 17
THE CHALLENGE OF ECONOMIC DEVELOPMENT

Consider this...*Argentina was once one of the richest countries in the world. Until 1989, however, it offered one of the twentieth-century's most visible examples of negative development. In 1900, New Zealand and Argentina, with growth fueled in part by agricultural exports to Europe, had the two highest GDPs in the world. Wage rates in Argentina in 1910 were 25 percent higher than in Paris and 80 percent higher than in Marseilles. Europeans were migrating to Argentina in large numbers. From 1864 to 1914, Argentina's economy grew by an average rate of 5 percent per year, an impressive achievement. At the turn of the century, the Argentine rancher played much the same role in French plays as Texas oil tycoon J.R. Ewing did in the TV series* Dallas. *Between 1965 and 1987, Argentina's real per capita GDP did not grow at all. By 1987, Argentina's per capita GDP was $2,767, and New Zealand's was $10,000. New Zealand was classed as a high-income country, Argentina an upper middle-income country. Only in the last few years has Argentina reversed its economic decline of almost a century.*

At different times in history, Egypt, Rome (Italy), Greece, Ethiopia (home of the Queen of Sheba), and Babylonia (now Iraq) were highly developed by the standards of their time. All are relatively poor today. Other countries that were poor in the past, like Taiwan, Thailand, and Mexico, are now prospering. Is there some explanation of why certain countries prosper while others decline? This chapter attempts to unravel the secrets to success in the economic sphere for those countries classified as "Third World," less developed, or developing nations.

LEARNING OBJECTIVES
1. Describe the distinctive characteristics of less developed countries.
2. Analyze the role of population growth and lack of investment in human capital in creating a vicious circle of poverty.
3. Explain the following theories and strategies for economic development: classical laissez-faire, Rostow's stages of growth, big push versus leading sectors, and export promotion versus import substitution.
4. Summarize the opposing views on the role of the national government in promoting economic development.
5. Discuss the role of the developed countries in promoting and encouraging development through foreign aid, the World Bank, the New International Economic Order, and multinational corporations.

CHARACTERISTICS OF LESS DEVELOPED COUNTRIES

Growth is a matter of concern for developed, industrial countries like the United States. However, it is closer to a life-or-death matter for many less developed countries (sometimes referred to as LDCs). The problems facing these countries encompass the whole operation of the economy. The term *economic*

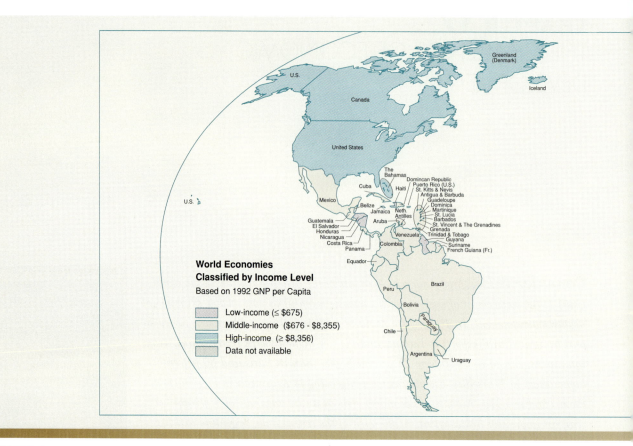

FIGURE 1

DISTRIBUTION OF COUNTRIES BY INCOME LEVELS

This map shows the world's nations divided into three economic groups based on income levels. Low-income economies have per capita incomes below $370. Lower middle-income countries range from $370 to $600, and upper middle-income from $600 to $2,400 in per capita income. High-income countries have per capita incomes of $7,000 and above.

Source: *World Development Report 1993* (New York: Oxford University Press, 1993). Copyright © 1993 by the International Bank for Reconstruction and Development/The World Bank.

growth used in Chapter 16 is too narrow to describe the goal of most of the poorer nations of the world. Economic development is a total process of transformation. It means not only raising current standards of living but also building a solid foundation of human and physical capital, technology, infrastructure, and economic institutions that will support continued improvement in the future.

It is easy to blame the poor countries themselves for their failure to attain a high standard of living, or to blame the rich for the problems of the poor. Here is a summary of both views from one development economist:

One says that we are so rich and they so poor because we are so good and they so bad; that is, we are hardworking, knowledgeable, educated, well-governed, efficacious, and productive, and they are the reverse. The other says that we are so rich and they so poor because we are so bad and they so good; we are greedy, ruthless, exploitative, aggressive, while they are weak, innocent, virtuous, abused, and vulnerable.[1]

Neither of these "good guys, bad guys" versions fully captures the extent to which relations between rich and poor countries affect the growth and devel-

1. David S. Landes, "Why Are We So Rich and They So Poor?" *American Economic Review Papers and Proceedings* (May 1990): 1.

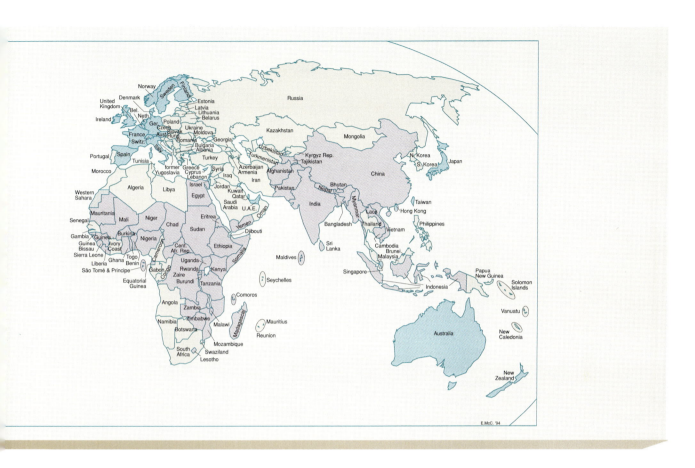

opment of both partners. This quotation does suggest, however, that the industrial world has a role to play in determining the future of the less developed countries.

LEVEL OF PER CAPITA INCOME

Although less developed countries are diverse, they have some important similarities. The most obvious characteristic of a less developed country is low per capita income. The World Bank considered any country with a GDP of less than $650 per capita (in 1991 U.S. dollars) as a low-income country. Forty countries were categorized as low-income in 1991. Another forty-three countries were classed as lower middle-income, with per capita GDP ranging from $650 (Bolivia) to $2,520 (Malaysia). Seventeen countries were classed as upper middle-income, with a range from $2,530 (Botswana) to $7,820 (Saudi Arabia). Only twenty-two countries made the list of high-income countries, including both industrial market economies and high-income oil exporters. Among this prosperous group, per capita incomes ranged from $11,120 (Ireland) to $33,610 (Switzerland). Figure 1 identifies the World Bank's low-, middle-, and high-income economies. Table 1 presents per capita GDP and growth rates of GDP for selected countries at various income levels.

TABLE 1 GDP AND GDP GROWTH, SELECTED COUNTRIES

	PER CAPITA GDP, 1991	AVERAGE ANNUAL GROWTH RATE OF PER CAPITA GDP, 1980–1991
LOW-INCOME COUNTRIES	350	3.9%
Ethiopia	120	–1.6
Bangladesh	220	1.9
Lesotho	580	–0.5
Indonesia	610	3.9
LOWER MIDDLE-INCOME COUNTRIES	1,590	0.3
Philippines	730	–1.2
Morocco	1,030	1.6
Paraguay	1,270	–0.8
Chile	2,160	1.6
Malaysia	2,520	2.9
UPPER MIDDLE-INCOME COUNTRIES	3,530	0.6
South Africa	2,560	0.7
Venezuela	2,730	–1.3
Brazil	2,940	0.5
Portugal	5,930	3.1
Korea	6,330	8.7
HIGH-INCOME COUNTRIES	21,050	2.3
United Kingdom	16,550	2.6
France	20,380	1.8
Canada	20,440	2.0
United States	22,240	1.7
Japan	26,930	3.6

Source: *World Development Report, 1993* (New York: Oxford University Press, 1993). Copyright © 1993 by the International Bank for Reconstruction and Development/The World Bank.

Table 1 both exhibits and conceals a great deal of diversity. The high-income oil-exporting countries are subject to the fluctuations of the world oil market and must eventually find other economic activities to replace dwindling oil reserves. Oil is part of the story of Venezuela's declining per capita GDP. Although the table indicates that Bangladesh is very poor and its growth in per capita GDP has been slow because of a high birth rate, it has made progress in agricultural production. Bangladesh may have more hope of development than some of the poor and largely desert nations of sub-Saharan Africa. Mexico graduated from lower middle-income to upper middle-income in the last few years, partly as a result of good policy choices.

The figures in Table 1 must be used with caution. Per capita GDP is not very reliable for comparison purposes. The problems of accurately measuring income and production are even greater in less developed countries than in developed ones. Less developed countries cannot use sophisticated methods of gathering and processing data. In addition, a much larger share of output in these countries is produced outside the market. In rural areas especially, a family is likely to grow its own food, build its own house, and make its own clothes. This output is difficult to estimate and value at market prices.

Finally, a major problem is the use of exchange rates to convert figures into a common currency, the U.S. dollar. Fluctuations in the value of the dollar can create impressions of faster or slower growth than actually took place. The International Monetary Fund prepared revised estimates of per capita GDP using purchasing power comparisons rather than exchange rates to convert the figures into U.S. dollars. The results of that conversion offer some very different figures. China, whose per capita GDP is only $370 using market exchange rates, comes in as a middle-income country at $2,460 using the IMF's method. In general, the developing counties look a lot better on this method relative to the industrial countries.[2]

The spread in growth rates among the groups in the table is quite narrow. Compare the 2.3 percent per year for the high-income group to the 3.1 percent for the low-income group. However, this narrow spread in rates of growth does not imply that income gaps are closing. First, the averages conceal the fairly wide country-to-country variation within each group, including some rates that are negative. Second, starting from a lower base of per capita income, it is possible for one country to grow at a faster rate than another and still fall further behind in absolute dollars. If country A starts at $100 per capita and grows at 5 percent a year while country B starts at $1,000 and grows at 3 percent a year, at the end of ten years, country A will have a per capita income of $163, and country B will have a per capita income of $1,344. The gap between the two will have widened from $900 to $1,181.

Even very small differences in growth rates can matter a great deal. Consider the growth rate of 2.3 percent for the lower middle-income group versus 3.1 percent for the low-income group. A country starting out at a per capita income of $1,000 will see its income rise to $1,243 in ten years at a 2.3 percent growth rate. The same per capita income will rise to $1,450 in ten years at a growth rate of 3.1 percent.

Are income differences among countries growing or shrinking? Economist William Baumol looked at historical evidence on convergence of incomes among countries from 1870 to 1979. He found the highest convergence among the industrialized countries, with much less convergence between rich and poor countries. Other economists, however, have criticized his findings because the strong convergence of the later years covered in his study overstates the long-term trend.[3]

AGRICULTURE

Most less developed countries devote a large share of resources to agriculture. Some of this agriculture is large-scale and relatively modern, producing export

---

2. "Chinese Puzzles," *The Economist* (May 15, 1992).
3. William J. Baumol, "Productivity Growth, Convergence, and Welfare: What the Long Run Data Show," *American Economic Review* (December 1986): 1072–1085. See also J. Bradford DeLong, "Productivity Growth, Convergence, and Welfare: Comment," *American Economic Review* (December 1988): 1138–1154, for some reservations about whether Baumol's results really demonstrate convergence.

TABLE 2 ROLE OF AGRICULTURE AT VARIOUS LEVELS OF DEVELOPMENT

	SHARE OF GDP FROM AGRICULTURE, 1991	SHARE OF GDP FROM MERCHANDISE EXPORTS, 1991
Low-income countries	29%	20%
Lower middle-income countries	21	27
Upper middle-income countries	12	13
Industrialized countries	4	11

Source: Adapted from *World Development Report, 1993* (New York: Oxford University Press, 1993).

crops such as cocoa, coffee, and bananas. Most of it, however, is basically subsistence agriculture. Simple, labor-intensive technology is used to produce food for individual families rather than crops to be sold for cash. Rural overcrowding, small land holdings that preclude modern cultivation, and low agricultural yields per acre are typical. A dominant role for the agricultural sector is strongly linked to low levels of per capita income. In order to escape poverty, a country must have some resources left over after feeding itself, either directly (by producing enough food for home use and export) or indirectly (by exporting enough nonfood items to import needed foodstuffs).

Table 2 shows significant differences in the agricultural sector at various levels of development. In the low-income group, about one-third of GDP is derived from agriculture. In both low-income and lower middle-income countries, the agricultural sector is a major source of exports. In low-income countries, an average of 70 percent of the population is in agriculture, compared to 44 percent in middle-income countries and 7 percent in high-income countries. In the United States, only 2 percent of the labor force produces enough to feed the entire nation, with a surplus for export. In general, agriculture tends to be much more productive in upper middle-income and high-income countries. In those countries, agriculture is highly mechanized and a small part of the population produces an abundant harvest, including some for export. The table shows a consistent pattern of declining reliance on agriculture as a nation becomes wealthier.

As a producing sector, agriculture faces certain problems in both developed and less developed countries. Supply is unpredictable, depending on the weather. Demand is not very responsive to price changes. Thus, a bumper crop will lead to a big price drop. A poor harvest will command high prices, but high prices are little comfort to farmers with little or nothing to sell. These problems are more serious when agriculture is a large share of GDP. For this reason, reducing dependence on agriculture is a goal of every development program. Development of new high-yield dwarf varieties of rice and wheat in the 1970s, with the support of the Rockefeller Foundation, helped to make some developing countries more nearly self-sufficient in food and to increase their agricultural productivity. However, the new varieties also had drawbacks, including lower resistance to pests and greater need for fertilizer, irrigation, and use of machinery.

CLIMATE

Almost all the poorest countries are in tropical climates. Conversely, all industrialized countries are in temperate climates. This relationship between climate and development is so strong that it seems unlikely to be a coincidence. In fact, the gap between levels of development between the regions is sometimes referred to by development economists as the "north-south problem." Some development economists have suggested that warmer climates produce lower human effort, more diseases, and unfavorable agricultural conditions. There is no winter to wipe out large numbers of disease-bearing pests and parasites. In addition, many tropical countries are largely jungle or desert, neither of which is hospitable to agriculture.

DUALISM

Almost all less developed countries are really two societies in the same country—one modern, urban, and market-oriented and the other made up of rural peasants who are illiterate, largely employed in agriculture, and with very little of their economic activity passing through the market. This coexistence is called **dualism**.

Cities in less developed countries contain many poor people, but also have modern transportation and plumbing, manufacturing and service jobs, culture, a concentration of educated people, and a modern market economy. Birth rates are lower and women are more likely to have access to education and market opportunities. Rural areas, in contrast, tend to maintain traditional lifestyles with centuries-old farming methods, early marriage with many children, and much home production with few market transactions. Most citizens in rural areas live in poverty or near poverty, generating little saving and investment and little interest in innovation.

Dualism can be a major handicap to development. The urban population in a dual economy is too small to provide a market for manufacturing and services or to generate enough saving and investment in human and physical capital. Dualism also complicates the challenge of development, because growth is not enough; it must also include increases in well-being for the rural as well as the urban poor.

Dualism
The coexistence of a modern, urban, market-oriented society and a rural, agriculture-based, traditional peasant society, characteristic of many less developed countries.

POVERTY AND INEQUALITY

Like developed countries, the distribution of income in developing countries shows great inequality. Typically there are greater extremes of wealth and poverty in LDCs, with a small wealthy elite, a large mass of poor people in both urban and rural areas, and a very small middle class. This distribution of income makes it difficult to save and invest, because the wealthy group is so small and most of the rest of the population is at a subsistence level of income.

The World Bank has established a poverty line of $US370 (1985 dollars) as the threshold for absolute poverty. This figure was arrived at from studies of thirty-one countries which include 80 percent of the population of the developing world, but it represents a much lower standard of poverty than is used in industrial countries. Even so, almost one-third of the population of developing countries are classed as poor. Other measures such as illiteracy and infant mortality suggest that the poor make up about 40 to 60 percent of the population in the developing world.

In recent years, a number of developing countries have succeeded in reducing poverty, some primarily through economic growth, others by investing in health and education for the poor, or by guaranteeing their access to basic services, or some combination of these strategies.[4] Economic growth does not automatically translate into poverty reduction. Some countries that have had high rates of economic growth, such as Brazil and Pakistan, have not improved such indicators as health and educational attainment. Growth can and does generate resources with which to address some of the problems of the poor. On the other hand, there are countries with low incomes and slow growth, such as Sri Lanka, which have made significant gains in life expectancy, infant mortality, and literacy. Poverty programs can be pro-growth if they involve investing in the health and skills of the poor, anti-growth if they increase dependency and discourage work. Ideally, growth and reduction in poverty will go hand in hand, but the combination is not automatic. Experience at the World Bank indicates that providing basic social services, specifically in health and education, has been the most effective way to work toward both growth and poverty relief.[5]

DEMOGRAPHICS

One striking difference between less developed and more developed countries is in demographics—the birth rate, the population growth rate, and the age distribution of the population. Table 3 shows some important differences in population characteristics between less developed and more developed countries.

The **crude birth rate** is the number of births per thousand of population. As Table 3 shows, there is a large difference in the crude birth rates of poor and industrialized countries. A high birth rate means a high **dependency ratio**, or the percentage of the population not of working age (under fifteen or over sixty-four). Low-income countries have much higher dependency ratios. Forty percent of the population of low-income countries is not of working age, compared to less than 33 percent in the industrial economies. A high dependency ratio means that a smaller proportion of the population is available to engage in productive labor. More resources must be used to meet the needs of dependent persons (a few of them elderly, but mostly children) for food, clothing, shelter, medical care, and basic education. Those resources will not be available to promote economic development through building factories and power plants, providing worker training, and developing transportation systems.[6]

Why are birth rates so high? Women marry soon after puberty in many poor countries, because they have few economic alternatives to marriage. They bear children early because children, especially sons, are useful as labor and for old-age insurance.

People in poorer countries also die younger. A shorter life expectancy reflects poor health care, poor nutrition, and high infant mortality. A shorter life expectancy means that the productive work life of the average adult is not as

Crude birth rate
The number of births per thousand population.

Dependency ratio
The percentage of the population not of working age (under fifteen or over sixty-five).

---

4. Lyn Squire, "Fighting Poverty," *American Economic Review Papers and Proceedings* (May 1993): 377–382.
5. Ibid., 377–382.
6. Allen C. Kelley, "Economic Consequences of Population Changes in the Third World," *Journal of Economic Literature* (December 1988): 1685–1728.

TABLE 3 STRUCTURE OF POPULATION

	CRUDE BIRTH RATE, 1991	CRUDE DEATH RATE, 1990	AVG. ANNUAL POPULATION GROWTH RATE, 1980–1991	PERCENTAGE OF POPULATION AGED 0–14, 1991
	(PER 1,000 POPULATION)			
Low-income countries	30	10	2.0%	35.4%
Lower middle-income countries	28	8	1.8	35.4
Upper middle-income countries	21	8	1.5	33.5
Industrialized countries	13	9	0.6	19.7

Source: Adapted from *World Development Report, 1993* (New York: Oxford University Press, 1993).

long. The consequence of a short life expectancy and a high birth rate in less developed countries is a large number of children with relatively few adults to support them. A growing population with a high dependency ratio is a major barrier to achieving the goal of increasing output and raising the standard of living.

POPULATION, HUMAN CAPITAL, AND ECONOMIC DEVELOPMENT

In 1800, the estimated world population was about 1 billion. In 1990, it was 5.3 billion. By the year 2000, it will have swelled to 6 billion. By 2050, there could be 10 billion citizens on the planet. The world's population is growing by 250,000 people per day, or 90 million people per year. The good news is that the growth rate is slowing down. The key to controlling population growth is the total fertility rate (TFR), or the number of children a woman will bear during her childbearing years. A TFR of 2.1 keeps population constant. In 1960–1965, the world TFR was 5.0. By 1990, it had fallen to 3.3—only 1.9 in the industrial countries. Even in LDCs, there has been some progress in reducing fertility rates.

The problem for development is that most of the projected growth will still occur in the less developed countries. Among countries with a population of 5 million or more, there are twenty-three countries with population growth rates of 3 percent or more per year. Only one (Israel) is classed as high-income, and most of Israel's population growth is due to immigration. Three more are upper middle income (Saudi Arabia, Libya, and Iraq), while the other nineteen are lower income or lower middle income. At the other extreme, there are twenty-four countries of 5 million or more population with growth rates ranging from negative to 1 percent a year. Among this group, fifteen are high-income (including the United States at 0.9 percent a year), 8 are upper middle-income, and only one (Hungary) is lower middle income. Population is growing fastest in those countries least able to provide their citizens with basic services and good opportunities.

CHANGING BIRTH RATES AND DEATH RATES

During the Industrial Revolution in Western Europe and the United States, populations grew rapidly but not at the explosive rates of today's less developed countries. As the standard of living began to rise during the Industrial Revolution, the birth rate increased, and death rates slowly began to decline. After incomes increased to higher levels, the birth rate also declined. Today, medical advances, inoculations, and many life-lengthening techniques have spread throughout the world, reducing death rates even in less developed countries. Those countries have high birth rates and declining death rates, resulting in an exploding population.

Birth rates didn't decline in the developed world until most countries had attained relatively high levels of per capita income. In most nations, death rates fell first as better health care, better nutrition, and higher standards of living lengthened life spans. After a time, birth rates fell. A nation that has bridged the developmental gap from falling death rates to falling birth rates, thus slowing population growth and reducing the dependency ratio, has made the demographic transition.

Recent health care advances have greatly lowered the death rate in most poorer countries, while it has remained almost constant in industrialized countries. The crude death rate fell from 1970 to 1991 in the low-income and lower middle-income countries: from 14 per 1,000 to 10 per 1,000 in low-income countries and from 12 to 8 in lower middle-income countries. The **crude death rate** is the number of deaths per thousand of population. The consequence of the declining death rate and the high and stable birth rate has been a population explosion in many less developed countries. This population growth means that these countries must grow rapidly in productive capacity just to stay *even* in per capita income.

Crude death rate
The number of deaths per thousand population.

COSTS AND BENEFITS OF POPULATION GROWTH

The effect of exploding population on per capita income is shown in Figure 2. The average annual growth rate of GDP is not that different in low-income, lower middle-income, upper middle-income, and high-income countries. But the picture is very different for growth in per capita GDP, also shown in Figure 2. The poorest countries have managed to stay ahead of population growth, largely because of a slowdown in birth rates in China and India. (Outside of those two countries, the population growth rate for the low-income countries has been 2.4 percent.) High rates of population growth have meant that both groups of middle-income countries have had slower than average growth rates of per capita GDP.

Most economists consider a large number of dependent children as a drag on economic development. Population growth due to high birth rates may, however, have positive consequences. A larger population can result in more specialization and economies of scale. Julian Simon has been one of the few voices in favor of population growth as a development strategy. In his book, *The Ultimate Resource,* Simon argues that the negative aspects of growth and develop-

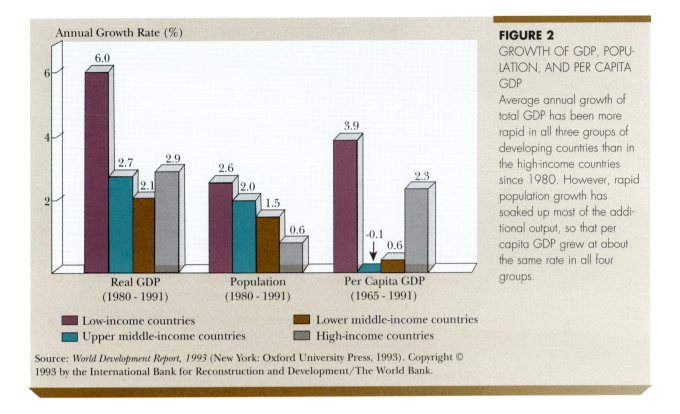

FIGURE 2
GROWTH OF GDP, POPULATION, AND PER CAPITA GDP
Average annual growth of total GDP has been more rapid in all three groups of developing countries than in the high-income countries since 1980. However, rapid population growth has soaked up most of the additional output, so that per capita GDP grew at about the same rate in all four groups.

ment—pressure on limited food supplies, land, and energy, slow growth of per capita income, and increasing pollution—are vastly overstated. An additional person is a productive resource who will ultimately add more to production than society had to invest in his or her care, feeding, and education up to maturity.[7]

Less developed countries are feeling pressure from both within and abroad to try to reduce their birth rates. In the present developed countries, a demographic transition occurred naturally. Most efforts to deliberately encourage or even enforce population control have occurred in communist countries, although India has made some strong efforts toward voluntary sterilization and birth control. In China, the Communist authorities have instituted a get-tough campaign that denies many state-supplied benefits to couples with more than one child. This "planned" approach has slowed China's population growth rate to 1.3 percent. It has had many unintended side effects, however, including claims of female infanticide and a very high number of late-term abortions.

INVESTMENT IN HUMAN CAPITAL

As a productive resource, population requires investment in health, education, and training. Most low-income countries invest very little in human capital, or the health, education, and skills of their citizens. One reason why low-income

---

7. Julian Simon, *The Ultimate Resource* (Princeton NJ: Princeton University Press, 1981).

TABLE 4 INVESTMENT IN HUMAN CAPITAL BY LEVELS OF INCOME

	NUMBER OF PEOPLE PER PHYSICIAN, 1990	SCHOOL ENROLLMENT RATE, 1990*		
		PRIMARY	SECONDARY	HIGHER EDUCATION
Low-income countries	6,760	105%	41%	4%
Lower middle-income countries	2,060	100	172	16
Upper middle-income countries	640	106	54	17
High-income countries	420	104	93	33

Source: Adapted from *World Development Report, 1993* (New York: Oxford University Press, 1993).
*For countries with universal primary education, the gross enrollment ratios exceed 100 percent, since some pupils are below or above the official primary school age.

Vicious circle of poverty A trap in which many low-income countries are caught, in which there is little investment because of a low level of income, and a low level of income because of lack of investment.

countries invest little in human capital is that they have little to invest. One reason they have little to invest is that they have had such low levels of investment in human and other kinds of capital in the past. This trap is called the **vicious circle of poverty**—little investment because there is a low level of income, and a low level of income because there has been little investment.

Table 4 gives some indicators of the levels of investment in human capital at different levels of development. Investment in health care is reflected in the number of people per physician. There are many more persons per physician in less developed countries than in high-income countries. Another important area of investment is in education, which is measured in Table 4 by school enrollment data. Low school enrollments in the low-income countries reflect a need for everyone to work to support the family in a subsistence economy. Education is a luxury that the family can rarely afford, especially for more than one child. Girls are less likely than boys to be enrolled in school. The effect of low school attendance is an uneducated and therefore less productive work force.

KEY IDEAS

CHARACTERISTICS OF LESS DEVELOPED COUNTRIES
- Low levels of per capita GDP
- Larger role for agriculture
- Tropical climate
- Rapid population growth
- Dualism
- Poverty/inequality
- Lower levels of educational enrollment/attainment

GLOBAL OUTLOOK: A DEVELOPMENT SUCCESS STORY—THE NEW ASIAN (AND LATIN AMERICAN) TIGERS

The most remarkable story in economic development in recent decades is a group of Asian countries that have been reclassified from less developed countries to newly industrializing countries (NICs). These four countries—Hong Kong, Taiwan, South Korea, and Singapore—have been nicknamed "The Asian Tigers." They have grown rapidly in the last twenty years in a climate of private enterprise, hard work, minimal regulation, and open trade. Two more Asian countries, Thailand and Indonesia, appear to be repeating the success of the other four.

All of these nations have seen rapid growth of both GDP and exports with low inflation rates and high employment. There is a consistent pattern of high levels of saving and investment relative to GDP and a strong emphasis on development of exports and export markets. In some ways, all four have followed the Japanese model. In other ways, each of them is unique. What they have in common are average growth rates from 1981 to 1988 ranging from 5.4 to 9.9 percent, per capita GDPs ranging from $3,600 (South Korea) to $9,070 (Singapore), and bright prospects for the future. All of them have deliberately embarked on a strategy involving a strong private sector and a government that plays a supporting rather than directing role in the growth process.

Even as attention was focused on success in Asia, the scene has shifted to Latin America, with three emerging success stories—Mexico, Brazil, and Argentina. Like the Asian Tigers, these countries have strengthened their private sectors and reduced the heavy role of government in the development process. They have also succeeded at taming inflation, a chronic problem in this region of the world. Mexico's turnaround was typical of the three. Change in Mexico was precipitated by a 1982 debt crisis that followed a decade of heavy deficit spending and four decades of protectionism and growth of large, state-owned enterprises. An eight-year adjustment program included renegotiation of the debt, reducing the number of state enterprises from 1,155 to less than 300, opening markets to foreign trade, encouraging competition, and trimming the public sector deficit. The government continues to play an important, if smaller, role in the Mexican economy in providing infrastructure (roads, water supply, and sewers) and in providing basic social services to the poor (education, health care, and poverty relief).[a]

These experiences suggest a need to carefully rethink the role of government in the development process. Both sets of development success stories make a powerful case for a market-oriented approach to development. At the same time, the government as a responsible manager of its own fiscal and monetary affairs and a supporting partner with appropriate trade and competition policies, protection for the poor, investment in human capital, and provision of infrastructure can provide a strong and essential ingredient to economic progress.

a. Benedicte Larre, "Mexico," *OECD Observer* (October/November 1992): 39–42.

THEORIES AND STRATEGIES OF ECONOMIC DEVELOPMENT

The basic elements of the development process are the same as those outlined in Chapter 16 for economic growth in developed countries. The production possibilities curve and the aggregate supply curve must both be shifted to the right. To do that, either existing resources must be used more effectively or additional resources must be created or acquired. Technology and cultural change are the keys to better resource use. Additional resources can come from within (through sacrificing consumption today to invest in physical and human capital for tomorrow) or from other countries.

CLASSICAL ECONOMICS AND ECONOMIC DEVELOPMENT

The original theorist of economic development was also the person who is regarded as the founder of market economics. The complete title of Adam Smith's *Wealth of Nations* (1776) was *An Inquiry into the Nature and Causes of the Wealth of Nations*. In that book, Smith set forth the classical principles of economic development. These principles rested on a laissez-faire governmental policy of nonintervention toward private industry and commerce. The division of labor and the resulting increase in productivity were limited only by the size of the market. Smith advocated free trade as a way to promote this division of labor by exploiting each nation's comparative advantage in production.

Some of Smith's successors in the classical tradition were less optimistic about the development process. David Ricardo developed the theory of diminishing marginal productivity. This theory suggested that as an economy grew, additional resources would add less and less to total output. Thomas Robert Malthus is best known for his dismal predictions about the race between population and the food supply. He saw population growth as the surest way to slow down or even reverse the growth of per capita output and the rise in the standard of living.

STAGES OF ECONOMIC GROWTH?

W. W. Rostow, in a book entitled *Stages of Economic Growth*, drew on the experience of modern industrial countries to identify five stages of economic growth.[8] The first stage is the traditional society, in which economic decisions are made on the basis of custom and obligation. The second stage develops the preconditions for takeoff. In this stage, cultural barriers to development are overcome, advances in agriculture take place, and an entrepreneurial class of risk takers begins to emerge. Takeoff is the third stage, during which there is a large increase in the rate of saving. Increased saving finances capital investment in the leading sectors (the industries that are developing most quickly). The leading sectors grow rapidly, and their growth pulls other sectors along. The takeoff is, of course, the key to emerging as an industrialized country. The Industrial Revolution in Western Europe and the United States marked the takeoff in these countries.

The final two stages are the drive to maturity and high mass consumption. During the drive to maturity, lagging sectors of the economy catch up to the leading sectors. The takeoff is consolidated into sustained growth. The fifth stage, high mass consumption, describes the present level of development in the United States and Western Europe. In this stage, the economy settles into a steady pace of growth that provides a high level of consumption for most members of the society. Rostow's theory of stages implies that all countries follow a (roughly) similar path to development.

Although the stages might describe the development process of the present industrialized nations, critics point out that the present less developed countries will not necessarily follow the same sequence. Economist Simon Kuznets, a Nobel Prize winner, noted many differences between conditions in today's less

---

8. W. W. Rostow, *Stages of Economic Growth*, 2e. (New York: Cambridge University Press, 1971).

developed countries and the preindustrial phase of today's developed countries.[9] Among the most important of these differences is agricultural production. Per capita agricultural output in today's less developed countries is about one-fourth the level it was in preindustrial stages of the present developed countries. Another significant difference is that population is still growing much more rapidly in less developed countries than it was in today's developed countries at a similar stage in their development. Social and political obstacles are also more formidable in many less developed countries. The dualism in the typical less developed country makes it very different from seventeenth-century England, where the level of technological development was similar in all sectors of the economy.

BIG PUSH OR LEADING SECTORS?

Development economists in the field are less interested in broad theories than in workable strategies. One specific approach is the **big push strategy**. It calls for a major thrust on all fronts in the economy by government or by private enterprise with the government's support. This strategy is based on the classical notion that growth in the output of an industry is limited by the extent of the market. At low levels of economic development, it is futile for any one industry to expand its output to a larger scale. It would be unable to sell its added product. But if all industries expand in a big push, the inputs needed for the production of one commodity become the demands for other industries' output. Also, the incomes generated will create a large demand for the final products. A big push must be orchestrated by the government, its proponents argue, because no single entrepreneur or group of entrepreneurs has the incentive to expand production unless there is expansion in other industries at the same time. However, there is much room for private sector involvement in a big push strategy, both from domestic firms and foreign multinationals.

Big push strategy
A development strategy calling for a major thrust on all fronts with government leadership and public-private partnership.

Albert O. Hirschman, a development economist with a great deal of field experience, takes a different tack from the big push strategy.[10] Hirschman supports a **leading sectors strategy** for economic growth. He argues that a country should concentrate on developing successful sectors that will then influence other sectors in the chain of production through backward and forward linkages.

For example, if there is a successful sardine fishing industry, it could be linked forward to a canning operation, which in turn could be linked forward to a packing and shipping industry. Backward linkages could develop effective demand for cans and shipping cartons, stimulating a mining industry and a paper industry. In this view, if the government is to be involved in the development process, it should concentrate its efforts on encouraging those sectors or industries that maximize the number of potential linkages. Private entrepreneurs would then take over in response to the demand created through the linkages. The role of the government would be limited. The market would play the primary role in allocating productive resources.

Leading sectors strategy
A development strategy calling for concentration on a few promising sectors, which will then pull along the other sectors in the development process.

---

9. Simon Kuznets, *Economic Growth and Structure* (New York: W. W. Norton, 1965).
10. Albert O. Hirschman, *The Strategy of Economic Development* (New Haven CT: Yale University Press, 1958).

IMPORT SUBSTITUTION OR EXPORT PROMOTION?

Import substitution
A development strategy that concentrates on becoming self-sufficient by replacing imported goods with domestic production.

Export promotion
A development strategy that calls for developing export industries in order to earn foreign exchange to purchase consumer goods, capital equipment, raw material, and food from abroad.

Economist Anne Krueger has examined two alternative trade strategies in relation to development. **Import substitution** is a strategy of becoming more self-sufficient and less dependent on other countries by developing domestic industries to produce goods that had previously been imported. **Export promotion** calls for developing export industries in order to earn foreign exchange to purchase consumer goods, capital equipment, raw material, and food from abroad. Both strategies have been used with mixed success, and both strategies have drawbacks. These strategies are largely mutually exclusive, since one concentrates on developing production for domestic buyers, while the other focuses on products to be sold abroad in order to earn the foreign exchange with which to import goods for domestic consumers.

IMPORT SUBSTITUTION. Import substitution, or self-sufficiency, has been a productive development strategy in a few countries, notably Japan. Import substitution usually requires high trade barriers in order to protect fledgling domestic industries from foreign competition until they get established. It is a strategy that requires governments to select industries to develop, protect, and subsidize.

The most successful form of import substitution for many LDCs has been improving domestic agriculture to reduce dependence on imported food. The result of this successful strategy has been, unfortunately, hard times for farmers in Canada, the United States, and Western Europe, which have seen shrinking markets for grains and other foodstuffs as countries like Bangladesh have become nearly self-sufficient.

Other strategies of import substitution have been less successful. For decades, developing countries have poured resources into ill-considered developments like steel factories in India and automobile production in Brazil. The economic rationale for this strategy is the hope that the linkages from a domestic steel or auto industry would produce other industrial development. In practice, import substitution has typically resulted in an inefficient domestic industry that requires continued government subsidies and continued protection from more efficient competitors abroad.

EXPORT PROMOTION. An export-oriented strategy, in contrast, calls for free and open trade, although government may still play a useful role in getting those industries started. This strategy develops those industries in which the country has a comparative advantage or can develop one. For example, Chile built on its copper resources to develop copper refining and manufacturing industries with various incentives for copper-based industries as well as penalties for the export of unprocessed copper. The advantage of export promotion over import substitution is that the country is developing and encouraging its most promising industries, those with the greatest potential for growth. Often export industries also offer linkages to other types of industries.

The biggest drawback to export promotion as a development strategy is that the current comparative advantage of many LDCs lies in the production of primary products—food, timber, and raw materials. These industries offer low wages, unstable world prices, and little opportunity to develop high-skill, high-wage jobs that have been associated with growth in the industrial countries.

THE ROLE OF GOVERNMENT

The choice of strategies and their implementation implies conscious choices by governments. Yet the United States and other industrial nations have been moving in a direction of less government involvement in economic activity. The role of government in economic development is a challenging issue.

CAN DEMOCRATIC GOVERNMENTS SUCCEED?

The debate over democracy and growth has concerned industrial and developing countries alike. A recent article in *Business Week* poses the question "Is Democracy Bad for Growth?"[11] This article points out that some of the more successful cases of development have occurred under political systems that are dictatorial, dominated by a single party, or in other ways not fully democratic. Among rapidly growing countries, China, South Korea, Singapore, and Chile all have had little democracy, while Mexico has had four decades of one-party rule. In contrast, industrial democracies have not fared as well, with Spain, Greece, Portugal, and Italy (all with unstable democratic coalition governments) ranking high on inflation and unemployment for the last decade.

Business Week cites the work of Canadian economist John F. Helliwell, who studied results for nearly 100 nations from 1960 and 1985 and concluded that authoritarian governments that guarantee private property rights can produce good growth performance. The article also notes, however, that growth tends to produce democracy as economic success leads to demands for greater political freedom.

Jagdish Bhagwati, a noted development economist, suggests the reason why it may be more difficult to develop under democratic conditions:

> *No policy of economic development can be carried out unless the government has the capacity to adhere to it. . . . Quite often, however, democratic governments lose equanimity and determination in the face of opposition. . . . This is the dilemma of most democratic governments. It is here that socialist countries . . . have an immense advantage: their totalitarian structure shields the government from the rigorous and reactionary judgments of the electorate. Another advantage of the socialist countries is their passionate conviction and dedication to the objective of economic growth—which contrasts visibly with the halting and hesitant beliefs and actions of most democracies. The firm and purposive sense of direction . . . is in pointed contrast to the extensive revisions and changes in policies and methods which are prompted by minor setbacks in most democratic governments and which produce a sense of drift and helplessness. The political economy of development appears to pose a cruel choice between rapid (self-sustained) expansion and democratic processes.*[12]

A contrary finding comes from a 1988 study by Gerald Scully exploring the role of the economic and political environment in development. Scully classified 115 economies on the basis of political rights, individual rights, and use of a free market. He found that those that most strongly emphasized political and individual rights and the use of markets had been growing at a rate 2.7 times as

---

11. (June 7, 1993): 84–88.
12. Jagdish Bhagwati, *The Economics of Underdeveloped Countries* (New York: McGraw-Hill, 1966): 203–204.

fast as those that did not.[13] Thus, he argues that the institutions of democratic capitalism can make a significant contribution to the development process.

LAISSEZ-FAIRE OR DIRIGISTE?

These two French expressions capture two opposing views of the role of government. Laissez-faire means let it be, while *dirigiste* means directing. Which role should government take in the development process? There is no clear-cut answer. Countries have succeeded or failed with democracy: most of the present high-income countries are democratic, but so is India, a spectacularly unsuccessful case of development. They have also succeeded or failed under totalitarian regimes: contrast South Korea and China with Uganda or Ethiopia. The key is not the political apparatus or the size of the public sector but what government does and does not do.

Most approaches to development are at neither the totalitarian nor the laissez-faire extreme. Government is usually expected to play some role. One important role it can play is to create a set of taxes and regulations that is favorable to development of private enterprise. Another important role for government is the development of human capital through health and education. Government also needs to provide infrastructure, such as roads, water systems, and airports. Finally, it is important for government not to become an obstacle to development by squandering scarce and valuable resources on political goals or as favors to special-interest groups.

Especially important roles of government in a market system are to define and protect property rights, and to encourage competition and discourage monopoly. The experience of developed, industrial nations offers evidence that private ownership of property and competition play important roles in economic development. Private property—the ability to buy and sell and exchange the products of one's labor—is an essential condition for individual incentives to work, save, invest, and take risks. When governments restrict property rights, they can reduce these work and investment incentives, slowing the economic growth process.

Governments influence the amount of competition that exists in both positive and negative ways. Government monopolies, or government-sponsored monopolies, can prevent competition from developing. Monopolies have less incentive to expand output, innovate, or take risks because there are no competitors nipping at their heels. Many African countries that were formerly under British rule inherited colonial policies that created government monopolies in many export industries, licensing of private sector producers, and state enterprises that spawned huge bureaucracies. With established public monopolies, or government-created private monopolies, it is difficult to create the kind of competitive environment in which economic growth is more likely to occur.

MACROECONOMIC MANAGEMENT

Regardless of how involved the government is in the development process, its macroeconomic management actions will have an important impact on devel-

---

13. Gerald W. Scully, "The Institutional Framework and Economic Development," *Journal of Political Economy*, 1988, 96(3): 652–662.

opment. Large fiscal deficits, heavy tax burdens, or monetary laxness will result in inflation and high interest rates. Monetary and fiscal mismanagement discourage investment, work effort, and enterprise. A stable economic environment, in which tax burdens are moderate and rewards to productive work are greater than rewards to lobbying and the political process, is an important component of a development program.

MILITARY SPENDING

In many less developed countries, a large share of public expenditure is devoted to military uses. Several African countries, including Ethiopia and the Sudan, have been fighting guerrilla wars for many years. Somalia became a battleground between competing warlords. Other ongoing battles are in Sri Lanka, the Philippines, and Central America. The Middle East is home to a number of middle-income countries that find it necessary to maintain a large military establishment for sporadic wars. Prior to the fall of communism, military spending also consumed a large share of GDP in Eastern Europe, ranging from 8.8 percent in former East Germany to 11.9 percent in Bulgaria.

According to the World Bank, world military expenditures in the 1980s accounted for about 5 percent of total world income. Developing countries spent $173 billion on defense in 1987, which accounted for 5.1 percent of GDP and 19.2 percent of central government budgets in those countries. Defense takes a much larger share of GDP in some countries. Pakistan, with a per capita GDP of only $380, spent 6.8 percent of GDP on defense in 1989. Yemen spends almost 10 percent. On the other hand, Costa Rica, which has attained exceptionally high levels of literacy and life expectancy compared to its Central American neighbors, has no standing army at all.

In addition to the domestic resources used, another problem created by defense spending in less developed countries is that much of that spending is for imported arms. These imports use scarce foreign exchange that could be used for industrial and agricultural development. Even if these countries do not actually go to war, their military spending is taking resources badly needed in other sectors. If military spending increases the likelihood of war, there is an additional potential loss of lives and infrastructure. On the positive side, the military often maintains domestic law and order, builds roads, and offers employment and training opportunities for poor youth. Since this issue has received limited attention from economists, there is really no clear evidence as to whether a high level of military spending helps or hinders development.[14]

HELP FROM OUTSIDE: DEVELOPMENT ASSISTANCE

An important resource for economic development in many countries is a flow of economic aid from governments and investments from companies in already developed countries. One element of the vicious circle of poverty is a low level of investment. It seems logical, then, that one way to break this circle would be for both the public and private sectors in less developed countries to borrow from the developed world.

14. Jurgen Brauer, "Perilous Information Gap: Third World Military Expenditures," *Challenge* (May–June 1991): 54–58.

Aid may come in the form of grants, loans, or technical assistance, or even in the form of foreign profit-seeking investments. The Marshall Plan for the recovery of Europe consisted mainly of grants, as did early development assistance. However, as it became apparent that the process of development would be slow and gradual, grants were used more for emergency relief, with the bulk of aid coming in the form of low-interest, long-term loans (with conditions attached) and technical assistance.

BILATERAL AND MULTILATERAL AID

In 1990, almost $90 billion in aid flowed from the developed countries to the LDCs. About one-sixth flowed through multilateral agencies; almost one-third consisted of investments and commercial loans. Most of the rest was country-to-country grants and some loans. A small part, about 5 percent, came through private voluntary agencies such as CARE, Church World Relief, and the Red Cross.

The United States concentrates its official development assistance through the **Agency for International Development (AID)**, which is part of the State Department and is in charge of U.S. aid to foreign countries. A publication of AID states:

Agency for International Development (AID)
The U.S. government agency in charge of U.S. bilateral assistance to foreign countries.

> *Programs to assist these people reflect an American tradition of sharing and helping the needy as well as enlightened national self-interest. In part, foreign aid is an expression of the American people's sense of justice and compassion. It also plays an important role in the continuing effort to achieve an enduring structure of world peace. This role is essential to the quest for global tranquility, freedom and progress. There are many things, however, that foreign aid cannot do. Experience has shown that it cannot right all social wrongs or solve every economic problem in a developing country. It cannot bring about instant progress. Some economists even claim that it has not been very effective in promoting economic development. Economic aid must be considered as a complement to other elements of foreign policy.*[15]

The United States is a major contributor to the development programs of low-income countries. In 1992, the United States contributed 24 percent of all aid given by Western industrialized countries and gave far more than any one of the other countries. However, as a percentage of GDP, thirteen countries gave a much larger share to low-income countries than the 0.25 percent contributed by the United States. France, for example, gave more than 1 percent of GDP to development aid. A significant part of economic assistance flows through multilateral agencies such as the World Bank and the United Nations. Politicians tend to prefer bilateral aid, over which they can exercise more control, while recipients prefer multilateral aid.

By the early 1990s, pressures for renewed and expanded foreign aid came mainly from fledgling democracies in Eastern Europe. They looked to the West for aid in rebuilding their economies. East Germany received aid mainly from West Germany before and after reunification. While Yugoslavia disintegrated into ethnic warfare, Poland, Hungary, Rumania, Czechoslovakia, and Bulgaria looked to Japan, the United States, Canada, and Western Europe for equipment, technical assistance, and other forms of aid.

---

15. Agency for International Development, Office of Public Affairs, *AID's Challenge in an Interdependent World* (Washington DC: U.S. Government Printing Office, 1978): 3.

POLICY FOCUS: THE DEVELOPED WORLD AND THIRD WORLD DEBT

Until the 1970s, LDCs borrowed mainly from the World Bank and foreign governments. In the 1970s, private banks began to lend to both governments and private firms in LDCs to allow them to undertake a variety of projects. These projects were expected to boost GDP enough to allow the borrowing country to make interest and principal payments and still be better off.

By 1982, problems began to surface. Many loans were not being used for capital investment to generate income. Some loans financed current consumption (especially oil imports) or ill-conceived investment projects. Other loans lined the pockets of corrupt politicians. Some U.S. banks had made so many risky loans to developing countries that default by borrowers could lead to bank failure. Some nations were unable to service their debts (to meet scheduled payments of interest and/or principal). As a result, banks were increasingly reluctant to extend or renew existing loans to those countries.

By 1987, when the debt crisis reached its peak, the total external public debt of Third World countries exceeded $911 billion. Brazil topped the list in debt size, with total debt of almost $90 billion. Seven countries had annual payments of principal and interest amounting to more than 10 percent of GDP.

Solutions to excessive debt are basically the same for individuals as for countries. Cut spending for consumption. Earn more income. Sell some assets. Renegotiate the terms of the loan. Or declare bankruptcy. All of these choices are painful. Cutting consumption spending is difficult in low-income nations like Ethiopia, with a 1990 debt of over $3 billion and a per capita GDP of only $120. Earning more income means not only expanding domestic production but also coming up with hard currency to repay the debt. The debtor nations would have to improve their trade balances to earn hard currency, which means expanding exports or reducing imports—both solutions that not only limit home consumption but are also unpopular in the industrial countries that would have to accept more imports or see their exports shrink.

In some cases, LDCs have agreed to a debt-equity swap, whereby debt is exchanged for ownership of local assets—much like an individual selling the car or the boat to cover his or her debts. A variant of that solution is a debt-for-nature swap; environmental groups in developed countries buy some of the debt at a discount and forgive the debt in exchange for establishing nature preserves or protecting endangered species in the debtor country.[a]

A partial solution for some indebted countries was developed by U.S. Treasury Secretary Nicholas Brady in 1990. Countries that met certain criteria (such as efforts to control inflation and reduce budget deficits) could swap a portion of their bank loans for marketable bonds—a procedure known as the Brady plan. The prices of Brady bonds have ranged from 10 percent of the value of the original debt to almost full value. Banks took some losses but also managed to recover more than they might have otherwise. The estimated value of the deals under this plan was over $100 billion in 1993. Some bonds that originally traded at a very low percentage of face value have appreciated, particularly bonds from Latin American countries that have experienced strong growth and reduced inflation. Lower interest rates in developed countries have also helped some countries to refinance their debt and reduce their debt service burdens.

Like home builders and automakers in the United States, developed countries do not want potential trading partners burdened by debt. It slows their growth and reduces their ability to purchase exports. A mutually acceptable deal on reducing the debt burden while still salvaging some payment and allowing countries to get a fresh start was in the interests of all countries concerned.

a. Huntington Williams, III, "Banking on the Future," *Nature Conservancy* (May/June 1992): 23–27.

THE WORLD BANK AND STRUCTURAL ADJUSTMENT LENDING

The **World Bank** is primarily a lending institution that makes long-term loans to promote economic growth in less developed countries. The World Bank, located in Washington DC, receives its funds from wealthier member countries as well as loan repayments and borrowing in world financial markets in order to make long-term, low-interest loans to less developed nations. It is the primary

World Bank
A multinational development lending agency that makes low-interest long-term loans to developing countries and provides technical assistance and economic advice.

multilateral foreign aid agency. The United Nations offers some more specialized multilateral aid programs in health, education, and services to children. Both the World Bank and its partner institution, the International Monetary Fund, were created when representatives of the major nations met in Bretton Woods, New Hampshire, in 1944 to make plans for international economic coordination in the postwar period. The World Bank's first charge was to assist Europe in recovering from World War II. Today, its primary role is as a long-term lender and technical adviser to developing nations.

Originally, most of the World Bank's loans were used for such developmental projects as roads, dams, electric power plants, and water systems. As these loans were repaid, the World Bank recycled the funds to other nations and other projects. By the early 1980s, however, the Bank was becoming increasingly frustrated with such projects. After a review of past experience, the Bank concluded that dropping infrastructure projects on a poorly functioning economy was not getting at the root of the problem. Since that time, a majority of the World Bank's funds have gone into **structural adjustment lending** (SALs). These loans are generally paid in three stages as countries meet conditions imposed by the Bank. Typical conditions include reducing monetary expansion, increasing domestic tax effort, providing more basic services for the poor, and selling off or significantly improving the performance of inefficient state-owned enterprises.

Structural adjustment lending
World Bank lending to developing countries that requires specific policy adjustments as a condition of the loan.

Economist Lawrence Summers evaluated effectiveness of the structural adjustment program and some of the criticisms leveled at it just before leaving the World Bank in 1993 to join the Clinton Administration.[16] He observes that it is difficult to make a scientific assessment because there is no control group. Structural adjustment loans go to countries whose economies are performing badly; those that are doing well are not a fair comparison group. Nevertheless, the evidence indicates that the countries with the greatest participation in structural adjustment lending had faster growth, higher exports, greater savings, and lower budget deficits than other countries or in comparison to their pre-loan performance. Structural adjustment lending was more successful in middle-income countries than in very poor countries.

HELP FROM THE PRIVATE SECTOR: MULTINATIONALS

In addition to aid from government to government, many countries' development efforts benefit from direct foreign investment by private firms and individuals, which supply scarce capital. Both private loans and multinational corporations (MNCs) transfer capital to these countries. A multinational corporation is a firm with headquarters in one country and one or more branch plants in other countries. There has been a foreign corporate presence in most less developed countries at least since World War II, and in many cases going back to the beginning of the century. The impact of multinational corporations on development is hotly disputed. Multinational corporations often choose locations in less developed countries for access to raw materials or to local and regional markets for products they cannot easily export from home, because of either distance, perishability, or trade barriers. They do benefit host countries

---

16. Lawrence H. Summers and Lant H. Pritchett, "The Structural Adjustment Debate," *American Economic Review Papers and Proceedings* (May 1993): 383–389.

by bringing in capital, providing job opportunities, and increasing foreign exchange. The fact that developing countries actively encourage multinationals to locate there suggests that there are substantial benefits.

However, good jobs are often filled by foreign nationals, not local workers. A multinational corporation may have no meaningful linkages to the rest of the host economy. It will then fail to act as a leading sector that spreads development to other sectors. A multinational corporation that is the largest taxpayer, largest export earner, and major employer in a small country may wield more real power than the host government.

Some multinational corporations simply transplant technology developed in their home country, usually a nation with abundant capital and skilled labor, but scarce unskilled labor. Many of these firms fail to adapt their methods of production to make the best use of local resources. Modifying production methods to suit local conditions is called technology adaptation, and its result is **appropriate technology**. In addition, multinationals do not usually make their technology available to other companies in related fields in the less developed countries. While some multinationals develop supplier and customer relationships in host countries, in many cases the multinationals fail to create the linkage effects necessary to promote development.

Appropriate technology
Adapting methods of production to take advantage of the mix of resources available in less developed countries.

THE NEW INTERNATIONAL ECONOMIC ORDER

Economic aid and trade are two major issues underlying a call by many Third World countries for a **New International Economic Order (NIEO)**. The NIEO was proposed by a group of less developed countries in the United Nations called the Group of 77. This agenda, first floated in 1974 and repeated frequently since, calls for changes in international economic policy in order to benefit poorer nations. In particular, it calls for developed nations to assume more responsibility for speeding up the development process.

NIEO calls for increased foreign aid and price stabilization programs for tropical agricultural products, much like the farm price support programs in the United States and Europe. It also calls for preferential tariff treatment and reduced regulations to allow less developed countries to export more to the developed nations. The main success of the NIEO has been increased attention to the problems of less developed countries in trade negotiations in the last two decades.

New International Economic Order
A proposal from developing nations calling for changes in international economic arrangements so as to benefit poorer nations through trade references, increased aid, and price stabilization for tropical agricultural products.

KEY IDEAS

EXTERNAL HELP FOR LESS DEVELOPED COUNTRIES
- Multilateral aid (World Bank, United Nations)
    Grants, loans (including SALs), technical assistance
- Bilateral aid (United States—Agency for International Development)
    Grants, loans, technical assistance
- Investment by multinational corporations
- New International Economic Order
    Access to markets for exports
    Increased financial assistance
    Price stabilization for primary products

Consider again... *What happened to Argentina from 1914 until its recent turnaround? Argentina taxed its exports heavily. Very little was invested. Argentines spent—Buenos Aires became the center of high living. Elvio Baldinelli, an Argentine trade expert, explained it well: "Argentina despised its export industries and taxed them very heavily, yet lived off them very well until markets closed and prices fell." Norman Gall wrote in* Forbes *magazine that Baldinelli's lament and the explanation for the decline of Argentina can be summed up in one sentence: "To succeed in the modern world, a country needs economic policies that encourage, not hamper, economic initiative."*[17]

Argentina is a country rich in possibilities—natural resources, climate, agricultural land, location, educated people. Unlike Chad, it is not burdened with an inland desert location with little potential for natural resource-based development. Unlike Bangladesh, it is not burdened with overpopulation or frequent and regular natural disasters. There is no reason for Argentina to be poor except mismanagement.

Since 1989, a combination of changes have turned Argentina around—a democratically elected government, reduced military spending, freer trade, privatization of many inefficient public enterprises, and stringent monetary reform. The inflation rate has fallen sharply from 200 percent in 1989 before the reforms began. Deregulation and free trade have given industry the opportunity and the challenge to become competitive. Strict tax enforcement has increased revenues to eliminate the budget deficit. Argentina, for long the example of how not to develop, is rapidly becoming a showcase of how to do it right.

SUMMARY

1. Less developed countries are characterized by low per capita income, high population growth, dualism, and a large part of productive activity in the agricultural sector. A tropical climate and a culture that is not favorable to economic activity are common in these countries.

2. Low-income countries invest little in human capital, that is, in the health, vigor, and education of the population. An unhealthy and uneducated labor force is relatively unproductive. Population growth creates problems for economic development because of the diversion of resources into caring for those too young or too old to be productive workers. While development can alleviate poverty, gains to the poorest citizens are not automatic. A conscious effort must be made to ensure their access to employment, training, and basic services.

3. Classical economists such as Smith and Ricardo called for a laissez-faire policy to free up private efforts to promote output growth. Rostow's theory of economic development, based on patterns observed in industrial countries, sees each country passing through stages of growth. The big push strategy suggests that government can speed the process of economic development through a major coordinated thrust on all fronts of the economy. The leading sectors strategy calls for efforts to be concentrated in some key sectors that will develop linkages to pull along the other sectors. An export promotion strategy concentrates on developing those industries with potential foreign markets, while an import substitution strategy focuses on developing domestic industries to reduce dependence on imported goods.

17. Norman Gall, "The Four Horsemen Ride Again," *Forbes* (July 28, 1986): 96.

4. Governments can play an important role in development by defining and protecting property rights, promoting competition, providing infrastructure, and making investment in human capital. Good macroeconomic management of taxes, spending, and money supply is an essential role. A laissez-faire approach relies more on private sector decisions, while a *dirigiste* approach sees a larger role for government in planning and implementing growth strategies. Excessive diversion of resources to military uses can be an obstacle to development.

5. Developing countries receive external assistance in development in the forms of grants, loans, and technical assistance. Much U.S. aid is channeled through the Agency for International Development (AID) as well as multilateral agencies such as the World Bank and the United Nations. Multinational corporations also channel capital to less developed countries, but the effects of MNCs on development are mixed. The New International Economic Order (NIEO) is a call for a new international economic system that gives preference to less developed countries in international trade and involves greater aid from the industrial countries.

NEW TERMS

dualism
crude birth rate
dependency ratio
crude death rate
vicious circle of poverty

big push strategy
leading sectors strategy
import substitution
export promotion

Agency for International Development (AID)
World Bank
structural adjustment lending

appropriate technology
New International Economic Order

QUESTIONS: REVIEW, APPLICATIONS, AND POLICY

REVIEW

1. Why are demographic trends so important to economic development?
2. What is the New International Economic Order (NIEO)? How would it help less developed countries?
3. What do development economists have in mind when they speak of linkages?
4. What is the vicious circle of poverty?
5. What is dualism? Does it exist in the United States?

APPLICATIONS

6. Suppose you were in charge of development for a less developed country and were approached by a multinational corporation interested in locating in your country. What kinds of concerns might you have?
7. Suppose the multinational corporation in Question 5 was in the business of printing books to ship abroad. What kinds of linkages might be involved?
8. Which of the following pieces of data are useful in determining whether countries are less developed countries: GDP (or GNP); per capita GDP; population growth rate; death rate; share of GDP derived from agriculture? Why?
9. Suppose you visited a less developed country and the local officials told you that they were pursuing a big push strategy instead of a leading sectors strategy. How could you tell if this was true?

POLICY

10. What role should government play in the development process? How does this differ from what governments actually do?
11. If you were to advise the government of a less developed country on steps to take toward development, what would be your top four priorities? Why?
12. If you were in charge of foreign aid for an industrial nation such as Canada or Sweden, would you choose to give your assistance to other nations in the form of (a) bilateral or multilateral aid?, (b) grants or loans? Justify your recommendation.

SUGGESTIONS FOR FURTHER READING

Kang, T. W. *Is Korea the Next Japan? Understanding the Structure, Strategy, and Tactics of America's Next Competitor.* New York: Free Press, 1989. Examines the reasons for Korea's rapid economic development in the 1980s.

Rostow, Walt Whitman. *Rich Countries and Poor Countries: Reflections on the Past, Lessons for the Future.* Boulder CO: Westview Press, 1987. This collection of essays on the world economy includes some comments on the development process from one of the best-known twentieth-century development economists.

Colclough, Christopher, and James Manor (eds). *States and Markets: Neo-Liberalism and the Development Policy Debate.* London: Oxford University Press, 1993. Explores the role of government in development and the success of market-oriented reform ideas.

Lissakers, Karin. *Banks, Borrowers, and the Establishment: A Revisionist Account of the International Debt Crisis.* New York: Basic Books, 1992. A helpful summary of the events that led up to the Brady plan for restructuring Third World debt.

PART 6

DEMAND AND CONSUMER CHOICE

The next three chapters cover the basic principles of supply and demand. We begin with an analysis of policy issues in Chapter 18, using the basic microeconomic models and theories developed in Part 1. These economic tools can yield profound insights into a variety of social issues. We look at such diverse issues as crime, rent control, the minimum wage, and U.S. agricultural policy.

Chapter 19 enriches demand and supply analysis by developing another tool of microeconomics—the elasticity measurement. We will develop several elasticity measures and then demonstrate their usefulness in the analysis of public policy.

The concept of demand is developed in theoretical detail in Chapter 20. Since individual demand curves form the bedrock of microeconomic analysis, we need to consider the factors that underlie them. We will first use an approach based on measurable utility to examine some problems and suggest some applications for demand analysis. The second approach to consumer demand—indifference curve analysis—is discussed in an appendix to this chapter.

CHAPTER 18
POLICY APPLICATIONS OF SUPPLY AND DEMAND

LEARNING OBJECTIVES

1. Demonstrate a simple economic model by calculating the expected cost of a crime given the probability of arrest and conviction, and the penalty.
2. Describe and diagram the economic effects of rent control, the minimum wage, and price supports in agriculture.
3. Discuss how markets allocate scarce resources.
4. Use U.S. agricultural policy to illustrate how intervention in markets creates incentives that further modify the market process.

Consider this... *In a recent issue of the* Chronicle of Higher Education, *the trade newspaper of colleges and universities, there was an interesting article about book publishing.[1] The story was about Andre Schiffrin, who has started a new publishing company that competes with university presses. University presses have historically published esoteric books that commercial publishers shy away from for economic reasons. These books aren't a good economic risk because so few people are interested in buying them. University presses, subsidized by their universities, stepped in and filled the void. In recent years, as university budgets have tightened, subsidies have fallen and university presses have tried to become economically successful. Therefore, they now avoid books they think have a low market demand.*

Schiffrin has stepped into this arena. The story stated that he started his company, New Press, to publish books in the public interest. Schiffrin stated that "publishing in the public interest means publishing books because they are inherently important, not for financial reasons." Schiffrin has financed his press with donations from foundations, much like public radio and public television do. Why would some university press people think that Schiffrin's remarks about university press managers are a bit self-serving?

When you finish this chapter, you will be able to analyze the Schiffrin situation with a new perspective. This chapter uses real world examples to illustrate the use of some of the basic microeconomic models and theories developed in the first three chapters of the text. You will find that these economic tools can yield profound insights into a variety of social and policy issues. Using these tools of analysis will increase your ability to understand and unravel other diverse issues.

---

1. Liz McMillen, "A Publisher Attempts to Fill the Niche Between Commercial and Academic Publishing," *The Chronicle of Higher Education* (June 13, 1993): A8.

THE ECONOMICS OF CRIME: USE OF THE SELF-INTEREST ASSUMPTION

We can use the self-interest assumption (described in Chapter 1) to analyze crime and its prevention. Assume that criminals are rational people who commit crimes when it is in their self-interest to do so. This type of simplifying assumption bothers some people who argue that some criminals are not rational. Addicts who commit crimes while on drugs are a case in point. Are they rational? Probably not, in a psychological sense. Yet, as you will see, this assumption allows us to develop a model with testable implications.

The critical point for the economic model of crime is whether criminals make decisions to commit more crimes if the cost of committing crimes goes down or is perceived to be lower. The model says that a criminal calculates the costs and benefits of each crime and commits those crimes for which the benefits exceed the costs. The hypothesis is that a criminal calculates costs (C) and benefits (B) of criminal activities and commits those for which B is greater than C. According to this hypothesis, crime is an economic activity, and the criminal behaves like any entrepreneur.

The benefits are what the criminal hopes to realize by the activity. For crimes involving the theft of property, it is relatively easy to determine a value. The anticipated benefit is the market value of the take. For other crimes, such as vandalism, illegal parking, or littering, we have to impute some value to the activity. This value may not be monetary. For example, it may consist of time saved due to parking illegally rather than searching for a legal parking spot.

The cost is the penalty (P) adjusted for the probability (π) that the criminal will be caught and the penalty will be imposed. The penalty for illegal activity is not imposed every time a crime is committed. Thus, adjusting the penalty by the probability of incurring it produces an expected cost of committing the crime. The prospective criminal compares B to $P \times \pi$. For example, suppose the fine for littering is \$500, but on the average one will be caught and fined only once every 500 times. The expected cost of littering is then \$1 ($= \$500 \times 1/500$). The economic model of crime thus suggests that if some people get more than \$1 worth of benefit from littering, they will litter.

There are three elements to the simple model just developed. First, the model says that crime depends on the benefits from the activity, so, *ceteris paribus*, as the value of those benefits goes up, so will the amount of criminal activity. Second, it says that as the penalty goes down (with no change in the probability of being caught), the criminal activity will increase. Third, it says that if the probability of being caught goes down, *ceteris paribus*, the amount of criminal activity will go up. This simple model can now be applied to crimes more serious than littering, such as armed robbery.

THE ECONOMICS OF ROBBERY

The economic model of crime can be used to advise policy makers on how to decrease the amount of armed robbery. Policy makers have three options. One possibility is to decrease the potential take, or profit. This is difficult to do, but you have probably noticed that most convenience stores and gas stations open late at night advertise that they don't keep much cash on hand. That's one way of reducing the take. Private citizens in New York City have also exercised this option by placing signs reading "no radio" in their parked cars.

The second possibility for reducing robbery is to increase the penalty. In one suburb of Washington, DC, the local police chief recently announced that squad cars would be equipped with rifles with exploding shells (outlawed by the United Nations as being too inhumane for warfare). In addition, officers had been instructed to shoot first and ask questions later when investigating robberies. Almost immediately, the robbery rate fell in this town and increased in adjacent areas. This result is predicted by the model, which says as the potential penalty rises, criminal activity will fall. Of course, some people object to such a policy even if it does reduce crime. Remember that economic models are positive, not normative. They only indicate what the consequences of a policy will be. They don't say if it's good or bad in a moral sense.

The third option for reducing the robbery rate would be to increase the probability that robbers will be arrested and convicted. This might be accomplished by adding more police, improving the court system, putting television cameras in banks, or other similar measures.

In an economic study of crime, William Trumbull shows that the probability of punishment and the severity of the punishment both have an effect on the crime rate.[2] He shows that the certainty of punishment has a greater deterrent effect than the severity of punishment, but both have significant effects. His research also shows that when the returns to legal activity increase (the outlook for jobs improves), illegal activity declines. Illegal activity is a substitute for regular employment when jobs are scarce.

THE ECONOMICS OF THE DEATH PENALTY

The preceding analysis may have led you to conclude that economists would argue that the death penalty deters crime by increasing the expected cost. At least one economist, Isaac Ehrlich, has argued that the death penalty does act to reduce the amount of murder.[3] If you are a doubter, answer this question: Would you ever litter if the probability of getting caught was 1 in 500, and the penalty was death? To answer yes, you would have to place a high value on being able to litter or a low value on your own life. However, some people argue that murderers have such a distorted view of reality that they underestimate the probability of being caught, convicted, and sentenced to death. These people argue that the death penalty provides little deterrence. More importantly, just because positive economic theory says that the death penalty deters crime, that does not mean that you, or anyone else, has to support the death penalty if you object on moral (normative) grounds. You can still be opposed to the death penalty on humanitarian grounds even if you accept the implications of the model.

THE ECONOMICS OF ILLEGAL PARKING

Some of you may still be skeptical about this simple economic model of crime. Let's apply it to an action that you have probably committed, or at least thought

---

2. William N. Trumbull, "Estimations of the Economic Model of Crime Using Aggregate and Individual Level Data," *Southern Economic Journal* (October 1989): 423–439.
3. Isaac Ehrlich, "The Deterrent Effect of Capital Punishment: A Question of Life and Death," *American Economic Review* (June 1975).

about committing: illegal parking on campus. On almost all college campuses, the quantity of parking spaces supplied is less than the quantity demanded at a zero price. As a result, there are benefits to parking in an illegal space. Suppose the fine for illegal parking is $10, and you find from experience that you get a ticket one out of every four times you park illegally. The expected cost of the crime is thus $2.50 ($10 × $1/4$). It is difficult to estimate the benefits that accrue to those who park illegally. Since there are many violators, however, it's clear that those benefits are substantial.

Assume that you are appointed to a committee formed by the college president to solve the parking problem. Using the simple economic model, your committee identifies three options: (1) The college could lower the benefits of illegal parking by buying shuttle buses to transport students from parking areas to the classroom buildings. (2) The college could increase the likelihood of being caught by hiring more police and increasing the number of times they check the parking areas. (3) The college could raise the cost of the crime by having illegally parked cars towed away. This last solution raises the cost of the crime in two ways. Violators would have to pay towing fees in addition to the parking fine. Also, recovering a towed vehicle involves a great deal of time and trouble.

If you still don't think the model works, there is an empirical test you can carry out. Observe the amount of illegal parking on your campus on a nice sunny day. Then the next time it rains, observe that activity again. What does the model predict? On rainy days, the benefits of the crime go up, *ceteris paribus*; they include being closer to class plus arriving to class dry. The probability of being caught also goes down, *ceteris paribus*, because campus police don't like to get wet either. The model thus predicts that there will be more illegal parking on rainy days. Check it out—test the model!

THE ECONOMICS OF BASKETBALL "CRIME"

Economists Robert E. McCormick and Robert D. Tollison applied a similar economic model for criminal activity to the game of basketball.[4] They picked college basketball as a subject of analysis because there is a great deal of data available and the number of referees (police) increased from two to three in 1978. Their empirical test showed that increasing the number of officials from two to three caused the number of fouls (crimes) to decline.

PRICE CEILINGS AND PRICE FLOORS

Chapter 3 described how free markets reach equilibrium. It is possible for this market process to be interfered with. Such interference is usually the result of governmental action. **Price ceilings** are upper limits on prices imposed by a governmental unit. The ceiling is a price that cannot be exceeded. **Price floors** are minimum limits on prices established by a governmental unit. The floor is a minimum price that cannot be undercut. Price ceilings and price floors disrupt the market-clearing process. Microeconomic tools make it possible to see the effects of these disruptions.

---

4. Robert E. McCormick and Robert D. Tollison, "Crime on the Court," *Journal of Political Economy* (April 1984): 223–235.

Price ceilings
Upper limits on prices imposed by a governmental unit. The ceiling is a price that cannot be exceeded.

Price floors
Minimum limits on prices established by a governmental unit. The floor is a price that cannot be undercut.

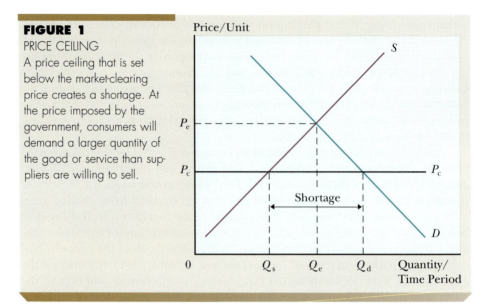

FIGURE 1
PRICE CEILING
A price ceiling that is set below the market-clearing price creates a shortage. At the price imposed by the government, consumers will demand a larger quantity of the good or service than suppliers are willing to sell.

PRICE CEILINGS

A price ceiling that is set below the equilibrium price prevents the market from clearing. The amount that consumers wish to purchase at the imposed price is greater than the amount suppliers are willing to supply at that price. Figure 1 demonstrates this problem. In Figure 1, the equilibrium price is P_e and equilibrium quantity is Q_e. The government imposes a price ceiling at P_c. The amount that consumers wish to consume at price P_c is Q_d. The amount suppliers are willing to supply at that price is Q_s. The result is a shortage.

A **shortage** exists when the amount that consumers wish to purchase at some price exceeds the amount suppliers wish to supply. When a price ceiling is in effect, a shortage can occur on a lasting basis. Keep in mind that supply and demand do not shift when a ceiling is in place. It is important to realize that the shortage is caused by the ceiling. Without the ceiling, the price would rise. The quantity demanded would decrease and the quantity supplied would increase until the price reached P_e and the market cleared.

If a price ceiling is to be maintained, government officials must replace the market with some other way of allocating the good or service. Consumers will be frustrated as they try to obtain the good or service at the lower price. Some means other than price must be used to determine who will get the available supply of the good or service. The means might be ration coupons, a first-come, first-served rule, or other nonmarket allocating mechanism. Nonmarket methods of allocation waste resources in unproductive activities as consumers attempt to obtain goods in roundabout ways. People might spend hours waiting in line for goods that are priced below market-clearing prices, or they might invest resources in political activity aimed at gaining an advantage in the allocation scheme.

This allocation problem was common in the planned economies of the former Soviet Union and Eastern Europe before the recent reforms. Price ceilings were maintained on many consumer goods. There were shortages of these goods and long lines of consumers waiting for a chance to purchase. Consumers would often get into any line when they saw it developing, knowing that a line meant there was some good in short supply available.

Shortage
The amount by which the quantity consumers wish to purchase at some price exceeds the quantity suppliers wish to supply at that price. A shortage can occur on a lasting basis only when a price ceiling is in effect.

POLICY FOCUS: PRICE CONTROLS AND BLACK MARKETS

If a government is going to control prices, it must also develop a policy option for allocating the scarce goods. Intervening in the market does not eliminate the need for allocating goods and services; it simply means another method must be developed.

During World War II, the U.S. government tried to control the prices of some basic commodities, such as gasoline and sugar. Ration tickets were distributed to determine who got the limited supplies. These ration tickets then were sold (illegally) on black markets, undermining the policy decision to control prices. Since governments at all levels usually refrain from trying to set price ceilings, there has been little black market activity in the United States except for that episode. About the only direct experience you might have with a black market is the scalping of tickets to athletic events and concerts.

However, you may be aware of black markets that exist in other countries. One important black market is in currencies. Many countries attempt to control the price of their currency in terms of other currencies. Economists refer to this price as the exchange rate. Attempts to control the exchange rate always produce black markets for foreign currencies. If you have been in Russia, or some parts of Asia, you were probably approached on the street by furtive individuals who wanted to exchange their currency for dollars at a much better exchange rate than any bank provides.

Currency exchange is not the only kind of black market exchange abroad. You have probably heard stories about the black market for jeans in China. If you travel to China, pack a couple of extra pairs of jeans. You can finance part of your trip with all the yen you can get for them on the black market. But don't get caught!

Governments usually attempt to control a broad range of prices during and after wars. This effort is made more difficult by the fact that consumer goods are usually more scarce at those times. Equilibrium prices would therefore be rising rapidly while the government was trying to control them. Perhaps the extreme examples of such controls happened in Germany and Japan after World War II.

Both countries had enormous national debts that were financed by monetary expansion. These large increases in the money supply led to severe inflation. At the same time, their governments imposed strict controls on food prices, even rationing the caloric intake of individuals. These strict controls led to black markets and the phenomenon of "trekking." Urban residents would leave town to go to the countryside to make black market deals with farmers. The stricter the controls, the more the trekking grew. Reports say that on one day more than 900,000 residents of Tokyo left town for the countryside. In Germany, the controls came to an end with the Erhard reforms of 1948. Without the controls, the incentive to trek evaporated. As with most economic forces, there was a secondary effect. Railroad passenger traffic in Germany fell immediately to less than 40 percent of the prereform level. This drop in rail traffic was evidence of the amount of trekking that had been taking place.

In almost all cases where price ceilings are imposed, black markets spring up. **Black markets** are markets in which people illegally buy and sell goods or services at prices above government-imposed price ceilings. We'll have more to say about black markets later.

RENT CONTROL. Price ceilings are used by various levels of government. Let's look at the effect of price ceilings on apartment rentals. The governments of many cities, including New York City and Washington, DC, have imposed price ceilings on apartment rents. This kind of ceiling, imposed by governmental units, is referred to as **rent control**. At first glance, the goal of rent control seems admirable. This goal is to keep rents low so that everyone, including those who are poor, can find a place to live at a reasonable price.

To see the effect of rent control, refer again to Figure 1. At a price less than the market-clearing price, there will be a shortage of rental units. More people will be looking for rental units than the number of units available. Something other than market forces will determine who gets the rental units. Landlords

Black markets
Markets in which people illegally buy and sell goods and services at prices above government-imposed price ceilings.

Rent control
A price ceiling imposed by a governmental unit on housing rents.

may impose criteria for prospective tenants because, for any vacancy, there will be a number of people eager to rent the apartment. Without rent control, a landlord is more likely to rent to any prospective tenant rather than leave the apartment vacant, because the market is clearing. With rent control, the landlord can choose from the backlog of prospective tenants. The landlord can exclude those who are young (or old) or those who have pets or children. Since landlords cannot raise rents, they will instead choose tenants who seem likely to cost the least in terms of damage, noise, complaints, or hassles. Interference in the market has replaced impartial market forces with a system that encourages discrimination.

Rent control, like many other governmental interventions in the market, has outcomes other than those intended by the well-meaning politicians who advocate them. This is certainly true of rent-controlled housing in New York. Some of the richest members of society gain from rent control, and some of the poorest are left with no housing. Donald Trump reports in his book that the actress Mia Farrow had a rent-controlled apartment for $2,000 per month that would have had a market rent of about $10,000 per month.[5] Trump thought that the most notorious example of the inequity of rent control is that Ed Koch, former mayor of New York City, has a very nice three-bedroom apartment with a terrace in a beautiful part of Greenwich Village, for $350 per month. The market rent would be close to $1,800 per month.

Rent-control laws live on even though their effects are apparent. A case study of the experience in Santa Monica, California, shows the political appeal of rent control. Santa Monica enacted rent control in 1979. The city rolled back rents and limited increases to about two-thirds of the increase in the Consumer Price Index. The original law was promoted by its sponsors as a way to preserve the existing population mix, which included large numbers of blacks, Hispanics, the elderly, and low-income families. Since 1979, many apartment complexes have been abandoned by their owners, who would rather have them vacant than rent them at the controlled rents. Abandoned rent-controlled apartments sit adjacent to homes selling for more than $500,000.

The problem is worsened because the owners of the abandoned apartment buildings find them very difficult to sell. Many want to tear down the buildings and build new office or residential space. But the city passed a law to prevent such reconstruction. In order to tear down any rental unit, the owner must pay to build replacement units in the city. One apartment owner had his building spray-painted with the words, "We want *perestroika* now."

The irony of the situation in Santa Monica is that the rent-controlled units have become a haven for rich young professionals. The parking lots outside these $350-per-month, two-bedroom apartments are filled with BMWs and Audis. The population mix that Tom Hayden wanted to preserve has not been preserved. So why isn't the law being changed? Perhaps the fact that 75 percent of the voters of Santa Monica are tenants offers a hint.

These examples show the impacts of rent control on the distribution of income and the production of new housing. The short-run effects of rent control are mainly distributional. Landlords in rent-controlled areas choose to rent to richer tenants because they may cause fewer problems and "know the right peo-

---

5. Donald J. Trump (with Tony Schwartz), *Trump: The Art of the Deal* (New York: Warner Books, 1987), 255–256.

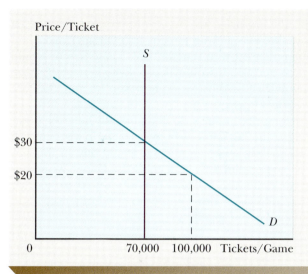

FIGURE 2
ORANGE BOWL TICKETS
A price ceiling is often imposed by universities in selling tickets to popular events. If such a price ceiling is below the market-clearing price, it creates a black market for the underpriced tickets.

ple" to get in. In the long run, fewer housing units are built and the existing stock of housing units deteriorates. Rent control in Stockholm and Cairo has the same result as rent control in Santa Monica; market forces work the same in every country.

BLACK MARKETS. As mentioned earlier, black markets tend to develop when price ceilings are imposed. In Santa Monica, it has been reported that "key money," an up-front payment of up to $5,000, was required of some prospective tenants. This practice was one form of black market.

Assume that Figure 2 represents the market for tickets to one of the biggest college football games of the year, the Orange Bowl. The stock of tickets is completely fixed in the short run because the stadium has a seating capacity of 70,000. The athletic departments of the two colleges are selling the tickets at a price ceiling of $20 per ticket. For this game, the market-clearing price would be $30. The price ceiling creates a shortage of 30,000 tickets. At that price, there is going to be a larger quantity of tickets demanded than exist. The athletic departments have to allocate the tickets by some other means than the market. Tickets will be sold to those fans who are willing to wait in line or those who donate to the booster club. The shortage of tickets will produce a black market. Some of those who are able to get the tickets for $20 will be willing to sell them. These people will engage in black market activity by selling their tickets to those who are willing to pay more.

Black marketers dealing in tickets to sports or entertainment events are referred to as scalpers. Scalping generally has a bad connotation. Consider that a scalper is performing the service of transferring tickets from people who value other goods more highly than they value the tickets to people who value the tickets more highly than other goods. Thus, the scalper is being paid for performing a service. In most states, scalping has been outlawed. In Texas, it is legal, and organized reselling of tickets takes place. In Washington, DC, it is illegal to resell tickets—even at prices below the original price!

WHY CEILINGS? If price ceilings are so disruptive, why do they exist? One answer is that not all people are hurt by ceilings. Those who are able to purchase the good or service at the artificially low price are better off. As a result, they approve of the ceiling. For example, people who already have an apartment and don't want to move would be better off with rent control. These people would probably vote for rent control because it would make them better off. Also, those who don't mind waiting in line or those who get tickets because they are team boosters like low ticket prices.

It is important to realize that price ceilings do not generally help the poor. If there is one $20 ticket left for the big game, who do you think will get it—a poor fan who likes football more than anything else $20 would buy, or the governor who thinks it would be good politics to be seen at the game? Whenever the market is replaced, another mechanism must be substituted to allocate goods. This mechanism usually depends heavily on power and influence. Thus, the poor are not generally helped by price ceilings.

PRICE FLOORS

A price floor that is set above the equilibrium price keeps the market from clearing. The amount that suppliers offer for sale at the imposed price is greater than the amount consumers wish to purchase at that price. Figure 3 demonstrates this case. In Figure 3, the equilibrium price is P_e, and the equilibrium quantity is Q_e. The government imposes a price floor at P_f. The result is that the quantity supplied at price P_f is Q_s, and the quantity consumers demand at that price is Q_d. The higher price has attracted more suppliers into the market. At the same time, it has discouraged buyers or caused them to shift to substitutes. The result is a surplus equal to $Q_s - Q_d$.

A **surplus** exists when the amount that suppliers wish to supply at some price exceeds the amount that consumers wish to purchase. When a price floor is in effect, a surplus can occur on a lasting basis. The surplus is created by the price floor. It is important to remember that neither the market demand nor market supply curve will shift due to the price floor. If the floor didn't exist, the price

Surplus
The amount by which the quantity suppliers wish to supply at some price exceeds the quantity consumers wish to purchase at that price. A surplus can occur on a lasting basis only when a price floor is in effect.

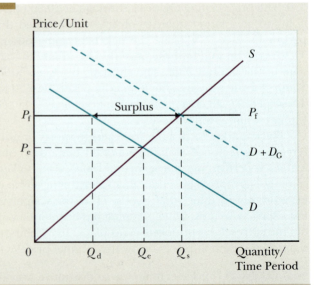

FIGURE 3
PRICE FLOOR
If the government imposes a price floor above the market-clearing price, a surplus will be created. At the price imposed by the government, suppliers will desire to sell more units than consumers will be willing to purchase. Demand would have to be artificially increased to $D + D_G$ to clear the market after the price floor is imposed.

would fall. The quantity demanded would increase and the quantity supplied would decrease until the market cleared.

It can be difficult for the governmental agency that imposes a price floor to keep prices from falling below the floor. Some suppliers will attempt to cut prices in order to sell the quantity they want to supply. The most effective way for the government to prevent this price cutting is to purchase the excess quantity supplied. By purchasing the surplus, the government in effect is shifting the demand curve outward to create a new equilibrium at the desired price. In Figure 3, the dashed demand curve represents the demand at the price floor (D) plus the added governmental demand (D_G). A shift to demand curve $D + D_G$ would allow the price to remain at P_f. Note that this is a "contrived" demand curve.

The best example of price floors that work in this way are the price supports operated by the Commodity Credit Corporation for some agricultural products in the United States. The **Commodity Credit Corporation (CCC)** is a U.S. government agency that makes loans to farmers as part of federal price support programs. Suppose the federal government wants to maintain a price for grain that is above the market-clearing price. To maintain this price floor, it is necessary for the CCC to purchase some grain. The effect of this is to shift the demand curve to the right (as with $D + D_G$ in Figure 3) so that the higher price can be maintained.

Commodity Credit Corporation (CCC)
A U.S. government agency that makes loans to farmers as part of federal price support programs.

THE MINIMUM WAGE

The **minimum wage** is a price floor imposed by the federal government in the labor market. Looking again at Figure 3, a minimum wage (P_f) set above the market wage (P_e) causes a surplus of labor ($Q_s - Q_d$). If the minimum wage is set above the market-clearing wage rate, the amount of labor that workers will supply at the minimum wage will be greater than the amount of labor that firms will wish to employ, resulting in unemployment.

Minimum wage
A price floor imposed by the federal government in the labor market.

In 1978, Congress raised the wage floor to $2.65 an hour, up from the $2.30 an hour that was set in 1974. In addition, a formula was adopted that ensured automatic increases up to $3.35 an hour in 1981. In 1989, Congress passed legislation to raise the minimum wage to $3.80 in 1990 and $4.25 in 1991. In late 1993, Robert B. Reich, President Clinton's Secretary of Labor, indicated that he planned to submit legislation to raise the minimum wage to $4.75, but that some of the increase could take the form of mandated health benefits.

Economists generally agree that minimum wage laws cause unemployment to be higher than it would be otherwise. Unemployment will especially affect young people, for whom the market-clearing wage might be much lower than the minimum wage. There is strong statistical evidence from a large number of economists that increases in the minimum wage result in higher youth unemployment. Robert Goldfarb and Edward Gramlich independently reviewed eight empirical studies by economists.[6] The studies agreed that increases in the mini-

---

6. Robert Goldfarb, "The Policy Content of Quantitative Minimum Wage Research," *Industrial Relations Research Association Proceedings* (December 1974): 261–268; and Edward M. Gramlich, "Impact of Minimum Wages on Other Wages, Employment and Family Incomes," *Brookings Papers on Economic Activity No. 2* (1976): 409–451.

mum wage cause increases in unemployment among teenagers. The studies predicted that a 15 percent increase in the minimum wage would increase teenage unemployment by 3.4 to 5.3 percentage points.[7]

If there is agreement among economists about the harmful effects of minimum wage laws, why are they enacted? The reason is very similar to the rationale for price ceilings. Not all people are hurt by the wage floor. Some workers receive pay increases when the legislation is enacted. Those who are laid off or who seek work but are unable to find it at the new minimum wage usually don't understand the role of the higher minimum wage in causing their problems. The result is that it is politically popular with some groups—organized labor, for example—to support minimum wage increases. Remember that the economic model only predicts that such laws cause decreased employment. It does not say that minimum wage legislation is a good or bad thing in other respects. Some groups may decide that it is better to have fewer people employed at a higher wage rate than to have a larger number employed at a lower, market-clearing wage rate.

During the Reagan administration, the minimum wage was not increased. Thus, its impact declined as market wages rose relative to the stable minimum wage. For most workers, the equilibrium wage was already above the floor, so it did not cause much, if any, unemployment. In fact, there is some evidence that the increase to $4.25 in 1991 had little impact, for two reasons. First, the legislation allowed a subminimum wage of $3.35 per hour for training purposes. This training wage can be paid for six months. Second, it appears that for most employers in most markets the equilibrium wage is already at or above $4.25. McDonald's, for example, pays an average of $4.65 per hour. Wendy's International pays $4.25. The only region where the higher minimum wage may cause some unemployment is in the south, where both wages and skill levels of employees tend to be lower. If the Clinton administration raises the minimum wage, this could change.

MARKETS AS ALLOCATION MECHANISMS

Auctions are markets in which there are few if any barriers to letting the price allocate scarce goods. If there are enough people bidding on the items offered, the price that results should be an equilibrium price. Auctions are, therefore, an efficient way to allocate scarce resources. Yet people often object to using auctions because they think that they will do better if some mechanism other than the market is used for allocation.

The case study from Arizona State University, which we referred to in Chapter 3, is a good example of this phenomenon.[8] When the university built a six-story addition to its business college, whole departments had to relocate to the new facility. As in most buildings, some offices were better than others (some had windows, some didn't, some were large, some were small). The departments faced the problem of allocating a scarce resource without a market.

---

7. These estimates were based on calculating the elasticity of supply and demand for teenage workers.
8. This case is drawn from William J. Boyes and Stephen K. Happel, "Auctions as an Allocation Mechanism in Academia: The Case of Faculty Offices," *Journal of Economic Perspectives* (Summer 1989): 37–40.

The chair of the management department adopted the allocation mechanism used most frequently in traditional societies—seniority (defined as the length of time spent on the faculty at Arizona State). The marketing and accounting departments followed the example of management and used a seniority system. Some of the younger assistant professors thought this to be very unfair, because they spent time in their offices doing research and preparing for classes while the full professors spent more time consulting and less in their offices. The chair of the finance department agreed that seniority allocation seemed unfair. A sign-up sheet was placed by the chair's office, and offices were allocated on a first-come, first-served basis. The result was that those professors who spent a lot of time roving the halls got the best offices. Those doing research, on sabbatical, or on a trip ended up with small offices and no windows. The chair of the statistics department decided to use a random drawing of names to allocate offices. This met with faculty approval because everyone would be treated equally. After the draw, senior faculty forced the chair to cancel the outcome and use seniority instead.

The chair of the economics department wanted to use the market to allocate the scarce resources. Being a good bureaucrat, he asked the faculty for suggestions. Surprisingly, in a department of economists, no one suggested using prices to allocate a scarce resource. Instead, the chair was advised by the most senior faculty member to use seniority, as is done at "all great institutions." Other suggestions were to allocate the offices based on research productivity, teaching effectiveness, height, race, sex, and religion. One member suggested office "wrestlemania"—a brawl. The chair decided on a sealed bid auction with the proceeds going to a scholarship fund. After three weeks, the twenty-four bids were opened. The highest bid was $500 and the second highest was $250. All twenty-four bids totaled $3,200. Offices were allocated in order of the sizes of the bids. The only complaint was from the person who bid $500, who overestimated the equilibrium price, bidding twice as much as the next highest bidder and almost four times the average bid.

KEY IDEAS

MARKET INTERVENTION
Any intervention into a market will distort the market outcome and prevent the market from reaching equilibrium.

REASONS FOR A SHORTAGE
A shortage can exist in a market only if there is a price ceiling below the market-clearing price. It could be called a price ceiling, price control, or rent control.
Result: A black market will always develop.

REASONS FOR A SURPLUS
A surplus can exist in a market only if there is a price floor set above the market-clearing price. It could be called a price floor, a minimum wage, or price supports.
Result: Someone or some governmental agency will have to absorb the surplus.

Trouble was brewing. A professor used the experiment as an example in a principles of economics course. The students thought it was a good idea. They even understood that it was only important that the price had to be paid. It did not matter where the money went. One student, who happened to be a reporter for the campus newspaper, thought that the office auction was such a good idea that it was reported on the front page. The story was then picked up by the Phoenix media and went out on the Associated Press wire service. The chair faced an onslaught of criticism from university administrators and local politicians who accused the chair of selling state property. Eventually, the publicity calmed down, largely because the money had gone to fund a scholarship. But the lesson was loud and clear: Many good opportunities to use the market as an allocation device are overlooked.

A LESSON FROM AGRICULTURE

U.S. agriculture presents a case study of what happens to well-intentioned government policy as the government becomes part of the problem. Even when it is recognized that policies are unsuccessful, it is politically very difficult to reduce or eliminate the government's role. In fact, the role of government often increases. In 1945 there were 10 million people employed on American farms, and the U.S. Department of Agriculture had 80,000 employees. In 1994 there were fewer than 3 million people employed on American farms, and there were 122,000 Department of Agriculture employees. Professor George Stigler has put it this way:

> *One finding has been that small groups do better in politics than large groups, certainly per capita and at times in the aggregate. Today American farmers and their families comprise a little over 2 percent of the population but they get about $40 billion in governmental outlays for income stabilization and all kinds of regulations and special programs (restrictions of crops, preferential interest rates, subsidized electrical utilities, etc.). As late as 1950 farmers and their families were about 15 percent of the population and received about $3 billion from total federal government outlays, as compared with $40 billion (about $9.5 billion in 1950 dollars) in the 1980s. That is about a sevenfold increase in payments per farm operator in dollars of stable purchasing power.*[9]

Government involvement in agriculture has a long history in the United States, beginning with the Homestead Act of 1862. During the Great Depression, direct income and price support programs began. Those who favored such government intervention believed that the market failed in agriculture in several ways. The structure of agriculture is very competitive, with a large number of firms (farms). Farmers face unstable prices for their products, so their incomes vary greatly from year to year. Unpredictable weather, international trading patterns that are subject to government influence, and technological changes aggravate the market instability.

---

9. George J. Stigler, *Memoirs of an Unregulated Economist* (New York: Basic Books, 1988), 118–119.

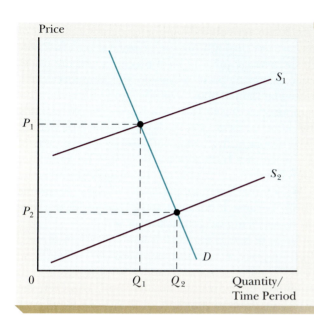

FIGURE 4
THE MARKET FOR FARM OUTPUT
The market for farm output has erratic supply (due to changes in the weather) and inelastic demand. Thus, the total revenue a farmer receives in any one year can be highly variable, and an increase in quantity supplied can reduce total farm income.

THE FARM PROBLEM

In the short run, the farm problem is simple enough to understand. First, agricultural production takes place in a very competitive market that closely resembles the basic supply and demand model we just developed. Second, the price of farm products does not affect the quantity demanded to a great extent. Third, weather plays a significant role in determining the yield of any crop. These conditions together mean that the revenue a farmer receives from year to year can be highly variable.

The irony is that in years of good harvests many farmers may be in worse shape than in years of poor harvests. This situation is depicted in Figure 4. Assume that in the first year farm output sold at a price of P_1, so Q_1 units were sold, and farmers received a total revenue of $P_1 \times Q_1$. The next year, the weather was very good and the crop was large, so the supply curve shifted to S_2. Price fell to P_2, and consumers purchased Q_2 units. Since demand is inelastic, farmers received less revenue than they did the year before ($P_2 \times Q_2$ is less than $P_1 \times Q_1$). The large fall in price brought only a small increase in sales.

The long-run problem for U.S. farmers is largely the result of huge increases in their productivity in the last century. It takes fewer and fewer farmers to produce the same amount of food. In the early nineteenth century, more than half of the U.S. labor force was engaged in farming. Now less than 2 percent of the work force is employed in agriculture.

Many of the arguments to save the family farm are intended to stop the trend toward fewer and fewer agricultural workers. Even some nonfarmers support maintaining the current number of farms. They argue that smaller farms are more environmentally benign than huge agri-industry. Farmers have political power, so there has been governmental response to their calls for action. Among the forms of this response have been agricultural price supports and managing production.

Agricultural support program
An attempt by the federal government to achieve parity for farmers through the use of price supports.

Parity
A one-to-one ratio between the average prices of farm products and the prices of what farmers buy.

Support prices
Price floors for agricultural products maintained by the government, which purchases any surplus to keep the price from falling.

SUPPORTING PRICES. Before 1973, the **agricultural support program** consisted of attempts to achieve parity for farmers through the use of price supports. **Parity** is a one-to-one ratio between the average price of farm products and the prices of what farmers buy. In practice, achieving parity means creating **support prices,** or price floors, which are prices maintained above equilibrium levels by the government. The idea behind support prices is to link farm prices to a parity index that maintains the purchasing power of farmers at the level of some base period. For example, if a bushel of wheat bought five gallons of gasoline or two pairs of shoes in the base period, the price of a bushel of wheat should be kept high enough to permit the same purchases today. Highly respected agricultural economist and Nobel laureate T. W. Schultz described parity as, "a vulgar economic concept."[10] It is vulgar to Schultz because it does not allow changes in the relative prices of agricultural and nonagricultural products over time.

You just saw the effect of price floors, so Figure 5 is familiar. When there is a price floor above the equilibrium price, the quantity supplied (Q_s) exceeds the quantity demanded (Q_d) at the imposed price (P_f), and a surplus develops. If the price floor is to be maintained, demand must be increased. However, the government can't sell the surplus on domestic markets, or the price will fall back to the equilibrium price (P_e). In the 1950s and early 1960s, the government reacted to this dilemma by building storage bins and storing farm products. The Department of Agriculture sold some of the surplus food to poor countries under the Food for Peace program and distributed some to school lunch programs and welfare recipients. Most of the surplus was just stored, however. At the high point of this storage activity in 1961, the U.S. government had 1.3 billion bushels of wheat and 1.7 billion bushels of corn in storage.

There are some steps that could be taken to dispose of such a surplus. The government could destroy the surplus, but this action would upset those who

---

10. T. W. Schultz, "Tensions between Economics and Politics in Dealing with Agriculture," *Agriculture Economics Paper No. 84:24,* Department of Economics, University of Chicago (August 10, 1985): 5.

FIGURE 5
PRICE FLOORS IN AGRICULTURE
If the government imposes a price floor (price support) above the market-clearing price, a surplus will result.

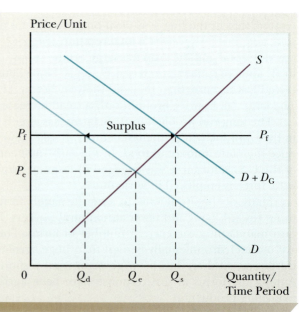

consider it wasteful.[11] The government could give the surplus away to poor countries, but this might anger other countries who are trying to sell their farm products. The government might distribute the surplus in its own country. In the 1980s, the Reagan administration distributed large amounts of surplus cheese to people over age 65. Some of this cheese went to people who were quite prosperous, including retirees with a great deal of accumulated wealth. The government could sell the surplus to other countries if customers could be found. Another alternative would be to retain the surplus for future emergency needs. Regardless of the disposal problems, it is absolutely necessary for the government to buy the surplus it has created.

MANAGING PRODUCTION. In the mid–1950s, the U.S. government decided that the purchase and storage of farm surpluses was too costly and that managing production was a better alternative. The new policy called for the government to maintain the price floor by keeping the quantity supplied at lower levels than would exist without government intervention. With this policy, the government was trying to shift the supply curve to the left in order to maintain the higher price without creating a surplus.

The first government attempt to limit production was known as the soil bank program. In the **soil bank program**, which was started under President Eisenhower in the 1950s, farmers were paid to let their land lie idle. A second attempt to reduce production was the acreage allotment. An **acreage allotment** sets a limit on the number of acres that can be used to produce a specific crop. The government must determine who gets what acreage allotment. For tobacco, for example, the decision is based on past levels of production. If your parents had a tobacco acreage allotment and you bought or inherited their farm, you would be entitled to an allotment based on their share of past production.

A long-term government program aimed at reducing supply is the **Conservation Reserve Program (CRP)**. This program pays farmers to remove land from production for ten years or more. In 1990, the total amount of farm land in this program was about 25 million acres. Payments to farmers in the program in that year were over $1.5 billion.[12]

The supplies of many crops that are not directly subsidized by the federal government are controlled by marketing orders. The system of marketing orders started in 1937 with the goal of maintaining farm income and stable marketing conditions. **Marketing orders** establish producer cartels that control the supply of certain agricultural commodities not subject to price supports. The federal government enforces these cartel agreements through a system of fines for growers. Marketing orders are very common in the fruit-growing industry. The influence of these cartels on supply can be enormous. For example, in 1983, 20 million cases of lemons were destroyed to keep them off the market. The amount of lemons destroyed in 1983 exceeded the amount sold to consumers.[13]

Soil bank program
The federal agricultural program that began in the 1950s under which farmers were paid to let their land lie idle in order to reduce their supply of farm products.

Acreage allotment
A limit set by the government on the number of acres that can be used to produce a specific crop, based on past production levels.

Conservation Reserve Program (CRP)
A federal program that pays farmers to remove land from production for ten years or more.

Marketing orders
A federal program that establishes producer cartels that control the supply of certain agricultural products not subject to price supports.

---

11. The Canadian government once destroyed 28 million eggs. See Patrick Howe, "Unscrambling the Egg Market: A Lesson in Economics," *Common Sense Economics 2* (Spring 1977): 42–47. For some ludicrous stories of price supports gone amok, see *Fortune* (November 25, 1985): 149, and (December 9, 1985): 150.
12. Jeffrey D. Karrenbrock, "The 1988 Drought: Its Impact on District Agriculture," *Review*, Federal Reserve Bank of St. Louis (May/June 1989): 8.
13. Doug Bandow, "Federal Marketing Orders: Good Food Rots While People Starve," *Business and Society Review* (Spring 1985): 41.

The transfer to farmers through marketing orders is a bit different from the transfer through support payments. In support programs, the payment from the government to the farmer represents a transfer from all taxpayers. Under marketing orders, the subsidy takes the form of a federally enforced artificially high price. This subsidy is a transfer from the consumers of specific products to the growers of those products.

Attempts to manage farm production directly by reducing inputs have not been very effective because most farmers are good entrepreneurs. Under the soil bank program, almost all farmers took their least productive land out of production with little decline in output. In the acreage allotment program, farmers had an incentive to cultivate the allowed acres very intensively in an effort to produce nearly the same output on fewer acres. Marketing orders have been more effective in reducing quantity supplied. Farmers cannot benefit by increasing productivity and output when the government specifies the maximum allowed output.

INCREASING DEMAND. In addition to trying to restrict supply, another way to raise prices for agricultural products is to increase demand. There have been some governmental attempts to do this. The Department of Agriculture (USDA) has engaged in export promotion. Programs have been created by the USDA and some land grant universities to assist companies in penetrating foreign markets. In other cases, the government has sold agricultural products directly to foreign countries, most often the former Soviet Union.

Another demand-increasing program is the food stamp program. In this program, the USDA gives food stamps to the poor to enable them to buy more agricultural products. This program redistributes income at the same time that it increases the demand for agricultural products.

RECENT FARM POLICY

Target prices
Prices the government considers to be fair for farmers; used to determine subsidy payments.

Since 1973, there have been some changes in the system of agricultural price supports. For some products, there are no longer price floors. Instead, the government sets target prices. **Target prices** are prices the government considers to be fair for farmers. The market is allowed to clear, and the USDA then compares the equilibrium price to the target price. The government then pays each farmer the difference between the target price and the market-clearing price. Target prices have less of a distorting effect than support prices because the relative prices of agricultural products are allowed to change. Also, the government does not have to purchase and store the surplus product. Finally, the subsidy aspect is more apparent with target prices than with support prices.

During the 1980s, the Reagan administration made some attempts to reduce the price support programs. The first attempt in early 1981 kept a scheduled rise in target prices for milk from going into effect. This move did not do away with supports, but did prevent an increase at that time.

Payment in kind (PIK) program
A federal agricultural program similar to the soil bank program, but with payments made in surplus commodities rather than in money.

In 1982, President Reagan initiated a **payment in kind (PIK) program**. The idea was to eliminate the overproduction (caused by the existing support prices) and deal with the huge stocks of farm surpluses. For example, the program gave a farmer 8,000 bushels of stored corn, which the farmer would sell, in exchange for idling a certain amount of land. The PIK program was similar to the soil bank program, but payment was made in surplus commodities rather than in money. The result was the same as for the soil bank program. Farmers idled 47 million

GLOBAL OUTLOOK: THE COMMON AGRICULTURAL POLICY

The European Community (EC) maintains a common agricultural policy (CAP) for its member nations. Unlike agricultural policy in the United States, which is based on paying not to produce, CAP says "pay for everything produced." This system of guaranteed payment has produced huge surpluses that are either rotting in storage or are sold to other countries at bargain basement prices.

CAP has resulted in what are jokingly referred to as the French wine lake, the European grain mountain, and the great olive oil sea. Great Britain has 150 storage depots that are stuffed full of grain and butter. A junior minister in Great Britain testified in the House of Commons that the cost of storing and disposing of stocks of cereals, sugar, wine, milk, and beef was about $25 million per day. A "rancher" with three or more cows is entitled to a subsidy from the EC. Many people have become cow ranchers; Bavaria, Germany, is full of cottages on small plots of land with three cows. Former Prime Minister Thatcher complained, "In Europe, believe it or not, the subsidy for every cow is greater than the personal income of half the people in the world."

The subsidy schemes in CAP are very intricate and bureaucratic. Many have come under attack in the British press because of their complexity. For example, one passage reads:

If you are claiming only Beef Special Premium and/or Suckler Cow Premium and *are exempted from the stocking density rules, you need not submit an area aid application. You are exempt from the stocking density rules if your total number of Livestock Units (LUs) is not more than 15. This total is based on any milk quota you hold on April 1, 1993, and cattle on which you are claiming Beef Special Premium or Suckler Cow Premium in 1993. Further details of the calculation of stocking density and LUs are set in paragraphs 44 to 57 of the explanatory booklet "CAP Reform in the Beef Sector." You will, however, need to submit an area aid application if you wish to claim extensification premium (see paragraphs 58 to 61 of "CAP Reform in the Beef Sector").*

Anyone want to try to translate this English into English?

Source: "Agriculture: The New Corn Laws", *The Economist* (December 12, 1992): 3–18.

---

acres of land in 1983, but they put aside their least productive land and worked the best land more efficiently. The percentage drop in production was much less than the percentage of land set aside.

THE FOOD SECURITY ACT OF 1985. In 1985, Congress passed the **Food Security Act.** The intent of the law was to make U.S. agricultural products more competitive on world markets. The law eliminated the price support programs that caused their prices to be above world market prices. The Food Security Act sets target prices and requires farmers to agree to keep part of their land idle. Thus, it combines elements of both the target price and soil bank programs. Farmers sell their products at world market prices, and the government pays them a deficiency payment equal to the difference between the target price and the world price. The target price is supposed to be related to the costs of production.

In 1986, the target price of wheat was $4.38 per bushel, and the world market price was around $2.75 per bushel. As a result, U.S. taxpayers had to make a payment of $1.63 for every bushel of wheat sold. As you might imagine, the cost of the Food Security Act is enormous. When Congress debated the bill in early 1985, the cost over its five-year life was estimated at $35 billion. When President Reagan signed the bill in November 1985, his advisers estimated that cost to be $52 billion. In November 1989, the Congressional Budget Office reported that the actual cost for only the first *three* years of the program was $70 billion.

Food Security Act
A 1985 federal law that sets target prices and requires farmers to agree to keep part of their land idle.

SAVE THE FAMILY FARM ACT. In 1987, Senator Tom Harkin of Iowa and Congressman Richard Gephardt of Missouri introduced the Save the Family Farm Act. The goal of this act was to raise farm prices by drastically decreasing farm output (by more than half). Farmers would be given the opportunity to control production by voting mandatory limits on the amount of farm land that could be put into production. Farmers would face penalties if they did not limit production. However, the bill did not specify what the penalties would be. *Business Week* commented that the Harkin-Gephardt bill sounded "borrowed from a Soviet economic plan."[14]

Supporters of the bill argued that, although prices to consumers would increase, taxpayers would save billions in subsidy payments. One difficulty with this proposal was that, if it were successful in raising U.S. prices, imports would be cheaper and import competition would drive the artificially high U.S. prices down to world market levels. Thus, the program could only achieve its goal with more restrictive tariffs and quotas on agricultural imports than existed at the time. The Save the Family Farm Act did not pass in 1987, but it may be introduced again in another form.

THE 1990S. Agriculture in the 1990s has to compete for attention with other high-visibility, high-priority issues such as crime, health care, welfare reform, and unemployment: The floods of summer 1993 did call attention to the issue of subsidized farming in high-risk areas, such as flood plains. With heavy past investments in farms and farmers, it is likely that the government will continue agricultural price support for some time to come.

CONFLICTING EFFECTS OF FARM POLICIES

Many of the federal government's farm policies work at cross purposes. Consider, for example, the price support program, which guarantees farmers an unlimited market for grains and dairy products. Farmers expand production because they know they have a buyer to generate the cash flow to meet their payments on expensive machinery and heavily mortgaged land. Thus, this policy works to stimulate production. Other programs, such as the soil bank and marketing orders, are intended to decrease production.

In 1986, the federal government set out to mop up the milk glut created by price supports and in the process created a new problem. In a sweeping offensive called the Dairy Termination Program, the government sought to eliminate 12.3 billion pounds of milk from the market by buying up dairy herds and selling the animals for beef. In order to participate in the program, farmers had to agree to stay out of the dairy business for five years. Almost $2 billion was spent to get 14,000 farmers out of the milk business. Groups representing beef producers were quick to respond. The program designed to increase milk prices by cutting supply had the opposite effect on beef prices. Prices fell as the supply of beef increased. The California Cattlemen's Association demanded compensation for their losses of from $25 to $60 per head of beef.

Under still another program, the **Soil Conservation Service**, grants were given to encourage farmers to conserve land (rather than produce full tilt) by

Soil Conservation Service
A federal program under which grants were given to encourage farmers to contract production by fallowing fields, contour plowing, and other conservation techniques.

---

14. Michael A. Pollock, "Farmers Will Reap a Bumper Crop of Supports," *Business Week* (January 12, 1987): 83.

fallowing fields, contour plowing, and other conservation techniques. (All of these techniques temporarily reduce crop yields.) The price support and the soil conservation programs, both costly to taxpayers, work in opposite directions. One creates incentives to expand production; the other offers incentives to contract production.

STATE REGULATION OF AGRICULTURE

A relatively new development in government intervention in the agricultural market has been at the state level. In the late 1980s, several states passed legislation that made it more difficult for large corporate farms to operate. Laws passed in Kansas, Iowa, Nebraska, South Dakota, and Minnesota prevent corporations with more than a certain number of stockholders (usually fifteen) from owning land. The intent of such legislation is to preserve the family farm. As Kansas state representative Bruce Larkin said, "The intent of these laws is to keep the family farm in place. Without a family farm structure, rural communities will dry up and wither away."[15] The legislation ignores the economic fact of life that family farms are disappearing. They are being replaced by large-scale corporate farming. Legislation is probably not going to change this trend.

One outcome of such state legislation has been an economic boon to adjacent states. National Farms, Inc. is building a 1,200-acre hog farm near Brush, Colorado. The company had originally planned to build this farm in South Dakota, but South Dakota passed anti-corporate farm legislation in 1988. The farm produces 300,000 hogs a year and employs 200 farm workers. Maybe some of the unemployed family farmers in South Dakota will move to Colorado to find work!

In early 1990, the state of Wisconsin passed a law prohibiting the sale of milk from cows that had been given a newly developed hormone that dramatically increases milk production. Supporters of the bill argued that health officials were concerned about possible effects of this hormone on humans. Wisconsin lawmakers maintained that they were worried about potential health risks from the hormone. Cynics argued that the lawmakers saw the bill as a way to reduce the potential supply of milk.

THE FUTURE OF FARM POLICY

U.S. agriculture policy is at a crossroads. The annual direct subsidy to the average American farmer is more than twice the mean family income in the United States. Two options are open to policy makers: the first is to follow a protectionist, supply management policy. The second option is to confront the challenge presented by other countries in recent tariff negotiations. These negotiations have developed an agreement to negotiate all barriers affecting trade in agricultural products. In 1991, the United States proposed an initiative that would eliminate all agricultural price supports in all member countries by the year 2000. Under this proposal, all government payments to farmers would be "decoupled" from farm production. This change would be drastic in that it would make the payments to farmers into direct welfare benefits rather than transfers through other mechanisms.[16]

---

15. This quote and the facts in the next paragraph are from Charles Siler, "Where Did All the Pigs Go?" *Forbes* (March 19, 1990): 152–156.
16. See E. C. Pasour, "Farm Programs Hurt Everyone—Even Farmers," *The Independent* (Vol. II, No. 1, 1989): 3.

Yet the position of U.S. negotiators in foreign trade conferences belies the action of officials at home. The truth is that farm subsidies are very difficult to end. In the federal budget discussions of 1993, the original Clinton cuts included many in agriculture. Consider the case of honey price support. Between 1989 and 1993, the federal government spent more than $230 billion subsidizing honey bee farmers. Republican Congressman Hank Brown of Colorado said, "If we cannot eliminate this program, we cannot eliminate anything." Beekeeper T. Ray Chancey of Dayton, TX, countered with, "We (beekeepers) have a lot of friends in Congress." Chancey was correct—the U.S. Senate voted fifty-six to forty-one to keep the honey subsidy. Perhaps Congressman Chancy is correct also when he says Congress can't eliminate any agriculture subsidy.[17]

Like many social problems, the farm problem cannot be resolved with the tools of economics. These tools can, however, point out some basic options. There are too many resources in the agricultural industry relative to the demand for its output. The resources are encouraged to stay there by transfer payments made to farmers out of general tax revenues. Taxpayers' income is being redistributed to farmers, keeping resources in the farm industry that would otherwise be attracted to other industries. In 1993, the direct budget costs of federal agriculture programs were more than $1,000 for every nonfarm family in the United States. These payments represent a significant share of federal tax revenues and do not include the off-budget transfers to farmers.

The basic tools of economics do not reveal whether this situation is good or bad or predict whether anything will be done to change it. The answer to the first question is a value judgment concerning whether society thinks it is good or bad to maintain the present level of resources in agriculture. The answer to the second question will, in part, depend on the political strength of farmers and the farm constituency relative to other groups.

***

Consider again...*We can now reflect back on the publishing venture of Andre Schiffrin. What does he mean when he says that he is publishing books in the "public interest"? You now know from looking at markets that public interest means the interest of consumers. If the interest of consumers are met, the market will bring the books that the public wants in production. What Schiffrin means by public interest is his interest, or, perhaps even more correctly, the interest of members of governing boards of foundations that will give him money. This use of the term* public *is one that is often used incorrectly from an economic perspective. Public radio and public television don't have anything to do with the public, if by public you mean most consumers. In that sense, commercial TV is what really should be called public TV. One final point: Is Schiffrin acting in his own self-interest, or, as the critic said, in a self-serving manner? You decide!*

As we have just seen, microeconomics is concerned with how incentives influence decision making and the ways in which institutions and changes in institutions in-

---

17. Doug J. Swanson, *The Dallas Morning News* (September 23, 1993).

fluence incentives and, in turn, the behavior of individuals. This method of looking at markets gives economists powerful insights into the impact that policies have.

SUMMARY

1. Crime can be modeled and analyzed as an economic activity resulting from a rational decision by the criminal. To decrease criminal activity, it is necessary to decrease the benefits the criminal receives or increase the costs the criminal must pay, or both. This holds for the entire range of crime, from illegal parking to armed robbery or murder.
2. Price ceilings are attempts to keep prices from rising to their equilibrium level. Price ceilings cause shortages, and black markets often develop in response to the shortages. Rent control is an example of a price ceiling. Price floors are attempts to keep prices from falling to their equilibrium level. Price floors cause surpluses that must be absorbed to prevent the price from falling. Agricultural price supports and minimum wages are examples of price floors. Rent control is a price ceiling in housing markets. Rent control will cause rental unit shortages. The minimum wage is a price floor in labor markets. Price floors cause surpluses to develop. In labor markets these surpluses are unemployed workers.
3. Prices and markets allocate goods and services by a process that allocates the good to the individual or group that is willing to pay the highest price. This allocative function can lead to policy arguments to change that market allocation.
4. The long-run problem for American farmers is the result of huge increases in productivity in the last century. In the short run, farmers' problems result from the fact that the farm sector is very competitive and is affected heavily by the weather. Most federal governmental farm policies are aimed at slowing the trend toward fewer agricultural workers. The various price support programs work primarily on the supply side of the agricultural market. The major programs have attempted to support prices or to manage production, often with conflicting results. The result of government intervention into agriculture has not been successful from an economic perspective.

NEW TERMS

price ceilings
price floors
shortage
black markets
rent control
surplus

Commodity Credit
  Corporation (CCC)
minimum wage
agricultural support
  program
parity

support prices
soil bank program
acreage allotment
Conservation Reserve
  Program (CRP)
marketing orders

target prices
payment in kind (PIK)
  program
Food Security Act
Soil Conservation Service

QUESTIONS: REVIEW, APPLICATIONS, AND POLICY

REVIEW

1. Why does a price ceiling that is set above the equilibrium price have no immediate effect on the market?
2. What are the short-term and long-term problems facing farmers? Why might these problems be considered market failures?
3. What is the distributional difference between support payments to farmers and marketing orders?
4. Why do programs such as the soil bank and acreage allotment programs have a smaller than expected influence on the supply of agricultural products?

APPLICATIONS

5. Can you formulate models like the simple economic model of crime for other decisions, such as having children, getting married, or getting a divorce?
6. How is the minimum wage maintained at higher than market-clearing rates? Why don't the unemployed workers agree to work for lower wages and thereby circumvent the imposed price floor?
7. Many price controls were used in the United States during World War II. Using the models developed in this chapter, how well do you think they worked?
8. Suppose you have an 8:00 A.M. economics class that is far away from the student parking lot. You learn over

time that if you park in a faculty spot but move your car by 9:15 A.M., you are ticketed every fourth time. The ticket cost is $15. What value are you implicitly placing on that illegal parking space? If the university raised the ticket price to $30, would you still park illegally? What effect would a towing policy have on your behavior?

9. Suppose that the price, total demand, and total supply of winter wheat on the Chicago grain market in March 1995 are as follows:

PRICE PER BUSHEL (DOLLARS)	BUSHELS DEMANDED (THOUSANDS)	BUSHELS SUPPLIED (THOUSANDS)
4.65	90	77
4.85	85	78
5.05	80	80
5.25	75	82
5.45	65	86

What is the equilibrium price? What is the equilibrium quantity? Why is this the equilibrium? Explain the forces that bring the market to this equilibrium, starting at a price of $5.25.

10. Draw the demand and supply curve for winter wheat using the data in Question 9.

11. What would happen if the federal government set a price floor (a support) for winter wheat of $5.45 per bushel? Draw this price floor on the diagram you produced in Question 10.

12. What would happen if the federal government set a price ceiling for winter wheat of $5.45 per bushel? Draw this price ceiling on the diagram from Question 10.

POLICY

13. Today farmers represent about 2 percent of the U.S. population, but they get more than $40 billion in governmental outlays. This is much more than farmers received in 1950, when they were a much larger segment of the population. Does it make sense for farmers to be getting more powerful politically as their share of the voting population decreases?

14. Nobel Prize-winning economist T. W. Schultz has referred to parity as "a vulgar economic concept." What did he mean?

15. Usury laws are laws that set maximum interest rates. These laws are price ceilings in the market for loanable funds. What will happen in states that have usury laws when the equilibrium interest rate exceeds the established ceiling? Why, then, are usury laws politically popular?

16. Even when many people know the negative impacts of rent control, rent control laws are hard to repeal. Why?

17. In 1991, the minimum wage in the United States increased to $4.25. This increase was not met with predictions by economists of dire consequences, as previous increases in the minimum wage were. Why?

18. Why do bureaucracies seldom make use of markets to allocate scarce resources?

SUGGESTIONS FOR FURTHER READING

Anderson, Robert M. "EP Seeks EP: A Review of *Sex and Reason*, by Richard Posner." *Journal of Economic Literature* (March 1993): 191–198. Posner's 1992 book, *Sex and Reason*, shows how basic economics has been applied to "other" human activities, such as sex. In this review, Anderson takes exception to Posner's approach.

Carr, Edward. "The New Corn Laws." *The Economist* (December 12, 1992): 3–18. A very readable review of the "absurd proportions" that farm subsidies have reached, complete with international comparisons.

Galston, William A. *A Tough Row to Hoe: The 1985 Farm Bill and Beyond*. New York: Hamilton Press, 1985. Covers the issues underlying the debate over the 1985 farm bill.

O'Rourke, P. J. "Manuregate." *Rolling Stone* (July 12, 1990): 45–48. A satirical view of the farm problem.

Scully, Gerald. *The Business of Major League Baseball*. Chicago: University of Chicago Press, 1989. Uses basic economic analysis to explain the economics of baseball.

CHAPTER 19
ELASTICITY: THE MEASURE OF RESPONSIVENESS

Consider this... *On the way to class you stumble across an old lamp. Instead of kicking it into the ditch, you pick it up and rub it; a genie jumps out and offers you three wishes. For one of your wishes, you ask to be the sole inventor, owner, and producer of Nintendo games. It is granted.*

You now are in a position to be very rich. What price should you charge for the Nintendo games? How many should you sell? For the sake of argument let's assume you want to be as rich as possible and that you can produce the games at no cost—they just appear like the genie. Now, what price should you charge and how many should you sell? You know that demand curves slope downward to the right, so in order to sell more you will have to lower your price. What a dilemma! This chapter will show you how to be as rich as possible!

LEARNING OBJECTIVES
1. Review the most important concepts in supply and demand analysis.
2. Define elasticity as a measure of responsiveness.
3. Define and calculate the coefficient of price elasticity of demand.
4. Define and calculate the income elasticity of demand and the cross elasticity of demand.
5. Define and calculate the price elasticity of supply.
6. Determine the incidence of an excise tax.

To do so we extend the concepts of supply and demand by developing another tool of the microeconomist—the elasticity measurement. **Elasticity** is the measure of the sensitivity, or responsiveness, of quantity demanded or quantity supplied to changes in price (or other conditions). We will develop several elasticity measures and then demonstrate their usefulness in the analysis of public policy and selling Nintendo games.

SUPPLY AND DEMAND REVISITED

Supply and demand are basic to economic analysis. It is worth reviewing them before beginning to expand your kit of economic tools.

When developing the concept of demand, we stressed the distinction between shifts in demand curves and movement along demand curves. Any movement along a demand curve occurs in response to a change in price and is referred to as a *change in quantity demanded*. Any shift of the demand curve is called

Elasticity
The measure of the sensitivity or responsiveness of quantity demanded or quantity supplied to changes in price (or other factors).

a *change in demand*. Changes in demand occur in response to changes in one or more of the *ceteris paribus* conditions that underlie the demand curve: the tastes of the group demanding the good or service, the size of that group, the income and wealth of that group, the prices of other goods and services, or expectations about any of these conditions.

Similarly, there is an important difference between changes in supply and changes in quantity supplied. The phrase *change in quantity supplied* indicates to the economist that the change that occurred was in response to a change in price. The phrase *change in supply* means that the change occurred in response to a change in one or more of the *ceteris paribus* conditions affecting supply: the prices of the productive factors, the number of sellers, the technology used to produce the good, or expectations about any of these conditions.

These principles and terms are useful in explaining economic events. Figure 1 is a diagram of supply and demand in the market for automobiles. Stable *ceteris paribus* conditions have been assumed, and differences in autos' quality, size, and gas mileage have been ignored, so that a demand curve for like units can be drawn. The market determines an equilibrium price of P_1 and quantity of Q_1. Now suppose the price of gasoline increases. Since gasoline and automobiles are complements, you know that the increase in the price of gasoline is going to cause the demand for automobiles to shift from D_1 to D_2 in Figure 1. That is, with gasoline being more expensive, people drive less, reducing the demand for automobiles. This decrease in demand for autos causes the price to fall to P_2 and the quantity supplied to decrease to Q_2. Remember that quality and other factors are held constant. Thus, the decrease in the demand for automobiles could represent a switch to smaller cars or less frequent trade-ins for newer models.

FIGURE 1

THE MARKET FOR AUTOMOBILES

Gasoline is a complementary good to automobiles. If the price of gasoline rises, there will be a decrease in the demand for automobiles. The price of autos will fall from P_1 to P_2, and the equilibrium quantity will decrease from Q_1 to Q_2. There has been a decrease in the quantity supplied.

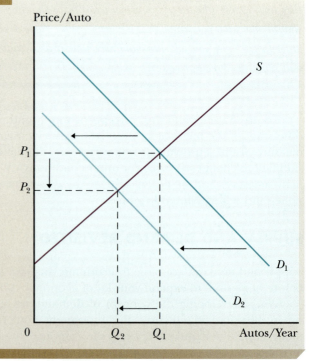

ELASTICITY AS A GENERAL CONCEPT

Elasticity measures the way one variable responds to changes in other variables. The dependent variable is the variable which depends or changes in response to some other variable, called the independent variable. The dependent variable (y) is written as a function of one or more independent variables (x_i):

(1) $\quad y = f(x_1, x_2, x_3, ..., x_n).$

Elasticity measures how the dependent variable responds to changes in any of the different independent variables. The formula to determine this responsiveness can be expressed as follows:

(2) $\quad E_1 = \dfrac{\%\Delta y}{\%\Delta x_1}, \; E_2 = \dfrac{\%\Delta y}{\%\Delta x_2}, \; E_n = \dfrac{\%\Delta y}{\%\Delta x_n}.$

This formula says that elasticity (E) is the percent change (the symbol Δ represents change) in the dependent variable (y) divided by the percent change in the particular independent variable (x) being examined.

In examining demand, economists are interested in how the quantity demanded responds to changes in price and to changes in certain other *ceteris paribus* conditions that affect demand. The quantity demanded of good A (Q_A^d) is thus the dependent variable, and the independent variables are the price of good A (P_A), income (I), tastes (T), the price of complements (P_c), and the price of substitutes (P_s). We can thus rewrite equation (1) as

$$Q_A^d = f(P_A, I, T, P_c, P_s).$$

It is now possible to determine how Q_A^d responds to change in any of the independent variables by holding all but one of them constant and calculating the elasticity coefficient using equation (2). For example, to see how quantity demanded responds to price, we use

$$E_d = \dfrac{\%\Delta Q_A^d}{\%\Delta P_A}.$$

where E_d is the coefficient of price elasticity of demand. This formula gives us the price elasticity of demand. **Price elasticity of demand** is the measure of the relative responsiveness of the quantity demanded to changes in price.

Price elasticity of demand The measure of the responsiveness of the quantity demanded to changes in price.

PRICE ELASTICITY OF DEMAND

In the late nineteenth century, the famous English economist Alfred Marshall developed the concept of elasticity to compare the demands for various products. When comparisons are made, it may be helpful to concentrate on the *relative* responsiveness of the quantity demanded to price changes rather than the absolute responsiveness, which is slope. Relative comparisons make it possible to measure and then describe the sensitivity of the demand relationship.

The **coefficient of price elasticity of demand** (E_d) is the numerical measure of price elasticity of demand. It is the percent change in quantity demanded of

Coefficient of price elasticity of demand (E_d) The numerical measure of price elasticity of demand, equal to the percent change in quantity demanded of a good divided by the percent change in its price.

a good divided by the percent change in price. That is, as you have seen, for good A,

$$E_d = \frac{\%\Delta Q_A^d}{\%\Delta P_A}.$$

Since percent change is the change in the variable divided by the base amount of the variable, this can be rewritten as

(3) $$E_d = \frac{\Delta Q_A^d / Q_A^d}{\Delta P_A / P_A}.$$

With most demand curves, the elasticity coefficient varies along the curve. However, some demand curves have a *constant* price elasticity of demand. We will examine three special cases before looking at more typical demand curves.

Figure 2 shows a vertical demand curve. With this curve, quantity demanded is totally unresponsive to changes in price. As price changes from P_1 to P_2, there is no change in the quantity demanded. The elasticity coefficient is

$$E_d = \frac{\Delta Q^d / Q_1}{\Delta P / P_1} = 0.$$

This vertical demand curve is a limiting case that violates the law of demand and is not known to exist in the real world. This curve is called a perfectly inelastic demand curve. **Perfectly inelastic demand** occurs when the coefficient of price elasticity of demand is zero. There is no response of quantity demanded to changes in price.

Figure 3 shows a horizontal demand curve, another limiting case. When price drops below P_1, an infinite increase in quantity of the good is demanded.

Perfectly inelastic demand Demand represented by a vertical demand curve with a coefficient of price elasticity of demand that is equal to zero. There is no response in quantity demanded to changes in price.

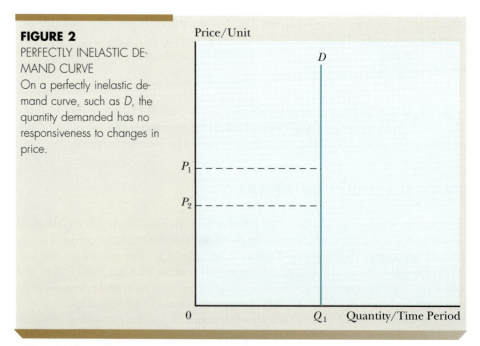

FIGURE 2
PERFECTLY INELASTIC DEMAND CURVE
On a perfectly inelastic demand curve, such as D, the quantity demanded has no responsiveness to changes in price.

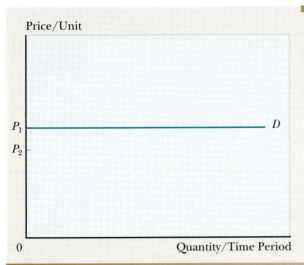

FIGURE 3
PERFECTLY ELASTIC DEMAND CURVE
On a perfectly elastic demand curve, such as D, the quantity demanded has an infinite response to changes in price. If price rises above P_1, no amount of the good will be purchased. If price falls to P_2, all that is available will be purchased.

If the price rises above P_1, quantity demanded drops to zero. Calculating the elasticity coefficient for a price change from P_1 to P_2 yields

$$E_d = \frac{\Delta Q^d / Q_1}{\Delta P / P_1} = \infty.$$

A horizontal demand curve is called a perfectly elastic demand curve because the response to changes in price is infinite. **Perfectly elastic demand** occurs when the coefficient of price elasticity of demand is infinite.

A third kind of demand curve is shown in Figure 4. The mathematical term for this curve is a *rectangular hyperbola*. Any percent decrease or increase in price causes the same percent increase or decrease in the quantity demanded. This means that the elasticity coefficient at any point along this demand curve is

Perfectly elastic demand Demand represented by a horizontal demand curve with a coefficient of price elasticity of demand that is equal to infinity. The quantity demanded is infinitely responsive to a change in price.

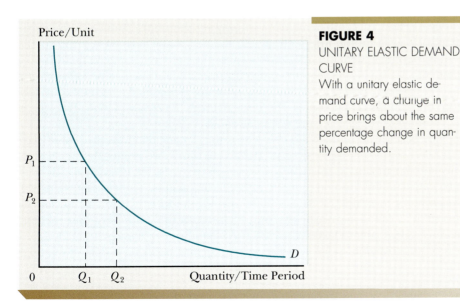

FIGURE 4
UNITARY ELASTIC DEMAND CURVE
With a unitary elastic demand curve, a change in price brings about the same percentage change in quantity demanded.

equal to 1. For example, if you calculated the elasticity coefficient for a price change from P_1 to P_2, you would find that

$$E_d = \frac{\Delta Q^d / Q_1}{\Delta P / P_1} = 1.$$

Such a demand curve is referred to as a unit elastic demand curve. **Unit elastic demand** occurs when the coefficient of price elasticity of demand is unitary (equal to 1).

Unit elastic demand
The situation where the coefficient of price elasticity of demand is unitary (equal to 1):

KEY IDEAS

A GUIDE TO ELASTICITY COEFFICIENT

NUMERICAL VALUE OF COEFFICIENTS	RESPONSIVENESS OF QUANTITY DEMANDED TO A CHANGE IN PRICE	TERMINOLOGY
• $E_d = 0$	No response	Perfectly inelastic
• $0 < E_d < 1$	Quantity demanded changes by a smaller percentage than the price changes	Inelastic
• $E_d = 1$	Quantity demanded changes by the same percentage as the price changes	Unit elastic
• $1 < E_d < \infty$	Quantity demanded changes by a larger percentage than the price changes	Elastic
• $E_d = \infty$	Quantity demanded becomes infinite, or all that is available is demanded	Perfectly elastic

Most demand curves are not shaped like those in Figures 2, 3, and 4. Most straight-line demand curves look like the one in Figure 5. Demand curve D has a *range* of elasticity coefficients from infinity (at the intersection with the vertical axis) to zero (at the intersection with the horizontal axis). When the coefficient is *less* than 1, demand is *inelastic* because the percent change in quantity demanded is less than the percent change in price. When the coefficient is *greater* than 1, demand is *elastic* because the quantity demanded changes relatively more than the price. Of course, there are degrees of responsiveness. The larger the coefficient, the greater the responsiveness.

The best way to understand elasticity is to calculate and interpret some elasticity coefficients. Before we do this, we need to clarify two points. Before an elasticity coefficient can be calculated, it is necessary to decide whether elasticity is to be calculated at a single point or between two points. The elasticity between two points is the value of the coefficient at the midpoint between the points. This value is called **arc elasticity**. Many economists use a different, but related, measure called **point elasticity**, which uses calculus to evaluate the responsiveness of quantity demanded to price at a particular point on a demand curve.[1]

Arc elasticity
The elasticity at the midpoint between two points on a demand curve.

Point elasticity
The elasticity at a particular point on a demand curve.

---

1. This concept relies on differential calculus. For those who have had calculus, elasticity at a particular point can be measured using the formula $E_d = dQ/dP \times P/Q$, where dQ/dP is the first derivative of the demand function $Q = f(P)$.

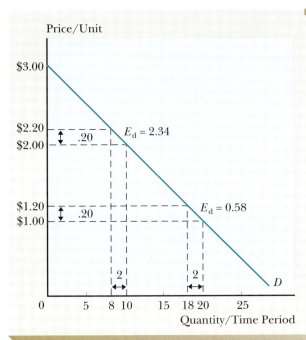

FIGURE 5
STRAIGHT-LINE DEMAND CURVE WITH VARYING ELASTICITY COEFFICIENTS
A straight-line demand curve has elasticity coefficients that vary from zero at the horizontal-axis intercept to infinity at the vertical-axis intercept.

Basically, the elasticity is measured at a point by assuming tiny changes in price and quantity demanded. However, we will use arithmetic to calculate particular coefficients and will be working with sizable changes. The numbers we will compute will be values of arc elasticity.

The second important point is that the formula for an elasticity coefficient will always produce a negative number because demand curves are negatively sloped. In practice, economists ignore the minus signs on coefficients of price elasticity of demand. An E_d value of −5 is considered to be larger than an E_d value of −4, for example. That is, these coefficients are treated as absolute values. It will be important later when considering other measures of elasticity to keep track of their signs, but the sign is not important for price elasticity of demand. Some economists put a negative sign in front of the formula to change the sign of the calculated coefficient.

The demand schedule of Table 1 can be used to calculate some coefficients of price elasticity of demand. Again, the formula is

$$E_d = \frac{\text{percent change in quantity demanded}}{\text{percent change in price}}.$$

For our purposes, this expression can be written as

$$E_d = \frac{\dfrac{\Delta Q}{\dfrac{Q_1 + Q_2}{2}}}{\dfrac{\Delta P}{\dfrac{P_1 + P_2}{2}}}.$$

Since we are calculating arc elasticity, we use averages. That is, we divide both the sum of the beginning price and the ending price and the sum of the begin-

TABLE 1 DEMAND SCHEDULE FOR STRAIGHT-LINE DEMAND CURVE IN FIGURE 5

PRICE	QUANTITY DEMANDED
$0.50	25
1.00	20
1.20	18
1.40	16
1.60	14
1.80	12
2.00	10
2.20	8
2.40	6
2.60	4
2.80	2
3.00	0

ning quantity and the ending quantity by two. If, instead of average values, we used the beginning or ending price and quantity as the bases, the formula would produce different elasticity measures between the same two points. By using this formula, we don't have to distinguish between price increases and decreases.

We can now compute the elasticity coefficients for two different price changes on the demand curve in Figure 5. First, the elasticity coefficient for the increase in price from $1.00 to $1.20:

$$E_d = \frac{\frac{20-18}{\frac{20+18}{2}}}{\frac{\$1.00-\$1.20}{\frac{\$1.00+\$1.20}{2}}} = \frac{\frac{2}{19}}{\frac{-.20}{\$1.10}} = \frac{0.105}{-0.182} = 0.58.$$

Recall that economists ignore the minus sign and just look at the absolute value of price elasticities of demand.

Now for the elasticity coefficient for the increase in price from $2.00 to $2.20:

$$E_d = \frac{\frac{10-8}{\frac{10+8}{2}}}{\frac{\$2.00-\$2.20}{\frac{\$2.00+\$2.20}{2}}} = \frac{\frac{2}{9}}{\frac{-.20}{\$2.10}} = \frac{0.222}{-0.095} = 2.34.$$

Note that the elasticity is different at different points along this demand curve, which has a constant slope. In fact, all linear demand curves except those that are vertical or horizontal have elasticity coefficients that range from zero through infinity. On a demand curve such as the one shown in Figure 6, all

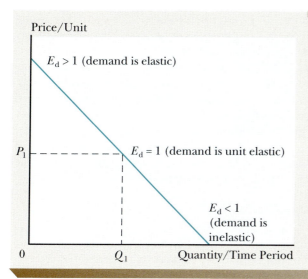

FIGURE 6
THE UNIT ELASTIC PRICE AND THE DEMAND CURVE
The point on the demand curve where $E_d = 1$ represents the unit elastic price (P_1) and divides the curve into two regions. At all prices above the unit elastic price, demand is elastic. At all prices below the unit elastic price, demand is inelastic.

points above price P_1 (which corresponds to the midpoint on a straight-line demand curve) have an elasticity coefficient greater than 1. At those points, demand is elastic. At price P_1, the elasticity coefficient is equal to 1. At that point, demand is unit elastic. All points below P_1 have an elasticity coefficient less than 1. In this region, demand is inelastic.

To see how important it is to average the quantity demanded and the price for the bases, you can calculate the effect of an increase in price from $1.00 to $1.20 and then of a decrease in price from $1.20 to $1.00 without averaging the P or Q in the denominator. If you do this, you will get two different elasticity coefficients, depending on whether the price is decreasing or increasing. When the average, or arc, elasticity between two points is found by averaging, the measure of elasticity will be the same in either direction.

The price elasticity of demand depends not only on the slope of the linear curve, but in addition, the size of quantity and price. Because the demand is a straight line, the demand curve in Figure 6 has a constant slope. However, the elasticity coefficients vary along this straight-line demand curve. The elasticity changes as we move along the curve. At the top of the curve price is high and quantity demanded is low. As a result, the elasticity coefficient will be high. As we move along the curve, price falls and quantity demanded increases; the coefficient therefore decreases as we move down the curve. Yet many students confuse the two. This confusion comes from the fact that economists sometimes use imprecise language. They often compare curves as to their elasticity, referring to one curve as being more inelastic than another. Be careful! All linear curves have portions that are elastic and portions that are inelastic, but some are more elastic at *each* price (or quantity) than others.

ELASTICITY AND SUBSTITUTABILITY

Price elasticity of demand depends, in large part, on the number of substitutes a good or service has. If a product, such as table salt, has relatively few substitutes, it will tend to have a relatively inelastic demand. This is just another way of saying that the quantity demanded of a good like table salt isn't very responsive to changes in price over a wide range of prices. The elasticity of demand for a broad category of goods will be lower than that for a specific good. For example, the elasticity of demand for salt in general will be lower than the elasticity of demand for Morton's salt.

Another determinant of the elasticity of demand is time. The longer the period of time consumers have to adjust, the more elastic the demand becomes. The reason for this is that a longer time period allows more opportunities to modify behavior and substitute different products. A good example is the elasticity of demand for natural gas. In the short run, the demand is likely to be very inelastic. Over time, however, as industry and homes convert to other sources of energy, the elasticity will increase. Table 2 lists estimated elasticities for some commonly purchased items in the range of their typical prices.

PRICE ELASTICITY OF DEMAND AND TOTAL REVENUE

Total revenue
The amount of money a firm takes in, equal to the quantity of the good or service sold multiplied by its price.

Demand curves illustrate price and quantity relationships. Quantity, or the number of items sold, multiplied by price equals the **total revenue** generated. The relationship between total revenue and price elasticity of demand explains how firms set and change prices. This relationship was first considered by French mathematician and economist Antoine Augustin Cournot (1801–1877). He wondered what the owner of a hypothetical mineral spring should charge for the spring's water, which was desired for its healing powers. Cournot made three assumptions: that the spring cost nothing to operate, that it produced an unlimited quantity of output, and that the owner wanted as much income as possible. If Cournot were writing today he would perhaps use Nintendo for an example rather than mineral water, although mineral springs have become very popular of late.

To determine the correct price, Cournot first recognized that a price change has two (opposite) effects on total revenue. The first effect is that a price decrease, by itself, will decrease total revenue. The other effect is that a price decrease causes quantity demanded to increase, thus increasing total revenue. The net effect of these two changes on total revenue depends on whether the relative price decrease exceeds the relative increase in quantity demanded, or vice versa. This is exactly the information that the price elasticity of demand provides.

For a concrete application of this principle, look again at Figure 5 and Table 1. At a price of $2.00, the total revenue (*TR*) is $20.00. An increase in price from

TABLE 2 SOME ESTIMATED ELASTICITIES

ITEM	E_d
Fresh tomatoes	4.60
Medical care	3.60
Canned tomatoes	2.50
Airline travel	2.40
Radios and televisions	1.25
Automobiles	0.80

Source: Adapted from Dean A. Worcester, Jr., "On Monopoly Losses: Comment," *American Economic Review* (December 1975): 1016.

$2.00 to $2.20 causes TR to fall from $20.00 to $17.60. TR drops because the 10 percent increase in price caused an even greater percent decrease in quantity demanded. The elasticity coefficient at that point was greater than 1. Conversely, if the price rises from $1.00 to $1.20, TR increases from $20.00 to $21.60 because the percent increase in price is greater than the percent decrease in quantity demanded. The elasticity coefficient at that point is less than 1.

Figure 7 illustrates the same principle. On both demand curves, the price falls from P_1 to P_2, and quantity demanded increases from Q_1 to Q_2D_1 and Q_2D_2 respectively. This price change causes the total revenue to change. Some revenue is lost and some revenue is gained. In Figure 7, the red area represents revenue that has been lost. The gold area represents revenue that has been gained on the relatively elastic demand curve, while the gold crosshatched area represents revenue gained on the relatively inelastic demand curve. With the more inelastic demand curve, the decrease in price brings about a decrease in total revenue. With the more elastic demand curve, the decrease in price brings about an increase in total revenue.

In other words, you can determine what will happen to total revenue when price changes if you know the elasticity of demand. A reduction in price will always cause an increase in quantity demanded, but total revenue will decrease with inelastic demand and increase with relatively elastic demand. Similarly, a rise in price will cause total revenue to fall when demand is relatively elastic and to rise when demand is relatively inelastic.

The answer to Cournot's question is that the owner of the mineral spring should not try to charge the highest possible price or sell the largest possible amount. The owner should set the price where the elasticity coefficient is 1. To see why, imagine that the price is where the elasticity coefficient is 0.5. Demand is inelastic. If the owner raises the price, quantity demanded will decrease, but

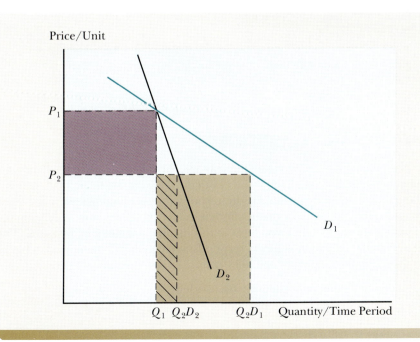

FIGURE 7
CHANGES IN TOTAL REVENUE
Equal price changes bring about different changes in total revenue, depending on the elasticity of the demand curve. If the demand curve is relatively inelastic, a decrease in price will bring about a decrease in total revenue. If the demand curve is relatively elastic, the same decrease in price will bring about an increase in total revenue.

by only half the rate of the price increase. Therefore, total revenue will rise. On the other hand, if the elasticity coefficient is 2 (or demand is elastic), the owner should decrease the price. If the price is lowered, the quantity demanded increases at twice the rate of the price. The owner will maximize total revenue when the demand coefficient is 1, or demand is unit elastic. So the mineral spring owner should set the price at P_1 in Figure 6. At price P_1, the area $P_1 \times Q_1$ represents maximum possible total revenue.

A good example of the importance of elasticity of demand is in setting prices occurred in the U.S. airline industry. The airline industry, believing that the demand for air travel was inelastic, had historically been against deregulation. The reason was that increased competition would result in lower fares. When deregulation occurred, the revenues of the airline companies increased dramatically despite the lower fares. The experience indicated that the demand for air travel was relatively elastic, or at least much more elastic than the airlines had thought. The airlines had set their prices based on incorrect estimates of the elasticity of demand. Now every summer the airlines run deep discounts to attract family travel, which has an elastic demand.

Perhaps the best example of the effect of price elasticity on total revenue is that of Henry Ford's Model T. When Ford entered the scene, automobiles were a curiosity for the rich. Ford's strategy was to make autos for the average person through mass production—but he had to sell them. He found that by reducing prices, he sold more autos and increased profits. In the process, Ford Motor Company revolutionized production. In the early years of the Model T, Henry Ford said, "Every time I reduce the charge for our car by one dollar, I get a thousand new buyers."[2]

KEY IDEAS

ELASTICITY AND TOTAL REVENUE

PRICE CHANGE	CHANGE IN QUANTITY DEMANDED	COEFFICIENT OF ELASTICITY	CHANGE IN TOTAL REVENUE
• Rise	Decrease	$E_d > 1$	Decrease
• Rise	Decrease	$E_d = 1$	Unchanged
• Rise	Decrease	$E_d < 1$	Increase
• Fall	Increase	$E_d > 1$	Increase
• Fall	Increase	$E_d = 1$	Unchanged
• Fall	Increase	$E_d < 1$	Decrease

OTHER DEMAND ELASTICITIES

Price elasticity of demand is not the only microeconomic measure of responsiveness. It is possible to calculate the elasticity of almost anything because what an elasticity coefficient measures is the responsiveness of one measurable quantity to another. Two other demand elasticities are quite common in economics.

The first of these other concepts is the **income elasticity of demand**. This measures the way in which demand responds to changes in income, assuming all other things, including price, are held constant. The formula is expressed as

$$E_I = \frac{\text{percent change in quantity demanded}}{\text{percent change in income}}.$$

Income elasticity of demand
The measure of the responsiveness of demand to changes in income.

---

2. *Forbes* (January 12, 1987): 26.

GLOBAL OUTLOOK: INCOME ELASTICITY OF DEMAND FOR CONSUMER GOODS

Many producers of consumer goods are looking to China and the Pacific Rim with great anticipation because of what they know about the income elasticity of demand for certain consumer products. For example, data shows that when per capita income is below $1,000, hardly any households buy color television sets. When incomes rise to over $1,000 per capita, almost all households have a color television. If you produce color television sets and you observe the rising levels of income in China, coupled with a population of over 1.2 billion, you can anticipate a significant increase in the world demand for color television sets.

The British magazine, *The Economist*, reports on the Malaysian experience with automobiles.[a] Between 1987 and 1991, per capita income rose to about $2,700. This was an increase of approximately 42 percent. The income threshold for automobile purchases seems to be about $4,000. A significant share of Maylasia's population passed this $4,000 threshold. Car purchases in Malaysia jumped 290 percent from 1987 to 1991, which means that the income elasticity of demand for automobiles was almost 7. For every 1 percent increase in income there was a 7 percent increase in automobile purchases.

Economic analysts speculate that by the turn of the century tens of millions of Chinese consumers will pass through the $4,000 threshold and hundreds of millions through the $1,000 threshold. Any wonder why TV producers and car manufacturers have been visiting China? If you want to go to work for General Motors, perhaps you should study Chinese!

a. "Chinese Consumers Next in Line," *The Economist* (January 23, 1993): 66.

The sign of the coefficient of the income elasticity of demand is important. If the sign is negative, indicating a negative relationship between income and demand, the good is said to be an inferior good. If the sign is positive, the good is a normal good.

For normal goods, if $E_I > 1$, demand for the good is income elastic. If $E_I < 1$, demand for the good is income inelastic. Goods that have high and positive income elasticities are classed as luxury goods. In fact, the concept of income elasticity of demand is used as a definition of what a luxury good is. Necessities, such as food, have a low but positive income elasticity. Luxuries, such as sports cars and foreign travel, have a high positive income elasticity.

Income elasticity is useful to producers in forecasting sales. If producers can forecast changes in consumer income and know the income elasticity of demand for their product, they can estimate how much more to produce. This planning is one of the reasons why firms are interested in economic forecasts.

The other common demand elasticity concept is the **cross elasticity of demand**. Cross elasticity measures the responsiveness of changes in demand of one good to changes in the price of another. The formula for the coefficient of the cross elasticity of demand is

$$E_{AB} = \frac{\text{percent change in quantity demanded of good } A}{\text{percent change in quantity demanded of good } B}.$$

Cross elasticity of demand The measure of the responsiveness of changes in the demand for one good to changes in the price of another.

If the cross elasticity is equal to anything but zero, the two goods are related. They are either complements or substitutes. Two goods that are completely unrelated (independent of one another) have a zero cross elasticity of demand. If the sign of the coefficient is negative, the relationship is an inverse one. An increase in the price of good *B* will bring about a decrease in the demand of good *A*. A negative cross elasticity coefficient thus indicates that good *A* and good *B* are complements. Complements are goods that are used together, such as coffee and cream or pens and paper. A positive cross elasticity coefficient indicates a substitute relationship between good *A* and good *B*. An increase in the price of good *B* will lead to an increase in the demand for good *A*. Substitute goods can be used in place of each other. Examples are coffee and tea, and beef and chicken. The size of the coefficient tells how strong the complementary or substitute relationship is between the two goods. As we will see in later chapters, cross elasticity is useful in defining markets and industries because it is a measure of how closely goods are related.

PRICE ELASTICITY OF SUPPLY

Price elasticity of supply
The measure of the responsiveness of the quantity supplied to changes in the price.

Coefficient of price elasticity of supply (E_s)
The numerical measure of price elasticity of supply, equal to the percent change in the quantity supplied of a good divided by the percent change in its price.

The concept of elasticity of demand is also applicable to supply schedules and supply curves. **Price elasticity of supply** is the measure of the responsiveness of the quantity supplied to changes in the price. The **coefficient of price elasticity of supply (E_s)** is the numerical measure of price elasticity of supply. The equation for the coefficient of price elasticity of supply is

$$E_s = \frac{\text{percent change in quantity supplied}}{\text{percent change in price}}$$

or, in a more workable form,

$$E_s = \frac{\Delta Q^s/Q^s}{\Delta P/P} \; .$$

As with the price elasticity of demand, when $E_s = 1$, supply is unit elastic. If $E_s > 1$, supply is elastic. If $E_s < 1$, supply is inelastic. The analogy to price elasticity of demand stops there. The coefficient of price elasticity of supply is usually positive because supply curves normally have positive slopes. Since supply curves are positively sloped, the relationship between elasticity and total revenue established for price elasticity of demand doesn't hold. Higher prices result in higher total revenue, regardless of whether supply is elastic or inelastic.

Special cases of supply curves are classified as perfectly inelastic, unit elastic, or perfectly elastic. With the vertical supply curve in Figure 8, the quantity supplied is totally unresponsive to changes in price. It is perfectly inelastic. Examples of perfectly inelastic supply curves are rare. In the short run, however, it is often impossible to produce more of a good regardless of what happens to price. This inability to produce more will affect the supply curve, which shows the amount producers are willing to supply at various prices. Consider the supply of Rembrandt paintings, for example, or of Rose Bowl tickets. A rise in the price of Rembrandt paintings (even in the long run) or Rose Bowl tickets (in the short run) does not cause the quantity supplied to increase. These supply curves are perfectly inelastic. This isn't quite correct because some individuals who own Rembrandt paintings will become suppliers if the price gets high enough. The price elasticity is actually zero only when the price gets high enough that all Rembrandt's are prospectively on the market. The example is, none the less, illustrative.

Figure 9 shows both a perfectly elastic supply curve and a unit elastic supply curve. S_1, a horizontal line, is a perfectly elastic supply curve. Any straight-line supply curve that is drawn through the origin, as is S_2 in Figure 9, is unit elastic

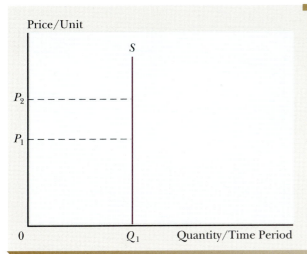

FIGURE 8
PERFECTLY INELASTIC SUPPLY CURVE
A perfectly inelastic supply curve is a vertical line. It would exist if suppliers offered a fixed amount of a good, regardless of any changes in its price.

over its entire range. Along such a curve, the percent changes of the two variables will always be equal to each other. Other linear supply curves are elastic at every price if they intersect the price (vertical) axis above the origin and inelastic at every price if they intersect the quantity (horizontal) axis to the right of the origin. This is true even though elasticity changes along both curves. Examples are shown in Figure 10.

PRODUCTION COSTS

Price elasticity of supply depends on the costs of production and how these costs change as the output of a good or service is increased. If costs rise rapidly as output is expanded, the quantity supplied will not be very responsive to changes in price. The supply curve is inelastic. On the other hand, if costs don't increase

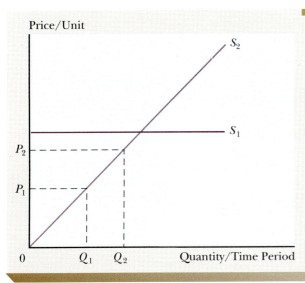

FIGURE 9
UNIT ELASTIC SUPPLY CURVE AND PERFECTLY ELASTIC SUPPLY CURVE
A perfectly elastic supply curve (S_1) is a horizontal line. With such a curve, a change in price produces an infinite response in the quantity supplied. A straight-line supply curve drawn through the origin (S_2) has a unitary coefficient of elasticity along the entire curve.

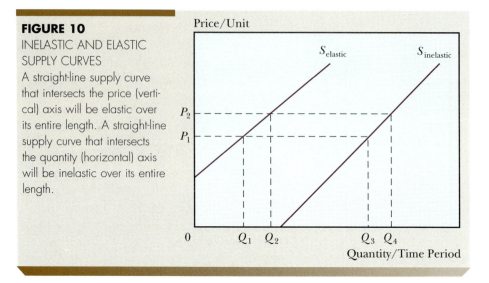

FIGURE 10

INELASTIC AND ELASTIC SUPPLY CURVES

A straight-line supply curve that intersects the price (vertical) axis will be elastic over its entire length. A straight-line supply curve that intersects the quantity (horizontal) axis will be inelastic over its entire length.

very much as output is increased, a rise in price will increase the profits of supplying firms and the output response could be substantial. The supply curve is elastic. Price elasticity of supply and the costs of production are so intertwined that we will postpone discussing them until a later chapter that examines costs.

RESOURCE AVAILABILITY AND TIME

Elasticity of supply is the measure of responsiveness of quantity supplied to changes in price. The major factor affecting this responsiveness is the availability of resources that can be attracted away from other uses. Another factor is the time period under consideration. As the time period increases, the possibility of obtaining new and different inputs to increase the supply increases. For the two earlier examples of fixed supply, you will recognize that in the long run the stadium could be expanded and the quantity of Rose Bowl tickets increased. These two factors—availability of inputs and time—affect elasticity of supply. Normally the elasticity of supply coefficient becomes larger with time and is larger for products that use relatively unspecialized or abundant inputs.

WHO PAYS THE EXCISE TAX?—AN EXERCISE IN THE ELASTICITY OF SUPPLY AND DEMAND

Debates over tax policy can be quite confusing. Consumers are often convinced that they ultimately pay all taxes, yet business firms often fight hard to prevent tax increases on their products. If consumers pay all taxes, why should a business firm care if its product is taxed or not? The answer is not simple. The correct answer to the question of who ultimately pays such a tax is, "It depends on supply and demand in the relevant market." This problem is an exercise that involves elasticity of both supply and demand.

An **excise tax** is a tax on the purchase of a particular good, such as liquor, cigarettes, or electricity, or a broad class of goods, such as food. Let's look at an example with normally sloped supply and demand curves. Figure 11 illustrates

Excise tax
A tax on the purchase of a particular good, such as liquor, cigarettes, or electricity, or a broad class of goods, such as food.

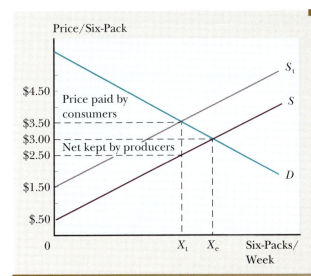

FIGURE 11
AN EXCISE TAX ON BEER
An excise tax on beer causes its supply curve to shift upward by the amount of the tax (from S to S_t). Less of the commodity is purchased at the higher price. Part of the tax is borne by consumers, and part of the tax is borne by producers.

the effect of an excise tax on the market for beer. Beer is a good example because excise taxes are often placed on items such as alcohol and cigarettes. These taxes are sometimes called "sin taxes."

Assume that the market settles on a price of $3.00 per six-pack, with X_e representing the equilibrium quantity of six-packs per week. Now suppose the government places an excise tax of $1.00 per six-pack on beer and collects this tax from producers. The costs of production have been increased by $1.00 per six-pack. The supply curve will shift up by the amount of the tax. One way to view the tax is that the producer must pay $1.00 per six-pack for the permission to produce beer. In terms of Figure 11, the supply curve shifts up at all points by $1.00. The post-tax supply curve is S_t. The equilibrium price will rise to $3.50 per six-pack, and the new equilibrium quantity is X_t.

Note that the new price is less than the sum of the old price and the tax. If the entire tax had been shifted onto consumers, the consumer would end up paying the old price of $3.00 plus the tax of $1.00, or $4.00 per six-pack. It is also clear that the amount of money the producer actually receives has fallen. Before the tax, the producer received $3.00 per six-pack, but now the producer receives $2.50 per six-pack ($3.50 price minus the $1.00 tax). The tax caused prices to rise, which caused the quantity demanded to fall. Because supply is relatively inelastic in this case, beer producers did not pass along the full amount of the tax in order to try to maintain sales. As a result, the producers sell a smaller quantity at a lower price than before. In this example, then, part of the tax was paid by consumers and part was paid by producers. Each paid half of the excise tax.

The amount of a tax paid by consumers or producers depends on the supply and demand elasticities for the goods being taxed. Figure 12 shows clearly how the elasticity of supply and the elasticity of demand affect the tax incidence. Tax incidence is the economist's term for who really pays the tax. **Tax incidence** is the place where the burden of a tax actually falls. It identifies those who pay the tax after all shifting has occurred.

Part (a) of Figure 12 shows a normally sloped supply curve and a perfectly inelastic demand curve. When the excise tax is placed on the good, the supply curve facing consumers shifts from S to S_{tax}. The result is that price rises from P_e

Tax incidence
The place where the burden of a tax actually falls after all shifting has occurred.

POLICY FOCUS: PRICE ELASTICITY OF DEMAND AND POLICY CHOICES—SMOKING

For many years, the U.S. government, primarily through the office of the Surgeon General, has pursued a policy of trying to discourage cigarette smoking. Many state and some local governments require public places, such as restaurants, to set up no-smoking sections and prohibit smoking in hospitals, doctors' offices, and public buildings. Most recently, the revenue from taxes on cigarettes has been suggested as a primary source of revenue for expanded national health care. We are not concerned with whether it is appropriate for government to try to intervene in personal decisions such as smoking, although it is interesting to note that the federal government has a domestic policy of discouraging cigarette smoking by Americans, subsidizing the growing of tobacco, and promoting the export of cigarettes to foreign countries.

The federal tax on cigarettes was $0.24 in 1993. In July 1993, insiders in the Clinton White House indicated that President Clinton could support a proposal pushed by the American Medical Association and The Coalition on Smoking and Health to increase the federal excise tax by $2.00 per pack and earmark the revenue for health care. The advocates of this tax argue that it would raise $35 billion yearly, enough to provide health insurance to 36 million Americans who have no health care insurance.

This forecast, however, assumes that there will be no response to the increased tax. But we know from studying elasticity that this is not the case. At the time this argument was made, the average price of a pack of cigarettes was about $2.00 and about 17.5 billion packs were sold annually on domestic markets. Thus the Clinton Administration official calculated that a $2.00 tax would raise $35 billion ($2.00 × 17.5 billion). Let's make a more realistic forecast based on the price elasticity of demand for cigarettes. The data on cigarette consumption and how it responds to changes in cigarette prices are not difficult to find. Suppose that you decide to use $E_d = 0.7$ from reviewing various studies of cigarette elasticities.[a] It is now a simple matter to compute the revenue that a $2.00 tax would generate and how it would impact on cigarette smoking. You know that the tax will increase $2.00 and that the present average price of a pack of cigarettes is $2.00. You can simply substitute into the elasticity formula to determine the effect of the tax:

$$E_d = \%\Delta Q / \%\Delta P$$

$$0.7 = \frac{\%\Delta Q}{(\$4 - \$2)/((\$2 + \$4)/2)}$$

$$0.7 = \%\Delta Q / 0.667$$

$$\%\Delta Q = 0.7 \times 0.667 = 46.7\%.$$

This calculation implies that cigarette consumption will fall from 17.5 billion packs annually to approximately 9.3 billion packs annually. Instead of generating $35 billion in tax revenue, the $2.00 tax will generate only $18.6 billion to be used to finance health care.

This result may at best be a lower estimate of the effect of the tax. We must qualify our policy advice. First, we must remember that elasticity estimates are for small changes in prices. This proposed tax increase is a huge increase in price, so our estimate may be quite inaccurate. The decrease in consumption might be more or less than 46.7 percent. Second, we must remind policy makers that this estimate is based on the assumption that all else remains the same. If it is proven that cigarette smoking is not bad for you, the estimate on the decline of smoking would be too high. On the other hand, if more evidence of the harmful effect of smoking is forthcoming, the estimate could be too low. But despite these qualifications, our estimate is more realistic than their estimate that did not use an elasticity calculation. These types of calculations are the essence of what economists do for policy advisers.

---

a. Many reports have reviewed studies of the price elasticity of demand for cigarettes. One study showed that the elasticity coefficient for smokers aged twelve to seventeen was 1.4. The elasticity coefficient for smokers as a whole was 0.7 [*Fortune* (February 13, 1989): 123]. Additional data on smoking and elasticity studies can be found in *Business Week* (June 18, 1990): 20–21; *Business Week* (March 14, 1993): 18; and *Fortune* (June 14, 1993): 138.

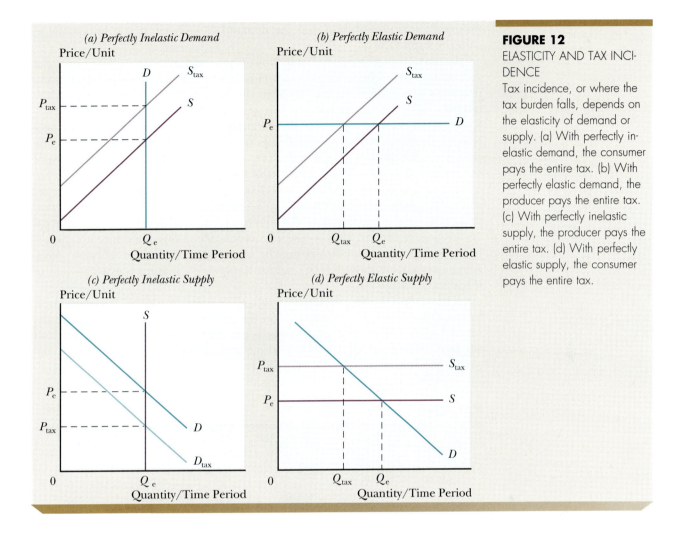

FIGURE 12

ELASTICITY AND TAX INCIDENCE

Tax incidence, or where the tax burden falls, depends on the elasticity of demand or supply. (a) With perfectly inelastic demand, the consumer pays the entire tax. (b) With perfectly elastic demand, the producer pays the entire tax. (c) With perfectly inelastic supply, the producer pays the entire tax. (d) With perfectly elastic supply, the consumer pays the entire tax.

to P_{tax}. Price has risen by the full amount of the tax, and the equilibrium quantity is unchanged. In this case, the incidence of the excise tax falls fully on the consumers of this good. The tax has been shifted forward to consumers by the full amount of the tax.

Part (b) of Figure 12 shows a normally sloped supply curve and a perfectly elastic demand curve. The post-tax supply curve is again S_{tax}. After the tax is imposed, price is unchanged at P_e, but the equilibrium quantity has fallen from Q_e to Q_{tax}. Since the price to consumers is unchanged, the producer is paying the entire tax. The incidence of the tax falls fully on the suppliers of this good.

The principle demonstrated by the first two parts of Figure 12 is clear. The more inelastic the demand for a good, the more any excise tax placed on the good will fall on consumers of that good. Conversely, the more elastic the demand, the more any excise tax placed on the good will fall on the producers.

In order to see the effects of different supply elasticities, it is necessary to refer to another graph. The usual way to represent a tax increase on a graph is by an upward shift in the supply curve. However, we can also represent a tax increase by a downward shift of the demand curve. In the case of perfectly inelastic supply, it is necessary to shift the demand curve because it is impossible to shift the supply curve.

In part (*c*) of Figure 12, *D* still shows what consumers are willing to pay for various quantities, including the tax. However, D_{tax} is the demand curve as the producer sees it, after the tax has been subtracted. The tax does not affect the quantity, which is determined by the perfectly inelastic supply curve. The industry views the demand curve as the curve with the amount of the tax subtracted from the price. The equilibrium quantity is unchanged by the shift. The price the firm receives falls from P_e to P_{tax}. In other words, the entire amount of the tax has been paid by the suppliers of the good.

Part (*d*) of Figure 12 shows a perfectly elastic supply curve. An excise tax shifts the supply curve from *S* to S_{tax} to account for the higher price at each output. After the shift, the price of the item has increased from P_e to P_{tax}, by the exact amount of the tax. In this case, consumers are paying the entire tax. Less is being sold, so some producers may be worse off in that sense. However, consumers are paying more for Q_{tax}, and this increased amount is exactly equal to the amount of the tax.

The complete answer to the question of who pays the excise tax should now be clear. The answer is, "It depends on the relative elasticities of supply and demand for the good on which the tax is placed." These elasticities depend on whether substitutes are available and on how consumers choose among competing goods when prices change. The next chapter will develop a theory of consumer choice that explains this process of adjustment.

KEY IDEAS

INCIDENCE OF AN EXCISE TAX
- The more inelastic the demand, the more price rises. The tax falls more heavily on consumers.
- The more elastic the demand, the less price rises. The tax falls more heavily on producers.
- The more inelastic the supply, the more the tax is paid by producers.
- The more elastic the supply, the more price rises. The tax is then paid mostly by consumers.

Consider again...*How would you price your Ninendo games? Having read Cournot's solution, you recognize that a price change has two (opposite) effects on total revenue. The first effect is that a price decrease, by itself, will decrease total revenue. The other effect is that a price decrease causes quantity demanded to increase, thus increasing total revenue. The net effect of these two changes on total revenue depends on whether the relative price decrease exceeds the relative increase in quantity demanded, or vice versa. This is exactly the information that the price elasticity of demand provides.*

You now know how to be as rich as possible. First, thank the genie. Second, set the price of your Nintendo games where the elasticity coefficient is 1.

SUMMARY

1. Movements along demand and supply curves are in response to a change in price. Shifts in demand and supply curves are in response to changes in *ceteris paribus* conditions.
2. Elasticity is the measure of the sensitivity or responsiveness of quantity demanded or quantity supplied to changes in price (and to changes in other *ceteris paribus* conditions).
3. Straight-line demand curves, except for those that are perfectly vertical or horizontal, have points on them that range from elastic to inelastic and one point that is unit elastic. Price elasticity of demand is higher when a good has many substitutes. The more substitutes an item has, the more elastic demand for it will be. Consumers will have more options and respond more readily to changes in price. Elasticity of demand is greater when the time period is longer because consumers have more opportunity to substitute between goods. Total revenue is closely related to elasticity because a demand curve is a price-quantity relationship, and total revenue is price times quantity. When price changes, the quantity demanded changes. This change affects total revenue. The amount of the change in total revenue will depend on the responsiveness of consumers to changes in price, or elasticity.
4. Income elasticity of demand measures the responsiveness of demand to changes in income. Cross elasticity of demand measures the responsiveness of changes in the demand of one good to changes in the price of another good.
5. Price elasticity of supply is the measure of the responsiveness of changes in quantity supplied to changes in price. As time passes, the elasticity of supply increases. The longer the time period, the more chance there is for adjustments to take place.
6. The concepts of supply, demand, and elasticity can be used to determine tax incidence. The more inelastic the demand for a good or service and the more elastic the supply, the greater is the amount of an excise tax on the good or service paid by consumers. The more elastic the demand and the more inelastic the supply, the greater is the amount of the tax paid by producers.

NEW TERMS

elasticity
price elasticity of demand
coefficient of price elasticity of demand (E_d)
perfectly inelastic demand
perfectly elastic demand
unit elastic demand
arc elasticity
point elasticity
total revenue
income elasticity of demand
cross elasticity of demand
price elasticity of supply
coefficient of price elasticity of supply (E_s)
excise tax
tax incidence

QUESTIONS: REVIEW, APPLICATIONS, AND POLICY

REVIEW

1. If the coefficient of the cross elasticity of demand for good *A* and good *B* is infinite, what kind of goods are *A* and *B*?
2. To demonstrate the importance of using average price and quantity changes when determining elasticity, use the correct formula for calculating the coefficient of price elasticity of demand for a change in price from $2.20 to $2.40 in Table 1. Then calculate the coefficient again for a price increase from $2.20 to $2.40, and a price decrease from $2.40 to $2.20, without using averaging. Explain the difference in your answers.
3. Would the elasticity of demand for Pepsi be higher or lower than that for soft drinks in general? Why?
4. Why is the value of the price elasticity of demand negative? Why do we ignore the negative sign?

APPLICATIONS

5. Which of the following pairs of products are complements and which are substitutes?
   a. men's suits and ties
   b. butter and margarine
   c. Pepsi and Coke
   d. gasoline and Cadillacs
   e. women's swimsuits and jackhammers
6. For each of the pairs in Question 5, is the coefficient of the cross elasticity of demand negative or positive? Do you expect the coefficient to be a large or small number? Why?
7. Many years ago, during the energy crisis, *The Wall Street Journal* ran a headline, "Europe's Drivers Don't Reduce Gasoline Use Despite Soaring Prices." Data from the article showed that gas prices were up 120 percent in Europe, and the general price level rose 140 percent during the same period. What was wrong with the headline?

493

8. The price of good X increases from $1.10 to $1.15, and the quantity of good Y consumed increases from 1,100 units to 1,750 units. What is the cross elasticity of demand? What does this imply about goods X and Y?

9. For the demand schedule below, calculate the values for the total revenue column by multiplying price times quantity demanded. Then use the formula to calculate the coefficients of price elasticity of demand based on the changes in price and total revenue.

PRICE	QUANTITY DEMANDED	TOTAL REVENUE (TR)	COEFFICIENT OF PRICE ELASTICITY OF DEMAND (E_d)
$0.50	25	_____	_____
1.00	20	_____	_____
1.20	18	_____	_____
1.40	16	_____	_____
1.60	14	_____	_____
1.80	12	_____	_____
2.00	10	_____	_____
2.20	8	_____	_____
2.40	6	_____	_____
2.60	4	_____	_____
2.80	2	_____	_____
3.00	0	_____	_____

10. Suppose one firm is the only seller of the product represented by the demand schedule in Question 9. What would you do if the price were $2.00 when you took over that firm's marketing department and if your bonus depended on maximizing total revenue for the firm?

11. Several years ago *The Wall Street Journal* ran an article entitled "Chicago's Troubled Transit System Takes Unorthodox Steps to Attract Commuters." The main unorthodox step was to reduce fares. What does this decision indicate about what the head of the Illinois State Department of Transportation thinks about the price elasticity of demand for the services of the transit system?

POLICY

12. If the government wants to place a tax on some good for the purpose of generating revenue, should it look for a good that has a relatively inelastic demand curve or a relatively elastic one?

13. If the elasticity of demand for cigarettes is 0.7 for all consumers and 1.4 for smokers aged twelve to seventeen, a 36 percent increase in price is needed to cut cigarette consumption for all consumers by 25 percent. If the 36 percent increase in price occurred, how much would the consumption of cigarettes by those aged twelve to seventeen change?

14. Why is the coefficient of the price elasticity of demand higher for those aged twelve to seventeen than for all smokers?

15. Why is public policy aimed at decreasing oil imports frustrated by the fact that demand for gasoline is income elastic and price inelastic?

SUGGESTIONS FOR FURTHER READING

Browning, Edgar K., and Jacquelene M. Browning. *Microeconomic Theory and Applications*, 4e. Boston: Little, Brown, 1992. This book contains a good treatment of elasticity, with problems to solve.

Pindyck, Robert S., and Daniel L. Rubinfeld. *Microeconomics.* New York: Macmillian, 1992. A well-written, intermediate textbook on price theory with elasticity applications.

CHAPTER 20
DEMAND AND CONSUMER CHOICE

Consider this... *Where you work, where you shop, and most certainly in the student union there is a vending area. In that area there are most likely coin-operated machines that supply everything from soft drinks, to snacks, to newspapers. If you think about it, you will notice a significant difference between the machines that dispense soft drinks and snacks and those that dispense newspapers. The food and drink machines provide one can or package through a chute of some sort, while the newspaper machine allows you to open a door and take one paper out. Why? Are readers more honest than eaters?*

This chapter will help provide an answer to this puzzle. To do this we will look at what determines consumer choice. Since individual demand curves form the bedrock of microeconomic analysis, we need to consider the factors that underlie them.

The first approach economists took in examining consumer demand, the classical approach, involved the concept of measurable utility. We will use this approach to examine some problems and suggest some applications for demand analysis. The second approach to consumer demand, indifference curve analysis, is discussed in an appendix to this chapter.

LEARNING OBJECTIVES
1. Discuss the importance of utility in explaining consumer choice.
2. Derive an individual demand curve for a good based on the equation for maximizing total utility and the principle of diminishing marginal utility.
3. Apply utility theory to explanations of consumer behavior.
4. Identify and describe the concept of consumer surplus.
5. Describe how advertising affects utility.

CHOICE, VALUE, AND UTILITY THEORY

The idea that households and firms must make choices because of scarcity is the fundamental notion of economic analysis. We now want to expand on that analysis to determine why consumers react in the way they do. Why does a person demand a certain good or service? An obvious answer is that the good or service is expected to satisfy some need or desire of the consumer. Economists, unlike other social scientists, are content with this simple answer.

There may be moral or ethical dimensions to the desires people have. Why do people want to buy guns, pornography, narcotics, sports cars, liquor, or cigarettes? These are questions to which psychologists, moralists, and many others devote a great deal of attention. But economists generally are not interested in why desires exist or why people should buy some goods and not others. It is not because they think such questions are unimportant. In fact, such questions may be more important than the questions economists try to answer: What would happen to the sales of Porsches if their price increased by $1,000? What would happen to the sales of potatoes if the price of wheat went up $1 per bushel? Economists accept the fact that people have a certain psychological or ethical makeup. Without approving or disapproving of it or asking where it came from, economists start their analysis from there.

Economists' view of consumer choice is based on five assumptions about the psychology of consumer behavior:

1. Consumers (or households) must make choices because they have limited income and are forced to choose which of their many wants to satisfy.
2. Consumers make rational choices when they make these consumption decisions. That is, they weigh costs and benefits and make the decision that gives them the most satisfaction.
3. Consumers make these choices with imperfect information. In other words, they don't know (with certainty) all the attributes of the goods they are choosing to consume.
4. As increasing amounts of a good are consumed, the additional satisfaction gained from an additional unit becomes smaller.
5. Many goods have qualities that make them satisfactory substitutes for other goods.

All of these statements may seem simple and obvious, but they will enable us to draw some powerful conclusions about the nature of demand.

THE HISTORY OF UTILITY THEORY: THE DIAMOND-WATER PARADOX

In the early development of economic theory, economists often posed questions that they then debated. One of the popular debate topics was what determined value. Adam Smith wrote that value could mean either "value in use" or "value in exchange." He posed (in 1776) what became known as the diamond-water paradox:

> *The things that have the greatest value in use have frequently little or no value in exchange; and on the contrary, those which have the greatest value in exchange have frequently little value in use. Nothing is more valuable than water, but it will purchase scarce anything; scarce anything can be had in exchange for it. A diamond, on the contrary, has scarce any value in use; but a very great quantity of other goods may frequently be had in exchange for it.*[1]

---

1. Mark Blaug writes in *Economic Theory in Retrospect* (Homewood IL: Irwin, 1968) that Adam Smith, in what may be the greatest understatement in the history of economic thought, conceded that his explanation of value was obscure.

The **diamond-water paradox** was the problem that classical economists used when they argued that value in use could not determine price (value in exchange). Diamonds, although less useful than water, are more expensive than water. The dialogue about the diamond-water paradox went on for a long time. Many famous mathematicians, economists, and philosophers took part in the debate. The confusion over the diamond-water paradox arose because of a lack of distinction between total units and marginal units and arguments over what the term *useful* meant. In the 1870s, William Stanley Jevons, Carl Menger, and Leon Walras, all writing separately, solved the paradox by developing a theory of value in which demand and utility came to the forefront. Their solution played a major role in developing the theory of consumer demand.

Another part of the debate underlying the diamond-water paradox was an argument over whether value (or price) was determined by supply or demand. In a famous analogy, Alfred Marshall, the great British economist, said that you could no more say whether supply or demand determined value than you could say which blade of a pair of scissors did the cutting. That is, value (or price) is determined by the interaction of supply and demand.

We'll consider the influence of demand on value first and leave supply for later chapters. Demand theorists use the notion of utility. If a consumer wants a good or service, then that good or service has utility for that person. **Utility** is the satisfaction a consumer expects to receive from consuming a good or service. The same good may have a great deal of utility for one person and none or very little for some other person. Like beauty, utility is in the eye (or mind) of the beholder.

Utility is a before-the-fact concept. That is, utility measures the way a consumer feels about a good *before* buying or consuming it. You may see a cake in a bakery window and have great desire for it—that's utility. If you buy and eat the cake, you may get sick and receive no satisfaction from its consumption—that's irrelevant, economically. Utility is the satisfaction you *expect* to get, not what you actually get. The reason for this distinction is that utility is used in the development of the demand curve, and the demand curve shows the amounts that people will buy based on anticipated satisfaction. It does not consider the amounts of satisfaction actually received after having made the purchase.

TOTAL UTILITY AND MARGINAL UTILITY

A good unit for the measurement of utility, like the pound or gallon or mile, does not exist. Since utility is unique to the individual, however, an arbitrary (and imaginary) unit called the **util** can be employed. As long as no attempt is made to compare the number of utils of different people, this is a satisfactory measuring device. Such comparisons between people are inappropriate because the number of utils is a subjective measure of a certain individual's satisfaction and as such is not subject to meaningful comparisons. (Some people prefer the beach to the mountains!)

A relationship that expresses a person's desire to consume differing amounts of a good is called a **utility function**. For example, suppose you try to construct your utility function for a certain brand of soft drink. First, choose a convenient time period, such as a day. Then, for one unit (one can) of Coke per day, assign a number of utils, say 20. (You can choose any number at all: 1, or 1,000, or 47½.) Ask yourself, if I get 20 utils from one can, how many would I get

Diamond-water paradox
The fact that diamonds, although less useful than water, are more expensive than water. That is, things with the greatest value in exchange (price) often have little value in use.

Utility
The satisfaction that a consumer expects to receive from consuming a good or service.

Util
An arbitrary unit used to measure individual utility.

Utility function
A relationship expressing a consumer's desire to consume differing amounts of a good.

if I consumed two cans per day? Suppose, after much reflection, you say 38. Ask yourself the same question about three cans per day, four, five, six, and so on. You use these figures to construct a utility schedule, as shown in Table 1.

Marginal utility (*MU*) is the amount of utility that one more or less unit consumed adds to or subtracts from total utility. It is the change in satisfaction provided by one more or one less unit of consumption. The formula for marginal utility is

$$MU = \frac{\text{change in total utility}}{\text{change in quantity consumed}}.$$

In Table 1, the marginal utility is determined by calculating how much each additional can of Coke adds to total utility. For example, the first can of Coke adds 20 utils to total utility. The fourth can of Coke adds 13 utils to total utility. Marginal utility is found by subtracting the total utility of consuming three Cokes from the total utility of consuming that number plus one (67 − 54 = 13).

PRINCIPLE OF DIMINISHING MARGINAL UTILITY

The important feature of the schedule shown in Table 1 is that, although the total utility becomes larger the more you consume per day (up to a point), the additions to total utility from each additional unit consumed become smaller. The fact that additional, or marginal, utility declines as consumption increases is called diminishing marginal utility.

The **principle of diminishing marginal utility** states that the greater the level of consumption of a particular good in a given time period, the lower the marginal utility of an additional unit. For some goods there may be increasing marginal utility in a short range. The advertisement for potato chips that says "Bet you can't eat just one" implies that the satisfaction from the second is greater than that from the first. Such examples of increasing marginal utility are

Marginal utility (*MU*)
The amount of utility that one more or one less unit of consumption adds to or subtracts from total utility.

Principle of diminishing marginal utility
The fact that the additional utility declines as quantity consumed increases. Less satisfaction is obtained per additional unit as more units are consumed.

TABLE 1 UTILITY SCHEDULE FOR COKE

CANS OF COKE PER DAY	TOTAL UTILITY (UTILS)	MARGINAL UTILITY (UTILS)
0	0	0
1	20	20
2	38	18
3	54	16
4	67	13
5	77	10
6	84	7
7	88	4
8	89	1
9	87	−2
10	82	−5

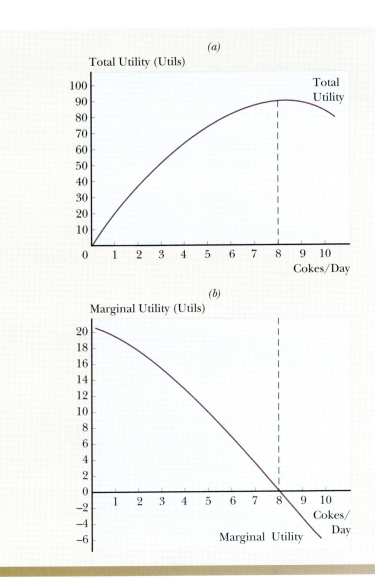

FIGURE 1

TOTAL AND MARGINAL UTILITY

Total utility increases as consumption increases to a certain level, in this case 8 Cokes per day, and then it declines. When total utility is increasing, marginal utility is declining, illustrating the principle of diminishing marginal utility. At the point where total utility begins to decline, marginal utility becomes negative.

exceptions that exist for only the first few units. In most cases, as you consume more units of a good, the later units yield less of an addition to total utility than the preceding units did. For instance, the seventh Coke is expected to provide less additional pleasure than the sixth Coke. This principle is reflected in Table 1. Marginal utility falls from 7 utils for the sixth Coke to 4 utils for the seventh.

Figure 1(*a*) shows the total utility curve plotted from Table 1. Figure 1(*b*) shows the marginal utility curve that corresponds to the table. Note that when the total utility curve reaches its maximum, marginal utility is zero. This makes sense because marginal utility must become negative for total utility to decline. In Table 1, total utility reaches a maximum at eight Cokes per day because the ninth Coke has a negative marginal utility. The only way a total of anything can decline is for changes in that total to be negative.

UTILITY AND CONSUMER BEHAVIOR

The concepts of utility and price can be combined to show how consumers make choices in the marketplace. Consumers are confronted with a range of items and also a range of prices. A consumer may not necessarily choose the item that has the greatest utility because its price and the consumer's income are also important factors. In other words, consumers don't always buy their first choice. You may prefer a Porsche to a Chevrolet, but you may purchase the Chevrolet. The explanation for this behavior lies in the relationship between price and utility.

Suppose, for example, you are considering purchasing a six-pack of soft drinks. You are presented with the three possibilities shown in Table 2. Coke is your first choice because it yields the most utility. But the relevant question is not which soft drink has the most utility, but which has the most utility *per dollar*. Therefore, you choose to buy a six-pack of Pepsi. This choice implies that the extra satisfaction of Coke over Pepsi is not worth $.75, but the extra satisfaction of Pepsi over 7-Up is worth $.25. There are other things you can do with the extra $.75. You are saying that $.75 spent on something other than Coke will yield more additional utils than the difference between the utility of Coke and the utility of Pepsi, but that $.25 spent on other goods will not yield more utils than spending it on Pepsi instead of 7-Up.

Thus, in deciding how to spend your money, you look at marginal utility per dollar rather than marginal utility alone. You do this because money is the common measure of what you have to give up. Dollars can be used to buy any available good. So for each dollar you spend, you want to choose the item with the highest utility per dollar. In doing so, you economize by getting the most satisfaction per dollar.

MAXIMIZING TOTAL UTILITY

The self-interest assumption implies that individuals will act to maximize their total utility. To see how marginal utility and price influence how a consumer maximizes total utility, consider an example with only two goods, Coke and pizza. A unit of Coke costs $.50 and a unit of pizza costs $1. The consumer's utility schedules for the two goods are presented in Table 3. The consumer has a

TABLE 2 HYPOTHETICAL UTILITY-PER-DOLLAR COMPARISONS

CHOICE	MARGINAL UTILITY (UTILS)	PRICE (DOLLARS)	MARGINAL UTILITY PER DOLLAR (UTILS)
Coke	30.0	3.00	10
Pepsi	27.0	2.25	12
7-Up	20.0	2.00	10

TABLE 3 UTILITY SCHEDULES FOR A CONSUMER OF TWO GOODS

	COKE				PIZZA		
QUANTITY PER WEEK (CANS)	MARGINAL UTILITY, MU (UTILS)	MU/P (P = $.50)	TOTAL UTILITY, TU (UTILS)	QUANTITY PER WEEK (PIECES)	MARGINAL UTILITY, MU (UTILS)	MU/P (P = $1.00)	TOTAL UTILITY, TU (UTILS)
1	15	30	15	1	32	32	32
2	14	28	29	2	31	31	63
3	13	26	42	3	28	28	91
4	12	24	54	4	24¾	24¾	115¾
5	11	22	65	5	20¼	20¼	136
6	10¾	21½	75¾	6	18	18	154
7	10¼	20½	86	7	17	17	171
8	10	20	96	8	16	16	187
9	9	18	105	9	14	14	201
10	8	16	113	10	12	12	213
11	7	14	120	11	11	11	224
12	6½	13	126½	12	9	9	233

given amount of income, called a budget constraint. A **budget constraint** is a given level of income that determines the maximum amount of goods that may be purchased by a consumer. Let's allow this consumer a budget constraint of $13, and see how that amount will be allocated between the two goods to achieve maximum utility.

The first dollar will be allocated to pizza because a dollar's worth of pizza (one piece) yields 32 utils of satisfaction compared with 29 utils for a dollar's worth of Coke (two cans). The next dollar will also be spent on pizza because it yields 31 utils, which is still greater than the first dollar's worth of Coke, the alternative purchase. In other words, the consumer buys two pieces of pizza before buying any Coke. The third dollar is spent on Coke because the 29 utils of satisfaction gained from purchasing two cans are greater than the 28 utils that are yielded by a third piece of pizza. The process continues until the entire income of $13 is spent. In maximizing total utility, the consumer will spend $5 on ten cans of Coke and $8 on eight pieces of pizza. This allocation produces 300 utils of satisfaction—the maximum total utility that can be purchased with $13 of income. You cannot find a different combination of Coke and pizza that will produce more satisfaction (try reducing Coke consumption by two cans and increasing pizza consumption by one piece, or vice versa).

The consumer's choices are based on a maximization rule that says that total utility is maximized when the last dollar spent on good A yields the same utility as the last dollar spent on good B. In algebraic form, total utility is maximized when

$$\frac{MU_A}{P_A} = \frac{MU_B}{P_B}.$$

Budget constraint
A given level of income that determines the maximum amount of goods that may be purchased by a consumer.

The marginal utility of a can of Coke, when ten cans per week are consumed, is 8 utils, and the price of a can is $.50. Thus,

$$\frac{MU_{cola}}{P_{cola}} = \frac{8}{\$.50} = 16 \text{ utils per dollar.}$$

For pizza, at the optimum consumption rate, the marginal utility is 16, and the price is $1. Thus,

$$\frac{MU_{pizza}}{P_{pizza}} = \frac{16}{\$1.00} = 16 \text{ utils per dollar.}$$

This can be generalized to include all goods by saying a consumer maximizes utility when

$$\frac{MU_x}{P_x} = \frac{MU_y}{P_y} = \ldots = \frac{MU_n}{P_n}.$$

Of course, individuals don't spend all their income on goods. Sometimes individuals hold money as they do any other commodity. Including money (symbolized by $), the equation for maximization of utility is

$$(1) \quad \frac{MU_A}{P_A} = \frac{MU_B}{P_B} = \frac{MU_\$}{P_\$}.$$

Utility maximization
The process by which a consumer adjusts consumption, given a budget constraint and a set of prices, in order to attain the highest total amount of satisfaction.

Utility maximization is the process by which a consumer adjusts consumption, given a budget constraint and a set of prices, in order to attain the highest total amount of satisfaction. Equation (1) is an expression for utility maximization. It includes all commodities, even money. This equation says that in order to maximize total utility, the marginal utilities per dollar of all goods consumed have to be equal and also have to equal the marginal utility of money. If this is not the case, a change in the consumption pattern can produce more satisfaction for a given budget constraint. This equation is just a formal way of saying that people allocate their income so as to yield the most satisfaction possible. When utility is being maximized, the additional satisfaction from any use of a dollar will equal the additional satisfaction from any other use of that dollar. When this is not the case, the consumer can reallocate personal income from one good to another and gain more satisfaction.

To see how a given consumption pattern can be adjusted to achieve maximum utility, look again at Table 3. Let's give Susan an income of $9 and say that she uses it to buy $3 worth of cola and $6 worth of pizza. The expression $MU_{cola}/P_{cola} = MU_{pizza}/P_{pizza}$ doesn't hold because

$$\frac{10\frac{3}{4}}{.50} > \frac{18}{1}.$$

Susan isn't maximizing her utility because the last dollar she spent on cola yielded more utils than the last dollar she spent on pizza. Susan should reallocate her consumption outlays. By giving up a dollar's worth of pizza, she will lose 18 utils. But she will gain $20\frac{1}{4}$ utils by spending that dollar on more cola. Her total utility will thus rise by 2 (rounded off), and

$$\frac{10}{.50} \approx \frac{20\frac{1}{4}}{1}.$$

By purchasing eight cans of cola and five pieces of pizza, Susan is maximizing utility with a $9 budget constraint.

MARGINAL UTILITY AND THE LAW OF DEMAND

Utility theory makes it possible to derive a consumer's demand curve for a good (good x). Suppose there are only two goods, x and y. Remember, demand curves are drawn using the *ceteris paribus* assumption. That is, income, tastes, and the prices of all other goods (good y) are held constant. The consumer is initially in equilibrium, maximizing utility when

$$\frac{MU_x}{P_x} = \frac{MU_y}{P_y}.$$

At this equilibrium, MU_{x1} corresponds to the consumption of x_1 units of good x in Figure 2. The price of x_1 units is represented by P_1 in Figure 2. The equation should now be written

$$\frac{MU_{x1}}{P_1} = \frac{MU_y}{P_y}.$$

Now suppose the price of good x falls to P_2. This change throws the expression out of equilibrium because the denominator on the left side is now smaller, making the left side of the expression larger:

$$\frac{MU_{x1}}{P_2} > \frac{MU_y}{P_y}.$$

To get back into equilibrium, the consumer has to lower the value of the left side of the expression and/or raise the value of the right side. How can this be done? If the individual consumes more of x, MU_x will decline because of the principle of diminishing marginal utility. As consumption moves to x_2 on Figure 2, the marginal utility of good x falls. Furthermore, consuming more of x will mean some reduction in the consumption of y. As consumption of y falls, MU_y rises. When this happens, the expression will move toward

$$\frac{MU_x}{P_x} = \frac{MU_y}{P_y}.$$

Utility-maximizing behavior requires that when the price of good x falls (as from P_1 to P_2 in Figure 2), the consumer will increase consumption of x. Since this is necessary for utility maximization, it demonstrates that the demand curves of individuals must have a negative slope. That is, the lower the price of a good, the greater the quantity demanded.

PROBLEMS WITH UTILITY THEORY

There are two major problems with a demand theory based on utility. The first problem is that some goods are not divisible. The second, more serious problem is that utility cannot be measured.

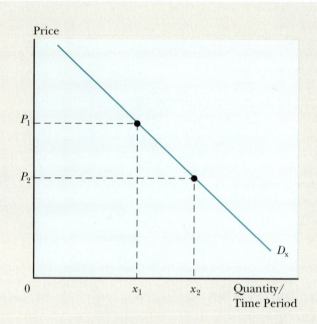

FIGURE 2

DEMAND CURVE FOR GOOD X

When price falls from P_1 to P_2, the consumer's utility maximization is thrown out of equilibrium. Equilibrium will be restored if the consumer increases consumption to X_2.

The theory works well enough to describe the consumption of certain kinds of goods, such as soft drinks or pizzas. When the good being consumed is an automobile or a home, however, it is difficult to talk about additional units because the purchase is "lumpy." It is very difficult to consume a part of a house or a part of a car, but it is common to consume part of a six-pack of cola. The theory is somewhat weakened, then, by the fact that the consumer can't always make continuous decisions about successive amounts of consumption.

This problem with utility theory is really not a major flaw. Consumers can still make adjustments with most lumpy purchases. Consider a house as an example. Suppose the consumer decides after the purchase that the house is too large and that other purchases would yield more marginal utility. Over time, expenditures on the house can be lowered by a lessening of routine maintenance so that more can be spent on the other goods that yield a higher marginal utility. Buying a smaller house, buying one at a less desirable location, and renting are also available alternatives.

A greater problem with utility theory is that it is impossible to measure utility. We have proceeded as if there were a way we could strap a meter to a consumer and exactly measure the utility expected from consuming one more unit, somewhat like measuring temperature or blood pressure. This is, of course, not possible. Psychology has not developed such sophisticated technology. But before you reject utility theory as useless, remember that it is a theoretical tool. It really isn't that important for the theory of demand to be able to measure utility. The purpose of utility theory is to develop a better understanding of why and how quantity demanded will change when prices change.

KEY IDEAS

UTILITY THEORY
- Assumptions of model
    - Individual has exogenous budget constraint
    - Prices are exogenous
    - Individual get utility from consumption
    - Marginal utility diminishes
- Maximization
    - Utility is maximized where the marginal utility per dollar spent on all goods (and the marginal utility of money) is equal.
- Testable implications
    - Quantity demanded is inversely related to price, *ceteris paribus*.
    - As the price of a good rises, the demand for substitutes will increase, *ceteris paribus*.
    - As income rises, the demand for normal goods will increase, *ceteris paribus*.

POLICY FOCUS: PROGRESSIVE INCOME TAXATION—ARE UTILITY FUNCTIONS INTERDEPENDENT?

Many noneconomists believe that money and income are subject to diminishing marginal utility. This idea is one of the main arguments (but not the only one) for a progressive income tax. A progressive tax takes a larger percentage of dollars from the rich because for them a dollar's marginal utility is thought to be low. A smaller percentage of dollars is taken from poorer taxpayers because for them a dollar's marginal utility is thought to be much higher. This argument assumes that it is possible to measure utility *and* to make interpersonal utility comparisons. Such comparisons are attempts to measure the utility of one individual relative to that of another. One way to avoid directly comparing utilities for different people is to assume that individuals all have the same utility schedule for given levels of income. With these two assumptions, proponents of the progressive income tax argue that society can maximize total utility by taking income away from high-income individuals who have lower marginal utilities of income and transferring it to low-income individuals who have higher marginal utilities of income.

Those who apply principles of individual utility maximization to a society as a whole are on very shaky ground, however. First, economists generally believe that interpersonal utility comparisons are not feasible. People are different. There is no way you can prove that an additional $100 of income gives less satisfaction to actress Julia Roberts than to an unemployed auto worker. In fact, Ms. Roberts may get more satisfaction because she is such an expert consumer. It is impossible to prove that one individual gets more or less satisfaction from an increment to income than any other individual does.

A second and more fundamental problem with this analysis is that it assumes a diminishing marginal utility for income, or goods and services in general. This proposition cannot be verified. The principle of diminishing marginal utility, you will remember, states that the marginal utility of a *particular good* declines as consumption is increased. Increased income, however, represents an increase in the consumption of all goods. If wants are insatiable, there is no reason to believe that the principle of diminishing marginal utility holds for money or income. Even so, it is probably the case that most people think that income has diminishing marginal utility. What about you?

There may be other arguments for progressive income taxes. Progressive income taxes may offset more regressive sales or property taxes to create an overall proportional tax system. In other cases, where income is very unequally distributed, the only substantial source of revenue for the government to tap may be income taxes on the very wealthy. There may be subjective interpretations of what is equitable or fair that go way beyond the scope of economics. All economics has to say on the subject is that diminishing marginal utility is *not* a valid argument for progressive income taxation.

INCOME AND SUBSTITUTION EFFECTS

The law of demand, which you studied in Chapter 3, states that as the price of a good or service declines, the quantity demanded increases, *ceteris paribus*. This law is true because of two effects that result from the price decline.

The first effect is called the **substitution effect**. When the price of a good (or service) falls, the good becomes less expensive relative to all other goods. As a result, consumers purchase more of it because it has become a better substitute for other goods as it has become cheaper. Steaks and ground beef provide a good example. As the price of steak falls, more people will switch from ground beef to steaks.

The second effect of a price decline is called the **income effect**. When the price of a good or service falls, *ceteris paribus*, the consumer's real income, or purchasing power, rises. That is, after buying the same amount as before (of the good for which price has fallen), the consumer has more income left over. With this higher real income, more of all normal goods will be consumed. Thus, the consumption of the good whose price declined also will increase (if it is a normal good). Income and substitution effects, along with diminishing marginal utility, explain why demand curves slope down from left to right.

Substitution effect
An increase in the quantity demanded of a good (or service) because its price has fallen and it becomes a better substitute for all other goods.

Income effect
An increase in demand for a good (or service) when its price falls, *ceteris paribus*, because the household's real income rises and the consumer buys more of all normal goods.

SOME APPLICATIONS OF UTILITY THEORY

You have practiced and observed utility maximization in your own life even though you may not have thought of it in the formal language of economics. Suppose, for example, you are organizing the beer concession for a fund-raising event. There are two ways to run the concession: you can charge an admission fee to the event and then allow unlimited consumption, or you can charge a set price for each beer, say $.50 per glass. Utility theory predicts different levels of consumption for these two alternatives and thus different requirements for planning the supply. In the first case, beer drinkers will consume beer until the marginal utility per glass is zero because the price per additional glass is zero. In the second case, beer drinkers will consume beer until the marginal utility per glass equals the marginal utility of $.50. You can predict, then, that there will be more drunken, rowdy behavior if the party is financed by an admission charge.

If you don't agree with this analysis, reflect back on parties you have observed. Were the most rowdy ones the pay-as-you-go type or the admission type? With the growing awareness of alcohol abuse on campus, student organizations on some campuses have outlawed keg beer parties ("all you can drink") and required that they be replaced with can-only beer parties (pay by the can). These campus rule-setters understand diminishing marginal utility whether they know it or not.

This example may seem insignificant because the consumption of beer isn't a very earth-shaking issue. Let's change the good from beer to medical services. If the government decides to provide free national health care, what do you predict will happen to the consumption of these services? Of course, people will consume them until the marginal utility of the last unit is zero. This is exactly what tends to happen with a prepaid or tax-financed health care system. If you have ever participated in such a program in the military, at a university, or under a health maintenance plan, you probably have consumed more medical services than before. Since there is no charge per visit, more services are consumed. You may also have noticed that with the free system, the waiting time is usually longer, the waiting rooms are less comfortable, and the workers are less congenial than with a fee-for-service system.

THE DIAMOND-WATER PARADOX EXPLAINED

Adam Smith (and others) argued that utility (and thus demand) could not be a determinant of price because diamonds, while less useful than water, are more expensive than water. The paradox disappears if we distinguish between total utility and marginal utility. The total utility of water is high. However, since there is a great deal in existence and large quantities are consumed, its marginal utility is low. The total utility of diamonds, on the other hand, is relatively low. However, since diamonds are rare, their marginal utility is high. Price, then, is determined by marginal utility, not total utility. Economists say that marginal utility determines value in exchange (price) and that total utility determines value in use. Price, then, is related to scarcity through utility. If something has a low marginal utility at all quantities consumed, it will have a low price, regardless of how scarce it is. If something is relatively scarce and has a high marginal utility, it will be valuable and thus expensive.

SHOPPING FOR BARGAINS

Economists have used the concept of utility-maximizing behavior to analyze shopping behavior. The idea is that a buyer will search for bargains until the expected savings in value or utility equals the cost of continued searching.

Several predictions can be made from this theory. The first is that the larger the amount individuals expect to save, the longer they will continue to search. In other words, the bigger the item in terms of your budget, the more you will shop around. You will search longer for a good price on a car than for a good price on a loaf of bread. You might even buy bread at a convenience store, where you know the price is higher, to save some shopping time. The second prediction is that, in percentage terms, the variation in prices for bigger budget items should be smaller than the variation in prices for smaller budget items. The search process will drive high-price sellers of large items out of business or force them to reduce their prices. The third prediction is that where search costs are higher, price differences between sellers could be higher without driving the high-priced sellers out of business. Have you ever noticed that prices of gasoline are higher near freeways than in towns? Utility-maximizing theory can explain this phenomenon. Users of freeways are going somewhere, often in a hurry. Their search costs are high. They therefore do less shopping around and as a result pay higher prices.

CONSUMER SURPLUS AND UTILITY

Consumers often benefit in a market economy because they are able to purchase a good or service by sacrificing something that is worth less to them than the value of what they receive. **Consumer surplus** is the extra utility derived from

Consumer surplus
The extra utility derived from a purchase that has a value to the consumer greater than the market price.

FIGURE 3

CONSUMER SURPLUS

The consumer surplus is the shaded area above the price P_1 and below the demand curve.

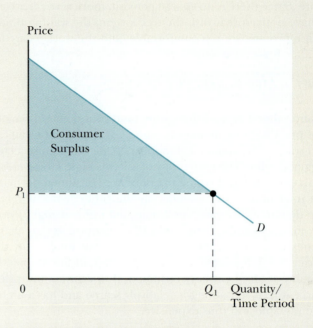

a purchase that has a value to the consumer greater than the market price. Utility theory provides a measure of consumer surplus.

Consider the demand curve for a single consumer (or group of homogeneous consumers) in Figure 3. At price P_1, the individual will consume Q_1 units of the good. According to the theory of utility-maximizing behavior, the marginal utility of the last unit purchased is equal to the price of the unit. This means that the marginal utility of each previous unit purchased was greater than price P_1. The consumer would have been willing to pay higher prices for those previous units, so at the market price of P_1, the consumer receives a bonus in terms of utility on all units but the last one. The total purchase is worth more to the consumer than the total amount (price times quantity) that is paid. This extra utility gained is called consumer surplus and is represented by the shaded area in Figure 3. Consumer surplus will be an important concept when we study monopoly. The Global Outlook describes an application of consumer surplus in international trade.

ADVERTISING, MARKETING, AND DEMAND

The theory developed in this chapter explains a great deal about demand and consumer equilibrium. It does not say anything about the role of advertising and marketing. Advertising and marketing are difficult topics for economists to deal with because economic analysis usually assumes that consumers are informed, rational utility maximizers who know their own tastes and preferences. Advertising and marketing are not, however, inconsistent with those basic assumptions.

GLOBAL OUTLOOK: PITY THE POOR JAPANESE CONSUMER!

Japan places high tariffs on food products to protect an efficient, but powerful political lobby in Japan. American beef ranchers, rice farmers, and citrus growers complain bitterly to the U.S. government about these tariffs. In fact, U.S. producers of goods that the Japanese export to the United States use these high tariffs in Japan as an argument that the United States should impose tariffs on Japanese goods to create a "level playing field." Let's examine the effect of Japanese tariffs on Japanese consumers.

Tariffs have many effects. They reduce the efficiency of resource allocation. They redistribute income between countries and between producers and consumers within countries. They raise revenue for the countries that impose them. All of the economic effects of tariffs are important and will be discussed in the chapter on international trade. It is possible, however, to use the concept of consumer surplus developed in this chapter to see how tariffs affect the well-being of Japanese consumers.

In Figure B1, S_d is the domestic supply curve and S_w is the world supply curve. World supply is perfectly elastic at the world price P_f. Consumers are demanding quantity Q, of which quantity A is sold by domestic producers and quantity $Q - A$ is imported. The triangle formed by S_w, D, and the vertical axis represents consumer surplus. What happens if the government imposes a tariff equal to t? The price rises by the amount of the tariff to P_t, creating a new world supply curve, S'_w. Consumers now purchase quantity B from domestic producers and $C - B$ from foreign producers. Consumer surplus is now represented by the triangle formed by S'_w, D, and the vertical axis. There has been a reduction in consumer surplus equal to the difference between the two triangles, or the shaded area. What this example demonstrates is that a tariff permits domestic producers to sell more of a product at a higher price and that government revenues rise by the amount of the tariff times the imported quantity. However, consumers experience a decline in consumer surplus.

The citizens that suffer the most from Japanese tariffs on beef, rice, and citrus are Japanese consumers. The problem is that they are not an effective lobbying group, while Japanese farmers are an effective lobbying group.

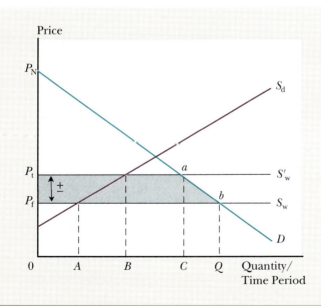

FIGURE B1
TARIFFS AND CONSUMER SURPLUS
Consumer surplus before the tariff is equal to triangle $P_f P_N b$. The loss of consumer surplus is area $P_f P_t ab$.

Advertisers spend a great deal of time trying to alter consumers' tastes and perceptions. If enough tastes and perceptions can be changed that the average consumer's utility from the firm's product can be increased, more will be demanded. Changes in tastes do not mean that the consumer is not rational. Even without advertising, tastes would change over time with changes in age, education, and other factors. Some tastes even change regularly with the change of season.

Advertisers also spend some time generating information for consumers about prices. This behavior of advertisers fits with the description of consumers' search behavior. If the cost of getting information falls, the cost of the search falls and consumers will do more searching. As a consequence, they may alter their purchasing patterns and buy from sellers offering lower prices.

Much advertising is directed toward making consumer demand more inelastic by convincing buyers that similar products are not satisfactory substitutes for the one being advertised. In other words, the advertiser attempts to widen the spread between the utility of its product and the utility of potential substitutes. From what you have learned in this chapter, you can see that if this strategy succeeds, an advertiser can charge a higher price for its product without losing many sales.

EXPERIMENTAL ECONOMICS: ECONOMICS ACCORDING TO RATS

Economics is beginning to borrow from experimental psychology. Some economists are carrying out work in lab settings to test some fundamental propositions in economics. At the University of Arizona, Vernon Smith has conducted research on market behavior using human subjects, usually students. At Texas A&M, economists Ray Battalio and John Kagel have experimented with human and animal subjects. These economists did experiments in mental hospitals with token economies. Patients were paid tokens for tasks and were free to spend these tokens on personal items. Some of the results of these investigations were fascinating. They found that the distribution of income earned was closely parallel to that in the U.S. economy. Perhaps even more startling was the fact that earning differences between male and female patients were similar to those between men and women in the U.S. economy.

This result led the two economists to experiment with rats. They found that rats trained to do "work for pay" (hit a bar for food) reduced their work effort after some point, choosing more leisure over additional income. They also found that among low-income rats (those that had to work hard for a little food), such work reduction patterns were more common. These experimental results are consistent with behavior patterns of individuals in real-life situations based on diminishing marginal utility.

Consider again... *You should now be able to explain why the vending machine technology is different for newspapers than it is for food and drink. It surely has nothing to do with technology. It would be easy to have the paper delivered to you in the same way a pack of Nabs comes out of the machine. The explanation is in* marginal utility analysis. Newspaper companies know that for most people the marginal utility of the second paper is zero—maybe even negative because you have to get rid of it. So most people will be honest. Have you ever taken a second paper when you only paid for one? If you did, we bet that the reason was that you were worried you would have to share the paper and as a result the second paper had positive utility. It is easy for newspapers to "trust" the honesty of people because the second unit of what they sell is "worthless."

SUMMARY

1. Total utility is the total amount of satisfaction expected from consuming an item. Marginal utility is the change in total utility from consuming one more or one less unit of a good.
2. Consumers, in deciding among items, choose those items with the highest marginal utility per dollar. An individual maximizes total utility by consuming all items so that their marginal utilities per dollar spent are equal. When the price of a good or service falls, the quantity demanded increases because of income effects and substitution effects.
3. Marginal utility determines value in exchange and total utility determines value in use.
4. Consumer surplus is the extra utility derived from a purchase that has a value to the consumer that is greater than the price paid. In this sense consumer surplus is bonus utility to the consumer.
5. If advertising can change tastes and perceptions, the utility a consumer gets from the advertised product will increase.

NEW TERMS

diamond-water paradox
utility
util
utility function

marginal utility (MU)
principle of diminishing marginal utility
budget constraint

utility maximization
substitution effect
income effect
consumer surplus

QUESTIONS: REVIEW, APPLICATIONS, AND POLICY

REVIEW

1. Does something have to be useful to have utility? What does it mean for a good or service to be useful?
2. What is happening when the price of a good such as petroleum is increasing without a decrease in consumption?
3. Does the fact that water is inexpensive and diamonds are expensive conflict with the theory developed in this chapter? Explain.

APPLICATIONS

4. A consumer is spending her entire weekly income on two goods. If the marginal utility of one good is 4 and its price is $2, and the marginal utility of another good is 5 and its price is $1, is the consumer maximizing total utility? If not, how could more utility be obtained?
5. The following table shows the marginal utility that Roger gets from buying various amounts of cola, pretzels, nuts, and pizza, and from holding dollars. Assume that Roger has an income of $106.

UNITS OF COLA (P = $18)	MU COLA	UNITS OF PRETZELS (P = $4)	MU PRETZELS	UNITS OF NUTS (P = $6)	MU NUTS	UNITS OF PIZZA (P = $24)	MU PIZZA	DOLLARS HELD	MU $
1	72	1	15	1	24	1	36	1	5
2	54	2	12	2	15	2	30	2	4
3	45	3	8	3	12	3	24	3	3
4	36	4	7	4	9	4	18	4	2
5	27	5	5	5	7	5	13	5	1
6	18	6	4	6	5	6	7	6	½
7	15	7	3½	7	2	7	4	7	¼
8	12	8	3	8	1	8	2	8	⅛

What quantities of cola, nuts, pretzels, and pizza will Roger purchase? How many dollars will he hold?

6. Observers of the wealthy often comment on the fact that they waste a lot of things, such as food, but are very careful in their use of time. Is this irrational behavior?

7. If you studied the appendix to this chapter, use a graph to explain how a demand curve can be derived from indifference analysis.

8. Given an indifference map, a set of indifference curves, and a budget line, where does the consumer maximize satisfaction? This question is only for those who studied the appendix to this chapter.

9. Suppose Kim Hagen's demand for escargot is represented by the following schedule (assume that the market price of escargots is $6 per ounce):

PRICE OF ESCARGOTS/OUNCE	OUNCES OF ESCARGOTS/MONTH
$10	1
8	2
7	4
6	6
5	9
4	11
3	13

What is the maximum amount that Kim would pay for the first ounce of escargots per month? By how much does this exceed the actual price? How much would Kim pay for the second ounce of escargots per month? By how much does this exceed the actual price? How much would Kim be willing to pay for the third and fourth ounces of escargots per month? By how much does this exceed the actual price? How much would Kim be willing to pay for the fifth and sixth ounces of escargots per month? By how much does this exceed the actual price?

10. According to the schedule in Question 9, how many ounces of escargots will Kim Hagen purchase per month? How large is Kim's consumer surplus?

11. Geno Hagen, Kim's husband, learns that the price of caviar has fallen significantly. If Kim's demand curve is their family demand curve, what will happen to their demand for escargot? What is the substitution effect? Do you think that it will be positive or negative? What is the income effect? Will it be significant in this example?

POLICY

12. Does advertising increase or decrease the utility you get from consuming certain goods? Is this good or bad? Should certain types of advertising be regulated by governmental policy?

13. What would you expect to happen to a normal consumer's total utility for bacon if the Surgeon General established a link between bacon and cancer? How would this announcement affect the consumer's demand curve for bacon?

14. The material in this chapter discusses rational consumer behavior. Is it ever rational to be irrational?

15. Some restaurants in Maryland advertise "all you can eat" crab feasts. How is this offer related to the theory in this chapter? Can you think of any restrictions a restaurant might make on the behavior of customers who buy this meal?

SUGGESTIONS FOR FURTHER READING

Blum, Walter J., and Harry Kalven, Jr. *The Uneasy Case for Progressive Taxation*. Chicago: University of Chicago Press, 1970. A classic piece of economic analysis that uses utility analysis to examine the policy case for progressive income taxes.

Stigler, George. *The Theory of Prices*, 4e. New York: Macmillan, 1988. Written by a Nobel Prize winner, this price theory book is considered a classic. Chapter 4 covers utility theory.

APPENDIX

INDIFFERENCE ANALYSIS: AN ALTERNATIVE APPROACH TO CONSUMER CHOICE

The marginal utility theory discussed in this chapter has the drawback that it requires precise numerical values to be assigned to alternatives (cardinal utility). A later innovation in the economic theory of choice was based on ordinal utility. Ordinal utility requires only that the utility of the choices can be ranked. Instead of saying, "The next slice of pizza has 30 units of utility," or, "The next Coke has 25 units of utility," the consumer needs only to be able to say, "I prefer another slice of pizza to another Coke."

In the late 1800s, Italian economist Vilfredo Pareto and British economist F.Y. Edgeworth, working separately, developed an approach to analyzing consumer behavior based on ordinal utility—**indifference analysis**. It wasn't until 1939, when Nobel Prize-winning British economist Sir John Hicks published his classic book, *Value and Capital*, that this technique became popular with economic theorists and teachers. The theory swept the economics profession, and, for a while, marginal utility analysis fell into disrepute.

Pareto, Edgeworth, Hicks, and others were not trying to discredit utility theory but rather were proposing an alternative way of viewing consumer behavior. The major improvement of their theory is that it does not require the measurement of units of utility. All that is necessary is that consumers be able to rank bundles of goods in the order, from low to high, in which they prefer them.

> **Indifference analysis**
> An approach to analyzing consumer behavior based on ranking the utility of choices relative to one another.

INDIFFERENCE OR PREFERENCE

Indifference and preference seem better than marginal utility for describing the way consumers actually make decisions. Individuals make choices between bundles, or collections, of goods. For example, you might choose between four tickets to a football game and two tickets to a concert. In indifference analysis, the consumer is viewed as making choices between collections of goods and services. The only assumption is that the consumer is able to state preferences for different collections or to profess indifference between some of them. In other words, confronted with a choice between going to a movie and going to a football game, the consumer might rank the football game as the preferred choice. Or the consumer might say, "I don't have a preference. I'm indifferent between the two choices."

Suppose Mary is considering different combinations of cans of Coke and slices of pizza, as indicated in Table 1A. Combination *A* consists of 16 cans of Coke and 3 slices of pizza, and combination *B* consists of 12 cans and 4 slices. When these two combinations are offered to Mary, she states that neither combination *A* nor combination *B* is preferred over the other. They are equal in the amount of satisfaction she expects to derive. Therefore, she is indifferent between the two. Offering Mary the choice among combinations *C*, *D*, and *E* yields the same response—indifference. Mary has indicated that all five combinations of pizza and Coke yield the same amount of satisfaction. These five combinations comprise an **indifference set** for her.

> **Indifference set**
> Any number of combinations of goods among which the individual consumer is indifferent (has no preference).

TABLE 1A MARY'S INDIFFERENCE SET

COMBINATION	GOOD X (CANS OF COKE)	GOOD Y (SLICES OF PIZZA)
A	16	3
B	12	4
C	0	5
D	8	7
E	6	9

An indifference set can be represented graphically by an indifference curve. An indifference curve corresponding to the indifference set in Table 1A is shown in Figure 1A. An **indifference curve** shows all combinations of two goods (or services) among which a consumer is indifferent.

Indifference curves are negatively sloped because for a consumer to be indifferent, all points on the curve must represent equal amounts of utility. If more of one good is added to the combination, some of the other must be removed. Each combination represents a trade-off. In Mary's case, if combination B has more pizza than combination A, it must have less Coke, since the combinations yield the same level of satisfaction. If one combination had more pizza and more Coke than any other, or if it had more of one without having less of the other, it would be preferred. The consumer would no longer be indifferent. This is yet another way of saying that more is preferred to less.

The indifference set represented by a higher indifference curve is preferred to that represented by a lower indifference curve. As Mary moves from I_1 to I_2 to

Indifference curve
A plot of all combinations of goods that the consumer is indifferent among.

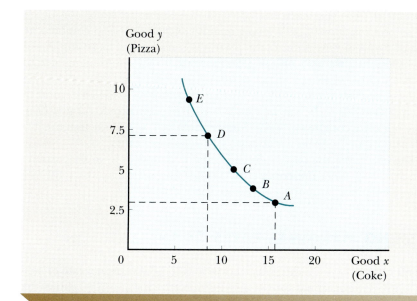

FIGURE 1A
INDIFFERENCE CURVE
An indifference curve represents combinations of two goods among which the consumer is indifferent. All combinations on the same indifference curve give the same level of satisfaction.

FIGURE 2A

INDIFFERENCE MAP

An indifference map is a set of indifference curves, each corresponding to a different level of satisfaction. Higher curves on the map represent higher levels of satisfaction.

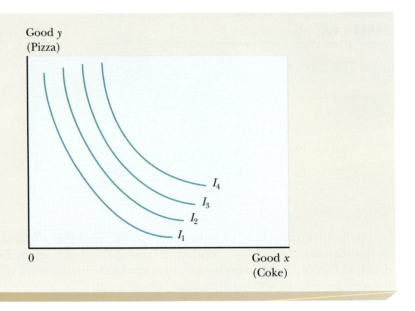

Indifference map
A set of indifference curves. Higher curves represent higher levels of utility.

I_3 to I_4 in Figure 2A, she receives more satisfaction. Such a series of indifference curves is called an **indifference map**. Every individual consumer has such a map, and movement to a higher curve on the map represents a gain in utility.

The shape of the typical indifference curve for two goods will be somewhat convex with respect to the origin. The convexity means that as a consumer gets more units of one good and fewer units of the other, it takes more and more units of the more abundant good to compensate for the loss of one unit of the good that is becoming more scarce. For example, at point A in Figure 3A, the individual is consuming relatively large amounts of good y and small amounts of good x. In order to compensate for a reduction in consumption of 1 unit of y, the person would only require 2 units of x in order to be satisfied with such a trade. At point B, however, since less of y and more of x are being consumed compared to point A, it will take a larger quantity of x (5 units) to compensate for the loss of 1 unit of y. At point C, the person is consuming a large amount of x and very little y. To give up 1 unit of y, 20 more units of x would be needed to have the same utility as before.

Why do economists expect such preference relations to hold? First, most of us would agree that this is the way we would behave in such a trade-off situation. Second, the opposite conclusion seems highly unlikely. It would say that the less you had of a good, the less you would want of it relative to other goods, and the more you had of a good, the more valuable additional units of it would become. Indifference curves reflect the concept of diminishing marginal utility for two goods without assigning numerical values to utility.

DIMINISHING MARGINAL RATES OF SUBSTITUTION

Marginal rate of substitution (MRS)
The trade-off ratio along an indifference curve.

The trade-off ratio along an indifference curve is called the **marginal rate of substitution (MRS)**. The marginal rate of substitution of x for y, MRS_{xy}, shows the willingness of the consumer to substitute between goods x and y:

$$MRS_{xy} = \frac{\text{number of units of } y \text{ given up}}{\text{number of units of } x \text{ gained}}.$$

In Figure 3A, the MRS_{xy} at point A is ½. That is, 1 unit of y must be sacrificed to gain 2 units of x. At point B, the MRS_{xy} is ⅕, and at point C it is 1/20. The declining value of MRS_{xy} is a reflection of the **principle of diminishing marginal rates of substitution**. That is, as more of one good (x) is substituted for the other good (y), the value of good x in terms of good y declines.

BUDGET CONSTRAINTS

An indifference map makes it possible to compare points representing combinations of two goods to determine whether the consumer prefers one such combination or feels indifferent among several. All points on any single indifference curve are equivalent to each other in utility, even if utility cannot be measured numerically. Points on indifference curves located to the right and above other indifference curves are preferred combinations.

Which combinations are actually attainable for the consumer? The answer depends on the income available and on the prices of the goods. Keep in mind that the consumer faces prices that are determined in markets and cannot influence them. Income constrains the consumer from buying all that might be desired. The income is the budget constraint and, when drawn on the indifference map, is called the budget line.

We limit the analysis to two goods (you could think of one of them as "all other goods"). Again assume that Mary can consume either slices of pizza or

Principle of diminishing marginal rates of substitution
The fact that as more of one good is consumed, more and more of the other must be given up to maintain indifference between the two.

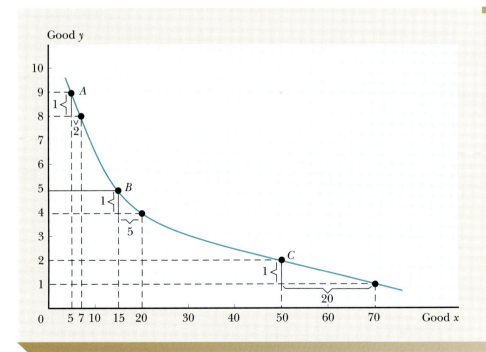

FIGURE 3A
CONVEXITY FEATURE OF INDIFFERENCE CURVES
A typical indifference curve is convex to the origin. This convexity means that it takes increasingly larger amounts of the abundant good to compensate for losses of the good that is becoming more scarce.

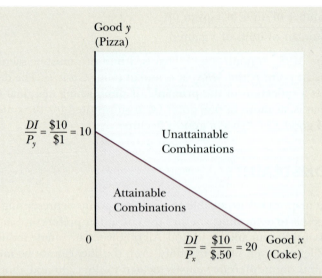

FIGURE 4A
BUDGET LINE
A budget line graphically depicts the consumption combinations that are attainable with a given level of income. Any combination above the line is unattainable.

cans of Coke. Suppose she has a disposable income (*DI*) of $10.00 and pizza (good *y*) and Coke (good *x*) sell for $1.00 and $.50, respectively, per unit. The construction of the budget line is illustrated in Figure 4A. If she spends her entire income (*DI*) on pizza, she can buy 10 slices. This number is determined by dividing income by the price of the good:

$$\frac{DI}{P_y} = \frac{\$10.00}{\$1.00} = 10 \text{ slices of pizza.}$$

Thus, 10 is the *y*-intercept. The *x*-intercept is calculated in the same manner:

$$\frac{DI}{P_x} = \frac{\$10.00}{\$.50} = 20 \text{ cans of Coke.}$$

A straight line connecting the two points that represent buying all good *y* (pizza) or all good *x* (Coke) shows all possible combinations that Mary can purchase with a given income level of $10. For example, $10 will buy 5 slices of pizza and 10 Cokes or 6 slices of pizza and 8 Cokes. Any combination outside (above) the line is unattainable at that income level. It is outside her budget constraint. In other words, the budget line is the dividing line between those combinations that are attainable and those that are unattainable at a given level of prices and a given level of income.

CHANGES IN INCOME AND CHANGES IN PRICES

The budget line is developed holding prices and income constant. How do changes in income and prices affect the budget line? An increase in income means that more of both goods can be purchased, if prices stay the same. A doubling of income means that twice as much of both goods can be purchased, if prices remain constant. An increase in income is represented by a parallel outward shift of the budget line. A decrease in income is represented by a parallel inward shift of the budget line. Such shifts are shown in Figure 5A.

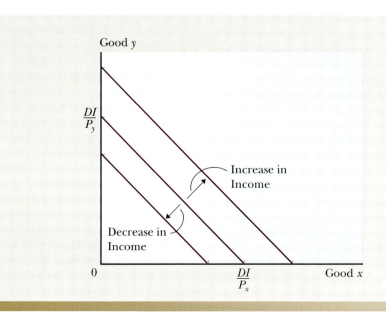

FIGURE 5A

THE EFFECT OF INCOME CHANGES ON BUDGET LINES

An increase in income is represented by an outward parallel shift of the budget line. A decrease in income is represented by an inward parallel shift of the budget line.

A change in the price of one good affects the maximum amount of that good that can be purchased, but does not affect the maximum amount of the other good that can be purchased. If the price of cola rises and Mary spends all her income on pizza, the price rise has no effect on the amount of pizza purchased. A price rise, then, will only affect the intercept of the budget line with the axis for the good that has experienced the price rise. Such a change is shown in Figure 6A. A price rise for good x from P_{x1} to P_{x2} causes the x-intercept of the

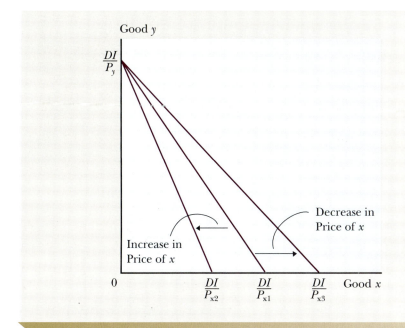

FIGURE 6A

THE EFFECT OF PRICE CHANGES ON BUDGET LINES

An increase in the price of one good changes the slope of the budget line because if all disposable income is spent on that good, less of it can be purchased. As a result, the intercept of the budget line will shift closer to the origin. The opposite holds for a decrease in price.

budget line to move closer to the origin, reflecting the fact that less of good *x* can now be purchased with constant income. A decrease in the price of good *x* from P_{x1} to P_{x3} means more of good *x* can be purchased. The *x*-intercept of the budget line moves away from the origin, reflecting increases in the potential consumption of good *x*.

Price changes cause the slope of the budget line to change. The slope of the budget line is $\Delta y / \Delta x$. Note that the slope is the negative of the ratio of the *y*-intercept to the *x*-intercept, or

$$-\frac{\frac{DI}{P_y}}{\frac{DI}{P_x}} = \frac{P_x}{P_y}$$

The slope of the budget line changes when the ratio of the prices of the two goods changes. A change in income, on the other hand, represents no change in relative prices. In that case, the slope of the budget line remains the same, but it shifts as described above.

MAXIMIZATION OF CONSUMER SATISFACTION

Adding a budget line to an indifference map makes it possible to demonstrate maximization of consumer satisfaction. In Figure 7A, at point *A*, the budget line is tangent to indifference curve I_2. Any point on I_3, such as point *B*, is preferred to point *A* because higher indifference curves represent higher levels of utility. However, point *B* is not attainable because it is outside the budget line. Point *C* on I_1 is attainable, but a point on I_2 is also attainable, and any point on I_2 represents more satisfaction than any point on I_1. The consumer wants to reach the

FIGURE 7A
MAXIMIZATION OF CONSUMER SATISFACTION
An individual maximizes consumer satisfaction at the point where the budget line is tangent to the highest attainable indifference curve.

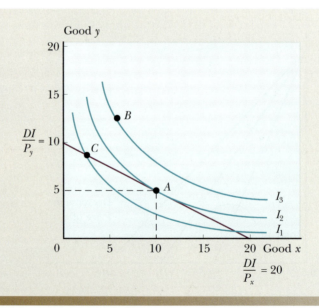

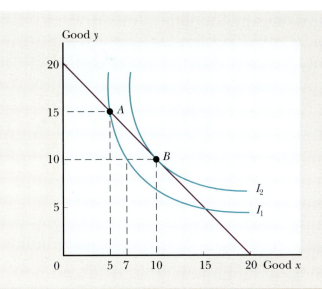

FIGURE 8A

TANGENCY ONCE AGAIN
Lower indifference curves that are within the budget constraint represent lower levels of utility than the highest, but still attainable, indifference curve.

highest attainable indifference curve. The highest attainable curve will be one that is tangent to the budget line because no higher curve can be reached with the given income and prices. In this example, the consumer is maximizing utility, or is in equilibrium, at point A on indifference curve I_2.

You should remember from geometry that two curves that are tangent have equal slopes at the point of tangency. At the point of tangency between the indifference curve and the budget line, the marginal rate of substitution is equal to the ratio of the price of x to the price of y.[a] That is,

$$MRS_{xy} = \frac{P_x}{P_y}$$

This expression means that the marginal rate of substitution expresses the willingness of the consumer to trade a certain amount of x for a certain amount of y, and the slope of the budget line reflects the market's willingness to trade a certain amount of x for a certain amount of y. The impersonal forces of the market impose the relative prices on the consumer, so the consumer adjusts consumption amounts in such a way that his or her trade-off is the same as the trade-off in the market.

Suppose you are consuming 15 units of y and 5 units of x (you are at point A in Figure 8A). According to your indifference curve (I_1), you would be willing to give up 5 units of y if you received 2 additional units of x. The market, however, is willing to give you 5 units of x in exchange for 5 units of y (note point B). You would probably consume less y and more x. In fact, you would be able to increase your utility by moving in the direction of the tangency of some higher indifference curve with the budget line.

---

a. Technically, MRS_{xy} is equal to the negative of the slope of the indifference curve. The price ratio, as we have seen, is the negative of the slope of the budget line. Therefore, at the (equilibrium) point of tangency between the indifference curve and the budget line, $MRS_{xy} = P_x/P_y$.

FIGURE 9A
INCOME CHANGES AND THE INCOME-CONSUMPTION CURVE

An income-consumption curve traces the response of consumption combinations to changes in income.

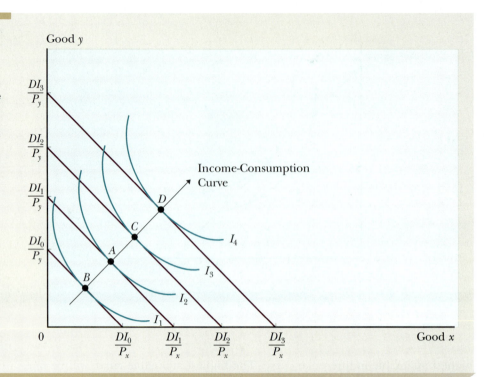

CONSUMER REACTION TO INCOME CHANGES.

The best feature of indifference curve analysis is that it allows us to analyze the reaction of consumers to price and income changes. Using the indifference map and the budget line, we can trace the adjustment process that takes place when a household experiences a change in income. In Figure 9A, for example, if the household's income is represented by the budget line DI_1, and x and y sell for P_x and P_y, respectively, the optimal utility is at point A. A decrease in income is represented by budget line DI_0, and two increases in income are represented by budget lines DI_2 and DI_3. The respective optimal positions representing tangencies of these budget lines with an indifference curve are points B, C, and D. Connecting points A, B, C, and D generates an **income-consumption curve**. This curve shows how consumption of the two goods changes as income changes. Recall the discussion of the income elasticity of demand in the preceding chapter. The income elasticities of both good x and good y in Figure 9A are positive because consumption of both goods increases as income increases. (Remember that a positive income elasticity indicates that a good is a normal good. An inferior good has a negative income elasticity since, in that case, as income increases, consumption of the good decreases.)

Figure 10A shows a case where one commodity, good x, is a normal good for a household until its income reaches DI_3. When income increases above DI_3, the household buys less of x. So x is a normal good up to point A and then becomes an inferior good as the income-consumption curve bends backward. There is nothing derogatory about the term *inferior*. A daily newspaper might be consid-

Income-consumption curve
A curve that uses parallel budget lines to show changes in consumer equilibrium when income changes.

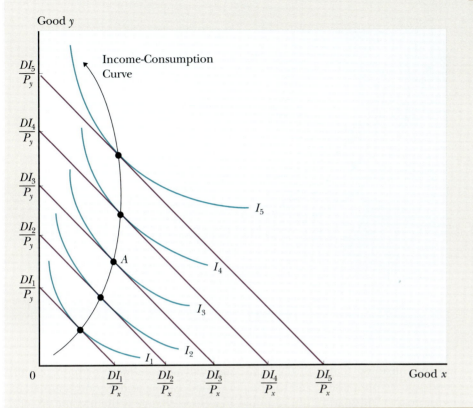

FIGURE 10A
INCOME-CONSUMPTION CURVE FOR AN INFERIOR GOOD
The income-consumption curve for an inferior good bends backward, indicating that less of the good is consumed as income increases beyond a certain level.

ered an inferior good for some buyers. As income falls, a person may buy the paper more often because it is a less expensive form of entertainment and also because it offers job listings. Remember, also, that a normal good to some people may be an inferior good to others.

CONSUMER REACTION TO PRICE CHANGES

Let's look at how the optimal consumption combination will be affected by price changes. Initially, the consumer is at the point of maximum utility (point A in Figure 11A). As the price of x falls from P_{x1} to P_{x2}, the budget line rotates out to intersect the x-axis at DI/P_{x2}, and the consumer now has a new optimum at point B on indifference curve I_2. Another decrease in price to P_{x3} allows the consumer to reach a still higher indifference curve, I_3, and a new optimum at point C. Connecting the points A, B, and C produces a **price-consumption curve**. This curve shows how consumption changes when relative prices change.

The theory behind this change in consumption patterns relies on the income and substitution effects again. When the price of a good falls, there are two forces at work to cause the consumer to increase purchases of that good. First, when the price of a good falls, the market trade-off between this good and other goods (or the substitution rate) changes. This part of the response to a price change is the substitution effect. Second, the consumer has a larger real

Price-consumption curve A curve that shows changes in consumer equilibrium when the price of one good on an indifference curve changes.

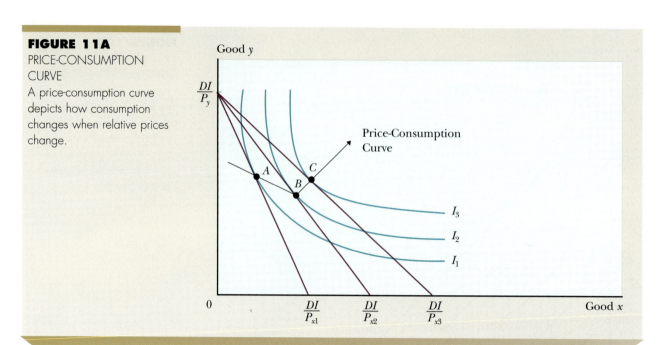

FIGURE 11A
PRICE-CONSUMPTION CURVE
A price-consumption curve depicts how consumption changes when relative prices change.

income, meaning that with the same nominal income, more of both (or all) goods can be purchased (and will be purchased as long as the good is not an inferior good). This part of the response to a price change is the income effect.

INDIFFERENCE ANALYSIS AND THE LAW OF DEMAND

Indifference analysis can be used to derive a consumer's demand curve and demonstrate the law of demand. This demonstration is a *ceteris paribus* experiment in which the price of one good is changed. Part (*a*) of Figure 12A shows an indifference map and a budget line for goods *x* and *y*. The consumer is at an optimum at point A. At point A, the individual consumes x_1 units of good *x* at a price of P_{x1}. Price and quantity demanded of good *x* are plotted in part (*b*). Now suppose the price of *x* falls to P_{x2}. As before, this decline in price causes the budget line to rotate outward. A new optimum is reached at point B, where the new budget line is tangent to indifference curve I_3. The change in price has caused the quantity demanded to increase from x_1 to x_2, as shown in part (*b*). The line connecting two price-quantity points in part (*b*) is a demand curve for good *x*, and it has the usual negative slope.

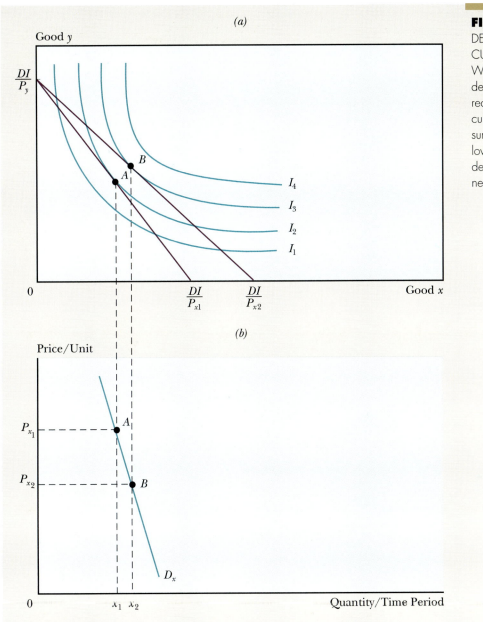

FIGURE 12A

DERIVING A DEMAND CURVE

When the price of good x decreases, the consumer can reach a higher indifference curve. This increased consumption of good x at a lower price means that the demand curve must have a negative slope.

PART 7

PRODUCT MARKETS

The next six chapters form the core of microeconomics and are often referred to as the *theory of the firm.* Before we can analyze firms as sellers of products in different types of markets, we must look at how firms organize the process of production. The firm buys productive resources and attempts to transform them into marketable outputs. Remember that the productive resources are land, labor, capital, and enterprise. Chapter 21 examines production, the process of transforming inputs into marketable outputs. Chapter 22 focuses on the cost relationships that result from production decisions.

Chapters 23, 24, and 25 look at four different models or market structures. The model discussed in Chapter 23 is perfect competition. It is important to keep in mind that this is a theoretical model and does not precisely describe reality. The model is useful, however, because it allows the development of tools that indicate what determines price and output quantity when conditions are close to those of perfect competition. The perfectly competitive market is the abstract ideal to which we will compare other market structures. Monopoly is at the other end of the continuum from perfect competition, and real-world examples of monopoly are also nonexistent. The theory developed in Chapter 24 is still useful, however, as a tool to examine real-world situations. Although there are no pure monopolies, many firms do have some degree of monopoly power.

The study of the theory of the firm is completed in Chapter 25 with development of the theory of imperfect competition. Market structures between the two extremes of monopoly and pure competition show imperfect competition. Economists divide the middle of the spectrum into monopolistic competition and oligopoly.

Chapters 23 through 25 examine four theoretical market structures. In Chapter 26 we apply these models to the real world and examine the extent of monopoly power in U.S. industry. This chapter will examine the theory and practice of regulation and the development of antitrust laws in the United States. It concludes with an assessment of the success of regulation and antitrust policy and an examination of recent trends in merger activity in U.S. industry.

CHAPTER 21
FIRMS AND PRODUCTION

LEARNING OBJECTIVES
1. Explain why firms come into existence.
2. Define the various types of firms and list the advantages and disadvantages of each business organization.
3. Describe the difference between a for-profit firm and a nonprofit firm.
4. Calculate the least-cost method of production to determine economic efficiency.
5. Use a production function to explain increasing and diminishing marginal returns.
6. Show how a firm chooses its mix of inputs to maximize output.

Consider this... Imagine that you and your friend Mark are seniors at the University of Miami. You have been going to restaurants and bars for five years and you think that you have a "better idea." You think you are a good manager and you believe Mark has good business sense, so you decide to team up. Your idea is to open a restaurant/bar that specializes in oysters and drinks, but serves hamburgers and other types of sandwiches too. You even have a name for your business. You are going to call it the Hurricane Oyster House. The first decision you have is how to organize your business: Do you want to be a partnership or a corporation? Imagine that it is so successful that you are going to start a chain of oyster houses. First you will move up the road and start the Gator Oyster House and the Seminole Oyster House. You then might skip to Texas and open the Aggie Oyster House. Then westward to California for the Trojan Oyster House. Start looking for a building near your campus where you can open the XOXOX Oyster House. How would these expansions affect your organizational plan? A good business plan might include these considerations before you go to City Hall to apply for a business license.

THE FIRM IN THEORY

It is easy to take the existence of firms for granted because we have all had dealings with many types of firms. We need to ask why firms exist. A firm buys or rents productive resources (also known as inputs) and attempts to transform them into marketable outputs. Remember that the productive factors are land, labor, capital, and enterprise. This chapter examines the process of transforming inputs into marketable outputs, which economists call **production**. Economic theory recognizes that firms exist to accomplish certain economic objectives and are organized in different ways to meet those objectives.

Production
The process of transforming inputs into marketable outputs.

HOUSEHOLDS AS FIRMS

In many ways, households compete with firms. Firms exist to organize production, and households also organize some production. Thus, there are aspects of household activities that are similar to the activities of firms. Firms put "things" together to make other "things" that have economic value. Households clearly do, too. Households cook meals, and so do restaurants. Households make clothes, and so do tailors. Households organize entertainment, and so do movie theaters.

An interesting economic question is why households don't do everything for themselves. Why don't they make their own cars, for example? That's an easy one. They don't make their own cars because it is more efficient for them to buy cars from firms that produce cars. It gets more difficult when we ask why households don't make their own granola or build their own homes. The answer is that some do. As the price of granola and homes produced by firms increases, more households may compete with organized business firms to produce their own products for consumption.

In fact, as relative market prices change, the kinds of production carried out by households change. In recent years, many households have started to grow their own vegetables in response to rising food prices and the lifestyle changes that emphasize gourmet cooking with high-quality, organically grown vegetables. This home production, in turn, has affected the demand for products of firms that produce canning equipment and related products.

WHAT BUSINESS FIRMS DO

First and foremost, firms in a market economy are organized by entrepreneurs to make profits. These firms are organizations that plan production. They assign tasks, monitor those tasks, and generate incentives that reward individuals for completing assigned tasks. An important point is that there are many different sizes of firms. At one extreme, households behave like very small firms. At the other, governments can be seen as extremely large, multipurpose firms. Until 1990 the government in the Soviet Union acted as a single firm in that it planned, organized, and provided incentives. As market reforms proceed in Russia and other former Soviet Republics, it will be interesting to watch how the relationship between firms and the government evolves. The former Soviet Republics have had central planning for so long that there are very few experienced entrepreneurs to take on the organizing function of business firms. This problem of reform in previously centrally planned economies will be discussed in detail in a later chapter.

Within the category of business firms, there is great diversity. Many firms in the U.S. economy are **vertically integrated firms**, which means they perform many steps in a production process. For example, a firm may grow cotton, weave cloth, dye the cloth, and finally sew it into garments. Firms that are not vertically integrated may simply weave cloth or make garments. Still others are **horizontally integrated firms**, which means that they perform many similar production operations in the same industry, operating many plants at the same stage of production—for example, Marriott Hotels, Domino's, or Kinko's. Many large firms are **conglomerates**, which means that they engage in many, often quite unrelated, activities. For example, G.E. produces light bulbs, dishwashers, and jet engines.

Vertically integrated firms
Firms that perform many sequential steps in a production process.

Horizontally integrated firms
Firms that perform many similar production operations in the same industry.

Conglomerates
Firms that perform many unrelated operations or produce in many different industries.

GLOBAL OUTLOOK: LABOR-MANAGED FIRMS AROUND THE GLOBE

In this chapter we discuss different forms of business organization with an eye on the types of firms we see in the United States and most other market-oriented economies. There is, however, a form of organization that grew up in the former Yugoslavia and spread to some of the other previously Soviet-type economies. This is the form of workers' self-management, a form of governance that comes close to what we find in many American universities.

In the United States, worker management exists in a few craft industries and has been attempted in a few instances when manufacturing plants were about to close, mostly in the steel industry. There are some companies in the United States where labor unions have become significant stock owners and have received an automatic seat on the board of directors in exchange for salary concessions to avoid bankruptcy. The most recent example of such an action was the union concession to Northwest Airlines in 1993. Perhaps the closest parallel in the United States is profit sharing by labor in some industries.

In other parts of the world workers actually own the plant and decide how it will be managed through workers' councils. The ownership rights end when a worker leaves the firm, so these ownership rights are different from stockholder rights in U.S. corporations. The labor-managed firm is an interesting concept for a socialist country because such worker democracy is closer to Marxist philosophy than the state-owned and -managed firms that existed in most communist countries. A policy issue to watch is how these worker-owned firms will develop in the market shift that is taking place in the former Soviet Union and its satellite countries.

Economists are interested in how such organization and control by workers' affects incentives and ultimately the economic development of the country. As we have seen, entrepreneurs try to maximize profits. If the firm is owned by workers, will something other than profit be maximized? Workers' self-management means that workers may seek to maximize wages and other benefits that they can capture while they are with the firm. Since workers have no ownership rights that they can sell, they may opt for a management policy that increases the short-term income of the firm over policies that would increase the firm's value over time. This bias would tend to reduce the firm's investments, which in turn (in the aggregate) would reduce the long-term economic growth of the country.

Transaction costs
Costs associated with gathering information about markets (prices and quantities supplied) for consuming or producing.

Economic theory helps explain why these different organizations can all coexist in a market economy. Part of the answer to this question can be found in the incentives that bring about such organizations. Ronald Coase, in a now famous article, showed that transaction costs create firms.[1] He argued that buying and selling imposes transaction costs. **Transaction costs** are costs associated with creating and running a business. For example, gathering and disseminating information involve costs. These transaction costs are minimized by the formation of firms. What Coase described was the effort that a buyer and seller in a market economy must make in continually exploring options. Buyers must search for quality and price. Sellers must monitor the changing demands of buyers.

The transactions cost of these activities can often be reduced by carrying out more research and exploration within a firm. Workers agree to join a firm that provides a workplace, incentives, and guidelines. The firm exists because it economizes on the transaction costs. But the firm also faces constraints. Some kinds of costs may rise as the size and complexity of the firm increase. Thus, smaller firms (maybe even households) will become potential competitors. In other words, firms exist in many organizational forms and sizes because various forms and sizes make the most efficient use of information and reduce transaction costs for different kinds of production activities.

1. Ronald Coase, "The Nature of the Firm," *Economica* (November 1937): 286–405.

Further developments in this theory of organization added other elements to the reasons why firms exist. Armen Alchian and Harold Demsetz added two important elements to this analysis.[2] First, firms exist because the production of many types of products is more efficiently carried out by teams than by individuals. **Teams** are groups of employees that work together to produce something. Firms exist to organize teams to produce goods or services efficiently. Second, when team production is not organized in a firm (as with volunteer activities), it is difficult to measure the contribution of the individual. There are incentives to **shirk**, to put forth less than the agreed-on effort.

The firm exists, then, to reward individuals for team effort and to monitor shirking behavior. Management is primarily responsible for developing organizational forms that use both negative and positive incentives in order to limit shirking.

Teams
Groups of employees that work together to produce something.

Shirk
To put forth less effort than agreed on.

THE BUSINESS FIRM IN PRACTICE

A **business firm** is organized by an entrepreneur (or group of entrepreneurs) to combine inputs of raw materials, capital, labor services, and technology in order to produce marketable outputs of goods and services.

Firms are parts of industries. There are many ways to define an industry. In general, what economists mean by an **industry** is a group of firms producing similar or related products. For example, the automobile industry might include just the big three—General Motors, Ford, and Chrysler. Or the industry might also include all foreign automakers selling in the U.S. market and all small domestic producers. It might also include firms that supply parts, materials, and services to automobile producers or automobile consumers. There are no absolute rules on how to define a specific industry. The definition usually depends on the purpose or the particular problem or issue being studied.

Business firm
An organization formed by an entrepreneur to combine inputs in order to produce marketable outputs.

Industry
A group of firms producing similar or related products.

FORMS OF ORGANIZATION

In the United States, firms are organized primarily in three ways. These categories are legal, not economic, and they differ mainly in the legal liability of the owners. Some interesting economic questions arise because of the different types of ownership and the different treatment under the law.

SOLE PROPRIETORSHIPS. A **sole proprietorship** is a form of enterprise in which no legal distinction is made between the owner and the firm. The financial resources of the firm are limited to those of the individual owner and what can be borrowed from friends or financial institutions. Thus, the profits and losses accrue solely to that individual. The owner also bears unlimited liability for any and all debts of the firm. Success of the firm is success of the owner; bankruptcy of the firm is bankruptcy of the owner. This close relationship usually means a constant involvement of the owner with the affairs of the firm. There are obviously great incentives for hard work and diligence in a sole proprietorship.

Sole proprietorship
A form of enterprise in which no legal distinction is made between the firm and its owner.

---

2. Armen A. Alchian and Harold Demsetz, "Production, Information Costs and Economic Organization," *American Economic Review* (December 1972): 777–795.

Compared to other forms of business enterprise, a sole proprietorship can be established or go out of business very easily. In certain lines of business, government approval is required, because licenses or permits are needed. Typically, however, the sole proprietor starts or ends a business by simply doing so. The IRS reported that, in 1990, 69 percent of the business firms in the United States were sole proprietorships. Most farmers and many small firms, especially in retailing and services, are sole proprietorships. Although dominant in numbers, sole proprietorships account for only 10 percent of annual business sales.

PARTNERSHIPS. **Partnerships** are similar to sole proprietorships except they have more than one owner. The firm does not have a legal existence separate from the owners (the partners). Like sole proprietorships, firms organized as partnerships tend to be quite small. They are typically found in professional services: medicine, law, consulting, and financial services.

There are more personal and financial resources available to a partnership than if only one person formed the firm. Besides improving finances, each partner may also bring special skills, knowledge, energy, or decision-making powers. Offsetting these advantages are the frictions that usually arise in operating the firm. Partners have to agree on the proportions of ownership owned by each partner, which may be dictated by the amounts of funds contributed, the amounts of work, or the amounts of other kinds of value contributed (such as ideas or patents). Partners also have to agree on joint rights and responsibilities. The partners share in any profits, but each partner bears unlimited liability for any debts incurred by the firm.

The disadvantages of a partnership arrangement apparently outweigh the advantages. The IRS reports that, in 1990, only 10 percent of the business firms and only 5 percent of annual business sales in the United States were accounted for by partnerships.

CORPORATIONS. The dominant form of business organization in the United States, measured in any way except absolute numbers, is the corporate form. A **corporation** is a form of enterprise in which persons who own shares of stock are the owners of the firm. Owners of a corporation are called **stockholders**. The legal liability of stockholders is limited. The IRS reports that, in 1990, corporations accounted for 21 percent of business firms and about 85 percent of annual business sales.

The number of stockholders may run into the hundreds of thousands, although some corporations have only a few stockholders. The stockholders vote, according to the number of shares they hold, for a board of directors. The board, in turn, appoints officers of the corporation to manage it along the guidelines set by the charter of incorporation and the directors. A **board of directors** consists of individuals elected by the stockholders of a corporation to select the managers and oversee the management of the corporation.

One of the strengths of the corporate form of business organization is the relative ease of acquiring financial assets. Money can be acquired by issuing shares of **stock**, which are certificates of ownership in a corporation. A corporation can borrow funds by issuing **bonds**, which are interest-bearing certificates issued by governments or corporations. A corporation can also borrow directly by taking out loans from banks or other financial intermediaries. Loans are the only option for obtaining outside funding available to partnerships and sole proprietorships.

Partnership
A form of enterprise in which there is more than one owner, and the firm does not have a legal existence separate from the owners.

Corporation
A form of enterprise in which stockholders are the owners of the firm but have limited liability.

Stockholders
The owners of a corporation.

Board of directors
The individuals elected by the stockholders of a corporation to select the managers and oversee the management of the corporation.

Stock
A certificate of ownership in a corporation.

Bond
An interest-earning certificate that is issued by a government or corporation in exchange for borrowed funds and has a fixed face value, annual interest payment, and maturity date.

The attractiveness of the corporation as a form of organization stems from the fact that the stockholders are the legal owners and have rights to the profits, but their legal liability is very limited. **Limited liability** means that the stockholders of a corporation cannot be sued for failure of the corporation to pay its debts. Only the corporation itself can be sued. This limited liability is a critical advantage of the corporate form of business. In many countries, corporations are referred to as limited liability companies, and the letters *Ltd.* appear after the name of the firm. The letters *Inc.* (Incorporated) after the name of a firm in the United States mean the same thing. Thus, a corporation, defined in law as a legal person in its own right, can go bankrupt without the owners going bankrupt. Of course, individuals who have most of their wealth in the stock of one corporation might go bankrupt because the stock would no longer have any value.

A second important advantage of corporate organization is the ease of transferring ownership. Ownership rights can be transferred through the sale of stocks, and markets (stock exchanges) have evolved to handle such transfers. The costs of transfer of ownership are significantly lower for corporations than for partnerships or sole proprietorships.

A major drawback of corporate organization is double taxation. Corporate income is subject to corporate income taxes, and then that income is taxed again when it is distributed to stockholders as dividends.

In the late 1980s, a hybrid type of corporation evolved very rapidly in the United States. The **S corporation** enjoys some of the advantages of a corporation, most notably limited liability, but is not subject to double taxation. The income of an S corporation is simply passed to the owners and only taxed once as personal income. Most S corporations tend to be relatively small. The S corporation is replacing sole proprietorships and partnerships as a form of business organization in many industries.

Different types of ownership cause managers of firms to behave in different ways. For instance, an owner-manager of a sole proprietorship may make decisions that are different from those of the hired manager of a large corporation, because the owner-manager benefits more directly from higher profits. For now, we will ignore such differences. We'll assume that business firms, however they are organized, exist for only one purpose—to increase the wealth of their owners. To do this, firms try to maximize profits. This assumption of profit maximization makes it possible to develop a powerful theory to predict the economic effects of different market structures.

Limited liability
The fact that the stockholders of a corporation cannot be sued for failure of the corporation to meet its obligations.

S corporation
A hybrid type of corporation that passes income directly to the owners, avoiding the double taxation of corporate profits.

ENTERPRISE, ENTREPRENEURS, AND THE FIRM

Enterprise is the productive resource provided by an entrepreneur. The entrepreneur is the founder and often the guiding spirit of a business firm. Many business schools now offer courses in entrepreneurship. What is it that entrepreneurs do? They identify consumer demands, organize production, allocate resources, and acquire assets. In the process, they take risks. Entrepreneurs are rewarded with profits if they have good hunches or go bankrupt if they are wrong. Many more go bankrupt than succeed, yet we read in the newspapers about the most successful. Biographies of rich entrepreneurs show that most successful entrepreneurs didn't start out as fortune seekers. Instead, they had an idea they wanted to follow; they were pursuing visions, not wealth.

KEY IDEAS

FORMS OF ORGANIZATION
- Sole proprietorship
    - No legal distinction between owner and firm
    - Financial resources limited to those of owner
    - Profits accrue solely to owner
    - Owner is liable for debts
- Partnership
    - More than one owner
    - Partners bring different skills and greater financial resources
    - Partners share profits and legal liability
- Corporation
    - The legal liability of stockholders is limited
    - Board of directors oversees management
    - Ownership is transferred with ease
    - Faces double taxation, except S corporation

THE NONPROFIT FIRM

Although economic models assume that business firms exist to maximize profits or wealth, an increasingly large number of firms are organized as nonprofit organizations. These firms differ from for-profit firms mainly in that they do not have a residual claimant. A **residual claimant** is an individual, or group of individuals, who shares in the profits (if any) of an enterprise. Thus, it is difficult to determine who owns a nonprofit organization. We can separate nonprofit firms into two categories: those in the private sector and those in the government sector.

NONPROFITS IN THE PRIVATE SECTOR

Nonprofit firms in the private sector are not part of, or sponsored directly by, a governmental unit. They exist for many reasons. Many of them (for example, health clinics and soup kitchens) are engaged in private forms of welfare. Some provide a type of welfare that cannot conveniently or effectively be provided through government.

The manager (organizer) of a private nonprofit firm usually receives a salary for managing the firm. Economists expect more shirking behavior to occur in these firms because the manager cannot convert increased efficiencies into profits that affect his or her salary. Such shirking behavior has been documented by economist Kenneth Clarkson.[3] He found that nonprofit hospitals had higher budgeted expenses for supervisory positions than for-profit hospitals did. The chief manager of a private nonprofit hospital was also much less concerned with the price and productivity of equipment. Automatic, across-the-board pay increases were more frequent in nonprofit hospitals. This method of giving raises is a type of shirking behavior. It would require more effort to separate good employees from bad employees.

Most economists would argue that nonprofit firms have significant organizational disadvantages that introduce inefficiencies. Yet, nonprofits have in-

Residual claimant
An individual, or group of individuals, who share in the profits of an enterprise.

---

3. Kenneth W. Clarkson, "Some Implications of Property Rights in Hospital Management," *Journal of Law and Economics* (October 1972): 363–384.

creased rapidly in recent years. Why have they become such a popular form of organization? Earl Thompson has suggested an answer.[4] He points out that most nonprofit firms are associated with charitable organizations. Contributors to these charitable organizations are usually remote from the production or use of the product or service they are supporting. These contributors would have a difficult time monitoring the managers of these firms. They wouldn't be able to determine easily whether a manager was using their gift to produce the charitable product or was simply "taking it home" in the form of higher wages. However, tolerating the inefficiencies caused by managers who are not profit seekers is less costly to contributors than is monitoring manager behavior. As a result, charitable donors accept some inefficiency in preference to supporting the provision of the products or services through the for-profit or governmental sector. Thompson argues that one way to lessen the problem is to specify certain salaries for the managers.

It is also true that tax laws play a role in encouraging the formation of nonprofit organizations. In some cases, individuals can create nonprofit firms that produce output for their own consumption. They can then support this production through tax-deductible "charitable" contributions. You might, for example, create a nonprofit organization to support the local theater in which you act and make tax-deductible gifts to this nonprofit organization.

NONPROFITS IN THE GOVERNMENT SECTOR

Everyone does business with some nonprofit governmental firms. Often these firms compete directly with private business firms. The U.S. Postal Service competes with United Parcel Service and Federal Express. City and county hospitals compete with private hospitals. Municipal golf and tennis clubs compete with private country clubs. City bus lines compete with private cab companies. Public and private colleges and universities compete for students. The list goes on and on.

What characterizes these governmental firms? To begin, like a private nonprofit firm, a governmental nonprofit has no profit and no residual claimants. Second, the manager of a governmental nonprofit usually has little control over price. If a price is charged, it is usually set by a board or some political entity. The price is often below the operating costs of the firm. In addition, the customers often have little influence over the behavior of the organization. Customers can express frustration with a private firm by switching to a competing firm. This is not always possible when dealing with a governmental firm.

The tendency to shirk is prevalent in governmental firms for the same reasons as in private nonprofits. In addition, a bureaucratic manager can get promoted by being "better" than other bureaucratic managers. In many instances, causing the agency to grow is taken as a sign of success and a cause for advancement. We will discuss this bureaucratic incentive in the chapter on market and government failure.

Some economists argue that the quality of products produced by governmental nonprofit firms is likely to be poorer than that of similar private, for-profit firms. This poorer quality results from the fact that prices charged by the

---

4. Earl Thompson, "Charity and Nonprofit Organizations," in *The Economics of Nonproprietary Organizations*, K.W. Clarkson and D.C. Martin, eds. (Greenwich CT: JAI Press, 1980): 125–128.

governmental organization are usually lower. Customers will often choose the low-priced product or service, even though it is of lower quality. Research on Veterans Administration hospitals in comparison to private, for-profit hospitals supports this observation.[5]

WHAT ABOUT THE PROFITS OF NONPROFIT FIRMS?

In recent years, many private and governmental nonprofit organizations have entered into profit-making activities. The profits from these activities are often referred to instead as "excess of revenues over expenses." Hospitals are selling health-related equipment, universities are selling in-company training programs, university presses are producing best sellers, alumni groups are selling tours, and religious organizations are selling condos at theme parks. Profits from such activities are not taxed because they are intertwined with the nonprofit firms' noncommercial activities.

In addition, nonprofit firms may have the advantages of access to referrals and free space for doing business. They can also use bulk mail instead of paying first-class rates, as the private sector must. These factors give a cost advantage to these firms over private sector firms in the same business.

Delegates to the 1990 White House Conference on Small Business voted that the second biggest problem facing small businesses was nonprofit organizations using their tax-exempt status to compete with the private sector. (This problem ranked after government-mandated employee benefits and before liability insurance.) This subsidized competition from nonprofit organizations has led private sector firms to pressure the U.S. Congress to change the law, as it relates to profit-making activities, of tax-exempt nonprofit organizations. In the last session of the Texas legislature, university bookstores were prohibited from granting "free" credit to students because this gave them an unfair advantage over private sector bookstores. The students were upset with the legislature because this also removed a benefit to students. We can expect more interest in this issue in state and federal legislative bodies in the next few years.

ECONOMIC EFFICIENCY

The firms that produce most of the U.S. output are private, profit-maximizing firms. An entrepreneur must combine resources efficiently if the firm is to maximize profits. To do this, entrepreneurs must decide among competing ways of producing a given product. Suppose, for example, that the printer producing this textbook is faced with the alternatives listed in Table 1. The production engineer tells the production manager that 100,000 copies can be produced in any of these four ways. The production manager informs the president and CEO of the firm, the entrepreneur, who must decide how to actually produce the textbooks. The entrepreneur must have a decision rule in order to select a production alternative. This is where profit maximization comes into play. Without profit maximization as a goal, the entrepreneur will have to choose on some other basis, such as physical units of input or output.

The method that would minimize the inputs in a physical sense would be method A, which uses the fewest inputs. The basis for choosing this method is

---

5. See C.M. Lindsay, "A Theory of Government Enterprise," *Journal of Political Economy* (October 1976): 1061–1077.

TABLE 1 ALTERNATIVE WAYS TO PRODUCE 100,000 COPIES OF THIS TEXTBOOK

METHOD	CAPITAL (MACHINES)	PRICE OF CAPITAL SERVICES (PER MACHINE)	LABOR (WORKER-YEARS)	PRICE OF LABOR SERVICES (PER WORKER-YEAR)	LAND (ACRES)	PRICE OF LAND SERVICES (PER ACRE)	TOTAL COST
A	5	$30,000	5	$4,000	1	$10,000	$150,000 + $20,000 +$10,000 = $180,000
B	4	30,000	10	4,000	1	10,000	$120,000 + $40,000 + $10,000 = $170,000
C	3	30,000	15	4,000	1	10,000	$90,000 + $60,000 + $10,000 = $160,000
D	2	30,000	25	4,000	1	10,000	$60,000 + $100,000 +$10,000 = $170,000

technical efficiency. **Technical efficiency** refers to the minimizing of the physical inputs to a production method according to some specific rule. It is an engineering concept with little economic relevance. The drawback of this decision rule is that it requires the decision maker to compare physical units of such diverse inputs as machines, acres of land, and worker-hours of labor.

Technical efficiency has been widely used as a production decision tool in planned economies, such as that of the former Soviet Union. The reforms in Russia and Eastern Europe have put this type of decision rule in question. In the 1990s, these countries are struggling to replace such calculations with more appropriate decision rules.

A market system puts the inputs into dollar terms and lets the entrepreneur choose the least-cost method of producing. The least-cost method, or the economically efficient method, is chosen by the entrepreneur because of the assumption of attempted profit maximization. **Economic efficiency** is therefore defined as the least-cost method of production. In Table 1, the entrepreneur would choose method *C* to produce the textbooks. Regardless of the price of the textbooks, method *C* helps to maximize profits (or minimize losses) because costs are less than the alternative ways to produce 100,000 units. However, the entrepreneur must know the prices of the various inputs in order to make this choice. This price information is not usually available in a command economy. Lack of market price information is one of the major problems facing the planned economies of Eastern and Central Europe as they try to make the transition to market economies.

Technical efficiency
The basis for minimizing the inputs to a production method according to some specific rule (an engineering concept).

Economic efficiency
The least-cost method of production.

PRODUCTION FUNCTIONS IN THE SHORT AND LONG RUN

A **production function** is a description of the amounts of output expected from various combinations of inputs. It is usually expressed in the form of a table or graph, but it also can be shown by a mathematical formula. The production function describes a technical or technological relationship. These technological relationships are sometimes simple and in other cases complex. It might be that engineers, agronomists, chemists, or other technical experts must be consulted to determine the relationships.

Production function
A description of the amounts of output expected from various combinations of inputs.

POLICY FOCUS: SHOULD A PUBLICLY HELD CORPORATION GIVE MONEY AWAY?

Economists view a firm, whether a sole proprietorship or a corporation, as existing to make profits for the owners. Some economists argue that it is therefore improper for a publicly held corporation to be involved in philanthropy (charity) because it is giving away the profits of its stockholders, who are not part of the decision to give the money away. They argue that the profits should be distributed to the stockholders, who can give it to charity themselves if they wish. However, corporations have been giving money to various causes for decades. For many years, this corporate giving was at the whim of the CEO, or whoever had the ear of the CEO. In recent years, the pattern has changed somewhat. Corporate giving is now more likely to be based on self-interest, accountability, and cause-related marketing.

Corporate philanthropy is big business. More than $6 billion was given away in 1994. American Express started cause-related marketing with its promise to earmark a portion of its revenue to the Statue of Liberty restoration program. That identified American Express with patriotism. Ben Cohen (of Ben & Jerry's Ice Cream) has set up a company that will give 40 percent of the revenue from the flavor Rainforest Crunch to protect the Amazon rain forest. Such gifts serve worthy causes while creating a good image and potential future customers. An investment in philanthropy may make a corporation even more profitable in the long run.

The biggest givers in corporate America are some of the biggest corporations. The table lists six of these and the main beneficiaries of their corporate largess. You will notice from the table that corporations tend to support universities. Often these gifts are to universities in the corporation's geographic area or to universities that do research of immediate benefit to the corporation. Other corporate gifts are made to promote affirmative action goals or community development in the region in which the corporation is located. In some cases, the tie between the company and the recipient is clearly business-related. Time Warner, Inc. combats illiteracy by selling its *Time to Read* program to other corporate sponsors.

CORPORATE GIVING

CORPORATION	RECIPIENTS
IBM	Not made public!
General Motors	University of Michigan
	GM Cancer Research Foundation
Exxon	New Jersey Science-Technology Center
	Community Summer Jobs Program
Hewlett-Packard	MIT, Stanford University Hospital
RJR/Nabisco	University of Delaware
	West End Neighborhood House
AT&T	Stanford University
	National Urban League

Source "What's in It for Me?" *Business Month* (November 1989).

Sometimes the link between a university and company is through the loyalty of the CEO and other top management to the university they attended. It would be an interesting research project to take the top public companies in your state and track their corporate donations. It would also be interesting to research contributions to the alma maters of the executives of these same companies. Should stockholders be "forced" to contribute to the alma maters of the CEOs of the companies in their stock portfolio? Is there anything they can do to control such contributions?

Only the technically efficient input combinations are included. For example, it might be that an output of 100 units could be produced by 5 units of capital, 20 units of labor, and 2 units of land; or by 6 units of capital, 30 units of labor, and 3 units of land. The second combination is inferior to the first because it takes more of all inputs to produce the same output. That method of production would be ignored. The production function reflects the most efficient technology available to produce a given level of output.

Usually entrepreneurs are interested in only a portion of the production function. For instance, it is often convenient to ask what would happen to total production if all but one of the inputs were at a given level. When considering a production function, it is possible to distinguish between fixed inputs and variable inputs. **Fixed inputs** are the productive resources that cannot be varied in the short run, such as the size of the plant. **Variable inputs** are the productive resources that can be increased or decreased in the short run. Which inputs are fixed and which are variable usually depends on the problem under consideration. In many cases, however, the land and the buildings of a firm (the physical plant) are considered fixed inputs and labor the variable input.

When economists distinguish between fixed and variable inputs, they are referring to a time period called the short run. In this context, the **short run** is the period of time that is too short to vary all the inputs. The **long run** is the period of time in which all inputs, including plant and equipment, can be varied. Short-run decisions are those concerning the profit-maximizing use of the existing (fixed) plant and equipment. The plant is used more intensively by increasing the amount of variable inputs, such as labor or new machines. Long-run decisions are those concerning the selection of a plant size that will maximize profits.

These time horizons cannot be defined in the calendar sense, because they are different in different industries. In some industries, firms may be able to increase in size very rapidly. In some cases, contractions can occur more quickly, depending on whether the plant and equipment are adaptable for other uses. It is primarily for convenience of analysis that decisions are classed as being either short-run or long-run. Keep in mind that such decisions are inherently interrelated. Once a long-run decision to build a plant of a certain size is made, a whole series of short-run decisions are affected because they must deal with that size of plant.

DIMINISHING RETURNS

As more and more units of a variable input are added to a set of fixed inputs, the resulting additions to output will eventually become smaller. This economic conclusion is referred to as the **principle of diminishing returns**. It is easy to see that returns must eventually diminish. Otherwise, all the wheat needed to feed the world could be produced on one acre of land by simply adding more seed, more fertilizer, more water, and more labor.

The principle of diminishing marginal returns is a fascinating and pervasive phenomenon. The principle is almost never contradicted by real-world observations. A tree grows more slowly as it grows larger. Little pigs put on more weight from a given amount of corn than big ones do. It is more costly to add a floor to a twenty-story building than to a ten-story building. Adding water to parched soil yields remarkable crop improvement, but adding the same amount of water to already moist soil has very little effect. If a firm adds a worker when its labor force is already large, the increase in output is less than if a worker is added at a time when the labor force is small. These are only a few examples of the principle of diminishing returns.

Note that the principle of diminishing marginal returns applies to the short run and says nothing about the long-run production function. It only says that if more and more variable input is added to a fixed input, after a while the additions to output will not be as large. Think of your own experience in studying for exams. The output is your test score, and the variable input is the time you spend studying. Assume that you could get a score of 55 percent without studying. One hour of studying would boost your score to 66 percent, two hours to 75

Fixed inputs
The productive resources that cannot be varied in the short run.

Variable inputs
The productive resources that can be increased or decreased in the short run.

Short run
The period of time that is too short to vary all the inputs.

Long run
The period of time in which all inputs, including plant and equipment, can be varied.

Principle of diminishing returns
The fact that as more and more units of a variable input are added to a set of fixed inputs, the resulting additions to output eventually become smaller.

percent, three hours to 80 percent, four hours to 84 percent, five hours to 86 percent, and so on. Each additional unit of variable input (hour spent studying) produces a smaller increment in output (improvement in test score). The first hour of studying produces an improvement of 11 percentage points, the second hour yields 9 points, the third hour 5 points, and so on. There is a diminishing marginal return to studying. It is up to you to decide when the return for an additional hour of studying is not worth the opportunity cost of that hour in terms of the other things you could be doing. So you see, even deciding how much to study is an exercise in rational economic choice.

AVERAGE AND MARGINAL RELATIONSHIPS

There is a technical relationship between average values and marginal values. Think of your grade point average. If your grade in this course (the marginal grade) is below your grade point average for all courses you have taken, your average will fall. If your grade in this course is above your grade point average, your average will rise. If a basketball player's lifetime shooting percentage (average) is higher this week than last week, you know that in the intervening games, the player has shot higher-than-average (marginal) percentages. If a marginal value is above average, it will pull the average up. If the average value is falling, the marginal value must be below the average.

In production, the relationship of marginal and average values is between marginal product and average product. In order to describe more precisely the relationship between inputs and outputs, economists use the concept of the marginal product. **Marginal product (*MP*)** is the change in total output that is produced by a unit change in an input. The marginal product of labor, for example, is the change in total output per unit change in the use of labor service. That is,

$$MP_L = \frac{\Delta TP}{\Delta L},$$

Marginal product (*MP*)
The change in total output that is produced by a unit change in an input.

where MP_L is the marginal product of labor, ΔTP is the change in the total product, and ΔL is the change in the number of units of labor employed. The **total product (*TP*)** is the amount of output that a firm produces in units. The **average product (*AP*)** of an input is simply the total product divided by the number of units of the input employed. For example, the average product of capital (AP_K) is

Total product (*TP*)
The amount of output that a firm produces.

Average product (*AP*)
The total product (output) divided by the number of units of input used.

$$AP_K = \frac{TP}{K},$$

where K is the number of units of capital used.

Table 2 illustrates these relationships for a short-run production function. All the inputs are fixed except labor. Labor, the variable input, can vary between zero and ten units. In Table 2, as more variable input is added to the fixed inputs, output goes through four distinct stages. When the first three units of labor are added, output increases at an increasing rate. That is, the marginal product of labor is increasing. Adding the fourth unit of labor causes output to increase but by a smaller amount than for the third unit of labor. The marginal product of labor is now declining, diminishing marginal returns has set in. The

TABLE 2 A SHORT-RUN PRODUCTION FUNCTION

VARIABLE INPUT (UNITS OF LABOR)	TOTAL PRODUCT (UNITS OF OUTPUT)	MARGINAL PRODUCT OF LABOR	AVERAGE PRODUCT OF LABOR
0	0	0	0.0
1	6	6	6.0
2	14	8	7.0
3	24	10	8.0
4	32	8	8.0
5	38	6	7.6
6	42	4	7.0
7	44	2	6.3
8	44	0	5.5
9	42	−2	4.7
10	36	−6	3.6

eighth unit of labor produces no increase in output, and the ninth and tenth units of labor actually cause total output to fall.

THE CHOICE OF INPUTS

We can use the concepts of production function and diminishing marginal returns to consider the choice of a production method. Earlier in this chapter, we demonstrated the concept of economic efficiency by showing how a printer might choose to produce this textbook. We can now add complexity and realism to this example.

Assume that we are again looking at the production of textbooks by a firm that is of a given size. This means that the firm is in the short run and, as a result, its size cannot be altered. Let's also assume that there are only two variable inputs: labor and printing presses. Table 3 shows the possible quantities of labor and printing presses and their corresponding marginal products. You can see from those values that this firm is in the range of diminishing returns.

The question facing the firm is to determine which combination of labor and presses will produce the largest amount of textbooks for a given expenditure of dollars. Let's say that presses cost $2 per unit per day, labor costs $1 per unit per day, and the firm has a budget of $26 per day.

The firm will maximize output by using labor and presses to the extent that will make their marginal products per dollar spent equal. This is written as follows:

$$\frac{MP_L}{P_L} = \frac{MP_K}{P_K}.$$

The firm would use 10 units of labor and 8 presses per day because 3/$1 = 6/$2.

You can easily see why this input combination maximizes output, given a spending constraint of $26. Add 2 units of labor to replace the eighth press, for

TABLE 3 INPUTS FOR PRINTING THIS TEXTBOOK AND THEIR MARGINAL PRODUCTS

VARIABLE INPUT—LABOR (UNITS)	MARGINAL PRODUCT OF LABOR (MP_L)	VARIABLE INPUT—PRESSES (UNITS)	MARGINAL PRODUCT OF PRESSES (MP_P)
7	6	5	10
8	5	6	9
9	4	7	8
10	3	8	6
11	1	9	3
12	0	10	0

example. This combination also costs $26. If presses are reduced from 8 to 7, 2 units of output will be lost, and if labor is increased from 10 to 12 units, only 1 unit of output will be added. The firm would lose a unit of output with this alternative mix of inputs.

We now can see that a firm maximizes output by choosing its mix of inputs so that the marginal product of a dollar's worth of each input is equal to the marginal product of a dollar's worth of every other input. If

$$\frac{MP_a}{P_a} > \frac{MP_b}{P_b}$$

the firm reallocates its inputs to use more of input *a* and less of input *b*. As the firm uses more of *a*, it will drive down the marginal product of *a* and bring about equality between MP_a/P_a and MP_b/P_b. This conclusion can be generalized to include all inputs by saying that the firm maximizes its production for a given cost outlay by using inputs (*a, b, ..., n*) so that

$$\frac{MP_a}{P_a} = \frac{MP_b}{P_b} = ... = \frac{MP_n}{P_n}.$$

You will note that the principles developed here are very similar to those developed for utility analysis. According to utility theory, the consumer maximizes utility for a given income, or budget constraint. Here, the firm maximizes output given a cost constraint. The principles of maximization are the same.

The principles of production are a foundation for analyzing costs. In the next chapter, we will see how production functions and the principle of diminishing marginal returns relate to the cost functions firms face.

KEY IDEAS

PRODUCTION FUNCTIONS AND INPUTS
- At least one input is fixed in the short run.
- All inputs are variable in the long run.
- The marginal product of an input is the change in output produced by a one-unit change in that input.
- Diminishing marginal returns is exclusively a short-run phenomenon.
- If the marginal product is negative, total product is declining.

Consider again... *It should be clear about how to organize your oyster bar business. You will want to be a corporation because you will want to limit liability. If one of your customers gets hepatitis, you don't want a lawsuit that would take your home from you. You also want to be an S corporation to avoid double taxation of your profits. A further policy decision will face you as you expand your business. There is a lot of risk in the bar and restaurant business. First, there is the normal market risk. Your bar may be popular with Texas Aggies, but will it be popular with Minnesota Gophers? In addition, there is increasing liability risk. If a patron gets drunk, drives home, and gets in an accident she may sue you for letting her drink too much! One way to insure yourself against such suits is to set up a separate S corporation for each of your businesses. That way, if you get sued, the limit on your liability will be set by the wealth of that separate business entity. That's why you picked Mark as a partner. He had that all figured out.*

SUMMARY

1. Firms are organized by entrepreneurs to produce outputs by combining inputs. The entrepreneur does this in such a way as to maximize profits.
2. Sole proprietorships are the dominant form of business organization by number. Corporations account for about 85 percent of annual business sales in the United States. S corporations have become popular because they are not subject to double taxation of corporate profits.
3. Nonprofit firms, both private and governmental, face different incentives than for-profit firms do because nonprofit firms have no residual claimants.
4. Economic efficiency is the basis for selecting that combination of resources that minimizes the cost of producing a certain level of output.
5. A production function is the technical relationship between inputs and outputs. In the short run, some inputs are fixed. In the long run, all inputs are variable.
6. Firms choose their input mix from the production function to maximize output subject to cost constraints.

NEW TERMS

production	business firm	bonds	variable inputs
vertically integrated firms	industry	limited liability	short run
horizontally integrated firms	sole proprietorship	S corporation	long run
	partnership	residual claimant	principle of diminishing returns
conglomerates	corporation	technical efficiency	marginal product (*MP*)
transaction costs	stockholders	economic efficiency	total product (*TP*)
teams	board of directors	production function	average product (*AP*)
shirk	stock	fixed inputs	

QUESTIONS: REVIEW, APPLICATIONS, AND POLICY

REVIEW

1. How does the short run differ from the long run? How long would the short run be for farming, for a lemonade stand, and for electricity generation?
2. Is there a parallel between diminishing marginal utility in consumption and diminishing returns in production? Describe any similarities you see.
3. Why must the marginal product of labor be equal to zero at the point where the total product is at its peak?
4. This question is for those who have read the appendix. The typical isoquant curve is curved and convex to the origin. What does this shape imply?

APPLICATIONS

5. Your grades on weekly quizzes are 90, 85, 75, 65, 90, and 95. What was your average grade after three weeks, four weeks, and five weeks? When your average fell, was the marginal grade below or above the average? What about when your average rose?
6. Suppose the following production function describes three ways to produce 1,000 shirts in a sewing factory.

METHOD	UNITS OF CAPITAL (SEWING MACHINES)	UNITS OF LABOR (SEWER-WEEKS)	UNITS OF LAND (ACRES)	UNITS OF OUTPUT (SHIRTS)
A	4	60	$1/5$	1,000
B	10	10	$1/5$	1,000
C	30	5	$1/5$	1,000

If you were the plant manager of this sewing factory, which method of production would you choose?

7. If the cost basis of the capital services of sewing machines in Question 6 is $3,000 per 1,000 shirts and the wage rate is $6.25 per hour (forty-hour week), which method of production will you choose?
8. What would happen to your choice of inputs if the sewing factory in Question 6 were successfully unionized and the union contract specified a wage rate of $10.65 per hour?
9. The price of land was irrelevant to your decision in Questions 6–8 because the plant uses one-fifth of an acre of land for all three methods of production. What would your reaction be (as plant manager) if the governor in a neighboring state offered you free land in an industrial park and forgave all property taxes on that land for ten years?

POLICY

10. List some of the differences you have observed between private for-profit firms and nonprofit firms that produce the same good.
11. In professional sports, there are very few player-coaches. Yet many players become coaches immediately after their playing days end. Can you think of any reasons why this may be the case, based on economic theories of why firms are formed and what managers do in these firms?
12. Classify the firm resulting from each of the following mergers as vertically integrated, horizontally integrated, or a conglomerate.
    a. An oil company buys a chain of gas stations.
    b. A cosmetics company buys a financial institution.
    c. An airline buys a travel agency.
    d. An airline buys an interstate bus line.
    e. A movie company buys a television studio.
    f. A supermarket chain buys a rental car company.
13. You may have heard about Deming Total Quality Management, quality circles, and similar techniques that increase worker involvement in the manufacturing process. These techniques are sometimes referred to as the Japanese style of management. How does such a style of management address the problem of shirking behavior?
14. Should corporate philanthropy be applauded or condemned from the standpoint of economic efficiency?
15. What is the advantage of an S corporation?

SUGGESTIONS FOR FURTHER READING

"The Entrepreneurs." *Business Week/Enterprise*, 1993. A section of a special edition of *Business Week* devoted to entrepreneurs; what makes them risk takers—how they are different and how they have common traits.

Moore, John H. *Growth With Self-Management*. Stanford CA: Hoover Institution Press, 1980. A very readable account of the economics of labor-managed firms.

Pindyck, Robert S., and Daniel L. Rubinfield. *Microeconomics*, 2e. New York: Macmillan, 1992. An intermediate text that goes into greater detail on some of the topics discussed in this chapter.

White, Michelle J., ed. *Nonprofit Firms in a Three Sector Economy*. Washington DC: Urban Institute Press, 1981. A collection of articles looking at the behavior of private nonprofit firms.

APPENDIX

PRODUCER CHOICE

If you have not already done so, you should study the preceding chapter's appendix, which describes indifference analysis and consumer choice. A similar approach can be used to analyze producer choice.

ISOQUANT CURVES

An **isoquant** (called a producer indifference curve by some economists) is a curve that shows all combinations of quantities of two inputs that can be used to produce a given quantity of output. (*Isoquant* means equal quantity.) Along an isoquant, the amount of output produced remains the same, but the combinations of inputs vary. There is a separate isoquant for each level of output.

isoquant
A curve that shows all combinations of two inputs that can be used to produce a given output.

TABLE 1A INPUT COMBINATIONS FOR PRODUCING 1,000 DOZEN SHIRTS

COMBINATION	INPUT X (LABOR)	INPUT Y (CAPITAL)
A	16	3
B	12	4
C	10	5
D	8	7
E	6	9

Suppose Eric, an entrepreneur, is considering the use of the different combinations of capital and labor shown in Table 1A. Combination *A* consists of 16 units of labor (measured in person-years) and 3 units of capital (measured in number of machines used per year). Combination *B* is 12 units of labor and 4 units of capital. Eric states that neither combination *A* nor combination *B* is preferred. They are equal with respect to the amount of output he expects to produce, and therefore, in the absence of prices, he is indifferent between these input combinations. When Eric considers input combinations *C*, *D*, and *E*, he has the same response because they all produce the same output, 1,000 dozen shirts. Such production choices can be plotted as an isoquant curve. An isoquant curve corresponding to the production choices in Table 1A is shown in Figure 1A. The isoquant curve shows all combinations of two inputs that produce a given output.

Input combinations lying on a higher isoquant curve are associated with larger quantities of output. As Eric moves from I_1 to I_2 to I_3 to I_4 in Figure 2A, he

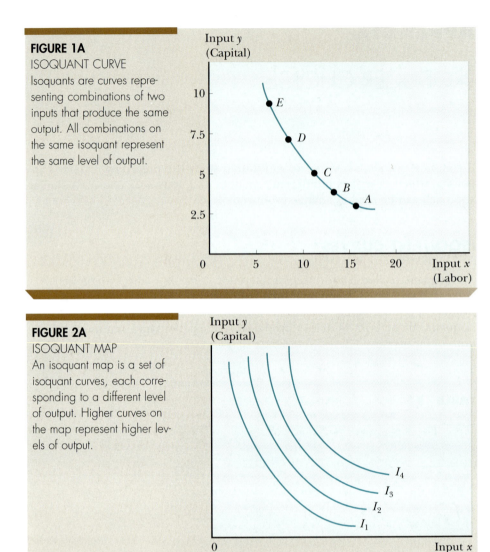

FIGURE 1A
ISOQUANT CURVE
Isoquants are curves representing combinations of two inputs that produce the same output. All combinations on the same isoquant represent the same level of output.

FIGURE 2A
ISOQUANT MAP
An isoquant map is a set of isoquant curves, each corresponding to a different level of output. Higher curves on the map represent higher levels of output.

is producing more output. Figure 2A is an isoquant map. An isoquant map makes it possible to compare points representing combinations of inputs x and y so as to determine whether the producer prefers one such combination. All points on any single isoquant curve represent the same level of output. Points on isoquant curves located to the right of and above a particular curve are combinations that produce greater levels of output.

The typical isoquant curve has a negative slope, which means that in order to produce the constant output, some extra amount of one input is necessary to compensate for the loss of some amount of the other. In other words, each combination of two inputs on the same isoquant curve has more of one of the inputs but less of the other compared to other combinations on that same isoquant curve.

DIMINISHING MARGINAL RATES OF SUBSTITUTION

The curvature of the isoquant is convex to the origin. The convexity means that as a producer uses more units of one input and fewer units of the other input, it takes more and more units of the more abundant input to compensate for the loss of one unit of the input that is becoming more scarce. Just as with indifference curves, the convexity of the isoquant reflects the principle of diminishing marginal rates of substitution.

The trade-off ratio along the isoquant curve is called (as before with indifference curves) the marginal rate of substitution. The marginal rate of substitution of input x for input y, MRS_{xy}, shows the willingness of the producer to substitute between the inputs:

$$MRS_{xy} = \frac{\text{number of units of } y \text{ released}}{\text{number of units of } x \text{ substituted}}.$$

As more of one input (x) is substituted for the other input (y), the value of input x in terms of input y declines.

COST CONSTRAINTS

Which combination of inputs should a producer choose? The answer depends on the budget of that producer and on the prices of the inputs. Keep in mind that the producer faces input prices that are determined in markets. The typical producer cannot influence these prices. Total costs constrain the producer from buying all the inputs that might be desired. For every possible value of total costs, there is an **isocost line**. (*Isocost* means equal cost.) This line identifies all combinations of inputs the firm can purchase for a given total cost. This concept is analogous to the budget line in indifference analysis.

A straight line connecting the two points that represent buying only input y or only input x will show all possible combinations that can be attained with a given cost outlay. Any combination outside (above) the line is unattainable at that cost outlay. It is outside the budget constraint. In other words, the isocost line is the dividing line between those input combinations that are attainable and those that are unattainable at a given level of prices and a given cost outlay. An isocost line is shown in Figure 3A. The intercept on the axis representing each input is determined by dividing the total cost outlay (TC) by the price of that input (P_x or P_y). The slope of the isocost curve is therefore the ratio of the per-unit costs of the two inputs.

isocost line
A line that shows the amounts of two inputs that can be purchased with a fixed sum of money (a firm's budget line).

CHANGES IN COST OUTLAY OR PRICES OF INPUTS

The isocost line is developed by holding prices of inputs and total cost outlay constant. How do changes in total cost outlay or prices affect the isocost line?

An increase in total cost outlay (or the firm's budget) means that more of both inputs can be purchased, if input prices stay the same. A doubling of cost outlay means that twice as much of both inputs can be purchased. Increases in cost outlay are represented by a parallel outward shift of the isocost line.

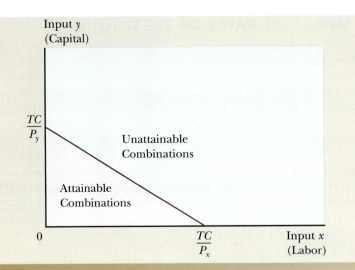

FIGURE 3A
ISOCOST LINE
An isocost line shows the input combinations that are possible at a given level of total cost outlay. Any combination outside (above) the line is unattainable.

Decreases in cost outlay are represented by a parallel inward shift of the isocost line. Such shifts are shown in Figure 4A.

A change in the price of one input only affects the amount of that input that can be employed, not the amount of the other input. A price rise, then, will affect only the intercept of the isocost line with the axis for the input that has experienced the price rise. The effect of such a change is shown in Figure 5A. A price rise for input x from P_{x1} to P_{x2} causes the x-axis intercept of the isocost line to move closer to the origin. This shift reflects the fact that less x can now be purchased with the same cost outlay. A decrease in the price of input x from P_{x1} to P_{x3} would mean that more of x could be purchased. The x-intercept moves away from the origin, reflecting increases in the potential employment of input x.

Price changes cause the slope of the isocost line to change. Note that the slope is the negative of the ratio of the prices of the two inputs, or $-(P_x/P_y)$. The

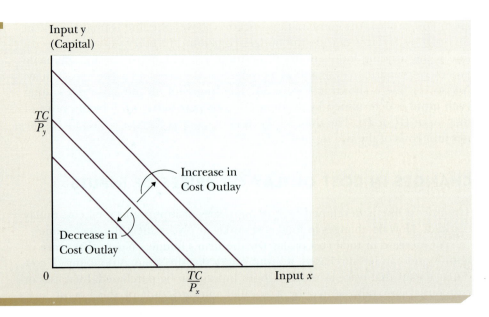

FIGURE 4A
THE EFFECT OF CHANGES IN TOTAL COST OUTLAY ON THE ISOCOST LINE
An increase in total cost outlay is represented by a parallel outward shift of the isocost line. A decrease in total cost outlay is represented by an inward parallel shift of the isocost line.

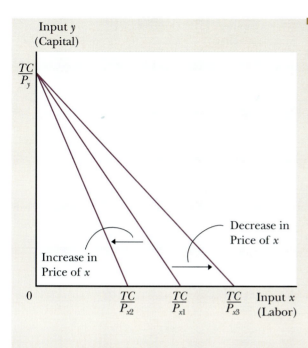

FIGURE 5A
THE EFFECT OF INPUT PRICE CHANGES ON THE ISOCOST LINE
An increase in the price of one input changes the slope of the isocost line. An increase in the price of an input means that if all of the firm's cost outlay is spent on that input, less of it can be purchased. As a result, the intercept of the isocost line with the axis for that input will shift closer to the origin. The opposite holds for a decrease in the price of an input.

slope of the isocost line changes when the ratio of the input prices changes. A change in total cost outlay, on the other hand, represents no change in relative prices. The slope of the isocost line remains the same in that case, shifting in a parallel fashion as described earlier.

CHOOSING THE OPTIMAL COMBINATION OF INPUTS

Drawing the isocost line on an isoquant map makes it possible to demonstrate the choice of input combination. In Figure 6A, at point A on isoquant I_2, the isocost line and isoquant I_2 are tangent. Any point on I_3, such as point B, is preferred to point A because higher isoquant curves represent higher levels of output. However, point B is not attainable because it is outside the isocost line. Point C on I_1 is attainable. Point A on I_2 is also attainable, however, and any point on I_2 represents more output than any point on I_1. The producer wants to reach the highest attainable isoquant. The highest attainable curve will be one that is tangent to the isocost line because no higher isoquant can be reached with the given cost outlay and prices.

You should remember from geometry that two curves that are tangent have equal slopes at the point of tangency. At the point of tangency between the isoquant curve and the isocost line, the marginal rate of substitution is equal to the ratio of the price of x to the price of y:[a]

---

a. Technically, MRS_{xy} is equal to the negative of the slope of the isoquant curve. The price ratio, as we have seen, is the negative of the slope of the isocost line. Therefore, at the (equilibrium) point of tangency between the isoquant curve and the isocost line, $MRS_{xy} = P_x/P_y$.

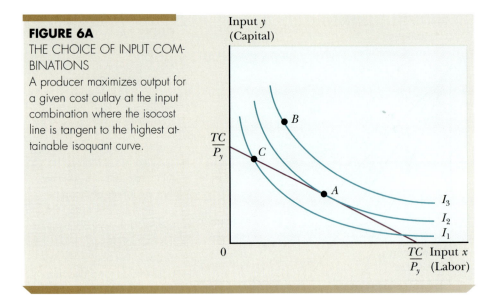

FIGURE 6A

THE CHOICE OF INPUT COMBINATIONS

A producer maximizes output for a given cost outlay at the input combination where the isocost line is tangent to the highest attainable isoquant curve.

$$MRS_{xy} = \frac{P_x}{P_y}.$$

The marginal rate of substitution expresses the willingness of the producer to substitute a certain amount of x for a certain amount of y. The slope of the isocost line reflects the market's willingness in terms of prices to trade a certain amount of x for a certain amount of y. The impersonal forces of the market impose the relative prices on the producer. The equation says that the producer adjusts the choice of inputs in such a way that his or her trade-off is the same as that of the market.

THE FIRM'S REACTION TO PRICE CHANGES

Figure 7A shows how changes in input prices affect the isocost line. We can now see how the optimal combination of inputs will be affected by price changes. Suppose a producer is initially at a point of maximum output at point A on isoquant I_1 in Figure 7A. As the price of output x falls from P_{x1} to P_{x2}, the isocost line rotates out to intersect the x-axis at TC/P_{x2}, and the producer now has a new optimum at point B on isoquant I_2. Another decrease in price to P_{x3} allows the producer to reach a still higher isoquant, I_3, and a new optimum at point C. Connecting points A, B, and C produces an expansion path, which shows how the input combination changes when relative input prices change.

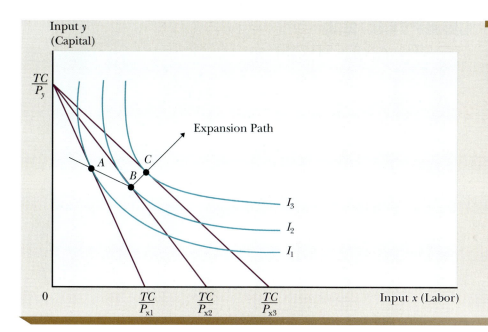

FIGURE 7A

THE FIRM'S EXPANSION PATH

An expansion path depicts how the firm's choice of inputs changes when relative prices change.

CHAPTER 22
COSTS AND PROFITS

LEARNING OBJECTIVES
1. Explain the difference between accounting profit and economic profit.
2. Calculate the various short-run cost measures and illustrate their relationships graphically.
3. List the reasons for economies and diseconomies of scale.
4. Determine the profit-maximizing level of production.
5. Calculate the present value of a future stream of income.
6. Discuss how risk and uncertainty affects decision making and determine what can be done to reduce this risk and uncertainty.

Consider this... *At the end of the Carter administration and the beginning of the Reagan administration, the U.S. airline industry was deregulated. The debate over the policy issue of airline deregulation was conducted between 1978 and 1982. The first observable result of this deregulation was the advent of competition in the industry. Price competition was observed for the first time. Other effects of competition were greater route frequency, better on-time performance, more baggage efficiency, and expanded frequent flyer programs.*

Between 1978 and 1993, 145 small airline operations were certified by the federal government to commercially haul passengers. In 1994, fewer than twenty-five of these airlines were still in business. Most simply went out of business; a few were taken over by the major airlines. Only two of the new entrants were viewed as major players in the industry. The first, Southwest Airlines, was the most profitable U.S. airline in the early 1990s. It carved out a niche by becoming the low-fare, no-frills alternative to the existing competitors. The second, America West, grew large by trying to become a traditional carrier. It was large by 1990, but was realizing huge losses from 1991 through 1993. Whether it will survive is anyone's guess. What happened to all the others? The discussion of costs and profits in this chapter will shed some light on this issue.

As we explained in the preceding chapter, entrepreneurs attempt to minimize costs in order to increase profit. But we need to be careful to define costs of inputs in terms of opportunity cost. You were introduced to opportunity cost earlier, and now you need to apply it with a vengeance. Measuring costs of inputs in this way can be a problem if you are not used to thinking in terms of opportunity cost and are more used to thinking in terms of explicit cost. Explicit costs are accounting costs or money outlays. Implicit costs are those additional costs implied by the alternatives given up. When economists talk of costs, they mean all opportunity costs—explicit and implicit.

Some examples can make this clearer. Suppose you have the option of working two hours of overtime at $10 an hour or going to a concert that costs $5. The cost of attending the concert is the $5 ticket charge plus the $20 you could have earned working overtime. Attending the concert will cost you $25. The explicit cost is $5. The implicit cost is $20. Or suppose your rich aunt in Great Britain sends you her "old" Rolls Royce that is worth $100,000. She doesn't care what you do with it. You are excited because now you can drive a classic car at very low cost. You need only pay for gas, oil, insurance, and repairs. Right? No! You have forgotten to include a calculation of the implicit cost. If you sold the car, you could invest the $100,000. You could put the money in a high-yield account that earns 10 percent per year. In other words, you are giving up $10,000 per year if you choose to drive the Rolls. The total cost is the implicit cost of that $10,000 plus the explicit costs of gas, oil, insurance, and repairs. Do you still want to drive the Rolls?

Explicit costs
Accounting costs or money outlays.

Implicit costs
Costs measured by the value of alternatives given up.

ACCOUNTING PROFIT AND ECONOMIC PROFIT

In Chapter 3, Susan's lemonade stand was used as an example of a firm as a supplier. Now suppose we can obtain Susan's account books in order to calculate her profits. Let's say she had total revenue of $15,000 for the summer. Her books say that she had accounting (explicit) costs of $11,500. Her **accounting profit** is $3,500, determined by subtracting her explicit costs from her total revenue. These are the profits she reported for tax purposes. Economists think that profits figured in this way are misleading because implicit costs are ignored. If Susan's skills and talents are worth $2,000, this is an opportunity cost. The total of her implicit costs plus her explicit costs is $13,500. She will be earning an economic profit of $1,500. **Economic profit** is the difference between total revenue and the total of explicit and implicit costs of production. An entrepreneur who does not earn a profit that is at least equal to his or her opportunity cost will quit the endeavor.

Accounting profit
The difference between total revenue and explicit costs.

Economic profit
The difference between total revenue and the total of explicit and implicit costs of production.

OPPORTUNITY COST AND NORMAL PROFIT

The opportunity cost of capital and enterprise is referred to as **normal profit**. A normal profit represents the rate of return that is necessary to keep capital and enterprise in an industry. Say, for example, the normal profit is 8 percent. Then a firm earning an 8 percent rate of return is earning zero economic profit because its capital and enterprise could earn 8 percent elsewhere. The concept of normal profit is used by regulators in setting prices for public utilities (such as electric and telephone companies). If an electric utility is not granted a price increase and the rate of return on its capital falls below the normal profit, capital will leave that industry to try to earn its opportunity cost elsewhere.

In other words, normal profit is part of the implicit cost structure of firms. Just like the "free" Rolls Royce, a firm's capital, even if it is paid for, represents wealth that could be sold and invested elsewhere. The calculation is, in principle, exactly the same as in the Rolls Royce example.

Figure 1 shows the relationships of the concepts of accounting profit, economic profit, and normal profit. Total revenue is the same in both bars, but the

Normal profit
The opportunity cost of capital and enterprise, or the rate of return that is necessary for a firm to remain in a competitive industry.

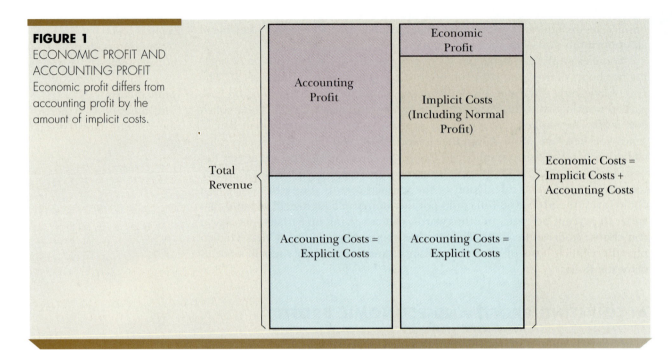

FIGURE 1
ECONOMIC PROFIT AND ACCOUNTING PROFIT
Economic profit differs from accounting profit by the amount of implicit costs.

difference between economic profit and accounting profit is the implicit costs, including normal profit.

A correct definition of costs is important because economists use costs and profits to predict behavior. When economic profits are positive, economists predict that new firms will enter an industry. When economic profits are negative, firms will leave the industry. When economic profits are zero, existing firms will remain and earn normal profits, but no new ones will enter. Economic profit serves as a signal, calling forth entry into or exit out of an industry. If a firm is not earning a normal profit in its present industry, its resources will flow to an industry where a higher rate of return can be earned. If more than a normal profit is being earned in an industry, resources will be attracted to it.

THE USE OF ACCOUNTING PROFITS IN ECONOMIC ANALYSIS

Economic theory is based on the concepts of economic costs and economic profit, but these data aren't usually available for real-world analyses. Economists are suspicious of accounting costs and accounting profits for at least two reasons. The first has to do with the way in which accounting costs are gathered. The second has to do with the discrepancy between accounting costs and economic costs.

Since federal income tax is paid on accounting profits, firms have incentives to make profits look as small as possible for the IRS and as large as possible for potential investors. There are techniques that can be used to manipulate accounting profits. Some flexibility in measuring profits comes from the very different ways in which firms can account for items whose value is estimated subjectively. These techniques fall into three categories: altering approved accounting methods, manipulating managers' estimates of costs, and changing the time periods in which costs are paid and revenues are received.

Even though economists argue that accounting profits do not reflect economic reality and can be manipulated, that data is all that is available for them to use in studying the economy. The use of accounting profits in economic research is subject to much debate. Some argue that studies that use accounting profits are meaningless. Others hold that accounting profits are the only data that is available, and as long as economists are careful, using such data can yield meaningful results.[1] This debate will go on as long as economists attempt to measure the performance of firms and industries.

COSTS IN THE SHORT RUN

The production function relates inputs to outputs. The inputs in the production function have prices and represent costs to the firm. These input prices, which are determined in resource markets, may or may not be affected by the actions of the firm itself. Given the prices of inputs and the production function, it is possible to develop cost schedules for the firm. Although the derivation can be done formally, we will show the relationship on a graph and then determine the costs in a simpler fashion.

DEFINING COSTS

An example of a cost profile for a firm is given in Table 1. **Total cost (*TC*)** is simply the sum of all the costs of production for a given level of output. Total cost is made up of two components: total fixed costs (*TFC*) and total variable costs (*TVC*). That is, *TFC* + *TVC* = *TC*. **Total fixed costs (*TFC*)** are the costs of the fixed inputs. Therefore, they can't be avoided or changed in the short run. These costs will be the same regardless of how many units of output the firm produces. **Total variable costs (*TVC*)** vary directly with output. Variable costs increase as more output is produced because more of the variable inputs have to be purchased if more output is to be produced. Total fixed costs and total variable costs are shown in the second and third columns in Table 1. In this cost schedule, we assume that the firm has already identified that combination of inputs that minimizes the total variable costs for each level of output. These figures represent the cost of the economically efficient input combinations. No firm will pay a higher total variable cost than it has to.

Given the information in the first four columns of Table 1, the rest of the columns are computed as follows. **Average fixed cost (*AFC*)** is total fixed costs of production divided by the quantity of output. **Average variable cost (*AVC*)** is total variable costs divided by the number of units of output. That is,

$$AFC = \frac{TFC}{Q}, \text{ and } AVC = \frac{TVC}{Q}.$$

Total cost (*TC*)
The sum of all the costs of production for a given level of output.

Total fixed costs (*TFC*)
The costs of the fixed inputs of production, which can't be avoided in the short run.

Total variable costs (*TVC*)
The total of costs that vary directly with the level of output, increasing as more output is produced.

Average fixed cost (*AFC*)
Total fixed costs of production divided by number of units of output.

Average variable cost (*AVC*)
Total variable costs of production divided by the number of units of output.

---

1. An interesting exchange in this debate was kicked off by George J. Benston, "The Validity of Profits-Structure Studies With Particular Reference to the FTC's Line of Business Data," *American Economic Review* (March 1985): 36–37. Thirteen economists responded to Benston's article in the March 1987 issue of the *American Economic Review*. See also Franklin M. Fisher and John J. McGowan, "On the Misuse of Accounting Rates of Return to Infer Monopoly Profits," *American Economic Review* (March 1983): 82–97. Comments in opposition to their position can be found in the June 1984 issue of the *American Economic Review*.

TABLE 1 COST PROFILE FOR A FIRM

OUTPUT PER WEEK (Q)	TOTAL FIXED COSTS (TFC)	TOTAL VARIABLE COSTS (TVC)	TOTAL COST (TC)	AVERAGE FIXED COST (AFC)	AVERAGE VARIABLE COST (AVC)	AVERAGE TOTAL COST (AC)	MARGINAL COST (MC)
0	$60	$ 0	$ 60	$ _	$ 0	$ _	$ 0
1	60	40	100	60	40	100	40
2	60	76	136	30	38	68	36
3	60	108	168	20	36	56	32
4	60	140	200	15	35	50	32
5	60	175	235	12	35	47	35
6	60	216	276	10	36	46	41
7	60	262	322	8 4/7	37 3/7	46	46
8	60	312	372	7 1/2	39	46 1/2	50
9	60	369	429	6 2/3	41	47 2/3	57
10	60	430	490	6	43	49	61

Average total cost (AC)
Total costs of producing a level of output divided by the number of units of output.

Average total cost (AC) is equal to the total costs of producing a quantity of output divided by that level of output. That is,

$$AC = \frac{TC}{Q}.$$

Marginal cost (MC)
The change in total cost from producing one more (or one less) unit of output.

Marginal cost (MC) is the change in total cost as a result of producing one more (or one less) unit of output. That is,

$$MC = \frac{\Delta TC}{\Delta Q} = \frac{\Delta TVC}{\Delta Q}.$$

Marginal costs are really marginal *variable* costs because there are no marginal fixed costs. When output changes, the change in fixed costs is zero.

COST CURVES

We can draw a series of cost curves from the data given in Table 1. The curves are drawn smoothly to better emphasize their relationships. Drawing the curves smoothly assumes that the output is divisible.

The total fixed costs, total variable costs, and total cost curves are shown in Figure 2. The shape of the production function determines the shape of the total variable cost curve and also the shape of the total cost curve because it is the summation of the fixed cost and the variable cost curve. As the amount of the variable input increases, both output and variable costs increase. If output increases more rapidly than input cost, variable cost increases at a decreasing rate. In Figure 2, decreasing costs are shown as output increases from zero to Q_1. From Q_1 to higher levels of output, output increases less rapidly than the input cost increases. Then variable costs increase at an increasing rate.

Consider this simple example. Suppose a firm hires one additional worker and output increases by ten units. The variable cost increases by the wage of that

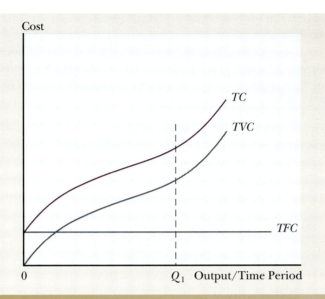

FIGURE 2

TOTAL COST CURVES
The shapes of the total cost (*TC*) curve and total variable costs (*TVC*) curve are a reflection of the production function. From zero output to an output level of Q_1, total cost and variable cost increase at a decreasing rate. Beyond output level Q_1, costs increase at an increasing rate.

worker (for a given time period). Now, if it takes two more workers to increase output by ten more units, total variable costs would increase by the wage rate times two. Clearly the cost would be increasing at an increasing rate.

Now let's look at average and marginal costs. Figure 3 shows the average fixed costs (*AFC*), average variable costs (*AVC*), average cost (*AC*), and marginal cost (*MC*) curves for a firm. The *AFC* curve declines continuously, getting closer and closer to the horizontal axis of the graph. This decline occurs because fixed costs are constant. Since average fixed costs are calculated by dividing that con-

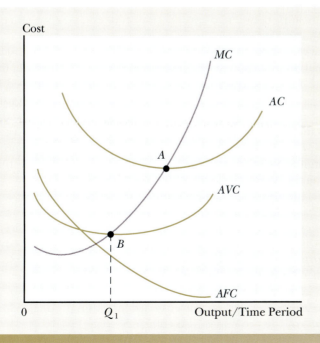

FIGURE 3

MARGINAL AND AVERAGE COST CURVES
The average fixed costs (*AFC*) curve declines continuously. The average variable costs (*AVC*) and average cost (*AC*) curves decline, reach a minimum, and then increase, resulting in a U shape. The marginal cost (*MC*) curve intersects the *AVC* and *AC* curves at their minimum points.

stant amount by an ever-increasing quantity (levels of output), the average fixed costs become smaller and smaller as output increases.

Average variable costs first decline and then increase, as does average cost. The U-shaped AVC curve represents returns to the variable inputs that at first increase and then diminish. The variable inputs are being added to a given quantity of fixed input, such as a fixed-size plant. Increasing returns occur for output levels up to Q_1 in Figure 3.

At output levels above Q_1, returns to the variable inputs decline. That is, returns are diminishing. The AVC and AC curves are U-shaped because of decreasing costs (increasing average product) for small levels of output and then increasing costs (decreasing average product) for higher levels of output. Average cost declines sharply at first because average fixed costs drop rapidly and then more slowly.

Note that the MC curve intersects the AC and AVC curves at their lowest points—points A and B in Figure 3. These points illustrate the relationship between average and marginal values, discussed in the preceding chapter. For the AC and AVC curves to be declining, the marginal cost must be below the average cost. For the AC and AVC curves to be rising, the marginal cost must be above the average cost. Thus, marginal cost and average cost must be equal where the AC curve is at its minimum point. Think about how your grade point average goes up or down depending on your grade in an added (marginal) course. Also, note that when the MC curve starts to rise as output is increased, it is still below the AVC curve. Thus, average variable costs are still falling. An average value falls as long as the marginal value is below it, regardless of whether the marginal value is falling or rising.

THE RELATIONSHIP BETWEEN PRODUCT CURVES AND COST CURVES

We have said that cost curves could be derived from production functions, because both show a relationship between inputs and outputs. Figure 4 shows the the relationship between a production function (represented by product curves) and cost curves.

Panel (*a*) of Figure 4 shows the marginal product (MP) and average product (AP) curves discussed in the preceding chapter. In this case, the variable input is labor. Panel (*b*) represents the cost curves that are derived from the production function that produced the product curves. The marginal cost (MC) curve is closely related to the MP_L curve. At those output levels where marginal product is increasing, reflecting increasing returns, marginal cost is decreasing. When the MP_L curve is at its maximum, the MC curve is at its minimum point. When marginal product is declining, reflecting diminishing returns, marginal cost is rising.

This relationship is based on simple logic. The cost curves simply measure the dollar value of inputs needed to produce a given output, and the production function measures outputs for a given amount of inputs. Given prices of resources, increasing returns have to mean decreasing marginal costs and diminishing returns have to mean increasing marginal costs.

Similar relationships hold for the AP and AVC curves. When average product is increasing, average variable costs are decreasing, and when average product is decreasing, average variable costs are increasing. The maximum and minimum points of the two curves also coincide.

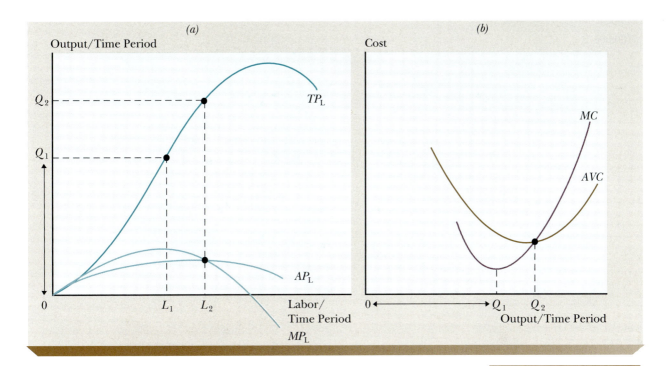

FIGURE 4
RELATIONSHIP BETWEEN PRODUCT CURVES AND COST CURVES
The cost curves are closely related to the respective product curves. When the product curve is increasing, the cost curve is decreasing, and vice versa. Q_1 on the vertical axis of part (a) is the same as Q_1 on the horizontal axis of part (b). L_1 in panel (a) represents the units of labor required to produce Q_1 units of output.

COSTS IN THE LONG RUN

In the long run, all productive resources are variable. Therefore, there are no fixed inputs in the long run. As a result, there are no fixed costs in the long run. All costs are variable in the long run. In fact, the long run is defined as the period long enough to vary all inputs.

Usually, the most important long-run decision is what size plant to build. Each possible size is represented by a short-run average cost (AC) curve. The long-run decision is based on the selection of the desired short-run average cost curve. That choice will be based on the output the firm expects to produce. Figure 5 illustrates this decision. Suppose the technological factors (given by the production function) are such that only three plant sizes are feasible. These plants are represented by curves AC_1, AC_2, and AC_3 in Figure 5. The long-run decision of which short-run curve to operate on will depend on the planned output of the firm. If output is to be less than Q_1, then the plant represented by AC_1 should be built because its size will produce any output level between zero and Q_1 at a per-unit cost that is lower than it would be for any other size. If an output level between Q_1 and Q_2 is planned, the plant represented by AC_2 should be built. If output is to be greater than Q_2, the plant represented by AC_3 should be built.

To expand our example, assume that more than three alternative plant sizes would be feasible. They would all be examined in the planning stage. The firm faces all the short-run average cost curves depicted in Figure 6. All these possible short-run curves are tangent to a curve that is sometimes referred to as a planning curve. A **planning curve** is the long-run average cost curve. It is called a planning curve because any point on the curve could be chosen in the planning stage by deciding to build a certain size of plant. Such a planning curve, more commonly called the long-run average cost curve, is shown in Figure 6. The **long-run average cost ($LRAC$) curve** represents the lowest attainable average

Planning curve
The long-run average cost curve used in the planning stage.

Long-run average cost ($LRAC$) curve
A curve tangent to all the possible short-run cost curves and representing the lowest attainable average cost of producing any given output.

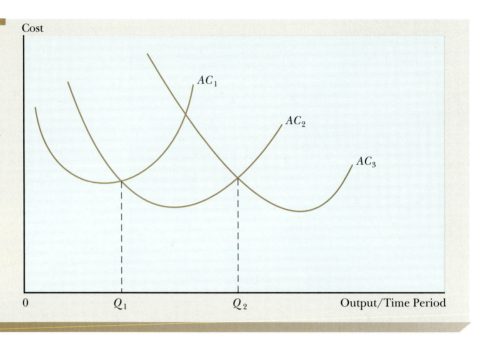

FIGURE 5
ALTERNATIVE PLANT SIZES
The determination of which size plant to build is a long-run decision of a firm. This decision is based on selection of the short-run cost curve that is optimal for the expected output level.

cost of producing any given output. It is a curve tangent to all the possible short-run average cost curves. For example, if you knew you were going to produce exactly Q_0 units of output, the plant size represented by AC_4 would have the lowest average cost.

Only at point A in Figure 6, which corresponds to an output of Q_1 units, is there tangency between the minimum point on a short-run AC curve and the minimum point on the $LRAC$ curve. This point indicates the optimal-size plant. The **optimal-size plant** is represented by the short-run average cost curve with the lowest attainable per-unit costs.

Optimal-size plant
The plant represented by the short-run average cost curve with the lowest attainable per-unit costs.

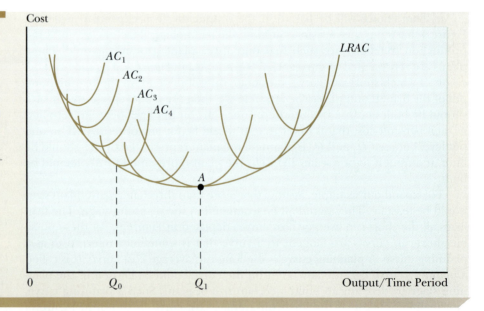

FIGURE 6
LONG-RUN AVERAGE COST CURVE
All the possible short-run cost curves are tangent to the planning curve. This planning curve is the long-run average cost ($LRAC$) curve and represents the lowest attainable average cost of producing any level of output. The optimal plant size is represented by point A, where the minimum point on a short-run average cost curve is tangent to the long-run average cost curve at its minimum point.

GLOBAL OUTLOOK: THE INFANT INDUSTRY ARGUMENT

Manufacturing is quite often subject to economies of scale over a relatively large output range. As a result of these large-scale economies, policy makers have often argued that manufacturing needs to be protected from foreign competition in order to get a toehold in domestic markets and someday be able to compete with industry in developed countries. This position, called the infant industry argument by economists, was strongly advocated by Alexander Hamilton (1755–1804), who served as the first Secretary of the U.S. Treasury in Washington's cabinet. Hamilton was a promoter of economic growth and a strong federal government.

Hamilton argued that it would be very difficult for the U.S. economy to develop in a system of free trade because Great Britain had entrenched manufacturers with established trade networks. He argued that the only way U.S. firms could compete with developed foreign firms was with the "interference and aid" of the federal government. These infant industries could stand on their own after a "nursing period." An important element of this argument is that the new firm needs to grow to a size at which it enjoys economies of scale before it faces foreign competition.

The infant industry argument is used by many countries today. In fact, many observers point to the sort of policy advocated by Hamilton when they examine the Japanese experience with industrialization in the postwar period. The Japanese government and business leaders defined a few key industrial sectors. They nurtured these key industries with subsidies and high tariff barriers until the industries attained economies of scale and low enough long-run average costs to be competitive in world markets. Japan maintains the high tariff barriers even after the protected industries mature. Japan may be the country that has used protection as a policy tool the most frequently, but it is by no means the only country to use this policy. France has used a similar policy to help develop the Airbus program.

The problems with the infant industry argument should be obvious. How can policy makers recognize promising industries in advance? Are they better equipped to discover these industries than private investors? Also, unless the infant industries have a domestic market that is large enough to attain economies of scale that make them cost-competitive on world markets, the government may have to protect the industries into old age.

ECONOMIES AND DISECONOMIES OF SCALE

The *LRAC* curve in Figure 6 is U-shaped. This shape means that, at first, as plant size and firm output increase, long-run average costs fall. After a certain point (point *A* on Figure 6), however, bigness becomes costly. As the plant continues to increase in size, average cost begins to rise. Economists refer to these changes in long-run average cost due to increased plant size as economies and diseconomies of scale. **Economies of scale** are declines in long-run average cost that are due to increased plant size. **Diseconomies of scale** are increases in long-run average cost that are due to increased plant size. As scale (plant size) increases, economies (cost savings) result. After a while, further growth results in diseconomies (higher average costs).

Economies and diseconomies of scale are distinct from increasing and decreasing returns. Increasing and decreasing returns are the result of using a given size plant more or less intensively in the short run. Economies and diseconomies of scale result from changes in the size of a plant in the long run.

It is easy to see how economies of scale result from an increase in plant size. As a firm increases its scale of operations, it usually can employ more specialized machinery. Also, jobs can be more specialized. Equipment can be used more efficiently. By-products of the operation that might be uneconomical to recover or

Economies of scale
Declines in long-run average cost that are due to increased plant size.

Diseconomies of scale
Increases in long-run average cost that are due to increased plant size.

exploit in a small-scale plant may become economical for a large operation. A large firm is often able to obtain quantity discounts on intermediate products from other firms. Political influence that has economic value is also more likely to accrue to a large, rather than a small, firm. These are just a few of the reasons for the negative slope of the *LRAC* curve as the scale of operations increases.

Diseconomies of scale are slightly harder to grasp. However, they are familiar to anyone who has dealt with giant bureaucracies, public or private. Diseconomies result from the fact that as an organization becomes very large, communication and coordination become more difficult and time consuming, and control from the top diminishes. After a firm has taken advantage of the gains to be achieved by growing larger, it becomes more difficult for upper management to monitor production activity and easier for some workers to shirk. With further growth, the *LRAC* curve turns upward.

OPTIMAL-SIZE PLANTS IN THE REAL WORLD

If you look at real-world industries, you see many different-sized firms operating side by side in the same industry. Steel, for example, is produced by both very large and very small firms. If there is a single, optimal size plant for each industry, why do firms of so many different sizes exist? Economists have spent much time investigating real economies of scale. Several different types of *LRAC* curves are represented in Figures 7, 8, and 9.

Figure 7 shows economies of scale over a large range of output. This situation occurs in the auto industry, where there are a few very large firms. The optimal-size plant in Figure 7 is that producing output level Q_1, which conceivably might represent the normal sales of the entire industry. In such industries, a natural monopoly can occur. A **natural monopoly** is a monopoly that emerges because of economies of scale. The size of the market is such that there is room for only one optimal-size firm. Many public utilities (such as gas and electric companies) need to have all the sales in a market in order to become large enough to be of optimal size.

Natural monopoly
A monopoly that emerges because economies of scale mean that there is room for only one firm in that market.

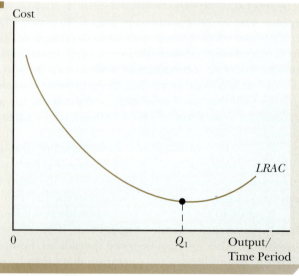

FIGURE 7
ECONOMIES OF SCALE AND A FEW VERY LARGE PLANTS
When economies of scale exist over large ranges of output, one large plant or a few large plants are most efficient.

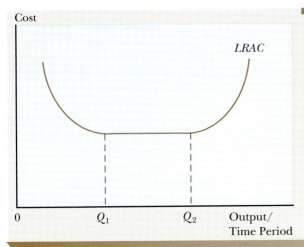

FIGURE 8

MANY OPTIMAL-SIZE PLANTS OF DIFFERENT SIZES

A range of outputs for the optimal-size plant can exist. When this situation exists, plants of distinctly different sizes can all produce efficiently in the same industry.

In Figure 8, a large number of plants of different sizes can be of optimal size. Firms in a range of sizes can all produce efficiently in the same industry at the same per-unit (or average) cost. In Figure 8, any firm producing an output between Q_1 and Q_2 would be efficient. If the demand for the product is large enough to support many firms in this size range, a very competitive situation exists. This situation prevails in many industries, such as textiles, publishing, and packaged food products.

Figure 9 illustrates an industry in which there are rapidly achievable economies of scale and diseconomies of scale. This kind of $LRAC$ curve occurs when all the firms in an industry are of a similar size. The optimal-size plant in Figure 9 is the one whose short-run average cost curve hits a minimum point at Q_1.

The benefit of economies of scale may not be passed along to consumers. Economies of scale mean that it is efficient to have production carried out by large firms. However, these large-scale firms may exert monopoly pricing power so that lower costs are not passed on to consumers in the form of lower prices. We will return to this problem in the chapter on monopoly.

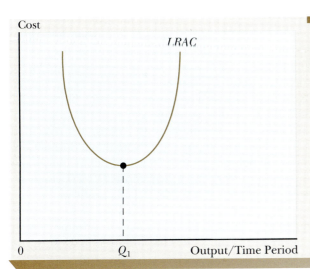

FIGURE 9

MANY OPTIMAL-SIZE PLANTS OF SIMILAR SIZES

If there is a unique minimum point on the long-run average cost curve, all the plants in an industry will be similar in size.

PROFIT MAXIMIZATION

The choice of plant size is one of several decisions that determine a firm's profits. The firms examined here and in the next three chapters are all profit-maximizing firms. What does profit maximization mean in terms of production decisions? It means that, in the short run, the firm will attempt to choose the output that maximizes the difference between total revenue and total cost. **Total revenue (*TR*)** is the price an item sells for multiplied by the number of units sold. **Marginal revenue (*MR*)** is the change in total revenue from selling one more (or one less) unit.

Profit will be maximized at the level of output at which marginal revenue equals marginal cost, or *MR* = *MC*. For any output level where marginal revenue is greater than marginal cost (*MR* > *MC*), total revenue is increasing faster than total cost when output and sales increase. This means that profit is increasing (or losses are decreasing) from selling more output. If output were reduced when marginal revenue was greater than marginal cost, total revenue would decline by more than total cost, so profit would fall. In other words, when marginal revenue is greater than marginal cost, if output is increased, total revenue will increase more than total cost, and profit will rise. On the other hand, if marginal cost is greater than marginal revenue (*MC* > *MR*), an increase in output and sales would cause total cost to increase more than total revenue. Profit would fall. A decrease in output and sales will reduce costs more than revenues, and profit will increase.

Therefore, if marginal revenue is greater than marginal cost, the firm should expand production and sales, and if marginal cost is greater than marginal revenue, the firm should decrease production and sales. If marginal revenue and marginal cost are equal, it would be unprofitable to either increase or decrease production. The decision rule for profit maximization, then, is to produce that level of output at which marginal revenue equals marginal cost (*MR* = *MC*). This rule is just another way of saying, "Produce where total profit is at its maximum" or; "Produce where total revenue exceeds total cost by the largest amount." Generally, the *MR* = *MC* rule is the most convenient to work with.

It's easy to see this relationship on a graph. In Figure 10, the firm is a price taker, which means that the price is given as far as this firm is concerned. Thus, the total revenue (*TR*) curve in Figure 10(*a*) is a straight line from the origin. The marginal revenue (*MR*) curve in panel (*b*) is a horizontal line at the level of the price of the product. The total cost (*TC*) curve is consistent with the law of diminishing returns beyond output level Q_1. (From zero output to Q_2, the *TC* curve represents decreasing average costs.) The vertical distance between *TR* and *TC* is greatest at output level Q_2. At that point the slopes of *TR* and *TC* are equal. The slope of *TR* is *MR*, and the slope of *TC* is *MC*. Thus, it is clear that *MR* = *MC* at output level Q_2, as can be seen in panel (*b*). Note that if output were decreased below Q_2, *MC* would fall below *MR*, and *TR* would fall by more than *TC*. Thus, profit would fall. If output were increased above Q_2, *TC* would increase more than *TR*, and *MC* would be above *MR*. Again, profit would fall. Profit is at a maximum at Q_2.

The decision to produce that output where marginal revenue equals marginal cost will come up again and again, so it is important to make sure you

---

Total revenue (*TR*)
The price an item sells for multiplied by the number sold.

Marginal revenue (*MR*)
The change in total revenue from selling one more (or one less) unit.

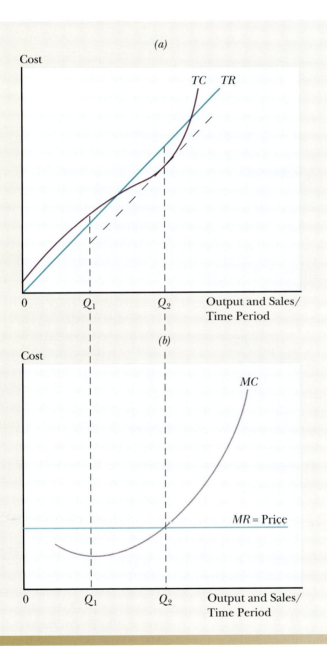

FIGURE 10

PROFIT MAXIMIZATION Profit is maximized where marginal cost is equal to marginal revenue. The vertical distance between total revenue (*TR*) and total cost (*TC*) is greatest in panel (*a*) at Q_2, the same level of output where marginal cost (*MC*) equals marginal revenue (*MR*) in panel (*b*).

understand it. It will always be true that maximum profit will be obtained by operating at the point where $MR = MC$, as long as the firm stays in business.

KEY IDEAS

RULES FOR PROFIT MAXIMIZATION
- $MR > MC$ Expand output
- $MR = MC$ Profits maximized, output unchanged
- $MR < MC$ Reduce output

PRESENT VALUE

The discussion of costs and the movement from the short run to the long run has ignored both uncertainty and differences between present and future income. It is important to keep in mind that when an entrepreneur makes the decision of which size plant to build, based on forecasted production, much uncertainty surrounds that decision. To make production forecasts, a great deal of information must be gathered and many factors must be considered. Production decisions (in fact, most economic decisions) affect costs and revenues over a number of periods of time. The decision maker needs a way of comparing revenues and costs in different time periods because a dollar cost or a dollar revenue today is not the same as a dollar cost or a dollar revenue next year or ten years from now.

To compare future dollars (costs or revenues) for different periods with present dollars, firms calculate the present value of the future dollars. **Present value (PV)** is the capitalized value of an item to be paid for or sold in the future. It is a future value discounted to the present. **Discounting** is the technique of calculating present values by adjusting for interest that would be earned between now and some specified future time. It works simply and has many important uses in daily life.

Present value is based on the fact that you can choose to save (refrain from consumption) and receive interest as a reward for your saving. As a result, you are always better off delaying a payment of a fixed sum that you must make and speeding up a payment of a fixed sum you are to receive. For example, suppose you owe a friend $100, and your friend doesn't care when you pay off the debt within the next year. If the interest rate is 10 percent, you could take $90.90, put it in the bank now, and in one year receive from the bank $100 to pay your friend—the $90.90 you deposited *plus* interest of $9.10. In other words, the present value of $100 to be paid in one year at 10 percent interest is only $90.90. Another way of saying this is that the $90.90 you put in the bank today will be equivalent to the $100 you pay to your friend a year from now. On the other hand, if you were owed $100, you would want the money now so you could put $100 in the bank and have $110 at the end of a year. Two principles emerge from this example of discounting.

Present value (PV)
The value of a future payment or series of future payments discounted to the present.

Discounting
The technique of calculating present values by adjusting for interest that would be earned between now and some specified future time.

TABLE 2 PRESENT VALUE OF $1.00

YEAR	3%	4%	5%	6%	7%	8%	10%	12%	15%	20%	YEAR
1	0.971	0.962	0.952	0.943	0.935	0.926	0.909	0.893	0.870	0.833	1
2	0.943	0.925	0.907	0.890	0.873	0.857	0.826	0.797	0.756	0.694	2
3	0.915	0.890	0.864	0.839	0.816	0.794	0.751	0.711	0.658	0.578	3
4	0.889	0.855	0.823	0.792	0.763	0.735	0.683	0.636	0.572	0.472	4
5	0.863	0.823	0.784	0.747	0.713	0.681	0.620	0.567	0.497	0.402	5
6	0.838	0.790	0.746	0.705	0.666	0.630	0.564	0.507	0.432	0.335	6
7	0.813	0.760	0.711	0.665	0.623	0.583	0.513	0.452	0.376	0.279	7
8	0.789	0.731	0.677	0.627	0.582	0.540	0.466	0.404	0.326	0.233	8
9	0.766	0.703	0.645	0.591	0.544	0.500	0.424	0.360	0.284	0.194	9
10	0.744	0.676	0.614	0.558	0.508	0.463	0.385	0.322	0.247	0.162	10
11	0.722	0.650	0.585	0.526	0.475	0.429	0.350	0.287	0.215	0.134	11
12	0.701	0.625	0.557	0.497	0.444	0.397	0.318	0.257	0.187	0.112	12
13	0.681	0.601	0.530	0.468	0.415	0.368	0.289	0.229	0.162	0.093	13
14	0.661	0.577	0.505	0.442	0.388	0.340	0.263	0.204	0.141	0.078	14
15	0.642	0.555	0.481	0.417	0.362	0.315	0.239	0.183	0.122	0.065	15
16	0.623	0.534	0.458	0.393	0.339	0.292	0.217	0.163	0.107	0.054	16
17	0.605	0.513	0.436	0.371	0.317	0.270	0.197	0.146	0.093	0.045	17
18	0.587	0.494	0.416	0.350	0.296	0.250	0.179	0.130	0.081	0.037	18
19	0.570	0.475	0.396	0.330	0.277	0.232	0.163	0.116	0.070	0.031	19
20	0.554	0.456	0.377	0.311	0.258	0.215	0.148	0.104	0.061	0.026	20
25	0.478	0.375	0.295	0.232	0.184	0.146	0.092	0.059	0.030	0.0105	25
30	0.412	0.308	0.231	0.174	0.131	0.0994	0.057	0.033	0.015	0.0042	30
40	0.307	0.208	0.142	0.0972	0.067	0.0460	0.022	0.011	0.0037	0.0006	40
50	0.228	0.141	0.087	0.0543	0.034	0.0213	0.008	0.003	0.0009	0.0001	50

1. The higher the interest rate, the lower the present value.
2. The longer the time period, the lower the present value.

The formula for calculating present value is

$$\text{P.V.} = \frac{V_t}{(1+i)^t}$$

where V_t is the value in year t, i is the interest rate, and t is the number of years. Table 2 shows the present value of $1 received in various future years (up to fifty years) at different interest rates. You can use the table to see that the present value of $100 for one year at a 10 percent interest rate is $90.90 (0.909 × $100).

Applications of present value surround you in your day-to-day life. Let's look at an example. Suppose that on your job as project manager, you are given the task of planning a new phase of operations. The engineer tells you the necessary equipment can be built in any of three ways over a period of three years. In each case, the firm's cash outlay will be spread out differently over the years. The alternatives are listed in Table 3. All alternatives are equal in the sense that each

TABLE 3 PRESENT VALUE OF THREE ALTERNATIVES AT A 10 PERCENT INTEREST RATE

ALTERNATIVE	COST IN YEAR 1	COST IN YEAR 2	COST IN YEAR 3	TOTAL COST
A	$200.00	$200.00	$200.00	$600.00
	(PV = 181.80)	(PV = 165.20)	(PV = 150.20)	(PV = 497.20)
B	$400.00	$100.00	$100.00	$600.00
	(PV = 363.60)	(PV = 82.60)	(PV = 75.10)	(PV = 521.30)
C	$100.00	$100.00	$400.00	$600.00
	(PV = 90.90)	(PV = 82.60)	(PV = 300.40)	(PV = 473.90)

POLICY FOCUS: STATE GAMBLING

For many years the only state in the United States that legalized gambling to generate tax revenue was Nevada. However in recent years most states have legalized or at least discussed the legalization of certain forms of gambling. When the idea is to generate revenue for public projects, the most common form of sanctioned gambling is a state-run lottery. It has even been suggested that the federal government run a lottery and use the profits to retire the federal debt! State governments usually earmark the proceeds from a lottery for some special purpose—most commonly, education.

In 1993, thirty-seven states had state-run lottery operations. The lottery generated net revenue of over $10 billion for the states. This $10 billion represented about 2 percent of the total state revenue in these lottery states. That doesn't seem like a lot, but it is a rapidly growing source of revenue and takes some pressure off taxes as a source of funds for state projects. In the 1980s, state revenue from lotteries grew almost 1,000 percent. Some of this growth came from the expansion of lottery activity. In 1980, only fourteen states had lotteries, but by 1990, the number had grown to thirty-three.

Some people feel that lotteries are a very regressive form of tax because the poor spend a higher percentage of their income in buying lottery tickets. Others, who support the lottery concept, argue that a lottery ticket is a voluntary purchase. Thus, a lottery cannot be viewed as a tax because people purchase the tickets of their own free will. Some advocates point out that people are going to gamble anyway so the state might as well get involved and make some profit to do "good things," such as spending more on education. However, the odds in state lotteries are much poorer than in other games of chance. The state keeps an average of 54 percent of lottery bets. That percentage is much higher than the house share in casino gambling or off-track betting. In addition, large winnings are usually paid in installments over 10 to 20 years, not all at once.

In many states, the newspapers on Sunday morning now carry a headline about the latest millionaire created by the lucky lottery drawing on Saturday night. The scene usually goes something like this: The newspaper reports that a local horse trainer, Margaret, was the co-winner of $4 million. "It hasn't hit me yet," she said, smiling broadly under the brim of a new lottery baseball cap. "But I wouldn't know what to do if I quit my job. I like to work."

Let's look at the present value of Margaret's jackpot using a 10 percent interest rate and assuming that she will be paid in one lump sum on December 31 of each year for 25 years. The newspaper reports that over the years $1.583 million of the $2 million will actually be paid out, after $417,000, or about 21 percent, is withheld in taxes. (We have rounded off these payments to simplify the arithmetic.) Table B1 shows what the reported $2 million is really worth. The present value of the $1.583 million at 10 percent is only $526,462. This low present value results from the fact that the payout is made over a long period of time and larger payouts are made in the most distant years.

In all, Margaret's payout adjusted for taxes and present value is only 26.3 percent of what the headlines reported. This is still a very nice prize, and most of us would be happy to be in her boots. But perhaps it is a good thing that Margaret "likes to work." A critic of lotteries referred to state-run lotteries as a "weekly tax on stupidity."

TABLE B1 LOTTERY PAYOUT

YEAR	PAYOUT IN DOLLARS	PRESENT VALUE IN DOLLARS	YEAR	PAYOUT IN DOLLARS	PRESENT VALUE IN DOLLARS
	$38,000	$38,000			
1	40,000	36,306	14	66,000	17,358
2	41,000	35,137	15	68,000	16,252
3	43,000	32,293	16	72,000	15,624
4	45,000	30,735	17	74,000	14,578
5	46,000	28,520	18	77,000	13,783
6	48,000	27,072	19	80,000	13,040
7	50,000	25,650	20	83,000	12,284
8	52,000	24,232	21	87,000	11,745
9	54,000	22,896	22	90,000	11,070
10	56,000	21,560	23	94,000	10,528
11	58,000	20,300	24	97,000	9,894
12	61,000	19,398			
13	63,000	18,207	Total:	$1,583,000	$526,462

costs $600, all have the same date of completion, and all payments are made at the end of the year. Which should you choose? The only way to determine which alternative will maximize profit is to use present value analysis and discount the future dollar amounts. Using Table 2, we calculate the present value of each amount in Table 3 at a 10 percent interest rate. We total the present value amounts to find the least-cost method of production, which turns out to be alternative *C*. The present value of the outlay for alternative *C* is 5 percent less than that of alternative *A* and 9 percent less than that of alternative *B*. Choosing *C* means a substantial savings for the firm.

A profit-making firm that expects to be in business for a while will try to maximize profits. However, it will maximize the present value of profits over a period of several years, not just the current period. The concept of present value is very important in business decisions but is *not* understood by many decision makers. It is often joked that the first year of an MBA program should be devoted solely to getting students to understand and make use of present value.

RISK, UNCERTAINTY, AND CHOICE

To this point in our discussion of how producers and consumers choose, we have assumed that prices, incomes, and other variables were known with certainty by the people doing the choosing. We all know from experience that this is not true in real life. We all know that our incomes could go up or down. We could even lose our jobs. Some of us might even get a huge bonus. We all live with risk and uncertainty. The questions we all face are how we can quantify the risk, how much risk we care to deal with, and how we can reduce the risk we face.

PROBABLE OUTCOMES

In any economic activity there is some probability of achieving (or not achieving) the benefits or bearing the costs. These objective probability measures may be based on past experience or research on the likelihood of certain outcomes. They often are based on the judgment of the consumer or the entrepreneur. In the example of illegal parking that we discussed earlier, the perpetrator of the crime "guessed" the probability of being caught at 20 percent, based on past experience. Using some method of determining the probability of certain events, the decision maker must make two important calculations to assess risk and uncertainty—the expected value and the variability of the possible outcomes.

EXPECTED VALUE

The expected value of any cost or benefit is the average of the possible outcomes. In the example of illegal parking that we used earlier, the "criminal" found that every five times the crime was committed the car was ticketed once. If the parking ticket was $100 the expected cost of each illegal parking venture was $20. We can approach benefits or incomes the same way. The expected value measures what we would expect to achieve on average. A salesperson learns that a certain number of calls will produce a predictable outcome in sales revenue. The salesperson has an expected value of a call.

Imagine that you are an oil wildcatter and that you are trying to determine if you should drill another well in a field that you have researched and know a great deal about. You know that on average a successful well produces a stream of income with a present value of $40 million and that nine out of ten holes you drill come up dry. The expected value of drilling another well is 10 percent of $40 million = $4 million. If it costs you $4.5 million in present value dollars to drill the well, you should look for another investment, because the present value of the expected costs exceeds the present value of the expected revenue.

VARIABILITY

The other important consideration in analyzing risk is the variability around the expected outcomes. This requires calculations of variance or standard deviation. Either provides a ranking of risk. We will leave the exact calculation of such risky outcomes to another course and instead offer an illustrative example. Suppose that two individuals, Rhondi and Paul, are offered jobs with an expected payoff of $45,000 per year. The two jobs are summarized in Table 4. The job of teaching pays $45,000 when all benefits are included. Since the job comes with

TABLE 4 COMPARATIVE JOBS

JOB	INCOME	PROBABILITY	EXPECTED VALUE	VARIABILITY
Teaching	$45,000	100%	$45,000	None
Sales	0–$250,000	18%	$45,000	High

tenure, the probability of receiving the $45,000 is 100 percent. There is no variability around the expected value. The sales job has a range of income from zero, being fired for lack of success, to $250,000. The average success rate is 18 percent so the expected value of the income is $45,000. There is also a great degree of variability around this expected value.

Let's assume that Rhondi looks at these calculations and decides to be a teacher. We would refer to Rhondi as being **risk averse**. She prefers a certain outcome to a risky outcome with the same expected value. By far, most people are risk averse. The greatest number of people choose occupations with stable salaries and job security. In addition, the huge markets for life insurance, health insurance, car insurance, and other forms of insurance (even vacation insurance) are all examples of risk aversion.

If Paul chooses the sales job we would refer to him as being risk neutral. A **risk neutral** person is indifferent between outcomes with the same expected value. A **risk seeking** person is one that chooses an expected value that has a higher variance. The risk loving person is looking for the chance of the big payoff. Risk loving behavior is typical of gamblers. But even risk seeking people act that way for only portions of their economic decision making, and even risk averse people may put aside a small amount of money to play the lottery.

Risk averse
The preference for a certain outcome to a risky outcome with the same expected value.

Risk neutral
Indifference between outcomes with the same expected values.

Risk seeking
Showing preference for an expected value with a higher variance.

RISK REDUCTION

We are all familiar with the common methods of reducing risk. All but the most risk seeking among us buy insurance. Insurance reduces risk because it pools the risk among large numbers of individuals.

A second way to avoid risk is to invest time and money to get more information. The value of information is the difference between the expected value of the decision when there is complete information and the expected value of the choice when there is incomplete information. We will return to this issue in a later chapter.

A third way to reduce risk is to diversify. You could take a job as a teacher and work part time as a salesperson to diversify your income risk. You could buy a mix of stocks, bonds, and other financial assets to diversify your investment portfolio. If your goal is to have a very successful child you could diversify your risk by having a dozen children!

Consider again... We may find a partial answer to the exit of over a hundred firms from the airline industry in the concept of economies and diseconomies of scale. Small airlines could not reach the size economies that are needed to spread some costly expenditures over large numbers of passengers. The first cost that can be spread is the cost of flight frequency. Most business passengers prefer frequent flights in order to accommodate schedule changes. If you are a business traveler, you prefer an airline that flies ten flights a day between two cities to one that flies two flights per day. The convenience of the more frequent flights is a cost to the airline. A second cost is the expense of maintaining sophisticated reservation systems that are well *staffed. Travelers want to get to the airline reservation system when they call. They do not want to be put on hold or face other types of inconvenience. Finally, small airlines could not offer enough service to establish "hub and spoke" service systems. In fact, most of the small carriers that were taken over by the major airlines were the "spoke" airlines, flying into "hubs." When these airlines were purchased, the service that they provided was available at lower cost because the larger carrier was able to take advantage of economies of scale.*

SUMMARY

1. Economists calculate both implicit and explicit costs of production. Implicit costs are those costs implied by alternatives given up. Explicit costs are money expenditures, or accounting costs. When total cost (both implicit and explicit costs) is equal to total revenue, economists say there is zero economic profit. This means the firm is covering all economic costs, including a normal profit. When costs exceed revenues, firms and resources will leave an industry in order to earn the opportunity cost associated with those resources.
2. In the short run, as variable inputs are added to the fixed inputs, the firm may experience increasing returns at low levels of output. Eventually, the firm will incur diminishing returns at some higher levels of output.
3. The U shape of the long-run average cost (*LRAC*) curve is due to economies and diseconomies of large-scale production.
4. Profit maximization means that an entrepreneur will produce that level of output that equates marginal cost and marginal revenue. Profits are the greatest when total revenue exceeds total cost by the largest possible amount.
5. Present value calculations are used to make dollar amounts to be received or paid in the future comparable with dollar amounts in the present.
6. Business policy makers must consider risk and uncertainty when making decisions. The expected value of an outcome in present value terms can be calculated. Insurance, diversity, and information are ways to cope with risk and uncertainty.

NEW TERMS

explicit costs
implicit costs
accounting profit
economic profit
normal profit
total cost (*TC*)
total fixed costs (*TFC*)

total variable costs (*TVC*)
average fixed cost (*AFC*)
average variable cost (*AVC*)
average total cost (*AC*)
marginal cost (*MC*)
planning curve

long-run average cost
 (*LRAC*) curve
optimal-size plant
economies of scale
diseconomies of scale
natural monopoly
total revenue (*TR*)

marginal revenue (*MR*)
present value (*PV*)
discounting
risk averse
risk neutral
risk seeking

QUESTIONS: REVIEW, APPLICATIONS, AND POLICY

REVIEW

1. Why are cost curves normally U-shaped in the long run? Are they U-shaped in the short run for the same reason?
2. What is a normal profit? Why is it necessary for a firm to earn at least a normal profit in the long run?
3. What is the difference between diminishing returns and diseconomies of scale?
4. Give an example of an explicit cost and an implicit cost

TOTAL OUTPUT PER DAY (Q)	TOTAL FIXED COSTS (TFC)	TOTAL VARIABLE COSTS (TVC)	TOTAL COST (TC)	AVERAGE FIXED COST (AFC)	AVERAGE VARIABLE COST (AVC)	AVERAGE TOTAL COST (AC)	MARGINAL COST (MC)
0	$10.00	$ 0	$10.00	$ —	$ —	$ —	$ —
1	___	___	15.00	___	___	___	___
2	___	___	___	___	___	9.00	___
3	___	___	___	___	3.33	___	___
4	___	___	21.00	___	___	___	___
5	___	___	___	___	___	___	2.00
6	___	16.00	___	___	___	___	___
7	___	___	___	___	___	___	4.00
8	___	___	___	___	3.13	___	___
9	___	___	41.00	___	___	___	___
10	___	___	___	___	___	___	7.00
11	___	___	56.00	___	___	___	___

of your college education. Why does enrollment in colleges and graduate schools increase when economic times are bad and unemployment rates are high?

5. What occurs when *MC* = *MR*? Why?

APPLICATIONS

6. Would you rather win $6 million in a lump sum or $1 million a year for ten years? Use a present value table to find an answer. What interest rate did you use? Why?
7. Complete the table at the top of the page. (You will be referring back to this table when you answer questions at the end of the next two chapters.)
8. Graph the values of *AFC*, *AVC*, *AC*, and *MC* from the table in Question 7. Why does *MC* cut *AVC* and *AC* at their low points?
9. In 1990, major league baseball salaries exploded. The large increases were the result of the end of salary collusion by the owners and greatly enhanced revenues. Each day a record salary was reported in the newspapers. Mark Langston, a pitcher with the California Angels, signed for a reported $16 million over five years. With the following table, calculate the present value of Langston's salary at the time of the contract (1989) using an 8 percent interest rate. (For ease of calculation assume the salary is paid in one lump sum on December 31 of each year.)

POLICY

10. The famous epigram of the Chicago School of Economics is, "There is no such thing as a free lunch." What does this mean in terms of opportunity cost?

11. At what size do universities start experiencing diseconomies of scale? What does the existence of many different sizes of universities indicate about the optimal-size university?
12. Does a university have to reach a certain size to have a winning sports program? How would you gather empirical evidence on this?
13. You are running a lottery and the current interest rate is 7 percent. Assume that you sell $10 million worth of tickets and that it costs you $40,000 for printing and other related expenses. If you make one payment of $10 million to the winner at the end of ten years, how much profit will you make?
14. In this chapter a distinction was drawn between short-run and long-run costs. What is the length of time that distinguishes between short-run and long-run costs? Can it be different for different firms?
15. What is the infant industry argument? How is it related to economies of scale?

YEAR	SALARY (MILLIONS OF DOLLARS)	PRESENT VALUE (MILLIONS OF DOLLARS)
1. 1990	3.2	___
2. 1991	3.2	___
3. 1992	3.2	___
4. 1993	3.2	___
5. 1994	3.2	___
Total	16.0	

SUGGESTIONS FOR FURTHER READING

Dung, Tran Hu, and Robert Premus. "Do Socioeconomic Regulations Discriminate Against Small Firms?" *Southern Economic Journal* (January 1990): 686–697. This article shows how federal regulations to hire the handicapped impact more significantly on smaller firms. The cost of complying with regulations is another element that impacts on the long-run average cost curves in an industry.

Kohler, Heinz. *Intermediate Microeconomics: Theory and Applications*, 3e. New York: HarperCollins, 1990. An intermediate price theory text that develops the material found in this chapter in much greater detail.

"The New Economies of Scale," *Business Week/Enterprise*, 1993. A special issue of *Business Week* that contains a very well written discussion of economies of scale in production and how they might be changing in the 1990s.

CHAPTER 23
PERFECT COMPETITION

Consider this... *Some firms, like convenience stores and grocery chains, are open twenty-four hours a day. Others close at 6:00 or 7:00 P.M. Some bars and restaurants open at 11:00 A.M. to cater to a lunch crowd, while others don't open until 4:00 P.M. for the happy hour crowd. Some resorts are open year-round, while others stop business in the off-peak season.*

How can you explain this distinctly different behavior in firms that are in the same industry, producing similar products? Any firm that makes production decisions will relate potential, or forecasted, revenues to costs in order to determine output levels. However, the forecasted revenues will depend on the market conditions faced by the firm. After studying the material in this chapter you will be able to explain why firms in the same industry make different choices.

This chapter and the next two look at four different models, referred to as market structures. The model discussed in this chapter is perfect competition. **Perfect competition** is the market structure in which there are many sellers and buyers, firms produce a homogeneous product, and there is free entry into and exit out of the industry. It is important to keep in mind that this is a theoretical model. Real data does not exist, and the model does not precisely describe reality. The model is useful, however, because it provides a point of reference. It allows the development of tools of analysis that indicate what determines price and quantity when conditions are close to those of perfect competition. The perfectly competitive market is the abstract ideal to which we will compare other market structures.

CHARACTERISTICS OF PERFECT COMPETITION

There are six basic assumptions for the model of perfect competition. In developing the theory, we assume that all firms in the market in which the product is sold possess these six characteristics.

LEARNING OBJECTIVES
1. List the assumptions of perfect competition.
2. Diagram the relationship between a firm and the total market. Calculate profits, given quantity, marginal revenue, marginal cost, average cost, and price. Identify the profit-maximizing level of output.
3. Define the shutdown point in terms of price and average variable costs or total fixed costs and losses.
4. Describe the long-run supply curve for a constant cost industry, an increasing cost industry, and a decreasing cost industry.
5. Identify the long-run equilibrium for the firm and the industry under perfect competition.
6. Explain how economic rent might exist in perfect competition, even in long-run equilibrium.

Perfect competition
The market structure in which there are many sellers and buyers, firms produce a homogeneous product, and there is free entry into and exit out of the industry.

Market power
The ability of buyers or sellers to affect price.

The first assumption is that there is a large number of sellers (producers) in the market. No specific number is indicated. A large number means there are so many sellers of the product that no single seller's decisions can affect price. For example, no single wheat farmer can influence the price of wheat. A farmer could sell the entire crop or none of the crop. The farmer's decision wouldn't affect the price of wheat in any perceptible manner because the market for wheat is so large relative to any single producer.

The second assumption is that there is a large number of buyers (consumers) in the market. No single purchaser has any **market power**. That is, a large number means that no one buyer can affect the price in any perceptible way.

The third assumption is that perfectly competitive firms produce a homogeneous product. Homogeneous means that the product of one firm is no different from that of other firms in the industry. Since this is the case, purchasers have no preference for one producer over another. If you are a miller and want to purchase wheat, you don't care if it was produced by Farmer Jones or Farmer Smith—a bushel of No. 1 winter wheat is a bushel of No. 1 winter wheat!

The fourth, and very important, assumption is that there is free entry into and free exit out of the market. This means that if one firm wishes to go into business or if another firm wishes to cease production, either can do so without any kind of constraint. This assumption is crucial in distinguishing perfect competition from monopoly, which we will examine in the next chapter.

The fifth assumption is that there is perfect knowledge. The sixth assumption is that workers and other resources can easily move in and out of the industry. These last two assumptions are even more unrealistic than the others because information is costly to acquire and resources are usually costly to move. The effect of these two assumptions is that when economic profits exist, firms will find out about these profits and enter the industry. Even though these assumptions are unrealistic, the resulting model is valuable because it shows what adjustments would take place in an ideal setting.

If these six assumptions are met, a market will be perfectly competitive. These assumptions create a model market in which no firm or individual has the power to exert control over the market. This means that neither buyer nor seller has any influence over price.

The six assumptions were first stated more than two centuries ago by Adam Smith in a general outline of the perfectly competitive model in his book, *An Inquiry into the Causes and Nature of the Wealth of Nations*. In the nineteenth century, the model of perfect competition was the main way of looking at how firms and markets determined price and output levels. The study of other market structures arose later.

LARGE NUMBERS ON THE BUYERS' SIDE

This chapter concentrates on developing a theory of firms in perfect competition, or competition on the sellers' side of the market. Keep in mind, however, that we also assume large numbers of buyers—so many that none possess market power.

Concentrating on the firm should not obscure the importance of competition on the buyers' side of the market. In order for markets to be competitive, there must be enough buyers that none can affect the price by withholding purchases or increasing purchases. A competitive market cannot be "cornered" by buyers with market power or wealth. A competitive market is too big and too impersonal to be influenced by single buyers. In most of your transactions as a buyer, you will find that you are a perfect competitor—too small to influence the price.

COMPETITIVE ADJUSTMENT IN THE SHORT RUN

Since the perfectly competitive firm is small relative to the market and its product is the same as that of other firms, this firm views itself as having no influence on market price. If the perfectly competitive firm wants to sell any of its output, it must sell at the market price. A firm in perfect competition is referred to as a **price taker** because it has no influence on price. It can sell any amount at the market-clearing price. The firm takes that price as its selling price. If it sets a higher price, none of its output will be sold because buyers will be able to purchase an identical product at the lower market price elsewhere. On the other hand, it makes no sense to sell below the market price because the firm can sell all it produces at that market price.

Price taker
A seller (or buyer) in perfect competition that has no influence on price and can sell any amount at the market-clearing price.

The market demand and supply curves and the firm's resultant demand curve are shown in Figure 1. (The graphs in this chapter are based on models first developed by nineteenth-century British economist Alfred Marshall.) Market demand (D) and supply (S) curves are such that the market equilibrium price is P_1. If the market is in equilibrium, the perfectly competitive firm can sell as much of its product as it wishes at price P_1. From the firm's viewpoint, the demand curve is perfectly elastic at price P_1.

The demand schedule a firm faces is also its average revenue schedule. If, for example, the price consumers pay in the market is $15, the average revenue a seller receives per unit sold is also $15. As price changes along a market demand curve, the average revenue that sellers receive will also change. Total revenue of a firm is the price times the quantity sold ($TR = P \times Q$). **Average revenue** (**AR**) is total revenue divided by the quantity sold. It is the revenue per unit sold,

Average revenue (AR)
Total revenue divided by the quantity sold, or the revenue per unit sold (the price).

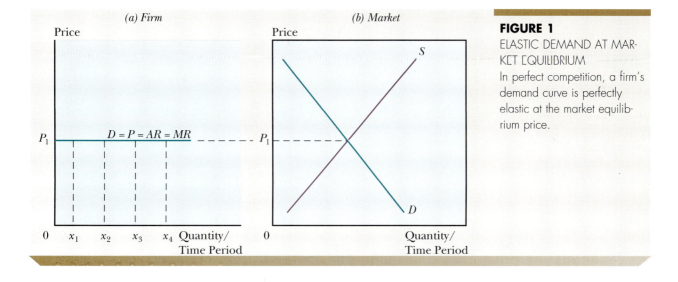

FIGURE 1

ELASTIC DEMAND AT MARKET EQUILIBRIUM
In perfect competition, a firm's demand curve is perfectly elastic at the market equilibrium price.

or the price of the product. A demand curve is an average revenue curve. With perfect competition, price does not vary with output. Thus, $AR = (P \times Q)/Q = P$ is a constant. The firm's perfectly elastic demand curve in Figure 1 is also a perfectly elastic average revenue curve.

THE LEVEL OF OUTPUT

Recall that a profit-maximizing firm always produces that quantity for which marginal revenue is equal to marginal cost. Thus, we need to determine what the competitive firm's marginal revenue curve looks like. Marginal revenue for the nth unit is the change in total revenue from selling one more unit:

$$MR_n = TR_n - TR_n - TR_{n-1}$$

In Figure 1, the change in total revenue if sales increase from x_1 to x_2 (where x_2 is one unit more than x_1) is $P_1(x_2 - x_1)$. If sales increase from x_2 to x_3, the change in total revenue is $P_1(x_3 - x_2)$. In other words, in the case of a perfectly elastic demand curve, such as the firm's demand curve in Figure 1, $D = P = AR = MR$. The marginal revenue curve associated with a perfectly elastic demand curve is the same as the demand curve. The demand curve is always the average revenue curve for any market structure. The demand curve is equal to the marginal revenue curve only in perfect competition. Remember the relationship between average and marginal values—if the average value doesn't change, the marginal value must be the same as the average.

Using marginal cost and marginal revenue, we now can determine how a perfectly competitive firm will adjust its output to changed prices in the short run. The demand curves for the market and a representative firm are depicted in Figure 2. A **representative firm** is a typical firm in perfect competition, one of the many similar firms in this market. In Figure 2, the representative firm's marginal cost curve is also shown. This firm maximizes profit by producing quantity x_1 when the price per unit is P_1 because at that output level, $MR_1 = MC$. Now assume the market demand increases to D_2. The market price rises to P_2. The firm's demand curve, average revenue curve, and marginal revenue curve change to $D_2 = AR_2 = MR_2$. The firm responds by increasing its output level to x_2, where $MR_2 = MC$.

Representative firm
A typical firm in perfect competition, one of the many identical firms in the market.

THE SUPPLY CURVE

In Figure 2, the firm's short-run marginal cost curve is the same as its short-run supply curve. A **short-run supply curve** is a supply curve for the period in which the size of the plant cannot be varied (the short run). In perfect competition, the short-run marginal cost curve is the short-run supply curve. As the market price rose, the firm in Figure 2 increased its output. The quantity which will be produced at each price is identified by the marginal cost curve. The marginal cost curve (above the shutdown point) is also the supply curve for a competitive firm.

Short-run supply curve
The supply curve for the period in which the size of the plant cannot be varied (in perfect competition, the same as the short-run marginal cost curve).

We can now look at the relationship between the firm's supply (marginal cost) curve and the market supply curve. The firm's supply curve represents its output response to increased market prices. If we were to add (horizontally) the

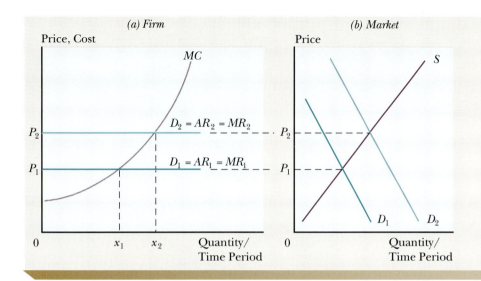

FIGURE 2

PROFIT MAXIMIZATION

An increase in market demand causes the equilibrium price to rise. The demand curve the firm faces adjusts by the amount of the increase in price, and the firm increases its output to equate MC and MR. The adjustment process is such that the firm's marginal cost curve is its short-run supply curve.

short-run supply curves for all firms, we would construct the short-run market (or industry) supply curve. The market supply curve is simply the aggregate of all the firms' supply curves. The short-run market supply curve then is the aggregate of the portions of all firms' marginal cost curves that lie above their average variable cost curves. In the long run, more firms can enter an industry as a response to economic profits. The market supply curve will shift to the right because it is made up of more individual supply curves. On the other hand, as firms leave an industry due to losses, the market supply curve will shift to the left, representing a decrease in supply. This decrease is due to the fact that there are fewer individual supply curves to be summed.

PROFITS AND LOSSES

We have just seen how a representative firm adjusts in the short run to changes in market demand. We don't yet know whether the firm has a profit or a loss, or how large this profit or loss is. To find out, we need to add the average cost curve to the graph. Also, in order to decide if the firm should continue to produce if losses are encountered, we need to add the average variable cost curve.

In Figure 3, the firm is maximizing profit by producing output x_1 at price P_1, where $P = MR = MC$. The average cost of producing x_1 is measured by distance x_1C in Figure 3. The total cost of producing x_1 is represented by the area of the rectangle $0P_1Cx_1$. Total revenue in Figure 3 is also the area of $0P_1Cx_1$, so $TR = TC$. This firm is therefore making zero economic profit, although it is meeting its opportunity costs. Remember that total cost includes normal profit, which is the return on capital and enterprise necessary to keep firms in an industry.

If the firm's average cost (AC) curve is the one drawn in Figure 4, the average cost of producing x_1 is the distance x_1A. Total revenue (TR) is still $P_1 \times x_1$, or the area of $0P_1Bx_1$. Total cost is now the area of $0CAx_1$. Since $TR > TC$, there is an economic profit equal to the area of CP_1BA in Figure 4. On the other hand, if the firm's average cost curve is the one drawn in Figure 5, the average cost of producing x_1 is the distance x_1A. Total revenue is the area of $0P_1Bx_1$, and total cost is the area of $0CAx_1$. In this case, $TC > TR$, so economic losses are being incurred. The economic loss is equal to the area of P_1CAB in Figure 5.

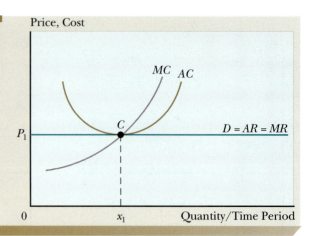

FIGURE 3

FIRM EARNING ZERO ECONOMIC PROFIT
The average cost (AC) curve is used to determine if a firm is making an economic profit. If average revenue (price) is equal to average cost, the firm is making zero economic profit.

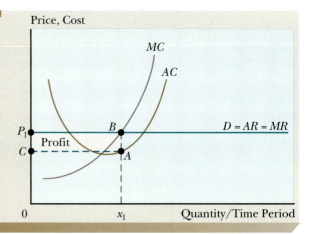

FIGURE 4

FIRM EARNING AN ECONOMIC PROFIT
If the firm's average revenue is greater than its average cost at the level of output being produced, the firm is making an economic profit.

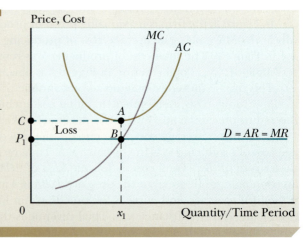

FIGURE 5

FIRM SUFFERING A LOSS
If the firm's average cost is greater than its average revenue at the level of output being produced, the firm is incurring a loss.

Should the firm of Figure 5 continue to produce and, if so, for how long? It is suffering a loss, which means the productive resources employed by this firm could earn more in some other use. Revenues are less than opportunity costs. But keep in mind that this diagram shows the short run, which means that some input is fixed. This fixed input means that there are fixed costs that cannot be eliminated. Fixed costs must be paid in the short run even if production ceases. We need to include the average variable cost (AVC) curve to determine the conditions under which the firm should cease production, because variable costs are the only ones under the firm's control in the short run.

THE SHUTDOWN DECISION

The short-run cost curves of a firm are depicted with several equilibrium points in Figure 6. At a price of P_1, which represents a marginal revenue of MR_1, the firm maximizes profits by producing x_1. At P_1, the firm is making an economic profit because total revenue (area of $0P_1Ax_1$) is greater than total cost (area of $0C_1Dx_1$). At price $P_2 = MR_2$, the firm would produce x_2 and make zero economic profit because total revenue (area of $0P_2Bx_2$) is equal to total cost (area of $0C_2Bx_2$).

Examine carefully what happens when price falls to P_3 and marginal revenue falls to MR_3. The profit-maximizing or loss-minimizing output is now x_3. At output level x_3, economic losses are incurred because total revenue is the area of $0P_3Sx_3$, and total cost is the area of $0C_3Ex_3$. Economic losses are thus represented by the rectangle P_3C_3ES. The firm needs to answer this question: Should

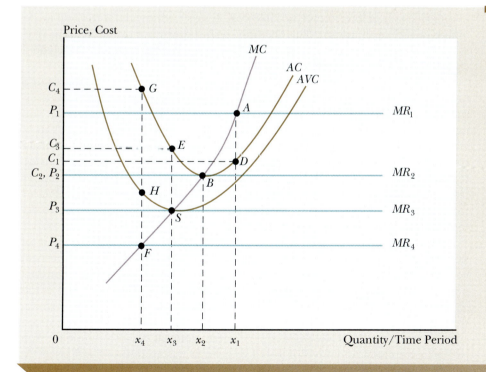

FIGURE 6
THE SHUTDOWN POINT
If a firm's average revenue is greater than its average variable cost, the firm will be able to cover total variable costs and make a payment toward total fixed costs. If price falls below average variable costs, the firm will lose less money if it shuts down than if it continues to produce. The shutdown point in this case is point S at a price of P_3.

it produce and incur this loss or should it cease production? Remember, if production is halted, fixed costs must still be paid. In Figure 6, if the market price is P_3, the firm is earning a total revenue equal to the area of $0P_3Sx_3$, and its total variable costs ($TVC = AVC \times Q$) are $0P_3Sx_3$. In other words, the firm is covering (exactly) its total variable costs and losing an amount equal to its total fixed costs. It must pay the fixed costs even if it shuts down, so at price P_3 the firm is indifferent about shutting down or continuing to produce. If the price falls below P_3, the firm will shut down in order to minimize losses. By shutting down, it will lose only total fixed costs, instead of total fixed costs plus some portion of variable costs if it continues to produce. The minimum or low point on the AVC curve (S in Figure 6) is called the **shutdown point** because if price falls below that point, the firm loses less by ceasing production.

Shutdown point
The minimum point on the average variable cost (AVC) curve, or the level of output at which a firm minimizes its losses by ceasing operation.

Consider price P_4 (or MR_4) in Figure 6. The $MR = MC$ rule tells the firm that at P_4 it should produce output level x_4. However, at x_4 the firm is losing P_4C_4GF ($0P_4Fx_4 - 0C_4Gx_4$). Total revenue of $0P_4Fx_4$ does not cover the total variable costs of producing x_4, which are x_4H times x_4. In other words, the firm is losing more than its total fixed costs. It is making variable cost outlays that it wouldn't have to make if it stopped production entirely. The firm would be better off to shut down and only incur its fixed costs.

Because the firm shuts down, we need to modify the earlier statement that the firm's marginal cost curve represents its short-run supply curve. That statement is not completely correct. A firm's short-run supply curve is represented by its marginal cost curve only *above* the shutdown point (point S in Figure 6). Below the shutdown point, the firm will produce no output, so only the part of the marginal cost curve above the minimum point on the average variable cost curve is the firm's supply curve.

The model has just told us that in the short run, the firm will shut down when price falls below average variable cost. It says nothing about the real-world timing of such a shutdown. The decision to shut down is more difficult in reality than in theory. It depends on many factors, including time and anticipated changes. A few examples may illustrate such problems.

First, imagine yourself the owner of a sporting goods store in a ski area or a beach resort. Shutdown may be a seasonal decision. If revenues fall below average variable costs (clerks' wages, electricity, and so on) in the off-season, you may close up, bearing only your fixed costs (such as rent on the store) until crowds return and your revenues increase. In this case, shutdown does not mean you are moving your investments in plant and equipment into other businesses. It simply means that you lose money in certain seasons and you lose less money if you shut down. You fully intend to reopen for business when the snow flies or the temperature sends people to the beaches. Past experience helps you to determine when to shut down and when to reopen.

Second, imagine yourself the owner-manager of a steel mill. The price of steel has fallen below your average variable costs of production. In the short run, you shut down (if laws and union contracts allow you to do so—a union contract might change labor from a variable to a fixed resource). The short run is too short a time period for you to vary your plant size (which is one way of saying that you can't move your fixed resources in this time period). However, if you are convinced that this low price is permanent, you will begin to liquidate. You will sell equipment and attempt to sell your buildings and other fixed assets. As you do this, you are moving to the long run.

KEY IDEAS

WHAT SHORT-RUN COST CURVES TELL US
- The minimum point on the average cost curve is the least-cost combination.
- The minimum point on the average variable cost curve is the shutdown point.
- The part of the marginal cost curve above the average variable cost curve is the perfectly competitive firm's supply curve.
- Profit or loss is measured as average revenue (price) times quantity minus average cost times quantity.

The short-run output decisions and profit determination for a perfectly competitive firm can be illustrated with a simple example. Table 1 presents some production cost data for a firm. Assuming that different market prices are the result of different market equilibrium situations, it is possible to determine the firm's response to different prices. In Table 2, six different market prices corresponding to different market conditions are assumed. When the market price is $61, the demand and marginal revenue curves the firm faces are perfectly elastic at $61. The firm produces 10 units (where $MR = MC = \$61$) and

TABLE 1 PRODUCTION COSTS FOR A FIRM

OUTPUT	AVERAGE VARIABLE COST (AVC)	AVERAGE COST (AC)	MARGINAL COST (MC)	TOTAL COST (TC)
1	$40	$100	$40	$100
2	38	68	36	136
3	36	56	32	168
4	35	50	32	200
5	35	47	35	235
6	36	46	41	276
7	37³⁄₇	46	46	322
8	39	46½	50	372
9	41	47⅔	57	429
10	43	49	61	490

TABLE 2 PRODUCTION DECISIONS AT VARIOUS MARKET PRICES

MARKET PRICE (MR)	FIRM'S OUTPUT	TOTAL REVENUE (TR)	TOTAL COST (TC)	FIRM'S PROFIT
$61	10	$610	$490	$120
50	8	400	372	28
46	7	322	322	0
41	6	246	276	−30
35	5	175	235	−60
32	4	128	200	−72

GLOBAL OUTLOOK: THE ORGANIZATION OF MARKETS IN DEVELOPING COUNTRIES

In many countries, markets are not as well developed as they are in the United States. In these countries, many nonmarket institutions have strong holds on culture in ways that affect production, distribution, and consumption. The laws of supply and demand still hold, but customs, systems of land tenure, village and family organization, religious practices, and corruption all have an impact on the functioning of markets.

Cultural differences affect the emergence of entrepreneurs and the profit motive. In poor countries, entrepreneurs may lack the help of markets to bring together materials, labor, and capital. If individuals are discouraged from being risk takers, their reaction may be to say "no" to new business opportunities. In fact, in some cultures, risk taking is viewed as unacceptable behavior, and minorities become the entrepreneurs. Jews played this role in medieval Europe, the Chinese in some countries in South America, and Indians in Africa. This kind of cultural obstacle makes economic development more difficult in many less developed countries, because development requires a strong entrepreneurial class. Also, if the ruling structure of a society does not encourage entrepreneurial development but supports the stability of a traditional society, the effect is to slow economic growth. In such traditional societies, a trauma often produces a spurt of economic growth. The trauma of World War II and its shakeup of the power structure in Japan is a case in point.

Another difference between the markets of less developed and industrialized countries is that retail markets are often less organized and products are less standardized. As a consequence, neither buyers nor sellers are price takers. Much time and effort is expended in negotiating prices. This time does not go into producing goods and services. Also, the market information widely available in industrialized countries is absent. The absence of this information adds to the cost of doing business in a traditional society and offers another cultural barrier to exchange, enterprise, and economic growth. It is easy for people in developed, industrialized countries to take markets and entrepreneurs for granted and overlook the role they play in creating and sustaining a high standard of living.

We saw some of these market interactions coming together the last few years in the formerly communist countries of East and Central Europe. There were many street scenes of people setting up places to bargain and exchange. These markets are very inefficient because information was scarce and people spent a lot of time in the simple acts of exchange. As these markets develop we will see growth in more traditional stores and shops that specialize in the sale of certain items. The scene in Moscow will change from one of street vendors to small shops, and eventually to stores that are similar to those found in other market economies. These changes will take place very quickly, if the political side of the equation remains stable.

---

earns an economic profit of $120. This situation corresponds to the graph in Figure 4. At a market price of $46, the firm maximizes profit where $MR = MC = 46, which is at an output of 7 units. Since $TR = TC$ at 7 units, there is zero economic profit. This situation corresponds to Figure 3. When market price falls to $41, the firm reacts by decreasing its output to 6 units (where $MR = MC = 41). At 6 units of output, it incurs a loss of $30. This economic loss corresponds to that shown in Figure 5.

The firm will continue to produce in the short run unless price falls below $35 because the minimum value of average variable costs (minimum point on the AVC curve) is at $35. To see why, look at how the firm responds when market price falls to $32. At $32, the firm produces 4 units. However, it loses $72 ($TR = 4 \times $32 = 128, $TC = 4 \times $50 = 200, and $128 - $200 = -$72$). If it shuts down, the firm loses only $60 in total fixed costs. The total variable cost (TVC) would have been $140 if production had taken place ($TVC = 4 \times $35 = 140 and $TFC = $200 - $140 = 60). So the firm loses less if it ceases production. At any price less than $35, the firm will shut down.

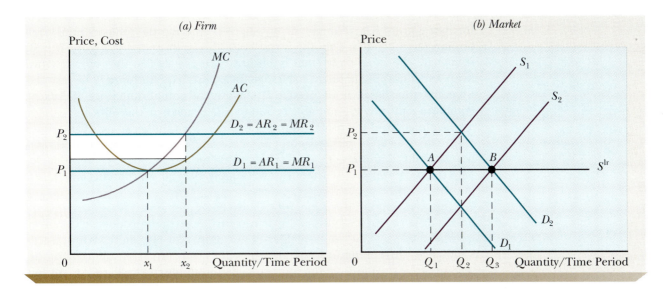

FIGURE 7
LONG-RUN ADJUSTMENT TO AN INCREASE IN MARKET DEMAND
An increase in market demand will cause the price to rise. The demand curve the representative firm faces will shift upward. Economic profit will result, and new firms will enter the industry in response to this profit. As new firms enter, the market supply curve shifts to the right, causing price to fall to the point at which the representative firm is again earning zero economic profit.

THE LONG RUN: CONSTANT, INCREASING, OR DECREASING COSTS

The process of determining price and output when firms have time to alter their fixed inputs and when new firms can enter the industry is illustrated in Figure 7. The D_1 and S_1 curves are the equilibrium demand and supply curves for the industry. The industry is in long-run equilibrium when no economic forces are working to cause it to expand or contract (or to cause the price to change). In part (a) of the figure, the firm is making zero economic profit at price P_1 and output x_1. Let's assume this firm is representative of 1,000 identical firms. Thus, the market supply curve (S_1) in part (b) is the summation of 1,000 MC curves (above the AVC curves). Since these firms are making zero economic profits at P_1, the industry is in equilibrium with an industry output of Q_1. Since each firm is producing x_1, $1,000 \times x_1 = Q_1$. Now suppose there is an increase in market demand to D_2, brought about by an increase in consumers' real income, and assume that the good under consideration is a normal good. When market demand shifts to D_2, market price rises to P_2. The demand curve for the firm rises to D_2 and is perfectly elastic at price P_2.

The firm's initial (short-run) response is to increase its output to x_2 because $MR_2 = MC$ at output level x_2. Thus, the increase in market demand from Q_1 to Q_2 is met by an increase in output by each of the 1,000 firms, from x_1 to x_2. Note, however, that each firm will then make an economic profit equal to the shaded area in Figure 7(a). Economic profit, you recall, means that productive resources are earning more than their opportunity cost. This profit means that the industry is out of equilibrium. Other firms are going to attempt to get some of this profit. The existence of profit is the signal for new firms to enter this industry.

Since free entry and perfect knowledge are assumed to be characteristics of perfect competition, entrepreneurs will be aware of this profit and will enter the industry. As firms enter the industry, the market supply curve will shift because it now is the summation of the 1,000 original MC curves plus the MC curves of the new entrant firms. In fact, firms will keep entering the industry until equilibrium (zero economic profit) is restored. This is illustrated in Figure 7. If all firms have the same costs (that is, all firms are exactly like the representative firm) and if nothing happens to change these costs, equilibrium will be restored when the price has been reduced to P_1, the original equilibrium price. If the new equilibrium price is P_1 and industry output is Q_3, each firm is producing x_1 units. The summation of the firms' output (1,000 plus the number of new firms times x_1) is equal to the industry output (Q_3). Connecting the market equilibrium points, points A and B in Figure 7(b), gives the industry's long-run supply curve, S^{lr}. This curve represents what firms will supply after all adjustments have taken place.

Just as profits are the signal for firms to enter an industry, losses are the signal for firms to exit an industry. Entrepreneurs move their productive resources to other uses, seeking to earn their opportunity cost elsewhere. With perfect knowledge, entrepreneurs will know where they can earn at least normal profit. As firms leave the industry, the short-run market supply curve will shift to the left because it is now derived by adding up the short-run supply curves of fewer firms. Firms will leave the industry until the remaining firms have zero economic profits and equilibrium is restored.

CONSTANT COST INDUSTRIES

Constant cost industry
An industry in which expansion of output does not cause average costs to rise in the long run.

The adjustments traced in Figure 7 assumed that input prices, and thus costs, were unaffected by the quantity of output the industry produced. As firms entered the industry (Figure 7) or exited the industry, the price of the productive resources did not change. As a result, the average and marginal cost curves did not change. When cost curves do not change as an industry expands or contracts, the industry is referred to as a constant cost industry. A **constant cost industry** is an industry in which expansion of output does not cause average costs to rise in the long run. In a constant cost industry, as more steel, labor, electricity, and other inputs are purchased, the price of those inputs does not increase. Constant costs are most likely to occur when the industry's purchase of inputs is small relative to the market supply of those inputs. If the industry's use of inputs is small relative to a very elastic market supply, increased demand for those inputs will not increase their prices (very much). For example, consider the home computer industry. If profits exist and firms enter, these firms will demand more inputs. They will demand more plastic, more labor, and more microchips. If all the computer-producing firms use a small fraction of the total supply of these inputs, the increase in demand will not cause the price of plastic, labor, and microchips to rise.

Figure 7 represents long-run expansions in constant cost industries. The short-run response to a contraction in demand is a decrease in price. An expansion in demand produces a short-run increase in price. The market adjustment, however, will return price to its original level, with fewer firms in the case of the contraction or more firms in the case of the expansion. The long-run supply curve in a constant cost industry is perfectly elastic, even though the short-run supply curve has a positive slope.

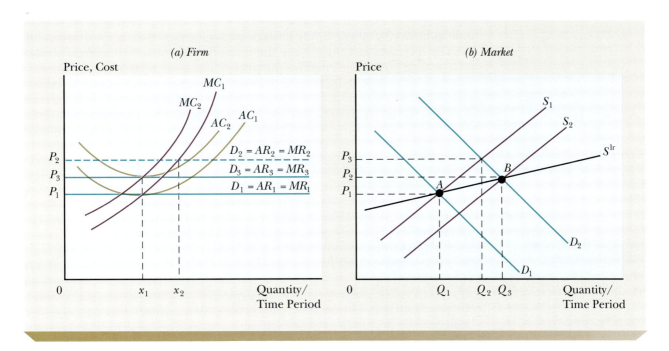

INCREASING COST INDUSTRIES

Sometimes an expansion in industry output will cause costs to increase in the long run. In this case, as an industry expands output and demands more inputs, the increased demand causes prices of inputs to rise. For example, an increase in demand for chicken causes new firms to enter the packing industry and to demand more chicken coops, chicken pluckers, land, and plastic bags. If the increased demand causes the price of chicken coops, chicken pluckers, land, or plastic bags to rise, the average production costs of the representative firm will increase as a result of the increased demand for chicken. Also, less productive inputs and firms may be drawn into the industry. These conditions describe an increasing cost industry. An **increasing cost industry** is an industry in which expansion of output causes average costs to rise in the long run.

Figure 8 illustrates the long-run adjustment process in an increasing cost industry. The industry is originally in equilibrium at price P_1 and output level Q_1. Each firm is producing x_1 units of output. Market demand increases to D_2. As a result, market price rises to P_2. The firm's demand is now represented by $D_2 = AR_2 = MR_2$. The firm's short-run response is to increase output to x_2, where $MC_1 = MR_2$. The industry's output is now at Q_2. At this increased output, two things will happen. First, new firms will enter the industry because of the economic profits that now exist. Second, costs will rise as a result of the increased demand for inputs. This rise in cost is represented by the upward shift in the marginal and average cost curves to MC_2 and AC_2 in Figure 8(a).

The upward shift of the marginal and average cost curves is based on the assumption that all costs increase at the same rate. In most cases, this would not be true, since the prices of some inputs (the scarcer ones) would rise faster. However, the example is clearer if we assume that all input prices rise proportionally, and this assumption does not seriously affect the analysis. Firms, as purchasers of inputs, are likely to have much influence in some input markets and

FIGURE 8

LONG-RUN ADJUSTMENT TO INCREASING DEMAND IN AN INCREASING COST INDUSTRY

When demand increases in an increasing cost industry, the firms that enter the industry bid up the prices of the productive resources for all firms in the industry. As a result, price does not return to the old equilibrium. Instead, a new equilibrium with the representative firm earning zero economic profit is established at a price above the old equilibrium price.

Increasing cost industry An industry in which expansion of output causes average costs to rise in the long run.

little influence in others. In the chicken-packaging example, as the demand for chicken increases and firms enter the industry, there may be no effect on the price of land but a large effect on the price of machines used to pluck chickens. This kind of cost increase is most likely when specific, rather than general, inputs are used in the production process. It is also possible that the new firms attracted to an industry will be less efficient at producing the good in question. In this case, the representative firm will have higher costs, indicating less efficient production.

The net result of an increased number of firms and increased costs is a rightward shift in the short-run market supply curve. The supply curve shifts to the right because it is the sum of the supply curves of more firms. However, it will not shift as far to the right as it did in the constant cost industry because costs have risen for every firm. The new short-run market supply curve will be S_2 in Figure 8(b). Equilibrium is reached at price P_3, where firms are no longer making profits. Industry output is now Q_3, and each firm is producing x_1 units, where $MR_3 = MC_2$.

As before, the long-run market supply curve connects the industry's equilibrium points on all of the short-run supply curves. Connecting points A and B in Figure 8(b) produces a long-run supply curve (S^{lr}) with a positive slope, indicating an increasing cost industry.

DECREASING COST INDUSTRIES

Decreasing cost industry An industry in which expansion of output causes average costs to fall in the long run.

To complete the analysis, consider a decreasing cost industry. A **decreasing cost industry** is an industry in which an expansion of output causes average costs to fall in the long run. In a decreasing cost industry, as more firms enter the industry causing the demand for inputs to increase, input prices fall. Falling input prices imply that there are economies of scale in an industry that is supplying an input to the decreasing cost industry. For example, as more electricity is demanded, more efficient generators are built and the price of this input falls.

KEY IDEAS

WHAT EQUILIBRIUM IN PERFECT COMPETITION MEANS
- $P = MC$ Production is at the level consumers indicate (through the market) they want. It is commonly called allocative efficiency.
- $P = AC$ Firms are earning normal profits. There is no movement into or out of the industry.
- $AC = MC$ Firms are using a least-cost method of production.

COMPETITIVE EQUILIBRIUM: WHAT'S SO GREAT ABOUT PERFECT COMPETITION?

The nature of perfect competition is such that the firm and industry are driven to equilibrium at zero economic profit. This equilibrium is the appeal of perfect competition as a standard against which to judge other market structures. Economists view this equilibrium as an ideal, or a social optimum. In equilibrium, resources are optimally allocated among competing uses. Figure 9 shows

POLICY FOCUS: FLOODS, SUBSIDIES, AND THE FARM PROBLEM

As we saw earlier, the "farm problem" is a very complex issue. Farmers face numerous problems. The market for farm products can be characterized as a competitive market. Many programs that are well-intended add to the problems of competitive, productive farmers. Some of the programs aimed at aiding farmers hit hard by flooding in the summer of 1993 are a case in point.

If the prices for farm products are "too low," meaning that farmers are suffering economic losses, the competitive solution is for some farms to exit the industry. That is what has been happening since 1900 in the United States. In the last decade the number of farms fell about 6 percent, while the average farm grew in size about 7 percent. As farm production falls, prices will rise to the point where existing farmers receive normal profits and remain in business.

Let's consider the impact of a well-intended flood policy that was put in place in the summer of 1993 to help Wisconsin dairy farmers. Even though the great flood of the summer of 1993 did not cause too much destruction in Wisconsin, it was a bad year for growing corn and hay to feed dairy cows that winter. Spring 1993 was very rainy and cold. The rain caused the Mississippi to swell and made the land unable to absorb the rain that came in June and July in Minnesota, Kansas, Iowa, and Missouri. The effect in Wisconsin was a very poor hay and corn crop. The government announced that dairy farmers could get a 3 percent loan in order to get them through this difficult time. One of the conditions for the 3 percent loan was that the farmer must be unable to get a conventional bank loan.

Consider now the case of Roddy, a very successful, very energetic dairy farmer. He has a very efficient, well-run operation and has been making profits for many years. He saw the rain every morning in April and May, but worked hard to get his corn planted and his hay made in July between the showers. He is in pretty good shape and stands to make at least a normal profit this year. The best thing for his long-term economic interest would be for some of the marginal farmers in his market area to go out of business, decreasing supply. Roddy has no trouble going to the bank and getting a loan to finance his dairy farm. He will get a farm loan and pay market rates of interest, about 7.5 percent in September 1993. Yet he is going to have to compete with the marginal farmer down the road who can't get a farm loan. That poor farmer will be able to get a 3 percent government loan. Now Roddy has to compete with a neighbor that has a lower cost of capital. A policy designed to help an unfortunate individual has disadvantaged an individual who worked hard and was successful.

One of the hardest things for governmental policy makers to understand is that competition requires relatively free entry *and* exit. If the price of farm products is insufficient to permit normal profit, the only solution is for some farmers and some farm production to *exit* the industry. But politicians want to help people, and many of those that are hurt by the governmental policy don't even know why they were hurt.

---

a perfectly competitive firm in equilibrium. At equilibrium, price (P) is equal to average cost (AC) and also is equal to marginal cost (MC).

First, consider $P = MC$. This means that allocative efficiency is being achieved and that the resources of the firm are being allocated exactly as consumers wish. It means that firms are expanding production exactly to the level desired by society. If P were greater than MC, it would mean that not enough resources were going into the production of the good in question. Consumers would be willing to pay a higher price (P) than it costs to produce another unit of the good (MC). If P were less than MC, too many resources would be devoted to the production of the good. Consumers would not be willing to pay as much as it costs to produce another unit of the good. In other words, where $P = MC$,

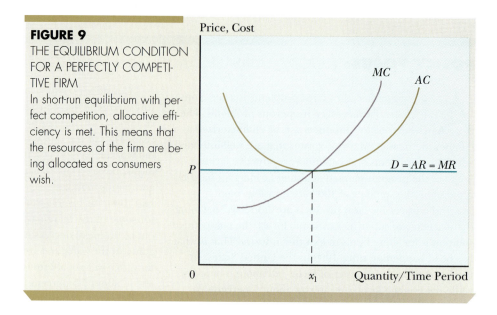

FIGURE 9
THE EQUILIBRIUM CONDITION FOR A PERFECTLY COMPETITIVE FIRM
In short-run equilibrium with perfect competition, allocative efficiency is met. This means that the resources of the firm are being allocated as consumers wish.

the socially optimal (or correct) amount of resources is being devoted to producing the good.

Second, consider $P = AC$. This means that firms are earning only normal profits. There is no incentive for firms to enter or leave the industry. It is important to note the role of profits in the perfectly competitive model. Economic profits serve as the signal for firms to move in or out of an industry. When profits exist, entrepreneurs rush in to attempt to capture them. The industry is forced to a new equilibrium. When losses are present, entrepreneurs leave to seek higher returns elsewhere. Equilibrium is attained because of the profit-seeking nature of firms. In equilibrium, there is efficiency. It is not because of some altruistic behavior on the part of entrepreneurs that firms are efficient. Entrepreneurs are assumed to be profit maximizers motivated by individual self-interest, and their response to changing profits brings about efficiency. In the competitive model, self-interest and the quest for profits produce the efficiency that benefits consumers. The firm is striving not for efficiency but for profits. When economic profits have served their signaling function, they disappear.

Third, consider $MC = AC$. This means that average cost (AC) is at a minimum. The variable resources are being combined as efficiently as possible.

In long-run equilibrium, as in Figure 10, the short-run average cost (AC) curve will be tangent with the long-run average cost ($LRAC$) curve at their respective minimum points. Also, short-run marginal cost, as well as long-run marginal cost, equals marginal revenue. In fact, $P = AR = AC = MC = LRAC = LRMC$. This means several things:

1. The firm has no further opportunities to improve or to enhance profitability.
2. Any larger or smaller plant size or production levels would be nonoptimal and result in economic losses.
3. Only the least-cost, most efficient firms will survive in a perfect competition.

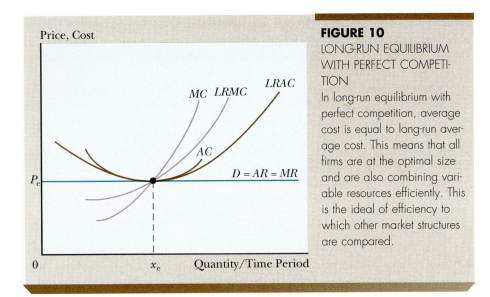

FIGURE 10
LONG-RUN EQUILIBRIUM WITH PERFECT COMPETITION
In long-run equilibrium with perfect competition, average cost is equal to long-run average cost. This means that all firms are at the optimal size and are also combining variable resources efficiently. This is the ideal of efficiency to which other market structures are compared.

The model of perfect competition is not meant to be a precise description of reality. Nor is it, in every case, the ideal state that society should be striving to reach. In certain industries, it may be too costly to bring about the necessary conditions for perfect competition. In that case, society can accept less than the ideal. The model of perfect competition is a tool for the economist. The economist can compare the real-world situation to the hypothetical world of perfect competition to determine what would be the case if perfect competition existed. In this sense, perfect competition is a benchmark, or yardstick, by which economists can measure the performance of other market structures.

ECONOMIC RENT IN PERFECT COMPETITION

According to the model of perfect competition, in industries in which free entry exists, profits will be driven to normal rates of return. Yet we all know of individuals who have become rich in industries that are very competitive and that have relatively free entry. How can this happen without totally invalidating this model? To explain how returns in excess of normal profits can exist in the long run, even under perfect competition, we must introduce some new concepts.

ECONOMIC RENT

Rent is a familiar term. You pay rent on your apartment. But economists have a special (and very different) meaning for this term. **Economic rent** is a payment to a productive resource in excess of the opportunity cost of that productive resource. Let's say, for example, you are trained as a teacher and could earn $30,000 per year in that profession. However, you also have beautiful teeth and can do toothpaste commercials, for which you earn $70,000 per year.

Economic rent
A payment to a productive resource in excess of its opportunity cost.

Economists would say that $40,000 of your income is economic rent because it is the amount by which your earnings exceed your opportunity cost. They would predict that you would do the commercials for $30,001 per year since you would then be earning more than your opportunity cost.

Economic rent, then, is more general than economic profit. Since economic profit is defined as revenue in excess of all the implicit costs (including normal profit) and explicit costs of production, economic profit is rent to entrepreneurs. Entrepreneurs will earn only normal profits in perfect competition because new entry will drive out higher rates of return. It is possible that economic rents to other productive resources will exist. Thus, we need to relate the concept of economic rent to the model of perfect competition.

REPRESENTATIVE FIRMS AND ECONOMIC RENTS

The theory of perfect competition uses a representative firm that is one of many firms with cost structures that are identical. This assumption is not always realistic. Consider agriculture as an example. Some farmland is far superior to other farmland. It is more fertile, gets more rainfall, or is located where the weather is warmer. The quality of the land will affect the farmer's costs of production. Economic rent will always be earned on the better land, and entry of new firms will not eliminate such rent. In other competitive industries, location, family connections, or talent will make firms' cost structures different, creating economic rents.

DIFFERENTIAL RENT THEORY

Economic rent does not weaken the theory of perfect competition. In 1817, classical economist David Ricardo reconciled the existence of economic rents with perfect competition by developing differential rent theory. He was interested in explaining the fact that fertile farmland earned a higher rent than poor farmland.

Consider, for example, the cost and revenue functions of two farms, shown in panels (a) and (b) of Figure 11. The market is represented in panel (c).

FIGURE 11
DIFFERENTIAL RENTS IN PERFECT COMPETITION
Farms A and B both face perfectly elastic demand curves at price P, determined in the market for their product, panel (c). Because its land is more fertile, farm B has lower average costs and earns a profit shown by the shaded area in panel (b). That profit will be converted to economic rent as competition for the fertile land bids up its price.

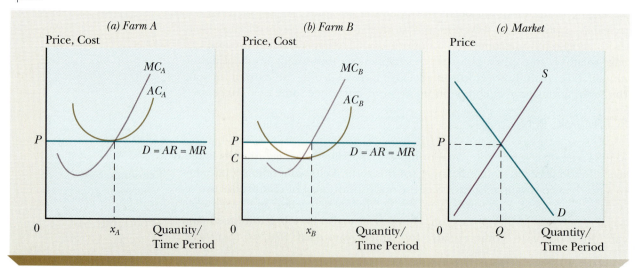

Supply and demand are such that market price for the farms' product is P. Farm A is earning zero economic profit ($P = AC_A$). Farm B has economic rent equal to the shaded area. This economic rent comes from the fact that the land used to produce the farm product is much more fertile for farm B. As a result, the costs of production are lower.

Other farmers would be willing to pay the owner of the land owned by farm B a higher price for being able to farm that land. This higher price becomes a cost of production to farm B because economic rent for the more fertile land will rise as farmers seek to either purchase or lease this land. Even if the owner of the land is also the farmer, economic rent is still an opportunity cost of production because the owner could lease the land to other farmers.

The result of differential rent to productive resources is because rents rise on more productive inputs. This rise equalizes the average cost of production among firms in perfect competition. In other words, the economic rent for farm B is a result of a superior productive resource, more fertile land. The user of the input (it could be the owner of the farm or someone else) will receive this rent. When the rent is paid, AC_B will, in fact, rise, as the shaded area for farm B is really an economic cost. We would expect the cost curves in Figure 11 (*a*) and (*b*) to equalize.

The point is that competitive firms may appear to earn economic profits (more than a normal rate of return), but these returns are often economic rents to unique inputs, not economic profits. In many cases, the firm's entrepreneur is the owner of the inputs. As a result, the rent looks like an economic profit. In fact, many times the entrepreneur has special skills that form the basis for the firm. The return to these skills is an economic rent to the productive resource enterprise. It is not an economic profit. The concept of economic rent is an important one and will be discussed in more detail in several upcoming chapters.

Consider again…*The question we began with is now easy to answer. Firms shut down in the short run when average revenue does not cover average variable costs. For many firms, the timing of the revenue flow determines hours of operation. One restaurant may open at 11:00 A.M. when one across the street opens at 5:00 P.M. For the firm that is closed more hours, the fixed cost is less than would be incurred if the firm were open for business.*

SUMMARY

1. Perfect competition is characterized by large numbers of buyers and sellers, homogeneous products, ease of entry into and exit out of the industry, perfect knowledge, and mobility of resources. Profits are the force that drives the perfectly competitive model to efficiency. The firm is seeking not efficiency but profits. This search for profits produces the efficiency that characterizes the model of perfect competition. Large numbers of buyers in a perfectly competitive market ensure that no single buyer can influence price.

2. A firm in a perfectly competitive market faces a perfectly elastic demand curve at the price determined by equilibrium in the market. The firm's short-run supply curve is the same as its short-run marginal cost curve.

3. Since the firm will shut down when price falls below average variable cost, the actual short-run supply curve is the marginal cost (MC) curve above the minimum point on the average variable cost (AVC) curve. This point of intersection is known as the shutdown point.

4. Long-run adjustments to changes in market demand are dependent on the cost characteristics for the industry. Since entry is easy, additional firms will enter an industry as long as economic profits are present. Thus, economic profits, brought about by an increase in demand, will lead to new entry. An industry can be characterized by constant, increasing, or decreasing costs. The slope of the long-run market supply curve will depend on which of these cost situations prevails.
5. At perfectly competitive equilibrium, $P = AC = MC = MR = LRAC = LRMC$. This condition describes the ideal allocative efficiency of perfect competition, to which other market structures are compared. From a society's perspective nothing can be done to improve the allocation of scarce resources.
6. Economic rent is a payment (return) to a productive resource over the opportunity cost of that input. Competitive firms may appear to be earning long-run economic profits, but these returns are actually economic rents to specific productive resources in the firms.

NEW TERMS

perfect competition
market power
price taker
average revenue (AR)
representative firm
short-run supply curve
shutdown point
constant cost industry
increasing cost industry
decreasing cost industry
economic rent

QUESTIONS: REVIEW, APPLICATIONS, AND POLICY

REVIEW

1. Explain how the long-run market supply curve will be determined by short-run supply adjustments in an increasing cost industry.
2. Draw the graphs for a decreasing cost industry in perfect competition, showing a market equilibrium and a representative firm. Then, for a decrease in market demand, trace through the short-run and long-run adjustments.
3. Why does profit maximization bring about economic efficiency?
4. What situations cause long-run supply curves to be positively sloped?
5. Explain in your own words why a firm might keep producing in the short run even if it were incurring a loss.
6. What does it mean to say that perfectly competitive equilibrium means that $P = AC = MC = MR = LRAC = LRMC$?
7. The assumptions of perfect competition include both large numbers of sellers and large numbers of buyers. Why is it important that there be large numbers of buyers?
8. Why do economists use the term *price taker* to discribe a firm in perfect competition?

APPLICATIONS

9. Assume that the data from the table in Question 7 in the last chapter represent the unit-cost data for a perfectly competitive firm in a constant cost industry. What will the firm produce in the short run if the market price is $7.00? Why? What is the economic profit or loss? If this is a representative firm, where is the market price going to settle?
10. What would happen to the firm in Question 9 if the market price fell to $2.50? Why?

POLICY

11. "If the price of wheat doesn't rise, farmers will lose money and the long-run price will be even higher." Analyze this statement.
12. Explain how the return to a good location for a firm (for instance, a gas station) in perfect competition does not violate the conclusion that economic profits are driven to zero by new entry.
13. What would happen to the price, output level, and profit for a firm in a perfectly competitive industry if the price of capital increased? Distinguish between short-run and long-run changes.
14. Why do some restaurants stay open all year and others are open only during certain times and/or certain seasons?
15. Assume for a moment that the health care industry is a perfectly competitive, increasing cost industry. If universal health care is passed, what will be the long-term effect on prices in the health care industry?

SUGGESTIONS FOR FURTHER READING

Mansfield, Edwin. *Microeconomics*, 8e. New York: W. W. Norton, 1994. An intermediate text that develops the graphical analysis in this chapter in greater detail.

Stigler, George J. "Perfect Competition, Historically Contemplated," *Journal of Political Economy* (1957). A very readable classical article that reviews the historical development of the theory of perfect competition.

Stigler, George J. *The Theory of Price*, 4e. New York: Macmillan, 1987, Chapter 10. A classic introductory price theory text by a Nobel Prize-winning economist.

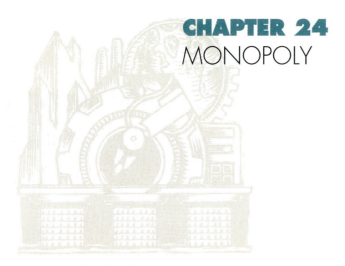

CHAPTER 24
MONOPOLY

LEARNING OBJECTIVES

1. Define monopoly and calculate average revenue and marginal revenue, given data on price and output. Diagram average revenue, marginal revenue, marginal cost, and average cost curves for a monopolistic firm making an economic profit, a loss, and finally, a normal profit.
2. Describe the economic role of natural and artificial barriers to entry into an industry.
3. Explain why firms practice price discrimination.
4. Discuss how a monopolist misallocates resources in terms of price and costs.
5. Describe the costs associated with monopoly.
6. Discuss why managers may pursue goals other than profit maximization.

Consider this...*Have you noticed that some people cut grocery coupons out of the paper and use them when they shop? Some shoppers have even been seen in grocery stores with their coupons organized into books and folders by product line so they can maximize the amount of money they can save. Some grocery stores promote double- and triple-coupon days. A recent article in a self-help magazine explained how you could save money on grocery shopping by being very organized in your coupon gathering. It described a woman with a family of seven children who saved 25 percent on a grocery budget of $400 per week. She spent sixteen hours cutting coupons, filing coupons, and organizing her shopping to save $100 per week. That seems like a lot of time and effort, but that comes to an equivalent wage of about $6.67 per hour take-home pay. There aren't many part-time jobs that pay that well! At that rate of return, it is surprising that we don't see more coupon clippers in the supermarket.*

After you study the material in this chapter you will be able to explain this behavior and analyze why the stores and the product makers use coupons as promotional tactics.

Monopoly is at the other end of the market continuum from perfect competition in the sense that perfect competition involves many firms and monopoly involves just one. The word *monopoly* is derived from the Greek words *mono* for "one" and *polein* for "seller." **Monopoly** is the market structure in which there is a single seller of a product that has no close substitutes.

Although there are no pure monopolies, there are many firms that have some degree of monopoly power. **Monopoly power** is the ability to exercise power over market price and output. As you learned in the last chapter, firms in perfect competition are price takers. In this chapter, you will see that, because it has some control over price, a monopoly is a price searcher. A **price searcher** is a firm that sets price in order to maximize profits. A price-searching firm has monopoly power. It searches for the price-quantity combination that will maximize its profit.

DEMAND, MARGINAL REVENUE, AND PRICE AND OUTPUT UNDER MONOPOLY

A perfectly competitive firm faces a perfectly elastic demand curve. As a result, price (or average revenue) and marginal revenue are equal. However, a monopolistic firm faces the *market* demand curve because the firm is the single seller and is, therefore, the industry. This distinction is very important because market demand curves have negative slopes. Since the monopolist's demand curve (which is also the average revenue curve) has a negative slope, its marginal revenue curve will lie below that curve. The commonsense reason why the marginal revenue curve lies below the average revenue curve is that the monopolist must lower price in order to sell more units of output. The price reduction applies to *all* units of output that the monopolist sells, not just the last, or marginal, unit. Each additional unit sold adds to total revenue by the amount it sells for (its price) but takes away from total revenue by the reduction in price on each unit sold. Thus, the change in revenue (the marginal revenue) must be less than the change in price.

Some data illustrating the relationship among average, total, and marginal revenue for a monopoly firm are presented in Table 1. When 3 units are sold, the total revenue is $186 (3 × $62). In order to sell 4 units, the monopolist must reduce the price from $62 to $60. Total revenue will then increase by $60 because an additional unit is being sold for $60. At the same time, it will decrease by $6 because the other 3 units now sell for $2 less each (for $60 each rather than for $62). The net result is that the monopolist has added $54 ($60 − $6) to total revenue by reducing the price from $62 to $60. Note that marginal revenue is $54 and price (average revenue) is $60 for 4 units. Marginal revenue has

7. Explain facts and fallacies of monopoly organization.
8. Evaluate the concept of contestable markets.

Monopoly
The market structure in which there is a single seller of a product that has no close substitutes.

Monopoly power
The ability to exercise some of the economic effects predicted in the model of monopoly by restricting output.

Price searcher
A firm that sets price in order to maximize profits and thus has monopoly power.

TABLE 1 AVERAGE, TOTAL, AND MARGINAL REVENUE FOR A MONOPOLIST

UNITS SOLD	PRICE (AVERAGE REVENUE)	TOTAL REVENUE	MARGINAL REVENUE
0	$65	0	
1	64	$64	$64
2	63	126	62
3	62	186	60
4	60	240	54
5	58	290	50
6	56	336	46
7	54	378	42
8	52	416	38
9	50	450	34
10	48	480	30

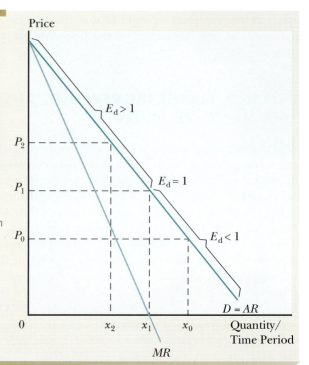

FIGURE 1

DEMAND AND MARGINAL REVENUE

The marginal revenue curve lies below the average revenue curve when there is a negatively sloped demand curve. In showing the relationship between average and marginal revenue. For a linear demand curve, the marginal revenue curve will intersect the x-axis exactly halfway between the origin and the point where the average revenue curve intersects the x-axis. Demand is elastic above P_1 and inelastic below P_1.

to be smaller than average revenue whenever units other than the marginal one suffer a price reduction.

The relationship between marginal revenue and demand is graphed in Figure 1. When demand is inelastic, decreases in price will cause total revenue to decline. If total revenue is declining, additions to total revenue must be negative. That is, marginal revenue is negative. In Figure 1, a reduction in price below P_1 will decrease total revenue because marginal revenue will be negative. This region corresponds to the inelastic portion of the demand curve. However, a reduction in price from P_2 to P_1 would increase total revenue because the demand curve is elastic in this range.

PROFIT MAXIMIZATION

Think back to the discussion of demand elasticity and Cournot's analysis of the mineral spring owner's situation. In that problem, the monopoly owner of a mineral spring with no production costs maximized profits by setting price where the price elasticity of demand was unitary. We can now apply the profit maximization rule $MR = MC$ to this case. If costs were zero, the MC curve would lie along the horizontal axis. In Figure 1, the monopolist would maximize profits by producing x_1 units (where $MR = MC = 0$) and selling them at price P_1. Since monopolists are profit maximizers, they produce the quantity where $MR = MC$ and sell the product for whatever the market will pay. The demand curve shows what price buyers will pay for any quantity of output. The mineral spring monopolist will increase sales of water as long as marginal revenue is positive, since it costs nothing more to produce another unit. You should note that this does *not* mean the mineral spring monopolist sells as much as possible. The monopolist sells the quantity that maximizes profit. In this case, it happens that the quantity at which profit is maximized is at a marginal revenue of zero, since costs are zero.

PRICE AND OUTPUT DECISIONS UNDER MONOPOLY

In the more general case, where costs are positive, the monopolist finds the profit-maximizing level of output by equating marginal cost and marginal revenue. The perfectly competitive firm is a price taker. The monopoly firm is a price searcher. A monopolist searches for the profit-maximizing price, not the highest price. This process can be seen by looking at the cost relationships graphically.

In Figure 2, a monopolist is producing a certain good for which the market demand curve is D. The marginal revenue curve (MR), derived from D, and the average cost (AC) and marginal cost (MC) curves are also given. The monopolist will maximize profit by producing x_1 units because at that level of output, $MR = MC$. If MR is greater than MC (that is, if output is less than x_1), the monopolist can increase profits by expanding output. Additions to output will cause total revenue to increase by more than the increase in total cost. On the other hand, if MR is less than MC (that is, if output is greater than x_1), the monopolist will reduce output because additions to output add more to total cost than to total revenue.

After choosing output level x_1, the monopolist will search for the highest price it can charge and still sell that amount of output. In Figure 2, this price is

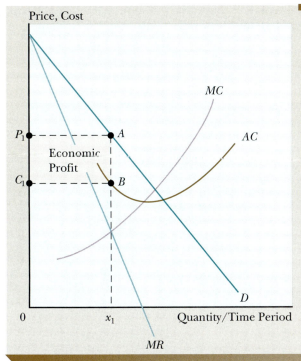

FIGURE 2

THE PROFIT-MAXIMIZING POSITION OF A MONOPOLIST

The profit-maximizing monopolist will produce x_1 units of output, where $MC = MR$. Since average cost (C_1) is less than average revenue (P_1) for output level x_1, this monopolist is making an economic profit.

P_1. The monopolist can sell x_1 units of output at price P_1 because the demand curve in Figure 2 shows that P_1 is the maximum that consumers will pay for that level of output.

At P_1 and x_1, the monopolist is making an economic profit. The average revenue (price) is P_1, and average cost is C_1. Since P_1 is larger than C_1, the monopolist is making a profit of $P_1 - C_1$ on each unit for a total profit of $(P_1 - C_1) \times x_1$. In Figure 2, total cost is represented by rectangle $0C_1Bx_1$, and total revenue is represented by rectangle $0P_1Ax_1$. Total revenue minus total cost equals economic profit, or rectangle C_1P_1AB. Since the cost curves include both explicit and implicit costs, the monopoly firm is making more than its opportunity cost. That is, the firm is earning more than is necessary to keep its resources employed in this industry—it is making an economic profit.

Table 2 shows the revenue and cost data for a monopolist. The monopolist would maximize profits at an output level of 7 units, where $MC = MR = \$46$. Price should be set at \$52 because the demand curve (AR) indicates that 7 units will sell for \$52 each. At a price of \$52, total revenue is \$364 ($7 \times \$52$) and total cost is \$322 ($\$46 \times 7$), which means that the monopolist is making a profit of \$42 (\$364 − \$322). If you don't believe this is maximum profit, calculate the profit at each level of output from 1 to 10 units. You will see profit is maximized at 7 units because at that level, $MR = MC$. Actually, in this numerical example, the firm would maximize profit at either 6 or 7 units. A unique point exists only when dealing with continuous functions that allow you to find a point somewhere between 6 and 7 units.

THE MONOPOLIST'S SUPPLY CURVE

A supply curve shows how much output will be offered for sale at various prices. In order to determine a supply curve, it is necessary to show that a firm will supply a unique quantity of output at any given price. This supply is by definition

TABLE 2 COST AND REVENUE DATA FOR A MONOPOLIST

OUTPUT AND SALES	TOTAL COST (TC)	AVERAGE COST (AC)	MARGINAL COST (MC)	AVERAGE REVENUE (AR)	TOTAL REVENUE (TR)	MARGINAL REVENUE (MR)	ECONOMIC PROFIT
0	\$60	\$—	\$—	\$0	\$0	\$0	\$60
1	100	100	40	58	58	58	−42
2	136	68	36	57	114	56	−22
3	168	56	32	56	168	54	0
4	200	50	32	55	220	52	20
5	235	47	35	54	270	50	35
6	276	46	41	53	318	48	42
7	322	46	46	52	364	46	42
8	372	46½	50	51	408	44	36
9	429	47⅔	57	50	450	42	21
10	490	49	61	49	490	40	0

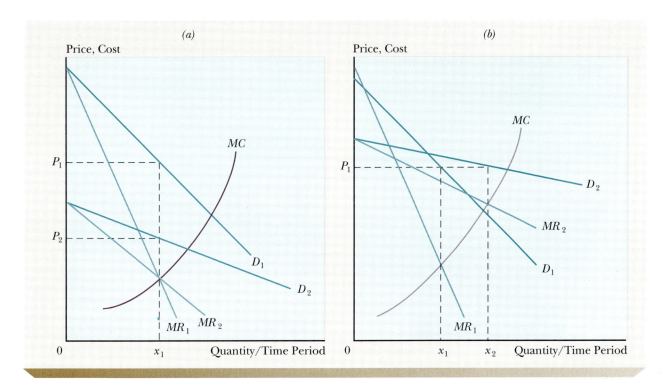

FIGURE 3

ONE OUTPUT WITH TWO PRICES OR ONE PRICE FOR TWO OUTPUTS

It is possible to trace out a supply curve only if a unique price is associated with a certain output. (a) Here there are at least two prices, P_1 and P_2, consistent with output x_1. (b) Here there are at least two outputs, x_1 and x_2, consistent with price P_1.

independent of demand. A monopoly firm does not have a supply curve in this sense. A monopolist sets the price at the profit-maximizing level of output, so it doesn't make sense to ask how much will be supplied at various prices. For a monopoly, the profit-maximizing output, where $MC = MR$, will depend on the location and shape of the demand curve. A monopoly firm therefore doesn't have a supply curve that is independent of demand.

To convince yourself that the monopolist does not have a supply curve, examine Figure 3. In part (a), two different prices, P_1 and P_2, are consistent with output x_1, depending on where the market demand curve is located (D_1 or D_2). The marginal revenue curves that are derived from the demand curves D_1 and D_2 both intersect the monopolist's marginal cost curve at the same level of output. In part (b), two different output levels, x_1 and x_2, can be produced at price P_1, depending on whether market demand is represented by D_1 or D_2.

Figure 3 shows that in the case of a monopolist you cannot discuss supply independent of demand. There is no way to predict what the monopolist will do without knowing the demand curve. The predictive powers of economists are, therefore, more limited in an analysis of monopoly. In this case, economists cannot say that an increase in demand will cause price to rise, *ceteris paribus*.

PROFITS AND BARRIERS TO ENTRY

If a monopolist is earning profits, other entrepreneurs will want some of those profits. As a result, there will be pressure from new firms entering the industry. But wait! A monopoly is a *single* seller producing a product that has no close substitutes. If there is new entry, there is no longer a monopoly. If a monopoly is to

Barriers to entry
Natural or artificial obstacles that keep new firms from entering an industry.

persist, there must be some forces at work to keep new firms from entering. **Barriers to entry** are natural or artificial obstacles that keep new firms from entering an industry. Without such barriers, monopoly cannot continue.

NATURAL BARRIERS

Economies of scale provide a natural barrier to entry. If the long-run cost curves are such that the optimal-size firm is very large relative to the size of the market, there may be room for only one cost-efficient firm in the industry. If there are great economies of scale, one firm that is bigger than any of the others will be able to undersell the rest. In such a case, the bigger firm will cut its price below that of its rivals and capture their customers. Eventually the large firm will become the only firm in the industry. When just one firm emerges in this way, the firm is called a natural monopoly. Natural monopolies exist in very few industries.

Public utilities such as telephone companies, electric companies, and cable television companies fit this category. The government recognizes that these are natural monopolies and therefore charters them and then regulates their prices and output levels. Problems associated with such regulation will be discussed in a later chapter. Some economists argue that even public utilities are not really natural monopolies. Since the occurrence of a natural monopoly is rare, most of the monopoly power that exists in our economy is due to artificial barriers.

ARTIFICIAL BARRIERS

An artificial barrier to entry is one that is contrived by the firm (or someone else) to keep others out. It doesn't take much imagination to come up with a list of such barriers. The least sophisticated, but perhaps the most effective example, would be the use of violence. Suppose you want to have a monopoly on the illegal numbers racket in South Chicago. If new entrepreneurs move in to reap some of these profits, you simply "do away" with them and hence establish a monopoly—very effective! This sort of tactic may sound barbaric, but business history contains many examples of the use of violence to keep out competitors. In the early history of oil exploration and drilling in the U.S., private armies were often essential.

On a more civilized level, it may be possible to erect artificial barriers that are legal, or at least quasi-legal. If exclusive ownership of all the raw materials in an industry could be captured, entry could be controlled by refusing to sell to potential new entrants. Alcoa enjoyed a monopoly before World War II because it controlled almost all the known sources of bauxite, the essential ore for the production of aluminum.

A current example of the use of artificial barriers occurs in the sale of diamonds. The de Beers Company of South Africa controls most of the world's diamond supply. This firm effectively controls the mining and marketing of new diamonds and has a great influence on price. In this case, there is still competition because all diamonds produced in the past are potential competitors. If de Beers manipulated production to drive price "too high," individuals might enter the market as suppliers, selling diamonds they presently own.

Another way to create artificial barriers is to own the patent on a process or machine that is vital in production. Patent rights give sole authority to use the process or machine to the holder of the patent. The problem with a patent, however, is twofold: First, it expires after seventeen years in the United States, and then everyone is entitled to use the idea. Second, to get a patent, detailed plans on how the item is produced must be provided, and these plans are available to potential competitors at the Library of Congress. So it appears a patent is not a very effective entry barrier to anyone who is willing to risk a lawsuit brought by the patent holder (and patent holders don't always win their cases). A good alternative to patents is secrecy. If a firm can keep its vital process or machine secret, it can keep new firms out of its industry. Now you know why there is barbed wire around some research and development offices, why you aren't told the formula for Pepsi-Cola, and why corporate spying is big business.

GOVERNMENTAL BARRIERS TO ENTRY

It is very difficult to be a monopolist because it is very hard to keep new entrants out of an industry—unless you can get the government to help you. Let's look briefly at two industries where firms have significant market power: the steel industry and the taxicab industry.

Suppose firms in the U.S. steel industry are earning economic profits. Firms that are producing steel in other countries see profits being earned and gear up to export steel to the United States to earn some of these profits. In effect, the foreign steel firms are entering the U.S. market. The domestic firms then appeal to Congress and/or the President to keep the foreign firms out (to block their entry). Tariffs or quotas may be put into effect. These tariffs or quotas serve as artificial barriers to entry for foreign firms by raising the price of foreign goods or prohibiting their sale in the United States.

Next, consider the taxicab industry. You probably consider this to be a competitive industry since in any large city there are cabs from many companies on the street every day. But, if you decide to start a cab business, you might be in for some trouble. Suppose you already own a car, so the entry costs are relatively small. All you need to do is to mark your car so that it can be recognized as a cab, and perhaps install a meter. However, you will need a permit, which in some cities will be very difficult and expensive to obtain. If you operate as a "gypsy," an underground cab that avoids city regulations, you will make the existing cab owners very unhappy. In many cities, cabs are a monopoly enterprise, and it is government that protects the monopoly.

In these examples, government supplied the artificial barriers to entry. Federal, state, and local governments all restrict entry and thereby ensure protected market positions. It should not be too surprising that many instances of corruption in government have centered on the granting of monopoly privileges. A government official or agency protects a monopoly by keeping competitors out. The monopolist is often willing to pay for this with campaign contributions, favors, or outright bribes, such as direct cash payments, free vacations, or jobs for relatives.

If monopoly power persists for a long period of time, there is very likely to be some explicit or implicit government role in creating barriers to entry. Monopoly profits are a very powerful and attractive force, and new entry is very difficult for the monopolist alone to block. As a result, monopolies usually try to enlist governmental support of one kind or another.

GLOBAL OUTLOOK: OF COMPANIES AND COUNTRIES

Many multinational corporations are very large relative to the countries in which they operate. It is conceivable that some companies may have worldwide net sales that are larger than the GDP of the country in which they are operating. Table B1 ranks countries by GDP and companies by gross sales. As you can see, General Motors is larger than Finland and Denmark. In the top 100, there are 47 companies and 53 countries. This ranking is based on 1991 data and there may now be fewer countries and more companies on the list. It is likely that Yugoslavia has dropped and that some of the companies have grown faster than some of the countries. These multinationals have a large amount of monopoly power in small host countries.

The political and economic dilemmas faced by multinational corporations and host governments have even come to the United States. For decades, U.S. policy makers were confronted with only one side of the problem, that of U.S. corporations in foreign countries. Recently, however, the United States has become a host country for foreign, primarily Japanese and European, investment.

Small, less developed countries face a political dilemma in bargaining with large multinational companies. At the onset, such a country may have very little bargaining power with the multinational because the company can "shop around" for hospitable governments. If the country's policy makers want to pursue economic growth, they may have to agree initially to the multinational's terms. As time passes and the company invests more fixed capital assets in the country, the host government can increase taxes and capture more of the monopoly profits. However, a delicate balance must be maintained. Taxes and government controls diminish the profitability of investment and future investment for the multinational. Other multinationals may be driven away by changes in a host country's business climate.

Host country controls on multinationals can take several forms. Some countries impose foreign exchange regulations that require the foreign firm to convert earnings at exchange rates that are different from market exchange rates. Another control is a rule requiring the foreign firms to use their earnings to buy local products and export them to countries with freely exchangeable currencies. Some countries (such as India) require foreign companies to divest their assets over time by selling them to native investors. This policy is a form of expropriation with compensation. Still other countries force foreign firms to purchase a certain percent of the components in a manufacturing process from domestic sources. Finally, although it may be illegal (or if not illegal, at least hushed), politicians in some countries may require bribes as a condition for doing business. This practice is not uncommon in countries with dictators.

In a small country, multinational companies not only exert monopoly power but also must confront monopoly power exerted by the host government. In this situation, with one monopoly confronting another, it is not always clear who wins.

MONOPOLY POWER AND PRICE DISCRIMINATION

Price discrimination
The practice of charging different prices to different consumers or to a single consumer for different quantities purchased.

In analyzing monopoly behavior, we have assumed that the monopolist charges the same price to all consumers and the same price for all units sold to a specific consumer. If, on the other hand, the monopolist is able to charge different consumers different prices or charge a given consumer different prices depending on the quantity purchased, the monopolist is practicing **price discrimination**. Price discrimination is a way to expand monopoly profits by extracting consumer surplus from consumers.

To see how price discrimination works, you need to recall the discussion of consumer surplus in the chapter on demand and consumer choice. Consumer surplus is the extra utility gained by consumers who end up paying less for an item than they would be willing to pay for it. Consumers purchase an item until the marginal utility of the last dollar spent on the item is equal to the marginal utility of spending the dollar on any other good or of holding the dollar. The

TABLE B1 THE TOP 100 ECONOMIES

Rankings based on countries' GDP and companies' gross sales

1. United States	35. Toyota Motor Co.	68. Toshiba Corp.
2. Japan	36. Hong Kong	69. Chevron Corp.
3. Germany	37. Yugoslavia	70. Nestle SA
4. France	38. General Electric Co.	71. United Arab Emirates
5. Italy	39. Greece	72. Nigeria
6. United Kingdom	40. Algeria	73. Singapore
7. Canada	41. Mobil Corp.	74. Renault
8. China	42. Hitachi Ltd.	75. ENI
9. Brazil	43. British Petroleum Co.	76. Hungary
10. Spain	44. IRI	77. Philips NV
11. India	45. Venezuela	78. Honda Motor Co.
12. Australia	46. Israel	79. BASF AG
13. Netherlands	47. Portugal	80. NEC Corp.
14. Switzerland	48. Matsushita Electric	81. Hoechst AG
15. Korea	49. Philippines	82. Amoco Corp.
16. Sweden	50. Daimler-Benz AG	83. Peugeot SA
17. Mexico	51. Pakistan	84. B.A.T. Industries
18. Belgium	52. New Zealand	85. ELF Aquitaine
19. Austria	53. Philip Morris Co.	86. Bayer AG
20. General Motors Corp.	54. Columbia	87. Peru
21. Finland	55. Malaysia	88. Chile
22. Denmark	56. Fiat S.P.A.	89. CGE
23. Ford Motor Co.	57. Chrysler Corp.	90. Morocco
24. Norway	58. Nissan Motor Co.	91. Imperial Chemical
25. Saudi Arabia	59. Unilever N.V.	92. Procter & Gamble Co.
26. Indonesia	60. DuPont	93. Mitsubishi Electric Co.
27. Exxon Corp.	61. Samsung Group	94. Asea Brown Boveri AB
28. South Africa	62. Volkswagen AG	95. Bulgaria
29. Royal Dutch/Shell Group	63. Kuwait	96. Nippon Steel Co.
30. Turkey	64. Siemens AG	97. Boeing Company
31. Argentina	65. Egypt	98. Puerto Rico
32. Poland	66. Texaco Inc.	99. Occidental Petroleum
33. Thailand	67. Ireland	100. Daewoo Corp.
34. IBM Corp.		

Source: *Across The Board* (December 1991): 18–19.

marginal utility of previously purchased units was greater than the price paid for those units because they were all purchased at the price of the last unit. The consumer would have been willing to pay higher prices for those units. Figure 4 illustrates this concept. At price P_1 in Figure 4, the consumer was receiving a "bonus" in terms of utility. This extra utility is called consumer surplus, represented by the shaded area in Figure 4.

A monopoly producer might be able to deal separately with consumers depending on the number of units purchased. In terms of Figure 5, the monopolist could say, "You may buy up to Q_1 units for P_1, from Q_1 to Q_2 units for P_2, from Q_2 to Q_3 units for P_3, and from Q_3 to Q_4 units for P_4." By doing this, the

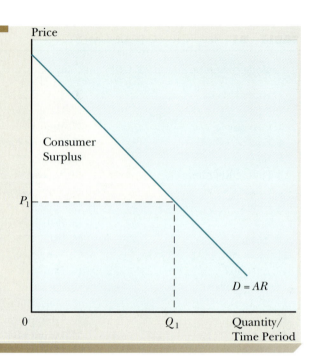

FIGURE 4
CONSUMER SURPLUS
Consumer surplus is the difference between the total utility received from the purchase of a product and the total revenue generated by the product. It exists because the marginal utility of each previous unit purchased was greater than price P_1.

monopolist extracts most of the consumer surplus and converts it into revenue for the firm. Compare the shaded areas in Figure 5 to the shaded area in Figure 4. Both represent consumer surplus. In Figure 5, by charging different prices for different amounts of consumption, the monopolist has expropriated much of the consumer surplus. It is theoretically possible for the monopolist to capture all of the consumer surplus by charging a different price for each unit.

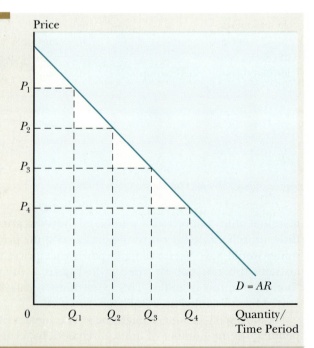

FIGURE 5
A PRICE-DISCRIMINATING MONOPOLIST
A price-discriminating monopolist can capture most of the consumer surplus by charging different prices for different amounts of consumption.

The second type of price discrimination occurs when a monopolist can separate markets and charge different prices to different groups of consumers. If the monopolist can separate the markets and prevent resale, it can price discriminate by adjusting output for the different demand elasticities in the two markets.

PRICE DISCRIMINATION IN PRACTICE

In practice, the first type of price discrimination is common. It requires that the seller have the power to separate sales on a unit-by-unit basis. This form of price discrimination is what is being practiced when multiples of a product can be purchased for a total that is less than the per-unit price times the number purchased. "Artichokes 40¢, two for 65¢" and "Coffee 50¢ a cup, refills a quarter" are examples of this type of price discrimination.

The second type of price discrimination requires that the seller be able to separate markets according to different elasticities of demand. Bookstores offer lower prices to professors than to students. Airlines charge lower fares to students and vacationers than to business people. University athletic departments offer lower-priced tickets to sports events to students and faculty. Medical doctors charge different patients different fees for the same service. Senior citizens get discounts on all kinds of items, from prescriptions to theater tickets. In each of these cases, the market with the greater elasticity gets lower prices. Let's see why.

Consider plane tickets. If you fly to Europe and stay for more than fourteen days, the fare is cheaper than if you stay for less than fourteen days. If you stay a month or longer, flights are even cheaper. Why? Which class of consumers of air transportation have the most inelastic demand? Business travelers, of course, who tend to travel on tight schedules and have bosses who don't want them sightseeing in France for fourteen days! With airline deregulation, major carriers have developed sophisticated techniques to set and change fares. Business magazines have reported that airline companies have had hundreds of traffic analysts working multiple shifts seven days a week. Their job was to juggle fares to match the bargain offerings of low-cost rivals while protecting their full-fare business.

It should be clear that two conditions are necessary in order to practice price discrimination. First, it must be possible to separate consumers into groups that have different demand elasticities. These groups need to be economically identifiable. If it costs too much to identify the groups, discrimination might not pay. When economists talk about price discrimination, they're not talking about discriminating on the basis of race, sex, or national origin, unless different races, sexes, or nationalities have different demand elasticities for certain products. Many times, age is used to identify groups with different demand elasticities. Senior citizens and students have more elastic demand curves because they typically have a tighter budget and more time to shop around than middle-aged people do. In the case of airfares, the classes of consumers are separated by length of stay. Business people seldom want to stay at a destination for more than a few days.

Time-of-day price discrimination includes matinee performances of cultural events and movies, bowling alley use, and lunch and dinner menus. In these cases, demand is more inelastic at night because some consumers are limited to night consumption. Magazine publishers charge higher prices for magazines purchased at newsstands than for subscriptions. Sometimes subscription prices are only a fraction of the newsstand prices. Newsstand demand is more inelastic because it is a spur-of-the-moment, unplanned purchase. Book publishers charge much higher prices for hardcover novels than for softcover versions of the same novel. They separate the markets by publishing the softcover version after the hardcover demand has been satiated. Some colleges charge in-state and out-of-state tuition because it is very easy to separate these two markets. Has your car ever broken down when you were out of town? Your demand is very inelastic in such a situation. You have little information about services available, and you are easy to identify as a one-time customer (you may have an out-of-state license plate). What do you think happens? You're right! You pay much more than a local person with car trouble would pay.

The second major requirement for price discrimination is that the monopolist *must* be able to prevent the resale of goods or the movement of customers between markets. Consider charging different prices to different classes of customers for tickets for a college football game. It only works if the customers paying the lower price are prohibited from reselling their tickets. If not, the college is no longer a monopolist in the sale of the higher-priced tickets. Is it any wonder that the athletic department requires you to show your picture I.D. card *and* your ticket at the gate? The higher-priced ticket holders are only required to present their tickets. Price discrimination works well where resale is very difficult. Services are good candidates for price discrimination because it is very difficult to resell a service. Medical doctors are very successful in practicing price discrimination because they have easily recognizable submarkets with different elasticities (by income and insurance category) *and* because resale is almost always ruled out.

The seller often justifies price discrimination as helping a group. For example, doctors might claim they practice price discrimination (charging less to some groups) in order to "help" the poor. Students or senior citizens might be charged less "to help them out." In reality, price discrimination is almost always practiced because it increases profit.

GAINERS AND LOSERS FROM PRICE DISCRIMINATION

Price discrimination does have a positive side effect. It will usually cause output under monopoly to increase. Earlier in this chapter, you learned that one of the disadvantages of monopoly is that it restricts output. If a monopoly can, however, sell output one unit at a time, output will be pushed to the point where price equals marginal cost. This is common sense because the monopolist only restricts output in order to keep price from falling on all units. If price falls only on the additions to output (not other units), then price equals marginal revenue, and output will be increased to the point where price equals marginal cost. This is the same conclusion as for perfect competition. The difference, of course, is that more of the benefit accrues to the monopolist. Price discrimination converts consumer surplus into monopoly profits, making monopolists wealthier and consumers worse off than if price discrimination did not exist.

Many people believe price discrimination is unfair because people pay different prices for the very same product. Why should an airplane ticket be cheaper because someone is a tourist rather than a business traveler? Why should professors get their books and pens for lower prices than students? Why should students pay less for a football ticket than nonstudents?

Interestingly, it is sometimes the group that benefits from price discrimination that complains. Price discrimination is common in international trade because the separation of national markets is often easy to maintain. Tariffs and transportation costs can help prevent resale. When firms in a country sell in a foreign market at a lower price than they do at home, they are engaging in price discrimination. Demand in the foreign country may be more elastic than domestic demand because there is more competition, and, therefore, more good substitutes are available. The foreign monopolist sells to foreigners at a lower price than at home. The U.S. Treasury calls this form of price discrimination **dumping**. Dumping occurs, for example, when the Japanese sell televisions in the United States at a lower price than they sell the same sets at home.

The odd thing is that dumping has a bad reputation. When the Japanese dump televisions in the United States, the U.S. government takes action against Japan. This is curious because Japanese firms are giving U.S. consumers a better deal than Japanese consumers. Complaining about being offered a lower price doesn't seem to make sense. Seen from the producer's angle, however, dumping is worth complaining about. You can understand why domestic manufacturers don't particularly approve of foreign competitors selling in this country more cheaply than in their own home market.

Dumping
The practice of selling in foreign markets at lower prices than in domestic markets (a form of price discrimination).

PRICE DISCRIMINATION AND MONOPOLY

We developed the concept of price discrimination in connection with the study of monopoly. Price discrimination is not limited to monopolies, however. It will never occur in perfect competition but could occur in monopolistic competition and oligopoly, which we will study in the next chapter. However, since the opportunity to use price discrimination is greater if consumers have few good substitutes, it is easiest to price discriminate under monopolistic conditions.

IS MONOPOLY BAD?

Any entrepreneur would prefer to sell in a monopoly rather than a perfectly competitive industry, because economic profit tends to zero in the perfectly competitive market. A firm that can create a successful monopoly will be rewarded with continuing profits. Monopoly is obviously good for the monopolist, but monopoly can be bad for society.

HOW MONOPOLY COMPARES TO PERFECT COMPETITION

To see what's so bad about monopoly, look at Figure 6. First, assume that Figure 6 represents a perfectly competitive industry. The market demand curve ($D = AR$) is that faced by the numerous sellers, and the marginal cost (MC) curve is the summation of all the individual firms' marginal cost curves. The competitive price and output are P_c and Q_c. Now suppose the industry is monopolized by one firm that has bought up all the competitive firms but still has the same cost curves. The monopoly firm, then, will face the same cost conditions that the ag-

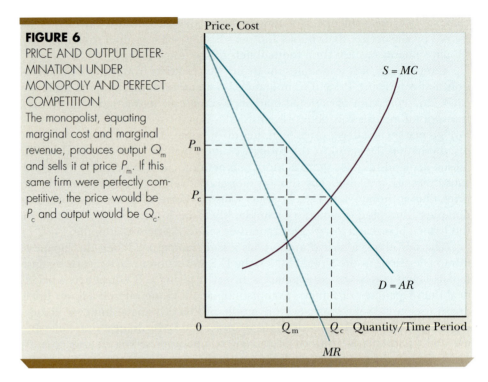

FIGURE 6
PRICE AND OUTPUT DETERMINATION UNDER MONOPOLY AND PERFECT COMPETITION
The monopolist, equating marginal cost and marginal revenue, produces output Q_m and sells it at price P_m. If this same firm were perfectly competitive, the price would be P_c and output would be Q_c.

gregate of competitive firms faced. The *market* supply curve becomes the monopolist's marginal cost curve because it is the summation of the purchased firms' marginal cost curves. The monopoly firm also faces the *market* demand curve and its corresponding marginal revenue curve. The monopoly firm will produce at Q_m and P_m. In this case, it is a very simple matter to contrast monopoly with perfect competition. The monopolist produces a smaller output ($Q_m < Q_c$) and charges a higher price ($P_m > P_c$) than the perfectly competitive firms did. This is possible because entry into the industry is blocked. Since new firms cannot enter, consumers are not getting the optimal amount of the good produced by the monopolist. Monopolies restrict output. This is the principal economic argument against monopoly.

The monopolistic output and price, then, represent misallocation of resources if the monopoly has the same cost conditions as the aggregate of the competitive firms. Note that the misallocation under monopoly could be even worse if, in buying up the individual firms, the monopoly introduced some inefficiencies of large-scale management. Such inefficiencies would cause an upward shift of the cost curves in Figure 6.

The misallocation of resources in a monopoly is illustrated in Figure 7. The monopoly is in equilibrium producing x_1 units at a price of P_1. The monopolist's profit, which is total revenue minus total cost, is represented by rectangle CP_1AB. Let's examine closely what is going on at this equilibrium. First, price P_1 is greater than average cost (which is x_1B per unit). That is, $P_1 > AC$, and economic profits are being earned. Second, price is greater than marginal cost ($P_1 > MC$), which means the value consumers place on the last unit (P_1) exceeds the opportunity cost of producing it (MC). From the society's (and the consumer's) point of view, more should be produced. The monopolist prevents output from increasing by restricting entry. Third, average cost at output x_1 is greater than

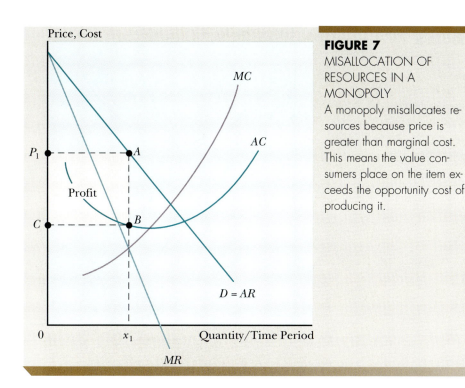

FIGURE 7
MISALLOCATION OF RESOURCES IN A MONOPOLY
A monopoly misallocates resources because price is greater than marginal cost. This means the value consumers place on the item exceeds the opportunity cost of producing it.

marginal cost at x_1. That is, $AC > MC$. This means that the technologically most efficient level of output is not being produced, because the monopolist is restricting output. You can easily see, therefore, what economists mean when they say that monopoly misallocates resources.

MONOPOLY PROFITS AND LOSSES

There is a common misconception that a monopoly situation guarantees profits. A monopoly is not a license to make profits. If the U.S. government granted you an absolute monopoly in the sale and manufacture of conestoga wagons, you would probably lose money. High costs or insufficient demand may cause a monopolist to lose money.

Figure 8 shows a monopoly suffering a loss. The monopoly is producing x_1 units and charging the loss-minimizing price, P_1. Average costs of producing are x_1A per unit. As a result, the monopolist is incurring losses equal to rectangle P_1CAB. Since the demand (or average revenue) curve is below the average cost curve, there is no way to avoid losses. Will the monopolist continue to produce? If price (or average revenue) is above average variable costs, as is the case in Figure 8, the monopolist will be better off in the short run if it continues producing. In the long run, if demand does not increase, the monopoly will go out of business. The presence of losses indicates that the productive resources are not earning their opportunity cost. Those inputs will move to more productive uses.

A monopolist can also earn only normal profits. Figure 9 illustrates this case. The monopoly is producing x_1 units and charges price P_1. Total revenue is equal to rectangle $0P_1Ax_1$. In this instance, the monopoly is earning its opportunity cost. There will be no incentive for other firms to try to enter this industry or for

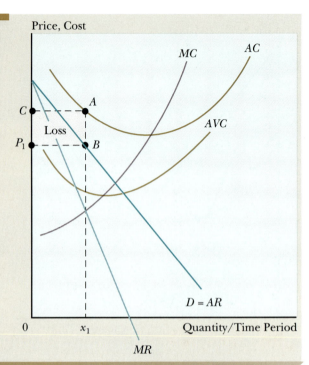

FIGURE 8

A MONOPOLY SUFFERING LOSSES

The monopolist might suffer losses in the short run. If average cost is greater than average revenue, the monopolist is suffering a loss.

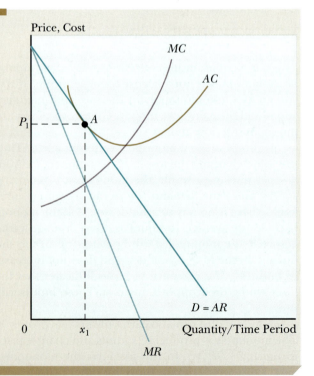

FIGURE 9

A MONOPOLY EARNING A NORMAL PROFIT

It is possible that a monopoly might earn only a normal profit. In this case, there is no incentive for other firms to enter the industry and no need for barriers to entry.

this firm to leave the industry. Price is equal to average cost, which means that producers are not earning economic profits. However, price is still greater than marginal cost, indicating that more units should be produced.

You can see, then, that monopolies don't always make profits. In fact, they might often incur losses and go out of business. Also, monopolists do not charge the highest price possible. Remember the mineral spring example? Monopolists charge the profit-maximizing price, and this price will depend on the demand conditions and costs in the industry.

KEY IDEAS

COMPARISON OF MONOPOLY AND PERFECT COMPETITION

MONOPOLY	PERFECT COMPETITION
One firm	Many firms
Barriers to entry	Free entry
$P > AC$, so economic profits exist	$P = AC$, only normal profit earned
$MC > AC$, the technologically most efficient level of production.	$MC = AC$, producing at least-cost combination

MONOPOLY IN THE LONG RUN

The monopolist, unlike the perfectly competitive firm, can continue to earn economic profits in the long run. As long as the barriers to entry remain, economic profits can be maintained. Sustaining these barriers in the long run is very difficult, however, because the economic profits will attract new firms, substitute products, and new processes. In principle, then, even with government help, the power of any single monopoly is likely to decline in the very long run.

REAL-WORLD MONOPOLIES

We have pointed out that there are no examples of true monopoly in the real world. A complete monopoly cannot exist, because all products or services have some substitutes with which they compete. There are, however, firms with some monopoly power. The model of monopoly is useful in explaining the behavior of these firms. Public utilities are allowed to operate as monopolies because they are considered natural monopolies. They are then regulated to reduce the ill effects of the monopoly power. Monopolies that are set up by some nations to engage in international trade are also monopolistic.

Local monopolies are another form of real-world monopoly. A **local monopoly** is a firm that has monopoly power in a geographic region. Even though close substitutes for the firm's product exist, the distance to other sources of supply creates a virtual monopoly. If you grew up in a small, remote town, there may have been only one movie theater or perhaps only one grocery store. If there is only one bookstore on or near your campus, it is a local monopoly. A firm in such a situation is a local monopoly because the substitutes are costly in the sense that you must travel to reach them. Economists use the model of monopoly to examine the effects of monopoly power in such real-world situations.

Local monopoly
A firm that has monopoly power in a geographic region because of the large distance from other suppliers of its product (or substitutes).

THE COSTS OF MONOPOLY

We have made the point that a monopoly misallocates resources by contriving shortages—producing less than the competitive output to create monopoly profits. There are, however, other costs associated with monopoly. Figure 10 depicts a monopoly firm with constant marginal costs and, thus, constant average costs. Constant marginal costs and average costs are assumed for simplicity.

The monopolist will produce output level Q_m and set price at P_m. A perfectly competitive structure would have produced an output of Q_c at price P_c. As a result of restricting output, the monopolist earns a monopoly profit equal to the shaded area in Figure 10. This shaded area represents a transfer from consumers (in terms of lost consumer surplus) to the monopolist (in terms of monopoly profit). This transfer, however, is not the only cost the monopoly creates.

DEADWEIGHT LOSS

The crosshatched triangle in Figure 10 represents lost consumer surplus that was not converted into monopoly profits. This lost consumer surplus is received by no one. Consumers have lost it because the monopoly has restricted output, but it has not been received by anyone in the economy. The lost consumer surplus is referred to as the deadweight loss of monopoly. The **deadweight loss** is the lost consumer surplus due to monopolistic restriction of output. It is a deadweight loss because nothing is received in exchange for the loss. It is equivalent to throwing a valuable resource away.

Deadweight loss
The lost consumer surplus due to monopolistic restriction of output.

Many years ago, Arnold C. Harberger attempted to measure this deadweight loss of monopoly.[1] He estimated that deadweight loss (he referred to it as the

---

[1]. See A. C. Harberger, "The Welfare Loss from Monopoly," *American Economic Review* (May 1954): 77–87. For a more recent study confirming Harberger's result and summarizing many other studies, see Micha Gisser, "Price Leadership and Welfare Losses in U.S. Manufacturing," *American Economic Review* (September 1986): 756–767.

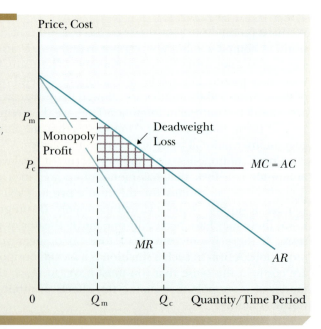

FIGURE 10
THE DEADWEIGHT LOSS OF MONOPOLY
A monopoly converts some consumer surplus to monopoly profit. The crosshatched area, however, represents consumer surplus that is lost. It is the deadweight loss associated with monopoly.

welfare loss from monopoly) was quite small. In 1954, for example, only about 0.1 percent of GDP was lost due to the deadweight loss effect. This small fraction of GDP amounted to about $1.50 for each U.S. citizen in 1954. Since Harberger's study, other economists have attempted to measure deadweight loss. Most of their estimates are also small and tend to congregate in the range of 1 percent of GDP. This is still a surprisingly low figure, although it is ten times larger than Harberger's original estimate. Harberger's work implies that, if the transfer from consumers to monopolists (the captured consumer surplus) is ignored, monopoly has little effect on welfare.

MONOPOLY RENT SEEKING

Gordon Tullock believes that deadweight loss estimates are likely to underestimate the costs of monopoly. Tullock argues that since the monopoly profits (the captured consumer surplus) are potentially huge, monopolists spend a great deal of time, effort, and resources in establishing a monopoly.[2] He developed his argument by drawing an analogy to theft. If thieves steal $100 million, they transfer that $100 million from victims to themselves. This transfer is just like the transfer of consumer surplus. But thieves invest time, effort, and resources in guns and getaway cars. In addition, victims invest money in protecting themselves from theft. Both of these costs are wasted from the viewpoint of society as a whole. Tullock argues that the same holds true for monopoly. Monopolists "waste" resources (from a societal viewpoint) in seeking to establish a monopoly. Society also expends resources trying to break up and prevent monopolies. The efforts and resources expended by those attempting to establish monopolies to earn monopoly profits have become known as **monopoly rent seeking**. This is a cost of monopoly because these resources are no longer available to produce goods and services. We will discuss monopoly rent seeking in greater detail in a later chapter.

Monopoly rent seeking The efforts and resources expended by those attempting to establish monopolies to earn monopoly profits.

MANAGERIAL INEFFICIENCY

Still another cost of monopoly has been identified by Harvey Leibenstein.[3] Leibenstein argues that competitive firms are forced to be efficient by the market, but this does not hold true for monopolies. Since the monopolist is not punished by the market for slack management, it will tend to have more managerial "looseness" than a competitive firm. This looseness will manifest itself in corporate jets, limousines, expense accounts, and golden parachutes. Leibenstein coined the term *x*-**inefficiency** to describe the inefficiency associated with the "slack" management of monopoly firms. The monopolist escapes the market discipline and is therefore less conscious of management efficiencies. Leibenstein estimated this cost to be as high as 2 percent of GDP.

***x*-inefficiency** The inefficiency associated with the "slack" management of monopoly firms because of the lack of market discipline.

WHO RUNS THE FIRM? ALTERNATIVES TO PROFIT MAXIMIZATION

We have consistently assumed that firms are profit maximizers. This assumption makes it possible to predict how a firm will adjust to changes in demand in the

---

2. G. Tullock, "The Welfare Costs of Tariffs, Monopolies and Theft," *Western Economic Journal* (June 1967): 224–232.
3. H. Leibenstein, "Allocative Efficiency vs. *x*-Inefficiency," *American Economic Review* (June 1966): 392–415.

Separation of ownership and control
The idea that large firms are run (controlled) by hired managers, not the owners, and the managers might have different goals than the owners.

market structure of perfect competition. What happens in the realm of giant firms run by professional managers? Corporations account for about 85 percent of the annual business sales in the United States. Corporations are run by hired managers, not owners. Managers might operate by some principle other than profit maximization. This idea is sometimes referred to as the **separation of ownership and control**, which simply means that managers who control corporations may behave differently than owner-managers would. Different behavior will occur only if the managers have different goals *and* if owners can't control managers. It has been argued that separation is part of the reason behind some of the takeovers in the 1980s. Leveraged buyouts occurred, according to this argument, because hired managers were not running their firms as profitably as owner-managers would have.

The hypothesis that managers' behavior deviates from profit maximization is based on organizational theory. (You may have studied that theory in a course on social psychology or management.) The hypothesis assumes that managers will follow standard procedures even if these procedures result in lower profits. Managers of big business firms are seen as bureaucrats who make conservative decisions to avoid mistakes and to minimize liability, like managers in the military, the federal bureaucracy, or any large organization. Those who argue that managers do not maximize profits offer several alternatives to that standard assumption. Let's look briefly at some of these.

Satisficing hypothesis
The argument that managers do not seek to maximize profits but rather seek target levels of output and profits that are satisfactory to the ownership interests.

The **satisficing hypothesis** argues that the management of a firm does not seek maximum profits but rather looks for certain target levels of output and profits that are satisfactory to the ownership interests. Owners' goals might include size or market share, altruism, or philanthropy. Unfortunately, in order to test this hypothesis and determine its validity, it would be necessary to specify a firm's target. Otherwise, any result that is found would be consistent with satisficing behavior. The proponents of the satisficing hypothesis have not as yet found a way to specify targets. As a result, the hypothesis cannot be proved or disproved.

Another goal that might be substituted in place of profit maximization is religious or racial discrimination. Firms with monopoly power and little threat of competition may sacrifice some of their profits in order to sell to, or hire, a particular group of people. A very interesting test of this hypothesis was conducted several years ago by Armen Alchian and Reuben Kessel.[4] They classified Jewish and non-Jewish graduates of the Harvard Business School according to the market structures of the industries in which they were employed. In the years examined, 36 percent of the school's graduates were Jewish. Alchian and Kessel discovered that 18 percent of Harvard MBAs employed in monopolized industries were Jewish, compared with 41 percent employed in competitive industries. This evidence is consistent with the hypothesis that monopoly power makes discrimination against minorities easier (less costly) and points to yet another cost of monopoly power.

Thomas DiLorenzo disagrees with the satisficing hypothesis and argues that rational profit-maximizing behavior of managers of private monopolies will not

---

4. A. Alchian and R. A. Kessel, "Competition, Monopoly, and the Pursuit of Money," in H. G. Lewis et al., *Aspects of Labor Economics* (Princeton NJ: Princeton University Press, 1962).
5. Thomas J. DiLorenzo, "Corporate Management, Property Rights, and the X-istence of *x*-Inefficiency," *Southern Economic Journal* (July 1981): 116–124.

be more lax than that of their counterparts in competitive firms.[5] He maintains that monopoly managers will try just as hard because they get to share in monopoly profits in the form of salary increases and added benefits.

Another hypothesis has been suggested by William Baumol. Baumol argues that given some level of profits, managers' primary goal is to increase the sales of the firm. In essence, Baumol is saying that managers are rewarded by stockholders, according to the relative size of the firm in the market, for increasing the firm's relative share of the market, say, from 15 to 20 percent. This hypothesis is called **constrained sales maximization**. The implication of this hypothesis is that monopoly might not be as bad as we concluded earlier. If sales, rather than profits, are the primary goal of a monopoly, the firm will charge lower prices and produce more output than a profit-maximizing monopolist. With lower prices and increased output, there will be less misallocation of resources than predicted with profit maximization.

A rejoinder to these competing hypotheses is the long-run profit maximization hypothesis. **Long-run profit maximization** says that even if managers seem to behave in accord with satisficing or constrained sales maximization, they do so only because it leads to higher profits in the long run. According to this hypothesis, if the firm maximizes sales, it is doing so because this will lead to higher profits in the long run. Also, if a firm demonstrates a concern for social responsibility or philanthropy, it may be doing so in the interest of long-run profits. The problem with the hypothesis of long-run profit maximization is that unless a distinct time period is specified, almost any behavior could be consistent with the hypothesis. There is no way to prove or refute this hypothesis.

Competing theories of monopoly behavior highlight our earlier discussion of what theory is and what it does. Theory abstracts from the real world by concentrating on the important aspects or effects of a phenomenon. If profit maximization is a valid assumption, it will yield reasonably accurate predictions about firms' behavior. Profit maximization is a cornerstone of many hypotheses that have been empirically tested and found to be valid. Alternative assumptions have yet to be rigorously tested.

Constrained sales maximization
The hypothesis that managers' primary goal is to increase the sales of the firm because they will be rewarded by stockholders for increasing the firm's relative share of the market.

Long-run profit maximization
The argument that even if managers seem to behave in accord with satisficing or constrained sales maximization, they only do so because it leads to higher profits in the long run.

FALLACIES AND FACTS ABOUT MONOPOLY

In this chapter, we have developed a model of monopoly. Although there is no such thing as a true monopoly in the real world, there are firms that have monopoly power. The model is useful in describing their behavior. Since there are so many misconceptions about monopoly, it is worthwhile to summarize a few fallacies and facts about monopolies.

FALLACY—MONOPOLIES CHARGE THE HIGHEST POSSIBLE PRICE

The public often believes that monopolies charge the highest possible price and "rip off" consumers. This view is often supported by the press and by consumer lobby groups. As you have seen in this chapter, however, monopolies produce the profit-maximizing output and then sell that output on the market at a price that is constrained by the market demand curve.

POLICY FOCUS: WHAT DO FIRMS MAXIMIZE?

Does corporate management differ greatly from the management of firms managed by a single owner? Until Herbert Simon began his research and writing, most economists would have said no. The assumption of profit maximization was the way business policy was set. Herbert Simon changed this notion and had a profound influence on the way economists view policy determination in corporate America.

Nobel Prize winner Herbert Simon was born in Milwaukee and educated at the University of Chicago. Simon has held teaching positions at the University of California, the Illinois Institute of Technology, and the University of Pittsburgh. He is presently at Carnegie-Mellon University. Simon has never held a teaching post in an economics department. Instead, he has held professorships in political science, administration, psychology, and information sciences. He is an economist in the broadest sense of the word, like the classical economists.

In awarding the 1978 Nobel Prize in Economics to Simon, the Royal Swedish Academy noted his work concerning the development of alternatives to profit maximization. The committee summarized his contribution in its official announcement:

> In his epoch-making book, Administrative Behavior (1947), and in a number of subsequent works, he (Simon) described the company as an adaptive system of physical, personal, and social components that are held together by a network of intercommunications and by the willingness of its members to cooperate and to strive towards a common goal. What is new in Simon's ideas is, most of all, that he rejects the assumption made in classic theory of the firm as an omnisciently rational, profit-maximizing entrepreneur.

Simon has had an impact on more academic disciplines than any other Nobel Prize winner in economics. His work in management science and public administration is credited with bringing scientific approaches to the study of management. Herbert Simon is perhaps the best example of an economic theorist who has made a major impact on business and public administration.

FALLACY—MONOPOLIES ALWAYS EARN (HIGH) PROFITS

A similar, but slightly different, fallacy is that monopolies always earn profits. You have seen in this chapter that some monopolies earn economic profits, some earn normal profits, and others suffer economic losses. To be sure, monopolists try to earn profits, but if demand changes, they might incur an economic loss. The key difference between monopoly and competition is that profits of a monopoly can persist because they don't lead to new entry. In cases where monopolies suffer losses, however, the resources will flow to other industries. In some cases, the government has tried to keep unprofitable monopolies from going out of business.

FALLACY—MONOPOLISTS DON'T HAVE TO WORRY ABOUT DEMAND

It is a commonly held belief that monopolists don't have to worry about demand. Having a monopoly on buggy whip production in 1996 and 1896 are quite different. Monopolists are constrained by the market demand for the good or service they produce. Their search for the price that maximizes their revenue is strictly tied to that demand curve. It might even be possible for the economist to increase demand by advertising the product. The decision to do so would depend on the cost of that advertising versus the revenue it could be expected to generate.

FACT—MONOPOLIES CHARGE A PRICE HIGHER THAN MARGINAL COST

You have seen in this chapter that a monopoly restricts output in order to earn economic profits. This restriction of output means that the price charged is greater than marginal cost. Compared to perfect competition, monopolies are less efficient in allocating resources to match consumer preferences.

FACT—MONOPOLISTS PRODUCE WHERE DEMAND IS ELASTIC

It is often mistakenly believed that a monopoly will produce where demand is inelastic. You have seen, though, that monopolies will always raise the price if demand is inelastic. Every monopoly will always be producing in an elastic portion of its demand curve.

FACT—MONOPOLIES DO NOT HAVE SUPPLY CURVES

As you have seen in this chapter, a monopoly is a price searcher. The monopoly establishes the profit-maximizing output and price is equal to average revenue. As a result, the concept of a unique supply curve is meaningless.

FACT—THE MONOPOLIST ULTIMATELY FACES COMPETITION

The model of monopoly assumes that the firm faces no competition because it defines a market structure consisting of a single firm producing a good with no close substitutes. In reality, however, the monopolist that earns an economic profit will be pursued by potential competitors, and the natural or artificial barriers to entry will be difficult to maintain. In a global economy, even if there are no domestic competitors, there is almost always a threat of competition from abroad.

As a closing note, it is appropriate to quote Alfred Marshall (1842–1924), the great neoclassical economist, on this subject:

> *It will in fact presently be seen that, though monopoly and free competition are really wide apart, yet in practice they shade into one another by imperceptible degrees: that there is an element of monopoly in nearly all competitive business: and that nearly all the monopolies, that are of any practical importance in the present age, hold much of their power by an uncertain tenure; so that they would lose it ere long, if they ignored the possibilities of competition, direct and indirect.*[6]

CONTESTABLE MARKETS

A number of economists have developed a new theory of industry structure called contestability theory.[7] **Contestable markets** are markets composed of

Contestable markets Markets composed of large firms that are nevertheless efficient because easily reversible entry into the market is possible.

---

6. Alfred Marshall, *Industry and Trade*, 4e. (London: Macmillan, 1923): 397.
7. William J. Baumol, John C. Panzar, and Robert D. Willig, *Contestable Markets and the Theory of Industry Structure* (New York: Harcourt, Brace, Jovanovich, 1982).

large firms that are nevertheless efficient because easily reversible entry into the market is possible. This theory attempts to bring more reality to microeconomics by analyzing large multiproduct firms. The theory is very complex because it relies heavily on mathematical models, but the insights produced are essentially quite simple.

The basic idea is that the ease of entry into their market constrains the behavior of large firms and makes them efficient. Using contestability theory, economists argue that it is no longer necessary to assume that there are large numbers of firms, each a price taker, acting as if their production had no impact on the market, in order to obtain efficiency. If easily reversible entry is possible, efficiency can be shown to coexist with large-scale production. In the past, this large-scale production might have been labeled monopoly.

Elizabeth Bailey, a proponent of contestability theory, was a commissioner at the Civil Aeronautics Board during the Carter administration. She suggested that contestability in the airline industry was enough to ensure efficiency because capital there consists mostly of aircraft, and capital costs can be recovered with little loss. In other words, entry into a particular air travel market is easy. She argued that even if a route were flown by only one airline, it is unlikely that monopoly prices would be charged because those prices would elicit entry by contesting airlines. According to Bailey, it is the recovery of capital costs rather than economies of scale that is important.

Critics of her theory argue that it says nothing new. They argue that the model is not much different from models that show that the possibility of entry limits the pricing behavior of monopolists. Regardless of who wins the debate, it is important to note that entry conditions are important in both theories. Monopoly cannot persist in open markets, and whether one refers to this threat as competition or contestability makes little difference for public policy.

Consider again... *The manufacturers' coupons that we brought to your attention at the start of this chapter are a vehicle for price discrimination. The manufacturer that prints those coupons in the paper or sends them in the mail is price discriminating because different groups of consumers have different elasticity of demand for these products. The producer reasons that the firm can separate these markets by the time cost of these different shoppers. Retired people and housewives have more time and will take the time to cut the coupons and organize them into a shopping strategy. Other shoppers, who have full-time jobs, don't have the time to spend on coupon activity and instead pay a higher price for the groceries.*

As we saw in this chapter, there are necessary conditions for this discrimination to succeed. The coupon issuer must have pricing power. Almost all coupons are for brand name products in concentrated markets—for example, soap and breakfast cereal. The second necessary condition is that resale must be prevented. This is done in the coupon market by limiting purchases and by the fact that there is no well-developed market for individuals to resell food. The practical reason is that most people do not resell items for a 25-cent profit.

SUMMARY

1. Monopoly is a market structure in which there is a single seller of a product with no close substitutes. The monopoly firm faces a negatively sloped demand curve and a marginal revenue curve that lies below that demand curve. The monopolist maximizes profits by producing the output level at which marginal revenue equals marginal cost. The price is the one on the demand curve at which exactly that amount of output can be sold. Since price is often greater than average cost for a monopoly, economic profits may exist.
2. A monopolist is sometimes able to erect barriers to entry that allow profits to persist in the long run. Such barriers are very difficult to maintain. As a result, monopolists often appeal to the government for help in maintaining entry barriers.
3. A monopoly can increase its revenues if it practices price discrimination. For price discrimination to be successful, customers must have different demand elasticities, and they must be separated and prohibited from reselling the product or service.
4. Monopolies produce a lower output at a higher price than do competitive industries. At equilibrium, the monopoly firm is producing at a level of output where price is not equal to marginal cost (and often not average cost).
5. Deadweight loss, rent seeking, and managerial inefficiency contribute to the cost of monopoly.
6. The satisficing hypothesis and the constrained sales maximization hypothesis are both derived from the idea of the separation of ownership and control. These hypotheses suggest that hired managers, as opposed to owner-managers, may attempt to meet satisfactory profit targets or to maximize sales rather than to maximize profits.
7. Monopolies charge the profit-maximizing price, they don't always earn profits, they worry about demand, they produce where demand is elastic, they charge a price higher than marginal cost, they do not have supply curves, and they ultimately face competition.
8. The concept of contestable markets is that if entry into an industry is easy, the firms will behave in a competitive fashion even if they look like monopoly firms. Critics argue that the idea is nothing new. However, the critical factor is the existance of barriers to entry. Monopoly cannot persist in open markets.

NEW TERMS

monopoly
monopoly power
price searcher
barriers to entry
price discrimination
dumping
local monopoly
deadweight loss
monopoly rent seeking
x-inefficiency
separation of ownership and control
satisficing hypothesis
constrained sales maximization
long-run profit maximization
contestable markets

QUESTIONS: REVIEW, APPLICATIONS, AND POLICY

REVIEW

1. Explain in your own words why marginal revenue is less than average revenue under conditions of monopoly.
2. Why will a monopolist never attempt to produce in the inelastic portion of its demand curve?
3. What is x-inefficiency?
4. How does a monopolist maximize profits?
5. In what ways is monopoly thought to be inefficient?

APPLICATIONS

6. The following table describes the demand curve faced by a monopoly firm. Complete the marginal revenue column.

PRICE	QUANTITY DEMANDED	MARGINAL REVENUE (MR)
$10	0	
9	1	
8	3	
7	4	
6	5	
5	6	
4	7	
3	8	

7. Assume that the cost data in the table you calculated for Question 7 in the chapter on costs and profits represent the cost data of the monopoly firm of Question 6. How much would the monopolist produce in the short run? Why? What price would the monopolist charge?

8. What is the monopolist's profit, again using the data from Question 7 in the chapter on costs and profits?
9. What will happen in the long run, based on the data used in the preceding two questions?

POLICY

10. Should government subsidize monopolies that are losing money to keep them in business?
11. Is some supermarkets' practice of giving trading stamps a form of price discrimination? If so, how does it work?
12. Should business firms be socially responsible? Respond to the argument that they should maximize profits and leave social responsibility to elected and appointed public officials.
13. List as many barriers to entry as you can. Which are the most effective?
14. Would a monopolist ever advertise? In what circumstances?
15. If you buy a round-trip airline ticket that includes a Saturday night stay at your destination city, the ticket price is often less than half that for the same round trip without a Saturday night stay. Is this price discrimination? Why is Saturday night the important night in this pricing scheme? Is this a "good" policy for the airline to pursue?

SUGGESTIONS FOR FURTHER READING

Browning, Edgar K., and Jacqueline M. Browning. *Microeconomic Theory and Applications*, 4e. Boston: Little, Brown, 1992. Chapters 11 and 12 present in-depth treatment of monopoly theory.

Bulow, Jeremy, and John Roberts. "The Simple Economics of Optimal Auctions." *Journal of Political Economy* (October 1989): 1060–1090. This article shows how the seller's problem in auctions is identical to the monopolist's problem of price discrimination.

Mansfield, Edwin. *Microeconomics*, 8e. New York: W. W. Norton, 1994. Chapter 10 of this intermediate micro book goes into greater detail on some of the topics covered here.

CHAPTER 25
MONOPOLISTIC COMPETITION AND OLIGOPOLY

Consider this... *What's in a brand name? Do you have a favorite soap, aspirin, breakfast food, cigarette, beer, or cola? When you get right down to it, a bar of soap is pretty much a bar of soap. An aspirin is pretty much an aspirin and a cola is pretty much a cola. Maybe including colas is taking it too far—to some people any cola is not the same as any other cola. Several years ago Coke introduced a new cola and some of its old cola customers revolted, forcing it to bring the old favorite back as Classic Coke. To these consumers any cola was not the same as any other.*

To the owner of a brand name, the important question is how much different is the product that has the brand identification. Is it a dime different? Would you pay ten cents more for a bar of the soap you use? Would you pay a dollar a bar more? How about ten dollars a bar more? Clearly the value of the brand disappears at some price. After you study this chapter you will understand these monopoly and competitive relationships in greater detail.

We have just seen that there are no perfect real-world examples of either perfect competition or monopoly. For many years, however, all real-world industries were analyzed in terms of these two models. In the 1930s, theories were developed that filled out the spectrum between monopoly and perfect competition. Market structures between the two extremes are called imperfect competition. Economists divide imperfect competition into monopolistic competition and oligopoly. We will study these two market structures in this chapter.

LEARNING OBJECTIVES
1. Describe the characteristics of monopolistic competition.
2. Explain why interdependence is unique to oligopoly.
3. Understand why government policy is often necessary to assure the success of a cartel.
4. Use game theory to understand oligopolistic behavior.
5. Describe how and why equilibrium price and output under monopolistic competition and oligopoly differ from that of perfect competition.

MONOPOLISTIC COMPETITION

The theory of monopolistic competition is usually associated with Edward Chamberlin and Joan Robinson. Chamberlin was a Harvard professor who published a book in 1933 entitled *The Theory of Monopolistic Competition.* Joan Robinson taught at Cambridge University in England and published *The Economics of Imperfect Competition,* also in 1933. (Robinson, who died in 1983, was only thirty years old when this classic was published.)

The model of **monopolistic competition** describes an industry composed of a large number of sellers. Each of these sellers offers a **differentiated product**, which is a good or service that has real or imagined characteristics that are different from those of other goods or services. This differentiation can take many forms. The salespeople may be nicer, the packaging prettier, the credit terms better, or the service faster. It could even be that a famous person is associated with the product, as Bill Cosby is with Jell-O gelatin and puddings. It is important to note that a product is differentiated if consumers perceive it as different. For example, chemists tell us that aspirin is aspirin, that there is no real difference among the various brands. Yet many consumers view the brands as different, so aspirin is a differentiated product.

In monopolistic competition, the industry consists of a large number of firms, each producing a differentiated product. A very important assumption is that entry into this industry is relatively easy. New firms can enter the industry and start selling products that are similar to those already being produced. In Chamberlin's original description of monopolistic competition, a market for a set of goods that were differentiated but had a large number of close substitutes was called a **product group**. Chamberlin characterized monopolistic competition as the large-group case where there was rivalry between many firms in a product group.

You may have recognized monopolistic competition as a familiar market structure, since retail firms often fit this model. Monopolistic competition is generally what comes to mind when people think of competition. Perfect competition, with its homogeneous products, simply does not fit the popular idea of competition in which firms are scrambling to make their products different.

SHORT-RUN EQUILIBRIUM

Short-run equilibrium of the monopolistically competitive firm is very similar to that of the monopolistic firm. Figure 1 shows the demand curve for a representative firm in monopolistic competition. When we depicted perfect competition, we started with the market and derived the representative firm's demand curve. In analyzing monopolistic competition, we begin with a representative firm, rather than with the market. With product differentiation, each firm faces a unique demand curve. The firm's demand curve in Figure 1 is negatively sloped, unlike the perfectly elastic demand curve faced by the perfectly competitive firm. The negative slope is a result of the differentiated nature of the firm's product. If the product's price is raised, the firm will not lose all its customers because some will continue to prefer this product to substitutes that are close but not perfect. Likewise, if the price is reduced, the firm will gain customers, but some customers will remain loyal to the products produced by other firms.

The relative elasticity of the demand curves is a measure of the degree of differentiation within the industry. If the products are only slightly differentiated, then they are close substitutes and each firm's demand curve will be very elastic. If the products are highly differentiated, the demand curve will be less elastic, indicating that the firm can more easily raise the price without losing many cus-

---

Monopolistic competition
The market structure in which a large number of firms sell differentiated products.

Differentiated product
A good or service that has real or imagined characteristics that are different from those of other goods or services.

Product group
A market for a set of goods that are differentiated but have a large number of close substitutes.

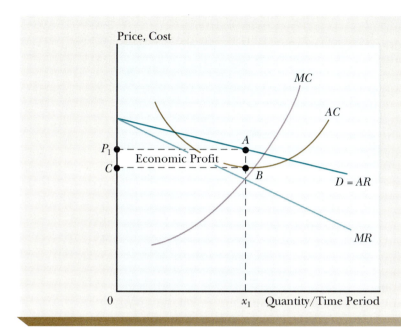

FIGURE 1

SHORT-RUN PROFITS IN MONOPOLISTIC COMPETITION

In the short run, an economic profit can exist for firms in monopolistic competition. Such profits will cause new firms to enter the industry.

tomers. Its customers don't change products because they don't view them as substitutes. Think of aspirin, for example. Some people are willing to pay more for Bayer than for Brand X because they think it is different. The makers of Bayer are able to charge a higher price without losing a large number of customers. Bayer will be limited in price flexibility by the amount of differentiation it is able to create. As price goes higher and higher, fewer people will be willing to pay for the differentiation. Some people may be willing to pay 10 cents more for Bayer than for a different brand, but if the price of Bayer is increased further, more and more people will shift to the other brands.

The demand curve in Figure 1 has a negative slope, indicating product differentiation. However, demand is very elastic, indicating that there are many good substitutes. Since the demand (average revenue) curve is negatively sloped, the marginal revenue curve will lie below it, for the same reasons it does in the case of monopoly. The firm will, of course, maximize profits at price P_1 and output x_1, where marginal revenue is equal to marginal cost. The firm in Figure 1 is earning an economic profit because average revenue, P_1, exceeds average cost, C. Total revenue is represented by rectangle $0P_1Ax_1$, and total cost is represented by rectangle $0CBx_1$. Economic profit is thus the area of the shaded rectangle CP_1AB.

This analysis is very similar to the one developed in the preceding chapter for monopoly in the short run. The most important difference is that the demand curve here is very flat. The key to whether it is more like a perfectly competitive firm or more like a monopoly depends on what happens in the long run in response to the economic profit.

LONG-RUN EQUILIBRIUM

What about long-run equilibrium in a monopolistically competitive industry? Figure 1 shows that a short-run equilibrium results in an economic profit.

FIGURE 2
LONG-RUN EQUILIBRIUM IN MONOPOLISTIC COMPETITION

Since entry into a monopolistically competitive industry is relatively easy, there can be no long-run economic profits. Firms will enter until all firms are earning only a normal profit.

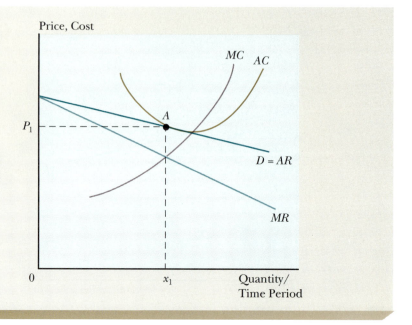

Robinson thought the analysis ended here, with the firms able to earn economic profits in the long run.

Suppose, instead, that new firms can respond to these economic profits. Entry into monopolistically competitive industries is assumed to be relatively easy. Thus, new firms will enter the industry in response to the economic profits. As firms enter the industry, the demand curve faced by any representative firm will shift to the left because the new firms will be attracting customers away from firms already in the industry. This shift of buyers is what happens, for example, when a new grocery store opens in an area. It draws some customers away from the existing stores. The existing firms' demand curves will continue to shift down and to the left as new firms enter, and new firms will enter as long as economic profits are to be made. Long-run equilibrium will occur when firms are earning zero economic profit (or normal profit). Such an equilibrium is depicted in Figure 2. Price is P_1 and output is x_1. Total revenue and total cost are represented by rectangle $0P_1Ax_1$. There are no economic profits being earned, and no additional firms will attempt to enter this industry.

Of course, too many firms might enter an industry due to a mistaken anticipation of economic profits. If this happens, firms will experience losses, and some firms will leave the industry as the long-run adjustment proceeds. Figure 3 shows a monopolistically competitive firm suffering a loss equal to rectangle P_1CBA. Firms would respond to such losses by leaving the industry. The demand curves faced by the remaining firms would shift up and to the right until the equilibrium shown in Figure 2 was restored. The long-run adjustment process under monopolistic competition produces an equilibrium with zero economic profits.

MONOPOLY AND COMPETITION

As you can see, the model of monopolistic competition borrows from the model of monopoly and the model of perfect competition. In the short run, the mo-

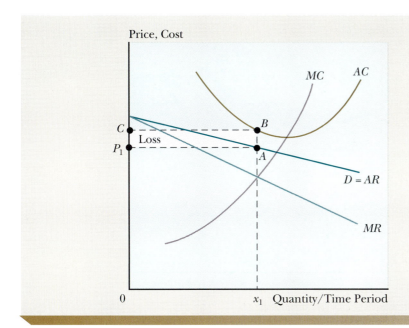

FIGURE 3
SHORT-RUN LOSSES IN MONOPOLISTIC COMPETITION
Short-run losses, indicated by the shaded area, will cause some firms to exit the industry. Firms will exit until the remaining firms are earning a normal profit, as in Figure 2.

nopolistically competitive firm is producing the profit-maximizing output and searching for the best price that can be charged for this output. In the long run, the economic profits disappear as new firms enter the industry. The demand curve of each firm then shifts to the left because market demand is shared by more firms. This result is similar to the long-run outcome in perfect competition. The market structure of monopolistic competition has some characteristics of monopoly and some of pure competition, which explains its name.

EXCESS CAPACITY

In long-run equilibrium, the monopolistically competitive firm chooses an output that does not fully utilize existing plant size. The unutilized part of the production facilities, called **excess capacity**, is depicted in Figure 4. The profit-maximizing output is x_1, where $MR = MC$. This level of output is not, however, the output that would have resulted under perfect competition. Under perfect competition, the firm would use the least-cost combination of inputs, where average cost is at a minimum. That output would be socially optimal because it represents maximum attainable allocative efficiency because $MC = P$. That output is represented by x_2 in Figure 4. In other words, in long-run equilibrium, the monopolistically competitive firm produces less than the quantity that would efficiently use its full productive capacity.

Is excess capacity a bad thing? To answer this question, it is necessary to consider what causes excess capacity. The firm is producing less than the socially ideal output because it maximizes profits by producing a lower output. This lower output results from the fact that the demand curve for the monopolistically competitive firm slopes downward. You can see this result by examining Figure 4. Begin with demand curve D_1. The monopolistically competitive firm is producing quantity x_1 at price P_1. Now make the demand curve more elastic by rotating it counterclockwise. As the demand curve becomes more and more elastic and finally perfectly elastic, at D_2 in Figure 4, the output will increase to-

Excess capacity
The unutilized part of existing production facilities by a monopolistically competitive firm.

FIGURE 4

EXCESS CAPACITY

Excess capacity results from the negative slope of the demand curve. As the demand curve becomes more elastic, the excess capacity diminishes. It disappears when the curve becomes perfectly elastic.

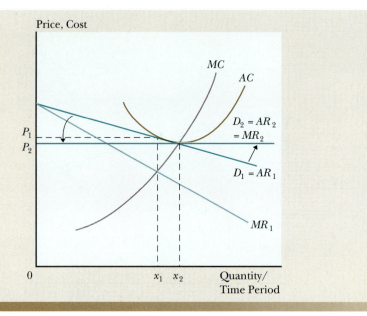

ward the socially efficient output x_2. Excess capacity is a result of the negative slope in the demand curve. This negative slope, you recall, is a result of the product differentiation. The excess capacity, therefore, results from product differentiation.

It can be argued that excess capacity is not necessarily a bad thing. Consumers may be willing to incur the extra cost in return for the perceived benefits of product differentiation. It would indeed be a very boring world without product differentiation. We might all be wearing khaki-colored shirts, for example.

The major problem with this argument lies in separating desired from undesired product differentiation. A consumer who is faced with a wide range of product choices but little price competition is not able to choose whether or not to pay extra to get the differentiated product. This problem isn't likely to be too important, however, when there are many firms, as in monopolistic competition. Consider aspirin. If the only products in the industry were Anacin, Bayer, Bufferin, and Excedrin, the consumer would probably not have a low-price choice, since these brands compete almost exclusively by advertising rather than by cutting prices. But the consumer actually does have a choice of lower-priced generic brands of aspirin. So in choosing Anacin over Brand X, the consumer voluntarily chooses product differentiation. In this case, product differentiation seems to be a good thing because the consumer making the choice is maximizing individual utility. If, on the other hand, there are no lower-priced products and the consumer must choose among products that compete only through advertising, then the consumer does not really have a choice about bearing the cost of the differentiation (unless, of course, he or she simply does without the product altogether).

PRODUCT DIFFERENTIATION AND ADVERTISING

The firm in monopolistic competition will try to differentiate its product in order to shift its demand curve to the right and to make demand relatively more inelastic by developing consumer loyalty. The firm will advertise as well as make changes in color, style, quality, and so on. Advertising can inform consumers about higher quality or develop brand loyalty. Either of these results creates product differentiation. Competing with rival firms through advertising, style changes, color changes, and techniques other than lowering price is referred to as **nonprice competition**.

If effective use of nonprice competition differentiates a firm's product enough that other firms' products do not seem to be good substitutes, the firm can earn an economic profit in the long run. Nonprice competition will often be gradual, so the firm can avoid a price war in which all firms will lose. A firm that is successful in such nonprice competition has in essence turned its share of the monopolistically competitive market into production with long-run economic profit. The profit of such a firm could exist in the long run and not be driven to zero by new entrants.

Fast-food preparation is usually a monopolistically competitive industry. In a small town, fast food could be a monopoly or an oligopoly. However, in metropolitan areas, there are large numbers of firms, and entry is relatively easy. If a firm is able to successfully differentiate its product so that consumers don't consider the products of other firms close substitutes, the firm will be able to earn a long-run economic profit because it can keep would-be competitors out of its segment of the market. For example, McDonald's can't keep firms out of the hamburger market, but it can keep firms out of the Big Mac market. If enough people believe there's nothing like a Big Mac, this persistent brand loyalty might allow McDonald's to maintain an economic profit in the long run. Remember—Robinson thought persistent profit would be the equilibrium state.

It is easy to determine how successful a firm is at product differentiation by examining the difference between its prices and its competitors' prices. The consumer may go to McDonald's if a Big Mac costs $0.15 more than the competition, but what if it cost $0.55 more or $1.15 more? There is some price at which the other products will become good substitutes. That price is a measure of the success of product differentiation. It may be that a Big Mac is worth more to the consumer because of higher quality or because McDonald's has a very successful advertising and public relations program. The point is that it doesn't matter what causes the differentiation. The economic impact is that McDonald's may be able to earn an economic profit in the long run.

Nonprice competition Competing with rival firms through advertising, style changes, color changes, and techniques other than lowering price.

KEY IDEAS

CHARACTERISTICS OF MONOPOLISTIC COMPETITION
- There are many sellers of similar but differentiated products.
- Economic profits can exist in the short run.
- Price is equal to average cost in the long run.
- Excess capacity exists in the long run (price is greater than marginal cost).
- Nonprice competition increases product differentiation.

RESOURCE ALLOCATION IN MONOPOLISTIC COMPETITION

The model of monopolistic competition has several implications for the allocation of resources. The resulting allocation will be different from the societal ideal achieved with perfect competition. First, even at the long-run equilibrium with zero economic profit, there will be excess capacity with monopolistic competition. This means that price will be greater than minimum average cost. Consumers are paying only the average cost of production, but this cost is higher than it would be with more competition.

Second, if costs are the same under perfect competition and monopolistic competition, prices will be higher with monopolistic competition because price is greater than marginal cost (or marginal revenue). Third, firms in monopolistic competition will provide a wider variety of styles, colors, qualities, and brands. These choices are, unfortunately, related to the product differentiation and excess capacity that cause average cost to be higher.

Fourth, in monopolistic competition, there will be advertising and other forms of nonprice competition. This outcome is not necessarily bad. To the extent that advertising adds to customer satisfaction and the product is voluntarily purchased, it can be a good thing. Some social critics consider any advertising that does more than convey information to be a bad thing. Economists would argue that one must compare the marginal benefits of advertising to the marginal costs of advertising to judge its worth.

OLIGOPOLY

The last of the four market structures is oligopoly. In 1934, German economist Heinrich von Stackelberg published a book entitled *Market Structure and Equilibrium*. It discussed the idea of firms' interdependence and formed the basis of the model of oligopoly. Oligopoly is the market structure in which a few firms compete imperfectly. The scarcity of sellers is the key to firms' behavior in oligopoly. In oligopoly, firms realize that their small number produces mutual interdependence. As a result, each firm will forecast or expect a certain response from its rivals to any price or output decision that it might make. Oligopoly is important because there are so many real-world examples of it. **Oligopoly** is the market structure in which there are only a few firms or a few firms dominate the market. Since there are few firms, the actions of the firms are interdependent.

In some people's minds, oligopoly and monopoly are essentially the same. This view was expressed by John Kenneth Galbraith. Galbraith argued, "So long as there are only a few massive firms in an industry, each must act with a view of the welfare of all."[1] This view, which is not widely held among economists, regards oligopoly as shared monopoly. **Shared monopoly** is the model of oligopoly that says that oligopolists coordinate decisions and share markets to act as a monopoly.

Most economists view oligopoly as more complex and more difficult to analyze than monopoly. There is no single model of oligopoly, as there is for the other three market structures. The difficulty stems from the interdependence that characterizes oligopoly. Because of the complexity of oligopoly, economic analysis of it often includes heavy doses of descriptive economics rather than formal models with graphs. We will follow this tradition and describe several types of oligopoly and forms of oligopolistic behavior.

Oligopoly
The market structure in which a few firms compete imperfectly and recognize their interdependence.

Shared monopoly
The model of oligopoly that says that oligopolists coordinate and share markets to act as a monopoly.

1. John K. Galbraith, *American Capitalism*, 2e. (Cambridge: Riverside Press, 1956), 83.

GLOBAL OUTLOOK: COMMODITY CARTELS IN THE REAL WORLD

The United States uses antitrust law to discourage cartel behavior, but many governments around the world actively encourage the formation of cartels. This is particularly the case with commodity cartels.

Commodity cartels have a long history of failure. In the 1950s, commodity agreements, which are essentially cartels for agricultural products and raw materials, existed for tin, coffee, sugar, and wheat. The countries forming these cartels were less developed countries of South America and Africa. The success of the Arab countries with OPEC in 1973 reenergized some of these cartels as many commodity-exporting countries tried to emulate OPEC. The result was a flurry of activity that produced the following official organizations:

- International Bauxite Association (IBA)
- International Coffee Organization (ICO)
- Intergovernmental Council of Copper-Exporting Countries (CIPEC)
- International Sugar Association (ISA)
- International Tin Council (ITC)
- Organization of Banana Exporting Countries (OBEC)

In addition, there were attempts in the late 1970s and early 1980s to organize cartels in iron ore, nickel, rubber, tungsten, molybdenum, cobalt, columbium, and tantalum. Very few of these cartels, however, enjoyed the success that OPEC had in the 1970s.

Several lessons can be learned from the experience of these commodity cartels and the success of OPEC. To be successful, a commodity cartel must:

1. have few members,
2. produce a product with few substitutes (have inelastic demand),
3. have buoyant world demand (have high income elasticity),
4. pursue a moderate pricing policy,
5. have at least tacit approval of consuming nations, and
6. have effective sanctions against chiselers.

Most cartels have great difficulty with the last three requirements and, as a result, break down rather quickly.

The effects of commodity cartels are often mixed up with economic development and world politics. Members tend to be less developed countries, and the consuming nations tend to be developed countries. The formation of a cartel is often justified in terms of a "fair" price that will redistribute wealth from rich to poor countries.

Cartels are anti-consumer. Although some of those consumers live in high-income countries, many are poor people in poor countries. The OPEC oil price hike caused more hardship in poor countries than it did in rich countries.

Oligopolies are sometimes categorized by the type of product they produce: homogeneous or differentiated. An oligopolistic industry that produces a homogeneous product is referred to as a **pure oligopoly** or a standardized oligopoly. The distinction is important because in pure oligopolies a single price is charged for the output of all the firms. An example of a pure oligopoly is the aluminum industry. As a manufacturer making aluminum furniture, you would be indifferent about which firm produced the bar of aluminum you purchase as an input.

In contrast, a **differentiated oligopoly** produces products that are different. The auto industry is a good example. In differentiated oligopolies, there are **price clusters**, which are groupings of prices for similar, but not homogeneous, products. The range of prices within a cluster will depend on the amount of product differentiation. The more differentiated the products, the greater the price divergence. Tight price clusters indicate very little product differentiation.

Pure oligopoly
An oligopolistic industry that produces a homogeneous product.

Differentiated oligopoly
An oligopoly that produces heterogeneous products that are very close substitutes.

Price clusters
Groupings of prices for similar, but not homogeneous, products.

COLLUSION AND OLIGOPOLIES

Perhaps the most useful classification tool for analyzing oligopolies is the system of definitions proposed by Fritz Machlup.[2] Machlup divided oligopolistic behavior into three classes based on the degree of communication, coordination, and collusion among the firms in the industry. **Communication** refers to the firms' ability to signal their intentions to one another. **Coordination** refers to the firms' ability to relate their production decisions to those of the other firms in the industry. **Collusion** refers to agreements between the firms in an industry to set a certain price or to share a market in certain ways. It should be obvious that the abilities to communicate, coordinate, and collude will depend on the number of firms in an industry. As the number of firms increases, the cost of these activities will increase.

Machlup's system identifies three categories of oligopolies: The first category is characterized by formal market coordination. The second is characterized by informal market coordination. The third category displays no market coordination.

FORMALIZED MARKET COORDINATION: CARTELS

Organized, collusive oligopolies are called cartels. **Cartels** are groups of independent firms that agree not to compete but rather to determine prices and output jointly. A perfect cartel, which is able to behave as a monopoly, corresponds to Galbraith's concept of a shared monopoly.

In striving for joint profit maximization, a cartel must set prices, outputs, and marketing areas. However, the cartel can't always set these variables so that each individual firm in the cartel is maximizing its own profit. Figure 5 shows this problem as a special case with two firms, a duopoly. In Figure 5, there are two firms, A and B, in a cartel that produces a homogeneous product. The marginal cost curves of these firms are MC_A and MC_B. MC_T is the horizontal summation (total) of MC_A and MC_B. The cartel will maximize profits, behaving exactly as a monopoly, by producing x_C, where $MR = MC_T$. This output level results in a price of P_C.

Now the cartel must enforce this decision by requiring firms A and B to produce x_A and x_B, respectively. The difficulty is that neither firm would be at its individual profit-maximizing output, because their marginal cost curves are different. If each firm views one-half of the market as its own, its demand curve is represented by MR in Figure 5. Remember that MR= 1/2D (measured horizontally). So if each firm views half of the market as its own, the demand curve that each firm faces would be identical to the marginal revenue curve for the market. The firms' profit-maximizing outputs are where $MC_A = MR_A$ and where $MC_B = MR_B$. Firm A would like to produce x_a, and Firm B would like to produce x_b.

In short, profit maximization for the cartel as a whole is not necessarily consistent with profit maximization for each individual member. In the example of Figure 5, firm A would prefer to produce *more* and sell it at a *higher* price, and firm B would prefer to produce *less* at a *lower* price. This example points out the most important problem faced by cartels. Joint profit maximization and indi-

---

Communication
Firms' ability to signal their intentions to each other.

Coordination
Firms' ability to relate their production decisions to those made by other firms in an industry.

Collusion
Agreements between firms in an industry to set a certain price or to share a market in certain ways.

Cartel
A group of independent firms that agree not to compete but rather to determine prices and output jointly.

---

2. Fritz Machlup, *The Economics of Sellers' Competition* (Baltimore: Johns Hopkins Press, 1952).

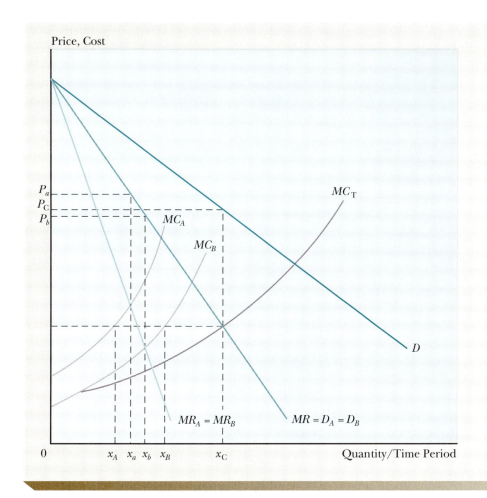

FIGURE 5

PROFIT MAXIMIZATION BY A CARTEL

Joint profit maximization by two firms occurs where MC_1 = MR. This quantity establishes a price of P_c and output of x_c. The cartel must then force firms A and B to produce output x_a and x_b, respectively. Assuming that each firm could view one-half of the market represented by the demand curve (D) as its own, individual profit maximization would establish a price of P_a and output of x_a for firm A and a price of P_b and output of x_b for firm B. To succeed, the cartel must compel firm A to produce less and firm B to produce more than its individual profit-maximizing output.

vidual profit maximization are often in conflict. As a result, a cartel is very unstable.

Perhaps the greatest threat to a cartel's existence is that members find it in their own self-interest to cheat on the cartel. **Chiseling** refers to cheating on a cartel agreement by lowering prices in an attempt to capture more of the market. If, for example, a cartel agrees on a set price, such as P_C in Figure 5, individual members may attempt to give secret price cuts and capture more of the market.

If any firm in a cartel believes the others to be untrustworthy, it will have more of an incentive to chisel. As the number of firms in a cartel increases, it becomes increasingly likely that individual firms will become suspicious of the other members. The amount of chiseling is thus closely related to the number of firms in a cartel. The fewer the firms, the more closely the cartel will be able to monitor their behavior to determine if any firm is chiseling. Other factors can help a cartel control chiseling. For example, if the number of buyers is small and if the price is widely publicized, the cartel will not worry so much about one of its members chiseling.

Another threat faced by cartels is new entry. If a cartel is successful in acting as a monopoly and earning higher than normal profits, it must create barriers

Chiseling
Cheating on a cartel agreement by lowering prices in an attempt to capture more of the market.

to entry. Otherwise, new firms might enter the market and compete with the cartel.

CARTELS IN THE REAL WORLD. The history of cartels is not impressive. Most have held together for only short periods of time, and have then fallen apart because of chiseling. In the few cases where cartels have had long-term success, there has usually been direct government support. Once a government is involved, it becomes more difficult to chisel because the government can police and penalize this behavior.

Organized, collusive activity in private industry in the United States has usually been invalidated by the courts. However, General Electric and Westinghouse engaged in a conspiracy in the late 1950s to act as a cartel. They decided on a scheme that allowed them to submit low bids alternately on government contracts. The scheme depended on the phases of the moon. At either full or new moon (every two weeks), the firm designated to be the low bidder would gain the contract because the other firm would submit an uncompetitively high bid. This plan worked well because there were only two firms dealing with one buyer, the federal government. Each firm would know if the other was cheating because the bids were later made public. In this case, the government was inadvertently helping the cartel overcome the chiseling problem.

Another example, involving a large number of firms, was an attempt to form a cartel known as the National Farm Organization (NFO). The industry for milk and beef production is composed of large numbers of firms (farms), and the NFO cartel only included about 10 percent of them. In 1967 and 1968, the NFO attempted two separate actions: one to raise milk prices and the other to raise beef prices. The cartel tried to organize farmers to keep production from the market. In order to raise prices, cartel members were to destroy milk and keep cattle away from the market. If the NFO members had been successful in raising prices, the nonmembers who continued to produce and sell would have benefited. They would have reacted to the higher prices by expanding output. Also, as prices began to rise, there would have been tremendous pressure on cartel members to chisel on the withholding action. In fact, the chiselers would have benefited much more than the members who refused to chisel. The attempt to organize the cartel resulted in violence. Cattle scales were blown up. NFO farmers sat in the roads to keep others from taking their products to market. Some farmers even resorted to taking cattle to market in house trailers to avoid detection. The lesson is clear: A cartel with many members will find it very difficult to succeed.

Cartels are much more common in Europe than they are in the United States. In Europe, cartels are permitted and often encouraged by governments. Before the 1950s, all major German industries operated as cartels. Currently in Western Europe, the Common Market Commission is actively promoting cartels in steel, textiles, and shipbuilding. In contrast, cartels are—with one exception—illegal in the United States. The one exception, based on the Webb-Pomerene Act of 1921, allows the formation of cartels when they are necessary to participate in foreign trade. These Webb-Pomerene cartels have not been successful in raising prices, primarily because of the large number of firms participating.

OPEC—A DECADE OF SUCCESS. The best-known cartel of recent years is the Organization of Petroleum Exporting Countries, known as OPEC. In the 1950s, international oil companies controlled a major portion of the world's oil supply. These companies frequently engaged in price competition. In an attempt to stop price cutting, some Arab governments and a few non-Arab governments formed OPEC in 1960. At first, OPEC enjoyed little success. But this changed in 1973, as the Arab-Israeli war heated up and the Arab countries banded together. On January 1, 1973, the price of oil was $2.12 per barrel. Of this $2.12, $1.52 went to the OPEC governments. By January 1, 1974, the price was $7.61 with $7.01 going to the governments. By January 1975, the price was about $10.50. By 1982, the price had risen to $35.00.

How did this cartel, which had been in existence since 1960, come to flex its muscles in 1973? At that time, importing governments helped by posting prices and dealing with OPEC in open forums, so individual members were less likely to chisel. More important, however, Saudi Arabia was willing to cut back its production of oil to allow other members to sell all they wanted to produce at the high prices set by the cartel.

In 1984, after production had to be cut back by 5 million barrels a day to prevent the cartel from collapsing, Saudi Arabia's willingness to bear this cost began to weaken. The price of oil began to fall. The January 1984 price was $29 per barrel, down from the 1982 high of $35. The slide continued. In January 1987, the price was $13 per barrel. In January 1990, it was under $12 per barrel. As prices fell, chiseling became more common. The predictions made by economists in the 1970s that the cartel would eventually weaken started to come true. Some of the Persian Gulf countries, notably Kuwait, the United Arab Emirates, and Qatar, were experiencing cash flow problems. These countries started grandiose development schemes when their oil revenues were in excess of $300 billion per year. Their revenues fell significantly because of the decreased price, but the development projects still had to be paid for. Kuwait began shipping more oil than allowed by OPEC agreements—one of the factors underlying the Gulf War. In 1986, Nobel Prize winner Milton Friedman wrote an editorial entitled, "Right at Last, an Expert's Dream," reminding readers that he had predicted in 1974 that OPEC would not last very long.[3]

As we pointed out earlier, all cartels face two problems. The first is chiseling, or secret price cutting. OPEC faced this problem in the presence of oil surpluses. The second problem a cartel faces is new entry. Large amounts of oil have been coming into the market from non-OPEC sources, such as the North Sea and Alaska. In addition, other sources of energy, such as solar and nuclear energy, which were uneconomical when oil was $2 per barrel, became profitable at the much higher prices. The new entry has been slow to develop, but the future should prove even more difficult for OPEC as new firms producing oil and other competing products enter the market and challenge the cartel's cohesiveness.

The impact of new oil supplies is evident in the statistics. In 1973, OPEC's share of world oil production was 56 percent. In 1975, its share was 51 percent. In 1980, it was 45 percent, and in 1984, it was 35 percent. In 1990, OPEC's share

---

3. Milton Friedman, "Right at Last, an Expert's Dream," *Newsweek* (March 10, 1986): 8.

had fallen to 28 percent. This declining share of production signaled the weakening of the cartel better than any other piece of data. If a cartel is going to set prices, it must control a large share of total production.

In addition to the new oil supplies, the high oil prices have also had an effect on quantity demanded. The decade of OPEC's dominance resulted in adjustments in consumer demand. Perhaps the most evident of these adjustments is the increased fuel efficiency of automobiles.

INFORMAL MARKET COORDINATION: PRICE LEADERSHIP

Tacit collusion
Unorganized and unstated attempts by informally coordinated oligopolies to practice joint actions.

Informally coordinated oligopolies engage in unorganized and unstated attempts to practice joint actions. Such **tacit collusion** is much weaker than the collusion among members of a cartel. It is weaker because all the incentives to chisel are still present, but organized vigilance against chiseling is not. Tacit collusion is found in U.S. industries because cartels are illegal under federal antitrust laws. Informal cooperation among oligopolistic firms can be viewed as an attempt to form cartels while avoiding antitrust laws. Such collusion usually takes the form of informal agreements to behave in certain ways. Often these agreements arise naturally, without any need for formal organization. The most common form of tacit, informal agreement is based on price leadership.

Price leadership
The form of tacit collusion in an oligopolistic industry in which one firm, the price leader, sets the price or initiates price changes and the other firms follow that lead.

PRICE LEADERSHIP. **Price leadership** is a form of tacit collusion in an oligopolistic industry in which one firm, the price leader, sets the price or initiates price changes and the other firms follow that lead. The firm that is the most influential in an industry is called the **dominant firm**. It may be either the largest firm or the lowest-cost firm. Price leadership is most effective where firms are few and have clearly similar products (for example, in the auto, cigarette, and steel industries). It helps if the demand for the product is price-inelastic since this will further discourage price cutting. If the demand curve for the product were perfectly inelastic, a firm that chisels on price would gain sales only at the expense of other firms. The lower price would not bring about additional sales for the industry. Thus, the conflict between firms will be sharper when demand is not very responsive to price cuts.

Dominant firm
The most influential firm in an industry, usually the largest firm.

Competitive fringe
The smaller competitors in informally coordinated markets with one large, dominant firm.

DOMINANT FIRM. In price leadership, the dominant firm sets a profit-maximizing price, and the other firms divide up the market at that price. The other firms, known as the **competitive fringe**, act much like firms in perfect competition. This result can be seen in Figure 6. The market demand curve for the product is D. The marginal cost curve of the dominant firm is MC_d, and the summation of all the other firms' marginal cost curves is S_f. Those firms (the fringe) will make production decisions as price takers and will always produce where price is equal to their marginal cost. The demand curve that the dominant firm faces can be derived by subtracting the amount supplied by the fringe firms (S_f) from the market demand curve (D_T). This subtraction gives the dominant firm's demand curve, D_d, and thus its marginal revenue curve, MR_d. The dominant firm will set a profit-maximizing price and output of P_1 and x_d. Once price P_1 is determined, the fringe firms view this price much as competitive firms view the market price. The fringe firms will produce x_f units at the market price P_1 because for them $P_1 = MR$ and they want to produce where $MR = MC_f$. The sum of

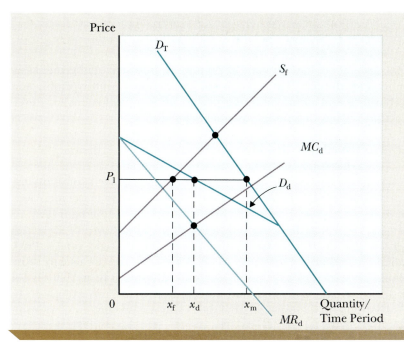

FIGURE 6
A DOMINANT FIRM WITH A COMPETITIVE FRINGE
The dominant firm views a part of the market, D_d, as its own. D_d is determined by subtracting the supply curve of the competitive fringe, S_f, from the market demand, D_T. The dominant firm produces where $MC_d = MR_d$, setting price P_1 and producing x_d units. The fringe firms face a perfectly elastic demand curve at P_1, and produce a combined output of x_f units (where $P_1 = MR = S_f$).

the production of the dominant firm (x_d) and the production of the fringe firms (x_f) satisfies the market demand of x_m at price P_1.

This model of price leadership is applicable to the oil refining industry in the United States. There is a small group of dominant firms and a large number of small fringe firms. Price leadership by a dominant firm also appears to have prevailed at one time or another in the aluminum, automobile, and cigarette industries in the United States.

HISTORICAL PRICE LEADERSHIP. In a few cases, especially in mature industries, it is possible for a firm to emerge as the price leader because it is convenient for the other firms in the industry to follow the leader and thus coordinate their pricing. This type of price leadership, called historical price leadership, is very similar to cartel behavior. Its intent is collusion—to achieve industry-wide profit maximization. Historical price leadership, however, is unorganized and thus not illegal in the United States. It was formerly rampant within U.S. oligopolies. General Motors was the recognized price leader in autos, U.S. Steel (now USX) in steel, and DuPont in chemicals. In the last ten years, the price leadership of these domestic oligopolies has been severely limited by foreign competition.

The way in which oligopolies can coordinate markets informally was clearly demonstrated by what have come to be known as the "Gary dinners." In 1901, U.S. Steel put together mergers that made it the dominant firm, supplying 65 percent of the domestic steel market. From 1907 to 1911, Judge Elbert H. Gary, chairman of the board of U.S. Steel, held a series of dinners for executives of competing companies. Gary explained that the close communication *and contact* developed at these dinners "generated such mutual *respect and affectionate regard* among steel industry leaders that all considered the obligation to cooperate and avoid destructive competition *more binding...than any written or verbal contract.*"[4] Efforts to prosecute U.S. Steel's behavior as an antitrust violation were unsuccessful.

In recent years, there haven't been any reported "informal" gatherings as effective as the Gary dinners. However, trade associations, country clubs, and other such business and social gathering places can serve as forums for developing cooperative behavior among potential competitors.[5]

SUCCESSFUL PRICE LEADERSHIP. In order to be successful—that is, in order to raise industry profit levels—price leadership must produce a kind of cartel but still avoid legal sanctions. This means walking a tightrope. As the tacit collusion embodied in price leadership becomes successful, the incentive to chisel increases. As a result, most successful price leadership not involving a dominant firm occurs in industries in which there are only a few firms. The record of such tacit collusion shows that such industries are characterized by rigid prices. Price changes, when they occur, are generally small. Such industries are usually those that can blame price increases on rising costs and can punish firms that do not follow the price increase. The steel and auto industries are two examples. In these industries, potential chiselers know they cannot easily get away with not following the price leader.

KEY IDEAS

CHARACTERISTICS OF OLIGOPOLY
- There are only a few sellers of homogeneous or differentiated products.
- Interdependence leads to attempts at communication, coordination, and collusion.
- Cartels may be formed to determine industry pricing and output.
- Price leadership may be used to coordinate industry pricing.
- The price leader may be a dominant firm.
- Nonprice competition increases product differentiation.

NO MARKET COORDINATION

Unorganized, uncollusive oligopolies are characterized by independent action. Firms in these oligopolies practice profit maximization independently but are affected by the actions and responses of their rivals. Each firm tries to anticipate the response of its rivals and then takes that prediction into account when making decisions. Economists tried to develop a model for this behavior in the early nineteenth century. In 1838, A. Augustin Cournot (1801–1877) published a theory of duopoly (a market with only two firms). His theory and those that followed (up to the post-World War II period) were unsatisfactory because they as-

---

4. F. M. Scherer, *Industrial Market Structure and Economic Performance* (Chicago: Rand McNally, 1980), 170. Italics indicate Judge Gary's actual words, taken from a government antitrust brief.
5. Adam Smith recognized the potential for such collusion. Here is his famous statement on this subject from *The Wealth of Nations*: "People of the same trade seldom meet together, even for merriment and diversion, but the conversation ends in a conspiracy against the public, or in some contrivance to raise prices."

POLICY FOCUS: OLIGOPOLY THEORY AND POLICY MAKING

The theory, or perhaps more correctly, the theory and descriptive economics in this chapter are part of a controversy between economists and economists as policy advisers. The late George Stigler was an impressive and articulate spokesman in this debate. His arguments with Paul Sweezy highlight the essence of the controversy. Economists, like Sweezy, developed the theory of imperfect competition because they felt it enriched and expanded on the theory of pure monopoly and perfect competition. Stigler argued the these embellishments didn't get us anywhere—that the results of the policy analysis were the same if you used the model of perfect competition. Stigler would argue the purpose of theory is to make the problem more simple. The models of pure monopoly and perfect competition do that simplifying, and policy analysis doesn't need to be complicated by using more "real world" models.

It is worth comparing George Stigler and Paul Sweezy as economists because they represent polar extremes in economic policy analysis. Both have written extensively in the field of industrial organization, but the similarities end there.

George Stigler, who died in 1991, was the personification of the Chicago School of free-enterprise capitalism. He received a bachelor's degree from the University of Washington, an MBA from Northwestern University, and a Ph.D. from the University of Chicago. In 1982, Stigler was awarded the Nobel Prize in economics. Paul Sweezy is an American Marxist. He has a B.A. degree and a Ph.D. in economics from Harvard University. Both economists were coeditors of prestigious journals that are at opposite ends of the ideological spectrum. Stigler was coeditor of the *Journal of Political Economy*, and Sweezy is coeditor of the *Monthly Review*. Stigler's views are best delineated in *The Theory of Price* (1966) and *Organization of Industry* (1968). Sweezy's views can be found in *The Dynamics of U.S. Capitalism* (1972), *Introduction to Socialism* (1968), and *Modern Capitalism and Other Essays* (1972).

Stigler and Sweezy have clashed over Sweezy's use of the kinked demand curve to explain why prices in oligopolies are more stable than prices in other market structures. This model has been severely criticized by Stigler, who argues that Sweezy's theory is wrong. Stigler says that Sweezy's claim that prices in an oligopoly are more stable than in other market structures does not stand up to real-world evidence.

---

sumed that the rival firm would not react to the action of the firm being analyzed. The post-World War II developments in oligopoly theory rest heavily on **game theory**. Game theory is a relatively new field of mathematics that can provide insights into oligopolistic behavior.

GAME THEORY: STRATEGY AND RIVALRY IN OLIGOPOLY

Life for the entrepreneur is simple in pure monopoly and pure competition. But most firms in the real world must make strategic decisions, based on how rival firms are likely to react to their own action. The just completed review of oligopoly and monopolistic competition demonstrated the interdependence in these market structures. A review of some elements of game theory will show how firms might make moves that could gain a competitive edge in the market place. Game theory applied to economic reasoning asks how management of a firm should act if it believes that the rival firm is rational and out to maximize its profits.

Game theory, a theory of rational decision making under conditions of uncertainty, was first developed by John von Neumann (1903–1957) and Oskar

Game theory
A mathematical theory about rational decision making under conditions of uncertainty that can provide insight into oligopolistic behavior.

Morgenstern (1902–1977) in a book entitled *The Theory of Games and Economic Behavior*.[6] Game theory says that players try to reach an optimal position through strategic behavior that takes into account the anticipated moves of other players. Game theory attempts to explain how a decision maker will make decisions based on the assumption that the competitors are rational and profit maximizing. This model describes very accurately how oligopolists behave.

Standard microeconomic decision-making theory is based on the assumption that the outcomes of various decisions are known with certainty. Game theory suggests rational solutions when the outcomes are uncertain. Games are usually described as being either zero-sum or non-zero-sum. Zero-sum games are those in which one player's gain is another player's loss. Non-zero-sum games open the door to collusion or cooperative action because all players may gain (or all may lose) from a certain course of action. This aspect of game theory has proved very useful in the study of oligopolies in which each firm must take into account the reactions of its competitors.

COOPERATIVE AND NONCOOPERATIVE GAMES. Games can be cooperative or noncooperative. A cooperative game is a game in which a contract is possible. You may, for example, enter into an agreement with a rival to share risk or bring complementary technologies together to solve a customer's problem. In both of these cases, it is possible for the parties to draw up a contract that divides the profits or losses. In a noncooperative game such a contract is not possible. An example of a noncooperative game would be an airline deciding to cut prices on some flights expecting that its rivals will match the cut. Most games of interest in examining business strategic behavior are noncooperative.

One of the most famous of non-zero-sum games is called the Prisoners' Dilemma. Two prisoners are interrogated separately. Each one knows that if neither confesses, both will go free. However, if one confesses and implicates the other, the one who confesses will receive a light sentence and the other will get a long prison term. The interrogator separately offers each prisoner the opportunity to confess and "get a better deal." The rational course of action for the self-interested prisoner is to confess and implicate the other. Since both face the same incentive and the same uncertainty about the other's action, both will confess. The outcome of the two rational decisions will make both of the prisoners worse off. They would both be better off if they could engage in collusion because if neither confesses, both will go free. This lesson holds for oligopolistic firms. Oligopolistic firms must decide to compete aggressively, attempting to take their competitors' market, or to cooperate and settle for the market share they have. Like the prisoners, each firm has an incentive to undercut the other *and* each knows the other has the same incentive.

Does the prisoners' dilemma mean that firms will be doomed to low profits and financial problems because they will always undercut one another? Experience in the airline industry in the past decade might lead to this conclusion. But, as we saw earlier, some oligopolies exist side by side over time and a form of price leadership or other cooperative behavior emerges. A major dif-

---

6. For a detailed and highly mathematical treatment of game theory, see John von Neumann and Oskar Morgenstern, *The Theory of Games and Economic Behavior* (Princeton NJ: Princeton University Press, 1949). For a survey of game theory, see R. S. Pindyck and D. L. Rubinfeld, *Microeconomics* (New York: Macmillan, 1992), Chapter 13.

ference between the prisoners' dilemma of theory and that faced by oligopolists is that the offer to the prisoners is made only once by the sheriff. In the real world of cartel behavior, the firm faces the prisoners' dilemma daily. Over time the firms can learn how their rival will react—most of the time!

THE KINKED DEMAND CURVE

One explanation of why prices in oligopolistic industries tend to be less flexible than prices in other market structures was presented by Paul Sweezy. Sweezy hypothesized that price rigidity exists because the firms in an oligopoly face a **kinked demand curve**. The demand curve has two sections because the firms come to believe that if they cut prices, their rivals will also do so. The price cut will not produce much of an increase in sales. A price increase, on the other hand, will not be imitated and will, therefore, result in a loss of sales for the firm making the increase. Since losses are likely from either higher or lower prices, once a price is reached in an oligopoly, it tends to remain in effect for long periods.

You can see the effect of a kinked demand curve by examining Figure 7. There is a kink in the demand curve D at point A (or at price P). Below point A, the other firms in the market will match any price decrease, making the demand curve relatively inelastic. A firm won't increase sales very much by decreasing price below P. Any increase in price above P will have the opposite effect. Competing firms will not match the increase. As a result, the demand curve above point A is relatively elastic. At the kink in the firm's demand curve, the corresponding marginal revenue curve, MR, is discontinuous. As you can see, MR has a break in it between B and C in Figure 7. This break allows a large vari-

Kinked demand curve A demand curve with a bend in it at the price settled on in an oligopolistic industry because other firms' price cuts, but not price increases, are matched.

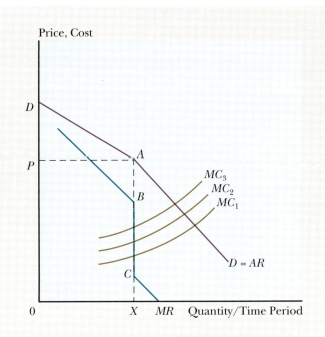

FIGURE 7

A KINKED DEMAND CURVE In this model, the firm faces a kinked demand curve (D) because price increases above P will not be matched and price decreases below P will be matched. The kink creates a discontinuity in the marginal revenue curve, which causes the price to be very rigid at the kink (P).

ation in marginal cost with no effect on the profit-maximizing price, P, or output, x. For example, marginal cost could change from MC_1 to MC_2 to MC_3 with no effect on price and output. Sweezy used this model to explain why prices were so rigid in oligopoly.

NONPRICE COMPETITION

All oligopolists compete in dimensions other than just the price dimension. In formulating models, economists tend to treat goods as homogeneous and view competition as occurring mostly through price adjustments. In the real world, however, competition can take other forms. Firms can change the quality, color, texture, design, size, advertising, and a host of other attributes of a product. Sometimes quality or quantity changes substitute for price changes. The size of a candy bar could be decreased while the price remained the same. This change is in effect a price increase, albeit a disguised price increase. Even an apparently homogeneous product can be differentiated by the quality of customer service.

Casual observation leads to the conclusion that a great deal of the advertising on television is done by firms in oligopolistic markets. Most informational advertising is done on radio or in the print media. Most of the major ads on television appear to be aimed at a goal other than informing consumers. There may be several economic goals of this advertising. George Stigler points out that institutional advertising, saying, for example, "our firm is the oldest or largest in the industry," is meant to convey to the consumer the comfort of reliability.[7] The idea is that the firm must treat consumers well or it wouldn't be large or old. **Name brand capital** is the value that consumers place on a product because of experience, reputation, or image. This name brand capital can be very important in terms of maintaining market share in the face of price (or quality) competition from new rivals that don't have it. In the extreme, name brand capital is a barrier to entry that may allow the firm to behave in a monopolistic fashion.

Robert Wills and Willard Mueller have examined the effect of brand advertising on pricing in oligopolistic markets.[8] They were motivated in part by the fact that in some markets consumers show a preference for high-priced brands even though competing brands are physically identical. Brands of lemon juice concentrate, evaporated milk, and household bleach, for example, are exactly the same in every respect except packaging. In addition, blind taste tests of some products, such as beer and cookies, show that consumers often cannot distinguish their preferred brand from competing brands. The research by Wills and Mueller showed that monopoly power in such markets produces price premiums and higher profits. This monopoly power was created by advertising. They conclude that large firms will tend to advertise more heavily, have higher prices, *and* have higher profits than their smaller competitors.

An oligopolistic firm may resort to nonprice competition in an attempt to increase its market share. We can apply the model of oligopoly to these other types of competition. For example, a firm contemplating a new advertising program has to consider whether the program will increase its market share or prompt a rival to undertake a similar program. In the first case, the program

Name brand capital
The value that consumers place on a product because of experience, reputation, or image.

---

7. George Stigler, *Memoirs of an Unregulated Economist* (New York: Basic Books, 1988), 81.
8. Robert L. Wills and William F. Mueller, "Brand Pricing and Advertising," *Southern Economic Journal* (October 1989): 383–395.

may be worthwhile. In the second, it would probably only increase costs without creating a larger market share. Thus, even with respect to advertising, firms in an oligopoly are interdependent and need to consider the reactions of rivals.

FACTORS DETERMINING MARKET COORDINATION BY OLIGOPOLIES

As you have seen, there are benefits to be gained by oligopolists who can coordinate output and pricing, whether such coordination is formal or informal. There are strong forces pulling in opposite directions. It is worthwhile to review some variables that facilitate or limit such market coordination.

THE NUMBER OF FIRMS. The number of firms in an oligopoly has the most obvious impact on the likelihood of formal or informal market coordination. As the number of firms increases, the incentive and ability to coordinate diminish. In addition, as the number of firms increases, the cost of coordinating and policing the agreement increases. It is obvious that as the size of the group increases, the probability that it will include a maverick also increases. As the number of firms increases, the likelihood of effective coordination diminishes rapidly. Some economists have suggested that after the number of firms in a market reaches ten, it is likely that they will ignore each other's actions, making coordination impossible.[9]

BARRIERS TO ENTRY. Barriers to entry play a key role in determining market coordination because they are related to the number of firms. An oligopoly will not be able to practice effective coordination if it can't limit entry. New firms will destroy market coordination and erode any economic profit created by it. The lesson is a simple one. If strong barriers to entry (including barriers created by government) exist, the possibility of coordination exists. If barriers to entry are weak, coordination is highly unlikely.

THE SIZE OF FIRMS. If the oligopolistic industry is dominated by one firm, or if several of the firms are large relative to the others, the possibility of market coordination is enhanced. In such a case, coordination would only require agreement by the dominant firm or firms.

SECRECY. Coordination requires the elimination of secrecy so that uncooperative behavior can be punished. Monitoring chiseling is easier in an environment in which secret deals don't stay secret long. Government has often aided in market coordination by requiring the full disclosure of contract details.

UNSTABLE OR FLUCTUATING DEMAND. If demand fluctuates or is otherwise unstable, a firm in an oligopoly will have difficulty determining if changes in its demand are the result of market forces or, alternatively, the competitive behavior of a rival. As a result, unstable or fluctuating demand will make market coordination more difficult.

---

9. See F. M. Scherer, *Industrial Market Structure and Economic Performance*, 3e. (Boston: Houghton Mifflin, 1990).

PRODUCT DIFFERENTIATION. The more homogeneous a product is, the easier it will be to coordinate the sale of that product. As product differences increase, firms will be unable to determine whether the price concessions of rivals are attempts to chisel or are due to actual differences in product characteristics.

INDUSTRY SOCIAL STRUCTURE. As you have already seen, the maturity of an industry can affect market coordination. The social structure of an industry is also important. Do the leaders know and trust each other? Do they get together at meetings? Do they play golf or engage in other recreational pursuits? If they do, coordination might be easier. Note, however, that socializing does not mean that entrepreneurs are not competitive. What appears to be cooperation may be a subterfuge for future chiseling on a coordinated effort. Remember, if an oligopolist can get all the others in the market to agree and then can chisel on the agreement, it can be very profitable.

ANTITRUST ACTIVITY. The U.S. antitrust laws make collusion illegal. If these laws are vigorously enforced, it will make coordination more costly. The antitrust laws will serve to limit attempts at coordination.

MARKET STRUCTURES IN REVIEW

This chapter concludes the discussion of the four theoretical market structures. Table 1 summarizes some of the important characteristics that differentiate these market structures. The key to understanding the theory of the firm is a solid understanding of monopoly and perfect competition. Oligopoly and monopolistic competition expand the models of monopoly and perfect competition and bring those models closer to real-world situations.

TABLE 1 SUMMARY OF MARKET STRUCTURES

TYPE	NUMBER OF FIRMS	PRODUCT DIFFERENTIATION	CONTROL OVER PRICE	TYPE OF NONPRICE COMPETITION	EXAMPLES
Perfect competition	Many	Homogeneous product	None	None	Agriculture
Monopolistic competition	Many	Slightly differentiated products	Some	Advertising and product differentiation	Retail trade and service industry
Oligopoly	Few	Homogeneous *or* differentiated products	Some to considerable (it depends)	Advertising and product differentiation	Auto and steel industries
Monopoly	One	Unique product (no close substitutes)	Considerable	Public relations, advertising can increase demand	Some utilities and aluminum industry before 1945

Consider again... *Now, what is the value of a brand name? The answer, of course, like all answers in economics, is, "it depends." Product differentiation and brand loyalty give the owners of that brand name monopoly power in a certain range. That range is determined by how much more consumers are willing to pay for the brand. In cigarettes, there is some evidence that brand loyalty is very strong. Full-priced brands sell for over $2.00 per pack, while generic or off-label brands sell for as little as $0.69 per pack. But even here there are problems for brand name owners. In April 1993, Philip Morris admitted that the world's most powerful and profitable cigarette brand, Marlboro, had lost significant market share to a cut-rate brand most people had never heard of. Philip Morris significantly reduced the price of Marlboros to compete with the lower-priced substitute. That same day the value of Philip Morris stock on the New York Stock Exchange fell $13.4 billion. That gives some idea of what investors felt about the value (or lack of value) of the Marlboro brand!*

SUMMARY

1. Monopolistic competition is a market structure characterized by many firms selling differentiated products. Key assumptions in the model of monopolistic competition are a large number of producers, product differentiation, and relative ease of entry. Economic profits can exist in the short run in this market structure, but entry of new firms will ensure a long-run equilibrium with zero economic profit.
2. Oligopoly is the market structure in which there are only a few firms competing imperfectly. Because there are so few firms in an oligopoly, they are interdependent. They take this interdependence into account in their economic decision making.
3. Cartels are threatened by chiseling behavior on the part of individual members and by new entry. The larger the number of firms in a cartel, the more difficult it is for the cartel to hold together. Barriers to entry are thus important in oligopoly, just as they are in monopoly. Successful cartels have often been supported by governments, which police chiseling behavior.
4. Game theory is a theory of rational decision making under uncertainty. It can give valuable insights into behavior in oligopoly.
5. Price leadership is common in oligopolies where formalized market coordination is not possible. The price leader can be a dominant firm or, in mature industries, a historical leader. Economic forces that work to limit coordination in oligopoly or to facilitate it pull in opposite directions. Because of product differentiation, monopolistically competitive firms produce a smaller output at a higher price than firms (with the same costs) engaged in perfect competition. In long-run equilibrium in monopolistic competition, marginal cost is not equal to average cost.

NEW TERMS

monopolistic competition
differentiated product
product group
excess capacity
nonprice competition
oligopoly
shared monopoly
pure oligopoly
differentiated oligopoly
price clusters
communication
coordination
collusion
cartel
chiseling
tacit collusion
price leadership
dominant firm
competitive fringe
game theory
kinked demand curve
name brand capital

QUESTIONS: REVIEW, APPLICATIONS, AND POLICY

REVIEW

1. What are the differences between the model of perfect competition and the model of monopolistic competition? What assumption is different?
2. What is excess capacity? Is it a good or a bad thing?
3. Explain how the expectation of new entry would limit cartel formation.
4. How would you expect the number of firms in a cartel to affect the probability of its success? Why?
5. In what sense is monopolistic competition like monopoly and in what sense is it like competition?
6. What does the kinked demand curve imply about the oligopolists' response to the pricing of rivals? What does the kinked demand curve say about prices in oligopolistic industries? On what grounds has this model been criticized?
7. How do oligopolies compete?

APPLICATIONS

8. Firms in monopolistic competition earn only normal profit in the long run, unless they can successfully convince consumers that their product is different. List four examples of product differentiation. Do you think the differences are real, imagined, or created? Does product differentiation make any economic difference?
9. How would you characterize the market in which the major television networks compete with each other? Are NBC, CBS, and ABC monopolists, oligopolists, or monopolistically competitive firms? How do they compete with one another?
10. Suppose advertising in an oligopolistic market does not increase the total volume of sales but only the distribution of sales among the oligopolistic firms. How does this fit with the Prisoners' Dilemma game?
11. Figure 2 depicts the long-run equilibrium for monopolistic competition.
    a. What is the equilibrium rate of output?
    b. What is the equilibrium price?
    c. What is the average cost?
    d. What is average revenue?
    e. What is the level of profit?
    f. What output level is necessary to reach the least-cost combination?
    g. What is the level of excess capacity?

POLICY

12. Would you consider the National Collegiate Athletic Association (NCAA) a cartel? How do some universities (firms) chisel on the agreement? Why do they do this?
13. How can changes in technology affect oligopoly?
14. Some experts have predicted that the energy crisis will be back to haunt the United States by 1997 and that OPEC will again be an effective cartel. How would each of the following events affect the probability of OPEC becoming as powerful as it was from 1974 to 1982?
    a. Reforms in the former Soviet Union permit the entry of Western oil companies to develop the vast oil reserves as joint ventures.
    b. Research on the accident at Chernobyl causes most Western governments to shut down all nuclear power plants.
    c. Environmental concerns over acid rain cause the United States to prohibit the burning of soft coal.
    d. The President authorizes an increase in California offshore drilling.
    e. The international debts of some members of OPEC grow significantly.
15. Twenty-five years ago, the U.S. steel industry was a coordinated oligopoly. New technology now allows smaller steel producers to compete with the larger firms. What effect do you think this change has had on labor unions in the steel industry?

SUGGESTIONS FOR FURTHER READING

"A Survey of the Airline Industry." *The Economist* (June 12, 1993): 4–22. An analysis of the airline industry that illustrates the interrelationships between the firms.

Friedman, James W. *Oligopoly Theory.* New York: Cambridge University Press, 1984. A thorough study of oligopoly theory using numerical examples.

Kanfer, Stephen. *The Last Empire: De Beers, Diamonds and the World.* New York: Farrar, Straus & Giroux, 1993. A very readable history of one of the most successful cartels of all time.

Scherer, F. M. *Industrial Market Structure and Economic Performance*, 3e. Boston: Houghton Mifflin, 1990. A reference work on industrial organization, market structure, and antitrust that contains a good review of monopolistic competition and oligopoly theory.

CHAPTER 26
REGULATION, DEREGULATION, AND ANTITRUST POLICY

LEARNING OBJECTIVES
1. Use the SIC system, a Herfindahl Index, and a Lerner Index to define an industry, describe the structure of an industry, interpret concentration ratios in U.S. industry, and discuss U.S. merger movements.
2. Describe the results of studies of the relationships between concentration and prices, and concentration and profits.
3. Diagram the regulation of monopoly power through price regulation and through taxation.
4. Identify and discuss the major events in the history of antitrust legislation and the economic consequences of this antitrust activity.

Consider this... *Imagine that you live in Galveston TX and it is July 1993. You are sitting on the jury for a case in the U.S. District Court of Judge Samuel Kent. Your involvement began in June 1993, when you were called to the district court and selected as a juror.*

The facts in the case are as follows. In April 1992, American Airlines introduced a four-tiered price structure. Regular coach fares were cut 40 percent. In May, Northwest countered the American price by offering a free ticket to an adult flying with a child. On June 8, 1992, Continental Airlines sued American in federal court in Galveston, alleging predatory pricing. Four days later Northwest filed a similar suit. A year later the case finally makes it into court and you are called to sit on the jury. On July 2, 1993, Judge Kent rejects American Airlines' argument to throw the case out of court. On July 12, the trial begins.

The nation's antitrust lawyers and economists watch this case with interest. Continental and Northwest paint American as an aggressor trying to drive them out of business by predatory pricing. They seek $3 billion in damages. Much of the colorful language of the testimony revolves around the tough-talking CEO of American, Robert Crandall. A decade earlier Crandall was recorded in a telephone conversation telling a rival airline executive, "Raise your #!# fares 20 percent. I'll raise mine the next morning. You'll make more money and I will too." That case was settled and Judge Kent has ruled that you will not hear that testimony. You will hear, however, that Continental countered by finding a loophole in American's pricing structure and internally dubbed their program "KickAAss," a play on American's use of AA* *in their advertising. Continental's pilots said that American pilots countered Continental's slogan, "one airline can make a difference," with buttons that said, "One LESS airline can make a difference."*

The question you need to ponder as you listen to the evidence produced by Continental and Northwest, is whether or not American used price cutting in an attempt to drive Continental and Northwest from the market. Was American engaging in predatory pricing, or was it just competing for customers in a free and open market? The plaintiffs try to portray CEO Crandall as a bellicose autocrat, and introduce profane memos that they claim were an extreme competitive response to drive them from the marketplace. This chapter may give you some help in deciding how to vote when the jury receives the case and begins deliberations on August 11.

5. Describe the public policy debate concerning competitiveness.
6. Evaluate the alternatives in public policy toward monopoly power.

WHAT IS AN INDUSTRY?

We have, up to this point, been using the term *industry* without carefully defining it. In general, an **industry** is a group of firms producing the same, or at least similar, products. The difficulty with this definition is that it does not specify how dissimilar products must be before they are thought of as being produced in different industries. Consider containers. Are firms producing glass bottles and aluminum cans similar enough to be included in the container industry? How about firms making paper cups or even pewter mugs? Most consumers regard pewter mugs and paper cups as quite different. If you are willing to pay substantially more for a pewter mug than for a paper cup, you regard them as being distinct products. What about a plastic Ronald McDonald glass? Is it closer to a paper cup or a pewter mug? These questions demonstrate that whatever scope is assigned to an industry will be arbitrary to some extent. Some people, even some economists, may disagree with a classification of two products as belonging to the same industry or to different industries.

Cross elasticity of demand, a concept we discussed earlier, can be useful in determining whether products belong to the same industry. If the cross elasticity of demand between two products is positive, the goods are substitutes. Goods that are close substitutes have a positive and very high cross elasticity of demand. If economists could agree on a value of this cross elasticity that would define goods as belonging to the same industry—again an arbitrary decision—they could use that number to draw the boundaries between industries.

The problem of assigning firms to industries is made even more difficult by the fact that some multiproduct firms produce a variety of goods that might be included in different industries. In which industry is a firm that produces coffee in addition to soap and cake mixes? General Electric produces goods as unrelated as jet engines and toasters. Informed judgments and somewhat arbitrary definitions are necessary in order to move from the world of theory into the real world of industry studies.

There is a standard set of data available from the U.S. government in which these judgments have already been made. The Commerce Department classifies

Industry
A group of firms producing similar or related products.

Standard Industrial Classification (SIC) system
A code devised by the U.S. Census Bureau for classifying industries using about 400 four-digit numbers.

firms according to the **Standard Industrial Classification (SIC) system**.[1] The SIC system divides the economy into about 400 industries and assigns them different four-digit code numbers. These four-digit industries can be combined into three-digit or two-digit industry groups or further differentiated into five-digit (or even seven-digit) product classes. Table 1 presents an example of how a code becomes more specific as more digits are added. The purpose of the SIC system is to provide a workable, consistent classification of U.S. industries. This system is used in studies cited in the remainder of this chapter.

This chapter looks at empirical industry studies to illustrate the real-world monopoly problem. **Industry studies** are investigations of specific industries to determine the degree of competitive behavior. This subfield of economics is sometimes referred to as industrial organization.

Industry studies
Investigations of specific industries to determine the degree of competitive behavior.

If an industry possesses some degree of monopoly power, it may be desirable to control or mitigate the worst effects of that power. Monopoly power could be reduced through antitrust action, monopoly profits could be taxed away, or the monopoly could be regulated and thus forced to behave in some prescribed fashion. In some cases, however, the answer might be to do nothing. This chapter will examine the theory and practice of regulation and the development of antitrust laws in the United States. It concludes with an assessment of the success of regulation and antitrust policy and an examination of recent trends in merger activity in U.S. industry.

INDUSTRY STRUCTURE

Once an industry has been defined, it is possible to determine its market structure, or where it lies on the spectrum from perfect competition to monopoly. The structure will depend on several characteristics of the industry. The degree of concentration and conditions of entry are especially important characteristics. Entry affects concentration because high barriers to entry result in a more concentrated industry.

CONCENTRATION RATIOS

Concentration ratio
A measure of the distribution of economic power among firms in an oligopolistic market.

Concentration refers to the extent to which a certain number of firms dominate sales in a given market. Measures of concentration have, for many years, been a major tool of industry studies. A **concentration ratio** is used by economists to provide a measure of the distribution of economic power among firms in an oligopolistic market. To calculate a concentration ratio, the economist lists all the firms having a particular four-digit SIC code in order of decreasing size. The next step is to calculate the percentage of that industry's total sales accounted for by a certain number of the largest firms. For example, a four-firm concentration ratio measures the percentage of sales accounted for by the four largest firms in an industry. Other commonly used concentration ratios are for the largest firm, the three largest firms, the eight largest firms, and so on. Most industry studies employ four-firm ratios. Table 2 gives four-firm concentration ratios for a few industries.

---

1. See U.S Bureau of the Census, *Standard Industrial Classification Manual* (Washington DC: U.S. Government Printing Office, 1988).

TABLE 1 SAMPLE CODES FROM THE SIC SYSTEM

CODE	EXAMPLE	DESIGNATION	NAME
Two-digit	20	Major Industry Group	Food and kindred products
Three-digit	201	Industry group	Meat products
Four-digit	2011	Industry	Meat-packing plants
Five-digit	20111	Product Class	Fresh beef

Source: U.S. Bureau of the Census, *Standard Industrial Classification Manual* (Washington, DC: U.S. Government Printing Office, 1988).

It could be argued that the percentage of sales accounted for by the largest firms is not the best measure of concentration in an industry. Concentration ratios might instead be calculated using percentage of assets, percentage of employees, or value of shipments. The various measures of concentration are all closely related, however, so the choice of a ratio isn't crucial.

The more concentrated an industry, the more likely it is that there will be a recognized interdependence and joint action of either a collusive or noncollusive nature. When the four-firm concentration ratio exceeds 50 percent, the degree of interdependence in the industry is likely to be very high.

BARRIERS TO ENTRY

Entry conditions are the second characteristic affecting market structure. If barriers to entry are high and the industry is highly concentrated, it is more likely that joint action can be undertaken to create monopoly profits. You saw earlier that cartels are very unstable and that economic profits will strongly attract new firms into the industry. If concentration is high and entry is blocked, the existing firms will be in a better position to restrict output, raise prices, and maintain persistent profits.

TABLE 2 FOUR-FIRM CONCENTRATION RATIOS FOR SELECTED INDUSTRIES

PRODUCT	CONCENTRATION RATIO
Automobiles	94%
Chewing gum	93
Window glass	89
Sewing machines	82
Detergent (household)	80
Tires	71
Canned beer	66

Source: Federal Trade Commission, *Selected Statistical Series* (Washington, DC: U.S. Government Printing Office, 1990).

The rapid internationalization of world markets makes the maintenance of entry barriers very difficult. It may be possible to limit entry in a domestic economy, but if free trade is allowed or if movements to increase trade exist, these barriers will fall. Almost all arguments against more liberal trade policies, such as the North American Free Trade Agreement (NAFTA), come from those firms and labor unions in those firms that enjoy some economic rents from the barriers to more open trade. One of the most effective antimonopoly policies is a policy of more open international trade.

THE HERFINDAHL INDEX

Herfindahl Index
A summed index of concentration that takes into account all the firms in an industry.

The U.S. Justice Department has been using the **Herfindahl Index,** a summed index of concentration, to replace the more traditional concentration ratios. The Herfindahl Index, which was developed in 1950 by Orris Herfindahl in his Ph.D. dissertation at Columbia University, takes into account the market shares of all of the firms in an industry, not just the market share of the few largest firms. Later in this chapter, we will look at how the Herfindahl Index was used by the Justice Department in the 1980s.

The Herfindahl Index is the sum of the squares of market shares in an industry. The formula for this sum is

$$H = (S_1)^2 + (S_2)^2 + ... + (S_n)^2,$$

where H is the Herfindahl Index and S_1 through S_n are the market shares of individual firms 1 through n. These market shares total 100 percent. An industry that had ten equal-sized firms each having 10 percent of the market would have a Herfindahl Index of 1,000.

Table 3 shows how the Herfindahl Index is calculated for two industries and compares each index to a four-firm concentration ratio. Note that both industries have four-firm concentration ratios of 96 percent, but industry A has a much higher Herfindahl Index (8,116) than industry B (2,308). These

TABLE 3 SAMPLE CALCULATIONS OF THE HERFINDAHL INDEX

	INDUSTRY A			INDUSTRY B	
FIRM	MARKET SHARE (%)	SQUARE OF MARKET SHARE	FIRM	MARKET SHARE (%)	SQUARE OF MARKET SHARE
1	90	8,100	1	24	576
2	2	4	2	24	576
3	2	4	3	24	576
4	2	4	4	24	576
5	1	1	5	1	1
6	1	1	6	1	1
7	1	1	7	1	1
8	1	1	8	1	1

Four-Firm Concentration Ratio = 96%.
Herfindahl Index = 8,116.

Four-Firm Concentration Ratio = 96%.
Herfindahl Index = 2,308.

POLICY FOCUS: CORPORATE COLLABORATION

Should American firms be allowed to collaborate in order to share technology and jointly bear the risk of new innovation? Historically, our antitrust laws have prohibited this type of undertaking, but some firms are already engaged in collaborative activity.

Fifteen U.S. and European pharmaceutical firms announced in 1993 that they plan to share information on AIDS research. The U.S. House has debated and may yet pass legislation that would lower antitrust barriers to joint manufacturing. The bill would reduce penalties on owners of joint ventures if they are later found guilty of antitrust behavior. It would also make it easier for the joint venture participants to defend themselves against the government. President Clinton has endorsed this bill. In 1993, a similar bill passed the U.S. Senate by a vote of ninety-six to one.

Firms in the U.S. auto industry, the Big Three, have begun to collaborate. General Motors, Ford, and Chrysler have set up ten consortia to research areas of interest to the automobile industry. They address such topics as less polluting automobile paint and more human-like crash dummies. One consortium also included the major oil companies. Researchers found that reducing sulfur in gasoline is the easiest way to reduce automobile pollution. The U.S. Advanced Battery Consortium, founded in 1991, has already spent more than $100 million in government and Big Three money to develop a battery to operate an electric car.

The experience from the last time the automakers collaborated does not offer an encouraging forecast for the benefits of future collaboration. In 1969, the U.S. Justice Department sued the Big Three and American Motors over their joint work on pollution controls. The Justice Department charged that they, the automakers, "collectively did all in their power to delay such research (on pollution devices), development, and installation." The automakers settled this civil suit without admitting to any wrongdoing by agreeing to stop all collaboration for eighteen years. This prohibition against collaborative work ended in 1987.

Are these developments good for the U.S. economy? Many think that the answer is yes, and the vote in the Senate seems to indicate that governmental policy will foster such cooperation. One can't, however, help recalling Adam Smith's famous statement: "People of the same trade seldom meet together, even for merriment and diversion, but the conversation ends in a conspiracy against the public, or in some contrivance to raise prices." What do you think Adam Smith would think of this proposed collaboration-permitting legislation?

Herfindahl Index values imply that industry A is 3.5 times more concentrated than is industry B. The table demonstrates that the Herfindahl Index has a much higher value for industries that have a firm or group of firms that are relatively large. This higher value is the result of squaring the individual market shares to construct the index.

THE NUMBER EQUIVALENT

M. A. Adelman has developed another way to interpret the Herfindahl Index. The **number equivalent** is the reciprocal of the Herfindahl Index (1 divided by the value of the Herfindahl Index times 10,000). It shows the theoretical number of equal-sized firms that should be found in an industry. Industry A in Table 3 should have 1.2 equal-sized firms, and industry B should have 4.3. Adelman would conclude that, *ceteris paribus*, industry B would be more competitive than industry A because A has a higher likelihood of collusion.

Number equivalent
A measure of the theoretical number of equal-sized firms that should be found in an industry (the reciprocal of the Herfindahl Index).

CONCENTRATION AND PERFORMANCE

It might seem that the number of concentrated, oligopolistic industries in the U.S. economy is high. But just how concentrated is U.S. industry? And does the concentration make any difference? In other words, would you as a consumer be better off if U.S. industry were generally less concentrated and, thus, perhaps more competitive?

STUDIES OF CONCENTRATION TRENDS

Given the difficulty of defining industries and the fact that any classification scheme requires arbitrary judgments, it is not surprising that studies have reached widely differing conclusions on the degree and trend of concentration in U.S. industry. The studies can be divided roughly into three groups.

One group of studies, which investigated trends in concentration in the first half of the twentieth century, concluded that there had been a pronounced increase in industrial concentration in the United States. This group of studies is associated with and represented by the work of Gardiner Means. Means found that the percentage of total assets controlled by the 200 largest nonfinancial corporations in the United States increased from 33.3 percent to 54.8 percent between 1909 and 1933. In contrast, a second group of studies done more recently by the Federal Trade Commission (FTC) using the same method that Means used showed that the percentage of assets controlled by the 200 largest nonfinancial corporations has not changed since 1950.[2]

The studies that found increased concentration in the early part of the century were challenged in a third group of studies begun by G. Warren Nutter. Nutter argued that industrial concentration declined in the United States between 1901 and 1937. His studies were attacked on the grounds that they relied heavily on data from 1899, which he took as a starting point. Critics argued that these early numbers were suspect because of the poor quality of data for that period. Later, Nutter's study was updated and extended by Henry A. Einhorn.[3] Einhorn used Nutter's data for 1939 as a benchmark and sought to determine if concentration had changed between 1939 and 1958. Einhorn concluded that between 1939 and 1958, roughly 60 percent of national income was generated by firms producing in a competitive structure. The monopolistic sector declined slightly, and the governmental sector increased slightly. The conclusion of Nutter and Einhorn's research is that market concentration in the twentieth century has been surprisingly stable.

William Shepherd looked at a later period using a method similar to Nutter and Einhorn's.[4] Shepherd divided firms in the economy into pure monopoly, dominant firm, tight oligopoly, and effective competition. He then categorized

---

2. Gardiner Means, National Resources Committee, *The Structure of the American Economy* (Washington DC: U.S. Government Printing Office, 1939); Norman R. Collins and Lee E. Preston, "The Size Structure of the Largest Industrial Firms," *American Economic Review* (December 1961); Adolf A. Berle and Gardiner C. Means, *The Modern Corporation and Private Property* (New York: Macmillan, 1933); and Richard Duke, "Trends in Aggregate Concentration," FTC Working Paper No. 61 (June 1982).
3. G. Warren Nutter and Henry A. Einhorn, *Enterprise Monopoly in the United States: 1899–1958* (New York: Columbia University Press, 1969).
4. William G. Shepherd, "Causes of Increased Competition in the U.S. Economy 1939–1980," *Review of Economics and Statistics* (November 1982): 601–631.

firms according to these in 1939, 1958, and 1980. Shepherd concluded that there was a slight increase in effectively competitive firms between 1939 and 1958. He found a significant increase in competitiveness between 1958 and 1980. The share of effectively competitive firms increased from 56.3 percent in 1958 to 76.7 percent in 1980. Shepherd attributed this growth in effectively competitive firms to increased competition from imports, deregulation of U.S. industries (airlines, banking, and trucking), and government antitrust activity.

Can we draw any conclusions from these seemingly conflicting studies? At one extreme in the debate is the position that the level of monopoly power has been stable. At the other extreme is the position that concentration in U.S. industry increased dramatically in the early part of this century and has increased at a much slower pace since World War II.

Keep in mind that these measures of concentration are all aggregate measures. That is, they measure concentration at the national level. These measures may understate the degree of monopoly power in U.S. industries because they ignore or understate the power of local and regional monopolies. The food distribution industry is a good example. At the national level, there is a good deal of competition among supermarket chains. However, in some regions, the concentration ratios are much higher. In some smaller markets, there is a virtual monopoly. Thus, the national figures might lead to the conclusion that the industry is competitive, but the regional or local figures might suggest that the industry consists of a series of local monopolies.

THE MERGER WAVE OF THE LATE 1980S

Beginning in 1983, U.S. industry experienced what many observers think is the greatest reshuffling of corporate assets in its history. Between January 1983 and January 1987, 12,200 companies worth at least $490 billion changed hands—and this was just the beginning. In 1989, the fifty largest acquisitions, mergers, and recapitalizations set a record of $144 billion in combined value. In the 1980s, $1.3 trillion in assets of U.S. corporations were acquired, merged, or purchased.[5]

For the most part, the public and political leaders thought the merger wave was bad for the economy. Most of the corporate raiders and many economists see the situation differently. They see takeovers as a catalyst that is necessary to shake up complacent managers. Often a company is completely restructured in the wake of a takeover or attempted takeover. Companies sometimes eliminate whole levels of management after they are victims of a takeover or in order to prevent a takeover.

Business journalist Leonard Silk points out that the boards of directors of most public companies are not looking out for the stockholders because inside directors owe their careers to the CEO and the outside directors are usually close friends of the CEO.[6] Indeed, Michael Jensen has argued: "The publicly held corporation, the main engine of economic progress in the United States for a century, has outlived its usefulness."[7] Jensen believes that the merger move-

---

5. A detailed report of the fifty largest mergers and acquisitions in the previous year can be in *Fortune* (in January). *Business Week* reported on the two largest deals in each year of the decade (January 15, 1990): 52–57. It also profiled the ten best and the ten worst deals of the 1980s.
6. Leonard Silk, "On Outside Directors," *Business Month* (November 1989): 11–13.
7. Michael C. Jensen, *Harvard Business Review* (September/October 1989): 43.

ment of the 1980s was not a merger movement in the usual sense but, instead, an organizational revolution. He believes that these mergers were a positive step, because they will resolve the conflict inherent in a public corporation. This conflict is due to the separation of ownership and control that we discussed in the chapter on monopoly. It is the conflict over the control of corporate resources and the use of those resources.

A study by Randall Morck, Andrei Shleifer, and Robert Vishny showed that corporate boards of directors have not been the main force behind removing unresponsive managers in industries that have been performing poorly.[8] Instead, these corporate managers have been removed through hostile takeovers. This academic study confirms the anecdotal stories offered by corporate raiders.

THE MERGER WAVE OF THE 1990S

As the decade of the 1980s ended, the activity in leveraged buyouts (LBOs) came to an end. The end was due to problems in the junk bond market, which meant that the raiders couldn't find financing for their deals. A second difficulty was the recession that began in 1990. The wave of LBOs required the confluence of a strong economy, lower interest rates, and a lower stock market. The years 1991 and 1992 were slow in the merger business when compared to every year in the 1980s. This changed in 1993 for a number of reasons. In the summer of 1993, AT&T bought McGraw Cellular for $12.6 billion. Merck bought Medco Containment for $6 billion and Mattel bought Fisher Price. These were just a few of the more visible 1993 mergers.

There were several suggested reasons for this uptick in merger activity. One is that business expected the Clinton administration to be more anti-merger, and was acting quickly while his administration was mired in tax reform and health care, and before it could turn its attention to business policy. A very important second reason is that interest rates were low and these low interest rates made financing costs lower. The LBO mania of the 1980s is being replaced in the 1990s by friendly mergers of big firms in related industries. The criteria for these friendly mergers are reported to be bigness and synergy. There are also signs that U.S. companies are becoming more interested in foreign acquisitions. Many of these friendly mergers have been transatlantic deals between U.S. firms and European firms in the same industry. Some of these mergers may be motivated by the fears of U.S. firms about being excluded from the European market after the European Community becomes more integrated.

THE MARKET CONCENTRATION DOCTRINE

Since the merger movement of the 1980s probably increased concentration in U.S. industry to some degree, we should examine the assumption that concentration, *per se*, is undesirable. Industrial organization economists typically see a sequence relating (1) the structure of the industry to (2) the behavior of firms in that industry (conduct) and then to (3) the performance of the industry itself. According to this line of thought, a highly concentrated structure will pro-

---

8. Randall Morck, Andrei Shleifer, and Robert W. Vishny, "Alternative Mechanisms for Corporate Control," *American Economic Review* (September 1989): 842–852.

duce the antisocial behavior and unsatisfactory performance of a monopoly. The industrial organization economist, therefore, examines the structure of an industry to predict price and output behavior. This structure-conduct-performance chain has been termed the market concentration doctrine.

The **market concentration doctrine** holds that the degree of concentration in an industry is a reliable index of monopoly power and that a high concentration ratio is likely to be associated with undesirable monopoly behavior. Strict application of this doctrine might lead policy makers to suggest antitrust action or some other form of control when concentration ratios reach a certain level. Before examining policy action against monopoly, let's first look at the observations underlying this doctrine.

Those who support the market concentration doctrine base their arguments primarily on two empirical observations. The first is that prices are more rigid (less flexible) in concentrated industries. The second is that profit rates and concentration are positively correlated. Supporters of this doctrine believe that both rigid prices and higher profit rates reflect the effects of the monopoly power that is associated with high degrees of concentration.

Market concentration doctrine
The hypothesis that the degree of concentration in an industry is a reliable index of monopoly power and that a high concentration ratio is likely to be associated with undesirable monopoly behavior.

ADMINISTERED PRICES. The lack of price flexibility in concentrated industries was first noted by Gardiner Means, whose findings were published in a famous monograph.[9] Looking at data from 1926 to 1933, he argued that price movements in different industries varied in frequency. In some industries, prices changed very often. In others, prices tended to be constant for relatively long periods of time. He labeled prices that were relatively rigid, or changed only infrequently, **administered prices**. Later he demonstrated that administered prices were related to the degree of concentration in the industry.[10]

This early work by Means had a significant influence on discussions of public policy toward industry. As is usually the case, the data and methods used by both sides in the debate have been criticized. Competing researchers criticized Means's study because his data were gathered from reports submitted by firms to the Bureau of Labor Statistics. Since firms reported at different intervals, his reported price flexibility (or inflexibility) might simply have reflected a different frequency of reporting.[11] Other researchers claimed that the Bureau's data were composed of prices *asked* by firms and that the relevant data are prices *paid* by consumers.[12] In order to hide their price cuts from their competitors, firms in oligopolies often grant buyers secret cuts on posted prices. For this reason, there could be significant discrepancies between prices asked and prices paid.

Administered prices
Prices that are relatively rigid, or changed only infrequently.

Even though this issue of administered prices has been scrutinized by economists for some time, there hasn't been a scientific conclusion. The conventional wisdom that has become part of public policy debates is that there is a loose association between concentration and price inflexibility. The

---

9. Gardiner Means, *Industrial Prices and Their Relative Inflexibility*, Senate Document 13, 74th Congress, 1st Session (January 17, 1935).
10. National Resources Committee, *The Structure of the American Economy* (Washington DC: U.S. Government Printing Office, 1939).
11. U.S. Congress, Joint Economic Committee, *Government Price Statistics*. Hearings before the Subcommittee on Economic Statistics of the Joint Economic Committee, 87th Congress, 1st Session (1961).
12. George J. Stigler and James K. Kindahl, *The Behavior of Industrial Prices* (New York: National Bureau of Economic Research, 1970).

economist, however, in the capacity of scientist, would be hard put to prove this relationship.

CONCENTRATION AND PROFIT LEVELS. The second observation underlying the market concentration doctrine is that profits and concentration ratios are positively correlated. The theoretical explanation for this relationship is that a small number of firms finds it easier to behave collusively. The empirical link between concentration and profits began with the work of Joe Bain.[13] Bain found that profit rates and concentration ratios were positively correlated for a sample of forty-two manufacturing industries. Bain also found that when the concentration ratio exceeded 70 percent, there was a significant increase in average profit rates. George Stigler, on the other hand, conducted similar research and found there was no clear-cut relationship between concentration ratios and profit rates.[14] In his study, Stigler defined an industry as concentrated if the four-firm concentration ratio for the value of output exceeded 60 percent. Other studies examining this link concluded that there is a weak, but positive, relationship between concentration and profit rates.[15]

There has been debate about the tendency for profits to be higher in concentrated industries over the years. In 1967, President Johnson's Task Force on Antitrust Policy concluded that such a correlation exists:

> *The adverse effects of concentration on output and price find some confirmation in various studies that have been made of return on capital in major industries. These studies have found a close association between high levels of concentration and persistently high rates of return on capital. It is the persistence of high profits over extended time periods and over whole industries rather than in individual firms that suggests artificial restraints on output and the absence of fully effective competition. The correlation of evidence of this kind with very high levels of concentration appears to be significant.*[16]

Bain's conclusion has also been challenged by Yale Brozen.[17] Brozen calculated more recent profit rates for the same industries considered in earlier studies. He found that, with the passage of time, there was a tendency for rates of profit in concentrated industries to converge with those of less concentrated industries. Rates of profit increased in the industries that previously had below-average profit levels and decreased in the industries with above-average profit levels.

DOES CONCENTRATION PREDICT PERFORMANCE? The relationship between concentration and profit levels, like the relationship between concentration and

---

13. Joe S. Bain, "Relation of Profit-Rate to Industry Concentration: American Manufacturing, 1936–1940," *Quarterly Journal of Economics* (August 1951).
14. George J. Stigler, *Capital and Rates of Return in Manufacturing* (Princeton NJ: Princeton University Press, 1963).
15. For a review of these studies, see Harold Demsetz, *The Market Concentration Doctrine* (Washington DC: American Enterprise Institute of Public Policy Research, 1975).
16. White House Task Force on Antitrust Policy, *Role of the Giant Corporation* (Washington, DC: U.S. Government Printing Office, 1967), 883.
17. Yale Brozen, "The Antitrust Task Force Deconcentration Recommendation," *Journal of Law and Economics* (October 1970): 279–292.

price rigidity, has been challenged. There appears to be some evidence to dispute the conventional wisdom that concentration ratios are a good predictor of monopoly performance, especially over time.

Why is this issue important? It is important because present policy proposals to reformulate antitrust law use market concentration as a guide. If concentration is made illegal because it is taken as an indicator of monopoly behavior and performance, many industries may be restructured by the courts simply because they are concentrated. If, instead, these industries are concentrated because there are economies of scale or because they have better, more aggressive managers or more innovation, why break them up? In such cases, antitrust activity would only serve to introduce inefficiencies into the market. In addition, many economists view the increase in concentration in the 1980s as a restructuring of corporate form rather than an increase in monopoly power.

In short, the challenges to the market concentration doctrine are significant enough to deserve closer examination. It is important that economists conduct further tests of this model so that they can provide scientifically grounded advice on this important issue. More research is needed before policy makers take any actions to restructure U.S. industry on the basis of a model that has not been adequately validated.

POLICIES AIMED AT REDUCING MONOPOLY POWER

In the remainder of this chapter, we will discuss policy aimed at correcting the problems associated with monopoly power. Even though there is disagreement over the connection between concentration and monopoly behavior, for most policy decisions, a high level of concentration is taken as implying monopoly behavior.

THE CASE FOR MONOPOLY

In the chapter on monopoly, we examined in detail the costs associated with monopoly. The arguments in favor of policy against monopoly are based on a perceived need to reduce those costs. You should review the chapter on monopoly if you are unclear as to what those costs are. At least two arguments have been made in support of monopoly power. These arguments concern countervailing power and the promotion of technological progress.

COUNTERVAILING POWER. John Kenneth Galbraith has developed the notion of **countervailing power**. He argues that monopoly produces power on both sides of the market, and these two kinds of power countervail, or offset, each other. According to Galbraith, the U.S. economy is made up of big unions, big government, and big firms. In bargaining with each other, these big units are equally powerful. Although Galbraith did not develop the concept of countervailing power as a defense of monopoly, other economists have used it for that purpose.

This argument seems to make some sense. Concentrated tire manufacturers deal with concentrated automobile producers. Large retail chains purchase from concentrated industries that manufacture the products they sell, and labor unions are most successful in concentrated industries, such as steel, autos, and

Countervailing power
The offsetting power possessed by both sides of the market in a monopoly.

mining. Consumers are, however, left out of this process, as Galbraith points out. The costs associated with monopoly still hold for them. In essence, countervailing power redistributes the monopoly profit only among monopoly sellers, monopoly buyers, and monopoly unions.

INNOVATION. Some economists, most notably Austrian-born economist Joseph Schumpeter and John Kenneth Galbraith, have argued that monopoly, or at least oligopoly, is more conducive to technological innovation than competition is. They argue that the costs of monopoly power are offset by the dynamic innovation that monopolistic firms introduce into the economy. Schumpeter called his conclusion that monopoly power leads to innovation "shocking," since traditional analysis showed that monopoly would not be innovative because it did not face the pressure of competition.[18]

Years later Galbraith sounded the same theme, that monopoly power and bigness promote innovation:

In the modern industry shared by a few large firms, size and the rewards accruing to market power combine to insure that resources for research and technical development will be available. The power that enables the firm to have some influence on prices insures that the resulting gains will not be passed on to the public by imitators (who have stood none of the costs of development) before the outlay for development can be recouped. In this way, market power protects the incentive to technical development.[19]

The argument that bigness allows a financial commitment to research and development seems logical. For years, General Electric advertised that progress was its most important product. But what are the facts? The facts, or more correctly the case histories, of invention and innovation are not so convincing. Researchers have found that the majority (as high as two-thirds) of important inventions are the products of individuals working independently and had no support from large research labs funded by giant corporations.[20]

MONOPOLY REGULATION

You have seen that monopoly power is present in the U.S. economy. Monopoly creates a suboptimal allocation of resources. Policy makers may decide that it is best to regulate rather than restructure a monopoly. Two common ways to regulate monopoly are through price regulation and taxation.

MARGINAL COST PRICING

Consider the monopoly represented in Figure 1. The monopoly is maximizing its profits by producing output level Q_1 at price P_1. Assume that the government

---

18. Joseph Schumpeter, *Capitalism, Socialism, and Democracy*, 2e. (New York: Harper and Row, 1942), 81–82.
19. John Kenneth Galbraith, *American Capitalism*, 2e. (Boston: Houghton Mifflin, 1956), 86–87.
20. John Jewkes, David Sawers, and Richard Stillerman, *The Sources of Invention* (New York: St. Martin's Press, 1959).

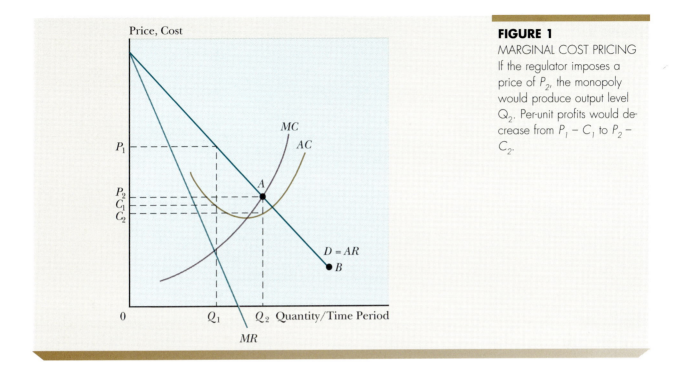

FIGURE 1
MARGINAL COST PRICING
If the regulator imposes a price of P_2, the monopoly would produce output level Q_2. Per-unit profits would decrease from $P_1 - C_1$ to $P_2 - C_2$.

wants to force the firm to produce the amount that would be produced if this were a purely competitive market, that is, to produce where the marginal cost curve intersects the demand curve. If the government set a price ceiling of P_2, the monopoly would react by producing Q_2 units of output because the demand curve the monopoly would face would be represented by line P_2AB. The firm, as always, would be expected to produce where $MR = MC$, and MR would be equal to line P_2A because demand is perfectly elastic for that line segment. The setting of such a price ceiling is sometimes called marginal cost pricing. **Marginal cost pricing** is a policy tool for forcing a monopoly to behave more like a competitive firm by regulating the monopoly price so that it is equal to marginal cost. Note that regulating monopoly in this way reduces per-unit profits from $P_1 - C_1$ to $P_2 - C_2$. Why not lower the price below P_2, since every decrease in price from P_1 to P_2 increases output even more? The problem is that for output levels greater than Q_2, every unit produced costs society more than it is willing to pay ($MC > P$). This larger output is just as inefficient as monopoly behavior when $MC < P$, and the cost of an extra unit is less than society is willing to pay.

Now let's look at a more realistic example, a natural monopoly. Remember, a natural monopoly is one that results from a constantly declining long-run average cost curve. In Figure 2, the profit-maximizing monopolist produces output level Q_1 at price P_1 and receives profit of $P_1 - C_1$ per unit. Now suppose a regulated price of P_2 is imposed on the monopolist. At P_2, it appears that the monopolist would increase output to Q_2. But note that at price P_2 and output level Q_2, the monopolist would lose $P_2 - C_2$ per unit sold. Price would be below average cost, so the monopolist would leave the industry. In other words, the optimal output from society's viewpoint would be where $AR = MC$, but this output would force losses on the monopolist.

Marginal cost pricing
A policy tool for forcing a monopoly to behave more like a competitive firm by regulating the monopoly price so that it is equal to marginal cost.

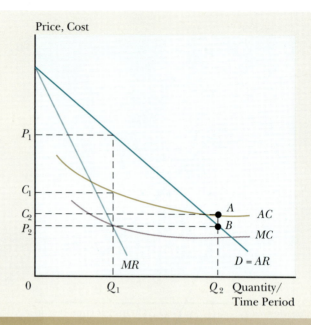

FIGURE 2

MARGINAL COST PRICING AND LOSSES

If the regulator sets a price of P_2, the monopolist would lose $P_2 - C_2$ per unit of output sold. The monopolist would thus only produce if the regulator subsidized it.

The output Q_2 could, however, be feasibly produced if the government would make up the loss, the area of rectangle P_2C_2AB in Figure 2. The monopolist would then produce output level Q_2 at price P_2. The problem with this solution is that if the government subsidizes an industry out of general tax revenues, it is transferring income from taxpayers in general to the consumers of the good produced by the monopoly. Most people (except consumers of the good) would view such a transfer as an unfair redistribution of income. The trick, then, for the would-be price regulator is to set price equal to marginal cost at the point where the MC curve intersects the demand curve, but only if price is equal to or greater than average cost for that level of output. This solution might not be possible in the case of a natural monopoly.

TAXATION OF MONOPOLISTS

Another approach is to use a tax to regulate monopoly power. Suppose government officials impose a license fee (tax) on the monopolist. In Figure 3, before the tax, the monopolist is producing output level Q_1 at price P_1. The average cost curve is AC_1. The monopolist is earning profits of $P_1 - C_1$ per unit. If the monopolist is charged a fee for the right to do business, the fee represents an increase in its fixed cost, but no change in variable or marginal cost. The AC curve shifts up by the amount of the fee, to AC_2 in Figure 3. The monopolist still maximizes profits by producing output level Q_1 at price P_1, but profits have been reduced to $P_1 - C_2$ per unit. Note that it is possible to set the fee so as to capture all the monopoly profit and shift average cost to AC_3 in Figure 3. However, no increase in output would occur.

There are practical difficulties with both methods of regulating monopoly, and they have quite different effects. Price regulation can cause the monopolist to produce the competitive output at a lower price. Taxation, on the other hand, leaves price and output unchanged. A tax simply captures the monopoly

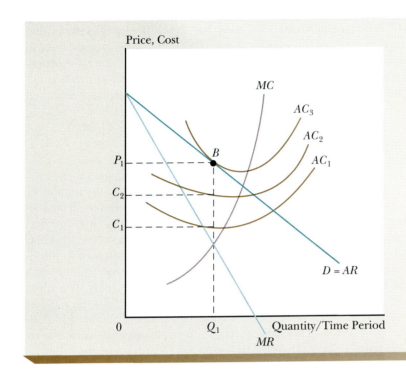

FIGURE 3
TAXING A MONOPOLIST
A license fee will be viewed by a monopolist as a fixed cost and will increase average cost but not marginal cost. The monopoly profit can be taxed away with no effect on output.

profit for the public coffers. It should be clear, then, that for optimal allocation of resources, price regulation is preferred because it increases output and lowers price. Taxation only corrects for the effect of monopoly on the distribution of income. The monopoly profit goes to the government instead of the monopolist and is spent on governmental projects. In this case, there is still an impact on the distribution of income because consumers will be paying "too much" for the product.

THE LERNER INDEX OF MONOPOLY POWER

The theory of regulation just discussed suggested a policy of marginal cost pricing as one way to correct for the misallocation of resources by a monopoly. That suggestion is based on the theoretical notion presented in the last two chapters that the degree of monopoly power is measured by the gap between marginal cost and price. Using this concept, Abba P. Lerner developed an index to measure monopoly power. The **Lerner Index of Monopoly Power (LMP)** evaluates the gap between price and marginal cost as a measure of monopoly power. The index is calculated as follows:

$$LMP = \frac{price - marginal\ cost}{price}$$

In a purely competitive industry, LMP would be zero because price would equal marginal cost. If monopoly power is present, LMP takes on positive values because price will exceed marginal cost. As the gap between price and marginal cost increases, the value of the index rises. Using LMP values permits a researcher to compare the monopoly power of firms.

Lerner Index of Monopoly Power (LMP)
An index that evaluates the gap between price and marginal cost as a measure of monopoly power.

The LMP is a valuable theoretical tool, but the difficulty of determining marginal cost limits its value in empirical work. If average cost data are used to approximate marginal cost data, the results will be misleading. Purely competitive firms might even appear to have monopoly power in the short run because price could be greater than average cost and at the same time equal to marginal cost.

REGULATION IN PRACTICE

Attempts at regulation often increase the power of oligopolies as the regulatory bodies are "captured" by the industry. The firms use the regulation to create barriers to entry, thus increasing their monopoly power. Even if regulators are pursuing the public interest in setting prices to regulate monopoly power, they may not be able to determine marginal costs. They must, in that case, turn to the alternative of regulating price on the basis of average cost information. Although it may not be the most efficient solution, such average cost pricing solves "the problem" of natural monopoly illustrated in Figure 2.

The usual practice is to allow the firm a markup that is a percentage of average costs of production. This most common form of price regulation is referred to as **cost-plus pricing**. This type of regulation creates some distortions. If the monopolist is allowed to charge a price, say, 10 percent above its average cost, it has less incentive to minimize costs. However, consumer demand gives the firm some incentive not to let price get too high.

Perhaps the best example of this form of regulation is in the present regulatory environment for utilities—electricity, gas, water, and so forth. Since utilities are considered natural monopolies, they are regulated for the public interest. Such regulation is based on cost-plus pricing. The markup is often called a fair rate of return. A **fair rate of return** is the normal profit that a regulated industry must earn in order to stay in business. Under such a regulatory policy, utilities have less incentive to cut costs than profit-oriented firms do. For those firms, profits increase whenever costs decrease.

Some communities have debated whether utilities should be allowed to advertise their products. The argument against such advertising is that it simply raises average costs and results in higher prices to consumers. The argument in favor of such advertising is that it usually increases demand, which leads to more output at lower average cost and thus lower prices. The analysis here tends to support the first argument. Interestingly, the assumption of self-interested behavior would predict that a certain group in the community would support utility advertising. Any guesses? Of course, it would be the news media. The news media have strongly supported utility advertising, often on the grounds of free speech.

Regulation not only makes a firm less cost-conscious, but can also raise the actual cost of doing business. The costs of compliance (and noncompliance) with regulation could mean that less is produced at higher prices because costs are higher. In this case, regulation does not promote the goal of making monopolies produce a larger output. Regulation is also rarely limited to price regulation. Most often, regulatory bodies interfere in a wide range of the firm's decisions. Regulation often changes the firm into a quasi-governmental firm, rather than a firm that is responsive to market forces.

Cost-plus pricing
The form of price regulation that allows firms a markup that is a percentage of average costs of production.

Fair rate of return
The normal profit that a regulated industry must earn in order to stay in business.

GLOBAL OUTLOOK: ANTITRUST ABROAD

Antitrust activity like that in the United States is not found in most other countries. Interestingly, after World War II, the U.S. government imposed antitrust policies on the defeated powers, Japan and Germany. Occupation forces set up new governments in Germany and Japan and imposed stringent antitrust measures aimed at deconcentrating industry. There were two stated goals: the first was to punish leading industrial groups for their wartime efforts, and the second was to weaken the German and Japanese industrial base so that those countries would be less able to pursue future wars.

This second objective was inconsistent with domestic antitrust policy in the United States at the time. Domestic policy was to pursue antitrust actions to limit monopoly power and make the U.S. economy *more* efficient. At the same time, foreign policy was to break up German and Japanese trusts to make them *less* efficient. After the United States decided that Japan and Germany should be allowed to grow economically, to counter Soviet expansion in the Cold War period, the first policy changed was the antitrust policy. One might legitimately ask what caused policy makers to view concentration as good for Germany and Japan and bad for the United States?

Except for the vigorous antitrust policy imposed temporarily on Germany and Japan, there have been no antitrust laws in other countries that are concentration-based and result in divestiture. In the mid–1970s, there was vigorous debate about proposed legislation for divestiture in Japan, but it was not enacted. Japan's trading conglomerates, called *sogo shosha*, are informal associations of industrial, financial, and commercial companies. These associations could not exist under U.S. antitrust laws.

Much of the relevant law in Europe is based on the Treaty of Rome, which established the European Economic Community. Individual countries tend to monitor the activities of "market-dominating" firms and regulate their price-setting ability. The emphasis is not on breaking up monopolies or potential monopolies but rather on preventing the abuse of any market power. A typical remedy is a price rollback and a requirement of government approval of future price increases. European governments often monitor the prices, costs, and profit rates of large firms.

ANTITRUST LAWS IN THE UNITED STATES

Toward the end of the nineteenth century, there was a substantial increase in the number of large business organizations in the United States. This period saw the establishment of legal arrangements such as **trusts**, which were organizations set up to control the stock of other companies through boards of trustees, and **holding companies**, which were firms set up for the sole purpose of owning and thus controlling other firms. Trusts and holding companies enabled robber barons, as they have been called by economic historians, to control and coordinate the activities of many previously independent firms. At first, these new types of companies were viewed as a natural outgrowth of the Industrial Revolution in the United States.

Eventually the public began to view some of these arrangements with suspicion. One of the earliest groups organized to oppose the trust movement was the National Grange. The Grange was a farm-based group organized in 1867 to oppose trusts. The efforts were mainly directed at the railroad trust because of the high monopoly prices it set, and also because it was able to practice price discrimination in the hauling of agricultural products.

In response to the Grange and other political movements against trusts, several states enacted antitrust statutes that regulated businesses chartered in those

Trusts
Organizations set up to control the stock of other companies through boards of trustees.

Holding companies
Firms set up for the sole purpose of owning and thus controlling other firms.

Sherman Antitrust Act
The first federal antitrust law in the United States, passed in 1890. Section 1 of the act declared every contract, combination, or conspiracy in restraint of trade to be illegal. Section 2 made it illegal to monopolize or attempt to monopolize.

Clayton Act
A federal law, passed in 1914, prohibiting the acquisition of the stock of a competing company if such an acquisition would "substantially lessen competition." It also prohibited tying contracts.

Tying contracts
Agreements between producers and retailers that call for the retailer to stock certain items in return for being allowed to stock other items.

Robinson-Patman Act
A federal law that amended the Clayton Act in 1936, making predatory pricing illegal.

Predatory pricing
The act of selling below cost to destroy competitors.

Celler-Kefauver Antimerger Act
A federal law that strengthened the Clayton Act in 1950 by making it illegal in certain circumstances for a firm to merge with another by purchasing its assets.

states. These state laws failed because corporations were able to obtain charters in less restrictive states. Two of the more lenient states were New Jersey and Delaware. By 1888, the antitrust sentiment had become so widespread and intense that both national political parties had an antitrust plank in their platforms.

In 1890, Congress passed the **Sherman Antitrust Act**, the first federal antitrust law. This act had two major provisions. Section 1 declared every contract, combination, or conspiracy in restraint of trade to be illegal. Section 2 made it illegal to monopolize or attempt to monopolize.[21] The language of the act is strong, but it is also vague, and the courts took years to determine its scope. We will trace some of the important decisions, after identifying the other major antitrust laws.

The **Clayton Act**, passed in 1914, made illegal certain business practices that could lead to monopoly. It prohibited a company from acquiring the stock of a competing company if such an acquisition would "substantially lessen competition." The act also prohibited tying contracts and price discrimination. **Tying contracts** are agreements between producers and retailers that call for the retailer to stock certain items in return for being allowed to stock other items. In 1936, the **Robinson-Patman Act** amended the Clayton Act to make predatory pricing illegal. **Predatory pricing** is selling below cost to destroy competitors. Although the Clayton Act prohibited the acquisition of competing firms through stock purchase, firms could get around this obstacle because the law did not prohibit acquisition of physical assets. The **Celler-Kefauver Antimerger Act**, passed in 1950, made it illegal in certain circumstances for a firm to merge with another by purchasing its assets. This act strengthened the Clayton Act.

In 1914, Congress passed the **Federal Trade Commission Act**. This act set up the Federal Trade Commission (FTC) to police unfair and deceptive business practices. Initially, the FTC had many powers, but in 1919 the Supreme Court denied it the power to issue cease and desist orders without judicial review. In 1938, the FTC Act was amended by the **Wheeler-Lea Act**, which added "unfair or deceptive acts or practices in commerce" to the list of transgressions. The **Hart-Scott-Rodino Antitrust Improvement Act** further amended the FTC Act in 1970. It required firms contemplating a merger or acquisition to notify the FTC and the Department of Justice before carrying it out.[22]

THE HISTORY OF ANTITRUST ENFORCEMENT

It took some time for the courts to determine the scope of the Sherman Act, in particular, and to form a legal definition of the phrase "in restraint of trade." Under a strict economic definition, a firm with any monopoly power (that is, power to restrict output or to increase price) would be guilty of restraint of trade. In two famous cases against Standard Oil and American Tobacco in 1911,

---

21. "Section 1: Every contract, combination in the form of trust or otherwise, or conspiracy, in restraint of trade or commerce among the several States, or with foreign nations, is declared to be illegal.... Section 2: Every person who shall monopolize, or attempt to monopolize, or combine or conspire with any other person or persons, to monopolize any part of the trade or commerce among the several States, or with foreign nations, shall be deemed guilty of a misdemeanor." (Sherman Antitrust Act, Sec. 1, 26 Stat. 209, 1890).

22. For more detail on all these laws, see J. G. Van Cise, *Understanding the Antitrust Laws* (New York: Practicing Law Institute, 1973).

KEY IDEAS

UNITED STATES ANTITRUST LAWS

ACT AND YEAR PASSED	MAJOR PROVISION(S)
• Sherman Antitrust Act (1890)	Makes it illegal to monopolize or attempt to monopolize. Makes contracts, combinations, or conspiracies in restraint of trade illegal.
• Clayton Act (1914)	Prohibits the acquisition of the stock of another company if that action will substantially lessen competition. Prohibits tying contracts and price discrimination.
• Robinson-Patman Act (1936)	Amendment to the Clayton Act that makes predatory pricing illegal.
• Celler-Kefauver Antimerger Act (1950)	Amendment to the Clayton Act that makes it illegal to purchase the assets of another company if that action will substantially lessen competition.
• Federal Trade Commission Act (1914)	Established the FTC to police unfair and deceptive business practices.
• Wheeler-Lea Act (1938)	Amendment to the FTC Act that makes unfair or deceptive trade practices illegal.
• Hart-Scott-Rodino Antitrust Improvement Act (1970)	Requires that the FTC and Justice Department be notified prior to mergers or acquisitions.

Federal Trade Commission Act A federal law passed in 1914 that set up the Federal Trade Commission (FTC) to police unfair and deceptive business practices.

Wheeler-Lea Act A 1938 federal law amending the FTC Act to make unfair or deceptive acts or practices in commerce illegal.

Hart-Scott-Rodino Antitrust Improvement Act A 1970 federal law amending the FTC Act to require firms to report mergers or acquisitions to the FTC and Department of Justice before the fact.

the Supreme Court interpreted the law using the rule of reason, which said that monopolies that behaved well were not illegal. In effect, the Court defined—some might say rewrote—the Sherman Antitrust Act to make only "unreasonable" restraints of trade illegal. The test of reasonableness was itself difficult to define. The Court held that the existence of competitors was sufficient to demonstrate reasonable behavior. In 1920, U.S. Steel, despite its dominance of the steel industry, was found not to be an unreasonable monopoly. The Court stated that the law did not make mere size an offense.

In 1945, after thirteen years of litigation, the rule of reason was dropped. Judge Learned Hand ruled in a case against Alcoa that size itself *was* enough to prove the exercise of monopoly power. The change was so fundamental that the ruling became known as the "new Sherman Act." The Alcoa case was based on estimates of market power and structural aspects of the industry. In such cases, the way in which an industry is defined is extremely important. In fact, to a large degree it determines defense and prosecution strategies. As you might guess, the defense would prefer the industry to be broadly defined, both geographically and by the number of products included, since that definition tends to reduce the importance of any one firm in any particular industry.[23]

---

23. For some examples of the ridiculous lengths to which defense lawyers will go in defining the relevant market, see Franklin M. Fisher, "Diagnosing Monopoly," *Quarterly Review of Economics and Business* (Summer 1979): 7–33.

The DuPont cellophane case in 1956 gave further indication of what the courts thought about markets. The Justice Department filed suit against DuPont for monopolizing the cellophane market because the company controlled 75 percent of U.S. sales. DuPont's lawyers successfully argued that the relevant market was not that for cellophane only, but rather that for flexible wrapping materials. These included waxed paper, aluminum foil, and vegetable parchment. The court said that products that are "reasonably interchangeable" must be included in the definition of a market. DuPont controlled only 20 percent of the market for a "reasonably interchangeable" set of wrapping products.

In 1982, the Justice Department's case against IBM, initiated in 1969, was dismissed. The case began when the Justice Department accused IBM of monopolizing the "general-purpose computer and peripheral-equipment industry." In 1969, IBM controlled 70 percent of the large mainframe computer market and 40 percent of the office equipment market. When the case was dismissed, IBM still controlled 70 percent of the mainframe computer market but was experiencing strong competition in office equipment and microcomputers. This case, like the others, centered on market share and the definition of the industry or market. The trend seems to be toward defining markets in a much broader way.

Another significant change in antitrust activity took place much more recently. The Sherman Antitrust Act provides that private parties who are victims of monopoly under Sections 1 and 2 are entitled to sue for treble damages. Section 7 of the Sherman Act provided for private treble damage actions. This provision was superseded by the more precise language of Section 4 of the Clayton Act, which *required* treble damages. Section 4 of the Clayton Act said ". . . and shall recover three-fold damages. . . ." In other words, if a firm is convicted under the Sherman or Clayton Acts, individuals will recover three times the damages they have sustained. Historically, it was seldom invoked. Recently, however, consumer groups have brought many class action lawsuits under the provisions of the antitrust laws. Consumer groups bring action on behalf of the entire class of consumers, and treble damages in these cases can be very large.

In recent years there has been a steady increase in antitrust cases brought by private parties. The courts can only rule on cases brought before them. This raises an important question: Who initiates most governmentally pursued antitrust cases? The decision on whether to bring charges or not rests largely with the Antitrust Division of the Department of Justice. This decision is made by a presidential appointee, the assistant attorney general for antitrust. Antitrust policy therefore reflects the wishes of the President. Theodore Roosevelt campaigned as the great "trust-buster." When he became president, he set up the Antitrust Division, and his administration brought the first cases.

Franklin Roosevelt's first term saw virtually no activity on the antitrust scene. On the contrary, in the early years of the Depression, the federal government actually fostered anticompetitive practices through the National Recovery Administration (NRA). The **National Recovery Administration (NRA)** was a major New Deal program aimed at business recovery. It allowed and encouraged agreements between firms. It set up cartels in virtually every industry, but they eventually were declared unconstitutional. In 1937, the Roosevelt administration changed its position and vigorously pursued antitrust cases, including the Alcoa case, which ultimately reversed the rule of reason.

National Recovery Administration (NRA) A major New Deal program that was aimed at business recovery but was anticompetitive since it allowed and encouraged agreements between firms. It was eventually declared unconstitutional.

Both the Eisenhower and Kennedy administrations pursued active antitrust programs. Johnson's administration retreated from vigorous antitrust policy, although the IBM case was filed at the end of his term in office. Nixon's first assistant attorney general, Richard McLaren, worked at restricting conglomerate mergers (in which a company buys a firm unrelated to its existing business). The Ford administration pursued an active antitrust policy. A major case was launched against AT&T, and many price-fixing cases were filed.

Carter appointees promised to use the antitrust laws to change the concentration of power. They also promised to attack shared monopolies (in which very few firms control an industry) and to speed up the litigation process so cases would not drag on for years. Very little was accomplished along these lines during Carter's tenure.

In 1980, Reagan's appointees made it clear that they did not equate big business with bad business practices. William Baxter, Reagan's first assistant attorney general for antitrust, believed that the purpose of antitrust activity should be to promote efficiency. To this end, Baxter argued that government should not interfere with most vertical mergers (mergers in which a company acquires other firms involved in different stages of production in the same production process). He also felt that conglomerate mergers should be allowed. Baxter argued that vertical mergers and conglomerate mergers seldom foster price fixing and do not reduce competition. On the other hand, Baxter approved of tough action against horizontal mergers (in which a firm acquires a competitor).

Baxter changed many of the practices of the Antitrust Division, dropping the Nixon administration's attack on conglomerates and the Carter administration's attack on shared monopoly. Reagan's first chair of the FTC, James C. Miller III, engineered a similar policy change there. These policy changes encouraged the merger movement of the 1980s. Most observers feel that many of those mergers would never have been permitted by previous administrations.

In 1986, the policies of the Reagan administration were supported by the Supreme Court, which ruled that antitrust laws were not meant to prevent mergers just because they create larger, more formidable competitors. The Supreme Court overturned two lower court decisions in allowing Cargill to buy Spencer Beef, combining the second and third largest beef packing companies.

When George Bush was elected president in 1988, it was believed that his administration would follow the laissez-faire policies of the Reagan administration. However, by 1990, it was clear that the policies of the Bush administration were decidedly different from those of the Reagan administration. President Bush's chief antitrust appointees, Janet D. Steiger, chair of the FTC, and James F. Rill, assistant attorney general for antitrust, openly expressed skepticism about the Reagan view that bigness means efficiency and would benefit consumers. They stepped up antitrust and regulatory activity.

In the Reagan era, the FTC stayed out of most merger proposals. In late 1988, after Bush was elected, executives at Winn-Dixie tried to increase their market share in Florida by buying U-Save Supermarkets. Under Reagan, this purchase would not have been challenged, but Steiger demanded so much data from Winn-Dixie that the merger was abandoned in early 1990. Increased FTC scrutiny will probably discourage mergers in the 1990s.

It is likely that antitrust and regulatory activity will be more aggressive in the Clinton administration than the Bush administration, further changing policy from the eight "hands-off" years of Reagan. President Clinton named Anne K. Bingaman as head of the Antitrust Division of the Department of Justice. Bingaman in early interviews claimed that she would return activism to the Justice Department. After being on the job only two months, Bingaman decided to investigate Microsoft, described in the business press as a "daunting foe." The case against Microsoft is that it offers unfair discount to customers, squeezing out competing makers of software. A second charge is that it designs its software so that the programs of competitors don't run properly.

Clinton's impact on the FTC was slow to develop. No seats at the FTC became open until late 1994. At that time Clinton could name his person and a new chair would be elected. However, FTC policy had already shifted away from the laissez-faire policy of the Reagan presidency under President Bush. It is likely that the Clinton FTC will be even more activist than the Bush FTC. Almost all of the economists Clinton has appointed to economic policy making positions believe in more regulation than those in the Bush and Regan administrations.

THE ROLE OF ECONOMIC VARIABLES IN FILING CASES

Economists and lawyers have used statistical analysis to study case-bringing activity of the Justice Department. The first such study, by Richard Posner, found that in the first eight decades of the Sherman Act, 1,551 cases were brought by the Justice Department.[24] Antitrust activity can also be initiated by the FTC and even by private citizens. Posner found that, contrary to popular belief, the antimonopoly activity of the FTC has not increased over time. However, the number of cases brought by private citizens has increased continuously since 1949.

Antitrust enforcement by the states has also been stepped up. This change, in part, resulted from a 1976 law that allows state attorneys general to sue suspected price fixers for treble damages on behalf of citizens. Politics often influence the use of this power. State attorneys general are often campaigning for reelection or for higher office. They will bring lawsuits for publicity value but will be careful to avoid suits against powerful groups that may help them in future elections. Cases are often brought against out-of-state firms. This approach creates good publicity but doesn't damage the attorney general's support from in-state businesses.

Although many antitrust cases last as long as five and six years, the success rate of the Justice Department is much higher than for FTC and private cases. However, the remedies the court imposes have been far from successful in terms of restoring competition. In civil cases, the remedy has often taken the form of regulation. The stated goal of antitrust activity is restoring competition, but regulation is in fact an admission that competition cannot be restored. The problems that regulation introduces make it a very unsatisfactory remedy. Criminal cases have resulted in very weak penalties for those found guilty. Not until the late 1950s was an individual sentenced to jail for price fixing. In 1960, seven more executives were sentenced to jail. In the few cases in which sentences have been imposed, the terms have been very short. In addition, the fines levied have been too small to have much of a deterrent effect.

Posner's study spawned some attempts to examine the determinants of antitrust activity. Posner pointed out that the level of antitrust activity and the

---

24. Richard A. Posner, "A Statistical Study of Antitrust Enforcement," *Journal of Law and Economics* (October 1970).

kinds of cases did not seem to be related to economic conditions in the country. He also found that the political party of the President does not seem to affect the number of cases initiated. This finding, of course, does not mean that politics does not affect the Justice Department's antitrust activity. It only means that the amount of political interference has not, on the average, been too much affected by which party holds the presidency.

William Long, Richard Schramm, and Robert Tollison analyzed case-bringing patterns of the Justice Department and found that cases were more likely to be brought in larger industries, measured by sales.[25] Other variables that may more meaningfully indicate monopoly power, such as profit rates on sales and concentration, were found to be less important in explaining Justice Department cases. John Siegfried has found that economic variables have little influence on the kinds of cases filed by the Justice Department.[26] The work of Siegfried and Peter Asch suggests that the case-bringing criteria of the Justice Department are complex and difficult to forecast using economic variables.[27]

THE ECONOMIC CONSEQUENCES OF ANTITRUST ACTIVITY

In addition to looking for an economic explanation of antitrust activity, economists have begun to examine its economic consequences. Several of these empirical studies are informative. Peter Asch and J. J. Seneca found that firms that were known to be engaged in collusion were, surprisingly, less profitable than firms that were not known to be in collusion.[28] Robert Feinberg argued that these results were actually due to the deterrent effect of antitrust cases.[29] Dosoung Choi and George Philippatos found that the filing of antitrust cases caused restraint in pricing but that this restraint decreased with the number of times the firm had been indicted.[30] This finding implies a diminishing return to bringing cases against a single firm, an implication that any beginning student of economics should be able to explain. Finally, and not too surprisingly, Kenneth Garbade, William Silber, and Lawrence White have found that the announcement of an antitrust suit against a firm has a negative impact on the stock price of that firm.[31]

ANTITRUST, GOVERNMENT-SPONSORED MONOPOLY, AND DEREGULATION

In recent years, the policy discussion about monopoly has shifted to looking at the role of government in fostering monopoly. Harold Demsetz has argued that

---

25. William F. Long, Richard Schramm, and Robert Tollison, "Economic Determinants of Antitrust Activity," *Journal of Law and Economics* (October 1973).
26. John J. Siegfried, "The Determinants of Antitrust Activity," *Journal of Law and Economics* (October 1975).
27. Peter Asch, "The Determinants and Effects of Antitrust Activity," *Journal of Law and Economics* (October 1975).
28. Peter Asch and J.J. Seneca, "Is Collusion Profitable?" *The Review of Economics and Statistics* (February 1976).
29. Robert Feinbert, "Antitrust Enforcement and Subsequent Price Behavior," *The Review of Economics and Statistics* (November 1980).
30. Dosoung Choi and George Philippatos, "The Financial Consequences of Antitrust Enforcement," *The Review of Economics and Statistics* (August 1983).
31. Kenneth Garbade, William Silber, and Lawrence White, "Market Reaction to the Filing of Antitrust Suits: An Aggregate and Cross Sectional Analysis," *The Review of Economics and Statistics* (November 1982).

there are two systems of belief about monopoly.[32] One system views private sector monopoly as a major threat to the economy. This view is held by supporters of the market concentration doctrine, who think such monopolies should be aggressively regulated and pursued by strictly defined antitrust policy. The other system, which Demsetz calls "the new learning," views the more serious economic threat as coming from monopolies that are sponsored and protected by government. Reducing the threat from this type of monopoly calls for deregulation and less governmental control. The new learning approach is helpful in understanding antitrust activity in the 1980s because it influenced the Reagan administration's view of monopoly.

THE ALPHABET SOUP OF REGULATORY AGENCIES

Regulation at the federal level has resulted in a host of regulatory agencies aimed at protecting consumer welfare. The acronyms for these agencies read like a can of alphabet soup: CAB, EEOC, EPA, FCC, FDA, FTC, ICC, NHTSA, OSHA, ITC, and SEC. The number of such agencies grew very rapidly in the 1960s and 1970s. The Reagan administration cut back their budgets and staffing. Presumably, lower budgets and fewer people meant less regulation. The Bush administration restored some of these cuts. The Clinton administration is very active on the regulatory front. This increased activity is especially apparent in the Environmental Protection Agency (EPA).

In many cases, regulatory agencies that were formed for consumer protection actually inhibited competition and innovation. Before airline deregulation, the Civil Aeronautics Board (CAB) set fares and prohibited entry. The Food and Drug Administration (FDA) still tightly controls innovation and entry in drug markets, forcing U.S. citizens to travel to foreign countries for access to certain medical procedures and drugs. On a local level, most cities regulate taxicabs by setting minimum prices, controlling entry, or both. Ironically, in many instances, regulatory agencies set up for consumer protection are responsible for the monopoly power that exists in the regulated market. Many companies defend the regulatory status quo because they have already met the regulations, and these regulations serve as an effective barrier to new entry and new competition. These firms are the government-supported monopolies that Demsetz identified.

COMPETITIVENESS

Those who propose a national economic policy to improve competitiveness seem to draw their ideas from the success of the Japanese economy. There is a belief that that success stems from the government's working closely with private industry to ensure that private industry is successful. The idea, in part, is that government should take steps to back industrial "winners" to make them even more successful. Such proposals rest on the premise that the U.S. economy is in serious decline and that other countries (notably Japan) have had a positive experience that is a result of industrial-governmental "partnerships."

---

32. Harold Demsetz, "Two Systems of Belief about Monopoly," in H. Goldschmid, H. M. Mann, and J. F. Weston, eds., *Industrial Concentration: The New Learning* (Boston: Little, Brown, 1974).

Regardless of the form that a policy fostering competitiveness may take at the federal level, it would represent an increased governmental role in making economic decisions. Proponents of such a policy are quick to point out that the United States already has a kind of industrial policy because every action of government in taxing and spending rewards some participants in the economy and penalizes others. Those individuals argue that a coordinated and intentional policy would be preferable to what exists at present. A competitiveness policy, however, would result in a more active role for government in the economy than most market-oriented economists would find acceptable.[33]

The latest argument for an industrial policy has come out of Silicon Valley in California. The high-tech manufacturers there want the United States to form a cohesive industrial policy to help them compete with what they refer to as "Japan, Inc." At the beginning of the Bush administration, their lobbyists in Washington were hopeful that the new administration would develop a plan to help them. They soon learned that Bush's advisers were opposed to industrial policy.

President Clinton, unlike Reagan and Bush, is an advocate of industrial policy, or "aiding specific industries," as he refers to it. His policy advisers have plans to help the auto industry develop a "clean" car, build the "information highway," aid oil and gas exploration, and help the shipbuilding industry, to name a few of their proposals.[34] Many of Clinton's economic policy advisers have been advocates of industrial policy for many years. Their influence will be seen in specific proposals to aid specific industries.

The competitiveness debate has a different focus at the state level. Policy makers at that level have become very involved in economic development activities. Almost every state has a state development board that aids the governor in recruiting new firms to the state from other states and foreign countries. Government officials use all types of tax breaks and other incentives to lure new firms to their states. In this context, fostering competitiveness can mean writing state tax laws, changing state regulatory activity, and examining state services, to make a state competitive with other states. Such competition puts constraints on state governments; if officials in one state create an environment that is hostile to business, firms will migrate to more friendly states.

ALTERNATIVES FOR CONTROLLING INDUSTRY

There is a great deal of monopoly power, or at least concentration, in U.S. industry, and monopoly power is undesirable from society's point of view. Unfortunately, attempts to control monopoly or to restore competition through antitrust actions have not always produced the desired results. Antitrust cases drag on for many years. The economic analysis in these cases is very complex and often conflicting. The arguments are difficult to present, and juries, judges, and even lawyers do not always understand them. Generally, the result is government intervention in the market that can introduce new inefficiencies.

---

33. For a thorough review of the industrial policy debate, see R. D. Norton, "Industrial Policy and American Renewal," *Journal of Economic Literature* (March 1986).
34. "Bill's Recipe: How He Plans to Help U.S. Business Cream Rivals," *Business Week*, (October 18, 1993): 30–31.

There does, however, seem to be at least one policy action that could increase competition without endangering the efficiency resulting from economies of scale. This policy is based on the benefits from the threat of new entry. If public policy could support new entry by dismantling artificial barriers to entry, competitive pressure would increase. These artificial barriers are both privately and publicly imposed. In many cases, the threat of new entry alone would be enough to alter the behavior of oligopolies.

Internationalization of the economy destroys many domestic barriers. As world markets become more integrated, the relevant market for antitrust activity becomes larger. If international trade is expanded, there may be less need to worry about domestic monopolies from an antitrust perspective.

Consider again... *You have been sitting in the jury box for four-and-a-half weeks. On August 10, Judge Kent reads the charge to the jury and sends you out to deliberate this very complicated, perhaps precedent-setting case. Judge Kent gives you twenty-seven pages of instructions and tells you that you have to be convinced that American "specifically intended" to monopolize the air markets served by Continental and Northwest. You and your fellow jurors return to the courtroom in less than an hour with a not guilty verdict. Some reporters note that this was not enough time to even read the Judge's instructions.*

American's CEO, Robert Crandall, indicated after the verdict that he was pleased with the outcome, but that it had cost American more than $20 million to defend itself. He indicated that, "My feelings are hurt. No one likes to be personally attacked." Crandall also had plenty of criticism for Continental and Northwest. He thought the suit was baseless and never should have been brought. Several weeks after the verdict, some of your fellow jurors were interviewed. The general consensus among them was that price wars benefit consumers and should not be illegal. In a period when new entry is not regulated, that is a very sound economic judgment. From an economic point of view, you and your fellow jurors did a very good job!

SUMMARY

1. Industries can be defined by SIC codes established by the Commerce Department. SIC codes can be used to calculate concentration ratios, which are measures of the degree to which markets are concentrated. The Herfindahl Index may be a better measure of monopoly power than a concentration ratio because it accounts for all of the firms in the industry. A Lerner Index of Monopoly Power (LMP) measures the percentage difference between price and marginal cost. It is perhaps the best measure of monopoly power, but limited availability of marginal cost data limits its use.

2. There is no conclusive evidence on the trend of concentration in U.S. industry. Some researchers have found the concentration level to be quite stable. Others have found an increase in competitive firms. The market concentration doctrine states that the structure of an industry determines its ultimate performance in terms of prices and profits. This model implies that concentrated industries should be restructured. There is, however, a good deal of debate concerning the degree to which concentration leads to higher profit rates and more rigid prices.

3. Regulation of monopoly leads to cost-plus pricing, which destroys the incentive to minimize costs. Taxation of monopoly is an alternative to regulation. It simply captures monopoly profits without affecting price or output.
4. U.S. antitrust law began with the Sherman Antitrust Act in 1890. The Sherman Act and later laws have been applied with varying degrees of vigor and success. The record of antitrust enforcement is not too impressive. Lawsuits take a long time and rarely restore competition. Politics plays an important role in antitrust activity. The merger movement of the 1980s may have increased the concentration of some U.S. industries. This movement involved $1.3 trillion in assets. Some economists believe that the business trend of the 1980s was more a restructuring of corporate management than a traditional merger movement. Mergers in the 1990s seem to be motivated by a desire to become internationalized, especially with respect to the European market.
5. Competitiveness became a major public concern in the late 1980s. At the federal level, it is an aspect of industrial policy, which has some proponents in the Clinton administration. At the state level, it relates to economic development.
6. Perhaps the most effective public policy tool in addressing monopoly power is to ease entry. Internationalization of the world's economies works to facilitate new entry.

NEW TERMS

industry
Standard Industrial Classification (SIC) system
industry studies
concentration ratio
Herfindahl Index
number equivalent
market concentration doctrine
administered prices
countervailing power
marginal cost pricing
Lerner Index of Monopoly Power (LMP)
cost-plus pricing
fair rate of return
trusts
holding companies
Sherman Antitrust Act
Clayton Act
tying contracts
Robinson-Patman Act
predatory pricing
Celler-Kefauver Antimerger Act
Federal Trade Commission Act
Wheeler-Lea Act
Hart-Scott-Rodino Antitrust Improvement Act
National Recovery Administration (NRA)

QUESTIONS: REVIEW, APPPLICATIONS, AND POLICY

REVIEW

1. Are profits a good measure of monopoly power? Is concentration a good measure of monopoly power? Discuss the advantages of using either or both.
2. Do concentration ratios provide any useful information about changes in conglomerate merger activity?

APPLICATIONS

3. The following data are for the soft drink industry in a certain country.

FIRMS	ANNUAL SALES (IN DOLLARS)
1	$400,000,000
2	300,000,000
3	200,000,000
4 1	50,000,000
5–35	300,000,000

What is the four-firm concentration ratio for this industry?
4. Now assume that the entire soft drink industry is made up of the first four firms listed in Question 3. What is the four-firm concentration ratio? What is the Herfindahl Index? What is the number equivalent? What does the number equivalent tell you?
5. What would happen to the concentration ratio in Question 3 if the industry were defined as the beverage industry? As the name-brand, nationally advertised soft drink industry?
6. A comprehensive study of the U.S. economy argued that it became more effectively competitive between 1958 and 1980. What are the three reasons for this increase in the number of competitive firms? How did each of these three reasons work to increase competitiveness?
7. Some economists argue that the merger movement of the 1980s was different from earlier movements because of the inherent problem of the separation of ownership and control in U.S. corporations. What do these economists have in mind?

POLICY

8. What would happen in a regulated industry if the price were set such that a representative firm could not earn a normal profit?

9. If prices charged by all firms in an industry are identical, is this evidence of an antitrust violation?
10. Why is it so difficult to regulate a natural monopoly?
11. Why do some economists favor deregulation as a way of dealing with monopoly rather than "better" or "tougher" regulation?
12. Imagine that the President has just appointed you the major national adviser on antitrust. Convince the cabinet that the government should pursue an active antitrust policy. After you have done that, take the opposite side and argue that monopoly is not so bad and the government shouldn't worry too much about it.
13. Why might U.S. firms want to merge with foreign firms, especially European firms?
14. Airlines were deregulated near the end of the Carter presidency and subjected to further competitive pressures in the Reagan years. In the last few years the airlines have suffered huge losses. Do you think they should be reregulated? Why or why not?
15. The term *competitiveness* is used increasingly in political campaigns. How does the meaning of the term differ when it is used by a candidate for federal office as opposed to a candidate for state office?

SUGGESTIONS FOR FURTHER READING

Adams, Walter, and James Brock. *Antitrust Economics on Trial: A Dialogue on the New Laissez-Faire.* Princeton NJ: Princeton University Press, 1991. A debate about the "new learning" by opponents to the new learning; it is conducted as a judicial hearing to determine the credibility of a new learning expert witness. Very readable; a must for would-be antitrust lawyers.

Asch, Peter. *Industrial Organization and Antitrust Policy.* New York: John Wiley and Sons, 1986. A textbook that gives detailed accounts of important antitrust cases.

Bauer, Paul W. "Airline Deregulation: Boon or Bust?" *Economic Commentary,* Federal Reserve Bank of Cleveland (May 1, 1989). A commentary on the issues surrounding airline deregulation.

Hermann, Werner, and G. J. Santoni. "The Cost of Restricting Corporate Takeovers: A Lesson from Switzerland." *Review,* Federal Reserve Bank of St. Louis (November/December 1989): 3–11. According to this article, the Swiss experience shows that restricting corporate takeovers has serious consequences on the wealth of stockholders.

Kim, E. Han, and Vijay Singal. "Mergers and Market Power: Evidence from the Airline Industry." *American Economic Review* (June 1993). An empirical paper that shows that mergers in the airline industry between 1985 and 1988 resulted in increased prices in those markets.

Reich, Robert B. *Tales of a New America.* New York: Random House, 1987. A book on competitiveness by one of the advocates of industrial policy.

Scherer, F. M. *Industrial Market Structure and Economic Performance,* 3e. Boston: Houghton Mifflin, 1990. A source book with detailed references to the literature on regulation and antitrust matters.

Winston, Clifford. "Economic Deregulation: Days of Reckoning for Economists." *Journal of Economic Literature* (September 1993): 1263–1289. A recent study that shows that the deregulation of the 1980s had significant positive economic impacts.

PART 8

RESOURCE MARKETS

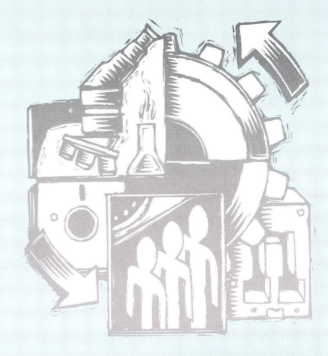

The next four chapters deal with productive resources. In the last few chapters, we described product markets, in which firms or individuals sell the goods and services they produce to consumers. Now we want to examine the labor market, the market in which firms buy—or rent—the services of labor from individuals. We can adopt many of the same analytical tools we used to study product markets. There are, however, some differences between labor and product markets, and we will concentrate on these differences.

Two of the chapters are theoretical and two discuss the way the real world operates. Chapter 27 explains how labor income is determined in a market system and why the distribution of income is what it is. Having looked at labor markets in theory, we examine the effect that unions have on those markets in Chapter 28. Unions in many countries have goals that are social and political as well as economic. However, for the most part, unions in the United States have concentrated on economic goals such as higher wages and benefits, job security, and good pensions. The chapter begins with a theoretical look at determining how unions attempt to raise wages. It then considers empirical evidence of the success of unions in raising wages and at whose expense these increased wages have come. Finally, we take a look at the history of the labor movement in the United States and examines some recent trends.

Chapter 29 extends marginal productivity theory to the other productive resources. Like the demand for labor, the demand for land and capital is derived from the demand for the products they help produce. The price that firms are willing to pay for the services of land and capital depends on their marginal productivity. The chapter highlights the important differences between the other resource markets and labor markets. We examine rent and interest, the payments to the owners of land and capital, and conclude with a discussion of profits, the payment to enterprise.

Finally, Chapter 30 looks at the distribution of income. No single topic in economics generates more controversy than income distribution and government policies for income redistribution. The chapter examines the actual distribution of income, the measures of income distribution and poverty, the effects of labor market discrimination, and the role of government in redistributing income.

CHAPTER 27
MARGINAL PRODUCTIVITY THEORY AND LABOR MARKETS

LEARNING OBJECTIVES
1. Explain what makes the demand for labor different from the demand for final goods.
2. Describe how a profit-maximizing firm in pure competition decides how much labor to employ in terms of its marginal revenue product and marginal resource cost.
3. Use a resource market diagram to illustrate and explain the difference between the use of labor under pure competition versus monopoly in the product market.
4. Define monopsony and discuss why monopsonistic exploitation may occur.
5. Determine the factors that effect the elasticity of demand for labor and describe possible causes for a shift in the demand for labor.

Consider this... *Every firm operates in two markets. It sells a product and it buys productive resources to produce that product. Nowhere is the firm purchasing labor in the labor market more in the news than in professional sports. At the beginning of each NFL season the sports pages provide a running tally of the unsigned players. In some cases, as in the summer of 1993 when Emmitt Smith went unsigned for months by the Dallas Cowboys, the issue became a public relations problem for management. The Dallas fans thought that Smith deserved more money and they wanted him signed. The team's owner, Jerry Jones, spent weeks on radio talk shows in the Dallas-Fort Worth area explaining that he had offered Smith $10 million and was not going to pay more than that. Smith's agents countered with evidence that other running backs, with much poorer statistics, were being paid much more. After all, Smith had been a key to the Dallas Cowboys winning the Super Bowl!*

Football is not alone in having the sports pages full of salary negotiations. Baseball salaries have increased more than those of any professional sport in recent years. Is there a reason for this? Are the owners more interested in harmony with their players in pro baseball than in pro football? The material in this chapter will help you understand the economics behind the headlines over player salaries that you read in the sports section of your newspaper.

SPECIAL FEATURES OF THE DEMAND FOR LABOR

Earlier in this book, we examined the circular flow as a starting point. It shows the firm involved in two markets: the product market and the resource market. Figure 1 reproduces the circular flow diagram from Chapter 2. We have studied the theory of the firm in the product market, the upper half of the circular flow diagram. We now turn our attention to the theory of the firm in the largest part of the resource market, the labor market.

The demand for labor is similar to other types of demand we have studied. In earlier chapters, we described product markets, in which firms or individuals sell the goods and services they produce to consumers. Now we want to examine the labor market, the market in which firms buy—or rent—the services of labor from individuals. We can adopt many of the same analytical tools we used to study product markets. There are, however, some differences between labor and product markets, and we will concentrate on these differences.

The demand for labor has three features that make it somewhat different from the demand for a product. The first is that the demand for labor is **derived demand**. A firm demands labor because the labor can be used to produce goods that consumers are demanding. The demand for labor is thus derived from the demand for the product it produces. If there were no consumer demand for products made from wood, there would be no demand for loggers. This principle holds for all productive resources. They are only valuable to a firm if they help to produce products that consumers value.

The second feature of the demand for labor is that it is **interdependent demand**. It depends on the demand for other inputs. In other words, the amount of labor demanded will depend on the amounts of other inputs a firm plans to use. The amount of labor a firm demands depends on the amounts of land, capital, and enterprise that will be used in combination with the labor. It is also true that the demand for most products is interdependent with the demand for other products. As you know, almost all goods have substitutes and many goods have complements. However, the interdependence of the demand for labor with the demand for other productive resources is unusual in that the other resources can be both complements and substitutes at the same time.

6. Explain the role of productivity, race, and comparable worth in determining labor income.

Derived demand
Demand for a productive resource that results from demand for a final good or service. For example, the demand for labor is derived from the demand for the product that the labor produces.

Interdependent demand
Demand that depends on another type of demand. For example, a firm's demand for labor depends on the amount of other resources that the firm plans to use.

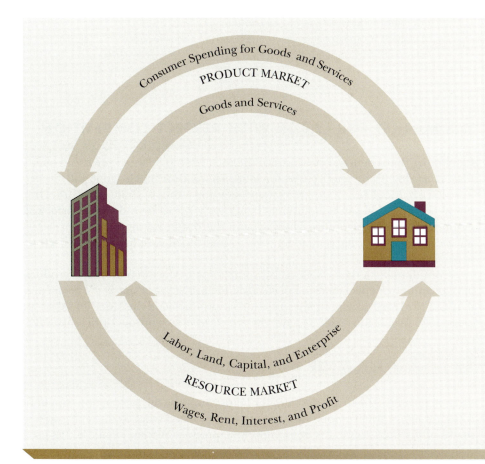

FIGURE 1

THE CIRCULAR FLOW OF INCOME
Households purchase goods and services and supply land, labor, capital, and enterprise. Firms buy these productive resources and supply goods and services. In the product market, buyers and sellers exchange goods and services. In the resource market, buyers and sellers exchange the services of productive resources.

Technologically determined demand
Demand that depends on techniques of production and technological progress. For example, the demand for labor will be affected by the introductions of new technology in a firm or industry.

Marginal productivity theory
An explanation of how the distribution of income is determined in a market system. Each input is paid according to its contribution, or its marginal productivity.

The third feature is that the demand for labor is in part **technologically determined demand**. That is, the demand for labor will depend on techniques of production and on technological progress, or the production function. Recall that the production function tells how much labor is needed to produce a certain level of output, given a certain production process and amounts of the other productive resources of production. This technological relationship can change with new inventions and new innovations. Any change resulting in a new technology or a new innovation will have an impact on the demand for productive resources, including labor.

These three elements are combined in marginal productivity theory, which was originally developed by John Bates Clark. **Marginal productivity theory** explains how the distribution of income is determined in a market system. Each input is paid according to its contribution, or its marginal productivity. The more productive inputs will be paid more. We will follow Clark's lead by developing marginal productivity theory in terms of labor supply and demand. The theory holds for all productive resources of production, but most interest centers on labor and the returns to labor.

KEY IDEAS

SPECIAL CHARACTERISTICS OF RESOURCE MARKETS
- Demand is derived from the demand for the final product.
- Demand is interdependent with demand for other inputs.
- Demand is technologically determined.

THE MARKET FOR LABOR WITH PERFECT COMPETITION

Remember that a demand curve shows the relationship between price and quantity demanded. A demand curve for labor shows how much labor will be demanded at various wage rates. In order to develop a theory about the market demand for labor, we start by asking how much labor an individual firm will employ at various wage rates. Then we sum the results for all firms in the same way we added individual demand curves to find the market demand for a product.

Consider a firm that is selling its product in a perfectly competitive product market and buying its labor in a perfectly competitive labor market. This means that the firm will take both the price of its product *and* the price of labor as given. The firm is too small to have any effect on either product prices or wage rates.

THE DEMAND FOR LABOR

What determines the firm's demand for labor? Suppose the production function is such that, as the firm increases the amount of labor employed, *ceteris paribus*, the resulting increases in the amount of total product become smaller. This pro-

TABLE 1 THE DEMAND FOR LABOR IN A PERFECTLY COMPETITIVE PRODUCT MARKET

UNITS OF LABOR	TOTAL PRODUCT	MARGINAL PRODUCT OF LABOR (MP_L)	PRODUCT PRICE	TOTAL REVENUE	VALUE OF MARGINAL PRODUCT OF LABOR (VMP_L)	MARGINAL REVENUE PRODUCT OF LABOR (MRP_L)
0	0		$2	$0		
		10			$20	$20
1	10		2	20		
		8			16	16
2	18		2	36		
		6			12	12
3	24		2	48		
		4			8	8
4	28		2	56		
		2			4	4
5	30		2	60		

duction function reflects the principle of diminishing marginal productivity, which we discussed in an earlier chapter. Holding constant the quantities of land and capital, it is possible to determine how the firm's output varies with the quantity of labor it uses. As the firm employs more labor in combination with fixed amounts of the other inputs, the additional amounts of output per additional unit of labor eventually decline. If this were not the case, it would be theoretically possible to grow the entire world's supply of wheat on one acre of land just by employing more workers.

The amount of total product associated with various amounts of labor inputs for the firm is given in the second column of Table 1. This output depends on the technical relationship defined by the production function. Once we know the total product, we can determine how much extra product is produced when labor inputs are added. That value is the marginal product of that unit of labor (MP_L). It is the marginal product because the output is in physical units, such as number of autos or tons of coal.

To put a market value on the additional output, we simply multiply the number of added units of the product by the price at which the firm can sell it. This value is called the **value of the marginal product of labor (VMP_L)**. It is listed in the sixth column of Table 1. The VMP_L, which is $P \times MP_L$, is a measure of the value of the additional output that each additional unit of labor adds to the firm's total. The **marginal revenue product of labor (MRP_L)** is the amount that an additional unit of labor adds to the firm's total revenue. It is found in the seventh column of Table 1. It is found by multiplying MR by MP_L. With perfect competition in the product market, $VMP_L = MRP_L$. These values are equal because the product price remains constant ($P = MR$). The firm can produce and sell as much as it wants at the market-determined price, which is $2 in this example. When the firm faces a given price, marginal revenue is exactly equal to that price in the model of perfect competition. Later in this chapter, we will look

Value of the marginal product of labor (VMP_L)
A measure of the value of the additional output that each unit of additional labor adds to a firm's total, found by multiplying the marginal product by the price at which the firm can sell the product.

Marginal revenue product of labor (MRP_L)
The amount that an additional unit of labor adds to a firm's total revenue.

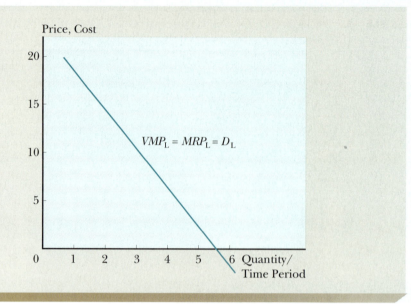

FIGURE 2

THE FIRM'S DEMAND FOR LABOR IN A PERFECTLY COMPETITIVE PRODUCT MARKET

The marginal revenue product of labor (MRP_L) curve is the firm's demand curve for labor. When the firm's product market is perfectly competitive, MRP_L and the VMP_L are identical.

at how the value of the marginal product and the marginal revenue product differ when there is monopoly power in the product market.

The values of VMP_L and MRP_L from Table 1 are plotted on a graph in Figure 2. The MRP_L curve is the firm's demand curve for labor. It shows the value of each additional unit of labor to the firm. Thus, it shows how much labor the firm will purchase at various prices (wage rates). If you know the price of labor, you will be able to determine how much labor this firm will demand.

THE SUPPLY OF LABOR

An individual's supply curve of labor looks like the other supply curves we have considered. As wage rates rise, the quantity of labor supplied increases. This supply curve of labor, like most supply curves, is upward sloping. As wage rates rise, an individual will want to work more hours. In general, as wages rise, more people will choose to give up leisure in favor of more income. This trade-off of income for leisure is the substitution effect of a wage increase. Individuals will substitute the increased consumption of goods and services that higher wages represent for leisure. This substitution effect occurs along the upward-sloping portion of Figure 3.

There is also an income effect associated with the increased income brought about by a wage increase. Individuals want to consume more leisure at higher incomes because leisure is a normal good. The income effect of a higher wage is that individuals want to supply a lower quantity of labor. At some point, the income effect of a wage increase could dominate the substitution effect. In that case, an increase in the wage rate would bring about a decrease in the quantity of labor supplied. This is represented by the crook in the individual's supply curve in Figure 3. For this individual, an increase in the wage rate above $15 per hour causes the quantity of labor supplied to decrease. Economists refer to a supply curve with this shape as a **backward-bending supply curve**. It is important

Backward-bending supply curve
A labor supply curve that slopes back to the left at the point where the income effect dominates the substitution effect.

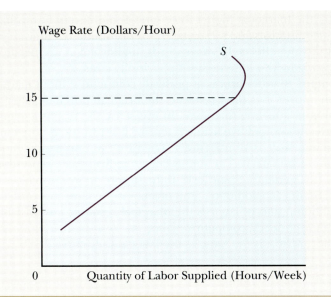

FIGURE 3
AN INDIVIDUAL'S LABOR SUPPLY CURVE
When the substitution effect of a wage increase for an individual exceeds the income effect, the quantity of labor supplied increases. Up to some wage ($15 per hour here), the income effect dominates. Above that wage, further increases in the wage rate cause the quantity of labor supplied to decrease.

to keep in mind that this is an individual supply curve. Where the bend occurs is an individual decision. Some entertainers perform less as they get more famous. Others appear to keep increasing the quantity of labor supplied as their wage rate increases.

The market supply curve of labor (S_L) is the aggregate of all the individual supply curves. It shows how much labor is available at different wage rates, as in Figure 4. This market supply curve is not backward-bending because more work-

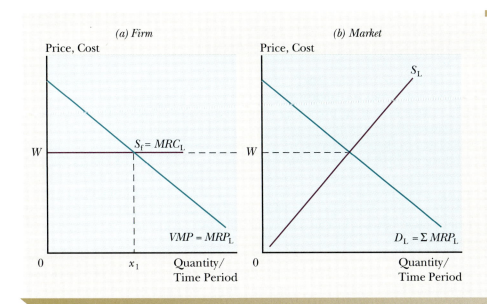

FIGURE 4
PERFECTLY COMPETITIVE LABOR MARKET
In a perfectly competitive labor market, the firm faces a perfectly elastic supply curve (S_f). If the supply curve is perfectly elastic, the marginal resource cost (MRC_L) curve is also perfectly elastic. The firm can purchase as much labor as it wants at the market-determined wage rate.

ers will enter the market at higher wage rates and different individuals have different opportunity costs and will make choices resulting in different substitution effects and income effects. In other words, higher wages are needed to attract additional workers who have higher opportunity costs.

We assumed that the firm is in perfectly competitive input markets. Perfect competition in the labor market means the firm can purchase labor at the market wage without affecting that wage. In this sense the firm is a wage taker, just like the perfectly competitive firm was a price taker in the product market. The equilibrium wage rate is W in Figure 4. The firm can purchase as much labor as it wants at the wage rate W. The supply curve the firm faces, represented by S_f in Figure 4, is thus perfectly elastic at W. If the supply curve a firm faces is perfectly elastic, the cost of each additional unit of labor is the same, or constant. The cost of each additional unit of labor is the **marginal resource cost of labor (MRC_L)**. For a firm in a perfectly competitive labor market, the marginal resource cost curve of labor, MRC_L, is the same as the labor supply curve.

Marginal resource cost of labor (MRC_L)
The cost of each additional unit of labor.

EQUILIBRIUM IN THE PERFECTLY COMPETITIVE LABOR MARKET

The MRC_L curve is the supply curve the firm faces because it shows the relationship between price and additional units of labor supplied. A profit-maximizing firm will employ or purchase labor until $MRP_L = MRC_L$. If a unit of labor adds more to revenue than to cost (if $MRP_L > MRC_L$), it will be profitable for the firm to purchase more units of labor. However, if a unit of labor adds more to cost than to revenue (if $MRP_L < MRC_L$), the firm should purchase fewer units. The firm will hire laborers until the amount they add to total cost (MRC_L) is exactly equal to the amount they add to revenue (MRP_L). In Figure 4, the firm would employ x_1 units of labor at wage rate W. In terms of the numbers in Table 1, the firm would employ 4 units of labor if the market wage was $8 per unit. If the market wage was $4 per unit, 5 units of labor would be employed.

A COMPETITIVE LABOR MARKET WITH A MONOPOLISTIC PRODUCT MARKET

Now consider a firm that sells its product under monopoly conditions. The monopolist's demand for labor is shown in Table 2. The difference between this case and the firm of the preceding section is that product price (fourth column) declines as the firm produces and sells more of its product. VMP_L and MRP_L are calculated in the same way as before. VMP_L is the value of the labor's marginal product, so $VMP_L = MP_L \times P$. MRP_L is found by calculating the change in total revenue due to additional units of labor. For example, when the third worker is added, total revenue rises from $162 to $192. Thus, MRP_L for the third worker is $192 − $162 = $30. Note that VMP_L is greater than MRP_L for all but the first unit of labor, because in a monopoly, product price is greater than marginal revenue.

Both the VMP_L curve and the MRP_L curve are graphed in Figure 5 using the data from Table 2. The MRP_L curve is the monopolist's demand curve for labor. This firm, like the perfectly competitive firm, will employ labor until $MRP_L = MRC_L$. Although this firm is selling its product in a monopolistic product market, it is purchasing labor in a competitive labor market.

TABLE 2 THE DEMAND FOR LABOR IN A MONOPOLISTIC PRODUCT MARKET

UNITS OF LABOR	TOTAL PRODUCT	MARGINAL PRODUCT OF LABOR (MP_l)	PRODUCT PRICE	TOTAL REVENUE	VALUE OF THE MARGINAL PRODUCT OF LABOR (VMP_l)	MARGINAL REVENUE PRODUCT OF LABOR (MRP_l)
0	0		$0	$0		
		10			$100	$100
1	10		10	100		
		8			72	62
2	18		9	162		
		6			48	30
3	24		8	192		
		4			28	4
4	28		7	196		
		2			12	−16
5	30		6	180		

The supply and demand curves for the monopolist in the competitive labor market are diagrammed in Figure 6. The market demand curve for labor is, as usual, found by summing the MRP_L curves for all firms purchasing this type of labor. The market supply curve (S_L) is the sum of individual supply curves of workers. The market-determined wage is W. This firm can purchase as much labor as it desires at W, since the supply curve it faces, S_F, is perfectly elastic at W.

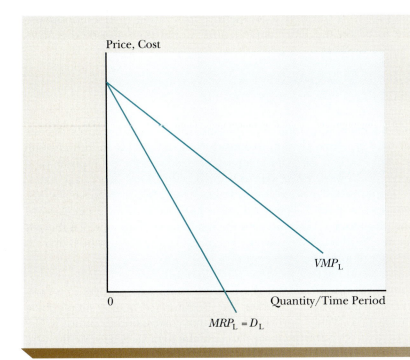

FIGURE 5
THE MONOPOLIST'S DEMAND FOR LABOR
When a firm has monopoly power in the product market, the MRP_L will lie below VMP_L. This is because product price is greater than marginal revenue under monopoly. Thus, $P \times MP_L$ is greater than $MR \times MP_L$.

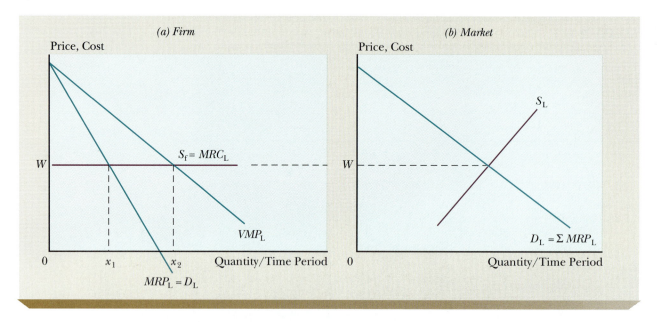

FIGURE 6

A MONOPOLISTIC FIRM FACING A PERFECTLY COMPETITIVE LABOR MARKET

A firm with monopoly power in the product market and in a perfectly competitive labor market will face a perfectly elastic supply curve. The firm will hire units of labor until the marginal revenue product of labor is equal to the marginal resource cost of labor ($MRP_L = MRC_L$).

Since S_f is perfectly elastic, MRC_L for this firm is constant. The firm maximizes profits where $MRC_L = MRP_L$, so it hires x_1 units of labor. Note from Figure 6 that the monopolist pays W, the market wage. The fact that MRP_L is less than VMP_L does not mean that the monopolist exploits labor by paying too little. The monopolist has to pay the market wage just like any other employer in this market. Because MRP_L is less than VMP_L, the monopolist *does* employ fewer workers than similar competitive firms would employ. Recall from the chapter on monopoly that the monopolist restricts output to keep price high. The result of this restriction of output in the resource market is that the monopolist uses fewer inputs, including labor. If this were a competitive firm rather than a monopolist, it would want to be on the VMP_L curve (which would then also be the MRP_L curve) and hire x_2 workers.

MONOPSONY

We have looked at competitive and monopolistic firms demanding labor in competitive labor markets. Now we want to consider a firm that has an influence on price in the labor market. We have assumed to this point that the purchasing firm has no effect on wage rates. But what if the firm does affect wage rates? What if the wage rate rises as the firm hires more labor? We refer to such a firm as having monopsony power. The word *monopsony* comes from a Greek word meaning "one purchaser." A monopoly is the market structure in which there is a single seller of a product. A **monopsony** is a market structure in which there is a single purchaser of a productive resource.

Monopsony
A market structure in which there is a single purchaser of a productive resource.

We begin by assuming that we know what the monopsonist's MRP_L curve is, shown in Figure 7. It doesn't matter if this firm is selling its product in a competitive market or a monopolistic market. We also know the market supply curve of labor to this firm, S_L. Table 3 provides values that correspond to Figure 7. The market supply curve, S_L, is the labor supply curve the firm faces because the firm

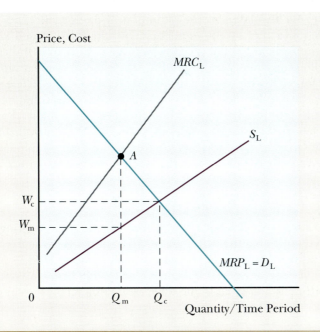

FIGURE 7
MONOPSONY
The monopsonist faces the market supply curve for labor (S_l). Since this curve has a positive slope, the marginal resource cost (MRC_l) curve lies above it. The monopsonist thus hires Q_m units of labor at a wage rate of W_m.

TABLE 3 THE DEMAND FOR LABOR IN A MONOPSONY

UNITS OF LABOR	WAGE RATE	WAGE COST	MARGINAL RESOURCE COST OF LABOR (MRC_l)
0		$0	
			$5
1	$5	5	
			7
2	6	12	
			9
3	7	21	
			11
4	8	32	
			13
5	9	45	
			15
6	10	60	
			17
7	11	77	
			19
8	12	96	
			21
9	13	117	
			23
10	14	140	

is the market for this labor by the definition of monopsony. In a competitive market, this situation of supply and demand would have resulted in a wage rate of W_c and employment level of Q_c. However, since the firm in this case faces the upward-sloping supply curve, S_L, the MRC_L curve lies above that supply curve, as shown in Figure 7. To see why this is the case, refer to Table 3. The supply curve is, of course, the graph of the values in the first and second columns of the table. Since the curve is upward sloping, the firm must pay a higher wage rate as it hires more labor. This result is different from that for a firm hiring in a competitive labor market. The total wage costs go up with additional workers in monopsony for two reasons. First, the wage must rise to attract more labor. Second, wage costs rise because all the other workers receive a higher wage as the firm hires more workers.

The amount that each additional worker adds to total wage cost is the marginal resource cost of labor (MRC_L). You can see by comparing the second and fourth columns that the MRC_L curve will lie above the S_L curve, as shown in Figure 7. The firm, as before, maximizes profits where $MRP_L = MRC_L$. Profit maximization occurs at point A in Figure 7, where the firm employs Q_m units of labor. But MRC_L is not equal to the wage rate. Remember, the supply curve indicates what has to be paid to hire Q_m units of labor. The firm will pay wage rate W_m.

Note that W_m is less than W_c, so the monopsonist is paying a lower wage than would have been paid in a competitive labor market. Economists refer to this situation as monopsonistic exploitation. **Monopsonistic exploitation** is the underpayment of wages by a firm that has monopsony power. Labor receives less than it would receive in a competitive market. This does not mean that workers are forced to work at wage rates below what they are willing to accept. The monopsonist simply restricts input, just as the monopolist restricts output.

MONOPSONY IN THE REAL WORLD

Are there any real-world examples of pure monopsony in a labor market? No, because all labor has some other possible employment. Pure monopsony, like pure monopoly, is a theoretical extreme. There are, however, real-world examples of some degree of monopsony power. You may have heard the song about the miner who "owes his soul to the company store." This song was written about mining companies when they dominated the labor market as the major employer in certain areas. Company towns—small towns with only one major employer—were common in the early twentieth century. An example was Pullman IL, where railroad sleeping cars were manufactured. A large college or university in a small town provides a more current example of monopsony power in a labor market. If you compare secretarial salaries at similar-sized schools in cities of varying size, you will find that where the college or university dominates the labor market, the salaries are lower. This lower pay may in part be due to monopsony power.

Perhaps the best example of monopsony in a labor market in the U.S. economy comes from professional sports. Congress has made sports leagues exempt from the federal antitrust laws. This exemption allows the leagues to hire as monopsonists by drafting players and maintaining control through reserve clauses. Players are not free to quit one team and go to work for another unless they become a free agent. As a result, wage rates for professional athletes are

---

Monopsonistic exploitation
The difference in wages paid by a firm that has monopsony power, compared to what would be paid in a competitive market.

lower than they would be if the teams competed for players in an open market. The recent settlement of an NFL player's antitrust suit against the owners made it much easier for players to become free agents. It is having a significant impact on salaries. Part of the settlement also involved a total salary cap per team. One of these actions reduces monopsony power, but the second acts to increase the monopsony power.

An early study of the economics of baseball by Gerald Scully found empirical evidence of monopsonistic exploitation in that sport.[1] Scully found that the typical MRP_L for star pitchers in 1969 was \$405,300, but the typical salary was only \$66,800. Think about basketball player Shaquille O'Neal. He receives a very high salary, but consider what he adds to his team's (and the league's) marginal revenue. He fills up the arena for practically every game he plays. His salary is surely less than his MRP_L.[2]

The formation of the United States Football League in the early 1980s had a profound effect on salaries in professional football. The new league introduced competition for players and the effect was startling. Rookie salaries in 1983 jumped an average of 52 percent over 1982 salaries. Many of football's general managers called this trend an "economic disaster" and blamed it on players, agents, and other teams. If they had studied economics, they would have realized it was due to the breakdown of monopsony power. When the new league folded, the upward pressure on football salaries declined.

Except for such special cases, where buyers are purchasing very specialized labor skills, there are few instances of real monopsony power. In general, improved transportation and communication in the United States have increased labor's mobility. With increased labor mobility, there is less monopsony power. If miners are aware of job possibilities in other areas and in other occupations, the mine will be forced to pay a competitive wage. Indeed, if even a small percentage of miners are willing to pull up stakes, the mine will be forced to pay competitive wages. Complete mobility of labor isn't necessary to reduce monopsony power. It's enough to have mobility at the margin.

MONOPSONY POWER AND MINIMUM WAGES

The minimum wage is a price floor set above the market-clearing price and, thus, generally causes a surplus of labor, or unemployment. However, if there is monopsony power, a minimum wage can cause employment to increase. In Figure 8, the monopsonist would employ Q_m units of labor at wage rate W_m. Now suppose a minimum wage of W_1 is imposed. Part of the market supply curve is replaced by a horizontal line at W_1, the imposed minimum wage. In effect, the monopsonist is forced to accept the minimum wage. The market supply curve is

---

1. Gerald W. Scully, "Pay and Performance in Major League Baseball," *American Economic Review* (December 1974): 915–930. Thomas H. Bruggink and David R. Rose, Jr. calculated the MRP_L of 103 major league baseball players and compared them to their salaries: "Financial Restraint in the Free Agent Labor Market for Major League Baseball: Players Look at Strike Three," *Southern Economic Journal* (April 1990): 1029–1043.
2. *Sports Illustrated* reported that the Milwaukee Bucks realized an additional \$700,000 profit during Kareem Abdul-Jabbar's first season. His salary was \$250,000. So, for Abdul-Jabbar's team, $MRP_L >$ MRC_L. *Sports Illustrated* reported in December 1987 that Michael Jordan brought in 276,996 more fans for the Chicago Bulls than had attended the previous season. At the average ticket price of \$14, that represented \$3.9 million in marginal revenue.

FIGURE 8

MONOPSONY POWER AND MINIMUM WAGES

A minimum wage of W_2 in a monopsonistic labor market changes the market supply curve from S_L to W_2B and the part of S_L above B. The marginal resource cost curve is the same as W_2B, the perfectly elastic portion of the supply curve.

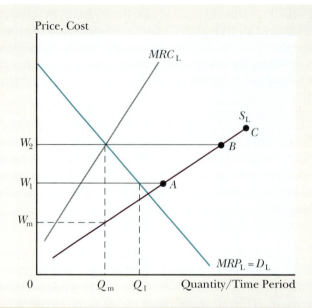

now represented by the line W_1AC_L. The marginal resource cost labor curve is now W_1A, because the supply curve is perfectly elastic in the range W_1A. At a wage rate of W_1, Q_1 units of labor would be employed. If the minimum wage imposed is W_2 instead of W_1, the supply curve the firm faces is W_2BC. The firm will face perfectly elastic supply and MRC_L curves in the range W_2B. In this case, the firm will employ Q_m units of labor at wage rate W_2. You can see that if the minimum wage that is imposed lies between W_m and W_2, more employment at a higher wage rate will result.

What we have just considered is an exception to the usual case where minimum wages result in unemployment. Be careful, though. This result only occurs when there is monopsony power in the labor market. A monopsony is relatively uncommon except in certain labor markets for specialized skills, such as the market for professional basketball players. Most empirical studies of the effects of minimum wages show that the monopsony exception to the negative effects of a minimum wage on employment is not very common.[3]

DETERMINANTS OF THE DEMAND FOR LABOR

At the beginning of this chapter, you learned that the demand for labor has three features making it somewhat different from the demand for a product. These features also influence the elasticity of the demand for labor, because they determine how the quantity of labor demanded will respond to changes in the wage rate. In other words, the demand for labor has a price elasticity just as

---

3. For a review of these empirical studies, see Jack Hirshleifer, *Price Theory and Applications*, 5e. (Englewood Cliffs NJ: Prentice-Hall, 1992), 336–340.

POLICY FOCUS: U.S. IMMIGRATION POLICY

Give me your tired, your poor,
Your huddled masses yearning to breathe free,
The wretched refuse of your teeming shore,
Send these, the homeless, tempest-tossed to me:
I lift my lamp beside the golden door.
—Inscription on the Statue of Liberty

The United States is a country of immigrants and descendants of immigrants—a "melting pot," as you learned in elementary school. In the early nineteenth century, Europeans, mostly from Western Europe, flooded into the United States. In the late nineteenth century, a wave of Chinese immigrated to California. In the early twentieth century, a huge flood of immigrants arrived from Southern and Eastern Europe. The most recent large waves of immigrants have been from Southeast Asia after the end of the Vietnam War, and from Central America. Many of those coming from Central America are illegal immigrants, making them distinct from most of the other waves of immigrants.

Each influx of immigrants caused a great debate among Americans who were already citizens. The issue was always the same—whether or not to shut the door to new immigrants. Often the answer was yes, and new restrictions were passed. Many legal restrictions on immigration are racist in origin. Many groups support immigration of those who are like themselves but are opposed to altering the racial mix of the country. (This motivation was clear in the 1924 Immigration Origins Act.)

There was the Chinese exclusion law in 1882, the "Gentlemen's Agreement" with Japan in 1907 (halting the immigration of Japanese), and the national origin quotas in 1921 and 1924. These quotas were designed to freeze the ethnic composition of the United States by limiting the entrance of any one nationality to a small percentage of the number of people of that nationality who were already here. The Quota Law of 1921 limited immigration from any Eastern Hemisphere country to 3 percent of the foreign-born persons from that country living in the United States in 1910. In 1924, the Immigration Origins Act set an annual quota of 2 percent of each country's U.S. residents in 1920. In 1965, Congress did away with the national-origin quotas and placed a yearly limit of 290,000 on all immigrants.

There is at least one economic motive for restricting immigration. Immigration makes the supply of labor much more elastic for each skill level, putting downward pressure on wage rates. It isn't surprising that organized labor groups are often opposed to liberalizing immigration. In fact, some states even prohibit the transfer of certain occupational skills within the United States. For example, a CPA in Wisconsin who plans to migrate to Arizona will not be licensed until he or she passes an Arizona exam. This requirement clearly reduces the supply of accounting services in Arizona. As a result, accountants in Arizona have higher incomes than they would otherwise.

In October 1986, the U.S. Congress passed an immigration reform bill that offered citizenship to illegal aliens who could prove they entered the United States before January 1, 1982. However, the law imposed strict penalties on employers who hire illegal aliens. If effectively enforced, this law would have put upward pressure on wage rates in the unskilled labor markets in the south and southwest, where illegal aliens are a large fraction of the work force. Shortly after the law was passed, there was evidence that the law was deterring illegal immigration. Illegal border crossings declined, and there were numerous reports of employers firing undocumented workers. By 1990, this trend seemed to have reversed. Field observations at the busiest illegal crossing point reported an increase in illegal crossing to the level recorded before the law went into effect. Data on the apprehension of illegal aliens confirms that this law did not substantially deter entry—nor is it likely to, as long as enforcement is weak and the wage pull is strong.

Most recently, policy to prevent illegal immigration has shifted to the state level. Governor Pete Wilson of California has led the policy debate. He has advocated strict enforcement of immigration policy by the federal government. He has also suggested that illegal immigrants and the children of illegal immigrants be denied state services, including education. The interesting twist on this state policy is that it is being driven by the fact that California's fiscal condition is poor, with rising spending demand outstripping state revenue. As school budgets have been drastically cut, the Governor is asking if the state should educate the children of illegal immigrants when it has had to cut funding for education to children of its taxpaying legal citizens.

the demand for products does. This elasticity is influenced by the distinguishing features of the demand for labor.

ELASTICITY OF THE DEMAND FOR THE PRODUCT

If the wage rate falls for all of the firms in the product market, the cost of producing the product will also fall. There will, as a result, be a decline in the selling price of the product. As the price of the product declines, consumers will increase their consumption of the product. The price elasticity of the demand for a product determines how much more of the product consumers will purchase in response to a decline in its price. Thus, the price elasticity of the demand for the product affects the price elasticity of the demand for labor. If the product demand is elastic, the firm will hire more labor in order to increase production to respond to the increased quantity demanded by consumers. The larger the increase in quantity demanded of the product, the larger the increase in quantity demanded of labor will be. As a result, labor demand is more elastic when the demand for the final product is more elastic.

SHARE OF LABOR IN INPUT COSTS

The second element that affects the elasticity of demand for labor is a bit more complex. First, assume that only labor is used to produce the product. Labor costs are 100 percent of product cost. If the price of labor falls 10 percent, the cost of production falls 10 percent, and price (in perfect competition) falls 10 percent. Now, more realistically, let labor costs constitute only 50 percent of product cost. Then if the price of labor falls 10 percent, the cost of production falls only 5 percent. In other words, the larger the share of labor cost in total production cost of a product, the more a change in the wage rate will affect the cost of production and the price of the product. As a result, the larger the share of the total cost of production that wages represent, the greater the elasticity of demand for labor will be.

OPPORTUNITIES FOR INPUT SUBSTITUTION

In actual production, a great deal of substitution among the productive resources is possible. We discussed this input substitution in detail in the chapter on production. The choice of which combination of productive resources to use depends, as you learned earlier, on the prices of those inputs. As the price of labor increases, entrepreneurs will substitute capital and land for labor to the extent that such substitution is feasible in the production function. Substitution can occur for all the productive resources. Perhaps it is most visible in the substitution that takes place among land, labor, and capital in urban versus rural areas. In urban areas, where land is expensive, labor and capital are substituted for land. High-rise structures, which use much more labor and capital, are built. In rural areas, low-rise office buildings and housing units are constructed. They use far less labor and capital than the high-rise structures of the central city.

Consider what happens when the wage rate falls. To the extent that labor can be substituted for other inputs, more labor will be hired. The greater the degree of substitutability in production, the greater will be the price elasticity of the demand for labor.

SHIFTS IN THE DEMAND FOR LABOR

The demand curve for labor, like the demand curve for products, can shift in response to changes in underlying conditions. Two of the most important causes of such shifts are changes in demand for the product and changes in the employment of the other productive resources.

CHANGES IN THE DEMAND FOR THE PRODUCT. The demand for labor is derived from the demand for the product it is used to produce. To see this more clearly, look again at Table 1 and Table 2, which show the situations for a competitive and a monopolistic firm, respectively. Suppose there is an increase in demand in the product market. The market demand curve will shift to the right. This shift will cause the product price to increase for the competitive firm, because the value of the marginal product of labor will be larger at all levels of production. That is, the values of MRP_L in Table 1 will increase in proportion to the increase in product price. In most cases, an increase in product demand will also increase the monopolist's values of MRP_L compared to those given in Table 2. The MRP_L curve shifts outward for either kind of firm, representing an increase in the demand for labor.

In a competitive labor market, each kind of firm will want to hire more labor at the existing wage rate. The market demand for labor could increase, raising both the level of employment and the wage rate. The amount by which the market wage increases will depend on how large the industry is relative to the labor market. If the industry is small, there may be only a very slight increase in wages. If it is large, however, the wage rate could rise significantly. Even in a monopsonistic labor market, the result will be an increase in wages and employment.

EFFECT OF CHANGES IN OTHER INPUTS. A second important cause of shifts in the demand for labor results from the fact that the demands for different inputs are mutually interdependent. Refer again to Table 1 and Table 2. Suppose the capital stock of the firm is doubled. If labor and capital used together are complementary in the sense that an increase in capital makes labor more productive, each unit of labor will have a larger product. Complementarity is a fairly general phenomenon. Consider an example. Suppose there is a great blizzard and you and your friends have a few days off because your school has been closed. Four of you decide to make some extra cash by pulling stranded vehicles out of snowdrifts. It turns out that the effort is profitable enough that instead of relying on your Jeep and a chain, your group invests the profits in a tow truck. When it snows the next time, how do you think your product will compare to the first experience?

If the capital stock is increased, the total product in Table 1 and Table 2 will increase. As a result, the values of MP_L will increase and the values of MRP_L will also increase. The MRP_L curve will shift outward, signifying that the demand for labor has increased. This is what is meant by complementarity: an increase in usage of one input raises the marginal revenue product of the other.

Increased productivity resulting from an increased capital stock can have several effects. Consider what happens if the capital stock expands in one firm but not the whole industry. The firm's demand curve (MRP_L) would shift to the right in Figures 4 and 6 without any (noticeable) effect on the market demand curve, because the firm is very small relative to the industry. The result would be that the firm would employ more units of labor at the market-determined price.

On the other hand, consider the effect of an industrywide increase in the capital stock. All firms in the industry have an increase in capital, causing their individual MRP_L curves and the industry MRP_L curve to shift outward. More labor is employed at a higher wage rate. Such a situation is depicted in Figure 9. The initial equilibrium occurs where the firm employs x_1 units of labor at the market wage of W_1. The industry is employing Q_1 units of labor. Now there is an industrywide increase in capital. The firm's MRP_L curve shifts to MRP_L'. Since all the firms in the industry experience this increase in MRP_L, the industry demand curve for labor will also shift, from D_L to D_L' in Figure 9. The market wage rises to W_2. As a result, the horizontal supply curve that the individual firm faces shifts from S_f to S_f'. The firm will now employ x_2 units of labor at wage rate W_2. Industry employment has risen from Q_1 to Q_2. The response of the firm to an increase in its capital stock was to hire more workers at higher wages because the increase in capital increased the marginal productivity of the workers. The demand for the two resources, labor and capital, can thus be seen to be interdependent.

Some U.S. manufacturing industries have hired more workers because of increases in the capital stock in recent years. The textile industry is a good example. The technology of weaving cloth has changed dramatically from shuttle looms to air jet and water jet shuttleless looms. Investment in this new technology has greatly increased the productivity of workers in the weaving sector of the textile industry. The result has been more output from fewer workers earning higher wages.

FIGURE 9

AN INDUSTRYWIDE INCREASE IN CAPITAL

An increase in the capital stock will increase the productivity of labor if capital and labor are complementary inputs. This increase in productivity will shift the marginal revenue product curve from MRP_L to MRP_L' and the market demand curve for labor from D_L to D_L'.

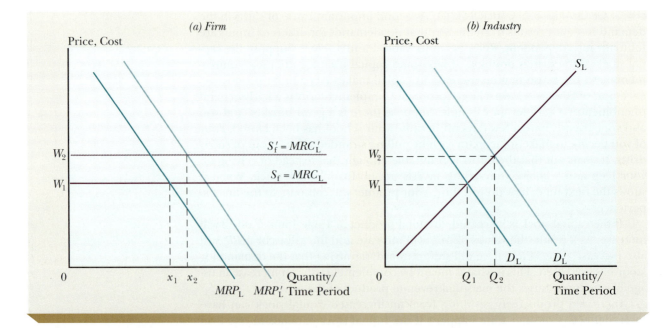

PRODUCTIVITY AND EARNINGS DIFFERENCES

In this chapter, we have applied marginal productivity theory to labor markets. We have shown that labor becomes more productive and wages rise when the labor is used with more capital. The notion of capital is, however, broader than simply tools. Capital is anything used to increase the flow of output. For example, economists define human capital as anything such as health, vigor, education, or training that (1) can be enhanced by "investment" and (2) increases the productivity of the individual.

Just as a firm can increase its investment in capital, an individual can invest in human capital. An individual's decision to seek additional education is similar to an entrepreneur's decision to purchase a new piece of equipment. In both cases, the investment is productive if the return (properly discounted) exceeds the cost (properly discounted).

HIGHER EDUCATION AS AN INVESTMENT

Your decision to pursue higher education is a form of investment. The costs are the direct costs (tuition, fees, books, and so on) plus the opportunity costs, primarily lost income (which you could earn instead of going to college). The return is the present value of the increased future earnings caused by the investment in education.

The anticipated future wage rate will have a profound impact on the type and amount of education that is pursued. For example, if wages of accountants rise relative to those of engineers, economists would expect more students to study accounting. Wages in professions that require long periods of study will have to be higher to attract new entrants, for three reasons. First, those in school for long periods of time (like medical doctors) incur greater current costs. Second, they sacrifice a great deal of present income. Third, their future income is a longer way off. As you know, income a long way into the future is worth a great deal less than income now. As we discussed in an earlier chapter, incomes of medical doctors have stopped rising as rapidly as they did decades ago. As a result of these declining (relative) incomes, applications to medical schools declined sharply in the 1980s.

This analysis does not deny that people attend universities and colleges for other reasons besides the return to investment in human capital. Some engage in education for its consumption value. For example, retired people returning to school are not investing in human capital, because their productive years (as workers) have ended. Instead, they are acquiring education for its consumption value. There are many consumption-related benefits to education, ranging from enjoyment of literature and fine arts to the thrill of solving a tricky problem in logic. There are also many consumption benefits related to being a student. If you are a member of a fraternity or a sorority or enjoy the "big game" or homecoming weekend, you are familiar with some of these consumption benefits.

Not everyone makes career decisions on a strictly economic basis, and we don't want to imply that you should. You are going to spend the rest of your life working. Why not pick out an occupation or profession that you find enjoyable? This discussion of human capital and education is similar to many policy debates in economics. An economic model of human capital formation may seem dehumanizing, but you shouldn't view it that way. It is just another way of analyzing a complex process, and it will give you important insights. These insights can help explain why workers enjoy different income levels or why two workers in the same occupation working for the same firm may receive different salaries.

HUMAN CAPITAL AND RACE

The idea that differences in human capital result in differences in wage rates is related to the issue of racial (or sexual) discrimination. The important economic question is how much of the income difference between whites and blacks in the United States is the result of discrimination and how much is a market phenomenon—the result of differences in human capital?

Many economists have examined income differences between blacks and whites from a human capital perspective. In 1955, Morton Zeman at the University of Chicago began the debate over the cause of such differences.[4] Zeman examined the effects of schooling and on-the-job training, two elements of human capital formation, on income differences. He reported that increases in schooling and training increased the incomes of both whites and blacks, but increased the earnings of whites more. In other words, the rate of return to this investment in human capital appeared to be higher for whites. Zeman's work implied that the income differences were the result of different pay for the same skill (that is, discrimination) and that increasing the schooling of blacks would do little to change these differences.

As more data became available in the 1960s, Zeman's result appeared to be confirmed. Blacks gained access to more schooling, yet income differences seemed to become more pronounced. However, in 1974, Finis Welch found support for a human capital explanation of the income differences.[5] Welch showed, using newly available and more extensive data, that rates of return to education were in fact as high for blacks as for whites.

James P. Smith of the Rand Corporation studied the effects of race on human capital formation using historical records.[6] Smith found that the increase in black education after the Civil War had important implications for income differences. This human capital approach also helped to explain the differences between the findings of Welch and those of other researchers. Before the Civil War, every southern state had laws prohibiting the schooling of slaves. As a result, 95 percent of all black southerners were illiterate in 1860. At the end of the Civil War, the difference in average schooling of blacks and whites was enormous. Smith reported that whites of either sex (on the average) finished four to five more years of schooling than blacks did. In the first two decades after the war, blacks began to close this gap. In the next two decades (1886 to 1906), however, black schooling made little progress, and human capital formation of whites outstripped that of blacks. This difference was the result of two factors: the disenfranchisement of blacks in the south and the increase in the number of whites in the north who finished high school. Finally, Smith found that the

---

4. Morton Zeman, "A Comparative Analysis of White and Non-White Income Differentials" (unpublished dissertation, University of Chicago, September 1955).
5. Finis Welch, "Education and Racial Discrimination," in Orley Ashenfelter and Albert Rees, eds., *Discrimination in Labor Markets* (Princeton NJ: Princeton University Press, 1974).
6. James P. Smith, "Race and Human Capital," *American Economic Review* (September 1984): 865–898.

differences in education between blacks and whites continually narrowed from 1906 to 1950.

Smith concluded that education, or human capital formation, profoundly affects race-related income differences, but with a great lag. Smith showed that interruptions in the progress of black schooling in the early 1900s are still influencing the income difference. The lesson of this research is that the key to further narrowing the income gap between the races (or sexes) will depend in large part on the availability of education and on-the-job training. It further shows that such changes are slow and evolutionary.

Discrimination is not the only explanation of male-female wage differences. Some observers claim that women bring less human capital to the market. Less human capital could be the result of less education and on-the-job training or the result of lower strength, vigor, dependability, and health of women in general. Historically, females have invested less in education and training than have males. As a result, the average market value of their skills is lower. However, like the educational gap between whites and blacks, the gap between male and female education levels is closing. Over the past thirty years, women have been enrolling in colleges and completing degrees at rates approaching those of men. The economics of this trend is simple. As human capital equalizes, wage differences between men and women should decline. We will explore this issue further in the chapter on income distribution.

COMPARABLE WORTH

A public policy area in which issues of perceived labor market inequities and human capital are important is the debate concerning comparable worth. **Comparable worth** is a standard for determining wages on the basis of equal pay for jobs that require similar levels of training, responsibility, skills, and so on. Support for such a standard is a response to the fact that women earn an average of about 67 percent of what men earn and are heavily concentrated in nursing, teaching, retail sales, and secretarial and clerical jobs. The political pressure for more comparable worth legislation almost died out during the Reagan and Bush years in the White House. Some labor experts expect it to surface with renewed vigor in the Clinton administration. The comparable worth standard is criticized heavily by many economists and is also politically controversial.

Advocates of using comparable worth to adjust wages argue that the Equal Pay Act of 1963 and the Civil Rights Act of 1964, which require equal pay for equal work, do not go far enough. They claim that these laws are inadequate because average female pay is only about 67 percent of average male pay. Comparable worth advocates argue that there should be equal pay for jobs requiring similar levels of training, responsibility, and abilities.

The argument for comparable worth is based on two observations: the existence of sex discrimination, and monopsony power in labor markets. If employers practice discrimination on the basis of race or sex and federal laws prohibit discrimination in pay in the same job category, then an indirect way to perpetuate discrimination is to separate jobs into categories. These categories would be predominately black or white, or male or female, and different wages would be offered for jobs with similar skills and responsibilities. Since competition would undermine such subtle discrimination, it could only persist if there were monopsony power in the labor market.

Comparable worth
A standard for determining wages that calls for equal pay for jobs that require similar levels of training, responsibility, and skills.

GLOBAL OUTLOOK: COMPARABLE WORTH IN CANADA: LESSONS FOR THE UNITED STATES?

The political popularity of comparable worth legislation rises and falls in the United States with elections. Some political observers expect an uptick in political activity with regard to comparable worth legislation during the Clinton administration. This issue is high on the agenda of some of Clinton's appointees such as Donna Shalala, Secretary of Health and Human Services. To date in the United States, comparable worth legislation has been limited to public sector employment and to various legal challenges, usually referred to as "gender equity." For example, U.S. universities have been under pressure, both political and legal, to equalize salaries and budgets for men's and women's sports, regardless of whether or not they are revenue-producing.

The United States can learn from the experience with comparable worth in our neighbor to the north. In Canada, a 1987 law extends comparable worth adjustments into the private sector. It could have an indirect impact on firms in the United States since many Canadian firms affected by the law are subsidiaries of U.S. firms.

The law was passed in the Province of Ontario and went into effect January 1, 1990. In the first phase, every firm that employs more than 500 persons must publish the results of a comparable worth study for the firm and solicit comments from employees. The pay-equity plan must reflect employees' comments and criticisms.

The law did not specify how the pay-equity plans were to be developed, but it did offer suggestions. It suggested that each job be allocated points on a scale of 1 to 100. The points should be based on the job's requirements, such as education, experience, physical exertion, mental exertion, money handling, personnel supervision, type of equipment operated, physical environment, stress, and working conditions. Employers should then identify any job classification in which more than 60 percent of the workers are female. The wages in these job classifications must then be compared to wages in male-dominated classifications with the same score. For example, if the secretarial job classification has a score of 50, the employer must compare wages in that classification with the wages for a male-dominated classification with a score of 50. If the male-dominated classification has a higher average wage than that of the female-dominated classification with the same score, the firm must raise the pay of the female-dominated group.

An interesting twist is that if the male-dominated classification is paid less than the female-dominated classification with the same score, the law says that the wages of the female-dominated group cannot be cut, *and* employers are not required to raise the pay of the male-dominated group. This plan not only applies to the notion of comparable worth, but to female workers.

The preliminary results of this law are starting to unfold. The Canadian headquarters of Campbell Soup Co. may have to raise the average salaries of secretaries by $3.00 per hour to make them comparable to earnings of janitors. This adjustment may, however, take some time. The law does not require firms to increase their payroll cost by more than 1 percent per year to meet these goals.

Some U.S. advocates of comparable worth think that the Canadian law may give women leverage in U.S. lawsuits. They believe that if discrimination is identified by the subsidiary of a U.S. corporation in Canada, that fact could be used as evidence in a sex discrimination case against the parent company in the United States.

The chief difficulty with comparable worth as a way of determining wages is that it substitutes bureaucratic judgments about job classifications for the forces of the marketplace. Shifts in supply and demand for products and services, subtle differences in skills, varying attractiveness of occupations, and other market determinants of wages are difficult to identify and can change more rapidly than a bureaucratic system could handle.

Peter F. Orazem and J. Peter Mattila highlight some problems of setting wages according to any comparable worth scheme. The fundamental problem is that the valuation of different jobs is subjective. Equally informed, unbiased, and qualified analysts can come up with very different results. Orazem and Mattila found that the potential gains for female state employees in Iowa under a proposed scheme were greatly modified by interest groups in the bureaucratic setting. Gains were shifted away from women and toward special-interest groups. "Through a series of modifications to the plan and through collective bargaining compromises, other interest groups such as unions, supervisors, and professionals were able to avoid potential losses in pay that would have accrued under the original plan. Indeed, these groups ended up with pay raises."[7]

MARGINAL PRODUCTIVITY AND INCOME

The analysis in this chapter leads to an important conclusion of marginal productivity theory. In a competitive labor market, the interaction of the value of the marginal product of labor and the supply of labor determines the wage rate. In turn, the productivity of labor depends on the inherent qualities of the labor, the quantity of labor employed, and the amounts of the other inputs that are used. In other words, the distribution of income is determined by the relative marginal revenue products of the different productive resources. Since wages make up the incomes of laborers, more productive workers will have higher incomes. Laborers that are less productive will have lower incomes.

John Bates Clark, who developed this theory, claimed that it presented a "morally correct" outcome of economic activity. Morality is not the province of economic theory, however. Economic theory is positive. The marginal productivity theory says nothing about whether the income distribution that results is a good one. Rather, the theory indicates that if labor markets are competitive, each worker will receive returns based on individual productivity. If people don't like the outcome, they can work to change it through political action (a topic that will be discussed in a later chapter). The theory also indicates that output will be maximized in societies in which labor is paid according to its marginal productivity.

*Consider again...*Having learned about monopsony and monopsony power, the issue of salaries in professional sports is clearer. A professional sports league—like the NBA, the NFL, or major league baseball—has monopsony power. A few players, like Bo Jackson or "Neon" Deon Sanders, who can play more than one professional sport, are immune to the monopsony power of the league, but most professional athletes have no such fallback option. In 1975, the "reserve clause" was abandoned in professional baseball, permitting free agentry. From 1903 to 1975, the reserve clause gave baseball owners complete control over a player's career. The player either played for the team that owned his contract or he could retire from baseball and coach Little League, tend bar, or whatever his next best alternative was. In 1975, this practice ended and players were able to market their skills to other teams.

---

7. Peter F. Orazem and J. Peter Mattila, "The Implementation Process of Comparable Worth: Winners and Losers," *Journal of Political Economy* (February 1990): 43.

This change reduced the monopsony power of the baseball owners. It did not eliminate their monopsony ownership altogether. This reduction in their monopsony power is responsible for the significant increase in baseball salaries since 1975. It has been estimated that the players' share of baseball total revenue increased from about 10 percent between 1903 and 1975 to about 33 percent after 1975.[8] That's clear evidence of a reduction in monopsony power.

8. Paul Wallich and Elizabeth Corcoran, "The MBAs of Summer," *Scientific American* (June 1992): 120.

SUMMARY

1. A firm is a supplier in the product market and a demander in the resource market. The demand for labor differs from the demand for a product in that it is derived, interdependent, and technologically determined. The demand for labor is derived from the demand for the product it produces. The amount of labor a firm demands depends on the amounts of land, capital, and enterprise that will be used in combination with the labor. And lastly, the demand for labor depends on techniques of production and on technological progress, or the production function.

2. A firm demands labor because labor is productive. The marginal revenue product of labor (MRP_L) curve is the firm's demand curve for labor. In a competitive labor market, the firm faces a perfectly elastic labor supply curve (S_L). When the labor supply curve is perfectly elastic, the marginal resource cost of labor (MRC_L) curve is the same as the labor supply curve. A profit-maximizing firm will employ or purchase labor until $MRP_L = MRC_L$.

3. A firm that is a monopolist in a product market uses less labor than a competitive firm would use, because the firm restricts inputs in the process of restricting output. The monopolist has to pay the market wage just like any other employer in this market. Because MRP_L is less than VMP_L, the monopolist *does* employ fewer workers than similar competitive firms would employ.

4. A monopsony is a market structure in which there is a single purchaser of a productive resource. Monopsony results in fewer units of labor being purchased at less than the perfectly competitive wage, because the marginal resource cost curve lies above the supply curve. The difference between the monopsonistic wage and the competitive wage is monopsonistic exploitation. Improved market information and mobility of workers greatly reduce monopsony power.

5. The elasticity of the demand for the product that labor produces, the share of the total cost of production that labor represents, and opportunity for input substitution all impact on the elasticity of demand for labor. Shifts in demand for a product will cause shifts in the demand for the labor used to produce that product. Also, increased usage of complementary inputs will raise the marginal revenue product of labor and cause the demand curve to shift outward.

6. The idea that differences in human capital result in differences in wage rates is related to the issue of racial (or sexual) discrimination. The decision to pursue more education can be viewed as an investment decision that adds to one's stock of human capital. As education rates of blacks and whites, and males and females, converge, the human capital argument predicts that income levels will also converge.

NEW TERMS

derived demand
interdependent demand
technologically determined demand
marginal productivity theory
value of the marginal product of labor (VMP_L)
marginal revenue product of labor (MRP_L)
backward-bending supply curve
marginal resource cost of labor (MRC_L)
monopsony
monopsonistic exploitation
comparable worth

QUESTIONS: REVIEW, APPLICATIONS, AND POLICY

REVIEW

1. How could the potential of career interruptions have an impact on starting salaries and create a difference between women's and men's earnings?
2. Firms operate in both the resource market and the product market. How does the market structure in the product market affect the market structure in the productive resource market? In other words, is a monopolist always a monopsonist, or vice versa?
3. Describe how an entrepreneur decides how much labor to employ.
4. How is a change in the quantity of labor demanded different from a change in the demand for labor?
5. How is equilibrium in the resource market different for a competitive firm and a monopsonistic firm? How are they the same?
6. Name three factors that could cause a firm's demand for labor to increase. How would such a shift affect the relative wages of the firm's employees?
7. What if the factors that caused the increase in demand in Question 14 affected the whole industry and not just the specific firm?

APPLICATIONS

8. Can you describe a situation that might involve monopsonistic exploitation? What would you recommend as a correction?
9. The demand for nurses has increased in recent years and the salaries of nurses have increased significantly. Is the demand for nurses a derived demand? If so, from what?
10. Why are professional athletes opposed to reserve clauses?
11. Discuss your decision to attend college in human capital terms. Include your opportunity costs and projected income. Will continued investment be required to keep your human capital from depreciating?
12. How can the elasticity of demand for the product that labor is producing affect the elasticity of demand for that labor?
13. Does the fact that undergraduate students with high grade point averages are recruited by "Big Eight" accounting firms have any impact on the supply of accounting professors?

POLICY

14. Do you think minimum wage legislation is a good idea? Why or why not?
15. Why might janitors earn higher wages than secretaries, even though the secretaries could do the janitors' job, but the janitors could not do the secretaries'?

SUGGESTIONS FOR FURTHER READING

Bergmann, Barbara R. *The Economic Emergence of Women*. New York: Basic Books, 1986. An argument for comparable worth made by an economist who chaired the Committee on the Status of Women in the Economics Profession of the American Economics Association for a number of years.

Choudhury, Sharmila. "Reassessing the Male-Female Wage Differential: A Fixed Effects Approach." *Southern Economic Journal* (October 1993): 327–340. An empirical study of wage differences that shows that the level of experience gathered on the job and overall labor market experience are the most important determinants of earnings. Marital status and schooling are not important determinants of earnings for women in this study.

Hill, John K., and James E. Pearce. "The Incidence of Sanctions against Employers of Illegal Aliens." *Journal of Political Economy* (February 1990): 28–44. A well-written analysis of the effects of the U.S. Immigration Bill of 1986, restricting illegal immigration.

Mansfield, Edwin. *Microeconomics*, 8e. New York: W.W. Norton, 1994. A standard intermediate theory text. Chapters 13 and 14 cover the material in this chapter in much greater detail.

CHAPTER 28
ORGANIZED LABOR IN THE UNITED STATES

LEARNING OBJECTIVES
1. List the economic goals of unions and the ways they can be achieved.
2. Diagram and analyze the economic effects of an exclusive union and an inclusive union.
3. Discuss the effects of unions on wages and productivity.
4. Trace the history of the U.S. labor movement.
5. Analyze the economic factors that strengthen unions and weaken unions.

Consider this... *If we look at the history of labor union activity in the United States, the present scene represents a low point for labor. Organized labor made an all out effort to prevent the passage of the North American Free Trade Agreement and lost even though Democrats held a large majority in Congress and unions traditionally have strong ties to the Democratic party. Only about one-sixth of all workers are unionized and the number unionized in the private sector has fallen to one-ninth. In 1993, only about 1/10,000 of all worker-hours were lost to work stoppages. In 1992, the number of unfair-labor-practice charges filed with the National Labor Relations Board was around 35,000. This number is significantly below the average number filed annually from 1955 to 1975. In addition, the NLRB reports that 90 percent of its cases were settled "amicably."*

From this story, one would predict that the union movement, as it relates to the political scene, would be quiet. Not so! Unions supported the presidential campaign of Bill Clinton and they want legislation to "close the book on an era of hostility and distrust," as Clinton's Labor Secretary Robert Reich, has described labor policy in the Reagan years. Specifically, organized labor seeks passage of the Cesar Chavez Workplace Fairness Act. This act, currently being debated in Congress, may become the defining labor policy legislation for the Clinton administration. This chapter will help you understand this act and why organized labor is working so hard for its passage.

This chapter examines the effect that unions have on labor markets. Unions in many countries have goals that are social and political as well as economic. However, for the most part, unions in the United States have concentrated on economic goals such as higher salaries, job security, and good pensions. The most important goal of unions in this country has been to raise wages, so we will concentrate on the effects unions have had on the wage rate.

THE ECONOMICS OF UNION GOALS

Labor unions have been formed for all sorts of reasons, many of which are social and political. However, the most successful labor unions in the United States have concentrated on economic goals. When we speak of economic goals, the bottom line is the real income of union members. It is largely correct, though oversimplified, to think of unions as existing to increase the wages of their members. Unions do pursue goals other than increasing wages, such as shorter hours and better working conditions. These goals also have the effect, *ceteris paribus*, of increasing the well-being of union workers. If wages are unchanged and working conditions have improved, the worker has received an increase in real income. In order to increase wage rates in a competitive labor market such as those shown in Figures 1 and 2, the union must do one of two things. It must either increase the demand for labor (from D_L to D'_L in Figure 1) or decrease the supply of labor (from S_L to S_U in Figure 2).

Increasing the demand for labor is very difficult for a union. In Figure 1, the demand curve for labor depends on both the demand for the product the labor produces and the productivity of the labor. One way for the union to increase the demand for labor is by increasing the demand for the product the firm produces. Unions have advertised in an attempt to influence people to "buy union-made." They have also lobbied to decrease imports through tariffs and quotas in an attempt to increase the demand for domestically produced (union) products. Unions have encouraged educational training programs aimed at increasing productivity and thus increasing the demand for labor. Unions have also tried to persuade the government to help by buying union-made goods and by using macroeconomic policy to increase the demand for such goods. In some instances, unions could keep demand from falling by preventing jobs from be-

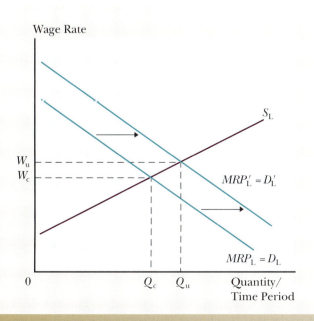

FIGURE 1

EFFECT OF INCREASED DEMAND FOR LABOR
One way in which a union can raise its members' wages above competitive levels is to increase the demand for union labor. An increase in demand from D_L to D'_L would increase wages from W_c to W_u. This increase in demand would cause employment to increase.

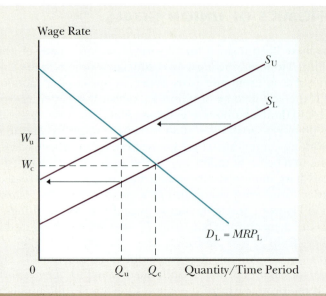

FIGURE 2

EFFECT OF DECREASED SUPPLY OF LABOR
Another way in which a union can raise its members' wages above competitive levels is to decrease the supply of labor. A decrease in the labor supply from S_L to S_U will cause wages to rise from W_c to W_u. This decrease in supply causes employment to decrease.

Featherbedding
The maintenance of jobs that management claims are unnecessary or redundant.

ing eliminated in declining or dying industries. All things considered, however, it is very difficult for unions to significantly increase the demand for labor.

One way to maintain jobs is the practice of **featherbedding**, or keeping jobs that management claims are unnecessary or redundant. Featherbedding does not increase the demand curve in Figure 1. Instead, it operates on the demand side by slowing a decrease in demand. The classic example of featherbedding involves railroad firemen. The advent of diesel and electric power made firemen obsolete, but railroad unions were successful in maintaining the job. Featherbedding has also been common in the newspaper industry, where typesetters' unions have forced the hand-setting of some layouts that could be prepared by computer. In the theater industry, Broadway producers are required to use a certain number of union members regardless of need. For example, a backstage crew of four union members is required no matter what kind of show is being staged. This kind of union success may be only temporary, however, because the added costs may speed the decline of an already dying industry, and the decline of the industry ultimately weakens the union.

Because of the difficulties of increasing demand, unions often focus on the supply side of the market, attempting to shift the supply curve leftward, as illustrated in Figure 2. Historically, many of the "social" goals of unions have had the effect of restricting the supply of labor. Unions have sought to reduce immigration, limit child labor, encourage compulsory and early retirement, enforce a shorter work week, and enact minimum wage legislation. Whatever else you may think of these goals, they all make economic sense for unions if the goal is to increase the wage rate of union members.

Regardless of whether unions focus on demand (Figure 1) or supply (Figure 2), their efforts have the same effect on wages. In both cases, successful union activity will cause the wage rate to rise. The effect on employment, however, is quite different. An attempt to increase demand, as shown in Figure 1, will cause employment in the industry to rise. If, however, the union tries to decrease supply, as in Figure 2, employment in the industry will decline. Since unions are much more effective at reducing supply than at increasing demand, a key economic consequence of unions is that they probably reduce employment in those industries that they organize most successfully.

TYPES OF UNIONS

From a theoretical point of view, we can class unions into two basic types: exclusive and inclusive.

EXCLUSIVE UNIONS

An **exclusive union** is a union that restricts the supply of labor and maintains a higher-than-competitive wage for its members by excluding workers from a trade or occupation. Because of this exclusion, the wage rate is higher in that part of the work force than it would be in the absence of the union. Figure 3 represents the labor market with such a union. Curve S_L represents the competitive supply of labor, and D_L represents the demand for labor. In the absence of any union organization, the wage rate would be W_c, and Q_c units of labor would be employed. The exclusive union attempts to exclude additional workers from the industry and thus shift the supply curve to S_U. If the union were to succeed in keeping new entrants out, the wage rate for union workers would be W_u, and the number of those workers hired would be Q_u.

The key, then, to an exclusive union is that it restricts entry into a job or occupation. The most familiar example of an exclusive union is a **craft union**, which is composed of specific kinds of skilled laborers, such as plumbers or carpenters. These unions very often require workers to serve apprenticeships and obtain a union sponsor in order to become members.

Exclusive union
A union that restricts the supply of labor and maintains a higher-than-competitive wage for its members by excluding workers from a trade or occupation. Craft unions are exclusive unions.

Craft union
A union composed of specific kinds of skilled workers, such as plumbers or carpenters.

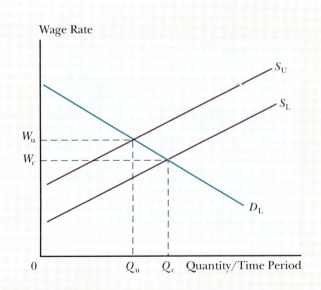

FIGURE 3
EFFECT OF AN EXCLUSIVE UNION
With an exclusive union, union membership is a precondition for employment. As a result, the union can exclude workers and decrease the supply of labor from S_L to S_U.

It should be obvious that a successful exclusive union is very powerful because increases in the wage rate result directly from the exclusionary tactics. The union doesn't need to bargain, coerce, or threaten to strike. Its power to exclude competing workers is sufficient to cause the market wage to increase. The power of the exclusive union is difficult to challenge once the union has been established.

It is also difficult to exclude workers from a union. When wages rise, there will be pressure from outside workers seeking employment in these trades. This natural economic force makes it necessary for the union to be able to control licensing. Many exclusive unions owe their success to getting the government to help them by requiring a worker to earn a license or permit to be a member of the trade. If the union can gain control of this licensing function, it has an automatic way of excluding labor. This gateway is one way in which plumbers and electricians have maintained their union power. Professional associations, such as the American Medical Association or the American Bar Association, are similar to craft unions in their effects on the labor market for their members. Entry is restricted through licensing and control over professional schools.

INCLUSIVE UNIONS

Inclusive union
A union that attempts to organize all the workers in an industry and to maintain a strong bargaining position with respect to management.

Industrial union
An inclusive union that gains power by organizing all (or a large share) of the workers in an industry.

The **inclusive union** attempts to organize all the workers in an industry and to maintain a strong bargaining position with respect to the management of firms in that industry. Inclusive unions, also referred to as **industrial unions**, include the United Steelworkers, the United Auto Workers, and the Teamsters. The goal of an inclusive union is to bring all workers in an industry into the union, resulting in a strong bargaining position. It is also important that an industrial union organize most of the firms in an industry. Otherwise, nonunionized firms will enjoy a cost advantage and be able to undersell union-organized firms. This competitive disadvantage will create an incentive for nonunionized firms to try to break the union. Inclusive union organization has been most successful in oligopolistic markets, where there are fewer firms in which the labor needs to be organized.

The labor market with an inclusive union is represented by Figure 4. The competitive wage and employment are W_c and Q_c, respectively. The union organizes the industry and bargains the wage rate, W_u. The bargained rate W_u has the same effect as a minimum wage in this industry, so employment will be Q_u. At W_u, however, the quantity of labor supplied will be Q_s. There will be a surplus of labor. Some extra workers would like to work at the bargained wage, and they may offer their services if a strike occurs. This surplus of labor is the so-called "scabs" you often see on television when management is trying to break a strike by hiring nonunion workers.

It should be clear that the ability of an inclusive union to raise wages depends on the strength of its bargaining position, which will, of course, depend on how large a share of the employment in the particular industry is held by its members. It is important that an inclusive union have a significant membership in the industry in which it operates because its success depends on its ability to threaten the firms in that industry.

Inclusive unions have been most successful in industries that are very concentrated. The firms in these industries may possess monopsony power in labor

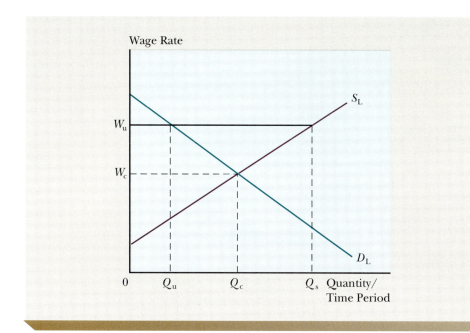

FIGURE 4

EFFECT OF AN INCLUSIVE UNION

An inclusive union attempts to organize all labor in an industry and then to bargain a wage. This bargained wage works like a price floor (or minimum wage) in this labor market.

markets, and an inclusive union can offset some of that power. **Bilateral monopolies** are market structures in which monopolies deal with each other as buyers and sellers, such as an inclusive union selling labor to a monopsonistic firm. Such bilateral monopolies may exist in the steel, auto, and farm machinery industries, where there are both big unions and big oligopolies. This situation is depicted in Figure 5. In the absence of the union, the monopsonistic firm would employ Q_f units of labor at a wage rate of W_f. The competitive wage rate and employment level would have been W_c and Q_c.

In the absence of monopsony power on the part of the purchaser, the union would want a wage of W_u because it faces a downward-sloping demand curve (D_L) for its product (labor). Since the demand curve is downward sloping, the marginal revenue curve lies below it. The union is a monopolist in the selling of its labor. The marginal revenue of the union is thus represented by MR in Figure 5. The union maximizes its gains where MR is equal to MC, at an employment level of Q_u. The result in terms of the wage rate is logically indeterminate. That is, the theoretical model will not say exactly where the resulting wage will fall. All it will say is that the wage will be between W_f and W_u. Whether it is closer to W_f or to W_u will depend on the relative bargaining strengths of the union and the monopsony firm. Note that if the wage is anywhere between W_m and W_f, unionization in a monopsonistic industry increases employment over the nonunion level, Q_f. The monopsonist hired fewer workers than would have been the case with competition. If the union is successful in bargaining a wage rate of W_c (the competitive rate), employment will rise to Q_c. Note that this result is very similar to the effect of a minimum wage in a monopsonistic labor market, which was discussed in the last chapter.

Bilateral monopoly
A market structure in which monopolies deal with each other as buyers and sellers, such as when an inclusive union sells labor to a monopolistic firm.

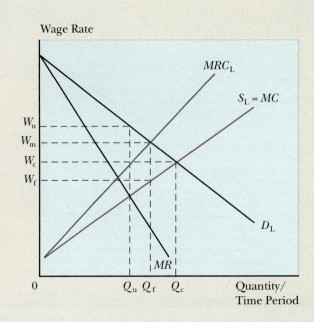

FIGURE 5

WAGES IN A BILATERAL MONOPOLY

In a bilateral monopoly, a monopolistic seller (the union) sells labor to a monopsony firm. The wage rate will depend on the relative bargaining strengths of the two participants.

ECONOMIC EFFECTS OF UNIONS

Much of the controversy over unions centers on their effects on wages, income distribution, productivity, stock prices, and inflation. We will examine each of these issues.

DO UNIONS RAISE WAGES?

Regardless of the power of a union, there are constraints on the degree to which it can influence wages. Competitive pressure from nonunion labor and the possibility of substituting other inputs will always put limits on union demands. For example, consider a union attempting to organize migrant workers. In response to higher wages resulting from the union, the farmer may substitute machinery for labor. A second powerful restraint on unions' demands exists in the product market. If unions raise wages, costs and prices rise. Consumers will react to an increased price by shifting consumption to nonunion products. The demand for union-made products, and thus for union labor, will then fall. These constraints are always present, and the union can do very little to offset them.

Given these limitations, how successful have unions been in increasing the wages of their members? The difficulty in answering this question lies in separating wage differences due to varying productivity from those based solely on union power. The path-breaking empirical study in this area was done by H. Gregg Lewis.[1] Lewis based his study on data from the 1940s and 1950s. He found

---

1. H. Gregg Lewis, *Union Relative Wage Effects: A Survey* (Chicago: University of Chicago Press, 1986), 56.

TABLE 1 EFFECT OF UNIONS ON WAGES

AUTHOR	TIME PERIOD OF DATA	INDUSTRY OR OCCUPATION	UNION/NON-UNION WAGE DIFFERENTIAL
Lewis (five studies)	1923–1958	Industrial workers	0–25%
Throop (two studies)	1950–1960	Selected industries	25–29.7%
Personick	1972	Construction	35–70%
Personick and Schwenk	1971	Shirt manufacturing	7–16%
Ashenfelter	1961–1966	Firefighters	6–16%
Schmenner	1962–1970	Public employees	12–15%
Weiss	1959	Craftsmen—operators	6–8%
Stafford	1966	Various occupations	–8–52%
Boskin	1967	Various occupations	–5.3–24.7%

Source: C. J. Parsley, "Labor Union Effects on Wage Gains: A Survey of Recent Literature," *Journal of Economic Literature* (October 1980); and H. Gregg Lewis, *Union Relative Wage Effects: A Survey, 1986* (Chicago: University of Chicago Press, 1986).

that union workers received on average from 10 to 15 percent higher wages than nonunion workers with similar productivity characteristics. Later studies using Lewis's techniques and more recent data indicate that union salaries are 15 to 25 percent higher for workers with similar productivity characteristics.[2] These same studies also indicate that craft unions are more successful in raising wages than industrial unions are.

In 1980, C. J. Parsley published an extensive review of empirical studies on the effects of unions on wages.[3] His survey of U.S. studies is summarized in Table 1. Parsley's review showed that wages are consistently higher in unionized sectors. The evidence seems to indicate that unions increase wages.

Where do union members' higher wages come from? Your first reaction may be that they come out of business profits, but can this be so? Recall the theory developed in earlier chapters. Wages are a cost of production. If markets are competitive, the increased cost of higher wages will result in higher prices because in the long run, with or without unions, the average firm will only be earning a normal profit. If the firm possesses some monopoly power, the higher labor costs might reduce monopoly profits, but part of the increased costs may also be passed forward in higher prices.

In addition, in any product market structure, the increased costs of union-made products will cause the quantity demanded to be lower than it would have been without a union. The reduction in sales in unionized industries means a loss of jobs in those industries. As unemployed workers from unionized industries seek jobs elsewhere, wage rates will fall in the nonunion sector.

This analysis implies that the higher wages of union workers are paid partly by consumers in the form of higher prices for union-made goods and partly by

---

2. See M. J. Boskin, "Unions and Relative Real Wages," *American Economic Review* (June 1972); and P. M. Ryscavage, "Measuring Union-Nonunion Earnings Differences," *Monthly Labor Review* (December 1974).
3. C. J. Parsley, "Labor Union Effects on Wage Gains: A Survey of Recent Literature," *Journal of Economic Literature* (October 1980).

nonunion workers in the form of lower wages. Research by H. Gregg Lewis concludes that nonunion wages are 3 to 4 percent lower because of union-increased wages in the organized labor sector.[4] There also appears to be some evidence that nonunion wages are higher in some sectors because nonunionized firms raise wages as a defensive tactic to keep unions out.[5]

UNIONS, WAGES, AND PRODUCTIVITY

As you saw earlier in this chapter, if unions could raise the marginal revenue product of labor, the demand for labor would increase and wage rates would rise. Increasing the demand for labor is difficult to do. In fact, some critics argue that unions are not only unsuccessful at raising worker productivity but, in fact, may introduce inefficiencies that decrease the marginal revenue product of labor.

Examples of these inefficiencies are well known. There are work rules requiring that certain jobs be performed by certain workers: a light bulb can't be changed by a custodian because the work rules require that the job be performed by an electrician, or a display for a convention must be unloaded by a teamster. Featherbedding, mentioned earlier, is another form of inefficiency. Unions can also introduce inefficiency into the production process through disruptive strikes. Strikes cause production to fall, and strikes in major industries can even cause production to be disrupted in related industries. Unions can also introduce inefficiency through the effects of wage increases. If unions raise wages in an industry above competitive levels, they must restrict entry into the jobs in that industry, and output is reduced.

Labor in a unionized industry might be more productive because of success in raising wages. If unions raise wages, there will be an incentive for firms to substitute capital for labor. As you learned in the last chapter, if more capital is employed in an industry, the labor in that industry will be more productive.

Economists Richard Freeman and James Medoff argue that unions can increase productivity because of their effect on worker turnover. They argue that unions give workers a "voice/response mechanism" that enables management and workers to iron out problems. This mechanism, they argue, "changes the employment relationship from a casual dating game, in which people look elsewhere at the first serious problem, to a more permanent marriage, in which they seek to resolve disputes through discussion and negotiation."[6] Freeman and Medoff go on to argue that unionization produces loyal employees who are more skilled and have higher levels of productivity. In fact, they argue, productivity is between 20 and 25 percent higher in the unionized sector of U.S. manufacturing.

STOCK PRICES OF UNIONIZED FIRMS

Another area where unions may have an economic impact is the stock prices of firms. Economists have increasingly looked to the stock market to analyze the ef-

---

4. Lewis, *Wage Effects*, 78.
5. See Barry Hirsch and John Addison, *The Economic Analysis of Unions* (Boston: Allen and Unwin, 1986).
6. Richard B. Freeman and James L. Medoff, *What Do Unions Do?* (New York: Basic Books, 1984), 38.

fect that economic events have on the value of a firm. The price of a firm's stock gives a measure of what an economic event has done to the value of the company.

A study by John M. Abowd examined the effect of union contracts on the value of the stock of the company that signs the contract. Abowd showed that shareholders' wealth moved in the opposite direction from union members' wealth.[7] There was a dollar-for-dollar trade-off between the two variables. This finding suggests that the union can negotiate a contract that extracts economic profit from a firm that has market power. This union contract then takes wealth away from the stockholders. This suggests that if unions are successful in raising wages, the increased wages come at the expense of owners of capital. The study also suggests that unions will only be successful in raising wages in industries where the firms have some degree of monopoly power. Abowd's results dispute Freeman and Medoff's conclusion that unions enhance productivity. A dollar-for-dollar loss of stockholders' wealth would mean that the stockholders could not expect to recoup any of the additional wage cost through productivity increases.

DO UNIONS CAUSE INFLATION?

You have just seen that unions cause wages and prices to be higher in unionized industries than in nonunionized ones. But do unions cause inflation? The answer is no! Unions are only affecting relative prices across industries—not the absolute level of prices. Of course, unions bargain for higher wages and businesses raise prices in inflationary times, but these are responses to inflation, not causes of it. In fact, most studies indicate that union wages rise less rapidly during the early stage of an inflationary period than do nonunion wages.[8] This is partly because unions are unaware in the beginning how high the inflation will be. Even if unions anticipate that inflation will occur, they may already have committed their members to long-term contracts with wage increases less than the inflation rate. When these contracts expire, the unions try to make up for the inflation in their wage demands. It sometimes appears as if unions are responsible for the inflation, rather than victims who are trying to catch up.

A HISTORY OF THE LABOR MOVEMENT

Around the turn of the century, the U.S. economy shifted from a largely agrarian base to an industrial one. By 1910, employment in industry exceeded employment in agriculture. The industrial labor force grew rapidly, and labor organizers became more successful. In 1914, about 7 percent of the work force was unionized. Growth in the labor force and growth in unionization were accompanied by a rapidly rising real wage rate. That rise in wages was largely due to rapid advances in technology and in the human capital of wage earners. Both union and nonunion labor received substantial wage increases during this period.

---

7. John M. Abowd, "The Effects of Wage Bargains on the Stock Market Value of the Firm," *American Economic Review* (September 1989): 774–800.
8. See Albert Rees, "Do Unions Cause Inflation?" *The Journal of Law and Economics* (October 1959).

THE EARLY UNSUCCESSFUL YEARS

The best way to understand the labor movement in the United States is to view it in historical perspective. In the early nineteenth century, the labor movement was unsuccessful in organizing large numbers of workers, and its operations were mostly limited to cities in the eastern United States. During this period, the workday changed from sunup to sundown to ten hours. Workers still spent twelve hours on the job but received two one-hour (mid-morning and mid-afternoon) breaks.

It became apparent by the middle of the century that a coordinated national effort to organize labor was necessary if unions were to be effective. Even if labor did successfully raise wages above the free market equilibrium wage in a certain area, the gains were short-lived. Labor from other regions of the country produced cheaper goods that could be shipped via the rapidly growing, low-cost transportation network. The U.S. Constitution forbids any interference with interstate commerce, so regions or states could not place tariffs on goods from other regions or states. Thus, all or most of the labor in the firms of an industry had to be organized if unionization was to be successful.

The first successful national union was organized by William H. Sylvis. Sylvis had been treasurer of the short-lived Iron Molders International Union. In 1867, he founded the National Labor Union. The **National Labor Union** was involved in political action and favored the eight-hour day, arbitration, and cooperatives (firms owned by the union members who worked there). The union published a journal, *The Workingman's Advocate*, to voice its political aims. The union grew rapidly to a membership of 600,000 but quickly fell apart after Sylvis's death in 1869.

In 1869, the **Knights of Labor** was organized by Uriah Stevens as a secret society. The secrecy was to protect members from reprisals by management, but it also led to suspicion of the union and bad public relations. As a result, the policy of secrecy was dropped in 1879. The Knights' greatest accomplishment was to win the first major strike in U.S. history. This strike was one against the Wabash, Missouri-Kansas-Texas, and Missouri Pacific railroads, which were owned by Jay Gould, one of the most famous of the robber barons. By the turn of the century, however, the Knights of Labor had become unimportant as a force for labor reform. The reasons for its decline were important for future labor organizations. The Knights' philosophical goal for labor reform was to abolish the wage system and replace it with worker cooperatives. It thus had a reformist political agenda rather than "bread and butter" economic goals. The focus on reformist political goals, coupled with some unsuccessful large strikes and some violent acts of sabotage (the Knights were linked to the infamous Haymarket bomb-throwing incident in Chicago), contributed to the union's failure.

The **American Federation of Labor (AFL)** was founded in 1886 by Samuel Gompers. Gompers actually founded the Federation of Organized Trades and Labor Unions, which is considered the precursor of the AFL. The AFL was an association of exclusive unions primarily made up of skilled workers. It was the first business union, which allowed it to overcome many of the problems earlier national unions had faced. A **business union** was defined by Samuel Gompers as a union that worked for economic goals without wanting to change or destroy the business organization or the political environment in which it worked.

National Labor Union
The first successful national union in the United States, founded in 1867 by William Sylvis.

Knights of Labor
Organized as a secret organization by Uriah Stevens in 1869, it won the first major strike in the United States against the railroad industry but had political reformist goals that led to its demise.

American Federation of Labor (AFL)
An exclusive union for skilled workers founded by Samuel Gompers in 1886 as the first business union.

Business union
According to Samuel Gompers, a union that works for economic goals without wanting to change or destroy the business organization or the political environment in which it functions.

Gompers was, above all, pragmatic. He set a single goal of economic gains for the union's members, with no political reformist goals. Gompers thought that national labor leaders had to have the sole authority to call strikes and control membership dues. This principle has remained important in the U.S. labor movement to the present.

Gompers was elected the first president of the AFL. By 1904, membership had grown to nearly 2 million. Much of the union's success was due to Gompers's abilities. Although Gompers had been a radical in his younger days, he realized that the labor movement had to shed its radical-socialist image in order to succeed in the United States. He worked hard to overcome organized labor's negative image, which was generated by the management of large corporations and fed by the activities and tactics of radical unions. Gompers joined the National Civic Federation, an association of wealthy eastern capitalists, editors, professional people, and corporation officers. This organization emphasized that labor unions' strength did not undermine U.S. business and that strong business was good for labor.

Perhaps the best evidence of Gompers's success was his acceptance by the political establishment. During World War I, President Wilson appointed Gompers to the advisory commission to the Council of National Defense. In 1919, at the Versailles Peace Conference, Gompers served as chairperson of the Commission of International Labor Legislation. He proved that labor leaders were respectable citizens, not communist radicals seeking to overthrow U.S. capitalism.

The early struggles of organized labor were understandable, since it was easy to break strikes and weaken labor organizations because there was a steady supply of eager workers pouring in from Europe. World War I brought prosperity and high labor demand and marked the beginning of success for American unions. Membership increased steadily during this period, and the image of unions started to improve. Much credit for this is due to Gompers. Unions flexed their muscles during the war period, and there were many strikes in 1917. These strikes were caused by the war-generated inflation and booming labor demand and the effect this inflation had on long-term union contracts. In 1918, labor was successful in negotiating an eight-hour day and collective bargaining rights in exchange for a no-strike agreement. As a result, labor emerged from World War I stronger than it had ever been.

The postwar period brought increased inflation and more strikes aimed at increasing wages. The **Industrial Workers of the World (IWW)** was an international union that organized steelworkers after World War I. These workers were unskilled laborers and thus not members of the AFL. The IWW had been associated with several prominent socialists and was regarded as a radical movement. At this time, after the Russian Revolution, the fear of a worldwide Bolshevik revolution gripped the United States. The IWW went on strike against U.S. Steel in 1920 and lost. The breaking of this strike was a major victory for steel companies, who successfully branded the union leaders as socialists who were attempting to overthrow capitalism. The IWW's failure, coupled with the recession of 1920 to 1922, halted what had been a steady rise in union prestige and membership.

The 1920s proved to be a difficult time for the labor movement. The Republican Presidents Harding, Coolidge, and Hoover were pro-business, and business at that time was aggressively opposed to organized labor. The federal

Industrial Workers of the World (IWW)
An international union that organized U.S. steelworkers after World War I and was viewed as a socialistic organization, which contributed to its demise.

Yellow-dog contracts
Contracts that require employees to agree to refrain from union activity as a precondition for employment and that allow firms to discharge workers who violate that agreement.

Injunction
A court order to cease some activity, such as ordering labor to end a strike or walkout.

Norris-La Guardia Act
A law passed in 1932 that vastly strengthened the power of labor unions by limiting the court's use of injunctions in labor-management disputes.

Wagner Act
A law passed in 1935 that gave employees the right to organize and bargain collectively and outlawed certain unfair labor practices by employers.

National Labor Relations Board (NLRB)
A board established by the Wagner Act in 1935 and empowered to investigate employer unfair labor practices and to determine the legitimate bargaining agent for labor when there are competing unions.

Congress of Industrial Organizations (CIO)
An affiliation of industrial unions that was organized when the AFL decided not to move into mass-production industries.

government sanctioned **yellow-dog contracts**, which required the employee to agree to refrain from union activity as a precondition of employment and which allowed the firm to discharge a worker for violation of that agreement. In addition, the courts were hostile to union activity. This hostility was apparent in the ease with which management was able to get court injunctions. An **injunction** is a court order to cease some action. In labor-management disputes, it was often used to order labor back to work. A section of the Clayton Act (1914), which had been hailed by Samuel Gompers as the Magna Carta of labor because it limited the use of injunctions against labor, was declared unconstitutional in 1926.

SUCCESS AND POWER

Bad times for unions ended with the election of Franklin D. Roosevelt in 1932. Roosevelt campaigned as the friend of the worker. The legislation that was proposed and passed during Roosevelt's terms established a bond between organized labor and the Democratic party that still exists today. The two key pieces of legislation were the Norris-La Guardia Act (1932) and the Wagner Act (1935). These acts vastly strengthened the power of labor unions and set the stage for their rapid development. They gave workers the right to organize and made it illegal to interfere with this right.

Under the **Norris-La Guardia Act**, yellow-dog contracts were outlawed. Injunctions against unions and their activities were limited to unlawful acts, and businesses were required to engage in collective bargaining and to bargain in good faith. Thus, the most common union-bashing tactic of employers was thwarted by the Norris-La Guardia Act. Court-issued injunctions had been used to stop strikes, boycotts, and other union activities. The intent of this act was to make the federal government neutral with respect to labor policy. Compared to past practices, this was a strong stimulus to union activity.

The **Wagner Act** made it federal policy that every worker should "have full freedom of association, self-organization, and designation of representatives of his own choosing, to negotiate terms and conditions of his employment." The act also established the **National Labor Relations Board (NLRB)**. The NLRB was empowered to investigate unfair labor practices by employers and to determine the legitimate bargaining agent for labor when there are competing unions. The Wagner Act was challenged in the courts and declared to be constitutional by the Supreme Court in 1937. Under this act, private sector workers were given the right to organize without interference from management. In practice, if organizers can get 30 percent of the work force in a place of employment to sign authorization cards, the NLRB steps in and conducts a vote. If the majority of the workers support the union in the vote, the management of the company must recognize the union and bargain with it.

During the early 1930s, a debate was going on within the AFL concerning whether it should organize unions in mass-production industries such as steel-working, automobile manufacturing, and mining. A number of the AFL-affiliated unions formed the Committee for Industrial Organization in 1935. The Executive Council of the AFL requested that the Committee disband immediately. The Committee refused to disband and the AFL Executive Council suspended the Committee unions. The suspension was ratified by a vote at the AFL convention. The Committee then formed the **Congress of Industrial**

Organizations (CIO). John L. Lewis, the colorful, forceful head of the United Mine Workers, became its first president.

WORLD WAR II AND THE 1950S

The boom economy of the World War II years brought a number of serious strikes. The Wagner Act had given unions more legal power, and the coffers of union treasuries were full. Unions flexed their muscles through a wave of work stoppages. Although the unions were successful in achieving sizable settlements, public sympathy began to shift away from organized labor. As a result, Congress passed the **Taft-Hartley Act** in 1947, which was designed to offset some of the labor gains created by the Wagner Act. President Truman vetoed the act, but Congress overrode the veto, an indication of the anti-union political atmosphere.

The Taft-Hartley Act shifted some legal rights back to employers. **Closed shops,** in which workers were required to become union members before employment, were made illegal. **Union shops,** in which union membership was necessary for a worker to remain employed, remained legal under the act. However, states were given the right to pass **right-to-work laws**, which allowed people to hold jobs without belonging to unions. These laws obviously undermined union power. As you saw earlier in this chapter, an inclusive union must present a united front if it is to be successful in bargaining with management. Right-to-work laws greatly undermined the ability of inclusive unions to present this united front.

The Taft-Hartley Act also required unions to bargain in good faith and outlawed featherbedding and secondary boycotts. **Secondary boycotts** are union actions to stop an employer from doing business with other firms. In other words, a union not only boycotts the firm it has a grievance against, which would be a primary boycott, but it also boycotts firms (and their products) who do business with that firm. A secondary boycott is more powerful than a picket line because it involves actions against and pressures on third parties. In certain instances, the Taft-Hartley Act empowers the President to call an eighty-day cooling-off period before a strike. During this period, mediation is attempted by a government-appointed fact-finding board.

Mediation is third-party intervention into a dispute. The mediator attempts to keep the parties together and talking by offering suggestions and clarifying issues. This process is different from arbitration. In **arbitration**, a third party hears the arguments of both sides in a dispute, studies their positions, and renders a decision. If the dispute has been submitted to binding arbitration, both parties must abide by that decision.

Union leaders fought the Taft-Hartley Act as a "slave labor law" every step of the way. They continue to campaign to reverse some of its provisions. Despite the Taft-Hartley Act, however, unions have continued to show great strength, which has been enhanced by careful and well-organized political activity.

Business and labor are not always at odds. Unions and management have often worked together to lobby for reduced pollution controls, to curb imports, and even to urge tax cuts for business. In some cases, union organization brings stability to an industry. An oligopolistic industry may even use labor power to help monopolize the industry. Before the days of the United Mine Workers, mine operators had a very difficult time with labor because miners were (and

Taft-Hartley Act
Act passed in 1947 to reverse some of the Wagner Act's favoring of labor by shifting some legal rights back to employers.

Closed shops
Firms where contract provisions require that workers must be union members before being employed.

Union shops
Firms where union membership is necessary for a worker to remain employed.

Right-to-work laws
State laws that allow people to hold jobs without belonging to unions.

Secondary boycotts
Union actions to stop an employer from doing business with other firms.

Mediation
Third-party intervention in a dispute consisting of attempts to keep the parties together and talking by offering suggestions and clarifying issues.

Arbitration
Third party intervention in a dispute, consisting of hearing the arguments of both sides, studying their positions, and rendering a decision. In binding arbitration, both sides must abide by the decision.

United Mine Workers (UMW)
The industrial union for mine workers.

Wildcat strikes
Local strikes that are unauthorized by the national union.

AFL-CIO
An organization formed by the merger of the American Federation of Labor and the Congress of Industrial Organizations in 1955, which gave labor a more unified political front.

Landrum-Griffin Act
An act passed in 1959, aimed at curbing union power by making unions more democratic, restricting Communist Party members and convicted felons from union leadership, and making picketing illegal under certain circumstances.

American Federation of State, County, and Municipal Employees (AFSCME)
A union of public employees that was one of the few unions that grew in the 1970s.

Humphrey-Hawkins Act
A 1978 amendment to the Employment Act of 1946 that set specific targets for output, employment, and prices.

are) a very independent lot. The **United Mine Workers (UMW)** is the industrial union for mine workers founded in 1890. Under the leadership of John L. Lewis, it brought organization *and* discipline to mine labor. When Lewis ordered the miners back to work, they went back to work! In more recent years, however, the leadership of the UMW has not been able to exercise such strong control, and **wildcat strikes**, which are local strikes unauthorized by the national union, have been frequent.

In 1955, the American Federation of Labor and the Congress of Industrial Organizations merged to form the **AFL-CIO**. This merger unified the labor movement under the leadership of Walter Reuther and George Meany. The **Landrum-Griffin Act**, passed in 1959, was a response to public concern over union power and certain questionable practices. The act made unions more democratic, prohibited Communist Party members and convicted felons from union leadership, and strengthened the Taft-Hartley Act by making picketing illegal under certain circumstances.

RECENT LABOR HISTORY

The real world of labor-management relations does not always run the way a review of the law would indicate. The NLRB is often slow to act and sometimes slow to rule in cases of unfair labor practices. The battleground of labor-management relations has shifted to the south, where much of recent industrial growth in the United States has taken place. It is also mainly in the south that right-to-work laws are found. Some economists attribute at least part of the growth of industry in the south to those laws.

The 1960s and 1970s saw a decline in the share of the labor force that was unionized. This trend was partly a result of the fact that the economy was becoming more service-oriented and less manufacturing-oriented. Thirty-five years ago, almost 40 percent of the U.S. labor force was unionized. Today, less than 20 percent is unionized.

One exception to this trend was a dramatic increase in the membership of public employee unions. The **American Federation of State, County, and Municipal Employees (AFSCME)** was one of the few unions that grew in the 1970s. In the early 1970s, AFSCME was politically active. However, in 1977 the union lost in a confrontation with Mayor Maynard Jackson of Atlanta. Garbage workers affiliated with the union struck the city of Atlanta. Jackson refused to bargain with the local AFSCME chapter and hired strike breakers. High unemployment in the city aided the strike breaking, and the jobs were quickly filled. In August 1981, President Reagan dealt the public sector union movement another blow when, in response to an unauthorized strike, he disbanded the Professional Air Traffic Controllers Organization (PATCO).[9] Is a turnaround occurring? After fourteen years of decline, the number of union members in the United States increased in 1993, according to the Department of Labor. Growth was concentrated in the public sector.

In late 1978, President Carter signed the Humphrey-Hawkins Act. The **Humphrey-Hawkins Act** was an amendment to the Employment Act of 1946 that set specific targets for output, employment, and prices. The original bill included increases in public sector jobs and was strongly supported by organized

---

9. For a review of the public sector union movement, see Richard B. Freeman, "Unionism Comes to the Public Sector," *Journal of Economic Literature* (March 1986).

labor. The version that finally passed Congress was viewed by many labor leaders as meaningless. The act set national goals to reduce unemployment to 4 percent in 1983, and to cut inflation to 3 percent in 1983 and to zero by 1988. Full employment was defined as the right to full opportunity for useful employment at fair rates of compensation for all individuals able and willing to work. The bill was regarded by labor as merely symbolic. It did not include any means to reach the goals specified, such as more public sector jobs, but left that to future legislation.

There has been little labor legislation since the Landrum-Griffin Act, except for an increase in the minimum wage approved in 1989, the first since 1981. Labor has campaigned vigorously to repeal some aspects of the Taft-Hartley Act. The two most important pieces of legislation that organized labor currently favors are the repeal of right-to-work laws and the common situs picketing bill. The latter bill grants any union the right to picket an entire construction job even when the union represents only a small part of the labor used on the project.

KEY IDEAS

SUMMARY OF MAJOR LABOR LAWS

STATUTE (YEAR)	MAJOR PROVISIONS
Norris-La Guardia Act (1932)	Outlawed yellow-dog contracts and made picket lines and secondary boycotts legal. Limited injunctions against labor to illegal acts and required management to bargain in good faith with unions.
Wagner Act (1935)	Established the right to form unions and set up the NLRB.
Taft-Hartley Act (1947)	Made closed shops illegal. Permitted union shops but also allowed states to pass right-to-work laws.
Landrum-Griffin Act (1959)	Strengthened the Taft-Hartley Act and made unions more democratic.
Humphrey-Hawkins Act (1978)	Set employment targets, but did not provide any implementation.

In the 1980s, the situation of organized labor was affected by President Reagan's policies toward the union movement. In his first term, the administration was antagonistic toward unions, an attitude perhaps best exemplified by the dismantling of PATCO in 1981. Reagan's appointees to the NLRB reversed earlier NLRB decisions that were favorable to organized labor. These reversals began in December 1983, when Reagan appointees gained a majority on the board. The effect of these reversals was to make it more difficult for labor to receive favorable rulings. For example, the board ruled that all grievance procedures must be exhausted before an appeal to the NLRB is allowed and that the

NLRB cannot force a company to bargain with a union unless the union proves it represents a majority of the workers.

The 1980s were a decade of decreased influence for labor unions. NLRB data show that unions won 60 percent of the certification elections they held in 1965. In 1989, they won less than 20 percent. This decline is the result of active policy on the part of many business firms to fight unionization. Also, firms have increasingly used sophisticated labor consultants who advise them on how to prevent union-forming activity. In 1990, the Bureau of Labor Statistics reported that union membership had declined by more than 3 million members between 1980 and 1990. This figure represented a drop in the unionized part of the labor force from 23 percent to 17.7 percent. This period also saw a decline in union strike activity. Strike activity put 454,000 workers on the picket line in 1990, compared to 432,000 workers in 1982.

The weakness of the labor movement was obvious in wage settlements in the 1980s. Because of increased pressure from imports and because of deregulation in some sectors, companies sought lower wage contracts with unions in attempts to be more competitive. What evolved was a system of two-tier labor contracts. In these contracts, which were very popular in the mid–1980s, the union agreed to accept lower wages for future employees as a way of maintaining the higher wages of existing members. These contracts created significant pay differences. A new pilot for TWA was paid $22,000, while a pilot with seniority on foreign routes was paid $110,000. The Giant Foods contract called for $6.96 per hour for "old hires" and $5.00 per hour for "new hires." The same type of contract at Briggs & Stratton produced a wage of $5.50 per hour for new workers and $8.00 per hour for old workers. The strategy started to backfire on union leaders in 1987. New union members eventually become old union members. They form powerful voting blocs. They pay the same union dues and resent being treated differently.

In 1989 the effect of years of Reagan appointees to the federal courts was evident in the Supreme Court's Beck decision. The Supreme Court ruled in favor of electrician Harry Beck's suit against the electricians' union. Beck's case centered around the contention that even if he could be forced to pay union dues in a union shop state, he should not be forced to pay the part of union dues that went to political activity. The Court held that under the collective bargaining agreement, union members could only be forced to pay that part of dues that went to collective bargaining. Further, the Courts ruled that the Labor Department and the NLRB had to force unions to notify their members of the law. President Bush did not move to enforce this Supreme Court decision until very late in his term when he was challenged to enforce it by Patrick Buchanan in a primary campaign in New Hampshire. There has been no attempt to enforce this law in the Clinton administration.[10]

PRESIDENT CLINTON AND ORGANIZED LABOR

The election of Bill Clinton as President in 1992 brought some hope to organized labor. The AFL-CIO traditionally supports Democrats and came out for Clinton early. Yet, labor's expectations were dashed early on by Clinton's inability to deal effectively with Congress, and suffered a major setback when the

---

10. Charles Kolb, *White House Daze: The Unmaking of Domestic Policy in the Bush Years* (New York: The Free Press, 1994). Chapter 2 contains an account of the Bush handling of the Beck decision. Kolb uses it as an example of how domestic policy changed from the Reagan to the Bush years.

President actively campaigned for the passage of the North American Free Trade Agreement, which labor bitterly opposed. In November 1993, labor was buoyed by the fact that, in a powerful show of presidential force, Clinton interceded in a strike between American Airlines and its flight attendants, persuading each to accept binding arbitration. This was the first presidential intersession in a labor dispute in more than two decades.

Much of Clinton's legislative agenda is supported by labor. The AFL-CIO has long been a proponent of a national health plan financed by a tax on employers.

The biggest hope for organized labor lies with Clinton's appointments to the Department of Labor and, perhaps most importantly, his appointees to the NLRB. President Clinton's appointment of Robert Reich as Secretary of Labor received rave reviews from organized labor. Reich says what labor wants to hear. Time will tell if the legislation needed to turn those words into action is forthcoming.[11] A key piece of legislation is the Cesar Chavez **Workplace Fairness Act (WFA)**. The WFA prohibits firms from permanently replacing striking workers. Reich has gone on the line for this act, claiming that, "Without a viable right to strike, employers have little incentive to engage in serious bargaining with their union, to hammer out mutually satisfactory solutions."[12]

Workplace Fairness Act (WFA). The WFA prohibits firms from permanently replacing striking workers.

The biggest change in presidential labor policy will be seen at the NLRB. President Clinton's choice to chair the NLRB was William B. Gould, IV, a Stanford University law professor and a former lawyer for the United Auto Workers. Gould has ambitious plans for the NLRB. In the Reagan years, employers were able to manipulate procedure to stall union formation elections for years. Gould plans to stop this with strict timetables for union elections. He has also proposed liberal use of court injunctions against labor violations to short-circuit lengthy appeals. In short, Gould has made it clear that he wants to revitalize unions. As he puts it, "The plight of many workers, coupled with the inability of unions to represent them at the bargaining table, erodes the fabric of democratic institutions and is profoundly worrisome to all who value a system of checks and balances in the workplace."[13] The AFL-CIO could not have asked for a better spokesman at the NLRB.

THE FUTURE OF UNIONS

Despite recent trends, many union leaders still think in terms of "old-style" unions. This attitude is revealed in an article by labor economist Audrey Freedman, reporting on an AFL-CIO gathering she attended. The chairperson broke the attendees into two groups by saying, "The real unions—steelworkers, boilermakers, etc.—go into the room next door. Pantywaist unions—communications workers, teachers—stay here."[14] However, the "pantywaist" unions have

---

11. Mike McNamee and Christina Del Valle, "Reich's Return to Those Thrilling Days of Labor's Yesteryear," *Business Week* (April 12, 1993): 45.
12. Louis Uchitelle, "Striker Replacement is Crucial Issue for Administration," *The New York Times* (June 19, 1993): B1.
13. Aaron Bernstein, "Labor's White Knight?" *Business Week* (August 16, 1993): 12–13.
14. Audrey Freedman, "What Has Happened to Unions?" *Bell Atlantic Quarterly* (Autumn 1985): 11; and Kevin G. Salwen, "What, Us Worry? Big Unions' Leaders Overlook Bad News, Opt for Status Quo," *The Wall Street Journal* (October 5, 1993): B1, B6. Salwen argues that what Freedman reported in 1985 apears to be alive and well in 1993—i.e., that union leaders are more interested in good jobs for union leaders than in labor issues.

POLICY FOCUS: UNPAID FAMILY LEAVE—WHO COULD OBJECT?

One of the first pieces of labor legislation to be signed by President Clinton was the Family and Medical Leave Act (FMLA). The FMLA had been passed in previous years, but the Democratic Congress did not have enough votes to overcome two vetoes by President Bush. During the election campaign, candidate Clinton indicated he would sign the act, so after the election it sailed through Congress and President Clinton signed it into law. It went into effect on August 5, 1993.

The FMLA is simple on its surface. It provides up to twelve weeks of unpaid leave for a child's birth, adoption, or foster care arrival. In addition, leaves may be taken to care for a spouse, parent, or child with a severe health problem. The federal law applies to all employees who have worked at least twenty-five hours per week in the last twelve months for the same company. It applies to all companies that have fifty or more employees. The firm must provide health benefits while the employee is on leave and must give the returning employee their prior or equivalent job back. Sounds simple enough, but let's look at some potential problems by reviewing the experience of similar state laws.

In 1988, Joe Clague asked General Electric Co. in Portland for ten weeks of unpaid leave to participate in the birth of his third child. He had asked at the time of the birth of his second child, but, as he reports, he was just "laughed at" by his boss. This time, Oregon had a law similar to FMLA on the books and he was entitled to the leave. But as Joe saw it, he should be able to get paid during part of the ten-week "unpaid leave." First, he had two weeks' vacation time coming. General Electric had no problem with this. Second, he had three "floating holidays" due. No problem. Third, he had seven-and-a-half weeks' sick leave accrued and he wanted that credited to his family leave. Putting all three together, Joe reasoned he was due a ten-week paid family leave. General Electric nixed the sick leave. They reasoned that Joe wasn't sick and substituting paid leave for unpaid leave changed the intent of the law. This case is yet to be decided by the Oregon courts.

Let's move on to Wisconsin. Wisconsin, like Oregon, had a state FMLA-type act that predated the federal law. In December 1988, Elizabeth Marquardt returned to work at the Kelly Co. after a family leave for maternity purposes. During her absence, Kelly Co. had gone through a reorganization and had eliminated her job. Her new job was 25 percent clerical and she only supervised one employee, rather than four. The new job was in the same location, had the same pay, and offered the same benefits as the old job. Elizabeth quit the next day and sued. The Wisconsin Appeals Court ruled that the new job was not equivalent to the old job and ordered a hearing to determine back pay. It is difficult to guess how the court would define back pay, as the pay in the two jobs was identical and she only held the new job one day. Kelly Co. settled with Marquardt out of court for an undisclosed amount.

So it's not so easy. We need to determine what constitutes an equivalent job. At some point the courts (or Congress) will need to define what a serious health condition is. Can you take leave if your mother has the flu? The courts will also need to determine if paid leave can be substituted for unpaid leave. If that is the case, the FMLA, which was supported by President Clinton as not costing a firm very much, could cost some employees a great deal.

One final thought: If you owned a firm that had forty-nine employees, would the FMLA be too costly to keep you from hiring an additional employee? If enough firms think this way, the FMLA could be more costly than anyone has figured! There could be many firms with exactly forty-nine employees.

Source: Michele Galen, "Sure Unpaid Leave Sounds Simple, But. . . ." *Business Week* (August 9, 1993): 32–33.

---

been growing, and the "real" unions have shrunk. This trend is exemplified by the Steelworkers of America. In 1981 they had over a million members; a decade later their membership stood at 570,000. In some unions the decline is even more rapid. The International Association of Machinists and Aerospace workers lost 221,000 members (23 percent of its membership) between 1991 and 1993. Many labor leaders are unaware of or unwilling to accept the fact that any growth in union membership will have to come in the white-collar and service trades. The most rapidly growing union has been the Service Employees International, which increased its membership 67 percent between 1981 and 1992.

The structure of the U.S. economy has been changing in such a way that there are fewer jobs in the industries that have traditionally been unionized. Union leaders were slow to grasp the implications of the changing structure and internationalization of the economy. At the beginning of the 1980s, many labor leaders argued that recruits from the expanding service sector of the economy would offset losses in the manufacturing industries. This growth has failed to happen, partly because firms in the service sector are usually smaller than firms in manufacturing and therefore harder to organize. Service workers accounted for 70 percent of the U.S. work force in 1993, but only 10 percent of them were unionized. In 1993, only 26 percent of manufacturing workers were unionized, compared to 38.7 percent of transportation, communication, and public utility workers and 35.7 percent of government employees. In the private sector, only 15.3 percent of the work force was unionized. These trends do not indicate an optimistic future for the union movement in the United States.

THE BROAD PICTURE

As the union movement developed in the United States, several motives for unionization were evident. These different motives were reflected in union goals. Some unions were welfare unions (the Knights of Labor, for example), which had lofty ideals of social welfare and sought these goals by advocating an end to the wage system and the establishment of worker cooperatives. Other unions were revolutionary unions (the International Workers of the World), which sought changes in the social order. Still others were business unions (the American Federation of Labor), which ignored social and political goals and sought only to better the economic status of their members. History indicates that only this third type has been successful and able to survive in the U.S. economic system.

The development of unions in the United States can be divided into several periods. The early period, from the late eighteenth century until 1930, might be called the repression phase because of the hostility of the government and the courts. This was a difficult time for union organization and one in which the successes of unions were few and far between. The period from 1930 to 1947 might be termed the encouragement phase. Government support and key labor legislation greatly increased the power and prestige of unions. Unions reached their peak of influence during this period. The period from the passage of the Taft-Hartley Act in 1947 to 1980 could be labeled the intervention phase. Government intervened in labor disputes, took away some of labor's earlier gains, and attempted to put big business and big labor on a more equal footing. The period since 1980 should perhaps be labeled the decline phase. The basic underpinnings of the labor movement are in a state of flux, the membership mix is changing, and unions are being challenged by government and business firms at all levels. In a sense, the labor movement is now at a turning point. Labor supported President Clinton early and expects to have a friend in the

White House. The next few years will determine if the political decline that organized labor has experienced in the last twelve years can be reversed

ECONOMIC FORCES AND THE FUTURE OF UNIONS

After more than a century of organized labor, the future of unions depends on the economic forces that work to make unions stronger, as well as those that weaken unions.

FORCES THAT STRENGTHEN UNIONS

MONOPOLY POWER. Market power in the product market means that the firm has some degree of control over the price of its product. As a result, the firm has less incentive to fight attempts at unionization. Therefore, unions should be more successful in monopolistic or oligopolistic industries.

ELASTICITY OF INPUT DEMAND. The preceding chapter discussed the determinants of the elasticity of input demand. The elasticity of demand for labor directly affects the strength of unions. The more inelastic the product demand, the more inelastic the demand for labor will be and the stronger the union can be.

The share of total cost that is labor cost is the second determinant of the elasticity of the demand for labor. The smaller the share of labor cost, the more inelastic the demand for labor will be and, as a result, the stronger the union will be.

The substitutability of inputs also affects elasticity of input demand. The fewer opportunities the firm has to substitute other productive resources for labor, the more inelastic the demand for labor will be and as a result, the stronger the union will be.

FORCES THAT WEAKEN UNIONS

Any input that increases the competitiveness in the economy (decreases monopoly power) or increases the elasticity of demand for labor will work to weaken union power. Such factors are simply the opposites of the factors that strengthen unions. However, there are a few additional forces that have weakened unions in recent years and deserve special mention.

CHANGING STRUCTURE OF U.S. INDUSTRY. The changing structure of U.S. industry has weakened the labor movement. More than 70 percent of the work force is now employed in service sector jobs. Fewer than 10 percent of these workers are unionized. As the economy becomes more service-oriented and less industrial, organized labor will suffer erosion of its membership.

RIGHT-TO-WORK LAWS. Twenty states, mostly southern and southwestern, have right-to-work laws. Right-to-work laws, coupled with favorable tax laws, abundant labor supply, and nice weather, attracted industry from the "Rust Belt" to the

GLOBAL OUTLOOK: THE DECLINE OF THE GERMAN UNION MOVEMENT?

Trade unions in Germany are the envy of labor leaders around the world. Almost half of all industrial workers and over 30 percent of all workers are unionized in Germany. Wage rates in manufacturing are the highest in the world and working hours are the shortest. Employers have for years worked cooperatively with the unions' leaders as the work force had high skills and perhaps the highest productivity in the world. But even in Germany, union power is waning.

The forces at work are in some ways similar to those in the United States, with one major exception. The forces that are similar to those in the United States are familiar. Germany, like many other industrialized countries, is moving toward a service economy. Service sector unions are weaker than trade unions and they are much harder to organize. Manufacturing is becoming leaner and more automated. Workers in a modern factory have more in common with technicians than with old-style blue-collar workers. They work in teams and have control over their own work methods. In some cases it is difficult to distinguish production workers from supervisory personnel. These workers are less likely to join unions and support old-style trade union leaders. In addition, the German economy faces the same worldwide competitive pressures that the United States faces. Competition through international trade works to weaken union strength.

The biggest challenge and the unique challenge to the German labor union movement comes from the integration of the two Germanys. The reunification immediately brought 4 million new union members from the former East Germany into German unions. These workers were not as productive as their counterparts in West Germany. They worked in outmoded factories, producing far less. Years of living under socialism with its distorted incentives had created a German worker that was not the match of the West German worker. Yet, these new union members felt that the wage rates and labor practices of West Germany should be brought to the primitive factories of East Germany (immediately). The wage and benefits packages for East German workers were about half that of their West German counterparts in 1994. The response of the unions has been to merge, on the belief that bigger unions are better than smaller unions. In 1994, the coal workers and the chemical workers merged.

The trend that is the most unsettling to German union leaders is that "rogue" contracts have been negotiated by some firms. These rogue contracts, which set wages below the level in the union contracts, are against German law, but have become a common practice. The fact of worker acceptance of such contracts suggests that the power of German labor unions is declining.

"Sun Belt" during the 1970s and 1980s. This movement presents a challenge to unions and undermines their strength. The products that these largely nonunionized workers produce compete with union-made products and weaken unionized firms. The unions have responded by attempting to unionize workers in right-to-work states, but firms there have successfully resisted these attempts. A study of organizing activity in right-to-work states concluded that union organizing is reduced by 50 percent in the first five years after passage of right-to-work legislation and that union membership is reduced by 5 to 10 percent.[15]

DEREGULATION. The increased deregulation of certain industries undermines the strength of unions in those industries. This trend is most obvious in the transportation industry, which underwent widespread deregulation in the early 1980s. Deregulation makes a previously regulated monopoly subject to compe-

---

15. David Ellwood and Glenn Fine, "The Impact of Right-to-Work Laws on Union Organizing," *Journal of Political Economy* (April 1987): 250–273.

tition, and firms may find it hard to compete if labor has previously bargained for higher-than-competitive wage rates. For example, before deregulation of the airline industry, salaries over $100,000 were common for airline captains. Post-deregulation airlines were offering much lower salaries. Continental Airlines, for example, declared bankruptcy, reorganized, tore up pilots' contracts, and offered starting salaries of $43,000. In addition, airlines increased work weeks for pilots to forty-hour, five-day weeks, and required them to do administrative work when not flying. American West Airlines, one of the new carriers that entered the industry in the competitive environment, offered pilots $32,500 and received 4,000 applicants for twenty-nine positions.

The lesson is an important one. Regulation protects not only businesses in regulated industries, but also unions. Don't be surprised to see unions fighting deregulation!

IMPORTS. Imports, like deregulation, undermine monopoly power and union power in some industries. The steel and auto industries are examples. The United Auto Workers (UAW) was successful over the years in negotiating wage contracts significantly above competitive wage rates. These high wages made the U.S. auto industry less competitive on world markets. Foreign autos have been a threat to union strength because they represent competition. As auto imports increased and auto profits fell in the early 1980s, the UAW found wage negotiations increasingly difficult. The unions and the automakers joined ranks and went to Washington to plead, successfully, for import restraints.

Consider again...*The key labor legislation issue of the Clinton Presidency is the Workplace Fairness Act (WFA). Clinton's Secretary of Labor, Robert Reich, and other appointees are anxious to pass the legislation. There are, however, unrealistic expectations about the impact of the bill. American employers have always had the right to replace striking workers with permanent replacements. This policy was not an invention of President Reagan when he replaced the striking air traffic controllers. The right to replace striking workers was elaborated by the Supreme Court in 1938 in the NLRB vs. Mackay Radio case. The U.S. electorate is not in favor of WFA. A 1993 CNN/Time poll showed that 60 percent of American voters were opposed to WFA. WFA will define the labor record of the Clinton presidency. It is a policy debate worth tuning in to.*

SUMMARY

1. The primary goal of unions in the United States is to increase the wages of their members.
2. Exclusive unions are more likely to be successful at raising wages than inclusive unions.
3. Evidence indicates that unions have been successful in raising wages and that these increases have been partly at the expense of consumers and nonunion labor and partly at the expense of business profits. Unions may add to productivity if they reduce employee turnover.
4. Early unions in the United States had reformist political goals and were largely unsuccessful. When Samuel Gompers turned the American Federation of Labor toward strictly economic goals, he was successful. Beginning in 1932, with the election of Franklin

Roosevelt, unions received active encouragement from government. The Norris-La Guardia Act (1932) and the Wagner Act (1935) greatly enhanced the power of unions. The Taft-Hartley Act (1947) and the Landrum-Griffin Act (1959) diminished the power and put unions and management on a more equal footing. Reagan appointees to the NLRB reversed several rulings favorable to unions. Organized labor is hoping to reverse the Reagan changes with Clinton appointees. In recent years, union membership has declined as a percentage of the U.S. labor force, except among public employees.

5. Factors that enhance monopoly power and make the demand for labor more inelastic increase the strength of unions. Factors that make the economy more competitive weaken union strength. Right-to-work laws, imports, and deregulation all fit in this category.

NEW TERMS

featherbedding
exclusive union
craft union
inclusive union
industrial unions
bilateral monopolies
National Labor Union
Knights of Labor
American Federation of Labor (AFL)
business union
Industrial Workers of the World (IWW)
yellow-dog contracts
injunctions
Norris-La Guardia Act
Wagner Act
National Labor Relations Board (NLRB)
Congress of Industrial Organizations (CIO)
Taft-Hartley Act
closed shops
union shops
right-to-work laws
secondary boycotts
mediation
arbitration
United Mine Workers (UMW)
wildcat strikes
AFL-CIO
Landrum-Griffin Act
American Federation of State, County, and Municipal Employees (AFSCME)
Humphrey-Hawkins Act
Workplace Fairness Act (WFA)

QUESTIONS: REVIEW, APPLICATIONS, AND POLICY

REVIEW

1. Do unions raise wages? If so, at whose expense?
2. Is there a difference in the way inclusive unions and exclusive unions organize an industry? Which is more difficult?
3. Explain how closed shops and union shops differ. What are right-to-work laws?
4. How do unions affect the distribution of labor income?
5. Why has union strength (measured as the percentage of the work force that is unionized) declined in the past twenty-five years?
6. What do labor unions maximize?

APPLICATIONS

7. Has union strength in the north had any impact on business activity in the south?
8. Is the American Medical Association (AMA) a union?
9. Unions are often viewed as existing simply to bargain for higher wages for their members. What other things do unions do?
10. Suppose the late Cesar Chavez had been successful in organizing the grape pickers in California. What would have been the likely effect on the price of California wine? What would have been the likely effect on the number of grape pickers employed? Would the fact that the border with Mexico is relatively easy to cross and that the supply of undocumented workers is relatively elastic have any impact on Chavez's organizing costs?

POLICY

11. Public employee unions have increased in strength, yet many states and the federal government forbid these unions from going on strike. Can you think of any reasons why this should be so? Is a police officer in Los Angeles any different from a bank guard there?
12. In the fall of 1987, the Players Association of the National Football League went on strike. The strike lasted four weeks and was unsuccessful from the players' point of view. Why?
13. Public employees who are union members should have (should not have) the right to strike. Which of these positions do you support? Defend it.
14. Why might labor union leaders and business leaders be in Washington lobbying for the same legislation? Can you think of any areas on which such legislation might focus?

SUGGESTIONS FOR FURTHER READING

Bluestone, Barry and Irving Bluestone. *Negotiating the Future: A Labor Perspective on American Business.* New York: Basic Books, 1993. This book calls for a new covenant between labor and management. It represents the thinking of many in the Clinton administration. Barry Bluestone was a member of Clinton's transition team and his father, Irving, is a former United Auto Workers official. The cover of the book has a glowing testimonial from President Clinton's Secretary of Labor, Robert Reich.

Case, John. "Perfect Union." *AUDACITY* (Fall 1993):55–62. A historical account of U.S. labor cooperatives of the 1920s that shows that many of the "innovations" of Japanese labor-management relations were tried in the early days of the United States.

Freeman, Richard B., and James Medoff. *What Do Unions Do?* New York: Basic Books, 1984. A study that claims unions are good for America because they increase productivity.

Gould, William B., IV. *Agenda for Reform: The Future of Employment Relationships and the Law.* Boston: MIT Press, 1993. A plan for revitalizing labor relations, written by a Stanford law professor named by President Clinton to chair the NLRB.

Hirsch, Barry T., and John T. Addison. *The Economic Analysis of Unions: New Approaches and Evidence.* Boston: Allen and Unwin, 1986. An evaluation of the literature on the economics of labor unions, with over thirty pages of bibliography.

Hughes, Jonathan. *American Economic History.* Glenview IL: Scott, Foresman, 1990. A well-written economic history of the United States with a good chapter (21) on the early years of the labor movement.

Neff, James. *Mobbed Up: Jackie Presser's High-Wire Life in the Teamsters, the Mafia, and the FBI.* New York: Atlantic Monthly Press, 1990. An interesting account of Presser's activities as president of the Teamsters Union.

Wendland, Michael F. "The Calumet Tragedy." *American Heritage* (April/May 1986): 38–48. A vivid account of union busting in northern Michigan in 1913, which resulted in deaths and ultimately the making of a ghost town.

CHAPTER 29
RENT, INTEREST, AND PROFIT

Consider this... *In recent years Japanese investors have purchased a great deal of property and many firms in the United States, making some Americans nervous and angry. When Columbia Pictures was purchased by Sony for $3.4 billion, Newsweek lamented that "a piece of America's soul" had been sold. When Mitsubishi purchased Rockefeller Center, The New York Times claimed that "a vital piece of American landscape" was sold.*

At present, Japanese direct investment in the United States represents less than 2 percent of all U.S. corporate assets. Although investment has grown significantly in the last decade, it is still lower than that of many other countries. British direct investment in the United States is five times the present level of Japanese direct investment. Japanese direct investment surpassed Dutch direct investment in the United States for the first time in 1989. When was the last time you heard someone complain about the Dutch? Furthermore, U.S. citizens still own more assets abroad than foreigners own in the United States.

So why all the fuss about the foreign investment in the United States, and by the Japanese in particular? After studying the material in this chapter you will be able to draw your own conclusions. In an earlier chapter, labor markets were used to illustrate the marginal productivity theory of input pricing. As you know, there are other productive resources that generate income for their owners. Most of the theory that describes labor markets holds for these other inputs. Rather than repeating the discussion of the marginal productivity model, this chapter discusses the important differences between the other input markets and labor markets.

LEARNING OBJECTIVES
1. Describe the productive resource land and explain economic rent.
2. Explain the relationship between interest and capitalized value, crowding out, and roundabout production.
3. Itemize the sources of profit and the role that profit plays in a market economy.
4. Discuss and analyze the influences that help determine the functional distribution of income.

LAND AND RENT

The property income that has generated the most political interest in the United States is rent. To begin, we must define the concepts of land and rent. To the British economists of the eighteenth and nineteenth centuries, land was

Demand-determined price
A price that is determined solely by changes in demand because supply is perfectly inelastic.

the input to the productive process that was fixed by nature. Such assets as arable acreage, water, oil, and coal all qualified as land. Recall that if something is fixed in supply, its supply curve is perfectly inelastic. If the supply of land is perfectly inelastic, as in Figure 1, its price is determined solely by changes in demand. Thus it is a **demand-determined price**. In Figure 1, if the demand curve is D_0, the price is zero. As the demand curve shifts to D_1, D_2, and D_3, the price rises to P_1, P_2, and P_3, respectively. These prices are not actually rent, but they are related to rent. *Rent* is the payment for the productive services of land, not the price of the land itself. The price of the land would be the present value of the expected future flow of rent payments for future years' productive services.

THE CAPITALIZATION OF RENT

Rent is an income flow to the owner of land in payment for its current use. Often, however, economists speak of the price of land as the lump sum at which the buyer and seller exchange title to the resource. There is a simple relationship between the value of a piece of land, or any resource, expressed as a lump sum or a flow. The market price of a piece of land is the capitalized value of the rent. **Capitalized value** is the present value of a stream of future rent payments. (You can review the concept of present value by returning to the earlier chapter on costs and profits.)

Capitalized value
The present value of a stream of future rent payments.

The capitalized value is the amount of money that would earn the annual rent if invested at the current market rate of interest. Changes in the stream of rent payments will thus have an impact on the capitalized value. A good example is the value of farmland. For a farmer, the rent from farmland is the income that is produced from farming the land. When farm income falls, the capitalized value of the farmland falls. In some midwestern states, the selling price of farm-

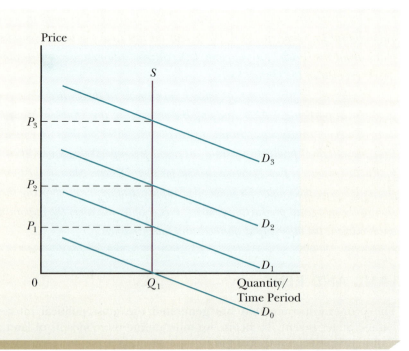

FIGURE 1
THE SUPPLY OF LAND
If the supply of land were perfectly inelastic, the price of land would be determined solely by the position of the demand curve.

land fell by over 50 percent in the mid–1980s. To compound the misery of some farmers (and their bankers), many had used their land, which was falling in value, as collateral for bank loans. They ended up owing banks more than the market value of their land.

ECONOMIC RENT

The idea of rent can be generalized to apply to any productive resource. Economic rent is technically a payment greater than the amount necessary to bring an input into productive use. In other words, in Figure 1, all the payments to land are rent because the amount Q_1 is fixed, and the payments don't bring any more land into existence. This supply curve is different from the labor supply curves described earlier. In the labor market, higher wage rates increase the quantity of labor supplied, and additional workers enter the market only at the higher wage rate. One essential difference between labor and land is that people have alternatives to work, such as leisure, which have utility.

Economic rent is a surplus paid to the owner of the productive resource. Because it is a surplus, this rent could be taken away with no effect on economic activity. For example, suppose actor Harrison Ford's skills are such that he has only two work alternatives: being a carpenter and earning $35,000 per year or being an actor and earning $2,500,000 per year. Assume that all other aspects of the two alternatives are equal. Under such circumstances, Ford is earning economic rent as an actor. If the two occupations are equally attractive to him, he could be paid $35,001 for being an actor, and he would continue to act. The reason his salary isn't $35,001 is that the competition among movie studios and producers for his services drives his salary up. By the same token, the government could tax away $2,464,999 of his earnings as an actor, and he would not change his behavior.

LOCATIONAL RENTS

In the chapter on perfect competition, we discussed differential rent theory. The topic arose because firms in perfect competition may appear to be earning economic profits that are actually economic rents to resources owned by the entrepreneur. Perhaps the most basic kind of such a rent is a *locational rent*. If the seller of a good or service can locate so that the cost of transportation for customers is lower at that location than at the competing locations, the seller can then charge a higher price. If you could find out the future location of the interchange on a new interstate highway, you could buy the land and make a huge profit after the highway is announced. Oceanfront property has a higher market price than does land next to a sewage plant. An acre of land is more expensive in New York City than in Fair Play, South Carolina. These price differences are due to differences in locational rents along interstate highways, on the ocean, and in urban areas.

CAPITAL AND INTEREST

The capital market is the market in which the productive resource capital is exchanged. The term *capital* is, however, used in a number of ways. The economic definition of capital is the tangible equipment (the machinery and buildings)

POLICY FOCUS: THE SINGLE TAXERS AND THE SINGLE TAX

In 1879, Henry George (1839–1897) wrote a book entitled *Progress and Poverty*, which advocated the policy of a single tax on land. The single tax would be a tax on land to capture its economic rent. George argued that the return to land was a surplus of unearned income and should be taxed away by the government. A social reformer, George felt that this land tax should be the only tax that government collects. His followers became known as the single taxers, and the George School of Social Science, which still promotes his policy ideas, can be found in New York City.

George's proposal rested on two basic ideas. First, the rent was unearned, and landowners were receiving the return simply because they held good land. If you think about this, it has political appeal. Why should someone get rich just because his or her grandfather happened to stake a claim on a piece of land that was located in a future population center? Second, George felt that taking this rent from landowners would not affect economic activity because the supply was perfectly inelastic. In other words, the tax wouldn't cause less land to be supplied.

George's single tax movement died for political reasons (landowners are a strong political force) as well as some serious theoretical flaws. The first weakness is the idea that the quantity of land is fixed. Remember, when economists draw a demand or supply curve, they hold quality constant. It is possible to make improvements in the quality of land, thus increasing the quantity of land of a given quality. Anyone who has seen agriculture in the Arizona or California deserts can attest to this fact. Increasing payments for land cause more land to be irrigated, increasing the quantity of arable land supplied. Similarly, swamps can be drained, and land can be reclaimed from the sea with dikes, as in the Netherlands. If the return to land were taxed away, this incentive to improve land would be gone.

The second problem with George's idea is that rents do serve a very important function, even if they have no influence on the quantity of land in existence. The rent payment made by the user of the land (the firm) ensures that the land is put to its highest-valued economic use. For example, suppose there is a choice acre of land now vacant near your school. What should this land be used for—a McDonald's, a day care center, a church, or a dump? In a market system, the use will be determined on the basis of who is willing to pay the most. In other words, the market decides between competing uses for the land. If payments to landowners were not received because they were taxed away, some kind of planning system would be needed to determine the allocation of land among competing uses.

From this discussion, you can see the policy role that zoning commissions or boards play in a mixed system of government. By planning the permitted uses of land they are taxing the owner's right to any rents from that land. Say you bought a piece of land on the beach and planned to sell ¼-acre beachfront lots for $1 million each. Now suppose your state's Department of Resources (these agencies have different names in many states) decides that in order to forestall beach erosion there must be a 300-yard setback (distance from the water's edge) for each lot. This policy means that you now have fewer lots to sell and the state has "taken" wealth from you. This has happened in recent years in states like South Carolina, and some lawsuits against the state's taking have been brought. In the most recent case, the U.S. Supreme Court ruled for the landowner and the state was forced to make compensation for the taken value.

---

that is used to produce goods and services for consumption. In popular usage, capital consists of the funds (money) borrowed and loaned for the purchase of capital. Markets for such loanable funds are close to the extreme of perfect competition. There are many lenders (sellers), many borrowers (buyers), and a well-publicized interest rate (market price).

ROUNDABOUT PRODUCTION

People produce goods so that they can consume. In a sense, therefore, the object of all production is consumption. It is clear, however, that even the most primitive societies make tools to use for production so that they can ultimately increase their output and consume more. These tools are capital. The production of physical capital to enhance production instead of final goods for consumption is sometimes referred to as **roundabout production**. That is, roundabout production is the creation of capital goods (such as tools) that enhance productive capacity and ultimately allow increased output. The capital goods that are produced are purchased or rented by firms as productive resources. The firm borrows the money it needs to acquire this capital in the market for loanable funds (the capital market).

Roundabout production The creation of physical capital (such as tools) that enhances productive capacity and ultimately allows increased output of consumer goods and services.

THE DEMAND FOR CAPITAL

Firms demand capital because it is productive. We can draw a marginal revenue product (MRP) curve for capital just as we did for labor. Such a curve is shown in Figure 2. Just as the demand for labor was a demand for units of input (hours worked), the demand in the market for capital is for physical units. In this example, it is a demand for computers. It is important to realize that the demand for capital is not a demand for money or loanable funds but rather a demand for physical capital.

We can aggregate a firm's demand for all the different types of physical capital it uses by converting this demand into a demand for loanable funds to purchase (or rent) that physical capital. The price of borrowing money in order to invest is the interest rate. Just as the quantity demanded of computers will increase as the price of computers falls, the quantity of dollars demanded to acquire physical capital will increase at lower rates of interest. The interest rate is relevant even if the firm uses its own funds instead of borrowing because the interest the firm could have earned is the opportunity cost of using those funds for capital investment. You can see this more clearly by examining Figure 3, which shows demand and supply of loanable funds for the firm and in the mar-

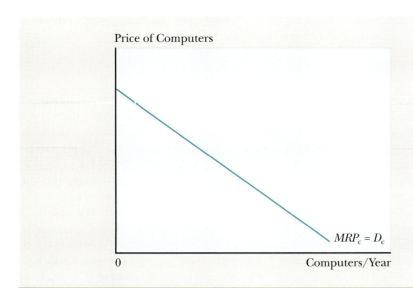

FIGURE 2
THE FIRM'S DEMAND FOR CAPITAL
The marginal revenue product of capital (computers in this case) is the firm's demand for capital.

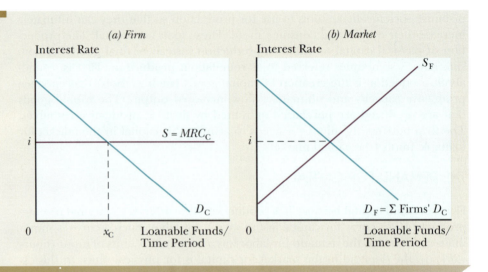

FIGURE 3

THE MARKET FOR LOANABLE FUNDS

The supply of capital to the firm is perfectly elastic at the interest rate set in the market for loanable funds. The firm invests in capital until the marginal revenue product of capital is equal to the market rate of interest.

ket for loanable funds. The supply of loanable funds comes from business and household saving. Firms build up a supply of funds out of profits in order to invest them, and individuals save in order to consume more in the future. At higher interest rates, people will save more because present consumption given up will allow greater consumption in the future. As a result, there is an upward-sloping supply curve in the market for loanable funds.

In Figure 3, the market demand curve for capital is the summation of all the individual firms' demand curves for capital expressed in the form of the demand for loanable funds. The firms' demands are based on their marginal revenue product curves for physical capital. The market rate of interest, i, determines the supply of capital available to firms in the competitive capital market. The firm can borrow all it wants to at the market rate of interest, which means that its marginal resource cost curve (and its supply curve) is perfectly elastic. We can thus determine the amount of borrowing by the firm, which in this case is x_C.

INTEREST RATES, INFLATION, AND RISK

The preceding analysis mentioned only one rate of interest. You know that there are in fact many interest rates, so which one is used for analyzing the capital market? This question is important in both microeconomic and macroeconomic policy because the interest rate is both a price (a micro variable) and an important aggregate that affects output and employment. In order to answer this question, we have to distinguish between the real rate of interest and the nominal rate of interest. The rate that is observed, or the market rate, is the nominal rate. Of course, we don't observe just one interest rate. We observe a whole family of interest rates. The various rates depend on who the borrower is, how much risk the lender perceives, and how long the repayment period is. Short-term loans ordinarily carry lower rates than long-term loans. Risky borrowers pay more than safe, dependable borrowers. Because there is a variety of interest rates, economists generally use the rate on U.S. Treasury bills (T-bills) as an indicator of how the market is doing. The T-bill rate is the interest rate the government, the least risky borrower possible, pays on its short-term borrowing.

Interest rates generally rise and fall together, so it's reasonable to pick out one important rate and use it to represent the overall level of interest rates. The spreads between rates, however, will vary over the course of the business cycle. As private borrowers begin to look riskier relative to the government, lenders will be more reluctant to lend to them and more inclined to buy T-bills. The rate to private borrowers rises relative to the T-bill rate. The difference between the T-bill rate and the rate to private borrowers for the same length of time is called the risk premium. Risk premiums generally rise during recessions and fall during expansions.

The real rate of interest isn't observed. The real rate of interest is the nominal rate of interest minus the expected rate of inflation. When lenders set an interest rate, they consider inflation as well as risk. If prices are rising, the dollars they are being repaid will be worth less and less with each successive payment. Lenders want to get back not the number of dollars they lent plus some interest, but the purchasing power they lent plus some interest. On the other side of the market, borrowers are also making calculations of what a loan really costs them, considering that they can repay with dollars that are declining in value. Thus, an inflation premium is included in the nominal interest rate.

KEY IDEAS

WHAT CAUSES HIGH INTEREST RATES?

Interest rates are higher:
- when inflation is expected to increase,
- with riskier loans,
- for longer time periods,
- when the demand for loanable funds increases,
- when the supply of loanable funds decreases.

COMPETITION FOR CAPITAL

The market interest rate allocates loanable funds among competing firms and competing uses exactly like the wage rate allocates labor services. Expanding on this idea a little will allow you to see why some economists are so concerned about federal budget deficits. Business firms are not the only demanders of loanable funds. There are two other important groups on the demand side of the market for loanable funds. Consumers demand loanable funds to finance the part of their consumption that is obtained on credit. They borrow to buy homes, furniture, automobiles, and college educations. The other demander of loanable funds is the government. At all levels—federal, state, and local—governments borrow loanable funds. The market for loanable funds is, therefore, composed of three important segments. Demand from all of these is added to give D_F in Figure 4. The market for loanable funds has a supply of S_F and a demand of D_F. The demand curve is the summation of the household demand, the busi-

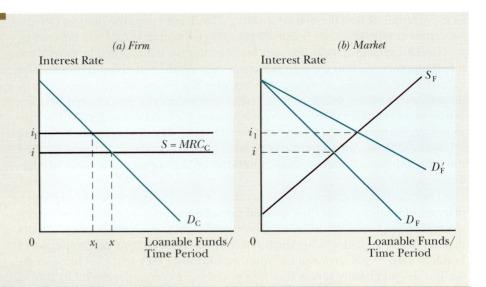

FIGURE 4

CROWDING OUT
The market demand for loanable funds is composed of household, business, and government demand. An increase in governmental borrowing will cause the market rate of interest to rise. Firms' response to this increased price of capital is to decrease the quantity demanded. Economists say that firms have been crowded out of the market for loanable funds.

ness demand, and the government demand for loanable funds. At the resulting interest rate, i, a representative firm adds x units of capital to its capital stock.

What happens, *ceteris paribus*, when the government increases its borrowing? Government demand for loanable funds increases, causing total demand to increase to D'_F. The interest rate rises to i_1. This higher interest rate means that the supply curve for the firm has shifted to the left. The firm will decrease its investment from x to x_1. The government has crowded some businesses (and households) out of the capital market. Interest rates allocate loanable funds among the three demanders. When the government bids interest rates up, households and businesses will get fewer of these funds.

Many policy makers and business leaders are concerned about crowding out. They believe that crowding out effect is a very real burden of the federal deficit. They argue that the large amounts of borrowing by the government bids up the interest rate and attracts investment funds away from business. When this happens, business investment does not grow as much as it would have and the productivity of the economy suffers. Recall that increases in the capital stock raise the overall demand for labor. Crowding out may also hold down the wages of workers by keeping the demand for labor from growing as fast as it otherwise would have. The Clinton administration's planned deficit reduction policy relies heavily on low interest rates (and hence lower interest payments) as the government tries to reduce borrowing.

ENTERPRISE AND PROFITS

Profits are a residual. They are what's left for the entrepreneur after land, labor, and capital have been paid. This is not to say that profits are not important. As you saw earlier, the quest for profit is the prime mover of a market economy. If profits are above normal levels, they will be a signal for firms to enter an industry. If below normal profit is earned, firms will leave the industry. In addition, potential profit is the incentive for innovative activity and risk taking. The entrepreneur takes chances and bets on the future because of the perceived chance to earn profit. Henry Ford installed the assembly line because he thought it would increase efficiency and lead to higher profit. The profit motive drove him to be innovative.

THE SOURCE OF PROFITS

As you have learned, monopoly power and other restrictions on markets are a source of profit. Entrepreneurs are therefore very likely to spend a great deal of time trying to monopolize their market. In fact, much of the curriculum in business schools is training in how to differentiate products, develop innovative products, and finance acquisitions. All of these actions are aimed at creating market power and generating profits. Any entrepreneur would choose to be a monopolist, rather than to be in competition. There is, of course, nothing wrong with the search for profit. It is Adam Smith's invisible hand at work. Most monopolies will be temporary, because new entry into the market will erode their success.

The entrepreneur engages in risky activities in search of profits. The entrepreneur assumes risk and is rewarded for his or her talent, wisdom, or luck with profit. There is a great deal of uncertainty in the economy. Many risks are insurable. You can buy auto insurance or fire insurance to protect yourself against risk because insurance companies are able to predict very accurately the average rate of occurrence of auto accidents or fires. The entrepreneur, however, is instead assuming uninsurable risks. These uninsurable risks are the uncertainties surrounding demand and supply. Will a product sell, and can it be sold for a price that is higher than the costs of production? If the answer is yes, the entrepreneur will make a profit for assuming the risk of this uncertain outcome. If the answer is yes *and* other firms can be kept from entering the market, the entrepreneur will have two sources of profit.

The entrepreneur is also involved in innovation. If the entrepreneur can produce a new or better product or find a way to produce an existing product faster or more efficiently, profit will result. Innovations can even include managerial techniques that give a firm a cost advantage. If such innovations can't be patented, and they usually can't, they will quickly be copied by competing firms. Competition forces entrepreneurs to make further innovations, if profits are to be maintained. This race after profits gives the market system its vitality.

ARE PROFITS TOO HIGH?

To much of the American public, profit is a four-letter word. It is often combined with an adjective to form phrases with a distinctly negative connotation, such as "windfall profit" or "obscene profit." This attitude toward profit arises from a very common misperception about how high profits really are for U.S. corporations.

Profit plays a very important role. First and foremost, profit is the signal of the market system. Second, they reward entrepreneurs for organizing production, monitoring shirking, and coordinating team production. Finally, profit generates the incentive to innovate and strive for greater efficiency.

GLOBAL OUTLOOK: THE PAY OF JAPANESE CEOS

In 1992, the pay of American CEOs (Chief Executive Officers) jumped some 56 percent, causing an uproar from the press and many in the American public. Part of the huge increase in CEO salaries occurred when American CEOs exercised stock options in 1992 because they expected (correctly) that President Clinton would raise income tax rates in 1993. The winner in this category was Thomas F. Frist, Jr., CEO of Hospital Corporation of America, who exercised $126 million of such stock options in 1993. Stock options increased his salary from $1 million to $127 million. Even without tax incentives, however, American CEOs are well paid. Concerns over such high compensation, especially when the firm's stock is losing value or the income statement shows losses, has caused stockholder protests at annual meetings. It has become an annual event in the business press to compare the earnings of CEOs to the performance of their company. In 1993, *Business Week* awarded the prize to the CEO whose company did the best, relative to his own compensation, to Raymond J. Noorda of Novell. The booby prize to the CEO whose company did the worst, relative to his own pay, went to Kenneth H. Olsen of Digital Equipment.

How does the pay of U.S. corporate leaders compare to other countries, like Japan. Comparisons are hard to make because Japanese companies are not required by law to divulge the pay of their executives. *Business Week* commissioned a consulting firm to estimate the pay of leading Japanese executives by going through their public tax records. This approach could, of course, overestimate their corporate compensation if Japanese executives had income from sources other than their corporate paycheck.

The study found that Japanese CEOs make only a fraction of what highly paid American CEOs make. Japanese CEOs' salaries averaged under $900,000, about 25 percent of the U.S. average. In relative terms, the average Japanese CEO makes 32 times more than the average Japanese factory worker, and 26 times what the average Japanese school teacher earns. The average CEO in the United States makes 157 times more than the average factory worker, and 113 times more than the average teacher.

American CEOs claim that their Japanese counterparts receive many perks and the perks help even the score. Perks may include golf club memberships, chauffeured limos, and even company-owned houses. The study indicates, however, that the value of these perks does not add up to much—and besides, U.S. CEOs get many of these same perks.

Perhaps the most revealing difference is that the pay of the Japanese CEO is often directly linked to the performance of his (there are no female CEOs in Japan) company. In 1992, executives at Hitachi Ltd. had their compensation cut 35 percent to match the 35 percent decline in profits. The managing director of Hitachi reported that, "When company results are down, managers have to take responsibility and accept such cuts."

There may be several explanations for this striking difference in executive compensation. First, executives in Japan do not change companies and thus there is virtually no market for chief executives. (Remember that the pay of baseball players was relatively low until the reserve clause was struck down by the courts.) Second, in Japan management is a team effort and the gains should be shared. In the United States, the CEO carries sole responsibility for much of the decision making that is shared in Japan.

Source: Robert Neff, "What Do Japanese CEOs Really Make?" *Business Week* (April 26, 1993): 60–61.

THE DISTRIBUTION OF INCOME

This chapter, in combination with the chapter on labor markets, provides a theory that explains why the distribution of income is what it is. Basically, the theory says that, given private property and competitive market conditions, market forces will produce a certain distribution of income. Labor will be paid according to its productivity, and the owners of capital and land will receive payments according to the productivity of the inputs they own. Any event that causes the marginal productivity of an input to increase will increase the payment that input receives.

The theory that productivity determines input income has received much criticism since it was first developed by John Bates Clark at the turn of the century. Clark was looking for a theoretical basis to explain how the distribution of income was determined. Most of the criticism of his marginal productivity theory has been on the grounds of **distributive justice**, a normative argument for a particular distribution of income. Critics argue that the market-determined income distribution is unfair because the old, the sick, the young, and the handicapped, among others, do not receive a fair share since they are not as productive as others. Another normative criticism of marginal productivity theory rests on the premise that social productivity rather than economic productivity should determine income. In a market system, a writer of pornographic novels often earns more than a writer of poetry. Some critics say this is undesirable.

You should recognize such criticisms for what they are—normative, ethical considerations and not positive criticisms of the theory. Think back to our early discussion of the role of theory. A theory is valuable if it provides a good explanation of some aspect of the real world. According to this test, marginal productivity theory stands up quite well.

Distributive justice
A normative argument for a particular distribution of income.

INCOME DISTRIBUTION AND THE MARKET

As you have seen, the distribution of income in a market economy is determined by the payments to productive resources, especially to labor. Wages are the largest component of income. However, ownership of other sources of income—rent from land, interest on capital, and profit for enterprise—often make the difference between an average income and a high one.

Assume that the market for the productive resources (land, labor, capital, and enterprise) is perfectly competitive. What then determines the distribution of income, and is this outcome just or equitable? The economic theory developed in this chapter offers a clear and positive answer to the first part of this question. Marginal productivity theory allows economists to analyze how input incomes change in response to changing market conditions. The second part of the question is normative. The distribution of income arising from the market may not be judged satisfactory. Decisions about changing the distribution of income involve value judgments about the "needs" of certain groups, as well as some positive statements about the effects of redistribution on incentives.

THE FUNCTIONAL DISTRIBUTION OF INCOME

The pattern of payments to the productive resources (rent, wages, interest, and profit) is called the **functional distribution of income**. This distribution (shown for the United States in Table 1) is determined by the supply of and demand for inputs of different kinds and qualities. Wages and salaries are the largest single component of income and have increased in relative importance compared to earlier periods.

Functional distribution of income
The pattern of payments to the productive resources (rent, wages, interest, and profits).

THE RETURN TO SPECIFIC INPUTS

The demand for any productive resource is derived from the demand for the goods and services that the input is used to produce. The value of any productive resource depends on the value of what it produces. Differences in input in-

TABLE 1 THE FUNCTIONAL DISTRIBUTION OF INCOME IN THE UNITED STATES

DECADE ENDING	SHARE OF TOTAL INCOME				
	WAGES AND SALARIES	PROPRIETORS' INCOME	CORPORATE PROFITS	INTEREST	RENT
1920	60.0%	17.5%	7.8%	6.2%	7.7%
1940	64.6	17.2	11.9	3.1	3.3
1960	69.9	11.9	11.2	4.0	3.0
1980	75.9	7.1	8.4	6.4	2.2
1990	73.6	8.9	6.8	10.4	0.3

Source: 1920 to 1980 data adapted from Irving Kravis, "Income Distributions: Functional Share," *International Encyclopedia of Social Sciences*, vol. 7; 1990 data from *Economic Indicators* (Washington, DC: U.S. Government Printing Office, February 1991).

comes result from differences in the inputs' productivity and in the demand for the final products.

Given inputs of equal productivity, the highest reward will go to those inputs employed in the industry whose products are most highly valued in the market. The return to an input will also be affected by the productivity of the other productive resources with which it is combined in a production process. Thus, it is possible that labor (or another input) of equal quality will receive different earnings when combined with different amounts and qualities of other productive resources.

Examples of productivity-related differences in input earnings are easy to find. A piece of land near a new interstate highway will be more valuable than a comparable piece of land elsewhere because of the highway. An engineer employed in a firm with a highly successful new product might receive a higher salary than an equally skilled engineer at another firm. A quarterback on a winning NFL team might receive a higher salary because he was at the right place at the right time with the right set of teammates.

MARGINAL PRODUCTIVITY AND EFFICIENCY

An important advantage of letting the market determine income distribution is that rewards will then be linked to efficiency of resource allocation. *Ceteris paribus*, inputs flow to those uses with the highest rewards, that is, those in which their productivity is most highly valued. The market system rewards and thus encourages higher productivity. In freely operating markets, the returns to inputs of equal productivity will tend to be equal (or nearly so). Over time, productive resources will tend to transfer to their highest-valued use.

The market-determined distribution of income may be unsatisfactory in other ways, however. Not only is this distribution very unequal, but it also involves a great deal of chance. Most individuals will avoid risk unless they can be compensated for assuming it. An individual's future income is subject to a high degree of uncertainty. Most of this uncertainty cannot be shifted or avoided through private effort. Risk aversion reduces the efficiency of allocation of productive inputs, especially labor. The situation creates a demand for government policies to reduce income uncertainty. Government may respond either by reducing the risk itself or by implementing various types of insurance plans. Policies to reduce the risk can take the form of education programs, various types of job security, or mandating of private pension and disability programs. Insurance plans include Social Security, unemployment insurance, deposit insurance on bank deposits, and welfare. All of these policies were instituted in the 1930s, a time of great economic misfortune, and are collectively known as the "social safety net."

In the next chapter we will consider the normative aspect of income redistribution. There is perhaps no other topic in economics or politics that generates more controversy. How and to what degree should government policies redistribute income?

Consider again... *Let's get back to the concern about foreign investment in the United States, and by the Japanese in particular. To the economist, this hostility seems strange. No vital piece of American landscape is going to be crated up and shipped to Tokyo. It would be hard to imagine that Columbia's new Japanese owners plan to stop making movies in the United States and turn all the firm's resources to making movies of sumo wrestlers. So why are so many Americans concerned? Does whether Mitsubishi or the Rockefeller family owns Rockefeller Center really matter? Some critics of Japanese ownership of real estate in Los Angeles seem to think that once the Japanese have the market cornered, they will raise rents and exploit the tenants. These critics don't seem to understand that the previous owners might go out and build some new buildings with the money they got from the Japanese. Another complaint against the Japanese is that they pay too much. This complaint must come from someone other than the sellers!*

The furor over Japanese direct investment in the United States may be indicative of political problems on the horizon. Foreign direct investment is not bad. It is not a sign of U.S. decline. Would you invest in a declining country? The United States is not losing its real estate or its soul. Americans are, however, losing their political patience with the Japanese. American exporters want to be treated fairly, and the evidence is that the Japanese do not "play fair" in terms of granting access to their markets. So Americans are really angry with Japanese trade policy. That anger should not cloud our attitude toward the purchase of U.S. assets.

SUMMARY

1. Land is the productive resource that is in fixed supply. Rent is the return to this fixed input. Economic rent is a payment above the amount necessary to bring an input into a given use.
2. Roundabout production is used to describe the production of physical capital to enhance productivity. Capital, like the other productive resources, is demanded by firms because it is productive. The payment to capital is interest. As interest rates rise, the quantity of capital that firms demand will decrease.

When an increase in the interest rate as a result of government borrowing reduces private borrowing, economists say that crowding out is taking place in the capital market.
3. Profits are the residual amount that entrepreneurs receive. They can exist because of monopoly power, risk taking, or innovation. In a market economy, profits serve as the signal for firms to either enter or leave a particular industry.
4. Income distribution is determined largely by forces in resource markets, described by marginal productivity theory. Wages and salaries are by far the largest component of income. Different types of labor, land, or capital earn different rewards depending on their productivities and the industries in which they are employed.

NEW TERMS

demand-determined price
capitalized value
roundabout production
distributive justice
functional distribution of income

QUESTIONS: REVIEW, APPLICATIONS, AND POLICY

REVIEW

1. What does it mean to say profits are a residual?
2. In what ways are economic rent and economic profit similar?
3. Why is the interest rate called the price of borrowing money?
4. What does roundabout production mean?
5. What is meant by the functional distribution of income?
6. What is meant by distributive justice?
7. What conditions determine wages? What causes some people with equal skills to receive different wages? Would more competitiveness in the economy reduce or increase these differences?
8. What purpose do profits serve? Why do some people think that they are too high?

APPLICATIONS

9. What is economic rent? Have you ever earned economic rent? How would taxation of this rent have caused you to behave differently?
10. Why do the activities of city and county zoning boards elicit such strong feelings?
11. The role of entrepreneurs in the production process is often misunderstood. What do entrepreneurs do that makes them so important in a market economy?
12. If your college raised your tuition by $1, would you drop out of school? If it raised tuition by $1,000, would you drop out? How about $10,000?

POLICY

13. Third World countries often complain that they are "ripped off" by multinational corporations because these corporations earn excessively high profits in host countries compared to their profits in their home countries. Can you think of any economic explanation for these higher profits?
14. When major airports are built in rural areas, commercial and residential buildings often spring up around them. The housing prices are often lower than for comparable houses in other areas. Why? If the residents band together and force planes to use noise abatement methods or follow different landing patterns, what is likely to happen? What does this likely happening represent to the homeowners?
15. If part of Harrison Ford's earnings as an actor is viewed as a rent, then this part of his pay could be taken away and he would still keep acting. Some people argue that it is necessary to pay such rents in order to ensure a future supply of actors (the same argument could hold for NFL running backs). Analyze this argument.

SUGGESTIONS FOR FURTHER READING

Aaker, David A., and Robert Jacobson. "The Role of Risk in Explaining Differences in Profitability." *Academy of Management Journal* (June 1987). A study that shows that risk, systematic and unsystematic, has significant impacts on the return on investment.

Lindholm, Richard W., and Arthur D. Lynn. *Land Value Taxation: The Progress and Poverty Centenary.* Madison WI: University of Wisconsin Press, 1982. This volume includes papers presented at a symposium commemorating the 100th anniversary of the publication of Henry George's book, *Progress and Poverty*. Many, but not all, of the papers are by present-day economists who support George's view.

Pindyck, Robert S., and Daniel L. Rubinfeld. *Microeconomics*, 2e. New York: Macmillan, 1992. An intermediate theory text that covers the material in this chapter in much greater detail.

"What Price Risk" *The Economist* (February 6, 1993): 81. A discussion of ways to measure risk.

CHAPTER 30
POVERTY, INEQUALITY, AND INCOME REDISTRIBUTION POLICIES

LEARNING OBJECTIVES
1. Describe the measurement of income distribution in the United States.
2. Explain how poverty is defined and the characteristics of those most likely to be poor.
3. Analyze the effects of discrimination on wage differences.
4. Summarize the arguments for and against the redistribution of income through government policy, and the advantages and disadvantages of equality of opportunity versus equality of results strategies, and redistribution in kind versus in cash.
5. Describe current government transfer programs and proposals for policy reform.

Consider this... *C.K. is a real person in her twenties, a college graduate who has been self-supporting but not earning much income. After working for about six years, part-time in college and full-time afterward, she was diagnosed with a chronic disease that makes it impossible to hold a regular, full-time job. She can work part-time and would like to do so. What should the social safety net do for C.K., and what does it actually do? What will it cost the taxpayers? What incentive does C.K. have to continue working part-time?*

J.T. is a hypothetical person, a twenty-year-old high school dropout and mother of two small children, ages two and four. She has never been married and has no real work experience. She has no means of support for herself and her children. What should the social safety net do for J.T., and what does it actually do? What will it cost the taxpayers? What incentive does J.T. have to acquire skills and work at least part-time?

This chapter is about the C.K.s and J.T.s of a market system. Some, like C.K., are unable to provide for themselves through no fault of their own. Others, like J.T., made foolish choices, in part because they knew that there was a social safety net to provide some minimal level of income. J.T. is the image most people have in mind when they attack the social welfare system, not C.K. But both represent a challenge to policy makers to design a system that helps those in need while preserving work incentives at a cost society is willing to pay.

The problem of defining a basic adequate standard of living and ensuring it to all without destroying work incentives is a challenge to all economic systems. It is a particular challenge to those systems that rely primarily on markets to allocate resources and encourage productive activities. This chapter examines the actual distribution of income, the measures of income distribution and poverty, the effects of labor market discrimination, and the role of government in redistributing income.

THE PERSONAL DISTRIBUTION OF INCOME

No single topic in economics generates more controversy than income distribution and policies for income redistribution. The market results in an unequal distribution of income. The government is a powerful tool for redistribution, although it does not always redistribute from the rich to the poor.

Economists are reluctant to propose schemes for the redistribution of income because value judgments are necessary to choose among alternative income distributions. However, many economists, philosophers, and politicians have developed normative standards for the distribution of income. Three widely used measures of how "fairly" income is distributed are need, equality, and productivity. The foundation of pure communism as stated by Karl Marx was "to each according to his needs, from each according to his abilities." The principle of pure equality would provide the same income for everyone. The productivity standard is based on the marginal productivity theory of resource earnings developed by John Bates Clark, which was discussed in an earlier chapter.

In the United States, productivity is the primary determinant of income. However, there is redistribution to the poorer members of society. Part of this redistribution is done privately through charitable giving and part is done publicly through governmental programs at all levels of government. The use of high marginal tax rates and the provision of certain basic services to all regardless of income are based on the equality notion. Social welfare programs are usually based on some indicators of need.

Income distribution in a market economy is determined primarily by ownership of the factors of production and by the prices those factors can command. The previous chapter described income distribution among the factors of production. Another way to describe income distribution is according to how income is divided, equally or unequally, among individuals or households. This measure is called the **personal distribution of income**.

LORENZ CURVES

A **Lorenz curve** is a graph showing the cumulative percentage of income received by a given percentage of households, whose incomes are arranged from lowest to highest. It is constructed by cumulating the percentage of households on the horizontal axis and the percentage of income on the vertical axis.

Figure 1 shows Lorenz curves for three societies. A perfectly egalitarian society would have the Lorenz curve labeled distribution *A*. If incomes were equally distributed, the lowest 10 percent of all households would receive 10 percent of total income, the highest 20 percent would receive 20 percent of total income, and so on.

When household incomes vary, the Lorenz curve diverges from the 45° line of perfect equality. Distribution *B* in Figure 1 shows a less egalitarian society. The greater the distance between the 45° line and the Lorenz curve, the greater the inequality in the income distribution. In Figure 1, distribution *C* represents more inequality than distribution *B*. Lorenz curves for different countries can be used to compare levels of income inequality. Sweden's Lorenz curve comes fairly close to the 45° line. Less developed countries tend to have curves that are farthest from the 45° degree line.

Personal distribution of income
A measure of how total income is divided among individuals or households.

Lorenz curve
A graph showing the cumulative percentages of income received by a given percentage of households.

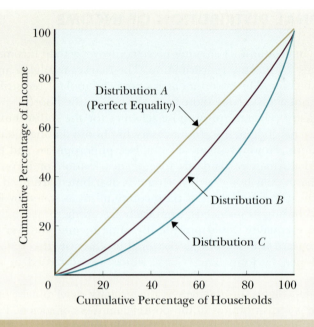

FIGURE 1

LORENZ CURVES

A Lorenz curve shows the percentage of income received by all percentages of households. A perfectly equal distribution would be represented by Lorenz curve A. Curves B and C represent more unequal distributions of income.

Lorenz curves can also be used to show how income distribution changes over time. The data in Table 1 show income distribution before taxes and transfer payments by quintiles, each representing 20 percent of the population. Data for 1980 and 1990 are graphed as Lorenz curves in Figure 2. Both Table 1 and Figure 2 indicate that the distribution of pretax income in the United States has become less equal since 1980, after moving slowly toward greater equality since 1967 (actually since 1929).

GINI COEFFICIENTS

A quick measure of inequality is the area between the diagonal and the Lorenz curve. The ratio of this area to the whole triangle below the diagonal is called the **Gini coefficient**. The Gini coefficient takes on values between zero and one. If all people have equal income shares, the Lorenz curve will lie along the diagonal, and the Gini coefficient will be zero. If one person has all the income and everyone else has nothing, the Lorenz curve will lie along the horizontal axis and the right vertical axis and the Gini coefficient will have a value of one. The closer the Gini coefficient is to one, the greater the degree of inequality.

The Gini coefficients for the United States tell the same story as Table 1. In 1967, the Gini coefficient was 0.399. From 1967 to 1980, it had a range of values from 0.388 to 0.403, rising in some years and falling in others. Since 1980, when the Gini coefficient was 0.406, the distribution of pretax income has become steadily more unequal, with a Gini coefficient in 1990 of 0.428.

Figure 3 shows the Lorenz curves for earnings in the United States, Canada, Australia, (West) Germany, and Sweden in the mid–1980s. As you can see, the United States had the largest degree of inequality of these five countries, while Sweden had the smallest, but differences are relatively small. Curves that show the effects of taxes and transfer programs would show a more pronounced dif-

Gini coefficient
A numerical measure of income inequality equal to the area between the diagonal and the Lorenz curve divided by the area of the triangle below the diagonal in the Lorenz curve diagram.

TABLE 1 DISTRIBUTION OF INCOME IN THE UNITED STATES

YEAR	LOWEST QUINTILE	SECOND QUINTILE	THIRD QUINTILE	FOURTH QUINTILE	FIFTH QUINTILE
1967	4.0	10.8	17.3	24.2	43.8
1972	4.1	10.5	17.3	24.5	43.5
1977	4.2	10.2	16.9	24.7	44.0
1980	4.2	10.2	16.8	24.8	44.1
1981	4.1	10.1	16.7	24.8	44.4
1982	4.0	10.0	16.5	24.5	45.0
1983	4.0	9.9	16.4	24.6	45.1
1984	4.0	9.9	16.3	24.6	45.2
1985	3.9	9.8	16.2	24.3	45.6
1986	3.8	9.7	16.2	24.3	46.1
1987	3.8	9.6	16.1	24.3	46.2
1988	3.8	9.6	16.0	24.3	46.3
1989	3.8	9.5	15.8	24.0	46.8
1990	3.9	9.6	15.9	24.0	46.6

Source: U.S. Department of Commerce, Bureau of the Census, *Studies in the Distribution of Income* (Washington DC: U.S. Government Printing Office, 1993).

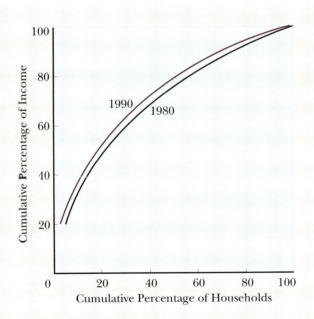

FIGURE 2
LORENZ CURVES FOR THE UNITED STATES, 1980 AND 1990
The distribution of pretax, pretransfer earnings became more unequal between 1980 and 1990.

Source: Source: U.S. Department of Commerce, Bureau of the Census, *Studies in the Distribution of Income*, 1993.

FIGURE 3

LORENZ CURVES FOR SELECTED INDUSTRIAL COUNTRIES

The distribution of pretax, pretransfer income in five industrial countries looks quite similar in the mid–1980s, with Sweden slightly more equal in distribution than other countries.

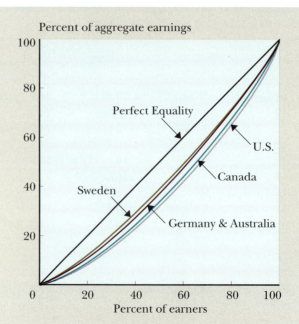

Source: U.S. Department of Commerce, Bureau of the Census, *Studies in the Distribution of Income* (Washington DC: U.S. Government Printing Office, 1992): 55.

ference, especially in Sweden, where the government collects high taxes and provides a broad array of social services to all citizens.

INTERPRETING THE DATA

Lorenz curves and Gini coefficients must be interpreted with caution for two reasons. First, Lorenz curves describe the *relative* distribution of income among households. A Lorenz curve might show the lowest 20 percent of households receiving only 5 percent of the income, but it doesn't say if this amount of income is high or low in an *absolute* sense. This 5 percent could be enough income to make everyone in the lowest 20 percent well fed, well housed, and well clothed. A Lorenz curve only shows the degree of inequality. By itself, it does not measure either wealth or poverty.

Second, Lorenz curves show how income is distributed among households at a given time. If the households in the lowest 10 percent change over time, the Lorenz curve will give an incorrect picture of relative poverty. The typical household's income changes in a predictable way over time. Income tends to be low when wage earners are young, increases as they reach middle age, and declines in their retirement years. This life-cycle pattern means that households will move around in the income distribution over time. Since the Lorenz curve shows an income distribution at a specific time, it may overstate income inequality over time.

One useful source of information on changes in income distribution over time is the Panel Study on Income Dynamics (PSID) prepared by the Institute for Social Research at the University of Michigan. The PSID has followed income and employment histories of 5,000 U.S. families since 1968. These data show considerable mobility among income levels. For example, of those who were at the top or the bottom of the income scale in 1971, only about half had been in the same relative position in 1968. Changes in family composition—births, deaths, divorces, marriages, and children leaving home—had the largest influence on relative economic well-being. This finding supports the life-cycle view of income distribution. The PSID data also suggest that the poor may not all be caught in a poverty trap. Many are temporarily rather than permanently poor.[1]

DISTRIBUTION OF INCOME AFTER TAXES AND TRANSFERS

What people are interested in, of course, is not pretax income but how much is available to spend or save, measured by income after taxes and transfer payments. (Transfer payments also include in-kind transfers such as subsidized housing and food stamps.) By this standard, the increase in inequality is even greater. In 1980, the Gini coefficient for income including taxes, cash transfers, and in-kind transfers was 0.347. In 1990, the Gini coefficient rose to 0.381—twice as much of an increase in inequality as was indicated by the pretax, pretransfer measure.

Why did the distribution of income, both before and after taxes and transfers, become more unequal in the United States in the 1980s? The change in pretax, pretransfer incomes goes back to the functional distribution of income. High interest rates throughout the decade benefited upper and upper-middle income households, not the poor or lower-middle income groups who have few interest-earning assets. Changes in the structure of jobs also affected wage earners. The decline in high-paying factory jobs and rise in service employment have reduced earnings at the bottom of the scale. Wages in service industries (such as fast food) are often at the bottom end of the wage scale. The growth in two-income households is also an important factor. Households with two or more adult earners increased their income dramatically, but the decline in real weekly wages meant that single-earner households fell behind.

Lower top-bracket tax rates increased the after-tax incomes of higher income groups. But higher Social Security taxes hit the working poor, further eroding the income position of those near the bottom of the ladder. Tax and transfer programs still helped to narrow the income gap between the top and the bottom, but they made less of a difference by the end of the 1980s than at the beginning.

POVERTY IN THE UNITED STATES

Income distribution is not just a relative concept. Data on starvation, malnutrition, homelessness, and disease show that poverty has an absolute meaning as well. Determining the level of income that marks the border between poverty and nonpoverty is difficult, because poverty is both absolute and relative. People who are relatively poor in one nation may be well off by the standards of another country or by the standards of the same nation at an earlier time.

---

1. Greg Duncan, et al., *Years of Poverty, Years of Plenty: The Changing Economic Fortunes of American Workers and Families* (Ann Arbor, MI: Institute for Social Research, 1984).

MEASURING POVERTY

The U.S. government first established an official definition of poverty in 1964. The definition was based on the cost of a minimally adequate diet. This figure was then multiplied by three, since the typical household spent one-third of family income on food. In 1964, the poverty income level for a family of four was $3,000 ($1,000 for food times three) or below. The poverty threshold has been adjusted each year for inflation. In 1993, the official poverty income level was $6,970 or below for a single individual and $14,350 or below for a family of four.

The poverty rate is a rather crude measure of poverty or changes in poverty because this number gives no indication of how poor people are. A person whose income is $1 below the threshold is counted as poor, and so is a person whose income is $3,000 below the threshold. If cash transfers bring the first person's income up by $2, the poverty rate falls. If transfer payments raise the second person's income by $2,000, the poverty rate is unchanged. However, even with these shortcomings, the poverty rate provides some indication of how much aggregate poverty exists and how it changes over time. Table 2 shows the poverty rate before and after taxes and transfer payments, which has remained relatively constant from 1980 to 1991 at 13 to 14 percent of the population. Transfers are particularly important at the bottom of the income ladder, reducing the poverty rate 3 to 5 percentage points each year.

The poverty rate shown in the third column of Table 2 has been criticized by some economists because it only counts cash transfer payments such as Social Security, unemployment compensation, and Aid to Families with Dependent Children. Since 1965, an increasing fraction of programs for the poor have taken the form of in-kind transfers. In 1989, the Bureau of the Census refigured the poverty rate by also counting as income the cash equivalent value of three major in-kind programs: food stamps, housing assistance, and Medicare. These adjustments produced a poverty rate of 10.5 percent in 1988 compared to the 13.1 percent official rate.[2] Transfer programs also increased economic well-being for other low-income families. In 1991, pretax earnings averaged $7,275 for the lowest quintile; after adjusting for taxes, transfers, employer-provided health insurance, return on homeowners' equity, and other resources, it rose to $9,416. For the highest quintile, pretax income averaged $88,101 before taxes, transfers, and other adjustments, and $78,825 after these adjustments were made.[3]

WHO ARE THE POOR?

In the United States, the poor come from all parts of the country and every age group. However, poverty is more common in certain geographic, demographic, and racial groups. Geographically, the poor tend to live in the rural south and in northern cities. Poverty is more common in rural areas than in cities. Table 3 points out other characteristics of people living below the poverty line in the United States. Almost 15 percent of the population fell below the poverty thresh-

---

2. Spencer Rich, "Defining Poverty: A Science or an Art," *The Washington Post National Weekly Edition* (November 12, 1989): 31. Rich summarizes how the poverty threshold was developed and some of the Congressional criticisms of it.
3. U.S. Department of Commerce, Bureau of the Census, *Measuring the Effects of Benefits and Taxes on Income and Poverty* (Washington DC: U.S. Government Printing Office, 1993).

TABLE 2 POVERTY RATES BEFORE AND AFTER TAXES AND TRANSFERS

YEAR	BEFORE TAXES AND TRANSFERS	AFTER TAXES AND TRANSFERS
1979	11.7%	8.2%
1980	13.0	8.7
1981	14.0	10.4
1982	15.0	9.9
1983	15.2	9.9
1984	14.4	9.9
1985	14.0	10.1
1986	13.6	9.7
1987	13.4	9.4
1988	13.0	9.7
1989	12.8	9.1
1990	13.5	9.8
1991	14.2	10.3

Source: U.S. Department of Commerce, Bureau of the Census, *Statistical Abstract of the United States: 1993* (Washington DC: U. S. Government Printing Office, 1993).

old in 1992. However, the poverty rate was above 25 percent for certain segments of the population. The poverty rate for nonwhites is higher than that for whites. Age is also an important factor; children represent a large fraction of those below the poverty level. In fact, poverty is now a less serious problem for the elderly than for female-headed households with small children.

Nonwhites are more likely to be poor than whites partly because of racial discrimination. In addition, nonwhites are also more likely to be poor because a higher percentage are under seventeen, have less education, or live in female-headed households. The nonwhite-white income difference has improved much more for females than for males. After some interim improvement, the black-white income ratio was about the same for males in 1988 as it was in the late 1950s.

Poverty in the United States is greatly influenced by labor force activity, education, and marriage. One encouraging sign is that the educational achievement of nonwhites has been increasing. This is especially true of black women; 1992 Census data show that about 14 percent of black women in the civilian labor force have bachelor or graduate degrees. This increase should eventually be reflected in higher income levels. Professor Thomas Sowell argues that monetary returns to education are much higher for minorities than for nonminorities.[4]

DISCRIMINATION AND THE DISTRIBUTION OF INCOME

How big a role does racial and sexual discrimination play in income distribution? Since the Civil Rights Act of 1964, discrimination in employment has been

4. Thomas Sowell, *Race and Economics* (New York: David McKay, 1975).

TABLE 3 CHARACTERISTICS OF THE POOR, MARCH 1992

CHARACTERISTIC	PERCENT BELOW POVERTY LEVEL
White	11.3%
Black	32.7
Hispanic	28.7
Asian	14.1
Household head 15–24 years old, all races	35.5
Household head 25–34 years old, all races	18.4
Household head 25–34 years old, black	40.9
Household head 25–34 years old, Hispanic	33.4
Household head 35–44 years old, all races	10.2
Household head 45–54 years old, all races	7.1
Household head 55–64 years old, all races	8.1
Household head 65+ years old, all races	6.5
Household head 65+ years old, black	23.7
No high school diploma, all races	24.2
High school graduate, all races	10.5
Some college (one year or more), all races	6.5
Employed (50–52 weeks), all races	4.0
Not employed, all races	24.5

Source: *Statistical Abstract of the United States: 1993.*

illegal. Many companies, in part to show their compliance with federal law, started affirmative action programs in the 1970s. Yet black-white and male-female wage (and income) differences remain high. These differences, however, do not mean that discrimination alone accounts for the income distribution pattern. Earning differences can be shown to depend at least partly on other influences.

THE DEMAND AND SUPPLY OF DISCRIMINATION

Labor market discrimination today rarely means setting wages or hiring on the basis of sex or race, which would violate federal laws. Discrimination usually takes more subtle forms, such as channeling workers by sex or race into occupations that are "more suitable" for females or nonwhites. As a result, certain work categories have a greater supply of workers and lower wage rates than they otherwise would. Traditionally, females have been directed into teaching and secretarial work. Many personal service occupations show a high proportion of minority workers. Table 4 shows concentrations of blacks and females in certain occupations. Females account for 45 percent of the labor force, and blacks account for 10 percent. Females are heavily concentrated in sales, clerical, and private household work. However, they have made progress in recent years in some higher-paying occupations, doubling their representation in medicine and showing impressive gains in law and management. Blacks have also broadened

POLICY FOCUS: THE NEGATIVE INCOME TAX AND THE EARNED INCOME CREDIT

The high cost of maintaining a bureaucracy to administer in-kind programs led economist Milton Friedman to propose replacing the current welfare system with a negative income tax. A negative income tax transfers income from the government to the poor based on a formula similar to the present personal income tax system. Friedman's proposal is popular among economists because of its simplicity and positive work incentive.

Under a negative income tax, everyone would be guaranteed some minimum income. The choice of a minimum is a normative decision: one approach could be to calculate a typical poverty-level budget at current prices as the standard, and adjust it for family size. The system would also require a negative tax rate, which is the rate at which transfer payments are reduced per additional dollar of earned income. The minimum guarantee and the negative tax rate then determine a third element, the break-even income, which is the level of income at which a household neither pays income taxes nor receives benefits.

Suppose that the negative income tax guarantees a family of four an income of $6,000, with a negative tax rate of 50 percent. When the household earns $12,000, it will lose its last dollar of benefits and live on earned income only. Since the household keeps part of its benefits when it earns a modest income, work incentives should be stronger than under the present welfare system.

The household's transfer payment $6,000 minus 50 percent of any income earned that is up to $12,000. The amount a household receives is determined by the formula

$$HT = IG - (t_n \times EI),$$

where HT is the household transfer payment, IG is the income guarantee, t_n is the negative tax rate, and EI is the earned income. For example, with a $6,000 guarantee and a 50 percent negative tax rate, a family with an income of $4,000 would receive a supplement of $2,000 for a total income of $6,000. After the household passes the break-even income level, it starts paying income taxes.

The relationship between the minimum income guarantee, the negative tax rate, and the break-even income creates some problems. In order to provide a guaranteed income high enough to ensure a minimum standard of living and a negative tax rate low enough to encourage work, the break-even income would be very high. It would reduce government income tax revenue because it would extend welfare benefits much higher up the income scale. The break-even income could be reduced by lowering the guaranteed income, but a low minimum income would penalize those who are unable to work—the aged and disabled, for example. Alternatively, it would be possible to combine a lower break-even income with an acceptable minimum guarantee by using a higher negative tax rate, but that higher tax on earnings would discourage work.

The negative income tax would be less costly to operate because funds would go directly to the poor rather than funneling them through a large welfare bureaucracy. The negative income tax is also attractive to recipients. It is objective and impersonal, allowing recipients to maintain a sense of dignity and entitlement. Instead of cutting off funds to those whose income is just above the guaranteed minimum, the negative income tax would provide aid to the nearly poor as well. Perhaps the most important advantage, however, is that the negative income tax would strengthen work incentives. The current welfare system reduces benefits by 100 percent of any earned income. A negative income tax would allow individuals to keep a portion of what they earn.

President Carter proposed a similar plan in 1978, the Program for Better Jobs and Income, but it was not enacted. It failed for three reasons: (1) the high cost (in lost tax revenue) of a program with an adequate income guarantee and a low enough negative tax rate, (2) the preference among potential voters for in-kind rather than cash transfer programs, and (3) the opposition of the "iron triangle" of congressional committees that oversee programs, beneficiaries, and government bureaucracies that administer existing programs.

Like most public policy debates, however, the negative income tax proposal did achieve some reform. The Earned Income Credit, which was added to the income tax in 1975, provided tax credits for low-income workers with at least one dependent. If the person owes no tax, the credit becomes a refund, much like the negative income tax. While the Earned Income Credit does not replace welfare, it does provide some poverty relief for the working poor. It also includes work incentives for those able to get off welfare. In 1993, the Earned Income Credit was expanded in size and extended to single-person, low-income households.

TABLE 4 EMPLOYED PERSONS IN SELECTED OCCUPATIONS BY SEX AND RACE

OCCUPATION	1983 FEMALE	1983 BLACK	1992 FEMALE	1992 BLACK
Child care workers	96.9%	7.9%	97.1%	10.2%
Kitchen workers	77.0	13.7	76.0	15.9
Textile operators	82.1	18.7	76.4	23.7
Retail sales clerks	69.7	6.7	65.5	9.1
Bank tellers	91.0	7.5	89.8	7.7
Computer operators	63.7	12.1	63.6	13.1
Computer programmers	32.5	4.4	33.0	6.8
Lawyers/judges	15.8	2.7	21.4	3.1
Economists	37.9	6.3	43.3	7.9
Physicians	15.8	3.2	20.4	3.3
Engineers	5.8	2.7	8.5	3.9

Source: *Statistical Abstract of the United States: 1993.*

their representation in higher-paying occupations but are still overrepresented in low-paying service and blue-collar occupations.

Figure 4 illustrates the effects of channeling on wage differences. If a majority of workers in some occupations are able to exclude other workers by sex or race, the supply curve of workers for exclusive occupations will be S_e' rather than S_e. Wage rates for workers in these jobs will be higher than otherwise (W_e rather than W_0). At the same time, the supply of workers in minority or female occupations shifts to the right (from S_m to S_m'). The result of channeling is a lower wage rate (W_m rather than W_0) in the minority or female occupations than otherwise. Such wage differences constitute discrimination only to the extent that they result from workers being excluded from one group of occupations and channeled into another. If there are real productivity differences between the two kinds of occupations in Figure 4 (reflected in different demand curves), market forces will produce different wage rates even with no racial or sexual discrimination. In practice, productivity differences and channeling effects may coexist in the same markets.

DOES LABOR MARKET DISCRIMINATION EXIST?

In the United States, discrimination in employment is illegal under the 1964 Civil Rights Act and the 1965 Equal Employment Opportunity Act, but there is some evidence that labor market discrimination still exists.[5] For example, a study by Michael Robinson and Phanindra Wunnava showed that female hourly earnings in full-time nonunion jobs would be 25 percent higher in the absence of "direct discrimination."[6]

---

5. Walter L. Updegrave, "Race and Money," *Money* (December 1989): 152–172.
6. Michael D. Robinson and Phanindra V. Wunnava, "Measuring Direct Discrimination in Labor Markets Using a Frontier Approach: Evidence from CPS Female Earnings Data," *Southern Economic Journal* (July 1989): 212–218.

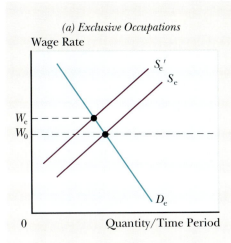
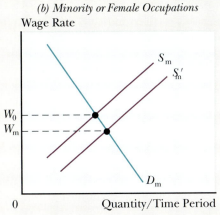

FIGURE 4

LABOR MARKET DISCRIMINATION

(a) If workers are excluded from certain occupations, the supply will shift from S_e to S_e'. The wage rate will rise to W_e in the exclusive occupations. The excluded workers will then be channeled into minority occupations. (b) The supply in the minority occupations will shift from S_m to S_m'. The wage rate will fall to W_m.

In order to measure discrimination, we must separate effects of productivity differences from other reasons for male-female or black-white earnings differences. Historically, females and minorities have invested less in human capital (education, training, and job experience) than white males and thus have lower average productivity. Studies suggest that about 75 percent of the earnings differences is due to differences in human capital, occupational choice, or other characteristics such as age, health, and geographic location. Do these studies mean that discrimination is not an important source of wage differences? No! Because discrimination affects the incentive to invest in human capital and channeling affects occupational choice, the gap in productivity that helps explain the gap in wages is itself related to discrimination. Thus, it is hard to tell exactly how much current wage differences reflect past and present discrimination and how much difference would persist even in a discrimination-free world.

OTHER EXPLANATIONS OF EARNINGS DIFFERENCES

Black-white earnings differences are fairly easy to explain as a mix of education, channeling, and past as well as present discrimination. The male-female gap is a little more complicated. In addition to gender discrimination, studies have identified career interruptions, role differentiation, relative number of hours worked, and geographic mobility as contributing factors.

CAREER INTERRUPTIONS. Many working females leave the labor force at least once during their working lives. Using data from Social Security records, Donald Cox found that lifetime earnings of females are lower because of these interruptions. Income growth is closely linked to job experience, which increases human capital. Interruptions disrupt the acquisition of experience. Cox also suggested that channeling is not entirely based on discrimination, at least for females. Some jobs more readily allow for career interruptions without loss of skills or continuity. Women may be attracted to such jobs because they fit better with childbearing and child care.[7]

---

7. Donald Cox, "Panel Estimates of the Effects of Career Interruptions on the Earnings of Women," *Economic Inquiry* (July 1984): 386–403.

ROLE DIFFERENTIATION. Economist Victor Fuchs argues that much of the pay inequality between males and females is the result of "role differentiation." Fuchs uses this term to indicate that society has different expectations for males and females. Fuchs contends that role differentiation begins in childhood. It influences decisions females make about education, job location, occupational choice, and time spent in the labor market. Role differentiation often encourages a female to choose a job location and job responsibilities that are compatible with her spouse's job choice or that lend themselves to career interruptions. Role differentiation is also reflected in hours worked and geographic mobility. Fuchs argues that lower salaries due to role differentiation are not really discrimination in a narrow sense. Instead, they result from choices made by females based on widely held social values. In the last twenty years more females have chosen to enter previously male-dominated occupations, and U.S. wage differences between the sexes have begun to fall.[8]

RELATIVE NUMBER OF HOURS WORKED. Females average fewer hours in paid employment than do males. Some comparisons of average earnings—such as the popular statement that females earn 59 percent as much as males—are not corrected for hours worked. And even that 59 percent ratio has gradually risen to 67 percent in recent years. After adjusting for differences in hours worked, the remaining sex-related difference in earnings is even less.

GEOGRAPHIC MOBILITY. When labor is immobile, firms enjoy greater monopsony power in local labor markets. Married females may refuse attractive job offers because of the geographic location of their spouse's job, and limit their job search to areas close to home.

One way to evaluate sex differences in earnings is to compare earnings of single males and single females. Some early studies showed that single females, who have the same incentives as males to invest in human capital, minimize career interruptions, work longer hours, and be geographically mobile, earn almost the same wages as males.[9]

DISCRIMINATION AND MARKET FORCES

Economic theory suggests that racial or sexual discrimination would not persist over time in a market system because it is costly to entrepreneurs. If employers discriminated, there would be large numbers of minority and female workers earning low salaries but having basically the same education and work skills as white male workers. A profit-motivated entrepreneur could hire these minority and female workers and produce goods and services more cheaply than other firms using the more expensive labor. As this activity spread, wages for the minority and female workers would be bid up closer and closer to the level of white male workers. Thus, the profit motive would work to undermine discrimination.

8. Victor Fuchs, "Recent Trends and Long-Run Prospects for Female Earnings," *American Economic Review Papers and Proceedings* (May 1984): 235–242.
9. Thomas Sowell, "Affirmative Action Reconsidered," *The Public Interest* (Winter 1976): 47–65; and James Gwartney and Richard Stroup, "Measurement of Employment Discrimination According to Sex," *Southern Economic Journal* (April 1973): 575–587.

Some economic historians argue that Jim Crow laws in the south in the late nineteenth and early twentieth centuries were a response to the threat that market forces would undermine racial discrimination. Jim Crow laws put the force of law behind segregation and discrimination. These laws were eventually overridden by federal legislation. In South Africa, apartheid was needed to maintain a racially segregated system that economic forces would otherwise have undermined.

If market forces and legal penalties work to undermine discrimination, why are there persistent white-black, female-male income differences? One reason is that different sectors of the economy and different occupations adjust to change with different speeds. It is clear that professional athletics has adjusted very quickly to changing laws and customs, while the medical profession has adjusted quite slowly. The presence of monopoly power and licensing as well as the length of time it takes to train for an occupation may influence the speed of adjustment.

Persistent discrimination also results from the interaction between discrimination and the determinants of worker productivity (education, training, experience, and occupational choice). Females or minorities, who expect to be offered lower salaries or to be excluded from desirable occupations, may invest less in human capital. As it became clear in the 1970s that jobs formerly closed to most females and minorities were now accessible, the numbers of females and minorities in those jobs began to rise. The information that provides the basis for such changes is disseminated and absorbed slowly.

Discrimination begets poverty, and poverty begets little investment in human capital. Although discrimination is not the sole source of poverty, it does contribute. Government can help combat discrimination both with antidiscrimination laws and with equal treatment for government employees regardless of race or sex. These policies by themselves, however, are not enough to eliminate poverty. The government may also be called on to make policy actions that change the income distribution determined by the market.

INCOME REDISTRIBUTION

Income redistribution in the United States, and many other countries, has been carried out by both the private sector and the public sector. Many public goods or goods with some public benefits are produced at least partly in the private sector. Some roads, schools, outdoor concerts, and other goods and services generate collective benefits but are privately produced. Income redistribution is another activity with public benefits produced at least in part by the private sector through charitable organizations.

Private redistribution alone is not likely to achieve the desired level of income transfers. Individuals in a large group recognize that their contribution is too small to significantly affect total redistribution. Each person has an incentive to leave the responsibility to contribute to others. People who give because of personal satisfaction gained from the act of charity do not experience this incentive to shirk their responsibility. However, for some people, the motive for giving is seeing less poverty in the world. For this group, giving by others diminishes their need to give. If everyone followed this strategy, there would be no private redistribution. Free riding explains why there is not enough private redistribution.

An important influence on the amount of private redistribution is the size of the group. In a relatively small, homogeneous group, there is likely to be relatively more private redistribution. Think about the Mormon church and Amish communities, for example, or small towns versus large cities. Greater charity in small groups is consistent with the view that the poverty is more visible when the group size is smaller.

The small-group influence is even present in public redistribution. A small country with a relatively homogeneous population, such as Sweden, practices more redistribution than a large "melting-pot" country, such as the United States. As Sweden has become host to more refugees in the 1990s, however, there has been a move away from the welfare state.

BENEFITS AND GOALS

Interdependent utility functions
Preference patterns in which the welfare of some individuals depends on the well-being of others.

Citizens may support income redistribution for many reasons. First, some people have **interdependent utility functions**, which means that their well-being is dependent on the well-being of others. These people support programs to redistribute income because such redistribution increases their utility. Second, some people might view poverty as a negative external effect, like air pollution—something that makes the environment less appealing. This group supports redistribution to improve their surroundings. They might, for example, support food stamp legislation to help keep hungry people from begging on the streets. Finally, redistribution can be viewed as an insurance policy. People might support redistribution as a safety net, realizing that they might become poor at some time.

EQUALITY OF OPPORTUNITY OR EQUALITY OF RESULTS?

Should the goal of redistribution be equality of opportunity or equality of results? A goal of equality of opportunity might mandate government investment in human capital through technical schools, student loans and grants, or training programs; or impose penalties on employers who discriminate.

Government or private programs that reduce unemployment and improve the match between workers and jobs are also indirect forms of poverty relief. Not only do these programs increase total output, they generally improve job opportunities and earnings for workers at the lower end of the wage scale. Anything that the government does to promote economic growth and reduce cyclical fluctuations will also reduce unemployment for all groups. Since the poor are so often the last hired and first fired, they would benefit more than most from such programs. Even programs that reduce the obstacles to working, such as those that improve public transportation or subsidize day care, help the poor who can work. The goal of equality of opportunity is to offer the working poor a chance to improve their earnings and escape from poverty.

Giving everyone an equal chance at success in the labor market is consistent with the values of freedom, incentives, and individual choice implicit in a market economic system. However, equality of opportunity does nothing to help those who are too old, too young, too sick, too disabled, or too unskilled to participate in the market as workers or those who have to care for very small children. The only programs that will reach these poor are programs that are aimed directly at equality of results.

The fraction of the poor outside the labor force, or not expected to work, has risen dramatically in the last fifty years. In 1939, less than one-third of poor households were composed of persons not able to work for one of the reasons listed above. Today, closer to two-thirds of poor households are headed by a person who is elderly, a student, disabled, or a female with one or more preschool children. These people do not benefit from the rising tide of economic growth and increased job opportunities unless there is a deliberate effort to share those gains through redistribution.

IN CASH OR IN KIND?

Once a society decides to alter the market-determined distribution of income, the next question is how to carry it out. Should the method be cash payments or in-kind transfers of goods and services, such as housing, food, or health care?

Both private and public redistribution rely heavily on in-kind transfers of specific goods or services. In-kind transfers by private charities take place through soup kitchens, shelters for the homeless, and Meals on Wheels for shut-ins. The motive for such transfers is often not a desire to reduce income inequality but rather to ensure provision of basic needs such as food and shelter. Nobel Laureate James Tobin describes people with this redistribution motive *specific egalitarians*.[10]

Economists, who tend to be *general egalitarians*, usually argue for giving cash instead of specific goods and services, because a cash transfer allows recipients more options and thus does more (per dollar) to increase the recipient's well-being. Economists also prefer cash transfers because such programs are much less costly to administer. Tobin argues that the majority of people are specific egalitarians who care about ill-clothed and ill-fed people, not inequality. The result of this widely-held preference is that a large share of government benefits for the poor are in kind rather than in cash.

Nobel laureate James Buchanan argues that a preference for in-kind rather than cash transfers simply means that voters are maximizing their own utility as donors rather than maximizing the utility of welfare recipients by allowing them freedom of choice. The donor/voter's motive for income redistribution may not be the welfare of the recipients but rather a desire to eliminate some perceived problem—homeless people on the streets, slum housing, or students who disrupt the learning process in public schools because of illness or hunger. Providing specific goods or services is a more direct way of accomplishing that goal.[11]

REDISTRIBUTION TO THE MIDDLE-INCOME CLASS

Not all income redistribution is to the poor. Nobel laureate George Stigler points out that people try to use government policy as a way to redistribute income to themselves rather than to others. The government has the power to ex-

---

10. James Tobin, "On Limiting the Domain of Inequality," *Journal of Law and Economics* (October 1970): 263–277.
11. James M. Buchanan, "What Kind of Redistribution Do We Want?" *Economica* (May 1968): 62–87.

tract resources that would not be provided voluntarily. Any group that can gain control of the government can use this power to its own benefit. Stigler argues that the group that controls government policy making is the middle class. Thus, most public expenditures and tax-breaks are made for the benefit of the middle class—programs such as college loans, tax deductions for mortgage interest, subsidies for highways and airports heavily used by the middle class, and grants to state and local governments to build water and sewer systems.[12]

While it is likely that a larger share of taxes will come from the rich, it does not necessarily follow that these taxes will be redistributed as transfers or services to the poor. Economist Gordon Tullock argues that only a small portion of government transfers go to the poor.[13] Since support of middle-income voters is necessary to obtain the authority needed to take resources from other members of society, Tullock expects that money will flow from both ends of the income ladder toward the middle. Certainly his predictions have been borne out by recent experience, at least on the tax side. In the 1980s the biggest tax increase was on the working poor in the form of higher Social Security taxes. In 1993 the tax gains to upper-income groups from the 1981 tax cut were largely reversed. The middle class paid more Social Security taxes in the 1980s, but less income taxes, and escaped largely untouched by the tax increases of 1990 and 1993.

GOVERNMENT TRANSFER PROGRAMS IN PRACTICE

Until the 1930s, programs to relieve poverty were small scale, provided mainly by local governments and private charities. During the 1930s Depression, state and local governments were swamped with demands, and the present system of federal and federally assisted income transfer programs was born. These programs include Social Security for workers who are retired or disabled, unemployment compensation for those temporarily unemployed, and welfare programs for those unable to work. Today, transfer programs are a federal-state partnership, with the larger share of the funding at the federal level.

SOCIAL SECURITY

Social Security was established in 1935 as an old-age pension system. It was later expanded to include survivors' benefits (1939) and disability insurance (1950). Social Security was designed to relieve poverty for three groups likely to be poor: the old, the dependent survivors of deceased workers, and the disabled. In 1965, a program of health care for the elderly (Medicare) was added to Social Security. Except for Medicare, Social Security is a cash transfer program with no in-kind benefits.

Social Security payments are financed by a tax on workers and employers; currently, each pay an equal amount. Workers do not have a choice about participating. With very few exceptions, everyone who earns more than $50 a quarter must pay Social Security tax, including self-employed individuals. While workers may believe that their employers actually pay the other half of their

---

12. George J. Stigler, "Director's Law of Public Income Redistribution," *Journal of Loaw and Economics* (April 1970): 1–10.
13. Gordon Tullock, *Economics of Income Distribution* (Boston: Klover-Nijhoff, 1983), Chapter 5.

GLOBAL OUTLOOK: INEQUALITY IN POST-COMMUNIST RUSSIA

Karl Marx was a big believer in income equality—distribution according to need, not according to contribution to production. Even in the communist days, Russians did not see that kind of equality. Political leaders had big, chauffeur-driven cars, dachas in the countryside for holidays, and other perks, while housing was crowded and life was hard for the average working family.

Since 1990, inequality has become even greater. *The Economist* reports:

> District hospital number 33 in a drab part of Moscow reports that, in an average month, 80–90 people claim they cannot afford to bury a relation who has died in the hospital. Meanwhile, in another part of the city, a shabbily dressed man walks into a new General Motors showroom in mid-January and buys seven Cadillacs, at a cost of $50,000 each, and an armored one for $300,000. He pays cash. For most Russians, the most striking result of 13 months of economic reform has been the widening gulf between rich and poor.[a]

Critics of the new order in Russia point to growing income inequality since the breakup of the former Soviet Union. The fall in output is not the primary source of the new poverty, because much of the output decline was in the defense industry, which was not producing consumer goods. More serious are the rising prices and more slowly rising wages that have reduced real earnings to the point where wages in February 1993 bought only 60 percent as much as they did at the end of 1991. Hardest hit are the elderly and unemployed living on pensions and unemployment compensation. In November 1992, 29 percent of the population fell below the Russian equivalent of the poverty threshold. Many have survived by using up savings and selling their possessions, but those assets are running low.

At the other extreme are the newly rich. Some are smart business dealers. In fact, Russia has borrowed the word *biznessmeni* (businessmen) from English since there is no Russian equivalent. A larger number of the new rich, however, are those who have been selling raw materials to the West and keeping the profits in Western banks. An estimated $17 billion in export earnings left the country in 1991–1993. The winners—smugglers, traders, and speculators—are members of the "old-comrade network," ripping off the best assets as state-owned assets are turned over to the private sector.[b] This open display of consumption financed by business activity, legal and illegal, is a sharp change for a country in which enterprise was defined as a criminal activity just a few years ago.

Russia is an interesting hodgepodge of frontier capitalism blended with the remains of the Soviet empire and a patchwork social welfare system that includes access to health care and housing for all (although the housing is old and crowded and the quality of the health care is very uneven). Once Russia passes the crisis, it has the potential to be a major industrial nation because it has great natural resources and an educated population. As Russia moves toward a modified market system, there will still be some extremes of wealth and poverty. But the 29 percent poverty rate should decline, while those who become wealthy through unscrupulous means will be subject to the same kinds of laws and regulations as they would be in the West.

a. "Getting Richer, Getting Poorer," *The Economist* (February 6, 1993): 52.
b. Mortimer B. Zuckerman, "How We Can Help Russia," *U.S. News and World Report* (March 29, 1993): 64.

Social Security payment, microeconomic theory suggests that at least part of the other half is borne by workers.

Figure 5 shows why this is the case. Before the Social Security tax, the supply of labor facing the firm is S_0, and the firm's demand is D. The equilibrium wage is W_0. Adding a Social Security tax equal to $B - A$ (or the length of line AB) shifts the supply curve facing this firm to S_1. If supply is fairly elastic but demand is relatively inelastic, most of the tax falls on the worker. The gross wage (including the tax) rises to W_g, but the net wage taken home by the worker falls to W_n. The actual division of the tax burden between worker and employer depends not on legislation that says half on each, but on the relative elasticities of

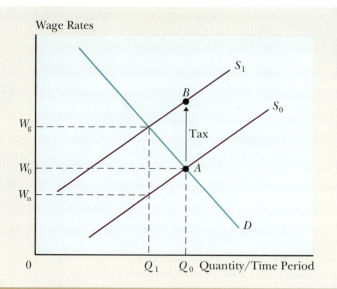

FIGURE 5

WHO PAYS SOCIAL SECURITY TAXES?
The higher price of labor, including the Social Security tax, reduces the number of workers employed from Q_0 to Q_1. The gross wage, including Social Security taxes, rises from W_0 to W_g, but the net wage falls to W_n.

supply and demand for labor. Economists believe that most of the tax falls on the worker because the market supply of labor is very inelastic.

Social Security is the largest income redistribution program in the United States. It also has some insurance features in the form of disability and survivors' benefits. Workers must contribute to the program for a specified minimum period of time in order to be eligible for benefits. The size of the benefit received is independent of any nonearned income such as interest, dividends, and private pensions. However, retirees under age seventy face a reduction of benefits if they *earn* above a certain wage income. This policy discriminates against poorer retirees, because the only way most of them can supplement their Social Security retirement income is with wages. Higher-income retirees collect interest, dividends, and private pensions without loss of Social Security benefits.

Until recently, Social Security benefits were not subject to federal income tax, and even now, most of these benefits are not taxed. Since 1985, Social Security recipients with adjusted gross incomes above $25,000 ($32,000 for married couples) have had to pay income taxes on one-half of their Social Security benefits. This rule affected 15 percent of the recipients. In 1993, the income ceilings were raised and 85 percent of benefits were made subject to income tax. Even with this change in the law, a large share of Social Security benefits still goes to people who are not poor. In fact, some of the taxes paid by the working poor are being transferred to middle- and upper-income households through Social Security.

Social Security taxes are paid into the Social Security Trust Fund. This name is misleading, because it is simply a fund into which current workers pay and from which current beneficiaries receive payments. Unlike private pensions and annuities, no money is held and invested for workers as the source from which they will later receive income. The Social Security System is a tax-and-transfer mechanism. Individuals are taxed during their working years to pay benefits to those who are currently retired, disabled, or surviving dependents of covered workers.

In the early years, funds coming in were more than adequate because there were many workers and few retirees. However, the age distribution of the U.S. population has changed greatly since that time. In 1950, an individual worker's taxes had to support only 6 percent of one recipient's benefits. In 1991, each worker had to be taxed enough to support 35 percent of one recipient's benefits. Coupled with the increased level of benefits, the changing ratio of workers to beneficiaries has created a heavy tax burden on workers. In 1980, Social Security taxes represented 30.5 percent of federal tax collections. By 1992, Social Security's share of federal tax revenues had grown to 38 percent.

Can today's workers rely on promised future Social Security payments? Many are concerned about whether they will receive those future benefits. Policy reforms made in 1985 did strengthen the stability of the system. The 1985 changes (1) reduced growth in benefit levels (by eliminating survivor benefits for children over eighteen and raising retirement ages in the future), (2) broadened categories of workers required to participate, so there will be more contributors, (3) raised the Social Security payroll tax rate, and (4) raised the level of income subject to the payroll tax. These last two changes increased Social Security revenues so much that the deficit turned into a temporary surplus. In 1993, Social Security collected $436 billion in payroll taxes and paid out $305 billion in benefits, a surplus of $131 billion. As more people retire in the next twenty years, however, that cushion of surplus funds will be needed to pay their benefits.

TRANSFERS TO THE ELDERLY. In the last several decades, the economic well-being of those over sixty-five has increased greatly in the United States. The largest segment of the poor in 1959 were people over sixty-five. By 1990, only 11 percent of those over sixty-five were below the poverty line. If in-kind transfers are counted, the number falls to 5 percent. Professor James Schulz observed, "Poverty among the elderly, as measured by the poverty index and adjusted for nonmoney income, has virtually disappeared."

Much of the decline is due to vast amounts of federal resources that are going to the elderly. However, another factor that has helped reduce poverty among the elderly is the dramatic increase in their wealth. In 1989, the average household in the sixty-five to seventy-four age range had assets of $278,300, compared to $131,900 for those under fifty-five. Unlike earlier generations, current retirees tend to have had smaller families, more years of relatively high earnings to build their assets, and considerable accumulation of wealth from increased values of owner occupied housing.

Social Security benefits represented 21 percent of federal spending in 1993. Benefits are given to all qualified individuals above a certain age, regardless of their financial situation. Medicare is another major transfer program benefiting the elderly. When it was established in 1965, Medicare was projected to cost $8.8 billion in 1990. Even after adjusting for inflation that estimate was far off the mark. In 1990, Medicare cost $111 billion in 1965 dollars.

THE SOCIAL SECURITY POLICY DEBATE. The policy trend toward transferring more resources to the relatively well-off elderly has begun to raise objections from the more numerous voters under age sixty-five. As demographer Samuel Preston observed, "The United States has become the first society in history in which the poorest group in the population is the children, not the aged." Economists argue that money spent on children is at least partly an investment in human capital and the future productivity of the economy. In contrast, money spent on the elderly generally goes into consumption to make their lives more comfortable.

There are no simple and politically acceptable policy solutions to the Social Security/Medicare problem. The Social Security System itself is financially secure for the present, except for Medicare. Medicare provides health care for the age group with the highest medical expenses, and medical costs in general have been rising more rapidly than the general rate of inflation. A solution to Medicare will have to be part of a larger health care reform policy. But whatever happens to Medicare, politicians will have to address the balance between the claims of the elderly and the needs of workers and children.

UNEMPLOYMENT COMPENSATION

Unemployment compensation is a transfer program financed by a tax on employers and administered by the states, which set benefit levels and eligibility requirements. Costs are shared between the states and the federal government. In 1992, there were about 2.5 million beneficiaries on average, receiving benefits that totalled $23 billion.

Unemployment compensation is intended to be a temporary replacement of lost income while a worker is between jobs or temporarily laid off. The program has been criticized as providing "paid vacations" while workers go through the motions of searching for jobs. It has also been praised as providing a safety net for unemployed workers while they match their skills to the best available jobs, making labor markets more efficient. Of all income transfer programs, this one is the least criticized because benefits are of a temporary nature.

WELFARE

The group of programs lumped together as "welfare" began in the 1930s with Aid to the Aged, Aid to the Disabled, and Aid to Dependent Children (later Aid to Families with Dependent Children, or AFDC). These programs identify groups of people not expected to work. Costs are shared between the federal and state governments. There are different eligibility requirements and benefit levels in different states. In the 1960s, these programs were expanded and new ones were added as part of President Johnson's War on Poverty. Aid to the Aged, Aid to the Disabled, and several smaller programs were merged into Supplemental Security Income, a federally funded program, in 1972.

In-kind welfare programs include food stamps, public housing, Medicaid, legal aid, Head Start for preschool children, and job training programs. These efforts to improve the welfare of the poor were designed to ensure that they consumed the "right mix" of goods and services, especially in the areas of health, nutrition, education, and training.

Although welfare policy gets a great deal of attention, these cash and in-kind programs are relatively small compared to Social Security. About 18 percent of households received some welfare benefit(s) in 1990 for a total federal expenditure of $152 billion. In the same year, $352 billion went to Social Security benefits.

THE WELFARE REFORM POLICY DEBATE. Welfare reform is, of course, high on the political agenda. The most recent series of welfare debates was started by the

1982 proposal to return the largest welfare program, Aid to Families with Dependent Children, to the states. About the same time, fuel was added to the debate fire by Charles Murray's controversial book, *Losing Ground*.[14] Murray argued that current welfare policy encourages people to do the wrong things—avoid working, have more children, and become welfare-dependent. Also, pressures of budget deficits led to a reexamination of all areas of federal spending, especially social welfare programs. The debate on welfare policy reform that has continued from 1982 through the 1992 election and beyond centers on two issues: work incentives and cost containment.

Critics of welfare programs argue that they discourage work. It is very likely that a welfare client who takes a job will actually be worse off. Welfare recipients who take jobs lose not only cash benefits but also medical help, subsidized housing, and other benefits from overlapping programs. Also, they have to pay Social Security taxes and possibly income taxes. Recent changes in income tax laws have provided some tax relief for the working poor, and they are able to keep food stamps until their income rises beyond a certain threshold.

In order to determine the effects of welfare programs on work incentives, the federal government sponsored four large-scale experiments to measure how various levels of benefits would affect individuals' work efforts. Households in New Jersey, Pennsylvania, rural areas of North Carolina and Iowa, Gary (Indiana), Seattle, and Detroit were studied at various times from 1969 to 1982. The researchers concluded that higher benefit levels did lead to some modest reductions in work effort, especially among females.[15]

WORKFARE PROGRAMS. Various states have developed a number of experimental programs aimed at providing work incentives while containing costs. These **workfare programs** encourage or require welfare recipients who are able to work to take jobs as a condition for continuing to receive benefits. Workfare programs appeal to both liberal and conservative politicians. They combine the liberal approach of giving where there is need with the conservative approach of giving to those who make an effort to support themselves.

State workfare programs involve job training, day care, and help with job searches as well as penalties for refusing to accept training or seek work. Sometimes the jobs are in the public sector, and some programs also include education programs that should lead to jobs.

During the 1980s, policy makers revisited the issue of work expectations for mothers of preschool children. Following the lead of nonwelfare working mothers, workfare programs have lowered the age at which children are expected to be placed in day care (so that their mothers can work) from six years to three. However, lack of day care at affordable prices has been a major obstacle to workfare programs.

INCOME SECURITY IN OTHER INDUSTRIAL COUNTRIES

Policy makers often explore what other countries do in order to find workable solutions to problems like welfare reform and growing Social Security costs. All governments provide some mix of transfer payments and social services in their

Workfare programs
State welfare programs requiring beneficiaries to take jobs or participate in training in order to remain eligible for benefits.

---

14. Charles Murray, *Losing Ground: American Social Policy, 1950–1980* (New York: Basic Books, 1984).
15. Alicia H. Munnell, ed., *Lessons from the Income Maintenance Experiments* (Proceedings of a conference sponsored by the Federal Reserve Bank of Boston and The Brookings Institution, 1986).

social welfare systems. Some of these programs are based on a means (needs-based) test and others go to all citizens. Children's allowances in Canada, for example, are provided to all families. Since these grants are taxable income, some funds are recovered in tax payments from higher-income families. Education up to a certain level is traditionally provided to all citizens in industrial countries regardless of income.

All major industrial countries have some type of publicly funded pension system, and some provision for unemployment and disability insurance. Health care is more likely to be provided at public expense in European nations. Public housing has been an important component of social welfare in Britain, where until recently 28 percent of the population lived in "council houses" (public housing rented at subsidized rates). In Scandinavian countries, the political consensus is that a basic standard of living is a right. Therefore, certain basic social services and social insurance programs (unemployment, disability, and so on) are provided to everyone without an income test.

Sweden's system has been under considerable stress lately because of a flood of refugees from Eastern Europe, all of whom are entitled to a full set of services. Financing this extensive social welfare system has required very high taxes on those who are working and earning incomes, and some of Sweden's big companies and higher earners have fled to more hospitable locations.

Support for the welfare state peaked in European countries and in the United States during the 1960s and 1970s. Today, U.S. social welfare expenditures are a lower share of GDP than in most other industrial countries, except for Japan. Japan spends a lower percentage of its total income on welfare programs because the family is expected to assume greater responsibility for both the young and the elderly.

In the 1990s, the emphasis on individualism and concern over work incentives that pervade the U.S. welfare policy debate have also received increased attention from policy makers elsewhere. The formerly communist nations of Eastern and Central Europe are struggling to dismantle their extensive welfare systems. As noted earlier, Sweden is being forced to reconsider how much it can afford to provide. Germany finds that the high payroll tax required to cover social welfare costs makes its labor very expensive and cuts into its global competitiveness. Under Prime Ministers Thatcher and Major, Britain made substantial cuts in its extensive system of welfare and unemployment benefits. Thus, those who debate fundamental changes in U.S. welfare policies are not alone. From Japan to Canada and the United States to Germany, Sweden, Hungary, and Russia, social welfare systems are one of the most pressing and difficult political and economic issues of the 1990s.

Consider again...*C.K. has worked long enough to be eligible for Social Security disability if she meets the stringent tests to ensure that she is genuinely unable to work. At 1993 rates, she will receive about $500 a month from Social Security, and may work part-time earning up to another $500 a month. The combined income will provide a modest but adequate standard of living. If she is not able to work at all, her income is low enough to make her eligible for food stamps. After two years, she will be eligible for Medicare to meet her medical expenses. C.K. is fortunate to qualify for a program designed specifically for workers who become un-*

able to work. About 7 million workers (6 percent of the labor force) received benefits in 1993.

C.K. still has an incentive to work part-time, but only up to a ceiling. The biggest work disincentive is in health care. If she recovers sufficiently to return to work full-time, she will lose not only her disability benefits but also her Medicare coverage. With a chronic disease, she will find it difficult to find other health care coverage.

J.T. is the typical AFDC recipient that most welfare reform has tried to reach. She is eligible for AFDC benefits, Medicaid for herself and her children, and food stamps. The combined value of AFDC and food stamps varies greatly from one state to another. Depending on the state, J.T. may be not only encouraged but pressured to obtain her high school diploma, get some job training, and look for work.

If she works, however, her standard of living may not improve very much. Remember, a full-time, year-round job at the minimum wage of $4.25 only pays $8,840 a year, which is still below the poverty level for a family of three. J.T., under present rules in most states, will lose one dollar in AFDC benefits for every dollar she earns from working. She will still receive food stamps, but will probably lose her eligibility for Medicaid. She will also incur child care costs and working expenses. Unlike C.K., J.T. has a powerful incentive not to work at all.

Designing a social welfare system that meets the needs of and provides appropriate incentives for both C.K. and J.T. is not easy, particularly in a nation with a patchwork system of health care coverage. The costs of checking out the eligibility of recipients is very high. It takes a lot of paperwork to separate the deserving from the undeserving poor, no matter what criteria are used. Welfare policy reform has been in every political platform of both major parties for twenty years. Thus far, the

SUMMARY

1. The Lorenz curve and the Gini coefficient measure the relative distribution of income in an economy. Neither measure, however, reflects the life-cycle pattern of income earning and may therefore give a false impression of how much income inequality exists over time.
2. The poverty threshold in the United States was established in 1965 and is adjusted regularly for inflation. This measure is used to determine changes in the amount of poverty in the United States. For families, the poverty threshold determines eligibility for certain kinds of benefits, such as food stamps. The poverty measures have been criticized because they fail to take into account the value of benefits other than cash payments.
3. Discrimination in labor markets channels certain groups into certain occupations. Some of the inequality that might appear to be the result of discrimination is actually due to differences in productivity or other objective characteristics. To the extent that discrimination exists in the labor market, total output is lower than it could be if all resources were used in the most efficient manner. Market forces will work against discrimination, because discrimination is costly and entrepreneurs can reduce the costs of production by not discriminating.
4. Income redistribution can be viewed as a public good that is under provided because of free-riding behavior. Critics of government redistribution argue that it crowds out private charity, destroys work incentives, and results in redistribution to the middle class and the rich rather than those who are truly needy. Programs that promote equality of opportunity encourage work and are less costly to taxpayers than those that promote equality of results. However, the latter programs are

more likely to reach the elderly, disabled, and children. Economists consider cash redistribution more efficient, but the public prefers in-kind redistribution to ensure that the program results in particular forms of consumption and reaches the intended beneficiary.

5. Poverty relief policies in the United States have taken three forms: training and job opportunities, social insurance, and direct assistance to those who are unable to work because of age and health problems.

Poverty among the elderly has largely been eliminated because of the Social Security System. Social Security, moreover, is now under some financial pressure because of the changing age distribution of the population. In-kind transfers have expanded in the last twenty-five years and reduced the incidence of poverty in the United States. Current welfare policy reform proposals center on cost control and work incentives.

NEW TERMS

personal distribution of income
Lorenz curve
Gini coefficient
interdependent utility functions
workfare programs

QUESTIONS: REVIEW, APPLICATIONS, AND POLICY

REVIEW

1. How is the official poverty level of income determined? Is it a meaningful measure?
2. Why are some people poor? What would you do if you were in a position to take some action?
3. Why do many economists feel that markets will work to undermine discrimination in labor markets?
4. Why does society redistribute income to the poor? Why is private charity likely to be inadequate?
5. Who really pays the Social Security tax, the employer or the employee?

APPLICATIONS

6. Public education is an in-kind transfer to all people in certain age groups. Who benefits more, the poor or the well-to-do?
7. How would George Stigler have explained the fact that transfers to the elderly have increased so significantly in the last two decades? Would Gordon Tullock find this surprising? Why or why not?
8. Why do AFDC recipients move? Does it surprise you that they do?
9. Do you favor equality of opportunity or equality of results? Why?

POLICY

10. Do you think a negative income tax would solve the problem of poverty in the United States? Why or why not?
11. Should society be concerned with relative poverty or absolute poverty? How would dealing with absolute poverty differ from dealing with relative poverty?
12. "The social safety net is intended to catch those who fall in, not those who jump in." Discuss the implications of this statement for designing an income support system.
13. Why are there long-term problems with the financial health of the Social Security System? Identify some possible solutions.
14. What problems with the welfare system are workfare programs designed to solve?
15. How do you think Congress should address the question of entitlement programs for the elderly?

SUGGESTIONS FOR FURTHER READING

Funicello, Theresa. *Tyranny of Kindness.* Atlantic Monthly Press, 1993. A former welfare mother takes a critical look at the welfare industry.

Hacker, Andrew. *Two Nations: Black and White, Separate, Hostile, Unequal.* New York: Scribners, 1992. Looks at changes in the economic status of black families from 1970 to 1990.

Jencks, Christopher. *The Dispossessed: America's Underclasses from the Civil War to the Present.* Cambridge: Harvard University Press, 1992. A collection of essays on poverty in terms of income, unemployment, culture, and values.

Levy, Frank, and Richard C. Michel. *The Economic Future of American Families: Income and Wealth Trends.* Washington DC: Urban Institute Press, 1991. A look at patterns of income inequality over the last two decades.

Murray, Charles. *In Pursuit: Of Happiness and Good Government.* New York: Simon & Schuster, 1988. The author of the controversial 1980 book, *Losing Ground,* argues that the poor can only be helped by local religious, social, and community organizations.

PART 9

MARKET FAILURE, GOVERNMENT FAILURE, AND PUBLIC CHOICE

The three chapters in this part represent the capstone to a course in microeconomics. The chapters evaluate the government's impact on allocation and efficiency. Many of the issues in these three chapters deal with property rights.

Since government (through the courts) ultimately defines the system of property rights, Chapter 31 begins with a discussion of the legal system as the most basic function of government. Then the chapter looks at market failure. Two market outcomes often viewed as unsatisfactory are the failure of markets to produce the optimal quantity (and price) of a good when there is monopoly power, and the poverty that is often the result of the market distribution of income. Additional instances of market failure exist because of externalities and public goods. This chapter examines the economic arguments for government intervention to correct for market failure.

Next we analyze some of the costs of intervention to solve the problems noted in Chapter 31. Public choice economists have identified ways in which government intervention introduces new problems and biases into the economic system. Chapter 32 examines these effects and how they might affect the growth of government. It also examines some other theories about the microeconomic role of government.

Chapter 33 applies the theories discussed in Chapters 31 and 32 to three real-world concerns: urban problems, the global environment, and health care. These are presented as case studies. The issues facing urban America are, in many instances, not unique to cities but are simply more severe there. Pollution, crime, and other negative externalities associated with living in cities are examples of market failures that government intervention has failed to solve.

The 1990s have already been labeled the decade of the environment. Critics of past environmental policies argue that environmental problems result from failure to plan far enough ahead or to consider the needs of future generations. Governments have attempted to intervene to protect the environment for future generations, but these attempts at correcting market failure bring their own problems.

Finally, health care is a page-one story in every newspaper in America. Chapter 33 presents the economic side of these issues in a way that should make you a better informed player in the policy issue debate.

CHAPTER 31
MARKET FAILURE AND GOVERNMENT INTERVENTION POLICIES

LEARNING OBJECTIVES
1. Describe the economic and policy impact of property law, tort law, and contract law.
2. Define externalities and explain how the Coase theorem can resolve some externality problems.
3. Explain how free-riding behavior results in the underproduction of public goods.
4. Evaluate the public goods aspects of income redistribution and education.

Consider this... *"Oh give me a home, where the buffalo roam, and the deer and the antelope play. Where seldom is heard a discouraging word and the skies are not cloudy all day." This old cowboy song no longer describes the west—if it ever did. Buffalo were almost shot into extinction in the days of the early west. If someone shot free-ranging cattle, the owner of those cattle expected compensation. But since nobody had property rights to the buffalo, no one objected when they were killed by the thousands.*

A similar situation now exists with wolves. Some environmentalists want to reintroduce wolves into Yellowstone and Glacier National Parks, areas located in the wolves' historical range. Many ranchers oppose this policy because they are convinced that wolves will kill their livestock, particularly during the calving season. Environmentalists argue that there is strong evidence that wolves would kill no more than 1 percent of the livestock. The problem is that any single rancher might have many calves killed, and thus ranchers have an incentive to kill the wolves. Can you suggest a simple answer to this dilemma? Economists have long recognized that when property rights are not well defined, markets fail to produce efficient outcomes. After studying this chapter you might find a solution as we examine the economic arguments for government intervention policies to correct for market failure.

LAW, ECONOMICS, AND GOVERNMENT POLICY

As Adam Smith noted, one of the basic roles of government is to define and enforce property rights. Thus, to an economist, law is the basic framework of any economy. In the United States, government's effect on the allocation of resources is defined by law and the interpretation of law. In recent years, economists have spent a great deal of time extending economic analysis to explain the purposes and effects of legislation (statute law) and judicial decisions (common law).[1] Both types of laws can be analyzed from an economic perspective, although in different ways. *Statute law* relates to laws that have been passed by legislative bodies, and is of interest because of the incentives statutes create and the way they alter existing property rights. *Common law* is law as defined by the courts. It changes through judicial interpretation and decisions, and these precedents alter incentives for decision making. Lawyers are interested in the applications of specific decisions to other cases. Economists are more concerned with how these decisions affect the economy by altering incentives.

In analyzing law, economists search for the economic reasoning implicit in legislation and judges' decisions. Laws are commonly divided into three major catagories. **Property law** relates to the enforcement of property rights. Enforcement of property rights is one of the basic requirements of any economic system. **Tort law** deals with intentional and unintentional wrongs imposed by one party on another. **Contract law** deals with the enforcement of voluntary exchanges.

The important relationships between economics and law have been studied intensively in recent years by both economists and lawyers. Economics deals with property rights and exchange, which are the most basic elements of a market system. Precedents in common law or changes in statute law will have profound effects on economic activity and government policy. Laws (more correctly, the courts' interpretation of laws) determine the private-public mix in our economy.

PROPERTY LAW

The law in the United States is generally compatible with the economic principle that the economy operates more efficiently under a system of exclusive, transferable property rights. The most important exceptions occur in two areas in which high transactions costs create market failure or interfere with the efficiency of market outcomes.

The first exception concerns incompatible uses of property. Incompatibility exists when the rights of the parties are in conflict. Noise, air, water pollution, and attractive hazards such as a swimming pool or a construction site are familiar examples. Cases involving incompatible uses are often treated as matters of nuisance. In many of these cases, the court will simply issue an injunction requiring that the party responsible for the nuisance cease and desist. This solution may appear to be the most fair or equitable approach, but it is not necessarily the best economic solution from an efficiency viewpoint.

The second exception to property law's compatibility with the principles of a free market is the doctrine of **eminent domain**. The principle here is that government has the legal right to purchase property at "fair market value" if it is deemed to be in the public interest. In these cases, the owner's property right is reduced in value because the owner cannot refuse to sell. Condemnation proceedings are court cases in which the government tries to take property away from an owner by arguing that the government's rights are more important. Governments often invoke eminent domain for construction of public facilities, such as parks, roads, or dams.

Property law
Law that concerns the enforcement of property rights.

Tort law
Law that deals with intentional and unintentional wrongs inflicted by one party on another.

Contract law
Law that deals with the enforcement of voluntary exchanges.

Eminent domain
A doctrine that gives government the right to buy property at "fair market value" if the purchase is in the public interest.

---

1. See Richard A. Posner, *Economic Analysis of Law* (Boston: Little Brown, 1972); and Werner Z. Hirsch, *Introduction to Law and Economics* (New York: McGraw-Hill, 1980).

TORT LAW

Tort
A wrongful action (or failure to act) that causes damage to the person or property of another individual.

A **tort** is a wrongful action (or failure to act) by an individual that causes damage to the person or property of another individual. For example, if reckless behavior on your part injures another person, that person may sue you for damages. Payment of these damages can be justified on the basis of *equity* (fairness). The payment restores the original distribution of income or assets. Payment of damages can also be justified on the basis of *efficiency*. It makes you bear the costs of your reckless action and thus increases the incentive to be more careful. For example, if you are responsible for any damage your dog may do by biting people or damaging property, you will be more likely to take precautions to keep your dog under control.

The equity principle requires a transfer payment from the wrongdoer to the individual who has been damaged. The impact of the efficiency principle is quite different. The law establishes a precedent for the ownership of property rights. Tort law is used to determine who has the property right when it is in dispute.

CONTRACT LAW

The economics of exchange and contract law are similar in the sense that individuals are presumed to enter into contracts only if they stand to gain. Parties to contracts may end up in court not because the contracts were bad (for either of the parties), but rather because one party failed to satisfy a provision. This most often happens when the contractual exchange fails to take place on time or when the cost/benefit calculation of one party changes.

Contracts usually are not set aside by the courts if the intent is reasonably clear. On the other hand, the courts have set contracts aside if (honest) mistakes have been committed. If one party has been induced to accept a contract through fraud, duress, or incapacity, the court will refuse to enforce the contract.

Contracts, and court decisions under the common law of contracts, are important in economics because contracts, whether they are expressed or implied, form the basis of exchange. Exchange is influenced by contract law, and contract law alters the incentives that affect exchanges. For example, the courts have ruled that a college catalog or a course syllabus represents a contract with a student. This ruling has altered the terms of the production and sale of higher-education services.

EXTERNALITIES

The principle of economic (allocative) efficiency states that the efficient level of production of a good or service is where the social marginal benefits equal social marginal costs. In saying "social" marginal benefits or costs, we mean the benefits and costs faced by society as a whole. "Society" includes those who are direct participants in the market transaction, but also others who may be affected by the transaction. Externalities and public goods cause market outcomes to deviate from the rule that social marginal benefits equal social marginal costs.

It is in this social optimum sense that markets have sometimes failed to allocate resources efficiently.

Externalities are costs or benefits associated with consumption or production that are not reflected in market prices. The cost or benefit is external because it falls on parties other than the buyer or seller. Externalities represent a form of market failure.

The most frequently cited example of an externality is pollution. For example, a firm producing steel must purchase iron ore, electricity, labor, and other inputs. The costs of these factors are embodied in the price of the steel. However, in producing steel, the firm also uses clean air and produces air pollution. Yet the firm doesn't compensate those individuals who give up the clean air. As a result, the cost of using the air is not embodied in the price of the steel. This cost is external to the production of the steel.

Many problems caused by externalities result from the fact that property rights to certain resources are not clearly defined. Clean air is a resource that is not owned by anyone. Therefore, the steel mill can use clean air and not compensate those who give it up, because there is no clearly defined owner to demand payment.

Externalities can be positive or negative. Air pollution is a negative externality; so is the noise resulting from the use of a snowmobile. The cost that this noise imposes on other individuals may not be taken into account in the price of snowmobiles or snowmobiling. It is external to any economic calculation.

Positive externalities are not so obvious. Inoculations against contagious diseases or spraying to control mosquitoes are examples of activities that generate positive externalities. Benefits accrue to others if enough people are inoculated or enough mosquito breeding areas are sprayed, but these benefits are not considered by those deciding on whether or not to incur the cost. Education is another good example of an activity that generates a positive externality. Society benefits from an individual's education. A person who is educated is likely to be a better citizen and to be less dependent on others. In addition, he or she is likely to be a more productive person, increasing national income. Yet individuals, in deciding how much education to pursue, do not consider these benefits because they are external to them. The individual is not able to charge those who enjoy the external benefit of his or her education.

To the extent that externalities exist, the market is likely to fail. Private market decisions will result in too little or too much of certain items being produced. Corrective action on a collective basis may be needed. Government policies can influence production or consumption that creates externalities through taxes, subsidies, outright prohibitions (like banning smoking within certain buildings), or by requiring citizens to consume certain goods, such as inoculations, education, and trash recycling.

In some cases it might be possible to organize advertising campaigns and appeal to "socially conscious" behavior or altruistic behavior to correct for the externality. There are many examples of such behavior in the real world. There are considerate smokers who go outside to smoke. Many environmentally conscious households recycle on their own. Indeed, in some communities the citizens have demanded that government make provisions for such recycling. If groups of people internalize externalities on their own, there is no need for government action.

Externalities
Costs or benefits associated with consumption or production that are not reflected in market prices and fall on parties other than the buyer or seller.

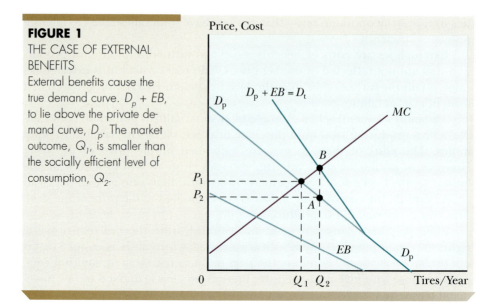

FIGURE 1
THE CASE OF EXTERNAL BENEFITS
External benefits cause the true demand curve, $D_p + EB$, to lie above the private demand curve, D_p. The market outcome, Q_1, is smaller than the socially efficient level of consumption, Q_2.

EXTERNAL BENEFITS

In order to analyze the economic implications of a positive externality, consider Figure 1, which represents the market for automobile tires. D_p represents the private demand for automobile tires, and MC represents the marginal cost. Consumers will purchase Q_1 tires at price P_1. Assume that EB represents the marginal external benefits arising from the consumption of new tires. External benefits exist when people consume more new tires, because their cars are safer and the chance of an accident involving others decreases. This greater safety creates a social benefit. EB can be viewed as the summation of the demand curves of people other than the immediate consumers of the product. It has a negative slope, like all demand curves.

Adding EB and D_p vertically gives the true demand curve, labeled $D_p + EB$. It is the true demand curve because its height represents the inclusion of marginal social benefits. The two demand curves are summed vertically instead of horizontally because we are interested in adding the benefits of all who gain at various quantities consumed. We are not summing the additional amounts consumers want to purchase but rather how much they value these units. If the external benefits are considered, the combined valuation ($D_p + EB$) indicates that Q_2 rather than Q_1 tires should be consumed. In other words, the existence of the positive externality resulted in this good being underproduced and underconsumed.

It is easy to see how government could correct this market failure. A subsidy to consumers equal to the length of line AB on the graph would reduce the price consumers pay to P_2 and bring about the socially optimal level of consumption, Q_2. This level is the social optimum because it includes the tire production demanded by those who are not counted by the market mechanism. Alternatively, government could require the purchase of Q_2 tires per year. Vehicle inspections, which some states require, are also attempts (rather crude ones) to reach this social optimum.

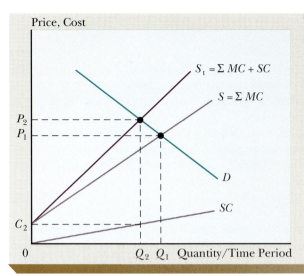

FIGURE 2
EXTERNALITIES AND MARKET EQUILIBRIUM
When the social cost of the negative externality (SC) is added to the marginal cost curves of the competitive firms (S), the true supply curve (S_t) is found. This true supply curve indicates that too much of the good is produced at too low a price, unless the externality is taken into account.

EXTERNAL COSTS

Earlier, we used air pollution as an example of an external cost. If you live near a steel mill, you are forced to breathe polluted air without being compensated for the fact that the mill is using the air as a place in which to dump some of its debris. The economic importance of this behavior is that the polluting firm avoids paying part of the costs of production. It is quite simple to determine the theoretical effects of such externalities. It is more difficult to determine how to correct them.

Pollution causes damage, or social costs, to those in the general area. **Social costs** are costs that are borne by society or some members of society without compensating benefits. In general terms, negative externalities impose damages, or social costs, on groups in the population external to the market transaction. This situation is represented in Figure 2. Assume that the polluter is in a competitive industry that is generating a negative externality. The demand curve is the usual market demand curve for the good or service. The supply curve is the summation of all the individual firms' marginal cost curves (above their average variable cost curves). This supply curve includes all private costs but not marginal social costs. Equilibrium is reached at price P_1 and output Q_1.

Now suppose we know the value of the marginal social costs generated by the externality, represented by the curve SC. The social costs are zero when no output is produced and are assumed to increase at a constant rate. If we add these marginal social costs to the supply curve, we get the true supply curve, S_t. This curve is the summation of the social costs and the private costs embodied in the firms' marginal cost curves. The socially optimal level of production is not Q_1 but the smaller Q_2. The price associated with efficient production is P_2, which is higher than P_1.

It is clear that when the social costs of production are included, the good becomes more expensive. It isn't that these costs weren't being borne before. They weren't being borne by the producers or the consumers of the good. Instead, they were being paid by those who live near where production is taking

Social costs
Costs that are borne by society or some group in society without compensating benefits.

place. In failing to take into account the social costs, the firm was producing too much of the good and charging the consumer too low a price because it was not paying some of the costs of production.

In the real world, when production or consumption of a good causes negative externalities, the people who bear those costs subsidize consumers of the product. For example, the people who live in Gary IN, where steel is produced, bear costs that allow consumers of steel to pay lower prices. A person who buys a steel and chrome table and chairs in Orlando FL is subsidized by someone who lives in Gary. If steel producers had to pay for the negative externalities they create, less steel would be produced, and it would be sold for a higher price. The general theoretical conclusion is that when negative externalities exist, the amount of production will not be optimal. Too much output will be produced at too low a price.

It is very important to understand that even if the cost of an externality such as pollution is placed on the buyer and seller of the good or service, this action does not cause the amount of pollution to fall to zero. Only if production of the good or service falls to zero will the resulting pollution fall to zero. In the example in Figure 2, the price paid by buyers rose from P_1 to P_2 when social costs were included, but some pollution and the costs associated with it continued. In other words, there is an efficient amount of pollution determined by the market process.

INTERNALIZING NEGATIVE EXTERNALITIES

Internalization
The incorporation of the social costs of negative external effects into the market price.

According to economists, the trick to controlling social costs of negative externalities is internalization of those externalities. **Internalization** means that producers are forced to take account of the costs they impose on other members of society in their production decisions. When internalized, the externality is incorporated into the market price.

In terms of Figure 2, the firm should have to bear the social costs SC so that S_t becomes the supply curve. How can this be done? It would be a simple matter if the social costs could easily be determined. It is easy to analyze the theoretical case, as in Figure 2, but in the real world it is very difficult to come up with a dollar value. You can determine the dollar value of having to paint your house more often because of air pollution, but what is the cost of a certain number of people dying because of respiratory problems? How much is not being able to have a cookout in the back yard worth? If government officials could determine these costs, they could place a tax on the industry that would shift the supply curve up just the right distance (to S_t in Figure 2). The market solution would then be an optimal price of P_2 and an optimal output level of Q_2.

Governmental policy makers could also charge firms for the amount of negative externalities they create. Each firm could be monitored and charged for air pollution on a monthly basis. It would be possible to put a meter on each smokestack and measure the pollutants. Then firms could be charged for the air they pollute just as they are charged for the electricity or labor they use. This pollution charge would cause costs to rise and move production toward the socially optimal level. This solution, however, has the same problem as taxation—determining the correct charge per unit of pollutant.

Although there are problems, it can be argued that there is a need for government to intervene in the market process under circumstances when there are negative externalities. When markets don't produce socially optimal results, it may be appropriate for government to step in with policies that attempt to correct for the market failure. It is not always necessary for government to correct for social costs, however. Private groups may form in an effort to prevent or limit negative externalities. A good example of such a group is a condominium association. Condo associations set up rules of behavior and upkeep of facilities that are designed to limit or prevent residents from creating certain types of negative externalities. By buying a condo, a person voluntarily limits his or her own behavior.

THE COASE THEOREM AND SMALL-NUMBER EXTERNALITIES. In a landmark study of externalities, economist and 1992 Nobel Prize winner, Ronald Coase, considered cases in which the number of affected parties is small. Coase concluded that, in such cases, individual maximizing behavior will correct for a negative externality without the need for government intervention.[2] The **Coase theorem** states that when there are small numbers of affected parties, a property right assignment is sufficient to internalize any externality that is present. Coase demonstrated that if property rights are clearly defined, the affected individuals will take action to internalize the externality. The only government intervention required to solve the problem is enforcement of property rights.

Consider, as Coase did in his paper, a case where there are only two parties involved in a dispute: a wheat farmer and a cattle rancher. The negative externality is the damage done by cattle roaming on unfenced land. As the rancher increases the size of the herd, the damage done by straying cattle will increase. To approach an optimal result, it is necessary to compel the rancher to take these costs into account. If government intervenes, it is likely to solve the problem with a policy of requiring the rancher to pay the farmer for the damage to the farmer's wheat. In this case, the rancher would restrict the number of cattle in the herd until marginal cost equaled marginal revenue (the marginal cost includes the damage to wheat).

In Figure 3, $D = MR$ represents the demand and marginal revenue curve of raising cattle, MC represents the marginal cost of raising cattle, and SC represents the marginal social cost, or the cost of the negative externality (the damage to the wheat). Without any internalizing of the social cost, the rancher would raise Q_1 cattle per year, and the farmer would incur a dollar loss to the wheat crop of W_1 for the last (marginal) cow raised. Government intervention would force the rancher to act on the basis of the joint $MC + SC$ curve through some tax scheme or direct regulation. As a result, the rancher would raise only Q_2 cattle.

Coase shows that even if government did not intervene, the same solution would result. According to Coase, all that is necessary is that property rights be defined and enforced. First, assume that the farmer's property rights include the right not to have the wheat harmed. The rancher will then be forced to pay damages, shown by the SC curve, and will add these to production costs. The rancher will then raise Q_2 cattle. On the other hand, suppose the rancher has the right to let the cattle roam. The important question then is how much the farmer will be willing to "bribe" the rancher to keep the cattle away. The farmer

Coase theorem
The idea that well-defined property rights are sufficient to internalize any external effect that is present, when there are small numbers of affected parties.

---

2. Ronald Coase, "The Problem of Social Cost," *Journal of Law and Economics 3*, (October 1960): 1–44.

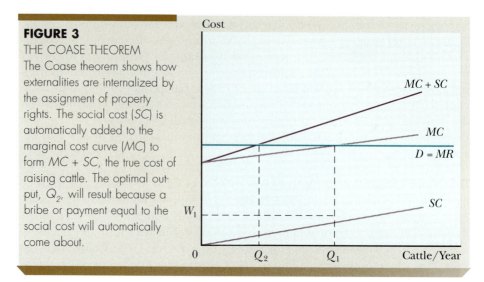

FIGURE 3

THE COASE THEOREM

The Coase theorem shows how externalities are internalized by the assignment of property rights. The social cost (SC) is automatically added to the marginal cost curve (MC) to form MC + SC, the true cost of raising cattle. The optimal output, Q_2, will result because a bribe or payment equal to the social cost will automatically come about.

will be willing to pay the rancher an amount just slightly less than the cost of the damage done by the cattle because this makes them *both* better off than allowing the cattle to damage the wheat. The farmer would pay W_1 for the last cow not raised. The rancher then must include these bribes as opportunity costs because if the cattle are raised, the bribes will not be paid. When these opportunity costs are added to the marginal cost curve, the rancher will raise Q_2 cattle. The result is that Q_2 cattle will be raised regardless of who has the property rights, as long as those rights are defined and the number of people involved is small. Small numbers are necessary because the farmer and rancher must get together and work out a solution.

Note that the Coase solution says only that the allocatively efficient results, or the number of cattle produced, will be the same whoever has the property rights. It says nothing about the distribution of income. Assigning property rights does affect who is better off. In the first case, the farmer's income is higher. In the second, the rancher's income is higher. The assignment of rights might have to be resolved by the law or through the political process since it involves an issue of equity, not economic efficiency. It's not really clear whether the rancher is imposing costs on the farmer (by damaging the wheat crop) or the farmer is imposing costs on the rancher (by restricting the grazing range of the herd). That uncertainty is the reason why there are legislatures to define property rights and courts to interpret and enforce them.

The importance of the Coase theorem is that it draws attention to the critical role of property rights. Many social problems result from ill-defined or nonexistent property rights. Consider air pollution as an example. If a copper mine dumped tailings on your yard, you would sue for damages or expect payment for the use of your land as a dump. Yet if the mine polluted the air, you would be helpless because you don't own the air above your land.

LARGE-NUMBER EXTERNALITIES. Even if property rights are well defined, there may still be problems from externalities. If there are large numbers of people sustaining damages or large numbers of firms doing the damage, the Coase theorem may not hold. The costs of organizing the involved parties may be too high

POLICY FOCUS: DOES A MARKET FAILURE ALWAYS REQUIRE A GOVERNMENTAL RESPONSE?

For years, apples and bees were used as a classic illustration of the externality problem. It was alleged that markets broke down because apple growers' orchards provided a positive externality (nectar) for bee farmers, but the orchard owners received no payment for this nectar. On the other hand, the bees provided pollinating services to orchard owners, but beekeepers were not compensated for this necessary service. As a result, a governmental policy of intervention would be needed to make orchard owners grow more nectar-yielding apple trees and beekeepers provide more pollinating bees.

Steven Cheung refused to take this classic illustration of market failure at its face value.[a] He went into apple orchards to determine if these two externalities did indeed produce market value. To everyone's surprise, except perhaps Cheung's, he found that the market worked quite well without government intervention. An active market for beehive placement was in operation. Where the nectar yield was great, beekeepers paid the orchard owner an "apiary rent" in order to place hives in these high-production spots. When the nectar yield was low, the orchard owner paid a "pollination fee" to induce beekeepers to place hives in these places. Cheung even found that beekeepers move hives to different states to pollinate crops in different seasons.

Cheung's study is important because it shows that markets can adapt well, and that market failure may be less widespread than might appear. The lesson for policy makers is that they should be very careful in determining whether market failure exists before proposing political or governmental solutions.

[a] See Steven N.S. Cheung, "The Fable of the Bees: An Economic Investigation," *The Journal of Law and Economics* (April 1973).

---

to make it worthwhile for the damaged individuals to sue for damages or organize a bribe. The individuals damaged would have to mount a door-to-door campaign, advertise in newspapers, and form a group for joint action. If the damaging firms are hard to identify, the problem is even greater. In an area with severe air pollution, it would be necessary to determine how much each of many firms contributes to this problem and who should be sued (or bribed). Because the information and transactions costs increase rapidly as the number of parties increases, it is often argued that the private actions embodied in the Coase theorem cannot fix the market failure that externalities create.

GOVERNMENT INTERVENTION AND EXTERNALITIES. Since the Coase theorem may not work, government intervention policies may be required to correct a negative externality. Policies usually take the form of direct controls, and such controls often lead to unfairness and inefficiency. Suppose the government requires all cars to have a pollution control device that costs $300. The outside salesperson who drives a great deal and, as a result, pollutes a great deal pays very little on a per-unit-of-pollution basis. In contrast, the retired couple who drives very little must pay the same $300, although they pollute very little. In addition, government policy affects the distribution of income. For example, as auto prices rise because of required pollution equipment, the poor are affected more than the rich because the poor spend a higher proportion of their income on cars.

Since government intervention almost always raises costs, it is important that policy makers are sure that the social costs are indeed worth correcting. Sometimes the government makes mistakes when it intervenes in markets, and these mistakes raise costs of production. Mistakes are to be expected because governmental decision making, like private decision making, is carried out by individuals with incomplete information, certain expectations, and facing certain incentives. Governmental decision makers aren't incentive-free; they simply face different incentives than private decision makers.

The federal government has often responded to calls to control negative externalities by creating regulations. These regulations impose costs on firms. The regulatory bodies themselves spend large amounts of money on enforcement. The costs imposed on firms are hard to estimate until the required action is actually taken. For example, a regulation to keep copper mines from polluting the air may cause them to close because of increased costs of production. In considering the costs of the regulation, an economist would examine its impact on the affected industry and region. Production may move to a state (or country) that has less stringent regulation. Some geographic regions may compete for industrial growth by offering fewer environmental regulations. Thus, in attempting to correct for the market distortions caused by negative externalities, government regulation can lead to other distortions.

Each call for regulation should be analyzed carefully. Some externalities may have already been corrected by market mechanisms. For example, houses near airports sell for lower prices because of airport noise. The people who buy these houses are freely choosing to do so because the lower price compensates for the noise. To change the law because these people don't like the noise would generate a windfall gain for them. It is not surprising that the residents should lobby for such a change, but it cannot be justified economically. The problem is complicated, however, by the fact that some residents may have purchased their homes before the noise became bad. These individuals lose twice. They suffer the cost of the noise and also a reduction in the value of their homes. It might make sense to compensate this group from an equity viewpoint.

A recent battle concerning negative externalities and the need for government intervention has taken place over cigarette smoking and the rights of nonsmokers. The issues involved in this political battle point once again to the property rights that are at the heart of most such questions. Most states and localities have passed laws prohibiting smoking in some areas (public buildings) and requiring nonsmoking areas in restaurants and other businesses that serve the public. Are such laws necessary? The laws are clearly necessary in the public buildings, but what about the private sector? If private demand for either smoke-free or smoking areas were high enough, some restaurants and other firms would fill the demand without the need for government action. In fact, some restaurants have done this without the pressure of laws because it meets a market demand. The recent opening of a motel chain for nonsmokers gives support to the feasibility of a private solution to some problems of negative externalities.

MARKETS FOR POLLUTION RIGHTS

More than a century ago, the famous economist John Stuart Mill wrote in his *Principles of Political Economy* (1862), "If from any revolution in nature the atmosphere became too scanty for the consumption,... air might acquire a very high marketable value." In the 1980s, he was proven correct as the market began to be used to allocate pollution rights. Economists have long argued for such a system rather than a regulatory approach. In 1970, Congress passed the **Clean Air Act**, which empowered the Environmental Protection Agency (EPA) to set stan-

Clean Air Act
A federal law passed in 1970 that empowered the EPA to set emission standards and impose standards on polluters.

dards for six pollutants and required each state to impose standards that would be met at each emission source. In other words, if emissions were to be reduced by 10 percent, all sources of the pollutant would have to be reduced by 10 percent. This act has since been renewed several times, most recently in 1990, and extended to more pollutants and greater reductions.

Some economists argued that it would be more efficient to allow the market to solve this problem. Marketing the right to pollute would make it possible to hold pollutants at the desired level and at the same time allocate them to the producers who were willing to pay the highest price. Firms that wished to expand production could do so only if the market value of their product enabled them to purchase the right to use the scarce commodity, air quality. In addition, if pollution rights had a value, firms would have the incentive to search for other ways to produce their products and for ways to control their emissions. If they discovered new methods of emission control, they could sell both the new technology and their pollution rights.

This idea came into use in the 1980s. In 1979, the EPA endorsed a "bubble" concept. The bubble concept measured pollution over a geographic area rather than individually for each polluter. It allows a group of plants in the same region to adjust their emissions to achieve regional clean-air standards. The economics of the idea is simple. If the plants in the bubble are all owned by the same company, the company achieves the desired level of pollution by shifting emission control from higher-cost to lower-cost sources until the marginal cost of control is the same at each source. This approach minimizes the total cost of pollution abatement. If the plants in the bubble belong to different firms, it is a bit more complicated, but the principle is the same. The plant manager with high costs of pollution control will look for savings by paying neighboring firms in the bubble whose costs are lower to cut their emissions more and sell some of their pollution rights. This approach achieves abatement in the bubble at the lowest cost.[3]

Such bargaining may seem difficult to achieve, but by 1987 there was evidence that a market in pollution rights was working. In California, several plants financed the installation of new technology that saved on emissions by selling their rights to pollute to other companies. These other companies found it less expensive to buy pollution rights than to purchase a more costly technology. In 1984, a private firm, AER*X, was formed to serve as a broker in pollution rights. In 1990, this firm had revenue of more than $1 million a year and was experiencing a rate of growth of more than 30 percent per year.[4]

The 1990 Clean Air Act makes use of the pollution rights concept. Acid rain is perhaps the biggest pollution problem the United States presently faces. The 1990 legislation proposed to solve this problem by setting annual limits on the emission of acid-producing pollutants. Under this act, 107 utilities, chiefly in the

---

3. For a more detailed discussion on the market for pollution rights and the bubble concept, see Bruce Yandle, "The Emerging Market in Air Pollution Rights," *Regulation* (July/August 1978): 21–28; M. T. Maloney and Bruce Yandle, "Bubbles and Efficiency," *Regulation* (May/June 1980): 49–52; and Bruce Yandle, "Community Markets to Control Agricultural Nonpoint Source Pollution," in Roger E. Meiners and Bruce Yandle, eds., *Taking the Environment Seriously* (Boston: Rowman & Littlefield, 1993).
4. For a discussion of AER*X, see Michael Weisskopf, "The Pollution Peddlers," *The Washington Post National Weekly Edition* (November 26, 1989): 9.

midwest, would be allowed to generate a certain level of sulfur dioxide every year based on the level of electricity generation. The utilities would be free to choose how to meet these standards. Those close to western sources of low-sulfur coal might switch fuels, and others might install anti-pollution technology. Still others might shut down. Beginning in 1995, the utilities would be free to sell their "allowances," regardless of how they had met them. By the year 2000, utilities in areas where more electricity was needed could purchase "allowances" from utilities in slow-growth areas. The Clinton administration can be expected, because of the environmental interests of Vice President Al Gore, to be active in the extension of the Clean Air Act. Early budget, health care, and NAFTA policy issues diverted attention from environmental legislation.

PUBLIC GOODS

Public goods have two important characteristics. First, once they are produced, no one can be excluded from consuming them. Second, they are not depleted by consumption. If someone consumes a public good, this action does not reduce the amount of the good available for others to consume. Economists refer to these two characteristics of public goods as *nonexcludability* and *nonrivalry*. Public goods were first introduced in Chapter 2. We expand on that discussion here because of the close relationship between public goods and externalities. These concepts are not really two separate and distinct arguments for government intervention policies. The arguments are actually the same. A public good is simply a good that has very strong external benefits that are nonexcludable and nonrival.

KEY IDEAS

MARKET FAILURE AND GOVERNMENTAL REMEDIES

MARKET FAILURE	EXAMPLE	GOVERNMENTAL REMEDY
Positive externality	Well-maintained houses	Zoning Fines Subsidies Deed restrictions
Negative externality	Pollution	Prohibitions Fines Selling pollution rights User fees
Public goods	National defense	Provision
Natural monopoly	Electric company	Regulation Taxation

PURE PUBLIC GOODS VERSUS PURE PRIVATE GOODS

A pure public good is one that is consumed (automatically) by all members of a community simultaneously. It is impossible to exclude individuals from consumption, and the good is perfectly nonrival. In contrast, a pure private good has a price equal to the full opportunity cost of production, and its consumption provides benefits only to the person (or group) that purchases the good.

It is difficult to come up with examples of pure public or pure private goods. No good is purely public because no good can be perfectly nonrival in consumption. Almost any public good, such as a road, a park, or a library, gets congested at some point and loses the characteristic of nonrivalry. At the other extreme, the more private a good is, the easier it is to exclude consumption. The more any individual consumes, the less there is for others to consume. A bottle of orange soda is a good example of a private good. A wilderness park might be an example of a public good if citizens consume the idea of wilderness it embodies, even though most of them don't ever visit it. Many of the appeals for the preservation of certain species or habitats are based on this idea. The spotted owl or the rain forest has an appeal for people, even those who do not go out and see the owl or walk in the forest. However, a theme park, such as Disneyland, can clearly be private, and an empty soda bottle on the side of the road is a public good in a negative sense—a public bad.

THE FREE-RIDER PROBLEM

Since nonexcludability is an essential feature of a public good, it is possible for individuals to consume such a good without paying for it. Economists call this behavior *free riding*. Since it is impossible (or at least costly) to exclude you from consumption of a public good whether you pay or not, you may choose to hide your demand for the good, let others pay for it, and still consume it. Thus, free riding makes it difficult for the market to measure actual demand. An example of a free rider would be a weekend sailor using Coast Guard markers to locate a safe channel into a busy harbor.

It is difficult to free ride in a small group, where everyone knows how much each person contributes and social pressure makes it costly for individuals not to contribute. In many rural communities, this type of social pressure is a way of overcoming the free-rider problem. If you don't help rebuild a barn that has been burned, you can't expect help from your neighbors if you run into problems. The free-rider problem, however, increases as the size of the group increases.

Because a public good is nonrivalrous and nonexcludable over a large group, it is likely that the market will not provide enough of the good. The free-rider problem can be better understood by examining Figure 4. For simplicity, assume that there are only two demanders of national defense. The two demand curves reflect the amount each is willing to pay for a given "quantity" of defense. If MC represents the marginal cost of national defense, the private market will produce Q_1 units of defense, which will be purchased by consumer b and consumed by both consumers a and b. However, the marginal benefits of additional units of national defense are determined by a vertical summation of the two individual demand curves. The result is a demand curve, $D_a + D_b$, for the public good national defense. This public demand curve reflects the combined

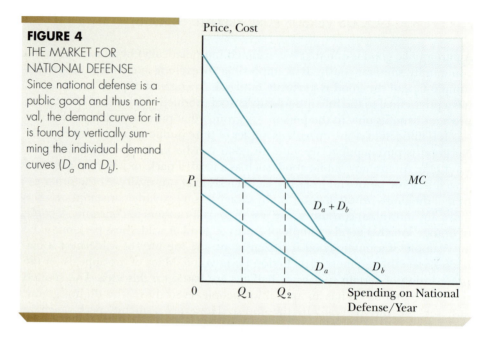

FIGURE 4

THE MARKET FOR NATIONAL DEFENSE
Since national defense is a public good and thus nonrival, the demand curve for it is found by vertically summing the individual demand curves (D_a and D_b).

marginal social benefits. We can now determine the optimal level of production of national defense. At price P_1, Q_2 units of national defense represent the efficient level of production. This public good solution is identical to the positive externality case examined earlier. Public goods are just a special type of externality problem. In this case, individuals have every incentive to hide their demand for national defense and consume amount Q_1.

Government financing of a public good overcomes the strategic holdout part of the free-rider problem. Forced tax collection compels the free rider to pay. It does, however, lead to another problem. In Figure 4, the two individual demand curves are summed to determine the "correct" demand for a public good such as defense. In reality, this demand is the demand of millions of people for the good. How could all their demand curves be measured? The answer to this difficult problem is that the political process reveals the demand for public goods. Voting for candidate x over candidate y is, at best, a very imperfect mechanism for determining the "correct" level of public good provision.

Volunteer groups can be more successful than governments in overcoming the free-rider problem and providing public goods under certain conditions. The group must be small—such as a small town, where peer pressure and visibility make free riding difficult. Volunteer fire departments and volunteer recreation programs flourish in small towns. In addition, clubs and associations can be formed to provide public goods. The condo association mentioned earlier provides public goods for its members. A second condition that allows volunteer groups to overcome the free-rider problem is the existence of private benefits blended with the social benefits. For example, members of a garden club working for city beautification may derive private benefits from both the companionship of other members and the personal enjoyment of a more beautiful town.

GLOBAL OUTLOOK: CHARGING FOR POLLUTION RIGHTS IN EUROPE

Among the nations that use a pollution rights approach to controlling water pollution are France, Germany, and the Netherlands. France uses a sewage tax on households and commercial enterprises to fund pollution abatement programs. Because the tax is based on the amount of water used, there is some link between the amount of tax paid and the amount of demand that a customer places on the waste treatment system. Charges to firms, which are also used to raise revenue for pollution abatement, are not linked as closely to the amount of waste discharged. France also uses fees for pollution abatement. By introducing the system through low charges on a few pollutants and gradually expanding coverage and increasing the rates, the French government has encountered very little political opposition to this program.

The German system is similar, except that it is administered by local governments. Charges depend on the type and size of the industry. Like France, Germany earmarks the revenues to pay for water quality improvement. However, economic efficiency only requires that the tax or charge be set so as to reduce the level of emissions to the socially optimal level. It says nothing about how the revenue should be used.

The Netherlands has a system of effluent charges that has been in use for more than three decades. Like France and Germany, the Netherlands earmarks the revenue for pollution abatement. Because effluent charges in this country are much higher than in the other two, however, it appears that the charges have had a significant effect on improving water quality. It is interesting to note that in the Netherlands, environmental groups have supported charges as a method of reducing pollution and industry has lobbied for a regulatory approach. These preferences seem to suggest that the market can be a very effective method of pollution control!

PUBLIC GOODS IN PRACTICE

Economists use the distinction between private and public goods to attempt to determine what projects and activities should be undertaken by the government when efficiency in the allocation of resources is the concern. The idea is to try to determine which markets might show a more nearly optimal level of output if government intervened in the process. This type of analysis is distinctly different from asking what projects and activities *will* be undertaken by government. In truth, the economic distinction between public goods and private goods has little to do with what goods and services government actually provides. Governments supply many goods that have the characteristics of private goods. At the same time, many goods that at least partly fit the definition of public goods are privately supplied by volunteer groups, nonprofit organizations, and clubs.

Politicians often incorrectly classify goods as public or private based on who supplies them. For example, trash removal may be considered a local public good even though it might be better classified in theory as a private good with some positive external effects. In fact, many goods supplied through local governments (such as recreation, education, trash removal, and police protection) could be supplied either privately or by government. The supplier may vary from one jurisdiction to another. The economist can ask what determines which goods a political unit will choose to supply, but this is a different question from whether these are public or private goods. An analysis of the political process as an interest-group activity is developed in the next chapter to address this question.

INCOME REDISTRIBUTION AS A PUBLIC GOOD

The argument for government redistribution of income is often based on viewing the activity as a public good, as we noted in the previous chapter. If a society decides that the income distribution resulting from the market is unsatisfactory, it can pursue deliberate redistribution. If income redistribution is a public good, less than the optimal amount of redistribution will take place in the absence of government intervention. Free riders will think that there is no need to help the poor because others will give. Voters, as a result, may decide to redistribute income through government and tax all citizens to achieve a more acceptable outcome than the market-produced outcome. The fact that government does some redistribution of income in most market economies suggests that such redistribution is widely viewed as having at least some characteristics of a public good.

EDUCATION AS A PUBLIC GOOD

It is easy to see how getting a college degree is an investment in human capital. Your income will be higher because you have developed marketable skills that make you more productive. Economists argue that most schooling is investment in human capital. According to this argument, education increases the productivity of the work force. This claim has been supported with a great deal of research that has shown the positive effects of education on economic growth.

If some of the return to education does not go to the individual student, individuals will not invest enough in education. This argument is based on the fact that trained and educated workers cannot directly capture all the gain from their education. Some of the benefits spill over to society in general. There is economic research supporting the view that primary and secondary education in particular appear to produce externalities that are not solely captured by the student. Much of this theory and empirical work is used to support an argument that education is a public good and should receive increased public financing. This funding argument is harder to make for higher education because much, perhaps most, of the benefits are captured by the student in terms of higher income levels. However, all states support colleges and universities that in turn charge lower tuitions to state residents.

WELFARE ECONOMICS

The body of economic theory that concentrated on market failures and sought remedies for them was developed in the 1930s, 1940s, and 1950s in the United States. This body of theory is part of a larger and older branch of economic theory that deals with normative policy prescriptions and is called *welfare economics*. Welfare economics was very optimistic in that it showed how these market failures could be solved by government action. It suggested the policy approach that government could and should intervene to correct for market failures. Collective choice through the political process would ensure that the society would (1) correct the externality, (2) produce the "correct" amount of the public good, (3) create an "equitable" distribution of income, and even (4) "fine-tune" the economy to a desired level of employment and price stability. This very optimistic theory envisioned collective choice and government operating to make the world a much better place through the use of enlightened economic policies. Practice showed that these policy actions were more difficult in practice than in theory. The next chapter will examine some of the problems associated with government intervention to correct market failure.

Consider again... Let's get back to the wolves, the ranchers, and the environmentalists. We could, of course, like Coase, just define the property rights. The government could arrest ranchers who shot wolves. But wolves live in out-of-the-way places. A ban on killing wolves is very difficult to enforce. A market solution is being attempted by one environmental group, Defenders of Wildlife. Defenders of Wildlife held a benefit concert featuring James Taylor and sold limited-edition prints of a family of wolves. They raised $100,000. In the first year of the program, they paid out $11,000 to ranchers who suffered losses due to wolf damage. To limit the potential damage, Defenders of Wildlife is educating farmers on how to protect their calves from wolves. They even bought a guard dog for one rancher. The lesson is clear. There must be some kind of compensation to remove the incentive that ranchers have to protect their valuable property. Environmentalists can provide that compensation by taking ownership in the endangered species they hope to protect. This lesson is not new. Ducks Unlimited and the Nature Conservancy have for years demonstrated how to internalize specific externalities, just like the ones caused by wolves.

SUMMARY

1. Laws, and changes in laws due to court decisions, have important impacts on economic incentives and thus on policy actions. Laws and their interpretation affect the allocation of resources in a market economy.
2. Externalities distort market outcomes because a cost or a benefit of the production process is not included in the economic decision-making process. This cost (or benefit) results in underproduction (or overproduction) of the good. The Coase theorem shows that natural market forces can solve problems of externalities if few people are involved and property rights are well defined.
3. Public goods are characterized by nonrivalry and collective consumption. Public goods can be produced by private groups. Not all goods produced by governments are public goods. Public goods are underproduced because some individuals will free ride.
4. Income redistribution and education are often viewed as public goods. Positive externalities are generated and individuals have incentives to free ride on the provision of redistribution and education.
5. Welfare economics is a body of economic theory that concentrates on market failure and develops a policy response to correct for the market failure.

NEW TERMS

property law
tort law
contract law
eminent domain
tort
externalities
social costs
internalization
Coase theorem
Clean Air Act

QUESTIONS: REVIEW, APPLICATIONS, AND POLICY

REVIEW

1. Distinguish between public goods as defined by economists and goods that governments provide for the public.
2. Why are tennis courts sometimes provided as public goods even though it would be relatively easy to exclude free-riding behavior?
3. Does football at Big Ten schools generate any externalities for students who attend these universities?
4. Why are the individual demand curves for public goods summed vertically rather than horizontally like those for a private good?
5. Why do indefinite or poorly defined property rights generate externalities?
6. What is welfare economics?

APPLICATIONS

7. Which of the following are public goods and which are private goods?
   a. National defense
   b. A lighthouse
   c. Income redistribution
   d. Education
   e. A Macintosh computer
   f. A Buick
   g. Medical care
8. Is education a public good? If not, why should taxes help to pay for the college education of some individuals?
9. What is free-riding behavior? Have you ever practiced free riding? Did it work? How could it have been prevented?
10. A main idea of the Coase theorem is that parties to a dispute have incentives to settle the dispute through negotiation. This idea has become standard fare in law school discussions of torts, property, and contracts. Professor Coase, in fact, wound up teaching in the law school at the University of Chicago. Can you think of reasons why some lawsuits would end up in court rather than being settled through negotiation?

POLICY

11. Does air or water pollution exist where you live? What should be done about it? Should the pollution be done away with entirely? How much more in taxes or higher prices for goods would you be willing to pay in order to have less pollution?
12. If you happen to live in a dorm or in an apartment populated by students, there is most likely a great deal of noise. Is there a Coase solution to this problem?
13. Suppose you were in charge of a government program to charge firms for the right to pollute. How *should* you set the price?
14. Which business firms will take action to reduce the amount they are polluting and which business firms will pay the fee you set in Question 13?
15. Will any of the firms on which you placed fees in Questions 13 and 14 be forced out of business? Which ones?

SUGGESTIONS FOR FURTHER READING

Mansfield, Edwin. *Microeconomics*, 8e. New York: W.W. Norton, 1991. An intermediate textbook with a solid chapter on externalities and public goods.

Posner, Richard A. *Economic Analysis of Law*, 4e. Boston: Little, Brown, 1992. The standard reference for the application of economics to legal issues.

Stigler, George J. *Memoirs of an Unregulated Economist*. New York: Basic Books, 1988. The memoirs of the Nobel Prize-winning economist provide a witty overview of the impact of theory on policy. Chapter 5 contains a delightful account of the development of the Coase theorem.

Tietenberg, Thomas H. *Environmental and Natural Resource Economics*, 3e. Boston: HarperCollins, 1992. A well-written textbook that deals with solutions to environmental pollution.

CHAPTER 32
GOVERNMENT FAILURE AND PUBLIC CHOICE

Consider this...*Imagine for a moment that you are the chief administrator of a public entity that has just received approval from its board of directors for a significant enlargement of its mission. The difficulty you face is that growth requires significant physical expansion: You need to build buildings. In order to build these buildings, you have to sell bonds to finance the construction. And in order to sell these bonds, the citizens in your area must vote themselves a tax increase. You are well aware that tax increases are hard to pass—just ask President Clinton. Is there anything you can do, besides the normal advertising and explaining of how important this expansion will be, that will increase your chance of success? This chapter might suggest a strategy. We will examine the effect of economic incentives on governmental policy decisions.*

LEARNING OBJECTIVES
1. Examine the implications of self-interested behavior in the public sector (public choice) as a cause of government failure.
2. Develop the concept of rent seeking.
3. Analyze the effects of rent defending.
4. Explain why government grows in terms of logrolling and bureaucratic incentives and why regulation creates a bias against new products and new technology.
5. List some of the methods of privatization.
6. Identify the contributions of the Austrian school and radical economics to understanding government failure.

PUBLIC CHOICE THEORY

Public choice theory is relatively new. A useful definition is provided in the 1993 annual report of the Center for the Study of Public Choice at George Mason University:

> Choice *is the act of selecting from alternatives.* Public *refers to people. But* people do not choose. Choices are made by individuals, and these may be private *or* public. *A person makes private choices as he goes about his ordinary business of living. He makes* public choices *when he selects among the alternatives for others as well as for himself.... While traditional economic theory has been narrowly interpreted to include only the private choices of individuals in the market process, traditional political science has rarely analyzed individual choice behavior. Public choice theory is the intersection of these two disciplines; the institutions are those of political science and the method is that of economic theory.*

Public choice theory is not as optimistic as traditional welfare economics (discussed in the last chapter) about the potential for government intervention to improve market outcomes. Public choice economists apply the same tools of analysis and assumptions to the collective choice process and to the private market. These economists recognize that there are market failures. They do not ignore externalities, public goods, unequal income distribution, and macroeconomic cycles. They do, however, demonstrate that collective choice and the intervention of government in the market do not work perfectly either. The weaknesses of the political process mean that government intervention does not work in the ideal way suggested by welfare economists. Public choice analysis begins with the assumption that people who act in a self-interested way when making personal economic decisions are the same people who vote, run for office, or are employed in the bureaucracy. Individuals bring their self-interest to the political process.

Public choice theory is as much political science as it is economics. Public choice analysis seeks to understand how economic incentives and individual self-interest affect political outcomes. For example, public choice economists expect the voter to be ill-informed because the cost of informed voting is extremely high. They view the politician as a vote maximizer, putting coalitions together to attract a majority of voters. Bureaucrats are not profit maximizers but seek instead to maximize budgets and/or to ensure the stability of their jobs. According to the public choice economist, the result of such self-interested behavior in the public sector is that government is an imperfect intervener in its attempt to correct for market failures. One of the most important insights that emerges from public choice theory is that small groups with strong interests will often get their way politically because it is irrational (unprofitable) for the majority to oppose them.

William C. Mitchell has succinctly summarized ten public sector biases that could produce this less-than-optimal intervention into the market.[1] This list provides a good foundation for understanding the thinking of public choice economists:

1. Proposals with long-delayed benefits are likely to be adopted only if their costs are unknown or can be deferred or concealed.
2. Proposals offering readily apparent short-term benefits and deferred costs stand a good chance of adoption.
3. Proposals that concentrate benefits and diffuse costs stand an excellent chance of adoption. (A direct majority voting system might induce the opposite, depending on the relative sizes of the individual tax share and benefit.)
4. Proposals to abolish programs or reduce public spending have a low probability of adoption. Electoral rewards go to politicians who propose new programs or expansions and extensions of existing programs.
5. Packages of reform proposals stand a better chance of adoption than individual reform proposals, even if none of the packages' components would be accepted by a majority of voters if considered separately.

---

1. William C. Mitchell, *The Anatomy of Public Failure: A Public Choice Perspective*, Original Paper No. 13 (Washington DC: International Institute for Economic Research, 1978).

6. Direct transfer programs, which clearly designate specific and limited benefits to certain persons or groups, stand little chance of adoption.
7. Proposals that rely on inefficient, complex, multiple revenue sources are preferred over those financed by simple, direct taxation.
8. Proposals that tax market efficiency stand a better chance of adoption than proposals that reward efficiency.
9. Proposals that limit consumption (such as price ceilings and rationing) as a response to product shortages are preferred over proposals that encourage increased production.
10. Policies that protect consumers by restraining producers are preferred over policies that simply improve the information level of consumers.

The implications of these biases for policy analysis are striking. Policy problems exist because two imperfect mechanisms are at work. The market fails because of externalities, underproduction of public goods, and business cycles. The collective political process fails because the participants are responding to incentives other than those assumed by the welfare economists. Policy makers must, therefore, choose between two imperfect mechanisms in attempting to solve any policy problem. The policy maker and voter must examine the biases inherent in both the market solution and the collective political solution. It will not always be clear that the cost of intervention is less than the cost of inactivity. Therefore, the public choice approach may lead to a prescription of no intervention in many cases, on the grounds that the cure could be worse than the disease.

RENT SEEKING

Economic rent is the economic return over opportunity cost. It was defined in the chapter on perfect competition as the payment to any productive resource greater than the amount necessary to bring that input into productive use. In the chapter on monopoly, we raised the issue of monopoly rent seeking, an additional economic cost incurred by firms seeking to establish monopolies. If you are uncertain about these two uses of the term *rent*, you should review the relevant sections of the earlier chapters.

We now want to look at the concept of rent seeking in a broader sense. **Rent seeking** is the commitment of scarce resources to capture returns created artificially (by government or quasi-government units). Rent-seeking analysis is used by economists to describe how people or firms compete for artificially contrived transfers. Consider the case in which a government decides to confer a monopoly privilege—for example, the contract for sole supplier of food services at a state university. A great deal of effort will be spent to obtain that contract. Lobbyists will work in the legislature, firms will make campaign contributions to legislators, and lawyers will draw up contracts. All these efforts are directed toward seeking a rent that has been artificially created by the state. None of this activity will cause the price of the contract to fall, as in the case in which rents are eroded by normal competitive forces. This rent seeking is a real cost to society because competition for governmentally created rents, unlike the "real" rents discussed earlier, does not generate increased supply.

Rent seeking
The commitment of scarce resources to capture returns created artificially.

FIGURE 1

THE COSTS OF RENT SEEKING

The deadweight loss of monopoly is the area of triangle ABC, but rent seeking could use up an amount equal to rectangle $P_c P_m AB$, as rent seekers compete for the monopoly right.

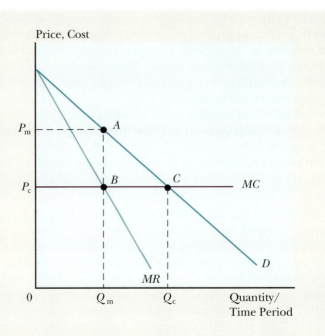

THE COST OF RENT SEEKING

Gordon Tullock, in attempting to measure the costs of rent seeking, was the first to develop the concept.[2] Figure 1 shows a market demand curve D yielding a competitive equilibrium (price P_c and quantity Q_c) and a monopolistic equilibrium (price P_m and quantity Q_m).

As you learned in the chapter on monopoly, the deadweight loss of monopoly is measured by the area of triangle ABC in Figure 1. The area of the rectangle $P_c P_m AB$ is supposed to be the transfer from consumers to monopolists in the form of monopoly profits. But Tullock argues that many of the resources represented by that area do not represent a transfer from consumers to producers. The spending to capture these profits turns them into a social cost of monopoly. In fact, if competition for the monopoly were vigorous, the area of rectangle $P_c P_m AB$ would be exactly equal to the resources wasted in competition for the monopoly privilege. The using up of economic rent in the "cost of capture" is unproductive in the sense that it uses scarce resources but does not generate any economic activity that lowers price or increases output.

LEGISLATION AND RENT SEEKING

Tullock's concept of rent seeking helps to explain government action as a form of self-interested behavior by politicians and voters. Many actions of people in government can be explained by this analysis. In fact, it might be argued that an

---

2. Gordon Tullock, "The Welfare Costs of Tariffs, Monopolies, and Theft," *Western Economic Journal* (now *Economic Inquiry*) (June 1967).

industry of rent seekers exists in most state capitals, and most certainly in Washington DC.

There are at least two broad applications of this rent-seeking theory to government actions. The first explains the types of government regulation. George Stigler described the benefits and costs to various interest groups of using the state as a vehicle to increase their own wealth.[3] Some groups, such as agricultural interests, seek income transfers from the state. Other groups, such as automobile producers, use the state to fend off regulation that would have a negative impact on costs and profit. In some cases, management and labor join together to use the state for their mutual benefit at a cost to consumers, such as in attempts to restrict imports.

The second application focuses on the economic behavior of legislatures. In this analysis, the politician is responsible for brokering transfers from one group to another. One can view the politician as an entrepreneur putting together coalitions of rent-seeking groups. Consider the public provision of education as an example. In the United States, education through the twelfth grade is mainly produced in the public sector. A public choice economist would argue that even if education is a public good, there is no reason to believe that representative democracy can create the incentives necessary to internalize the external benefits of education. Instead, such economists expect office holders to broker benefits to certain subsets of the population, including (but not limited to) members of the educational bureaucracy and organized student or parent groups. So, what started as a correction of market failure ends in a solution that is quite far removed from the optimal correction. It might reasonably be called government failure.

POLITICIANS AS RENT EXTRACTORS

In most of the literature on rent seeking, the politician is viewed as a broker for private rent seekers. Fred S. McChesney has focused on the politician as the rent extractor.[4] He sees the politician as an independent actor making demands to which the private sector responds. The politician first threatens to extract private rents through legislation that creates special taxes or new regulations. The private sector responds by striking bargains in the form of campaign contributions or other payments to protect its rent. As long as the cost of protecting the rent is less than the costs imposed by the threatened law, the incentive to strike such bargains exists. McChesney reports that this practice is so common that politicians even have a name for it. They refer to such legislation as "milker bills."

One example that McChesney used to support his argument was the Federal Trade Commission's used car rule. In 1975, Congress passed a law that ordered the FTC to initiate regulation of the warranties on used cars. The FTC developed a procedure that would have been costly for used car dealers. While the

---

3. George Stigler, "The Theory of Economic Regulation," *Bell Journal of Economics and Management Science* (Spring 1971).
4. Fred S. McChesney, "Rent Extraction and Rent Creation in the Economic Theory of Regulation," *Journal of Legal Studies* (January 1987): 101–118. For an interesting discussion of the rent extraction and rent defending that took place during the formulating of tax reform legislation, see Laura Saunders, "One Man's Problem Is Another's Opportunity," *Forbes* (March 7, 1988): 105–112.

procedure was being written, Congress legislated itself a veto over FTC action. After the FTC formulated its rule, Congress held hearings. Used car dealers and their trade associations descended on Congress. Congress in turn vetoed the FTC rule. What rent was extracted? McChesney reports that 89 percent of those in Congress who supported the veto and ran again in 1982 received contributions from the National Auto Dealers Association (NADA). The average contribution was over $2,300, and contributions were received by sixty-six members of Congress who had not previously been supported by NADA.

RENT DEFENDING

John T. Wenders has extended the analysis of rent seeking to how consumers also spend resources defending their consumer surplus from rent seekers.[5] Wenders recognizes that this activity might more correctly be called consumer surplus defending, but he prefers to label it **rent defending**. Consumers would be willing to pay an amount represented by the area of rectangle P_cP_mAC in Figure 1 to prevent the market from being monopolized. As you saw in an earlier chapter, that area represents consumer surplus. Consumer surplus is the extra utility that consumers gain because they pay less than they would be willing to pay for the item because all units are sold for the price of the last, or marginal unit.

Rent seekers and rent defenders are bidding for the same resources. Rent seekers are bidding for the monopoly privilege. Consumers are willing to spend a similar amount to prevent the rent seekers from acquiring a monopoly. Wenders shows that this situation is analogous to that of the Prisoners' Dilemma. If either party spends less, it will lose to the party spending more. This situation ensures that close to *double* the amount represented by P_cP_mAC in Figure 1 will be spent seeking the monopoly and defending the consumer surplus.

The concept of rent defending expands the analysis of rent seeking. The implication is that in some situations the cost of regulation is much higher than it is traditionally thought to be.

> **Rent defending**
> Actions by consumers to keep their consumer surplus from being captured by rent seekers.

ANALYSIS OF THE POLITICAL MARKET

According to the self-interest theory of government, the size of government increases due to rent-seeking activity by firms and individuals, and brokering activity by politicians. There are also other forces at work to influence the type of governmental programs that are created by politicians. Most of these forces tend to increase the size of government.

THE MEDIAN VOTER THEOREM

> **Median voter theorem**
> A theory that predicts that, under majority rule, politicians will reflect the positions of voters near the center of the political spectrum.

The **median voter theorem** predicts that under majority rule, politicians will adopt the positions of voters near the center of the political spectrum. To see why, refer to Figure 2. Assume that political preferences in society are continu-

---

5. John T. Wenders, "On Perfect Rent Dissipation," *American Economic Review* (June 1987): 456–459.

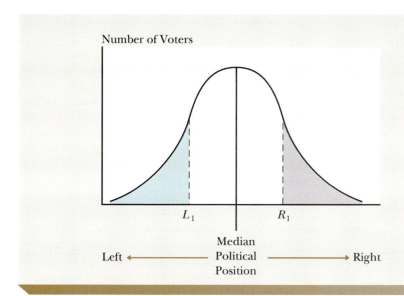

FIGURE 2

THE MEDIAN VOTER MODEL

If two politicians are running against one another, they will both move toward the median position to capture votes.

ous from left to right and distributed under the normal curve in the figure. If there are two candidates, R_1 and L_1, who are at equal distances from the center, they will get the number of votes represented by the area under the curve on their side of the median line. They tie at the polls. Candidate R_1 will realize that he can steal some votes by moving toward the median, because he can count on all the voters to his right. Candidate L_1 will realize what is happening, and she will also move toward the center in an attempt to get a majority of the votes cast. As a result, both politicians will end up near the median political position, where there are the same number of voters to the left and the right.

The median voter theorem can be used to explain why public spending is aimed at groups in the middle of the political stream, especially in a two-party system. Why, for example, do politicians promote programs to spend more money on education in general than they do for education for poor kids? The median voter theorem is also the basis of Stigler's and Tullock's argument presented in the chapter on income distribution—that most of the redistribution of income will be from the rich and the poor to the middle class.

LOGROLLING

When many issues are before a legislative body at the same time, the outcome most preferred by voters on some issues may not result. This failure is due to **logrolling**, which is a form of exchange in which politicians trade support on one issue for support on another issue. Logrolling is the direct exchange of support. The senator from Oklahoma votes for the military base in South Carolina in exchange for a vote by the senator from South Carolina for the water project that will make Tulsa a seaport.

Economists can't say much about the properties of logrolling except that it does not necessarily produce optimal levels of public output. The size of the budget is likely to be too large and its content may be altered as a result of logrolling. The overall outcome depends on the coalitions that surface. It is

Logrolling
Vote trading in the legislative process.

POLICY FOCUS: WHY ARE VOTER TURNOUTS SO LOW?

When election time rolls around, voters are bombarded with messages concerning their civic responsibility to vote. These statements are often accompanied by complaints about low voter turnouts for U.S. elections. You may even be told by your local newspaper's editorial writer that, "If you don't vote, you can't complain."

But think about it rationally for a minute. What are the costs of voting? You must register to vote. You must spend time getting to the polls. You must wait in line at the polls. Most importantly, you must spend time becoming informed on the issues and the candidates. What are the benefits of voting? It is possible that you might be able to affect the outcome, but the probability of your vote being important is tiny, especially in national elections. Perhaps you vote because you get a feeling that you have done your duty, or you receive satisfaction from participating in civic affairs. These feelings must be important, or even fewer people would vote. This is a consumption motivation for voting.

If we really wanted more people to vote, we would need to make it less costly to vote. In Europe, most countries vote on Sunday. Some states make election day a legal holiday to encourage voting. It's not clear whether this increases or decreases the cost of voting! If you don't think costs affect turnout, answer this question: Do more people vote when the weather is nice or when it is bad?

How could the cost of voting be lowered or the benefits increased? Some methods are postcard registration, transportation to the polls, and more voting places so that lines are shorter. Coffee and doughnuts at the polls might lure a few hungry voters, or rock bands might bring in younger voters (but perhaps keep older ones away). Recently, Texas has introduced what it calls, "No Excuse Voting." The polls are open for two weeks before the election. You can stop in anytime during these two weeks and cast your vote. This greatly reduces the cost of voting by making it more convenient.

If you think about it, perhaps you can suggest even more voter-luring techniques to your local election board. We might even reach the point where you could vote at home by using your touch-tone telephone. After all, if you can register for classes over the phone, why can't you vote over the phone? Maybe there are some people out there who are happy with low turnouts! Who might they be?

---

probably safe to infer that logrolling does not enhance the efficient use of resources.

It often is argued by economists that geographically based representative democracy and logrolling produce too much "pork barrel" government spending. This excess spending results because citizens see the cost of their local projects being shifted to citizens of other states or districts and reward their elected officials for delivering such projects. As most representatives attempt to be successful at this political game, logrolling creates larger than desired levels of government spending.

BUREAUCRATS AND BUREAUS

Once a governmental unit has decided how much of a public good to produce and how to pay for it, the legislature and the executive branch (president, governor, mayor) usually turn the job of supplying the good over to a bureau—a government agency or department. In a few cases, governmental units simply purchase privately supplied goods with tax revenue. A classic case of using private suppliers exists in Scottsdale AZ, where part of the fire protection is privately supplied and part is provided by the local government. Garbage removal is privately supplied in many communities. Often, however, a bureau is responsible for production of a good in the public sector.

The role of bureaus and bureaucracy creates many problems in supplying public goods. It is extremely difficult, if not impossible, to monitor the efficiency of a bureau. Bureaus do not usually produce measurable outputs. Instead, they produce activities. For example, a bureau might produce fire protection, education, or defense. When legislatures monitor these activities, they tend to examine spending rather than measure outputs. Citizens, however, are more interested in output levels. Sometimes there is a partial measure of output, such as the number of students educated or length of response time for fire-fighting units. But how can the value of the output of the Department of Defense be measured? The value of output must usually be inferred from the activity of the bureau, and that activity is most often measured by the level of expenditure. Thus, complaints about the quality and quantity of education or defense are generally reduced to calls for increased spending on the activity itself.

MONOPOLY PROBLEMS. The problem of monitoring bureaus is further complicated by the fact that bureaus are almost always monopoly suppliers dealing with a single purchaser, the government. This relationship makes the monitoring function of the government committee charged with oversight of the bureau difficult at best. The rationale for a monopoly supplier is that it avoids inefficient duplication. This reasoning may or may not be valid. However, the monitoring committee has no competing information by which to judge the bureau's efficiency.

This point has become a hot topic in debates concerning the public funding of education. Some leading policy critics suggest a voucher system as a way to introduce competition into public education. Under a voucher system, each student receives a "ticket" that can be used for tuition at any school. The hope is that the resulting competition will improve the quality and quantity of publicly financed education. Teachers as a group are opposed to the voucher system concept. If you think about it, a voucher system in primary and secondary education would be a lot like state support of higher education. The state "pays" public colleges and universities based on their enrollment, and the state colleges and universities compete with each other (and with private colleges) for students. It isn't a perfect analogy, but a fairly close one.

BUDGET MAXIMIZING. Still another problem in monitoring bureaus is created by the way in which bureaucrats are rewarded. As we discussed in a previous chapter, entrepreneurs or hired managers in the private sector generally lay claim to any profit and, therefore, have ample incentive to increase efficiency. In a public bureau, the manager has no such stake. In fact, it may even be that the bureau manager's salary is inversely related to efficiency. This perverse situation can result when salary increases are tied to the size of the budget and the budget grows (in part) because of inefficiency.

There are many possible goals that bureaucrats substitute for the private manager's goal of profit maximization. Among these other motivations are salary, perquisites of the office, power, public reputation, patronage, bureau output, ease of management, or investment in future private sector employment. Government officials need to keep these competing motivations in mind when they establish bureaus and when they evaluate bureau managers' behavior. There is an internal contradiction in expecting a government official to try to control the size of a bureau.

THE INHERENT BIAS AGAINST INNOVATION

Government regulation has a built-in bias against new products and new technology. This bias clearly exists in the area of food and drugs, and holds generally for any product that faces regulatory approval. The reason is that old products are on the market until they are proven too harmful, but new products cannot be introduced until they are proven safe. This requirement greatly retards innovation in some areas of the U.S. economy. For example, many U.S. citizens routinely travel to Europe or Mexico to receive innovative medical treatment. The list of innovative drugs not available in the United States is very long. Somatotropin for pituitary deficiency, disopyramide for heart patients, propranolol for blood pressure, and sodium valprote for epilepsy were all available in Europe five to ten years before they could be used in the United States.

Similar biases have existed for other products and techniques. For six years, Chemical Waste Management has sought permission to burn waste 140 miles at sea. The technique has been used in Europe for more than fifteen years. CBS's *60 Minutes* reported on a similar incident in Texas. A firm used a harmless predatory insect to keep harmful bugs out of stored grain. The insect replaced previously approved pesticides that some consumers found unacceptable. The FDA shut the firm down, ruling that the insect was an unapproved additive to the grain, even though its use was recommended by the Department of Agriculture.

Perhaps the most illuminating story about old versus new products relates to sugar substitutes. In 1977, the FDA proposed a ban on saccharin because it had been linked to cancer. Saccharin had been sold in the United States for almost a hundred years. The makers of saccharin fought the ban in Congress, and it was overruled. At the same time, it took G.D. Searle eight years and large sums of money to win FDA approval of an alternative sweetener, aspartame.

The moral of such stories is a simple one: Regulation has slowed the introduction of new products. Regulation may be having a significant impact on U.S. competitiveness in global markets. Peter Huber commented:

> *I strongly suspect that if Henry Ford had to bring out his Model T in today's environment, the courts and the regulators would have stopped him. Darn thing was dangerous; why you could break your arm cranking it. Of course, horses were dangerous, too, but as an established technology, horse transportation would have fared better in the courts and regulatory halls than transportation by new fangled flivver.*[6]

WHAT IS THE ANSWER?

These problems of government intervention lead to disturbing conclusions. You saw in previous chapters, especially the one on monopoly, that markets do not always produce ideal results. The chapter on market failure and government intervention added externalities and public goods to the list of market failures. But this chapter has shown that political action designed to correct market failure introduces a whole new set of problems. The net result is a messy one.

---

6. Peter Huber, "Who Will Protect Us from Our Protectors?" *Forbes* (July 13, 1987): 23.

Markets may fail, but governments also can fail. Government and government representatives do not always work in the public interest.

In fact, the conclusion of public choice theory is that there is no such thing as the public interest. It is instead correct to say the self-interest of groups working in the public sector. As we said in the beginning, this conclusion is not as optimistic as a political science approach that assumes that certain political actors have high "public interest" positions. Contrast, for example, what you have learned in this chapter to a traditional political statement such as, "It is time we start thinking about the common good and the national interest, instead of just individuals in this country."[7]

This view of government failure as a parallel to market failure has been widely accepted among policy makers and voters. The important point is that economists can attempt to identify market failure and government failure and allow policy makers to sort out the least harmful solution to policy problems that affect everyone.

PRIVATIZATION

One policy movement, often referred to as privatization, has worked against the tendency of governments to grow. **Privatization** is the transfer of governmental activities and/or assets to the private sector. Privatization has been increasing not only in the United States but worldwide. In England, the Thatcher government had a major program of privatizing numerous state-owned industries. In the People's Republic of China, "the reform of the basic tenets of the system" involves elements of privatization. In the United States, privatization has been done mostly by local governments, but the concept may spread to state and federal governments. U.S. cities and localities have used five methods to privatize services.

Privatization
The transfer of governmental activities and/or assets to the private sector.

KEY IDEAS

METHODS OF PRIVATIZATION

METHOD	OPERATION	EXAMPLE
Contracting	Government bids out activity	Cabs and buses
Franchising	Government grants franchise	Garbage pickup
Vouchers	Government gives "tickets" and public buys	Education
Subsidies	Government gives grants	Cultural activities
Tax Incentives	Government grants tax credits	Child care

The advantages of privatization are that it reduces government spending and is politically feasible because it does not eliminate the service. The spending reductions come from several sources:

---

7. Hillary R. Clinton, in a speech to the Association of American Medical Colleges, *The Chronicle of Higher Education* (November 17, 1993): 1.

1. Privatization introduces competition and the resulting efficiencies.
2. It permits smaller localities to join together into more efficiently sized units for purchasing services.
3. It removes government from labor negotiations and retirement commitments.
4. It transfers revenue-consuming activities to private firms that pay taxes and produce revenues.

Privatization can also result inadvertently from failure of governments to deliver a quality service. United Parcel Service's (UPS) success in competing with the U.S. Postal Service in delivering packages and overnight mail is perhaps the best example of such a governmental default. Privatization can be expected to be an important policy topic for state and local governments in the 1990s. The concept of reinventing or reengineering government makes heavy use of privatization. Federal government interest in this option may grow because "reengineering" government is a favorite policy topic of Vice President Al Gore.

AUSTRIAN AND RADICAL ECONOMISTS AND GOVERNMENTAL FAILURE

Public choice economists, whose ideas were outlined earlier in this chapter, apply microeconomic analysis to the political process. We now draw your attention to two other schools of economic thought. Both offer some useful insights on the appropriate role of government, policy making, and the nature of government failure.

THE AUSTRIAN SCHOOL

The Austrian school has its roots in the work of Ludwig von Mises and Nobel laureate F.A. Hayek.[8] Economists of this school start their analysis from the assumption that policy makers make economic decisions in a state of partial ignorance. Individual consumers and producers plan with incomplete and/or incorrect knowledge of the future. Markets play the role of providing feedback, which coordinates actions as individuals adjust their incorrect plans to changing relative prices. Individuals are frustrated, but by adjusting to changes in relative prices they are better off than they would have been before the adjustment.

The Austrian school is in many ways very close to public choice theory. Economists of the Austrian school argue that political manipulation of the economy is microeconomic in nature, rather than macroeconomic. In their view, politicians do not seek to influence the unemployment rate or the inflation rate, but rather try to influence certain markets for their own gain. For example, one politician may work to create subsidies for farmers. Another may work for aid to urban slum dwellers. The result of these actions is that the size of government increases, with many programs that are difficult to control, much less to reduce.

Economists of this school take a strong stand against governmental planning. This stand is based on four points made by one of the best-known mem-

---

8. A very good survey of the Austrian school can be found in Thomas Sowell's *Knowledge and Decision* (New York: Basic Books, 1981). In the United States, this school of thought is embodied in the Ludwig von Mises Institute, which has its offices at Auburn University.

GLOBAL OUTLOOK: RETURN TO SENDER IN GREAT BRITAIN

The British government is considering privatizing the post office, but they are treading very slowly. In 1980, Prime Minister Margaret Thatcher decided to distribute social security checks fortnightly (every two weeks) instead of weekly. The checks were distributed by post offices. Reducing the frequency of distribution would cut the preparation and distribution costs in half. Although it sounded like a sensible, cost-saving idea, the sub-postmasters, owners of small franchised post offices, balked because it would reduce their income. The Parliament panicked and Margaret Thatcher, perhaps the greatest privatizer of all time, retreated with the lame excuse that it was inappropriate to privatize something known as the Royal Mail.

Despite this earlier setback, the junior minister of the industry department, Edward Leigh, is back for another try. Over half of the sub-post offices lose money. The government hopes to convince them that privatization would permit them to pursue other money-making activities.

The problem is a simple one and one faced in all technologically advanced countries. The post office faces competition, even where it has a monopoly on the delivery of mail. There is competition from fax, competition from direct electronic data transmission, and, in England, from foreign bulk-mail service.

The issue is not a simple one. The delivery of mail by government has a long history. In England, the Royal Mail has delivered the post for centuries. It has existed by cross-subsidization of services. As the law now stands, private postal carriers can compete with the Royal Mail as long as they charge 1£ ($1.43) per item delivered. It is estimated that the cost of delivery of a letter in London is 12 pence (17 cents) per letter. So many private firms are interested in competing with the Royal Mail in the London market. But the cost of delivering an item to Barra is estimated to be 7£ ($10); there are not too many local firms interested in this business for $1.43 per item. So the issue, like so many public sector policy issues, is equity and income redistribution. Should businesses in London have to pay $1.43 per letter so the citizen in Barra can pay $1.43 rather than $10? Most of the public (64 percent in a recent poll) like the idea of a nationwide single-priced letter delivery service. So keep the monopoly, don't privatize!

The dilemma is that Londoners will stop using the Royal Mail and use other competing communication methods, such as the fax. The result will be that the monopoly will lose even more money, and the subsidy for the citizens of Barra will have to come from general tax revenue, rather than stamp fee cross-subsidies. The conservative government wants to privatize the postal service; the unions and the labor party are opposed. The most likely outcome is a slow movement to privatization, by allowing the price at which private carriers can deliver mail to decrease very slowly.

Source: "Post Office Privatization: Return to Sender," *The Economist* (February 13, 1993): 60.

---

bers of the school, F. A. Hayek. The first is that planning always results in more planning because people will circumvent the rules of the planner. As a result, the planner will devise more rules, which lead to more circumvention, which produces still more rules. Hayek referred to this process as "the road to serfdom." Hayek's second point about governmental planning is that no matter how detailed the plan, it can't cover all the specific cases. A bureaucracy will be needed to implement the plan. This bureaucracy will grow powerful and corrupt. Hayek's third point is that high morale is so important to the success of governmental planning that any critics of the plan must be silenced. Hayek's last point is that "the worst get to the top," that governmental planning leads to a dictator.

One of the great appeals of Hayek's work is that it describes the path followed by many countries that have tried central planning. The Austrian school would argue that the problems of the former Soviet Union and the People's Republic of China were caused by planning, and reforms such as those proposed by Gorbachev in the late 1980s were doomed to fail.

Perhaps the leading spokesman of the Austrian school in the United States is Murray Rothbard, who is a professor at the University of Nevada, Las Vegas. Professor Rothbard views conservative economists who are suspicious of government intervention as "wimpy moderates" because they do not view *all* government intervention as "not only ineffectual, but also pernicious, and counterproductive." Rothbard and the Austrian school are opposed to any intervention in the macroeconomy. Although they believe that money matters in the economy, they don't think that monetary policy can be carried out because it requires impossibly precise assumptions about the economy.

RADICAL ECONOMIC THOUGHT

Unlike the Austrian school, radical economists are critical of both the market and government in a capitalistic system. Radical economists in the United States draw on the tradition of Karl Marx and Marxist thought. These economists do add several new lines of attack on capitalism.[9] The basic difference between radical economics and other schools of economic thought is that most other economists see a basic harmony in the economic system and believe that most problems can be solved by relying on market forces. However, radicals contend that solutions to the problems of modern capitalism can only be found by restructuring industrial capitalism. In addition, radical economists regard orthodox economists as being much too narrow in their analyses.

The main themes of radical economics are monopoly power, state power, exploitation, imperialism, and waste and alienation. Radicals believe that the U.S. economy is dominated by large corporations and that small firms play an insignificant role. They believe that these large corporations set arbitrary prices and manipulate consumer wants. The state is viewed as the protector and fostering agent of the powerful monopolies. The radicals see the federal government as controlled by big companies. They believe that the state sets economic policy, including defense spending, in the interest of big business.

Radicals, unlike Austrians, are very critical of the private sector. For example, they challenge the marginal productivity theory of income determination (discussed in an earlier chapter). Radicals argue that monopolistic firms, unequal opportunity, and the unjustifiable private ownership of capital make this theory defective. They base their description of incomes on dual, or segmented, labor markets. **Dual labor markets** result from artificial barriers in labor markets that trap some workers in jobs with low wages. Radicals argue that these two labor markets consist of one in which pay is good and advancements are possible, and a second in which pay is low and opportunities for advancement are nonexistent. These dual labor markets are a result of a conscious effort on the part of capitalists to restrict advancement to certain groups in the labor force. As a result, a large fraction of the labor force is doomed to dead-end jobs for life, with low pay, little job security, and no opportunities for advancement.

Finally, radicals argue that resources are wasted in a capitalistic system. This waste is the amount of money spent on such items as expensive autos, furs, alcohol, and drugs, as well as the billions of dollars spent on advertising, which

Dual labor markets
The existence of two separate labor markets because of artificial barriers that keep some workers earning low wages.

---

9. Most radical economists in the United States are members of the Union of Radical Political Economy (URPE). URPE publishes a journal, *The Review of Radical Political Economics*, which you can check if you are interested in learning more about radical economics.

radicals claim is used to manipulate consumer wants. Radicals argue that this waste and the power of monopolies contribute to alienation. Since individuals have little control over their destiny, they consume high levels of unnecessary consumer goods and feel alienated from society.

Radical economists have challenged the mainstream to examine more closely some of the weaknesses of capitalism. The response of most economists has been to not take the radicals too seriously (or to ignore them completely). Radical ideas have, however, led to suggestions for "tinkering" with capitalism in some areas, especially in control of monopoly power. The radicals have also provided useful insights into how special-interest groups use government to serve their own self-interests. These insights are not unlike those of public choice economists. The most serious weakness of the radical economic critique of capitalism is that it has concentrated on criticism without offering feasible solutions.

***

Consider again... *Return to the public bond issue that you are in charge of getting passed. Is there anything you might do to help your own cause? A good example of what you might do just occurred in Tarrant County TX. Tarrant County Junior College (TCJC) wanted to build an additional campus. They received approval from their governing board and then had to go to the voters in a bond election to have them approve a tax increase to pay for the campus. Tax increases are not easy to pass! There are a few people who will gain from the tax increase. Students who will attend certainly will gain. But most potential students aren't even of voting age yet. Faculty and staff will gain. Most of them haven't been hired yet. Certainly there are enlightened business people and citizens who favor education and will come to the polls and support the bond issue. There are, however, a lot of people who will lose through higher taxes. They will lose only a little because it is a very small tax increase and it is spread over a very large county.*

Therein lies a strategy. Pick a time for the election when the bond issue is the only item on the ballot. That is exactly what the administration of TCJC did. They could have picked a special election held in Texas to pick a new U.S. senator. They could have picked a time when there were city and county elections all over Tarrant County. But they didn't; they picked a Saturday in July when the bond issue was the only thing on the ballot. Those people who had a direct interest in the expansion of TCJC turned out and voted for the bond issue. The larger group of voters who would have had an interest in the U.S. Senate election and/or had an interest in the city elections did not go to the polls. They were uninterested or maybe didn't even know there was a special bond election.

So you see, voter turnout is a double-edged sword. It depends who's side you are on. Sometimes policy makers might be just as happy if some voters stayed home!

SUMMARY

1. Public choice theory identifies biases in the political process and applies economic analysis to political processes and outcomes.
2. Rent seeking is the economic description of individuals' use of the political process to generate income transfers to themselves or to groups they support. Politicians can threaten to pass taxes or regulations in order to extract rents from private parties.
3. Rent defending is the process by which consumers attempt to defend their consumer surplus from rent seekers.
4. The median voter theorem suggests that, under majority rule, politicians will adopt positions near the middle of the political spectrum. Logrolling in a legislature increases the size of budgets. Legislators agree to vote for a colleague's project in return for a vote on their project. Bureaucratic decision making is different from firm decision making because bureau managers face a different set of incentives than private sector managers do. All of this type of behavior tends to increase the size of government. Government regulation introduces a bias against new products and new technology.
5. Privatization of government assets or activities permits provision of goods and services to be done more efficiently by relying on market (and other) forces.
6. The Austrian school of economic thought assumes that decision makers proceed on the basis of incorrect and/or incomplete information. The school makes a strong case against economic planning by governments. Radical economics, which is related to Marxism, is based on the belief that monopoly capitalism, protected by government, is manipulative and exploitative. Both groups have added to our understanding of government failure.

NEW TERMS

rent seeking
rent defending
median voter theorem
logrolling
privatization
dual labor markets

QUESTIONS: REVIEW, APPLICATIONS, AND POLICY

REVIEW

1. Why do bureaucracies not always serve the public interest?
2. What is the Austrian school's argument against governmental planning?
3. How do radical economists challenge the marginal productivity theory of income distribution?
4. What is public choice theory?
5. Why do public choice economists argue that direct transfer programs that clearly target a limited group stand little chance of adoption?
6. Why is it so hard to cut public programs once they are started?

APPLICATIONS

7. Why, according to public choice theory, is it not rational to vote?
8. Why do members of the Austrian school take such a strong stand against central planning?
9. How can politicians be rent extractors?
10. How can logrolling increase the size of government?
11. Is public choice theory pessimistic? What is its criticism of welfare economics (discussed in the preceding chapter)?
12. Is it possible for interest groups in Washington to engage in logrolling? How would they do it?

POLICY

13. When the late Governor George Wallace of Alabama was campaigning for the U.S. presidency, he was fond of saying that there wasn't a "dime's worth of difference between the other candidates." Does his claim make any economic sense?
14. Should the government intervene in every case in which an externality exists?
15. Why do government programs that concentrate benefits and diffuse costs have a better chance of being enacted than those that benefit many and impose costs on a few?

SUGGESTIONS FOR FURTHER READING

Buchanan, James M., and Robert D. Tollison. *The Theory of Public Choice-II*. Ann Arbor: University of Michigan Press, 1984. This book contains a series of articles related to applications of public choice theory in various policy questions.

Frey, Bruno S. *International Political Economics*. New York: Basil Blackwell, 1984. This book applies public choice theory in an international setting.

Heilbroner, Robert L. *The Nature and Logic of Capitalism*. New York: Norton, 1985. A critical look at capitalism from a (traditional) liberal perspective.

Lindbeck, Assar. *The Political Economy of the New Left: An Outsider's View*, 2e. New York: Harper & Row, 1977. Presents a critical review of the radical economics movement.

Osborne, David, and Ted A. Gaebler. *Reinventing Government*. New York: Addison-Wesley, 1992. A book on making government more efficient that captured the minds of many in state government and motivated Vice President Gore's program to reengineer government. Gore calls it his bible.

Saporita, Bill. "The Most Dangerous Job in America." *Fortune* (May 31, 1993): 131–140. A report on crab fishing in Alaska and how governmental regulation makes the work more risky, rather than less risky.

Vickers, John, and George Yarrow. "Economic Perspectives on Privatization." *Journal of Economic Perspectives* (Spring 1991): 111–132. A very thorough review of the reasons and methods for privatization of public firms and activities.

CHAPTER 33
POLICY STUDIES: CITIES, THE ENVIRONMENT, AND HEALTH CARE

LEARNING OBJECTIVES

1. Explain optimal city size in terms of economies and diseconomies of agglomeration and demonstrate how the provision of local public goods is complicated by spillovers.
2. Use housing and transportation to explore various blends of private and public roles in the provision of urban services.
3. Explain the role of the tragedy of the commons, inadequate information, and sovereignty issues in making some kinds of environmental issues difficult to address and solve.
4. Identify the economic issues in health care cost increases.
5. Evaluate the Clinton proposal for policy reform of health care.

Consider this... *In August 1993, two seemingly unrelated events were covered in television news programs every evening and in the newspaper every morning. One story concerned the emerging Clinton health care policy being developed under the direction of Hillary Rodham Clinton. The second involved the story of seven-weeks old Amy and Angela Lakeberg. Amy and Angela were Siamese twins born in Wheatfield IN. The twins shared a defective heart and liver tissue. Doctors at Children's Hospital of Philadelphia performed very costly experimental surgery to separate the twins. The doctors knew one would die on the operating table and the other had less than a 1 percent chance of surviving. Amy died in surgery.*

For several days the public was bombarded with news of Angela's progress. Her parents were regulars on morning talk shows. After a short period, Angela also died. The total cost of the hospital stays and surgery was estimated to be about half a million dollars. The Lakeberg family had no insurance and local fundraisers stepped in to help with their mounting medical bills. In the first few days, more than $15,000 was put in a local bank account. About the time of Amy's funeral, news coverage revealed that the twins' father, Kenneth Lakeberg, had spent $8,000 of the donations on a car and a three-day cocaine binge. Lakeberg went on television and said he was sorry and admitted that those who gave money were "probably disappointed and upset, probably a little mad."

In the weeks that followed, many reporters, editorial writers, and citizens reflected on the ethics involved in this case. Who should decide who gets expensive medical treatment? One critic argued that it wasn't fair to spend that kind of money on the twins when the chance of survival was so low. The same money spent on vaccinations would have saved hundreds of children.

The policy dilemma is an important issue. And the two events are related. Health care policy is about who gets expensive health treatments and who doesn't get them. After studying this chapter you will better understand these difficult trade-offs. This chapter applies the theories discussed in the last two chapters to three real-world concerns: urban problems, the environment, and health care.

URBAN ECONOMICS AND POLICY ISSUES

The issues facing urban America are often not unique to cities but are simply more severe there. For example, pollution and crime are found in all parts of the world, but they are more serious problems in urban areas. Pollution, crime, and other negative externalities associated with living in cities are examples of market failures that government intervention policies have failed to solve. Government failure occurs when policy responds to market failures in a less-than-optimal way. In this case, market failure consists of the negative externalities associated with population density. These externalities include crime, traffic congestion, environmental pollution, and noise pollution, to name a few. In addition, provision of public goods in many urban areas is complicated by the large number of political divisions.

In the 1970s, population growth in cities was slower than that in rural areas and in suburbs. The 1980s saw a reversal of this trend, with population growth in cities exceeding growth in areas outside of cities. Also during the 1980s, the Reagan administration sharply reduced the amount of federal government transfers that had been going to U.S. cities. In 1992 the urban problem again came to the forefront with the Los Angeles riots that followed the Rodney King beating trial. Much was promised by politicians, but little was accomplished and the L.A. situation has evaporated into the background. The election of Bill Clinton was cheered by most big-city mayors, as they expected him to be an advocate of federal spending for city problems.

HOW LARGE SHOULD A CITY BE?

Cities come in all sizes, both in population and in land area. There are very small cities that seem to offer their residents a satisfactory collection of public and private goods and services. Very large cities often offer a greater variety of services and attractions to residents and visitors. The most desirable size for a city depends on the balance between the advantages and disadvantages of a large population.

ECONOMIES OF AGGLOMERATION. Urban areas develop because of economies of scale. Urban economists use the more specific term **economies of agglomeration** to describe the cost savings that people enjoy when enough of them locate in one relatively small area. The reasons are similar to the reasons for cost savings to a firm when economies of scale exist. The savings result because the size of the city yields enough local demand for highly specialized suppliers. In addition, large pools of specialized labor exist in urban areas, again because the demand is large enough to attract enough workers.

The broadcasting industry is a good example of this principle at work. Broadcasting is concentrated in New York City and Los Angeles. This concentration represents demand for writers, actors, musicians, dancers, technicians,

Economies of agglomeration
The cost savings that individuals enjoy when enough of them locate close together in or near a large city.

807

directors, designers, and for firms that specialize in the equipment these people use. Start-up costs for new firms are lower because suppliers are close at hand. New artists locate in these areas in order to take advantage of the large number of job opportunities.

Economies of agglomeration usually take the form of efficiencies in production and information gathering. However, agglomeration can also result in a wider variety of consumption alternatives—more variety of restaurants, entertainment, and shopping. This wider range of choices can attract residents and lead to further agglomeration. Although some costs are lower as agglomeration takes place, others increase because of **diseconomies of agglomeration**. There are both negative and positive externalities associated with urban growth. The two most obvious negative externalities are crime and pollution.

Diseconomies of agglomeration
The additional costs that individuals must pay when too many of them locate in one city (thus creating negative external effects for one another).

OPTIMAL CITY SIZE. Since there are economies and diseconomies associated with agglomeration, there should be some optimal city size. This optimum is the size at which the value of the benefits exceeds the total cost of the negative externalities by the greatest amount. In terms of microeconomic theory, the optimal size is that for which the marginal agglomeration benefits are equal to the marginal agglomeration (congestion) costs. The optimal size of a city changes as these costs and benefits change. For example, if new technology made crime prevention cheaper, the model would predict an increase in optimal city size. If technology reduced the diseconomies of agglomeration, optimal city size would increase. In addition, to the extent that demand for the consumption activities supplied by cities is income-elastic, the incomes of residents and potential residents will affect the optimal size of that city. An increase in income will increase the optimal size of urban areas, *ceteris paribus*.

The decision about optimal size will be made by thousands of individuals. Migration into and out of cities is driven by individual decisions about the value of the positive and negative externalities associated with city size. Differences in tastes and preferences ensure a variety of sizes of cities. Most economists would argue that such a decentralized process is superior to some governmental decision about how large a city should be. Policy makers can, however, have some influence on city size through zoning, taxes, and transportation systems. They may move a city's size toward or away from the optimum by changing the costs and benefits people face in locating there. Both market forces and policy decisions determine the optimal size for each city, and the optimum is always in a state of flux.

SMALL TOWNS AND LARGE CITIES. Large cities in the United States continue to grow, but much of the U.S. population still lives in smaller towns and cities that lack both the attractions and the problems of New York, Detroit, or Houston. Many of these smaller towns have lost population. The booming main streets of the first half of the twentieth century have given way to many empty storefronts as retail outlets have moved to malls that serve a cluster of small towns in a single central location. Economies of agglomeration in retailing have led to the centralization of shopping at the expense of small-town main streets.

NEW SUBURBS. Historically, suburbs grew outside the central city, but most suburban residents commuted there for work, entertainment, and shopping. This pattern has changed as the information age is decentralizing cities, and it is no longer as necessary to commute. All kinds of businesses have moved out of the city and into the suburbs, where, among other things, the rents are cheaper. Barbara Boggs Sigmund, the mayor of Princeton NJ, refers to these new suburbs as "urbanoid villages." Sigmund is critical of urbanoid villages, arguing that they breed traffic, fail to deliver services, and hinder rather than promote community.[1]

URBAN PUBLIC GOODS AND THE SPILLOVER PROBLEM

Public policy to solve urban problems is complicated by the number of political entities involved in these areas. For example, metropolitan Atlanta has fifty-three separate local governments. These governments do not always cooperate and are often in direct competition for projects and development funds. This competition can lessen the potential for government failure by making governments more sensitive to voter demand. But it can also contribute to government failure by making it harder to overcome the free-rider problem when supplying public goods.

Supplying public goods is more difficult when there are many local governments in an urban area. With many political subdivisions, the external benefits of the provision of a public good may spill over into different jurisdictions, making it harder to collect payments from all who benefit. Urban public spending combines public goods and externality problems. For example, Figure 1 represents the demand for crime prevention by two groups of citizens in a political subdivision of an urban area. D_a represents the demand of group a, and D_b the demand of group b. Since crime prevention is a public good, it is subject to the free-rider problem discussed earlier. The true demand curve, which represents

1. Betsy Morris, "New Suburbs Tackle City Ills While Lacking a Sense of Community," *The Wall Street Journal* (March 26, 1987): 1.

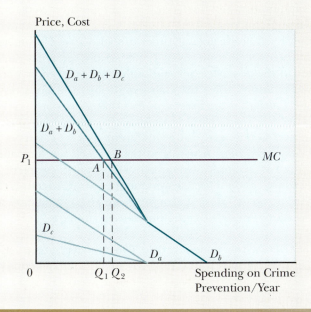

FIGURE 1

THE MARKET FOR CRIME PREVENTION
Crime prevention is a local public good. If D_a and D_b represent the demand of two groups within a jurisdiction, the optimal amount of crime prevention is Q_1. However, if some of the benefits spill into other jurisdictions and the demand of residents in the other jurisdictions is represented by D_c, the optimal amount of the public good is Q_2.

social marginal benefits, is found by vertically summing the two demand curves. The socially optimal provision of the public good is amount Q_1 at price P_1. Assume for a moment that it is possible to overcome the free-rider problem and that the citizens of the subdivision vote to tax themselves an amount equal to rectangle $0P_1AQ_1$ and supply the optimal amount of crime prevention.

The optimal amount of crime prevention will still not occur if some of its benefits spill into other jurisdictions. Figure 1 illustrates the spillover problem. D_c represents the demand of people who live in the urban area but outside the political subdivision for crime prevention. They have a demand because they come to work and/or shop in the subdivision. In addition, they live close enough to fear that criminal activity might easily spread to where they live. Since they do not vote and pay taxes in the subdivision, their demand is not incorporated into the political decision to supply amount Q_1. If it were, the demand curve (again a vertical summation) would be $D_a + D_b + D_c$ and the optimal amount of spending on crime prevention would be equal to rectangle $0P_1BQ_2$. The conclusion of this analysis is that internalizing externalities within a political subdivision becomes much more difficult when benefits spill over to adjacent political units.

SOLVING THE SPILLOVER PROBLEM. Revenue sharing, or grants from higher to lower levels of government, is one way to overcome the spillover problem and increase the provision of goods with positive externalities. The state or federal government can help overcome such local urban problems through the use of grants. In the 1970s, this type of grant was very popular. In 1979, 38 percent of the revenue of U.S. cities came from higher levels of government, mostly the federal government. The Reagan administration reduced such grants, forcing urban governments to rely increasingly on their own sources of revenue.[2] By 1990, grants accounted for only 22 percent of local revenues.

Fiscal conservatives are critical of grants from higher to lower levels of government for two reasons. First, they argue that the federal government should not transfer such funds when the federal budget has huge deficits. Second, they argue that these grants make local officials less fiscally accountable than they would be if they had to raise taxes in order to spend. Proponents argue that such grants can redistribute income from richer to poorer areas and compensate cities for some of the positive externalities that are enjoyed by nonresidents.

User charges
Fees that cover part or all of the cost of a public service.

One possible way to solve the spillover problem without resorting to revenue sharing is through **user charges**, or fees that cover part or all of the cost of a local public service. User charges can finance some public goods, at least partially. Local governments can charge different fees to residents and nonresidents. This type of payment schedule works very well for recreational and cultural programs. For example, Greenbelt MD requires proof of residence in order to pay a lower resident fee for swimming lessons and tennis classes at community recreation areas. Most state universities have a tuition schedule that charges less to state residents than to out-of-state students.

THE TIEBOUT SOLUTION. In a famous article, Charles Tiebout argued that the provision of local public goods is best done by small homogeneous jurisdictions.[3]

---

2. See Richard P. Nathan and Fred C. Doolittle, "Federal Grants: Giving and Taking Away," *Political Science Quarterly* (Spring 1985): 53–74.
3. Charles M. Tiebout, "A Pure Theory of Public Expenditures," *Journal of Political Economy* (October 1956): 416–424.

The smaller the jurisdiction, the more responsive the government will be to its citizens. Citizens in an urban area will choose to live in a certain jurisdiction by buying into its package of local public goods and tax prices. For example, in the Washington, DC, area, households can choose to live in the District or five adjacent counties—two in Maryland and three in Virginia. Each offers different tax levels, transportation services, housing quality, and local public goods.

Tiebout argues that a market exists for local public goods in which consumers "vote with their feet" by moving to areas that provide satisfactory combinations of taxes and services. Further, he argues, the price of housing in an area will reflect the relative desirability of what is offered to the voter-consumers. The **Tiebout hypothesis** is that voters will influence local public goods through their choice of locations. This idea is closely related to the concept of privately supplied public goods discussed in the chapter on market failure. Competition among suppliers of local public services (local governments) forces them to offer more desirable combinations of spending and taxing, since people will migrate to those jurisdictions that have the most attractive mix. In such a situation, elements of markets (competition and choice) blend with elements of government (tax-financed services) to overcome some of the problems of both government and governmental failure.

Tiebout hypothesis The idea that competition among local governments as suppliers of local public services will force them to offer the desired combination of spending and taxing to voters, who will migrate to those jurisdictions that produce that combination.

PRIVATE-PUBLIC POLICY MIX: HOUSING AND TRANSPORTATION

Housing and transportation are two policy issues that face most cities. Both issues present valuable case studies of the difficulty of solving urban economic problems.

PRIVATIZING: THE CASE OF LOW-INCOME HOUSING.
One strategy used by some cities to hold down their tax burdens is privatization, or shifting production of some services to the private sector. Low-income housing is an example. Federally funded programs to provide public housing in the 1960s and 1970s produced very unsatisfactory results in most cities. It was usually easy to identify "the project" by its many boarded-up windows and slumlike appearance. Indeed, in many cities the housing projects built in the late 1960s have been abandoned. Some have even been torn down.

The Local Initiative Support Corporation (LISC), with financing from the Ford Foundation, has tried a different approach—privatizing the process of supplying low-cost housing. The result is low-income housing that has a blend of public and private financing. LISC works with local community groups to determine what is needed in housing. These local groups use public money, foundation grants, and loans from private mortgage lenders to rebuild an area. The group then takes ownership of and manages the housing units. The results have been impressive. Pride of ownership (due to transferable property rights) has meant better maintenance, and these rebuilt areas have become models that other cities can emulate. The key element has been incentives at the tenant level, resulting in tenant associations that maintain and police the areas.

IS MASS TRANSPORTATION A PUBLIC GOOD?
Many cities are expanding or building new mass transportation systems. These systems can cover an entire metropolitan area, in some cases crossing city or even county lines. For example, the Metropolitan Atlanta Rapid Transit Authority (MARTA) runs bus and train service from distant suburbs into downtown Atlanta. Perhaps the "snazzi-

est" urban mass transportation system is the Metro in Washington DC. The system features clean facilities (in contrast to the subway in New York City) with a space-age look. In 1994, the Washington Metro was a forty-seven-mile system. It will have cost more than $6 billion when it is complete. Some critics have joked that it would have been cheaper to buy every citizen of the District of Columbia a new Mercedes automobile![4]

Are such systems worth the cost? Proponents argue that mass transportation is a public good. Positive externalities are produced by urban bus and subway systems. Low-cost transportation increases population density, which increases the urban tax base. Economic development increases because the dense population attracts businesses. The transportation network also allows the labor force easier access to work sites. Finally, mass transportation reduces air pollution, congestion on the roads, and parking problems. During the energy crisis, an important argument for building mass transportation networks was that they use less of scarce energy resources. Proponents claim that all these positive externalities are of sufficient value to make the benefits of mass transportation exceed the costs of construction.

Critics disagree. They argue that subsidized public transportation transfers income from taxpayers to users of the system. The systems represent a subsidy to riders. Critics say that proponents have exaggerated the benefits of such systems and that the costs actually exceed the benefits. For example, the benefits of low-cost transportation in allowing the density of the population to increase are often offset by higher land prices as the demand for urban housing increases. As a result, those who benefit most from public transportation are land owners in the urban area. There is also little evidence that road congestion and air pollution are much improved by such systems. In fact, after the Metro opened, some studies showed that rush-hour traffic into the District of Columbia actually increased.

Transportation, parking, and road congestion are problems facing all urban policy makers. The debate over mass transportation hinges on determining a value for its positive externalities. These benefits must then be weighed against the costs of the project. Conflicting views arise even among economists because it is very difficult to put an accurate monetary value on a positive externality.

The majority of Americans now live in an urban environment. Many are concerned about the spillovers that occur when people live close together: noise, pollution, crime, congestion, and other urban problems. As urban populations have grown in the United States and throughout the world, total world population and economic activity have also grown. This growth has created more pressures on scarce resources and more external effects that spread over greater distances of time and space. Concern about these issues has led economists and others to expand their focus beyond rural and urban environments to the global environment.

ENVIRONMENTAL POLICY ISSUES

The 1990s have already been labeled the decade of the environment. Concerns exist about massive oil spills, depletion of the ozone layer, exhaustion of nonre-

---

4. See David M. Steward, "Rolling Nowhere," *Inquiry* (July 1984): 18–23.

newable resources, acid rain, the greenhouse effect, destruction of tropical rain forests, and the pressure of world population on a fragile ecological system. Critics argue that environmental problems result from failure to plan far enough ahead or to consider the needs of future generations. The market system does not plan for the long term. Governments have attempted to intervene to protect the environment for future generations, but these policies to correct market failure bring their own problems.

Many forms of pollution have market-based solutions based on assignment of property rights. When the negative externalities and the number of people affected are small, it is easier to apply the Coase theorem and resolve those problems through assignment of property rights and negotiation. However, for larger problems, such as acid rain, depletion of the ozone layer, and global climate change, it becomes more difficult to find simple market-based solutions. These problems often extend across national boundaries and over several generations.

THE TRAGEDY OF THE COMMONS

One of the most famous articles in the field of environmental economics, "The Tragedy of the Commons," written by Garrett Hardin, was published in 1948 in *Science* magazine.[5] Hardin addressed the overuse of a **common access resource**, the common grazing land that was found in English villages before enclosure laws assigned such land to specific owners. He pointed out that private owners use their resources at an optimal rate so as to maximize their benefits over time. The same is not true of resources held in common. Because the marginal cost is zero, each user has an incentive to overuse the common property to the point where the marginal benefits are zero. This overuse is the **tragedy of the commons**.

For example, if a farmer does not put an extra cow to graze on the commons, he does not benefit by having more forage for his other cows or less exhaustion of the common grazing land. The space that farmer doesn't use will be occupied by some other farmer's cow. Since everyone faces the same incentives, the commons will be overgrazed and eventually become useless for all the owners. The benefits from overuse go to the individual, but the costs are spread among the entire group.

The only solution to the overuse of common property resources is to either assign property rights to individuals or have the government or other authority regulate the use in the common interest. If one farmer owns the commons, that farmer will use it at the optimal rate, because all of the costs and benefits will be internalized. If the farmer puts an extra cow to graze, it is that farmer's private property that is being depleted. The future costs will all fall on the farmer and the farmer's heirs rather than on the entire community. Assigning property will thus result in an efficient solution.

As you learned in an earlier chapter, opportunities to assign property rights are more widespread than might be expected. Air pollution rights have been assigned, bought, sold, and traded in the United States. Charging fines or fees for polluting is quite similar to the purchase and sale of property rights to use the air or water for disposal of wastes. In this case, the property rights have been as-

Common access resource A resource that is not owned by any individual but is available for all to use.

Tragedy of the commons The overuse of common access resources.

---

5. Garrett Hardin, "The Tragedy of the Commons," *Science* (August 1948): 16–48.

signed to the government, which charges for the use of the property. Some common access resources do not lend themselves to assignment of property rights, however. Sometimes it is difficult to identify the individuals who create the problem, the people who are hurt, or the possible long-term effects of certain uses of common resources. In other cases, the commons extends across national boundaries, making it difficult for governments to intervene because several governments with different constituents and agendas are involved.

The air, the water, the ozone layer—all of these are common access resources for everyone on earth. The concern about these global commons is expressed in a variety of ways. Is there a greenhouse effect resulting from too much carbon dioxide emission? If so, the result might be global warming with catastrophic results, such as flooding of coastal cities and creation of deserts where there had been forests and fields. Are human actions destroying the ozone layer that provides protection from the most harmful effects of the sun's rays? Are nonrenewable resources being exploited at a rate that will inflict suffering on future generations? Are renewable resources—trees, fish, whales—being used up at rates faster than they can be replaced? Are humans going to suffocate in their wastes as they pollute the air and water and pile up trash faster than places can be found to put it? These are the major questions posed by those concerned with the use and misuse of the global commons.

THE INFORMATION PROBLEM. Managing the global commons is complicated by two important problems. One problem is lack of adequate information. For example, in the case of global warming, scientists can determine changes in atmospheric gases. However, it is harder to predict precisely how much warming will result and what its impact will be on specific regions. For nonrenewable resources, it is difficult to forecast improvements in extraction technology and development of substitutes. The same is true to some extent for renewable resources. In the case of hazardous wastes, long delays are common between the disposal of wastes and the recognition of their hazardous effects. In one of the most famous cases of delayed impact in U.S. history, Love Canal in New York, residents ultimately had to abandon their homes because of hazardous wastes beneath their sites.

Inadequate information allows two types of errors: accepting a hypothesis as true when it is false, and rejecting a hypothesis as false when it is in fact true. Scientists tend to pay more attention to avoiding the first type of error, because in their work it is generally more damaging or costly. In the case of the global environment, however, both types of error are significant. If the dangers of global warming are real and imminent, and this true hypothesis is rejected because it cannot be verified, the costs will be large and irreparable. Suppose, however, that the hypothesis is accepted, and governments act to restrain economic activity, save the rain forest, and reduce carbon dioxide emissions. Then the forecasts turn out to be wrong, or the forecasts are right but scientists develop a technological solution, or the forecasts are right but the damage is very minimal. In this case, we will have unnecessarily given up output, economic growth, and present consumption.

Many economists point to past experiences to show that the first kind of error, acting on a prediction that turns out to be false or at least overstated, is very common. In the 1930s, the fertile farmlands of the midwest turned into a dust bowl, and some observers thought that farm practices were creating a new

POLICY FOCUS: RESEARCH AS ENVIRONMENTAL POLICY—THE CASE OF SCIENCE AT INTERIOR

When Bruce Babbitt, former governor of Arizona and 1988 presidential candidate, was appointed Secretary of Interior by President Clinton, a cheer went up among environmentalists. So far, Babbitt has not disappointed his constituency. As soon as Babbitt took over Interior, he set out to reorganize the department's biological research structure. The reorganization took effect October 1, 1993.

The National Biological Survey (NBS) will take over the biological research at Interior. Its goal is to look at the "big picture," starting with an inventory of every animal and plant species in the United States. Babbitt argues that this inventory will allow scientists (and regulators) to develop better plans to protect endangered species from extinction. Babbitt could create the survey without legislation, but he wants legislation passed to create legal standing for the survey. Once the survey is legislated, it could only be undone by the Congress, protecting it from a future Secretary of Interior who might not share Babbitt's goals.

In hearings before Congress on the reorganization bill, Babbitt predicted that the survey will be successful; that in a decade, "I would hope the Endangered Species Act has been virtually forgotten, not abolished," because we "will have reached a biological balance."

Critics of the survey policy are not so sure that Babbitt is on the right track. Some members of Congress feel that the research may be a threat to property rights. They are concerned that once endangered species are identified by the plant and animal census, regulators will use the data to prevent land owners from developing their property. Myron Ebell, of the Multiple-Use Land Alliance, argued, "We consider this the greatest threat to property rights since the Endangered Species Act. Why would (the government) want to gather information without using it?" Babbitt disagreed with Ebell, and testified, "There's no chance (the survey) would turn out to be a regulatory nightmare." Two representatives, Billy Tauzen (Democrat from Louisiana) and Charles Taylor (Republican from North Carolina), presented an amendment to the bill that would prohibit the NBS from surveying private property without the owner's consent.

The policy debate over this bill is interesting because it demonstrates the battle over environmental policy and economic development. The proponents of environmental activism claim that they only want information on biodiversity. Others, more concerned with economic growth, fear that the data will be used by government and environmental activists to prevent economic growth. They fear the data will be used to "take" property rights by limiting how types of property in certain areas can be used. Regardless of which side is right, you can expect that the Department of Interior will be actively involved in many environmental policy issues during the Clinton administration.

Source: "Babbitt Shakes Up Science at Interior," *Science* (August 20, 1993): 976–977.

---

desert. Today this land is again highly productive. Even the energy crisis of the 1970s disappeared as higher oil prices led to discovery of new reserves and more conservation. However, the fact that disasters have been averted in the past through technological change or discoveries does not necessarily mean that such solutions will arise in the future. People's positions on environmental issues depend on their faith in technological innovation.

THE SOVEREIGNTY PROBLEM. The second problem that complicates managing the global commons is the fact that the air and water span many nations. The assignment of property rights and the regulation of the commons are responsibilities of governments. However, some of the most important conflicts over the use of common access resources cross national boundaries. By burning fossil fuels, Britain exports sulfur dioxide to Scandinavia, where acid rain damages the forests. Brazil is chopping down its tropical rain forests, which absorb a great deal of carbon dioxide and help to slow the greenhouse effect around the world. The Brazilian government argues that if it were not for the emissions from industrial nations that consume most of the fossil fuels, the rain forest would not be an issue. The United States consumes fossil fuels at a higher rate than any other nation and has been criticized for failing to restrain such consumption with high taxes, as most other industrialized nations do. Even the huge oceans that girdle the globe have shown some serious damage from the disposal of wastes by many nations. Some cooperation between governments in either assigning property rights or developing policies to regulate use of common access resources is essential to finding solutions for these problems.

THE RAIN FOREST, CARBON DIOXIDE, AND GLOBAL WARMING

It is difficult to determine whether global warming is occurring. Data on weather and climate collected over decades, even centuries, indicate that weather is highly variable. Some climatologists have argued that the earth is headed for ecological disaster because of clear cutting of the forests—especially tropical rain forests—that absorb carbon dioxide. Figure 2 shows the recent increase in the concentration of carbon dioxide in the atmosphere, due mainly to the heavy use of fossil fuels in the twentieth century. The increased carbon dioxide traps the earth's radiated heat in the atmosphere rather than allowing it to escape. Scientists know that higher levels of carbon dioxide should result in global warming. However, the amount of increase in global temperature and the resulting effects on weather and climate patterns are uncertain. Effects will be stronger in temperate zones than in tropical zones. The danger of melting the polar ice caps and flooding coastal cities is an extreme possibility. The impact of global warming on world food production could also be serious.

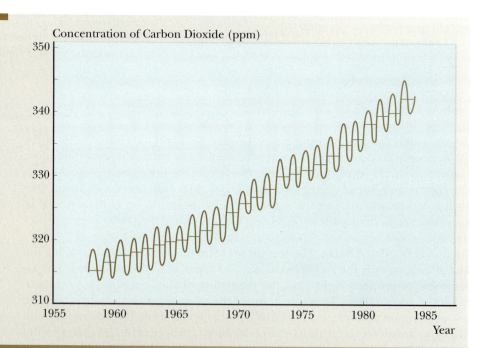

FIGURE 2

CARBON DIOXIDE IN THE ATMOSPHERE, 1958–1984 This diagram, based on samples taken at Hawaii's isolated Mauna Loa observatory, shows that there has been a steady increase of about 0.5 percent per year in the concentration of carbon dioxide in the earth's atmosphere.

Changing weather patterns would dry up some areas and provide other, previously dry, areas with more water than they could effectively use.

In the United States, there has been no great reduction in forest lands that absorb carbon dioxide, but there has been increased production of carbon dioxide from burning fossil fuels (especially gasoline). Throughout the world, however, population pressures have led to loss of forests. Tropical rain forests are especially effective in absorbing carbon dioxide from the atmosphere, so concerns have focused on those forests rather than on other facets of the problem.

Market mechanisms have a role in both the problem and potential solutions. The demand for tropical hardwoods as building materials in developed countries and the need for more agricultural and grazing land have been powerful incentives for cutting down rain forests. One possible market force for maintaining the rain forests lies in the discovery of valuable natural substances that can be used to produce medicines, food additives, and cosmetics. Yet another market force has been the purchase of tracts of rain forest by citizens' groups in developed countries. The new owners preserve the trees rather than cut them down. The overall impact of such private efforts has been very modest, however.

Individual governments can certainly act to reduce carbon dioxide emissions or to preserve forests. However, just as no individual has enough incentive to preserve the commons, no individual government has an incentive to act to prevent global warming unless other governments also act. In the absence of a single sovereign government to regulate the use of the rain forest as a global commons, the role of governments has been limited to efforts to negotiate preservation. The United States and other developed nations that have made loans to tropical nations such as Brazil have offered to forgive part of that debt in exchange for a commitment to preserve the rain forest. Such efforts have met with little response. Since the problem of carbon dioxide in the atmosphere is linked to both destruction of forests and use of fossil fuels, it is difficult to identify a single cause or a single nation that is responsible.

ACID RAIN

Closely related to global warming is the problem of acid rain. Sulfur dioxide and nitrous oxide combine with water in the atmosphere to create sulphuric acid and nitric acid. When it rains, the rain has a strong acid component that is damaging to plant and animal life. Scientists have documented the negative impact of acid rain on fish and plant life in lakes. The effect of acid rain on forests is not as clearly established.

Acid rain is part of a broader problem of air quality that has been addressed by governments in many nations. Within nations, there is an incentive to clean up air in order to improve the immediate environment and reduce health risks. The battle lines within a country are drawn between those who wish to use the air for the disposal of wastes and those who wish to preserve its quality. What makes acid rain different from other kinds of air pollution is that spillovers between nations are more evident with acid rain than with other types of air pollution.

Certain countries are net exporters of sulfur emissions. Britain, for example, imports one-fifth of its sulfur and exports two-thirds of its sulfur-based emissions to Western Europe. Net importers of pollutants include West Germany, Austria, and the Scandinavian countries. Within the United States, emissions in the midwest have their greatest impact in the northeastern states. Efforts to control acid rain within the country have pitted the producers and users (mainly electric utilities) of high-sulfur coal against environmentalists and residents and firms in the affected areas. Within the United States, the battle over amendments to the Clean Air Act is waged in Congress almost annually. These amendments represent the current trade-offs between the interests of these two conflicting groups. In Europe, the European Community has provided a broader base for discussion and resolution of acid rain spillovers between countries.

MOUNT TRASHMORE IN YOUR BACK YARD: WASTE DISPOSAL

The disposal of household and industrial wastes has become a major policy problem for local governments in the United States. Wastes can be grouped into three classes: hazardous, recyclable, and other. Each type presents different disposal problems and potential solutions.

RECYCLABLE AND OTHER NONHAZARDOUS WASTES.
Americans—and others—discard an enormous amount of waste each year. Some of this waste has no recoverable value and must be burned or buried in a commons—the local landfill or city dump. New Jersey has an above-ground landfill with the picturesque name of Mount Trashmore! Some household waste is disposed of through the sewer system, especially for households with garbage disposals. A large part of household waste can in fact be reused. Recycling recovers valuable nonrenewable resources (aluminum cans and petroleum-based plastics, for example), reduces the pressure on renewable resources (newspapers and glass), and lowers the amount of space and effort that must be devoted to disposal.

Until recently, most households had little incentive to recycle. It took time and effort to separate the trash and take recyclable items to an appropriate place. There was no penalty for failure to recycle and no rewards for cooperation. In recent years, this situation has changed. Trash disposal is largely the responsibility of local governments. Local and state governments have developed innovative and effective policies that change the costs and benefits people face in recycling. Local governments took this initiative because of the incentives they faced. Rising land prices, increasing federal regulations on site preparation, and hauling of trash over greater distances created an immediate and powerful incentive to act.

Figure 3 shows the shift in costs and benefits facing the individual household. MB_1 is the marginal benefit curve for recycling in the first year. Perhaps there were a few deposit bottles that could be returned, a small payment for aluminum cans, and some sense of contributing to community well-being. However, the marginal cost of recycling was high, because of the distance the recycler had to travel. Under these circumstances, the representative household only engaged in amount Q_1 of recycling. Then the local government established a recycling center. This act reduced the cost of recycling and shifted the marginal cost curve downward. The local government also started a campaign of education and persuasion that changed preferences, increasing the perceived benefits (MB_1 shifts to MB_2). These actions were typical for local governments in the 1970s and early 1980s. They had an effect on some households, but did not greatly reduce the amount of waste disposal (in the diagram, recycled material

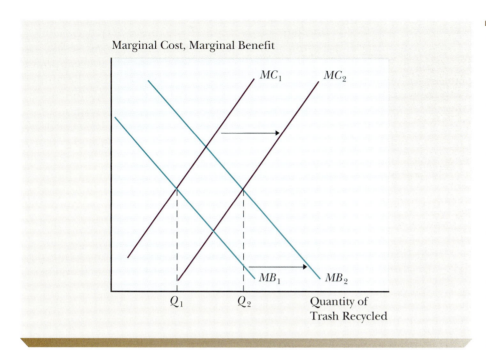

FIGURE 3

MARGINAL COSTS AND BENEFITS OF RECYCLING With the original marginal cost curve, MC_1, and the original marginal benefit curve, MB_1, the costs of recycling were too high and the perceived benefits too low to result in a very large volume of recycling. The combination of lower costs (a recycling center) and higher perceived benefits (result of an education campaign) shifts the curves. The result is some increase in recycling, from Q_1 to Q_2. Further increases in recycling can be brought about by making it more convenient to recycle (separation containers, curbside pickup) and more expensive not to recycle (higher pickup fees for unsorted trash).

rose only from Q_1 to Q_2). Effective waste reduction and recycling required more powerful incentives for both governments and citizens.

Further increases in land costs, higher payments for recycled materials, and other pressures caused some local governments to step up their efforts. These efforts shifted both the marginal benefit curve and the marginal cost curve to the right. One city in Oregon uses a combination of carrot and stick to promote recycling. Households are given two kinds of containers for waste pickup. The first, general and unsorted waste, carries a fee that increases sharply with added pickups each month. The second container is separated into color-coded sections for plastics, glass, aluminum, and paper. Pickups from the color-coded containers are free. This policy combines a substantial cash benefit for not using the unsorted pickup with much lower costs of recycling because of the sorting bins and curbside pickup.

Following this example, Seattle established a very aggressive recycling plan that has a goal of recycling 60 percent of all waste. By 1993, a remarkable 42 percent of all Seattle's trash was being recycled and 90 percent of all households were participating. But city officials admitted that the program was running out of steam and tougher measures, like fining nonparticipants, would be needed to reach the 60 percent goal. The chief motivation for Seattle was a warning that landfills would not be available. In fact, this proved to be inaccurate, as regional landfills in Oregon and Washington were opened, creating another century of capacity.[6]

Other cities use similar combinations of positive and negative incentives. Recycling is an excellent illustration of how local governments can use policy to increase market incentives to reduce overuse of a local commons, the city dump.

---

6. Bill Richards, "Recycling in Seattle Sets a National Standard But is Hitting Snags," *The Wall Street Journal* (August 3, 1993): 1.

HAZARDOUS WASTES. Hazardous wastes represent a more serious problem. There is no easy way of disposing of such wastes without endangering the air, water, or soil in the area. No one wants to live near the refuse of a nuclear power plant or a chemical plant. In fact, this reluctance to accommodate hazardous waste disposal sites produced a new acronym, NIMBY, which stands for "not in my back yard." Some states have resisted disposal of hazardous wastes, sometimes not even allowing such wastes to pass through en route to another destination. Many states have raised their fees for disposal of such wastes as both a deterrent and a revenue source. As firms find it increasingly difficult and costly to dispose of hazardous wastes, they are forced to seek other solutions. Reuse of waste materials or changes in technology that reduce the amount of hazardous wastes produced are alternatives.

Most of the horror stories about hazardous wastes result from past dumping, when there was less knowledge of the dangers and less government regulation. Hazardous waste problems, chiefly due to industrial wastes, are present in every state and will be costly to clean up. The Environmental Protection Agency's Superfund is earmarked for correcting such past mistakes. Unlike global warming and acid rain, hazardous wastes represent a problem that can be addressed through a combination of market incentives and government regulation.

CHALLENGES FOR THE FUTURE

We have not exhausted the list of environmental issues. For example, the ocean is the ultimate common access resource, and little progress has been made in conserving its bounty or controlling its use as a waste dump. Problems of conserving common access resources, whether local or global, represent a serious and substantial challenge to policy makers. Imperfect information, lack of coordination between nations, and a natural tendency to overuse and exhaust common access resources complicate the problem. It will require a combination of market incentives, technological innovation, government regulation, and intergovernmental cooperation to protect the environment for generations to come.

THE HEALTH CARE POLICY ISSUE

Because of rapidly rising costs, health care has gained increased attention from journalists and politicians in recent years. Bill Clinton made health care a major issue in his campaign for the presidency. Shortly after being elected, he designated First Lady Hillary Rodham Clinton to head the efforts to develop a health care reform plan.

Interest has also increased because health care has become one of the fastest growing industries in the United States. Between 1950 and 1980, total annual spending on health care increased from $11 billion to more than $200 billion. A significant change in demand occurred with the passage of Medicare/Medicaid legislation in 1965. Using present estimates for 1995, annual spending more than tripled between 1985 and 1995 (adjusted for inflation). In 1950, health care expenditures represented 4.5 percent of total national income. In l995, health spending will represent more than 14 percent of national income.

Another economic issue is the impact of the cost of health care on a firm's desire to employ more workers. If firms are required to provide health care insurance for employees, they will experience an increase in the cost of the resource, labor. Firms will respond by trying to substitute other inputs for labor and by substituting part-time workers for full-time workers.

SUPPLY AND DEMAND ANALYSIS

Let us analyze the potential problems of the health care industry using the basic economic tools of supply and demand. Figure 4 illustrates what has happened in the health care industry. The market in 1950 is represented by supply curve S_{1950} and demand curve D_{1950}. Equilibrium is at P_1 and Q_1. It is important to note that between 1950 and 1995, there were some drastic changes in the *ceteris paribus* conditions in the health care market. On the supply side there have been dramatic changes. We have more physicians, drug suppliers, hospital beds, and nurses. These changes should have increased the supply. On the other hand, the sophistication of the care supplied by hospitals and doctors has greatly increased. There has been a virtual explosion of technological advances in the industries that make diagnostic, surgical, and therapeutic equipment. This technology is expensive and increases the cost of supplying health care (even as it improves that care). The net effect of this more expensive care has been to shift the supply curve leftward from S_{1950} to S_{1995} in Figure 4. Note that this diagram, like all supply and demand diagrams, holds quality constant.

On the demand side, the changes have been equally significant. First and foremost, the income of U.S. citizens rose over this period. The demand for health care increased rapidly as incomes increased. Second, there has been an

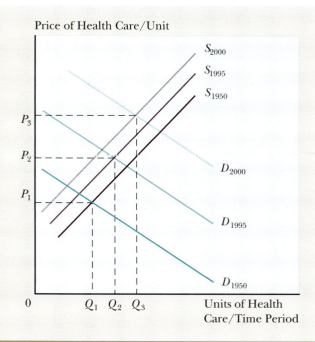

FIGURE 4

THE MARKET FOR HEALTH CARE

The health care market is characterized by decreasing supply due to increasing costs, and increasing demand due to rising incomes and the aging of the population. As a result, the equilibrium price of health care has been rising rapidly.

increase in Medicare, Medicaid, and employer-provided health insurance. Since payment would be made by a third party, many demanded more health care. Third, the age distribution of the U.S. population has shifted upward. Demand will increase further as baby boomers age. Fourth, the very success of health care delivery creates more future demand for health care. As health care improves, the population lives longer. More health care is then demanded because the population is now older, and older people have more health problems. Fifty years ago, many people died giving birth, or from acute infections, heart disease, or stroke before they would have been old enough to develop the chronic maladies now associated with older age. The increased demand for health care is represented by the shift from D_{1950} to D_{1995} in Figure 4.

The result of these changes in supply and demand has been for the price of health care to rise to P_2 and a new level of consumption to be established at Q_2. The magnitude of the shift from P_1 to P_2 can be understood by comparing the price index for medical services to the consumer price index. Between 1950 and 1995, the price index for medical services rose over 1,000 percent. This increase was more than 2.25 times the change in the consumer price index (CPI).

What about the future? It is likely that the supply curve for health care will continue to shift leftward with increases in the cost of the resources used to produce that service. It is also likely that demand will continue to increase as incomes rise and the population ages. Thus, in response to a shift in demand from D_{1995} to D_{2000} and a shift in supply from S_{1995} to S_{2000} in Figure 4, there should be an increase in price to P_3 and an increase in the equilibrium quantity to Q_3.

This prediction supposes that the government does not intervene in this market. A quick review of Congressional interest in the health care industry would be enough to convince you that this is not a realistic assumption. The most likely governmental response to the rapidly rising price of health care is twofold: some form of national health insurance and/or price controls.

THE CLINTON HEALTH CARE PROPOSAL

On September 22, 1993, with much fanfare, President Clinton outlined his proposal for health care reform on national TV to a joint session of Congress. Clinton told the American people that the system of health care in the United States was "badly broken" and the system was the "costliest and most wasteful" system in the world. Fixing it would be "our most urgent priority."[7]

The Clinton plan, called the Health Security Act, is complex and will very likely emerge from Congress in a form quite different from the original proposal. Essentially, the Clinton plan sets up a new set of institutions. A *National Health Board* (seven presidential appointees) would set standards and benefits, and oversee the system. *Regional alliances,* which are agencies of each state government, would serve as purchasing co-ops. Within each regional alliance, *health plans,* which are similar to current health insurance plans, would provide basic health care benefits. The health plans can offer whatever coverage they want, but must provide at least the basic package as defined by the National Health Board. Providers are the doctors, clinics, and hospitals that are part of one or more health plans.

---

7. *The Washington Post* (September 23, 1993) contains the complete text of President Clinton's health care reform address to Congress.

Everyone in the United States would join one of these health plans and be entitled to at least minimal benefits. A plastic health security card (the President even showed one of these during his speech) would guarantee entrance. Patients would have their choice of primary-care providers within the health plan, but the choice could be made only once a year. The health security card would represent a prepaid credit card for health care, under a certain health plan with a selected provider, for the one-year period.

Workers would be issued their health security cards by their employer. Employers would be required to pay 80 percent of their employees' plan premiums according to a formula based on a weighted average of all regional premiums. Employees would then choose their own plan and pay the rest of the premium. The employee's share would be deducted from his or her paycheck just like social security taxes. Companies that have more than 5,000 employees would be permitted to set up their own health plan and provider outside of the regional alliance.

The government would subsidize the cost of health care for small employers (50 employees or fewer) and low-wage workers. The self-employed and unemployed would be issued health security cards by health alliance management. The government would also subsidize the plan for low-income individuals.

The Clinton administration estimated in September 1993 that the cost of health insurance under this program would be about $1,800 per individual and $4,200 for a family. The cost would be covered by employer and employee premiums, and government subsidies. (The government subsidies would come from revenues previously used for Medicaid.)

Each health care provider that joins a regional alliance would know at the beginning of the year how much money it had to operate. A provider (doctor, hospital, or clinic) would not be allowed to join the alliance if it had "poor quality" or if its prices were 20 percent above average prices for particular services. Each provider accepted into the regional alliance would have to agree to provide the defined basic services to all patients and be subject to federal controls on annual price increases. There might be some rationing to "schedule" the provision of the health care. Most importantly, it would be open to everyone with a health care card. Finally, health care providers would have to set up one fee-for-service health plan. It would be available to all subscribers with higher co-payments and deductibles.

ECONOMICS OF THE CLINTON PLAN. In essence, the President's program does two things. First, it provides access to health care for those people who presently are denied or have limited access. This access, however, is limited to a basic package of no-frills health care services. Second, it imposes price controls on the providers of this basic health care. The simple supply and demand of this program is easy to put on a graph. The program works to increase demand and potentially establish price ceilings. As you learned in an earlier chapter, an increase in demand with a price ceiling will create a shortage.

The Clinton plan calls for everyone to shoulder some of the cost of health care. Even the poor will have to pay something. This price is seen as a way to control some of the increase in demand. A second important element is that those who choose to spend more on health care will be allowed to do so, but they will be required to pay proportionally more if they consume outside their regional alliance. This is an interesting issue, because wealthy consumers will always have the option of purchasing health care in other countries. If the Clinton proposals become too binding and health care becomes substandard or rationed, one would predict that private entrepreneurial hospitals will spring up in Mexico or on cruise ships so that higher income people can get what they want.

ALTERNATIVE PERSPECTIVES. Before the President finished his speech to Congress, opponents began to offer counter arguments. One group of critics argue that the U.S. health care system is the best in the world, not the "badly broken" system the President described. This argument insists that everyone in the United States gets health care and that the Clinton plan, with its inevitable price controls, will certainly reduce the amount of health care available to Americans.

Opponents argue that having no health insurance is not the same thing as having no health care. Persons without health insurance go to hospital emergency rooms for treatment. In fact, the American Hospital Association estimates that its members provided more than $10 billion in uncompensated health care in 1993. This system for providing health care to the poor may be inefficient, but it is not the same thing as saying the poor do not get health care. Indeed, the American Medical Association (AMA) estimates that the cost of lifetime care provided to an AIDS patient is over $100,000, and very few have health insurance. The costs of providing health care to the poor are borne by society through federal and city taxes, higher premiums for private medical insurance, and higher fees for services. To absorb the uncompensated share of costs, hospitals must make choices and may offer fewer services.

A second point of contention is how best to measure the quality of health care. Clinton and other critics of the quality of U.S. health care often point to life expectancy at birth and the infant mortality rate as measures of the quality of health care. By those measures the United States is not the best in the world—it is not even *among* the best in the world. In 1992, life expectancy in the United States was behind that in Canada, France, Germany, Italy, Japan, and Britain. Infant mortality was worse, with the United States ranking nineteenth in the world. Opponents claim that these are misleading measures of the quality of health care because they reflect many other things than the health care system. Indeed, the federal government's own *Health Care Financing Review* in 1992 indicated some social reasons for the difference in life expectancy. The homicide rate in the United States is ten times higher than in Great Britain. For every U.S. homicide there are 100 assault cases reported by emergency rooms; 25 percent of all spinal injuries in the United States come from assaults. AIDS statistics are

KEY IDEAS

BASIC ECONOMIC ISSUES IN HEALTH CARE POLICY REFORM

• Access	Increasing access increases the number of demanders.
• Rationing	Who determines who gets what service and at what time?
• Redistribution	Who pays?
• Price Controls	Price ceilings for some services will create shortages.
• Ultimate Outcome	Richer Americans are going to pay more to assure health care for poorer Americans.

GLOBAL OUTLOOK: CANADIAN-STYLE NATIONAL HEALTH INSURANCE

Many people in the United States are examining Canadian health care policy to see if there are any lessons that might be learned. Most Canadians seem to be very happy with the quality of the health care they receive. The Canadian health care system has some important differences from the system in the United States. Everyone is covered for hospital and medical services from the first dollar, with no limits. This health care is available to all Canadians under the same terms and conditions. The cost of the system is covered primarily from income tax revenue and it is the second most costly system in the world. A final point is that the system is not national. Each province or territory has its own plan.

The basic policy elements of the Canadian system are a series of controls on costs and payments. The first control is at the patient-doctor level. Doctors receive the same payment for all patients for the same service. A physician is barred by law from accepting money from a patient to supplement the government payment. This feature represents a significant difference from the U.S. system, where a physician might receive $100 for an office visit from an insured patient who pays $10, and the insurance company the other $90. This same U.S. doctor might receive $40 from Medicare for this same kind of visit or $30 from Medicaid for a similar visit from a low-income patient. You can see the economic incentives of this first control. In Canada, physicians compete for patients. In the United States, physicians compete for wealthy, insured patients first and Medicare patients second. Medicaid patients are a distant third. Successful doctors are too busy in the United States to take Medicare and Medicaid patients.

The second control (in most, but not all provinces) is on the doctors' income. The maximum payment a doctor can receive from the government for treating patients is $450,000 per year. The incentive here is also pretty simple. Once a Canadian doctor receives $450,000 from the government, there is no incentive to keep working, although very few doctors reach this level. There is a joke in Toronto that the only way to see a Canadian dermatologist in October, November, or December (the last quarter of governmental payments) is to go to Florida.

Canadian hospitals are also paid by the government. They receive a single annual budget. Costs can be contained by not giving the hospitals what they request, although this rarely happens. In 1992, Canadian hospitals asked for a 9 percent increase in their budgets. They got 1 percent as part of a cost containment effort. The result was that almost 30 percent of the acute care beds in Toronto were closed. This budgetary policy produces a much different kind of hospital than those found in the United States. Most Canadian hospitals invest very little in high-tech care. There is also very little difference between hospitals in Canada, while in the United States there is a great deal of difference between "rich" and "poor" hospitals.

The differences between the two systems can be seen by comparing Toronto to Washington DC, two cities that are very similar in size. In 1992, Toronto had fifty-one hospitals with a budget of $485 million. Washington DC had fourteen hospitals with a budget of $566 million. The difference in funding creates some striking differences.

In Toronto, only eleven of the fifty-one hospitals are equipped for bypass surgery, total capacity is about 2,200 bypass operations a year. Because of the controls on the number of hospitals that can do bypass surgery; those facilities are fully booked and very efficient. A bypass in Toronto costs about $14,350. The bad news is that the rationing creates a waiting list. It can take up to six months to get the surgery done. In Washington DC, 4,000 bypass operations are done annually; a wealthy or well-insured patient would look for a new cardiologist if it took more than a week to get a bypass. DC has bypass on demand, but it costs more than twice as much as a Canadian bypass. What is the effect on the population of half the bypass surgeries at half the cost?

The statistics are revealing. Canadian cardiac mortality rates are no different than cardiac mortality rates in the United States. What if half the DC bypass surgeries were eliminated? At roughly $30,000 per bypass, that would save $6 million per year in DC alone. But, let's look behind the statistics. Quentin Macmanus, a DC cardiologist, describes the typical U.S. bypass patient as an active, self-sufficient, 70-year-old male who plays golf. His major difficulty is controlling his chest pain. He has bypass on demand and is back on the golf course in no time flat. In Canada, he quits golf and slows down. For Dr. Macmanus, it is not mortality, but quality of life that is important.

Look at the difference in technology. In the Washington DC area there are thirty-five magnetic resonance imagers (MRIs); Toronto has five. Each MRI machine costs $2 million. In the United States, MRIs are used about 12 times a day, so the DC daily total is 420 MRIs. In Toronto, the machines are used about 16 times a day, which means about 80 patients are sent to the MRI. Who are the "extra" 340 Washington area patients who get an MRI? A patient with a knee injury in Washington can get an MRI the next morning. In Canada, there is a nine-month wait. In DC, if your doctor thinks you have a herniated disk, you go to the MRI immediately. The MRI is painless and takes seconds. In Toronto, your doctor orders a myelogram. A myelogram requires an overnight hospital stay, is painful, and can have serious side effects. U.S. doctors rarely use myelograms anymore. Dr. Walter Kucharzyk, Chief of Radiology at the University of Toronto, complains that he is forced to operate with too few MRIs. "I can point to a dozen cases a year at my hospital where someone's health was directly jeopardized because they couldn't get an MRI."

So which health system is better? It probably depends on who you are. If you are an uninsured patient needing standard care you are certainly better off living in Canada. If you are an insured worker with lower back pain you should hope you live in Alexandria, VA, rather than Toronto. And if you are a highly trained brain surgeon in Toronto, you probably are thinking about emigrating to the United States!

Source: Malcolm Gladwell, "Can Canada's Health Plan Cure America?" *The Washington Post National Weekly Edition* (April 5, 1992): 10–11.

---

even more compelling. In 1992 there were more than 450,000 AIDS cases reported in the United States, while in Japan there were fewer than 500.

WHERE IS HEALTH CARE POLICY HEADED?

Health and health care is a very complex interaction of income, social, and market forces. As one critic put it, the health care crisis in America would not be an issue if we could get people to buckle up, drive the speed limit, turn in all handguns, stop smoking, practice safe sex, eat less beef, get three hours of vigorous exercise weekly, give up all illegal drugs, and lose twenty pounds! Easier said than done.

Currently, medical care in the United States is essentially a mixed market system. Those who are wealthy or have insurance and can afford the expensive treatments are treated first. Second in line are those who qualify for government assistance through Medicare or Medicaid. These people are either old or poor. Next in line are those like Amy and Angela Lakeberg who can't pay for their care, but are interesting cases. Many times doctors are interested in these cases because they are experimental and advance the research and knowledge of health professionals. Finally, there are millions of Americans with very little access to health care. These people can wait in line at hospital emergency rooms, but treatment is often too little, too late.

Certain facts about health care policy issues are clear. The United States spends a very large share of GDP on health care. Some poor people are denied access to medical services and others must choose between buying medicine and food. Some physicians refuse to treat Medicare and Medicaid patients. Some towns and areas in the United States have no doctors. People are turned down for health insurance because of preexisting conditions. Workers are losing health insurance when their jobs are eliminated in corporate restructurings. Those still employed are finding that their insurance and choices are lessened through benefit cutbacks. These are some of the reasons the health care policy issue has attracted so much attention. It is important to keep in mind that the debate about health care policy has just begun. The final legislation will likely be quite different from that proposed by the Clinton administration. Indeed, the political battle lines are already drawn.

ECONOMICS OF POLICY REFORM. Reform of the market for health care is not as complicated as it appears. At least, the economics is not complicated; it is the politics that are very complicated. The issues are access, price controls, rationing, and redistribution. Giving more people access to health care is going to increase the demand for health care. We learned this economic fact of life in Chapter 1. If demand increases, price is going to rise. No amount of health care planning or political rhetoric is going to change this economic fact. If demand increases and price controls are in place, shortages are going to occur. If shortages occur, someone has to ration the scarce resource. Are the old, the young, the potentially productive, those who wait in line, or those who are politically powerful going to have the first access? Under the national health plan in Britain, physicians in part make this choice. That is one way to ration; it may not even be a bad way to ration. It is, however, different from the way Americans are used to rationing scarce resources—through higher prices.

Finally, a major part of the debate over health care reform is really about income redistribution. It is about equity, the fairness of a system that rations scarce health care by income. Economics is not very well equipped to deal with these equity issues, another lesson we learned in Chapter 1. The ultimate outcome of health care policy is that richer Americans are going to help pay for the health care of poorer Americans.

WINNERS AND LOSERS IN POLICY REFORMS. As the debate over health care reform plays out, political positions will be determined by economic interests. As you have learned, economic interests are really the self-interest of the economic actors in any debate. The press often refers to these economic interests as "special interests" (usually with a negative connotation), but we should expect political interests to pursue their self-interest. This is the main point of public choice theory.

Table 1 spells out probable winners and losers in the health care reform issue. You can use this table to predict the political positions of those who look out for the votes of these groups, or special interests. Some of the groups in each category have organized lobbies in Washington DC working on their behalf. These groups are the rent seekers and the rent defenders that we discussed in the previous chapter. Other groups do not have organized lobbies.

Winners and losers among physicians are also apparent in the political positions they are taking on the Clinton health plan (see Table 1). In late 1993, the AMA opposed Clinton's plan to finance expanded health coverage through employer mandates. Within days the White House assembled some other physician groups to say to the press that the AMA was off base. Who was right? Both groups of physicians took political positions that protected their own self-interest. The AMA's policy-making group is dominated by medical specialists. A shift in the present fee-for-service system to a managed system envisioned by Clinton would turn physicians from self-employed professionals into employed professionals. This would hit medical specialists particularly hard, which explains some of the AMA opposition to the Clinton plan. The group the White House assembled represented general practitioners, who might stand to gain from the Clinton plan. At least it is not as clear that the general practitioners would be losers.[8]

---

8. David Broder, "Health Care Winners, Losers," *The Honolulu Advertiser* (January 5, 1994): A10.

TABLE 1 A SELF-INTEREST GUIDE TO HEALTH REFORM

WINNERS	WHY? WHAT GAIN?
Retiree groups (AARP)	Expanded drug and long-term health coverage, paid for by transfers from younger, working people
Organized labor	Preservation of their high quality health care benefits, which are currently under pressure
Consumer groups	Health coverage for all Americans
Primary health care providers and general practitioners	Increase in demand for their product
Major insurance companies	Forces fringe competitors out of business
Large unionized industries (e.g. steel and autos)	Lower labor costs by transferring part of their contract obligations to governmental programs

LOSERS	WHY? WHAT COST?
Small business firms	Increased labor costs due to mandated cost for employer-provided insurance
Pharmaceutical companies	Price controls (ceilings)
Hospitals	Price controls (ceilings)
Medical specialists	Price controls (ceilings)
Small insurance companies	(1) Forced out of business by big insurers (2) Mandated limits on risk management and premiums (price ceilings)
Insurance agents	Health alliances take over their role
Trial lawyers	Malpractice reforms and settlement limitations
Tobacco industry	Increased federal excise taxes
Liquor industry	Increased federal excise taxes
Fiscal conservatives	Big governmental spending program
Young and healthy people	Have to pay for transfers to old and sickly

Consider again...*Let's return to Hillary Clinton and the Lakeberg twins. Should the expensive surgery have been performed on Amy and Angela? Who should decide? That is an ethical question. And who should pay? That is a question of redistribution and one that positive economics dodges. Remember, in Chapter 1 we learned that positive economics says what is, not what ought to be. But in Chapter 1 we also noted the need to ration in every society. So in essence we have come full circle. The health dilemma is essentially a problem of rationing. We have scarce resources and unlimited needs.*

The current U.S. system uses prices, and thus income, as the rationing device. Those who are wealthy and those who have private or public insurance coverage get the health care services. Those who do not have insurance or sufficient income wait in emergency rooms or do without. As health care costs continue to increase, more and more government spending will go to health care, and access will become more of a problem.

Someone, or some policy, is going to have to decide who gets what. The lessons in some other systems of health care are informative. In Norway, patients of a certain age are not eligible for treatment for cardiac arrest. The same week that the Lakeberg girls were news in the United States, a story ran about Harry Elphick from Manchester, England. Elphick needed bypass surgery after a heart attack. His doctor refused treatment because Elphick smoked more than a pack of cigarettes daily. Elphick died. When his widow was asked by a reporter if the doctors weren't "tending to play God," she replied, "Haven't they always?"[9] If you think about it, Elphick's story and the story of the twins are two sides of the same dilemma.

9. Jennifer Fisher, "Smoke and Croak," *U.S. News & World Report*, (September 6, 1993): 15.

SUMMARY

1. Cities are formed and grow because of economies of agglomeration. The optimal city size is where the total benefits of agglomeration exceed the diseconomies of agglomeration by the greatest amount. Supplying local public goods in urban areas is complicated by the division of the area into many political subdivisions. The Tiebout hypothesis is that voters will solve the spillover problem by choosing to live in the jurisdiction that provides the desired combination of services and taxes.
2. Some cities have attempted to address the housing issue by privatizing public housing projects. These efforts have met with modest success. Mass transportation has elements of a public good. The policy issue lies in determining the value of the positive externality.
3. The tragedy of the commons is the overuse of common access resources. Each user of such a resource has the incentive to use that resource to the point where marginal benefits are zero. Common access resources must be regulated or assigned to individuals in order to attain efficient use of these resources. Managing the global commons is even more complicated because of jurisdictional and informational problems.
4. The health care industry in the United States is one of the fastest-growing industries. Prices have risen because of increasing demand and increasing costs. These increasing prices and the rapidly growing share of GNP that is devoted to health care expenditures have attracted the attention of politicians.
5. The Clinton proposal calls for increased access to health care by individuals who have not been insured. It also calls for cost containment through price regulation and more cost sharing by users. Critics see it as a demand-increasing program with a redistributive effect on the economy.

NEW TERMS

economies of agglomeration
diseconomies of agglomeration
user charges
Tiebout hypothesis
common access resource
tragedy of the commons

QUESTIONS: REVIEW, APPLICATIONS, AND POLICY

REVIEW

1. How is a common access resource different from a private resource?
2. In what way is the Tiebout solution for the provision of local public goods similar to the Coase theorem (discussed in the preceding chapter) for dealing with negative externalities?
3. Should mass transportation be viewed as a public good?
4. What is causing the demand for health care to increase? What is causing the supply of health care to decrease? If supply decreases and demand increases, what will happen to the equilibrium price of health care?
5. It has been argued that with universal health care someone must "play God." What does this mean in economic terms?

APPLICATIONS

6. Health care reform produces economic winners and losers. Table 1 shows that the elderly and sickly are winners and the young and healthy are losers. What does the public choice theory we studied in the previous chapter tell you about the likely political outcome of the political process if these were the only two groups affected?
7. Suppose you were sent to a city you had never visited before to determine whether that city needed more residents or already had too many. What criteria would you use to answer that question?
8. Is a city park a common access resource? How can crowding be controlled?
9. Suppose you belong to a sailing club, which owns a dock and a boat. Will these be kept in better or worse shape than an individually owned boat and dock? Why or why not?
10. If the graduate student in the mechanical engineering lab invented a new technology that reduced the marginal cost of cleaning the air at factory smokestacks, what would happen to the optimal level of pollution?
11. How do technological innovations like the fax machine, the information super highway, and satellite-assisted communication affect the size of cities?
12. It has been said that the debate over health care reform is really a policy debate over redistribution. Comment on this statement by saying what economic theory brings to this debate over redistribution.

POLICY

13. A global environmental problem is the depletion of the ozone layer of the atmosphere, which screens out cancer-causing ultraviolet radiation. The ozone layer is being depleted by the use of chlorofluorocarbons (CFCs) in air conditioners, refrigerators, and spray cans (these spray cans are now illegal in the United States). How is this an example of the tragedy of the commons? How can markets and governments contribute to a solution?
14. Cattle and buffalo are very similar animals, yet buffalo were shot almost to extinction, while cattle were left alone in the same habitat. Why?
15. When mayors and city council members of adjacent cities get together to "cooperate" on tax policy increases, what are they really up to?

SUGGESTIONS FOR FURTHER READING

Faltermayer, Edmund. "A Health Plan that Can Work." *Fortune* (June 14, 1993): 88–96. Claims that health care reform is underway without the Clinton plan and questions whether the Clinton reform will impede the beneficial change that is taking place.

Feshbach, Murray, and Alfred Friendly, Jr. *Ecocide in the USSR*. New York: Basic Books, 1992. Shows that the environmental legacy of communist rule in the former Soviet Union is dying land, dead rivers, and sick people.

Gordon, John Steele. "How America's Health Care Fell Ill." *American Heritage* (May/June, 1992): 49–65. A very readable history of health care provision in the United States.

Helms, Robert B., ed. *Health Care and Politics: Lessons From Four Countries*. Washington DC: AEI Press, 1993. A review of health care policy in Canada, Germany, the Netherlands, and the United Kingdom.

Mieszkowski, Peter, and Edwin S. Mills. "The Causes of Metropolitan Surburbanization." *Journal of Economic Perspectives* (Summer 1993): 135–147. An empirical study of central city decline.

Norton, Rob. "History's Lessons for Health Care Costs." *Fortune* (January 10, 1994): 86–87. Reviews the history of political attempts to keep prices from rising from the Roman emperor Diocletian (A.D. 245–313) through Richard Nixon's price controls to Clinton and health care prices.

Ray, Dixie Lee. *Environmental Overkill: What Ever Happened to Common Sense?* Washington DC: Regentry Gateway, 1993. The late Dixie Lee Ray, former Governor of Washington, argues that good stewardship of the environment, scientific honesty, and our constitutional liberties are being threatened by environmental extremists.

Ridley, Matt, and Nobbi S. Low. "Can Selfishness Save the Environment?" *The Atlantic Monthly* (September 1993). A very readable article that shows how an economic approach to solving environmental problems can be successful, while attempts to persuade people to change their selfish habits are likely to fail.

The Journal of Economic Perspectives (Fall 1993). An entire issue of this journal devoted to environmental issues. Five articles relate to global climate change and three articles are devoted to local commons issues.

PART 10

THE WORLD ECONOMY

The chapters in this section represent an extension of many of the concepts developed and issues raised in earlier chapters to a global environment. As technological innovations in transport and communications have linked the world more closely together, the competitors that workers and firms face are no longer in the next city or state but are likely to be in another country. Trade flows, capital flows, and the exchange rate have much more impact on the lives of individual citizens in the 1990s than they did in earlier times. At the same time, these stronger global links enable us to observe each other more closely and reexamine some basic questions about the roles of government and the private sector in the light of the experiences of other nations.

The first chapter in this part explores the impact of international trade on the domestic economy. Also covered are the various policies that nations use to influence or control trade with other countries, including the formation of trading blocs such as NAFTA. The second chapter looks at the macroeconomic impact of international economic relations, and particularly at the role of the exchange rate and the balance of payments in balancing domestic policy concerns with the need to settle accounts between nations.

The final chapter takes yet a third approach to putting what you have learned into a global context. It explores the evolving role of government and the market in other national economies, with special emphasis on changes taking place in the former Soviet Union. Together, these three chapters serve as a firm reminder that much of what Americans may take for granted as "how a mixed market economy works" is in fact how a particular economy works at a particular time.

CHAPTER 34
TRADE AMONG NATIONS

LEARNING OBJECTIVES

1. Describe the benefits of free trade based on comparative advantage.
2. Analyze the effects of tariffs, quotas, and other trade restrictions.
3. Evaluate the arguments for tariff protection.
4. Discuss the costs and benefits of forming free trade areas and common markets.
5. Evaluate the impact of immigration and direct foreign investment.

Consider this... *Ross Perot, 1992 presidential candidate, said that NAFTA is the source of "that great flushing sound" we hear as American jobs go south of the border. President Bush said that NAFTA would bring great benefits to the U.S. economy in terms of jobs and exports. President Clinton took a more cautious stand, endorsing the treaty with qualifications and a call for side agreements. Who was right? Is it a boon, a disaster, or something in between?*

The debate over NAFTA began in the mid–1980s and will continue long after the treaty has been signed. NAFTA represents all the fears, hopes, and uncertainties that firms and workers have about foreign competition. Will we export more to Mexico? Will cheap Mexican labor undercut American workers? Will better job opportunities in Mexico slow the tide of immigrants, legal and illegal, from Mexico to the United States? We know there will be gainers and losers. Who will gain and who will lose?

The issues surrounding NAFTA are much the same as the questions surrounding trade policy in general. Economic relations with the rest of the world are increasingly important to the American economy. You may drive a Japanese car, drink coffee from Brazil, eat Mexican tomatoes and Honduran bananas, or take pictures with a German camera. Chances are there is a plant of a foreign-owned multinational corporation close to where you live.

Even for a country as large as the United States, where trade with other countries is a relatively small fraction (about 10 to 12 percent) of GDP, international trade has an increasing impact on the domestic economy. The percentage of output and sales entering into international trade has doubled in the last fifteen years. Foreign competition is important to major industries such as textiles, steel, and autos. Immigration (both legal and illegal), foreign investment in the United States, and American investment abroad all play a big role in the political debate and the daily news.

WHY NATIONS TRADE

The reasons for international trade are really no different from the reasons for trade between individuals who live in the same country. It is important to realize that in most cases international trade takes place between individuals and firms. When we speak of trade between the United States and Japan, we are really talking about trade between individuals and firms in these countries. These individuals and firms trade for the same reasons that individuals and firms within a country trade. Trade takes place because of the availability of a better product or a better price or because of an opportunity for profit. Exactly what determines the patterns of trade between nations and how much each nation benefits have been important concerns to economists as long as there have been nation-states and economists.

Before Adam Smith, the dominant view was that government should direct many spheres of economic activity, especially international trade. This view, called mercantilism, put heavy emphasis on control of shipping, maintaining colonies, discouraging imports, and promoting exports. Two famous economists are responsible for developing the arguments for a policy of free trade. Adam Smith's *Wealth of Nations* in 1776 made a strong case for freedom in every sphere of economic activity. David Ricardo, a nineteenth-century British economist and member of Parliament, was very interested in the practical question of what trade policy England should pursue. He developed the principle of comparative advantage in his classic 1814 book, *Principles of Political Economy and Taxation*.

THE BENEFITS OF EXCHANGE

It is easier to envision the processes at work in international trade by focusing first on exchange rather than production. Consider Heather and Peter, who are both stamp collectors. Like most stamp collectors, they expand their collections by trading duplicates of stamps they have. Let's say that Heather has the complete 1938 presidential series and several extras. Peter has some gaps in that series, but has some extra Canadian stamps that he would like to trade and that Heather would like to have. They work a deal. She trades three presidential stamps for five Canadian stamps. As an outside observer, you might say that the trade was one of "equal values." That may be true in a market sense, but the stamps weren't of equal value to Peter and Heather. Heather wanted the Canadian stamps more than she wanted the extra presidential stamps, and Peter felt just the opposite. They both were better off as a result of the trade.

Economists who look at international trade emphasize the **gains from trade**, or the higher level of economic well-being that comes partly from greater production when nations specialize and partly from mutually beneficial exchange. While people do occasionally trade out of existing stocks of goods, like Heather and Peter, most of the time they produce in order to trade. The explanation of how people and nations decide what to produce for trade is based on the concepts of absolute advantage and comparative advantage.

Gains from trade
The increase in economic well-being resulting from specialization and trade.

ABSOLUTE ADVANTAGE

Suppose Heather and Peter are sister and brother, and their parents want the twelve windows in the house washed and the twenty-four square yards of leaves raked. Heather and Peter estimate their output as shown in Table 1.

TABLE 1 AN EXAMPLE OF ABSOLUTE ADVANTAGE

	WINDOWS PER HOUR	SQUARE YARDS OF LEAVES PER HOUR
Heather	4	6
Peter	2	8

If this brother and sister divided the tasks equally, they would each have to wash half the windows (6 for Heather, which would take her 1½ hours, and 6 for Peter, which would take him 3 hours) and rake 12 square yards of leaves (which would take Heather 2 hours and Peter 1½ hours to complete). At the end of a long afternoon, Heather would have worked 3½ hours, and Peter would have worked 4½ hours. On the other hand, if they each specialized in what they do better, Heather could have all of the windows washed in just 3 hours and Peter could have all of the leaves raked in 3 hours. There would be a clear gain of a valuable ½ hour for Heather and 1½ hours for Peter.

Both Heather and Peter are better off if they specialize, because each has an **absolute advantage**. Heather is more efficient than Peter at washing windows, and Peter is more efficient than Heather at raking leaves. It's not difficult to convince anyone of the benefits of specialization and trade when there is a clear absolute advantage for each partner.

Absolute advantage
The ability to produce something using fewer resources than other producers use.

COMPARATIVE ADVANTAGE

Suppose, however, that one partner is better at both. Assume that Heather is better at *both* window washing and leaf raking. The production rates for Heather and Peter in this case are shown in Table 2. If they continue to divide the tasks equally, Heather will spend 1½ hours on her 6 windows and 2 hours on 12 square yards of raking. She's through in just 3½ hours. Poor Peter, however, has to spend 6 hours on windows and 3 hours on leaves, for a total of 9 hours of work. Can Heather do something to make Peter better off without spending any more of her own time working?

If they decide to specialize, it's not quite as obvious who should specialize in what as it was in the previous example. The concept of opportunity cost provides an answer. When Heather rakes 6 square yards of leaves, she's giving up 4 clean

TABLE 2 AN EXAMPLE OF COMPARATIVE ADVANTAGE

	WINDOWS PER HOUR	SQUARE YARDS OF LEAVES PER HOUR
Heather	4	6
Peter	1	4

windows she could have "produced" in that time. A clean window costs her $1\frac{1}{2}$ square yards of raking. For Peter, a clean window costs 4 square yards of raking. Clearly, Heather's window washing is cheaper than Peter's in terms of alternatives. Heather has a **comparative advantage** in window washing because her opportunity cost is lower in that activity than in the other one. Peter also has a comparative advantage in raking, even though he has an absolute disadvantage in both activities. His opportunity cost of raking leaves is only $\frac{1}{4}$ of a clean window per square yard, and Heather's is $\frac{4}{6}$ or $\frac{2}{3}$. So Peter should specialize in that activity in which he has a comparative advantage, that is, in which his opportunity cost is lower.

Even though Heather is more efficient than Peter at both tasks, they can increase their productivity by specializing on the basis of comparative advantage. Heather washes all the windows, which takes her 3 hours. Peter rakes all the leaves, which takes him 6 hours. By specializing on the basis of comparative advantage, both of them are better off! They have produced the same "output" (clean windows and a leaf-free yard) with considerably less input. Heather saved $\frac{1}{2}$ hour, and Peter saved 3 hours. Both parties gained from specialization. They can use the time saved for leisure, or they can use the extra time to wash the neighbors' windows and rake the neighbors' leaves, getting more output out of the same amount of time spent.

The same principles that determine specialization for two individuals in simple situations apply to more complex situations involving individuals and firms in groups, regions, or nations. Trade between nations is also based on comparative advantage. By specializing, both parties can gain from trade.

Suppose there are two countries called Inland and Outland. Before they discover one another, they are producing the products shown in Table 3. Outland, like Peter, is able to produce less of both commodities. This lack of absolute advantage may be due to Outland's resources being less efficient, or Outland may just be a smaller or poorer country with fewer resources. The reason for absolute advantage or absolute disadvantage makes no difference for comparative advantage and the gains from trade.

The output numbers for Inland and Outland in Table 3 represent points on their production possibilities curves. (To keep things simple, both production possibilities curves are assumed to be straight lines as in Chapter 3.) One more piece of information is needed in order to draw the straight-line production possibilities curve for each country. Assume that each country is devoting two-thirds of its resources to steel and one-third of its resources to cloth. This assumption makes it possible to calculate the end points of their production possibilities curves.

Comparative advantage
The ability to produce something at a lower opportunity cost than other producers face.

TABLE 3 PRODUCTION IN THE ABSENCE OF TRADE

COUNTRY	STEEL (TONS)	CLOTH (BOLTS)
Inland	50	75
Outland	20	60
World Total	70	135

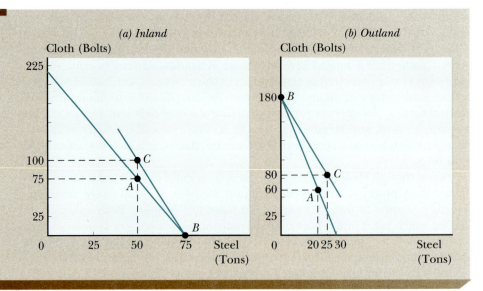

FIGURE 1
PRODUCTION POSSIBILITIES CURVES FOR INLAND AND OUTLAND
The production possibilities curve illustrates the gains from specializing on the basis of comparative advantage. Each country moves from pre-trade production and consumption (point A) to output with specialization (point B) and then to consumption after trade (point C).

If Inland specializes in cloth, the country can produce 225 bolts. If it specializes in steel, it can produce 75 tons. If Outland specializes in cloth, the country can produce 180 bolts. If it specializes in steel, it can produce 30 tons. These points give the production possibilities curves in Figure 1.

Which country should specialize in which product? The answer lies in the two countries' opportunity costs. For Inland, the opportunity cost of producing 75 tons of steel is 225 bolts of cloth not produced, or 3 bolts of cloth per ton of steel. For Outland, the same calculation says that 1 ton of steel costs 6 bolts of cloth. Inland's steel is cheaper in terms of cloth forgone. Measuring the cost of cloth in terms of steel, on the other hand, gives these results: One bolt of Inland cloth costs $1/3$ of a ton of steel, and one bolt of Outland cloth costs only $1/6$ of a ton of steel. Measured in terms of opportunity costs, Outland's cloth is cheaper. The result of specialization is shown in Table 4.

Total world output has increased, without using additional resources, by 5 tons of steel and 45 bolts of cloth. Are the two countries better off? Not yet. After all, they could have been producing those combinations anyway. It is only after trade that they can be better off.

TABLE 4 PRODUCTION BEFORE AND AFTER SPECIALIZATION

COUNTRY	BEFORE SPECIALIZATION		AFTER SPECIALIZATION	
	STEEL (TONS)	CLOTH (BOLTS)	STEEL (TONS)	CLOTH (BOLTS)
Inland	50	75	75	0
Outland	20	60	0	180
World Total	70	135	75	180

THE TERMS OF TRADE

The rate at which Inland and Outland trade steel for cloth is called the **terms of trade**. Inland will not accept less than 3 bolts of cloth for a ton of steel, because this country can do that well producing its own cloth. Outland will not offer more than 6 bolts of cloth per ton of steel, because more than that would make it cheaper not to specialize. Anywhere between 3 and 6 bolts of cloth per ton of steel should be a mutually acceptable trading ratio. Let's make the terms of trade 4 bolts of cloth for 1 ton of steel. The terms of trade will always lie somewhere between the two trading parties' opportunity costs. Exactly where the terms of trade fall between those limits depends on the relative strength of demand for both products in both countries.

There are numerous after-trade combinations of steel and cloth that could make both countries better off. One possibility is to let Inland take all of its gains from trade in extra cloth, keeping its steel consumption at the original level of 50 tons and trading away the other 25 tons to Outland for 100 bolts of cloth. That exchange leaves Outland with 25 tons of imported steel and 80 bolts of domestic cloth, a consumption combination that represents more of both goods. The results of trade are summarized in Table 5.

These new consumption points are shown in Figure 1. Point C in part (a) shows Inland consuming 50 tons of steel and 100 bolts of cloth. Point C in part (b) represents a consumption combination of 25 tons of steel and 80 bolts of cloth for Outland. In each graph, this point lies along a "terms of trade" line, or a **consumption possibilities curve**, beginning at point B (total production with specialization) and having a slope of $\frac{1}{4}$ (1 steel to 4 cloth). Each country is able to get beyond its production possibilities curve by separating production (at point B) from consumption (at point C). The gains from trade are the same kinds of improvements in well-being that a country gets from having additional economic resources. Point C in each case represents one of many trade and consumption combinations that makes that partner better off.

THE SOURCES OF COMPARATIVE ADVANTAGE

What makes Inland better at producing steel and Outland better at producing cloth? For some products, the reasons are obvious. Climate determines the cheapest place to produce bananas, potatoes, and other agricultural products.

Terms of trade
The ratio at which one product is exchanged for another.

Consumption possibilities curve
A line showing the consumption combinations attainable through trade.

TABLE 5 GAINS FROM TRADE

COUNTRY	BEFORE SPECIALIZATION		AFTER SPECIALIZATION		AFTER TRADE	
	STEEL	CLOTH	STEEL	CLOTH	STEEL	CLOTH
Inland	50	75	75	0	50	100
Outland	20	60	0	180	25	80
World Total	70	135	75	180	75	180

Mineral resources determine other production patterns. Some products use a high proportion of unskilled labor relative to capital and other inputs. These products will be produced in countries with relatively large amounts of low-cost, unskilled labor. Other products require relatively more skilled labor, capital, or fertile land. These products will be produced in countries where those resources are more abundant. The basis of comparative advantage in resource endowments (relative amounts of capital and labor) and input requirements (whether goods are capital-intensive or labor-intensive) was stated in the 1930s by Swedish economist Bertil Ohlin and German economist Eli Heckscher. This idea is known as the Heckscher-Ohlin proposition.

Resource endowments and input requirements do not explain all of the patterns of trade. Some products follow what economist Raymond Vernon called the **product cycle**. When the product is introduced, it will be exported by the country in which it was developed. But as the product and the production process become standardized, production will eventually migrate to other countries with a suitable resource mix. Automobiles, whose production technology was developed in the United States, are now produced almost everywhere. Textiles were originally developed in England, but the production of simple cotton textiles (the most standardized part of the industry) has migrated around the globe in search of the inexpensive, low-skill labor that is used heavily in their manufacture.

Product cycle
A series of stages, from development through standardization, through which a new product passes.

Sometimes the explanation for comparative advantage lies in historical accident. A product starts being produced in country *A* because that is where it was invented, or because its citizens want such a product. Country *A* develops the skills and resources needed to produce that product, including related industries that supply inputs or use the product in making other goods. If *A*'s resources are suited to the production of the good, *A* is likely to have a comparative advantage that it can retain for some time. As *A* specializes more and more in the production of a particular good, its costs continue to fall, unlike the constant cost examples we have used earlier. Access to a large world market instead of a smaller domestic one may enable a small number of firms in just a few countries to operate at a more efficient scale.

For many products, economies of scale are an important factor in being able to compete in a global market. If the world market is not large, there may be room only for a few suppliers who take advantage of cost savings in large-scale production. The first producer may enjoy a lasting advantage for that reason. Scale economies are especially important for large durable goods such as mainframe computers, aircraft, and heavy machinery. Consumers also benefit from economies of scale because lower costs mean lower prices.

All these factors may explain the existence of comparative advantage. Regardless of the source of comparative advantage, the important point is that it is possible for both partners to increase output and reduce prices to consumers by specializing on the basis of comparative advantage.

TRADE AND COMPETITION

Another important benefit from trade is increased competition. Trade increases the number of competing firms from whom consumers can buy, widening their range of choices of goods and suppliers. This benefit of trade can be very important if the domestic industry has only a few firms. For example, car buyers in the United States have a wide range of choices because of international trade, although there are only a few domestic producers. As a result of foreign competition, domestic producers have responded to demands of some car buyers for smaller, more fuel-efficient cars.

TARIFFS AND QUOTAS

With all of these good reasons for free trade, why are some U.S. firms and industries protected from foreign competition? Many arguments are offered by firms that have to compete with imports, but most of these arguments come down to one reason—income distribution. A country as a whole benefits from free trade, but not everyone in the country benefits equally.

Protection of domestic industries is accomplished with two main tools: tariffs and quotas. A **tariff** is a tax on imported goods or services. The tariff can be specific (based on weight, volume, or number of units) or *ad valorem* (figured as a percentage of the price). The average U.S. tariff is less than 5 percent. Many items bear no tariff at all, and a few items have large tariffs.

A **quota** is a quantity limit. It specifies the maximum amount of a good or service that can be imported during a given time period (usually a year). Quotas can be global (limiting total imports of widgets from all foreign suppliers to 1,000 widgets per year) or geographic (assigning quotas to specific countries). Quotas also can be combined with tariffs in a **tariff quota**. In this case, a certain amount of a good from one country is allowed to enter another country without a tariff. For amounts in excess of that limit, a tariff is applied.

EFFECTS OF A TARIFF

Figure 2 illustrates the effects of a specific tariff. In this figure, Inland produces, consumes, and imports cheese. The domestic supply curve is S_d. The domestic demand curve is D_d. Because Inland is a small country, its purchases of imported goods do not affect the world price of those goods. Inland can buy all the cheese it wants at the world price, P_w. At P_w, domestic producers are producing A pounds and consumers are buying B pounds. The difference between production and consumption is imports of $B - A$ pounds of cheese.

P_t is the price of imported cheese after Inland imposed a tariff equal to T. Since the tariff drives up the price, consumers buy less. Cheese consumption falls to C. Domestic producers move up along their supply curve to E. They get a bigger share of the smaller market. Imports decrease from $B - A$ to $C - E$.

Who gains? Domestic producers, including their owners, workers, and suppliers. These firms can charge a higher price and have a larger market share, which benefits everyone connected with them. Government also gains some tariff revenue. Who loses? Domestic consumers are paying more and getting less, so they lose. Foreign producers have lost sales. Also, the country imposing the tariff has given up some of the benefits of free trade noted earlier—more output, competition, and economies of scale. Since foreign cheese producers are more efficient than most of Inland's domestic cheese producers, this country is switching from more efficient to less efficient producers.

Tariff
A tax on an imported good or service.

Quota
A limit on the amount of a good or service that can be imported during a given time period.

Tariff quota
A combination of a quota and a tariff that allows a certain amount of a good or service to be imported without paying a tariff and imposes the tariff on further imports.

EFFECTS OF A QUOTA

Quotas are similar to tariffs. In fact, they can be represented by the same diagram. The main difference is that quotas restrict quantity, and tariffs work through prices. If, in Figure 2, the government imposed a quota in the amount of $C - E$ on cheese, the effects on price, domestic production, consumption, and imports would be the same as those of the tariff $T = P_t - P_w$.

Quotas come in a number of forms. The limit may be placed on the physical quantity imported or the value of the product imported. A quota may be combined with a tariff so that a certain amount enters tariff-free, and imports over that amount are subject to a tariff. Or a quota may be negotiated with the exporting country on a "voluntary" basis in the form of voluntary export restraints, which is the kind of protection that the United States provided for steel and autos in the 1980s. Other than these two products, most U.S. quotas are for agricultural products, such as beef and sugar, and are linked to domestic farm programs.

DIFFERENCES BETWEEN TARIFFS AND QUOTAS

Although Figure 2 seems to suggest that tariffs and quotas are very similar, there are some important differences. First, a tariff raises revenue for the government, in the amount of the nonshaded area in Figure 2. A quota generates no government revenue. All the benefits of a quota go to protected domestic producers and to those importers who manage to get the scarce and valuable import permits used to implement quotas. Permit holders can buy the good at the low foreign price and resell it at the higher domestic price. The difference between the price the importer pays the foreign supplier and the price the importer can charge the domestic consumer $(P_t - P_w)$ times the number of units imported is a monopoly profit that comes from having a license to import. Note that this

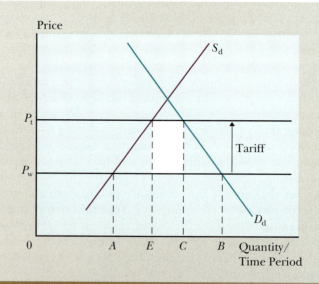

FIGURE 2
EFFECTS OF A TARIFF OR QUOTA
A tariff $(T = P_t - P_w)$ or an equivalent quota $(C - E)$ raises prices for domestic consumers (from P_w to P_t), reduces imports (from $B - A$ to $C - E$), lowers consumption (from B to C) and increases domestic output and sales (from A to E).

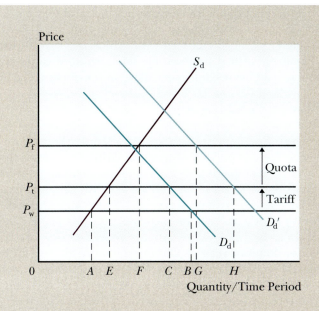

FIGURE 3

EFFECTS OF A TARIFF OR QUOTA WHEN DEMAND INCREASES

Under a tariff, an increase in demand increases the quantity of imports (from $C - E$ to $H - E$) and consumption (from C to H) but leaves price unchanged at P_t. With a quota, increased demand leads to a rise in price for domestic consumers (from P_t to P_f) and an increase in domestic production (from E to F). Consumption rises slightly (from B to G). Imports are unchanged ($G - F = C - E$).

monopoly profit is equal to the revenue the government would have received under a tariff.

Second, suppose demand increased in the country. With a tariff, the quantity of imports would increase. With a quota, only the price would increase. Originally, the tariff (T) and the quota ($C - E$) had the same effect on prices and quantities. As Figure 3 shows, however, when demand shifts from D_d to D'_d under a tariff, imports rise to $H - E$ and consumption rises to H. With a quota, price rises to P_f. Imports remain the same ($C - E = G - F$). Domestic production rises to F, and consumption rises slightly to G.

Most economists prefer a policy of free trade to either tariffs or quotas. If they have to choose, they usually consider a tariff less harmful in terms of effi-

KEY IDEAS

TARIFFS VERSUS QUOTAS

A TARIFF	A QUOTA
• Raises prices	• Raises prices
• Reduces imports and consumption	• Reduces imports and consumption
• Increases domestic output	• Increases domestic output
• Produces government revenue	• Creates monopoly profits for those with import licenses
• Lets imports rise when demand increases	• Makes prices rise when demand increases

ciency than an equivalent quota for some rather practical reasons. A tariff does allow imports to increase in response to increases in demand. Also, at least some of the tariff revenue goes to the government, which uses it to further the general welfare. Finally, a tariff is more visible and therefore easier to eliminate. Because a quota is less obvious, it is more likely to remain in place indefinitely.

NONTARIFF BARRIERS TO TRADE

In addition to tariffs and quotas, there are other kinds of government barriers to trade. Domestic laws or policies other than tariffs and quotas that interfere with the free exchange of goods and services across national borders are called **nontariff barriers**. Some of these barriers are intentional. One example is *domestic preference laws* (known as "Buy American" in the United States). These laws require the government to favor domestic suppliers when making purchases for government agencies and programs. Other nontariff barriers are laws or regulations enacted for domestic reasons that make it more difficult for foreign suppliers to compete. For example, it may be difficult for a foreign supplier to comply with U.S. safety standards and labeling requirements. A common form of nontariff barrier is requiring excessive paperwork that adds to costs and reduces profits for foreign suppliers and domestic importing firms. In France, a shortage of customs inspectors constitutes a nontariff barrier because it creates long delays and thus discourages imports.

Sometimes nontariff barriers work the other way. Some U.S. laws and regulations make it more difficult for domestic firms to sell abroad. If American products must meet higher safety standards, for example, the American firm may not be able to compete with foreign producers who do not have to incur those costs.

An important nontariff barrier is antidumping codes. Dumping consists of selling a good at a lower price in a foreign country than in the firm's home country. Firms may dump abroad to get rid of surpluses, to take advantage of differences in elasticity of demand (price discrimination), or to establish a foothold in a competitive market. Most countries, including the United States, have antidumping regulations that forbid this practice as unfair competition. If a foreign firm is accused of dumping (usually by a competing firm in the importing country), the International Trade Commission will hear the case and may impose a duty on the dumped good to counteract the price difference. American firms often charge foreign firms with dumping in order to make selling in the United States more difficult for foreign competitors.

Since 1985, there have been more than 320 government investigations of dumping claims filed by U.S. firms. Other countries also have antidumping regulations. Canada filed a complaint about dumping by American steel firms and beer brewers in 1993; India has claimed dumping in polyvinyl chloride, Mexico in telephone connections, and the EC in soda ash and artificial sweeteners.[1] Reduction in other trade barriers both through negotiated tariff reductions and formation of free trade areas means that domestic producers increasingly turn to claims of dumping, valid or not, as their last defense against foreign competition.

Nontariff barriers
Trade restrictions other than tariffs or quotas.

1. "Now the Tables Are Turning," *Newsweek* (August 9, 1993): 43.

U.S. COMMERCIAL POLICY

The set of actions that a country undertakes to deliberately influence trade in goods and services is its **commercial policy**. For most of its history, the United States has had high tariffs and other trade restrictions. The highest U.S. tariff ever was imposed by the Smoot-Hawley Act of 1930, an average charge of 53 percent.

Since 1934, the United States has greatly reduced tariffs and other trade barriers by negotiating treaties with other countries. Trade barriers were reduced under a series of Congressional acts, beginning with the Reciprocal Trade Agreements Act of 1934. Regular trade negotiations led to reductions in tariffs by the United States and its major trading partners through GATT (General Agreement on Tariffs and Trade), a multilateral process started in 1947. As more nations have joined free trade areas and other trading blocs, the multilateral trade negotiations have declined in importance.

The latest complete series of trade negotiations, which took place from 1974 to 1979, was called the Tokyo Round. After the tariff cuts agreed to in that round were finally implemented, the average U.S. tariff was only about 4.2 percent. The Tokyo Round also involved some agreements on reducing nontariff barriers. In 1986, a round of negotiations called the Uruguay Round began. They were scheduled to end in December 1990, but because of disagreements over trade in agricultural products between the United States and Europe, that round dragged on several years beyond the deadline before finally resulting in a modest agreement to cut tariffs, reduce barriers to trade in financial services, and resolve some conflicts over agricultural issues.

> **Commercial policy**
> The set of actions that a country undertakes to deliberately influence trade in goods and services.

THE RATIONALE FOR PROTECTION

The reduction in tariffs over the last sixty years does not mean that the United States, or other GATT members, have arrived at free trade. Quotas still protect autos, steel, textiles, and other industries. Nontariff barriers are still an important impediment to free trade.

The battle between free trade and protectionism is an ongoing one. Most demands for protection come from industries that once had a comparative advantage but lost it when other industries developed even greater relative efficiency. Such demands also come from industries where monopoly or oligopoly conditions allowed them to ignore the need to improve technology and productivity. Shoes, clothing, steel, and automobiles are U.S. industries that have asked for protection because they lost a comparative advantage. Part of the problem with steel and automobiles is that they have been slow to modernize and to respond to changes in consumer preferences. More recently, however, both of these industries have become more competitive. Small, worker-owned steel mills have had some success in regaining their share of the U.S. market, while Detroit's Big Three have outstripped Japanese cars to reestablish their dominance in the U.S. car market. Protectionists credit these gains to the breathing space provided by temporary protection from foreign competition. Free traders argue that these improvements would have happened faster under the stimulus of free trade and foreign competition.

ECONOMIC ARGUMENTS FOR PROTECTION

When workers and owners from import-competing firms go to Washington to lobby for protection, they use some tried and true arguments. Some of these arguments have some economic validity. Others have strong political or emotional appeal, but weak economic foundations.

INFANT INDUSTRY. One theoretically valid argument for protection is the infant industry argument. An infant industry is a new industry that is not yet ready to compete with established foreign producers. Given some time (and sheltered conditions) to master the technology, establish a reputation, train workers, and reach economies of scale, the infant industry may eventually be competitive. Comparative advantage can change over time. Temporary protection could give an infant industry the chance to acquire a comparative advantage and "catch up" with established foreign firms.

This argument is only valid if the protected industry will be competitive in time. There is no reason to protect industries that will never be competitive, wasting scarce resources that could be better used elsewhere. There should be no need to protect industries that will quickly become competitive, because entrepreneurs (and lenders) should be able to see past the early losses to profits. The only industries that really qualify are those that generate some kinds of external benefits to society that they are unable to recoup in the early years. Examples of such external benefits include developing roads and power sources that are then available to other industries, training a labor force that may migrate to other firms, or producing a low-cost input that other industries can use. Thus, the few deserving infant industries are those that are not profitable by simple cost and revenue calculations, but are worth protecting because they meet two tests:

1. They will eventually be able to compete in the market without protection.
2. They generate benefits to society that are worth the cost of a tariff.

Infant industry as an argument for protection usually appears in other guises, such as a period of restructuring, or industrial policy. Many advocates of protection point to the success of Japan and Korea, which experienced economic growth with very restrictive trade barriers, developed along infant industry lines. They argue that the same could be true of the United States. However, the external benefits that are the basis of the infant industry argument are likely to be created in less developed countries. It's difficult to make a convincing case for protecting an infant industry in a developed country such as the United States. Even in less developed countries, this argument is easily abused by overstating external benefits and underestimating how long it will take for the industry to become competitive.

NATIONAL DEFENSE. Another common and economically valid argument for protection is national defense. The product of this industry may be needed in wartime, the argument goes, but the domestic producer can't compete with cheaper foreign producers. Without protection during peacetime, the firm may not be here when war comes and foreign supplies are cut off. This argument gained merit after the War of 1812. England had been the United States's main trading partner and then became an enemy who successfully blockaded the U.S. coast. Again, during World War II, German interference with shipping created problems in obtaining some needed supplies.

However, this argument makes little sense for the United States, especially since the end of the Cold War. The government stockpiles strategic raw materials, and most products needed in wartime are those in which the United States has a comparative advantage, such as heavy machinery, sophisticated electronics, and aircraft. Economists Leland Yeager and David Tuerck argue that the national defense claim only applies in the case of another World War II, what they describe as a "prolonged nonnuclear war of attrition."[2] But, they argue, the more likely kinds of wars—the kind the Pentagon seems to be preparing for—are either "brush fire" wars, such as the Panamanian invasion of 1990 and other localized battles, which do not affect U.S. access to supplies, or else all-out nuclear war, in which case there would be no time to resupply. Even the 1991 Gulf War, which was somewhat larger than a brush fire war, did not affect U.S. access to shipping and supplies.

OFFSETTING DISTORTIONS. Another argument offered for protection is that such distortions may be needed to offset other distortions. Monopoly, government policies, and externalities often cause a divergence between private and social costs and benefits, and governmental policy may not be able to eliminate this divergence in order to pursue the first-best policy of free trade. Then a second-best policy of tariffs may improve economic well-being by introducing new distortions that negate the effects of existing distortions.

The theory of the second best can be used to justify import restrictions on a selective basis when external effects make the private costs to a domestic producer higher than the social costs to the country. Consider, for example, an excise tax on a domestically produced good, automobile tires, that is an input into another good, cars. This tax raises the cost of producing cars because the price of cars will include the excise tax. As a result, domestic production of cars is lower, and imports of cars are higher than they would be without the excise tax on tires. The country is importing cars at a higher social price than it would cost to produce them at home. An import duty on cars equal to the excise tax on a set of tires would increase the domestic production of cars to the point where the marginal social cost of imported cars and the marginal cost of domestic production are equal.

If government created cost differences or foreign trade restrictions affected all industries equally, they would not affect comparative costs and distort the efficient pattern of specialization and trade. It is only when these factors affect different industries differently that there may be a distortion of relative prices that justifies some kind of protection. For example, the minimum wage has more impact on costs for industries that use large amounts of unskilled labor than for industries that use primarily highly skilled labor and capital. Thus, the minimum wage raises the costs of the first type of industry more than the second.

The theory of the second best is not limited to trade theory. It recognizes that whenever market prices fail to reflect real opportunity costs, a second-best policy may be appropriate. You should remember, however, that the first-best policy is free trade.

2. Leland B. Yeager and David G. Tuerck, *Foreign Trade and U.S. Policy* (New York: Praeger, 1976).

EMPLOYMENT. The employment argument suggests that reducing imports can create jobs producing import substitutes. However, the cost of doing so is high. Tariffs encourage the development of domestic industries producing import substitutes, usually products in which the nation has a comparative disadvantage. This policy encourages inefficient use of scarce resources. Furthermore, tariffs usually lead to retaliatory tariffs on the exports of the country imposing the tariff. The tariff-imposing country may gain jobs in import-competing industries and lose them in more efficient exporting industries.

CHEAP FOREIGN LABOR. The cheap foreign labor argument popular among protectionists goes something like this: "We're just as efficient as the foreign competition—we use the same machinery and technology and produce at least as high a quality product. However, U.S. labor costs are at least $8.00 an hour, and firms in some foreign countries have to pay only $1.00 an hour. How can we possibly compete?"

There are several possible answers. One is that cheap labor often means lower productivity. Another is that labor, especially unskilled labor, may be cheap in some countries, but other inputs such as capital and skilled labor are relatively expensive. A country such as the United States should concentrate on producing those products that use relatively more of its abundant (and, therefore, relatively less expensive) resources—capital and skilled labor.

THE POLITICS OF PROTECTION

Fair trade
The idea that the United States should impose trade barriers equivalent to those that its trading partners place on U.S. exports.

If there are so few valid economic arguments for protection, why does protection exist? There is a group of politically appealing arguments labeled **fair trade**. The concept of fair trade is often described as a "level playing field." If foreign countries erect tariff barriers, nontariff barriers, or quotas that limit U.S. firms' exports to those countries, protectionists argue that the United States should do the same. For example, if the Japanese make it very difficult or expensive for their citizens to buy U.S. automobiles or beef, protectionists say that Americans should treat Japanese exports the same way.

Some protectionists argue that it is more costly to operate in the U.S. market than in other markets. U.S. firms pay high corporate taxes, face strict environmental and safety standards, and have to comply with employment regulations such as affirmative action, minimum wage, and overtime pay. Many foreign producers, especially in less developed countries, do not incur similar costs. They can participate in the U.S. market without incurring the costs of maintaining it. This issue has received considerable attention recently because of the proposed free trade area between the United States and Mexico. Mexico has lax environmental standards and few employment regulations. These fair trade arguments are usually put forward by organized lobbies for industries that are losing sales to foreign competitors. The appeal makes sense to the average voter, because it is couched in terms of fair play and equal treatment. International trade differs from domestic trade in that the political dimension carries much more weight. Political concerns help to explain why the economically sound practice of free trade is rarely implemented.

The politics of protectionism is about winners and losers, like most political issues. It is easy to identify gainers and losers from tariffs and quotas. Consumers lose. Foreign producers lose sales. Domestic competitors gain. One loser who

POLICY FOCUS: "I LIFT MY LAMP BESIDE THE GOLDEN DOOR"

These words by Emma Lazarus, inscribed on the Statue of Liberty, represented the immigration policy of the United States in the eighteenth and much of the nineteenth century. Today, immigration policy is hotly debated, legal immigration is subject to quotas, and the Immigration and Naturalization Service (INS) is trying to cope with a steady stream of illegal immigrants from all parts of the globe. Should the United States still have an open door? Is there a limit to the number of immigrants we can absorb? If we limit immigration, how many should we take, and from where, and for what reason? Political refugees? Skilled workers? What about the Haitian boat people, the refugees from former Yugoslavia, the boatloads of Chinese?

While politicians debate, Western Europe is trying to cope with a flood of refugees, especially from Russia and Bosnia, and the United States is invaded by an estimated 1.5 million illegal immigrants a year. France and Germany have responded with new restrictions on working without a permanent visa and tighter border patrols.

The United States thought that the Immigration Reform and Control Act in 1986 would solve the problem with larger quotas, legalization of illegal aliens already here, and tighter checks on work permits with stiff penalties for employing illegal aliens. But with only 350 INS employees available to police industries, the odds of getting caught are very small.

In 1992 and 1993, *National Review* opened its pages to a debate on the issue. An article by Peter Brimelow in 1992 opposing immigration resulted in replies from Julian Simon, George Borjas, Ben J. Wattenberg, Dan Stein, and Robert L. Bartley, a group of economists and economic journalists with a variety of perspectives.[a] Brimelow's arguments were based on the effects on wages for those already here and the cultural impact of absorbing large numbers of citizens at once—especially immigrants from a non-European background.

Simon supports immigration because he believes that the additional resources in the form of labor will enhance our standard of living, while cultural diversity will enrich our lives. Wattenberg points to low birth rates in the United States that would actually result in a declining U.S. population in the absence of immigration. In fact, some advocates of open immigration see a need for young workers to fund the Social Security System when the baby boomers start to retire in 2012!

On the negative side, Borjas argues that even low welfare benefits are attractive compared to the income that can be earned in many source countries, and our income redistribution policies are acting as a magnet. Stein points out that other countries, such as Australia, are restricting immigration. Those countries that remain open will be attracting even larger flows of immigrants if they do not undertake defensive restrictions.

Behind the rhetoric on both sides are some fairly straightforward issues. One is the cost of immigration enforcement—patrolling the borders, verifying work status, holding hearings, and deporting illegal aliens. How much are we willing to spend to keep people out of the country? A second is the role of welfare benefits and public services in attracting immigrants. A third issue is "absorptive capacity." How quickly can we settle immigrants into jobs and housing, teach them the language, and prepare them for citizenship? Are we placing an undue share of the costs of absorbing immigrants on a few points of entry, like Florida, California, and Texas?

The overriding issue, however, is the costs and benefits of new citizens and workers. They add to production. They take jobs American citizens refuse, as day laborers, agricultural laborers, domestics, and assembly line workers. They pay taxes and expand our consumer market. On the negative side, they crowd schools in many areas with students that cost more to teach because they come from a different culture and speak no English at home. Some of them receive welfare benefits and other services provided by the taxpayer. They compete with workers at the bottom of the skill ladder, who are the ones already most likely to suffer from prolonged spells of unemployment. Those who favor free and open immigration point to the benefits, while those opposed focus on the costs. The debate is as old as the Constitution, and immigration will continue to be a divisive public issue in decades to come.

---

a. "Why Control the Borders?" *National Review* (February 1, 1993): 27–33.

does not show up in Figures 2 and 3 is the U.S. exporter. When one country raises tariffs, other countries are likely to do so in response, and the first country's exports fall. Another group that suffers are firms that use imported goods subject to trade restrictions who have to pay more for their inputs. Thus, political support for free trade should come from a coalition between exporting firms and consumers, with help from wholesalers and retailers of imported goods and importers of raw materials and semifinished goods. However, such a diverse group is not easy to organize and hold together.

Firms that gain from protection spend large sums of money in lobbying to get or keep a tariff or quota. Consider a tariff on shoes. As a consumer, you may find that the tariff only costs you a few more dollars a year, so it's hardly worthwhile to lobby against the tariff. But if you are a worker whose job in a shoe factory depends on protection, or a shoe manufacturer losing sales to imports, you will work much harder to get and keep protection. Even though the total benefits of free trade would exceed the costs, complaints from a few big losers tend to generate far more noise and attention than the lobbying for free trade. If the losers are concentrated in certain regions, the American system of representation by states and districts makes it easier for them to develop "client" relationships with their members of Congress.

PART WAY TO FREE TRADE: FREE TRADE AREAS AND COMMON MARKETS

In the last few decades the move toward lowering tariff barriers has taken a turn toward the formation of regional trading blocs. While the GATT negotiations have encouraged each nation to lower its barriers uniformly for all its trading partners, a trading bloc eliminates trade barriers only for selected countries. A **free trade area** consists of a group of countries that have agreed to eliminate trade barriers—tariffs, quotas, and nontariff barriers—among themselves, while retaining their own barriers to trade with the rest of the world. A **common market** is a much more closely knit trading bloc, in which nations eliminate not only trade barriers but also barriers to the flow of labor and capital among themselves. They also adopt a common external set of tariffs and quotas, and agree on other common policies, such as unemployment insurance, tax policy, and professional licensing.

TRADE CREATION AND TRADE DIVERSION

From an economic perspective, there are some important differences between cutting your tariffs or quotas for all potential sellers and cutting barriers for just one or two countries. Suppose that the United States eliminates a tariff on imported shoes from Mexico as a result of a free trade area. Before, the United States may have been producing its own expensive shoes. Now, U.S. consumers have a choice of cheaper Mexican shoes. This gain in consumer welfare is the same as the gain from free trade. It results from changing suppliers from a higher-cost to a lower-cost source. When this happens, a free trade area or common market results in **trade creation**, which means shifting from a higher cost to a lower cost source of supply as a result of forming a trading bloc.

Free trade area
An agreement between two or more countries to eliminate tariffs and other trade barriers on trade among themselves, while each country maintains its existing trade barriers to outside countries.

Common market
A free trade area with a common external tariff, free movement of capital and labor, and harmonization of social and economic policies.

Trade creation
Shifting from a higher-cost supplier to a lower-cost supplier as a result of forming a free trade area or common market.

Trading blocs also can reduce welfare by limiting access to cheaper outside suppliers. Suppose, again, that the United States eliminates a tariff on Mexican shoes as a result of a free trade area. However, the United States keeps its tariff on shoes from other sources, such as Brazil, or may even adopt the higher Mexican tariff on shoes from outside the free trade area. Suppose, further, that Brazil is even more efficient than Mexico at producing shoes. Before the free trade area, the United States was buying shoes from Brazil, even with the tariff. Now, Mexican shoes are artificially cheaper, and the United States switches suppliers to the higher-cost producer because of the free trade area. When a free trade area or common market results in shifting from a higher cost to a lower-cost source of supply as a result of forming a trading bloc, there is **trade diversion**.

Trade diversion
Shifting from a lower-cost supplier to a higher-cost supplier as a result of forming a free trade area or common market.

NAFTA

The North American Free Trade Area is a large single market made up of the United States, Canada, and Mexico, in which tariffs, quotas, and nontariff barriers on trade with each other will be gradually eliminated. The NAFTA treaty is the second stage of a process that began in November 1989, when Canadian voters approved the Canada-U.S. Trade Agreement (CUSTA) establishing a free trade area between the United States and Canada.

CUSTA called for a ten-year phase-in of complete free trade. Before the pact, about 75 percent of the markets between the two countries had free trade. Autos have been freely traded since 1965. The beneficiaries of this agreement were predicted to be primarily Canadian consumers and U.S. producers, because Canadian tariffs were about three times higher than U.S. tariffs. A number of Canadian producers, especially along the U.S. border, are unhappy with the agreement.

A second precursor of the NAFTA agreement was *maquiladoras*, or border plants, which have been booming along the U.S.-Mexican border since 1965. Nearly half a million Mexicans are employed in almost 2,000 plants. These plants receive shipments of parts from U.S. manufacturers and assemble the parts into complete products. Any tariffs are due only on the value added. General Motors, Ford, and General Electric are among the many firms that produce parts in the United States and ship them to *maquiladoras* for assembly. In 1986, this trade amounted to more than $65 billion.

The NAFTA agreement will greatly expand the range of products that are traded freely between the United States and Mexico (also Canada and Mexico). Organized labor in the United States, as well as in Canada, was strongly opposed to such an agreement. Labor leaders argued that Mexican firms enjoy an unfair advantage because they do not have to meet the environmental and safety standards that U.S. firms do. They have pressed for supplementary agreements covering these issues.

Most economists feel that the worries over the impact of NAFTA on U.S. jobs and investment in Mexico are overstated. The Mexican economy is small relative to that of the United States—a GDP of $334 billion in 1992 compared to the United States at $5,950 billion. The incentive to invest in Mexico will be less under NAFTA than before for firms who located there in order to avoid Mexican tariffs. A prosperous and successful neighbor to the south will benefit

American firms who are already seeing increased exports of both consumer and producer goods and services to Mexico.

THE EUROPEAN COMMUNITY

Supporters of NAFTA pointed to the success of the European Community (EC) in revitalizing Europe in the last two decades. The European Community began with six nations in 1957 and has expanded to take in twelve nations in a common market. In the 1960s, the original six nations eliminated tariffs and other trade barriers, merged their agricultural price support systems, and adopted a common domestic tax, the tax on value added. Gradually, other policies were brought into line, making it easy for capital and labor to move freely without worrying about such differences as health and safety standards and social insurance benefits. EC citizens have a common passport and do not have to wait in long lines when going from one country to another.

In the 1970s and 1980s, the EC grew larger, adding six more countries. This addition slowed the process of welding the nations into a single economic unit. In 1992, after lengthy preparation, EC92 took a leap forward. Three hundred directives reduced other barriers to a unified market, such as different labelling requirements and professional licensing standards.

One goal that has eluded the EC is a common currency. Because of differences in national monetary policies, the attempt to establish a single currency has been put on hold. The reunification of Germany in 1990 also slowed the process of unifying the EC because Germany is now so large in area, population, and GDP relative to the other member states that some of them fear German domination. Another obstacle to further integration is that there are several other countries that would like to join. Austria is the most likely addition in the near future, but Turkey has applied, and most of the formerly communist nations of Central Europe from Poland to Bulgaria would like to be considered. If the EC expands again, absorbing these new members will divert energy from further unification and also create more differences to be resolved just because the union has more partners.

Overall, the experience with the EC has been positive. The large single market has increased trade both within the EC and between the EC and the outside world. This market has attracted investment and promoted growth, although there is still considerable unemployment in several member nations. The EC is comparable in population and wealth to the United States, making it an attractive export market, an appealing place to invest, and a player with considerable clout on the world stage. The EC's successes have been the inspiration for trading blocs in other parts of the world, especially in the Americas.

MOVEMENT OF RESOURCES: IMMIGRATION AND DIRECT INVESTMENT

If trading countries benefit from the flow of goods and services, what about benefits from the flow of inputs? Labor, capital, and raw materials also move between countries. In general, the movement of inputs between countries can substitute for free movement of goods. If a country is poor in raw materials, capital, or skilled labor, it has two possible remedies: It can import goods that incorpo-

GLOBAL OUTLOOK: THE OTHER FREE TRADE AGREEMENT

While North America has been focused on NAFTA, south of the Panama Canal another large free trade area has been taking shape. This free trade area, called Mercosur, takes in four nations in South America—Brazil, Argentina, Uruguay, and Paraguay. Together, they make up a market of 190 million people with a combined GDP of $427 billion.[a] Under the Asunción treaty of March 1991, tariffs are being reduced rapidly, with total elimination scheduled for December 1994. The new free trade area is a major destination for exports from the United States ($8.8 billion in 1991) and the European Community, but trade within Mercosur is also growing rapidly.

Mercosur is the latest in a series of attempts to organize free trade areas in Latin America. In the late 1960s, four small nations of Central America organized the Central American Common Market, which lasted until political problems and guerrilla warfare tore the relationship apart in the early 1970s. An earlier attempt to form a Latin American Free Trade Area (LAFTA) struggled along for about ten years in the 1960s and 1970s before giving up. The NAFTA agreement, which was in development since the early 1980s, was a spur to yet further efforts. In 1990, President Bush proclaimed a dream of a free trade area from Anchorage, Alaska, to Tierra del Fuego (the southern tip of South America). Already, Chile had taken steps to liberalize trade with Mexico, and has recently signed agreements with both Argentina and Bolivia. Colombia is opening its markets to Venezuela and Ecuador on a reciprocal basis. As a result of that agreement, trade between Colombia and Venezuela increased from $525 million in 1990 to $932 million in 1992.[b]

The two large nations in Mercosur, Brazil and Argentina, see the new free trade area as one step in a series aimed at turning their economies around. The area is rich in natural resources and has great potential for economic growth. Both countries have been working hard to bring inflation under control and to sell off their inefficient state-owned industries. Competition within the free trade area should provide a larger market and more competition in order to stimulate productivity and investment. Already, Eastman Kodak, Ford-Volkswagen, and Monsanto have made major investment commitments in response to the new free trade area.

Like all free trade agreements, these trade blocs have a downside. There is some diversion of trade from outside partners to partners within the union. Members have to compromise their national sovereignty in order to accommodate the policies of other members. But for a continent with a long history of protectionism, Mercosur and the other trade agreements are an important step in the direction of open trading markets.

a. "The New World's Newest Trading Bloc," *Business Week* (May 4, 1992): 50–51.
b. "Latin American Trade: Patchwork," *The Economist* (May 15, 1993): 85–86.

---

rate large quantities of those inputs, or it can import those inputs and produce its own final products. Both kinds of trade should bring benefits. In the absence of artificial barriers, market considerations determine which choice is more efficient—to move the final product or to move the input.

When labor and capital move from country to country, you can count on objections from those who are threatened by foreign competition. Foreign competition is unpopular with the owners of productive resources, whether the competition is in product markets or in resource markets. Thus, these owners seek restrictions on the movement of resources as well as on the movement of goods.

Organized labor, for example, opposes immigration of workers and construction of plants abroad. Newly arrived workers compete for jobs and depress wages. An offshore plant of a U.S. firm means more jobs for foreign workers and fewer jobs for American workers. Domestic firms oppose letting their foreign competitors locate inside the country with no tariff wall for protection. Canada is cautious about letting U.S. firms build new plants in that country, and countries such as Kuwait and Japan have even tighter restrictions. Emotional and political arguments are sometimes stronger than economic concerns. Many U.S. citizens are unhappy about the purchase of U.S. banks, farmland, and resort islands by foreign firms and individuals, even when there are no obvious adverse consequences.

The United States puts fewer restrictions than most countries on the inflow or outflow of capital. Except for strategic raw materials (those needed for national defense), there are no restrictions on the flow of natural resources. Exports of natural resources such as oil and copper are often restricted by countries with some market power as suppliers. Some of these countries use controls on exports of these resources to generate revenue for their governments or to attract industries that use the resources as raw materials in manufacturing. Cartels are sometimes formed to take advantage of such market power when that power is shared among a small number of countries.

IMMIGRATION

Immigration policy has been a source of much debate in the United States. After several previous attempts, Congress finally passed a new immigration bill in 1986. The most controversial provisions of that bill centered on illegal aliens, who have come to the United States in large numbers in the last twenty years. The bill made it possible for illegal aliens who resided in the United States prior to 1982 to become citizens, but also imposed stiff penalties on employers who hire illegal aliens. The large number of illegal aliens who were residing in the United States when the law was passed was the result of past restrictive immigration quotas. However, there still is a substantial flow of illegal aliens to the United States, especially through Mexico.

Organized labor has generally opposed raising or eliminating immigration quotas because it wants to protect jobs for U.S. citizens. Owners of small manufacturing firms, large-scale farmers, hotel chains and other service establishments, and professionals in need of household help and child care see immigrants as a real boon because they are willing to work long hours for low wages. The immigrants themselves, for the most part, find a low-wage, unskilled job in the United States a significant improvement over the situation they left behind—especially if the situation they left was war-torn Yugoslavia, dire poverty in Haiti, or the hard life of a rural peasant in Central America.

In general, when unskilled workers migrate to the United States or other industrial countries, the gainers are owners of capital or firms in the United States and skilled workers in the United States. These two groups will experience higher returns to their past investment in physical and human capital because unskilled labor is complementary to these other productive resources. Unskilled workers in the country of origin should also gain because they face less competition and may be able to earn higher wages. Owners of other productive resources in the country of origin are losers if they have less unskilled labor available. Finally, if the migrants are more productive in the new country than the old one, and if these gains are not eaten up in the costs of getting the worker there and overcoming the cultural gap, the world as a whole may enjoy a higher standard of living.

THE FLOW OF CAPITAL AND TECHNOLOGY: MULTINATIONAL CORPORATIONS

An important influence on the movement of inputs as well as outputs is the multinational firm. A **multinational corporation** is a firm with headquarters in one country and plants in one or more other countries. Many large and well-known multinationals are headquartered in the United States, including Ford, General Motors, IBM, and AT&T. (So are many smaller and less-known ones.) Other large multinationals are headquartered in other countries, especially Japan (Honda and Mitsubishi) and European countries (Shell Oil, Nestlé, Michelin, and BASF). Multinationals have been around for a long time, but most of their growth has occurred since World War II. Building a plant in another country involves a flow of capital, and often a flow of high-skill labor and technology as well, from the parent country to the host country.

Multinational corporation A firm with headquarters in one country and one or more subsidiaries in other countries.

WHY FIRMS GO ABROAD. Why do firms build plants in foreign countries? Why not just export or invest in a local firm that can produce the product? Exporting may not be feasible because of trade barriers, perishability, or a need to produce a product tailored to the local market. Investing in a local firm by purchasing stock or making a loan is sometimes feasible. Often, however, the investing firm wants more control over management, product quality, or patented processes. Sometimes the only way to get access to local resources, especially raw materials, is to build a plant.

Labor unions oppose building plants abroad, arguing that firms are in search of cheap foreign labor. Unions would rather see plants built in the United States and goods exported. However, trade barriers or the unique needs of foreign markets are much more common reasons for building foreign plants than the attraction of cheap labor. Furthermore, U.S. workers have found jobs in the many plants in the United States owned by foreign multinationals, especially Japanese-owned firms. The lower wages and different management style of Japanese companies have meant adjustments not only for their American employees but also for their American competitors.

Multinationals get mixed reviews from citizens and local firms in most countries where they build or buy plants, even the United States. Labor Secretary Robert Reich thinks that nationality of firms doesn't matter, as long as they create jobs and behave like good corporate citizens in the United States or wherever their plants are located. Laura D'Andrea Tyson, chair of President Clinton's Council of Economic Advisers, is more concerned about the kinds of jobs created and the importance of maintaining technological leadership. She has been particularly critical of Japanese firms building in the United States for hiring American workers for production-line jobs but not for higher-paying positions.[3]

EFFECTS OF MULTINATIONALS. Multinationals are accused by their critics of stifling competition in the countries in which they locate, creating balance of payments problems, and leading to unhealthy concentrations of economic and political power. Advocates argue that multinationals often increase competition,

---

3. Paul Magnusson, "Why Corporate Nationality Matters," *Business Week* (July 12, 1993): 142–143.

speed up the transfer of capital and technology, and help counteract artificial barriers to trade.

In some cases, the multinational "shakes up" domestic competitors, forcing them to try harder when they can no longer hide behind a protective tariff wall. On the other hand, multinationals often simply buy out local competitors or keep local competition from developing. Sometimes multinationals increase competition, and sometimes they reduce it. Japanese multinationals and others have generally been regarded as beneficial in the United States. They compete for resources and markets with established American firms that must adjust or decline.

Multinationals expedite the flow of technology between countries. They make available to their foreign subsidiaries processes and methods that they would be reluctant to share with competitors. Less developed countries sometimes argue, however, that this transfer doesn't spill over to other industries for maximum benefit. They also argue that multinationals, which are generally from developed industrial countries, don't try very hard to adapt technology to the local mix of available resources. The process of technology transfer is made more difficult by the fact that developed countries resist the flow of technology to other countries through multinationals and other channels, because technology is often the basis for their fragile comparative advantage.

Probably the most serious concern about multinationals is that small countries are at a disadvantage in dealing with these large firms. Such a firm may have an annual revenue much larger than the host country's GDP. The multinational may be the largest employer, land owner, and taxpayer in a small country. A multinational represents a threat to the sovereignty of a host country when the firm is larger and more powerful than the government.

Despite these problems, there are real benefits to having multinationals. They provide a way for resources and technology to flow around trade and cultural barriers, which has been very beneficial to the world economy. In most cases, they promote the free trade goals of more output with less effort that were the concern of classical economists two centuries ago when they formulated the theory of comparative advantage.

Consider again...*The answers to the questions about NAFTA may not be clear for ten or twenty years. Many of the same questions were raised about the effects of the EC thirty years ago, and some countries—notably the United Kingdom—chose to stay out, only to join later. The success of the EC in growth, investment, and trade has been impressive, although it is difficult to decompose the gains into those caused by the common market and those attributable to other factors.*

NAFTA will probably be neither the disaster its opponents predict nor the bonanza that some of its boosters claim. Mexico is small relative to the U.S. market, in population and in GDP. Mexicans have been migrating to the United States and would continue to come, with or without NAFTA. Much of the investment headed for Mexico has already gone, encouraged by the maquiladoras and the opportunity to get inside the Mexican trade barriers to produce for sale in the Mexican market. That incentive will be smaller under free trade. There will certainly be some short-

term dislocations in particular industries, regions, and occupations. But twenty years from now, if economic theory and past experience are any guide, we will see some modest gains to both the United States and Mexico from NAFTA, and wonder what the fuss was all about in the early 1990s.

SUMMARY

1. Trade takes place because both parties benefit. Trade is based on the principle of comparative advantage, which means that each country produces that product for which its opportunity cost is lower in terms of other production. Specialization increases total output, and trade allows that increase to be shared. Trade also increases competition and allows countries to take advantage of economies of scale for some products.
2. Tariffs, quotas, and nontariff barriers interfere with free trade. A tariff or quota will raise the price, reduce imports, reduce consumption, and increase domestic production of the protected good.
3. Arguments for protection include protecting infant industries, national defense, balance of payments, employment, and cheap foreign labor. The first two have some validity but must be applied with caution. Most arguments for protection are really thinly disguised requests for income redistribution. The optimal tariff and the theory of the second best are two sophisticated arguments for tariffs.
4. Countries form free trade areas and common markets in order to get the benefits of limited free trade, especially benefits resulting from a larger market. Economic integration represents a movement toward free trade when there is trade creation, and a movement away from free trade when there is trade diversion.
5. Movements of resources can substitute for trade in goods and services. Immigrants usually gain, and world output increases when workers migrate from areas where the productivity of labor is low to areas where it is higher. Multinational corporations increase the flow of technology and capital among nations. MNCs increase competition in some cases and decrease it in others.

NEW TERMS

gains from trade
absolute advantage
comparative advantage
terms of trade

consumption possibilities
   curve
product cycle
tariff
quota

tariff quota
nontariff barriers
commercial policy
fair trade
free trade area

common market
trade creation
trade diversion
multinational corporation

QUESTIONS: REVIEW, APPLICATIONS, AND POLICY

REVIEW

1. Who gains and who loses from a tariff? How do the effects of tariffs differ from the effects of quotas?
2. Why do multinational firms go abroad?
3. Why do economists generally prefer tariffs to quotas?
4. Why is an economy's consumption possibilities curve different from the production possibilities curve? How does a consumption possibilities curve help explain the benefits of trade as similar to the benefits of economic growth?
5. At what stage in the product cycle is a product likely to shift from exported to imported?

APPLICATIONS

6. Consider the following situation for Upland and Downland. Each country devotes half of its resources to

producing bananas and half to producing apples, and the figures given are what they produce in the absence of trade.

COUNTRY	APPLES (TONS)	BANANAS (TONS)
Upland	40	80
Downland	60	60

Do these figures indicate an absolute advantage, a comparative advantage, or both? What is each country's opportunity cost of producing apples? By how much will total output rise when they specialize? Can you find a better consumption combination for each country through trade?

7. Represent the information in Question 6 on a graph as a pair of production possibilities curves.
8. A tariff is proposed on imported pineapple. Economists calculate that 1 million pineapple buyers will incur additional costs of $2 each. Five thousand pineapple workers will earn an additional $100 a year. One hundred unemployed workers will find jobs at an average salary of $10,000. One hundred owners of pineapple packing firms will experience an average income increase of $5,000. What are the total gains to the gainers and the total losses to the losers? Are there other losses not counted in these figures? Do you think the tariff is likely to be enacted?
9. Can the government completely eliminate imports of some goods even if there is general agreement that such restrictions are appropriate? How does the experience with illegal immigration and illegal drugs support your argument?
10. Assume that the United States can produce 3 mainframe computers or 3,000 pairs of shoes with one unit of resource, and Italy can produce 1 mainframe computer or 2,000 pairs of shoes with one unit of resource. Could specialization and trade increase world output and consumption?
11. Given the data in Question 10, how will firms in the United States and Italy know what to produce? Who or what will tell them what to produce and what to import?

POLICY

12. If you were running a small country, why might you have mixed feelings about the building of a plant there by a big multinational?
13. Among the U.S. industries that have received tariff protection in recent years are textiles and autos. Use one or more of the arguments in this chapter to present a case for protection of one of these industries.
14. Write a criticism of the case you made in Question 13, citing the benefits of free trade.
15. Why do nations join free trade areas and common markets? What costs might they incur?

SUGGESTIONS FOR FURTHER READING

King, Philip. *International Economics and International Economic Policy: A Reader.* New York: McGraw-Hill, 1990. A collection of readings on trade policy issues, Including Japan's trade policy, strategic trade, Europe 1992, and multinational companies.

Lustig, Nora, Barry P. Bosworth, and Robert Z. Lawrence, eds. *North American Free Trade: Assessing the Impact.* Washington DC: Brookings Institution, 1991. Summarizes studies on the impact of the NAFTA agreement on the three partner countries.

Root, Franklin R. *International Trade and Investment,* 7e. Cincinnati: South-Western, 1994. An intermediate-level textbook covering both international trade and international finance.

Yeager, Leland B., and David G. Tuerck. *Foreign Trade and U.S. Policy.* New York: Praeger, 1976. Presents the case for free trade and a criticism of protectionism in theory and practice, with many examples and illustrations from Congressional hearings.

CHAPTER 35
INTERNATIONAL FINANCE AND EXCHANGE RATES

Consider this...*If you have ever visited a foreign country, even for a short time, you are probably aware of the ups and downs of currency prices. An American who visited Germany in the late 1960s received almost 4 marks per dollar. In the early 1990s, the exchange rate was only 1.5 marks per dollar. Clearly, the American tourist needed to bring a lot more money to Germany in the 1990s than in the 1960s in order to enjoy the same experience! Even over shorter periods the price of one currency in terms of another can change a great deal, and the generous supply of dollars you took abroad may suddenly and unexpectedly shrink in value.*

Suppose, instead of being a tourist for just a few days, you have a more permanent interest in exchange rates because you are in the importing business. Let's say that you import twenty music boxes from Switzerland. Your supplier bills you for $300 each, payable in Swiss francs, but he also gives you six months credit—time to sell those music boxes. You look in the paper and see that the dollar is selling for 1.38 Swiss francs, so you calculate the bill and figure that your bill for $6,000 will mean 8,280 Swiss francs at the current exchange rate (20 boxes times $300 per box times 1.38 Swiss francs per dollar). Then you call your friendly neighborhood economist and ask what her forecast is. She tells you that the dollar is going to fall in price, perhaps dropping to only 1.25 Swiss francs in the next six months. You haul out your calculator and refigure your bill. You will still owe 8,280 Swiss francs in six months, but if the exchange rate falls that much, it will cost you $6,624 to buy that many francs. There goes your profit!! What can you do to protect yourself from a fluctuating exchange rate? Would you be better off if the United States went back on a fixed exchange rate like the system before 1973?

LEARNING OBJECTIVES
1. Identify the components of the balance of payments accounts and discuss the uses of balance of payments information.
2. Explain the relationship between the foreign exchange market and the trade and capital flows on the balance of payments.
3. Explain how the foreign exchange market works and how the market for currencies is different from other kinds of markets.
4. Discuss the operation of floating rates since 1973.
5. Analyze the advantages and disadvantages of various types of fixed exchange rate systems, including the gold standard, Bretton Woods, and the European Monetary Union.

One important difference that distinguishes trade *between* nations from trade within nations is that people in different countries use different currencies. To pay for goods purchased abroad, a buyer must acquire foreign currency. This chapter looks at the market for foreign currencies and what determines the price of one currency in terms of another (the exchange rate). It also describes the accounting statement for the foreign sector—the balance of payments—and its links to the domestic economy. Finally, we will return to the issue of fixed versus floating exchange rates to see how different kinds of international monetary systems to see how different kinds of monetary systems affect transactions between countries.

THE BALANCE OF PAYMENTS

Balance of payments
An annual summary of transactions between residents of one country and residents of the rest of the world.

Every month in the newspaper you will see reports of the most recent trade surplus or trade deficit. Policy makers and economic journalists follow these figures very closely, because they have an important impact on both the exchange rate and the domestic economy. The trade surplus or trade deficit is part of a larger financial statement, the balance of payments. A country's **balance of payments** is a yearly summary of the transactions between residents of one country and residents of the rest of the world. The balance of payments is an income statement—a summary of the flows of goods, services, and assets in and out of a country in a given year. Table 1 presents a simplified summary of the U.S. balance of payments for 1992.

The pluses and minuses in the table have important meanings. A transaction that gives rise to a payment to the United States or a claim to future payment is entered with a plus sign. A transaction resulting in a payment by the United States or a claim for future payment is entered with a minus sign. Thus, the figure for foreign investment in the United States means that the sum of foreign purchases of U.S. stocks and bonds, foreign deposits in U.S. bank accounts, and foreign expenditures on building plants and facilities in the United States was positive; these purchases exceeded any withdrawals from U.S. bank accounts or sales of U.S.-based financial assets by foreigners. The negative figure for private foreign investment by U.S. citizens abroad means that the same kinds of purchases by Americans abroad exceeded any reduction in such assets by bringing the money home.

CURRENT ACCOUNT

Current account
The part of the balance of payments that summarizes transactions in currently produced goods and services.

Balance of trade
Difference between the value of a country's merchandise exports and imports.

The **current account** is the part of the balance of payments that summarizes transactions in currently produced goods and services, including merchandise, services, investment income, and several smaller items. Investment income is included in this account because it is the payment for the current year's use of your financial capital. In 1993, the United States had a $109 billion deficit for this account, reflecting an excess of imports over exports. The current account measures the impact of trade on output and employment because it represents (with a few adjustments) net foreign demand for U.S. goods and services, or $X - M$ in the GDP accounts.

The sum of merchandise exports and imports (the **balance of trade**) is usually taken as an indicator of how competitive U.S. exports are. The deficit in the

TABLE 1 U.S. BALANCE OF PAYMENTS, 1993
(BILLIONS OF DOLLARS)

CURRENT ACCOUNT	
Merchandise exports	456.7
Merchandise imports	−589.2
Balance of Trade	−132.5
Service transactions, net	56.7
Military transactions, net	−1.0
Investment income, net	0.1
Transfers, public and private	−32.3
Balance on Current Account	−109.2
CAPITAL ACCOUNT	
Change in U.S. Government assets abroad	−1.5
Change in foreign government assets in United States	71.2
U.S. private investment abroad	−142.4
Foreign private investment in the United States	155.2
Balance on Capital Account	82.5
STATISTICAL DISCREPANCY	26.7

(Should add to zero: difference is due to rounding errors.)
Source: Adapted from U.S. Department of Commerce, *Economic Indicators* (Washington DC: U.S. Government Printing Office, March 1994).

balance of trade in the last decade has been a matter of great concern to policy makers. The buzzword "competitiveness" reflects concern for the big gap between U.S. merchandise exports and imports. This figure receives more attention than it deserves in the press, because exports and imports of services are an increasingly important component of trade flows. Notice the $58 billion surplus in the services part of the current account. The current account balance is a better indicator of competitiveness because it includes net exports of services as well as merchandise, along with investment income and a few other items. Table 2 shows the balances on current account and capital account as well as statistical discrepancy for 1980–1993.

CAPITAL ACCOUNT

The **capital account** is the part of the balance of payments that summarizes purchases and sales of financial assets, such as bonds, short-term debts, bank deposits, stocks, and foreign plants. This category showed a surplus of about $82 billion in 1993, including about $155 billion in foreign private investment in the United States. This level of foreign private investment in the United States is enormous compared to past experience, while the outflow of private U.S. investment of $142 billion is also large compared to levels of investment abroad in previous years. A pattern of a large net inflow of foreign private capital has existed only since 1982, largely because of the attraction of high real interest rates in the United States for the last decade.

Capital account
The part of the balance of payments that summarizes purchases and sales of financial assets.

TABLE 2 SUMMARY BALANCE OF PAYMENTS DATA, 1980–1993 (BILLIONS OF DOLLARS)

YEAR	CURRENT ACCOUNT BALANCE	CAPITAL ACCOUNT BALANCE	STATISTICAL DISCREPANCY
1980	2.3	−28.9	25.4**
1981	5.0	−31.1	25.0
1982	−11.4	−29.9	41.4
1983	−43.6	24.5	19.1
1984	−98.8	72.8	26.0
1985	−121.7	96.9	24.8
1986	−147.5	132.1	15.4
1987	−163.5	167.6	−4.1
1988	−126.7	126.8	−0.1
1989	−101.1	98.8	2.4
1990	−90.4	43.1	47.4
1991	−3.7*	4.8	−1.1
1992	−62.3	75.5	−13.1
1993	−109.2	82.5	26.7

Source: Council of Economic Advisors, *Economic Report of the President* (Washington DC: U.S. Government Printing Office, 1994).
*This unusual figure reflects foreign contributions to help pay for the Gulf War.
**Figures for 1980 and 1981 do not add to zero because of a special allocation by the International Monetary Fund. Other years show small discrepancies due to rounding errors.

STATISTICAL DISCREPANCY

The sum of the current account and the capital account should be approximately zero. When they are not, the gap between them is called statistical discrepancy. The **statistical discrepancy** is the part of the balance of payments that reflects unrecorded transactions (such as workers' remittances, smuggling, and other illegal activities) and inaccurate estimates of spending by U.S. tourists abroad or by foreign tourists in the United States. There is a good reason for this entry. Balance of payments accountants do not have perfect information. When the discrepancy is large, it is believed to consist mainly of unrecorded bank deposits. A positive discrepancy suggests an outflow of funds not recorded, while a negative value implies an inflow that went unrecorded.

The category of statistical discrepancy is often rather large—$27 billion in 1993. The large positive statistical discrepancy for 1993 implies that there were additional (unrecorded) capital outflows in that year.

USING BALANCE OF PAYMENTS DATA

The data in the balance of payments are useful for a number of purposes. Exports of goods and services are added to aggregate demand, and imports are a reduction in aggregate demand, impacting on output, employment and the price level. The sum of merchandise, services, and military transactions in 1993

Statistical discrepancy
The part of the balance of payments that reflects unrecorded transactions and inaccurate estimates of spending by tourists.

came to −$76.8 billion, so that aggregate demand was to the left of where it would be with balanced trade in goods and services. Investment income and private transfers add to personal income and affect consumption and saving. Capital inflows help to keep interest rates lower and allow firms to invest more. A large statistical discrepancy may signal a growth of illegal activities—smuggling, drug running, or tax evasion. The balance of payments is a useful source of valuable macroeconomic data that helps to predict the course of domestic economic activity. It also is a summary of the transactions that influence the price of a nation's currency. It is to currency markets that we turn next.

THE BALANCE OF PAYMENTS AND THE MARKET FOR CURRENCIES

The transactions in the balance of payments all require that buyers and sellers go through different national currencies in order to carry out their trade and financial investing activities. Figure 1 represents the market for foreign currencies as it appears to U.S. buyers and sellers. In this figure, foreign currencies are represented by the German mark (DM). The price of foreign currency is measured in dollars. Citizens of other countries supply their currencies in order to buy U.S. exports, to travel or invest in the United States, or to purchase U.S. services or assets. All of these sources of supply of foreign currencies correspond to the "+" entries in the U.S. balance of payments. U.S. citizens demand foreign currencies in order to import foreign goods and services (including traveling abroad) and to invest in foreign assets. All of these sources of demand for foreign currencies correspond to the "−" entries on the balance of payments.

In Figure 1, the equilibrium price of the mark is 50 cents, and the equilibrium quantity is 100 million. At a price of 70 cents per mark (equivalent to 1.4 marks per dollar), there would be a surplus of foreign currencies of 60 million marks. Quantity supplied is 130 million marks, and quantity demanded is only 70 million. At 30 cents per mark (equivalent to 3.3 marks per dollar), there

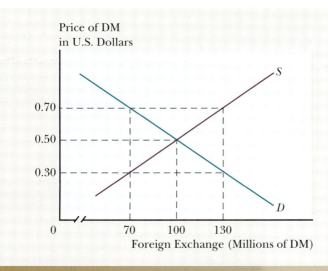

FIGURE 1
THE FOREIGN EXCHANGE MARKET
The foreign exchange market shows the supply of foreign exchange (German marks) from abroad, the demand for foreign exchange by U.S. citizens, and the equilibrium price (50 cents) and quantity (100 million marks).

would be a shortage of foreign currencies of 60 million marks (130 million marks demanded less 70 million marks supplied).

The U.S. balance of payments for 1992 was in balance because the United States has a floating exchange rate, so the price adjusts to eliminate a surplus or deficit. Some countries, however, have fixed exchange rates, and are likely to have a gap between quantity demanded and quantity supplied at that fixed price. This gap must be filled by sales or purchases of foreign exchange by the government in order to bring the balance of payments into accounting balance. A shortage of foreign currencies is equivalent to a balance of payments deficit. A **balance of payments deficit** is an excess of a country's foreign spending over its foreign earnings for a given year. In Figure 2, that difference amounts to 50 million marks. (At 2 marks per dollar, 50 million marks translates into $25 million.) A nation can instead have a balance of payments surplus (foreign earnings exceed foreign spending) or a balance of payments equilibrium (inflows and outflows are equal).

While balance of payments deficits or surpluses have no meaning under floating exchange rates, they are important for countries on fixed exchange rates. Accountants working in such a system would identify those transactions in foreign currencies or in a nation's own currency abroad that appear to have occurred in order to make the accounts balance, not just because of the normal course of business. Usually these transactions would be undertaken by the government, or by cooperating foreign governments, in order to control the currency's price. The sum of these transactions would constitute the balance of payments surplus or deficit.

Balance of payments deficit
An excess of a country's foreign spending over its foreign earnings for a given year.

THE FOREIGN EXCHANGE MARKET AND THE EXCHANGE RATE

The network of banks and financial institutions through which buyers and sellers exchange national currencies is called the **foreign exchange market**. The foreign exchange market works much like the market for wheat, apples, or roller

Foreign exchange market
The network of banks and financial institutions through which buyers and sellers exchange national currencies.

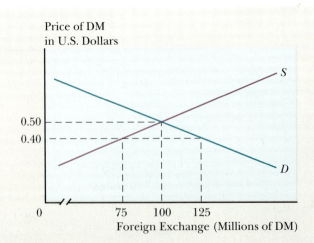

FIGURE 2
DISEQUILIBRIUM IN THE FOREIGN EXCHANGE MARKET
At 40 cents per mark, the quantity of foreign exchange demanded exceeds the quantity supplied by 50 million marks. This gap between supply and demand corresponds to a balance of payments deficit.

blades. As we have just seen, there is a supply curve, a demand curve, and an equilibrium price and quantity. There are also conditions that are held constant (*ceteris paribus* conditions). When these conditions change, the curves shift and the equilibrium price and quantity change. A market-determined rise in the price is called **appreciation**, and a market-determined fall is called **depreciation**.

MEASURING CURRENCY PRICES

The price of a nation's currency is measured in terms of the number of units of other currency it can buy. In 1995, the U.S. dollar might be worth .6 British pounds, 110 Japanese yen, 5.5 French francs, and 1.28 Canadian dollars. One problem of a floating rate system is the difficulty of measuring changes in the price of one currency when others are moving around at the same time. If changes in the price of the dollar are measured in French francs instead of Japanese yen, the picture of what is happening to the dollar may look very different.

Currency market-watchers obtain a consistent measure of what is happening to a currency's price by using an index called the **trade-weighted dollar**. This index measures the value of the dollar in terms of a market basket of other major currencies, with the weights determined by their relative share of trade with the United States. Canada, for example, would have a relatively high weight, while Italy's weight would be much smaller. The trade-weighted dollar is a fairly accurate reflection of changes in the price of the dollar. From 1971 to 1985, the trade-weighted dollar rose from 117.8 to 143.0 (1973=100). During that same period, the U.S. dollar rose more than that amount relative to the French franc, even as it fell sharply with respect to the Japanese yen. Other factors besides trade with the United States were affecting the value of both the franc and the yen during that period. By using a multi-currency measure, some of those factors wash out. The index gives a better measure of what happens to the dollar than just looking at the price in terms of one currency.

Another factor in measuring exchange rates is to correct for changes in the domestic price level. If the price of the dollar increases, but domestic prices are stable in the United States while they have risen in our trading-partner countries, then the dollar has not necessarily risen in purchasing power. When the exchange rate is adjusted for changes in relative price levels, the adjusted exchange rate is called the **real exchange rate**. If R represents the exchange rate for the U.S. dollar, P_{US} represents the U.S. price index, and P_{ROW} represents the price index in the rest of the world, then the real exchange rate (REX) is given by

$$REX = R \times (P_{US} / P_{ROW}).$$

Table 3 shows the trade-weighted dollar in nominal terms for 1971 to 1993 and in real terms from 1973 to 1993. As you can see, the price of the dollar rose quite sharply from 1980 to 1985, then returned to its original level by the early 1990s. The change is a little less dramatic in real terms but the pattern is the same.

SHIFTS IN SUPPLY AND DEMAND

Demand for foreign exchange will increase if something causes U.S. citizens to want to import more foreign goods and services or to invest more abroad. The

Appreciation
A market-determined increase in a currency's price.

Depreciation
A market-determined decrease in a currency's price.

Trade-weighted dollar
A price index for the dollar that measures changes in its value in terms of a market basket of currencies of major trading partners.

Real exchange rate
The foreign currency exchange rate after adjustment for changes in relative price levels.

TABLE 3 NOMINAL AND REAL TRADE-WEIGHTED DOLLAR

	NOMINAL	REAL
1971	117.8	
1972	109.1	
1973	99.1	98.9
1974	101.4	99.4
1975	98.5	94.1
1976	105.7	97.6
1977	103.4	93.3
1978	92.4	84.4
1979	88.1	83.2
1980	87.4	84.9
1981	103.4	100.9
1982	116.6	111.8
1983	125.3	117.3
1984	138.2	128.8
1985	143.0	132.4
1986	112.2	103.6
1987	96.9	90.9
1988	92.7	88.2
1989	98.6	94.4
1990	89.1	86.0
1991	89.8	86.5
1992	86.6	83.3
1993	93.2	89.9

Source: Council of Economic Advisors, *Economic Report of the President* (Washington DC: U.S. Government Printing Office, 1994).

supply of foreign exchange will increase if foreigners want to buy more U.S. goods and services or invest more in the United States. Recall from Chapter 3 that demand curves shift when the *ceteris paribus* conditions change. Some of those demand shifters, including changes in tastes, population, and income, apply here. Others work a little differently because the foreign exchange market is heavily influenced by macroeconomic conditions.

INCOME. Changes in a country's income have no direct effect on its exports, but there is a fairly consistent relationship between imports and the level of income. In fact, imports appear to be quite sensitive to changes in income in the United States; on average, a 1 percent rise in income results in a 1.1 percent increase in imports. Exports are sensitive to changes in income in the rest of the world, but the response tends to be smaller (a 0.8 percent increase in U.S. exports for every 1 percent increase in world income). This income sensitivity means that the current account balance tends to worsen when the U.S. economy comes out of a recession or grows more rapidly than the rest of the world.

PRICES OF RELATED GOODS. The price of a good is affected by changes in the prices of related goods. For example, demand for orange juice is affected by the price of tomato juice. In the foreign exchange market, it is aggregate rather than individual prices that matter. Aggregate price changes that can affect foreign exchange are changes in the price level in the United States relative to the price level abroad, or changes in the prices of U.S. exports in general relative to prices of foreign goods. Note that the price on the vertical axis in Figure 1 is the price of foreign exchange. Changes in other prices, including the domestic price level, can shift the supply and demand curves for foreign exchange.

If the U.S. price level rises more than foreign price levels, imports become cheaper relative to domestic goods, and Americans will want to buy more imported goods. Rising domestic prices shift the U.S. demand curve for foreign exchange rightward. U.S. citizens demand more foreign exchange to buy more imported goods. At the same time, the U.S. supply curve for foreign exchange shifts to the left because foreigners want to buy fewer American exports at higher prices. In fact, economists who forecast changes in exchange rates find that changes in relative price levels are the most significant determinant.

INTEREST RATES. Changes in relative interest rates also shift demand for foreign exchange. If interest rates are higher abroad, Americans will demand more foreign exchange to buy foreign financial assets, such as bonds or bank deposits. From 1981 to 1985, interest rates in the United States were higher than in most other countries, attracting an inflow of foreign capital. This increased supply of foreign exchange drove the price of foreign currencies down, or the price of the dollar up. As U.S. interest rates fell after 1985, the price of the dollar also fell (that is, the prices of marks, yen, and pounds began to rise).

GOVERNMENT RESTRICTIONS. Another source of shifts in demand for foreign exchange is changes in government restrictions on trade, such as tariffs, quotas, and nontariff barriers. These commercial policy tools are often used intentionally to shift the demand for foreign exchange, either to change the currency price or to "cure" a shortage of foreign exchange (balance of payments deficit). Export subsidies and promotions encourage foreign purchases and shift the

KEY IDEAS

SOURCES OF SHIFTS IN SUPPLY AND DEMAND FOR FOREIGN EXCHANGE

Changes in:
- relative price levels
- relative incomes
- relative interest rates
- tastes and preferences
- population
- technology
- input cost and availability
- tariffs, quotas, and nontariff barriers
- export subsidies

supply of foreign exchange to the right. Finally, demand for foreign exchange shifts when there are changes in technology or input costs, which can change demand for foreign inputs or foreign products.

The same kinds of factors that shift one nation's demand for foreign exchange also operate to shift other countries' supply of foreign exchange. Changes in a country's relative price level or income, tastes, population, technology, interest rates, and tariffs and quotas all affect the supply of foreign exchange from other countries.

UNIQUE FEATURES OF THE FOREIGN EXCHANGE MARKET

The foreign exchange market has several unique features. First, the operations of this market have important macroeconomic implications. What happens in the market for foreign exchange affects (and is affected by) interest rates, output, and price levels. Second, governments are often heavily involved in setting the price, often in an attempt to limit its fluctuations. Third, a well-developed forward market exists for foreign exchange, where people make contracts for future deliveries of currency at a fixed price. Finally, the foreign exchange market sometimes suffers from persistent disequilibrium.

MACROECONOMIC IMPLICATIONS. U.S. exports and imports, which are heavily influenced by changes in exchange rates, each constitute about 12 to 13 percent of GDP—much higher than thirty years ago, when each was about 5 percent of GDP. In addition, the foreign exchange market supports some large transactions in financial assets, such as stocks and bonds. Exports, imports, and capital transactions affect the domestic economy in many ways. A rise in exports can increase output, but expanding output puts upward pressure on the price level. Rising imports can reduce domestic output but will also reduce inflationary pressures. An inflow of foreign capital can drive down interest rates, while the opposite is true for a capital outflow. Thus, any macroeconomic model of the U.S. economy must incorporate the foreign sector in order to predict output, employment, prices, and interest rates accurately.

Domestic events also affect exports, imports, and trade in capital assets. Changes in output, prices, and interest rates spill over into the foreign sector. Rising output means rising income, some of which will be spent on more imports. This effect helped to account for the decline in the current account balance in 1992 and 1993 as the U.S. economy recovered from recession while several of its major trading partners were still in recession. A fall in output and income will reduce imports, as it did in the 1990–1991 recession.

Rising U.S. prices (relative to foreign prices) encourage U.S. citizens and foreigners to substitute cheaper goods made in other countries for more expensive American products. When the price level rises faster in the United States than abroad, exports fall and imports rise. Falling prices, or prices rising more slowly than in the rest of the world, stimulate exports and discourage imports. Higher interest rates attract capital from abroad, but lower interest rates encourage U.S. capital owners to try to earn a higher return in other countries. All these changes shift the supply and demand for foreign exchange, and thus change currency prices under the present floating exchange rate system.

POLICY FOCUS: HOLDING THE DOLLAR DOWN

The value of the dollar fell steadily from 1985 to 1993. By the end of 1992, the trade-weighted dollar was at its lowest level since the dollar began to float. There were predictions of 100 yen to a dollar—compared to 360 yen in the 1960s and 250 yen ten years earlier. Does anyone care? Does it have any impact on Americans? Who gains and who loses?

There are Americans who suffer from a weak dollar. People who travel abroad have to offer more dollars to get the same amount of foreign currency. Importers have to pay more for their merchandise, including wholesalers, retailers, and manufacturers using imported parts or raw materials.

Political power, however, lies with those who gain from a cheaper dollar. Exporters find it easier to sell their products abroad. Import-competing industries, like autos, find that they have a price advantage over foreign competitors. American tourist destinations discover that they not only have more foreign visitors attracted by the cheap dollar, but also bring in more American tourists who decide to travel at home where their dollars go farther.

Can the U.S. government influence the price of the dollar? To the extent that actions by the government to reduce interest rates—lower budget deficits and expansionary monetary policy—are effective, the answer is yes. Beginning in 1990, the government has been aggressively pursuing lower interest rates in order to stimulate housing, auto sales, and business investment. An important and intended side effect was a falling dollar.[a] Lower interest rates make the United States a less attractive haven for foreigners looking for attractive yields on financial assets. As less financial capital flows into the country, and more flows out, demand for the dollar falls and supply rises. The result is a falling price for the dollar, bringing joy to the hearts of exporters, U.S. tourist destinations, and import-competing industries.

Net export sales are an important factor in recovery from recession. The normal pattern is for imports to rise as the economy recovers, so exports must grow even faster in order to keep the foreign sector from being a drag on the recovery. When the United States began to recover from the 1990–1991 recession, exports were initially a contributing factor; but as Japan and Europe slid into recession, net exports began to decline. Under these conditions, falling interest rates and a declining dollar were important factors in keeping international trade from putting too severe a damper on the U.S. recovery.

a. "Why Washington Likes its Dollar Weak," *Business Week* (October 21, 1991): 31.

GOVERNMENT INTERVENTION. Governments have always been heavily involved in the market for their own currencies. Governments set and maintain prices in many markets, including minimum wages, farm price supports, and rent controls. In these markets, however, the government usually sets either a floor price or a ceiling price. In the market for foreign exchange, governments historically have set both a floor and a ceiling.

Even with floating rates, governments don't always allow the market to completely determine the prices of their currencies. A government may want to keep the price of its currency from falling because of the short-run effects on export revenue, particularly if sales of the nation's principal exports are not very sensitive to price changes in the short run. Alternatively, a government may want to keep the price of the currency from rising too high because such an increase would make it more difficult for the country's exporters to compete and easier for imports to undersell domestic goods. In small countries where foreign trade is a large part of total economic activity, monetary authorities may be concerned about the effects of changes in the currency's price on the volume of the country's monetary reserves and the money supply. Finally, a government may want to keep the price of the currency stable in order to encourage trade and foreign investment by minimizing risk and uncertainty.

THE FORWARD MARKET. Another special feature of the foreign exchange market is a well-developed **forward market,** in which contracts are made for future delivery of specific amounts of currency at a specified price. Forward (or futures) markets also exist in other goods and services. Probably the best-known forward market is the commodities market, where contracts for the future delivery of corn, wheat, pork bellies, copper, tin, gold, and other metals and agricultural goods are traded.

Traders who try to reduce their risk by buying or selling contracts for future delivery are called **hedgers**. Those who are willing to assume risk in return for the chance of a profit are called **speculators**. Let's look at a simple illustration of how hedgers and speculators interact in the foreign exchange market. Suppose a Honda dealer in the United States receives a shipment of Hondas from Japan. The dollar cost of the shipment is $100,000, but the contract calls for payment in six months in yen. The yen is trading for 125 yen per U.S. dollar, so the dealer owes 12.5 million yen. What the dealer needs in six months is not $100,000, but however many dollars it takes at that time to buy 12.5 million yen. Suppose the dealer thinks the price of a dollar in six months will be only 100 yen. Then the payment will cost the dealer more dollars—$125,000, to be precise. There goes the profit! If the dealer can find someone now who will guarantee a reasonably attractive price, say 120 yen to the dollar, that will eliminate the exchange risk. The dealer can concentrate on the business of selling cars and motorcycles.

What about the opposite situation—that of the speculator? Chances are the speculator is a large commercial bank, with many forward transactions in many directions. There is probably some Japanese firm in need of dollars that can be matched with the U.S. car dealer's need for yen. Some speculators are gambling on changes in currency prices. Perhaps the speculator who offered the car dealer 120 yen per dollar expects the price of the yen to go to 135 yen per dollar. The dealer would be delighted to buy dollars at 120 yen per dollar and sell them at 135, making a profit of 15 yen on each dollar bought and sold.

The forward market in foreign exchange has been around for a long time. Since 1973, when most countries adopted floating exchange rates, the forward market has played an important role in encouraging foreign exchange by reducing risk.

PERSISTENT DISEQUILIBRIUM. Although the United States and most major industrial countries allow their currency prices to float, many other countries maintain a fixed price for their currencies. If the price of currency is set by the government, it may not be a market-clearing price. If it isn't, there will be a persistent disequilibrium—that is, constant surpluses or shortages of foreign exchange. Figure 2 showed a disequilibrium situation for the United States. The market shows a shortage of foreign exchange because the price of 40 cents per mark is too low for equilibrium. The quantity of marks demanded exceeds the quantity supplied by 50 million marks.

One way to deal with this problem is to change the price of the currency. When changing the price is the usual answer, a country has a floating currency. If the price must remain constant, the government must intervene in response to a persistent shortage or surplus. The government might try to shift supply or

---

Forward market
The market in which contracts are made for future deliveries of specific amounts of a currency at a specified price.

Hedgers
People who try to reduce their risk by buying or selling contracts in the forward market for currency.

Speculators
People who assume risk in the forward market for currency in return for a chance of a profit.

demand for foreign exchange in order to make the curves intersect at the official price. This method was the basis of the gold standard. Alternatively, if the government has some foreign exchange reserves, it may draw on those reserves to meet the shortage, hoping that the shortage will eventually disappear of its own accord. This method was the basis of the Bretton Woods system from 1945 to 1971.

FLOATING EXCHANGE RATES

A system of floating exchange rates represents a pure market approach to foreign exchange, in which any shift in supply or demand will change the price of a currency. This system had been tried by some countries, such as Canada, but was not widely adopted until 1973. In February 1973, the United States totally abandoned its commitment to fixed exchange rates. Japan quickly followed suit and allowed the yen to float against the dollar. Within a month, the finance ministers of the European Economic Community announced that they would allow their currencies to float. Most major industrial countries have had floating exchange rates since 1973.

Floating exchange rates work on the basic principles of supply and demand. Floating rates support all of the suggested goals for an international monetary system except stable exchange rates. If exchange rate adjustments clear the market, then the balance of payments should always be at or near equilibrium. Thus, there will be no need to shift the curves to intersect at a fixed price or to use restrictions in order to make international payments balance.

When countries first began to use floating exchange rates, there was widespread fear that the volume of trade would shrink because exchange rates would be very unstable. Traders would incur high costs to protect themselves against losses from exchange rate fluctuations. Although exchange rates have been unstable, well-developed forward markets have ensured that this instability does not discourage international trade. One serious problem has been that a currency's exchange rate may fall *below* its ultimate equilibrium before rising back to that equilibrium. In the interim, the exchange rate is still incorrect, but is too low instead of too high. During this time, price signals to importers, exporters, consumers, and producers are distorted. Decisions are made that would not be profit-maximizing at the correct exchange rate.

Floating rates have not resulted in annual balance of payments equilibrium. Why? Part of the problem is measurement, but another part reflects a basic truth about market equilibrium. Equilibrium is never where the market is, but rather the direction in which it is headed. If supply and demand shift often, the market may always be in the process of moving from one equilibrium to another. However, deficits and surpluses generally have been much smaller under floating rates than they were under fixed rates. In fact, the floating rate system has worked well during severe shocks (major supply and demand shifts), such as the OPEC oil price hike that created large deficits and surpluses and the 1981–1982 recession. There are some substantial lags between changes in exchange rates and improvements in the current account balance, but overall the adjustment process has been successful.[1]

---

1. Paul R. Krugman, *Has the Adjustment Process Worked?* (Washington DC: Institute for International Economics, 1991).

The floating rate system established in 1973 is not a completely free market in practice. A floating rate can be either clean or, more commonly, dirty. A clean float means that there is no government intervention to influence the currency's price. A dirty float implies some government involvement in the market to limit fluctuations. Governments continue to intervene in the market, buying and selling their own currency to limit swings in the price. Countries have not allowed the market alone to completely determine exchange rates, but they are closer to doing so than ever in the past. Although there is still some unhappiness with floating rates, there is little pressure to return to a fixed rate system. Many government officials are reluctant to go back on the gold standard or to return to the Bretton Woods system because both would limit their flexibility of action.

FIXED RATES: THE GOLD STANDARD, BRETTON WOODS, AND THE EMU

Although most industrial countries have floating rates, some countries have fixed rates. Others have a blend of the two, fixing the price of their currency with respect to one or more other currencies but then floating this "package" of currencies with respect to the rest of the world. Historically, there were two fixed-rate systems that were adopted by a large number of countries and lasted for some time: the gold standard and the Bretton Woods system. More recently, the nations of the European Community have attempted to establish a fixed relationship among member country currencies called the European Monetary Union.

There are still economists, policy makers, traders, and bankers who advocate a return to some form of fixed rates.[2] They argue that stable rates reduce much of the uncertainty and the need for hedging in international transactions, making foreign trade more like domestic trade. The majority view, however, is that the system of floating rates in place for the last twenty years has worked quite well. Supporters of this system point to the breakdown of the gold standard in 1914, of the Bretton Woods system in 1971, and of the European Monetary Union in 1993 as evidence that fixed-rate systems eventually fail.

THE GOLD STANDARD

Gold standard
An international monetary system in which currencies were defined in terms of gold, money supplies were linked to gold, and balance of payments deficits were settled in gold.

From the late nineteenth century until the 1930s, most industrial countries were on the gold standard. The **gold standard** was an international monetary system in which currencies were defined in terms of gold, money supplies were tied to gold, and balance of payment deficits were settled in gold. Gold served as money in most of the world for centuries. Thus, gold was a logical choice for settling accounts between countries with different national currencies. A country on the gold standard was supposed to observe three rules:

1. To define the value of its currency in terms of gold content. Under the gold standard, the dollar price of an ounce of gold was $20.67 from 1837 to 1934, and the price of gold in British pounds was £4.25. The price of each cur-

---

2. For example, Princeton economist Peter B. Kenen, who sets forth his arguments in *Managing Exchange Rates* (Council on Foreign Relations Press, 1988).

rency in gold automatically determined the exchange rates between the two countries. The British pound was worth $4.86 ($20.67 divided by £4.25).

2. To have its money supply consist of gold or be tied to the gold stock in some fixed ratio. For example, the ratio of gold to currency in the United States was 1:4 in the nineteenth century. The nation's supply of currency could not exceed four times its gold stock. The money supply could be less than the maximum, however.

3. To require its central bank or monetary authority to buy gold from anyone or to sell gold to anyone at the official price.

CORRECTING DEFICITS AND SURPLUSES. These rules, if followed, automatically corrected deficits and surpluses in the balance of payments. When there was a deficit (surplus of U.S. dollars offered for foreign exchange), the price of foreign exchange would tend to rise. As the dollar price of foreign exchange started to rise, U.S. citizens would find that they could get more pounds or francs per dollar by exchanging their dollars for gold at the Fed, shipping the gold abroad, and exchanging it there for pounds or francs. As gold flowed out of the country, the U.S. money supply would shrink, and prices and output would fall.

When prices fall in the United States, exports rise and imports fall. There is a shift in demand and supply for foreign exchange. Foreigners supply more of their currencies to buy more of relatively cheaper U.S. exports. At the same time, U.S. citizens demand less foreign exchange because they want to buy less of other countries' relatively more expensive products. Also, as U.S. output and national income fall, Americans buy less of everything, including imports.

Figure 3 shows these effects. Again, German marks (DM) represent all foreign currencies. The official price of the mark is 40 cents, and the cost of shipping 1 mark's worth of gold is 5 cents. In a free market, the equilibrium price of

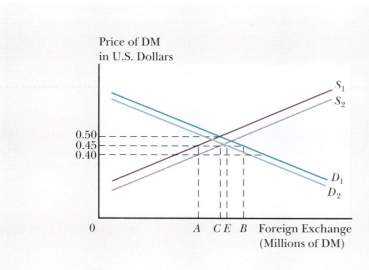

FIGURE 3

AUTOMATIC ADJUSTMENT UNDER THE GOLD STANDARD

At 45 cents per mark, gold flows out of the country to cover the deficit, $B - A$. The gold outflow shrinks the money supply, reducing income and prices. Lower income and prices reduce demand for imports (from D_1 to D_2) and increase the supply of foreign currency to buy U.S. exports (from S_1 to S_2). The deficit shrinks from $B - A$ to $E - C$.

the mark would be 50 cents. Because the United States is on the gold standard, the price of foreign exchange cannot rise above the official price plus the cost of shipping the gold to Germany. Thus, at the maximum price of 45 cents, amount $B - A$ of gold flows out of the United States. That outflow shrinks the U.S. money supply, lowering national income and the price level and shifting supply and demand for foreign exchange to S_2 and D_2. The deficit falls to $E - C$. This process of gold flows and shifts in supply and demand continues until the official price is restored and the deficit is eliminated. This automatic correction of deficits (and surpluses) was recognized in the early eighteenth century by David Hume.

The effects of the gold flow are reinforced by events in the other country into which gold is flowing. The other country's money supply expands, raising income and prices and further shifting supply and demand in the correct direction.

HISTORICAL EXPERIENCE. The gold standard worked fairly well in the late nineteenth and early twentieth centuries. Numerous discoveries of gold in California, Colorado, Alaska, Canada, and South Africa provided an adequate supply of gold for stock. The gold standard meant that governments could not control their money supplies, but nineteenth-century governments didn't pursue an active monetary policy anyway. There were few major disturbances, such as wars and revolutions, that might have caused shifts in supply and demand so great that they would have been difficult and painful to correct.

World War I marked the beginning of the end of the gold standard, although some countries (including the United States) remained on it until the 1930s. The gold standard's main attractions were fixed exchange rates and automatic correction. The slow growth in the supply of gold in the twentieth century and the gold standard's restrictions on monetary policy were serious problems that could not be resolved.

THE GOLD BUFFS. The idea of returning to the gold standard has never died. It just went underground, surfacing as regularly as the groundhog every February. Why does this idea keep returning? In part, it is because gold seems to offer a degree of certainty that paper money does not. When governments have gone down in revolutionary flames, new governments have usually restored faith in the currency by tying it to gold. When refugees leave countries in turmoil, the safest way to transport their wealth is in the form of gold. Fifty years after the gold standard was abandoned, some people still think of gold as the only universal money.

Gold buffs, however, are not sentimental. Most of them are hardheaded profit seekers. Many invested in gold as its price made its dramatic rise from $35 an ounce in 1967 (the official price, maintained by central banks) to over $1,000 an ounce in the mid–1970s in a free market. (Some also had the foresight to get out of gold before its price dropped sharply to under $400 an ounce in the early 1980s.) They didn't invest because of the demand for gold to use for jewelry and dental work. They invested because gold was, is, and probably always will be considered money by a substantial part of the world. The gold buffs would like gold to be *the* money of the world again in the same way it was in earlier centuries.

Gold buffs usually want to return to the gold standard because they do not trust the government to control the money supply. They would rather have the

GLOBAL OUTLOOK: EXCHANGE CONTROL

While industrial countries use floating rates to varying degrees, less developed countries are more likely to rely on a system of exchange control. Some degree of exchange control is practiced by all but a few industrialized countries, but the stronger forms exist only in less developed countries. Exchange control means that a country's government requires all earnings of foreign exchange to be turned over to it and then sells the foreign currencies to those who want to import, travel abroad, or invest in other countries.

Usually, a country adopts exchange control because the currency price is too high and the country doesn't want to change it. Without exchange control, the balance of payments would be in deficit. Typically, the country that uses exchange control has limited reserves and little international credit. By insisting that everyone turn in their foreign currency to the government, which then sells it, the country can make its balance of payments accounts balance.

In some countries, such as China, exchange control has involved two kinds of currency. One is used solely by foreigners, such as tourists and approved traders, and the other is used by ordinary citizens. Some stores and service institutions, such as hotels, accept only the first kind. In this way, the government can closely control the use of foreign exchange, deciding who buys imports and who gets the currency that foreigners spend in the country. With this type of exchange control, black markets are less likely, because the country's citizens are not allowed to hold exchangeable currency.

Exchange control gives a country stable exchange rates, independent monetary and fiscal policy, and no apparent deficit in the balance of payments. However, free trade is sacrificed. In addition, black markets almost always exist. People make side deals in foreign exchange in order to bypass the government. Bribery, smuggling, and falsified reporting of earnings from exports and the cost of imports are regular events in countries with exchange control.

However, exchange control can accomplish other objectives. Often there are multiple exchange rates—different rates for buying, selling, and other uses. Suppose the government wants to encourage factory construction and discourage luxuries. It can charge a low price for foreign exchange to people who want to import machinery and a high price to those who want to buy air conditioners and yachts. Thus, the government can promote specific consumption and production goals. Also, the government can gain revenue for public purposes by buying foreign currencies at a low price and selling them at a higher price. Despite the leaks, the confused market signals, and the long-term distortions of exchange control, this system has a lot of short-run appeal to governments in crisis situations.

---

money supply determined by the impersonal forces of the marketplace and the supply of monetary gold. Give governments the freedom to print money, they argue, and political pressures will sooner or later run up the money supply and the price level.

The main reason why gold buffs are unlikely to get their way is that governments don't like to tie their own hands. Returning to the gold standard would mean giving up any sort of stabilization policy and letting the inflow and outflow of gold determine changes in the money supply. No elected government is going to be willing to give up that option. The argument will go on, but as nations adapt to floating rates, the likelihood of going back on the gold standard gets smaller and smaller each year.

BRETTON WOODS

From 1945 to 1973, international monetary arrangements were governed by the **Bretton Woods system**, named for the small New Hampshire town where delegates from major countries met to create a new international monetary system.

Bretton Woods system
The international monetary system in effect from 1945 to 1973, based on infrequent changes in currency prices, ample reserves, and the dollar as key currency.

The Bretton Woods system had some of the characteristics of the gold standard and some of the advantages of floating rates.

OPERATING RULES. Under the Bretton Woods system, a country defined a par value for its currency in terms of gold. The government was then obliged to keep its currency price within 1 percent of that par value. Central banks bought and sold their countries' currencies in exchange for gold, dollars, or other foreign currencies in order to maintain the currency's price at par value.

The Bretton Woods system differed from the gold standard in that there was no connection between gold, deficits, and the money supply. Countries could pursue independent monetary policies instead of linking their money supply to their holdings of gold. Since there was no automatic correction for deficits and surpluses, a balance of payments disequilibrium might last indefinitely. Because of this problem, the designers of the Bretton Woods system created a pool of **international monetary reserves**, or funds that countries could borrow to settle deficits and repay when they ran surpluses. Reserves consisted of gold, dollars, and other currencies. These reserves were kept at a newly created institution, the International Monetary Fund (IMF). The **International Monetary Fund (IMF)** was the agency that supervised the operation of the Bretton Woods system by recording par values, consulting on devaluations and revaluations, and maintaining a pool of reserves.

International monetary reserves
The pool of gold and major currencies created under the Bretton Woods system, from which countries could borrow to settle deficits and replenish from surpluses.

International Monetary Fund (IMF)
The agency that supervised the operation of the Bretton Woods system and maintained a reserve pool, and which continues to assist countries with currency and monetary management problems.

What happened if a country kept running deficits and borrowing from the IMF? The pool of reserves was not intended to sustain deficits forever—just long enough for the situation to get back to normal. If a disequilibrium continued, the Bretton Woods system had a second method for coping with deficits (or surpluses). A country with a persistent deficit could change the currency's price, or the exchange rate. Thus, the Bretton Woods system did not mandate unchangeable currency prices, a central feature of the gold standard. In this respect, the Bretton Woods system was more like floating rates, except that currency prices changed infrequently by large amounts instead of frequently by small amounts.

WHY THE BRETTON WOODS SYSTEM FAILED. The key to the failure of the Bretton Woods system lay in the difficulty of finding enough reserves. Since there was not enough gold, the next choice was the U.S. dollar, for two reasons. First, at the end of World War II, the United States had two-thirds of the world's monetary gold stock and was the only nation willing to redeem its currency in gold. Second, the United States dominated world trade as the biggest supplier and the biggest customer. Because dollars were so popular and so useful, they were even used to make payments when no U.S. citizens or firms were involved. A currency that serves as a major reserve asset and is used in transactions between third-party nations is called a **key currency.** The dollar, as the most popular key currency, joined gold as the second major form of international reserves.

Key currency
A currency that serves as a major reserve asset and is used in transactions between third-party nations.

Unfortunately, since the Bretton Woods system provided for no built-in corrections, deficits became large and persistent for many countries. Demand for reserves grew rapidly. The United States obliged by creating reserves. To create reserves, the United States ran deficits. The bigger and more frequent these deficits were, the more reserves were created. But the more dollars that were outstanding, the less likely it became that the United States would be able to redeem them from its dwindling gold stock. It became more likely that a devaluation of the dollar would be necessary to correct the deficits. No one wanted to be holding dollars when they were devalued, because of the financial loss. The pending crisis came to a head in 1971, when foreigners started turning in dollars for gold. After a long period of increased reluctance to redeem foreign-held dollars for gold, the United States finally suspended the redemption of dollars for gold in August 1971—an event known as the "closing of the gold window." In December 1971, the dollar was devalued by about 8 percent, raising the dollar price of gold from $35 to $38. In February 1973, the dollar was devalued again, raising the dollar price of gold to $42. After the second devaluation, the United States and its major trading partners all switched to floating rates.

CURRENCY AREAS AND THE EMU

Many countries still maintain a fixed exchange rate or "peg" their currency to a major currency. For example, many former French colonies in Africa keep a fixed relationship between the price of their currency and the French franc. Since France is still their major trading partner, this link creates a fixed exchange rate for most of their transactions. If the price of the franc falls 10 percent relative to the dollar, the price of a currency pegged to the franc will also fall by 10 percent relative to the dollar. The pegged currency will still have the same relationship to the franc.

The best-known currency area of the last decade is the **European Monetary Union (EMU)**, which is a currency area among the member countries of the European Community. Member countries establish a par value between their currency and other members' currencies, and buy and sell currencies to keep it within a certain percentage of that par value. The long-range goal of the EMU was a common European currency, to accompany the common passport, common labelling and professional standards, common external tariff, and other elements of a closely knit common market.

A monetary union is not a necessary part of a free trade area or common market. Neither NAFTA nor Mercosur, described in the preceding chapter, involves any kind of exchange rate coordination. Furthermore, membership in the European Community did not automatically entitle a country to membership in the EMU. Countries had to demonstrate their ability to sustain the price of their currency by showing past exchange rate stability, fiscal responsibility (low budget deficits), and adequate foreign exchange reserves. By 1992, only three countries met the conditions.

The EMU came into being in a loose sense in the late 1980s as the EC member countries agreed to a "joint float"—keeping their currencies stable internally while allowing them to float as a group with respect to other currencies. The EMU was to be formalized by the Maastricht treaty in 1992, which addressed a number of steps to be taken to further integrate the economic and political systems of the twelve member countries. However, two events kept the EMU from ever really coming into being in a formal sense. The first was opposition to some of the provisions of the treaty in several countries, notably France, Denmark, and the United Kingdom. The second event was the recession in Europe that was precipitated in large part by high German interest rates.

Germany is the dominant economy in the EC, especially since reunification. It overshadows its partners in terms of land mass, population, and GDP. The reunification of East and West Germany in 1990 put great pressure on the central

European Monetary Union (EMU)
A currency area of members of the European Community in which exchange rates are fixed among members within narrow bands, but float together with respect to other currencies; broke up in 1993.

government budget, which has run large deficits since that time. Germany has always had a very conservative monetary and fiscal policy, stressing price stability. Faced with large budget deficits, the Bundesbank (the German central bank) pursued a tight monetary policy that drove interest rates up to record highs. Capital began to flow into Germany. Other countries in the EMU found that they were running balance of payments deficits. In order to protect the price of their currencies, they had to allow interest rates to rise. All of the EC was following Germany into recession. Dropping out of the EMU allowed countries to break the link to Germany. As currency prices fell, interest rates returned to more normal levels and export sales began to improve.

The EMU has been the subject of the same kind of controversy that surrounded the Bretton Woods system. Economist Martin Feldstein, a former chair of the U.S. Council of Economic Advisers, argued that the EMU was neither necessary nor useful.[3] He argues that there is no evidence to support the notion that a fixed exchange rate will increase the volume of trade, and expresses concern about the impact of losing independent monetary policy in a monetary union. Supporters see the EMU as one of a number of essential steps toward creation of a United States of Europe with political as well as economic integration. The experience of 1993 makes it unlikely the EMU will be a full-fledged reality in the near future. The EMU appears to be yet another experiment in a fixed-rate system that was unable to endure.

Consider again...*This chapter probably didn't solve your problem with the Swiss music boxes, but at least you can now identify your choices. You can ignore the six months credit and pay immediately—a good solution if you have the cash and if the interest forgone for six months is not too high. Most importers, however, count on selling some of their imported goods before the credit period ends in order to generate the cash flow to meet their payment to the supplier. You could take a chance on what the exchange rate will be in six months; you might come out ahead, or you might come out behind. Now you are gambling not only on conditions in the music box industry, which you know something about, but also on conditions in the foreign exchange market.*

Finally, you could become a hedger, buying an insurance policy in the form of a forward contract. For a small fee, a bank or other foreign exchange dealer will guarantee a price for Swiss francs in six months—not the current price of SF1.38 per dollar, but not the SF1.25 you were having nightmares about. More likely, it will be a little below the current price, perhaps SF1.35—less for a small transaction or if the dollar is really expected to drop sharply and soon. For a relatively small fee, you can trade your worries to a professional speculator and concentrate on the business you know. Should you do it? Most importers would say yes.

---

3. Martin Feldstein, "The Case Against EMU," *The Economist* (June 13, 1992): 19–22.

SUMMARY

1. The balance of payments is a summary of transactions between U.S. residents and foreigners. There are two main accounts, the current account and the capital account. The difference between them is the statistical discrepancy. Current account includes exports and imports of goods and services, income on investments, and grants or transfers. Capital account consists of transactions in assets, including stocks, bonds, bank accounts, factories, land, and foreign currencies.
2. The items accounting for inflows of currency, such as exports of merchandise and services and sales of capital assets, are the sources of demand for a nation's currency in the foreign exchange market. The items accounting for outflows of currency, such as imports of merchandise and services and purchases of capital assets by U.S. residents, are the sources of supply for a nation's currency in the foreign exchange market.
3. Unique features of the foreign exchange market are the forward market, government price setting, and effects on important macroeconomic variables. The forward market reduces the risk connected with changing currency prices. Shifts in supply and demand for foreign exchange result from changes in relative prices, incomes, interest rates, tastes, population, technology, and input cost and availability. Such shifts can result in short-run or long-run disequilibrium in the foreign exchange markets. Disequilibrium often persists in the foreign exchange market if the monetary system involves fixed exchange rates.
4. Floating exchange rates, determined in the market, have been widely used since 1973. Those who oppose floating rates complain about the high cost of hedging. However, world trade has continued to grow rapidly under floating rates. A major disadvantage is lagged response of trade to changes in currency prices.
5. The gold standard relied on movements of gold to settle deficits. Gold flows changed money supplies, affecting prices and income and shifting supply and demand for currency. The Bretton Woods system (1945–1973) relied on reserves to settle deficits. It broke down because it was too dependent on a single currency—the dollar—which could not be devalued. The European Monetary Union (EMU) provided relatively stable exchange rates between members of the European Community but broke down in 1993 because of differences in monetary policy.

NEW TERMS

balance of payments
current account
balance of trade
capital account
statistical discrepancy
balance of payments deficit

foreign exchange market
appreciation
depreciation
trade-weighted dollar
real exchange rate
forward market

hedgers
speculators
gold standard
Bretton Woods system
international monetary reserves

International Monetary Fund (IMF)
key currency
European Monetary Union (EMU)

QUESTIONS: REVIEW, APPLICATIONS, AND POLICY

REVIEW

1. Why is the forward market especially important with floating exchange rates?
2. How do changes in prices and incomes in one country affect the supply and demand for its currency? What about changes in prices and incomes in other countries?
3. Why do some people want to return to the gold standard? What drawbacks does the gold standard have?
4. If interest rates rise in the United States, what happens to the supply, demand, and price of the dollar? Why? How might this affect U.S. exports and imports of goods and services?
5. How does a recession in one country affect economic conditions in another country?
6. Why is there a statistical discrepancy in the balance of payments?
7. How would you describe the current international monetary system? How did it evolve?
8. Stories in the press often draw attention to the fact that the balance of trade between the United States and Japan is in deficit. In itself, is this bilateral deficit a meaningful number?

APPLICATIONS

9. Look up the balance of payments for the United States for the last year in the *Federal Reserve Bulletin*. See if you

can put it into the simplified format of Table 1. How has it changed since 1993?

10. In what part of the U.S. balance of payments (Table 1) would each of the following transactions be incorporated?
    a. Sale of tractors to Poland
    b. Gift of tractors to Mexico
    c. U.S. citizen's purchase of a restaurant meal in Canada
    d. British resident's purchase of U.S. government bonds

11. How would each of the following be likely to affect supply or demand for the U.S. dollar? What should happen to its price?
    a. A recession in Japan, Canada, and Western Europe, the major trading partners of the United States
    b. A fall in the U.S. interest rate relative to that in the rest of the world
    c. More rapid inflation in the United States than in the rest of the world
    d. An export boom in U.S. movies and television shows

12. Graph the foreign exchange market for the zloty, the currency of Poland, to indicate an equilibrium price of 20 cents and an equilibrium quantity of 50 million. Is there a surplus or a shortage at prices of 40 cents and 10 cents?

POLICY

13. Which groups are likely to prefer a fixed exchange rate in their own self-interest? Which are likely to prefer floating rates? Which is better for an effective domestic monetary policy?

14. If NAFTA becomes a reality, should it be accompanied by a currency union between the three member countries? Why or why not?

SUGGESTIONS FOR FURTHER READING

Krugman, Paul R. *Has the Adjustment Process Worked?* Washington DC: Institute for International Economics, 1991. One of the best-known younger American economists offers a careful evaluation of how well exchange markets have worked under floating exchange rates.

Melamed, Leo, ed. *The Merits of Flexible Exchange Rates: An Anthology.* Fairfax VA: George Mason University Press, 1988.

A collection of articles by eminent economists in support of flexible exchange rates.

Root, Franklin R. *International Trade and Investment*, 7e. Cincinnati: South-Western, 1994. An intermediate textbook on international trade and international finance.

CHAPTER 36
ECONOMIES IN TRANSITION

Consider this... *The early 1990s have seen staggering and revolutionary changes in the formerly communist world. Indeed, only three countries still identify themselves as communist (North Korea, China, and Cuba). Of these three, both China and Cuba have moved in the direction of reliance on markets.*

The transition in the formerly communist countries has been painful, exciting, and challenging. Poland and the tiny Baltic republic of Estonia have come through the worst of it and seem to be emerging as healthy market economies, although Poland is still fighting a rear-guard action with former communists. Yugoslavia has disintegrated, while East Germany has been reunited with its Western half. Czechoslovakia has separated into two countries; the Soviet Union into fifteen separate nations. Hungary and the Czech Republic have made progress in privatizing industries, while Bulgaria and Romania have reelected Communist majorities in their parliaments and are moving slowly toward liberalization. The industrial democracies have been less helpful than they expected to be. Western countries know how to run a market-based economic system, but they don't know much about how to make the transition from a centrally planned economy to one in which most decisions are made in decentralized markets.

How long will the transition take, and what kinds of economies can we expect at the end of the transition? This chapter will examine the events of the recent past and speculate on what might occur as these economic and political changes mature. The introduction of markets and market mechanisms means choice and uncertainty in countries where security and sameness ruled. To some people, this change will be very unsettling. To others, it represents an opportunity. To the West, the transition in Eastern and Central Europe means a welcome end to the Cold War and demands for trade, aid, and patience while these nations develop a new system to replace their old command economies.

LEARNING OBJECTIVES
1. List the factors used to classify economies as market-oriented, socialist, and hybrid.
2. Distinguish among capitalism, socialism, and communism as theoretical economic systems and discuss the advantages and disadvantages of each.
3. Describe the events leading up to the collapse of communism in the former Soviet Union and Central Europe.
4. Discuss the process of transition from a centrally planned to a market economy and the difficulties being encountered in Eastern and Central Europe.
5. Evaluate the changes currently taking place in China, Japan, and Mexico as examples of economies in transition.

MARKETS, PLANNING, AND OWNERSHIP OF PROPERTY

Until 1990, economists described different economic systems by classifying them as capitalist, socialist, communist, or mixed. With only a handful of communist countries remaining, and with many countries moving away from the extremes of both socialism and capitalism, these categories do not describe contemporary reality. All economies blend elements of the old systems in different combinations. For modern economies, the array of economic arrangements reflects two criteria: the ownership of productive resources (private or public) and the locus of economic decision-making (market or government). These two factors determine the process by which the society answers the basic economic questions of what to produce, how to produce, and for whom to produce.

All economies are mixed to some degree. They contain varying combinations of central planning and government ownership with markets and private property. Sweden has primarily private ownership of resources, but a large share of economic decisions are made by the government. China is still nominally communist and has substantial public ownership, but decision-making is increasingly being turned over to the market. More typically, the two criteria move together. Extensive private ownership of resources means that most decisions are made through the market, while primarily public ownership of productive resources means that planners and other government officials make most economic decisions.

A shorthand way to combine these two criteria is to look at the share of economic activity passing through government. Table 1 gives two measures of the share of economic activity passing through the central government for selected countries. Included are countries at all income levels, but with emphasis on upper-middle-income and high-income countries.

The first measure in Table 1 indicates how much of income passes through government. However, this measure does not really capture some important aspects of the division of labor between the public and private sectors. In many countries, such as the United States, a large share of government activity is simply a transfer of income from one group to another through Social Security, unemployment insurance, and welfare programs. Economic decisions and property ownership are still primarily left to the private sector. On the other hand, for countries with extensive roles for state or provincial and local governments (such as the United States and Canada), this figure understates the total role of government by limiting the measure to the central government.

The second measure in Table 1 is a better indicator of the production role of government, since it measures government spending in the same way that G is measured in the GDP accounts. It is a better measure of direct government allocation activity and includes all levels of government. This measure shows a consistent pattern; a larger share of GDP is devoted to government consumption (which is also production) in higher-income countries, except for Japan. However, at every income level there is still much diversity.

Neither figure captures the indirect ways in which governments influence private production decisions. Governments at all levels place restrictions on the use of private property. Firms must meet health, safety, environmental, and financial accountability standards. Residential property owners are constrained in how they can use their property. In addition, tax systems are usually designed to

TABLE 1 CENTRAL GOVERNMENT SHARE OF ECONOMIC ACTIVITY, 1990

COUNTRY	(1) GOVERNMENT EXPENDITURES AS SHARE OF GDP	(2) GOVERNMENT CONSUMPTION AS SHARE OF GDP	(3) INCOME LEVEL
Japan	16.7%	9%	High
Venezuela	23.1	9	Upper middle
Sri Lanka	28.4	9	Low
Chile	32.8	10	Lower middle
Egypt	40.2	10	Low
Mexico	18.4	11	Upper middle
Hungary	54.8	11	Upper middle
India	18.1	13	Low
Turkey	24.6	14	Lower middle
Belgium	49.3	14	High
Bolivia	18.8	15	Lower middle
Pakistan	23.9	15	Low
Spain	33.5	15	High
Brazil	36.0	16	Upper middle
Ireland	54.5	16	High
United States	24.0	18	High
Australia	25.8	18	High
United Kingdom	34.8	20	High
Canada	23.4	20	High
Sweden	2.3	27	High

Source: *World Development Report 1992* (Washington DC: The World Bank). Low-income countries have per capita GDP less than $US600 per year, lower-middle $600-$2,500, upper-middle $2,500 to $6,000, and high-income over $6,000.

encourage certain kinds of activities and discourage others. Thus, government's involvement in private decisions in most countries is both larger and smaller than either measure in Table 1 would indicate.

CAPITALISM, SOCIALISM, AND COMMUNISM

An essential distinction between economic systems lies in who directs production, who makes decisions, and who bears the costs for wrong decisions or receives the rewards for correct decisions. The question is not whether planning should take place, but rather, who should do the planning? General Motors plans, home builders plan, wheat farmers plan—and so do you. The key question is the degree of centralization of planning and control. At the market extreme, the answer would be that only individual consumers and entrepreneurs should plan. Pure capitalism describes this extreme. At the command extreme, the answer would be that only governmental authorities should plan. Socialism is a system in which all planning is done by government.

Capitalism and socialism are the two polar extremes of real-world economic systems. Communism is more a political philosophy or a theory of history than an actual system for a national economy, although many of the ideas of communism are expressed in socialism.

CAPITALISM

Capitalism is an economic system characterized by private ownership of the productive resources by individuals or groups of individuals. In pure capitalism, individuals would be free to use their property as they see fit. Any limitations on the use of the property diminish its value to the owner. Private property rights are an important feature of capitalism because they create incentives and make exchange possible. In capitalism, property rights to productive resources, including labor, are vested with the individual. Individuals seeking profits make investment decisions. Workers are free to move about, but they are not guaranteed jobs. In pure capitalism, individuals are also not guaranteed any basic income if they are unable or unwilling to work. A system based on private ownership is one in which individuals maximize their own well-being, in terms of either profit or utility.

Most capitalist countries (but not all) are politically democratic. Political democracy smoothes some of the rough edges of capitalism by restraining the excesses of monopoly, providing basic public services through government, and alleviating poverty and inequality. However, democracy also tends to weaken the power of the market and the security of property rights, because a majority of the population can use the government to redistribute income or to change property rights to their own benefit.

SOCIALISM

Under pure **socialism**, all nonhuman means of production are owned by society or the state. Socialism has theoretical roots in the work of Marx and real-world roots in various twentieth-century revolutions and their leaders. The central authority makes the major economic decisions. Utopian socialists see this central authority as promoting the "common good," usually greater equality and/or economic development. In some socialist countries this authority has developed into a centralist, personal dictatorship, such as that of Stalin in the former Soviet Union or Nicolae Ceausescu in Romania. In other cases, however, countries are socialist but at least nominally democratic, even though one party may dominate the political system for long periods (such as the PRI in Mexico).

Under socialism, especially in China, people are often assigned jobs in certain geographic locations and do not have the freedom to switch occupations or geographic location. Workers under socialism typically have greater job security but less freedom to choose jobs than in a market system. In socialist countries, a central plan determines the level and composition of investment. Production decisions and decisions that affect the distribution of income are also made by the central planning authority under socialism. These decisions answer the *what* and *for whom* questions of Chapter 2.

Capitalism
An economic system in which private individuals own the means of production and are free to use them in response to economic incentives.

Socialism
An economic system in which the nonhuman means of production are owned by the state.

KEY IDEAS

ESSENTIAL DIFFERENCES BETWEEN CAPITALISM AND SOCIALISM	
CAPITALISM	SOCIALISM
Property Rights Resources are owned by individuals or groups of individuals.	Resources are owned by the state.
Labor Workers have a property right to their own labor. They are self-employed or work for private firms.	Workers are employed by the government and are usually not allowed to change jobs.
Investment Investment is determined and undertaken by entrepreneurs.	Investment is determined and undertaken by government.
Production Mix What is produced is determined by market forces.	What is produced is determined by central plan.
Distribution Distribution of income is determined by market forces, productivity, and ownership patterns.	Distribution of income is determined by central plan.
Incentives Labor, management, and entrepreneurs respond to wages, prices, and profits.	Often many nonmaterial incentives are used.

COMMUNISM

Perhaps no other economist has had more effect on shaping the political world than Karl Marx, who, with Friedrich Engels, published the *Communist Manifesto* in 1848. This book, along with Marx's *Das Kapital*, is the philosophical basis for a widely divergent group of economic-political systems. In recent years, almost all communist governments have claimed to be Marxist. China still claims to adhere to the tenets of Karl Marx.

To Karl Marx, **communism** was the final stage in a progression from capitalism, with socialism representing the middle stage. Under communism, Marx foresaw the end of scarcity, the end of conflict among classes, and creation of a new social order. An ideal member of this new order would no longer be the self-interested individual on which most economic analysis is based. The true communist would put the interest of the larger community above personal self-interest. In the final stage, individuals would receive goods and services according to their needs, and the state would wither away until all it did was administer the economy. The organizational structure that Marx foresaw under communism is not at all clear. Presumably everyone would contribute labor in exchange for goods and services needed.

Communism
The final stage of social evolution according to Marx, in which the state has withered away and economic goods are distributed according to need.

Marx believed that every society would evolve through historical stages of tribal communism, slavery, feudalism, capitalism, socialism, and, finally, communism. The most important transition would come when capitalism decayed because of internal conflict and was succeeded by socialism. The regular cyclical ups and downs of a capitalist economy (the business cycle) would become more and more severe until capitalism finally collapsed. Marx saw the empire building of European countries in the nineteenth century as an attempt to postpone the inevitable failure of capitalism. He believed that when socialism was replaced by communism, scarcity would disappear, and workers would produce without material incentives.

The countries that adopted communism have been those in which there was little industrial development. This pattern is inconsistent with what Marx predicted. What, then, is the significance of Marx's writings? It lies not in the accuracy of his predictions but rather in the theoretical, philosophical, and political movements spawned by his work. Communist parties in many countries consider themselves Marxists and appeal to the writings of Marx to justify their views on various issues. They all condemn the "exploitation" of workers under capitalism and believe that the pursuit of profit is an inappropriate goal.

Socialism, to Marx, was an intermediate stage between capitalism and communism. Under socialism, decision-making authority shifts from individual entrepreneurs to a central authority, which Marx called the "dictatorship of the proletariat." In practice, the central authority has almost always been personified by a dominant individual. It is thus possible to view many of the offshoots of Marxism as the products of the interaction of Marxist ideas with the personalities of strong-willed leaders—Mao Zhe-Dong in China, Lenin and Stalin in Russia, Tito in former Yugoslavia, and Castro in Cuba. Of these various efforts to implement Marxism in practice, the longest and best-known experiment took place in the Soviet Union from 1917 to 1990.

FROM THE SOVIET UNION TO THE RUSSIAN REPUBLIC

Vladimir Lenin (1870–1924) was active in developing the Communist Party in Russia and led that country's successful Bolshevik Revolution in 1917–1918. He claimed to be a follower of Marx, but developed new directions for the achievement of communism. Lenin refused to wait for the maturation of capitalism and instead developed a different model for revolution based on four essential ingredients: (1) a small, revolutionary elite, (2) economic underdevelopment (the opposite of Marx's industrialization), (3) a discontented peasantry, and (4) war against an outside force. Lenin's formula worked in Russia, North Korea, China, Vietnam, and Cuba. In Eastern and Central Europe, communism was imposed on more modern economies by the Soviet Union after World War II.

Lenin was the first communist to be faced with the task of setting up an economic system after the political system was secure. After the 1917 revolution, Lenin nationalized industry and outlawed private trading. All labor mobility was rigidly controlled, and money as an exchange mechanism almost disappeared. By 1921, the economy had seriously deteriorated. Lenin responded by instituting a program called the New Economic Policy (NEP). This policy limited nationalization and planning to the key industries in the economy. The remainder of the economy was left to respond to market forces. There was very rapid economic growth during this period, and the Soviet economy quickly recovered from the protracted civil war. However, the NEP greatly reduced the power of the Communist Party to channel and direct the course of economic development.[1]

After Lenin's death, there was open dispute in the Soviet Communist Party over the direction of development between those who favored rapid industrialization with central planning and investment in industry, and those who supported a more decentralized, market approach. When Stalin came to power, he set up a system of five-year plans that persisted for more than sixty years. The first five-year plan involved very centralized planning, investment in heavy industry, and forced collectivization in the agricultural sector. Industrialization was very rapid, but the costs of this policy in human terms were great.

CENTRAL PLANNING

Central planning and control was the most basic feature of the Soviet-style economy. Everything was controlled from the center until the late 1980s, when some discretionary authority was delegated to some enterprise managers. Even municipalities turned their revenues over to the central government and operated under a budget handed down by a central ministry.

In the Soviet system, as well as the communist nations of Central Europe, the state owned all natural resources (including land), most of the physical capital (plant and equipment), 75 percent of urban housing and 25 percent of rural housing; it produced 88 percent of agricultural output (1986) and controlled 98 percent of retail trade. The only lawful private activities were family farm plots, housing, arts and crafts, and some professional and personal services (although there was considerable illegal private activity, especially in more recent years).

The planning process was centralized in a Council of Ministers and twenty state committees, under which there were fifty branch ministries (five for food and agriculture, nine for construction, nine for the military, etc.). These branch ministries were in turn divided into departments along either product or regional lines. A similar structure existed in each of the fifteen republics. At the bottom of the structure were the associations and enterprises that actually produced and distributed goods and services. In 1986, there were over a million wholesale and retail outlets, 47,000 construction firms, 23,000 state farms, 27,000 collective farms, and 46,000 industrial enterprises.[2]

FIVE-YEAR PLANS AND ANNUAL PLANS. While the five-year plan is the most famous, detailed plans were made annually with precise production targets. These targets were developed through bargaining as the flow of directives from above crossed reports and requests for resources from below. Money and financial considerations played little role. Money functioned mainly to pay wages and allow consumers to make purchases. Prices, which are a crucial signal in Western economies, were used for measurement, accounting, and control, and were set

---

1. This brief summary cannot do justice to the complexities of 75 years of Soviet communism. For a history of the first 50 years, see Alec Nove, *An Economic History of the USSR* (London: Penguin, 1975).
2. Bergson, Abram, "The USSR Before the Fall: How Poor and Why," *Journal of Economic Perspectives* (Fall 1991): 29–44.

on a cost-plus basis to allow enterprises to be self-financing. The plus included "profit", turnover tax, and handling costs.

STRENGTHS AND WEAKNESSES. The critical features of this system were a hierarchy with upward accountability, lack of horizontal supplier-customer relationships, rationing, rigidity, and incentives to respond to superiors rather than to workers, customers, or suppliers. With separation of operations and information from the authority and the incentive to use it, the system was resistant to change and unable to respond to new conditions or needs. The incentive at the bottom (the manager of the plant, store, or farm) was to lie, to bargain, to get an easy target, to appear to do well rather than to actually produce a large quantity of high-quality product at minimum cost. The Soviet system divorced information from authority and incentives.

A centralized, hierarchical system like this can do certain things well, and the Soviet system did accomplish some specific goals from the 1930s to the 1970s. Accomplishments included collectivization of agriculture (albeit at high cost in both lives and output), development of heavy industry, recovery from World War II, and development of the Soviet military. The Soviet Union enjoyed the "advantage of backwardness" in being able to catch up by borrowing ideas and technology.

However, weaknesses were ultimately more powerful than strengths as the Soviets attempted to make the leap from a Third World, just-above-subsistence economy to a modern, technologically sophisticated superpower. Successful development means increased diversity in inputs, outputs, and processes, which is difficult to achieve in a rigid hierarchical system. In the West, already decentralized in its reliance on markets for the bulk of economic decisions, further decentralization has been the watchword of the last fifteen years—from shifting government responsibility to the local level, to worker quality circles and very flat corporate organizational structures, to privatization of public services.

MISSING MARKET FEATURES

Certain features of a market system make it more efficient in allocating resources into those uses where they are most productive and in ensuring that output of the system matches what households need or want. Two features that are particularly important in a market system were weak or nonexistent in centrally planned economies. One is the use of a rate of return/interest to allocate capital. The other is private ownership of resources, which creates incentives that reward efficiency (especially the profit motive). Both characteristics are feedback mechanisms that diagnose problems, failures, and bottlenecks in the system and call forth a response.

INTEREST AND CAPITAL. Charging interest has a bad press, not only in socialism; Greek, Roman, and medieval Christian writers also regarded interest as extortion or exploitation. However, in a system where there is a good deal of physical capital—factories, tools, equipment, power supplies, and so on—the interest rate plays an important role in ranking projects and deciding which ones to undertake. The market rate of interest is determined by the interaction of borrowers and lenders. Would-be borrowers compare the interest rate to their best estimates of the rate of return on investment to determine whether or not to

POLICY FOCUS: THE FUTURE OF PLANNING

In 1922, a professor at the University of Vienna, Ludwig von Mises, wrote a famous article, "Economic Calculation in the Socialist Commonwealth."[a] He claimed that rational economic calculations were impossible under socialism. If the state owned the productive resources (other than labor), it would have to allocate them among competing uses. Without a market to determine prices, planners would have to use shadow prices, or simulated market prices used by economic planners when actual market prices are not available. A simulated market with shadow prices could not supply correct information because of the absence of the profit motive.

Polish economist Oskar Lange responded to von Mises with a model of a socialist economy using a combination of central *and* local decision-making. Lange tried to prove that such an economy can arrive at the same efficient result as perfect competition.[b] Prices are set by the central authority. Local managers are told to maximize profits, although they cannot keep these profits. If shortages or surpluses develop, the price is changed until an equilibrium price is finally reached. While Lange's solution is clever, however, he ignores the role of profits in a market system as not merely a measure of success but the *incentive* to succeed.[c]

Nobel laureate F.A. Hayek joined the debate by pointing to the differences in how information is used in socialist and capitalist systems.[d] Information is costly to develop and spread, using scarce resources that must be taken away from other uses. Hayek argued that market systems are superior because they need less information than centrally planned systems.

Suppose there is a shortage of an important input (e.g., electricity) in a market economy. As the price of electricity rises, profit-minded entrepreneurs will substitute other energy sources or try to improve operating efficiency. In a planned economy, the response is more complicated. In Bulgaria, a shortage of electricity due to problems with nuclear power plants in the 1990s was addressed with rolling blackouts. Power was shut off one hour in four for each of four sectors of the country. This mandated solution bore no relation to the relative productivity of electricity in varying parts of the country or in different uses.

In general, the process of adaptation is much slower. Planners must first be informed of the shortage. They then inform each user of electricity to substitute other inputs because less electricity will be available. Planners must also notify producers of other energy sources to supply the enterprises with replacements. In addition, planners will have to set priorities for use of electricity. In a market system, the increase in price lets the private sector set priorities.

Hayek argues that central planning can never be as efficient as a market system because it requires the use of so many resources to transmit information. A market system minimizes the amount of information needed. In 1989, there were severe earthquakes in both San Francisco and Soviet Armenia. The response to the earthquake was much faster in San Francisco, reflecting the positive role that the market can play in speeding the process of economic recovery. The transitions now underway in most planned economies suggest that almost every country is willing to rely on the market for a significant share of economic decisions because markets offer a faster response and a more

a. Ludwig Von Mises, "Economic Calculation in the Socialist Commonwealth," in F. A. Hayek (ed.), *Collectivist Economic Planning* (Clifton NJ: Augustus M. Kelley, 1967), 103.
b. A thorough discussion of this controversy is provided in Paul R. Gregory and Robert C. Stuart, *Soviet Economic Structure and Performance* (New York: Harper & Row, 1974).
c. Paul C. Roberts, "Oskar Lange's Theory of Socialist Planning," *Journal of Political Economy* (May-June 1971): 562–568.
d. F. A. Hayek, "The Use of Knowledge in Society," *American Economic Review* (September 1945): 519–528.

---

borrow and invest. In this way, capital is allocated in a decentralized fashion using locally generated information to those uses where it is most productive.

Without interest rates, and without market-generated prices for capital, labor, and raw materials, it is not possible to make calculations about where to allocate capital so as to maximize its productivity. There were some internal rate of return calculations in the Soviet economy, but without related prices and direct use of interest rates, allocation of capital was somewhat haphazard and arbitrary.

PRIVATE OWNERSHIP AND INCENTIVES. Private ownership of resources in a market economy increases the likelihood that those resources will be used where they are most productive. At the most basic level, workers own their labor resources; they decide how much to invest in themselves or their children, and what job to take in order to earn a return on those resources. Market signals limit the number of people getting advanced degrees in comparative literature and classical languages, compared to engineers and accountants. Households also own land and buildings, and are faced with competing uses for those resources. The market encourages resource owners to put those resources to their best and highest use, partly signalled by market prices.

Private ownership is closely linked to incentives—higher salaries, profits, and other tangible rewards for good performance and penalties for failure. Taking risks is two-sided. In order to make workers, resource owners, and enterprises responsive to changes in resource availability, technology, consumer preferences, and other information, there must be immediate and tangible rewards for good performance and immediate and tangible penalties for poor performance. In the East, the right to a job carries with it a guarantee of worker indifference. The incentive of an enterprise manager in the Soviet system was to hoard resources, hide capabilities, and simulate desirable outcomes in order to please an often distant and harried superior.

Recognition of these problems led to several attempts to reform the system, especially during the Gorbachev era. Some reforms aimed at improving central planning through use of computers; others attempted to decentralize with more enterprise discretion and various incentive schemes. However, in the context of the Soviet planning bureaucracy, more local discretion often made behavior at the enterprise level worse instead of better.

REASONS FOR COLLAPSE

There are many factors that contributed to the collapse of the Soviet system, but it is possible to single out a few major contributing factors. In addition to a series of special problems, collapse was hastened by the effects of liberalization, events in Central Europe, the failure of halfway reforms, and performance failures.

SPECIAL PROBLEMS. Gorbachev inherited, in 1985, an economy that was performing worse than in earlier decades.[3] In short order, he encountered the following economic shocks, some of his own making, others not. First, the nuclear accident at Chernobyl in 1986 was costly in power production, cleanup, and health care and relocation costs. The estimated cost was 25 billion rubles at a time when the local value of the ruble was about $1.

Second, the earthquake in Armenia in 1988 was another costly blow. This natural disaster caused 25,000 deaths, 530,000 homeless, and loss of 10 percent

---

3. Noren, James H., "The Economic Crisis: Another Perspective," in E. A. Hewett and V. H. Winston (eds.) *Milestones in Glasnost and Perestroika: The Economy* (Washington DC: Brookings Institution, 1991), 360–406.

of Armenia's industrial base and 11 percent of the housing as well as schools, hospitals, and other facilities. The estimated recovery cost was 13 billion rubles.

Third, the decline in world oil prices after 1985 cost the Soviet Union about $24 billion in hard currency needed to finance imports of consumer goods and machinery, putting further pressure on supplies and increasing consumer frustration.

Fourth, the weather contributed to worsening conditions. The winters and springs of 1985 and 1987 were among the coldest in two decades, while 1984 and 1986 saw the hottest and driest springs. Estimated weather losses for those four years were about 30 billion rubles, or 6 percent of total output.

Finally, restricting the supply of alcohol was a Gorbachev policy decision with unexpected secondary effects. His crackdown on vodka resulted in a run on sugar and other ingredients of homemade vodka. In conjunction with reduced imports because of the loss of oil revenues, limits on availability of vodka contributed to a situation where consumers were flush with cash but found little to buy. As lines got longer, consumers got angrier.

GLASNOST AND PERESTROIKA. Gorbachev's policy of openness raised expectations that could not be fulfilled and brought the failures of the economic system into the open. **Glasnost** is the Russian term for openness, which meant political freedom and open dissent. **Perestroika** referred to restructuring of the economy with more decentralization. Perestroika reduced the role of the Communist Party in managing the economy. The party became demoralized, and the leadership vacuum was not filled by other groups. Glasnost, allowing open dissent, resulted in demonstrations, strikes, and ethnic unrest. The eruption of long-suppressed frustrations and hostilities among the diverse ethnic groups in the Soviet Union ultimately led to its dissolution.

Declining party morale, consumer frustration, and general pessimism led to increased strikes and absenteeism. A sharp rise in worker absenteeism reflected not only morale but longer queues to purchase consumer goods. With more absenteeism, production began to fall.

Glasnost (Russian, openness): Political reforms involving free speech and tolerance of dissent in the former Soviet Union in the Gorbachev era.

Perestroika (Russian, restructuring): Economic reforms in the former Soviet Union in the Gorbachev era.

THE CENTRAL EUROPE FACTOR. Perestroika and glasnost fed into a long history of unrest and partial reforms in Central Europe, especially in Poland and Hungary. Hungary had been working on reform and decentralization for more than three decades. Poland, Czechoslovakia, and East Germany all moved away from the traditional Soviet model in the last half of the 1980s in response to closer links to the West and citizen unrest. Much of the impact of these changes on the USSR was transmitted via COMECON, the Warsaw Pact's common market. COMECON's assignment of industries and other responsibilities among countries was vital to the Soviet Union, which sold raw materials and energy to other countries in exchange for consumer goods and machinery. Once these countries broke loose from the orbit, a combination of lower prices for Soviet exports and loosening of trade ties meant that Soviet exports fell by 10 percent from 1989 to 1990. Imports fell even further because these countries were no longer willing to finance a continued Soviet trade deficit.

FAILURE OF HALFWAY REFORMS. Perestroika represented an attempt to reorganize the planning process, shift the mix of output toward consumer goods, and impose higher quality standards. Firms were no longer provided with detailed plans or fixed production targets, but had some leeway in locating their own customers and suppliers. As enterprises became self-financing (pouring their "profits" back into the enterprise instead of sending them up the chain of command), they stopped producing unprofitable items and shifted to higher-priced consumer goods. With incomplete freeing of prices, market forces were not in place to lead to corrections in the output mix. Some enterprises were also making foreign contracts without making sure that they had access to needed foreign exchange, resulting in a growing trade deficit.

PERFORMANCE FAILURES. Bad economic news is clearly not enough to overthrow a dictatorial government. After all, Castro is still in power. But poor performance can contribute to a change in policy in a system that has created just a modest amount of openness.

For years, reported Soviet growth rates were well above those of the industrial West. Some of this apparent success was overreporting, which declined with glasnost beginning in 1985.[4] Some of the growth was real, but quality measures were ignored. Some of the growth in the early postwar period was easy to attain because, like Germany and Japan, the Soviet Union was in a war recovery mode. With the production base so depressed, higher growth rates were easier to generate.

By the late 1980s, some of the negative economic results of the Soviet system were becoming increasingly visible both at home and abroad: an obsolete capital stock, abuse of the resource base and the natural environment, technological backwardness, and a maze of construction projects that had remained half-finished for years. Measures of performance were difficult to determine, but estimates could be made for certain aspects of performance. Western standards of performance call for comparison measures of per capita GDP, inflation, unemployment, consumer welfare, and environmental quality.

Per capita GDP in the Soviet Union in 1987 was about 29 percent of the U.S. figure, higher than Turkey but lower than Portugal (the poorest nation in Western Europe). The standard of living is reflected more accurately by per capita consumption, which excludes investment, military spending, and so forth. The U.S. Central Intelligence Agency developed estimates of Soviet consumption per capita. Allowing for the problems of comparing noncomparable goods and services (Soviet goods were notorious for poor quality and lack of variety), these estimates still confirm a relatively low standard of living and a deterioration in the immediate pre-Gorbachev era. Compared to the United States, Soviet citizens consumed 31 percent as much per capita in 1980, 29 percent in 1985. Other estimates from Central European sources (Hungary and Poland) of Soviet consumption show more decline between 1980 and 1985, from 30 percent to 26 percent of U.S. consumption (Hungarian estimate) or from 33 percent to 22 percent (Polish estimate). All other measures of output also showed a decline in 1988 and 1989—industrial production, freight transportation, production of consumer durables and processed foods, fuels, and electric power.[5]

Measures of per capita GDP or consumption neglect some important dimensions of quality of life. One is leisure; this includes not only the length of the work week but also time spent in line to make consumer purchases. Soviet work-

---

4. Noren, "The Economic Crisis," 360–406.
5. Bergson, "The USSR Before the Fall," 29–44.

ers have had a reputation for slackness on the job (a consequence of a job guarantee), but already long lines for consumer goods increased under Gorbachev for a variety of reasons (including the alcohol ban, import restrictions, poor harvests, and growth of the black market). Leisure was more apparent than real, especially for Soviet women, who shouldered all of the household responsibilities. Often it was the grandmother who kept the family going by tending the children and waiting in line at stores.

Another dimension of economic welfare is environmental quality, an area in which Soviet and Eastern European performance is appalling by Western standards, perhaps even by Third World standards. Market systems often perform poorly in environmental quality because of the lack of clearly defined property rights to air, water, and other common property resources. However, the Soviet system did much worse. In emphasizing output goals, there was no charge to use the environment as a waste dump or a cesspool. In addition, Western technology has made significant advances in nuclear safety, air filtration, and other environment-friendly methods of production that were not known or implemented in Eastern and Central Europe.

A third dimension of economic performance and quality of life is inflation and unemployment. Historically, centrally planned economies appear to be successful in fighting these two demons of capitalism by repressing inflation (which shows up in long lines and empty shelves instead) and attaining full employment (even if the worker is highly unproductive, he or she is guaranteed a job). Unemployment did not begin to appear until 1990, but is now rising rapidly in the former Soviet republics, as well as in Central Europe, as enterprises are given much more authority and autonomy to get rid of excess workers. Inflation began to surface as a problem during the Gorbachev reforms of the late 1980s with the freeing of some prices, and surged to 1,200 percent in 1992 before slowing down in 1993.

Much of current measured inflation, however, is the result of decades of price controls. Soviet-style systems are inherently inflationary. Prices are set below their equilibrium levels to guarantee that everything will be sold. If the plan is in danger of not being fulfilled, cutbacks always fall on consumer goods, not industrial goods. Wages always exceed the goods available to buy, resulting in shortages, long lines, and consumer frustration—all symptoms of masked inflation. Some inflation was also the result of overexpansion of the money supply to finance government budget deficits as the economy declined while expenditure obligations mounted.

THE RUSSIAN REPUBLIC

Recent changes in the former Soviet Union and the other communist nations of Eastern and Central Europe have been staggering. In 1989, radical change swept Eastern Europe. To the surprise of the West, the Soviet Union chose not to intervene. The most dramatic events occurred in East Germany, where the Berlin Wall came down, and in Romania, where a military coup led to the Christmas Day execution of the former dictator, Ceausescu Political and economic reforms also took place rapidly in the three small Baltic states (Estonia, Latvia, and Lithuania) as well as Poland, Czechoslovakia, and Hungary, and finally in Bulgaria and Albania. A coup against Gorbachev in 1991 was thwarted, but it was followed shortly by the rise of Yeltsin to the top position, free elections, and the breakup of the Soviet Union into fifteen independent republics. The largest of these republics, headed by Yeltsin, is the Russian Republic.

Yeltsin came to power under very difficult circumstances. The old order had collapsed, but there were no market institutions to replace the old central direction. Other problems included ethnic unrest, widespread pollution, political corruption, labor unrest, rising unemployment, high inflation rates, and strong resistance from unreformed communists. Some old central planners are still on the job, including several former executives of Gosplan, the Soviet central planning agency.[6] Ironically, because of problems related to political turmoil and the breakup of the Soviet Union, the first European nation to declare itself communist will probably be one of the last to make a successful transition to a mixed market economy.

TRANSITION TO A MARKET SYSTEM

The stated goal of Eastern and Central European governments is to move in the direction of a market-based system with freely determined prices, competition, profits, private ownership, and other features of capitalism. The degree of government involvement in the economy, particularly in social welfare, will vary greatly from country to country. The reason for the shift is the demonstrated superiority of a market system in satisfying consumer wants, providing incentives, and minimizing the need for bureaucratic controls. At the same time, many citizens are concerned about problems of insecurity and inequality that they see as the failings of a market system. Vaclev Havel, president of the Czech Republic, captured this notion as "capitalism with a human face." He also warned that, "Popular disenchantment with the shortcomings of central planning does not automatically translate into a broad-based acceptance of market economics."

Other Eastern and Central European countries have moved much faster than the Russian Republic in economic reform. For most of these countries, the main obstacle to reform was the Soviet Union. Reform took off when opposition leaders in these countries realized that the Soviet Union was not going to intervene militarily, as it had in Hungary (1956) and Czechoslovakia (1968). East Germany's reform has been greatly helped by its reunification with West Germany, but at a high cost to West Germans. Poland moved toward capitalism rapidly, and, after a painful transition, is seeing growth, low inflation, well-stocked stores, and hope for the future, although unemployment remains high and the social welfare system is much weaker. Czechoslovakia (now two separate countries) and Hungary are moving steadily toward reform. Progress is slower in Bulgaria and Romania, where the communists still have considerable influence in government.

The fifteen republics that made up the former Soviet Union and the countries of Eastern Europe have some advantages to build on. All of them have a highly educated and well-trained labor force. Many of the former Soviet republics, in particular, are rich in natural resources; some countries, especially Bulgaria and Ukraine, have rich and fertile agricultural land. Several have locational advantages: Bulgaria in access to the near East, Poland as the link between

---

6. "Hard Pounding," *The Economist* (May 15, 1993): 60–62.

Germany and Russia, all of Central Europe in easy access to the European market. Between that potentially bright future and the untidy present, however, lies the transition.

PRIVATIZATION

An important first step in moving to a market economy is to transfer ownership of enterprises from the government to the private sector. This transfer is called **privatization**. In the Western industrial countries, including France and the United Kingdom, and also in Latin America, privatization has been in vogue for about twelve years. It involves not only sale of state enterprises to the private sector (Amtrak in the United States, British Leyland Motors in the United Kingdom, Pemex in Mexico) but also contracting out certain kinds of public services paid for with taxes to private firms (such as management of prisons and hospitals). The scale of privatization in Central and Eastern Europe is much larger, however, since virtually all productive assets other than labor were owned by the government prior to the 1990s.[7]

Privatization
Transferring assets from public to private ownership in order to increase the share of economic decisions made through the market.

COSTS AND BENEFITS. There are several benefits associated with privatizing those enterprises that produce goods and services for sale to private consumers without any special public element. These benefits are those you have learned in microeconomics—efficiency, incentives, prices, and variety. If there is room for competition, benefits should include lower prices and more variety. If the firm needs to operate on a very large scale to be efficient, there may be a continued need for some regulation of the firm as a private monopoly. Even in this case, however, privatization will offer better incentives for workers and owners to be efficient. Private firms are generally more responsive than government enterprises to the needs and desires of their customers and suppliers because the income of workers and owners depends on those relationships.

The costs of privatization are greater income inequality, uncertainty, and unemployment. A centrally planned economy guarantees a job, which reduces the incentive for the worker to try harder, but also reduces insecurity and uncertainty facing households as they plan for their futures. A centrally planned economy can result in greater equality, a value that is deeply ingrained in Eastern European culture. Concern about equality and economic security will play an important role in defining the relative spheres of the public and private sectors in these nations in the future.

PROBLEMS OF PRIVATIZATION. Typically, in a Western privatization a firm is prepared for sale. It may have its capital restructured (e.g., debt reduction), it may spin off some of its lesser activities, its financial position and pricing policies may be thoroughly reviewed, and there may be management changes or restructuring. When these steps have been completed to make the shares in the enterprise attractive to buyers, a public offering is made in the stock market. Some shares may be sold to foreigners, but in most Western economies there is a substantial domestic market that will absorb most of the shares.

---

7. Transition issues in Eastern and Central Europe were the subject of a symposium in the *Journal of Economic Perspectives* (Fall 1991). Eleven contributors examine theoretical and practical issues of privatization in the former Soviet Union and Eastern/Central Europe.

Such a procedure does not meet the needs of Central and Eastern Europe for three reasons: First, these countries have not had stock markets until very recently. Second, there is no substantial pool of domestic private capital with which to purchase shares. Third, there are too many enterprises to proceed so slowly.

Lack of a banking system and stock exchange has been a serious obstacle to privatization. Transactions under communism were generally made in cash; credit cards are still rare, except in places serving foreigners, and checks are unknown. Poland and the Czech Republic have developed a stock exchange and others are working on it. Still in development are such related features of capitalism as insurance, bond markets, bond ratings services, consumer credit, and securities disclosure regulations. An important function of a banking system is to gather up the pool of savings by individuals and firms to a critical mass and use it to make loans to businesses, individuals, cities, and even the central government. At the time of collapse or revolution, most of these countries had very little accumulated domestic savings, although saving has risen in anticipation of an opportunity to invest in enterprises.

Finally, a market system will require a legal structure for the enforcement of contracts, bankruptcy rules, and definition and enforcement of property rights. Along with creating a legal system based on private property, public education on legal rights and obligations will be an important part of the process of change. There are mistaken notions of the meaning of "free" in "free enterprise" or "free market." Eastern Europe is just discovering the value and necessity of a certain amount of regulatory control in protecting both parties to transactions as well as third-party interests.

EXPERIENCE WITH PRIVATIZATION. Several special procedures have been developed in Central Europe to speed up the privatization process. Farmland is being privatized by restitution to the original owners or their descendants or division among members of collective farms. The easiest enterprises to privatize are retail shops and services—auto repair, taxis, restaurants, beauty parlors, jewelry stores, bookstores, bakeries—as well as small enterprises (defined in Russia as those with fewer than 200 employees). Usually, retail operations are owned by the municipalities and are restored to private hands by lease (often by auction), outright sale, or, in some cases, restitution to original owners. Leasing does not require a new private entrepreneur to put up a lot of initial capital and thus keeps the enterprises largely in domestic hands. However, it also limits the entrepreneur's willingness to invest further in the enterprise, since someone else may win the lease when it is up for renewal, usually after five years.[8]

A greater challenge has been privatizing large-scale enterprises in the absence of well-developed financial markets. Of the Central European countries, only Poland and the Czech Republic have anything close to a workable stock market. The approach to privatizing large enterprises has been somewhat similar from country to county in Central Europe. Most countries have stressed methods that allow a large number of citizens with little capital to participate as owners in the transfer of enterprises—even though some may wind up with worthless shares in noncompetitive, bankrupt firms. Although saving is increas-

---

8. For a typical experience, see "Pioneers of Privatization," *U.S. News and World Report* (March 29, 1993): 37–38.

ing sharply, the pool of funds is still quite small, so various kinds of coupon or voucher systems have been used in Poland, the Czech Republic, Hungary, and Russia. For example, each Russian citizen received a voucher for 10,000 rubles at the end of 1992 (worth about $25 at that time) which could be resold or used to purchase shares in some 6,000 enterprises.[9] Worker and manager participation in ownership is another common feature of privatization programs. For citizens who do not know how to invest, mutual funds have developed in Poland and Hungary. To protect the nation's assets during a time when the exchange rate may not correctly reflect values, there are usually restrictions on foreign ownership.

Russia has made some progress in selling off private firms (those with less than 200 employees) via auctions. In larger enterprises, workers get 25 percent of the stock—it is currently nonvoting, but there is pressure to change that to voting stock. Five percent is sold to managers with voting rights, and the rest is to be marketed with vouchers. Collective farms are being privatized, but the process is slow; most workers regard themselves as hourly employees rather than risk-taking farm entrepreneurs, and there is much jealousy and resentment of those who have actually taken advantage of the opportunity to enlarge the scale of their small private plots and become business farmers.

Ripoffs by the *nomenklatura* (former Communist Party leaders) are an important issue in Russia and elsewhere. The *Washington Post* described Russia in 1992 as "Wild West capitalism," in which some people interpret privatizing as looting the state. The *Post* reported sales of public assets for private gain—computers from a research institute, timber from state forests, military equipment from the army. Now that profit is legitimate, Russians are having a hard time distinguishing between enterprise and corruption.[10]

BIG BANG OR GRADUALISM?

How rapidly should the transition take place? Jeffrey Sachs, who has advised the governments of Russia and Poland, is a strong advocate of the "big bang"—a rapid transition to a private economy with lifting of controls on production and prices, budget reform, freeing the currency price to find its own level relative to other currencies, and rapid privatization of most enterprises.[11] Despite his advice, the process has gone slowly because these countries lacked necessary preconditions such as a financial and legal system to support a market economy. In addition, the continued presence of semireformed communists in government and in the management of enterprises has led to a considerable amount of foot-dragging in the transition.

Sociologist Amitai Etzioni argues for the benefits of gradualism, giving the culture a chance to change and institutions time to evolve.[12] Havel shares his preference for a slow road. Etzioni points out that there is no basis in economic theory for Sachs's argument that "You cannot leap a chasm in two steps."

---

9. "Bargain Debasement," *The Economist* (May 8, 1993): 79.
10. Hiatt, Fred, "In Russia, Take the Ruble and Run," *Washington Post National Weekly Edition* (May 25–31, 1992): 15–16.
11. Sachs, Jeffrey D., *Challenge* (September/October 1991): 26–32.
12. Etzioni, Amitai, "Eastern Europe: The Wealth of Lessons," *Challenge* (July/August 1991): 4–10.

GAINERS AND LOSERS

Like any change, reforms in Eastern and Central Europe will create losers as well as gainers—some short-term, some long-term. A favorite comment of unreformed communists critical of the new order is to point out that before the change "we were all poor but we were all equal" (a statement many citizens would challenge, pointing to the affluent lifestyle of party bosses.) In the new economy, there is visible inequality between prosperous entrepreneurs, displaced workers, fixed-income pensioners, and newly land-rich peasants. The entire social order is being shaken up. There is resentment at the "ripoff" of public assets by the communists. Unemployment is a new experience, even though most of these countries do provide unemployment benefits. Whole ranges of skills have been made useless. For example, teachers of Marxist philosophy are looking for useful alternative employment in a system where their skills are no longer in demand. There is a surplus of scientists and economists (who are production or enterprise managers, not economists in the Western sense), an emerging merchant class, and a shortage of accountants and lawyers, who had little to do in a Soviet-style economy but are the workhorses of a market system. Constructing a workable social safety net is a major challenge for countries just getting used to unemployment and economic insecurity.

THE ROLE OF THE WEST

The process of transition will be long, slow, and painful, and many unreformed ex-communists are waiting to say, "We told you so," and, "Weren't things really better before?" To counter this threat to the stability of some of these new governments, is there anything useful that the United States, Japan, Canada, and Western Europe could contribute to ensure continued reform?

One form of aid has been technical assistance. Western business and academic experts, sent by the World Bank as well as individual governments and private organizations, have visited these countries to describe how a market system works, what some of the options are, and how to restructure government and carry out privatizations. Advice has also been offered in areas where the East has been closed off from technological advances in industry and agriculture. Teams have visited Eastern and Central Europe from numerous countries, under various auspices, working on agriculture, industry, law, local government, privatization, enterprise development, financial systems, instruction in English and economics, educational reform, and even religious revival.

A second need is markets for their products. Open trade will speed up the process of transition. Experience in the Third World suggests that willingness to open markets to exports and to sell these countries what they need is one of the most effective and lasting forms of assistance. Welcoming these new members to GATT (General Agreement on Trade and Tariffs) was an important step in this direction, ensuring them all most-favored-nation treatment by Western countries.

A third need is financial capital. Large amounts of capital have not been forthcoming because of other problems and priorities in the principal donor nations. Japan and Western Europe have been suffering from slow growth and high unemployment, the United States is preoccupied with its budget deficit, and Germany is fully occupied with reunification. Large amounts of either pub-

GLOBAL OUTLOOK: CASTRO'S CUBA: READY FOR CHANGE?

The Castro revolution in Cuba in 1958 followed a pattern set by Lenin in the Soviet Union. Like Lenin, Castro led a small group of committed revolutionaries in a country with a large, discontented peasant class and an underdeveloped economy. The United States served as an outside enemy used to unify the diverse elements within Cuba. Until the collapse of the Soviet system in 1990, Castro's Cuba was dependent on Soviet aid, particularly as a market for its sugar and a source of petroleum. A trade embargo cut off exchange with a more natural trading partner, the United States, which had been the main market for exports and source of imports before the 1960s.

Rather than attempt to industrialize the Cuban economy rapidly, Castro concentrated on agriculture and sought to exploit the export potential of the sugar industry. This policy required the transfer of labor from cities to rural areas, the exact opposite of what occurred under European communist regimes. The Cuban economy remains heavily dependent on agriculture.

As one of the few nations still adhering to a Marxist philosophy, Castro faces severe problems. The loss of the $5 billion in annual subsidies from the Soviet Union resulted in a sharp decline in Cuba's GDP, from $US32 billion in 1989 to about $US20 billion in 1992. Castro sent 100,000 "volunteers" into the countryside to plant and harvest crops and called on Cubans to tighten their belts. As changes continued in the former Soviet Union, Cuba began to adapt. While communism is still the official policy, there are now joint-stock companies as well as "autonomous" state-owned enterprises that are dealing with foreigners and earning foreign exchange to pay for badly needed imports of oil, food, and other necessities. Encouraging tourism (before Castro, Cuba was a favorite vacation spot for Americans and Europeans) has been an important part of the strategy, and hotel owners have been allowed a great deal of freedom in making deals and setting prices.[a]

Like many communist countries, Cuba has followed a path dictated by a strong leader. As Castro ages, and the world changes around Cuba, this nation is likely to be forced to join the mainstream, allowing a greater role for markets, opening its economy to trade with the West, and shedding much of its Marxist ideology, state ownership, and central planning.

a. "Capitalism, Castro Style," *Business Week* (August 3, 1992): 36.

---

lic or private capital are not required. The model of reconstruction aid, the Marshall Plan for Europe after World War II, offered only about 2 percent of GDP per recipient country per year for four years. Countries that have developed or rebuilt successfully have relied mainly on domestic savings supplemented by modest amounts of foreign aid and private investment. Private investment as a source of capital has also run into problems. Formerly communist countries don't want to sell too many of their assets abroad, and foreign investors are reluctant to lend or invest in firms with an uncertain future.

OTHER ECONOMIES IN TRANSITION: CHINA, MEXICO, AND JAPAN

While the world's attention has been focused on the changes in Europe, important changes have been taking place in other economies around the world. We have chosen three examples to suggest the variety of institutions that coexist with increasing roles for markets in economic decisions. The three countries are China, Japan, and Mexico.

THE PEOPLE'S REPUBLIC OF CHINA

China became communist in the late 1940s under the leadership of Chairman Mao (Zhe Dong). Factories, land, shops, and other enterprises were nationalized. A system similar to that of the Soviet Union was imposed on the world's most populous nation. The centerpiece of Mao's policy was the 1958 Great Leap Forward, which was aimed at rapid growth through industrialization and collectivized agriculture.

In 1966–1969, Mao undertook a second major policy change, called the Cultural Revolution. He called for a radical restructuring of the economy. The Cultural Revolution honored peasants and workers, while former landlords and intellectuals were sent to work in the countryside and denied access to good schools. There was no relief through the courts, because Mao had removed all laws. Laws, he claimed, interfered with the "dictatorship of the proletariat."

ECONOMIC AND POLITICAL REFORM, 1978–1990. After Mao's death in 1976, there was rapid reform in China, affecting almost every aspect of the economy. Much of this reform was due to the efforts of Deng Xiaoping, Party General Secretary since December 1978. Changes in the 1980s made life easier for China's intellectuals, who were encouraged to debate and exchange ideas with Western scholars. The results were sweeping demands for political freedom that culminated in large demonstrations. A new system of laws replaced the arbitrary power of party secretaries and brought some stability to the country.

Economic reform (the "readjustment" of some priorities) accompanied Deng's political reforms. The key to Deng's reforms was better production incentives. To satisfy consumption demands, Deng set lower production targets for heavy industries and increased investment in light, consumer-oriented industries. Once production goals were met, industrial enterprises could sell any surplus on the open market, or they could barter for other goods. Profits and losses were used to reward or penalize managers, and some factories that had been making losses were turned over to workers. In addition, the state started to charge industrial enterprises interest on the investment capital it supplied. Trade with the rest of the world was greatly expanded; from 1975 to 1985, China's international trade increased from 3.5 percent to 16 percent of GDP.

In agriculture, the "household responsibility system" assigned land that had been held in communes to individual families. In exchange, these farmers assumed contractual obligations to provide a certain amount of food to the state, but were allowed to sell the excess privately. Production increased sharply, and some peasant farmers became very wealthy.

PROTEST AND BACKLASH. The changes brought about by Deng Xiaoping injected a great deal of Western influence into the Chinese economy. There was rising interest in Western dress, music, and ideas about democracy. Deng encountered the same kinds of problems that Gorbachev had with partial reforms, especially glasnost. Economic reform produced economic gains, which in turn led to political demands. Political conservatives began to complain about the "excesses" of the reforms and called for a return to central planning, thrift, and reduced consumption.

Student demonstrations for freedom of expression united the police and military elements in the party leadership to reverse some of the changes. In June 1989, students gathered in Tiananmen Square demanding democracy. On June 4, 1989, the military opened fire on the students. Thousands of students died. The commander of the 38th Army who refused to attack the students received a ten-year prison sentence. During the crisis, Jian Zemin emerged as General Secretary of the Chinese Communist Party. He told *U.S. News & World Report,* "We do not regret or criticize ourselves for the way we handled the Tiananmen event because if we had not sent in the troops then, I would not be able to sit here today."[13]

GROWTH AND REFORM. As Deng allowed greater autonomy to local governments and state enterprises and more freedom to engage in private enterprise in the early 1990s, China experienced real growth rates as high as 12 percent. Earlier estimates of per capita GDP were revised as it became apparent that China was much more of a middle-income country than previously supposed. The influence of Hong Kong and contacts with the West, growing since President Nixon's 1973 trip to China, have allowed a gradual change in management of production that has paid off in spectacular ways. A stock market has appeared in Shanghai and Shenzhen. Substantial foreign investment has added to the growth based on domestic enterprises and a large pool of private savings. In 1993, the boom began to cool, as inflation took hold and as China's limited infrastructure of roads, banking, and telecommunications began to show the strains of trying to service a rapidly growing private sector. Even such basic business skills as accounting are in short supply, as the government is requiring new private enterprises to produce income statements and balance sheets.

Inevitably, economic reforms offering greater freedom to earn, experiment, take risks, and make choices will spread to the political sphere. Thus far, Deng has managed to maintain tight political control while permitting increasing economic freedom, but after his death (Deng is 88) the political system is likely to change. In spite of the crackdown in Tiananmen Square in 1989, China thus far has pursued a smoother and more successful transition to a modified market system than the chaotic shifts in Central Europe and the former Soviet Union.

CHINA AND HONG KONG. China's contacts with the West have greatly increased as both China and Hong Kong prepare for 1997, when the 100-year lease that the British have for Hong Kong expires and the territory reverts to Chinese rule. Hong Kong greatly influenced the changes in mainland China. Guadong Province, adjacent to Hong Kong, experienced 19 percent economic growth in 1992. Foreign investment has poured in and private firms have multiplied.

There are virtually no government impediments to doing business in Hong Kong. A corporation can be started for a fee of only $250, and there are no reporting requirements. Hong Kong has no currency exchange controls, no tariffs, and no quotas. Entrepreneurs in this prosperous capitalist state are casting a wary eye on 1997 and the arrival of the communist Chinese, but some of their fears have been assuaged by movements toward reliance on markets and decentralization in China.

13. Emily MacFarquhar, "Back to the Future in China," *U.S. News & World Report* (March 12, 1990): 41.

MEXICO

Mexico's transition is very different from the experiences of China or Russia. Mexico has never been communist, but it has had a long history of one party rule as a poor nation with all the characteristics of less developed countries. Mexico's problems included too many resources in agriculture, budget deficits, runaway inflation (almost 100 percent in 1982), substantial foreign debt, inefficient state-owned monopolies, high population growth, and urban squalor. Mexico's problems were intensified by the fact that it lay just south of the prosperous United States, its major trading partner and a main destination for Mexicans leaving their country in search of better opportunities elsewhere. Yet Mexico clearly had advantages that indicated great economic potential, including tourist attractions, oil resources, and an educated populace.

In just ten years, Mexico has made remarkable progress in economic growth—containing inflation, reducing the budget deficit, and providing better living conditions and opportunities for its citizens. The crisis in Mexico occurred in 1982, when growth ground to a halt because foreign lenders were not willing to advance any more credit or refinance existing debt. Six painful years of reform began to pay off by the end of the decade with higher growth, less inflation, foreign investment, and enough resources to relieve poverty for the poorest groups in the population.[14] By 1992, Mexico had made the transition to an upper-middle-income country, comparable to Greece, Turkey, or Portugal in per capita income, although problems of inequality, inflation, and environmental quality are still high on the agenda.

The key to Mexico's transition lay in reduced public spending and privatization. Mexico reduced the number of state enterprises from 1,115 in 1982 to fewer than 300 in 1992. Even the giant state oil monopoly, PEMEX, was restructured and some of its operations were privatized. Revenues from the sale of public enterprises helped to close part of the budget gap during the transition. Trade policy also played an important role. A prior policy of import substitution was replaced with trade liberalization and emphasis on exports and on attracting foreign investment.

Spending cuts meant reductions in infrastructure development and social programs (education, health care, and poverty relief) in the early part of the reform period. As GDP grew, attention turned to both those areas. Mexico now hopes that NAFTA, granting preferential access to the huge U.S. market, will help to keep the momentum alive. Although Mexico still has problems to overcome, it provides an example of success for other developing countries to emulate.

JAPAN

The Japanese "miracle" has attracted attention in both developing countries and other industrial nations searching for the secret of success and hoping it can be transplanted elsewhere. The miracle dates back to 1950, when Japan was starting to recover from the devastation of World War II. Per capita income in 1950 was only about an eighth of that in the United States. Forty-two years later, in 1992, Japan's per capita income level was four-fifths of that of the United States. In the 1950s, the phrase "Made in Japan" implied cheap, shoddy copies of U.S.

---

14. "Mexico," *OECD Observer* (October/November 1992): 39–42.

products. In the 1990s, "Made in Japan" implies the finest of automotive and high-tech products. This rapid economic growth occurred in a country smaller than the state of California, with few natural resources and a population half that of the United States.

Compared to Western Europe and the United States, Japan has very low taxes. Japan's taxes are around 25 percent of national income, compared to 30 percent in the United States, 35 percent in the United Kingdom, and almost 40 percent in West Germany. The tax structure in Japan is not used to redistribute income. Until very recently, there was no social insurance system, and even now it is very limited. The pretax distribution of income is about the same as the post-tax distribution. As a result, there are powerful incentives to save, invest, and take risks. With no mandatory retirement system and low taxes on earnings from savings, the Japanese people save about 20 percent of their annual incomes. These savings find their way into capital investment, creating future income.

Since 1990, some of the shine has worn off the miracle as Japan has undergone some adjustments. Japanese exports have dropped and industrial production has fallen. A stock market crash and falling land prices after speculation drove prices to incredible heights left many Japanese with depleted savings. Consumer purchases in Japan began to fall, with increasingly price-conscious shoppers and an expansion of discount retailers. The Japanese Ministry of International Trade predicts that Japan will lose 560,000 manufacturing jobs by the year 2000. Some of this loss is the result of decisions by Japanese firms to produce in foreign countries rather than exporting from Japan. Approximately 20 percent of Japanese manufacturing is expected to be "offshore" in 2000, compared to 5 percent in 1987. Other losses are due to increased competition from other successful nations of Southeast Asia—South Korea, Singapore, Thailand, Indonesia, and, increasingly, China.

The Japanese recession coincided with a different kind of transition from a production-focused economy to one in which there is more emphasis on consumption and quality of life. Until very recently, Japanese workers had great loyalty to their firms. Many workers in the manufacturing sector enjoyed lifetime employment to age fifty-five, when mandatory retirement occurs. Since the recession of 1991–1993, however, Japan has had to adjust to layoffs, forced early retirements, and unemployment. Increasing publicity about deaths from overwork among Japanese men in their forties also led to calls for shorter work weeks, more leisure, and less pressure on workers. These changes will take a toll of Japanese growth and productivity. Younger workers in Japan have grown restless because of long working hours, crowded living conditions, long commutes, and high consumer prices. They are demanding higher standards of living, rather than increased investment and production through higher levels of saving. Japanese women have also begun to protest their lack of access to higher level positions and opportunities in a male-dominated society. While Japan remains a success story, with useful lessons for other countries, the miracle appears to have run its course.

Consider again... *The transformation of Eastern and Central Europe is proceeding at a slow and uneven pace, but early signs are encouraging. There are new shops and enterprises. Unemployment and inflation remain high, but a few coun-*

tries—Estonia and Poland in particular—appear to have weathered the worst of the transition. Large state enterprises are being sold to stockholders in a massive move toward "people's capitalism." At the same time, these nations are trying to preserve a social safety net and some of the economic security that was an important value under communism. Each country will develop a slightly different variation on a mixed economy with a strong private sector, a defined role for government, and its own particular set of rules for operating business enterprises, redistributing income, and protecting the poor from the most severe risks of free markets while strengthening incentives to work, invest, and succeed.

SUMMARY

1. The basic difference between economic systems lies in whether productive resources are publicly or privately owned and whether the majority of economic decisions are made by government planners or through the market.
2. Capitalism involves primarily private ownership of resources and decisions through markets. Socialism calls for government ownership of nonhuman productive resources and decision making by government planning. Socialism is a real-world system, while communism is a largely theoretical system based on the writings of Marx. Marx developed a theory of evolution of economic systems in which capitalism and socialism represent stages en route to communism, in which there is no need for the state and self-interested economic motivations have been replaced by the "new man" who serves the common good.
3. The Soviet system was based on central planning in great detail, but lacked important incentives, particularly for those who had to carry out production decisions. This system collapsed in Europe as a result of special problems, the effects of partial reforms, and performance failure.
4. The transition to markets in Eastern and Central Europe is slow and painful because of the lack of basic market features such as a banking system, a stock exchange, private savings, and organized markets. The process of privatization of state-owned industries involves such diverse methods as vouchers, coupons, and worker buyouts.
5. China has moved rapidly in the direction of decentralization and the use of markets while retaining central control politically. The use of markets has led to remarkable achievements in Chinese economic growth. Mexico has gone through successful major structural reforms in a largely one-party political system and has had good economic performance while reducing the scope of government involvement in production activities. Japan's economic system offers powerful incentives to save and invest that accounted for its impressive economics performance for decades.

NEW TERMS

capitalism
socialism

communism
glasnost

perestroika
privatization

QUESTIONS: REVIEW, APPLICATIONS, AND POLICY

REVIEW

1. What are the characteristics used to classify economies as capitalistic or socialistic? Based on Table 1, which countries would you put on the capitalistic end of the spectrum? The socialist end?
2. Why is central government spending as a share of GDP not an accurate measure of the size and scope of government involvement in the economy?
3. Describe the decision-making process in a capitalistic economy. Contrast that process with that of a socialist economy.
4. According to Marx, what stages would a country pass through en route to communism?
5. List the factors contributing to the collapse of the Soviet Union.
6. Historically, communist countries seemed to perform better in containing inflation and unemployment than capitalist economies. Why might one question that performance?
7. What are the obstacles encountered in moving from a centrally planned to a primarily market economy?
8. What are the benefits of privatization?
9. Why has China grown so rapidly in recent years?
10. In what ways is the Japanese economic system different from other industrial market systems?

APPLICATIONS

11. What common features are there in the recent experiences of China, Japan, Mexico, and Russia? How are their transitions different?
12. Based on the description of the Russian economy, what factors would you consider in evaluating a country's economic performance? Looking through some of the data in other chapters, how good is the performance of the United States on those measures?

POLICY

13. Suppose you were placed in charge of selling off state-owned enterprises for a developing nation like Mexico that was moving toward a more market-directed economy. How would you proceed? How would your answer affect the distribution of benefits and losses among different groups in society?
14. If you were advising a government on the transition from centrally planned to market, would you recommend the "big bang" approach or a more gradual method? Why?
15. What can Western countries do to help the transition in Eastern and Central Europe?

SUGGESTIONS FOR FURTHER READING

Aslund, Anders, and Richard Layard, eds. *Changing the Economic System in Russia.* Pinter Publishers/St. Martin's Press, 1993. A collection of papers by Russian reformers and Western advisers that is very critical of the slow and uneven pace of change in Russia.

Carson, Richard L. *Comparative Economic Systems.* M.E. Sharpe, Inc., 1992. A contemporary textbook in three parts that stresses the role of the state and property rights in different economic systems, examining both socialist countries and capitalist alternatives.

Gerlach, Michael L. *Alliance Capitalism: The Social Organization of Japanese Business.* University of California Press, 1993. A thorough exmaination of the Japanese *keiretsu* system and how it promotes efficiency and long-term success.

Remnick, David. *Lenin's Tomb: The Last Days of the Soviet Union.* New York: Random House, 1993. A widely acclaimed history of the end of the Soviet Union by an American journalist who spent 1988 to 1991 in Moscow.

"The Strange Death of Soviet Communism." *The National Interest,* special issue (Spring 1993). Fifteen articles look at why communism collapsed and examine some of the ideological implications of the change.

GLOSSARY

Absolute advantage The ability to produce something using fewer resources than other producers use.

Accommodating monetary policy Monetary expansion that is undertaken to help the Treasury to finance deficits without driving interest rates up too much.

The Accord The 1951 agreement between the Fed and the Treasury that the Fed was no longer obliged to hold interest rates low in order to assist with the Treasury's debt financing.

Accounting profit The difference between total revenue and explicit costs.

Acreage allotment A limit set by the government on the number of acres that can be used to produce a specific crop, based on past production levels.

Adaptive expectations Expectations about the future that are formed by economic actors on the basis of current and recent past experience and that adjust slowly to changing conditions.

Administered prices Prices that are relatively rigid, or changed only infrequently.

AFL-CIO An Organization formed by the merger of the American Federation of Labor and the Congress of Industrial Organizations in 1955, which gave labor a more unified political front.

Agency for International Development (AID) The U.S. government agency in charge of U.S. bilateral assistance to foreign countries.

Aggregate demand curve A graph showing the amounts of total real output that all buyers in an economy wish to purchase at various price levels.

Aggregate expenditure (*AE*) Total planned spending for an economy's total output.

Aggregate production function A graph showing the relationship between total real output and the number of workers employed.

Aggregate supply curve A graph showing the amounts of total real output that all producers in an economy will offer for sale at various price levels.

Aggregates Quantities whose values are determined by adding across markets.

Agricultural support program An attempt by the federal government to achieve parity for farmers through the use of price supports.

Allocation Any activities by government or its agents that affect the distribution of resources and the combination of goods and services produced.

American Federation of Labor (AFL) An exclusive union for skilled workers founded by Samuel Gompers in 1886 as the first business union.

American Federation of State, County, and Municipal Employees (AFSCME) A union of public employees that was one of the few unions that grew in the 1970s.

Appreciation A market-determined increase in a currency's price.

Appropriate technology Adapting methods of production to take advantage of the mix of resources available in less developed countries.

Arbitration Third party intervention in a dispute consisting of hearing the arguments of both sides, studying their positions, and rendering a decision. In binding arbitration, both sides must abide by the decision.

Arc elasticity The elasticity at the midpoint between two points on a demand curve.

Asset demand for money Demand for money to hold in order to protect the value of one's assets against changes in interest rates. The asset demand for money is negatively related to the interest rate.

Auction markets Markets characterized by good information, many buyers and sellers, and rapid adjustment of prices to changing conditions.

Automatic stabilizers Changes in tax collections and transfer payments that are automatically triggered by changes in national income and tend to reduce changes in output and employment.

Average fixed cost (*AFC*) Total fixed costs of production divided by number of units of output.

Average product (*AP*) The total product (output) divided by the number of units of input used.

Average revenue (*AR*) Total revenue divided by the quantity sold, or the revenue per unit sold (the price).

Average total cost (*AC*) Total costs of producing a level of output divided by the number of units of output.

Average variable cost (*AVC*) Total variable costs of production divided by the number of units of output.

Backward-bending supply curve A labor supply curve that slopes back to the left at the point where the income effect dominates the substitution effect.

Balance of payments An annual summary of transactions between residents of one country and residents of the rest of the world.

Balance of payments deficit An excess of a country's foreign spending over its foreign earnings for a given year.

Balance of trade Difference between the value of a country's merchandise exports and imports.

Balance on goods and services The difference between the value of exports and the value of imports for a country in any given year.

Balance sheet A statement of assets owned, liabilities owned, and the difference between them at a particular point in time.

Bank panics Sudden waves of fear that banks will not be able to pay off their depositors.

Bar chart A graphic representation that expresses data using columns of different heights.

Barriers to entry Natural or artificial obstacles that keep new firms from entering an industry.

Barter Direct exchange of one good or service for another without the use of money.

Big push strategy A development strategy calling for a major thrust on all fronts with government leadership and public-private partnership.

Bilateral monopoly A market structure in which monopolies deal with each other as buyers and sellers, such as when an inclusive union sells labor to a monopolistic firm.

Black markets Markets in which people illegally buy and sell goods and services at prices above government-imposed price ceilings.

Board of directors The individuals elected by the stockholders of a corporation to select the managers and oversee the management of the corporation.

Board of Governors The central governing body of the Federal Reserve System.

Bond An interest-earning certificate that is issued by a government or corporation in exchange for borrowed funds and has a fixed face value, annual interest payment, and maturity date.

Bond market A market in which the debt instruments of governments and corporations are traded.

Bretton Woods system The international monetary system in effect from 1945 to 1973, based on infrequent changes in currency prices, ample reserves, and the dollar as key currency.

Budget constraint A given level of income that determines the maximum amount of goods that may be purchased by a consumer.

Business cycle Fluctuations in economic activity measured by the ups and downs in real output, employment, and prices.

Business cycle theorists A group of economists in the nineteenth and early twentieth centuries who tried to develop explanations for cyclical patterns in economic activity.

Business firm An organization formed by an entrepreneur to combine inputs in order to produce marketable outputs.

Business inventories Stocks of goods held by businesses from which they can make sales to meet demand.

Business union According to Samuel Gompers, a union that works for economic goals without wanting to change or destroy the business organization or the political environment in which it functions.

Capital The durable inputs into the production process created by people. Machines, tools, and buildings are examples of capital.

Capital account The part of the balance of payments that summarizes purchases and sales of financial assets.

Capital consumption allowance (depreciation) The national income accountants' estimate of the amount of the nation's capital stock used up in production during the current year.

Capital gain An increase in the market price of an asset.

Capitalism An economic system in which private individuals own the means of production and are free to use them in response to economic incentives.

Capitalized value The present value of a stream of future rent payments.

Cartel A group of independent firms that agree not to compete but rather to determine prices and output jointly.

Celler-Kefauver Antimerger Act A federal law that strengthened the Clayton Act in 1950 by making it illegal in certain circumstances for a firm to merge with another by purchasing its assets.

***Ceteris paribus* assumption** The assumption that everything else will remain constant, used for most economic models. (*Ceteris paribus* is Latin for "all else being equal.")

Checkable deposits Balances in accounts at depository institutions against which checks can be drawn.

Chiseling Cheating on a cartel agreement by lowering prices in an attempt to capture more of the market.

Circular flow model A visual representation of the relationships between the resource market (in which income is obtained) and the product market (in which income is used to purchase goods and services).

Classical school A group of economists in the eighteenth and nineteenth centuries who believed that the economy automatically tended toward the full-employment level of output.

Clayton Act A Federal law, passed in 1914, prohibiting the acquisition of the stock of a competing company if such an acquisition would "substantially lessen competition." It also prohibited tying contracts.

Clean Air Act A federal law passed in 1970 that empowered the EPA to set emission standards and impose standards on polluters.

Closed shop Firms where contract provisions require that workers must be union members before being employed.

Coase theorem The idea that well-defined property rights are sufficient to internalize any external effect that is present, when there are small numbers of affected parties.

Coefficient of price elasticity of demand (E_d) The numerical measure of price elasticity of demand, equal to the percent change in quantity demanded of a good divided by the percent change in its price.

Coefficient of price elasticity of supply (E_s) The numerical measure of price elasticity of supply, equal to the percent change in the quantity supplied of a good divided by the percent change in its price.

Collusion Agreements between firms in an industry to set a certain price or to share a market in certain ways.

Command economy An economy in which the three basic questions are answered through central planning and control (also called a planned economy).

Commercial policy The set of actions that a country undertakes to deliberately influence trade in goods and services.

Commodity Credit Corporation (CCC) A U.S. government agency that makes loans to farmers as part of federal price support programs.

Common access resource A resource that is not owned by any individual but is available for all to use.

Common market A free trade area with a common external tariff, free movement of capital and labor, and harmonization of social and economic policies.

Communication Firms' ability to signal their intentions to each other.

Communism The final stage of social evolution according to Marx, in which the state has withered away and economic goods are distributed according to need.

Comparable worth A standard for determining wages that calls for equal pay for jobs that require similar levels of training, responsibility, and skills.

Comparative advantage The ability to produce something at a lower opportunity cost than other producers face.

Comparative statics A technique of comparing two equilibrium positions to determine the changing relationships between variables.

Competitive fringe The smaller competitors in informally coordinated markets with one large, dominant firm.

Complementary goods Goods that are jointly consumed. The consumption of one enhances the consumption of the other.

Concentration ratio A measure of the distribution of economic power among firms in an oligopolistic market.

Conglomerates Firms that perform many unrelated operations or produce in many different industries.

Congress of Industrial Organizations (CIO) An affiliation of industrial unions that was organized when the AFL decided not to move into mass-production industries.

Conservation Reserve Program (CRP) A federal program that pays farmers to remove land from production for ten years or more.

Constant cost industry An industry in which expansion of output does not cause average costs to rise in the long run.

Constrained sales maximization The hypothesis that managers' primary goal is to increase the sales of the firm because they will be rewarded by stockholders for increasing the firm's relative share of the market.

Consumer durables Goods that last, on average, a substantial length of time.

Consumer nondurables Goods that last, on average, only a short period of time.

Consumer Price Index (CPI) A measure of the year-to-year increase in the price level based on the cost of a representative market basket of consumer goods.

Consumer services That part of household consumption composed of nontangible activities.

Consumer surplus The extra utility derived from a purchase that has a value to the consumer greater than the market price.

Consumption expenditures Sales to the household sector.

Consumption function Any equation, table, or graph that shows the relationship between income received by consumers and the amount they plan to spend on currently produced final output.

Consumption possibilities curve A line showing the consumption combinations attainable through trade.

Contestable markets Markets composed of large firms that are nevertheless efficient because easily reversible entry into the market is possible.

Contract law Law that deals with the enforcement of voluntary exchanges.

Contract markets Markets characterized by imperfect information, few buyers and sellers, long-term contracts, and sluggish price adjustments.

Contractionary fiscal policy Raising taxes, lowering transfer payments, or reducing government purchases in an attempt to reduce the equilibrium level of output to one that is attainable with available resources.

Coordinates The values of x and y that define the location of a point in a coordinate system.

Coordination Firms' ability to relate their production decisions to those made by other firms in an industry.

Corporation A form of enterprise in which stockholders are the owners of the firm but have limited liability.

Cost-plus pricing The form of price regulation that allows firms a markup that is a percentage of average costs of production.

Countervailing power The offsetting power possessed by both sides of the market in a monopoly.

Craft union A union composed of specific kinds of skilled workers, such as plumbers or carpenters.

Credit market The aggregate market consisting of financial institutions that channel household saving to business firms that want to invest.

Cross elasticity of demand The measure of the responsiveness of changes in the demand for one good to changes in the price of another.

Crowding out The negative effect on borrowing for private investment due to competition from the federal government in the credit market.

Crude birth rate The number of births per thousand population.

Crude death rate The number of deaths per thousand population.

Currency Paper money with a specified value, issued by the government or a central bank.

Currency drain An increase in currency holdings by the public that causes a dollar-for-dollar decline in bank reserves.

Current account The part of the balance of payments that summarizes transactions in currently produced goods and services.

Cyclical deficit The part of a deficit that is due to a downturn in economic activity.

Cyclical unemployment Unemployment caused by fluctuations in the level of total output, or GNP.

Deadweight loss The lost consumer surplus due to monopolistic restriction of output.

Decrease in demand A shift in the demand curve indicating that at every price, consumers demand a smaller amount than before.

Decrease in supply A shift in the supply curve indicating that at every price, a smaller quantity will be offered for sale than before.

Decreasing cost industry An industry in which expansion of output causes average costs to fall in the long run.

Deficit The difference between the federal government's revenues and expenditures in a given year (the fiscal year), when the government spends more than it collects in taxes.

Demand The desire and ability to consume certain quantities of a good at various prices over a certain period of time.

Demand-based growth strategies Policies attempting to increase the level of output over time by shifting the aggregate demand curve to the right.

Demand curve A graph representing a demand schedule and showing the quantity demanded at various prices in a certain time period.

Demand-determined price A price that is determined solely by changes in demand because supply is perfectly inelastic.

Demand for money The amount of money that people want to hold in currency or checking accounts.

Demand schedule A table that shows quantities demanded at various prices during a specific time period.

Dependency ratio The percentage of the population not of working age (under fifteen or over sixty-five).

Dependent variable The variable, usually plotted on the vertical axis, that is affected or influenced by the other variable.

Deposit multiplier The ratio between the maximum increase in the money supply and a given increase in excess reserves. It equals the reciprocal of the reserve ratio.

Depreciation A market-determined decrease in a currency's price.

Depression A very severe recession.

Derived demand Demand for a productive resource that results from demand for a final good or service. For example, the demand for labor is derived from the demand for the product that the labor produces.

Diamond-water paradox The fact that diamonds, although less useful than water, are more expensive than water. Things with the greatest value in exchange (price) often have little value in use.

Differentiated oligopoly An oligopoly that produces heterogeneous products that are very close substitutes.

Differentiated product A good or service that has real or imagined characteristics that are different from those of other goods or services.

Discount rate The interest rate the Fed charges on loans to banks.

Discounting The technique of calculating present values by adjusting for interest that would be earned between now and some specified future time.

Discretionary fiscal policy Deliberate changes in tax rates, transfer programs, or government purchases designed to change the equilibrium level of national income.

Diseconomies of agglomeration The additional costs that individuals must pay when too many of them locate in one city (creating negative external effects for one another).

Diseconomies of scale Increases in long-run average cost that are due to increased plant size.

Disposable income Income received by households and available to spend or save; equals personal income less personal taxes.

Dissaving Consuming by drawing on accumulated stocks (inventories) or financial assets.

Distributive justice A normative argument for a particular distribution of income.

Dominant firm The most influential firm in an industry, usually the largest firm.

Dual labor markets The existence of two separate labor markets because of artificial barriers that keep some workers earning low wages.

Dualism The coexistence of a modern, urban, market-oriented society and a rural, agriculture-based, traditional peasant society, characteristic of many less developed countries.

Dumping The practice of selling in foreign markets at lower prices than in domestic markets (a form of price discrimination).

Economic efficiency The least-cost method of production.

Economic growth An increase in the level of real per capita output.

Economic profit The difference between total revenue and the total of explicit and implicit costs of production.

Economic rent A payment to a productive resource in excess of its opportunity cost.

Economics The study of how people and institutions make decisions about production and consumption and how they face the problem of scarcity.

Economies of agglomeration The cost savings that individuals enjoy when enough of them locate close together in or near a large city.

Economies of scale Declines in long-run average cost that are due to increased plant size.

Elasticity The measure of the sensitivity or responsiveness of quantity demanded or quantity supplied to changes in price (or other factors).

Eminent domain A doctrine that gives government the right to buy property at "fair market value" if the purchase is in the public interest.

Endogenous variables Variables that are explained or determined within a model.

Enterprise The input to the production process that involves organizing, innovation, and risk taking.

Equation of exchange An identity based on the quantity theory of money that states that the money supply times the velocity of money is equal to the price level times the level of real output.

European Monetary Union (EMU) A currency area of members of the European Community in which exchange rates are fixed among members within narrow bonds, but float together with respect to other currencies; broke up in 1993.

Excess capacity The unutilized part of existing production facilities by a monopolistically competitive firm.

Excess reserves Reserves above the level required by law.

Excise tax A tax on the purchase of a particular good,

such as liquor, cigarettes, or electricity, or a broad class of goods, such as food.
Exclusive union A union that restricts the supply of labor and maintains a higher-than-competitive wage for its members by excluding workers from a trade or occupation. Craft unions are exclusive unions.
Exogenous variables Variables that are determined outside a model and affect endogenous variables.
Expansion A period of growth in real output following a recession.
Expansionary fiscal policy Cutting taxes, raising transfer payments, or increasing government purchases to try to increase the level of income and employment.
Expectations Feelings that individuals have about future conditions.
Expected yield The rate of return on an asset that includes expected interest or dividends and the expected increase or decrease in price.
Expenditure multiplier Measure of the impact of a given initial change in total expenditures on equilibrium national income; equal to $1/(1 - MPC)$.
Explicit costs Accounting costs or money outlays.
Export promotion A development strategy that calls for developing export industries in order to earn foreign exchange to purchase consumer goods, capital equipment, raw material, and food from abroad.
Exports Goods and services sold to foreign buyers.
Externalities Costs or benefits associated with consumption or production that are not reflected in market prices and fall on parties other than the buyer or seller.

Fair rate of return The normal profit that a regulated industry must earn in order to stay in business.
Fair trade The idea that the United States should impose trade barriers equivalent to those that its trading partners place on U.S. exports.
Featherbedding The maintenance of jobs that management claims are unnecessary or redundant.
Federal funds market The market in which banks borrow reserves from each other.
Federal funds rate The interest rate charged in the federal funds market.
Federal Open Market Committee (FOMC) The committee that supervises the conduct of monetary policy.
Federal Reserve System (Fed) The central bank of the United States.
Federal Trade Commission Act A federal law passed in 1914 that set up the Federal Trade Commission (FTC) to police unfair and deceptive business practices.
Fiat money Money that is not a commodity and not redeemable in a commodity.
Final goods Goods that do not have to be further processed or resold before final sale.
Fiscal policy The use of government spending and taxes to try to influence the levels of output, employment, and prices.
Fixed inputs The productive resources that cannot be varied in the short run.

Fixed investment The part of investment that does not add to inventories; consists of business plant and equipment and residential construction.
Flow variable A variable that is defined over a period of time.
Food Security Act A 1985 federal law that sets target prices and requires farmers to agree to keep part of their land idle.
Foreign exchange market The network of banks and financial institutions through which buyers and sellers exchange national currencies.
45° line A line in the first quadrant, passing through the origin, with a slope of +1, which divides the quadrant in half. If the scales on the axes are the same, the value of the *x*-variable is equal to the value of the *y*-variable along the 45° line.
Forward market The market in which contracts are made for future deliveries of specific amounts of a currency at a specified price.
Fractional reserve banking The practice of holding a fraction of money deposited as reserves and lending the rest.
Free reserves Excess bank reserves minus loans from the Fed to member banks.
Free riders People or business firms who consume collective goods without contributing to the cost of their production.
Free trade area An agreement between two or more countries to eliminate tariffs and other trade barriers on trade among themselves, while each country maintains its existing trade barriers to outside countries.
Frictional unemployment Unemployment caused by workers temporarily between jobs or new entrants to the labor force.
Full-bodied money Money that has a value in other uses equal to its monetary value.
Full employment The level of employment at which approximately 94 to 95 percent of those who want to work are employed.
Full-employment level of output The level of real output associated with full use of all resources, especially labor.
Functional distribution of income The pattern of payments to the productive resources (rent, wages, interest, and profits).

Gains from trade The increase in economic well-being resulting from specialization and trade.
Game theory A mathematical theory about rational decision making under conditions of uncertainty that can provide insight into oligopolistic behavior.
GDP deflator A current-weights index used to correct for price changes in the GDP.
GDP targeting A monetary policy that calls for the Fed to aim at some level of nominal GDP by influencing a number of variables that affect GDP.
Gini coefficient A numerical measure of income equality equal to the area between the diagonal and the Lorenz curve divided by the area of the triangle below the diagonal in the Lorenz curve diagram.
Glasnost (Russian, openness): Political reforms involving free speech and tolerance of dissent in the former Soviet Union in the Gorbachev era.

Gold standard An international monetary system in which currencies were defined in terms of gold, money supplies were linked to gold, and balance of payments deficits were settled in gold.

Gross Domestic Product (GDP) The total market value of all final products produced by a country's residents in a given year.

Gross private domestic investment Business sector purchases of final output in the GDP.

Hart-Scott-Rodino Antitrust Improvement Act A 1970 federal law amending the FTC Act to require firms to report mergers or acquisitions to the FTC and Department of Justice before the fact.

Hedgers People who try to reduce their risk by buying or selling contracts in the forward market for currency.

Herfindahl Index A summed index of concentration that takes into account all the firms in an industry.

Holding companies Firms set up for the sole purpose of owning and thus controlling other firms.

Horizontally integrated firms Firms that perform many similar production operations in the same industry.

Human capital The investment made to improve the quality of people's labor skills through education, training, health care, and so on.

Humphrey-Hawkins Act A 1978 amendment to the Employment Act of 1946 that set specific targets for output, employment, and prices.

Impact lag The time that elapses between implementation of a fiscal policy and its full effect on economic activity.

Implementation lag The time it takes after a problem is recognized to choose and enact a fiscal policy in response.

Implicit costs Costs measured by the value of alternatives given up.

Import substitution A development strategy that concentrates on becoming self-sufficient by replacing imported goods with domestic production.

Imports Purchases of goods and services from foreign sellers.

Inclusive union A union that attempts to organize all the workers in an industry and to maintain a strong bargaining position with respect to management.

Income-consumption curve A curve that uses parallel budget lines to show changes in consumer equilibrium when income changes.

Income effect An increase in demand for a good (or service) when its price falls, *ceteris paribus*, because the household's real income rises and the consumer buys more of all normal goods.

Income elasticity of demand The measure of the responsiveness of demand to changes in income.

Income gap The difference between the equilibrium level of output and the full employment level of output; equal to the recessionary gap times the multiplier.

Income statement Measures the total flow of revenues to an economic unit, such as a household, individual, or firm over a particular period of time.

Increase in demand A shift in the demand curve indicating that at every price, a larger quantity will be offered for sale than before.

Increase in supply A shift in the supply curve indicating that at every price, a larger quantity will be offered for sale than before.

Increasing cost industry An industry in which expansion of output causes average costs to rise in the long run.

Increasing opportunity cost The principle that as production of one good rises, larger and larger sacrifices of another are required.

Independent variable The variable, usually plotted on the horizontal axis, that affects or influences the other variable.

Indifference analysis An approach to analyzing consumer behavior based on ranking the utility of choices relative to one another.

Indifference curve A plot of all combinations of goods that the consumer is indifferent among.

Indifference map A set of indifference curves. Higher curves represent higher levels of utility.

Indifference set Any number of combinations of goods among which the individual consumer is indifferent (has no preference).

Industrial policy A growth strategy consisting of government programs to identify and encourage promising industries and to ease the decline of old industries.

Industrial union An inclusive union that gains power by organizing all (or a large share) of the workers in an industry.

Industrial Workers of the World (IWW) An international union that organized U.S. steelworkers after World War I and was viewed as a socialistic organization, which contributed to its demise.

Industry A group of firms producing similar or related products.

Industry studies Investigations of specific industries to determine the degree of competitive behavior.

Inferior good A good for which demand decreases as income increases.

Inflation A rise in the general, or average, level of prices.

Injections Spending added to the circular flow that is not paid for out of resource income, such as business investment, government expenditures, and exports.

Injunction A court order to cease some activity, such as ordering labor to end a strike or walkout.

Innovation The translation of inventions into products and processes that are commercially feasible and cost-effective.

Insider-outsider model An explanation of labor market behavior that assumes that insiders (employed union members) will negotiate for higher wage rates for themselves at the expense of outsiders, thus worsening the inflation-unemployment trade-off.

Institutional investors Large investors, including insurance companies, mutual funds, and pension funds, whose purchases and sales have a significant impact on the prices of investment assets.

Interdependent demand Demand that depends on another type of demand. For example, a firm's demand for labor depends on the amount of other resources that the firm plans to use.

Interdependent utility functions Preference patterns in which some people's well-being is dependent on the well-being of others.

Interest The return to capital, one of the productive resources.

Intermediate goods Goods sold to be further processed into final goods.

Internalization The incorporation of the social costs of negative external effects into the market price.

International Monetary Fund (IMF) The agency that supervised the operation of the Bretton Woods system and maintained a reserve pool, and which continues to assist countries with currency and monetary management problems.

International monetary reserves The pool of gold and major currencies created under Bretton Woods system, from which countries could borrow to settle deficits and replenish from surpluses.

Investment Purchase of real tangible assets, such as machines, factories, or inventories, that are used to produce goods and services.

Investment demand schedule A graph that ranks possible investment projects for a firm in order of decreasing expected rate of return.

Key currency A currency that serves as a major reserve asset and is used in transactions between third-party nations.

Keynesian revolution The change in macroeconomic theory and policy that occurred when Keynes's ideas displaced the classical theory of how output and employment are determined.

Keynesians Twentieth century economists who share the views of Keynes that there could be persistent unemployment and low levels of production that could be corrected only with government intervention.

Kinked demand curve A demand curve with a bend in it at the price settled on in an oligopolistic industry because other firms' price cuts, but not price increases, are matched.

Knights of Labor Organized as a secret organization by Uriah Stevens in 1869, it won the first major strike in the United States against the railroad industry but had political reformist goals that led to its demise.

Labor The physical and mental exertion that human beings put into production activities.

Labor force Those who are working or actively seeking work.

Labor force participation rate The fraction of the population over 16 years of age who are employed or actively seeking work.

Land Natural resources that can be used as inputs to production.

Landrum-Griffin Act An act passed in 1959, aimed at curbing union power by making unions more democratic, restricting Communist Party members and convicted felons from union leadership, and making picketing illegal under certain circumstances.

Law of demand The quantity demanded of a good or service is negatively related to its price, *ceteris paribus*.

Leading sectors strategy A development strategy calling for concentration on a few promising sectors, which will then pull along the other sectors in the development process.

Leakages Flows out of the circular flow that occurs when resource income is not spent directly on purchases from domestic firms, but goes to savings, taxes, and imports.

Legal tender Money that, by law, must be accepted by private parties and governments in payment of debts and obligations.

Lender of last resort A source of funds for rescuing sound banks by lending them funds to meet temporary high demands from depositors.

Lerner Index of Monopoly Power (LMP) An index that evaluates the gap between price and marginal cost as a measure of monopoly power.

Limited liability The fact that the stockholders of a corporation cannot be sued for failure of the corporation to meet its obligations.

Liquidity The measure of how quickly a financial asset can be converted into the medium of exchange.

Local monopoly A firm that has monopoly power in a geographic region because of the large distance from other suppliers of its product (or substitutes).

Logrolling Vote trading in the legislative process.

Long run The period of time in which all inputs, including plant and equipment, can be varied.

Long-run average cost (*LRAC*) curve A curve tangent to all the possible short-run cost curves and representing the lowest attainable average cost of producing any given output.

Long-run profit maximization The argument that even if managers seem to behave in accord with satisficing or constrained sales maximization, they only do so because it leads to higher profits in the long run.

Lorenz curve A graph showing the cumulative percentages of income received by various percentages of households.

M1 money supply The total of all financial assets in the United States that function as a medium of exchange: currency, traveler's checks, demand deposits, and other checkable deposits.

M2 money supply The total of M2 and small-denomination time and savings deposits at all financial institutions, money market accounts, and a few other items.

M3 money supply The total of M2 and large-denomination time and savings deposits and a few other items.

Macroeconomic equilibrium The level of output at which there is no tendency to change. The amount that buyers wish to buy is exactly equal to what is being produced.

Macroeconomics The study of the economy as a whole or of economic aggregates, such as the level of employment and the growth of total output.

Marginal analysis A technique for analyzing problems by examining the results of small changes.

Marginal cost (MC) The change in total cost from producing one more (or one less) unit of output.

Marginal cost pricing A policy tool for forcing a monopoly to behave more like a competitive firm by regulating the monopoly price so that it is equal to marginal cost.

Marginal efficiency of investment (MEI) curve A graph that represents the combined investment demand schedules for all firms in the economy, showing the volume of investment demand as a function of the expected rate of return.

Marginal product (MP) The change in total output that is produced by a unit change in an input.

Marginal productivity theory An explanation of how the distribution of income is determined in a market system. Each input is paid according to its contribution, or its marginal productivity.

Marginal propensity to consume (MPC) The fraction of any change in income that is consumed; the MPC is greater than zero and less than one.

Marginal propensity to save (MPS) The fraction of any change in income that is saved; the MPS is greater than zero and less than one, and MPC + MPS = 1.

Marginal rate of substitution (MRS) The trade-off ratio along an indifference curve.

Marginal resource cost of labor (MRC_L) The cost of each additional unit of labor.

Marginal revenue (MR) The change in total revenue from selling one more (or one less) unit.

Marginal revenue product of labor (MRP_L) The amount that an additional unit of labor adds to a firm's total revenue.

Marginal utility (MU) The amount of utility that one more or one less unit of consumption adds to or subtracts from total utility.

Market A place where buyers and sellers meet to exchange goods, services, and productive resources.

Market-clearing price The equilibrium price, which clears the market because there are no frustrated consumers or suppliers.

Market concentration doctrine The hypothesis that the degree of concentration in an industry is a reliable index of monopoly power and that a high concentration ratio is likely to be associated with undesirable monopoly behavior.

Market demand curve The sum of all of the individual demand curves. A market demand curve shows what quantities will be demanded by all consumers in a specific time frame in a certain market at various prices.

Market economy An economy in which the three basic questions are answered through the market, by relying on self-interested behavior and incentives.

Market equilibrium A point at which quantity demanded by consumers is equal to quantity supplied by producers. The price at which this occurs is the equilibrium price, or market-clearing price.

Market for loanable funds The market in which transactions between borrowers and lenders determine the interest rate and the volume of loans.

Market power The ability of buyers or sellers to affect price.

Market supply curve The sum of all of the individual supply curves. A market supply curve shows what quantities will be supplied by all firms at various prices during a specific time period.

Marketing orders A federal program that establishes producer cartels that control the supply of certain agricultural products not subject to price supports.

Maximum The point on a graph at which the *y*-variable, or dependent variable, reaches its highest value.

Median voter theorem A theory that predicts that under majority rule, politicians will reflect the positions of voters near the center of the political spectrum.

Mediation Third-party intervention in a dispute consisting of attempts to keep the parties together and talking by offering suggestions and clarifying issues.

Medium of exchange A function of money in simplifying transactions by allowing people to exchange the goods and services they produce for money and then exchange money for other goods and services they want.

Microeconomics The study of individual market interactions, focusing on production and consumption by the individual consumer, firm, or industry.

Minimum The point on the graph at which the *y*-variable, or dependent variable, reaches its lowest value.

Minimum wage A price floor imposed by the federal government in the labor market.

Mixed economy An economy in which the three basic questions are answered partly by market forces and partly through government.

Model A set of assumptions and hypotheses that is a simplified description of reality.

Monetarists Economists who emphasize the role of money and monetary policy as the important influence on the price level and inflation.

Monetary base The currency in the hands of the public plus reserves held by banks.

Monetary rule A proposed regulation requiring the Fed to make the money supply grow at some predetermined, steady rate.

Money Any financial asset that serves as a medium of exchange, a standard of value, and a store of wealth.

Money multiplier The ratio of the actual money supply to the monetary base.

Money stock The amount of financial assets in existence at a particular time that perform the function of money as a medium of exchange.

Monopolistic competition The market structure in which a large number of firms sell differentiated products.

Monopoly The market structure in which there is a single seller of a product that has no close substitutes.

Monopoly power The ability to exercise some of the economic effects predicted in the model of monopoly by restricting output.

Monopoly rent seeking The efforts and resources expended by those attempting to establish monopolies to earn monopoly profits.

Monopsonistic exploitation The difference in wages paid by a firm that has monopsony power, compared to what would be paid in a competitive market.

Monopsony A market structure in which there is a single purchaser of a productive resource.

Moral suasion Attempts by the Fed to convince depository institutions to do what the Fed favors.

Multinational corporation A firm with headquarters in one country and one or more subsidiaries in other countries.

Mutual fund A financial institution that pools money from many individuals in order to invest in a diversified portfolio of assets.

Name brand capital The value that consumers place on a product because of experience, reputation, or image.

National debt The total of all past budget deficits minus all past surpluses, or the net amount owed to bondholders by the federal government.

National income (NI) Income earned by the resources; consists of wages, rent, interest, profit, and proprietors' net income.

National Labor Relations Board (NLRB) A board established by the Wagner Act in 1935 and empowered to investigate employer unfair labor practices and to determine the legitimate bargaining agent for labor when there are competing unions.

National Labor Union The first successful national union in the United States, founded in 1867 by William Sylvis.

National Recovery Administration (NRA) A major New Deal program that was aimed at business recovery but was anticompetitive since it allowed and encouraged agreements between firms. It was eventually declared unconstitutional.

Natural monopoly A monopoly that emerges because economies of scale mean that there is room for only one firm in that market.

Natural rate of unemployment The rate of unemployment that is determined by frictional and structural factors and toward which the economy tends to return.

Near money Highly liquid financial assets that are very similar to those assets that are included in the money stock.

Negative externalities Harmful spillovers to third parties that result from production or consumption of certain goods.

Negative relationship A relationship between two variables in which an increase in the value of one is associated with a decrease in the value of the other.

Net National Product (NNP) Equal to GNP less capital consumption allowance and adjustments (depreciation).

Net private domestic investment Gross private domestic investment less capital consumption allowances and adjustments (depreciation).

Net worth The difference between assets and liabilities for a particular person or firm at a point in time.

New International Economic Order A proposal from developing nations calling for changes in international economic arrangements so as to benefit poorer nations through trade references, increased aid, and price stabilization for tropical agricultural products.

Nominal rate of interest The rate of interest actually charged, without correction for inflation (also known as the market rate of interest).

Nonprice competition Competing with rival firms through advertising, style changes, color changes, and techniques other than lowering price.

Nontariff barriers Trade restrictions other than tariffs or quotas.

Normal good A good for which demand increases as income increases.

Normal profit The opportunity cost of capital and enterprise, or the rate of return that is necessary for a firm to remain in a competitive industry.

Normative statements A set of propositions about what ought to be (also called value judgments).

Norris-La Guardia Act A law passed in 1932 that vastly strengthened the power of labor unions by limiting the court's use of injunctions in labor-management disputes.

(Not quite) law of supply The quantity supplied of a good or service is usually a positive function of price, *ceteris paribus*.

Number equivalent A measure of the theoretical number of equal-sized firms that should be found in an industry (the reciprocal of the Herfindahl Index).

Oligopoly The market structure in which a few firms compete imperfectly and recognize their interdependence.

Open market operations Purchases and sales of U.S. Treasury securities on the open market by the Fed in order to affect bank reserves.

Opportunity cost The value of the other alternatives given up in order to enjoy a particular good or service.

Optimal-size plant The plant represented by the short-run average cost curve with the lowest attainable per-unit costs.

Origin The intersection of the vertical and horizontal axes of a coordinate system, at which the values of both the *x*-variable and the *y*-variable are zero.

Parity A one-to-one ratio between the average prices of farm products and the prices of what farmers buy.

Partnership A form of enterprise in which there is more than one owner, and the firm does not have a legal existence separate from the owners.

Payment in kind (PIK) program A federal agricultural program similar to the soil bank program, but with payments made in surplus commodities rather than in money.

Peak The highest output level in a business cycle: the upper turning point.

Perestroika (Russian, restructuring): Economic reforms in the former Soviet Union in the Gorbachev era.

Perfect competition The market structure in which there are many sellers and buyers, firms produce a homogeneous product, and there is free entry into and exit out of the industry.

Perfectly elastic demand Demand represented by a horizontal demand curve with a coefficient of price elasticity of demand that is equal to infinity. The quantity demanded is infinitely responsive to a change in price.

Perfectly inelastic demand Demand represented by a vertical demand curve with a coefficient of price elasticity of demand that is equal to zero. There is no response in quantity demanded to changes in price.

Permanent income hypothesis The view that consumption

does not depend on current income alone, but on past income and expected future income as well.

Personal distribution of income   A measure of how total income is divided among individuals or households.

Personal income   Equals NI after the subtraction of corporate profits taxes and undistributed corporate profits, Social Security contributions, and the addition of net transfer payments.

Phillips curve   A graph showing the relationship between the rates of inflation and unemployment for a country over a specified period of years.

Pie chart   A graphic representation in the shape of a pie that expresses actual economic data as parts of a whole. The sizes of the slices of the pie correspond to the percentage shares of the components.

Planning curve   The long-run average cost curve used in the planning stage.

Point elasticity   The elasticity at a particular point on a demand curve.

Political business cycle   A business cycle that results from the use of fiscal (or monetary) policy to influence the outcome of elections.

Positive externalities   Spillover benefits to third parties (free riders) that result from production or consumption of certain goods.

Positive relationship   A relationship between two variables in which an increase in one is associated with an increase in the other and a decrease in one is associated with a decrease in the other.

Positive statements   A set of propositions about what is, rather than what ought to be.

Potential output   The output an economy could produce if all of its resources were fully employed.

Predatory pricing   The act of selling below cost to destroy competitors.

Present value (*PV*)   The value of a future payment or series of future payments discounted to the present.

Price ceilings   Upper limits on prices imposed by a governmental unit. The ceiling is a price that cannot be exceeded.

Price clusters   Groupings of prices for similar, but not homogeneous, products.

Price-consumption curve   A curve that shows changes in consumer equilibrium when the price of one good on an indifference curve changes.

Price discrimination   The practice of charging different prices to different consumers or to a single consumer for different quantities purchased.

Price elasticity of demand   The measure of the responsiveness of the quantity demanded to changes in price.

Price elasticity of supply   The measure of the responsiveness of the quantity supplied to changes in the price.

Price floors   Minimum limits on prices established by a governmental unit. The floor is a price that cannot be undercut.

Price index   A measure of changes in price levels from year to year.

Price leadership   The form of tacit collusion in an oligopolistic industry in which one firm, the price leader, sets the price or initiates price changes and the other firms follow that lead.

Price searcher   A firm that sets price in order to maximize profits and thus has monopoly power.

Price taker   A seller (or buyer) in perfect competition that has no influence on price and can sell any amount at the market-clearing price.

Primary effect   The dominant or immediate effect of a change in an economic variable.

Principle of comparative advantage   The idea that output will be maximized if people specialize in producing those goods or services for which their opportunity costs are lowest and engage in exchange to obtain other things they want.

Principle of diminishing marginal rates of substitution   The fact that as more of one good is consumed, more and more of the other must be given up to maintain indifference between the two.

Principle of diminishing marginal utility   The fact that the additional utility declines as quantity consumed increases. Less satisfaction is obtained per additional unit as more units are consumed.

Principle of diminishing returns   The fact that as more and more units of a variable input are added to a set of fixed inputs, the resulting additions to output eventually become smaller.

Privatization   Transferring assets from public to private ownership in order to increase the share of economic decisions made through the market.

Producer Price Index   A group of three indexes for raw materials, semifinished goods, and finished goods that shows what is happening to prices paid by producers and wholesalers.

Product cycle   A series of stages, from development through standardization, through which a new product passes.

Product group   A market for a set of goods that are differentiated but have a large number of close substitutes.

Product market   Set of markets in which goods and services produced by firms are sold.

Production   The process of transforming inputs into marketable outputs.

Production function   A description of the amounts of output expected from various combinations of inputs.

Production possibilities curve   A graph that depicts the various combinations of two goods that can be produced in an economy with the available resources.

Productivity   A measure of year-to-year changes in output per worker hour.

Profit   The return to enterprise, one of the productive resources of production. Profit is whatever remains after all other resources have been paid.

Progressive tax   A tax that takes a larger share (percentage) of income as income rises.

Property law   Law that concerns the enforcement of property rights.

Property rights   The legal rights to a specific piece of property, including the rights to own, buy, sell, or use in specific ways. Markets can exist and exchanges can occur only if in-

dividuals have property rights to goods, services, and productive resources.
Proportional tax   A tax that takes the same share (percentage) of income from all taxpayers.
Public bads   Negative external effects of production or consumption that impact a large number of individuals—for example, acid rain.
Public choice economics   A branch of economic theory that attempts to integrate economics and politics by examining the motives and rewards facing individuals in the public sector.
Public goods   Goods that are nonrival in consumption and not subject to exclusion.
Pure oligopoly   An oligopolistic industry that produces a homogeneous product.

Quantity theory of money   The theory that changes in the price level will be proportional to changes in the money supply.
Quota   A limit on the amount of a good or service that can be imported during a given time period.

Real business cycle   A cyclical pattern of economic activity resulting from changes in aggregate supply rather than aggregate demand.
Real deficit   A measure of the federal budget deficit as the change in the real (inflation-adjusted) value of the national debt from one year to the next.
Real exchange rate   The foreign currency exchange rate after adjustment for changes in relative price levels.
Real income   Income measured in terms of the goods and services it will buy.
Real rate of interest   The nominal rate of interest minus the expected rate of inflation.
Recession   A decline in real output for two or more successive quarters.
Recessionary gap   The difference between aggregate expenditure and the full-employment level of output.
Recognition lag   The length of time it takes to determine that an economic problem exists.
Redistribution   Actions by government that transfer income from one group to another.
Regressive tax   A tax that takes a smaller share (percentage) of income as income rises.
Rent   The return to land, one of the productive resources.
Rent control   A price ceiling imposed by a governmental unit on housing rents.
Rent defending   Actions by consumers to keep their consumer surplus from being captured by rent seekers.
Rent seeking   The commitment of scarce resources to capture returns created artificially.
Representative firm   A typical firm in perfect competition, one of the many identical firms in the market.
Representative money   Money that is redeemable in a commodity such as gold.
Reserve ratio   The fraction of deposits that banks are required to hold in reserves.
Reserves   Bank assets that can be used to pay depositors when checks are presented for payment, consisting of currency and reserve deposits at the central bank.

Residual claimant   An individual, or group of individuals, who share in the profits of an enterprise.
Resource market   Set of markets in which owners of productive resources sell these to producers.
Resources   The inputs of land, labor, capital, and enterprise that a firm uses to produce outputs.
Right-to-work laws   State laws that allow people to hold jobs without belonging to unions.
Risk   A measure of how much the actual yield on an asset may vary from the expected yield.
Risk averse   The preference for a certain outcome to a risky outcome with the same expected value.
Risk neutral   Indifference between outcomes with the same expected values.
Risk premium   The difference between the interest rate charged the safest borrowers and those charged to less safe borrowers for the same length of time.
Risk seeking   Showing preference for an expected value with a higher variance.
Robinson-Patman Act   A federal law that amended the Clayton Act in 1936, making predatory pricing illegal.
Roundabout production   The creation of physical capital (such as tools) that enhances productive capacity and ultimately allows increased output of consumer goods and services.

S corporation   A hybrid type of corporation that passes income directly to the owners, avoiding the double taxation of corporate profits.
Satisficing hypothesis   The argument that managers do not seek to maximize profits but rather seek target levels of output and profits that are satisfactory to the ownership interests.
Saving   The part of an income flow not spent on purchases of goods and services.
Savings rate   The ratio of combined business, household, and government saving to GDP.
Scarcity   The central economic problem that there are not enough resources to produce everything that individuals want.
Scatter diagram   A graph that plots actual pairs of values of two variables to determine whether there appears to be any consistent relationship between them.
Secondary boycotts   Union actions to stop an employer from doing business with other firms.
Secondary effects   Effects indirectly related to the immediate effect, often smaller and felt after some time.
Self-interested behavior   A basic assumption of economic theory that individual decision makers do what is best for themselves.
Self-regulating markets   Markets that quickly resolve problems of shortage and surplus through price changes, quantity adjustments, or a combination of the two.
Separation of ownership and control   The idea that large firms are run (controlled) by hired managers, not the owners, and the managers might have different goals than the owners.
Shared monopoly   The model of oligopoly that says that oligopolists coordinate and share markets to act as a monopoly.

Sherman Antitrust Act The first federal antitrust law in the United States, passed in 1890. Section 1 of the act declared every contract, combination, or conspiracy in restraint of trade to be illegal. Section 2 made it illegal to monopolize or attempt to monopolize.

Shirk To put forth less effort than agreed on.

Short run The period of time that is too short to vary all the inputs.

Short-run supply curve The supply curve for the period in which the size of the plant cannot be varied (in perfect competition, the same as the short-run marginal cost curve).

Shortage The amount by which the quantity consumers wish to purchase at some price exceeds the quantity suppliers wish to supply at that price. A shortage can occur on a lasting basis only when a price ceiling is in effect.

Shutdown point The minimum point on the average variable cost (AVC) curve, or the level of output at which a firm minimizes its losses by ceasing operation.

Slope The ratio of the change in the dependent variable (y) to the change in the independent variable (x).

Social costs Costs that are borne by society or some group in society without compensation.

Social science An academic field that studies the behavior of human beings, individually and in groups, and examines their interactions.

Socialism An economic system in which the nonhuman means of production are owned by the state.

Soil bank program The federal agricultural program that began in the 1950s under which farmers were paid to let their land lie idle in order to reduce their supply of farm products.

Soil Conservation Service A federal program under which grants were given to encourage farmers to contract production by fallowing fields, contour plowing, and other conservation techniques.

Sole proprietorship A form of enterprise in which no legal distinction is made between the firm and its owner.

Specialization Limiting production activities to one or a few goods and services that one produces best in order to exchange for other goods.

Speculators People who assume risk in the forward market for currency in return for a chance of a profit.

Spread The difference between the average interest rate earned on bank loans and the average interest rate paid on deposits.

Stabilization Actions by the government to reduce changes in output, employment, and prices.

Stabilization policy Government actions designed to dampen fluctuations in output, employment, and prices.

Stagflation An economic condition of slow growth, high unemployment, and inflation.

Standard Industrial Classification (SIC) system A code devised by the U.S. Census Bureau for classifying industries using about 400 four digit numbers.

Standard of value A function of money in providing a measuring unit in which goods can be valued and compared with each other and in providing a medium in which to write contracts for future payment.

Statistical discrepancy The part of the balance of payments that reflects unrecorded transactions and inaccurate estimates of spending by tourists.

Stock A certificate of ownership in a corporation.

Stock market A financial market in which ownership claims on corporations are bought and sold.

Stock variable A variable that is defined at a point in time.

Stockholders The owners of a corporation.

Store of wealth A function of money in providing purchasing power in a generalized form that can be held in order to buy goods and services in the future.

Structural adjustment lending World Bank lending to developing countries that requires specific policy adjustments as a condition of the loan.

Structural deficit The part of a deficit that would persist even if the economy were at the full-employment level of output.

Structural unemployment Unemployment caused by a mismatch of the skills or location of unemployed workers and the skills required or locations of available jobs.

Substitute goods Goods that can be interchanged. The consumption of one replaces the consumption of the other.

Substitution effect An increase in the quantity demanded of a good (or service) because its price has fallen and it becomes a better substitute for all other goods.

Supply The quantity of a good offered for sale at various prices during a certain time period.

Supply curve A graph representing a supply schedule and showing the quantities supplied at various prices in a certain time period.

Supply schedule A table that shows quantities offered for sale at various prices over a particular time period.

Supply side economics A branch of economics that advocates a specific group of policies relating to deregulation, tax incentives, and work incentives.

Support prices Price floors for agricultural products maintained by the government, which purchases any surplus to keep the price from falling.

Surplus The amount by which the quantity suppliers wish to supply at some price exceeds the quantity consumers wish to purchase at that price. A surplus can occur on a lasting basis only when a price floor is in effect.

T-accounts Partial balance sheets showing changes in assets and/or liabilities resulting from a transaction or group of transactions.

Tacit collusion Unorganized and unstated attempts by informally coordinated oligopolies to practice joint actions.

Taft-Hartley Act Act passed in 1947 to reverse some of the Wagner Act's favoring of labor by shifting some legal rights back to employers.

Tangent line A straight line just touching a curve (nonlinear graphic relationship) at a single point. The slope of the tangent line is equal to the slope of the curve at that point.

Target prices Prices the government considers to be fair for farmers, used to determine subsidy payments.

Tariff A tax on an imported good or service.

Tariff quota A combination of a quota and a tariff that allows a certain amount of a good or service to be imported without paying a tariff and imposes the tariff on further imports.

Tax incidence The place where the burden of a tax actually falls after all shifting has occurred.
Tax wedge The gap between prices paid by buyers and the prices received by sellers.
Teams Groups of employees that work together to produce something.
Technical efficiency The basis for minimizing the inputs to a production method according to some specific rule (an engineering concept).
Technologically determined demand Demand that depends on techniques of production and technological progress. For example, the demand for labor will be affected by the introductions of new technology in a firm or industry.
Terms of trade The ratio at which one product is exchanged for another.
Testable hypothesis An inference from a theory that can be subjected to real-world testing.
Theory A set of principles that can be used to make inferences about the world.
Tiebout hypothesis The idea that competition among local governments as suppliers of local public services will force them to offer the desired combination of spending and taxing to voters, who will migrate to those jurisdictions that produce that combination.
Token money Money whose monetary value is greater than its commodity value.
Tort A wrongful action (or failure to act) that causes damage to the person or property of another individual.
Tort law Law that deals with intentional and unintentional wrongs inflicted by one party on another.
Total cost (TC) The sum of all the costs of production for a given level of output.
Total fixed costs (TFC) The costs of the fixed inputs of production, which can't be avoided in the short run.
Total product (TP) The amount of output that a firm produces.
Total revenue (TR) The amount of money a firm takes in, equal to the quantity of the good or service sold multiplied by its price.
Total variable costs (TVC) The total of costs that vary directly with output, increasing as more output is produced.
Trade creation Shifting from a higher-cost supplier to a lower-cost supplier as a result of forming a free trade area or common market.
Trade diversion Shifting from a lower-cost supplier to a higher-cost supplier as a result of forming a free trade area or common market.
Trade-weighted dollar A price index for the dollar that measures changes in its value in terms of a market basket of currencies of major trading partners.
Traditional economy An economy in which the three basic questions are answered by custom, or how things have been done in the past.
Tragedy of the commons The overuse of common access resources.
Transaction costs Costs associated with gathering information about markets (prices and quantities supplied) for consuming or producing.

Transactions demand for money Demand for money in order to make purchases and carry out other day-to-day market activities. The transactions demand for money is positively related to income.
Transfer payments Income payments to individuals who do not have to provide any goods or services in exchange.
Transmission mechanism The process by which a change in the money supply is transformed into changes in demand, output, and the price level.
Trough The lower turning point in a business cycle.
Trusts Organizations set up to control the stock of other companies through boards of trustees.
Tying contracts Agreements between producers and retailers that call for the retailer to stock certain items in return for being allowed to stock other items.

Unemployment rate The percentage of the labor force that wants to work but is not currently employed.
Union shops Firms where union membership is necessary for a worker to remain employed.
Unit elastic demand The situation where the coefficient of price elasticity of demand is unitary (equal to 1).
United Mine Workers (UMW) The industrial union for mine workers.
Unlimited wants The needs and desires of human beings, which can never be completely satisfied.
User charges Fees that cover part or all of the cost of a public service.
Util An arbitrary unit used to measure individual utility.
Utility The satisfaction that a consumer expects to receive from consuming a good or service.
Utility function A relationship expressing a consumer's desire to consume differing amounts of a good.
Utility maximization The process by which a consumer adjusts consumption, given a budget constraint and a set of prices, in order to attain the highest total amount of satisfaction.

Value of the marginal product of labor (VMP_L) A measure of the value of the additional output that each unit of additional labor adds to a firm's total, found my multiplying the marginal product by the price at which the firm can sell the product.
Variable inputs The productive resources that can be increased or decreased in the short run.
Vertically integrated firms Firms that perform many sequential steps in a production process.
Vicious circle of poverty A trap in which many low-income countries are caught, in which there is little investment because of a low level of income, and a low level of income because of lack of investment.

Wages The return to labor, one of the productive resources.
Wagner Act A law passed in 1935 that gave employees the right to organize and bargain collectively and outlawed certain unfair labor practices by employers.
Wheeler-Lea Act A 1938 federal law amending the FTC

Act to make unfair or deceptive acts or practices in commerce illegal.

Wildcat strikes Local strikes that are unauthorized by the national union.

Workfare programs State welfare programs requiring beneficiaries to take jobs or participate in training in order to remain eligible for benefits.

Workplace Fairness Act (WFA) The WFA prohibits firms from permanently replacing striking workers.

World Bank A multinational development lending agency that makes low-interest long-term loans to developing countries and provides technical assistance and economic advice.

X-axis The horizontal line in a coordinate system that shows the values of the independent variable; the horizontal axis.

X-inefficiency The inefficiency associated with the "slack" management of monopoly firms because of the lack of market discipline.

Y-axis The upright line in a coordinate system that shows the values of the dependent variable; the vertical axis.

Yellow-dog contracts Contracts that require employees to agree to refrain from union activity as a precondition for employment and that allow firms to discharge workers who violate that agreement.

Yield The return on funds invested in an asset measured as a percentage of the price paid for the asset.

INDEX

Absolute advantage, 835–36
Accommodating monetary policy, 378
Accord, The, 358–59
Accounting, basic concepts of, 111–14
Accounting balance, 165
Accounting profit, 553–54
Acid rain, 817
Acreage allotment, 465–66
Actual deficit, 258–59
Adaptive expectations, 391–92
Administered prices, 657–58
Advertising, 508–10, 628–30, 664
AFDC (Aid to Families with Dependent Children), 102, 763
AFL-CIO, 716, 718–19
Agglomeration, 807–8
Aggregate demand (*AD*), 133–36
    and aggregate expenditure, 211–13
    and fiscal policy, 223
    Keynesian model and, 211–13
    Keynesian view of, 183–84
    monetary policy and, 343–49
    and money supply and demand, 289–90
    shifts in, 142–45
Aggregate demand (*AD*) curve, 133–35, 141–42
Aggregate expenditure (*AE*)
    and aggregate demand, 210–13
    changes in, 206–10, 223
    components of, 222
    in Keynesian model, 190–201
Aggregate expenditure model. *See* Keynesian model
Aggregate production function, 147–48
Aggregates, 2–3
Aggregate supply, 137–40
    classical view of, 138–40, 149–52, 162–63
    economic growth and, 401–2
    Keynesian view of, 139–40, 149–50, 152–55, 190
    shifts in, 145–47, 404–18

Aggregate supply curve, 137–42
Aggregate supply and demand model, 133–55, 162–63, 211–13, 245
Agricultural support program, 464
Agriculture
    floods of 1993, 589
    government policy on, 459, 462–70, 589
    in LDCs, 427–28, 438
AID (Agency for International Development), 442
Airlines, deregulation of, 484, 552, 571–72, 724
Alchian, Armen, 531, 616
Allocation, 44–47
    market, 76–77, 460–62
    in monopolistic competition, 629–30
    nonmarket, 76–77, 454–60
Allocative efficiency. *See* Economic efficiency
American Federation of Labor (AFL), 712–13
American Federation of State, County, and Municipal Employees (AFSCME), 716
Antitrust laws, 653, 659, 665–72
Appreciation, 865
Appropriate technology, 445
Arbitration, 715
Arc elasticity, 478
Asia, development in, 435
Asset demand for money, 181, 283
Assets
    accounting definition of, 112
    and inflation, 90–91
    and price level changes, 135–36
Auction markets, 392–93
Austrian school of economic thought, 800–801
Automatic stabilizers, 231–34
Average fixed costs (*AFC*), 555
Average product (*AP*), 540

Average revenue (*AR*), 577–78
Average total cost (*AC*), 556
Average values, and marginal values, 540
Average variable costs (*AVC*), 555

Backward-bending supply curve, 682–83
Balanced budget multiplier, 227–28
Balance of payments, 860–64
Balance of trade, 263, 860
Balance of trade deficit, 262–63, 860–61, 864
Balance on goods and services, 109–10, 120
Balance sheet, 112–13
    of banks, 295–96
    of Fed, 307–8
Banking
    central, 301–4
    crisis in late 1980s, 307, 320–24
    development of, 278–80, 294–95, 301–4
    legislation on, 323–24
Bank notes, 279
Bank panics, 302
Banks
    creation of money by, 278–79, 294–98
    deregulation of, 320–23
    failures and safety of, 306–7
    operations of, 295–301
    state, 303
Bar chart, 29
Barriers to entry, 601–3, 643, 651–52, 674
Barro, Robert, 264, 379–80
Barter, 273–74
Basketball "crime," economics of, 453
Baumol, William, 427, 617
"Big bang" transition strategy, 897
Big push strategy, 437
Bilateral monopoly, 707
Black markets, 56, 455, 457
Board of directors, 532

I-1

Board of Governors (Federal Reserve System), 305–6, 359
Bond market, 334–35
Bonds, 331, 334–35, 532
Bretton Woods system, 872, 875–77
Buchanan, James, 240, 757
Budget, debate over balancing, 256–66
Budget constraints, 501, 517–20
Budget line, 517–20
Budget maximizing, 797
Bulgaria, banking in, 303–4
Bureaucracy, 796–97, 801
Bush, George, 237, 255, 669–70, 672–73
Business cycle, 89, 97–99
    political, 243
    real, 403
Business cycle theorists, 150, 152–53, 176–78
Business firm. *See* Firms
Business inventories, 117, 119
Business union, 712

Canada, 100–102, 253–54, 698, 825–26
Capital, 33, 695
    allocation in Soviet Union, 888–90
    international flow of, 852–56
    market for, 729–34
Capital account, 861
Capital consumption allowance, 122
Capital gains, 335, 406, 416
Capitalism, 802–3, 883–84
Capitalized value, 728–29
Cartels, 631–36
Carter, Jimmy, 244, 359, 669, 751
Castro, Fidel, 899
Celler-Kefauver Antimerger Act, 666
Central planning. *See* Planning
CEO pay, 736
Ceteris paribus conditions, 13–14, 59–65, 71
Checkable deposits, 278
Checking accounts, 279–80
China, 140–41, 900–901
Chiseling, 633
Choice. *See* Consumer choice; Producer choice; Public choice theory
Cigarettes, elasticity of demand for, 490
Circular flow model, 39–42
    credit market in, 331
    foreign sector in, 109–10, 202–3
    four-sector, 201–6
    government in, 40–42, 108–9, 201–2
    with leakages and injections, 40–42, 200–201, 205–6
    and macroeconomics, 106–10
    with saving and investment, 40–42, 107, 200–201
    taxes in, 201–2
    two-sector, 107, 197–98
Civil Rights Act of 1964, 697
Clark, John Bates, 680, 699, 737, 743
Classical economics, 162–76
    aggregate supply theory of, 138–40, 149–52, 162–63

Classical economics *(Contd.)*
    critiques of, 176–81
    economic development principles of, 436
    and government borrowing, 375–78
    on government intervention, 395
    on labor, 163, 166
    macroeconomic standpoints of, 394–97
    and monetary policy, 344, 347–49
    unemployment-inflation relationship in, 386–91
Clayton Act, 666, 668, 714
Clean Air Act, 780–82, 818
Clinton, William J., 229, 241, 259
    antitrust policy of, 669–70, 672
    deficit reduction policies of, 237–38, 255
    environmental issues and, 815
    health care reform and, 820, 822–24
    industrial policy and, 673
    labor policies of, 718–20, 722
Closed shops, 715
Coase, Ronald, 530, 777
Coase theorem, 777–79
Coefficient
    Gini, 744–46
    of price elasticity of demand (E_d), 475–76
    of price elasticity of supply (E_s), 486
Collaboration, 653
Collusion, 632
Commercial policy, 845
Commodity Credit Corporation (CCC), 459
Common access resource, 813–14
Common markets, 850
Common situs picketing, 717
Communication, 632
Communism, 884–86
Comparable worth, 697–99
Comparative advantage, 51–52, 836–40
Comparative statics, 69–70
Competitive fringe, 636
Competitiveness, national, 672–73
Complementarity, 693
Concentration of industry, 654–59
Concentration ratio, 650
Conglomerates, 529
Congressional Budget Office, 258–59
Congress of Industrial Organizations (CIO), 714–15
Conservation Reserve Program (CRP), 465
Conservative, 151
Constant cost industry, 586
Constrained sales maximization, 617
Consumer choice
    indifference analysis of, 514–25
    utility theory of, 495–507
Consumer durables, 118
Consumer nondurables, 118
Consumer Price Index (CPI), 89–90, 93–96, 121
Consumer services, 118

Consumer surplus, 507–8, 614, 794
Consumption, changes in, 209–10
Consumption function, 190–96
Consumption possibilities curve, 839
Consumption spending, 117–18, 142–43, 184–85
Contestable markets, 619–20
Contractionary fiscal policy, 235–36, 242, 245
Contract law, 771–72
Contract markets, 393
Coordinates, 23
Coordination, 632
Corporations, 532–33, 538, 618, 655–56
Cost constraints, 547–49
Cost curves, 556–60
Cost-plus pricing, 664
Costs, of production, 552–63
Council of Economic Advisers, 241, 258–59
Countervailing power, 659–60
Coupons, 596
Cournot, Antoine Augustin, 482, 638
Craft union, 705
Credit markets, 107, 168–69, 320, 331, 343–44
Credit supply. *See* Loanable funds
Crime, economics of, 451–53
Cross elasticity of demand, 485–86
Crowding out, 261–62, 376–80, 734
Cuba, 899
Currency, 277–78
    black market in, 455
    key, 876
Currency areas, 877–78
Currency drain, 300
Current account, 263, 860–61
CUSTA (Canada-U.S. Trade Agreement), 851
Cyclical deficit, 257–58
Cyclical unemployment, 85

Dairy Termination Program, 468
Deadweight loss, 614–15
Death penalty, economics of, 452
Decreasing cost industry, 588
Defense conversion, 410–11
Defense spending, 230, 410, 441
Deficit(s), 108, 249–50
    in current account, 263
    cyclical versus structural, 257–58
    and exchange rate, 379
    and fiscal policy, 252–53
    growth of, 250–55
    Keynesian view of, 256
    problems attributed to, 261–66
    projected versus actual, 258–59
    real, 265
    reduction of, 255, 266–67, 734
    role of Social Security in, 259–61
    state and local governments and, 265–66
    "third," 262

I-2

Demand, 57–63
  for capital, 731–32
  changes in, 59–63, 71–73, 473–74
  cross elasticity of, 485–86
  derived, 679
  for foreign exchange, 865–68
  income elasticity of, 484–85
  indifference analysis and, 524
  Keynesian view of, 190–91
  for labor, 678–82, 690–94, 703–4, 722
  law of, 57, 503, 507, 524
  for money, 174–76
  in monopolistic competition, 624–26
  in monopoly, 597–98
  nonprice determinants of, 59–63
  in oligopoly, 632, 636, 641–43
  price elasticity of, 475–84, 490
  utility theory and, 495–96, 503
Demand-based growth strategies, 400–401
Demand curve, 57–58
  kinked, 641–42
Demand-determined price, 728
Demand schedule, 57
Demographic transition, 432
Demsetz, Harold, 531, 671–72
Deng Xiaoping, 900–901
Dependency ratio, 430–31
Dependent variable, 23
Deposit multiplier, 299
Depreciation, 122, 865
Depression, 99–100
Deregulation, 320–23, 414–15, 484, 552, 571–72, 672, 723–24
Derived demand, 679
Development assistance, 441–45
Diamond-water paradox, 496–97, 506
Differential rent theory, 592–93
Differentiated oligopoly, 631
Differentiated product, 624
Diminishing returns, principle of, 539–40
Dirigiste economics, 440
Discounting, 313–15, 566–67
Discount rate, 313–14
Discretionary fiscal policy, 234–38
Discrimination, 616, 696–97, 752–53
Diseconomies of agglomeration, 807–8
Diseconomies of scale, 561–62
Disequilibrium, 67–69
Disposable income, 124–25, 192
Dissaving, 196
Distributive justice, 737
Dollar, value of, 869
Dominant firm, 636–37
Dow-Jones Industrial Average, 332
Dualism, 429
Dual labor market, 802
Dumping, 609, 844

Earned Income Credit, 751
Eastern Europe, 387, 881, 887, 891, 893–99
Economic decision-making, in modern economies, 882–83

Economic development, 424–25
  and agriculture, 427–28, 438
  culture and, 584
  and dualism, 429
  international assistance for, 441–45
  and political environment, 439–40
  and population growth, 430–33
  and poverty, 429–30, 433–34
  role of government in, 439–41
  of states, 673
  strategies for, 435–38
Economic efficiency, 536–37, 615, 772
Economic fluctuations, 97–103
Economic forecasting, 89, 115, 333
Economic growth, 10–12, 106–7, 400–401
  costs of, 128–29
  defense and, 410–11
  demand-based strategies for, 400–403
  industrial policy strategy for, 418–20
  in investment and savings, 404–7
  in labor force, 407–8
  measurement of, 126–29
  in natural resources, 408–9
  and productivity, 411–13
  rate of, 127–28
  rates in LDCs, 427
  and research and development, 409–11
  stages theory of, 436
  supply-based sources of, 404–13
  supply side policies to promote, 413–18
Economic models, 68–70
Economic policy analysis, 639
Economic profit, 553–54
Economic rent, 591–93, 729
Economics, 2–3, 15–17, 34–38
  Austrian school, 800–801
  environmental, 813–16
  experimental, 510
  and public policy, 17–18
  radical school, 802–3
  schools of thought in, 16, 102–3, 138–40, 149–55, 800
  urban, 807–12
  welfare, 786–87
Economic systems, 35–38, 882
Economic well-being, 82–83, 115
Economies of agglomeration, 807–8
Economies of scale, 561–62
Economy
  changes in, 37–38
  types of, 35–38, 40
Education
  individual investment in, 695–96
  in LDCs, 434
  as public good, 786
  public investment in, 230, 262, 407–8
  voucher system for, 797
Efficiency
  economic (allocative), 536–37, 615, 772
  technical, 537
Eisenhower, Dwight D., 669

Elasticity, 473–75, 478
Elderly, transfers to, 761
Eminent domain, 771
Employment
  classical view of, 163, 166
  effect of unions on, 704–5
  fluctuations in, 97–103
  full, 83, 147–49, 224
  Keynesian view of, 180, 182–85
  productivity and, 86
  protectionism and, 847
Employment Act of 1946, 235, 241, 716
Enterprise, 33–34, 533
Entrepreneur, 533
Environment
  economic growth and, 128–29
  policy issues of, 812–20
  in Soviet Union and Eastern Europe, 893
Environmental economics, 813–16
Environmental Protection Agency (EPA), 780–81
Equal Pay Act of 1963, 697
Equation of exchange, 170–71, 174, 180
  money supply and, 280–81
Equilibrium, 67–69
  aggregate, 141–42
  changes in, 141–47
  in four-sector model, 204
  in IS-LM model, 366–69
  macroeconomic, 165
  in money market, 287
  in monopolistic competition, 624–26
  in perfect competition, 588–91
  in perfectly competitive labor market, 684
  in two-sector model, 197–98
Europe
  acid rain in, 817–18
  cartels in, 634
  Great Depression in, 100–102
  industrial policy in, 419
  pollution rights in, 785
European Community (EC), 356, 467, 852
European Monetary Union (EMU), 872, 877–78
Excess capacity, 627–28
Excess reserves, 298, 347
Exchange control, 869, 875
Exchange rate(s), 144, 864–65, 870–71
  and deficit, 379
  fixed, 872–78
  floating, 871–72
  multiple, 875
  real, 865
Excise tax, 488
Exclusive union, 705–6
Expansion, 98
Expansionary fiscal policy, 241, 245
Expectations
  adaptive, 391–92
  and aggregate supply, 391–92
  demand and, 63

Expectations *(Contd.)*
   influence on investment, 143
   and Phillips curve, 386, 390
   supply and, 66
Expected value, 570
Expected yield, 329
Expenditure multiplier, 206–10
Experimental economics, 510
Explicit costs, 552–53
Export promotion, 438
Exports, 40–41, 204. *See also* Net exports
Externalities, 772–82

Faculty office allocation, 77, 460–62
Fair rate of return, 664
Fair trade, 847
Family and Medical Leave Act (FMLA), 720
Featherbedding, 704
Federal Deposit Insurance Corporation (FDIC), 306–7, 323
Federal funds market, 314
Federal funds rate, 314
Federal National Mortgage Association, 334
Federal Open Market Committee (FOMC), 305–6, 353
Federal Reserve Act, 303–4
Federal Reserve System, 301, 359
   balance sheet of, 307–8
   bank deregulation and, 320
   and Great Depression, 357–58
   on inflation, 92
   monetary policy and, 343, 349–50, 353–54
   money supply and, 308–16
   policies from 1914 to 1993, 357–61
   political independence of, 311
   structure and functions of, 304–8
Federal Savings and Loan Insurance Corporation (FSLIC), 306–7, 323
Federal Trade Commission (FTC), 654, 670
Federal Trade Commission Act, 666–67
Fertility rate, total, 431
Fiat money, 276
Final goods, 117
Firms, 528–38, 550–51
Fiscal policy, 221–23
   aggregate demand and, 223
   automatic stabilizers in, 231–34
   business tax cuts as tool of, 228
   changing output level with, 226
   contractionary, 235–36, 242, 245
   and deficits, 252–53
   discretionary, 234–38
   effectiveness of, 375–80
   examples of, 231–32, 235–38
   expansionary, 225–26, 241, 245
   and government spending, 223–24, 229–30, 240–41
   international impact of, 222, 241
   Keynesian, 221, 252

Fiscal policy *(Contd.)*
   limitations of, 238–40
   versus monetary policy, 375–76
   multiplier and, 226–28
   supply side effects of, 228–29
   taxes as tool of, 226, 229–30
   time lags in, 242–43
   tools of, 229–30
Fixed exchange rate, 872–78
Fixed inputs, 539
Fixed investment, 118
Floating exchange rate, 871–72
Flow, in macroeconomics, 107, 114
Flow variable, 113–14
Food Security Act, 467
Food stamp program, 466
Forbes price index, 94
Ford, Gerald R., 236, 669
Foreign exchange, 863–71
Foreign sector
   benefits of trade with, 49–52
   in circular flow model, 40–42, 109–10, 202–3
   costs of trade with, 49
   and GDP, 119–20
   and recession, 222
45° line, 28
Forward market, 870
Fractional reserve banking, 295
Free reserves, 359
Free riding, 45, 783–84
Free trade, as policy issue, 50
Free trade areas, 850–51, 853
Frictional unemployment, 83, 85
Friedman, Milton, 15–17, 76, 238–39, 358, 361, 386, 390, 396, 635, 751
Full-bodied money, 278
Full employment, 83, 147–49, 224
Functional distribution of income, 737

Gains from trade, 835
Galbraith, John Kenneth, 630, 659–60
Game theory, 639–41
GATT (General Agreement on Tariffs and Trade), 204, 845, 898
Gender, and income, 697–99, 749–54
General Theory of Employment, Interest, and Money, The (Keynes), 103, 155, 177–79
George, Henry, 730
Germany, 231–32, 356, 723, 877–78
Ghana, Keynesian model applied to, 211
Gini coefficient, 744–46
Glasnost, 891
Global warming, 816–17
Gold standard, 872–75
Gompers, Samuel, 712–13
Goods
   complementary, 61
   final, 117
   inferior, 61
   intermediate, 117
   normal, 61
   substitute, 61–63

Gorbachev, Mikhail, 890–91, 893
Government
   allocation function of, 44–47
   bias against innovation in, 798
   borrowing by, 376–80
   bureaucracy in, 796–97
   in circular flow model, 40–42, 108–9, 201–2
   classical view of, 150–51, 176, 395
   and economic development, 439–41
   economic intervention by, 43–49, 76–77, 394–95
   exchange control by, 867–70
   and exports, 204
   externalities and, 773, 776–77, 779–80
   federal system of, 47
   growth of, 240, 261
   income redistribution by, 47–48
   industrial policy and, 673
   and inflation, 91
   and interest rates, 143
   Keynesian view of, 151, 155, 185, 395
   logrolling in, 795–96
   market failure and, 76–77, 773, 779, 786, 790, 798–99
   median voter theorem of, 794–95
   modern economies and, 882–83
   nonprofits in, 535–36
   purchases by, 108–9, 119, 143
   rent seeking and, 792–94
   revenue sources for, 230
   spending by, 136, 201–2, 223–24, 229–30, 240–41, 252–53, 261, 376–80, 796
   stabilization and, 48–49, 97, 102
Government failure, 793–99
Gradualism, 897
Gramm-Rudman-Hollings Act, 255
Graphs, 21–31
Great Britain, 45, 799, 801
Great Depression, 99–103, 178–79, 181–83, 185–86, 357–58
Greenspan, Alan, 92, 354, 359–60
Gross domestic product (GDP), 96, 126–27, 353–54
   and growth rate, 141
   international comparisons of, 121
   measurement of, 114–20
   and national income, 120–23
   nominal, 126
   omissions from, 125–26
   per capita. *See* Per capita income
   real, 126–27
Gross national product (GNP), 115, 120–22
Gross private domestic investment, 118–19

Hart-Scott-Rodino Antitrust Improvement Act, 666–67
Hayek, F. A., 800–801, 889
Hazardous wastes, 820
Health care
   and growth of deficit, 266

I-4

Health care *(Contd.)*
    LDC investment in, 434
    policy reform movement, 806, 820–28
Heckscher-Ohlin proposition, 840
Hedgers, 870
Herfindahl Index, 652–53
Holding companies, 665
Hong Kong, 901
Horizontally integrated firms, 529
Households, as firms, 529
Housing
    and inflation, 91
    privatization of low-income, 811
How to Lie with Statistics (Huff and Geis), 31
Human capital, 33, 113, 695–97
    investment in, 406–8, 416, 433–34
Hume, David, 171, 874
Humphrey-Hawkins Act, 350, 716–17
Hyperinflation, 170

Immigration, 691, 849, 853–54
Impact lag, 243
Implementation lag, 243
Implicit costs, 552–53
Imports, 40–41, 109
    and aggregate demand, 143–44
    as automatic stabilizer, 234
    effects of changes in, 143–44
    fiscal policy to limit, 222
    and income, 866
    unions and, 724
Import substitution, 438
Inclusive union, 706
Income
    and changes in demand, 61
    disposable, 124–25
    imports and, 866
    personal, 124
    real, 94–95
    total, 107
Income-consumption curve, 522
Income distribution, 47–48, 736–39
    and discrimination, 749–55
    in LDCs, 429–30
    and macroeconomic schools of thought, 395–96
    marginal productivity theory and, 699
    personal, 743–47
Income effect, 507
Income elasticity of demand, 484–85
Income gap, 225
Income redistribution, 755–58
    and inflation, 90
    as public good, 786
Income statement, 111–12
Income Tax Credit, 228
Increasing cost industry, 587–88
Independent variable, 23
Indifference analysis, 514–25
Indifference curve, 515
Indifference map, 516
Indifference set, 514–15

Industrial policy, 418–20, 673
Industrial union, 706
Industrial Workers of the World (IWW), 713
Industry, 531, 649–53, 722
    concentration of, 654–59
    constant cost, 586
    decreasing cost, 588
    increasing cost, 587–88
Industry studies, 650
Infant industry argument, 561, 846
Inflation, 89–96
    and currency stability, 285
    effect on loanable funds market, 327–29
    examples of, 170–73, 893
    and expansionary monetary policy, 389–90
    hedges to, 284
    and net exports, 135
    relationship to unemployment, 380–91
    unions and, 711
    zero-rate of, 92–93
Inflation premium, 327
Inflation psychology, 92
Infrastructure, investment in, 262, 406
Injections, 107–8
Injunction, 714
Innovation, 409–11, 798
Inputs, combination of, 541–42, 547–50
Insider-outsider model, 385
Institutional investors, 336
Insurance companies, 336–37
Interdependent demand, 679
Interdependent utility functions, 756
Interest, 33–34
    lack in Soviet economy, 888–90
Interest rates, 324–27
    bonds and, 334–35
    and budget and trade deficits, 263
    capital market and, 732–34
    classical view of, 169
    effect of deficit on, 261–62
    foreign exchange and, 867
    in global economy, 330
    influence on government purchases, 143
    and investment, 143, 337–40
    in Keynesian model, 185, 345–47
    loanable funds and, 324, 327–30
    as monetary policy target, 353–54
    and money demand, 283
    and money supply and demand, 287
    and price level changes, 136
    since 1979, 255
Intermediate goods, 117
Internalization, 776
International Monetary Fund (IMF), 427, 444, 876
International monetary reserves, 876
International monetary systems, 871–78
International trade, 834–35
    barriers to, 841–45

International trade *(Contd.)*
    benefits of, 49–52, 835–41
    cartels and, 634
    dependence on, 41–42
    effect on monopoly power, 673–74
    price discrimination in, 609
Interpersonal utility comparisons, 505
Inventories, 117, 119, 198–99
Investment, 33–34, 40, 107
    changes in, 208–9
    classical theory on, 164
    demand for, 190, 197, 338–40
    in education, 230, 262, 407–8
    fixed, 118
    gross private domestic, 118–19
    growth in, 404–7
    in human capital, 406–8, 416
    influences on, 143, 184–85
    and interest rates, 337–40
    in Keynesian economics, 190, 196–97, 346–47
    net private domestic, 122
    private, 406–7
    public, 406–7
    in research and development, 409–11
    supply side economics and, 415–16, 418
Investment demand curve, 338–40
Investment demand schedule, 337–38
Investment Tax Credit, 419
IS curve, 365–66
IS-LM model, 365–71
Isocost line, 547–49
Isoquant curve, 545–47

Japan, 231–32, 323, 419, 509, 736, 902–3
Jevons, William Stanley, 98, 497
Johnson, Lyndon B., 12–13, 235–36, 762
Just in time production, 199

Kennedy, John F., 235, 241, 669
Key currency, 876
Keynes, John Maynard, 3–4, 17, 103, 139, 162, 178–80, 189
Keynesian economics, 102–3, 139–40, 177
    aggregate demand in, 183–84, 190
    aggregate expenditure approach in, 191–213
    aggregate supply in, 139–40, 149–50, 152–55, 190–91, 391–92
    algebra of, 217–20
    and balanced budget, 256
    building blocks of, 182–83
    critique of classical model, 179–82
    and government borrowing, 377–78
    and government intervention, 151, 155, 185, 395
    macroeconomic standpoints of, 394–97
    and monetary policy, 344–50
    and national debt, 252
    unemployment-inflation relationship in, 380, 385–86
Keynesian model, 189–213, 245

Keynesian revolution, 178–79
Kinked demand curve, 641–42
Knights of Labor, 712
Kondratieff, Nikolai, 98–99

Labor, 32–33
    demand for, 678–82, 690–94, 703–4, 722
    supply of, 682–84, 704
Labor force, 87–88, 407–8, 695
Labor force participation rate, 88
Labor market, 678–79
    classical view of, 166–68
    discrimination in, 752–53
    dual, 802
    Keynes on, 180
    in monopoly, 684–86
    in perfect competition, 680–84
Labor movement, 711–22
Laissez-faire economics, 16, 150, 440
Land, 33, 727–29
Landrum-Griffin Act, 716
Latin America, 435, 853
Law, 770–72
Layoffs, 200
Leading indicators, 89
Leading sectors strategy, 437
Leakages, 107–8
Legal tender, 276
Lender of last resort, 302
Lenin, Vladimir, 886–87
Lerner Index of Monopoly Power (LMP), 663–64
Less developed countries (LDCs), 423–33
    exchange control in, 875
    Keynesian model and, 211
    market organization in, 584
    multinational corporations and, 444–45, 604, 856
Level playing field concept, 50
Leveraged buyouts, 616, 656
Lewis, H. Gregg, 708–10
Lewis, John L., 715–16
Liabilities, 112
Liberal, 151
Liberal school, 16
Life expectancy, in LDCs, 430–31
Limited liability, 533
Lindahl, Erik, 102–3
Liquidity, 275
LM curve, 366–70
Loanable funds, 168–69
    and interest rates, 324, 327–30
    supply of, 377
Local Initiative Support Corporation (LISC), 811
Local monopoly, 613
Logrolling, 795–96
Long run, 539
    costs in, 559–63, 585–88
    in monopolistic competition, 625–26
    in monopoly, 613
    in perfect competition, 585–88

Long-run average cost ($LRAC$) curve, 559–60
Long-run profit maximization, 617
Long-run supply curve, 586
Lorenz curve, 743–44, 746
Lotteries, 568–69

Maastricht treaty, 877
Macroeconomic equilibrium, 165
Macroeconomics, 2–3, 81–82, 138, 394–97
Malthus, Thomas Robert, 152, 177, 436
Managers, profit maximization and, 616–18
Mao Zhe Dong, 900
maquiladoras, 851
Marginal analysis, 16, 70
Marginal cost (MC), 556
Marginal cost pricing, 660–62
Marginal efficiency of investment (MEI) curve, 338
Marginal product (MP), 540
Marginal productivity, theory of diminishing, 436
Marginal productivity theory, 680, 699, 737–38, 802
Marginal propensity to consume (MPC), 193–95
Marginal propensity to save (MPS), 193–94
Marginal rate of substitution (MRS), 516–17
    principle of diminishing, 517, 547
Marginal resource cost of labor (MRC_L), 684
Marginal revenue (MR), 564
    for monopoly, 597–98
Marginal revenue product of labor (MRP_L), 681
Marginal utility (MU), 497–99, 503
    principle of diminishing, 498–99, 505
Marginal values, and average values, 540
Market(s), 34
    auction, 392–93
    black, 56, 455, 457
    bond, 334–35
    capital, 729–34
    contestable, 619–20
    contract, 393
    efficiency of, 75
    federal funds, 314
    foreign exchange, 863–65, 868–71
    forward, 870
    loanable funds, 324, 327–29
    money, 287
    political, 794–99
    pollution rights, 780–82
    product, 39
    self-regulating, 166–69, 180
Market-clearing price, 67
Market concentration doctrine, 656–59, 672
Market demand, 58–59
Market demand curve, 58, 597

Market equilibrium, 67–70
Market failure, 772–73, 782, 786
Marketing, 508–10
Marketing orders, 465–66
Market power, 576
Market structures, 644
Market supply, 64
Market supply curve, 64, 579
    of labor (S_L), 683–84
Market system, 73–77
Marshall, Alfred, 4, 174–76, 178, 282, 497, 577, 619
Marshall Plan, 442
Marx, Karl, 152, 743, 802, 884–86
Mass transportation, 811–12
Maximum, 26–27
Means, Gardiner, 654, 657
Measure of Economic Welfare (MEW), 115
Median voter theorem, 794–95
Mediation, 715
Medicare, 266, 758, 762
Menu cost of inflation, 92
Mercosur, 853
Mergers, 324, 655–56
Mexico, economic growth in, 902
Microeconomics, definition of, 2–3
Midwestern floods of 1993, 589
Minimum, 27
Minimum wage, 419, 459–60, 689–90
Mitchell, Wesley C., 177, 403
M1 money supply, 280–81
M2 money supply, 280–81
M3 money supply, 280–81
Model, 12–13
Monetarists, 140, 348–51, 353, 360, 375, 396
Monetary base, 350–52
Monetary policy
    accommodating, 378
    and aggregate demand, 343–49
    classical view of, 344
    effectiveness of, 375–76
    expansionary, 387–91
    Fed and, 308–15, 343, 349–50, 353–54
    in global economy, 355–57
    Keynesian view of, 344–47
    monetarist view of, 348–49, 375
    sectoral effects of, 355
    targets of, 349–54
    time lags in, 355
    from 1914 to 1993, 357–61
    tools of, 308–15
Monetary rule, 360–61
Money, 272–80
    asset demand for, 181, 283
    creation of, 278–79, 294–98
    inflation and, 285
    quantity theory of, 169–76, 180–81
    in seventeenth-century Europe, 171–73
    transactions demand for, 181, 282–83
    velocity of, 170–71, 283–84

Money demand, 174–76, 282–86
    changes in, 282–90
    and interest rates, 283, 347–48
Money market, 287
Money multiplier, 351–52
Money stock, 278
Money supply
    changes in, 170–76, 180–81, 288–90
    classical view of, 170–76
    contraction of, 300–301, 310–11
    and equation of exchange, 280–81
    expansion of, 298–300, 309–11, 378
    as monetary policy target, 350–52
Monopolistic competition, 623–30
Monopoly, 596–97
    alternative theories of, 615–17
    arguments in favor of, 659–60
    bilateral, 707
    costs of, 614–15
    economic development and, 440
    by government bureaus, 797
    and international trade, 673–74
    labor market for, 684–86
    local, 613
    long run in, 613
    natural, 562
    and perfect competition, 609–11
    price and output decisions in, 599–601
    price discrimination and, 604–9
    profits and losses in, 611–13
    regulation of, 660–72
    rent seeking in, 615
    shared, 630, 632
Monopoly power, 596–97
    policies to reduce, 659–74
    unions and, 722
Monopsonistic exploitation, 688
Monopsony, 686–90
Monthly Labor Review, 94
Moral suasion, 315
Multinational corporations, 444–45, 604, 855–56
Multiplier, 226–28, 238–39
Municipal bonds, 334
Murray, Charles, 416, 763
Mutual fund, 336
Myrdal, Gunnar, 102–3

NAFTA (North American Free Trade Agreement), 50, 73–75, 204, 719, 834, 851–52
Name brand capital, 642
National Banking System, 303
National Biological Survey, 815
National debt, 249–55, 263–64
    of LDCs, 443
National defense argument, 846–47
National Farm Organization (NFO), 634
National income, fiscal policy target of, 224
National income (NI), 120–25
National Labor Relations Board (NLRB), 714, 717–18

National Labor Union, 712
National Recovery Administration (NRA), 668
Natural monopoly, 562
Natural rate of unemployment hypothesis, 386–91
Natural resources, growth of, 408–9
Near money, 280
Negative externalities, 45–46, 773–75
Negative income tax, 751
Negative relationship, 24
Negative statements, 15
Net exports, 109
    and aggregate demand, 143–44, 222
    effects of changes in, 143–44
    and price level changes, 135
    and trade deficit, 262–63
Net National Product (NNP), 122–24
Net private domestic investment, 122
Net worth, 112
New International Economic Order (NIEO), 445
New York Stock Exchange, 332
Nixon, Richard M., 669
Nominal rate of interest, 326
Nonbank financial institutions, 335–37
Nonprice competition, 629, 642–43
Nonprofits, 534–36
Nontariff barriers, 844
Normal profit, 553–54
Norris-LaGuardia Act, 714
Number equivalent, 653

Ohlin, Bertil, 840
Oil, price fluctuations in, 321, 384, 409, 635–36
Oligopoly, 630–44
OPEC, 631, 635–36
Open market operations, 309–11
Opportunity costs, 5–7, 552–53
    increasing, 8–10
Optimal-size plant, 560, 562–63
Organ donations, 76–77
Origin, 22
Output
    fluctuations in, 97–103
    full employment level of, 138
    measurement of, 106–30
    potential, 257
    total, 107

Panel Study on Income Dynamics (PSID), 746–47
Parity, 464
Partnership, 532
Payment in kind (PIK) program, 466–67
Peak, 98
Pension funds, 336–37
Per capita income
    in LDCs, 425–27, 432
    in Soviet Union, 892
Perestroika, 891–92

Perfect competition, 575–77
    compared to monopoly, 609–11
    economic rent in, 591–93
    equilibrium in, 588–91
    labor market for, 680–84
Perfectly elastic demand, 477
Perfectly inelastic demand, 476
Permanent income hypothesis, 238–40
Personal distribution of income, 743–47
Personal income (PI), 124
Phillips curve, 382–86
Pie chart, 29
Planning
    versus market allocation, 889
    in modern economies, 882–83
    in Soviet Union and Eastern Europe, 887
Planning curve, 559
Plant size, 559–63
Point elasticity, 478
Political economy, 151
Political systems, and economies, 439–40, 884
Pollution, 773, 775–76, 778–82, 785
Population growth, 430–33, 436
Positive externalities, 45–46, 773–74
Positive relationship, 24
Positive statements, 15
Potential output, 257
Poverty, 747–49
    in LDCs, 429–30, 433–34
    measurement of, 748
    price ceilings and, 458
    vicious circle of, 434
Predatory pricing, 666
Present value (*PV*), 566–69
Price(s)
    as determinant of demand, 59–60
    as determinant of supply, 64–67
    fluctuations in, 97–103
    functions of, 75
    relative, 91–92
Price ceilings, 453–58
Price clusters, 631
Price-consumption curve, 523
Price discrimination, 604–9
Price elasticity of demand, 475–84, 490
Price elasticity of supply, 486–88
Price fixing, 670
Price floors, 453, 458
Price formation, theory of, 71–73
Price indexes, 89, 93–96, 126–27
Price inflexibility, 657–58
Price leadership, 636–38
Price level, 91
    aggregate, 134
    classical view of, 170–71, 173
    effects of changes in, 135–36
Price regulation, 660–62, 664
Price searcher, 596–97
Price stability, 89
Price supports. *See* Support prices
Price taker, 577

Primary effect, 70
Prisoners' Dilemma, 640
Private property. *See* Property ownership; Property rights
Privatization, 45, 799–801, 895–97
Producer choice, 545–51
Producer Price Index (PPI), 96
Product cycle, 840
Product differentiation, 624, 628–29, 644
Product group, 624
Production, 528
Production function, 537–42, 555, 558
Production possibilities curve, 7–12
Productivity, 86, 97–98
    effect of unions on, 710
    growth of, 86, 411–13
    income distribution and, 736–38, 743
    theory of diminishing marginal, 436
Productivity index, 86
Product market, 39, 107, 166–68, 180
Profit(s), 33–34, 553–55, 734–35
    in monopoly, 598–600, 611–13
    in perfect competition, 579–81, 590
Profit maximization, 533, 536, 564–66, 598–99
    alternatives to, 615–17
Progressive tax, 233, 415–16, 505
Projected deficit, 258–59
Property law, 771
Property ownership, 440, 882–83, 890
Property rights, 37, 770
    environmental problems and, 813–15
    externalities and, 777–78, 780
Proportional tax, 232
Protectionism, 845–50
Public bads, 46
Public choice theory (economics), 240, 789–91
Public goods, 44–46, 782–86
    urban, 809–11
Pure oligopoly, 631

Quantity theory of money, 169–76, 180–81, 282, 344
Quick response management, 199
Quotas, 222, 841–44, 848–49

Race, and income, 696–97, 749–52
Radical economic thought, 802–3
Reagan, Ronald, 221, 229, 244, 359
    agricultural policies of, 466–67
    antitrust policy of, 669
    deregulation and, 414
    labor policies of, 716–18
    supply side policies of, 414, 417–18
    tax cut under, 236–37, 254
    urban policy of, 810
Real business cycle, 403
Real deficit, 265
Real exchange rate, 865
Real income, 94–95
Real rate of interest, 326–27

Recession(s), 98–99, 129, 178, 189, 222, 240, 333
    of 1980-1982, 213–14, 221, 254
    of 1990-1991, 213, 255
    in Europe in 1990s, 356
    in Germany and Japan in 1990s, 231–32
Recessionary gap, 224–26
Recognition lag, 242
Recycling, 818–19
Regressive tax, 232
Regulation, 672, 793
    of monopoly, 660–72
    unions and, 724
Reich, Robert B., 420, 459, 719, 855
Relative prices, 91–92
Rent, 33, 727–29
Rent control, 455–57
Rent defending, 794
Rent seeking, 615, 791–92
Representative firm, 578
Representative money, 276
Research and development, economic growth and, 409–11
Reserve ratio, 299–300, 312–14
Reserves, 295
    excess, 298
Resolution Trust Corporation (RTC), 323–24
Resource availability, and aggregate supply, 145
Resource market, 39, 107, 166
Resources, 5, 32–33
Revenue sharing, 810
Ricardian equivalence, 265
Ricardo, David, 17, 436, 592, 835
Right-to-work laws, 715, 717, 722–23
Risk, 329–30, 569–71, 735
Risk premium, 326
Robinson-Patman Act, 666
Roosevelt, Franklin D., 101–2, 668, 714
Roosevelt, Theodore, 668
Rostow, W. W., 436
Roundabout production, 730–31
RTC. *See* Resolution Trust Corporation
Russia, 170, 759, 881, 893–99

Sachs, Jeffrey, 897
Samuelson, Paul, 15–17, 383
Satisficing hypothesis, 616
Save the Family Farm Act, 468
Saving, 107
    changes in, 210
    classical theory on, 164
    growth in, 405–7
    supply side economics and, 415–16, 418
Savings and loan bailout. *See* Bank bailout
Savings rate, 405–6
Say's law, 164, 179
Scalping, 56, 457
Scarcity, 4–5
Scatter diagram, 23–24

Schumpeter, Joseph, 177, 403, 660
S corporation, 533
Scully, Gerald, 439, 689
Secondary boycotts, 715
Secondary effects, 70
Self-interest, 14, 76, 451–53
Self-regulating markets, 166–69, 180
Separation of ownership and control, 616
Services, shift to, 200
Sex. *See* Gender
Shared monopoly, 630, 632
Sherman Antitrust Act, 666–68, 670
Shirking, 531
Shortage, 454
Short run, 539
    competitive adjustment in, 577–81
    costs in, 555–58
    in monopolistic competition, 624–25
Short-run supply curve, 578–79, 582
Shutdown point, 581–82
Simon, Julian, 432–33, 849
Single tax, 730
Slopes, 24–25
Smith, Adam, 17, 51, 75, 150, 436, 496, 505, 576, 653, 835
Smoking, 490, 780
Smoot-Hawley Act of 1930, 845
Social costs, 775
Socialism, 883–84, 886
Social science, 3
Social Security, 102, 230, 758–62
    and deficit, 259–61, 266
Social welfare, non-U.S., 764
Soil bank program, 465–66
Soil Conservation Service, 468–69
Sole proprietorship, 531–32
Soviet Union, 886–93
Specialization, 50–51
Speculators, 870
Spillover problem, 810
Sports, monopsony in, 688–89
Spread, 321
Stabilization, 48–49
Stabilization policy, 97, 102–3
Stalin, Joseph, 887
Standard and Poor's 500, 332
Standard Industrial Classification (SIC) system, 650
Statistical discrepancy, 862
Stigler, George, 75, 462, 639, 658, 757–58, 793
Stock(s), 91, 114, 331–32, 532
Stockholders, 332, 532
Stock market, 331–34
Stock prices, effect of unions on, 710–11
Stock variable, 113–14
Structural adjustment lending, 444
Structural deficit, 257–58
Structural unemployment, 84–85
Substitutability, elasticity and, 481–82
Substitution, marginal rate of (*MRS*), 516–17, 547
Substitution effect, 507

I-8

Sunspot theory, 98
Supply, 57, 63–67
    changes in, 64–67, 71–73, 474
    fiscal policy effects on, 228–29
    of foreign exchange, 866–68
    of labor, 682–84, 704
    (not quite) law of, 63
    price elasticity of, 486–88
Supply and demand, 3, 68–77
    health care industry and, 821–22
    NAFTA and, 73–75
Supply curve, 63
    backward-bending, 682–83
    of individual, 682–83
    long-run, 586
    market, 579
    monopoly and, 600–601
    short-run, 578–79, 582
Supply schedule, 63
Supply side economics, 221, 228–29, 254, 413–18
Supply siders, 229, 254, 413–14
Support prices, 464
Surplus, 108, 458
    consumer, 507–8, 614, 794
    of state and local governments, 265–66
Symbols, glossary of, 159–60

T-accounts, 296–98
Tacit collusion, 636
Taft-Hartley Act, 715, 717
Tangent line, 25–26
Target prices, 466
Tariff(s), 841–44, 848–49
Tariff quota, 841
Tax(es), 47–48, 201–2
    in circular flow model, 108
    corporate income, 228, 233–34
    effect on work effort, 415, 417
    elasticity of supply and demand and, 488–92
    excise, 488
    as fiscal policy tool, 226, 229–30
    and inflation, 91
    in Japan, 903
    negative income, 751
    policies of five presidents, 235–38
    and price level changes, 135
    progressive, 233, 415–16, 505
    proportional, 232
    regressive, 232
    to regulate monopoly power, 662–63
    resource allocation and, 416
    and saving and investment, 415–16, 418
    supply side economics view of, 415–17
    supply side effects of, 229
Tax incidence, 489
Tax wedge, 415

Teams, 531
Technical efficiency, 537
Technological change, 145–46, 409–11
Technologically determined demand, 680
Technology, international flow of, 856
Technology adaptation, 445
Terms of trade, 839
Testable hypothesis, 12
Thatcher, Margaret, 45, 799, 801
Theory, 12
Theory of the second best, 847
Tiebout hypothesis, 810–11
Tobin, James, 115, 235, 240, 757
Token money, 278
Tollison, Robert D., 453, 671
Tort law, 771–72
Total cost (TC), 555
Total fixed costs (TFC), 555
Total product (TP), 540
Total revenue (TR), 482–84, 564
Total utility, 497–99
Total variable costs (TVC), 555
Trade, terms of, 839
Trade creation, 850
Trade deficit. *See* Balance of trade deficit
Trade diversion, 851
Trade ratio, 41–42
Trade-weighted dollar, 865
Tragedy of the commons, 813
Transaction costs, 73, 530
Transactions demand for money, 181, 282–83
Transfer payments, 47–48, 119
    effect on productivity, 416–17
    as fiscal policy tool, 225–26, 229–30, 234
Transfer programs, 748, 757–64
Transmission mechanism, 344–48
Trough, 98
Truman, Harry, 715
Trusts, 665
Tullock, Gordon, 615, 758, 792
Tying contracts, 666
Tyson, Laura D'Andrea, 241, 855

Unemployment, 10, 83–88
    in aggregate supply and demand model, 148–49
    cyclical, 85
    and expansionary monetary policy, 387–90
    in former Soviet Union and Eastern Europe, 893
    frictional, 83, 85
    and minimum wage, 459–60, 689–90
    natural rate hypothesis of, 386–91
    relationship to inflation, 380–91
    structural, 84–85
Unemployment compensation, 102, 762

Unemployment rate, 87–88
Unions, 702–8, 721–24, 851
Union shops, 715
United Auto Workers (UAW), 724
United Mine Workers (UMW), 715–16
United Nations, 444
Unit elastic demand, 478
Urban economics, 807–12
User charges, 810
Util, 497
Utilities, 664
Utility, 497
Utility function, 497–98
Utility maximization, 502–3
Utility theory, 495–508

Value
    determination of, 496–97, 506
    expected, 570
Value of the marginal product of labor (VMP_l), 681
Variable inputs, 539
Variables, 21–24
    endogenous versus exogenous, 70
    flow versus stock, 113–14
    macroeconomic, 114
Velocity of money, 170–71, 283–86
Vertically integrated firms, 529
Volcker, Paul, 353, 359–60
von Mises, Ludwig, 800, 889
Voting, costs of, 796

Wages, 32–33
    effect of unions on, 703–4, 708–10
    and inflation, 91
Wagner Act, 714
Wants, 5
Waste disposal, 818–20
Wealth of Nations, The (Smith), 51, 150, 436, 576, 835
Webb-Pomerene Act, 634
Welfare economics, 786–87
Welfare programs, 762–63
Wheeler-Lea Act, 666–67
Wildcat strikes, 716
Work effort, effect of taxes on, 415, 417
Workfare programs, 763
Workplace Fairness Act (WFA), 719
World Bank, 129, 425, 443–44
World Resources Institute, 123

x-axis, 21
x-inefficiency, 615

Yap, money of, 272
y-axis, 21
Yellow-dog contracts, 714
Yeltsin, Boris, 893–94
Yield, 329

YEAR	PERSONAL INCOME (BILLIONS OF DOLLARS)	PER CAPITA DISPOSABLE INCOME ($)	CONSUMER PRICE INDEX	PER CAPITA DISPOSABLE INCOME (1982 DOLLARS)	MEDIAN FAMILY INCOME (1992 DOLLARS)	POVERTY RATE (%)
1960	409.2	1,994	29.6	7,264		
1961	426.5	2,048	29.9	7,382		
1962	453.4	2,137	30.2	7,583		
1963	476.4	2,210	30.6	7,718	27,258	15.9
1964	510.7	2,389	31.0	8,140	38,383	15.0
1965	552.9	2,527	31.5	8,508	29,448	13.9
1966	601.7	2,699	32.4	8,822	20,996	11.8
1967	646.7	2,861	33.4	9,114	31,731	11.4
1968	709.9	3,077	34.8	9,399	33,136	10.0
1969	773.7	3,274	36.7	9,606	34,363	9.7
1970	831.0	3,521	38.8	9,875	33,500	10.1
1971	893.5	3,779	40.5	10,111	33,480	10.0
1972	980.5	4,042	41.8	10,414	35,030	9.3
1973	1,098.7	4,521	44.4	11,013	35,821	8.8
1974	1,205.7	4,893	49.3	10,832	34,560	8.8
1975	1,307.3	5,329	53.8	10,906	24,249	9.7
1976	1,496.3	5,796	56.9	11,192	35,305	9.4
1977	1,601.3	6,316	60.6	11,406	35,539	9.3
1978	1,807.9	7,042	65.2	11,851	36,665	9.1
1979	2,033.1	7,787	72.6	12,039	37,136	9.2
1980	2,265.4	8,576	82.4	12,005	35,839	10.3
1981	2,534.7	9,455	90.9	12,156	34,862	11.2
1982	2,090.9	9,989	96.5	12,146	34,390	12.2
1983	2,862.5	10,642	99.6	12,349	34,757	12.3
1984	3,154.6	11,672	103.9	13,029	35,693	11.6
1985	3,379.8	12,339	107.6	13,258	36,164	11.4
1986	3,590.4	13,010	109.6	13,552	37,709	10.9
1987	3,802.0	13,545	113.6	13,545	38,249	10.7
1988	4,075.9	14,477	118.3	13,890	38,177	10.4
1989	4,380.3	15,307	124.0	14,005	38,710	10.3
1990	4,073.8	16,205	130.7	14,101	37,950	10.7
1991	4,850.9	16,721	146.2	13,965	37,021	11.5
1992	5,144.9	17,615	140.3	14,219	36,812	11.7
1993	5,387.6	18,222	144.5	14,329	NA	NA